Peterson's Four-Year Colleges 2020

PETERSON'S®

PETERSON'S®

About Peterson's®

Peterson's® has been your trusted educational publisher for over 50 years. It's a milestone we're quite proud of, as we continue to offer the most accurate, dependable, high-quality educational content in the field, providing you with everything you need to succeed. No matter where you are on your academic or professional path, you can rely on Peterson's for its books, online information, expert test-prep tools, the most up-to-date education exploration data, and the highest quality career success resources—everything you need to achieve your education goals. For our complete line of products, visit **www.petersons.com**.

For more information about Peterson's range of educational products, contact Peterson's, 8740 Lucent Blvd., Suite 400, Highlands Ranch, CO 80129, or find us online at **www.petersons.com**.

© 2019 Peterson's

Previous editions published as *Peterson's Annual Guide to Undergraduate Study* © 1970, 1971, 1972, 1973, 1974, 1975, 1976, 1977, 1978, 1979, 1980, 1981, 1982 and as *Peterson's Four-Year Colleges* © 1983, 1984, 1985, 1986, 1987, 1988, 1989, 1990, 1991, 1992, 1993, 1994, 1995, 1996, 1997, 1998, 1999, 2000, 2001, 2002, 2003, 2004, 2005, 2006, 2007, 2008, 2009, 2010, 2011, 2012, 2013, 2014, 2015, 2016, 2017, 2018

Contents

A Note from the Peterson's® Editors

For over fifty years, Peterson's® has given students and parents the most comprehensive, up-to-date information on undergraduate institutions in the United States and Canada. *Peterson's® Four-Year Colleges 2020* features advice and tips on the college search and selection process, such as how to consider the factors that truly make a difference during your search, how to understand the application process, and how to get financial aid. Each year, Peterson's researches the data published in *Peterson's® Four-Year Colleges*. The information is furnished by the colleges and is accurate at the time of publishing.

Opportunities abound for students, and this guide can help you find what you want in a number of ways:

- For application and admissions advice and guidance, just head to **THE ADVICE CENTER.** The "College Admissions Countdown Calendar" outlines pertinent month-by-month milestones. "Choosing Your Top Ten Colleges" gets you started on putting together the most important Top Ten list you have ever made. You'll find some excellent advice in the article, "Planning is Essential on the Road to College," by Sarah E. Gibbs, Director of Admissions at Grove City College. Next, "Surviving Standardized Tests" describes frequently used tests and what you need to know to succeed on them. Of course, part of the college selection process involves visiting the schools themselves, and "The Whys and Whats of College Visits" is the planner you need to make those trips well worth your while. Be sure to check out the articles on specific institutions and programs that may be just right for you, including "Honors Programs and Colleges: Smart Choices for an Undergraduate Education," "Public and Private Colleges and Universities—How to Choose," "Distance Education—It's Closer than You Think," and "Why Not Women's Colleges?" Next, "Applying 101" provides advice on how best to approach the application phase of the process. If you can't make sense out of the early decision/early action conundrum, "The 'Early Decision' Decision" may help clarify it for you. The article "Coming to America: Tips for International Students Considering Study in the U.S." offers helpful information and expert tips from professionals who work with international students at colleges and universities throughout the United States. For essential information on how to meet your education expenses, you'll find the "Financial Aid Countdown Calendar" followed by the articles "Who's Paying for This? Financial Aid Basics" and "Middle Income Families: Making the Financial Aid Process Work." Finally, you'll want to read through the "How to Use This Guide" section, which explains the information pre-

sented for each individual college, how Peterson's collects its data, and how Peterson's determines eligibility for inclusion in this guide.

- Next up is the **PROFILES** section. Here you'll find our unparalleled college profiles, arranged alphabetically by state, U.S. territories, and by country. They provide need-to-know information about accredited four-year colleges—including entrance difficulty, campus setting, total enrollment, student-faculty ratio, application deadlines, expenses, most frequently chosen baccalaureate fields, and academic programs. The contact information appears at the conclusion of each college profile. Display ads, which appear near some of the institutions' profiles, have been provided and paid for by those colleges or universities that wished to supplement their profile data with additional information about their institution. A star ★ next to the name of a school signifies that the school also has an expanded profile on Peterson's website at **www.petersons.com**.

- Nearly 100 two-page narrative descriptions appear as **COLLEGE CLOSE-UPS**—descriptions written by admissions or college officials that provide great detail about each school. They are edited to provide a consistent format across entries for your ease of comparison.

- If you already have specifics in mind, such as a particular major or institution, turn to the **INDEXES** section. Here you can search for a school based on major, entrance difficulty, cost ranges, and geography. If you already have colleges in mind that pique your interest, you can use the "Alphabetical Listing of Colleges and Universities" to search for these schools. Page numbers referring to all information presented about a college are conveniently referenced.

Peterson's publishes a full line of books—college and grad guides as well as books on education exploration, test preparation, financial aid, and career preparation. Peterson's® publications can be found at high school guidance offices, college libraries and career centers, and your local bookstore and library. Peterson's books are also available at **www.petersons.com**.

We welcome any comments or suggestions you may have about this publication. Your feedback will help us make educational dreams possible for you—and others like you.

Colleges will be pleased to know that Peterson's helped you in your selection. Admissions staff members are more than happy to answer questions, address specific problems, and help in any way they can. The editors at Peterson's wish you great success in your college search!

The Advice Center

College Admissions Countdown Calendar

This practical month-by-month calendar is designed to help you stay on top of the process of applying to college. For most students, the process begins in September of the junior year of high school and ends in June of the senior year. You may want to begin considering financial aid options, reviewing your academic schedule, and attending college fairs before your junior year.

FRESHMAN YEAR

- **Remember that college admissions decisions are most often based on a six semester transcript (your grades your Freshman, Sophomore, and Junior years) so instead of having four years to create your best GPA, you really only have three.**

- Get organized! Using a paper or digital planner, begin keeping up with your assignments in your classes, note when you have tests or quizzes coming up, and plan ahead. Staying organized in high school will help you continue these good study habits into your college years.

- Begin keeping records of your accomplishments and awards now to create your resume your senior year.

- You should begin evaluating your interests and join clubs and organizations specifically for those interests.

- Explore community service opportunities in your area. Most nonprofits will be glad to have a volunteer that works from a few hours a month to multiple hours a week and anywhere in between. Your continued participation in volunteer activities throughout your high school career speaks volumes about your character that a 30-minute interview might not provide.

SOPHOMORE YEAR

- Continue the above activities you started your freshman year.

- Begin building your preliminary college preference list

- Register for the PSAT®. This test provides a a great practice experience for the SAT, **but your PSAT test score only qualifies for the National Merit Scholarship Qualifying Competition in your JUNIOR year.**

- Check in with your counselor frequently and make sure you're signed up for classes that challenge you and will help you prepare for college. Sometimes the rigor of the curriculum on your high school transcript can mean the difference in receiving scholarships or even gaining admission into a college.

- For extra practice, sign up for the ACT® and/or the SAT® anytime this year and begin prepping for those tests using resources found at **actstudent.org**, **collegeboard.org**, and **petersons.com.**

- In the summer, spend time visiting colleges, interning, working, and/or volunteering. Depending on how busy you are during the school year, sometimes the summer months provide a valuable "break" for you to participate more in these activities.

- Ask your counselor about any **concurrent enrollment** opportunities available at your school. Most of these courses can be taken your Junior or Senior year in high school and are offered in partnership with local colleges or universities. Concurrent enrollment courses allow you to receive both high school and college credit for these courses.

JUNIOR YEAR

September

- Create an account at **www.commonapp.org** to begin adding your personal information and accomplishments to a Common Application that is accepted by many colleges and universities around the U.S.
- Check again with your counselor to make sure your course credits will meet college requirements.
- Be sure you are involved in one or two extracurricular activities.
- Explore opportunities to add community service hours to your list of activities for applications.
- Begin building your preferred college list (if you haven't already). Ideally, you should have fifteen to twenty colleges and/or universities on this list.
- If you plan to play college sports, register with the NCAA.

October

- Register for and take the PSAT/NMSQT®.

November

- Strive to get the best grades you can. A serious effort will provide you with the most options during the application process.

December

- If you haven't already, get involved in a community service activity.
- To familiarize yourself with current events, begin to read newspapers, reputable online news sources, and news magazines. This will prepare you for admissions and/or scholarship interviews where you might be asked your opinion on important happenings in the U.S. and around the world.
- Buy *Peterson's® SAT® Prep Guide*, or *Peterson's® ACT® Prep Guide* and begin to study for the tests.

January

- With your school counselor, decide when to take the ACT®, SAT®, and SAT Subject Tests™ (and which Subject Tests to take). If English is not your primary language and you are planning on attending a college in North America, decide when to take the TOEFL®.
- Keep your grades up!

February

- Plan a challenging schedule of classes for your senior year.
- Think about which teachers you will ask to write recommendations.
- Check **www.nacacfairs.org/exhibit/national-college-fairs/** and click on "College Fairs" for up-to-date schedules and locations of college fairs.

March

- Register for the tests you will take in the spring (ACT®, SAT®, SAT Subject Tests™, or the TOEFL®).
- Meet with your school counselor to discuss college choices.
- Review your transcript and test scores with your counselor to determine how competitive your range of choices should be.
- Narrow down your preferred colleges list to ten to fifteen colleges and universities.
- Start scheduling campus visits. The best time is when school is in session (but never during final exams). Summers are OK but will not show you what the college is really like. If possible, save your top college choices for the fall. Be aware, however, that fall is the busiest visit season, and you will need advance planning. Don't forget to write thank you letters to your interviewers.

April

- Take any standardized tests for which you have registered.
- Create a list of your potential college choices and begin to record personal and academic information that can be transferred later to your college applications.

May

- Plan college visits and make appointments.
- Structure your summer plans to include advanced academic work, travel, volunteer work, or a job.
- Confirm your academic schedule for the fall.

Summer

- Write to any colleges on your list that do not accept the Common Application to request application forms.
- Begin working on your application essays.

SENIOR YEAR

September

- ❑ Continue any appropriate activities from your freshman, sophomore, and junior years.

- ❑ DEADLINES! Note in your planner your preferred colleges' admissions deadlines, financial aid application due dates, ACT®/SAT® registration deadlines for testing, scholarship application deadlines, and any other related important dates in your planner.

- ❑ Begin asking your Junior year teachers for letters of recommendation now because they're the most familiar with your work and abilities.

- ❑ Register for the ACT®, SAT®, SAT Subject Tests™, or the TOEFL®, as necessary.

- ❑ Check with your school counselor for the fall visiting schedule of college reps.

- ❑ Ask appropriate teachers if they would write recommendations for you. Don't forget to write thank you letters when they accept.

- ❑ Meet with your counselor to compile your final list of colleges.

October

- ❑ Prepare the Free Application for Federal Student Aid (FAFSA®), available at **www.fafsa.ed.gov** or through your school counseling office. An estimated income tax statement (which can be corrected later) can be used. The sooner you apply for financial aid, the better your chances. For academic year 2019–2020, the FAFSA® application window opens October 1, 2018, and closes June 30, 2020.

- ❑ Mail or send early applications electronically after carefully checking them to be sure they are completely filled out.

- ❑ Photocopy or print extra copies of your applications to use as a backup.

- ❑ Take the tests for which you have registered.

- ❑ Don't be late! Keep track of all deadlines for transcripts, recommendations, financial aid, etc.

November

- ❑ Be sure that you have requested your ACT® and SAT® scores be sent to your colleges of choice.

- ❑ Complete and submit all applications. Print or photocopy an extra copy for your records.

December

- ❑ Take any necessary tests: ACT®, SAT®, SAT Subject Tests™, or the TOEFL®.

- ❑ Meet with your counselor to verify that all is in order and that transcripts were sent to colleges.

February

- ❑ Submit your FAFSA® either online or via U.S. mail.

- ❑ Be sure your midyear report has gone out to the colleges to which you've applied.

- ❑ Let colleges know of any new honors or accomplishments that were not in your original application.

March

- ❑ Register for any Advanced Placement® (AP®) tests you might take.

- ❑ Be sure you have received a FAFSA® acknowledgment.

April

- ❑ Review the acceptances and financial aid offers you receive.

- ❑ Go back to visit one or two of your top-choice colleges.

- ❑ Notify your college of choice that you have accepted its offer (and send in a deposit by May 1).

- ❑ Notify the colleges you have chosen not to attend of your decision.

May

- ❑ Take AP® tests.

- ❑ Graduate! Congratulations and best of luck.

Choosing Your Top Ten Colleges

By using all the information in the various sections of this guide, you will find colleges worthy of the most important top-ten list on the planet—yours.

The first thing you will need to do is decide what type of institution of higher learning you want to attend. Each of the thousands of four-year colleges and universities in the United States is as unique as the people applying to it. Although listening to the voices and media hype around you can make it sound as though there are only a few elite schools worth attending, this simply is not true. By considering some of the following criteria, you will soon find that the large pool of interesting colleges can be narrowed down to a more reasonable number.

SIZE AND CATEGORY

Schools come in all shapes and sizes, from tiny rural colleges of 400 students to massive state university systems serving 100,000 students or more. If you are coming from a small high school, a college with 3,500 students may seem large to you. If you are currently attending a high school with 3,000 students, selecting a college of a similar size may not feel like a new enough experience. Some students coming from very large impersonal high schools are looking for a place where they will be recognized from the beginning and offered a more personal approach. If you don't have a clue about what size might feel right to you, try visiting a couple of nearby colleges of varying sizes. You do not have to be seriously interested in them; just feel what impact the number of students on campus has on you.

Large Universities

Large universities offer a wide range of educational, athletic, and social experiences. Universities offer a full scope of undergraduate majors and award master's and doctoral degrees as well. Universities are usually composed of several smaller colleges. Depending on your interest in a major field or area of study, you would likely apply to a specific college within the university. Each college has the flexibility to set its own standards for admission, which may differ from the overall average of the university. The colleges within a university system also set their own course requirements for earning a degree.

Universities may be public or private. Some large private universities, such as Harvard, Yale, Princeton, University of Pennsylvania, New York University, Northwestern, and Stanford, are well-known for their high entrance standards, the excellence of their education, and the success rates of their graduates. These institutions place a great deal of emphasis on research and compete aggressively for grants from the federal government to fund these projects. Large public universities,

such as the State University of New York (SUNY) System, University of Michigan, University of Texas, University of Illinois, University of Washington, and University of North Carolina, also support excellent educational programs, compete for and win research funding, and have successful graduates. Public universities usually offer substantially lower tuition rates to in-state students, although their tuition rates for out-of-state residents are often comparable to those of private institutions.

At many large universities, sports play a major role on campus. Athletics can dominate the calendar and set the tone year-round at some schools. Alumni travel from far and wide to attend their alma mater's football or basketball games, and the campus—and frequently the entire town—grinds to a halt when there is a home game. Athletes are heroes and dominate campus social life.

What are some other features of life on a university campus? Every kind of club imaginable, from literature to bioengineering and chorus to politics, can be found on most college campuses. You will be able to play the intramural version of almost every sport in which the university fields interscholastic teams and join fraternities, sororities, and groups dedicated to social action. You can become a member of a band, an orchestra, or perhaps a chamber music group or work on the newspaper, the literary magazine, or the website. The list can go on and on. You may want to try out a new interest or two or pursue what you have always been interested in and make like-minded friends along the way.

Take a look at the size of the classrooms in the larger universities and envision yourself sitting in that atmosphere. Would this offer a learning environment that would benefit you?

Liberal Arts Colleges

If you have considered large universities and come to the conclusion that all that action could be a distraction, a small liberal arts college might be right for you. Ideally tucked away on a picture-perfect campus, a liberal arts college generally has fewer than 5,000 students. The mission of most liberal arts schools is learning for the sake of learning, with a strong emphasis on creating lifelong learners who will be able to apply their education to any number of careers. This contrasts with objectives of the profession-based preparation of specialized colleges.

Liberal arts colleges cannot offer the breadth of courses provided by the large universities. As a result, liberal arts colleges try to create a niche for themselves. For instance, a college may place its emphasis on its humanities departments, whose professors are all well-known published authors and international presenters in their areas of expertise. A college may highlight its science departments by providing state-of-the-art-facilities where undergraduates conduct research side by side with top-notch professors and co-publish their findings in the most prestigious scientific journals in the country. The personal approach is very important at liberal arts colleges. Whether in advisement, course selection, athletic programs tailored to students' interests, or dinner with the department head at her home, liberal arts colleges emphasize that they get to know their students.

If they are so perfect, why doesn't everyone choose a liberal arts college? Well, the small size limits options. Fewer people may mean less diversity. The fact that many of these colleges encourage a study-abroad option (a student elects to spend a semester or a year studying in another country) reduces the number of students on campus even further. Some liberal arts colleges have a certain reputation that does not appeal to some students. You should ask yourself questions about the campus life that most appeals to you. Will you fit in with the campus culture? Will the small size mean that you go through your social options quickly? Check out the activities listed on the Student Center bulletin board. Does the student body look diverse enough for you? Will what is happening keep you busy and interested? Do the students have input into decision making? Do they create the social climate of the school?

Small Universities

Smaller universities often combine stringent admissions policies, handpicked faculty members, and attractive scholarship packages. These institutions generally have undergraduate enrollments of about 4,000 students. Some are more famous for their graduate and professional schools but have also established strong undergraduate colleges. Smaller universities balance the great majors options of large universities with a smaller campus community. They offer choices but not to the same extent as large universities. On the other hand, by limiting admissions and enrollment, they manage to cultivate some of the characteristics of a liberal arts college. Like a liberal arts college, a small university may emphasize a particular program and go out of its way to draw strong candidates in a specific area, such as premed, to its campus. Universities such as The Johns Hopkins University, University of Notre Dame, Vanderbilt University, Washington University in St. Louis, and Wesleyan University in Connecticut are a few examples of small universities.

Technical or Specialized Colleges

Another alternative to the liberal arts college or large university is the technical or otherwise specialized college. Its goal is to offer a specialized and saturated experience in a particular field of study. Such an institution might limit its course offerings to engineering and science, the performing or fine arts, or business. Schools such as California Institute of Technology, Carnegie Mellon University, Massachusetts Institute of Technology, and Rensselaer Polytechnic Institute concentrate on attracting the finest math and science students in the country. At other schools, like Bentley College in Massachusetts or Bryant College in Rhode Island, students eat, sleep, and breathe business. These institutions are purists at heart and strong believers in the necessity of focused, specialized study to produce excellence in their graduates' achievements. If you are certain about your chosen path in life and want to immerse yourself in subjects such as math, music, or business, you will fit right in.

Religious Colleges

Many private colleges have religious origins, and many of these have become secular institutions with virtually no trace of their religious roots. Others remain dedicated to a religious way of education. What sets religious colleges apart is the way they combine faith, learning, and student life. Faculty members and administrators are hired with faith as a criterion as much as their academic credentials.

Single-Gender Colleges

There are strong arguments that being able to pursue one's education without the distraction, competition, and stress caused by the presence of the opposite sex helps a student evolve a stronger sense of her or his self-worth; achieve more academically; have a more fulfilling, less pressured social schedule; and achieve more later in life. For various historic, social, and psychological reasons, there are many more all-women than all-men colleges. A strict single-sex environment is rare. Even though the undergraduate day college adheres to an all-female or all-male admissions policy, coeducational evening classes or graduate programs and coordinate facilities and classes shared with nearby coed or opposite-sex institutions can result in a good number of students of the opposite sex being found on campus. If you want to concentrate on your studies and hone your leadership qualities, a single-gender school is an option.

LOCATION

Location and distance from home are two other important considerations. If you have always lived in the suburbs, choosing an urban campus can be an adventure, but after a week of the urban experience, will you long for a grassy campus and open space? On the other hand, if you choose a college in a rural area, will you run screaming into the Student Center some night looking for noise, lights, and people? The location—urban, rural, or suburban—can directly affect how easy or how difficult adjusting to college life will be for you.

Don't forget to factor in distance from home. Everyone going off to college wants to think he or she won't be homesick, but sometimes it's nice to get a home-cooked meal or to do the laundry in a place that does not require quarters. Even your kid sister may seem like less of a nuisance after a couple of months away.

Here are some questions you might ask yourself as you go through the selection process: In what part of the country do I want to be? How far away from home do I want to be? What is the cost of returning home? Do I need to be close to a city? How close? How large of a city? Would city life distract me? Would I concentrate better in a setting that is more rural or more suburban?

ENTRANCE DIFFICULTY

Many students will look at a college's entrance difficulty as an indicator of whether or not they will be admitted. For instance, if you have an excellent academic record, you might wish to primarily consider those colleges that are highly competitive.

Although entrance difficulty does not translate directly to quality of education, it indicates which colleges are attracting large numbers of high-achieving students. A high-achieving student body usually translates into prestige for the college and its graduates. Prestige has some advantages but should definitely be viewed as a secondary factor that might tip the scales when all the other important factors are equal. Never base your decision on prestige alone!

The other principle to keep in mind when considering this factor is to not sell yourself short. If everything else tells you that a college might be right for you, but your numbers just miss that college's average range, apply there anyway. Your numbers—grades and test scores—are undeniably important in the admissions decision, but there are other considerations. First, lower grades in honors or AP® courses will impress colleges more than top grades in regular-track courses because they demonstrate that you are the kind of student willing to accept challenges. Second, admissions directors are looking for different qualities in students that can be combined to create a multifaceted class. For example, if you did poorly in your freshman and sophomore years but made a great improvement in your grades in later years, this usually will impress a college. If you are likely to contribute to your class because of your special personal qualities, a strong sense of commitment and purpose, unusual and valuable experiences, or special interests and talents, these factors can outweigh numbers that are weaker than average. Nevertheless, be practical. Overreach yourself in a few applications, but put the bulk of your effort into gaining admission to colleges where you have a realistic chance for admission.

THE PRICE OF AN EDUCATION

The price tag for higher education continues to rise, and it has become an increasingly important factor for people. While it is necessary to consider your family's resources when choosing a list of colleges to which you might apply, never eliminate a college solely because of cost. There are many ways to pay for college, including loans, and a college education will never depreciate in value, unlike other purchases. It is an investment in yourself and will pay back the expense many times over in your lifetime.

Surviving Standardized Tests

WHAT ARE STANDARDIZED TESTS?

Colleges and universities in the United States use tests to help evaluate applicants' readiness for admission or to place them in appropriate courses. The tests that are most frequently used by colleges are the ACT® Exam and the College Board's SAT® Exam. In addition, the Educational Testing Service (ETS) offers the TOEFL® test, which evaluates the English-language proficiency of nonnative speakers. The tests are offered at designated testing centers located at high schools and colleges throughout the United States and U.S. territories and at testing centers in various countries throughout the world.

Upon request, special accommodations for students with documented visual, hearing, physical, or learning disabilities are available. Examples of special accommodations include tests in Braille or large print and such aids as a reader, recorder, magnifying glass, or sign language interpreter. Additional testing time may be allowed in some instances. Contact the appropriate testing program or your guidance counselor for details on how to request special accommodations.

THE ACT® EXAM

The ACT® exam is a standardized college entrance examination that measures knowledge and skills in English, mathematics, reading comprehension, and science reasoning and the application of these skills to future academic tasks. The ACT® exam consists of four multiple-choice tests. The four tests and the content covered in each is as follows:

English Test (75 questions; 45 minutes)
- Usage and mechanics
- Rhetorical skills

Mathematics Test (60 questions; 60 minutes)
- Pre-algebra
- Elementary algebra
- Intermediate algebra
- Coordinate geometry
- Plane geometry
- Trigonometry

Reading Test (40 questions; 35 minutes)
- Literary narrative/Prose fiction
- Humanities
- Social studies
- Natural sciences

Science (40 questions; 35 minutes)
- Data representation
- Research summaries
- Conflicting viewpoints

Each section is scored from 1 to 36 and is scaled for slight variations in difficulty. Students are not penalized for incorrect responses. The composite score is the average of the four scaled scores. The ACT® Plus Writing includes the four multiple-choice tests and the 40-minute Writing Test, which measures writing skills emphasized in high school English classes and in entry-level college composition courses and does not count toward your final score.

To prepare for the ACT® Exam, ask your guidance counselor for a free guidebook, *Preparing for the ACT® Test*, or download it at **http://www.act.org/content/dam/act/unsecured/documents/Preparing-for-the-ACT.pdf**. Besides providing general test-preparation information and additional test-taking strategies, this guidebook provides a full-length practice exam including the Writing Test, instructions for taking the Writing Test, test-preparation strategies, and what to expect on test day.

DON'T FORGET TO . . .

- ❑ Take the SAT® Exam or ACT® Exam before application deadlines.
- ❑ Note that test registration deadlines precede test dates by about six weeks.
- ❑ Register to take the TOEFL® test if English is not your native language and you are planning on studying at a North American college.
- ❑ Contact the College Board or ACT, Inc., in advance if you need special accommodations when taking tests.

THE SAT® EXAM

The SAT® has these sections: Evidence-Based Reading and Writing, Math, and the SAT® Essay. It is based on 1600 points—the top scores for the Math section and the Evidence-Based Reading and Writing section will be 800, and the SAT® Essay score is reported separately.

Reading Test (52 questions; 65 minutes)
Passages in U.S. and world literature, history/social studies, and science are used to test the following skills:
- Command of Evidence
- Words in Context
- Analysis in History/Social Studies and in Science

Writing and Language Test (44 questions; 35 minutes)
Passages in careers, history/social studies, humanities, and science are used to test the following skills:
- Command of Evidence
- Words in Context
- Analysis in History/Social Studies and in Science
- Expression of ideas
- Standard English conventions

Math Test (58 questions; 80 minutes)

This test is divided into two sections: the no-calculator section (25 minutes) and the calculator section (55 minutes).

- Content includes algebra, problem solving and data analysis, advanced math, area and volume calculations, trigonometric functions, and lines, triangles, and circles using theorems.

SAT® Essay (Optional)

* 50 minutes

- Argument passage written for a general audience
- Analysis of argument in passage using text evidence
- Score: 3–12 (Reading: 1–4 scale, Analysis: 1–4 scale, Writing: 1–4 scale)

According to the College Board's website, the following are the "Key Content Features" of the SAT® exam:

- **Relevant Words in Context:** Students need to interpret the meaning of words based on the context of the passage in which they appear. The focus is on "relevant" words—not obscure ones.

- **Command of Evidence:** In addition to demonstrating writing skills, students need to show that they're able to interpret, synthesize, and use evidence found in a wide range of sources.

- **Essay Analyzing a Source:** Students read a passage and explain how the author builds an argument and supports their claims with actual data from the passage.

- **Math Focused on Three Key Areas:** Problem Solving and Data Analysis (using ratios, percentages, and proportional reasoning to solve problems in science, social science, and career contexts), the Heart of Algebra (mastery of linear equations and systems), and Passport to Advanced Math (more complex equations and the manipulation they require).

- **Problems Grounded in Real-World Contexts:** All of the questions are grounded in the real world, directly related to work performed in college.

- **Analysis in Science and in Social Studies:** Students need to apply reading, writing, language, and math skills to answer questions in contexts of science, history, and social studies.

- **Founding Documents and Great Global Conversation:** Students will find an excerpt from one of the Founding Documents—such as the Declaration of Independence, the Constitution, and the Bill of Rights—or a text from the "Great Global Conversation" about freedom, justice, and human dignity.

- **No Penalty for Wrong Answers:** Students earn points for the questions they answer correctly, and like the ACT® optional writing test, the optional SAT® Essay section does not count toward your final score.

Check out the College Board's website at **https://collegereadiness.collegeboard.org/sat-subject-tests/about/at-a-glance** for the most up-to-date information.

Top 10 Ways NOT to Take the Test

1. Cramming the night before the test.
2. Not becoming familiar with the directions before you take the test.
3. Not becoming familiar with the format of the test before you take it.
4. Not knowing how the test is graded.
5. Spending too much time on any one question.
6. Second-guessing yourself.
7. Not checking spelling, grammar, and sentence structure in essays.
8. Writing a one-paragraph essay.
9. Forgetting to take a deep breath—
10. and finally—Don't lose it!

SAT SUBJECT TESTS™

SAT Subject Tests™ are required by some institutions for admission and/or placement in freshman-level courses. Each Subject Test measures one's knowledge of a specific subject and the ability to apply that knowledge. Students should check with each institution for its specific requirements. In general, students are required to take three Subject Tests (one English, one mathematics, and one of their choice).

Subject Tests are given in the following areas: biology, chemistry, Chinese, French, German, Italian, Japanese, Korean, Latin, literature, mathematics, modern Hebrew, physics, Spanish, U.S. history, and world history. These tests are 1 hour long and are primarily multiple-choice tests. Three Subject Tests may be taken on one test date.

On the subject tests, students gain a point for each correct answer and lose a fraction of a point for each incorrect answer. The raw scores are then converted to scaled scores that range from 200 to 800 For more details about SAT Subject Tests™, visit **https://collegereadiness.collegeboard.org/sat-subject-tests/about/at-a-glance**.

THE TOEFL (IBT)® INTERNET-BASED TEST

The Test of English as a Foreign Language Internet-Based Test (TOEFL iBT®) is designed to help assess a student's grasp of English if it is not the student's first language. Performance on the TOEFL® test may help interpret scores on the critical reading sections of the SAT® exam. The test consists of four integrated sections: speaking, listening, reading, and writing. The TOEFL iBT® emphasizes integrated skills. The paper-based versions of the TOEFL® test will continue to be administered in certain countries where the internet-based version has not yet been introduced. For further information, visit **www.ets.org/toefl**.

WHAT OTHER TESTS SHOULD I KNOW ABOUT?

The AP® Program

The AP® program allows high school students to try college-level work and build valuable skills and study habits in the process. Subject matter is explored in more depth in AP courses than in other high school classes. A qualifying score on an AP test—which varies from school to school—can earn you college credit or advanced placement. Getting qualifying grades on enough exams can even earn you a full year's credit and sophomore standing at more than 1,500 higher-education institutions. There are more than thirty AP courses across multiple subject areas, including art history, biology, and computer science. Speak to your guidance counselor for information about your school's offerings. For more information about the AP® program, **visit www.apstudent.college board.org/home**.

College-Level Examination Program (CLEP®)

The CLEP® exam enables students to earn college credit for what they already know, whether it was learned in school, through independent study, or through other experiences outside of the classroom. More than 2,900 colleges and universities now award credit for qualifying scores on one or more of the 33 CLEP exams. The exams, which are 90 minutes in length and are primarily multiple choice, are administered at participating colleges and universities. For more information, check out the website at **www.clep.college board.org**.

WHAT CAN I DO TO PREPARE FOR THESE TESTS?

Know what to expect. Get familiar with how the tests are structured, how much time is allowed, and the directions for each type of question. Get plenty of rest the night before the test and eat breakfast that morning.

There are a variety of products, from books to software to videos, available to help you prepare for most standardized tests. Find the learning style that suits you best. As for which products to buy, there are two major categories—those created by the test-makers and those created by private companies. The best approach is to talk to someone who has been through the process and find out which product or products he or she recommends.

Some students report significant increases in scores after participating in coaching programs. Longer-term programs (40 hours) seem to raise scores more than short-term programs (20 hours), but beyond 40 hours, score gains are minor. Math scores appear to benefit more from coaching than critical reading scores.

Resources

There is a variety of ways to prepare for standardized tests—find a method that fits your schedule and your budget—but you should definitely prepare. Far too many students walk into these tests cold, either because they find standardized tests frightening or annoying or they just haven't found the time to study. The key is that these exams are standardized. That means these tests are largely the same from administration to administration; they always test the same concepts. They have to, or else you couldn't compare the scores of people who took the tests on different dates. The numbers or words may change, but the underlying content doesn't.

So how do you prepare? At the very least, you should review relevant material, such as math formulas and commonly used vocabulary words, and know the directions for each question type or test section. You should take at least one practice test and review your mistakes so you don't make them again on the test day. Beyond that, you know best how much preparation you need. You'll also find lots of material in libraries or bookstores to help you: books and software from the test-makers and from other publishers (including Peterson's) or live courses that range from national test-preparation companies to teachers at your high school who offer classes.

Planning is Essential on the Road to College

Sarah E. Gibbs, Director of Admissions
Grove City College

The road to college is much like an expedition. It can appear overwhelming, exciting, and at times too far away to be tangible. However, much like planning a trip out of town or across the globe, there is preparation involved, and it is always best to start that planning early. First, you must figure out where you want to go, then how you want to get there, and finally, what you want to do once you arrive. Each decision will require a different route—a route that may or may not look the same as that of your friends.

The same is true when considering college planning. If you start early—making short-term and long-term goals—it will help you determine your next steps. For instance, if you start your freshman year determining you want to graduate with a certain GPA, that decision will dictate your next steps, like studying, choosing to take harder curriculum, and prioritizing your involvement in activities.

Once you establish your short-term and long-term goals, you need to make wise decisions about those goals. For instance, if you do not do well in a certain class, don't make a rash decision to withdraw from that subject area. You may want to continue in that subject knowing that you may need to seek out help or tutors to help you achieve your goal.

In addition to thinking through your academic goals, you must also consider your personal interests and activities. Your interests may determine the type of college you would like to attend. Decide early on what your passion(s) are, and invest your time wisely in those pursuits. If you know those activities are ones you want to pursue in college, then visit college campuses that fulfill your desire to march in the band, compete in a varsity or intramural sport, or participate in a service organization.

Ask yourself the question that most students do not: Am I ready for college? If the answer is no, then ask yourself what you need to do to be ready, and work towards that goal.

When looking at applicants, most private colleges will look holistically at the student, taking into consideration his or her commitment, dedication, and character. These attributes, along with academic performance and specific major pursuit, indicate whether the student may succeed at a campus. Also, make sure you participate in any interview process through an admissions office. Interviewing with an Admission Counselor allows him/her to get to know you and become your advocate.

Ultimately, the sooner you start planning, the better prepared you will be for the journey you are about to take. Not only will you be prepared for the college planning process, you will be well equipped for attending college and achieving your goals and dreams for a successful future.

Sarah E. Gibbs has been serving families in higher education for several decades. She is currently the Director of Admissions at Grove City College in Grove City, Pennsylvania.

The Whys and Whats of College Visits

Dawn B. Sova, Ph.D.

The campus visit should not be a passive activity for you and your parents. Take the initiative and gather information beyond that provided in the official tour. You will see many important indicators during your visit that will tell you more about the true character of a college and its students than the tour guide will reveal. Know what to look for and how to assess the importance of such indicators.

WHAT SHOULD YOU ASK AND WHAT SHOULD YOU LOOK FOR?

Your first stop on a campus visit is the visitor center or admissions office, where you will probably have to wait to meet with a counselor. Colleges usually plan to greet visitors later than the appointed time in order to give them the opportunity to review some of the campus information that is liberally scattered throughout the visitor waiting room. Take advantage of the time to become even more familiar with the college by arriving 15 to 30 minutes before your appointment to observe the behavior of staff members and to browse through the yearbooks and student newspapers that will be available.

If you prepare in advance, you will have already reviewed the college catalog and map of the campus. These materials familiarize you with the academic offerings and the physical layout of the campus, but the true character of the college and its students emerges in other ways.

Begin your investigation with the visitor center staff members. As a student's first official contact with the college, they should make every effort to welcome prospective students and project a friendly image.

- How do they treat you and other prospective students who are waiting? Are they friendly and willing to speak with you, or do they try their hardest to avoid eye contact and conversation?

- Are they friendly with each other and with students who enter the office, or are they curt and unwilling to help?

- Does the waiting room have a friendly feeling or is it cold and sterile?

If the visitor center staff members seem indifferent to prospective students, there is little reason to believe that they will be warm and welcoming to current students. View such behavior as a warning to watch very carefully the interaction of others with you during the tour. An indifferent or unfriendly reception in the admissions office may be simply the first of many signs that attending this college will not be a pleasant experience.

Look through several yearbooks and see the types of activities that are actually photographed, as opposed to the activities that colleges promise in their promotional literature. Some questions are impossible to answer if the college is very large, but for small and moderately sized colleges the yearbook is a good indicator of campus activity.

- Has the number of clubs and organizations increased or decreased in the past five years?

- Do the same students appear repeatedly in activities?

- Do sororities and fraternities dominate campus activities?

- Are participants limited to one sex or one ethnic group, or is there diversity?

- Are all activities limited to the campus, or are students involved in activities in the community?

Use what you observe in the yearbooks as a means of forming a more complete understanding of the college, but don't base your entire impression on just one facet. If time permits, look through several copies of the school newspaper, which should reflect the major concerns and interests of the students. The paper is also a good way to learn about the campus social life.

- Does the paper contain a mix of national and local news?

- What products or services are advertised?

- How assertive are the editorials?

- With what topics are the columnists concerned?

- Are movies and concerts that meet your tastes advertised or reviewed?

- What types of ads appear in the classified section?

The newspaper should be a public forum for students, and, as such, should reflect the character of the campus and of the student body. A paper that deals only with seemingly safe and well-edited topics on the editorial page and in regular feature columns might indicate administrative censorship. A lack of ads for restaurants might indicate either a lack of good places to eat or that area restaurants do not welcome student business. A limited mention of movies, concerts, or other entertainment might reveal a severely limited campus social life. Even if ads and reviews are included, you should still balance how such activities reflect your tastes.

You will have only a limited amount of time to ask questions during your initial meeting with the admissions counselor, for very few schools include a formal interview in the initial campus visit or tour. Instead, this brief meeting is often just a nicety that allows the admissions office to begin a file for the student and to record some initial impressions. Save your questions for the tour guide and for students on campus you meet along the way.

HOW CAN YOU ASSESS THE TRUE CHARACTER OF A COLLEGE AND ITS STUDENTS?

Colleges do not train their tour guides to deceive prospective students, but they do caution guides to avoid unflattering topics and campus sites. Does this mean that you will see only a sugarcoated version of life on a particular college campus? Not at all, especially not if you are observant.

Most organized campus visits include such campus facilities as dormitories, dining halls, libraries, student activity and recreation centers, and the health and student services centers. Some may only be pointed out, while you will walk through others. Either way, you will find that many signs of the true character of the college emerge if you keep your eyes open.

Bulletin boards in dormitories and student centers contain a wealth of information about campus activities, student concerns, and campus groups. Read the posters, notices, and messages to learn what *really* interests students. Unlike ads in the school newspaper, posters put up by students advertise both on-and off-campus events, so they will give you an idea of what is also available in the surrounding community.

Review the notices, which may cover either campus-wide events or events that concern only small groups of students. The catalog may not mention a performance group, but an individual dormitory with its own small theater may offer regular productions. Poetry readings, jam sessions, writers' groups, and other activities may be announced and show diversity of student interests.

Even the brief bulletin board messages offering objects for sale and noting objects that people want to purchase reveal a lot about a campus. Are most of the items computer-related? Or do the messages specify audio equipment or musical instruments? Are offers to trade goods or services posted? Don't ignore the "ride wanted" messages. Students who want to share rides home during a break may specify widely diverse geographical locations. If so, then you know that the student body is not limited to only the immediate area or one locale. Other messages can also enhance your knowledge of the true character of the campus and its students.

As you walk through various buildings, examine their condition carefully.

- Is the paint peeling, and do the exteriors look worn?

- Are the exteriors and interiors of the building clean?

- Is the equipment in the classrooms up-to-date or outdated?

Pay particular attention to the residence halls, especially to factors that might affect your safety. Observe the appearance of the structure and ask about the security measures in and around the residence halls.

- Are the residence halls noisy or quiet?

- Do they seem crowded?

- How good is the lighting around each residence hall?

- Are the residence halls spread throughout the campus or are they clustered in one main area?

- Who has access to the residence halls in addition to students?

- How secure are the means by which students enter and leave the residence hall?

While you are on the subject of dormitory safety, you should also ask about campus safety. Don't expect that the guide will rattle off a list of crimes that have been committed in the past year. To obtain that information, access the recent year of issues of *The Chronicle of Higher Education* and locate its yearly report on campus crime. Also ask the guide about safety measures that the campus police take and those that students have initiated.

- Can students request escorts to their residences late at night?

- Do campus shuttle buses run at frequent intervals all night?

- Are "blue-light" telephones liberally placed throughout the campus for students to use to call for help?

- Do the campus police patrol the campus regularly?

If the guide does not answer your questions satisfactorily, wait until after the tour to contact the campus police or traffic office for answers.

Campus tours usually just point out the health services center without taking the time to walk through. Even if you don't see the inside of the building, you should take a close look at the location of the health services center and ask the guide questions about services.

- How far is the health center from the residence halls?

- Is a doctor always on call?

- Does the campus transport sick students from their dormitories or must they walk?

- What are the operating hours of the health center?

- Does the health center refer students to a nearby hospital?

If the guide can't answer your questions, visit the health center later and ask someone there.

Most campus tours take pride in showing students their activities centers, which may contain snack bars, game rooms, workout facilities, and other means of entertainment. Should you scrutinize this building as carefully as the rest? Of course. Outdated and poorly maintained activity equipment contributes to your total impression of the college. You should also ask about the hours, availability, and cost (no, the activities are usually not free) of using the bowling alleys, pool tables, air hockey tables, and other amenities.

As you walk through campus with the tour, also look carefully at the appearance of the students who pass. The way in which both men and women groom themselves, the way they dress, and even their physical bearing communicate a lot more than any guidebook can. If everyone seems to conform to the same look, you might feel that you would be uncomfortable at the college, however nonconformist that look might be. On the other hand, you might not feel comfortable on a campus that stresses diversity of dress and behavior, and your observations now can save you discomfort later.

- Does every student seem to wear a sorority or fraternity t-shirt or jacket?
- Is everyone of your sex sporting the latest fad haircut?
- Do all of the men or the women seem to be wearing expensive name-brand clothes?
- Do most of the students seem to be working hard to look outrageous with regards to clothing, hair color, and body art?
- Would you feel uncomfortable in a room full of these students?

Is appearance important to you? If it is, then you should consider very seriously if you answer *yes* to any of the questions above. You don't have to be the same as everyone else on campus, but standing out too much may make you unhappy.

As you observe the physical appearance of the students, also listen to their conversations as you pass them. What are they talking about? How are they speaking? Are their voices and accents all the same, or do you hear diversity in their speech? Are you offended by their language? Think how you will feel if surrounded by the same speech habits and patterns for four years.

WHERE SHOULD YOU VISIT ON YOUR OWN?

Your campus visit is not over when the tour ends because you will probably have many questions yet to be answered and many places to still be seen. Where you go depends upon the extent to which the organized tour covers the campus. Your tour should take you to view residential halls, health and student services centers, the gymnasium or field house, dining halls, the library, and recreational centers. If any of the facilities on this list have been omitted, visit them on your own and ask questions of the students and staff members you meet. In addition, you should step off campus and gain an impression of the surrounding community. You will probably become bored with life on campus and spend at least some time off campus. Make certain that you know what the surrounding area is like.

The campus tour leaves little time to ask impromptu questions of current students, but you can do so after the tour. Eat lunch in one of the dining halls. Most will allow visitors to pay cash to experience a typical student meal. Food may not be important to you now while you are living at home and can

simply take anything you want from the refrigerator at any time, but it will be when you are away at college with only a meal ticket to feed you.

- How clean is the dining hall? Consider serving tables, floors, and seating.
- What is the quality of the food?
- How big are the portions?
- How much variety do students have at each meal?
- How healthy are the food choices?

While you are eating, try to strike up a conversation with students and tell them that you are considering attending their college. Their reactions and advice can be eye-opening. Ask them questions about the academic atmosphere and the professors.

- Are the classes large or small?
- Do the majority of the professors only lecture or are tutorials and seminars common?
- Is the emphasis of the faculty career-oriented or abstract?
- Are the teaching methods innovative and stimulating or boring and dull?
- Is the academic atmosphere pressured, lax, or somewhere in between?
- Which are the strong majors? The weak majors?
- Is the emphasis on grades or social life or a mix of both at the college?
- How hard do students have to work to receive high grades?

Current students can also give you the inside line on the true nature of the college social life. You may gain some idea through looking in the yearbook, in the newspaper, and on the bulletin boards, but students will reveal the true highs and lows of campus life. Ask them about drug use, partying, dating, drinking, and anything else that may affect your life as a student.

- Which are the most popular club activities?
- What do students do on weekends? Do most go home?
- How frequently do concerts occur on campus? Who has recently performed?
- How can you become involved in specific activities (name them)?
- How strictly are campus rules enforced and how severe are penalties?
- What counseling services are available?
- Are academic tutoring services available?
- Do they feel that the faculty really cares about students, especially freshmen?

You will receive the most valuable information from current students, but you will only be able to speak with them after the tour is over. And you might have to risk rejection as you try to initiate conversations with students who might not want to reveal how they feel about the campus. Still, the value of this information is worth the chance.

If you have the time, you should also visit the library to see just how accessible research materials are and to observe the physical layout. The catalog usually specifies the days and hours of operation, as well as the number of volumes contained in the library and the number of periodicals to which it subscribes. A library also requires accessibility, good lighting, an adequate number of study carrels, and lounge areas for students. Many colleges have created 24-hour study lounges for students who find the residence halls too noisy for studying, although most colleges claim that they designate areas of the residences as "quiet study" areas. You may not be interested in any of this information, but when you are a student you will have to make frequent use of the campus library so you should know what is available. You should at least ask how extensive their holdings are in your proposed major area. If they have virtually nothing, you will have to spend a lot of time ordering items via interlibrary loan or making copies, which can become expensive. The ready answer of students that they will obtain their information from the internet is unpleasantly countered by professors who demand journal articles with documentation.

Make a point of at least driving through the community surrounding the college because you will be spending time there shopping, dining, working in a part-time job, or attending events. Even the largest and best-stocked campus will not meet all of your social and personal needs. If you can spare the time, stop in several stores to see if they welcome college students.

- Is the surrounding community suburban, urban, or rural?

- Does the community offer stores of interest, such as bookstores, craft shops, and boutiques?

- Do the businesses employ college students?

- Does the community have a movie or stage theater?

- Are there several types of interesting restaurants?

- Do there seem to be any clubs that court a college clientele?

- Is the center of activity easy to walk to, or do you need other transportation?

You might feel that a day is not enough to answer all of your questions, but even answering some questions will provide you with a stronger basis for choosing a college. Many students visit a college campus several times before making their decision. Keep in mind that for the rest of your life you will be associated with the college that you attend. You will spend four years of your life at this college. The effort of spending several days to obtain the information to make your decision is worthwhile.

Dawn B. Sova, Ph.D., is a former newspaper reporter and columnist, as well as the author of 22 books and numerous magazine articles. She teaches creative and research writing, as well as scientific and technical writing, newswriting, and journalism.

Honors Programs and Colleges: Smart Choices for an Undergraduate Education

Dr. Joan Digby

In general, students and their parents are guided toward a narrow selection of colleges and universities based on reputation, conversations with friends, or promotional material. Few people think to approach the college search focused on honors opportunities. As a result, students with extraordinary talents and interests miss out on a rich variety of untapped financial resources and exciting college experiences.

The smarter approach is to seek out a distinctive education that caters to students' great diversity of intellectual and creative strengths. If you are a strong student filled with ideas, longing for creative expression and ready to take on career-shaping challenges, then an honors education is just for you. Honors programs and colleges offer some of the finest undergraduate degrees available at U.S. colleges and do it with students in mind. The essence of honors is personal attention, top faculty, enlightening seminars, illuminating study-travel experiences, research options, and career-building internships—all designed to enhance a classic education and prepare you for life achievements. And here is an eye-opening bonus: Honors programs and colleges may reward your past academic performance by giving you scholarships that will help you pay for your higher education!

Take your choice of institutions: community college, state or private, two- or four-year, college or large research university. There are honors opportunities in each. What they share is an unqualified commitment to academic excellence. Honors education teaches students to think and write clearly, be excited by ideas, and become independent, creative, self-confident learners. It prepares exceptional students for professional choices in every imaginable sphere of life: arts and sciences, engineering, business, health, education, medicine, theater, music, film, journalism, media, law, politics—invent your own professional goal and honors will guide you to it! Whichever honors program or college you choose, you can be sure to enjoy an extraordinarily fulfilling undergraduate education.

WHO ARE HONORS STUDENTS?

Who are you? Perhaps a high school junior filling out your first college application, a community college student seeking to transfer to a four-year college, or possibly a four-year college student doing better than you had expected. You might

be an international student, a varsity athlete, captain of the debate team, or second violin in the orchestra. Whether you are the first person in your family to attend college or an adult with a grown family seeking a new career, honors might well be right for you. Honors programs admit students with every imaginable background and educational goal.

How does honors satisfy students and give them something special? Read what students in some honors programs and colleges say. Although they refer to particular honors colleges or programs, their experiences are typical of what students find exciting about honors education on hundreds of campuses around the country.

"Being an honors program student has been a life-changing experience for me. I have gained tremendously in knowledge, experience, and self-esteem. I have learned so much more in the program than any textbook could teach about the value of encouraging support and positive thinking."

—*Cheri, Mount Wachusett Community College*

"I've been in a healing ceremony in Ecuador and have performed music on stage. I've guided my peers and Navajo children, hiked the Grand Canyon, and so much more. Sometimes, experience speaks for itself; always, it creates paths, opens eyes, and helps us find our places. Thanks to my honors program, I've experienced these wonders and accomplishments. Now I know that there are no greater lessons than how to learn and love discovery."

—*April, University of North Florida*

"The Honors College has been my home away from home. In the midst of a diverse, fairly large university, it has provided me with the intimacy that I needed... My freshman-year living situation on the honors floor... allowed me to find like-minded students early in my college career."

—*Brian, Davidson Honors College, University of Montana*

"I was able to transition from an honors program at a two-year institution into an honors program at a four-year institution without any reservations or tribulations."

—*Rachel, Harrisburg Area Community College*

"Every single professor is in love with what they do and it shows in their research, their amazing teaching, and their interaction with students outside of the classroom. The undergraduate journey can be very difficult at times, but as an Honors College student, you're sure to have plenty of support every step of the way."

—*Walteria, Wilkes Honors College, Florida Atlantic University*

"The class size is perfect, and I've been able to make some of my closest relationships with students and teachers through the program. The majority of honors faculty I have encountered have been overwhelmingly helpful... and my favorite courses have been honors classes."

—*Ellen, Eastern Illinois University*

"Our professor met us at a local restaurant the last evening of class, and we shared a wonderful dinner. It had such a familiar feel to it because these are students I have known throughout my four years in the program."

—*Betsy, University of La Verne*

"For the last two years, I have investigated new synthetic methods under the direction of a professor emeritus. Through the University Honors College, I am able to pursue this interest in chemistry and other academic endeavors... that have allowed me to develop my academic potential and contribute to the scientific body of knowledge."

—*Justin, University of Pittsburgh*

"The most rewarding part of being a member of the honors program is the joy of doing creative, meaningful projects with faculty I love."

—*Meleia, Hartwick College*

"I would... like to add a word of praise for the way the curriculum is structured. It has deepened and enriched my thinking and helped me develop tools to negotiate the complex world we live in."

—*Monideepa, Southeastern Louisiana University*

"We have a better time... our discussions get rather heated. In a lot of classes, only one or two students will speak up, but in the honors classes, it's a free-for-all."

—*Jonathan, Reinhardt College*

"My internship at a major international bank gave me an in-depth look into the world of investment and accounting. Funded by the Honors College, I was able to study business and culture in Shanghai, China, for a month. These valuable experiences are helping me to develop professionally, academically, and personally."

—*Jenny, Honors College, The College of Staten Island, CUNY*

"The honors thesis was the key factor during the selection process at my future employer.... It helped me to get the job and have an advantage over others. It is a lot of work but, in the end, it is worth it."

—*Olgierd, Lee Honors College, Western Michigan University*

These portraits don't tell the whole story, but they should give you a sense of what it means to be part of an honors program or college. One of the great strengths of honors programs and colleges is that they are nurturing environments that encourage students to be well-rounded and help students make life choices.

WHAT IS AN HONORS PROGRAM?

An honors program is a sequence of courses designed specifically to encourage independent and creative learning. For more than half a century, honors education—given definition by the National Collegiate Honors Council—has been an institution on U.S. campuses. Although honors programs have many different designs, there are typical components. At two-year colleges, the programs often concentrate on special versions of general education courses and may have individual capstone projects that come out of students' special interests. At four-year colleges and universities, honors programs are generally designed for students of almost every major in every college on campus. In growing numbers, they are given additional prominence as honors colleges. Whether a program or a college, honors often includes a general education or "core" component followed by advanced courses (often called colloquia or seminars). Some programs have honors contracts that shape existing courses into honors components to suit the needs of individual students. Many have interdisciplinary or collaborative seminars that bring students of different majors together to discuss a complex topic with faculty members from different disciplines. A good number have final thesis, capstone, or creative projects, which may or may not be in the departmental major. Almost always, honors curriculum is incorporated within whatever number of credits is required of every student for graduation. Honors very rarely requires students to take additional credits. Students who complete an honors program or honors college curriculum frequently receive transcript and diploma notations as well as certificates, medallions, or other citations at graduation ceremonies.

In every case, catering to the student as an individual plays a central role in honors course design. Most honors classes are small (fewer than 20 students); most are discussion-oriented, giving students a chance to present their own interpretations of ideas and even teach a part of the course. Many classes are interdisciplinary, which means they are taught by faculty members from two or more departments, providing different perspectives on a subject. All honors classes help students develop and articulate their own perspectives by cultivating both verbal and written style. They help students mature intellectually, preparing them to engage in their own explorations and research. Some programs even extend the options for self-growth to study abroad and internships in science, government, the arts, or business related to the major. Other programs encourage or require community service as part of the honors experience. In every case, honors is an experiential education that deepens classroom learning and extends far beyond.

Despite their individual differences, all honors programs and honors colleges rely on faculty members who enjoy working with bright, independent students. The ideal honors faculty members are open-minded, encouraging master teachers. They want to see their students achieve at their highest capacity and are glad to spend time with students in discussions and laboratories, on field trips and at conferences, or online in e-mail. They often influence career decisions, are inspiring role models, and remain friends long after they have served as thesis advisers.

WHERE ARE HONORS PROGRAMS AND HONORS COLLEGES LOCATED?

Because honors programs and honors colleges include students from many different departments or colleges, they usually have their own offices and space on campus. Some have their own buildings. Most programs have honors centers or lounges, where students gather together for informal conversations, luncheons, discussions, lectures, and special projects.

Many honors students have cultivated strong personal interests that have nothing to do with classes. They may be multilingual; they may be fine artists or poets, musicians or racing car enthusiasts, mothers or fathers. Some volunteer in hospitals or do landscape gardening to pay for college. Many work in retail stores and in catering. Some are avid sports enthusiasts, while others collect antiques. When they get together in honors lounges, there is always an interesting mixture of ideas!

In the honors center, you will also find the honors director or dean. The honors director often serves as a personal adviser to all of the students in the program. Many programs also have peer counselors and mentors who are upperclass honors students and know the ropes from a student's perspective and experience. Some have specially assigned honors advisers who guide honors students through their degrees, assist in registration, and answer every imaginable question. The honors office area usually is a good place to meet people, ask questions, and solve problems.

In general, honors provides an environment in which students feel free to talk about their passionate interests and ideas knowing that they will find good listeners and, sometimes, even arguers. There is no end to conversations among honors students. Like many students in honors, you may feel a great relief in finding a sympathetic group that respects your intelligence and creativity. In honors, you can be eccentric; you can be yourself! Some lifelong friendships, even marriages, are the result of social relationships developed in honors programs.

ARE YOU READY FOR HONORS?

Admission to honors programs and honors colleges is generally based on a combination of several factors: high school or previous college grades, experience taking AP or IB courses, SAT or ACT scores, personal essay, and extracurricular achievements. To stay in honors, students need to maintain a certain grade point average (GPA) and show progress toward the completion of the specific honors program or college requirements. Since you have probably exceeded admissions standards all along, maintaining your GPA will not be as big a problem as it sounds. Your professors and your honors director are there to help you succeed in the program. Most honors programs have very low attrition rates because students enjoy classes and do well.

Of course, you must be careful about how you budget your time for studying. Honors encourages well-rounded, diversified students, so you should play a sport, work at the radio station, join clubs of interest, or pledge a sorority or fraternity. You might find a job in the student center or library that will help you pay for your car expenses and that also is reasonable. But remember, each activity takes time, and you must strike the balance that leaves you enough time to do your homework, write papers, prepare for seminar discussions, do your research, and do well on exams. Choose the jobs and activities that attract you, but never let them overshadow your primary purpose—which is to be a student.

Sometimes even the very best students who apply for admission into an honors program or college are frightened by the thought of speaking in front of a group, giving seminar papers, or writing a thesis. But if you understand how the programs work, you will see that there is nothing to fear. The basis of honors is confidence in the student and building the student's self-confidence. Admittance to an honors program means you have already demonstrated your academic achievement in high school or college classes. Once in the honors environment, you learn how to formulate and structure ideas so that you can apply critical judgment to sets of facts and opinions. In small seminar classes, you practice discussion and arguments, so by the time you come to the senior thesis or project, the method is second nature. For most honors students, the senior thesis, performance, or portfolio presentation is the project that gives them the greatest fulfillment and pride. In many honors programs and colleges, students present their work either to other students or to faculty members in their major departments. Students often present their work at regional and national honors conferences. Some students even publish their work jointly with their faculty mentors. These are great achievements, and they come naturally with the training. There is nothing to fear. Honors will prepare you for life.

Dr. Joan Digby is Director of the Honors Program and Professor of English at Long Island University, C.W. Post Campus. She was also President of the National Collegiate Honors Council from 1999 to 2000, and she received NCHC's prestigious Founders Award in 2018.

Public and Private Colleges and Universities— How to Choose

Debra Humphreys

As you survey the thousands of four-year colleges in the country and weigh the options before you, it is important to be aware of how colleges differ and what kind of educational experience each college offers you. In every state in the country, you will find both public and private colleges and universities. What are the differences between public and private colleges, and how should you approach the decision to attend one or the other? What are some common misconceptions regarding both public and private colleges that you should know about before you eliminate an entire category of institution from your list of prospective schools?

WHAT ARE THE BASIC CHARACTERISTICS OF PUBLIC AND PRIVATE INSTITUTIONS?

Over the course of the nation's history, what began as a small group of mostly church-affiliated colleges has grown in both size and complexity. Over the years, education in the United States became increasingly democratized, and more and more state-sponsored institutions and state systems of higher education emerged. These included small colleges, sometimes called "normal schools," designed to train school teachers for the expanding public school system; land-grant colleges and universities brought into existence with federal support in the mid-nineteenth century in order to prepare workers to expand the nation's agricultural and technological capacity; and large state systems that evolved in the twentieth century and now include two-year colleges, basic four-year institutions, and large research universities, all supported at least in part by state revenues.

While there are some clear distinctions to be made, even some of the core characteristics of public and private colleges vary from state to state. In general, a public institution receives at least part of its operating budget from state tax revenues, operates with a mandate and mission from the state where it is located, and is accountable to the elected officials of that state. Most private colleges and universities are independent, not-for-profit institutions. They operate with revenues from tuition; income from endowments; private gifts and bequests; and federal, private, or corporate foundation grants. These institutions are primarily accountable to a board of trustees,

usually made up of local or national business and community leaders and esteemed alumni.

There are also a small but growing number of for-profit colleges whose operating revenues include tuition dollars but also might include investor financing. Some of these colleges are owned and operated by publicly traded corporations. Most of the following generalizations about private institutions however refer to the more familiar not-for-profit independent college previously described.

While the distinction between public and private institutions might seem clear at first, these two kinds of colleges and universities actually share many characteristics. All accredited colleges and universities in the country—whether public or private, for profit or not—are entitled to receive public funds from the federal government in the form of direct grants and loans for eligible students, support for student work-study programs, and competitive grants to support research or campus programs. In exchange for this federal support, all schools undergo a peer-reviewed accreditation process by a regional accreditor authorized by the federal government's Department of Education.

Whether a college is public or private, you should know if it is accredited and therefore an institution whose students are eligible for all available federal financial aid. Accreditation status also provides you with assurance that the school operates in a fiscally responsible manner and that its academic programs have been deemed sound by an outside group of educators from its peer institutions.

HOW ARE PUBLIC AND PRIVATE COLLEGES AND UNIVERSITIES RUN?

In many ways, your experience as a student will not differ significantly based on what type of governance system a college or university uses. However, some knowledge of this might be useful in making choices among the various options. Private colleges and universities tend to have more independence and autonomy in how they are run, with boards of trustees that oversee financial and other programs and life on campus at these schools. Public colleges and universities often have more complex governing structures with boards of regents or other types of oversight committees made up of politically appointed or elected officials exercising more or less oversight and intrusion into their day-to-day operations. New York, for instance, has a board of regents that oversees the system's campuses and is more actively involved in reviewing and revising curricular requirements that apply to institutions throughout the system. Other states have multiple public colleges, each with its own board overseeing each campus' operations with more or less intrusion into day-to-day operations.

Whether an institution is public or private, you will want to ask lots of questions about campus climate and academic programs in order to help you determine if a school is right for you. Being aware of some facts about public and private institutions will help you frame these questions to get truly useful answers.

ARE ALL PUBLIC COLLEGES AND UNIVERSITIES BIG AND IMPERSONAL?

Like private institutions, public colleges come in all shapes and sizes. Some are large institutions offering multiple degrees and majors to both undergraduate and graduate students alike. These institutions offer students many curricular options as well as access to leading scholars and an environment where cutting-edge academic research is conducted. While an institution of this size and scope might seem intimidating at first, remember that there are large institutions that do take very seriously their undergraduate programs. While you may receive less customized attention at a larger institution, many large public and private research universities offer options such as smaller honors programs, academic learning communities with smaller cohorts of students, or theme residence halls that can minimize the potential that you will get lost in the crowd.

If you are considering a large research institution—whether it is public or private—you should ask questions about the undergraduate program. What is the student-faculty ratio for undergraduates? What is the average class size, especially for introductory first-year courses? How many courses are taught by graduate students, and what sort of teacher training do those students receive? Are there opportunities for undergraduate students to participate in research projects with university faculty members?

In addition to the large, public research universities, there are many other smaller, state-funded regional institutions that still offer a wide range of both liberal arts and sciences fields as well as professional fields of study. Many states also offer small, public liberal arts colleges that share many of the defining characteristics of traditional, private liberal arts colleges. In 1987, some of these institutions formed the Council of Public Liberal Arts Colleges (COPLAC). COPLAC schools pride themselves on providing students of high ability and from all backgrounds access to a quality liberal education. These colleges and universities have been nationally recognized as outstanding in many ways. They offer small classes, innovations in teaching, personal interactions with faculty members, opportunities for faculty-supervised research, and supportive atmospheres. Most of them are located on campuses in rural or small-town settings. In addition to offering rigorous and well-integrated undergraduate programs, these

institutions often charge far less tuition than many private colleges do. More information can be found at www.coplac.org.

These public liberal arts colleges, along with more traditional private liberal arts institutions, do offer unique learning environments that research suggests often lead to higher levels of student achievement. Liberal arts colleges tend to offer a high degree of student-faculty interaction, high levels of student engagement with both in-class and out-of-class experiences, and lots of opportunities for collaborative and innovative learning practices. Businesses are also increasingly asking for exactly the set of skills and capacities that a liberal education provides, whether offered in a traditional liberal arts college setting or within a larger university that grants degrees in both liberal arts and other fields. Many public liberal arts and more comprehensive colleges and universities also now offer students a rigorous liberal education while integrating liberal learning into professional degree programs, for instance in health sciences, engineering, or education.

ARE PUBLIC COLLEGES CHEAPER THAN PRIVATE COLLEGES?

The cost of college is not easy to calculate and is not limited simply to the advertised price of tuition. It is absolutely not the case that attending a public college will always cost a student less money than attending a private institution. It is true that the basic tuition for in-state or out-of-state students attending public colleges is on average less expensive than the advertised tuition rate at private institutions. It is very important, however, to note that many private colleges and universities offer significant amounts of financial aid—often beyond the basic federal loans and grants available to all students. Many, but not all, private colleges have large endowments that allow them to effectively discount the standard, published tuition rates for a great number of their students. The National Association of College and University Business Officers sampled a small group of private colleges and discovered that only 10 percent of entering students were paying the full, advertised tuition. Ninety percent of their students received price discounts in the form of scholarships or financial aid. In other words, don't write off a college simply because its tuition looks extremely high relative to other institutions.

Both private and public institutions, however, have been fiscally stressed in recent years because of declining values of stock portfolios in endowments or because of declining state revenues. It is safe to say that for many students in the coming years, it will become increasingly difficult to get large amounts of financial aid. Many institutions, however, remain committed to widening access to more students from less economically privileged backgrounds. In addition, students demonstrating high levels of academic achievement are being rewarded at both private and public institutions—both in terms of admission and financial aid.

It is important to look carefully at the tuition and the financial aid requirements and availability at each school you are considering, private or public. In-state and out-of-state tuitions and the difference between them varies substantially from state to state. Out-of-state tuition also varies from state to state but still tends to be lower than average private tuition levels.

Policies vary as well for determining state residency status. In many states, the policy for dependent students requires that their parents must have lived in the state for at least twelve months prior to attendance in order to qualify for in-state tuition. For independent students, the requirement of twelve months residence prior to enrollment applies to the student. Independent status must be verified and generally entails proof that a student receives no support from parents or other relatives living in or out of the state in question. As budgets have increasingly tightened, states have over the past several years made it increasingly difficult to establish in-state residence after matriculating at a school. Exceptions are sometimes made, however, for students from migrant, refugee, or military families.

IS IT EASIER TO GAIN ADMISSION TO A PUBLIC INSTITUTION ESPECIALLY AS A STATE RESIDENT?

Few public colleges and universities automatically admit students who graduate from a public high school in their state. Many, however, give preference in admissions and financial assistance to in-state residents. Moreover, some states have implemented policies that guarantee admission to at least one of the state's public institutions for all students graduating in a top percentage of their high school classes.

There are, indeed, more highly selective private than public institutions. Many public colleges and universities, however, do admit very few applicants. These highly selective institutions might draw their students from a national pool of applicants and can be among the most selective in the country. However, the national universities and liberal arts colleges with the lowest acceptance rates in the country are mostly all private institutions.

While some public institutions offer virtually open admissions to state residents, it is important for all prospective students to realize that even an open-admission institution will require incoming students to meet certain academic standards before being admitted to credit-bearing courses. In most cases, public and private institutions give incoming students a series of placement exams that determines at what level the student can begin his or her course work. Depending on the results of these exams, a student may be required to take and pass one or more remedial courses before being admitted to courses that will actually count towards a degree.

Since each state's requirements are different and shift often, you should not assume that, regardless of your academic background, admission is automatic to your local state college. In the current climate—with costs rising and competition across systems tightening—admission rates are dropping at many public institutions.

IS THE CLIMATE ON A PUBLIC COLLEGE CAMPUS SIGNIFICANTLY DIFFERENT THAN THAT ON A PRIVATE COLLEGE CAMPUS?

The social and academic climate at colleges and universities varies substantially, and public institutions do not necessarily offer a distinctively different climate than private institutions do. You can find, at some public institutions, the small, residential environment traditionally associated with private liberal arts colleges. You will also find the presence of fraternities and sororities at both public and private institutions. You should look carefully at whether a school in which you are interested has fraternities and sororities and how much influence the Greek system has on college life. At some institutions, fraternities and sororities dominate the entire social life of the campus.

One campus environment that can only be found at a private institution is a highly religious environment. Many early colleges and universities were founded by churches or religious orders. Some of these institutions no longer retain a strong affiliation with one church or denomination. Others do retain a strong affiliation, and church traditions can heavily influence the climate of these institutions. Usually, these campuses will admit a student from any religious background, but they may require students to attend chapel services and/or take religion or theology courses to graduate. In addition, some college missions and curricula are influenced by their religious affiliations. For instance, many Catholic institutions have a strong commitment to community service and social justice. Students may find, at these institutions, curricula related to social justice issues and requirements that they complete a community-service learning activity or course to graduate. Institutions with a strong mission are also often able to develop more coherent, cohesive, and innovative curricula for their students.

Finally, other important climate factors to consider include whether a college or university is in an urban or rural setting; what the diversity of the student body is in terms of geographic, religious, or racial/ethnic background; if most students live on campus or commute from home; and finally if the college dominates the life of the community in which it is located. Each of these options has advantages and disadvantages you will want to weigh in making your decisions.

ARE PRIVATE COLLEGES MORE ACADEMICALLY RIGOROUS THAN PUBLIC COLLEGES?

Private colleges and universities are not necessarily more academically rigorous than public institutions. You will find rigorous, intellectually challenging, and innovative academic programs at both private and public institutions. There is also a common misconception that schools that are more highly selective have the most effective or engaging academic programs. Research suggests that there is no connection between the selectivity of an institution and the presence of effective or innovative teaching and learning practices. There is, however, preliminary research that suggests that the academic quality of

Questions to Ask as You Evaluate Prospective Colleges and Universities

- Does the college offer a distinctive first-year experience?
- Does the college offer a small-size freshman seminar for all students?
- Are all students required to complete a senior project or assignment that allows them to integrate all that they have learned and demonstrate acquired skills and knowledge?
- Are students encouraged or required to complete internships and/or service-learning courses?
- Are students encouraged to study abroad? Is support for study abroad provided to all students and are study abroad experiences integrated into a student's overall curricula?
- Does the college offer learning communities, especially in the student's early years?
- Are students required to complete rigorous writing courses not only in the freshman year but also across the curriculum in whatever major he or she chooses to pursue?
- Are there opportunities for students to pursue independent research or creative projects under the supervision of a senior faculty member?

one's peers does seem to have an impact on the grade point averages of fellow students.

Nothing could be more important in your decision-making process than evaluating the nature of academic programs at prospective colleges or universities. Across both public and private institutions, there have been exciting and important changes in how colleges and universities are organizing undergraduate curricula. Many promising programs have been

proven to result in higher levels of student retention, graduation, satisfaction, and academic achievement.

Many colleges and universities also now participate in the National Survey of Student Engagement. This survey asks students in both their first and last years about a series of effective educational practices and the degree to which they are engaged in the academic life of their school. Issues that are examined in the survey include the level of academic challenge, active and collaborative learning opportunities, the nature of student-faculty interactions, the number of enriching educational experiences available, and the supportive nature of the campus environment. Ask if the school you are considering participates in this survey and if you can see the results from recent classes of students.

THE PRIVATE/PUBLIC CHOICE

While there are distinct differences between public and private colleges and universities you should not limit your choice—whatever your background—to only one type of institution. There are wonderful opportunities at many different kinds of schools. The availability of many kinds of financial aid may bring private institutions with high-tuition levels within reach for you, whatever your financial background. Whether a school is highly selective or has open admissions, you should also be able to find a college or university that will challenge you academically and provide you with a supportive environment in which to live, learn, and pursue a college degree of lasting value.

Debra Humphreys is the Vice President of Strategic Engagement at the Lumina Foundation for the Association of American Colleges and Universities.

Distance Education— It's Closer Than You Think

You may not realize it, but as an incoming college student, you are joining a revolution that is radically changing education. It's called distance learning. From kindergarten up to postgraduate degrees, distance learning is fast becoming an essential teaching tool. Most of the colleges and universities you are considering for a bachelor's degree offer distance learning in one form or another. Most likely you will be a distance learner at some point, whether during college or graduate school or throughout your career.

In case you're not familiar with distance learning—or asynchronous learning, online learning, or distance education—it means you don't sit in a classroom facing a teacher. You can be hundreds of miles or minutes from the teacher and other students. Most often you connect through the internet to the teacher, fellow students, and study materials. However, increasingly sophisticated technologies, such as virtual laboratories, simulations, and interactive multimedia, are also used. You may run across the term "blended learning." Many institutions incorporate online learning into their face-to-face classes. In fact, a number of colleges require that a part of all classes is online.

FROM SNAIL-MAIL COURSES TO LEADING-EDGE TECHNOLOGY

Talk about change. Distance education began in the late 1800s, when schools mailed correspondence courses to farmers who wanted to learn how to grow better crops. As technology has advanced, distance learning has become accessible and widespread. At first educators were skeptical, but as name-plate universities began to incorporate it into their teaching methodology, distance education became accepted.

When brick-and-mortar colleges and universities first considered distance education, the goal was to make it as good as face-to-face education. Now, says Ray Schroeder, Professor Emeritus of Communication and Director of the Center for Online Learning, Research, and Service (COLRS), at the University of Illinois at Springfield, "Field research shows that online learning technologies are better than face-to-face learning in a number of ways." Having taught online, he has seen firsthand how students participate more in discussions and learn from one another. Peg Miller, Ph.D., former Coordinator of Academic Support for Distributed Learning, University of Central Florida, cites a survey she conducted every other semester that compares face-to-face and distance learners at her institution. She has found that students from face-to-face and online classes were almost identical in the grades they earned and in their satisfaction with the classes.

ON THE UPSWING

Today, a third of all college and university students are enrolled in at least one online course. Many reasons have caused the phenomenal growth of distance education. It's convenient and user-friendly, plus the scope of classes is stunning. Not that you'll likely begin your college years with classes in forensics or grading diamonds, but they are offered and indicate the enormous variety of courses. Along with many others in education, Michael P. Lambert, former executive director of the Distance Education Training Council, feels that online learning has transformed how people learn. "You no longer sit in a box with 35 other people where you might never raise your hand," he says. Adds Gerald Heeger, former President of the University of Maryland University College (UMUC), "Online learning gets rid of the limitations of geography and time. And as bandwidth increases, we will do more and more."

PROCEED WITH CAUTION

Now that you're convinced that distance education sounds great, and you're ready to say "sign me up," it's only fair to warn you that perhaps you shouldn't start your bachelor's degree totally online. Distance learning changes how you study, respond to your teachers, participate in class discussions, and take exams. If you're not prepared for the differences, you can easily fall behind and even fail. Though the age of online students continues to drop, many are older, have had some life experience since graduating from high school, and have the self-discipline, maturity, and self-motivation, that distance education demands. They know what they want from college and are willing to meet the rigors of online learning, which are considerable.

Of course, some students straight from high school do successfully start college as distance learners because they've already had some online learning experience. Some take online classes in high school or advanced-placement and college courses. At Stevens Institute of Technology's Web Campus, incoming freshmen brush up on math and precalculus online before their first fall semester. At first, Nathan Kahl, former instructor for the Euclid Program at Stevens Institute of Technology Web Campus, was skeptical that high school graduates could succeed in the online courses he taught, but he saw that "everyone quickly got into the swing of things." He admits that he underestimated the students' ability to learn online. Heeger agrees "There's no reason why a bright junior in high school who is ready to take college freshmen courses can't do it."

The University of Phoenix Online (parent company: Apollo Group, Inc.) has developed a bachelor's degree program specifically for incoming freshmen of any age—including those just out of high school. In today's job market, a college education is a necessity, yet many students have life situations that prevent them from attending. Notes former president of Apollo Group, Inc., Brian Mueller about the accommodations their program makes for students who are new to higher education, "It is our experience that if you create an online classroom, it must have all the features that incoming students need, which are small, highly interactive, and collaborative classes." Their freshman classes average 15 and require that the instructor has consistent contact with the students. New freshmen also get a tremendous amount of support in writing, math, and online research skills and have the help of an academic counselor who closely tracks them for ten weeks into their first semester. "We think there are more students coming out of high school who must have jobs, so we took the model for working adults and created an environment for traditional students that combines education and work," says Mueller.

However, not all educators have the same experience with incoming freshmen. Jimmy Reeves, Ph.D., Professor of Chemistry and Coordinator of the Tablet PC Initiative at the University of North Carolina at Wilmington, teaches both online and face-to-face classes and knows how students can react. Freshmen who fail his face-to-face class sometimes ask to take his class online. He says no because the discipline required is rare among 19-year-old students. "Junior and senior college students do well, but it has more to do with their level of maturity and the reasons why they're in college," he says, referring to the fact that many incoming college students want to experiment or come because their parents demand it. "Without any real desire to learn or sense of why they're in college, it's easy to get distracted in online classes," he notes. You can't hide in the back of a lecture hall half asleep on Monday morning and hope for the best on multiple-choice questions. In online classes, your active participation is noticed and taken into account for final grades.

Attending college isn't just about acquiring knowledge in a particular field in order to get a job. It's also about learning social skills and meeting people with different ideas from diverse backgrounds. "If you want to live in a dorm and have bull sessions on the meaning of life with the kids down the hall, then being a fully online freshman student isn't for you," advises Cynthia Davis, Acting Vice Provost and Dean of the Undergraduate School at the University of Maryland University College (UMUC). She adds that sometimes students mistakenly think getting a bachelor's degree online will take less time than physically attending classes or won't require as much work. But as she points out, online classes demand the same amount of effort, if not more, than face-to-face classes.

WHAT'S IT GOING TO BE LIKE?

Blended learning or mixed-mode classes, combining face-to-face and online instruction, are becoming a permanent fixture in higher education. Students might sit in a classroom on Monday but take the remaining two classes for that week online. Professors routinely post the syllabus, class calendar, or PowerPoint lectures online. Reeves says that it's rare to see college classes without some web-based materials. Davis com-

ments that UMUC routinely enhances all of its face-to-face classes with companion online classrooms. Students can have optional online discussions or print copies of class materials.

"We find more students use online technology to enhance their studies and get better grades," comments Schroeder. Educators see a trend of students enrolling in one university and taking courses from other institutions. For instance, say you're in an art class but want to study German cathedral architecture, which your university doesn't have but another one offers online. It's only a matter of time before this will be a standard option for college students.

LOTS TO LOOK FOR, LOTS TO AVOID, LOTS TO ASK

Though much of distance education depends on the internet, you can't just type in "distance education" and see what comes up in a search for a college. You must seriously research and do background checks to make sure a diploma mill doesn't hand you a bachelor's degree that isn't credible. There are plenty of places to get information. Petersons.com offers a database of colleges and universities that have online courses, as well as totally online distance education providers. "You have to be a good consumer," recommends Heeger. "It's no different from getting a loan. You don't borrow money from people you never heard of. You shouldn't get degrees from people you never heard of." Schroeder suggests checking the course completion of online programs, their enrollment, and growth of programs. "Just as one checks with friends and colleagues about the quality of consumer services, such as computers and cars, one should check with students who are enrolled in online programs," he advises.

Is the Institution Accredited by a Valid Accrediting Body?

There are several kinds of accrediting organizations:

- The six regional accrediting agencies recognized by the U.S. Department of Education
- The Council for Higher Education Accreditation (**www.chea.org**)
- Other institutional accrediting agencies, such as the Accrediting Council for Independent Colleges and Schools and the Distance Education and Training Council
- Specialized accrediting agencies that cover schools offering everything from acupuncture to veterinary medicine
- Other discipline-based accrediting organizations, such as those for law and business schools

Can You Transfer Credits Received Online from One Institution to Another?

Policies vary greatly among universities and colleges. Though distance education is widely accepted, there are so many places where students can take bogus online courses that institutions are justifiably cautious. If students do decide they want to get a bachelor's degree completely online, they need to be sure the campus-based program and distance education program offer the same degree. At most institutions, both on-campus and online degrees are the same, but others do differentiate in the degrees conferred, and it will show up on your diploma.

Test-Drive an Online Class

Just like face-to-face instruction, online classes are different, depending on the course material and how each teacher chooses to structure the course, but here's a typical scenario of what it's like to be a distance learner.

Getting started. First you'll want to get to the general information page for the class, which you'll visit often. The professor's contact information, the class calendar, the syllabus, and announcements on quizzes and tests or links to other pages on which you'll find posted discussion questions may be found here. Some teachers will ask you to tell something about yourself to the other students in the class. Be sure to read the syllabus, which will outline the course and tell you when assignments are due and how grades are determined.

Responding to discussion questions. Those students who never raised their hands in face-to-face classes will get a shock in online courses. Responding with thoughtful answers to online discussion groups is mandatory. Usually the teacher will assign reading material and then post a discussion question. The material might be from your textbook or websites. You must respond to the question and possibly to the postings of other students in the class. Teachers will gauge your participation in the class and how well you learn the material.

Interacting with fellow students and your teacher. Ray Schroeder, Professor Emeritus of Communication and Director of the Center for Online Learning, Research, and Service (COLRS) at the University of Illinois at Springfield, gives talks about distance education. Often he'll ask his audience to recall their favorite class from elementary school up to college and what made it so memorable. Was it the textbook? The actual classroom? The view out the window? When he asks if it was the interaction among students and with the teacher, the audience realizes that's what made the class good. "Both in person and online, learning takes place in the interaction," says Schroeder. "Otherwise, we would do just as well to read a book or watch a video to learn." In online classes, interaction between you and the professor and other students is an enormous part of your success.

Nathan Kahl, former instructor for the Euclid Program at Stevens Institute of Technology Web Campus, explains, "Distance students expect that their teachers will be online at least as much as they are." The level of interaction expected from you will vary by school and course, but you should know that in online courses, you must be an active participant. On the flip side, teachers carefully monitor discussions to make sure the more talkative students don't dominate. Keith W. Miller, Professor of Computer Science at the University of Illinois at Springfield, interacts with his students in a variety of ways. "I make announcements to the whole class on the homepage. I send e-mails to the whole class. I enter into the electronic discussions on the bulletin board forums and post daily reminders and assignments to the course calendar. The students interact with me using e-mail, notes in their assignments, and via the bulletin boards. Now and then someone calls me at my office on the phone, but that's rare." He likes to answer his e-mails at least once a day, which means that his students get much more feedback than they would if he were physically in a classroom with them.

As do most online teachers, Cynthia Davis, Associate Dean of Academic Affairs in the School of Undergraduate Studies at the University of Maryland University College, gets students to participate with a weekly discussion topic. "If we're reading a novel," she says, "I ask them to discuss the role of the narrator or analyze a passage. The students respond individually and then respond to other students' comments."

Attending virtual lectures. Some online courses allow you to hear and see the professor or other guest speakers who are also online. If you want to ask a question, there's a button to indicate you want to speak. Everyone else can hear you as if you all were in the same room. Other professors add voice to PowerPoint lectures, which you can view when you want to, not at some prearranged time.

Taking quizzes and tests. No more waiting weeks to get your tests back. Online technology in some courses instantly zaps back the corrected test and notes that you missed question six and need to study page 54 of the textbook. Just like in face-to-face classes, you have an allotted amount of time to take the quiz. Some online courses may have automated components, such as instant quizzes and animated and interactive practice sessions. Others have mandatory proctored exams at a nearby community college or learning center for students who are off campus.

What Kind of Refund Policy Does the University Have for Distance Learners?

It might become painfully apparent for students that online learning is not for them, and they want to drop out. Find out ahead of time about the refund policy for online classes. What happens if you're ill during an online class? How can you make up the work? Even before taking any classes, you should find out if you're suited for online learning. Many institutions offer self-assessment tests on their websites.

What Online Services Does the College Provide?

Is the dorm wired? Can you get an e-mail address from the university? What about browsers and computer compatibility? Ask how the internet is part of face-to-face classes. To what extent is the library online, and is it available 24/7 for research? Ask about writing and math labs and help-desk support. Look for online tutorials that show students how to use the school's specific software. Is there a tech fee?

IF YOU'RE LEARNING ONLINE, YOU BETTER HAVE THESE

Since online learning is part of college, it's helpful to know what to expect ahead of time, rather than three weeks into the class, when you feel like throwing your laptop out the window and would happily settle for sitting in the back row of the nearest classroom. Here are the five skills and abilities that successful online students must have:

1. You must have the self-discipline to do things you don't want to do when you don't want to do them.

If you're a procrastinator, you'll find the catch-up tactics that served you well in face-to-face classes won't work online. "Students get the idea they can whiz by without studying, or they came from high schools where they weren't pushed," cautions Heeger. "Maybe they never got Fs in high school, but they do here." That's because they don't realize they're responsible for learning the material on their own. The burden is on you to keep up with the homework. It doesn't take long to fall far behind in online classes.

Typically, students in face-to-face and online classes need 2 hours for work outside of class for every hour in class. But online students often forget to add that hour. For every hour they would have to sit in a traditional classroom, they should be listening, studying, thinking, writing, responding to discussions, and getting ready for tests, plus the 2 hours outside of class. Three classes a week—that's 9 to 10 hours for one class. Online teachers keep students on track with weekly quizzes and homework assignments. If students start lagging, they're likely to get an e-mail from the professor asking what's going on. Claudine SchWeber, Ph.D., Chair of the Doctor of Management Program at the University of Maryland University College, has taught online for years and states, "My classes are structured by weekly readings, activities, and discussions. Students can't decide to get around to doing the work when they feel like it. It must be done at the instructor's pace. The first shot of online can be a shock to their system."

2. You must have the ability to manage your time without anyone telling you to do your homework NOW.

In high school, students usually can put off studying until the weekend. "That doesn't work in college. You can't write complex papers the night before," says Karen L. Kirkendall, Ph.D., Associate Professor of Liberal and Integrative Studies and Director of the Capitol Scholars Honors Program at the University of Illinois at Springfield. She teaches both online and face-to-face classes and has seen first-time online students who have never failed before start to slip and suddenly realize they are in big trouble. "My online classes are extraordinarily structured so I pretty much know when students aren't engaged, which I monitor by seeing how much they participate in online discussions," she notes.

3. You must have the skills to communicate your thoughts in writing.

"Online participation in class discussions isn't instant messaging. You are what you write in online classes," advises SchWeber. Most of the work in online classes is written,

Distance Learning Myths

Myths regarding distance learning continue to persist even as distance education becomes more widely accepted and offered.

Distance learning is for people on ranches 200 miles from the nearest freeway. Geography is not a factor. Many distance learners who are located across the campus or a few miles away just don't want to deal with the commute or have a work schedule that conflicts with being in a class at a certain time. They appreciate the flexibility that distance education gives them.

Distance learning is easier than face-to-face classes. Once you start an online class, you'll knock that myth off the list. Still, some students think it will be easier. When they realize they must not only respond to discussion questions but also comment on the responses from other students, they wonder why they ever thought distance education was going to be easy. Online teachers normally keep track of how their students progress with frequent monitoring and quizzes.

I'll get a better education in face-to-face classes. Much research has been conducted comparing the two and consistently, online learning is equivalent or better. Teachers of online courses now have plenty of precedents to follow, training and research to help them teach better, and technology to prepare for classes and keep up with their students' progress.

I'll talk to a computer all day. Yes, you are in front of a computer as a distance learner, but you also interact with professors and other students much more than you ever would in a core freshman class of 200. Teachers have sophisticated software to facilitate interaction. Even though you don't physically see your teachers, they put a great deal of effort into class preparation and reading e-mails. Some get as many as 3,000 e-mails in a ten-week class. Distance learners often get to know fellow students much more easily online than they would walking in and out of a class.

I need to be a computer geek. If you can handle the simplest maneuvers around a computer, such as attaching documents to e-mails or going to a specified web address, you can be a distance learner. And you'll have tech support to help out if you run into problems.

Distance education is cheaper than face-to-face. Too bad this is a myth. It costs the same as a traditional college if you attend a recognized institution. Most students pay for distance education through student loans.

whether it's participation in discussions, homework, quizzes, papers, or tests.

Since you'll communicate by e-mail and post your thoughts, netiquette is essential. You need to think differently online than when speaking on the phone or face-to-face. "You can't write a report that sounds like you are hanging out with friends," advises SchWeber. "When you are totally online, the only image people (including your professor) have of you is how you write." Kirkendall has reprimanded students who sent e-mails showing disrespect to the teacher because they were upset about something. Probably they would never respond that way if face-to-face. "Never hit the submit button when you're angry," Kirkendall cautions.

4. You must have the ability to research worthwhile information on the web.

You need to know what's junk and what's reliable. In addition, professors take plagiarism very seriously, especially because it's so easy to do.

5. You must have some computer skills and know some computer-speak.

Those who design the software and set up how a distance learning class is taught are careful to make sure the technology doesn't get in the way of learning; however, you should know the basics. "In some classes, certain downloads are required, such as Adobe Acrobat, but in general, the skills are not beyond the abilities used daily by most elementary school children," says Schroeder, pointing out that if distance programs use expensive or exotic technology, they defeat the purpose. He reports that most computers that are five years old have the speed, memory, and capability to support online learning. Some classes might require a microphone. You should be familiar with some of the computer jargon so that if you're asked to post something or use a drop box, add an attachment, or take part in a threaded discussion, you'll know what you need to do. Just about every distance learning provider has online tutorials to familiarize you with their particular online software. If you run into technical problems, help-desk support is available.

Why Not Women's Colleges?

Before we start talking about the many advantages that women's colleges offer, let's get some myths out of the way. It is almost certain that the minute you hear "women's colleges" in the same sentence with "choosing colleges" you immediately think: no boys, no fun, no way!

Maybe that is why some girls who visit Joan Jaffe's office at Mills College in San Francisco, California, rush in to tell her that they just saw some guys on the campus of this women's college. Jaffe, Associate Dean of Admission, frequently gets this reaction from the young women who visit the campus. That's because many think that if they go to a women's college they are never going to see a guy within 2 miles of the campus gates, which, by the way, will clang shut behind them, leaving them secluded inside a heavily guarded male-free zone.

KISS MYTH NUMBER ONE GOOD-BYE

Forget iron gates. The first myth to get rid of is the one that assumes attending a women's college means kissing your social life good-bye. In fact, as Patricia Gibbs, Vice President for Student Affairs, Dean of Students at Wesleyan College in Macon, Georgia, points out, "If you were a guy looking for a date, where would you go?" Not only that, the majority of women's colleges are near, if not next to, coed campuses. Most share activities with other colleges and universities, and many have reciprocal agreements so that guys can take classes at the women's college and vice versa.

When it comes to dating, women's colleges offer the best of both worlds. You can hang out with guys when you want to and then retreat to your own lovely environment (women's dorms usually are beautiful) and hang out with the girls. Julie Binder, who transferred from the University of Wisconsin to all-women's Barnard College in New York City, notes that there is open registration with Columbia University, which just happens to be right next door. "Campus life is shared. Sports are shared," she says.

As you dig deeper into this myth, you will find that attending a women's college is not about isolation, it's about options. You get to choose if you want to be in classes, clubs, and organizations only with women or mingle with the men.

SCRATCH MYTH NUMBER TWO

Women's colleges are just a bunch of catty, competitive females waiting for the right moment to claw each other's eyes out. Scratch that myth, too. Instead, women's colleges cultivate an environment of sisterhood—women who look out for one another. Most women's colleges encourage women in the upper-level classes to help their younger classmates. Talking to their "big sisters," newcomers can find out what classes to take and which professors are best, and they find a sympathetic ear for the problems that most first-year college students face.

The Rich Traditions in Women's Colleges

Tradition plays an important part of the experience women have in women's colleges. They run the gamut from solemn ceremonies of passing along the bond of sisterhood to the fun of secret surprises. "Women's colleges have a strong sense of tradition," says Amy Shaver, former Academic Dean at Stephens College in Columbia, Missouri. It's also a wonderful way to help women from all social, economic, religious, and ethnic backgrounds to share a common experience and pass it on to the next generation of students. "Traditions bond women over the generations," says Jennifer Rickard, former Dean of Admissions and Financial Aid at Bryn Mawr College, who notes that it's not unusual at all to have students today singing songs and participating in ceremonies that the class of 1945 did and which will be the same when today's students have their twenty-year reunion.

Here's a sampling of the many traditions you'll find on women's college campuses:

Lantern Night At Bryn Mawr's Lantern Night, women gather around a fountain on campus. Each woman is given a lantern as a symbol of knowledge and learning. Each class has a color, and as the lanterns are passed from the sophomores to the first-year students, songs are sung in Greek that are the same as the ones sung 100 years ago around the same fountain.

Senior Paint Night Mills College seniors get the okay to paint the campus in their class color. Along with brushes and cans of paint, they are given a few guidelines as to what can and cannot be painted, but the rest is up to them.

The Crossing of the Bridge As women students come to Stephens to begin their college education, they cross over a bridge on campus in a ceremony symbolizing their entrance into the world of academia. At graduation, they cross over another bridge on campus and are welcomed into the alumnae society.

Candlelight Induction Ceremony Spelman students dressed in white dresses and black shoes light candles and hear the charge to be the best they can be. While the candles are still lit, they sing the Spelman hymn.

Midnight Breakfast At Barnard, the night before finals, the president of the college, deans, and professors make breakfast for the students.

"The sense of community is very strong at women's colleges," observes Fran Samuels, former Director of College Counseling at The Master's School in Dobbs Ferry, New York. "The myth is that a women's college will be cliquish. In truth, the women are supportive of each other." The strong bonds of sisterhood that naturally develop connect students to their college, its history, and its students—past, present, and future. Many women's colleges designate a rotating color for each incoming class. For example, if the freshman class you enter is dubbed the golden hearts, by the time you graduate, you are connected to all the golden hearts who graduated ahead of you and all the golden hearts who will graduate after you.

TOSS MYTH NUMBER THREE

Another myth that should be tossed out is that women's colleges don't prepare you for the "real world." Well, try saying that to the 12 women members of Congress who graduated from women's colleges. Or to the 15 women on *Business Week*'s list of the rising stars in corporate America. Although you are not in a totally coed situation, on the other hand you are in an environment in which you can gain skills to think critically and learn to meet challenges. Becky Marsh, Director of Communications and Marketing at Whitfield School, in St. Louis, Missouri, points out that when you first ride a bike, training wheels allow you to learn how to balance. Once you are ready to race down the street, you take them off. Same with women's colleges. The focus is on your education and your strengths, and who you are. You graduate ready to take on the obstacles of the real world. "In high school, I had the feeling that boys were given more opportunities to share their knowledge. It was harder and more intimidating for me to share my opinions in a coed class," says Brittany Johnson, from Spelman College in Atlanta, Georgia. "Now I feel like I can do anything."

Graduates of women's colleges feel empowered and willing to confront any limits to their abilities. While in college, they have many opportunities to assume leadership roles and see women in leadership positions as professors and deans. "They don't doubt whether they can do anything. Instead, they ask, 'Why can't I do it now?'" reports Amy Shaver, former Academic Dean at Stephens College in Columbia, Missouri. Women can find their own voices and establish their own ways of approaching things that will ultimately make them successful in a male-dominated world. They learn from seeing other women students and professors engaged in the intellectual process.

THE ADVANTAGES

As more young women find out about the advantages that women's colleges offer them, they like what they see. Maybe that is why attendance at women's colleges is growing. Learning leadership skills tops the list of advantages. Says Shaver, "Women in a same-sex environment are more likely to take risks and speak up in class. They are more willing to stand up and voice an opinion." If you think about it, students get plenty of practice at a women's college because all the leadership roles go to women. From day one, you will see women leading the entire college or involved in interesting and significant research. You get more exposure to what leadership is and what to expect as a leader. "Leadership becomes ingrained," notes Jennifer Fondiller, Dean of Enrollment Management at Barnard College in New York City.

You might not realize it, but women react differently in classrooms with all women. They tend to speak up with confidence and test their ideas more readily when they are not competing with men. Researchers find that even as early as the fifth grade, girls are taught differently than boys. Teachers call on boys more frequently and don't ask girls the more thought-provoking questions or to critically analyze problems. In coed situations, the more aggressive and competitive guys take over, whereas in all-female classes, research indicates there is much more give-and-take and exchange of ideas.

Coming from a coed public school, Johnson realized that more attention was given to the guys in her classes, but at Spelman, she says, "Everyone is on the same path." Arlene Cash, former Vice President for Enrollment Management at Spelman, notes that women don't have to vie for attention or retreat into the intellectual background in all-women classes. In a coed class, the environment becomes more adversarial. "Women feel they have to perform. In women's colleges they become more academically involved and interact with faculty members more frequently," says Debbie Greenberg, former College Counselor at Whitfield School. Speaking of the rich interaction that occurs in her classes at Barnard, Binder says, "The diversity of experience around the discussion table is unparalleled."

YOU CAN SUCCEED

Shaver characterizes the environment in women's colleges as one in which there is no fear of failing when the social pressures and dynamics of men and women are removed from the classroom. Women's colleges give women the opportunity to explore different avenues without the fear of failing. "We challenge them to become what they want to become," says Gibbs from Wesleyan. "No one says, 'You can't do that because you are a woman.'" At the same time, you are interacting with other women who have the same goals as you, which reinforces who you are. Or, as Jennifer Rickard, former Dean of Admissions and Financial Aid at Bryn Mawr College, in Bryn Mawr, Pennsylvania, points out, women are not just sitting in classes to do well on exams and get good grades. They also are figuring out what they want to do with their education. "There's less expectation to conform to an external measure," she says.

Many women's colleges foster self-government and give their students responsibilities they might not find in a coed institution. At Bryn Mawr, for instance, students pay a self-government association fee as part of their tuition. This is put into a fund that is controlled by a student government that takes ownership of how the students want to govern themselves. "This isn't student government making only recommendations to the administration as to how to allocate the budget to the different student groups vying for funds," notes Rickard. "You have students dealing with real-world management issues, such as resource allocation."

Since women's colleges are smaller than big coed universities, women receive all the benefits that students get from a small liberal arts college in addition to the advantages that only a women's college offers. A big plus is interaction with professors and staff, which is hard to achieve when you are one of

What Made You Choose a Women's College?

When she got to the point of choosing which college to attend, Wisambi Loundu had plenty of options. Coming from San Diego, the California universities were a logical choice. Women's colleges were not on her list. In fact, she hardly knew they existed. Her first thought when someone suggested a women's college to her was, "I'm not going to a school full of girls minus boys." Her second thought was just as negative. "If it's all girls, they will always be fighting." The third and fourth thoughts assumed that a women's college wouldn't prepare her for the real world, plus she would be isolated.

But then her math teacher's daughter told her about Bryn Mawr, and as Wisambi started exploring the possibility, the advantages of a women's college started lining up. However, it wasn't until she visited Bryn Mawr that she really began to see herself there. "I fell in love with the campus," says Wisambi. "It was like nothing I'd ever seen before." Her stay in the dorm added to her steadily growing thoughts that Bryn Mawr might be it. "The girls I stayed with in the dorm were so friendly. At first I was suspicious, but I saw it was not a front. Plus, there were girls from all over the world."

But Wisambi didn't make her final decision just yet. She decided to look at other schools, like Wellesley and the University of California schools, as well as Stanford. Meanwhile, her friend told her more about Bryn Mawr. "She said I'd make lasting friends and she talked about how the academics would train me for the outside world even if there were no men on campus. Bryn Mawr would build my identity as a woman."

She still wasn't convinced and made a second visit, along with visits to Wellesley and Stanford, which she says were nice, but too big. It would be too hard to make friends there, she thought. When the time came to make her final selection, she chose Bryn Mawr.

Now at Bryn Mawr, how does Wisambi feel about her choice? The academics are more challenging than she anticipated but doable, and she is excited about the internships she will be able to access. She also finds that the staff and teachers at Bryn Mawr go out of their way to make her feel at home. "They match us up with a mentor and professor," she says.

How about dating? Since Bryn Mawr is part of a tri-college community, guys are around, though Wisambi says you have to make an effort to meet people on other campuses.

Talking to seniors who are getting ready to head out to the "real world," Wisambi can see that they are full of confidence and don't think for a minute that they won't do well. "And that's a positive," she says.

200 students in a lecture hall taught by a graduate student. Women's colleges tend to foster seminar-style classes taught by full professors, many of them women. "You have an expert teaching you," says Gibbs. Faculty members get to know their students and can challenge them intellectually on an individual basis. "Within two days, all my teachers knew my name," recalls Johnson, who says she was given each professor's e-mail address, home phone number, and all the contact information she needed and was encouraged to reach out to them.

Women are encouraged to achieve their intellectual goals. Professors often will point out specific programs that they know suit the student's interests. Add to this the opportunities to conduct research with a professor, and in many cases actually present research findings to a professional society, and you can see why women graduate with a terrific resume before they even start their careers. Rickard mentions the opportunity that Bryn Mawr students have to work on funded projects with professors during the summer and then present the results along with them at conferences. "It's a window into the academic world and the world of the intellectual," she notes. It's no surprise that women in women's colleges major in math and science at a higher national average than women in coed institutions.

Paid and unpaid internships, too, are more available for women at women's colleges, mainly because of the network of women graduates in business and industry who want to help their "sisters" at their alma maters. "I'm getting my professional edge now," says Binder, who is interested in TV production and had a paid internship as a production assistant while a sophomore at Barnard. "You will have an amazing resume by the time you graduate," she says.

Peggy Hock, Ph.D., former College Counselor at Notre Dame High School in San Jose, California, points out that colleges naturally rely on their alumni to come forward with networking opportunities for students; however, the alumnae of women's colleges tend to be more loyal and willing to give of their time. This translates into many more opportunities for internships, mentoring, and job possibilities. At Barnard, for example, the career office has an alumna mentor network. Students can call, ask questions, and get advice about career choices. At alumnae events, current students mix with the graduates. Binder takes full advantage of the web log of women who are working all over the world and willing to spend time online with Barnard students. She applied for a job at a public relations firm in New York after contacting a fellow Barnard graduate working there. She met with her and subsequently got a letter of recommendation.

HOW TO CHOOSE

Choosing a women's college isn't any different from choosing a coed college. You should definitely visit the campus and don't be afraid to ask lots of questions—even the ones that might make you uncomfortable. Because women's colleges are similar to small coed liberal arts colleges, make sure that you don't compare a women's campus to a big university.

Janet Ashley, former Interim Director for Admissions at Spelman College, advises high school women to ask what a women's college can give them academically. "Their choice depends on what their goals are," she says.

If you're worried about the dating scene, ask about the levels of interaction with guys and how close the relationships are with neighboring institutions.

"Look at the individuality of each women's college," suggests Rickard, "because each has its own personality."

Look at the school before looking at the fact that it's a women's college, and on the flip side, don't rule out a school just because it is a women's college. "So many students make quick decisions about where to apply," warns Fondiller, noting that sometimes the decision hinges on what schools a friend is applying to rather than if that institution really fits the student. Many women's colleges specialize in certain fields like science, math, or theater.

Famous Firsts from Women's Colleges

Do you know which college the first woman to be named Secretary of State graduated from? Or the woman scientist who identified the Hong Kong flu? Or the first woman executive vice president of the American Stock Exchange? Here's a big clue. They were all graduates of women's colleges.

SENATORS
- Barbara Mikulski (MD)—Mount Saint Agnes College
- Tammy Baldwin (WI)—Smith College

REPRESENTATIVES (Current and Former)
- Tammy Baldwin (WI)—Smith College
- Donna Christian-Christensen (VI)—St. Mary's College
- Rosa DeLauro (CT)—Marymount College
- Jane Harman (CA)—Smith College
- Gabrielle Giffords (AZ, 2007–12)—Scripps College
- Eddie Bernice Johnson (TX)—Saint Mary's College
- Barbara Lee (CA)—Mills College
- Nita Lowey (NY)—Mount Holyoke College
- Betty McCollum (MN)—College of Saint Catherine
- Nancy Pelosi (CA), first woman elected as Speaker of the House of Representatives—Trinity College
- Allyson Schwartz (PA)—Simmons College

FORMER SECRETARY OF STATE
- Hillary Rodham Clinton (NY)—Wellesley College

OTHER FAMOUS WOMEN FIRSTS
- Madeleine Albright, first woman to be named Secretary of State in the United States, appointed in 1997—Wellesley College
- Jane Amsterdam, first woman editor, the New York Post—Cedar Crest College
- Emily Green Balch, first woman to receive the Nobel Peace Prize in 1946—Bryn Mawr College
- Catherine Brewer Benson, first woman to receive a college bachelor's degree—Wesleyan College
- Earla Biekert, first scientist to identify the Hong Kong flu virus—Wesleyan College
- Cathleen Black, first woman leader of the American Newspaper Publishers Association—Trinity Washington University
- Sarah Porter Boehmler, first woman executive vice president of American Stock Exchange—Sweet Briar College
- Jane Matilda Bolin, first African American woman judge in the United States—Wellesley College
- Dorothy L. Brown, first African American woman general surgeon in the South—Bennett College for Women
- Pearl S. Buck, first American woman to win the Nobel Prize in Literature—Randolph-Macon Woman's College
- Ila Burdett, Georgia's first female Rhodes Scholar—Agnes Scott College
- Dorothy Vredenburgh Bush, first woman secretary of the Democratic National Party—Mississippi University for Women
- Hon. Audrey J. S. Carrion, first Hispanic woman judge Circuit Court for Baltimore City—College of Notre Dame of Maryland
- Rachel Carson, first environmentalist who awakened public consciousness through her book, *Silent Spring*—Chatham University
- Barbara Cassani, first woman CEO of a commercial airline—Mount Holyoke College
- Elaine L. Chao, U.S. Secretary of Labor, 2001; First Asian American woman appointed to a President's cabinet—Mount Holyoke College

Adapted from the website of the Women's College Coalition at http://www.womenscolleges.org.

Applying 101

The words "applying yourself" have several important meanings in the college application process. One meaning refers to the fact that you need to keep focused during this important time in your life, keep your priorities straight, and know the dates that your applications are due so you can apply on time. The phrase might also refer to the person who is really responsible for your application—you.

You are the only person who should compile your college application. You need to take ownership of this process. The guidance counselor is not responsible for completing your applications, and neither are your parents. College applications must be completed in addition to your normal workload at school, college visits, and SAT®, ACT®, or TOEFL® testing.

THE APPLICATION

The application is your way of introducing yourself to a college admissions office. As with any introduction, you want to make a good first impression. The first thing you should do in presenting your application is to find out what the college or university needs from you. Read the application carefully to find out the application fee and deadline, required standardized tests, number of essays, interview requirements, and anything else you can do or submit to help improve your chances for acceptance.

FOLLOW THESE TIPS WHEN FILLING OUT YOUR APPLICATIONS

- **Follow the directions to the letter.** You don't want to be in a position to ask an admissions officer for exceptions due to your inattentiveness.
- **Proofread all parts of your application,** including your essay. Again, the final product indicates to the admissions staff how meticulous and careful you are in your work.
- **Submit your application as early as possible,** provided all of the pieces are available. If there is a problem with your application, this will allow you to work through it with the admissions staff in plenty of time. If you wait until the last minute, it not only takes away that cushion but also reflects poorly on your sense of priorities.
- **Keep a copy of the completed application,** whether it is a photocopy or a copy saved on your computer. *(For more hands-on help with your application essays, pair up with a professional editor who can provide you with proofreading services as well as full critiques: www.essayedge.com)*

Completing college applications yourself helps you learn more about the schools to which you are applying. The information a college asks for in its application can tell you much about the school. State university applications often tell you how they are going to view their applicants. Usually, they select students based on GPAs and test scores. Colleges that request an interview, ask you to respond to a few open-ended questions, or require an essay are interested in a more personal approach to the application process and may be looking for different types of students than those sought by a state school.

In addition to submitting the actual application, there are several other items that are commonly required. You will be responsible for ensuring that your standardized test scores and your high school transcript arrive at the colleges to which you apply. Most colleges will ask that you submit teacher recommendations as well. Select teachers who know you and your abilities well and allow them plenty of time to complete the recommendations. When all portions of the application have been completed and sent in, whether electronically or by mail, make sure you follow up with the college to ensure their receipt.

THE APPLICATION ESSAY

Whereas the other portions of your application—your transcript, test scores, and involvement in extracurricular activities—are a reflection of what you've accomplished up to this point, your application essay is an opportunity to present yourself in the here and now. The essay shows your originality and verbal skills and how you approach a topic or problem and express your opinion.

Some colleges may request one essay or a combination of essays and short-answer topics to learn more about who you are and how well you can communicate your thoughts. Common essay topics cover such simple themes as writing about yourself and your experiences or why you want to attend that particular school. Other colleges will ask that you show your imaginative or creative side by writing about a favorite author, for instance, or commenting on a hypothetical situation. In such cases, they will be looking at your thought processes and level of creativity.

Admissions officers, particularly those at small or mid-size colleges, use the essay to determine how you, as a student, will fit into life at that college. The essay, therefore, is a critical component of the application process. Here are some tips for writing a winning essay:

- Colleges are looking for an honest representation of who you are and what you think. Make sure that the tone of the essay reflects enthusiasm, maturity, creativity, the ability to communicate, talent, and your leadership skills.
- Be sure you set aside enough time to write the essay, revise it, and revise it *again.* Running "spell check" will only

detect a fraction of the errors you probably made on your first pass at writing it. Take a break and then come back to it and reread it. You will probably notice other style, content, and grammar problems—and ways that you can improve the essay overall.

- Always answer the question that is being asked, making sure that you are specific, clear, and true to your personality.

- Enlist the help of reviewers who know you well—friends, parents, teachers—since they are likely to be the most honest and will keep you on track in the presentation of your true self.

THE PERSONAL INTERVIEW

Although it is relatively rare that a personal interview is required, many colleges recommend that you take this opportunity for a face-to-face discussion with a member of the admissions staff. Read through the application materials to determine whether or not a college places great emphasis on the interview. If they strongly recommend that you have one, it may work against you to forego it.

In contrast to a group interview and some alumni interviews, which are intended to provide information about a college, the personal interview is viewed both as an information session and as further evaluation of your skills and strengths. You will meet with a member of the admissions staff who will be assessing your personal qualities, high school preparation, and your capacity to contribute to undergraduate life at the institution. On average, these meetings last about 45 minutes—a relatively short amount of time in which to gather information and leave the desired impression—so here are some suggestions on how to make the most of it.

Scheduling Your Visit

Generally, students choose to visit campuses in the summer or fall of their senior year. Both times have their advantages. A summer visit, when the campus is not in session, generally allows for a less hectic visit and interview. Visiting in the fall, on the other hand, provides the opportunity to see what campus life is like in full swing. If you choose the fall, consider arranging an overnight trip so that you can stay in one of the college dormitories. At the very least, you should make your way around campus to take part in classes, athletic events, and social activities. Always make an appointment and avoid scheduling more than two college interviews on any given day. Multiple interviews in a single day hinder your chances of making a good impression, and your impressions of the colleges will blur into each other as you hurriedly make your way from place to place.

Preparation

Know the basics about the college before going for your interview. Read the college catalog and website in addition to this guide. You will be better prepared to ask questions that are not answered in the literature and that will give you a better understanding of what the college has to offer. You should also spend some time thinking about your strengths and weaknesses and, in particular, what you are looking for in a college education. You will find that as you get a few interviews under your belt, they will get easier. You might consider starting with a college that is not a top contender on your list, so that the stakes are not as high.

Asking Questions

Inevitably, your interviewer will ask you, "Do you have any questions?" Not having one may suggest that you're unprepared or, even worse, not interested. When you do ask questions, make sure that they are ones that matter to you and that have a bearing on your decision about whether or not to attend that college. The questions that you ask will give the interviewer some insight into your personality and priorities. Avoid asking questions that are answered in the college literature—again, a sign of unpreparedness. Although the interviewer will undoubtedly pose questions to you, the interview should not be viewed merely as a question-and-answer session. If a conversation evolves out of a particular question, so much the better. Your interviewer can learn a great deal about you from how you sustain a conversation. Similarly, you will be able to learn a great deal about the college in a conversational format.

Separate the Interview from the Interviewer

Many students base their feelings about a college solely on their impressions of the interviewer. Try not to characterize a college based only on your personal reaction, however, since your impressions can be skewed by whether you and your interviewer hit it off. Pay lots of attention to everything else that you see, hear, and learn about a college. Once on campus, you may never see your interviewer again.

In the end, remember to relax and be yourself. Your interviewer will expect you to be somewhat nervous, which will relieve some of the pressure. Don't drink jitters-producing caffeinated beverages prior to the interview, and suppress nervous fidgets like leg-wagging, finger-drumming, or bracelet jangling. Consider your interview an opportunity to put forth your best effort and to enhance everything that the college knows about you up to this point.

THE FINAL DECISION

Once you have received your acceptance letters, it is time to go back and look at the whole picture. Provided you received more than one acceptance, you are now in a position to compare your options. The best way to do this is to compare your original list of important college-ranking criteria with what you've discovered about each college along the way. In addition, you and your family will need to factor in the financial aid component. You will need to look beyond these cost issues and the quantifiable pros and cons of each college, however, and know that you have a good feeling about your final choice. Before sending off your acceptance letter, you need to feel confident that the college will feel like home for the next four years. Once the choice is made, the only hard part will be waiting for an entire summer before heading off to college!

The "Early Decision" Decision

Maybe a senior you knew last year didn't get into the college he wanted. He said it was because he didn't apply "early decision." Maybe your friend's mom told your mom that unless students apply early decision, their chances of getting into top schools are slim to none, even though they have great grades and spectacular essays. Maybe you figure you'd better get in on the early decision action.

All of the above are true—well, sort of—because many students applying to college get the term "early decision" backwards. High school guidance and college counselors run into this kind of thinking all the time and suggest putting "decision" before "early"—as in making a wise decision about committing to a college before applying early. For some students, early decision is a great option. For others, early decision is loaded with pitfalls and dangers.

"When students come back in the fall of their senior year, I often hear 'I know I want to apply early. Can you help me choose the school?'" says Kathy Cleaver, Co-Director of College Counseling at Durham Academy in Durham, North Carolina. She compares that to saying, "I know I want to get married, please help me pick the man." Continues Cleaver, "First you have to fall in love with the school and know it's your first choice and then join the circus for early decision." She's referring to the media hype flying around high school halls about early decision—it's easy to fall prey to the early decision madness. Hot competition to get into "top" schools creates early decision anxiety. Michael "Mickey" Gilbert, Guidance Counselor at Passaic High School in Passaic, New Jersey, throws out some scary numbers that confirm that, yes, the competition for admittance to top schools is white-hot. There are about 30,000 high schools in the United States, and although the majority of high school seniors apply to institutions in their own states, there are still limited spaces in the "top" schools and the eight Ivy League schools. "No wonder kids think that early decision is the way to go," speculates Gilbert. Early decision panic sets in because students are convinced that if they get their applications in early, they have an edge. Sometimes early decision might make the difference, but there are many issues to consider before taking the early decision leap.

EARLY THIS, EARLY THAT

With all the buzz about early decision, do you really know what it means along with all the other early options, such as early action and early notification? And what about the variations of early decision? Each institution can have its own version of early decision, meaning that deadlines and criteria are different. There's the early decision that notifies students by December, there's the early decision round two, and then there is the early action/single choice.

Seeing the confusion, the National Association for College Admission Counseling (NACAC) developed a standard set of definitions. NACAC is an education association of secondary school counselors, college and university admissions and financial aid officers, counselors, and other individuals who work with students as they transition from high school to college. While each institution has its own variations of each early option, an understanding of the basic differences can help. The list that follows was adapted from the definitions found on the NACAC website (**www.nacacnet.org**).

Early Decision

- Early decision is the application process in which students make a commitment to a first-choice institution where, if admitted, they definitely will enroll. Should a student who applies for financial aid not be offered an award that makes attendance possible, the student may decline the offer of admission and be released from the early decision commitment.

- While pursuing admission under an early decision plan, students may apply to other institutions, but may have only one early decision application pending at any time.

- The institution must notify the applicant of the decision within a reasonable and clearly stated period of time after the early decision deadline. Usually, a nonrefundable deposit must be made well in advance of May 1.

- A student applying for financial aid must adhere to institutional early decision aid application deadlines.

- The institution will respond to an application for financial aid at or near the time of an offer of admission.

- The early decision application supercedes all other applications. Immediately upon acceptance of an offer of admission, a student must withdraw all other applications and make no subsequent applications.

- The application form will include a request for a parent and a counselor signature, in addition to the student's signature, indicating an understanding of the early decision commitment and agreement to abide by its terms.

Early Action

- Early action is the application process in which students make application to an institution of preference and receive a decision well in advance of the institution's regular response date. Students who are admitted under early action are not obligated to accept the institution's offer of admission or to submit a deposit until the regular reply date (not prior to May 1).

- A student may apply to other colleges without restriction.

- The institution must notify the applicant of the decision within a reasonable and clearly stated period of time after the early action deadline.

- A student applying for financial aid must adhere to institutional aid application deadlines.

- A student admitted under an early action plan may not be required to make a commitment prior to May 1 but may be encouraged to do so as soon as a final college choice is made. Colleges that solicit commitments to offers of early action admission and/or financial assistance prior to May 1 may do so provided those offers include a clear statement that written requests for extensions until May 1 will be granted, and that such requests will not jeopardize a student's status for admission or financial aid.

Regular Decision

- Regular decision is the application process in which a student submits an application to an institution by a specified date and receives a decision within a reasonable and clearly stated period of time, but not later than April 15.

- A student may apply to other colleges without restriction.

- The institution will state a deadline for completion of applications and will respond to completed applications by a specified date.

- A student applying for financial aid must adhere to institutional aid application deadlines.

- A student admitted under a regular decision plan may not be required to make a commitment prior to May 1 but may be encouraged to do so as soon as a final college choice is made. Colleges that solicit commitments to offers of admission and/or financial assistance prior to May 1 may do so provided those offers include a clear statement that written requests for extensions until May 1 will be granted, and that such requests will not jeopardize a student's status for admission or financial aid.

Rolling Admission

- Rolling admission is the application process in which an institution reviews applications as they are completed and renders admission decisions to students throughout the admission cycle.

- A student may apply to other colleges without restriction.

- The institution will respond to completed applications in a timely manner.

- A student applying for financial aid must adhere to institutional aid application deadlines.

- A student admitted under a rolling admission plan may not be required to make a commitment prior to May 1 but may be encouraged to do so as soon as a final college choice is made. Colleges that solicit commitments to offers of admission and/or financial assistance prior to May 1 may

do so provided those offers include a clear statement that written requests for extensions until May 1 will be granted, and that such requests will not jeopardize a student's status for admission or financial aid.

Wait List

- Wait list is an admission decision option utilized by institutions to protect against shortfalls in enrollment. Wait lists are sometimes made necessary because of the uncertainty of the admission process, as students submit applications for admission to multiple institutions and may receive several offers of admission. By placing a student on the wait list, an institution does not initially offer or deny admission, but extends to a candidate the possibility of admission in the future before the institution's admission cycle is concluded.

- The institution will ensure that a wait list, if necessary, is of reasonable length and is maintained for a reasonable period of time, but never later than August 1.

- In the letter offering a wait list position, the institution should provide a past wait list history, which describes the number of students placed on the wait list(s), the number offered admission from the wait list, and the availability of financial aid. Students should be given an indication of when they can expect to be notified of a final admission decision.

- An institution must resolve final status and notify wait list candidates as soon after May 1 as possible.

- The institution will not require students to submit deposits to remain on a wait list or pressure students for a commitment to enroll prior to sending an official offer of admission in writing.

There is one more option, called early action/single choice (EASC), that some highly selective schools such as Harvard, Yale, Princeton, and Stanford have begun using. Early action/single choice is a nonbinding early admission option for freshman applicants that replaces early decision. With this change, students learn about their admission decision in December without being required to reply until May 1. This option allows students to apply to as many colleges as they want under a regular admission time frame. The difference is that the early action/single choice option does not allow a candidate to apply to other schools under any type of early action, early decision, or early notification program. Students are asked to sign a statement in their application agreeing to file only one early application.

Each of these options has variations, depending on the institution using them. Some schools have a November 1 deadline for early decision round one. Smaller schools have a deadline of November 15, while others have a December 1 deadline. Then there's an early decision round two. To make matters even more complicated, some schools with early decision say that students can't apply to other institutions if they've sent in an early decision application to their admissions office. Others say it's okay to apply to other schools at the same time you're

PARENTS, SOME ADVICE FOR YOU

Though guidance counselors stress that high school students should make the final decision about which college to attend, they also say that parents are a very important part of the decision equation. Parents can help as organizers of all the information and provide the support needed to make a good choice. "Little things like setting up file folders and keeping track of deadlines can keep a student on track," advises David Gibson, former College Advisor at St. Mary's Parish in Annapolis, Maryland.

Along with their children, parents also need to understand the basics of early option terminology as it applies to each institution being considered. Five different colleges might have five different early decision criteria. Read the fine print and make note of deadlines.

What really will help—you, your child, and your wallet—is to understand the basics about financial aid. Says Shawn Leftwich, Director of Undergraduate Admissions at Wheaton College in Illinois, "Have an in-depth discussion with the financial aid officer so that you are aware of the ramifications, restrictions, and implications of the financial aid offer."

If possible, make an appointment to visit with a financial aid officer at the college while your child is visiting the campus. Bring your tax forms and discuss the prospects of financial aid. "Financial aid people are straight shooters. It's not in their best interest to tell you one thing to get your foot in the door and then turn around and pull the rug out from under you," says Bill McClintick, Dean of College Relations and Outreach at Mercerburg Academy. "Parents might not like the answer they get from the financial aid officer, but they will get a candid assessment of their eligibility for financial aid."

Leftwich suggests having an honest discussion with your child early in the college selection process. Talk about what you can realistically afford, what colleges will appropriately challenge him or her, if location is a factor, and what kind of environment best suits your child. Whichever option your child uses to apply, you both will know the decision is an informed one.

applying early decision to them, but if they send you an acceptance, you must withdraw the other applications.

Just because two institutions have an application process called early decision or early action doesn't mean that their policies are identical. "There is no common terminology, even among the colleges that have early decision," says Christoph Guttentag, Dean of Undergraduate Admissions at Duke University in Durham, North Carolina. He also points out that just when you think you've got the definitions figured out, institutions change them. "Colleges are always balancing the needs of their institution and the needs of students," he comments.

EARLY DECISION: A MATCHMAKING TOOL OR A CLEVER STRATEGY?

Despite the differences in what actually constitutes early decision, it has become more of a strategy than a matchmaking tool, according to Bill McClintick, Director of College Relations and Outreach at Mercersburg Academy in Mercersburg, Pennsylvania. He also chairs the national steering committee on admissions standards for NACAC. The focus of early decision used to be on matching the student with the college and letting the admissions office know that that institution is where the student wants to be above all others. Today, early decision is misunderstood and misused. High school seniors think that they must use the early decision tactic to get an edge. The result, says McClintick is "at many of the top places, early decision applications have gone through the roof."

Though high school students may have exaggerated ideas of how much early decision can really help them, it is true that it does give a small segment of students applying at highly selective schools an advantage. Generally, the more selective the institution, the more small differences matter. "Even if it's a small increase, you need everything you can get," states John Latting, Ph.D., Emory University's Assistant Vice Provost for Undergraduate Enrollment and Dean of Admission.

"Remember," cautions McClintick, "we're only talking about a small slice of kids in the grand scheme of things." He mentions 5 percent of high school seniors nationally who aspire to the "top" institutions. State colleges and universities fill a much lower percentage of their freshman class with early decision applications. "I don't believe that more kids are chasing the same number of spots," says Jon Reider, Director of College Counseling at San Francisco University High School in San Francisco, California. "Students are applying to more and more schools, even with the early decision option on the side. This is inflating the selectivity of some colleges beyond what it used to be." In reality, 90 percent of students apply regular admission. Interest in early decision comes from a relatively small segment of the college applicant pool.

THE BENEFITS OF EARLY DECISION

There are clear benefits for students who apply for early decision. Aside from the fact that early decision does play a role in acceptance rates for a relatively small percentage of students at a small number of schools, early decision is a good option. The caveat is that students must know, without a shred of doubt, that one institution, above all others, is the best match for their goals and their likes and dislikes, and that based on grades and test scores, they solidly match the institution's criteria for admission. The option to go early decision should be taken after extensive research, multiple visits to the campus, and talking to a lot of people. "Early decision is for those who can put their hearts and souls into one application," advises Cleaver.

There are other advantages. You have to make only one choice, and you will know by December if you've been accepted. You have to fill out only one application. You are not chewing your nails over your list of possibilities during the winter break. Instead, you know where you're going and can sit back and enjoy the rest of your senior year, while others in your class are madly filling out applications, writing essays, and agonizing over the thin envelopes that arrive in the mail. Says Guttentag, "The advantage of having that challenging process over with is not insignificant."

Early decision is helpful for admissions officers at selective colleges because it allows them to make decisions between well-qualified students and select those who really want to be at their institution. As Shawn Leftwich, Director of Undergraduate Admissions at Wheaton College in Illinois, points out, early decision is for the students who are strongly committed. "We like you. You like us. We know you're coming, and we can fill our freshman class." However, on the flip side, she adds that some students aren't so sure about which college they want to attend, and early decision only makes the process more stressful.

Before you decide to go with early decision, consider early action. Many high school counselors lean toward early action, which is another good option. With early action you're able to apply later in the process. This means you will be able to take the SATs again. Your first-semester grades and AP classes taken in the first semester of your senior year can be used to evaluate your eligibility. You have September and October to visit several campuses while they are in session and plenty of time to do the research to put more than one school on your list.

THE PITFALLS OF EARLY DECISION

Though early decision has benefits, before you jump into it, look at the ramifications of that option. Advises Gilbert, "Early decision might give you an edge, but the tradeoff is not so great."

Perhaps the most compelling reason why students should seriously examine early decision before jumping at it is because they are bound by an agreement to attend that school if accepted. Students sign a pledge to attend that institution and are required to withdraw applications from all other schools. They also are obligated to accept the financial aid award that the institution gives them. An early decision is a binding decision. "Regardless," advises David Gibson, of David Gibson College Advising, LLC, in Annapolis, Maryland, "students don't learn about their financial aid awards until March or April, and if the award funding is not at all acceptable because the family's financial need was not met, they need to decline the offer and begin searching for a new college. March or April is not a good time to start applying to new colleges."

How binding is binding? Though no school can force a student to attend if they've signed an early decision agreement, students who decide not to attend that school hurt others with that decision. High school counselors have to sign the binding agreement, along with parents, and must state that they will not send out transcripts to other institutions. Many institutions will not accept the application of a student who applied early decision elsewhere and backed out of the agreement. Admissions officers may find out in May that an

QUESTIONS TO ASK YOURSELF BEFORE APPLYING EARLY DECISION

What if you don't get accepted early decision—then what? Speaking from the experience of seeing students deal with early decision rejection letters, Reider says, "Some of your friends are getting acceptance letters, and you get one thin envelope and the pain of rejection. You've given the early decision institution your best shot and you lost." Cleaver has seen kids in her high school end up thinking they won't get in anywhere. "This is the first time they've faced a big rejection and news they don't want to hear," she says, noting that because of the timetable of early decision, letters often come right around exam time in December.

When students apply regular decision, meaning they wait until well into their senior year and apply to several different institutions, it's "all or some," quips Latting. "With early decision, it's all or nothing." Many application deadlines for regular decision are in January. If you get that rejection letter from the school you were counting on, that doesn't give you much time to apply to other schools, much less visit them.

Are you ready to make such a drastic decision so early in your senior year? A lot can change in how you think about your future between the beginning of your senior year and graduation. With six or seven months behind you as a senior, you might be in a better position to compare colleges in April than you were back in September. Think about it—you're making the decision about where you want to spend the next four years of your life in early October of your senior year!

Have you given yourself enough time to pick one college above all others? If you want to apply early decision, you should start making plans to do so in your junior year. In order to apply early decision, you must have your ACT®s or SAT®s taken, campus visits done, a final choice made, a dynamite essay written, a stellar application filled out, and teacher recommendation letters collected. That's a lot to cram into the end of your junior year and a few months into your senior year.

Have you given an admissions office enough information to make a decision about you? The more information the admissions office has about grades and classes you took and activities and leadership positions you held, the better they can decide if you're a good match for them. Do you really want decisions being made about you based on sophomore and junior grades and activities? What happens to that AP English class you finally felt ready to take the beginning of your senior year? What about that calculus class you aced in the first semester of your senior year? Admissions won't be able to assess that on an early decision application.

early decision student is not coming, so they'll call the counselor and ask if the student applied to another school. If so, often a phone call to the other institution is made and acceptance denied. Sometimes the counselor loses a good reputation with that institution, putting applicants who follow in subsequent years at a disadvantage.

After the consequences of signing a binding agreement, the financial aspect of early decision is the next biggest pitfall. "You can't compare financial aid offers," says Latting. "You have only one offer." Students won't know if they're eligible for Pell grants or merit scholarships. Government FAFSA forms are not submitted until January, and students might not find out how much aid they can get until March or April, long after the early decision agreement was signed and sealed. "This means that if they are accepted, they are then obligated to a college that might not fund them to the level of their financial need," says Gibson. Students who apply early action or regular decision are in a better position to negotiate financial aid packages.

EARLY DECISION REJECTION

In case you haven't heard, "fat" is good, "thin" is bad. Thin envelopes from college admissions offices usually mean a single-page letter saying good luck, we wish you the best, but you're not going to be attending our school next fall. However stated, it's hard to be rejected, especially when you've applied early decision, which states to the college and to yourself that this is the college you've decided is the only one you really, really want to attend above all others.

But thin envelopes don't mean the end of the world. Cleaver advises to not let early decision get control of you. "There are too many choices of colleges for you not to get into college. You might not get into Princeton, but there are many other wonderful schools if you do the research to look for a good match. Early decision is a tool to use to apply, but it is not always the best tool."

Objecting to the term "perfect match," Reider asks, "Does it really matter what kind of car you drive? There are twenty different colleges that can get you where you want to go. You'll be successful in most places."

HOW TO DO EARLY DECISION THE RIGHT WAY

Taking the early decision option requires more than gathering information, filling out an application, writing an essay, and waiting for an envelope to come in the mail or an e-mail to hit your Inbox. If you're going to be serious about early decision, the time to start is in your junior year.

Research the institutions at the top of your list. Think through what you want out of college—not just in terms of a future career, but also factors such as location, size, distance from home, sports, and other activities. Think about who you want to be. "It has to be a love connection," says Cleaver. Tune out all the early decision talk and do your homework about each college. Then ask yourself if one stands out above all the others you've researched. Is this the one to which you can commit to a binding agreement? Are you in the competition to be admitted? Will you have the funds to attend this college?

"Admissions can tell if your application is from the heart," Cleaver cautions. Students ask her how to make their applications "look like they want to go there." She replies that what they put on an application and in an essay has to pour out of their hearts. Students who visit the campus and sit in on a class or a campus organization have the edge if something really clicked with them. They will write a convincing application. Perhaps they'll tell about how exciting the professor they heard was or how wonderful it is that the college has a chess club. Cleaver observes that kids usually write about an institution's sports team or about the ivy-covered walls of the campus on their application essay instead of writing about some interesting aspect of the university that spoke to them, which takes research, time, and reflection. "Don't make the mistake of chasing a name and not being a good consumer," cautions McClintick. Part of being a good consumer is to make sure you are a reasonably competitive applicant. This means looking at the school's admission criteria and statistics. What percentage of the freshman class is filled with early decision and early action students? If it's a high percentage, then you might want to reconsider where that school falls on your wish list. How many students return for their sophomore year? If more than 10 percent leave after their freshman year, that should tell you something about student satisfaction—and ultimately yours.

One of the most important ways to choose the right school is to visit the campus, perhaps multiple times and preferably with students on campus. "Campus visits are a critical time to talk with undergraduates and to find out what the academic, social, and physical climate is like," advises Guttentag. If you're staying in a dorm on Tuesday night during a visit, you can tell how serious kids are about their work. What kinds of conversations are they having? "Are these the kind of kids you want to spend four years of your life with?" asks McClintick.

After you've thoroughly investigated all the aspects of a college and decided it's at the absolute top of your list, after you are familiar with the early decision requirements at that institution, and after you've determined that you have a good chance of getting into that institution, then you can say early decision is for you. For those who are not so sure, fortunately, colleges and universities have plenty of other options for admission.

Coming to America: Tips for International Students Considering Study in the U.S.

Introduction:
Why Study in the United States?

Are you thinking about going to a college or university in the United States? If you're looking at this book, you probably are! All around the world, students like you who are pursuing high education are considering that possibility. They envision themselves on modern, high-tech campuses in well-known cities, surrounded by American students, taking classes and having fun. A degree from a U.S. school would certainly lead to success and fortune, either back in your home country or perhaps even in the United States, wouldn't it?

It can be done—but becoming a student at a college or university in the U.S. requires academic talent, planning, time, effort, and money. While there may be only a small number of institutions of higher learning in your country, there are more than 2,900 four-year colleges and universities in the United States. Choosing one, being accepted, and then traveling and becoming a student in America is a big undertaking.

If this is your dream, here is some helpful information and expert tips from professionals who work with international students at colleges and universities throughout the United States.

Timing and Planning

The journey to a college or university in the U.S. often starts years in advance. Most international students choose to study in the U.S. because of the high quality of academics. Your family may also have a lot of input on this decision, too.

"We always tell students they should be looking in the sophomore year, visiting in the junior year, and applying in the senior year," says Father Francis E. Chambers, OSA, D.Min., Associate Director of International Admission at Villanova University. He stresses that prospective students need to be taking challenging courses in the years leading up to college. "We want to see academic rigor. Most admission decisions are based on the first six semesters—senior year is too late."

Heidi Gregori-Gahan, Assistant Provost for International Programs at the University of Southern Indiana agrees that it's important to start early. "Plan ahead and do your homework. There is so much to choose from—so many schools, programs, degrees, and experiences. It can be overwhelming."

While students in some countries may pay an agent to help them get into a school in the United States, Gregori-Gahan often directs potential international students to EducationUSA (**https://educationusa.state.gov**), a U.S. State Department network of over 400 international student advising centers in more than 170 countries. "They are there to provide unbiased information about studying in the United States and help you understand the process and what you need to do."

Two to three years of advance planning is also recommended by Daphne Durham, who has been an international student adviser at Harvard, Suffolk University, Valdosta State University, and the University of Georgia. She points out that the academic schedule in other countries is often different than that of the United States, so you need to synchronize your calendar accordingly.

You will have to take several tests in order to gain admission to a U.S. school, so it's important to know when those tests are given in your country, then register and take them so your scores will be available when you apply. Even if you have taken English in school, you will probably have to take The Test of English as a Foreign Language (TOEFL®), but some schools also accept the International English Language Testing System (IELTS). You will probably also have to take the SAT® or ACT® tests, which are achievement or aptitude tests, and are usually required of all students applying for admission, not just international students.

"Make sure you understand how the international admissions process works at the school or schools you want to attend," says Durham. "What test scores are needed and when? Does the school have a fixed calendar or rolling admissions?" Those are just some of the many factors that can impact your application and could make a difference in when you are able to start school.

"Every university is unique in what's required and what they need to do. Even navigating each school's different website can be challenging," explains Gregori-Gahan.

Searching for Schools

This book contains information on thousands of four-year colleges and universities, and it will be a valuable resource for you in your search and application process. But with so many options, how do you decide which school you should attend?

"Where I find a big difference with international students is if their parents don't recognize the school, they don't apply to the school," says Fr. Chambers. "They could be overlooking a lot of great schools. They have to look outside the box."

The school Gregori-Gahan represents is in Evansville, Indiana, and it probably isn't familiar to students abroad. "Not many people have heard of anything beyond New York and California and maybe Florida. I like to tell students that this is 'real America.' But happy international students on our campus have recruited others to come here."

She points out that internet technology has made a huge difference in the search process for international students. Websites full of information, live chat, webinars, virtual tours, and admission interviews via video chat have made it easier for potential students to connect with U.S. institutions, get more information, and be better able to visualize the campus.

One thing that will help narrow your search for a school is knowing specifically what you want to study. You need to know what the course of study is called in the United States, what it means, and what is required in order to study that subject. You also need to consider your future plans. What are your goals and objectives? What do you plan to do after earning your degree?

"If you're going to overcome the hurdles and get to a U.S. school, you have to have a directed path chosen," says Durham.

The other thing that could help your search process is finding a school that is a good fit.

Fit Is Important

You want your clothing and shoes to fit you properly and be comfortable, so a place where you will spend four or more years of your life studying should also be comfortable and appropriate for you. So how can you determine if a particular school is a good fit?

"We really recommend international students visit first. Yes, there are websites and virtual tours, but there's still nothing that beats an in-person visit," says Fr. Chambers. He estimates that 50 to 60 percent of Villanova's international students visited the campus before enrolling.

"It can be hard to get a sense of a place—you're so far away and you're probably not going to set foot on campus until you arrive," says Gregori-Gahan. "There is a high potential for culture shock."

You need to ask yourself what is important to you in a campus environment, then do some homework to ensure that the schools you are considering meet those needs. Here are some things to consider when it comes to fit:

- **Location:** Is it important for you to be in a well-known city or is a part of the United States that is unfamiliar a possibility? "Look at geographic areas, but also cost of living," recommends Durham. "Be sure to factor in transportation costs also, especially if you plan to return to your home country regularly."
- **Student population:** Some small schools have 1,000 students while larger ones may have 30,000 students or more.
- **Familiar faces:** Is it important for you to be at a school with others from your home nation or region?

- **Climate:** Some students want a climate similar to where they live now, but others are open and curious about seasons and weather conditions they may not have ever experienced. "We do have four seasons here," says Gregori-Gahan. "Sometimes students who come here from tropical regions are concerned about the winters. The first snow is so exciting, but after that, students may not be aware of how cold it really is."
- **Amenities:** Do you want to find your own housing or choose a school where the majority of students live on campus? Is there public transportation available or is it necessary to walk or have a bicycle or car? Does the school or community have access to things that are important to you culturally and meet the traditions you want to follow?
- **Campus size:** Some campuses are tightly compacted into a few city blocks, but others cover hundreds of acres of land. "International students are amazed by how green and spacious our campus is, with blooming flowers, trees, and lots of grass," says Gregori-Gahan.
- **Academic offerings:** Does this school offer the program you want to study? Can you complete it in four years or perhaps sooner? What sort of internship and career services are available?
- **Finances:** Can you afford to attend this school? Is there any sort of financial assistance available for international students?
- **Support services:** Durham suggests students look carefully at each school's offerings for international students. "Does the school have online guidance for getting your visa? Is ESL tutoring available? Does the school offer host family or community friend programs?" She also suggests you look for campus support groups for students from your country or region.

Looking at the listings and reading the in-depth descriptions in this book can help you search for a school that is a good fit for you.

Government Requirements

The one thing that every international student must have in order to study in the United States is a student visa. Having accurate advice and following all the necessary steps regarding the visa process is essential to being able to enter this country and start school.

As you schedule your tests and application deadlines, you must also consider how long it will take to get your visa. This varies depending on where you live; in some countries, extensive background checks are required. The subject you plan to study can also impact your visa status; it does help to have a major rather than be undeclared. The U.S. State Department website, **https://travel.state.gov/content/travel/en/us-visas/study.html**, can give you an idea of how long it will take.

In addition to the visa, you will also need a Form I-20, which is a U.S. government immigration form. You must have this form when you get to the United States.

"It's very different from being a tourist. You need to be prepared to meet with an immigration officer and be interviewed about your college," explains Durham. "Where you are going, why you are going, where the school is located, what you are studying, and so on."

You also need to keep in mind that there are reporting requirements once you are a student in the United States. Every semester, your adviser has to report to the government to confirm that you are enrolled in and attending school in order for you to stay.

Finances

Part of the visa process includes having the funds to pay for the cost of your schooling and support yourself. Finances are a huge hurdle in the process of becoming a college student in the United States.

"It's crucial. So many foreign systems offer 'free' higher education to students. How is your family going to handle the ongoing expense of attending college for four years or longer in the United States?" Durham reiterates that planning ahead is key because there are so many details. Student loans require a U.S.-based cosigner. Each school has its own financial aid deadlines. You have to factor in your own government's requirements, such currency exchange and fund transfers.

The notion that abundant funds are available to assist international students is not true. Sometimes state schools may offer diversity waivers or there may be special scholarship opportunities for international students. But attending school in the U.S. is still a costly venture.

"We do offer financial aid to international students, but they still have to be able to handle a large portion of the costs. Full-need scholarships are not likely," explained Fr. Chambers. "Sometimes students think that once they get here, it will all work out and the funds will be there. But the scenario for the first year has to be repeated each year they are on campus."

Once You Arrive…

You've taken your tests, researched schools, found a good fit, applied, got accepted, arranged the financing, gotten your visa and I-20, and made it to the campus in the United States. Now what?

You can expect the school where you have enrolled to be welcoming and helpful, but within reason. If you arrive on a weekend, or at a time outside of the time when international students are scheduled to arrive, the assistance you need may not be available to you.

Every school offers different levels of assistance to international students. For instance, Villanova offers a full-service office that can assist students with everything from visas, to employment, to finding a place for students to stay over breaks.

Fr. Chambers attends the international student orientation session to greet the students he's worked with through the recruitment and application process. "But I rarely see an international student after that. I think that bodes well for them being integrated into the entire university."

"Those of us who work with international students are really working to help them adjust," says Gregori-Gahan. "International students get here well before school starts so they can get over jet lag. We have orientation sessions and pair them with peer advisers who help them navigate the first few days, and we assure them that we are there for them."

Students should be open to their new setting, but they should be prepared that things may not be at all how they had envisioned during their planning and searching process. "While you may think you'll meet lots of Americans, don't underestimate the importance of community with your traditional home culture and people," says Durham.

Don't Make These Mistakes

The journey to college attendance in the United States is a long one, with many steps. Experts warn about avoiding common mistakes along the way and offer the following helpful advice:

"Not reading through everything thoroughly and not understanding what the program of study really is and what will it cost. You have to be really clear on the important details," says Gregori-Gahan.

"Every school does things differently," cautions Fr. Chambers. "International students must be aware of that as they are applying."

Durham stresses that going to school in the United States is too big a decision to leave to someone else. "Students need to know about their school—they have to be in charge of their application."

"It involves a lot of work to be successful and happy and not surprised by too many things," Gregori-Gahan says.

Hopefully now, you are more informed and better prepared to pursue your dream of studying at a college or university in the United States.

Financial Aid Countdown Calendar

JUNIOR YEAR

Fall

Now is the time to get serious about the colleges in which you are interested. Meet with your guidance counselor to help you narrow down your choices. Hopefully by the spring, your list will have five to ten solid choices. College visits are always a great idea—remember this will be the place you will call home for four years, so start your campus visits soon!

- ❑ Register for the PSAT/NMSQT®.
- ❑ Check out local financial aid nights in the area. Be sure to attend these valuable sessions, especially if this is the first time your family is sending someone off to college. Try to become familiar with common financial aid terms. Start reviewing the literature available and begin to familiarize yourself with the various programs. A good booklet is published by the U.S. Department of Education, "Do You Need Money for College or Career School? Apply for Federal Student Aid 2019–20" and is available at any financial aid office or on the web at **https://studentaid.ed.gov/sa/sites/default/files/2019-20-do-you-need-money.pdf**
- ❑ In October, take the PSAT/NMSQT®.
- ❑ Do some web browsing! There are many free scholarship search engines, such as **Petersons.com**. Also, head to the bookstore or library and pick up a copy of *Peterson's® Scholarships, Grants & Prizes,* which features details on aid from private sources, or *Best Scholarships for the Best Students,* which offers great info on scholarships, fellowships, and experiential learning programs for top students.
- ❑ Ask your parents to contact their employers, unions, and any religious and fraternal organizations with which they have a connection to learn about possible scholarship opportunities.
- ❑ Check with your high school guidance counselor for the qualifications and deadlines of local scholarship awards. Many guidance counselors report that there are few applicants for these awards.

Winter

- ❑ Keep checking for scholarships! Remember that this is the one area over which you have control. The harder you work, the better your chances for success!
- ❑ Register and study for the ACT® or SAT® and SAT Subject Tests™.

Spring

- ❑ Spring Break—a great time to visit colleges. Remember your top ten list? Time to start narrowing it down.
- ❑ Review the requirements for local scholarships. What can you do now and over the summer to improve your chances?
- ❑ Take the ACT® or SAT®. Good luck!
- ❑ Look for a summer job, especially one that ties in with your college plans. For example, if you want to major in premed, why not try to get a job at a hospital or with a laboratory?

Summer

- ❑ College visit time! Ask: Is this where I see myself getting my undergraduate degree? Can I adjust to the seasons, the town surrounding the campus, the distance from home, the college size? Does this school feel right for me?
- ❑ Why not get a jump on college (and maybe save some money!) and enroll for a college course at the local community college? Or, better yet, do some extra prep work for the ACT® or SAT®!

SENIOR YEAR

Fall

How's the college list coming? Can you get your list down to five or six choices? Your guidance counselor can help with this process. Once you have your top choices, make a list of what each college requires for admission and financial aid. Be sure your list includes all deadlines. Attend a financial aid night presentation with your parents. Some of these sessions offer help in completing forms; others offer a broader view of the process. Contact the presenter (usually a local college financial aid professional) to be sure you are getting the information you need.

❏ Do any of these colleges require the CSS/Financial Aid PROFILE® financial aid application? Many private colleges use this form for institutional aid. You need to file this comprehensive form in late September or early October. For more information or to find out which colleges use this supplemental form, go to **https://cssprofile.collegeboard.org/**. (Website registration is free; however, PROFILE® is a fee-based application).

❏ If you are planning on applying for federal student aid, you should complete and submit your FAFSA® Application as soon as possible. The application can be submitted as early as October 1 every year.

❏ Don't falter now in your scholarship search. Get the applications filed by the published deadlines.

❏ Register now if you are planning to retake the SAT®.

❏ Most important, start completing your college applications—the earlier, the better! If you are interested in early decision or early action, now is the time! Remember, accuracy and completeness are a must!

Winter

❏ Ensure all college applications are completed.

❏ Do you have questions? Call the local financial aid office. Many states have special toll-free call-in programs in January and February (Financial Aid Awareness Month). Be sure that you have completed each school's required forms.

❏ As the letters of admission start to arrive, the financial aid award letters should be right behind them. Important question for parents: What is the bottom line? Remember, aid at a lower-cost state school will be less than a higher-cost private college. But what will you be required to pay? This can be confusing, so consider gift aid (scholarships and grants), student loans, and parent loans. The school with the lowest sticker price (tuition, fees, and room and board) might not be the best bargain when you look at the overall financial aid package.

Spring

❏ Still not sure where to go? The financial aid package at your top choice just not enough? Call the financial aid office and the admissions office. Talk it over. While schools don't like to bargain, they are usually willing to take a second look. Is there something unusual about your family's financial situation that might impact your parents' ability to pay?

❏ By May 1, you must make your final decision. Notify your chosen college and find out what you need to do next. Tell the other colleges you are not accepting their offers of admission and financial aid.

Summer

❏ Time to crunch the numbers. Parents, get information from the college on the total charges for the coming fall term. Deduct the aid package and then plan for how the balance will be paid. Contact the college financial aid office for the best parental loan program. If you want to arrange for a payment plan, contact the business office for further information. Most schools have deferred payment plans available for a nominal fee.

Congratulations! Remember that you need to reapply for aid every year!

Who's Paying for This?
Financial Aid Basics

A college education can be expensive—costing over $250,000 for four years at some of the higher priced private colleges and universities. Among the 10 most expensive private schools, the average tuition and fees in 2018-2019 was almost $56,900. Even at the lower-cost state colleges and universities, the cost of a four-year education can approach $60,000. Determining how you and your family will come up with the necessary funds to pay for your education requires planning, perseverance, and learning as much as you can about the options that are available to you. But before you get discouraged, College Board statistics show that 53 percent of full-time students attend four-year public and private colleges with tuition and fees less than $12,000, while 20 percent attend colleges that have tuition and fees more than $48,000. College costs tend to be less in the western states and higher in New England.

Paying for college should not be looked at as a four-year financial commitment. For many families, paying the total cost of a student's college education out of current income and savings is usually not realistic. For families that have planned ahead and have financial savings established for higher education, the burden is a lot easier. But for most, meeting the cost of college requires the pooling of current income and assets and investing in longer-term loan options. These family resources, together with financial assistance from state, federal, and institutional sources, enable millions of students each year to attend the institution of their choice.

FINANCIAL AID PROGRAMS

There are three types of financial aid:

1. Gift-aid—Scholarships and grants are funds that do not have to be repaid.

2. Loans—Loans must be repaid, usually after graduation; the amount you have to pay back is the total you've borrowed plus any accrued interest. This is considered a source of self-help aid.

3. Student employment—Student employment is a job arranged for you by the financial aid office. This is another source of self-help aid.

The federal government has four major grant programs—the Federal Pell Grant, the Federal Supplemental Educational Opportunity Grant, Academic Competitiveness Grants (ACG), and National SMART (Science and Mathematics Access to Retain Talent) grants. ACG and SMART grants are limited to students who qualify for a Pell Grant and are awarded to a select group of students. Overall, these grants are targeted to low-to-moderate income families with significant financial need. The federal government also sponsors a student employment program called the Federal Work-Study Program, which offers jobs both on and off campus, and several loan programs, including those for students and for parents of undergraduate students.

There are two types of student loan programs: subsidized and unsubsidized. The subsidized Federal Direct Loan and the Federal Perkins Loan are need-based, government-subsidized loans. Students who borrow through these programs do not have to pay interest on the loan until after they graduate or leave school. The unsubsidized Federal Direct Loan and the Federal Direct PLUS Loan Program are not based on need, and borrowers are responsible for the interest while the student is in school. These loans are administered by different methods. Once you choose your college, the financial aid office will guide you through this process.

After you've submitted your financial aid application and you've been accepted for admission, each college will send you a letter describing your financial aid award. Most award letters show estimated college costs, how much you and your family are expected to contribute, and the amount and types of aid you have been awarded. Most students are awarded aid from a combination of sources and programs. Hence, your award is often called a financial aid "package."

SOURCES OF FINANCIAL AID

Millions of students and families apply for financial aid each year. Financial aid from all sources exceeds $143 billion per year. The largest single source of aid is the federal government, which will award more than $100 billion this year.

The next largest source of financial aid is found in the college and university community. Most of this aid is awarded to students who have a demonstrated need based on the Federal Methodology. Some institutions use a different formula, the Institutional Methodology (IM), to award their own funds in conjunction with other forms of aid. Institutional aid may be either need-based or non-need based. Aid that is not based on need is usually awarded for a student's academic performance (merit awards), specific talents or abilities, or to attract the type of students a college seeks to enroll.

Another source of financial aid is from state government. All states offer grant and/or scholarship aid, most of which is need-based. However, more and more states are offering substantial merit-based aid programs. Most state programs award aid only to students attending college in their home state.

Other sources of financial aid include:

- Private agencies
- Foundations
- Corporations

Who's Paying for This? Financial Aid Basics

THE ADVICE CENTER

- Clubs
- Fraternal and service organizations
- Civic associations
- Unions
- Religious groups that award grants, scholarships, and low-interest loans
- Employers that provide tuition reimbursement benefits for employees and their children

More information about these different sources of aid is available from high school guidance offices, public libraries, college financial aid offices, directly from the sponsoring organizations, and online at **https://www.petersons.com/scholarship-search.aspx**.

HOW NEED-BASED FINANCIAL AID IS AWARDED

When you apply for aid, your family's financial situation is analyzed using a government-approved formula called the Federal Methodology. This formula looks at five items:

1. Demographic information of the family
2. Income of the parents
3. Assets of the parents
4. Income of the student
5. Assets of the student

This analysis determines the amount you and your family are expected to contribute toward your college expenses, called your Expected Family Contribution, or EFC. If the EFC is equal to or more than the cost of attendance at a particular college, then you do not demonstrate financial need. However, even if you don't have financial need, you may still qualify for aid, as there are grants, scholarships, and loan programs that are not need-based.

If the cost of your education is greater than your EFC, then you do demonstrate financial need and qualify for assistance. The amount of your financial need that can be met varies from school to school. Some are able to meet your full need, while others can only cover a certain percentage of need. Here's the formula:

> Cost of Attendance
> − Expected Family Contribution
> = Financial Need

The EFC remains constant, but your need will vary according to the costs of attendance at a particular college. In general, the higher the tuition and fees at a particular college, the higher the cost of attendance will be. Expenses for books and supplies, room and board, transportation, and other miscellaneous items are included in the overall cost of attendance. It is important to remember that you do not have to be low-income to qualify for financial aid. Many middle and upper-middle income families qualify for need-based financial aid.

APPLYING FOR FINANCIAL AID

Every student must complete the Free Application for Federal Student Aid (FAFSA) to be considered for financial aid. The FAFSA is available from your high school guidance office, many public libraries, colleges in your area, or directly from the U.S. Department of Education.

Students are encouraged to apply for federal student aid on the web. The electronic version of the FAFSA can be accessed at **http://www.fafsa.ed.gov**.

The NEW Federal Student Aid ID

In order for a student to complete the online FAFSA®, he or she will need a Federal Student Aid (FSA) ID. You can get this online at **https://fsaid.ed.gov/npas/index.htm**. Since May 2015, the FSA ID has replaced the previously used PIN system. Parents of dependent students also need to obtain their own FSA ID in order to sign their child's FAFSA® electronically online.

The FSA ID can be used to access several federal aid-related websites, including FAFSA.gov and StudentLoans.gov. It consists of a username and password and can be used to electronically sign Federal Student Aid documents, access your personal records, and make binding legal obligations. The FSA ID is beneficial in several ways:

- It removes your personal identifiable information (PII), such as your Social Security number, from your log-in credentials.
- It creates a more secure and efficient way to verify your information when you log in to access to your federal student aid information online.
- It gives you the ability to easily update your personal information.
- It allows you to easily retrieve your username and password by requesting a secure code be sent to your e-mail address or by answering challenge questions.

It's relatively simple to create an FSA ID and should only take a few minutes. In addition, you will have an opportunity to link your current Federal Student Aid PIN (if you already have one) to your FSA ID. The final step is to confirm your e-mail address. You will receive a secure code to the e-mail address you provided when you set up your FSA ID. Once you retrieve the code from your e-mail account and enter it—to confirm your e-mail address is valid—you will be able to use this e-mail address instead of your username to log in to any of the federal aid-related websites, making the log-in process EVEN simpler for you and your parents.

When you initially create your FSA ID, your information will need to be verified with the Social Security Administration. This process can take anywhere from one to three days. For that reason, it's a good idea to take care of setting up your FSA ID as early as possible, so it will be all set when you are ready to begin completing your FAFSA.

IMPORTANT NOTE: Since your FSA ID provides access to your personal information and is used to sign online documents, it's imperative that you protect this ID. Don't share it with *anyone* or write it down in an insecure location—you could place yourself at great risk for identify theft.

If Every College You're Applying to for Fall 2020 Requires the FAFSA

. . . then it's pretty simple: Complete the FAFSA after October 1, 2019, being certain to send it in before any college-imposed deadlines. Students will be required to report income information from an earlier tax year. For example, on the 2019-20 FAFSA, students (and parents, as appropriate) will report their 2018 income information, rather than their 2018 income information.

After you send in your FAFSA, you'll receive a Student Aid Report (SAR) that includes all of the information you reported and shows your EFC. If you provided an e-mail address, the SAR is sent to you electronically; otherwise, you will receive a SAR or SAR Acknowledgment in the mail, which lists your FAFSA information but may require you to make any corrections on the FAFSA website. Be sure to review the SAR, checking to see if the information you reported is accurately represented. If you used estimated numbers to complete the FAFSA, you may have to resubmit the SAR with any corrections to the data. The college(s) you have designated on the FAFSA will receive the information you reported and will use that data to make their decision.

The CSS/Financial Aid PROFILE®

To award their own funds, some colleges require an additional application, the CSS/Financial Aid PROFILE® form. The PROFILE asks supplemental questions that some colleges and awarding agencies feel provide a more accurate assessment of the family's ability to pay for college. It is up to the college to decide whether it will use only the FAFSA or both the FAFSA and the PROFILE. PROFILE applications are available from the high school guidance office and on the Web. Both the paper application and the website list those colleges and programs that require the PROFILE application.

If a College Requires the PROFILE

Step 1: Register for the CSS/Financial Aid PROFILE in the fall of your senior year in high school. You can apply for the PROFILE online at **https://cssprofile.collegeboard.org/**. Registration information with a list of the colleges that require the PROFILE is available in most high school guidance offices. There is a fee for using the Financial Aid PROFILE application ($25 for the first college, which includes the $9 application fee, and $16 for each additional college). You must pay for the service by credit card when you register. If you do not have a credit card, you will be billed. A limited number of fee waivers are automatically granted to first-time applicants based on the financial information provided on the PROFILE.

Step 2: Fill out your customized CSS/Financial Aid PROFILE. Once you register, your application will be immediately available online and will have questions that all students must complete, questions which must be completed by the student's parents (unless the student is independent and the colleges or programs selected do not require parental information), and *may* have supplemental questions needed by one or more of your schools or programs. If required, those will be found in Section Q of the application.

In addition to the PROFILE application you complete online, you may also be required to complete a Business/ Farm Supplement via traditional paper format. Completion of this form is not a part of the online process. If this form is required, instructions on how to download and print the supplemental form are provided. If your biological or adoptive parents are separated or divorced and your colleges and programs require it, your noncustodial parent may be asked to complete the Noncustodial PROFILE.

Once you complete and submit your PROFILE application, it will be processed and sent directly to your requested colleges and programs.

IF YOU DON'T QUALIFY FOR NEED-BASED AID

If you are not eligible for need-based aid, you can still find ways to lessen your burden.

Here are some suggestions:

- Search for merit scholarships. You can start at the initial stages of your application process. College merit awards are increasingly important as more and more colleges award these to students they especially want to attract. As a result, applying to a college at which your qualifications put you at the top of the entering class may give you a larger merit award. Another source of aid to look for is private scholarships that are given for special skills and talents. Additional information can be found at **www.finaid.org**.

- Seek employment during the summer and the academic year. The student employment office at your college can help you locate a school-year job. Many colleges and local businesses have vacancies remaining after they have hired students who are receiving Federal Work-Study Program financial aid.

- Borrow through the unsubsidized Federal Direct Loan program. This is generally available to all students. The terms and conditions are similar to the subsidized loans. The biggest difference is that the borrower is responsible for the interest while still in college, although the government permits students to delay paying the interest right away and add the accrued interest to the total amount owed. You must file the FAFSA to be considered.

- After you've secured what you can through scholarships, working, and borrowing, you and your parents will be expected to meet your share of the college bill (the Expected Family Contribution). Many colleges offer monthly payment plans that spread the cost over the academic year. If the monthly payments are too high, parents can borrow through the Federal Direct PLUS Loan Program, through one of the many private education loan programs available, or through home equity loans and lines of credit. Families seeking assistance in financing college expenses should inquire at the financial aid office about what programs are available at the college. Some families seek the advice of professional financial advisers and tax consultants.

How to Use This Guide

PROFILES

The **PROFILES** section contains basic data in capsule form for quick review and comparison. Organized by state, more than 2,700 colleges and universities are listed alphabetically, followed by their city and state and website URL. Those schools that offer a special, detailed listing at **www.petersons.com**, will also have a ★ next to their name.

The following outline of the format shows the section headings and the items that each section covers. Any item that does not apply to a particular college or for which no information was supplied is omitted from that college's listing. Display ads, which appear near some of the institutions' profiles, have been provided and paid for by those colleges and universities that chose to supplement their profile with additional information.

Category Overviews

Type of Institution

Private institutions are designated as *independent* (nonprofit), *proprietary* (profit-making), or *independent with a specific religious denomination or affiliation*. Nondenominational or interdenominational religious orientation is possible and would be indicated. Public institutions are designated by the source of funding. Designations include *federal, state, province, commonwealth* (Puerto Rico), *territory* (U.S. territories), *county, district* (an educational administrative unit often having boundaries different from units of local government), *city, state and local* (local may refer to county, district, or city), or *state-related* (funded primarily by the state but administratively autonomous). *Religious affiliation* may follow, along with year founded. Each institution is classified as one of the following:

- Primarily two-year: Awards baccalaureate degrees but majority of students are enrolled in two-year programs.

- Four-year: Awards baccalaureate degrees; may also award associate degrees; does not award graduate (postbaccalaureate) degrees.

- Five-year: Awards a five-year baccalaureate in a professional field such as architecture or pharmacy; does not award graduate degrees.

- Upper-level: Awards baccalaureate degrees but entering students must have at least two years of previous college-level credit; may also offer graduate degrees.

- Comprehensive: Awards baccalaureate degrees; may also award associate degrees; offers graduate degree programs, primarily at the master's, specialist's, or professional level, although one or two doctoral programs may be offered.

- University: Offers four years of undergraduate work, plus graduate degrees through the doctorate in more than two academic or professional fields.

Setting

Designated as *urban* (located within a major city), *suburban* (a residential area within commuting distance of a major city), *small town* (a small but compactly settled area not within commuting distance of a major city), or *rural* (a remote and sparsely populated area).

Endowment

The total dollar value of funds and/or property donated to the institution or the multicampus educational system of which the institution is a part.

Student Body

An institution is *coed* (coeducational—admits men and women), *primarily* (80 percent or more) *women, primarily men, women only,* or *men only.* A few schools are designated as *undergraduate: women only; graduate: coed* or *undergraduate: men only; graduate: coed.*

Entrance

The five levels of entrance difficulty (*most difficult, very difficult, moderately difficult, minimally difficult,* and *noncompetitive*) are based on the percentage of applicants who were accepted for fall 2018 freshman admission (or, in the case of upper-level schools, for entering-class admission) and on the high school class rank and standardized test scores of the accepted freshmen who actually enrolled in fall 2018. The colleges were asked to select the level that most closely corresponds to their entrance difficulty, according to these guidelines.

UNDERGRAD STUDENTS

Number of full-time or part-time undergraduates. Number of states and territories that students come from; percentages of undergraduates who are out-of-state; live on campus; Black or African American, non-Hispanic/Latino; Hispanic/Latino; Asian, non-Hispanic/Latino; Native Hawaiian or other Pacific Islander, non-Hispanic/Latino; American Indian or Alaska Native, non-Hispanic/Latino American Indian or Alaska Native, non-Hispanic/Latino; two or more races, non-Hispanic/Latino; race/ethnicity unknown; international; and percentage of students who transferred in are given.

Freshmen

Admission: Figures are given for the number of students who applied for fall 2018 admission, the number of those who were admitted, and the number who enrolled. *Average high school GPA:* Freshman statistics include the average high school GPA. *Test scores:* Percentage of freshmen who took the SAT® (not the Redesigned SAT) and received critical reading, math, and writing scores above 500, above 600, and above 700; as well as percentage of freshmen taking the ACT® who received a composite score of 18 or higher, 24 or higher, and 30 or higher.

Retention: The percentage of full-time freshmen who returned the following year for the fall semester/term.

FACULTY

Total: The total number of faculty members; percentage of full-time faculty members as of fall 2018; and percentage of total faculty members who hold terminal degrees. *Student/ faculty ratio:* School's estimate of the ratio of matriculated undergraduate students to faculty members teaching undergraduate courses.

ACADEMICS

Calendar: Most colleges indicate one of the following: 4-1-4, 4-4-1, or a similar arrangement (two terms of equal length plus an abbreviated winter or spring term, with the numbers referring to months); semesters; trimesters; quarters; 3-3 (three courses for each of three terms); modular (the academic year is divided into small blocks of time; courses of varying lengths are assembled according to individual programs); or standard year (for most Canadian institutions). *Degrees:* This names the full range of levels of certificates, diplomas, and degrees, including prebaccalaureate, baccalaureate, graduate, and professional, that are offered by this institution.

Special study options: Details on study options available at each college, such as accelerated degree program, academic remediation for entering students, Advanced Placement credit, cooperative education programs, distance learning, double majors, English as a second language (ESL), and external degree programs. *ROTC:* Army, Naval, or Air Force Reserve Officers' Training Corps programs offered either on campus, at a branch campus [designated by a (b)], or at a cooperating host institution [designated by (c)].

Unusual degree programs: Information is offered here on any unique programs at the institution, such as 3-2 engineering, computer science, or business administration programs.

Computers: Information is provided on the numbers of computers/terminals available on campus for general student use, what computer technology is accessible to students, and availability of a campus-wide network and wireless campus network.

STUDENT LIFE

Housing options: Institution's policy about whether students are permitted to live off-campus or are required to live on campus for a specified period; whether freshmen only, coed, single-sex, cooperative, and disabled student housing options are available; whether campus housing is leased by the school and/or provided by a third party; whether freshman applicants are given priority for college housing. "College housing not available" indicates that no college-owned or -operated housing facilities are provided for undergraduates and that noncommuting students must arrange for their own accommodations.

Activities and organizations: Information on clubs and organizations, including sororities and fraternities.

Athletics: Membership in one or more of the following athletic associations is indicated by initials: NCAA: National Collegiate Athletic Association; NAIA: National Association of Intercollegiate Athletics; NCCAA: National Christian College Athletic Association; USCAA: United States Collegiate Athletic Association; and CIS: Canadian Interuniversity Sport. The overall NCAA division in which all or most intercollegiate teams compete is designated by I, II, or III. All teams that do not compete in this division are listed as exceptions.

Sports offered by the college are divided into two groups: *Intercollegiate* ("M" or "W" following the name of each sport indicates that it is offered for men or women) and *Intramural.* An "s" in parentheses following an "M" or "W" for an intercollegiate sport indicates that athletic scholarships (or grants-in-aid) are offered for men or women in that sport, and a "c" indicates a club team as opposed to a varsity team.

Campus security: Campus safety measures including 24-hour emergency response devices (phones and alarms) and patrols by trained security personnel, student patrols, late-night transport-escort service, and controlled dormitory access (key, security card, etc.).

Student services: Information indicates services offered to students by the college, such as legal services, health clinics, personal-psychological counseling, and women's centers.

COSTS & FINANCIAL AID

Costs: Costs are given for the 2019–20 academic year or for the 2018–19 academic year if 2019–20 figures were not yet available. *Tuition:* Annual expenses may be expressed as a comprehensive fee (including full-time tuition, mandatory fees, and college room and board) or as separate figures for full-time tuition, fees, room and board, or room only. For public institutions where tuition differs according to residence, separate figures are given for area or state residents and for nonresidents. Part-time tuition is expressed in terms of a per-unit rate (per credit, per semester hour, etc.).

The tuition structure at some institutions is complex in that freshmen and sophomores may be charged a different rate from that for juniors and seniors, a professional or vocational division may have a different fee structure from the liberal arts division of the same institution, or part-time tuition may be prorated on a sliding scale according to the number of credit hours taken. Tuition and fees may vary according to academic program, campus/location, class time (day, evening, weekend), course/credit load, course level, degree level, reciprocity agreements, and student level. *Room and board* charges are reported as an average for one academic year and may vary according to the board plan selected, campus/ location, type of housing facility, or student level. *Payment plans* may include tuition prepayment, installment payments, and deferred payment. A tuition prepayment plan gives a student the option of locking in the current tuition rate for the entire term of enrollment by paying the full amount in advance rather than year by year. *Waivers:* availability of full or partial undergraduate tuition waivers to minority students, children of alumni, employees or their children, adult students, and senior citizens may be listed.

Financial Aid: This information represents aid awarded to undergraduates for the available academic year. Figures are given for the number of undergraduates who applied for aid, the number who were judged to have need, and the number who had their need met. The number of Federal Work-Study

Programs and/or part-time jobs and average earnings are listed, as well as the number of non-need-based awards. The *Average percent of need met* for those determined to have need, *Average financial aid package* awarded to undergraduates (the amount of scholarships, grants, work-study payments, or loans in the institutionally administered financial aid package divided by the number of students who received any financial aid-amounts used to pay the officially designated Expected Family Contribution (EFC), *Average need-based loan, Average need-based gift aid,* and *Average non-need-based aid* are given. *Average indebtedness upon graduation,* which is the average per-borrower indebtedness of the last graduating undergraduate class from amounts borrowed at this institution through any loan programs, excluding parent loans, is listed last.

APPLYING

Standardized Tests

The most commonly required standardized tests are the ACT®, SAT®, and SAT Subject Tests™. These and other standardized tests may be used for selective admission, as a basis for counseling or course placement, or for both purposes. This section notes if a test is used for admission or placement and whether it is required, required for some, or recommended. In addition to the ACT and SAT, the following standardized entrance and placement examinations are referred to by their initials: ABLE (Adult Basic Learning Examination); ACT ASSET (ACT Assessment of Skills for Successful Entry and Transfer); ACT PEP (ACT Proficiency Examination Program); CAT (California Achievement Tests); CELT (Comprehensive English Language Test); CPAt (Career Programs Assessment); CPT (Computerized Placement Test); DAT (Differential Aptitude Test); LSAT (Law School Admission Test); MAPS (Multiple Assessment Program Service); MCAT (Medical College Admission Test); MMPI (Minnesota Multiphasic Personality Inventory); OAT (Optometry Admission Test); PAA (Prueba de Aptitud Académica—Spanish-language version of SAT); PCAT (Pharmacy College Admission Test); PSAT/NMSQT® (Preliminary SAT/National Merit Scholarship Qualifying Test); SCAT (Scholastic College Aptitude Test); TABE (Test of Adult Basic Education); TASP (Texas Academic Skills Program); TOEFL® (Test of English as a Foreign Language); WPCT (Washington Pre-College Test).

Options: This includes the following: Early admission—(highly qualified students may matriculate before graduating from high school); Early action—admission plan that allows students to apply and be notified of an admission decision well in advance of the regular notification dates (if accepted, the candidate is not committed to enroll; students may reply to the offer under the college's regular reply policy); Deferred entrance—practice of permitting accepted students to postpone enrollment, usually for a period of one academic term or year; Early decision deadline—plan that permits students to apply and be notified of an admission decision (and financial aid offer, if applicable) well in advance of the regular notification date, and applicants agree to accept an offer of admission and to withdraw their applications from other colleges.

Application fee: The fee required with an application is noted.

Required, Required for some, and Recommended: Other application requirements are grouped into three categories and may include an essay, standardized test scores, a high school transcript, a minimum high school grade point average (expressed as a number on a scale of 0 to 4.0, where 4.0 equals A, 3.0 equals B, etc.), letters of recommendation, an interview on campus or with local alumni, and, for certain types of schools or programs, special requirements such as a musical audition or an art portfolio.

Application deadlines and notification: Admission application deadlines and dates for notification of acceptance or rejection are given either as specific dates or as rolling and continuous. Rolling means that applications are processed as they are received, and qualified students are accepted as long as there are openings. Continuous means that applicants are notified of acceptance or rejection as applications are processed up until the date indicated or the actual beginning of classes. The application deadline and the notification date for transfers are given if they differ from the dates for freshmen. Early decision and early action application deadlines and notification dates are also indicated when relevant.

CONTACT

The name, title, mailing address, and phone number of the person to contact for further information are given at the end of the profile. The fax number and e-mail address may also be provided.

Additional Information

Each school that has a College Close-Up and a half-page display in this guide will have a cross-reference with the page numbers of the half-page display and Close-Up.

COLLEGE CLOSE-UPS

These two-page descriptions are more in-depth and provide an inside look at several colleges and universities. The descriptions provide a wealth of information that is crucial in the college decision-making process—components such as tuition, financial aid, and major fields of study. Prepared exclusively by college officials, the descriptions are designed to help give students a better sense of the individuality of each institution, in terms that include campus environment, student activities, and lifestyle. The absence of any college or university does not constitute an editorial decision on the part of Peterson's. In essence, these descriptions are an open forum for colleges and universities, on a voluntary basis, to communicate their particular message to prospective college students. The colleges included have paid a fee to Peterson's to provide this information. The College Close-Ups are edited to provide a consistent format across entries for your ease of comparison.

INDEXES

Here you'll find easy-to-use breakdowns of schools' majors, entrance difficulty, and cost ranges. In addition, you'll find an "Advertisers Index," a "Geographical Listing of College Close-Ups," and an "Alphabetical Listing of Colleges and Universities."

Majors

This listing presents hundreds of undergraduate fields of study that are currently offered, according to the colleges' responses on *Peterson's® Annual Survey of Undergraduate Institutions*. The majors appear in alphabetical order, each followed by an alphabetical list of the schools that offer a bachelor's-level program in that particular field. Liberal Arts and Sciences/ Liberal Studies indicates a general program with no specified major.

The terms used are those of the U.S. Department of Education Classification of Instructional Programs (CIP). Many institutions, however, use different terms. Although the term major is used in this guide, some colleges may use other terms, such as concentration, program of study, or field.

Entrance Difficulty

This listing groups colleges by their own assessment of their entrance difficulty level. The colleges were asked to select the level that most closely corresponds to their entrance difficulty. Institutions for which high school class rank and/or standardized test scores do not apply as admission criteria were asked to select the level that best indicates their entrance difficulty as compared to other institutions.

Cost Ranges

Colleges are grouped into ten price ranges, from under $2,000 to $30,000 and over.

DATA COLLECTION PROCEDURES

The data contained in the **PROFILES** and **INDEXES** sections were researched between winter 2018 and spring 2019 through *Peterson's® Annual Survey of Undergraduate Institutions*. Questionnaires were sent to the more than 4,500 colleges and universities that met the outlined inclusion criteria. All data included in this edition have been submitted by officials (usually admissions and financial aid officers, registrars, or institutional research personnel) at the colleges. Some of the institutions that submitted data were contacted directly by the Peterson's research staff to verify unusual figures, resolve discrepancies, or obtain additional data. All usable information received in time for publication has been included. The omission of any particular item from the **PROFILES** and **INDEXES** sections signifies that the information is either not applicable to that institution or not available. Because of Peterson's comprehensive editorial review and because all material comes directly from college officials, we believe that the information presented is accurate. You should check with a specific college or university at the time of application to verify such figures as tuition and fees, which may have changed since this guide's publication.

CRITERIA FOR INCLUSION IN THIS BOOK

The term "four-year college" is the commonly used designation for institutions that grant the baccalaureate degree. Four years is the expected amount of time required to earn this degree, although some bachelor's degree programs may be completed in three years, others require five years, and part-time programs may take considerably longer. Upper-level institutions offer only the junior and senior years and accept only students with two years of college-level credit. Therefore, "four-year college" is a conventional term that accurately describes most of the institutions included in this guide but should not be taken literally in all cases.

To be included in this guide, an institution must have full accreditation or be a candidate for accreditation (preaccreditation) status by an institutional or specialized accrediting body recognized by the U.S. Department of Education or the Council for Higher Education Accreditation (CHEA). Institutional accrediting bodies, which review each institution as a whole, include the six regional associations of schools and colleges (Middle States, New England, North Central, Northwest, Southern, and Western), each of which is responsible for a specified portion of the United States and its territories. Other institutional accrediting bodies are national in scope and accredit specific kinds of institutions (e.g., Bible colleges, independent colleges, and rabbinical and Talmudic schools). Program registration by the New York State Board of Regents is considered to be the equivalent of institutional accreditation, since the board requires that all programs offered by an institution meet its standards before recognition is granted. A Canadian institution must be chartered and authorized to grant degrees by the provincial government, affiliated with a chartered institution, or accredited by a recognized U.S. accrediting body. This guide also includes institutions outside the United States that are accredited by these U.S. accrediting bodies. There are recognized specialized or professional accrediting bodies in more than forty different fields, each of which is authorized to accredit institutions or specific programs in its particular field. For specialized institutions that offer programs in one field only, we designate this to be the equivalent of institutional accreditation. A full explanation of the accrediting process and complete information on recognized, institutional (regional and national) and specialized accrediting bodies can be found online at **www.chea.org** or at **www2.ed.gov/admins/finaid/accred/ index.html**.

A Note from the Peterson's® Editors

NOTICE: Certain portions of or information contained in this book have been submitted and paid for by the educational institution identified, and such institutions take full responsibility for the accuracy, timeliness, completeness and functionality of such content. Such portions or information include (i) each display ad in the "Profiles" section from pages 55 through 1272 that comprises a half or full page of information covering a single educational institution, and (ii) each two-page description in the "College Close-Up" section from pages 1273 through 1606.

THE ADVICE CENTER

Institutional Changes Since *Peterson's*® Four-Year Colleges 2019

The following is an alphabetical listing of institutions that have closed, merged with other institutions, or changed their names or status since *Peterson's*® *Four-Year Colleges 2019*.

Argosy University, Dallas (Farmers Branch, TX): *closed.*
Argosy University, Denver (Denver, CO): *closed.*
Argosy University, Inland Empire (Ontario, CA): *closed.*
Argosy University, Nashville (Nashville, TN): *closed.*
Argosy University, Salt Lake City (Draper, UT): *closed.*
Argosy University, San Diego (San Diego, CA): *closed.*
Argosy University, San Francisco Bay Area (Alameda, CA): *closed.*
Argosy University, Sarasota (Sarasota, FL): *closed.*
Argosy University, Schaumburg (Schaumburg, IL): *closed.*
Arlington Baptist College (Arlington, TX): *name changed to Arlington Baptist University.*
Armstrong State University (Savannah, GA): *name changed to Georgia Southern University–Armstrong Campus.*
Art Center College of Design (Pasadena, CA): *name changed to ArtCenter College of Design.*
The Art Institute of California–San Francisco, a campus of Argosy University (San Francisco, CA): *closed.*
Augsburg College (Minneapolis, MN): *name changed to Augsburg University.*
Bristol University (Anaheim, CA): *closed.*
Claremont McKenna College (Claremont, CA): *merged into The Claremont Colleges (Claremont, CA).*
Coleman University (San Diego, CA): *closed.*
Digital Media Arts College (Boca Raton, FL): *closed.*
Everest University (Tampa, FL): *no longer offers graduate degrees.*
Fairleigh Dickinson University, College at Florham (Madison, NJ): *name changed to Fairleigh Dickinson University, Florham Campus.*
Faith Evangelical College & Seminary (Tacoma, WA): *name changed to Faith International University.*
Frank Lloyd Wright School of Architecture (Scottsdale, AZ): *name changed to School of Architecture at Taliesin.*
Future Generations Graduate School (Franklin, WV): *name changed to Future Generations University.*
Georgia Christian University (Atlanta, GA): *not accredited by an agency recognized by USDE or CHEA at the time of publication.*
Grace University (Omaha, NE): *closed.*
Greenville College (Greenville, IL): *name changed to Greenville University.*
Hazelden Graduate School of Addiction Studies (Center City, MN): *name changed to Hazelden Betty Ford Graduate School of Addiction.*
Henley-Putnam University (San Jose, CA): *name changed to Henley-Putnam School of Strategic Security.*
Huntington College of Health Sciences (Knoxville, TN): *name changed to Huntington University of Health Sciences.*
The Institute for the Psychological Sciences (Arlington, VA): *name changed to Divine Mercy University.*
International College of the Cayman Islands (Newlands, Cayman Islands): *not accredited by an agency recognized by USDE or CHEA at the time of publication.*
Johnson State College (Johnson, VT): *name changed to Northern Vermont University–Johnson.*
John Wesley University (High Point, NC): *closed.*
Kaplan University, Davenport Campus (Davenport, IA): *name changed to Purdue University Global.*

Knowledge Systems Institute (Skokie, IL): no longer degree granting.
Long Island University–Hudson at Westchester (Purchase, NY): *name changed to Long Island University–Hudson.*
Lutheran Theological Seminary at Gettysburg (Gettysburg, PA): *name changed to United Lutheran Seminary.*
Lynchburg College (Lynchburg, VA): *name changed to University of Lynchburg.*
Lyndon State College (Lyndonville, VT): *name changed to Northern Vermont University–Lyndon.*
Marylhurst University (Marylhurst, OR): *closed.*
McNally Smith College of Music (Saint Paul, MN): *closed.*
Memphis College of Art (Memphis, TN): *closed.*
Mirrer Yeshiva (Brooklyn, NY): *name changed to Mirrer Yeshiva Central Institute.*
Moody Theological Seminary–Michigan (Plymouth, MI): *name changed to Moody Theological Seminary Michigan.*
Mount Ida College (Newton, MA): *closed.*
National American University (Rapid City, SD): no longer offers graduate degrees.
The Ohio State University–Mansfield Campus (Mansfield, OH): *name changed to The Ohio State University at Mansfield.*
The Ohio State University–Newark Campus (Newark, OH): *name changed to The Ohio State University at Newark.*
Our Lady of the Lake College (Baton Rouge, LA): *name changed to Franciscan Missionaries of Our Lady University.*
Philadelphia University (Philadelphia, PA): *closed.*
Rudolf Steiner College (Fair Oaks, CA): *not accredited by an agency recognized by USDE or CHEA at the time of publication.*
Sacred Heart School of Theology (Hales Corners, WI): *name changed to Sacred Heart Seminary and School of Theology.*
Sewanee: The University of the South (Sewanee, TN): *name changed to The University of the South.*
Shepherd University (Los Angeles, CA): *closed.*
Silicon Valley University (San Jose, CA): *closed.*
South University (Novi, MI): *closed.*
South University (High Point, NC): *closed.*
South University (Cleveland, OH): *closed.*
University of Great Falls (Great Falls, MT): *name changed to University of Providence.*
University of Phoenix–Atlanta Campus (Sandy Springs, GA): *closed.*
University of Phoenix–Augusta Campus (Augusta, GA): *closed.*
University of Phoenix–Central Florida Campus (Orlando, FL): *closed.*
University of Phoenix–Charlotte Campus (Charlotte, NC): *closed.*
University of Phoenix–Colorado Campus (Lone Tree, CO): *closed.*
University of Phoenix–Colorado Springs Downtown Campus (Colorado Springs, CO): *closed.*
University of Phoenix–Columbus Georgia Campus (Columbus, GA): *closed.*
University of Phoenix–Jersey City Campus (Jersey City, NJ): *closed.*
University of Phoenix–New Mexico Campus (Albuquerque, NM): *closed.*
University of Phoenix–North Florida Campus (Jacksonville, FL): *closed.*
University of Phoenix–Southern Arizona Campus (Tucson, AZ): *closed.*
University of Phoenix–Southern California Campus (Costa Mesa, CA): *closed.*
University of Phoenix–South Florida Campus (Miramar, FL): *closed.*
University of Phoenix–Utah Campus (Salt Lake City, UT): *closed.*

University of Phoenix–Washington D.C. Campus (Washington, DC): *closed.*

University of Phoenix–Western Washington Campus (Tukwila, WA): *closed.*

University of Puerto Rico, Mayagüez Campus (Mayagüez, PR): *name changed to University of Puerto Rico–Mayagüez.*

University of Puerto Rico, Medical Sciences Campus (San Juan, PR): *name changed to University of Puerto Rico–Medical Sciences Campus.*

University of Puerto Rico, Río Piedras Campus (San Juan, PR): *name changed to University of Puerto Rico–Río Piedras.*

The University of South Dakota (Vermillion, SD): *name changed to University of South Dakota.*

Urbana University (Urbana, OH): *name changed to Urbana University–A Branch Campus of Franklin University.*

Virginia College in Birmingham (Birmingham, AL): *closed.*

Warner Pacific College (Portland, OR): *name changed to Warner Pacific University.*

Wheelock College (Boston, MA): *merged into Boston University (Boston, MA).*

Wright Institute (Berkeley, CA): *name changed to The Wright Institute.*

Yeshiva Karlin Stolin Rabbinical Institute (Brooklyn, NY): *name changed to Yeshiva Karlin Stolin.*

Profiles

A ★ *indicates that the school has detailed information with a Premium Profile on Petersons.com.*

ALABAMA

Alabama Agricultural and Mechanical University

Huntsville, Alabama
http://www.aamu.edu/

CONTACT
Dr. Evelyn Ellis, Interim Director of Admissions, Alabama Agricultural and Mechanical University, 4900 Meridian Street, Huntsville, AL 35811. *Phone:* 256-372-5245. *Toll-free phone:* 800-553-0816. *Fax:* 256-851-9747.

Alabama State University

Montgomery, Alabama
http://www.alasu.edu/
- **State-supported** university, founded 1867, part of Alabama Commission on Higher Education
- **Urban** 172-acre campus
- **Endowment** $89.3 million
- **Coed** 3,903 undergraduate students, 93% full-time, 63% women, 37% men
- **Minimally difficult** entrance level, 98% of applicants were admitted

UNDERGRAD STUDENTS
3,643 full-time, 260 part-time. Students come from 41 states and territories; 24 other countries; 34% are from out of state; 94% Black or African American, non-Hispanic/Latino; 0.9% Hispanic/Latino; 0.4% Asian, non-Hispanic/Latino; 0.1% Native Hawaiian or other Pacific Islander, non-Hispanic/Latino; 0.1% American Indian or Alaska Native, non-Hispanic/Latino; 1% Two or more races, non-Hispanic/Latino; 1% Race/ethnicity unknown; 1% international; 4% transferred in; 34% live on campus.

Freshmen:
Admission: 7,588 applied, 7,412 admitted, 1,042 enrolled. *Average high school GPA:* 3.1. *Test scores:* SAT evidence-based reading and writing scores over 500: 39%; SAT math scores over 500: 36%; ACT scores over 18: 43%; SAT evidence-based reading and writing scores over 600: 6%; SAT math scores over 600: 5%; ACT scores over 24: 5%.
Retention: 59% of full-time freshmen returned.

FACULTY
Total: 409, 56% full-time, 57% with terminal degrees.
Student/faculty ratio: 17:1.

ACADEMICS
Calendar: semesters. *Degrees:* certificates, bachelor's, master's, doctoral, post-master's, and postbachelor's certificates.
Special study options: academic remediation for entering students, advanced placement credit, cooperative education, distance learning, double majors, freshman honors college, honors programs, independent study, internships, part-time degree program, student-designed majors, summer session for credit. *ROTC:* Army (c), Air Force (b).
Computers: 805 computers/terminals and 805 ports are available on campus for general student use. Students can access the following: computer help desk, free student e-mail accounts, online (class) grades, online (class) registration, online (class) schedules. Campuswide network is available. 100% of college-owned or -operated housing units are wired for high-speed Internet access. Wireless service is available via entire campus.
Library: Levi Watkins Learning Center plus 1 other. *Books:* 437,312 (physical), 69,796 (digital/electronic); *Serial titles:* 1,607 (physical), 6,084 (digital/electronic); *Databases:* 192. Weekly public service hours: 78; study areas open 24 hours, 5–7 days a week; students can reserve study rooms.

STUDENT LIFE
Housing options: men-only, women-only, special housing for students with disabilities. Campus housing is university owned.

Activities and organizations: drama/theater group, student-run newspaper, radio station, choral group, marching band, Alabama State University Marching Band, Alpha Kappa Alpha Sorority Inc, Empower Ministry, Nu Alpha Nu Service Fraternity Inc, Delta Sigma Theta Sorority Inc, national fraternities, national sororities.
Athletics Member NCAA. All Division I. *Intercollegiate sports:* baseball M(s), basketball M(s)/W(s), bowling W(s), cheerleading M(s)/W(s), cross-country running M(s)/W(s), football M(s), golf M(s)/W(s)(c), soccer W(s), softball W(s), tennis M(s)/W(s), track and field M(s)/W(s), volleyball W(s). *Intramural sports:* basketball M, football M.
Campus security: 24-hour emergency response devices and patrols, late-night transport/escort service.
Student services: health clinic, personal/psychological counseling.

COSTS & FINANCIAL AID
Costs (2018–19) *One-time required fee:* $150. *Tuition:* state resident $8328 full-time, $347 per credit hour part-time; nonresident $16,656 full-time, $694 per credit hour part-time. Full-time tuition and fees vary according to class time, course level, course load, degree level, program, and student level. Part-time tuition and fees vary according to class time, course level, course load, degree level, program, and student level. *Required fees:* $2740 full-time, $446 per term part-time. *Room and board:* $6050. Room and board charges vary according to board plan and housing facility. *Payment plan:* deferred payment. *Waivers:* employees or children of employees.
Financial Aid Of all full-time matriculated undergraduates who enrolled in 2018, 3,587 applied for aid, 3,513 were judged to have need, 1,728 had their need fully met. In 2018, 55 non-need-based awards were made. *Average percent of need met:* 83. *Average financial aid package:* $16,925. *Average need-based loan:* $3948. *Average need-based gift aid:* $5606. *Average non-need-based aid:* $9478. *Average indebtedness upon graduation:* $3376.

APPLYING
Standardized Tests *Required:* SAT or ACT (for admission).
Options: electronic application, early admission, deferred entrance.
Application fee: $25.
Required: high school transcript, minimum 2.0 GPA. *Recommended:* essay or personal statement, interview.
Notification: continuous (freshmen), continuous (transfers).

CONTACT
Mr. Freddie Williams, Director of Admissions and Recruitment, Alabama State University, 915 South Jackson Street, Montgomery, AL 36101-0271. *Phone:* 334-229-4291. *Toll-free phone:* 800-253-5037. *Fax:* 334-229-4984. *E-mail:* fwilliams@alasu.edu.

Amridge University

Montgomery, Alabama
http://www.amridgeuniversity.edu/
- **Independent** university, founded 1967, affiliated with Church of Christ
- **Urban** 10-acre campus
- **Endowment** $8.0 million
- **Coed** 356 undergraduate students, 49% full-time, 68% women, 32% men
- **Minimally difficult** entrance level

UNDERGRAD STUDENTS
176 full-time, 180 part-time. Students come from 46 states and territories; 48% are from out of state; 79% Black or African American, non-Hispanic/Latino; 2% Hispanic/Latino; 0.6% Asian, non-Hispanic/Latino; 0.6% American Indian or Alaska Native, non-Hispanic/Latino; 2% Race/ethnicity unknown.

Freshmen:
Admission: 3 enrolled.

FACULTY
Total: 56, 64% full-time, 75% with terminal degrees.
Student/faculty ratio: 12:1.

ACADEMICS

Calendar: semesters. *Degrees:* associate, bachelor's, master's, and doctoral.

Special study options: academic remediation for entering students, accelerated degree program, adult/continuing education programs, advanced placement credit, distance learning, double majors, external degree program, independent study, internships, part-time degree program, services for LD students, summer session for credit.

Computers: 5 computers/terminals are available on campus for general student use. Students can access the following: computer help desk, free student e-mail accounts, online (class) grades, online (class) registration, online (class) schedules. Campuswide network is available. Wireless service is available via entire campus.

Library: Southern Christian University Library. *Books:* 90,000 (physical); *Databases:* 12. Weekly public service hours: 50.

STUDENT LIFE

Housing options: college housing not available.

Activities and organizations: Amridge University Student Advisory Committee.

Campus security: 24-hour emergency response devices, security guards.

FINANCIAL AID

Financial Aid Of all full-time matriculated undergraduates who enrolled in 2018, 77 applied for aid, 77 were judged to have need, 69 had their need fully met. *Average financial aid package:* $8734. *Average need-based loan:* $5423. *Average need-based gift aid:* $2871. *Average indebtedness upon graduation:* $11,179.

APPLYING

Standardized Tests *Required:* ACT (for admission). *Required for some:* SAT or ACT (for admission).

Options: electronic application, early admission.

Application fee: $50.

Required: high school transcript, minimum 2.0 GPA.

Application deadlines: rolling (freshmen), rolling (transfers).

CONTACT

Mrs. Elaine Tarence, Registrar, Amridge University, 1200 Taylor Road, Montgomery, AL 36117. *Phone:* 334-387-3877 Ext. 7528. *Toll-free phone:* 888-790-8080. *Fax:* 334-387-3878. *E-mail:* registrar@amridgeuniversity.edu.

Athens State University

Athens, Alabama

http://www.athens.edu/

- **State-supported** upper-level, founded 1822
- **Small-town** 45-acre campus
- **Coed**
- **Noncompetitive** entrance level

FACULTY

Student/faculty ratio: 17:1.

ACADEMICS

Calendar: semesters. *Degrees:* certificates, bachelor's, and master's.

Library: Athens State University Library. *Books:* 83,092 (physical), 255,950 (digital/electronic); *Serial titles:* 289 (physical), 296,023 (digital/electronic); *Databases:* 23,955. Students can reserve study rooms.

STUDENT LIFE

Housing options: college housing not available.

Activities and organizations: drama/theater group, student-run newspaper, SGA, Accounting, Art, PE.

Campus security: 24-hour emergency response devices and patrols.

Student services: personal/psychological counseling, veterans affairs office.

COSTS & FINANCIAL AID

Costs (2018–19) *Tuition:* state resident $6060 full-time; nonresident $12,120 full-time. *Required fees:* $750 full-time.

Financial Aid Of all full-time matriculated undergraduates who enrolled in 2016, 1,003 applied for aid, 909 were judged to have need, 27 had their need fully met. In 2016, 11 non-need-based awards were made. *Average*

percent of need met: 47. *Average financial aid package:* $10,201. *Average need-based loan:* $3326. *Average need-based gift aid:* $4110. *Average non-need-based aid:* $2603.

APPLYING

Options: electronic application, deferred entrance.

Application fee: $30.

CONTACT

Athens State University, 300 North Beaty Street, Athens, AL 35611. *Phone:* 256-233-8151. *Toll-free phone:* 800-522-0272.

Auburn University

Auburn University, Alabama

http://www.auburn.edu/

- **State-supported** university, founded 1856
- **Small-town** 1875-acre campus with easy access to Atlanta, Birmingham
- **Endowment** $768.1 million
- **Coed** 24,628 undergraduate students, 91% full-time, 48% women, 52% men
- **Moderately difficult** entrance level, 75% of applicants were admitted

UNDERGRAD STUDENTS

22,460 full-time, 2,168 part-time. Students come from 52 states and territories; 67 other countries; 36% are from out of state; 5% Black or African American, non-Hispanic/Latino; 3% Hispanic/Latino; 2% Asian, non-Hispanic/Latino; 0.1% Native Hawaiian or other Pacific Islander, non-Hispanic/Latino; 0.4% American Indian or Alaska Native, non-Hispanic/Latino; 2% Two or more races, non-Hispanic/Latino; 0.3% Race/ethnicity unknown; 7% international; 5% transferred in; 19% live on campus.

Freshmen:

Admission: 20,742 applied, 15,645 admitted, 4,783 enrolled. *Average high school GPA:* 3.9. *Test scores:* SAT evidence-based reading and writing scores over 500: 98%; SAT math scores over 500: 98%; ACT scores over 18: 100%; SAT evidence-based reading and writing scores over 600: 66%; SAT math scores over 600: 60%; ACT scores over 24: 85%; SAT evidence-based reading and writing scores over 700: 8%; SAT math scores over 700: 13%; ACT scores over 30: 33%.

Retention: 90% of full-time freshmen returned.

FACULTY

Total: 1,606, 86% full-time, 85% with terminal degrees.

Student/faculty ratio: 19:1.

ACADEMICS

Calendar: semesters. *Degrees:* bachelor's, master's, doctoral, post-master's, and postbachelor's certificates.

Special study options: accelerated degree program, adult/continuing education programs, advanced placement credit, cooperative education, distance learning, double majors, English as a second language, freshman honors college, honors programs, independent study, internships, off-campus study, part-time degree program, services for LD students, study abroad, summer session for credit. *ROTC:* Army (b), Navy (b), Air Force (b).

Unusual degree programs: 3-2 engineering.

Computers: 1,722 computers/terminals are available on campus for general student use. Students can access the following: computer help desk, free student e-mail accounts, online (class) grades, online (class) registration, bursar payments, course materials. Campuswide network is available. 100% of college-owned or -operated housing units are wired for high-speed Internet access. Wireless service is available via entire campus.

Library: R. B. Draughon Library plus 3 others. *Books:* 4.6 million (physical), 1.0 million (digital/electronic); *Serial titles:* 76,345 (physical), 94,890 (digital/electronic); *Databases:* 245. Study areas open 24 hours, 5–7 days a week.

STUDENT LIFE

Housing options: coed, men-only, women-only, special housing for students with disabilities. Campus housing is university owned.

Activities and organizations: drama/theater group, student-run newspaper, radio and television station, choral group, marching band, Student Government Association, University Program Council, IMPACT (volunteer opportunities), International Student Organization, student media (AU Plainsman newspaper, WEGL radio, Glomerata yearbook, Eagle Eye television, AU Circle literary journal), national fraternities, national sororities.

Athletics Member NCAA. All Division I except football (Division I-A). *Intercollegiate sports:* baseball M(s), basketball M(s)/W(s), cheerleading M/W, cross-country running M(s)/W(s), equestrian sports W(s), golf M(s)/W(s)(c), gymnastics W(s), soccer W(s), softball W(s), swimming and diving M(s)/W(s), tennis M(s)/W(s), track and field M(s)/W(s), volleyball W(s). *Intramural sports:* basketball M/W, crew M(c)/W(c), football M, golf M/W, ice hockey M(c)/W(c), lacrosse M(c)/W(c), racquetball M/W, rugby M(c), sailing M(c)/W(c), sand volleyball M(c)/W(c), skiing (downhill) M(c)/W(c), soccer M/W, softball M/W, swimming and diving M/W, table tennis M/W, tennis M/W, track and field M/W, ultimate Frisbee M/W, volleyball M/W, water polo M(c)/W(c), wrestling M(c)/W(c).

Campus security: 24-hour emergency response devices and patrols, late-night transport/escort service, controlled dormitory access.

Student services: health clinic, personal/psychological counseling, veterans affairs office.

COSTS & FINANCIAL AID

Costs (2018–19) *Tuition:* state resident $9624 full-time, $401 per semester hour part-time; nonresident $28,872 full-time, $1203 per semester hour part-time. Full-time tuition and fees vary according to program and reciprocity agreements. Part-time tuition and fees vary according to course load, program, and reciprocity agreements. *Required fees:* $1652 full-time, $826 per term part-time. *Room and board:* $13,332; room only: $7860. Room and board charges vary according to board plan and housing facility. *Payment plan:* installment. *Waivers:* employees or children of employees.

Financial Aid Of all full-time matriculated undergraduates who enrolled in 2017, 14,199 applied for aid, 7,804 were judged to have need, 1,024 had their need fully met. 148 Federal Work-Study jobs (averaging $4448). In 2017, 4337 non-need-based awards were made. *Average percent of need met:* 45. *Average financial aid package:* $11,344. *Average need-based loan:* $4551. *Average need-based gift aid:* $8295. *Average non-need-based aid:* $7421. *Average indebtedness upon graduation:* $29,331.

APPLYING

Standardized Tests *Required:* SAT or ACT (for admission).

Options: electronic application, early admission, early action.

Application fee: $50.

Required: essay or personal statement, high school transcript, minimum 2.0 GPA. *Required for some:* minimum 3.0 GPA. *Recommended:* minimum 3.0 GPA.

Application deadlines: 1/15 (freshmen), 6/1 (transfers), 11/1 (early action).

Notification: 2/1 (freshmen), continuous (transfers).

CONTACT
Cindy Singley, Director, University Recruitment, Auburn University, Quad Center, Auburn, AL 36849. *Phone:* 334-844-4080. *Toll-free phone:* 800-AUBURN9. *E-mail:* admissions@auburn.edu.

Auburn University at Montgomery
Montgomery, Alabama
http://www.aum.edu/

- **State-supported** comprehensive, founded 1967, part of Auburn University
- **Urban** 500-acre campus
- **Endowment** $50.1 million
- **Coed** 4,632 undergraduate students, 77% full-time, 65% women, 35% men
- **Moderately difficult** entrance level, 93% of applicants were admitted

UNDERGRAD STUDENTS
3,554 full-time, 1,078 part-time. 6% are from out of state; 41% Black or African American, non-Hispanic/Latino; 1% Hispanic/Latino; 2% Asian, non-Hispanic/Latino; 0.1% Native Hawaiian or other Pacific Islander, non-Hispanic/Latino; 0.4% American Indian or Alaska Native, non-Hispanic/Latino; 4% Two or more races, non-Hispanic/Latino; 1% Race/ethnicity unknown; 5% international; 11% transferred in; 25% live on campus.

Freshmen:
Admission: 5,941 applied, 5,514 admitted, 757 enrolled. *Average high school GPA:* 3.4. *Test scores:* SAT evidence-based reading and writing scores over 500: 87%; SAT math scores over 500: 62%; ACT scores over 18: 100%; SAT evidence-based reading and writing scores over 600: 9%; SAT math scores over 600: 11%; ACT scores over 24: 20%; SAT math scores over 700: 6%; ACT scores over 30: 1%.

Retention: 67% of full-time freshmen returned.

FACULTY
Total: 330, 64% full-time, 70% with terminal degrees.
Student/faculty ratio: 15:1.

ACADEMICS
Calendar: semesters. *Degrees:* bachelor's, master's, doctoral, and post-master's certificates.

Special study options: academic remediation for entering students, advanced placement credit, cooperative education, distance learning, double majors, English as a second language, honors programs, independent study, internships, off-campus study, part-time degree program, services for LD students, study abroad, summer session for credit. *ROTC:* Army (b), Air Force (c).

Computers: 500 computers/terminals are available on campus for general student use. Students can access the following: computer help desk, free student e-mail accounts, online (class) grades, online (class) registration, online (class) schedules. Campuswide network is available. 100% of college-owned or -operated housing units are wired for high-speed Internet access. Wireless service is available via entire campus.

Library: Auburn University at Montgomery Library. *Books:* 340,819 (physical), 1.2 million (digital/electronic). Weekly public service hours: 84; students can reserve study rooms.

STUDENT LIFE
Housing options: coed, special housing for students with disabilities. Campus housing is university owned.

Activities and organizations: drama/theater group, student-run newspaper, television station, choral group, Student Government Association, Campus Activities Board, Panhellenic Association, Accounting Club, national fraternities, national sororities.

Athletics Member NCAA. All Division II. *Intercollegiate sports:* baseball M(s), basketball M(s)/W(s), cheerleading M(s)/W(s), cross-country running M(s)/W(s), soccer M(s)/W(s), softball W(s), tennis M(s)/W(s), volleyball W(s). *Intramural sports:* badminton M/W, golf M(c)/W(c), table tennis M/W, tennis M/W, ultimate Frisbee M/W, volleyball M/W.

Campus security: 24-hour emergency response devices and patrols, student patrols, late-night transport/escort service, controlled dormitory access.

Student services: health clinic, personal/psychological counseling, veterans affairs office.

COSTS & FINANCIAL AID
Costs (2019–20) *One-time required fee:* $125. *Tuition:* state resident $7752 full-time, $323 per credit part-time; nonresident $17,424 full-time, $726 per credit part-time. *Required fees:* $868 full-time. *Room and board:* $7090; room only: $4690.

Financial Aid Of all full-time matriculated undergraduates who enrolled in 2017, 2,516 applied for aid, 2,213 were judged to have need, 215 had their need fully met. 59 Federal Work-Study jobs (averaging $204,468). In 2017, 343 non-need-based awards were made. *Average percent of need met:* 62. *Average financial aid package:* $8943. *Average need-based loan:* $3323. *Average need-based gift aid:* $4427. *Average non-need-based aid:* $3262. *Average indebtedness upon graduation:* $28,464.

APPLYING
Standardized Tests *Required:* SAT or ACT (for admission).
Options: electronic application, early admission.
Required: high school transcript, minimum 2.3 GPA.
Notification: continuous (freshmen), continuous (transfers).

CONTACT
Ronnie McKinney, Director of Admissions and Recruiting, Auburn University at Montgomery, PO Box 244023, Montgomery, AL 36124-4023. *Phone:* 334-244-3615. *Toll-free phone:* 800-227-2649. *Fax:* 334-310-5589. *E-mail:* admissions@aum.edu.

Birmingham-Southern College

Birmingham, Alabama
http://www.bsc.edu/
- **Independent Methodist** 4-year, founded 1856
- **Urban** 196-acre campus with easy access to Birmingham
- **Endowment** $51.7 million
- **Coed**
- **Moderately difficult** entrance level

FACULTY
Student/faculty ratio: 13:1.

ACADEMICS
Calendar: 4-1-4. *Degree:* bachelor's.
Library: Charles Andrew Rush Learning Center/N. E. Miles Library. Students can reserve study rooms.

STUDENT LIFE
Housing options: on-campus residence required for freshman year; coed, men-only, women-only, special housing for students with disabilities. Campus housing is university owned. Freshman campus housing is guaranteed.

Activities and organizations: drama/theater group, student-run newspaper, choral group, marching band, Student Government Association, Quest II Event Programming, Black Student Union, Multi-Cultural Awareness Organization, Reformed University Fellowship, national fraternities, national sororities.

Athletics Member NCAA. All Division III.

Campus security: 24-hour emergency response devices and patrols, late-night transport/escort service, controlled dormitory access, vehicle safety inspections for students, emergency phone stations throughout campus.

Student services: health clinic, personal/psychological counseling.

COSTS & FINANCIAL AID
Costs (2018–19) *One-time required fee:* $300. *Comprehensive fee:* $29,950 includes full-time tuition ($16,353), mandatory fees ($1297), and room and board ($12,300). *College room only:* $6950. Room and board charges vary according to board plan, housing facility, and location.

Financial Aid Of all full-time matriculated undergraduates who enrolled in 2017, 680 applied for aid, 757 were judged to have need, 225 had their need fully met. In 2017, 492 non-need-based awards were made. *Average percent of need met:* 74. *Average financial aid package:* $33,234. *Average need-based loan:* $4318. *Average need-based gift aid:* $6247. *Average non-need-based aid:* $22,998. *Average indebtedness upon graduation:* $28,007.

APPLYING
Standardized Tests *Recommended:* SAT or ACT (for admission).

Options: electronic application, early admission, early decision, early action, deferred entrance.

Application fee: $50.

Required: high school transcript, minimum 2.5 GPA, 1 letter of recommendation. *Required for some:* interview. *Recommended:* essay or personal statement, interview.

CONTACT
Birmingham-Southern College, 900 Arkadelphia Road, Birmingham, AL 35254. *Toll-free phone:* 800-523-5793.

Columbia Southern University

Orange Beach, Alabama
http://www.columbiasouthern.edu/
- **Proprietary** comprehensive, founded 1993
- **Small-town** campus
- **Coed** 15,245 undergraduate students, 55% full-time, 37% women, 63% men
- **Noncompetitive** entrance level

UNDERGRAD STUDENTS
8,397 full-time, 6,848 part-time. Students come from 58 states and territories; 17% Black or African American, non-Hispanic/Latino; 5% Hispanic/Latino; 2% Asian, non-Hispanic/Latino; 0.1% Native Hawaiian or other Pacific Islander, non-Hispanic/Latino; 1% American Indian or Alaska Native, non-Hispanic/Latino; 3% Two or more races, non-Hispanic/Latino; 21% Race/ethnicity unknown; 0.1% international; 12% transferred in.

Freshmen:
Admission: 364 enrolled.

FACULTY
Total: 477, 34% full-time, 67% with terminal degrees.
Student/faculty ratio: 70:1.

ACADEMICS
Calendar: Non-standard Term: 9-weeks of instruction, LifePace Learning: 10-week courses that are self-paced. *Degrees:* certificates, associate, bachelor's, master's, doctoral, post-master's, and postbachelor's certificates (offers only distance learning degree programs).

Special study options: academic remediation for entering students, adult/continuing education programs, distance learning, off-campus study, part-time degree program, services for LD students.

Computers: Students can access the following: computer help desk, online (class) grades, online (class) registration, online (class) schedules, student portals for learning modules, policy updates, and other institutional information. Wireless service is available via entire campus.
Library: CSU Online Library.

STUDENT LIFE
Housing options: college housing not available.

Activities and organizations: Student Veteran Association, American Criminal Justice Association, Delta Epsilon Tou (DET) - Alumni Honor Society.

Campus security: 24-hour emergency response devices, On-line Institutions.

COSTS
Costs (2019–20) *One-time required fee:* $135. *Tuition:* $5520 full-time, $235 per credit hour part-time.

APPLYING
Options: electronic application.

Application deadlines: rolling (freshmen), rolling (transfers).

CONTACT
Columbia Southern University, 21982 University Lane, PO Box 3110, Orange Beach, AL 36561. *Toll-free phone:* 800-977-8449.

Faulkner University

Montgomery, Alabama
http://www.faulkner.edu/
- **Independent** university, founded 1942, affiliated with Church of Christ
- **Urban** 75-acre campus with easy access to Montgomery
- **Endowment** $20.4 million
- **Coed**
- **Minimally difficult** entrance level

FACULTY
Student/faculty ratio: 12:1.

ACADEMICS
Calendar: semesters. *Degrees:* associate, bachelor's, master's, and doctoral.
Library: Gus Nichols Library System plus 4 others. *Books:* 121,708 (physical), 159,003 (digital/electronic); *Serial titles:* 2,098 (physical), 142,578 (digital/electronic); *Databases:* 134. Weekly public service hours: 74.

STUDENT LIFE
Housing options: on-campus residence required through junior year; men-only, women-only, special housing for students with disabilities. Campus housing is university owned. Freshman campus housing is guaranteed.

Activities and organizations: drama/theater group, student-run newspaper, choral group, marching band, Student Government, Marching Band, Dinner Theatre, Acappella Chorus, Phi Lambda/Kappa Social Clubs.

Athletics Member NAIA.

Campus security: 24-hour emergency response devices and patrols, late-night transport/escort service, controlled dormitory access.

Student services: health clinic, personal/psychological counseling, veterans affairs office.

COSTS & FINANCIAL AID

Costs (2018–19) *Comprehensive fee:* $29,240 includes full-time tuition ($19,880), mandatory fees ($1810), and room and board ($7550). Full-time tuition and fees vary according to class time, course load, location, and program. Part-time tuition: $675 per semester hour. Part-time tuition and fees vary according to class time, course load, location, and program. *Required fees:* $375 per term part-time. *College room only:* $3600. Room and board charges vary according to board plan and housing facility. *Payment plans:* installment, deferred payment.

Financial Aid Of all full-time matriculated undergraduates who enrolled in 2016, 1,482 applied for aid, 1,482 were judged to have need, 86 had their need fully met. 208 Federal Work-Study jobs (averaging $1271). In 2016, 80 non-need-based awards were made. *Average percent of need met:* 52. *Average financial aid package:* $11,980. *Average need-based loan:* $3789. *Average need-based gift aid:* $4691. *Average non-need-based aid:* $6701. *Average indebtedness upon graduation:* $33,622. *Financial aid deadline:* 8/1.

APPLYING

Standardized Tests *Required for some:* SAT or ACT (for admission).

Options: electronic application, early admission, deferred entrance.

Required: high school transcript, minimum 2.0 GPA. *Recommended:* essay or personal statement, 2 letters of recommendation, interview.

CONTACT

Mr. Neil Scott, Director of Admissions, Faulkner University, 5345 Atlanta Highway, Montgomery, AL 36109-3398. *Phone:* 334-386-7200. *Toll-free phone:* 800-879-9816. *Fax:* 334-386-7137. *E-mail:* nscott@faulkner.edu.

Heritage Christian University
Florence, Alabama
http://www.hcu.edu/

CONTACT
Mr. Brad McKinnon, Dean of Students, Heritage Christian University, PO Box HCU, Florence, AL 35630. *Phone:* 256-766-6610 Ext. 305. *Toll-free phone:* 800-367-3565. *Fax:* 256-766-9289. *E-mail:* bmckinnon@hcu.edu.

Herzing University
Birmingham, Alabama
http://www.herzing.edu/birmingham/

CONTACT
Ms. Tess Anderson, Admissions Coordinator, Herzing University, 280 West Valley Avenue, Birmingham, AL 35209. *Phone:* 205-916-2800. *Toll-free phone:* 800-596-0724. *E-mail:* admiss@bhm.herzing.edu.

Huntingdon College
Montgomery, Alabama
http://www.huntingdon.edu/
- **Independent United Methodist** 4-year, founded 1854
- **Suburban** 70-acre campus with easy access to Birmingham
- **Endowment** $48.2 million
- **Coed**
- **Moderately difficult** entrance level

FACULTY
Student/faculty ratio: 15:1.

ACADEMICS
Calendar: semesters. *Degree:* bachelor's.

Library: Houghton Memorial Library. *Books:* 91,034 (physical), 103,891 (digital/electronic); *Serial titles:* 187 (physical), 41,336 (digital/electronic); *Databases:* 114. Students can reserve study rooms.

STUDENT LIFE
Housing options: on-campus residence required through junior year; coed, men-only, women-only, special housing for students with disabilities. Campus housing is university owned. Freshman campus housing is guaranteed.

Activities and organizations: drama/theater group, student-run newspaper, choral group, marching band, Student Government Association, Campus Activities Board, Voice of Justice, Freshman Forum, Exchange Club, national fraternities, national sororities.

Athletics Member NCAA. All Division III.

Campus security: 24-hour emergency response devices and patrols, late-night transport/escort service, controlled dormitory access, electronic video surveillance, weather alert broadcasts.

Student services: health clinic, personal/psychological counseling.

COSTS & FINANCIAL AID

Costs (2018–19) *Comprehensive fee:* $36,900 includes full-time tuition ($25,900), mandatory fees ($1500), and room and board ($9500). Full-time tuition and fees vary according to course load and program. Part-time tuition: $1080 per credit hour. Part-time tuition and fees vary according to course load and program. *Room and board:* Room and board charges vary according to housing facility.

Financial Aid Of all full-time matriculated undergraduates who enrolled in 2017, 755 applied for aid, 675 were judged to have need, 87 had their need fully met. 149 Federal Work-Study jobs (averaging $910). In 2017, 191 non-need-based awards were made. *Average percent of need met:* 67. *Average financial aid package:* $19,156. *Average need-based loan:* $4197. *Average need-based gift aid:* $15,593. *Average non-need-based aid:* $11,673. *Average indebtedness upon graduation:* $32,201.

APPLYING

Standardized Tests *Required:* SAT or ACT (for admission).

Options: electronic application, deferred entrance.

Required: high school transcript. *Required for some:* essay or personal statement, 3 letters of recommendation, interview, audition required for music majors; portfolio recommended for art majors.

CONTACT
Office of Admission, Huntingdon College, 1500 East Fairview Avenue, Montgomery, AL 36106-2148. *Phone:* 334-833-4497. *Toll-free phone:* 800-763-0313. *Fax:* 334-833-4347. *E-mail:* admiss@hawks.huntingdon.edu.

Huntsville Bible College
Huntsville, Alabama
http://www.huntsvillebiblecollege.org/

CONTACT
Huntsville Bible College, 904 Oakwood Avenue, Huntsville, AL 35811-1632.

Jacksonville State University
Jacksonville, Alabama
http://www.jsu.edu/

CONTACT
Mr. Andrew Green, Director of Admission, Jacksonville State University, 700 Pelham Road North, Jacksonville, AL 36265. *Phone:* 256-782-5363. *Toll-free phone:* 800-231-5291. *Fax:* 256-782-5291. *E-mail:* info@jsu.edu.

Judson College
Marion, Alabama
http://www.judson.edu/

CONTACT
Ms. Layne Hoggle, Executive Director of Enrollment Services, Judson College, 302 Bibb Street, Marion, AL 36756. *Phone:* 334-683-5110. *Toll-free phone:* 800-447-9472. *Fax:* 334-683-5282. *E-mail:* admissions@

Miles College
Fairfield, Alabama
http://www.miles.edu/

CONTACT
Mr. Christopher Robertson, Director of Admissions and Recruitment, Miles College, 5500 Myron Massey Boulevard, Bell Building, Fairfield, AL 35064. *Phone:* 205-929-1657. *Toll-free phone:* 800-445-0708. *Fax:* 205-929-1627. *E-mail:* admissions@miles.edu.

Oakwood University
Huntsville, Alabama
http://www.oakwood.edu/

CONTACT
Mr. Jason McCracken, Director of Enrollment Management, Oakwood University, 7000 Adventist Boulevard, NW, Huntsville, AL 35896. *Phone:* 256-726-7354. *Toll-free phone:* 800-824-5312. *Fax:* 256-726-7154. *E-mail:* admission@oakwood.edu.

Remington College–Mobile Campus
Mobile, Alabama
http://www.remingtoncollege.edu/

CONTACT
Remington College–Mobile Campus, 828 Downtowner Loop West, Mobile, AL 36609. *Phone:* 251-343-8200. *Toll-free phone:* 800-323-8122.

Samford University
Birmingham, Alabama
http://www.samford.edu/

- **Independent Baptist** university, founded 1841
- **Suburban** 212-acre campus
- **Endowment** $297.5 million
- **Coed** 3,535 undergraduate students, 98% full-time, 67% women, 33% men
- **Moderately difficult** entrance level, 82% of applicants were admitted

UNDERGRAD STUDENTS
3,453 full-time, 82 part-time. Students come from 40 states and territories; 24 other countries; 68% are from out of state; 6% Black or African American, non-Hispanic/Latino; 3% Hispanic/Latino; 1% Asian, non-Hispanic/Latino; 0.1% American Indian or Alaska Native, non-Hispanic/Latino; 2% Two or more races, non-Hispanic/Latino; 0.4% Race/ethnicity unknown; 1% international; 4% transferred in; 67% live on campus.

Freshmen:
Admission: 3,884 applied, 3,188 admitted, 958 enrolled. *Average high school GPA:* 3.8. *Test scores:* SAT evidence-based reading and writing scores over 500: 94%; SAT math scores over 500: 85%; ACT scores over 18: 99%; SAT evidence-based reading and writing scores over 600: 51%; SAT math scores over 600: 33%; ACT scores over 24: 73%; SAT evidence-based reading and writing scores over 700: 7%; SAT math scores over 700: 5%; ACT scores over 30: 23%.
Retention: 91% of full-time freshmen returned.

FACULTY
Total: 549, 66% full-time, 74% with terminal degrees.
Student/faculty ratio: 12:1.

ACADEMICS
Calendar: 4-1-4. *Degrees:* certificates, bachelor's, master's, doctoral, post-master's, and postbachelor's certificates.
Special study options: accelerated degree program, adult/continuing education programs, distance learning, double majors, honors programs, independent study, internships, off-campus study, part-time degree program, services for LD students, study abroad, summer session for credit. *ROTC:* Army (c), Air Force (b).

Unusual degree programs: 3-2 engineering with The University of Alabama at Birmingham, Auburn University, Mercer University.
Computers: 330 computers/terminals and 400 ports are available on campus for general student use. Students can access the following: campus intranet, computer help desk, free student e-mail accounts, online (class) grades, online (class) registration, online (class) schedules, free online storage and tech support. Campuswide network is available. 100% of college-owned or -operated housing units are wired for high-speed Internet access. Wireless service is available via entire campus.
Library: University Library plus 2 others. *Books:* 574,434 (physical), 299,458 (digital/electronic); *Serial titles:* 6,045 (physical), 117,199 (digital/electronic); *Databases:* 296. Weekly public service hours: 99; students can reserve study rooms.

STUDENT LIFE
Housing options: on-campus residence required through sophomore year; men-only, women-only. Campus housing is university owned. Freshman campus housing is guaranteed.
Activities and organizations: drama/theater group, student-run newspaper, radio station, choral group, marching band, Student Government Association, Greek Chapters and councils, Campus Ministries, national fraternities, national sororities.
Athletics Member NCAA. All Division I except football (Division I-AA). *Intercollegiate sports:* baseball M(s), basketball M(s)/W(s), cross-country running M(s)/W(s), golf M(s)/W(s), soccer W(s), softball W(s), tennis M(s)/W(s), track and field M(s)/W(s), volleyball W(s). *Intramural sports:* basketball M/W, crew M(c)/W(c), equestrian sports M(c)/W(c), football M/W, golf M(c)/W(c), lacrosse M(c)/W(c), sand volleyball M/W, soccer M/W, softball M/W, table tennis M/W, ultimate Frisbee M/W, volleyball M/W.
Campus security: 24-hour emergency response devices and patrols, late-night transport/escort service.
Student services: health clinic, personal/psychological counseling, veterans affairs office.

COSTS & FINANCIAL AID
Costs (2019–20) *Comprehensive fee:* $43,830 includes full-time tuition ($32,000), mandatory fees ($850), and room and board ($10,980). Part-time tuition: $1070 per credit. *Required fees:* $355 per term part-time. *College room only:* $5970.
Financial Aid Of all full-time matriculated undergraduates who enrolled in 2017, 1,940 applied for aid, 1,371 were judged to have need, 329 had their need fully met. In 2017, 1512 non-need-based awards were made. *Average percent of need met:* 70. *Average financial aid package:* $20,510. *Average need-based loan:* $3901. *Average need-based gift aid:* $16,387. *Average non-need-based aid:* $11,163. *Average indebtedness upon graduation:* $32,146.

APPLYING
Standardized Tests *Required:* SAT or ACT (for admission).
Options: electronic application, early admission, deferred entrance.
Application fee: $40.
Required: essay or personal statement, high school transcript, 1 letter of recommendation. *Required for some:* interview.
Application deadlines: 4/30 (freshmen), 4/30 (out-of-state freshmen), rolling (transfers).
Notification: continuous until 11/1 (freshmen), continuous until 11/1 (out-of-state freshmen), continuous (transfers).

CONTACT
Mr. Brian L. Kennedy, Director of Recruitment, Samford University, 800 Lakeshore Drive, Samford Hall, Birmingham, AL 35229-0002. *Phone:* 205-726-4176. *Toll-free phone:* 800-888-7218. *E-mail:* blkenned@samford.edu.

Selma University
Selma, Alabama
http://www.selmauniversity.edu/

CONTACT
Selma University, 1501 Lapsley Street, Selma, AL 36701-5299. *Phone:* 334-872-2533 Ext. 116.

South University

Montgomery, Alabama

http://www.southuniversity.edu/montgomery/

CONTACT
South University, 5355 Vaughn Road, Montgomery, AL 36116-1120. *Phone:* 334-395-8800. *Toll-free phone:* 866-629-2962.

Spring Hill College

Mobile, Alabama

http://www.shc.edu/

- **Independent Roman Catholic (Jesuit)** comprehensive, founded 1830
- **Suburban** 450-acre campus
- **Coed** 1,270 undergraduate students, 99% full-time, 62% women, 38% men
- **Moderately difficult** entrance level, 66% of applicants were admitted

UNDERGRAD STUDENTS
1,257 full-time, 13 part-time. 58% are from out of state; 16% Black or African American, non-Hispanic/Latino; 3% Hispanic/Latino; 1% Asian, non-Hispanic/Latino; 0.2% Native Hawaiian or other Pacific Islander, non-Hispanic/Latino; 0.6% American Indian or Alaska Native, non-Hispanic/Latino; 4% Two or more races, non-Hispanic/Latino; 4% Race/ethnicity unknown; 5% international; 2% transferred in; 71% live on campus.

Freshmen:
Admission: 8,587 applied, 5,648 admitted, 309 enrolled. *Average high school GPA:* 3.6. *Test scores:* SAT evidence-based reading and writing scores over 500: 81%; SAT math scores over 500: 83%; ACT scores over 18: 95%; SAT evidence-based reading and writing scores over 600: 26%; SAT math scores over 600: 23%; ACT scores over 24: 39%; SAT evidence-based reading and writing scores over 700: 3%; SAT math scores over 700: 5%; ACT scores over 30: 6%.
Retention: 72% of full-time freshmen returned.

FACULTY
Total: 137, 64% full-time, 74% with terminal degrees.
Student/faculty ratio: 14:1.

ACADEMICS
Calendar: semesters. *Degrees:* certificates, bachelor's, master's, post-master's, and postbachelor's certificates.
Special study options: academic remediation for entering students, accelerated degree program, adult/continuing education programs, advanced placement credit, distance learning, double majors, honors programs, independent study, internships, off-campus study, part-time degree program, services for LD students, student-designed majors, study abroad, summer session for credit. *ROTC:* Army (c), Air Force (c).
Unusual degree programs: 3-2 engineering with Marquette University, University of Alabama at Birmingham, University of Florida, Auburn University, Texas A&M University, University of South Alabama.
Computers: Students can access the following: campus intranet, computer help desk, free student e-mail accounts, online (class) grades, online (class) registration, online (class) schedules. Campuswide network is available. 100% of college-owned or -operated housing units are wired for high-speed Internet access. Wireless service is available via computer centers, computer labs, dorm rooms, libraries, student centers.
Library: Marnie and John Burke Memorial Library plus 1 other.

STUDENT LIFE
Housing options: on-campus residence required through senior year; coed. Campus housing is university owned. Freshman campus housing is guaranteed.
Activities and organizations: drama/theater group, student-run newspaper, choral group, Fraternities and sororities, SHAPe, National Society of Leadership and Success, Peer One Project, Chemistry Club, national fraternities, national sororities.
Athletics Member NCAA. All Division II. *Intercollegiate sports:* baseball M(s), basketball M(s)/W(s), cross-country running M(s)/W(s), golf M(s), soccer M(s)/W(s), softball W(s), tennis M(s)/W(s), track and field M(s)/W(s), volleyball W(s). *Intramural sports:* basketball M/W,
bowling M(c)/W(c), football M/W, racquetball M/W, rugby M(c)/W(c), soccer M/W, ultimate Frisbee M/W, volleyball M/W.
Campus security: 24-hour emergency response devices and patrols, late-night transport/escort service, controlled dormitory access.
Student services: health clinic, personal/psychological counseling.

COSTS & FINANCIAL AID
Costs (2018–19) *Comprehensive fee:* $52,926 includes full-time tuition ($37,078), mandatory fees ($2386), and room and board ($13,462). Full-time tuition and fees vary according to course load. Part-time tuition: $1104 per credit hour. Part-time tuition and fees vary according to course load. *Required fees:* $57 per credit hour part-time. *College room only:* $7108. Room and board charges vary according to board plan and housing facility. *Payment plan:* installment. *Waivers:* employees or children of employees.
Financial Aid Of all full-time matriculated undergraduates who enrolled in 2018, 1,245 applied for aid, 910 were judged to have need, 362 had their need fully met. In 2018, 321 non-need-based awards were made. *Average percent of need met:* 81. *Average financial aid package:* $35,052. *Average need-based loan:* $4392. *Average need-based gift aid:* $8757. *Average non-need-based aid:* $22,662.

APPLYING
Standardized Tests *Required:* SAT or ACT (for admission).
Options: electronic application, early admission, deferred entrance.
Application fee: $25.
Required: essay or personal statement, high school transcript, 1 letter of recommendation. *Recommended:* minimum 2.5 GPA, interview.
Notification: continuous (freshmen), continuous (out-of-state freshmen), continuous (transfers).

CONTACT
Ms. Britney Finley, Admissions Counselor, Spring Hill College, 4000 Dauphin Street, Mobile, AL 36608-1791. *Phone:* 251-380-3032. *Toll-free phone:* 800-SHC-6704. *Fax:* 251-460-2186. *E-mail:* bfinley@shc.edu.

Stillman College

Tuscaloosa, Alabama

http://www.stillman.edu/

CONTACT
Stillman College, PO Drawer 1430, 3600 Stillman Boulevard, Tuscaloosa, AL 35403-9990. *Phone:* 205-366-8837. *Toll-free phone:* 800-841-5722.

Strayer University–Birmingham Campus

Birmingham, Alabama

http://www.strayer.edu/alabama/birmingham/

CONTACT
Strayer University–Birmingham Campus, 3570 Grandview Parkway, Suite 200, Birmingham, AL 35243. *Toll-free phone:* 888-311-0355.

Strayer University–Huntsville Campus

Huntsville, Alabama

http://www.strayer.edu/alabama/huntsville/

CONTACT
Strayer University–Huntsville Campus, 4955 Corporate Drive, Huntsville, AL 35805. *Toll-free phone:* 888-311-0355.

Talladega College

Talladega, Alabama

http://www.talladega.edu/

- **Independent** 4-year, founded 1867
- **Small-town** 130-acre campus with easy access to Birmingham
- **Endowment** $3.3 million
- **Coed**
- **Moderately difficult** entrance level

FACULTY
Student/faculty ratio: 20:1.

ACADEMICS
Calendar: semesters. *Degrees:* associate and bachelor's.
Library: Savery Library. *Books:* 100,000 (physical); *Serial titles:* 1,922 (digital/electronic); *Databases:* 244. Weekly public service hours: 77; students can reserve study rooms.

STUDENT LIFE
Housing options: men-only, women-only. Campus housing is university owned. Freshman campus housing is guaranteed.

Activities and organizations: choral group, marching band, Student Government Association, Crimson Ambassadors, Students in Free Enterprise (SIFE), Talladega College Choir, Social Work Club, national fraternities, national sororities.

Athletics Member NAIA.

Campus security: 24-hour patrols, late-night transport/escort service, campus police.

Student services: health clinic, personal/psychological counseling.

FINANCIAL AID
Financial Aid Of all full-time matriculated undergraduates who enrolled in 2003, 407 applied for aid, 375 were judged to have need, 100 had their need fully met. 141 Federal Work-Study jobs (averaging $691). *Average percent of need met:* 90. *Average financial aid package:* $5000. *Average need-based loan:* $5335. *Average need-based gift aid:* $3025. *Average non-need-based aid:* $5774. *Average indebtedness upon graduation:* $12,790. *Financial aid deadline:* 6/30.

APPLYING
Standardized Tests *Required:* SAT or ACT (for admission).

Options: electronic application, early admission.

Application fee: $25.

Required: high school transcript, minimum 2.0 GPA.

CONTACT
Talladega College, 627 West Battle Street, Talladega, AL 35160-2354. *Phone:* 256-761-6175. *Toll-free phone:* 866-540-3956.

Troy University
Troy, Alabama
http://www.troy.edu/

- **State-supported** comprehensive, founded 1887, part of Troy University System
- **Small-town** 906-acre campus
- **Endowment** $104.4 million
- **Coed**
- 90% of applicants were admitted

FACULTY
Student/faculty ratio: 15:1.

ACADEMICS
Calendar: semesters. *Degrees:* certificates, associate, bachelor's, master's, doctoral, post-master's, and postbachelor's certificates.
Library: Lurleen B. Wallace Library (Troy Campus) plus 2 others. *Books:* 603,904 (physical), 277,690 (digital/electronic); *Serial titles:* 213 (physical), 134,396 (digital/electronic); *Databases:* 261.

STUDENT LIFE
Housing options: on-campus residence required for freshman year; coed, men-only, women-only. Campus housing is university owned. Freshman campus housing is guaranteed.

Activities and organizations: drama/theater group, student-run newspaper, television station, choral group, marching band, T-Day/Athletic Events (Homecoming), Activities Council, Pep Rallies, national fraternities, national sororities.

Athletics Member NCAA. All Division I except football (Division I-A).

Campus security: 24-hour emergency response devices and patrols, student patrols, late-night transport/escort service, controlled dormitory access.

Student services: health clinic, personal/psychological counseling.

COSTS & FINANCIAL AID
Costs (2018–19) *Tuition:* state resident $10,415 full-time, $325 per credit hour part-time; nonresident $20,830 full-time, $650 per credit hour part-time. Full-time tuition and fees vary according to location and program. Part-time tuition and fees vary according to location and program. *Required fees:* $2045 full-time, $43 per credit hour part-time, $50 per term part-time. *Room and board:* $8185; room only: $4592. Room and board charges vary according to board plan and housing facility.

Financial Aid Of all full-time matriculated undergraduates who enrolled in 2017, 6,538 applied for aid, 6,538 were judged to have need. In 2017, 1795 non-need-based awards were made. *Average financial aid package:* $5664. *Average need-based loan:* $2965. *Average need-based gift aid:* $3118. *Average non-need-based aid:* $6423. *Average indebtedness upon graduation:* $28,363.

APPLYING
Standardized Tests *Required:* SAT or ACT (for admission).

Options: electronic application, deferred entrance.

Application fee: $30.

Required: high school transcript, rigor of secondary school record.

CONTACT
Mr. Buddy Starling, Associate Vice Chancellor for Enrollment Management, Troy University, University Avenue, Troy, AL 36082. *Phone:* 334-670-3243. *Toll-free phone:* 800-551-9716. *Fax:* 334-670-3733. *E-mail:* bstar@troy.edu.

Tuskegee University
Tuskegee, Alabama
http://www.tuskegee.edu/

CONTACT
Hon. Courtney L. Griffin, Executive Director of Enrollment Management, Tuskegee University, 1200 Old Montgomery Road, Margaret Murray Hall, Admissions, Tuskegee, AL 36088. *Phone:* 334-724-4828. *Toll-free phone:* 800-622-6531. *Fax:* 334-727-5750. *E-mail:* cgriffin@mytu.tuskegee.edu.

United States Sports Academy
Daphne, Alabama
http://www.ussa.edu/

- **Independent** upper-level, founded 1972
- **Suburban** 10-acre campus
- **Coed**

FACULTY
Student/faculty ratio: 41:1.

ACADEMICS
Calendar: continuous. *Degrees:* bachelor's, master's, and doctoral.
Library: United States Sports Academy Library plus 1 other. Weekly public service hours: 5.

STUDENT LIFE
Activities and organizations: Alumni Association.

Campus security: Electronically operated building entrances.

COSTS & FINANCIAL AID
Costs (2018–19) *Tuition:* $14,652 full-time, $407 per credit hour part-time. *Required fees:* $1320 full-time.

Financial Aid Of all full-time matriculated undergraduates who enrolled in 2017, 36 applied for aid, 36 were judged to have need, 31 had their need fully met. *Average percent of need met:* 86. *Average financial aid package:* $4124. *Average need-based loan:* $4610. *Average need-based gift aid:* $2242.

APPLYING
Options: electronic application.

CONTACT
United States Sports Academy, One Academy Drive, Daphne, AL 36526-7055. *Phone:* 251-626-3303 Ext. 7147. *Toll-free phone:* 800-223-2668.

The University of Alabama

Tuscaloosa, Alabama
http://www.ua.edu/

- **State-supported** university, founded 1831, part of University of Alabama System
- **Suburban** 1026-acre campus with easy access to Birmingham
- **Endowment** $683.2 million
- **Coed**
- **Moderately difficult** entrance level

FACULTY
Student/faculty ratio: 23:1.

ACADEMICS
Calendar: semesters. *Degrees:* bachelor's, master's, doctoral, and post-master's certificates.
Library: Amelia Gayle Gorgas Library plus 8 others. *Books:* 3.3 million (physical), 1.5 million (digital/electronic); *Serial titles:* 419 (physical), 199,096 (digital/electronic); *Databases:* 589. Weekly public service hours: 146; study areas open 24 hours, 5–7 days a week; students can reserve study rooms.

STUDENT LIFE
Housing options: on-campus residence required for freshman year; coed, men-only, women-only, special housing for students with disabilities. Campus housing is university owned and leased by the school. Freshman campus housing is guaranteed.

Activities and organizations: drama/theater group, student-run newspaper, radio station, choral group, marching band, ABXY Gaming Network, Residence Hall Association, International Student Association, Student Government Association, Black Student Union, national fraternities, national sororities.

Athletics Member NCAA. All Division I except football (Division I-A).

Campus security: 24-hour emergency response devices and patrols, late-night transport/escort service, controlled dormitory access, 24-hour patrols by University of Alabama Police (UAPD), certified law enforcement personnel.

Student services: health clinic, personal/psychological counseling, women's center, legal services, veterans affairs office.

COSTS & FINANCIAL AID
Costs (2018–19) *Tuition:* state resident $10,780 full-time; nonresident $29,230 full-time. Full-time tuition and fees vary according to course load. Part-time tuition and fees vary according to course load. *Room and board:* $10,102; room only: $6300. Room and board charges vary according to board plan, housing facility, and location. *Payment plans:* installment, deferred payment.

Financial Aid Of all full-time matriculated undergraduates who enrolled in 2017, 16,792 applied for aid, 13,136 were judged to have need, 2,715 had their need fully met. 646 Federal Work-Study jobs (averaging $2891). In 2017, 7935 non-need-based awards were made. *Average percent of need met:* 55. *Average financial aid package:* $15,346. *Average need-based loan:* $4341. *Average need-based gift aid:* $13,718. *Average non-need-based aid:* $16,706. *Average indebtedness upon graduation:* $35,005.

APPLYING
Standardized Tests *Required:* SAT or ACT (for admission).

Options: electronic application, early admission.

Application fee: $40.

Required: high school transcript, minimum 3.0 GPA. *Required for some:* essay or personal statement, 2 letters of recommendation, interview.

CONTACT
Dr. Rick Barth, Assistant Vice President for Enrollment Management, The University of Alabama, Box 870132, Tuscaloosa, AL 35487. *Phone:* 205-348-8666. *Toll-free phone:* 800-933-BAMA. *Fax:* 205-348-9046. *E-mail:* admissions@ua.edu.

The University of Alabama at Birmingham

Birmingham, Alabama
http://www.uab.edu/

- **State-supported** university, founded 1969, part of University of Alabama System
- **Urban** 323-acre campus with easy access to Birmingham
- **Endowment** $424.5 million
- **Coed**
- **Moderately difficult** entrance level

ACADEMICS
Calendar: semesters. *Degrees:* certificates, bachelor's, master's, doctoral, post-master's, and postbachelor's certificates.
Library: Mervyn Sterne Library plus 2 others. *Books:* 1.3 million (physical). Students can reserve study rooms.

STUDENT LIFE
Housing options: coed, special housing for students with disabilities. Campus housing is university owned and is provided by a third party. Freshman applicants given priority for college housing.

Activities and organizations: drama/theater group, student-run newspaper, radio station, choral group, marching band, campus ministries, service-oriented groups, sports-affiliated groups, national fraternities, national sororities.

Athletics Member NCAA. All Division I.

Campus security: 24-hour emergency response devices and patrols, late-night transport/escort service, controlled dormitory access.

Student services: health clinic, personal/psychological counseling, women's center.

COSTS & FINANCIAL AID
Costs (2018–19) *Tuition:* state resident $10,710 full-time, $357 per credit hour part-time; nonresident $24,630 full-time, $821 per credit hour part-time. Full-time tuition and fees vary according to course load, degree level, program, and reciprocity agreements. Part-time tuition and fees vary according to course load, degree level, program, and reciprocity agreements. *Room and board:* $11,682; room only: $7532. Room and board charges vary according to board plan and housing facility.

Financial Aid Of all full-time matriculated undergraduates who enrolled in 2018, 7,303 applied for aid, 5,945 were judged to have need, 859 had their need fully met. In 2018, 2196 non-need-based awards were made. *Average percent of need met:* 55. *Average financial aid package:* $7131. *Average need-based loan:* $3919. *Average need-based gift aid:* $4809. *Average non-need-based aid:* $7771. *Average indebtedness upon graduation:* $31,129.

APPLYING
Standardized Tests *Required:* SAT or ACT (for admission).

Options: electronic application, early admission, deferred entrance.

Application fee: $30.

Required: high school transcript.

CONTACT
The University of Alabama at Birmingham, 1720 2nd Avenue South, Birmingham, AL 35294. *Toll-free phone:* 800-421-8743.

The University of Alabama in Huntsville

Huntsville, Alabama
http://www.uah.edu/

CONTACT
Ms. Peggy Masters, Director of Undergraduate Admissions, The University of Alabama in Huntsville, Enrollment Services, 301 Sparkman Drive, Huntsville, AL 35899. *Phone:* 256-824-2771. *Toll-free phone:* 800-UAH-CALL. *Fax:* 256-824-4539. *E-mail:* uahadmissions@uah.edu.

University of Mobile

Mobile, Alabama

http://www.umobile.edu/

- **Independent Southern Baptist** comprehensive, founded 1961
- **Suburban** 880-acre campus
- **Endowment** $23.2 million
- **Coed**
- **Moderately difficult** entrance level

FACULTY
Student/faculty ratio: 14:1.

ACADEMICS
Calendar: semesters. *Degrees:* associate, bachelor's, and master's.
Library: J. L. Bedsole Library. *Books:* 66,089 (physical), 157,420 (digital/electronic); *Serial titles:* 153 (physical), 151,115 (digital/electronic); *Databases:* 80.

STUDENT LIFE
Housing options: on-campus residence required through sophomore year; men-only, women-only. Campus housing is university owned. Freshman campus housing is guaranteed.

Activities and organizations: drama/theater group, choral group, Campus Activity Board, Campus Ministry, Student Government Association, Student Nurse Organization.

Athletics Member NAIA.

Campus security: 24-hour emergency response devices and patrols, controlled dormitory access, text alerts.

Student services: personal/psychological counseling, veterans affairs office.

COSTS & FINANCIAL AID
Costs (2018–19) *Comprehensive fee:* $32,730 includes full-time tuition ($21,620), mandatory fees ($1410), and room and board ($9700). Full-time tuition and fees vary according to course load and program. Part-time tuition: $772 per credit hour. Part-time tuition and fees vary according to course load and program. *Room and board:* Room and board charges vary according to board plan and housing facility.

Financial Aid Of all full-time matriculated undergraduates who enrolled in 2016, 970 applied for aid, 888 were judged to have need, 887 had their need fully met. 55 Federal Work-Study jobs (averaging $1575). In 2016, 163 non-need-based awards were made. *Average percent of need met:* 66. *Average financial aid package:* $17,739. *Average need-based loan:* $2175. *Average need-based gift aid:* $5279. *Average non-need-based aid:* $10,158. *Average indebtedness upon graduation:* $30,029.

APPLYING
Standardized Tests *Required:* SAT or ACT (for admission).
Options: electronic application, deferred entrance.
Application fee: $25.
Required: high school transcript, minimum 2.8 GPA.

CONTACT
Mrs. Hali Givens, Director of Enrollment, University of Mobile, 5735 College Parkway, Mobile, AL 36613-2842. *Phone:* 251-442-2222. *Toll-free phone:* 800-946-7267. *E-mail:* hgivens@umobile.edu.

University of Montevallo

Montevallo, Alabama

http://www.montevallo.edu/

- **State-supported** comprehensive, founded 1896
- **Small-town** 160-acre campus with easy access to Birmingham
- **Endowment** $20.6 million
- **Coed** 2,285 undergraduate students, 90% full-time, 67% women, 33% men
- **Moderately difficult** entrance level, 48% of applicants were admitted

UNDERGRAD STUDENTS
2,063 full-time, 222 part-time. Students come from 36 states and territories; 26 other countries; 13% are from out of state; 17% Black or African American, non-Hispanic/Latino; 5% Hispanic/Latino; 1% Asian, non-Hispanic/Latino; 0.2% Native Hawaiian or other Pacific Islander, non-Hispanic/Latino; 0.4% American Indian or Alaska Native, non-Hispanic/Latino; 4% Two or more races, non-Hispanic/Latino; 2% Race/ethnicity unknown; 3% international; 8% transferred in; 48% live on campus.

Freshmen:
Admission: 3,882 applied, 1,852 admitted, 490 enrolled. *Average high school GPA:* 3.6. *Test scores:* ACT scores over 18: 98%; ACT scores over 24: 48%; ACT scores over 30: 10%.
Retention: 76% of full-time freshmen returned.

FACULTY
Total: 230, 66% full-time, 72% with terminal degrees.
Student/faculty ratio: 14:1.

ACADEMICS
Calendar: semesters. *Degrees:* bachelor's, master's, and post-master's certificates.

Special study options: academic remediation for entering students, accelerated degree program, advanced placement credit, distance learning, double majors, honors programs, independent study, internships, part-time degree program, services for LD students, study abroad, summer session for credit. *ROTC:* Army (c), Air Force (c).

Unusual degree programs: 3-2 engineering with Auburn University, University of Alabama at Birmingham.

Computers: 340 computers/terminals are available on campus for general student use. Students can access the following: campus intranet, computer help desk, free student e-mail accounts, online (class) grades, online (class) registration, online (class) schedules. Campuswide network is available. 100% of college-owned or -operated housing units are wired for high-speed Internet access. Wireless service is available via classrooms, computer centers, computer labs, dorm rooms, libraries, student centers.
Library: Carmichael Library. Students can reserve study rooms.

STUDENT LIFE
Housing options: on-campus residence required for freshman year; coed, men-only, women-only. Campus housing is university owned. Freshman campus housing is guaranteed.

Activities and organizations: drama/theater group, student-run newspaper, television station, choral group, Student Government Association, University Programming Council, Campus Ministries, Greek Life, Environmental Club, national fraternities, national sororities.

Athletics Member NCAA. All Division II except golf (Division I). *Intercollegiate sports:* baseball M(s), basketball M(s)/W(s), cheerleading W, cross-country running M/W, golf M(s)/W(s), lacrosse M/W, soccer M(s)/W(s), softball W, swimming and diving M/W, tennis M/W(s), track and field M/W, volleyball W(s). *Intramural sports:* basketball M/W, bowling M, football M, golf M, tennis M/W, volleyball M/W.

Campus security: 24-hour emergency response devices and patrols, late-night transport/escort service, controlled dormitory access.

Student services: health clinic, personal/psychological counseling.

COSTS & FINANCIAL AID
Costs (2018–19) *Tuition:* state resident $12,090 full-time, $403 per credit hour part-time; nonresident $25,110 full-time, $837 per credit hour part-time. *Required fees:* $670 full-time. *Room and board:* $7836; room only: $4906. Room and board charges vary according to housing facility. *Payment plan:* installment. *Waivers:* employees or children of employees.

Financial Aid Of all full-time matriculated undergraduates who enrolled in 2018, 1,673 applied for aid, 1,433 were judged to have need, 302 had their need fully met. 119 Federal Work-Study jobs (averaging $1800). In 2018, 476 non-need-based awards were made. *Average percent of need met:* 57. *Average financial aid package:* $12,240. *Average need-based loan:* $4013. *Average need-based gift aid:* $9905. *Average non-need-based aid:* $12,350. *Average indebtedness upon graduation:* $29,391.

APPLYING
Standardized Tests *Required:* SAT or ACT (for admission).
Options: electronic application, early admission, deferred entrance.
Application fee: $30.
Required: high school transcript, minimum 2.0 GPA. *Recommended:* interview.
Application deadlines: 8/15 (freshmen), rolling (transfers).
Notification: 9/1 (freshmen).

CONTACT
Audrey Crawford, Director of Admissions, University of Montevallo, Office of Admissions, Station 6030, Montevallo, AL 35115-6030. *Phone:* 205-665-6030. *Toll-free phone:* 800-292-4349. *Fax:* 205-665-6032. *E-mail:* admissions@montevallo.edu.

University of North Alabama
Florence, Alabama
http://www.una.edu/
- **State-supported** comprehensive, founded 1830
- **Urban** 200-acre campus with easy access to Huntsville
- **Endowment** $32.6 million
- **Coed**
- **Minimally difficult** entrance level

FACULTY
Student/faculty ratio: 19:1.

ACADEMICS
Calendar: semesters. *Degrees:* bachelor's, master's, post-master's, and postbachelor's certificates.
Library: Collier Library plus 3 others. *Books:* 225,076 (physical), 469,260 (digital/electronic); *Serial titles:* 4,070 (physical), 55,929 (digital/electronic); *Databases:* 182. Weekly public service hours: 98; students can reserve study rooms.

STUDENT LIFE
Housing options: on-campus residence required for freshman year; coed, men-only, women-only. Campus housing is university owned and is provided by a third party. Freshman campus housing is guaranteed.

Activities and organizations: drama/theater group, student-run newspaper, choral group, marching band, Phi Mu, Alpha Gamma Delta, Zeta Tau Alpha, Alpha Delta Pi, Student Government Association, national fraternities, national sororities.

Athletics Member NCAA. All Division II.

Campus security: 24-hour emergency response devices and patrols, student patrols, late-night transport/escort service, controlled dormitory access.

Student services: health clinic, personal/psychological counseling, women's center, veterans affairs office.

COSTS & FINANCIAL AID
Costs (2018–19) *Tuition:* state resident $8310 full-time, $277 per credit hour part-time; nonresident $16,620 full-time, $554 per credit hour part-time. Full-time tuition and fees vary according to course load and program. Part-time tuition and fees vary according to course load and program. *Required fees:* $2060 full-time, $238 per credit hour part-time. *Room and board:* $7700. Room and board charges vary according to board plan, housing facility, and student level.

Financial Aid Of all full-time matriculated undergraduates who enrolled in 2017, 3,958 applied for aid, 3,911 were judged to have need, 144 had their need fully met. In 2017, 427 non-need-based awards were made. *Average percent of need met:* 50. *Average financial aid package:* $8629. *Average need-based loan:* $3852. *Average need-based gift aid:* $3677. *Average non-need-based aid:* $2870. *Average indebtedness upon graduation:* $28,283.

APPLYING
Standardized Tests *Required:* SAT or ACT (for admission).
Options: electronic application, early admission, deferred entrance.
Application fee: $35.
Required: high school transcript, minimum 2.0 GPA, 13 approved units from high school academic core.

CONTACT
Mrs. Julie Taylor, Interim Director of Admissions, University of North Alabama, One Harrison Plaza, Florence, AL 35632-0001. *Phone:* 256-765-4680. *Toll-free phone:* 800-TALK-UNA. *Fax:* 256-765-4329. *E-mail:* admissions@una.edu.

University of South Alabama
Mobile, Alabama
http://www.southalabama.edu/
- **State-supported** university, founded 1963
- **Suburban** 1225-acre campus
- **Endowment** $152.6 million
- **Coed** 10,293 undergraduate students, 84% full-time, 59% women, 41% men
- **Moderately difficult** entrance level, 79% of applicants were admitted

UNDERGRAD STUDENTS
8,637 full-time, 1,656 part-time. Students come from 41 states and territories; 67 other countries; 18% are from out of state; 23% Black or African American, non-Hispanic/Latino; 4% Hispanic/Latino; 3% Asian, non-Hispanic/Latino; 0.2% Native Hawaiian or other Pacific Islander, non-Hispanic/Latino; 0.6% American Indian or Alaska Native, non-Hispanic/Latino; 4% Two or more races, non-Hispanic/Latino; 2% Race/ethnicity unknown; 3% international; 7% transferred in; 22% live on campus.

Freshmen:
Admission: 6,688 applied, 5,259 admitted, 1,910 enrolled. *Average high school GPA:* 3.7. *Test scores:* SAT evidence-based reading and writing scores over 500: 85%; SAT math scores over 500: 79%; ACT scores over 18: 98%; SAT evidence-based reading and writing scores over 600: 40%; SAT math scores over 600: 29%; ACT scores over 24: 49%; SAT evidence-based reading and writing scores over 700: 5%; SAT math scores over 700: 7%; ACT scores over 30: 12%.
Retention: 74% of full-time freshmen returned.

FACULTY
Total: 1,038, 57% full-time, 60% with terminal degrees.
Student/faculty ratio: 18:1.

ACADEMICS
Calendar: semesters. *Degrees:* certificates, bachelor's, master's, doctoral, post-master's, and postbachelor's certificates.

Special study options: academic remediation for entering students, accelerated degree program, adult/continuing education programs, advanced placement credit, cooperative education, distance learning, double majors, English as a second language, freshman honors college, honors programs, independent study, internships, part-time degree program, services for LD students, student-designed majors, study abroad, summer session for credit. *ROTC:* Army (b), Air Force (b).

Computers: Students can access the following: campus intranet, computer help desk, free student e-mail accounts, online (class) grades, online (class) registration, online (class) schedules. Campuswide network is available. 100% of college-owned or -operated housing units are wired for high-speed Internet access. Wireless service is available via entire campus.
Library: Marx Library plus 5 others.

STUDENT LIFE
Housing options: coed, special housing for students with disabilities. Campus housing is university owned and is provided by a third party.

Activities and organizations: drama/theater group, student-run newspaper, radio and television station, choral group, marching band, Student Government Association, African American Student Association, Council of International Student Organizations, Alpha Epsilon Delta Pre-Health Professions, Panhellenic Council, national fraternities, national sororities.

Athletics Member NCAA. All Division I. *Intercollegiate sports:* baseball M(s), basketball M(s)/W(s), cross-country running M(s)/W(s), football M(s), golf M(s)/W(s), soccer W(s), softball W(s), tennis M(s)/W(s), track and field M(s)/W(s), volleyball W(s). *Intramural sports:* archery M(c)/W(c), basketball M/W, cheerleading M(c)/W(c), football M(c)/W(c), rock climbing M(c)/W(c), rugby M(c), soccer M/W, softball M/W, ultimate Frisbee M(c)/W(c), volleyball M/W, water polo M/W.

Campus security: 24-hour emergency response devices and patrols, late-night transport/escort service, controlled dormitory access.

Student services: health clinic, personal/psychological counseling, women's center, legal services, veterans affairs office.

FINANCIAL AID

Financial Aid Of all full-time matriculated undergraduates who enrolled in 2015, 7,167 applied for aid, 5,829 were judged to have need, 487 had their need fully met. In 2015, 1146 non-need-based awards were made. *Average percent of need met:* 50. *Average financial aid package:* $9708. *Average need-based loan:* $4348. *Average need-based gift aid:* $6606. *Average non-need-based aid:* $5321.

APPLYING

Standardized Tests *Required for some:* SAT or ACT (for admission).

Options: electronic application, early admission, deferred entrance.

Application fee: $45.

Required: high school transcript. *Required for some:* essay or personal statement, minimum 3.5 GPA, 1 letter of recommendation, minimum high school GPA of 3.0 for Accelerated College Enrollment Program, minimum high school GPA of 3.5 for Early Admission. *Recommended:* minimum 2.5 GPA.

Application deadlines: 7/15 (freshmen), 7/15 (out-of-state freshmen), 7/15 (transfers).

Notification: continuous (freshmen), continuous (out-of-state freshmen), continuous (transfers).

CONTACT

Mrs. Kristin Odom, Director, New Student Recruitment, University of South Alabama, 390 Alumni Circle, 2500 Meisler Hall, Mobile, AL 36688-0002. *Phone:* 251-460-7834. *Toll-free phone:* 800-872-5247. *Fax:* 251-460-7876. *E-mail:* recruitment@southalabama.edu.

The University of West Alabama
Livingston, Alabama
http://www.uwa.edu/

- **State-supported** comprehensive, founded 1835
- **Small-town** 514-acre campus
- **Endowment** $38,085
- **Coed** 2,159 undergraduate students, 85% full-time, 58% women, 42% men
- **Minimally difficult** entrance level, 40% of applicants were admitted

UNDERGRAD STUDENTS

1,836 full-time, 323 part-time. Students come from 30 states and territories; 24 other countries; 19% are from out of state; 43% Black or African American, non-Hispanic/Latino; 2% Hispanic/Latino; 0.3% Asian, non-Hispanic/Latino; 0.4% American Indian or Alaska Native, non-Hispanic/Latino; 3% Two or more races, non-Hispanic/Latino; 3% Race/ethnicity unknown; 5% international; 16% transferred in; 41% live on campus.

Freshmen:
Admission: 8,870 applied, 3,518 admitted, 415 enrolled. *Test scores:* ACT scores over 18: 80%; ACT scores over 24: 19%; ACT scores over 30: 1%.

Retention: 62% of full-time freshmen returned.

FACULTY

Total: 302, 39% full-time, 60% with terminal degrees.

Student/faculty ratio: 13:1.

ACADEMICS

Calendar: semesters. *Degrees:* certificates, associate, bachelor's, master's, and post-master's certificates.

Special study options: academic remediation for entering students, accelerated degree program, advanced placement credit, cooperative education, distance learning, double majors, English as a second language, freshman honors college, honors programs, independent study, internships, part-time degree program, services for LD students, student-designed majors, study abroad, summer session for credit. *ROTC:* Air Force (c).

Unusual degree programs: 3-2 engineering with Auburn University, The University of Alabama at Birmingham, Mississippi State University, The University of Alabama; forestry with Auburn University; social work with University of Alabama; wildlife with Auburn University.

Computers: 600 computers/terminals are available on campus for general student use. Students can access the following: campus intranet, computer help desk, free student e-mail accounts, online (class) grades, online (class) registration, online (class) schedules. Campuswide network is available. 100% of college-owned or -operated housing units are wired for high-speed Internet access. Wireless service is available via entire campus.

Library: Julia Tutwiler Library plus 1 other. *Books:* 176,910 (physical), 1,789 (digital/electronic); *Serial titles:* 11 (physical); *Databases:* 39. Weekly public service hours: 96; students can reserve study rooms.

STUDENT LIFE

Housing options: on-campus residence required for freshman year; coed. Campus housing is university owned. Freshman campus housing is guaranteed.

Activities and organizations: drama/theater group, student-run newspaper, television station, choral group, marching band, Student Government Association, RHA, Phi Mu, Alpha Sigma Alpha, Blue Key, national fraternities, national sororities.

Athletics Member NCAA. All Division II. *Intercollegiate sports:* baseball M(s), basketball M(s)/W(s), cross-country running M(s)/W(s), football M(s), soccer M(s)/W(s), softball W(s), tennis M(s)/W(s), track and field M(s)/W(s), volleyball W(s). *Intramural sports:* badminton M/W, baseball M/W, football M/W, soccer M/W, softball M/W, table tennis M/W, tennis M/W, ultimate Frisbee M/W, volleyball M/W.

Campus security: 24-hour emergency response devices and patrols, student patrols, late-night transport/escort service, controlled dormitory access.

Student services: health clinic, personal/psychological counseling.

COSTS & FINANCIAL AID

Costs (2018–19) *Tuition:* state resident $8450 full-time, $325 per hour part-time; nonresident $16,900 full-time, $650 per hour part-time. Full-time tuition and fees vary according to course load. Part-time tuition and fees vary according to course load. *Required fees:* $1590 full-time. *Room and board:* $7316; room only: $4620. Room and board charges vary according to board plan, housing facility, and student level. *Payment plan:* installment. *Waivers:* employees or children of employees.

Financial Aid Of all full-time matriculated undergraduates who enrolled in 2017, 1,628 applied for aid, 1,421 were judged to have need, 95 had their need fully met. 76 Federal Work-Study jobs (averaging $1800). In 2017, 73 non-need-based awards were made. *Average percent of need met:* 21. *Average financial aid package:* $10,969. *Average need-based gift aid:* $5258. *Average non-need-based aid:* $6765. *Average indebtedness upon graduation:* $21,562.

APPLYING

Standardized Tests *Required:* SAT or ACT (for admission).

Options: electronic application, deferred entrance.

Application fee: $40.

Required: high school transcript, minimum 2.0 GPA.

Application deadlines: rolling (freshmen), rolling (transfers).

Notification: continuous (freshmen), continuous (transfers).

CONTACT

Mrs. Brenda Edwards, Coordinator of Admissions Operations, The University of West Alabama, Station 4, Livingston, AL 35470. *Phone:* 205-652-3699. *Toll-free phone:* 888-636-8800. *Fax:* 205-652-3881. *E-mail:* belliott@uwa.edu.

ALASKA

Alaska Bible College
Palmer, Alaska
http://www.akbible.edu/

- **Independent nondenominational** 4-year, founded 1966
- **Small-town** 2-acre campus with easy access to Anchorage, AK
- **Coed**
- **Minimally difficult** entrance level

FACULTY

Student/faculty ratio: 4:1.

ACADEMICS
Calendar: semesters. *Degrees:* certificates, associate, and bachelor's.
Library: Alaska Bible College Ball Memorial Library. *Books:* 32,000 (physical); *Serial titles:* 46 (physical). Weekly public service hours: 40.

STUDENT LIFE
Housing options: men-only, women-only. Campus housing is university owned. Freshman applicants given priority for college housing.
Student services: veterans affairs office.

COSTS & FINANCIAL AID
Costs (2018–19) *Comprehensive fee:* $15,300 includes full-time tuition ($9000), mandatory fees ($600), and room and board ($5700). Part-time tuition: $375 per credit hour. *Required fees:* $50 per term part-time.
Financial Aid Of all full-time matriculated undergraduates who enrolled in 2018, 4 Federal Work-Study jobs (averaging $1250).

APPLYING
Standardized Tests *Required:* SAT or ACT (for admission).
Options: electronic application, deferred entrance.
Application fee: $35.
Required: essay or personal statement, high school transcript, minimum 2.0 GPA, 3 letters of recommendation.

CONTACT
Justin Archuletta, Director of Admissions, Alaska Bible College, 248 E. Elmwood Avenue, Palmer, AK 99645. *Phone:* 907-745-3201 Ext. 111. *Toll-free phone:* 800-478-7884. *Fax:* 907-745-3210. *E-mail:* admissions@akbible.edu.

Alaska Pacific University
Anchorage, Alaska
http://www.alaskapacific.edu/
- **Independent** comprehensive, founded 1959
- **Urban** 170-acre campus
- **Coed**
- **Minimally difficult** entrance level

FACULTY
Student/faculty ratio: 10:1.

ACADEMICS
Calendar: semesters. *Degrees:* certificates, associate, bachelor's, master's, doctoral, and postbachelor's certificates.
Library: Consortium Library. Students can reserve study rooms.

STUDENT LIFE
Housing options: on-campus residence required through sophomore year; coed. Campus housing is university owned. Freshman campus housing is guaranteed.
Activities and organizations: drama/theater group, student-run newspaper, choral group, ASAPU (Associated Students of Alaska Pacific University), Photography Club, Dive Club, Basketball club, Spectrum Club.
Campus security: 24-hour emergency response devices, student patrols, late-night transport/escort service, controlled dormitory access.
Student services: personal/psychological counseling.

COSTS
Costs (2018–19) *Comprehensive fee:* $29,060 includes full-time tuition ($20,350), mandatory fees ($480), and room and board ($8230). Full-time tuition and fees vary according to course load, degree level, program, and reciprocity agreements. Part-time tuition and fees vary according to course load, degree level, and program. *Room and board:* Room and board charges vary according to board plan and housing facility. *Payment plans:* installment, deferred payment.

APPLYING
Options: electronic application, deferred entrance.
Application fee: $25.
Required: high school transcript, minimum 2.5 GPA.

CONTACT
Ms. Kate Hillenbrand, Director of Admissions, Alaska Pacific University, 4101 University Drive, Anchorage, AK 99508. *Phone:* 907-564-8300. *Toll-free phone:* 800-252-7528. *Fax:* 907-564-8317. *E-mail:* admissions@alaskapacific.edu.

Charter College
Anchorage, Alaska
http://www.chartercollege.edu/

CONTACT
Ms. Lily Sirianni, Vice President, Charter College, 2221 East Northern Lights Boulevard, Suite 120, Anchorage, AK 99508. *Phone:* 907-277-1000. *Toll-free phone:* 888-200-9942.

University of Alaska Anchorage
Anchorage, Alaska
http://www.uaa.alaska.edu/

CONTACT
Enrollment Services, University of Alaska Anchorage, PO Box 141629, 3901 Old Seward Highway, Anchorage, AK 99508-8046. *Phone:* 907-786-1480. *Fax:* 907-786-4888. *E-mail:* enroll@uaa.alaska.edu.

University of Alaska Anchorage, Kenai Peninsula College
Soldotna, Alaska
http://www.kpc.alaska.edu/

CONTACT
Mrs. Julie Cotterell, Admission and Student Records Coordinator, University of Alaska Anchorage, Kenai Peninsula College, 156 College Road, Soldotna, AK 99669-9798. *Phone:* 907-262-0311. *Toll-free phone:* 877-262-0330. *E-mail:* jmcotterell@kpc.alaska.edu.

University of Alaska Fairbanks
Fairbanks, Alaska
http://www.uaf.edu/
- **State-supported** university, founded 1917, part of University of Alaska System
- **Small-town** 2250-acre campus
- **Endowment** $98.9 million
- **Coed**
- **Minimally difficult** entrance level

FACULTY
Student/faculty ratio: 8:1.

ACADEMICS
Calendar: semesters. *Degrees:* certificates, associate, bachelor's, master's, doctoral, and postbachelor's certificates.
Library: Rasmuson Library plus 1 other. *Books:* 533,679 (physical), 324,260 (digital/electronic); *Serial titles:* 222,847 (physical), 30,490 (digital/electronic); *Databases:* 175. Weekly public service hours: 87; students can reserve study rooms.

STUDENT LIFE
Housing options: coed, special housing for students with disabilities. Campus housing is university owned. Freshman applicants given priority for college housing.
Activities and organizations: drama/theater group, student-run newspaper, radio station, choral group, Chi Alpha, Yoga Club, Aurora Aerial Arts, Festival of Native Arts, Gender and Sexuality Alliance.
Athletics Member NCAA. All Division II except ice hockey (Division I).
Campus security: 24-hour emergency response devices and patrols, student patrols, late-night transport/escort service, controlled dormitory access, ID check at door of residence halls, crime prevention and safety workshops.
Student services: health clinic, personal/psychological counseling, legal services, veterans affairs office.

COSTS & FINANCIAL AID
Costs (2018–19) *Tuition:* state resident $7020 full-time, $212 per credit hour part-time; nonresident $23,190 full-time, $751 per credit hour part-time. Full-time tuition and fees vary according to course level, course load, location, program, and reciprocity agreements. Part-time tuition and fees vary according to course level, course load, location, program, and reciprocity agreements. *Required fees:* $1780 full-time. *Room and board:*

A ★ indicates that the school has detailed information with a Premium Profile on Petersons.com.

www.petersons.com **69**

COLLEGES AT-A-GLANCE

$8930; room only: $4200. Room and board charges vary according to board plan, housing facility, and location. *Payment plans:* installment, deferred payment.

Financial Aid *Average indebtedness upon graduation:* $22,155. *Financial aid deadline:* 7/1.

APPLYING
Standardized Tests *Required:* SAT or ACT (for admission).
Options: electronic application, deferred entrance.
Application fee: $50.
Required: high school transcript, minimum 2.5 GPA.

CONTACT
University of Alaska Fairbanks, PO Box 757500, Fairbanks, AK 99775-7520. *Toll-free phone:* 800-478-1823.

University of Alaska Southeast

Juneau, Alaska
http://www.uas.alaska.edu/

CONTACT
Ms. Deema Ferguson, Admissions Clerk, University of Alaska Southeast, 11120 Glacier Highway, Juneau, AK 99801-8625. *Phone:* 907-796-6294 Ext. 6100. *Toll-free phone:* 877-465-4827. *Fax:* 907-796-6365. *E-mail:* admissions@uas.alaska.edu.

University of Alaska Southeast, Sitka Campus

Sitka, Alaska
http://www.uas.alaska.edu/sitka/

CONTACT
Ms. Teal Gordon, Admissions Representative, University of Alaska Southeast, Sitka Campus, UAS Sitka, 1332 Seward Avenue, Sitka, AK 99835. *Phone:* 907-747-7726. *Toll-free phone:* 800-478-6653. *Fax:* 907-747-7731. *E-mail:* ktgordon@uas.alaska.edu.

ARIZONA

Argosy University, Phoenix

Phoenix, Arizona
http://www.argosy.edu/phoenix-arizona/default.aspx

CONTACT
Argosy University, Phoenix, 2233 West Dunlap Avenue, Phoenix, AZ 85021. *Phone:* 602-216-2600. *Toll-free phone:* 866-216-2777.

Arizona Christian University

Phoenix, Arizona
http://arizonachristian.edu/
- **Independent Conservative Baptist** 4-year, founded 1960
- **Urban** 19-acre campus with easy access to Phoenix
- **Coed**
- 99% of applicants were admitted

FACULTY
Student/faculty ratio: 16:1.

ACADEMICS
Calendar: semesters. *Degrees:* associate and bachelor's.
Library: R. S. Beal Library. *Books:* 28,496 (physical), 19,581 (digital/electronic); *Serial titles:* 471 (physical), 32 (digital/electronic); *Databases:* 18. Weekly public service hours: 76.

STUDENT LIFE
Housing options: on-campus residence required through sophomore year; coed. Campus housing is university owned. Freshman campus housing is guaranteed.

Activities and organizations: choral group, Joseph Story Pre-Law Society, International Student Association, Pre-Medicine Club, Flock Council and Flock Leaders, Reason and Religion.
Athletics Member NAIA, NCCAA.
Campus security: 24-hour emergency response devices, student patrols, late-night transport/escort service, controlled dormitory access, 20-hour patrol with a guard on call on weekdays, 24-hour patrol by trained security personnel on weekends.
Student services: personal/psychological counseling.

COSTS & FINANCIAL AID
Costs (2018–19) *Comprehensive fee:* $36,150 includes full-time tuition ($25,476) and room and board ($10,674). Full-time tuition and fees vary according to class time, course load, and program. Part-time tuition: $1062 per credit hour. Part-time tuition and fees vary according to class time, course load, and program. *College room only:* $5400. Room and board charges vary according to board plan.

Financial Aid Of all full-time matriculated undergraduates who enrolled in 2017, 460 applied for aid, 422 were judged to have need, 64 had their need fully met. In 2017, 179 non-need-based awards were made. *Average percent of need met:* 28. *Average financial aid package:* $9685. *Average need-based loan:* $3822. *Average need-based gift aid:* $8478. *Average non-need-based aid:* $12,439.

APPLYING
Standardized Tests *Required:* SAT or ACT (for admission).
Application fee: $30.
Required: essay or personal statement, high school transcript, minimum 2.0 GPA, 1 letter of recommendation.

CONTACT
Lambert Cruz, Registrar and Assistant Dir Enrollment Management, Arizona Christian University, 2625 E. Cactus Road, Phoenix, AZ 85032. *Phone:* 602-386-4160. *Toll-free phone:* 800-247-2697. *Fax:* 602-404-2159. *E-mail:* lambert.cruz@arizonachristian.edu.

Arizona College–Mesa

Mesa, Arizona
http://www.arizonacollege.edu/

CONTACT
Arizona College–Mesa, 163 N Dobson Road, Mesa, AZ 85201.

Arizona State University at the Downtown Phoenix campus

Phoenix, Arizona
http://campus.asu.edu/downtown/
- **State-supported** university, founded 2006
- **Urban** 18-acre campus with easy access to Phoenix
- **Coed**
- **Moderately difficult** entrance level

FACULTY
Student/faculty ratio: 19:1.

ACADEMICS
Calendar: semesters. *Degrees:* certificates, bachelor's, master's, doctoral, post-master's, and postbachelor's certificates.
Library: Downtown Phoenix campus Library. *Books:* 3.9 million (physical), 963,136 (digital/electronic); *Serial titles:* 72,649 (physical), 73,043 (digital/electronic); *Databases:* 650. Weekly public service hours: 149; study areas open 24 hours, 5–7 days a week; students can reserve study rooms.

STUDENT LIFE
Housing options: on-campus residence required for freshman year; coed, special housing for students with disabilities. Campus housing is leased by the school and is provided by a third party. Freshman campus housing is guaranteed.
Activities and organizations: drama/theater group, student-run newspaper, radio and television station, Student Nurses Association, American Medical Student Association, Exercise and Wellness Organization, Student Nutrition Council, Physical Therapy Club.

Athletics Member NCAA. All Division I.

Campus security: 24-hour emergency response devices and patrols, late-night transport/escort service, controlled dormitory access, LiveSafe smart phone application, surveillance camera in some residence halls.

Student services: health clinic, personal/psychological counseling, veterans affairs office.

COSTS & FINANCIAL AID

Costs (2018–19) *Tuition:* state resident $10,104 full-time, $702 per credit hour part-time; nonresident $27,618 full-time, $1151 per credit hour part-time. *Required fees:* $718 full-time. *Room and board:* $14,584; room only: $9536. Room and board charges vary according to board plan.

Financial Aid Of all full-time matriculated undergraduates who enrolled in 2016, 6,691 applied for aid, 5,766 were judged to have need, 1,011 had their need fully met. 431 Federal Work-Study jobs (averaging $2689). 1,321 state and other part-time jobs (averaging $3390). In 2016, 1181 non-need-based awards were made. *Average percent of need met:* 58. *Average financial aid package:* $14,667. *Average need-based loan:* $4030. *Average need-based gift aid:* $10,233. *Average non-need-based aid:* $8125. *Average indebtedness upon graduation:* $24,368.

APPLYING

Standardized Tests *Required for some:* SAT or ACT (for admission), SAT Subject Tests (for admission). *Recommended:* SAT or ACT (for admission).

Options: electronic application, deferred entrance.

Application fee: $50.

Required: high school transcript, minimum 3.0 GPA. *Required for some:* essay or personal statement, letters of recommendation, additional requirements for Honors College and certain majors.

CONTACT

Admission Services, Arizona State University at the Downtown Phoenix campus, PO Box 870112, Tempe, AZ 85287-0112. *Phone:* 480-965-7788. *Fax:* 480-965-3610. *E-mail:* admissions@asu.edu.

Arizona State University at the Polytechnic campus

Mesa, Arizona
http://campus.asu.edu/polytechnic
- **State-supported** university, founded 1996
- **Suburban** 575-acre campus with easy access to Phoenix
- **Coed**
- **Moderately difficult** entrance level

FACULTY
Student/faculty ratio: 21:1.

ACADEMICS
Calendar: semesters. *Degrees:* certificates, bachelor's, master's, and doctoral.
Library: Polytechnic campus Library. *Books:* 3.9 million (physical), 963,136 (digital/electronic); *Serial titles:* 72,649 (physical), 73,043 (digital/electronic); *Databases:* 650. Weekly public service hours: 149; study areas open 24 hours, 5–7 days a week; students can reserve study rooms.

STUDENT LIFE
Housing options: on-campus residence required for freshman year; coed, special housing for students with disabilities. Campus housing is university owned and is provided by a third party. Freshman campus housing is guaranteed.

Activities and organizations: drama/theater group, student-run newspaper, Pre-Health Club, AIGA Polytechnic, Environmental Resource Management Club, Computer Science, Disc Golf Club.

Athletics Member NCAA. All Division I.

Campus security: 24-hour emergency response devices and patrols, late-night transport/escort service, controlled dormitory access, LiveSafe smart phone application, surveillance camera in some residence halls.

Student services: health clinic, personal/psychological counseling, veterans affairs office.

COSTS & FINANCIAL AID

Costs (2018–19) *Tuition:* state resident $9613 full-time, $667 per credit hour part-time; nonresident $26,238 full-time, $1094 per credit hour part-time. *Required fees:* $718 full-time. *Room and board:* $11,683; room only: $6635. Room and board charges vary according to board plan and housing facility.

Financial Aid Of all full-time matriculated undergraduates who enrolled in 2016, 2,491 applied for aid, 2,102 were judged to have need, 414 had their need fully met. 197 Federal Work-Study jobs (averaging $2581). 777 state and other part-time jobs (averaging $3900). In 2016, 435 non-need-based awards were made. *Average percent of need met:* 58. *Average financial aid package:* $13,973. *Average need-based loan:* $4155. *Average need-based gift aid:* $9309. *Average non-need-based aid:* $6948. *Average indebtedness upon graduation:* $26,797.

APPLYING

Standardized Tests *Required for some:* SAT or ACT (for admission), SAT Subject Tests (for admission). *Recommended:* SAT or ACT (for admission).

Options: electronic application, deferred entrance.

Application fee: $50.

Required: high school transcript, minimum 3.0 GPA. *Required for some:* essay or personal statement, letters of recommendation, additional requirements for Honors College and certain majors.

CONTACT

Admission Services, Arizona State University at the Polytechnic campus, PO Box 870112, Tempe, AZ 85287-0112. *Phone:* 480-965-7788. *Fax:* 480-965-3610. *E-mail:* admissions@asu.edu.

Arizona State University at the Tempe campus

Tempe, Arizona
http://www.asu.edu/
- **State-supported** university, founded 1885
- **Urban** 661-acre campus with easy access to Phoenix
- **Coed**
- **Moderately difficult** entrance level

FACULTY
Student/faculty ratio: 22:1.

ACADEMICS
Calendar: semesters. *Degrees:* certificates, bachelor's, master's, doctoral, post-master's, and postbachelor's certificates (profile includes data for the West, Polytechnic and Downtown Phoenix campuses).
Library: Hayden Library plus 3 others. *Books:* 3.9 million (physical), 963,136 (digital/electronic); *Serial titles:* 72,649 (physical), 73,043 (digital/electronic); *Databases:* 650. Weekly public service hours: 149; study areas open 24 hours, 5–7 days a week; students can reserve study rooms.

STUDENT LIFE
Housing options: on-campus residence required for freshman year; coed, special housing for students with disabilities. Campus housing is university owned, leased by the school and is provided by a third party. Freshman campus housing is guaranteed.

Activities and organizations: drama/theater group, student-run newspaper, choral group, marching band, Sun Devil Ski Club, Residence Hall Association, Alpha Epsilon Delta, American Medical Student Association, Software Developers Association, national fraternities, national sororities.

Athletics Member NCAA. All Division I.

Campus security: 24-hour emergency response devices and patrols, late-night transport/escort service, controlled dormitory access, LiveSafe smart phone application, surveillance cameras in some residence halls.

Student services: health clinic, personal/psychological counseling, veterans affairs office.

COSTS & FINANCIAL AID

Costs (2018–19) *Tuition:* state resident $10,104 full-time, $702 per credit hour part-time; nonresident $27,618 full-time, $1151 per credit hour part-time. *Required fees:* $718 full-time. *Room and board:* $12,648; room only: $7600. Room and board charges vary according to board plan and housing facility.

Financial Aid Of all full-time matriculated undergraduates who enrolled in 2016, 25,918 applied for aid, 20,975 were judged to have need, 4,088 had their need fully met. 1,136 Federal Work-Study jobs (averaging $2470). 6,382 state and other part-time jobs (averaging $3322). In 2016, 8547 non-need-based awards were made. *Average percent of need met:* 62. *Average financial aid package:* $14,940. *Average need-based loan:* $4004. *Average need-based gift aid:* $10,528. *Average non-need-based aid:* $8329. *Average indebtedness upon graduation:* $23,237.

APPLYING
Standardized Tests *Required for some:* SAT or ACT (for admission), SAT Subject Tests (for admission). *Recommended:* SAT or ACT (for admission).

Options: electronic application, deferred entrance.

Application fee: $50.

Required: high school transcript, minimum 3.0 GPA. *Required for some:* essay or personal statement, letters of recommendation, additional requirements for Honors College and certain majors.

CONTACT
Admission Services, Arizona State University at the Tempe campus, PO Box 870112, Tempe, AZ 85287-0112. *Phone:* 480-965-7788. *Fax:* 480-965-3610. *E-mail:* admissions@asu.edu.

Arizona State University at the West campus

Glendale, Arizona
http://campus.asu.edu/west

- **State-supported** university, founded 1984
- **Urban** 278-acre campus with easy access to Phoenix
- **Coed**
- **Moderately difficult** entrance level

FACULTY
Student/faculty ratio: 14:1.

ACADEMICS
Calendar: semesters. *Degrees:* certificates, bachelor's, master's, doctoral, and postbachelor's certificates.
Library: Fletcher Library at the West campus. *Books:* 3.9 million (physical), 963,136 (digital/electronic); *Serial titles:* 72,649 (physical), 73,043 (digital/electronic); *Databases:* 650. Weekly public service hours: 149; study areas open 24 hours, 5–7 days a week; students can reserve study rooms.

STUDENT LIFE
Housing options: on-campus residence required for freshman year; coed, special housing for students with disabilities. Campus housing is university owned and is provided by a third party. Freshman campus housing is guaranteed.

Activities and organizations: drama/theater group, student-run newspaper, choral group, Hispanic Honor Society, Teachers of the Future, Business to Business, W. P. Carey MBA Association, American Medical Student Association.

Athletics Member NCAA. All Division I.

Campus security: 24-hour emergency response devices and patrols, late-night transport/escort service, controlled dormitory access, LiveSafe smart phone application, surveillance camera in some residence halls.

Student services: health clinic, personal/psychological counseling, veterans affairs office.

COSTS & FINANCIAL AID
Costs (2018–19) *Tuition:* state resident $9613 full-time, $667 per credit hour part-time; nonresident $26,238 full-time, $1094 per credit hour part-time. *Required fees:* $718 full-time. *Room and board:* $11,588; room only: $6540. Room and board charges vary according to board plan.

Financial Aid Of all full-time matriculated undergraduates who enrolled in 2016, 2,238 applied for aid, 1,981 were judged to have need, 293 had

their need fully met. 169 Federal Work-Study jobs (averaging $2277). 506 state and other part-time jobs (averaging $3380). In 2016, 234 non-need-based awards were made. *Average percent of need met:* 59. *Average financial aid package:* $12,895. *Average need-based loan:* $4137. *Average need-based gift aid:* $9034. *Average non-need-based aid:* $6743. *Average indebtedness upon graduation:* $24,498.

APPLYING
Standardized Tests *Required for some:* SAT or ACT (for admission), SAT Subject Tests (for admission). *Recommended:* SAT or ACT (for admission).

Options: electronic application, deferred entrance.

Application fee: $50.

Required: high school transcript, minimum 3.0 GPA. *Required for some:* essay or personal statement, letters of recommendation, additional requirements for Honors College and certain majors.

CONTACT
Arizona State University at the West campus, PO Box 870112, Tempe, AZ 85287-0112. *Phone:* 480-965-7788. *Fax:* 480-965-3610. *E-mail:* admissions@asu.edu.

Brookline College
Phoenix, Arizona
http://brooklinecollege.edu/

CONTACT
Ms. Theresa Dean, Director of Admissions, Brookline College, 2445 West Dunlap Avenue, Suite 100, Phoenix, AZ 85021. *Phone:* 602-242-6265. *Toll-free phone:* 800-793-2428. *Fax:* 602-973-2572. *E-mail:* tdean@ brooklinecollege.edu.

Brookline College
Tempe, Arizona
http://brooklinecollege.edu/

CONTACT
Ms. Cheryl Kindred, Campus Director, Brookline College, 1140-1150 South Priest Drive, Tempe, AZ 85281. *Phone:* 480-545-8755. *Toll-free phone:* 888-886-2428. *Fax:* 480-926-1371. *E-mail:* ckindred@ brooklinecollege.edu.

Brookline College
Tucson, Arizona
http://brooklinecollege.edu/

CONTACT
Ms. Leigh Anne Pechota, Campus Director, Brookline College, 5441 East 22nd Street, Suite 125, Tucson, AZ 85711. *Phone:* 520-748-9799. *Toll-free phone:* 888-292-2428. *Fax:* 520-748-9355. *E-mail:* lpechota@ brooklinecollege.edu.

Chamberlain College of Nursing
Phoenix, Arizona
http://www.chamberlain.edu/

CONTACT
Admissions, Chamberlain College of Nursing, 2149 West Dunlap Avenue, Phoenix, AZ 85021. *Phone:* 602-331-2720. *Toll-free phone:* 877-751-5783.

CollegeAmerica–Flagstaff
Flagstaff, Arizona
http://www.collegeamerica.edu/

CONTACT
CollegeAmerica–Flagstaff, 399 South Malpais Lane, Flagstaff, AZ 86001. *Phone:* 928-213-6060 Ext. 1402. *Toll-free phone:* 800-622-2894.

CollegeAmerica–Phoenix
Phoenix, Arizona
http://www.collegeamerica.edu/

CONTACT
CollegeAmerica–Phoenix, 9801 North Metro Parkway East, Phoenix, AZ 85051. *Toll-free phone:* 800-622-2894.

DeVry University–Phoenix Campus
Phoenix, Arizona
http://www.devry.edu/

CONTACT
DeVry University–Phoenix Campus, 2149 West Dunlap Avenue, Phoenix, AZ 85021. *Phone:* 602-870-9222. *Toll-free phone:* 866-338-7934.

Dunlap-Stone University
Phoenix, Arizona
http://www.dunlap-stone.edu/

CONTACT
Dunlap-Stone University, 19820 North 7th Street, Suite #100, Phoenix, AZ 85024. *Phone:* 602-648-5750. *Toll-free phone:* 800-474-8013.

Embry-Riddle Aeronautical University–Prescott
Prescott, Arizona
http://www.prescott.erau.edu/

- **Independent** comprehensive, founded 1978
- **Small-town** 547-acre campus with easy access to Phoenix
- **Endowment** $40.6 million
- **Coed** 2,726 undergraduate students, 95% full-time, 25% women, 75% men
- **Moderately difficult** entrance level, 67% of applicants were admitted

UNDERGRAD STUDENTS
2,592 full-time, 134 part-time. Students come from 51 states and territories; 39 other countries; 76% are from out of state; 2% Black or African American, non-Hispanic/Latino; 13% Hispanic/Latino; 6% Asian, non-Hispanic/Latino; 0.6% Native Hawaiian or other Pacific Islander, non-Hispanic/Latino; 0.4% American Indian or Alaska Native, non-Hispanic/Latino; 6% Two or more races, non-Hispanic/Latino; 3% Race/ethnicity unknown; 6% international; 4% transferred in; 44% live on campus.

Freshmen:
Admission: 2,859 applied, 1,922 admitted, 609 enrolled. *Average high school GPA:* 3.7. *Test scores:* SAT evidence-based reading and writing scores over 500: 93%; SAT math scores over 500: 96%; ACT scores over 18: 97%; SAT evidence-based reading and writing scores over 600: 66%; SAT math scores over 600: 67%; ACT scores over 24: 74%; SAT evidence-based reading and writing scores over 700: 16%; SAT math scores over 700: 21%; ACT scores over 30: 25%.
Retention: 81% of full-time freshmen returned.

FACULTY
Total: 185, 67% full-time.
Student/faculty ratio: 17:1.

ACADEMICS
Calendar: semesters. *Degrees:* bachelor's and master's.
Special study options: accelerated degree program, advanced placement credit, cooperative education, distance learning, double majors, English as a second language, freshman honors college, honors programs, internships, part-time degree program, services for LD students, study abroad, summer session for credit. *ROTC:* Army (b), Air Force (b).
Computers: Students can access the following: campus intranet, computer help desk, free student e-mail accounts, online (class) grades, online (class) registration, online (class) schedules. Campuswide network is available. 100% of college-owned or -operated housing units are wired for high-speed Internet access. Wireless service is available via entire campus.
Library: Christine & Steven F. Udvar-Hazy Library & Learning Center. *Books:* 26,008 (physical), 249,693 (digital/electronic); *Serial titles:* 137 (physical), 54,540 (digital/electronic); *Databases:* 90. Students can reserve study rooms.

STUDENT LIFE
Housing options: on-campus residence required for freshman year; coed. Campus housing is university owned. Freshman campus housing is guaranteed.
Activities and organizations: student-run newspaper, choral group, Hawaii Club, Strike Eagles, Theta XI, American Institute of Aeronautics and Astronautics (AIAA), Arnold Air Society, national fraternities, national sororities.
Athletics Member NCAA, NAIA. All NCAA Division II. *Intercollegiate sports:* basketball M(s)/W(s), cross-country running M(s)/W(s), golf M(s)/W(s), soccer M(s)/W(s), softball W(s), track and field M(s)/W(s), volleyball W(s), wrestling M(s). *Intramural sports:* archery M(c)/W(c), baseball M(c), basketball M/W, bowling M(c)/W(c), fencing W(c), field hockey M(c), football M/W, ice hockey M(c), racquetball M/W, rock climbing M/W, rugby M(c)/W(c), skiing (cross-country) M(c)/W(c), soccer M(c)/W(c), softball W(c), table tennis M/W, tennis M/W, ultimate Frisbee M(c)/W(c), volleyball M(c)/W(c).
Campus security: 24-hour emergency response devices and patrols, student patrols, late-night transport/escort service, controlled dormitory access.
Student services: health clinic, personal/psychological counseling, women's center, veterans affairs office.

COSTS & FINANCIAL AID
Costs (2019–20) *One-time required fee:* $150. *Comprehensive fee:* $48,426 includes full-time tuition ($35,424), mandatory fees ($1284), and room and board ($11,718). Part-time tuition: $1476 per credit hour. *Required fees:* $642 per term part-time. *College room only:* $6882.
Financial Aid Of all full-time matriculated undergraduates who enrolled in 2018, 1,788 applied for aid, 1,523 were judged to have need. In 2018, 656 non-need-based awards were made. *Average financial aid package:* $19,115. *Average need-based loan:* $4242. *Average need-based gift aid:* $16,568. *Average non-need-based aid:* $15,683.

APPLYING
Standardized Tests *Recommended:* SAT or ACT (for admission).
Options: electronic application, deferred entrance.
Application fee: $50.
Required: high school transcript, minimum 2.0 GPA, medical examination for flight students. *Recommended:* essay or personal statement, minimum 3.0 GPA, 2 letters of recommendation, interview.
Application deadlines: rolling (freshmen), rolling (out-of-state freshmen), rolling (transfers).
Notification: continuous (freshmen), continuous (out-of-state freshmen), continuous (transfers).

CONTACT
Ms. Sara K. Bofferding, Director, Prescott Admissions, Embry-Riddle Aeronautical University–Prescott, 3700 Willow Creek Road, Prescott, AZ 86301-3720. *Phone:* 800-888-3728. *Toll-free phone:* 800-888-3728. *Fax:* 928-777-6606. *E-mail:* prescott@erau.edu.

Grand Canyon University
Phoenix, Arizona
http://www.gcu.edu/

CONTACT
Enrollment, Grand Canyon University, 3300 West Camelback Road, PO Box 11097, Phoenix, AZ 86017-3030. *Phone:* 800-486-7085. *Toll-free phone:* 800-800-9776. *E-mail:* admissionsonline@gcu.edu.

International Baptist College and Seminary

Chandler, Arizona
http://www.ibcs.edu/

CONTACT
Director of Admissions, International Baptist College and Seminary, 2211 West Germann Road, Chandler, AZ 85286. *Phone:* 480-245-7970. *Toll-free phone:* 800-422-4858. *E-mail:* admissions@ibconline.edu.

National Paralegal College

Phoenix, Arizona
http://nationalparalegal.edu/
- **Proprietary** comprehensive, founded 2003
- **Coed** 776 undergraduate students, 97% full-time, 89% women, 11% men
- 85% of applicants were admitted

UNDERGRAD STUDENTS
752 full-time, 24 part-time. Students come from 51 states and territories; 4 other countries; 96% are from out of state; 7% Black or African American, non-Hispanic/Latino; 5% Hispanic/Latino; 1% Asian, non-Hispanic/Latino; 0.6% Native Hawaiian or other Pacific Islander, non-Hispanic/Latino; 0.4% American Indian or Alaska Native, non-Hispanic/Latino; 0.1% Two or more races, non-Hispanic/Latino; 56% Race/ethnicity unknown; 15% transferred in.

Freshmen:
Admission: 2,331 applied, 1,979 admitted, 91 enrolled.
Retention: 58% of full-time freshmen returned.

FACULTY
Total: 33, 15% full-time, 97% with terminal degrees.
Student/faculty ratio: 28:1.

ACADEMICS
Calendar: continuous new session each month. *Degrees:* certificates, associate, bachelor's, and master's.

Special study options: academic remediation for entering students, accelerated degree program, distance learning, part-time degree program, summer session for credit.

Computers: Students can access the following: online (class) grades, online (class) registration, online (class) schedules.
Library: Jones eGlobal Library. *Books:* 27,803 (digital/electronic); *Databases:* 56. Weekly public service hours: 168.

COSTS
Costs (2018–19) *One-time required fee:* $195. *Tuition:* $7800 full-time, $325 per credit part-time. Full-time tuition and fees vary according to course load. Part-time tuition and fees vary according to course load. No tuition increase for student's term of enrollment. *Payment plans:* tuition prepayment, installment. *Waivers:* employees or children of employees.

APPLYING
Options: electronic application.
Required for some: high school transcript. *Recommended:* essay or personal statement, interview.
Application deadlines: rolling (freshmen), rolling (transfers).
Notification: continuous (freshmen), continuous (transfers).

CONTACT
Ms. Dana Wasserstrom, Admissions Director, National Paralegal College, 717 East Maryland Avenue, Phoenix, AZ 85014. *Phone:* 800-371-6105 Ext. 126. *Toll-free phone:* 800-371-6105. *E-mail:* danielle@nationalparalegal.edu.

Northern Arizona University

Flagstaff, Arizona
http://www.nau.edu/
- **State-supported** university, founded 1899, part of Arizona University System
- **Small-town** 683-acre campus
- **Endowment** $30.5 million
- **Coed**
- **Moderately difficult** entrance level

FACULTY
Student/faculty ratio: 19:1.

ACADEMICS
Calendar: semesters. *Degrees:* certificates, bachelor's, master's, doctoral, post-master's, and postbachelor's certificates.
Library: Cline Library plus 1 other. *Books:* 574,711 (physical), 237,606 (digital/electronic); *Serial titles:* 6,264 (physical), 93,756 (digital/electronic); *Databases:* 146. Weekly public service hours: 117; students can reserve study rooms.

STUDENT LIFE
Housing options: coed, special housing for students with disabilities. Campus housing is university owned and is provided by a third party. Freshman campus housing is guaranteed.

Activities and organizations: drama/theater group, student-run newspaper, radio and television station, choral group, marching band, Louie's Cupboard, Feral Cat Alliance, American Medical Student Association, National Alliance on Mental Illness local chapter, National Society of Collegiate Scholars, national fraternities, national sororities.

Athletics Member NCAA. All Division I.

Campus security: 24-hour emergency response devices and patrols, late-night transport/escort service, controlled dormitory access.

Student services: health clinic, personal/psychological counseling, legal services, veterans affairs office.

COSTS & FINANCIAL AID
Costs (2018–19) *Tuition:* state resident $10,390 full-time, $742 per credit hour part-time; nonresident $24,654 full-time, $1027 per credit hour part-time. Full-time tuition and fees vary according to course load, location, and reciprocity agreements. Part-time tuition and fees vary according to course load, location, and reciprocity agreements. No tuition increase for student's term of enrollment. *Required fees:* $1174 full-time, $14 per credit hour part-time, $343 per term part-time. *Room and board:* $10,334; room only: $7100. Room and board charges vary according to board plan and housing facility. *Payment plans:* installment, deferred payment.

Financial Aid Of all full-time matriculated undergraduates who enrolled in 2017, 16,625 applied for aid, 13,722 were judged to have need, 1,580 had their need fully met. In 2017, 3972 non-need-based awards were made. *Average percent of need met:* 62. *Average financial aid package:* $12,446. *Average need-based loan:* $4077. *Average need-based gift aid:* $7052. *Average non-need-based aid:* $6635. *Average indebtedness upon graduation:* $23,685.

APPLYING
Standardized Tests *Recommended:* SAT (for admission), SAT Subject Tests (for admission).

Options: electronic application, deferred entrance.

Application fee: $25.

Required: high school transcript, minimum 2.5 GPA, 16 college preparatory courses with minimum 2.0 in each subject.

CONTACT
Undergraduate Admissions, Northern Arizona University, Box 4084, Flagstaff, AZ 86011. *Phone:* 928-523-5511. *Toll-free phone:* 888-628-2968. *Fax:* 928-523-6023. *E-mail:* admissions@nau.edu.

See previous page for display ad and page 1062 for the College Close-Up.

Penn Foster College
Scottsdale, Arizona
http://www.pennfostercollege.edu/

CONTACT
Admissions, Penn Foster College, 14300 North Northsight Boulevard, Suite 120, Scottsdale, AZ 85260. *Phone:* 888-427-1000. *Toll-free phone:* 800-471-3232.

Pima Medical Institute
Mesa, Arizona
http://www.pmi.edu/

CONTACT
Admissions Office, Pima Medical Institute, 957 South Dobson Road, Mesa, AZ 85202. *Phone:* 480-644-0267 Ext. 225. *Toll-free phone:* 800-477-PIMA.

Pima Medical Institute
Tucson, Arizona
http://www.pmi.edu/

CONTACT
Admissions Office, Pima Medical Institute, 3350 East Grant Road, Tucson, AZ 85716. *Phone:* 520-326-1600 Ext. 5112. *Toll-free phone:* 800-477-PIMA.

Prescott College
Prescott, Arizona
http://www.prescott.edu/

CONTACT
Nancy Simmons, Admissions Coordinator, Prescott College, 220 Grove Avenue, Prescott, AZ 86301. *Phone:* 928-350-2100. *Toll-free phone:* 877-350-2100. *Fax:* 928-776-5242. *E-mail:* admissions@prescott.edu.

Southwest University of Visual Arts
Tucson, Arizona
http://www.suva.edu/

CONTACT
Robert Mairs, Director of Admissions, Southwest University of Visual Arts, 2525 North Country Club Road, Tucson, AZ 85716-2505. *Phone:* 520-325-0123. *Toll-free phone:* 800-825-8753. *Fax:* 520-325-5535.

University of Advancing Technology
Tempe, Arizona
http://www.uat.edu/

CONTACT
Admissions Office, University of Advancing Technology, 2625 West Baseline Road, Tempe, AZ 85283-1042. *Phone:* 602-383-8228. *Toll-free phone:* 800-658-5744. *Fax:* 602-383-8222. *E-mail:* admissions@uat.edu.

The University of Arizona
Tucson, Arizona
http://www.arizona.edu/
- **State-supported** university, founded 1885, part of Arizona Board of Regents
- **Urban** 392-acre campus
- **Endowment** $754.4 million
- **Coed**
- **Moderately difficult** entrance level

FACULTY
Student/faculty ratio: 15:1.

ACADEMICS
Calendar: semesters. *Degrees:* certificates, bachelor's, master's, doctoral, post-master's, and postbachelor's certificates.
Library: University of Arizona Main Library plus 4 others. *Books:* 3.1 million (physical), 1.8 million (digital/electronic); *Serial titles:* 6.3 million (physical), 101,171 (digital/electronic); *Databases:* 835. Weekly public service hours: 94; study areas open 24 hours, 5–7 days a week; students can reserve study rooms.

STUDENT LIFE
Housing options: coed, women-only, special housing for students with disabilities. Campus housing is university owned and leased by the school. Freshman applicants given priority for college housing.

Activities and organizations: drama/theater group, student-run newspaper, radio and television station, choral group, marching band, Alpha Epsilon Delta, Wildcats Committed to Animal Rescue and Education, Physiology, Psi Chi Chapter, Investments Club, national fraternities, national sororities.

Athletics Member NCAA. All Division I.

Campus security: 24-hour patrols, student patrols, late-night transport/escort service, controlled dormitory access, emergency telephones.

Student services: health clinic, personal/psychological counseling, women's center, legal services, veterans affairs office.

FINANCIAL AID

Financial Aid Of all full-time matriculated undergraduates who enrolled in 2016, 18,155 applied for aid, 14,902 were judged to have need, 1,578 had their need fully met. 1,117 Federal Work-Study jobs (averaging $2581). 7,384 state and other part-time jobs (averaging $2892). In 2016, 6555 non-need-based awards were made. *Average percent of need met:* 58. *Average financial aid package:* $13,288. *Average need-based loan:* $5160. *Average need-based gift aid:* $10,555. *Average non-need-based aid:* $7974. *Average indebtedness upon graduation:* $23,956.

APPLYING

Standardized Tests *Recommended:* SAT or ACT (for admission).

Options: electronic application, deferred entrance.

Application fee: $50.

Required: high school transcript. *Required for some:* minimum 3.0 GPA. *Recommended:* essay or personal statement, interview.

CONTACT

The University of Arizona, Tucson, AZ 85721. *Phone:* 520-621-3705.

University of Arizona South

Sierra Vista, Arizona

http://www.uas.arizona.edu/

CONTACT

University of Arizona South, 1140 North Colombo Avenue, Sierra Vista, AZ 85635.

University of Phoenix–Online Campus

Phoenix, Arizona

http://www.phoenix.edu/

CONTACT

Marc Booker, Senior Director, Office of Admissions and Evaluation, University of Phoenix–Online Campus, 4035 South Riverpoint Parkway, Mail Stop CF-L101, Phoenix, AZ 85040. *Phone:* 602-557-4609. *Toll-free phone:* 866-766-0766. *Fax:* 480-643-1156.

University of Phoenix–Phoenix Campus

Tempe, Arizona

http://www.phoenix.edu/

CONTACT

Marc Booker, Senior Director, Office of Admissions and Evaluation, University of Phoenix–Phoenix Campus, 4035 South Riverpoint Parkway, Mail Stop CF-L101, Phoenix, AZ 85040. *Phone:* 602-557-4609. *Toll-free phone:* 866-766-0766. *Fax:* 480-643-1156.

ARKANSAS

Arkansas Baptist College

Little Rock, Arkansas

http://www.arkansasbaptist.edu/

CONTACT

Arkansas Baptist College, 1621 Dr. Martin Luther King, Jr. Drive, Little Rock, AR 72202-6067. *Phone:* 501-244-5104 Ext. 5124.

Arkansas State University

Jonesboro, Arkansas

http://www.astate.edu/

CONTACT

Ms. Tracy Finch, Director of Admissions, Records, and Registration, Arkansas State University, PO Box 1570, State University, AR 72467. *Phone:* 870-972-2031. *Toll-free phone:* 800-382-3030. *Fax:* 870-972-3406. *E-mail:* admissions@astate.edu.

Arkansas Tech University

Russellville, Arkansas

http://www.atu.edu/

- **State-supported** comprehensive, founded 1909
- **Small-town** 559-acre campus
- **Endowment** $37.4 million
- **Coed** 11,151 undergraduate students, 57% full-time, 54% women, 46% men
- **Moderately difficult** entrance level, 90% of applicants were admitted

UNDERGRAD STUDENTS

6,396 full-time, 4,755 part-time. 4% are from out of state; 7% Black or African American, non-Hispanic/Latino; 7% Hispanic/Latino; 1% Asian, non-Hispanic/Latino; 0.1% Native Hawaiian or other Pacific Islander, non-Hispanic/Latino; 0.6% American Indian or Alaska Native, non-Hispanic/Latino; 4% Two or more races, non-Hispanic/Latino; 4% international; 4% transferred in; 28% live on campus.

Freshmen:

Admission: 5,122 applied, 4,622 admitted, 1,022 enrolled. *Average high school GPA:* 3.3. *Test scores:* SAT math scores over 500: 78%; ACT scores over 18: 84%; SAT math scores over 600: 39%; ACT scores over 24: 40%; SAT math scores over 700: 13%; ACT scores over 30: 7%.

Retention: 70% of full-time freshmen returned.

FACULTY

Total: 605, 61% full-time, 46% with terminal degrees.

Student/faculty ratio: 19:1.

ACADEMICS

Calendar: semesters. *Degrees:* certificates, associate, bachelor's, master's, doctoral, post-master's, and postbachelor's certificates.

Special study options: academic remediation for entering students, accelerated degree program, adult/continuing education programs, advanced placement credit, distance learning, double majors, English as a second language, honors programs, independent study, internships, off-campus study, part-time degree program, services for LD students, study abroad, summer session for credit. *ROTC:* Army (c).

Computers: 1,190 computers/terminals are available on campus for general student use. Students can access the following: campus intranet, computer help desk, free student e-mail accounts, online (class) grades, online (class) registration, online (class) schedules. Campuswide network is available. 100% of college-owned or -operated housing units are wired for high-speed Internet access. Wireless service is available via classrooms, computer centers, computer labs, dorm rooms, learning centers, libraries, student centers.

Library: Ross Pendergraft Library and Technology Center. *Books:* 154,336 (physical), 386,793 (digital/electronic); *Serial titles:* 5,478 (physical), 73,489 (digital/electronic); *Databases:* 279. Students can reserve study rooms.

STUDENT LIFE

Housing options: on-campus residence required through sophomore year; coed, men-only, women-only, special housing for students with disabilities. Campus housing is university owned. Freshman campus housing is guaranteed.

Activities and organizations: drama/theater group, student-run newspaper, radio and television station, choral group, marching band, national fraternities, national sororities.

Athletics Member NCAA. All Division II except golf (Division I). *Intercollegiate sports:* baseball M(s), basketball M(s)/W(s), cheerleading M(s)/W(s), cross-country running W(s), football M(s), golf M(s)/W(s), softball W(s), tennis W(s), volleyball W(s). *Intramural sports:* basketball M/W, bowling M/W, golf M(c)/W(c), racquetball M/W, soccer M/W, softball M/W, table tennis M/W, tennis M/W, ultimate Frisbee M/W, volleyball M/W.

Campus security: 24-hour emergency response devices and patrols, student patrols, late-night transport/escort service, controlled dormitory access.

Student services: health clinic, personal/psychological counseling.

COSTS & FINANCIAL AID

Costs (2018–19) *Tuition:* state resident $6780 full-time, $226 per credit hour part-time; nonresident $13,560 full-time, $452 per credit hour part-time. Full-time tuition and fees vary according to course load and location. Part-time tuition and fees vary according to course load and location. *Required fees:* $2288 full-time, $76 per credit hour part-time. *Room and board:* $7870; room only: $4542. Room and board charges vary according to board plan, housing facility, and location. *Payment plans:* installment, deferred payment. *Waivers:* senior citizens and employees or children of employees.

Financial Aid Of all full-time matriculated undergraduates who enrolled in 2017, 6,089 applied for aid, 4,673 were judged to have need, 433 had their need fully met. In 2017, 937 non-need-based awards were made. *Average percent of need met:* 60. *Average financial aid package:* $10,188. *Average need-based loan:* $3604. *Average need-based gift aid:* $4845. *Average non-need-based aid:* $6893. *Average indebtedness upon graduation:* $23,417.

APPLYING

Standardized Tests *Required:* SAT or ACT (for admission).

Options: electronic application, early action, deferred entrance.

Required: high school transcript, minimum 2.0 GPA.

Notification: continuous (freshmen), continuous (transfers).

CONTACT

Ms. Jessica Brock, Director of Admissions, Arkansas Tech University, Brown Hall, Suite 104, 105 West O Street, Russellville, AR 72801. *Phone:* 479-968-0343. *Toll-free phone:* 800-582-6953. *Fax:* 479-964-0522. *E-mail:* tech.enroll@atu.edu.

Central Baptist College

Conway, Arkansas
http://www.cbc.edu/

CONTACT

Central Baptist College, 1501 College Avenue, Conway, AR 72032. *Toll-free phone:* 800-205-6872.

Crowley's Ridge College

Paragould, Arkansas
http://www.crc.edu/

- **Independent** 4-year, founded 1964, affiliated with Church of Christ
- **Small-town** 150-acre campus
- **Coed**
- **Noncompetitive** entrance level

ACADEMICS

Calendar: semesters. *Degrees:* associate and bachelor's.

Library: Learning Center.

STUDENT LIFE

Housing options: on-campus residence required through sophomore year; men-only, women-only. Campus housing is university owned.

Activities and organizations: drama/theater group, choral group.

Athletics Member NAIA.

COSTS & FINANCIAL AID

Costs (2018–19) *Comprehensive fee:* $19,250 includes full-time tuition ($11,250), mandatory fees ($1650), and room and board ($6350). Part-time tuition: $375 per hour. Part-time tuition and fees vary according to course load. *Required fees:* $42 per hour part-time. *College room only:* $2800. Room and board charges vary according to board plan and housing facility.

Financial Aid Of all full-time matriculated undergraduates who enrolled in 2017, 78 Federal Work-Study jobs (averaging $500).

APPLYING

Options: electronic application.

Required: high school transcript, recommendation form filled out by high school. *Required for some:* interview.

CONTACT

Crowley's Ridge College, 100 College Drive, Paragould, AR 72450-9731. *Toll-free phone:* 800-264-1096.

Ecclesia College

Springdale, Arkansas
http://www.ecollege.edu/

CONTACT

Ecclesia College, 9653 Nations Drive, Springdale, AR 72762. *Phone:* 479-248-7236 Ext. 223.

Harding University

Searcy, Arkansas
http://www.harding.edu/

- **Independent** university, founded 1924, affiliated with Church of Christ
- **Small-town** 350-acre campus with easy access to Little Rock
- **Endowment** $128.7 million
- **Coed** 3,974 undergraduate students, 94% full-time, 54% women, 46% men
- **Moderately difficult** entrance level, 68% of applicants were admitted

UNDERGRAD STUDENTS

3,742 full-time, 232 part-time. Students come from 54 states and territories; 49 other countries; 72% are from out of state; 4% Black or African American, non-Hispanic/Latino; 4% Hispanic/Latino; 0.8% Asian, non-Hispanic/Latino; 0.3% American Indian or Alaska Native, non-Hispanic/Latino; 3% Two or more races, non-Hispanic/Latino; 0.1% Race/ethnicity unknown; 6% international; 3% transferred in; 91% live on campus.

Freshmen:

Admission: 1,927 applied, 1,309 admitted, 857 enrolled. *Average high school GPA:* 3.6. *Test scores:* SAT evidence-based reading and writing scores over 500: 90%; SAT math scores over 500: 86%; ACT scores over 18: 96%; SAT evidence-based reading and writing scores over 600: 52%; SAT math scores over 600: 42%; ACT scores over 24: 64%; SAT evidence-based reading and writing scores over 700: 11%; SAT math scores over 700: 9%; ACT scores over 30: 21%.

Retention: 85% of full-time freshmen returned.

FACULTY

Total: 403, 76% full-time, 61% with terminal degrees.

Student/faculty ratio: 14:1.

ACADEMICS

Calendar: semesters. *Degrees:* bachelor's, master's, doctoral, and post-master's certificates.

Special study options: academic remediation for entering students, accelerated degree program, adult/continuing education programs, advanced placement credit, cooperative education, distance learning, double majors, English as a second language, freshman honors college, honors programs, independent study, internships, part-time degree program, services for LD students, student-designed majors, study abroad, summer session for credit. *ROTC:* Army (c).

MORE THAN YOU IMAGINED

At Harding, we believe who you learn with and who you learn from are vitally important. Our Christian faculty and high-quality degree programs equip graduates with an exceptional education and a Christ-centered worldview. Visit harding.edu to learn more. Or better yet, come visit and see for yourself.

NCAA Division II sports including baseball, basketball, golf, football, soccer, tennis, track & field, and volleyball

Eight conference championships in 2017. Football (No. 6) and women's basketball teams (No. 4) attained national rankings and finals play

World class fitness center with sports courts and suspended track

More than 100 social, musical, religious and academic clubs and organizations, on-campus radio and television stations and a student newspaper

harding.edu • 501-279-4000

Computers: 512 computers/terminals and 3,200 ports are available on campus for general student use. Students can access the following: campus intranet, computer help desk, free student e-mail accounts, online (class) grades, online (class) registration, online (class) schedules. Campuswide network is available. 100% of college-owned or -operated housing units are wired for high-speed Internet access. Wireless service is available via entire campus.

Library: Brackett Library plus 1 other. *Books:* 187,838 (physical), 382,577 (digital/electronic); *Serial titles:* 925 (physical), 82,048 (digital/electronic); *Databases:* 185. Students can reserve study rooms.

STUDENT LIFE

Housing options: on-campus residence required through senior year; men-only, women-only, special housing for students with disabilities. Campus housing is university owned. Freshman campus housing is guaranteed.

Activities and organizations: drama/theater group, student-run newspaper, radio and television station, choral group, marching band, Bisons for Christ, Harding in Action, Spring Break Campaigns, HUmanity.

Athletics Member NCAA. All Division II except golf (Division I). *Intercollegiate sports:* baseball M(s), basketball M(s)/W(s), cheerleading W, cross-country running M(s)/W(s), football M(s), golf M(s)/W(s), lacrosse M(c), rugby M(c), soccer M(s)/W(s), tennis M(s)/W(s), track and field M(s)/W(s), ultimate Frisbee M(c)/W(c), volleyball W(s). *Intramural sports:* basketball M/W, cross-country running M/W, football M/W, golf M/W, racquetball M/W, soccer M/W, softball M/W, swimming and diving M/W, table tennis M/W, tennis M/W, track and field M/W, ultimate Frisbee M/W, volleyball M/W, weight lifting M/W.

Campus security: 24-hour emergency response devices and patrols, student patrols, late-night transport/escort service, controlled dormitory access.

Student services: health clinic, personal/psychological counseling, veterans affairs office.

COSTS & FINANCIAL AID

Costs (2018–19) *Comprehensive fee:* $26,644 includes full-time tuition ($19,140), mandatory fees ($500), and room and board ($7004). Full-time tuition and fees vary according to course load. Part-time tuition: $638 per credit hour. Part-time tuition and fees vary according to course load. *Required fees:* $25 per credit hour part-time. *College room only:* $3658. Room and board charges vary according to board plan and housing facility. *Payment plans:* tuition prepayment, installment. *Waivers:* senior citizens and employees or children of employees.

Financial Aid Of all full-time matriculated undergraduates who enrolled in 2017, 3,066 applied for aid, 2,533 were judged to have need, 335 had their need fully met. 603 Federal Work-Study jobs (averaging $1279). 1,268 state and other part-time jobs (averaging $1349). In 2017, 1142 non-need-based awards were made. *Average percent of need met:* 76. *Average financial aid package:* $13,086. *Average need-based loan:* $4947. *Average need-based gift aid:* $9795. *Average non-need-based aid:* $7270. *Average indebtedness upon graduation:* $33,954.

APPLYING

Standardized Tests *Required:* SAT or ACT (for admission).

Options: electronic application, early admission, early action, deferred entrance.

Application fee: $50.

Required: essay or personal statement, high school transcript, 3 letters of recommendation.

Application deadlines: rolling (freshmen), rolling (transfers).

Notification: continuous (freshmen), continuous (transfers).

CONTACT

Mr. Scott Hannigan, Senior Director of Admissions, Harding University, 915 E. Market Avenue, Box 12255, Searcy, AR 72149-5615. *Phone:* 501-279-4407. *Toll-free phone:* 800-477-4407. *Fax:* 501-279-4129. *E-mail:* admissions@harding.edu.

See this page for display ad and page 1018 for the College Close-Up.

Henderson State University
Arkadelphia, Arkansas
http://www.hsu.edu/

CONTACT
Dr. Brandie Benton, Associate Provost Enrollment Services and Admissions, Henderson State University, 1100 Henderson Street, PO Box 7560, Arkadelphia, AR 71999-0001. *Phone:* 870-230-5203. *Toll-free phone:* 800-228-7333. *Fax:* 870-230-5066. *E-mail:* bentonb@hsu.edu.

Hendrix College
Conway, Arkansas
http://www.hendrix.edu/
- **Independent United Methodist** comprehensive, founded 1876
- **Suburban** 180-acre campus with easy access to Little Rock
- **Endowment** $185.5 million
- **Coed**
- **Very difficult** entrance level

FACULTY
Student/faculty ratio: 11:1.

ACADEMICS
Calendar: semesters. *Degrees:* bachelor's and master's.
Library: Olin C. and Marjorie H. Bailey Library plus 1 other. Weekly public service hours: 83; study areas open 24 hours, 5–7 days a week.

STUDENT LIFE
Housing options: on-campus residence required through senior year; coed, men-only, women-only, special housing for students with disabilities. Campus housing is university owned. Freshman campus housing is guaranteed.
Activities and organizations: drama/theater group, student-run newspaper, radio station, choral group.
Athletics Member NCAA. All Division III.
Campus security: 24-hour emergency response devices and patrols, late-night transport/escort service, controlled dormitory access.
Student services: health clinic, personal/psychological counseling.

COSTS & FINANCIAL AID
Costs (2018–19) *Comprehensive fee:* $58,074 includes full-time tuition ($45,440), mandatory fees ($350), and room and board ($12,284). Full-time tuition and fees vary according to course load. Part-time tuition: $5680 per course. Part-time tuition and fees vary according to course load. *College room only:* $6324. Room and board charges vary according to board plan and housing facility.
Financial Aid *Average indebtedness upon graduation:* $27,786.

APPLYING
Standardized Tests *Required:* SAT or ACT (for admission).
Options: electronic application, early action.
Application fee: $40.
Required: essay or personal statement, high school transcript. *Required for some:* interview. *Recommended:* 1 letter of recommendation.

CONTACT
Hendrix College, 1600 Washington Avenue, Conway, AR 72032. *Phone:* 501-450-1362. *Toll-free phone:* 800-277-9017. *Fax:* 501-450-3843. *E-mail:* adm@hendrix.edu.

John Brown University
Siloam Springs, Arkansas
http://www.jbu.edu/
- **Independent interdenominational** comprehensive, founded 1919
- **Small-town** 200-acre campus
- **Endowment** $113.3 million
- **Coed**
- **Moderately difficult** entrance level

FACULTY
Student/faculty ratio: 14:1.

ACADEMICS
Calendar: semesters. *Degrees:* associate, bachelor's, master's, and post-master's certificates.
Library: Arutunoff Learning Resource Center plus 4 others. *Books:* 105,116 (physical), 329,913 (digital/electronic); *Serial titles:* 1,032 (physical), 67,078 (digital/electronic); *Databases:* 144. Weekly public service hours: 110; students can reserve study rooms.

STUDENT LIFE
Housing options: on-campus residence required through junior year; coed, men-only, women-only, special housing for students with disabilities. Campus housing is university owned. Freshman campus housing is guaranteed.
Activities and organizations: drama/theater group, student-run newspaper, radio and television station, choral group, Student Government Association, Student Ministries Organization, Student Activities Club, Student Missionary Fellowship, Enactus.
Athletics Member NAIA.
Campus security: 24-hour emergency response devices and patrols, late-night transport/escort service, controlled dormitory access.
Student services: health clinic, personal/psychological counseling.

COSTS & FINANCIAL AID
Costs (2018–19) *Comprehensive fee:* $36,152 includes full-time tuition ($25,750), mandatory fees ($1178), and room and board ($9224). Full-time tuition and fees vary according to course load and degree level. Part-time tuition: $858 per credit hour. Part-time tuition and fees vary according to course load and degree level. *Required fees:* $295 per term part-time. *College room only:* $4424. Room and board charges vary according to board plan and housing facility.
Financial Aid Of all full-time matriculated undergraduates who enrolled in 2017, 1,198 applied for aid, 1,048 were judged to have need, 175 had their need fully met. In 2017, 448 non-need-based awards were made. *Average percent of need met:* 69. *Average financial aid package:* $19,615. *Average need-based loan:* $3419. *Average need-based gift aid:* $13,272. *Average non-need-based aid:* $11,048. *Average indebtedness upon graduation:* $27,732.

APPLYING
Standardized Tests *Required for some:* SAT or ACT (for admission).
Options: electronic application, deferred entrance.
Application fee: $25.
Required: essay or personal statement, high school transcript, minimum 2.5 GPA, 2 letters of recommendation. *Recommended:* interview.

CONTACT
Mr. Jared Burgess, Director of Visitation Program, John Brown University, 2000 West University, Siloam Springs, AR 72761. *Phone:* 479-524-7190. *Toll-free phone:* 877-JBU-INFO. *Fax:* 479-524-4196. *E-mail:* jburgess@jbu.edu.

Lyon College
Batesville, Arkansas
http://www.lyon.edu/
- **Independent Presbyterian** 4-year, founded 1872
- **Small-town** 136-acre campus
- **Coed**
- **Moderately difficult** entrance level

FACULTY
Student/faculty ratio: 14:1.

ACADEMICS
Calendar: semesters. *Degree:* bachelor's.
Library: Mabee-Simpson Library.

STUDENT LIFE
Housing options: on-campus residence required through junior year; coed. Campus housing is university owned. Freshman campus housing is guaranteed.
Activities and organizations: drama/theater group, student-run newspaper, choral group, Wesley Fellowship, Gay-Straight Alliance, Alpha Xi Delta Sorority, Fellowship of Christian Athletes, Young

Democrats/Japanese Culture Club, national fraternities, national sororities.

Athletics Member NAIA.

Campus security: 24-hour patrols, late-night transport/escort service, controlled dormitory access.

Student services: health clinic, personal/psychological counseling.

COSTS & FINANCIAL AID

Costs (2018–19) *Comprehensive fee:* $37,900 includes full-time tuition ($28,200), mandatory fees ($590), and room and board ($9110). Full-time tuition and fees vary according to course load. Part-time tuition: $930 per credit hour. Part-time tuition and fees vary according to course load. *Required fees:* $590 per year part-time. *Room and board:* Room and board charges vary according to board plan and housing facility.

Financial Aid Of all full-time matriculated undergraduates who enrolled in 2017, 552 applied for aid, 485 were judged to have need, 121 had their need fully met. In 2017, 99 non-need-based awards were made. *Average percent of need met:* 73. *Average financial aid package:* $22,842. *Average need-based loan:* $4207. *Average need-based gift aid:* $20,056. *Average non-need-based aid:* $15,710. *Average indebtedness upon graduation:* $26,353.

APPLYING

Standardized Tests *Required:* SAT or ACT (for admission).

Options: electronic application, early admission, early action, deferred entrance.

Required: high school transcript, minimum 2.5 GPA. *Required for some:* essay or personal statement, 2 letters of recommendation.

CONTACT

Office of Enrollment Services, Lyon College, 2300 Highland Road, Batesville, AR 72501. *Phone:* 870-307-7250. *Toll-free phone:* 800-423-2542. *Fax:* 870-307-7542. *E-mail:* admissions@lyon.edu.

Ouachita Baptist University

Arkadelphia, Arkansas

http://www.obu.edu/

- **Independent Baptist** 4-year, founded 1886
- **Small-town** 200-acre campus with easy access to Little Rock
- **Endowment** $118,705
- **Coed** 1,660 undergraduate students, 92% full-time, 55% women, 45% men
- **Moderately difficult** entrance level, 64% of applicants were admitted

UNDERGRAD STUDENTS

1,529 full-time, 131 part-time. Students come from 28 states and territories; 22 other countries; 32% are from out of state; 8% Black or African American, non-Hispanic/Latino; 5% Hispanic/Latino; 0.4% Asian, non-Hispanic/Latino; 0.1% Native Hawaiian or other Pacific Islander, non-Hispanic/Latino; 0.6% American Indian or Alaska Native, non-Hispanic/Latino; 3% Two or more races, non-Hispanic/Latino; 2% international; 3% transferred in; 97% live on campus.

Freshmen:

Admission: 2,162 applied, 1,375 admitted, 443 enrolled. *Average high school GPA:* 3.7. *Test scores:* SAT evidence-based reading and writing scores over 500: 81%; SAT math scores over 500: 81%; ACT scores over 18: 95%; SAT evidence-based reading and writing scores over 600: 42%; SAT math scores over 600: 34%; ACT scores over 24: 57%; SAT evidence-based reading and writing scores over 700: 14%; SAT math scores over 700: 5%; ACT scores over 30: 15%.

Retention: 83% of full-time freshmen returned.

FACULTY

Total: 170, 64% full-time, 65% with terminal degrees.

Student/faculty ratio: 12:1.

ACADEMICS

Calendar: semesters. *Degrees:* associate and bachelor's.

Special study options: academic remediation for entering students, accelerated degree program, adult/continuing education programs, advanced placement credit, cooperative education, distance learning, double majors, English as a second language, honors programs, independent study, internships, off-campus study, part-time degree program, study abroad, summer session for credit. *ROTC:* Army (b).

Unusual degree programs: 3-2 engineering with University of Arkansas.

Computers: 275 computers/terminals and 1,375 ports are available on campus for general student use. Students can access the following: campus intranet, computer help desk, free student e-mail accounts, online (class) grades, online (class) schedules, student Web portal. Campuswide network is available. 100% of college-owned or -operated housing units are wired for high-speed Internet access. Wireless service is available via entire campus.

Library: Riley-Hickingbotham Library plus 2 others. *Books:* 160,398 (physical), 12,821 (digital/electronic); *Serial titles:* 1,723 (physical), 41,230 (digital/electronic); *Databases:* 150. Weekly public service hours: 80; students can reserve study rooms.

STUDENT LIFE

Housing options: on-campus residence required through senior year; men-only, women-only, special housing for students with disabilities. Campus housing is university owned and leased by the school. Freshman campus housing is guaranteed.

Activities and organizations: drama/theater group, student-run newspaper, television station, choral group, marching band, Phi Beta Lambda, Student Foundation, Student Education Association, Campus Activities Board, International Club.

Athletics Member NCAA. All Division II. *Intercollegiate sports:* baseball M(s), basketball M(s)/W(s), cheerleading M/W, cross-country running W(s), football M(s), soccer M(s)/W(s), softball W(s), swimming and diving M(s)/W(s), tennis M(s)/W(s), volleyball W(s), wrestling M(s). *Intramural sports:* basketball M/W, football M/W, soccer M, softball M/W, table tennis M/W.

Campus security: 24-hour emergency response devices and patrols, controlled dormitory access.

Student services: health clinic, personal/psychological counseling.

COSTS & FINANCIAL AID

Costs (2019–20) *Comprehensive fee:* $35,900 includes full-time tuition ($27,280), mandatory fees ($620), and room and board ($8000). Part-time tuition: $725 per credit hour. *College room only:* $6280.

Financial Aid Of all full-time matriculated undergraduates who enrolled in 2018, 1,249 applied for aid, 1,007 were judged to have need, 397 had their need fully met. 353 Federal Work-Study jobs (averaging $608,103). 142 state and other part-time jobs (averaging $258,017). In 2018, 463 non-need-based awards were made. *Average percent of need met:* 85. *Average financial aid package:* $24,312. *Average need-based loan:* $3436. *Average need-based gift aid:* $16,442. *Average non-need-based aid:* $14,042. *Average indebtedness upon graduation:* $22,983. *Financial aid deadline:* 5/1.

APPLYING

Standardized Tests *Required:* SAT or ACT (for admission).

Options: deferred entrance.

Required: high school transcript, minimum 2.8 GPA. *Recommended:* interview.

Notification: continuous (freshmen), continuous (transfers).

CONTACT

Mrs. Lori Motl, Director of Admissions Counseling, Ouachita Baptist University, OBU Box 3776, Arkadelphia, AR 71998-0001. *Phone:* 870-245-5110. *Toll-free phone:* 800-342-5628. *Fax:* 870-245-5500. *E-mail:* motll@obu.edu.

Philander Smith College

Little Rock, Arkansas

http://www.philander.edu/

CONTACT

Mr. Maurice Osbourne, Director of Admissions, Philander Smith College, 900 West Daisy Bates Drive, Little Rock, AR 72202. *Phone:* 501-370-5221. *Toll-free phone:* 800-446-6772. *Fax:* 501-370-5225.

Southern Arkansas University–Magnolia

Magnolia, Arkansas
http://www.saumag.edu/

- **State-supported** comprehensive, founded 1909, part of Southern Arkansas University System
- **Small-town** 1390-acre campus
- **Endowment** $38.5 million
- **Coed** 3,542 undergraduate students, 85% full-time, 55% women, 45% men
- **Moderately difficult** entrance level, 69% of applicants were admitted

UNDERGRAD STUDENTS
3,018 full-time, 524 part-time. Students come from 38 states and territories; 7 other countries; 23% are from out of state; 26% Black or African American, non-Hispanic/Latino; 4% Hispanic/Latino; 1% Asian, non-Hispanic/Latino; 0.2% Native Hawaiian or other Pacific Islander, non-Hispanic/Latino; 0.7% American Indian or Alaska Native, non-Hispanic/Latino; 2% international; 5% transferred in; 54% live on campus.

Freshmen:
Admission: 3,552 applied, 2,443 admitted, 900 enrolled. *Average high school GPA:* 3.3. *Test scores:* SAT evidence-based reading and writing scores over 500: 75%; SAT math scores over 500: 75%; ACT scores over 18: 83%; SAT evidence-based reading and writing scores over 600: 33%; SAT math scores over 600: 23%; ACT scores over 24: 34%; SAT evidence-based reading and writing scores over 700: 10%; SAT math scores over 700: 4%; ACT scores over 30: 5%.

Retention: 65% of full-time freshmen returned.

FACULTY
Total: 296, 56% full-time, 46% with terminal degrees.
Student/faculty ratio: 18:1.

ACADEMICS
Calendar: semesters. *Degrees:* certificates, associate, bachelor's, and master's.

Special study options: academic remediation for entering students, accelerated degree program, adult/continuing education programs, advanced placement credit, distance learning, double majors, English as a second language, freshman honors college, honors programs, independent study, internships, part-time degree program, services for LD students, study abroad, summer session for credit.

Computers: 199 computers/terminals and 199 ports are available on campus for general student use. Students can access the following: campus intranet, computer help desk, free student e-mail accounts, online (class) grades, online (class) registration, online (class) schedules. Campuswide network is available. 100% of college-owned or -operated housing units are wired for high-speed Internet access. Wireless service is available via computer centers, computer labs, dorm rooms, libraries, student centers.

Library: Magale Library. *Books:* 138,050 (physical), 10,973 (digital/electronic); *Serial titles:* 130 (physical), 86 (digital/electronic); *Databases:* 187. Weekly public service hours: 87.

STUDENT LIFE
Housing options: on-campus residence required through sophomore year; coed, men-only, women-only. Campus housing is university owned and is provided by a third party. Freshman campus housing is guaranteed.

Activities and organizations: drama/theater group, student-run newspaper, radio station, choral group, marching band, Student Government Association, Student Activities Board, Resident Hall Association, Residential College, International Student Association, national fraternities, national sororities.

Athletics Member NCAA. All Division II except golf (Division I). *Intercollegiate sports:* baseball M(s), basketball M(s)/W(s), cheerleading M(s)(c)/W(s)(c), cross-country running M(s)/W(s), football M(s), golf M/W, softball W(s), tennis W(s), track and field M(s)/W(s), volleyball W(s). *Intramural sports:* badminton M/W, basketball M/W, football M, golf M/W, soccer M/W, softball M/W, swimming and diving M/W, table tennis M/W, tennis M/W, ultimate Frisbee M/W, volleyball M/W.

Campus security: 24-hour emergency response devices, student patrols, late-night transport/escort service, controlled dormitory access.
Student services: health clinic, personal/psychological counseling, veterans affairs office.

COSTS & FINANCIAL AID
Costs (2018–19) *Tuition:* state resident $6840 full-time, $228 per credit hour part-time; nonresident $10,950 full-time, $365 per credit hour part-time. Full-time tuition and fees vary according to course load. Part-time tuition and fees vary according to course load. *Required fees:* $1836 full-time. *Room and board:* $6240; room only: $3110. Room and board charges vary according to board plan and housing facility. *Payment plan:* installment. *Waivers:* children of alumni, senior citizens, and employees or children of employees.
Financial Aid *Average indebtedness upon graduation:* $22,616.

APPLYING
Standardized Tests *Required:* SAT or ACT (for admission). *Recommended:* ACT (for admission).
Options: electronic application, early admission, deferred entrance.
Required: high school transcript. *Required for some:* interview.
Application deadlines: 8/27 (freshmen), 8/27 (transfers).

CONTACT
Ms. Sarah Jennings, Dean of Enrollment Services, Southern Arkansas University–Magnolia, 100 East University, Magnolia, AR 71753. *Phone:* 870-235-4040. *Toll-free phone:* 800-332-7286. *E-mail:* sejennings@saumag.edu.

Strayer University–Little Rock Campus

Little Rock, Arkansas
http://www.strayer.edu/arkansas/little-rock/

CONTACT
Strayer University–Little Rock Campus, 10825 Financial Centre Parkway, Suite 400, Little Rock, AR 72211. *Toll-free phone:* 888-311-0355.

University of Arkansas

Fayetteville, Arkansas
http://www.uark.edu/

- **State-supported** university, founded 1871, part of University of Arkansas System
- **Urban** 718-acre campus
- **Coed** 23,386 undergraduate students, 90% full-time, 53% women, 47% men
- **Moderately difficult** entrance level, 77% of applicants were admitted

UNDERGRAD STUDENTS
21,005 full-time, 2,381 part-time. Students come from 47 states and territories; 85 other countries; 46% are from out of state; 4% Black or African American, non-Hispanic/Latino; 9% Hispanic/Latino; 2% Asian, non-Hispanic/Latino; 0.1% Native Hawaiian or other Pacific Islander, non-Hispanic/Latino; 0.9% American Indian or Alaska Native, non-Hispanic/Latino; 4% Two or more races, non-Hispanic/Latino; 0.6% Race/ethnicity unknown; 3% international; 6% transferred in; 25% live on campus.

Freshmen:
Admission: 18,732 applied, 14,512 admitted, 5,005 enrolled. *Average high school GPA:* 3.7. *Test scores:* SAT evidence-based reading and writing scores over 500: 97%; SAT math scores over 500: 95%; ACT scores over 18: 100%; SAT evidence-based reading and writing scores over 600: 56%; SAT math scores over 600: 47%; ACT scores over 24: 75%; SAT evidence-based reading and writing scores over 700: 9%; SAT math scores over 700: 9%; ACT scores over 30: 24%.

Retention: 84% of full-time freshmen returned.

FACULTY
Total: 1,401, 85% full-time, 78% with terminal degrees.
Student/faculty ratio: 19:1.

ACADEMICS

Calendar: semesters. *Degrees:* certificates, bachelor's, master's, doctoral, post-master's, and postbachelor's certificates.

Special study options: academic remediation for entering students, accelerated degree program, advanced placement credit, cooperative education, distance learning, double majors, English as a second language, freshman honors college, honors programs, independent study, internships, off-campus study, part-time degree program, services for LD students, student-designed majors, study abroad, summer session for credit. *ROTC:* Army (b), Air Force (b).

Unusual degree programs: 3-2 business administration; law.

Computers: 675 computers/terminals and 24 ports are available on campus for general student use. Students can access the following: computer help desk, free student e-mail accounts, online (class) grades, online (class) registration, online (class) schedules. Campuswide network is available. 100% of college-owned or -operated housing units are wired for high-speed Internet access. Wireless service is available via entire campus.

Library: David W. Mullins Library plus 4 others. *Books:* 2.0 million (physical), 593,016 (digital/electronic); *Serial titles:* 60,187 (physical), 147,231 (digital/electronic); *Databases:* 331. Weekly public service hours: 109; students can reserve study rooms.

STUDENT LIFE

Housing options: on-campus residence required for freshman year; coed, women-only, special housing for students with disabilities. Campus housing is university owned. Freshman campus housing is guaranteed.

Activities and organizations: drama/theater group, student-run newspaper, radio and television station, choral group, marching band, Associated Student Government, Catholic Campus Ministry, Chinese Students and Scholars, Alpha Lambda Delta, Student Alumni Association, national fraternities, national sororities.

Athletics Member NCAA. All Division I except football (Division I-A). *Intercollegiate sports:* baseball M(s), basketball M(s)/W(s), cross-country running M(s)/W(s), golf M(s)/W(s)(c), gymnastics W(s), soccer W(s), softball W(s), swimming and diving W(s), tennis M(s)/W(s), track and field M(s)/W(s), volleyball W(s). *Intramural sports:* badminton M/W, baseball M(c), basketball M/W, cross-country running M(c)/W(c), golf M(c)/W(c), ice hockey M(c), lacrosse M(c)/W(c), racquetball M(c)/W(c), riflery M(c)/W(c), rugby M(c)/W(c), sand volleyball M/W, soccer M(c)/W(c), softball M/W, swimming and diving M(c)/W(c), table tennis M/W, tennis M(c)/W(c), track and field M/W, triathlon M(c)/W(c), ultimate Frisbee M(c)/W(c), volleyball M(c)/W(c), water polo M(c)/W(c).

Campus security: 24-hour emergency response devices and patrols, student patrols, late-night transport/escort service, controlled dormitory access.

Student services: health clinic, personal/psychological counseling, women's center, legal services, veterans affairs office.

COSTS & FINANCIAL AID

Costs (2018–19) *Tuition:* state resident $7384 full-time, $246 per credit hour part-time; nonresident $23,422 full-time, $781 per credit hour part-time. Full-time tuition and fees vary according to course load, location, and program. Part-time tuition and fees vary according to course load, location, and program. *Required fees:* $1746 full-time, $58 per credit hour part-time. *Room and board:* $11,020; room only: $7090. Room and board charges vary according to board plan, housing facility, and location. *Payment plan:* installment. *Waivers:* senior citizens and employees or children of employees.

Financial Aid Of all full-time matriculated undergraduates who enrolled in 2018, 13,475 applied for aid, 8,947 were judged to have need, 1,197 had their need fully met. 1,147 Federal Work-Study jobs (averaging $2783). In 2018, 3004 non-need-based awards were made. *Average percent of need met:* 56. *Average financial aid package:* $9896. *Average need-based loan:* $5196. *Average need-based gift aid:* $7799. *Average non-need-based aid:* $5378. *Average indebtedness upon graduation:* $25,778.

APPLYING

Standardized Tests *Required:* SAT or ACT (for admission).

Options: electronic application, early action.

Application fee: $40.

Required: high school transcript, minimum 3.0 GPA, minimum ACT Composite score of 20 or SAT total (math and EBRW only) of 1030, completion of 16 core academic units. *Required for some:* essay or personal statement.

Application deadlines: 8/1 (freshmen), 8/1 (out-of-state freshmen), 8/1 (transfers), 11/1 (early action).

Notification: continuous until 9/1 (freshmen), continuous until 9/1 (out-of-state freshmen), continuous (transfers), 12/15 (early action).

CONTACT

Wendy Stouffer, Associate Vice Provost for Enrollment Services and Assistant Dean of Admissions and Financial Aid, University of Arkansas, 232 Silas H. Hunt Hall, Office of Admissions, Fayetteville, AR 72701-1201. *Phone:* 479-575-3806. *Toll-free phone:* 800-377-8632. *Fax:* 479-575-7515. *E-mail:* uofa@uark.edu.

University of Arkansas at Little Rock
Little Rock, Arkansas
http://www.ualr.edu/

CONTACT

Ms. Tammy Harrison, Director of Admissions, University of Arkansas at Little Rock, 2801 South University Avenue, Little Rock, AR 72204-1099. *Phone:* 501-569-3127. *Toll-free phone:* 800-482-8892. *Fax:* 501-569-8956. *E-mail:* twharrison@ualn.edu.

University of Arkansas at Monticello
Monticello, Arkansas
http://www.uamont.edu/

CONTACT

Ms. Mary Whiting, Director of Admissions, University of Arkansas at Monticello, 346 University Drive, Monticello, AR 71656. *Phone:* 870-460-1026. *Toll-free phone:* 800-844-1826. *E-mail:* admissions@uamont.edu.

University of Arkansas at Pine Bluff
Pine Bluff, Arkansas
http://www.uapb.edu/

CONTACT

University of Arkansas at Pine Bluff, 1200 North University Drive, Pine Bluff, AR 71601-2799. *Phone:* 870-575-8492. *Toll-free phone:* 800-264-6585.

University of Arkansas for Medical Sciences
Little Rock, Arkansas
http://www.uams.edu/

CONTACT

University of Arkansas for Medical Sciences, 4301 West Markham, Little Rock, AR 72205-7199.

University of Arkansas–Fort Smith
Fort Smith, Arkansas
http://uafs.edu/

CONTACT

Ms. Kelly Westeen, Director of Admissions, University of Arkansas–Fort Smith, 5210 Grand Avenue, PO Box 3649, Fort Smith, AR 72913-3649. *Phone:* 479-788-7106. *Toll-free phone:* 888-512-5466. *Fax:* 479-424-6106. *E-mail:* kelly.westeen@uafortsmith.edu.

University of Central Arkansas

Conway, Arkansas
http://www.uca.edu/

- **State-supported** university, founded 1907
- **Small-town** 356-acre campus
- **Coed** 9,425 undergraduate students, 83% full-time, 60% women, 40% men
- **Moderately difficult** entrance level, 91% of applicants were admitted

UNDERGRAD STUDENTS
7,863 full-time, 1,562 part-time. Students come from 45 states and territories; 72 other countries; 10% are from out of state; 16% Black or African American, non-Hispanic/Latino; 5% Hispanic/Latino; 2% Asian, non-Hispanic/Latino; 0.1% Native Hawaiian or other Pacific Islander, non-Hispanic/Latino; 0.5% American Indian or Alaska Native, non-Hispanic/Latino; 4% Two or more races, non-Hispanic/Latino; 0.4% Race/ethnicity unknown; 5% international; 7% transferred in; 40% live on campus.

Freshmen:
Admission: 5,541 applied, 5,048 admitted, 2,033 enrolled. *Average high school GPA:* 3.5. *Test scores:* ACT scores over 18: 97%; ACT scores over 24: 55%; ACT scores over 30: 14%.
Retention: 74% of full-time freshmen returned.

FACULTY
Total: 723, 77% full-time.
Student/faculty ratio: 16:1.

ACADEMICS
Calendar: semesters. *Degrees:* certificates, bachelor's, master's, doctoral, post-master's, and postbachelor's certificates.
Special study options: academic remediation for entering students, accelerated degree program, advanced placement credit, cooperative education, distance learning, double majors, English as a second language, freshman honors college, honors programs, independent study, internships, part-time degree program, services for LD students, study abroad, summer session for credit. *ROTC:* Army (b).
Unusual degree programs: 3-2 engineering with Arkansas Tech University.
Computers: 610 computers/terminals are available on campus for general student use. Students can access the following: campus intranet, computer help desk, free student e-mail accounts, online (class) grades, online (class) registration, online (class) schedules. Campuswide network is available. 100% of college-owned or -operated housing units are wired for high-speed Internet access. Wireless service is available via entire campus.
Library: Torreyson Library plus 1 other. *Books:* 326,160 (physical), 16,245 (digital/electronic); *Serial titles:* 2,955 (physical), 368,249 (digital/electronic); *Databases:* 143. Study areas open 24 hours, 5–7 days a week; students can reserve study rooms.

STUDENT LIFE
Housing options: on-campus residence required for freshman year; coed, men-only, women-only, special housing for students with disabilities. Campus housing is university owned and leased by the school. Freshman campus housing is guaranteed.
Activities and organizations: drama/theater group, student-run newspaper, radio and television station, choral group, marching band, Bears Den, Greek Organizations, national fraternities, national sororities.
Athletics Member NCAA. All Division I. *Intercollegiate sports:* baseball M(s), basketball M(s)/W(s), cheerleading M(s)(c)/W(s)(c), cross-country running M(s)/W(s), football M(s), golf M(s)/W(s)(c), soccer M(s)/W(s), softball W(s), tennis W(s), track and field M(s)/W(s), volleyball W(s). *Intramural sports:* basketball M/W, soccer M/W, softball M/W, tennis W, track and field M/W, volleyball M/W.
Campus security: 24-hour emergency response devices and patrols, student patrols, late-night transport/escort service, controlled dormitory access.
Student services: health clinic, personal/psychological counseling, women's center, veterans affairs office.

COSTS & FINANCIAL AID
Costs (2018–19) *Tuition:* state resident $6523 full-time, $217 per credit hour part-time; nonresident $13,046 full-time, $435 per credit hour part-time. Full-time tuition and fees vary according to course load. Part-time tuition and fees vary according to course load. *Required fees:* $2228 full-time. *Room and board:* $6854. Room and board charges vary according to board plan and housing facility. *Payment plan:* installment. *Waivers:* senior citizens and employees or children of employees.
Financial Aid *Financial aid deadline:* 7/1.

APPLYING
Standardized Tests *Required:* SAT or ACT (for admission).
Options: electronic application, early admission, deferred entrance.
Application fee: $25.
Required: high school transcript. *Required for some:* minimum 2.75 GPA, minimum ACT score of 21 or SAT score of 1450.
Application deadlines: rolling (freshmen), rolling (transfers).
Notification: continuous (freshmen), continuous (transfers).

CONTACT
Ms. Courtney Bryant, Director of Admissions, University of Central Arkansas, 201 Donaghey Avenue, Conway, AR 72035-0001. *Phone:* 501-450-3185. *Toll-free phone:* 800-243-8245. *E-mail:* cbryant13@uca.edu.

University of the Ozarks

Clarksville, Arkansas
http://www.ozarks.edu/

CONTACT
Ms. Jana Hart, Dean of Admission and Financial Aid, University of the Ozarks, 415 North College Avenue, Clarksville, AR 72830-2880. *Phone:* 479-979-1227. *Toll-free phone:* 800-264-8636. *Fax:* 479-979-1417. *E-mail:* admiss@ozarks.edu.

Williams Baptist College

Walnut Ridge, Arkansas
http://www.wbcoll.edu/

CONTACT
Mr. Andrew Watson, Director of Admissions, Williams Baptist College, PO Box 3737, Walnut Ridge, AR 72476. *Phone:* 870-759-4118. *Toll-free phone:* 800-722-4434. *Fax:* 870-759-4163. *E-mail:* awatson@wbcoll.edu.

CALIFORNIA

Abraham Lincoln University

Los Angeles, California
http://www.alu.edu/

CONTACT
Abraham Lincoln University, 3530 Wilshire Boulevard, Suite 1430, Los Angeles, CA 90010.

★ Academy of Art University

San Francisco, California
http://www.academyart.edu/

- **Proprietary** comprehensive, founded 1929
- **Urban** 3-acre campus
- **Coed** 7,406 undergraduate students, 55% full-time, 58% women, 42% men
- **Noncompetitive** entrance level, 100% of applicants were admitted

UNDERGRAD STUDENTS
4,090 full-time, 3,316 part-time. Students come from 50 states and territories; 99 other countries; 44% are from out of state; 6% Black or African American, non-Hispanic/Latino; 11% Hispanic/Latino; 6% Asian, non-Hispanic/Latino; 0.7% Native Hawaiian or other Pacific Islander, non-Hispanic/Latino; 0.5% American Indian or Alaska Native, non-Hispanic/Latino; 3% Two or more races, non-Hispanic/Latino; 28%

Race/ethnicity unknown; 28% international; 14% transferred in; 14% live on campus.

Freshmen:
Admission: 2,363 applied, 2,363 admitted, 570 enrolled.
Retention: 78% of full-time freshmen returned.

FACULTY
Total: 1,138, 21% full-time, 18% with terminal degrees.
Student/faculty ratio: 14:1.

ACADEMICS
Calendar: semesters. *Degrees:* certificates, associate, bachelor's, master's, and postbachelor's certificates.

Special study options: academic remediation for entering students, adult/continuing education programs, distance learning, English as a second language, independent study, internships, part-time degree program, services for LD students, study abroad, summer session for credit. *ROTC:* Army (c).

Computers: 900 computers/terminals are available on campus for general student use. Students can access the following: free student e-mail accounts, online (class) grades, online (class) registration, online (class) schedules, support for students taking online courses. Campuswide network is available. 100% of college-owned or -operated housing units are wired for high-speed Internet access. Wireless service is available via entire campus.

Library: Academy of Art University Library. *Books:* 38,441 (physical), 9,675 (digital/electronic); *Serial titles:* 185 (physical), 400,000 (digital/electronic); *Databases:* 22. Weekly public service hours: 83; students can reserve study rooms.

STUDENT LIFE
Housing options: coed, men-only, women-only. Campus housing is university owned and leased by the school. Freshman campus housing is guaranteed.

Activities and organizations: drama/theater group, student-run newspaper, radio and television station, choral group, Tea Time Animation, Beyond the Front Row, Drawaholics Anonymous Crew, Comics and Concept Art Club, Chinese Student Association, national fraternities, national sororities.

Athletics Member NCAA. All Division II except golf (Division I). *Intercollegiate sports:* baseball M(s), basketball M(s)/W(s), cross-country running M(s)/W(s), golf M(s)/W(s), soccer M(s)/W(s), softball W(s), tennis W(s), track and field M(s)/W(s), volleyball W(s).

Campus security: 24-hour emergency response devices and patrols, late-night transport/escort service, controlled dormitory access.

COSTS & FINANCIAL AID
Costs (2019–20) *Comprehensive fee:* $46,700 includes full-time tuition ($28,890), mandatory fees ($300), and room and board ($17,510). Part-time tuition: $963 per credit. *Required fees:* $963 per credit part-time. *College room only:* $11,740.

Financial Aid Of all full-time matriculated undergraduates who enrolled in 2017, 1,930 applied for aid, 1,798 were judged to have need, 57 had their need fully met. In 2017, 106 non-need-based awards were made. *Average percent of need met:* 35. *Average financial aid package:* $12,705. *Average need-based loan:* $3921. *Average need-based gift aid:* $11,761. *Average non-need-based aid:* $6985. *Average indebtedness upon graduation:* $35,862.

APPLYING
Options: electronic application, early admission, deferred entrance.
Application fee: $50.
Required: high school transcript. *Recommended:* interview.
Application deadlines: rolling (freshmen), rolling (transfers).
Notification: continuous (freshmen), continuous (transfers).

CONTACT
Academy of Art University, 79 New Montgomery Street, San Francisco, CA 94105-3410. *Toll-free phone:* 800-544-ARTS.

See below for display ad and page 964 for the College Close-Up.

Alliant International University–San Diego

San Diego, California
http://www.alliant.edu/

- **Independent** university, founded 1952, part of Alliant International University
- **Suburban** 60-acre campus with easy access to San Diego
- **Coed**
- **Minimally difficult** entrance level

FACULTY
Student/faculty ratio: 15:1.

ACADEMICS
Calendar: semesters. *Degrees:* certificates, bachelor's, master's, doctoral, and postbachelor's certificates.
Library: Walter Library.

STUDENT LIFE
Housing options: college housing not available.

Activities and organizations: Residence Hall Association, Latino Students Association, Finance Club, Student Government, Sigma Iota Epsilon.

Campus security: 24-hour patrols.

Student services: health clinic, personal/psychological counseling, veterans affairs office.

FINANCIAL AID
Financial Aid Of all full-time matriculated undergraduates who enrolled in 2018, 44 applied for aid, 44 were judged to have need, 2 had their need fully met. 8 Federal Work-Study jobs (averaging $3750). *Average percent of need met:* 64. *Average financial aid package:* $13,545. *Average need-based loan:* $5350. *Average need-based gift aid:* $9670.

APPLYING
Options: electronic application, deferred entrance.
Application fee: $65.
Required: high school transcript, minimum 2.0 GPA.

CONTACT
Ms. Ashley Carter, Director of Admissions, Alliant International University–San Diego, 10455 Pomerado Road, San Diego, CA 92131-1799. *Phone:* 866-825-5426. *Toll-free phone:* 866-825-5426. *E-mail:* admissions@alliant.edu.

★ AMDA College and Conservatory of the Performing Arts, Los Angeles Campus

Los Angeles, California
http://www.amda.edu/

CONTACT
Mr. Joseph Siriano, Director of Admissions, AMDA College and Conservatory of the Performing Arts, Los Angeles Campus, 6305 Yucca Street, Los Angeles, CA 90028. *Phone:* 323-603-5999. *Toll-free phone:* 888-474-9444. *E-mail:* admissionsteam@amda.edu.

See below for display ad and page 968 for the College Close-Up.

America Evangelical University

Los Angeles, California
http://www.aeu.edu/

CONTACT
America Evangelical University, 1818 South Western Avenue, Los Angeles, CA 90006.

American University of Health Sciences

Signal Hill, California
http://www.auhs.edu/

- **Proprietary** comprehensive
- **Coed**
- **Moderately difficult** entrance level

Unparalleled Performing Arts Education in the USA

AMDA
NEW YORK CITY CAMPUS
LOS ANGELES CAMPUS

+1 (323) 490.1284
amda.edu

Bachelor of Fine Arts Degree Programs

Professional Conservatory Programs

Talent Scholarships and International Grants Available

A ★ *indicates that the school has detailed information with a Premium Profile on Petersons.com.*

ACADEMICS
Degrees: bachelor's and master's.
Library: AUHS Library.

STUDENT LIFE
Activities and organizations: student-run newspaper.
Student services: personal/psychological counseling.

APPLYING
Options: early admission, deferred entrance.
Application fee: $80.
Required: essay or personal statement, high school transcript, interview.

CONTACT
American University of Health Sciences, 1600 East Hill Street, Building #1, Signal Hill, CA 90755.

Angeles College
Los Angeles, California
http://www.angelescollege.edu/

CONTACT
Angeles College, 3440 Wilshire Boulevard, Suite 310, Los Angeles, CA 90010.

Antelope Valley College
Lancaster, California
http://www.avc.edu/
- **District-supported** primarily 2-year, founded 1929, part of California Community College System
- **Suburban** 135-acre campus with easy access to Los Angeles
- **Endowment** $4.6 million
- **Coed**
- **Noncompetitive** entrance level

FACULTY
Student/faculty ratio: 24:1.

ACADEMICS
Calendar: semesters. *Degrees:* certificates, associate, and bachelor's.
Library: Antelope Valley College Library. *Books:* 54,721 (physical), 8,152 (digital/electronic); *Serial titles:* 10 (physical); *Databases:* 65. Weekly public service hours: 58; students can reserve study rooms.

STUDENT LIFE
Housing options: college housing not available.
Activities and organizations: drama/theater group.
Campus security: 24-hour emergency response devices and patrols, late-night transport/escort service.
Student services: health clinic, personal/psychological counseling, veterans affairs office.

APPLYING
Options: electronic application, early admission.

CONTACT
Welcome Center, Antelope Valley College, 3041 West Avenue K, SSV Building, Lancaster, CA 93536. *Phone:* 661-722-6300 Ext. 6331.

Antioch University Los Angeles
Culver City, California
http://www.antioch.edu/los-angeles/
- **Independent** upper-level, founded 1972, part of Antioch University
- **Urban** 1-acre campus with easy access to Los Angeles
- **Coed**
- **Moderately difficult** entrance level

ACADEMICS
Calendar: quarters. *Degrees:* bachelor's, master's, doctoral, post-master's, and postbachelor's certificates.

STUDENT LIFE
Housing options: college housing not available.

Activities and organizations: student-run newspaper, radio and television station.
Campus security: 24-hour emergency response devices, late-night transport/escort service.
Student services: personal/psychological counseling.

COSTS
Costs (2018–19) *Tuition:* $27,160 full-time, $679 per credit hour part-time. Full-time tuition and fees vary according to course load and program. Part-time tuition and fees vary according to course load and program. *Required fees:* $400 full-time.

APPLYING
Options: electronic application, deferred entrance.
Application fee: $60.

CONTACT
Admissions, Antioch University Los Angeles, 400 Corporate Pointe, Culver City, CA 90230. *Phone:* 310-578-1080 Ext. 100. *Toll-free phone:* 800-726-8462. *Fax:* 310-822-4824. *E-mail:* admissions@antiochla.edu.

Antioch University Santa Barbara
Santa Barbara, California
http://www.antioch.edu/santa-barbara/
- **Independent** upper-level, founded 1977, part of Antioch University
- **Urban** campus
- **Coed**
- **Moderately difficult** entrance level

ACADEMICS
Calendar: quarters. *Degrees:* certificates, bachelor's, master's, and doctoral.
Library: Sage Library.

STUDENT LIFE
Housing options: college housing not available.
Activities and organizations: student-run newspaper.
Campus security: late-night transport/escort service.

COSTS
Costs (2018–19) *Tuition:* $17,820 full-time, $495 per credit hour part-time. Full-time tuition and fees vary according to course load, degree level, and program. Part-time tuition and fees vary according to course load, degree level, and program. *Required fees:* $400 full-time.

APPLYING
Standardized Tests *Required for some:* TOEFL for international students.
Options: electronic application, deferred entrance.
Application fee: $60.

CONTACT
Jessica Grater, Research Analyst, Antioch University Santa Barbara, 602 Anacapa Street, Santa Barbara, CA 93101-1581. *Phone:* 407-967-6547. *Toll-free phone:* 866-526-8462. *E-mail:* jgrater@antioch.edu.

Argosy University, Los Angeles
Los Angeles, California
http://www.argosy.edu/locations/los-angeles/

CONTACT
Argosy University, Los Angeles, 5230 Pacific Concourse, Suite 200, Los Angeles, CA 90045. *Phone:* 310-531-9700. *Toll-free phone:* 866-505-0332.

Argosy University, Orange County
Orange, California
http://www.argosy.edu/locations/los-angeles-orange-county/

CONTACT
Argosy University, Orange County, 601 South Lewis Street, Orange, CA 92868. *Phone:* 714-620-3700. *Toll-free phone:* 800-716-9598.

ArtCenter College of Design
Pasadena, California
http://www.artcenter.edu/
- **Independent** comprehensive, founded 1930
- **Suburban** 163-acre campus with easy access to Los Angeles
- **Coed**
- **Very difficult** entrance level

FACULTY
Student/faculty ratio: 9:1.

ACADEMICS
Calendar: semesters. *Degrees:* bachelor's and master's.
Library: James Lemont Fogg Memorial Library plus 1 other. *Books:* 101,955 (physical), 1.0 million (digital/electronic); *Serial titles:* 592 (physical), 36,738 (digital/electronic); *Databases:* 46. Weekly public service hours: 63.

STUDENT LIFE
Housing options: college housing not available.
Activities and organizations: ACSG, Christian Fellowship, Stop Motion Club, Art Center Business Club, Fine Art Society.
Campus security: 24-hour emergency response devices and patrols, late-night transport/escort service.
Student services: personal/psychological counseling.

COSTS & FINANCIAL AID
Costs (2018–19) *Tuition:* $42,816 full-time, $1785 per credit part-time. *Required fees:* $600 full-time.
Financial Aid *Average financial aid package:* $17,803. *Average need-based loan:* $10,169. *Average need-based gift aid:* $14,627.

APPLYING
Standardized Tests *Required for some:* SAT or ACT (for admission).
Options: electronic application, deferred entrance.
Application fee: $50.
Required: essay or personal statement, portfolio. *Required for some:* high school transcript.

CONTACT
Ms. Kit Baron, Vice President, Admissions and Enrollment Management, ArtCenter College of Design, 1700 Lida Street, Pasadena, CA 91103. *Phone:* 626-396-2322. *Fax:* 626-795-0578. *E-mail:* kit.baron@artcenter.edu.

The Art Institute of California–Hollywood, a campus of Argosy University
North Hollywood, California
http://www.artinstitutes.edu/hollywood/

CONTACT
The Art Institute of California–Hollywood, a campus of Argosy University, 5250 Lankershim Boulevard, North Hollywood, CA 91601. *Phone:* 818-299-5100. *Toll-free phone:* 877-468-6232.

The Art Institute of California–San Diego, a campus of Argosy University
San Diego, California
http://www.artinstitutes.edu/sandiego/

CONTACT
The Art Institute of California–San Diego, a campus of Argosy University, 7650 Mission Valley Road, San Diego, CA 92108. *Phone:* 858-598-1200. *Toll-free phone:* 866-275-2422.

Ashford University
San Diego, California
http://www.ashford.edu/

CONTACT
Ms. Waunita M. Sullivan, Director of Enrollment, Ashford University, 8620 Spectrum Center Boulevard, San Diego, CA 92123. *Phone:* 563-242-4023 Ext. 3401. *Toll-free phone:* 866-711-1700. *E-mail:* admissns@tfu.edu.

Azusa Pacific University
Azusa, California
http://www.apu.edu/
- **Independent nondenominational** university, founded 1899
- **Suburban** 60-acre campus with easy access to Los Angeles
- **Coed**
- **Moderately difficult** entrance level

FACULTY
Student/faculty ratio: 10:1.

ACADEMICS
Calendar: semesters. *Degrees:* certificates, bachelor's, master's, doctoral, post-master's, and postbachelor's certificates.
Library: Marshburn Memorial Library plus 3 others. Study areas open 24 hours, 5–7 days a week; students can reserve study rooms.

STUDENT LIFE
Housing options: on-campus residence required through sophomore year; coed, men-only, women-only. Campus housing is university owned and leased by the school. Freshman applicants given priority for college housing.
Activities and organizations: drama/theater group, student-run newspaper, radio and television station, choral group, marching band.
Athletics Member NCAA, NAIA. All NCAA Division II.
Campus security: 24-hour emergency response devices and patrols, student patrols, late-night transport/escort service, controlled dormitory access.
Student services: health clinic, personal/psychological counseling, women's center, veterans affairs office.

COSTS & FINANCIAL AID
Costs (2018–19) *Tuition:* $36,926 full-time, $1596 per unit part-time. Full-time tuition and fees vary according to course load and degree level. Part-time tuition and fees vary according to course load and degree level. *Required fees:* $580 full-time. *Room only:* $5770. Room and board charges vary according to board plan and housing facility.
Financial Aid Of all full-time matriculated undergraduates who enrolled in 2018, 4,658 applied for aid, 3,544 were judged to have need, 1,040 had their need fully met. In 2018, 1017 non-need-based awards were made. *Average percent of need met:* 61. *Average financial aid package:* $24,723. *Average need-based loan:* $3612. *Average need-based gift aid:* $5535. *Average non-need-based aid:* $10,296. *Average indebtedness upon graduation:* $24,867.

APPLYING
Standardized Tests *Required:* SAT or ACT (for admission).
Options: electronic application, early action.
Required: essay or personal statement, high school transcript, minimum 3.0 GPA, 1 letter of recommendation, SAT composite of 990 (writing excluded) or ACT composite 19. *Required for some:* interview.

CONTACT
Ms. Lynnette Barnes, Processing Coordinator, Azusa Pacific University, 901 East Alosta Avenue, PO Box 7000, Undergraduate Admissions, 7221, Azusa, CA 91702-7000. *Phone:* 626-815-6000 Ext. 3419. *Toll-free phone:* 800-TALK-APU. *E-mail:* admissions@apu.edu.

Bergin University of Canine Studies

Rohnert Park, California

http://www.berginu.edu/

CONTACT
Bergin University of Canine Studies, 5860 Labath Avenue, Rohnert Park, CA 94928.

Bethesda University

Anaheim, California

http://www.buc.edu/

CONTACT
Jacquie Ha, Director of Admission, Bethesda University, 730 North Euclid Street, Anaheim, CA 92801. *Phone:* 714-517-1945. *Fax:* 714-517-1948. *E-mail:* admission@bcu.edu.

Beverly Hills Design Institute

Beverly Hills, California

http://www.bhdi.edu/

CONTACT
Beverly Hills Design Institute, 8484 Wilshire Boulevard, Suite 730, Beverly Hills, CA 90211. *Phone:* 310-360-8888.

Biola University

La Mirada, California

http://www.biola.edu/

- **Independent interdenominational** university, founded 1908
- **Suburban** 95-acre campus with easy access to Los Angeles
- **Coed**
- **Moderately difficult** entrance level

FACULTY
Student/faculty ratio: 15:1.

ACADEMICS
Calendar: 4-1-4. *Degrees:* diplomas, bachelor's, master's, doctoral, post-master's, and postbachelor's certificates.
Library: Biola University Library plus 1 other. *Books:* 550,000 (physical); *Databases:* 259. Weekly public service hours: 100; students can reserve study rooms.

STUDENT LIFE
Housing options: coed, women-only, special housing for students with disabilities. Campus housing is university owned. Freshman campus housing is guaranteed.

Activities and organizations: drama/theater group, student-run newspaper, radio and television station, choral group, Adventure Club, Guerilla Film Society, Biola Cross-Fit, Xopoc Dance Team, Lacrosse Club.

Athletics Member NCAA, NAIA. All NCAA Division II.

Campus security: 24-hour emergency response devices and patrols, late-night transport/escort service, controlled dormitory access.

Student services: health clinic, personal/psychological counseling, veterans affairs office.

COSTS & FINANCIAL AID
Costs (2018–19) *Comprehensive fee:* $51,800 includes full-time tuition ($40,488) and room and board ($11,312). Full-time tuition and fees vary according to course load and degree level. Part-time tuition: $1687 per credit hour. Part-time tuition and fees vary according to course load and degree level. *College room only:* $6200. Room and board charges vary according to board plan and housing facility.

Financial Aid Of all full-time matriculated undergraduates who enrolled in 2017, 2,846 applied for aid, 2,555 were judged to have need, 196 had their need fully met. In 2017, 1193 non-need-based awards were made. *Average percent of need met:* 54. *Average financial aid package:* $23,820. *Average need-based loan:* $3512. *Average need-based gift aid:* $17,920. *Average non-need-based aid:* $10,230. *Average indebtedness upon graduation:* $34,687.

APPLYING
Standardized Tests *Required:* SAT or ACT (for admission).

Options: electronic application, early decision, early action, deferred entrance.

Application fee: $45.

Required: essay or personal statement, high school transcript. *Required for some:* interview. *Recommended:* minimum 3.0 GPA.

CONTACT
Mrs. Michelle Reider, Associate Director of Undergraduate Freshman Admissions, Biola University, 13800 Biola Avenue, La Mirada, CA 90639. *Phone:* 562-903-4752. *Toll-free phone:* 800-652-4652. *E-mail:* admissions@biola.edu.

Brandman University

Irvine, California

http://www.brandman.edu/

- **Independent** comprehensive, founded 1958, part of Chapman University System
- **Suburban** 7-acre campus with easy access to Greater Los Angeles Area
- **Coed**
- 79% of applicants were admitted

Freshmen:
Admission: 96 applied, 76 admitted.

FACULTY
Student/faculty ratio: 15:1.

ACADEMICS
Calendar: trimesters. *Degrees:* certificates, associate, bachelor's, master's, doctoral, post-master's, and postbachelor's certificates.

Special study options: academic remediation for entering students, accelerated degree program, adult/continuing education programs, advanced placement credit, cooperative education, distance learning, double majors, independent study, internships, off-campus study, part-time degree program, services for LD students, summer session for credit.

Computers: 769 computers/terminals and 769 ports are available on campus for general student use. Students can access the following: campus intranet, computer help desk, free student e-mail accounts, online (class) grades, online (class) registration, online (class) schedules. Campuswide network is available. Wireless service is available via entire campus.

Library: Leatherby Library plus 1 other. *Books:* 300,000 (physical), 17,000 (digital/electronic); *Serial titles:* 265 (physical), 71,000 (digital/electronic); *Databases:* 300. Weekly public service hours: 65; study areas open 24 hours, 5–7 days a week; students can reserve study rooms.

STUDENT LIFE
Housing options: college housing not available.

Activities and organizations: Social Work Student Association, Society for Human Resource Management, Nursing Honor Society, Early Childhood Education Leadership, Pi Alpha Honor Society for Social Workers.

Campus security: late-night transport/escort service.

Student services: personal/psychological counseling, veterans affairs office.

COSTS
Costs (2018–19) *Tuition:* $15,000 full-time, $500 per credit hour part-time. *Required fees:* $380 full-time, $95 per term part-time. *Payment plan:* deferred payment. *Waivers:* employees or children of employees.

APPLYING
Options: electronic application, deferred entrance.

Required: high school transcript, minimum 2.0 GPA. *Required for some:* essay or personal statement, 3 letters of recommendation, 3 letters of recommendation, CPR certification, immunizations, professional liability insurance, RN licensure, and prerequisite coursework for RN-BSN program.

Application deadlines: rolling (freshmen), rolling (out-of-state freshmen), rolling (transfers).

Notification: continuous (out-of-state freshmen), continuous (transfers).

CONTACT
Andy LeCompte, Admissions Office, Brandman University, 16355 Laguna Canyon Drive, Irvine, CA 92618. *Phone:* 949-341-9839. *Toll-free phone:* 800-746-0082. *E-mail:* lecompte@brandman.edu.

California Baptist University
Riverside, California
http://www.calbaptist.edu/
- **Independent Southern Baptist** comprehensive, founded 1950
- **Suburban** 160-acre campus with easy access to Los Angeles
- **Endowment** $41.8 million
- **Coed**
- **Moderately difficult** entrance level

FACULTY
Student/faculty ratio: 17:1.

ACADEMICS
Calendar: 2-4-4-2. *Degrees:* associate, bachelor's, master's, and doctoral.
Library: Annie Gabriel Library. *Books:* 130,837 (physical), 190,918 (digital/electronic); *Serial titles:* 59,915 (physical), 21,548 (digital/electronic); *Databases:* 83. Weekly public service hours: 101; students can reserve study rooms.

STUDENT LIFE
Housing options: on-campus residence required for freshman year; men-only, women-only. Campus housing is university owned. Freshman applicants given priority for college housing.

Activities and organizations: drama/theater group, student-run newspaper, choral group, International Service Projects, United States Service Projects, CBU Crazies (Campus Spirit), Summer of Service, Associated Students of California Baptist University (government and leadership).

Athletics Member NCAA. All Division II.

Campus security: 24-hour emergency response devices and patrols, late-night transport/escort service, controlled dormitory access.

Student services: health clinic, personal/psychological counseling.

COSTS & FINANCIAL AID
Costs (2018–19) *One-time required fee:* $310. *Comprehensive fee:* $45,638 includes full-time tuition ($31,668), mandatory fees ($1810), and room and board ($12,160). Full-time tuition and fees vary according to course load, location, and program. Part-time tuition: $1218 per unit. Part-time tuition and fees vary according to course load, location, and program. *Required fees:* $175 per term part-time. *College room only:* $5860. Room and board charges vary according to board plan and housing facility.

Financial Aid Of all full-time matriculated undergraduates who enrolled in 2018, 6,130 applied for aid, 5,538 were judged to have need, 712 had their need fully met. 392 Federal Work-Study jobs (averaging $1713). In 2018, 488 non-need-based awards were made. *Average percent of need met:* 60. *Average financial aid package:* $22,465. *Average need-based loan:* $4505. *Average need-based gift aid:* $17,469. *Average non-need-based aid:* $11,367. *Average indebtedness upon graduation:* $39,544.

APPLYING
Standardized Tests *Required:* SAT or ACT (for admission). *Recommended:* SAT and SAT Subject Tests or ACT (for admission).
Options: electronic application, early action, deferred entrance.
Application fee: $45.
Required: essay or personal statement, minimum 2.0 GPA. *Required for some:* high school transcript.

CONTACT
Mr. Dustin Lowe, Director of Undergraduate Admissions, California Baptist University, 8432 Magnolia Avenue, Riverside, CA 92504-3297. *Phone:* 951-343-4477. *Toll-free phone:* 877-228-8866. *Fax:* 951-343-4525. *E-mail:* admissions@calbaptist.edu.

California Christian College
Fresno, California
http://www.calchristiancollege.edu/
- **Independent Free Will Baptist** 4-year
- **Urban** campus
- **Endowment** $166,018
- **Coed**
- **Noncompetitive** entrance level

ACADEMICS
Calendar: semesters. *Degrees:* associate and bachelor's.
Library: Cortese Library. *Books:* 17,572 (physical); *Serial titles:* 12 (physical). Weekly public service hours: 15.

STUDENT LIFE
Housing options: men-only, women-only. Campus housing is leased by the school.

Student services: personal/psychological counseling.

COSTS & FINANCIAL AID
Costs (2018–19) *Tuition:* $8880 full-time, $370 per unit part-time. *Required fees:* $610 full-time, $305 per term part-time.

Financial Aid Of all full-time matriculated undergraduates who enrolled in 2017, 7 applied for aid, 7 were judged to have need. 2 Federal Work-Study jobs (averaging $2604). *Average percent of need met:* 51. *Average financial aid package:* $12,671. *Average need-based loan:* $4158. *Average need-based gift aid:* $6362.

APPLYING
Standardized Tests *Required:* math and English exams (for admission). *Recommended:* SAT or ACT (for admission).

Options: electronic application.

Application fee: $40.

Required: essay or personal statement, high school transcript, minimum 2.0 GPA, 2 letters of recommendation, statement of faith, moral/ethical statement. *Recommended:* interview.

CONTACT
Mr. Billy Parris, Admissions Recruiter, California Christian College, 5364 E. Belmont Avenue, Fresno, CA 93727. *Phone:* 559-251-4215 Ext. 1002. *Fax:* 559-385-2329. *E-mail:* admissions@calchristiancollege.edu.

California Coast University
Santa Ana, California
http://www.calcoast.edu/

CONTACT
California Coast University, 925 North Spurgeon Street, Santa Ana, CA 92701. *Phone:* 714-547-9625. *Toll-free phone:* 888-CCU-UNIV.

California College of the Arts
San Francisco, California
http://www.cca.edu/
- **Independent** comprehensive, founded 1907
- **Urban** 4-acre campus with easy access to San Francisco, Oakland
- **Endowment** $30.3 million
- **Coed**
- **70% of applicants were admitted**

FACULTY
Student/faculty ratio: 9:1.

ACADEMICS
Calendar: semesters. *Degrees:* bachelor's and master's.
Library: Meyer Library plus 1 other.

STUDENT LIFE
Housing options: coed, special housing for students with disabilities. Campus housing is university owned and leased by the school. Freshman applicants given priority for college housing.

Activities and organizations: student-run radio station, Student of Color Coalition, International Student Alliance, Chimera Council, Animation Resource Center, MyChina, national fraternities, national sororities.

Campus security: 24-hour emergency response devices and patrols, late-night transport/escort service, controlled dormitory access.

Student services: personal/psychological counseling.

COSTS & FINANCIAL AID
Costs (2018–19) *Tuition:* $48,648 full-time, $2027 per unit part-time. *Required fees:* $500 full-time, $170 per term part-time. *Room only:* $10,136. Room and board charges vary according to housing facility.

Financial Aid Of all full-time matriculated undergraduates who enrolled in 2018, 653 applied for aid, 594 were judged to have need, 49 had their need fully met. In 2018, 424 non-need-based awards were made. *Average percent of need met:* 68. *Average financial aid package:* $38,416. *Average need-based loan:* $4853. *Average need-based gift aid:* $31,113. *Average non-need-based aid:* $12,984. *Average indebtedness upon graduation:* $33,190.

APPLYING
Options: electronic application.

Application fee: $70.

Required: essay or personal statement, minimum 2.0 GPA, 1 letter of recommendation, portfolio of creative work. *Required for some:* high school transcript, interview.

CONTACT
Mr. Arnold Icasiano, Director of Admissions, California College of the Arts, 1111 Eighth Street, San Francisco, CA 94107. *Phone:* 415-703-9523 Ext. 9532. *Toll-free phone:* 800-447-1ART. *Fax:* 415-703-9539. *E-mail:* enroll@cca.edu.

California College San Diego
National City, California
http://www.cc-sd.edu/

CONTACT
California College San Diego, 700 Bay Marina Drive, Suite 100, National City, CA 91950. *Toll-free phone:* 800-622-3188.

California College San Diego
San Diego, California
http://www.cc-sd.edu/

CONTACT
Tana Sanderson, Director of Admission, California College San Diego, 6602 Convoy Court, Suite 100, San Diego, CA 92111. *Phone:* 619-295-5785. *Toll-free phone:* 800-622-3188. *E-mail:* tana.sanderson@cc-sd.edu.

California College San Diego
San Marcos, California
http://www.cc-sd.edu/

CONTACT
California College San Diego, 277 Rancheros Drive, Suite 200, San Marcos, CA 92069. *Toll-free phone:* 800-622-3188.

California Institute of Integral Studies
San Francisco, California
http://www.ciis.edu/
- **Independent** upper-level, founded 1968
- **Urban** campus with easy access to San Francisco
- **Endowment** $1.9 million
- **Coed**
- **Minimally difficult** entrance level

FACULTY
Student/faculty ratio: 11:1.

ACADEMICS
Calendar: semesters. *Degrees:* bachelor's, master's, doctoral, and postbachelor's certificates.
Library: The Laurance S. Rockefeller Library plus 1 other.

STUDENT LIFE
Housing options: college housing not available.

Activities and organizations: drama/theater group, Student Alliance, People of Color, Queer@CIIS, International Students and Friends, AWARE - Awaking to Whiteness and Racism Everywhere.

Student services: personal/psychological counseling, veterans affairs office.

COSTS & FINANCIAL AID
Costs (2018–19) *Tuition:* $19,792 full-time, $825 per unit part-time. *Required fees:* $430 full-time, $215 per term part-time. *Payment plans:* installment, deferred payment.

Financial Aid Of all full-time matriculated undergraduates who enrolled in 2015, 86 applied for aid, 86 were judged to have need, 4 had their need fully met. 6 Federal Work-Study jobs (averaging $3208). *Average percent of need met:* 22. *Average financial aid package:* $18,625. *Average need-based loan:* $5799. *Average need-based gift aid:* $6193.

APPLYING
Options: electronic application.

Application fee: $65.

CONTACT
Admissions Counselor, California Institute of Integral Studies, 1453 Mission Street, San Francisco, CA 94103. *Phone:* 415-575-6156. *Fax:* 415-575-1268. *E-mail:* admissions@ciis.edu.

California Institute of Technology
Pasadena, California
http://www.caltech.edu/
- **Independent** university, founded 1891
- **Suburban** 124-acre campus with easy access to Los Angeles
- **Endowment** $2.9 billion
- **Coed** 948 undergraduate students, 100% full-time, 45% women, 55% men
- **Most difficult** entrance level, 7% of applicants were admitted

UNDERGRAD STUDENTS
948 full-time. Students come from 46 states and territories; 23 other countries; 63% are from out of state; 1% Black or African American, non-Hispanic/Latino; 14% Hispanic/Latino; 40% Asian, non-Hispanic/Latino; 8% Two or more races, non-Hispanic/Latino; 9% international; 0.2% transferred in; 86% live on campus.

Freshmen:
Admission: 8,208 applied, 543 admitted, 231 enrolled. *Test scores:* ACT scores over 18: 100%; SAT evidence-based reading and writing scores over 600: 100%; SAT math scores over 600: 100%; ACT scores over 24: 100%; SAT evidence-based reading and writing scores over 700: 95%; SAT math scores over 700: 99%; ACT scores over 30: 100%.
Retention: 98% of full-time freshmen returned.

FACULTY
Total: 374, 89% full-time, 95% with terminal degrees.
Student/faculty ratio: 3:1.

ACADEMICS
Calendar: quarters. *Degrees:* bachelor's, master's, doctoral, and post-master's certificates.

Special study options: cooperative education, double majors, English as a second language, independent study, off-campus study, services for LD students, student-designed majors, study abroad. *ROTC:* Army (c), Air Force (c).

Unusual degree programs: 3-2 engineering with Bowdoin College, Bryn Mawr College, Grinnell College, Haverford College, Mt. Holyoke College, Oberlin College, Occidental College, Ohio Wesleyan University, Pomona College, Reed College, Spelman College, Wesleyan University, Whitman College.

Computers: 75 computers/terminals and 1,250 ports are available on campus for general student use. Students can access the following: campus intranet, computer help desk, free student e-mail accounts, online (class) grades, online (class) registration, online (class) schedules. Campuswide network is available. 100% of college-owned or -operated housing units are wired for high-speed Internet access. Wireless service is available via entire campus.

Library: Sherman Fairchild Library plus 5 others. *Books:* 276,995 (physical), 74,744 (digital/electronic); *Serial titles:* 6,183 (physical), 5,495 (digital/electronic); *Databases:* 197. Weekly public service hours: 168; study areas open 24 hours, 5–7 days a week; students can reserve study rooms.

STUDENT LIFE

Housing options: on-campus residence required for freshman year; coed, special housing for students with disabilities. Campus housing is university owned. Freshman campus housing is guaranteed.

Activities and organizations: drama/theater group, student-run newspaper, choral group, Instrumental music groups, Entrepreneur's Club, Glee Club, Theater Arts, Ultimate Disc Club.

Athletics Member NCAA. All Division III. *Intercollegiate sports:* baseball M, basketball M/W, cross-country running M/W, fencing M/W, soccer M/W, swimming and diving M/W, tennis M/W, track and field M/W, volleyball W, water polo M/W. *Intramural sports:* badminton M(c)/W(c), basketball M/W, soccer M/W, table tennis M/W, ultimate Frisbee M(c)/W(c), volleyball M/W.

Campus security: 24-hour emergency response devices and patrols, late-night transport/escort service, controlled dormitory access.

Student services: health clinic, personal/psychological counseling, women's center.

COSTS & FINANCIAL AID

Costs (2019–20) *One-time required fee:* $500. *Comprehensive fee:* $71,244 includes full-time tuition ($52,506), mandatory fees ($2094), and room and board ($16,644). *College room only:* $9615.

Financial Aid Of all full-time matriculated undergraduates who enrolled in 2018, 567 applied for aid, 503 were judged to have need, 503 had their need fully met. 233 Federal Work-Study jobs (averaging $3124). 45 state and other part-time jobs (averaging $2465). In 2018, 1 non-need-based awards were made. *Average percent of need met:* 100. *Average financial aid package:* $51,318. *Average need-based loan:* $3589. *Average need-based gift aid:* $47,564. *Average non-need-based aid:* $5000. *Average indebtedness upon graduation:* $16,337.

APPLYING

Standardized Tests *Required:* SAT or ACT (for admission), SAT and SAT Subject Tests or ACT (for admission), SAT Subject Tests (for admission).

Options: electronic application, early admission, early action, deferred entrance.

Application fee: $75.

Required: essay or personal statement, high school transcript, 2 letters of recommendation.

Application deadlines: 1/3 (freshmen), 2/15 (transfers), 11/1 (early action).

Notification: 4/1 (freshmen), 5/1 (transfers), 12/15 (early action).

CONTACT

Mr. Jarrid James Whitney, Executive Director of Admissions, California Institute of Technology, 383 South Hill Avenue, Mail Code 10-90, Pasadena, CA 91125. *Phone:* 626-395-6341. *Fax:* 626-683-3026.

California Institute of the Arts
Valencia, California
http://www.calarts.edu/

CONTACT
Molly Ryan, Director of Admissions, California Institute of the Arts, 24700 McBean Parkway, Valencia, CA 91355-2340. *Phone:* 661-255-1050. *Toll-free phone:* 800-545-2787. *Fax:* 661-253-7710. *E-mail:* admiss@calarts.edu.

California Intercontinental University
Irvine, California
http://caluniversity.edu/

CONTACT
John Ramsay, Director of Admission, California Intercontinental University, 17310 Red Hill Avenue, #200, Irvine, CA 92614. *Phone:* 909-396-6090. *Toll-free phone:* 866-687-2258. *Fax:* 909-804-5151. *E-mail:* admissions@caluniversity.com.

California Jazz Conservatory
Berkeley, California
http://www.cjc.edu/

CONTACT
California Jazz Conservatory, 2087 Addison Street, Berkeley, CA 94704.

California Lutheran University
Thousand Oaks, California
http://www.callutheran.edu/
- **Independent Lutheran** comprehensive, founded 1959
- **Suburban** 290-acre campus with easy access to Los Angeles
- **Endowment** $109.1 million
- **Coed** 3,059 undergraduate students, 96% full-time, 57% women, 43% men
- **Moderately difficult** entrance level, 71% of applicants were admitted

UNDERGRAD STUDENTS
2,942 full-time, 117 part-time. Students come from 39 states and territories; 32 other countries; 11% are from out of state; 4% Black or African American, non-Hispanic/Latino; 33% Hispanic/Latino; 5% Asian, non-Hispanic/Latino; 0.5% Native Hawaiian or other Pacific Islander, non-Hispanic/Latino; 0.3% American Indian or Alaska Native, non-Hispanic/Latino; 8% Two or more races, non-Hispanic/Latino; 3% Race/ethnicity unknown; 3% international; 8% transferred in; 52% live on campus.

Freshmen:
Admission: 5,752 applied, 4,111 admitted, 681 enrolled. *Average high school GPA:* 3.7. *Test scores:* SAT evidence-based reading and writing scores over 500: 93%; SAT math scores over 500: 91%; ACT scores over 18: 97%; SAT evidence-based reading and writing scores over 600: 43%; SAT math scores over 600: 36%; ACT scores over 24: 51%; SAT evidence-based reading and writing scores over 700: 6%; SAT math scores over 700: 6%; ACT scores over 30: 13%.
Retention: 83% of full-time freshmen returned.

FACULTY
Total: 458, 43% full-time, 59% with terminal degrees.
Student/faculty ratio: 16:1.

ACADEMICS
Calendar: semesters. *Degrees:* certificates, bachelor's, master's, doctoral, post-master's, and postbachelor's certificates.

Special study options: accelerated degree program, adult/continuing education programs, advanced placement credit, cooperative education, double majors, honors programs, independent study, internships, off-campus study, part-time degree program, services for LD students, student-designed majors, study abroad, summer session for credit. *ROTC:* Army (c), Air Force (c).

Unusual degree programs: 3-2 computer science, political public policy and administration.

Computers: 543 computers/terminals are available on campus for general student use. Students can access the following: campus intranet, computer help desk, free student e-mail accounts, online (class) grades, online (class) registration, online (class) schedules. Campuswide network is available. 100% of college-owned or -operated housing units are wired for high-speed Internet access. Wireless service is available via entire campus.

Library: Pearson Library. *Books:* 93,605 (physical), 250,900 (digital/electronic); *Serial titles:* 13 (physical), 75,211 (digital/electronic); *Databases:* 155. Weekly public service hours: 105; students can reserve study rooms.

STUDENT LIFE
Housing options: on-campus residence required through junior year; coed, special housing for students with disabilities. Campus housing is university owned. Freshman campus housing is guaranteed.

Activities and organizations: drama/theater group, student-run newspaper, radio and television station, choral group, Student Government, recreation, sports fan, or club sports related, service organizations, campus ministry or other religiously affiliated organization, multicultural organizations.

Athletics Member NCAA. All Division III except golf (Division II). *Intercollegiate sports:* baseball M, basketball M/W, cheerleading M/W, cross-country running M/W, football M, golf M/W, soccer M/W, softball W, swimming and diving M/W, tennis M/W, track and field M/W, volleyball M/W, water polo M/W. *Intramural sports:* basketball M/W, football M/W, ice hockey M(c)/W(c), lacrosse M(c)/W(c), rugby M(c), soccer M/W, swimming and diving M(c)/W(c), tennis M(c)/W(c), ultimate Frisbee M(c)/W(c), volleyball M/W, water polo M(c)/W(c), wrestling M(c)/W(c).

Campus security: 24-hour emergency response devices and patrols, late-night transport/escort service, controlled dormitory access, escort service, shuttle service.

Student services: health clinic, personal/psychological counseling, women's center, veterans affairs office.

COSTS & FINANCIAL AID
Costs (2019–20) *Comprehensive fee:* $58,483 includes full-time tuition ($43,900), mandatory fees ($483), and room and board ($14,100). *College room only:* $7590.

Financial Aid Of all full-time matriculated undergraduates who enrolled in 2017, 2,771 applied for aid, 2,065 were judged to have need, 452 had their need fully met. 260 Federal Work-Study jobs (averaging $2500). In 2017, 688 non-need-based awards were made. *Average percent of need met:* 79. *Average financial aid package:* $36,600. *Average need-based loan:* $4840. *Average need-based gift aid:* $27,600. *Average non-need-based aid:* $18,860. *Average indebtedness upon graduation:* $34,220.

APPLYING
Standardized Tests *Required:* SAT or ACT (for admission).

Options: electronic application, early action, deferred entrance.

Application fee: $25.

Required: essay or personal statement, high school transcript, minimum 2.8 GPA, 1 letter of recommendation. *Recommended:* minimum 3.0 GPA, interview.

Application deadlines: 1/1 (freshmen), 6/1 (transfers).

Notification: 4/1 (freshmen), continuous (transfers), 1/15 (early action).

CONTACT
Dr. Michael Elgarico, Dean of Undergraduate Enrollment, California Lutheran University, Office of Admission, #1350, Thousand Oaks, CA 91360. *Phone:* 805-493-3135. *Toll-free phone:* 877-258-3678. *Fax:* 805-493-3114. *E-mail:* cluadm@clunet.edu.

California Miramar University
San Diego, California
http://www.calmu.edu/

CONTACT
Jean Van Slyke, Director of Admissions, California Miramar University, 3550 Camino Del Rio North, Suite 208, San Diego, CA 92108. *Phone:* 858-653-3000. *Toll-free phone:* 877-570-5678. *Fax:* 858-653-6786. *E-mail:* admissions@calmu.edu.

California Polytechnic State University, San Luis Obispo
San Luis Obispo, California
http://www.calpoly.edu/

- **State-supported** comprehensive, founded 1901, part of California State University System
- **Suburban** 6000-acre campus
- **Coed** 21,037 undergraduate students, 96% full-time, 48% women, 52% men
- **Moderately difficult** entrance level, 30% of applicants were admitted

UNDERGRAD STUDENTS
20,272 full-time, 765 part-time. 14% are from out of state; 0.8% Black or African American, non-Hispanic/Latino; 17% Hispanic/Latino; 13% Asian, non-Hispanic/Latino; 0.2% Native Hawaiian or other Pacific Islander, non-Hispanic/Latino; 0.1% American Indian or Alaska Native, non-Hispanic/Latino; 8% Two or more races, non-Hispanic/Latino; 4% Race/ethnicity unknown; 2% international; 4% transferred in; 32% live on campus.

Freshmen:
Admission: 54,663 applied, 16,491 admitted, 4,398 enrolled. *Average high school GPA:* 4.0. *Test scores:* SAT evidence-based reading and writing scores over 500: 100%; SAT math scores over 500: 100%; ACT scores over 18: 100%; SAT evidence-based reading and writing scores over 600: 85%; SAT math scores over 600: 83%; ACT scores over 24: 91%; SAT evidence-based reading and writing scores over 700: 25%; SAT math scores over 700: 40%; ACT scores over 30: 48%.

Retention: 94% of full-time freshmen returned.

FACULTY
Total: 1,486, 64% full-time, 59% with terminal degrees.
Student/faculty ratio: 19:1.

ACADEMICS
Calendar: quarters. *Degrees:* bachelor's, master's, and postbachelor's certificates.

Special study options: academic remediation for entering students, advanced placement credit, cooperative education, distance learning, double majors, English as a second language, honors programs, internships, off-campus study, part-time degree program, services for LD students, study abroad, summer session for credit. *ROTC:* Army (b).

Computers: Students can access the following: campus intranet, free student e-mail accounts, online (class) grades, online (class) registration, online (class) schedules. Campuswide network is available. Wireless service is available via classrooms, computer centers, computer labs, dorm rooms, learning centers, libraries, student centers.
Library: Robert E. Kennedy Library.

STUDENT LIFE
Housing options: on-campus residence required for freshman year; coed, special housing for students with disabilities. Campus housing is university owned.

Activities and organizations: drama/theater group, student-run newspaper, radio and television station, choral group, marching band, national fraternities, national sororities.

Athletics Member NCAA. All Division I except football (Division I-AA). *Intercollegiate sports:* baseball M(s), basketball M(s)/W(s), bowling M(s)/W(s), cross-country running M(s)/W(s), golf M(s)/W(s)(c), soccer M(s)/W(s), softball W(s), swimming and diving M(s)/W(s), tennis M(s)/W(s), track and field M(s)/W(s), volleyball M(s)/W(s), wrestling M(s). *Intramural sports:* badminton M/W, basketball M/W, football M, racquetball M/W, sand volleyball M/W, soccer M/W, softball M/W, table tennis M/W, tennis M/W, volleyball M/W.

Campus security: 24-hour emergency response devices and patrols, student patrols, late-night transport/escort service.

Student services: health clinic, personal/psychological counseling, women's center, legal services, veterans affairs office.

COSTS & FINANCIAL AID
Costs (2018–19) *Tuition:* state resident $5742 full-time, $3330 per year part-time; nonresident $17,622 full-time, $8082 per year part-time. Full-time tuition and fees vary according to course load, degree level, and program. Part-time tuition and fees vary according to course load, degree level, and program. *Required fees:* $4074 full-time, $3307 per year part-time. *Room and board:* $13,796; room only: $8259. Room and board charges vary according to housing facility. *Payment plan:* installment. *Waivers:* employees or children of employees.

Financial Aid Of all full-time matriculated undergraduates who enrolled in 2017, 12,403 applied for aid, 8,266 were judged to have need, 672 had their need fully met. In 2017, 2600 non-need-based awards were made. *Average percent of need met:* 57. *Average financial aid package:* $10,770. *Average need-based loan:* $4052. *Average need-based gift aid:* $3648. *Average non-need-based aid:* $2205. *Average indebtedness upon graduation:* $22,298.

APPLYING
Standardized Tests *Required:* SAT or ACT (for admission).

Options: electronic application.

Application fee: $55.

Required: high school transcript.

Application deadlines: 11/30 (freshmen), 11/30 (transfers).

Notification: 4/1 (freshmen), 4/1 (transfers).

CONTACT
Mr. James Maraviglia, Vice Provost for Enrollment Development and Chief Marketing Officer, California Polytechnic State University, San Luis Obispo, Admissions Office, 1 Grand Avenue, San Luis Obispo, CA 93407-0031. *Phone:* 805-756-2913. *Fax:* 805-756-5911. *E-mail:* admissions@calpoly.edu.

California State Polytechnic University, Pomona

Pomona, California
http://www.cpp.edu/

- **State-supported** comprehensive, founded 1938, part of California State University System
- **Urban** 1400-acre campus with easy access to Los Angeles
- **Endowment** $96.1 million
- **Coed**
- **Moderately difficult** entrance level

FACULTY
Student/faculty ratio: 25:1.

ACADEMICS
Calendar: quarters. *Degrees:* bachelor's, master's, and doctoral.
Library: University Library. *Books:* 576,734 (physical), 246,874 (digital/electronic); *Serial titles:* 278,011 (physical), 13,335 (digital/electronic); *Databases:* 143. Weekly public service hours: 92; study areas open 24 hours, 5–7 days a week; students can reserve study rooms.

STUDENT LIFE
Housing options: on-campus residence required for freshman year; coed, special housing for students with disabilities. Campus housing is university owned and is provided by a third party. Freshman applicants given priority for college housing.

Activities and organizations: drama/theater group, student-run newspaper, choral group, Rose Float Club, Mexican American Student Association (MASA), Barkada - Filipino American Student Association, American Marketing Association, Cal Poly Society of Accountants, national fraternities, national sororities.

Athletics Member NCAA. All Division II.

Campus security: 24-hour emergency response devices and patrols, student patrols, late-night transport/escort service, controlled dormitory access, video camera surveillance.

Student services: health clinic, personal/psychological counseling, women's center, veterans affairs office.

COSTS & FINANCIAL AID
Costs (2018–19) *Tuition:* state resident $5742 full-time; nonresident $17,622 full-time, $396 per credit hour part-time. Full-time tuition and fees vary according to course load, degree level, and program. Part-time tuition and fees vary according to course load, degree level, and program. *Required fees:* $1611 full-time. *Room and board:* $17,358; room only: $9766. Room and board charges vary according to board plan and housing facility. *Payment plans:* installment, deferred payment.

Financial Aid Of all full-time matriculated undergraduates who enrolled in 2018, 17,237 applied for aid, 15,137 were judged to have need, 695 had their need fully met. 390 Federal Work-Study jobs (averaging $3404). In 2018, 20 non-need-based awards were made. *Average percent of need met:* 56. *Average financial aid package:* $11,161. *Average need-based loan:* $4820. *Average need-based gift aid:* $10,472. *Average non-need-based aid:* $2195. *Average indebtedness upon graduation:* $22,228.

APPLYING
Standardized Tests *Required:* SAT or ACT (for admission).
Options: electronic application.
Application fee: $55.
Required: high school transcript, minimum 2.0 GPA.

CONTACT
Ms. Deborah L. Brandon, Executive Director of Admissions and Enrollment Planning, California State Polytechnic University, Pomona, 3801 W. Temple Avenue, 98-T2, Pomona, CA 91768. *Phone:* 909-869-3427. *Fax:* 909-869-5315. *E-mail:* dlbrandon@cpp.edu.

California State University, Bakersfield

Bakersfield, California
http://www.csub.edu/

- **State-supported** comprehensive, founded 1970, part of California State University System
- **Urban** 575-acre campus
- **Coed** 9,196 undergraduate students, 86% full-time, 61% women, 39% men
- **100% of applicants were admitted**

UNDERGRAD STUDENTS
7,906 full-time, 1,290 part-time. 1% are from out of state; 5% Black or African American, non-Hispanic/Latino; 61% Hispanic/Latino; 6% Asian, non-Hispanic/Latino; 0.2% Native Hawaiian or other Pacific Islander, non-Hispanic/Latino; 0.5% American Indian or Alaska Native, non-Hispanic/Latino; 3% Two or more races, non-Hispanic/Latino; 6% Race/ethnicity unknown; 5% international; 13% transferred in; 4% live on campus.

Freshmen:
Admission: 5,429 applied, 5,429 admitted, 1,492 enrolled. *Average high school GPA:* 3.3. *Test scores:* SAT evidence-based reading and writing scores over 500: 46%; SAT math scores over 500: 55%; ACT scores over 18: 56%; SAT evidence-based reading and writing scores over 600: 14%; SAT math scores over 600: 11%; ACT scores over 24: 14%; SAT evidence-based reading and writing scores over 700: 3%; SAT math scores over 700: 2%; ACT scores over 30: 6%.
Retention: 77% of full-time freshmen returned.

FACULTY
Total: 678, 50% full-time, 42% with terminal degrees.
Student/faculty ratio: 26:1.

ACADEMICS
Calendar: semesters. *Degrees:* bachelor's, master's, and doctoral.
Special study options: adult/continuing education programs, external degree program, part-time degree program.
Computers: Students can access the following: online (class) registration. Campuswide network is available.
Library: Walter W. Stiern Library.

STUDENT LIFE
Housing options: coed.
Athletics Member NCAA. All Division II except wrestling (Division I). *Intercollegiate sports:* basketball M(s), golf M(s), soccer M(s), softball W(s), swimming and diving M(s)/W(s), tennis W(s), track and field M(s)/W(s), volleyball W(s), water polo W(s), wrestling M(s). *Intramural sports:* archery M/W, badminton M/W, baseball M/W, basketball M/W, fencing M, field hockey W, football M/W, golf M/W, gymnastics M/W, racquetball M/W, riflery M/W, soccer M, softball M/W, swimming and diving M/W, tennis W, volleyball M/W, weight lifting M/W, wrestling M/W.
Campus security: 24-hour emergency response devices and patrols, late-night transport/escort service.

FINANCIAL AID
Financial Aid Of all full-time matriculated undergraduates who enrolled in 2017, 6,638 applied for aid, 6,265 were judged to have need, 193 had their need fully met. In 2017, 31 non-need-based awards were made. *Average percent of need met:* 61. *Average financial aid package:* $11,440. *Average need-based loan:* $4114. *Average need-based gift aid:* $9996. *Average non-need-based aid:* $2265. *Average indebtedness upon graduation:* $18,143.

APPLYING
Standardized Tests *Required for some:* SAT or ACT (for admission).
Options: electronic application, deferred entrance.
Application fee: $55.
Required: high school transcript.

CONTACT
Debra Blowers, Assistant Director, Admissions and Evaluations, California State University, Bakersfield, 9001 Stockdale Highway, Balersfield, CA 93311-1099. *Phone:* 661-664-3036. *Toll-free phone:* 800-788-2782. *E-mail:* admissions@csub.edu.

California State University Channel Islands

Camarillo, California

http://www.csuci.edu/

CONTACT
Ms. Ginger Reyes, California State University Channel Islands, One University Drive, Camarillo, CA 93012. *Phone:* 805-437-8520. *Fax:* 805-437-8519. *E-mail:* prospective.student@csuci.edu.

California State University, Chico

Chico, California

http://www.csuchico.edu/

- **State-supported** comprehensive, founded 1887, part of California State University System
- **Small-town** 119-acre campus
- **Endowment** $64.7 million
- **Coed** 16,420 undergraduate students, 93% full-time, 53% women, 47% men
- **Moderately difficult** entrance level, 65% of applicants were admitted

UNDERGRAD STUDENTS
15,237 full-time, 1,183 part-time. 1% are from out of state; 3% Black or African American, non-Hispanic/Latino; 34% Hispanic/Latino; 5% Asian, non-Hispanic/Latino; 0.2% Native Hawaiian or other Pacific Islander, non-Hispanic/Latino; 0.5% American Indian or Alaska Native, non-Hispanic/Latino; 5% Two or more races, non-Hispanic/Latino; 8% Race/ethnicity unknown; 3% international; 9% transferred in; 2% live on campus.

Freshmen:
Admission: 23,964 applied, 15,639 admitted, 2,725 enrolled. *Average high school GPA:* 3.4. *Test scores:* SAT evidence-based reading and writing scores over 500: 79%; SAT math scores over 500: 78%; ACT scores over 18: 82%; SAT evidence-based reading and writing scores over 600: 27%; SAT math scores over 600: 21%; ACT scores over 24: 30%; SAT evidence-based reading and writing scores over 700: 2%; SAT math scores over 700: 3%; ACT scores over 30: 4%.
Retention: 85% of full-time freshmen returned.

FACULTY
Total: 987, 51% full-time, 58% with terminal degrees.
Student/faculty ratio: 24:1.

ACADEMICS
Calendar: semesters. *Degrees:* certificates, bachelor's, master's, post-master's, and postbachelor's certificates.

Special study options: academic remediation for entering students, adult/continuing education programs, advanced placement credit, cooperative education, distance learning, double majors, English as a second language, external degree program, honors programs, independent study, internships, off-campus study, part-time degree program, services for LD students, student-designed majors, study abroad, summer session for credit.

Computers: 1,328 computers/terminals and 1,328 ports are available on campus for general student use. Students can access the following: campus intranet, computer help desk, free student e-mail accounts, online (class) grades, online (class) registration, online (class) schedules, student account information, calendar, transcripts. Campuswide network is available. 100% of college-owned or -operated housing units are wired for high-speed Internet access. Wireless service is available via entire campus.
Library: Meriam Library plus 1 other. *Books:* 544,345 (physical), 306,440 (digital/electronic); *Serial titles:* 72,555 (physical). Study areas open 24 hours, 5–7 days a week; students can reserve study rooms.

STUDENT LIFE
Housing options: coed, women-only, special housing for students with disabilities. Campus housing is university owned. Freshman applicants given priority for college housing.

Activities and organizations: drama/theater group, student-run newspaper, radio station, choral group, Chico Snow Club, Chico State Nursing Club, Pre-Medical Association, Health Professionals Association, Exercise Physiology Majors Club, national fraternities, national sororities.

Athletics Member NCAA. All Division II except golf (Division I). *Intercollegiate sports:* baseball M(s), basketball M(s)/W(s), cross-country running M(s)/W(s), golf M(s)/W(s), soccer M(s)/W(s), softball W(s), track and field M(s)/W(s), volleyball W(s). *Intramural sports:* basketball M/W.

Campus security: 24-hour emergency response devices and patrols, student patrols, late-night transport/escort service, controlled dormitory access.

Student services: health clinic, personal/psychological counseling, women's center, legal services, veterans affairs office.

FINANCIAL AID
Financial Aid Of all full-time matriculated undergraduates who enrolled in 2016, 12,269 applied for aid, 10,577 were judged to have need, 1,606 had their need fully met. In 2016, 444 non-need-based awards were made. *Average percent of need met:* 74. *Average financial aid package:* $16,022. *Average need-based loan:* $4653. *Average need-based gift aid:* $10,134. *Average non-need-based aid:* $1429.

APPLYING
Standardized Tests *Required:* SAT or ACT (for admission).

Options: electronic application, deferred entrance.

Application fee: $55.

Required: high school transcript, GPA from 10th/11th grade college preparatory courses.

Notification: 3/1 (freshmen), 3/1 (transfers).

CONTACT
Kimberly Guanzon, Director, California State University, Chico, 400 West First Street, Chico, CA 95929-0722. *Phone:* 530-898-6322. *Toll-free phone:* 800-542-4426. *Fax:* 530-898-6456. *E-mail:* info@csuchico.edu.

California State University, Dominguez Hills

Carson, California

http://www.csudh.edu/

- **State-supported** comprehensive, founded 1960, part of California State University System
- **Urban** 350-acre campus with easy access to Los Angeles
- **Endowment** $11.0 million
- **Coed**
- **Moderately difficult** entrance level

FACULTY
Student/faculty ratio: 21:1.

ACADEMICS
Calendar: semesters. *Degrees:* bachelor's, master's, post-master's, and postbachelor's certificates.
Library: Leo F. Cain Educational Resource Center. *Books:* 457,885 (physical), 300,523 (digital/electronic); *Serial titles:* 6,542 (physical), 75,366 (digital/electronic); *Databases:* 94. Weekly public service hours: 81; students can reserve study rooms.

STUDENT LIFE
Housing options: men-only, women-only, special housing for students with disabilities. Campus housing is university owned. Freshman applicants given priority for college housing.

Activities and organizations: drama/theater group, student-run newspaper, radio station, choral group, American Marketing Association, Phi Sigma Sigma, Organization of African Studies, Latino Student Business Association, Circle K, national fraternities, national sororities.

Athletics Member NCAA. All Division II.

Campus security: 24-hour emergency response devices and patrols, student patrols, late-night transport/escort service.

Student services: health clinic, personal/psychological counseling, women's center, veterans affairs office.

COSTS & FINANCIAL AID
Costs (2018–19) *Tuition:* state resident $6937 full-time, $3330 per year part-time; nonresident $16,441 full-time, $396 per unit part-time. Full-

time tuition and fees vary according to course load, program, and reciprocity agreements. Part-time tuition and fees vary according to course load, program, and reciprocity agreements. *Required fees:* $1195 full-time, $1195 per year part-time. *Room and board:* $12,540. Room and board charges vary according to housing facility.

Financial Aid Of all full-time matriculated undergraduates who enrolled in 2018, 7,993 applied for aid, 7,738 were judged to have need, 100 had their need fully met. 208 Federal Work-Study jobs (averaging $2743). In 2018, 155 non-need-based awards were made. *Average percent of need met:* 31. *Average financial aid package:* $6131. *Average need-based loan:* $2364. *Average need-based gift aid:* $5210. *Average non-need-based aid:* $3765. *Average indebtedness upon graduation:* $15,512. *Financial aid deadline:* 5/10.

APPLYING
Standardized Tests *Required for some:* SAT or ACT (for admission).
Options: electronic application.
Application fee: $55.
Required: high school transcript.

CONTACT
Information Center, California State University, Dominguez Hills, 1000 East Victoria Street, Carson, CA 90747-0001. *Phone:* 310-243-3696. *E-mail:* info@csudh.edu.

California State University, East Bay
Hayward, California
http://www.csueastbay.edu/

- **State-supported** comprehensive, founded 1957, part of California State University System
- **Suburban** 343-acre campus with easy access to San Francisco Bay Area
- **Coed**
- **Minimally difficult** entrance level

FACULTY
Student/faculty ratio: 22:1.

ACADEMICS
Calendar: quarters. *Degrees:* certificates, bachelor's, master's, doctoral, and postbachelor's certificates.
Library: Hayward Campus Library. *Books:* 630,855 (physical), 233,485 (digital/electronic); *Serial titles:* 10,905 (physical), 107,791 (digital/electronic); *Databases:* 133. Weekly public service hours: 101; students can reserve study rooms.

STUDENT LIFE
Housing options: coed, special housing for students with disabilities. Campus housing is university owned and leased by the school. Freshman applicants given priority for college housing.

Activities and organizations: drama/theater group, student-run newspaper, choral group, marching band, Tau Sigma Hour Society, East Bay Student Nursing Association, Golden Key Honor Society, Black Student Union, Sigma Sigma Sigma Society, national fraternities, national sororities.

Athletics Member NCAA, NAIA. All NCAA Division II.

Campus security: 24-hour emergency response devices and patrols, student patrols, late-night transport/escort service, controlled dormitory access.

Student services: health clinic, personal/psychological counseling, veterans affairs office.

COSTS & FINANCIAL AID
Costs (2018–19) *Tuition:* state resident $5742 full-time, $3330 per term part-time; nonresident $18,714 full-time, $7290 per term part-time. Full-time tuition and fees vary according to program and reciprocity agreements. Part-time tuition and fees vary according to course load, program, and reciprocity agreements. *Required fees:* $1197 full-time, $364 per term part-time. *Room and board:* $13,980. Room and board charges vary according to board plan, housing facility, and student level.

Financial Aid Of all full-time matriculated undergraduates who enrolled in 2016, 7,847 applied for aid, 7,676 were judged to have need, 189 had their need fully met. *Average percent of need met:* 55. *Average financial aid package:* $10,778. *Average need-based loan:* $6352. *Average need-based gift aid:* $8545. *Average indebtedness upon graduation:* $19,149.

APPLYING
Standardized Tests *Required for some:* SAT or ACT (for admission).
Options: electronic application.
Application fee: $55.
Required: high school transcript, minimum 2.0 GPA, California State University eligibility index.

CONTACT
Dave Vasques, Associate Director for Admissions, California State University, East Bay, 25800 Carlos Bee Boulevard, Hayward, CA 94542-3000. *Phone:* 510-885-2029. *E-mail:* dave.vasquez@csueastbay.edu.

California State University, Fresno
Fresno, California
http://www.csufresno.edu/

CONTACT
Mr. Andy Hernandez, Admissions Officer, California State University, Fresno, 5150 North Maple Avenue, M/S JA 57, Fresno, CA 93740-8026. *Phone:* 559-278-6115. *Fax:* 559-278-4812. *E-mail:* andyhe@csufresno.edu.

California State University, Fullerton
Fullerton, California
http://www.fullerton.edu/

- **State-supported** comprehensive, founded 1957, part of California State University System
- **Suburban** 236-acre campus with easy access to Los Angeles
- **Endowment** $52.6 million
- **Coed** 34,751 undergraduate students, 80% full-time, 56% women, 44% men
- **Moderately difficult** entrance level, 43% of applicants were admitted

UNDERGRAD STUDENTS
27,907 full-time, 6,844 part-time. 1% are from out of state; 2% Black or African American, non-Hispanic/Latino; 44% Hispanic/Latino; 22% Asian, non-Hispanic/Latino; 0.2% Native Hawaiian or other Pacific Islander, non-Hispanic/Latino; 0.1% American Indian or Alaska Native, non-Hispanic/Latino; 4% Two or more races, non-Hispanic/Latino; 3% Race/ethnicity unknown; 6% international; 11% transferred in; 6% live on campus.

Freshmen:
Admission: 51,415 applied, 22,317 admitted, 4,408 enrolled. *Average high school GPA:* 3.7. *Test scores:* SAT evidence-based reading and writing scores over 500: 85%; SAT math scores over 500: 85%; ACT scores over 18: 86%; SAT evidence-based reading and writing scores over 600: 31%; SAT math scores over 600: 32%; ACT scores over 24: 32%; SAT evidence-based reading and writing scores over 700: 3%; SAT math scores over 700: 5%; ACT scores over 30: 4%.
Retention: 88% of full-time freshmen returned.

FACULTY
Total: 2,146, 46% full-time, 53% with terminal degrees.
Student/faculty ratio: 30:1.

ACADEMICS
Calendar: semesters. *Degrees:* bachelor's, master's, doctoral, post-master's, and postbachelor's certificates.

Special study options: academic remediation for entering students, adult/continuing education programs, advanced placement credit, cooperative education, distance learning, double majors, honors programs, independent study, internships, off-campus study, part-time degree program, services for LD students, student-designed majors, study abroad, summer session for credit. *ROTC:* Army (b).

Computers: 2,000 computers/terminals are available on campus for general student use. Students can access the following: campus intranet, computer help desk, free student e-mail accounts, online (class) grades, online (class) registration, online (class) schedules. Campuswide network is available. Wireless service is available via entire campus.
Library: Pollak Library.

STUDENT LIFE

Housing options: coed, men-only, women-only. Campus housing is university owned. Freshman applicants given priority for college housing.

Activities and organizations: drama/theater group, student-run newspaper, radio station, choral group, Pan-Hellenic Council, American Marketing Association, Lacrosse Club, Samaritans (volunteer service club), Human Services Student Association, national fraternities, national sororities.

Athletics Member NCAA. All Division I. *Intercollegiate sports:* archery M(c)/W(c), baseball M(s), basketball M(s)/W(s), bowling M(c)/W(c), cross-country running M(s)/W(s), equestrian sports M(c)/W(c), golf M(s)/W(s)(c), ice hockey M(c)/W(c), lacrosse M(c)/W(c), rugby M(c)/W(c), sailing M(c)/W(c), skiing (downhill) W(c), soccer M(s)/W(s), softball W(s), tennis W(s), track and field M(s)/W(s), ultimate Frisbee M(c)/W(c), volleyball M(c)/W(s), water polo M(c)/W(c). *Intramural sports:* badminton M/W, basketball M/W, bowling M/W, football M/W, racquetball M/W, soccer M/W, softball M/W, volleyball M/W.

Campus security: 24-hour emergency response devices and patrols, student patrols, late-night transport/escort service, controlled dormitory access.

Student services: health clinic, personal/psychological counseling, women's center, legal services.

COSTS & FINANCIAL AID

Costs (2019–20) *Tuition:* area resident $6895 full-time; state resident $6895 full-time; nonresident $16,399 full-time. *Required fees:* $1149 full-time.

Financial Aid Of all full-time matriculated undergraduates who enrolled in 2017, 22,093 applied for aid, 19,976 were judged to have need, 2,608 had their need fully met. In 2017, 814 non-need-based awards were made. *Average percent of need met:* 59. *Average financial aid package:* $10,978. *Average need-based loan:* $4328. *Average need-based gift aid:* $10,108. *Average non-need-based aid:* $1961. *Average indebtedness upon graduation:* $14,965.

APPLYING

Standardized Tests *Required:* SAT or ACT (for admission).

Options: electronic application.

Application fee: $55.

Required: high school transcript, minimum 2.0 GPA.

Application deadlines: 12/15 (freshmen), 11/30 (transfers).

Notification: continuous (freshmen), continuous (transfers).

CONTACT

Ms. Nancy J. Dority, Assistant Vice President of Enrollment Services, California State University, Fullerton, Office of Admissions and Records, PO Box 34080, Fullerton, CA 92834-9480. *Phone:* 657-278-3100. *Fax:* 657-278-7699. *E-mail:* admissions@fullerton.edu.

California State University, Long Beach

Long Beach, California

http://www.csulb.edu/

- **State-supported** comprehensive, founded 1949, part of California State University System
- **Suburban** 320-acre campus with easy access to Los Angeles
- **Endowment** $77.2 million
- **Coed** 31,447 undergraduate students, 87% full-time, 57% women, 43% men
- **Moderately difficult** entrance level, 31% of applicants were admitted

UNDERGRAD STUDENTS

27,462 full-time, 3,985 part-time. 1% are from out of state; 4% Black or African American, non-Hispanic/Latino; 43% Hispanic/Latino; 22% Asian, non-Hispanic/Latino; 0.3% Native Hawaiian or other Pacific Islander, non-Hispanic/Latino; 0.1% American Indian or Alaska Native, non-Hispanic/Latino; 5% Two or more races, non-Hispanic/Latino; 3% Race/ethnicity unknown; 6% international; 13% transferred in; 4% live on campus.

Freshmen:

Admission: 69,578 applied, 21,725 admitted, 4,912 enrolled. *Average high school GPA:* 3.6. *Test scores:* SAT evidence-based reading and writing scores over 500: 83%; SAT math scores over 500: 82%; ACT scores over 18: 88%; SAT evidence-based reading and writing scores over 600: 36%; SAT math scores over 600: 36%; ACT scores over 24: 46%; SAT evidence-based reading and writing scores over 700: 3%; SAT math scores over 700: 7%; ACT scores over 30: 8%.

Retention: 87% of full-time freshmen returned.

FACULTY

Total: 2,322, 45% full-time, 60% with terminal degrees.

Student/faculty ratio: 24:1.

ACADEMICS

Calendar: semesters. *Degrees:* bachelor's, master's, doctoral, and postbachelor's certificates.

Special study options: accelerated degree program, adult/continuing education programs, double majors, English as a second language, honors programs, independent study, internships, part-time degree program, student-designed majors, study abroad. *ROTC:* Army (b), Air Force (c).

Computers: 2,000 computers/terminals are available on campus for general student use. Students can access the following: campus intranet, computer help desk, free student e-mail accounts, online (class) grades, online (class) registration, online (class) schedules. Campuswide network is available. Wireless service is available via entire campus.

Library: CSULB University Library. *Books:* 681,649 (physical), 1.0 million (digital/electronic); *Serial titles:* 16,851 (physical), 105,038 (digital/electronic); *Databases:* 227. Weekly public service hours: 97.

STUDENT LIFE

Housing options: coed.

Activities and organizations: drama/theater group, student-run newspaper, radio and television station, choral group, national fraternities, national sororities.

Athletics Member NCAA. All Division I. *Intercollegiate sports:* archery M(c)/W(c), baseball M(s), basketball M(s)/W(s), bowling M(c)/W(c), cheerleading M(c)/W(c), crew M(c)/W(c), cross-country running M(s)/W(s), golf M(s)/W(s)(c), rugby M(c)/W(c), sailing M(c)/W(c), sand volleyball W(s), skiing (downhill) W(c), soccer M/W(s), softball W(s), tennis W(s), track and field M(s)/W(s), triathlon M(c)/W(c), ultimate Frisbee M(c)/W(c), volleyball M(s)/W(s), water polo M(s)/W(s), weight lifting M(c)/W(c), wrestling M(c)/W(c). *Intramural sports:* basketball M/W, cheerleading M/W, racquetball M/W, sand volleyball W, softball W, tennis W.

Campus security: 24-hour emergency response devices and patrols, student patrols, late-night transport/escort service, controlled dormitory access.

Student services: health clinic, personal/psychological counseling, women's center, legal services.

COSTS & FINANCIAL AID

Costs (2018–19) *Tuition:* state resident $5742 full-time, $3330 per year part-time; nonresident $16,038 full-time, $4752 per year part-time. Full-time tuition and fees vary according to course level, course load, degree level, and program. Part-time tuition and fees vary according to course level, course load, degree level, and program. *Required fees:* $1056 full-time, $1060 per year part-time. *Room and board:* $12,750; room only: $8200. Room and board charges vary according to board plan. *Payment plan:* installment. *Waivers:* senior citizens and employees or children of employees.

Financial Aid Of all full-time matriculated undergraduates who enrolled in 2018, 23,698 applied for aid, 21,943 were judged to have need, 9,879 had their need fully met. *Average percent of need met:* 78. *Average financial aid package:* $13,948. *Average need-based loan:* $4028. *Average need-based gift aid:* $7966. *Average indebtedness upon graduation:* $19,067. *Financial aid deadline:* 6/19.

APPLYING

Standardized Tests *Required:* SAT or ACT (for admission). *Recommended:* ACT (for admission).

Options: electronic application.

Application fee: $55.

Required: high school transcript. *Required for some:* minimum 3.0 GPA.

Notification: continuous (freshmen), continuous (transfers).

CONTACT
Mrs. Janice Miller, Director, Admin Ops and Policy, ES Admissions, California State University, Long Beach, Brotman Hall, 1250 Bellflower Boulevard, Long Beach, CA 90840. *Phone:* 562-985-7827. *E-mail:* janice.miller@csulb.edu.

California State University, Los Angeles

Los Angeles, California
http://www.calstatela.edu/

- **State-supported** comprehensive, founded 1947, part of California State University System
- **Urban** 175-acre campus with easy access to Los Angeles
- **Endowment** $32.9 million
- **Coed** 24,004 undergraduate students, 86% full-time, 57% women, 43% men
- **Moderately difficult** entrance level, 42% of applicants were admitted

UNDERGRAD STUDENTS
20,600 full-time, 3,404 part-time. 0.3% are from out of state; 3% Black or African American, non-Hispanic/Latino; 68% Hispanic/Latino; 13% Asian, non-Hispanic/Latino; 0.1% Native Hawaiian or other Pacific Islander, non-Hispanic/Latino; 0.1% American Indian or Alaska Native, non-Hispanic/Latino; 2% Two or more races, non-Hispanic/Latino; 2% Race/ethnicity unknown; 7% international; 12% transferred in; 10% live on campus.

Freshmen:
Admission: 39,854 applied, 16,548 admitted, 3,862 enrolled. *Average high school GPA:* 3.2. *Test scores:* SAT evidence-based reading and writing scores over 500: 47%; SAT math scores over 500: 48%; ACT scores over 18: 48%; SAT evidence-based reading and writing scores over 600: 9%; SAT math scores over 600: 8%; ACT scores over 24: 6%; SAT evidence-based reading and writing scores over 700: 1%; SAT math scores over 700: 1%; ACT scores over 30: 1%.
Retention: 82% of full-time freshmen returned.

FACULTY
Total: 1,712, 38% full-time, 3% with terminal degrees.
Student/faculty ratio: 24:1.

ACADEMICS
Calendar: quarters. *Degrees:* certificates, bachelor's, master's, doctoral, post-master's, and postbachelor's certificates.

Special study options: academic remediation for entering students, accelerated degree program, adult/continuing education programs, advanced placement credit, cooperative education, distance learning, double majors, English as a second language, freshman honors college, honors programs, independent study, internships, off-campus study, part-time degree program, services for LD students, student-designed majors, study abroad, summer session for credit. *ROTC:* Army (c), Air Force (c).

Unusual degree programs: 3-2 nursing.

Computers: 1,500 computers/terminals are available on campus for general student use. Students can access the following: campus intranet, computer help desk, free student e-mail accounts, online (class) grades, online (class) registration, online (class) schedules. Campuswide network is available. 100% of college-owned or -operated housing units are wired for high-speed Internet access. Wireless service is available via entire campus.
Library: John F. Kennedy Memorial Library. *Books:* 537,271 (physical), 86,220 (digital/electronic); *Serial titles:* 7,843 (physical), 83,822 (digital/electronic); *Databases:* 230. Weekly public service hours: 99.

STUDENT LIFE
Housing options: special housing for students with disabilities. Campus housing is university owned.

Activities and organizations: drama/theater group, student-run newspaper, radio and television station, choral group, Phi Alpha Theta History Honor Society, National Student Speech Language, Student Dietetic Association, Film Productions, Child Development Association, national fraternities, national sororities.

Athletics Member NCAA. All Division II. *Intercollegiate sports:* baseball M(s), basketball M(s)/W(s), cheerleading M(c)/W(c), cross-country running M(s)/W(s), golf W(s), sand volleyball W(s), soccer M(s)/W(s), tennis W(s), track and field M(s)/W(s), volleyball W(s). *Intramural sports:* basketball M/W, bowling M/W, football M/W, gymnastics M/W, racquetball M/W, skiing (cross-country) M/W, soccer M/W, softball M/W, swimming and diving M/W, volleyball M/W, water polo M/W, wrestling M.

Campus security: 24-hour emergency response devices and patrols, student patrols, late-night transport/escort service, controlled dormitory access.

Student services: health clinic, personal/psychological counseling, women's center, legal services, veterans affairs office.

COSTS & FINANCIAL AID
Costs (2019–20) *Tuition:* area resident $5742 full-time; state resident $5742 full-time; nonresident $17,622 full-time, $396 per unit part-time. *Required fees:* $1020 full-time. *Room and board:* $12,918; room only: $8785.

Financial Aid Of all full-time matriculated undergraduates who enrolled in 2017, 19,046 applied for aid, 18,495 were judged to have need, 941 had their need fully met. In 2017, 37 non-need-based awards were made. *Average percent of need met:* 70. *Average financial aid package:* $11,904. *Average need-based loan:* $4451. *Average need-based gift aid:* $11,560. *Average non-need-based aid:* $5495. *Average indebtedness upon graduation:* $17,024.

APPLYING
Standardized Tests *Required:* SAT or ACT (for admission).

Options: electronic application, early admission.

Application fee: $55.

Required: high school transcript.

Application deadlines: 11/30 (freshmen), 11/30 (out-of-state freshmen), 11/30 (transfers).

Early decision deadline: 11/30 (for plan 1), 11/30 (for plan 2).

Notification: 8/30 (freshmen), 4/1 (out-of-state freshmen), 8/30 (transfers).

CONTACT
Vince Lopez, Director of Outreach and Recruitment, California State University, Los Angeles, 5151 State University Drive, Los Angeles, CA 90032-8530. *Phone:* 323-343-3839. *E-mail:* admission@calstatela.edu.

California State University Maritime Academy

Vallejo, California
http://www.csum.edu/

- **State-supported** comprehensive, founded 1929, part of California State University System
- **Suburban** 64-acre campus with easy access to San Francisco
- **Coed**
- **Moderately difficult** entrance level

FACULTY
Student/faculty ratio: 16:1.

ACADEMICS
Calendar: semesters. *Degrees:* bachelor's and master's.

STUDENT LIFE
Housing options: on-campus residence required through senior year; coed. Campus housing is university owned. Freshman campus housing is guaranteed.

Activities and organizations: student-run newspaper, choral group, Sailing Club, Dive Club, drill team.

Athletics Member NAIA.

Campus security: 24-hour patrols, student patrols.

Student services: health clinic, personal/psychological counseling.

FINANCIAL AID
Financial Aid Of all full-time matriculated undergraduates who enrolled in 2018, 697 applied for aid, 499 were judged to have need, 34 had their need fully met. In 2018, 3 non-need-based awards were made. *Average*

financial aid package: $11,862. *Average need-based loan:* $4147. *Average need-based gift aid:* $8741. *Average non-need-based aid:* $6000. *Average indebtedness upon graduation:* $28,375.

APPLYING
Standardized Tests *Required:* SAT or ACT (for admission).
Options: electronic application, early action.
Application fee: $55.
Required: high school transcript, minimum 2.0 GPA, health form.

CONTACT
California State University Maritime Academy, 200 Maritime Academy Drive, Vallejo, CA 94590. *Phone:* 707-654-1330. *Toll-free phone:* 800-561-1945.

California State University, Monterey Bay

Seaside, California
http://www.csumb.edu/
- **State-supported** comprehensive, founded 1994, part of California State University System
- **Small-town** 1387-acre campus with easy access to San Jose
- **Coed** 6,717 undergraduate students, 90% full-time, 62% women, 38% men
- **Moderately difficult** entrance level, 59% of applicants were admitted

UNDERGRAD STUDENTS
6,052 full-time, 665 part-time. 2% are from out of state; 5% Black or African American, non-Hispanic/Latino; 41% Hispanic/Latino; 6% Asian, non-Hispanic/Latino; 1% Native Hawaiian or other Pacific Islander, non-Hispanic/Latino; 0.7% American Indian or Alaska Native, non-Hispanic/Latino; 8% Two or more races, non-Hispanic/Latino; 6% Race/ethnicity unknown; 6% international; 14% transferred in.

Freshmen:
Admission: 12,423 applied, 7,270 admitted, 1,000 enrolled. *Average high school GPA:* 3.4. *Test scores:* SAT evidence-based reading and writing scores over 500: 70%; SAT math scores over 500: 67%; ACT scores over 18: 72%; SAT evidence-based reading and writing scores over 600: 25%; SAT math scores over 600: 15%; ACT scores over 24: 23%; SAT evidence-based reading and writing scores over 700: 2%; SAT math scores over 700: 2%; ACT scores over 30: 2%.
Retention: 83% of full-time freshmen returned.

FACULTY
Total: 476, 35% full-time, 49% with terminal degrees.
Student/faculty ratio: 26:1.

ACADEMICS
Calendar: semesters. *Degrees:* bachelor's and master's.
Special study options: academic remediation for entering students, accelerated degree program, advanced placement credit, cooperative education, distance learning, double majors, independent study, internships, off-campus study, part-time degree program, services for LD students, student-designed majors, study abroad, summer session for credit. *ROTC:* Air Force (c).
Computers: Students can access the following: campus intranet, computer help desk, free student e-mail accounts, online (class) grades, online (class) registration, online (class) schedules. Campuswide network is available. 100% of college-owned or -operated housing units are wired for high-speed Internet access. Wireless service is available via entire campus.
Library: The Tanimura & Antle Family Memorial Library.

STUDENT LIFE
Housing options: on-campus residence required through sophomore year; coed, special housing for students with disabilities. Campus housing is university owned. Freshman applicants given priority for college housing.
Activities and organizations: drama/theater group, student-run newspaper, radio station, choral group, national fraternities, national sororities.
Athletics Member NCAA. All Division II. *Intercollegiate sports:* baseball M(s), basketball M(s)/W(s), cross-country running M(s)/W(s),

golf M(s), sailing M/W, soccer M(s)/W(s), softball W(s), volleyball W(s), water polo W(s). *Intramural sports:* basketball M/W, football M, soccer M/W, softball M/W, ultimate Frisbee M/W, volleyball M/W.
Campus security: 24-hour emergency response devices and patrols, student patrols, late-night transport/escort service, controlled dormitory access.
Student services: health clinic, personal/psychological counseling, women's center.

FINANCIAL AID
Financial Aid *Average indebtedness upon graduation:* $19,962. *Financial aid deadline:* 8/30.

APPLYING
Standardized Tests *Required:* SAT or ACT (for admission).
Options: electronic application, deferred entrance.
Application fee: $55.
Required: high school transcript, minimum 2.0 GPA.

CONTACT
California State University, Monterey Bay, 100 Campus Center, Seaside, CA 93955-8001.

California State University, Northridge

Northridge, California
http://www.csun.edu/
- **State-supported** comprehensive, founded 1958, part of California State University System
- **Urban** 356-acre campus with easy access to Los Angeles
- **Coed** 34,900 undergraduate students, 84% full-time, 54% women, 46% men
- **Moderately difficult** entrance level, 51% of applicants were admitted

UNDERGRAD STUDENTS
29,279 full-time, 5,621 part-time. 5% Black or African American, non-Hispanic/Latino; 49% Hispanic/Latino; 10% Asian, non-Hispanic/Latino; 0.1% Native Hawaiian or other Pacific Islander, non-Hispanic/Latino; 0.1% American Indian or Alaska Native, non-Hispanic/Latino; 3% Two or more races, non-Hispanic/Latino; 4% Race/ethnicity unknown; 8% international.

Freshmen:
Admission: 34,856 applied, 17,647 admitted, 4,804 enrolled. *Average high school GPA:* 3.4.
Retention: 80% of full-time freshmen returned.

FACULTY
Total: 2,093, 43% full-time.
Student/faculty ratio: 27:1.

ACADEMICS
Calendar: semesters. *Degrees:* bachelor's, master's, and doctoral.
Special study options: academic remediation for entering students, adult/continuing education programs, advanced placement credit, distance learning, double majors, English as a second language, independent study, internships, off-campus study, part-time degree program, services for LD students, student-designed majors, study abroad, summer session for credit. *ROTC:* Army (c), Air Force (c).
Computers: Students can access the following: online (class) registration. Campuswide network is available.
Library: Oviatt Library plus 1 other. Students can reserve study rooms.

STUDENT LIFE
Activities and organizations: drama/theater group, student-run newspaper, radio station, choral group, national fraternities, national sororities.
Athletics Member NCAA. All Division I except football (Division II). *Intercollegiate sports:* baseball M(s), basketball M(s)/W(s), cross-country running M(s)/W(s), football M(s), golf M(s), soccer M(s), softball W(s), swimming and diving M(s)/W(s), tennis W(s), track and field M(s)/W(s), volleyball M(s)/W(s). *Intramural sports:* baseball M, basketball M/W, bowling M(c)/W(c), cross-country running M/W, football M/W, golf M, ice hockey M(c), racquetball M/W, rugby M(c), sailing M(c)/W(c), skiing (downhill) M(c)/W(c), soccer M/W, softball W, swimming and diving

M/W, table tennis M(c)/W(c), tennis W, track and field M/W, volleyball M/W.

Campus security: 24-hour emergency response devices, late-night transport/escort service.

Student services: health clinic, personal/psychological counseling, women's center.

COSTS & FINANCIAL AID

Costs (2018–19) *Tuition:* state resident $6888 full-time; nonresident $396 per unit part-time. *Room and board:* $11,122. Room and board charges vary according to board plan and housing facility. *Payment plan:* installment. *Waivers:* senior citizens and employees or children of employees.

Financial Aid Of all full-time matriculated undergraduates who enrolled in 2018, 24,707 applied for aid, 24,011 were judged to have need. In 2018, 5015 non-need-based awards were made. *Average financial aid package:* $18,744. *Average need-based loan:* $5954. *Average need-based gift aid:* $16,923. *Average non-need-based aid:* $2445. *Average indebtedness upon graduation:* $16,876.

APPLYING

Standardized Tests *Required:* SAT or ACT (for admission).

Options: electronic application.

Application fee: $55.

Required: high school transcript.

Notification: continuous (freshmen), continuous (transfers).

CONTACT

David Dufault-Hunter, Director, Admissions and Records, California State University, Northridge, 18111 Nordhoff Street, Northridge, CA 91330. *Phone:* 818-677-3700. *Fax:* 818-677-7676. *E-mail:* admissions.records@csun.edu.

California State University, Sacramento

Sacramento, California

http://www.csus.edu/

- **State-supported** comprehensive, founded 1947, part of California State University System
- **Urban** 300-acre campus
- **Coed**
- **Moderately difficult** entrance level

FACULTY

Student/faculty ratio: 25:1.

ACADEMICS

Calendar: semesters. *Degrees:* bachelor's, master's, and doctoral.
Library: California State University, Sacramento Library. Students can reserve study rooms.

STUDENT LIFE

Housing options: coed, special housing for students with disabilities. Campus housing is university owned.

Activities and organizations: drama/theater group, student-run newspaper, radio station, choral group, marching band, national fraternities, national sororities.

Athletics Member NCAA. All Division I except football (Division I-AA).

Campus security: 24-hour emergency response devices and patrols, student patrols, late-night transport/escort service, controlled dormitory access.

Student services: health clinic, personal/psychological counseling, women's center, legal services, veterans affairs office.

COSTS & FINANCIAL AID

Costs (2018–19) *Tuition:* state resident $5742 full-time, $1665 per term part-time; nonresident $17,622 full-time, $396 per credit hour part-time. *Required fees:* $1192 full-time, $731 per term part-time. *Room and board:* $14,396; room only: $9774. Room and board charges vary according to board plan and housing facility.

Financial Aid Of all full-time matriculated undergraduates who enrolled in 2016, 19,743 applied for aid, 17,735 were judged to have need, 1,216

had their need fully met. In 2016, 37 non-need-based awards were made. *Average percent of need met:* 60. *Average financial aid package:* $10,572. *Average need-based loan:* $4136. *Average need-based gift aid:* $8712. *Average non-need-based aid:* $1675. *Average indebtedness upon graduation:* $20,052.

APPLYING

Standardized Tests *Required:* SAT or ACT (for admission).

Options: electronic application, early action.

Application fee: $55.

Required: minimum 2.0 GPA. *Required for some:* high school transcript.

CONTACT

Brian Henley, Director of Admissions and Outreach, California State University, Sacramento, 6000 J Street, Lassen Hall, Sacramento, CA 95819-6048. *Phone:* 916-278-7766. *Fax:* 916-278-5603. *E-mail:* admissions@csus.edu.

California State University, San Bernardino

San Bernardino, California

http://www.csusb.edu/

- **State-supported** comprehensive, founded 1965, part of California State University System
- **Suburban** 430-acre campus with easy access to Los Angeles
- **Coed** 17,854 undergraduate students, 90% full-time, 61% women, 39% men
- **Moderately difficult** entrance level, 55% of applicants were admitted

UNDERGRAD STUDENTS

16,110 full-time, 1,744 part-time. 5% Black or African American, non-Hispanic/Latino; 65% Hispanic/Latino; 5% Asian, non-Hispanic/Latino; 0.2% Native Hawaiian or other Pacific Islander, non-Hispanic/Latino; 0.2% American Indian or Alaska Native, non-Hispanic/Latino; 2% Two or more races, non-Hispanic/Latino; 4% Race/ethnicity unknown; 7% international; 14% transferred in; 6% live on campus.

Freshmen:
Admission: 16,042 applied, 8,798 admitted, 2,682 enrolled. *Average high school GPA:* 3.3. *Test scores:* SAT evidence-based reading and writing scores over 500: 52%; SAT math scores over 500: 52%; ACT scores over 18: 52%; SAT evidence-based reading and writing scores over 600: 9%; SAT math scores over 600: 7%; ACT scores over 24: 5%; SAT math scores over 700: 1%.

Retention: 86% of full-time freshmen returned.

FACULTY

Total: 1,022, 46% full-time, 46% with terminal degrees.
Student/faculty ratio: 28:1.

ACADEMICS

Calendar: quarters. *Degrees:* certificates, bachelor's, master's, doctoral, and postbachelor's certificates.

Special study options: academic remediation for entering students, accelerated degree program, advanced placement credit, cooperative education, distance learning, double majors, honors programs, independent study, internships, off-campus study, part-time degree program, services for LD students, student-designed majors, study abroad, summer session for credit. *ROTC:* Army (b), Air Force (b).

Computers: Students can access the following: computer help desk, free student e-mail accounts, online (class) grades, online (class) registration, online (class) schedules. Campuswide network is available. Wireless service is available via entire campus.
Library: Pfau Library.

STUDENT LIFE

Housing options: coed, women-only, special housing for students with disabilities. Campus housing is university owned and is provided by a third party. Freshman applicants given priority for college housing.

Activities and organizations: drama/theater group, student-run newspaper, radio and television station, choral group, national fraternities, national sororities.

Athletics Member NCAA. All Division II. *Intercollegiate sports:* baseball M(s), basketball M(s)/W(s), cross-country running W, golf M(s), soccer M(s)/W(s), softball W(s), track and field W, volleyball W(s).

Campus security: 24-hour emergency response devices and patrols, student patrols, late-night transport/escort service.

Student services: health clinic, personal/psychological counseling, women's center, legal services, veterans affairs office.

COSTS & FINANCIAL AID

Costs (2018–19) *Tuition:* state resident $5472 full-time; nonresident $11,880 full-time, $264 per credit hour part-time. *Required fees:* $1184 full-time. *Room and board:* $12,711. Room and board charges vary according to board plan and housing facility. *Payment plan:* installment. *Waivers:* senior citizens and employees or children of employees.

Financial Aid Of all full-time matriculated undergraduates who enrolled in 2018, 14,493 applied for aid, 13,679 were judged to have need, 1,866 had their need fully met. 366 Federal Work-Study jobs (averaging $3643). In 2018, 41 non-need-based awards were made. *Average percent of need met:* 66. *Average financial aid package:* $9569. *Average need-based loan:* $4091. *Average need-based gift aid:* $9611. *Average non-need-based aid:* $4637. *Average indebtedness upon graduation:* $21,605.

APPLYING

Standardized Tests *Recommended:* SAT or ACT (for admission).

Options: electronic application, early admission, early action.

Application fee: $55.

Required: high school transcript, minimum 2.0 GPA.

Application deadlines: rolling (freshmen), rolling (transfers).

Notification: continuous (freshmen), continuous (transfers).

CONTACT

Julie Rogers, Assistant Director of Admissions and Evaluations, California State University, San Bernardino, 5500 University Parkway, University Hall, Room 115, San Bernardino, CA 92407-2397. *Phone:* 909-537-5211. *Fax:* 909-537-7034. *E-mail:* moreinfo@mail.csusb.edu.

California State University, San Marcos

San Marcos, California

http://www.csusm.edu/

- **State-supported** comprehensive, founded 1990, part of California State University System
- **Suburban** 304-acre campus with easy access to San Diego
- **Coed** 13,962 undergraduate students, 82% full-time, 61% women, 39% men
- **Moderately difficult** entrance level, 58% of applicants were admitted

UNDERGRAD STUDENTS

11,400 full-time, 2,562 part-time. 4% are from out of state; 3% Black or African American, non-Hispanic/Latino; 47% Hispanic/Latino; 9% Asian, non-Hispanic/Latino; 0.2% Native Hawaiian or other Pacific Islander, non-Hispanic/Latino; 0.3% American Indian or Alaska Native, non-Hispanic/Latino; 5% Two or more races, non-Hispanic/Latino; 4% Race/ethnicity unknown; 5% international; 15% transferred in; 80% live on campus.

Freshmen:
Admission: 17,648 applied, 10,311 admitted, 2,472 enrolled. *Average high school GPA:* 3.4. *Test scores:* SAT evidence-based reading and writing scores over 500: 56%; SAT math scores over 500: 89%; ACT scores over 18: 71%; SAT evidence-based reading and writing scores over 600: 33%; SAT math scores over 600: 22%; ACT scores over 24: 15%; ACT scores over 30: 1%.
Retention: 77% of full-time freshmen returned.

FACULTY

Total: 907, 32% full-time.

Student/faculty ratio: 26:1.

ACADEMICS

Calendar: semesters. *Degrees:* bachelor's and master's.

Special study options: academic remediation for entering students, adult/continuing education programs, advanced placement credit, distance learning, double majors, English as a second language, independent study, internships, off-campus study, part-time degree program, services for LD students, student-designed majors, study abroad, summer session for credit. *ROTC:* Army (c), Navy (c), Air Force (c).

Computers: Students can access the following: computer help desk, free student e-mail accounts, online (class) registration. Campuswide network is available.

Library: Kellogg Library. *Books:* 215,402 (physical), 268,189 (digital/electronic); *Serial titles:* 3,130 (physical), 81,643 (digital/electronic); *Databases:* 100. Weekly public service hours: 100; students can reserve study rooms.

STUDENT LIFE

Housing options: special housing for students with disabilities. Campus housing is provided by a third party.

Activities and organizations: drama/theater group, student-run newspaper, choral group, national fraternities, national sororities.

Athletics Member NCAA. All Division I. *Intercollegiate sports:* baseball M, basketball M/W, cross-country running M/W, golf M/W(c), soccer M/W, softball W, track and field M/W, volleyball W.

Campus security: 24-hour emergency response devices and patrols, student patrols, late-night transport/escort service.

Student services: health clinic, personal/psychological counseling, women's center, veterans affairs office.

COSTS & FINANCIAL AID

Costs (2019–20) *Tuition:* state resident $5742 full-time; nonresident $15,246 full-time. *Room and board:* $13,227.

Financial Aid Of all full-time matriculated undergraduates who enrolled in 2017, 9,047 applied for aid, 8,017 were judged to have need, 413 had their need fully met. In 2017, 10 non-need-based awards were made. *Average percent of need met:* 42. *Average financial aid package:* $11,052. *Average need-based loan:* $4111. *Average need-based gift aid:* $9495. *Average non-need-based aid:* $3251. *Average indebtedness upon graduation:* $24,304.

APPLYING

Standardized Tests *Required:* SAT or ACT (for admission).

Options: electronic application.

Application fee: $55.

Required: high school transcript.

Notification: continuous (freshmen), continuous (transfers).

CONTACT

Scott Hagg, Director of Admissions, California State University, San Marcos, 333 South Twin Oaks Valley Road, San Marcos, CA 92096-0001. *Phone:* 760-750-4848. *Fax:* 760-750-3248. *E-mail:* apply@csusm.edu.

California State University, Stanislaus

Turlock, California

http://www.csustan.edu/

- **State-supported** comprehensive, founded 1957, part of California State University System
- **Suburban** 228-acre campus
- **Endowment** $11.6 million
- **Coed**
- **Moderately difficult** entrance level

FACULTY

Student/faculty ratio: 23:1.

ACADEMICS

Calendar: semesters. *Degrees:* bachelor's, master's, and doctoral.

Library: Vasche Library. *Books:* 514,045 (physical), 8,002 (digital/electronic); *Serial titles:* 634 (physical), 60,803 (digital/electronic); *Databases:* 187. Weekly public service hours: 90; students can reserve study rooms.

STUDENT LIFE

Housing options: coed. Campus housing is university owned and leased by the school.

Activities and organizations: drama/theater group, student-run newspaper, radio station, choral group, Alpha Xi Delta, Phi Sigma Sigma,

Kappa Sigma, Tau Kappa Epsilon, Theta Chi, national fraternities, national sororities.

Athletics Member NCAA. All Division II.

Campus security: 24-hour emergency response devices and patrols, student patrols, late-night transport/escort service, controlled dormitory access.

Student services: health clinic, personal/psychological counseling, women's center.

COSTS & FINANCIAL AID

Costs (2018–19) *Tuition:* state resident $5742 full-time; nonresident $18,956 full-time. Full-time tuition and fees vary according to reciprocity agreements. Part-time tuition and fees vary according to reciprocity agreements. *Required fees:* $1334 full-time. *Room and board:* $10,542; room only: $6827. Room and board charges vary according to board plan and housing facility.

Financial Aid Of all full-time matriculated undergraduates who enrolled in 2018, 6,463 applied for aid, 5,951 were judged to have need, 1,980 had their need fully met. 23 Federal Work-Study jobs (averaging $4000). In 2018, 259 non-need-based awards were made. *Average percent of need met:* 84. *Average financial aid package:* $17,568. *Average need-based loan:* $4008. *Average need-based gift aid:* $10,673. *Average non-need-based aid:* $3422. *Average indebtedness upon graduation:* $21,214.

APPLYING

Standardized Tests *Required for some:* SAT or ACT (for admission).

Options: electronic application.

Application fee: $55.

Required for some: high school transcript. *Recommended:* minimum 3.0 GPA.

CONTACT

Student Outreach, California State University, Stanislaus, One University Circle, Turlock, CA 95382. *Phone:* 209-667-3070. *Toll-free phone:* 800-300-7420. *Fax:* 209-667-3394. *E-mail:* outreach_help_desk@csustan.edu.

California University of Management and Sciences

Anaheim, California

http://www.calums.edu/

CONTACT

California University of Management and Sciences, 721 North Euclid Street, Anaheim, CA 92801.

Chamberlain College of Nursing

Rancho Cordova, California

http://www.chamberlain.edu/

CONTACT

Chamberlain College of Nursing, 10971 Sun Center Drive, Rancho Cordova, CA 95670.

Chapman University

Orange, California

http://www.chapman.edu/

- **Independent** comprehensive, founded 1861, affiliated with Christian Church (Disciples of Christ)
- **Suburban** 78-acre campus with easy access to Los Angeles
- **Endowment** $352.6 million
- **Coed**
- **Very difficult** entrance level

FACULTY

Student/faculty ratio: 14:1.

ACADEMICS

Calendar: 4-1-4. *Degrees:* bachelor's, master's, and doctoral.
Library: Leatherby Libraries plus 1 other. *Books:* 339,051 (physical), 17,371 (digital/electronic); *Serial titles:* 267 (physical), 69,372 (digital/electronic); *Databases:* 287. Weekly public service hours: 127; students can reserve study rooms.

STUDENT LIFE

Housing options: coed, special housing for students with disabilities. Campus housing is university owned. Freshman campus housing is guaranteed.

Activities and organizations: drama/theater group, student-run newspaper, radio station, choral group, national fraternities, national sororities.

Athletics Member NCAA. All Division III.

Campus security: 24-hour emergency response devices and patrols, late-night transport/escort service, controlled dormitory access, full safety education program.

Student services: health clinic, personal/psychological counseling.

COSTS & FINANCIAL AID

Costs (2018–19) *Comprehensive fee:* $68,552 includes full-time tuition ($52,340), mandatory fees ($384), and room and board ($15,828). Part-time tuition: $1625 per credit hour. Part-time tuition and fees vary according to course load. *College room only:* $10,900. Room and board charges vary according to board plan and housing facility. *Payment plans:* tuition prepayment, installment, deferred payment.

Financial Aid Of all full-time matriculated undergraduates who enrolled in 2017, 4,208 applied for aid, 3,711 were judged to have need, 491 had their need fully met. 2,167 Federal Work-Study jobs (averaging $2874). In 2017, 394 non-need-based awards were made. *Average percent of need met:* 72. *Average financial aid package:* $34,629. *Average need-based loan:* $4444. *Average need-based gift aid:* $18,322. *Average non-need-based aid:* $17,454. *Average indebtedness upon graduation:* $28,374.

APPLYING

Standardized Tests *Required:* SAT or ACT (for admission). *Recommended:* SAT Subject Tests (for admission).

Options: electronic application, early decision, early action.

Application fee: $70.

Required: essay or personal statement, high school transcript, 1 letter of recommendation. *Required for some:* audition for music, dance, and theatre majors; portfolio for art and film majors; supplemental application for all talent-based majors.

CONTACT

Ms. Marcela Mejia-Martinez, Director of Undergraduate Admission, Chapman University, One University Drive, Orange, CA 92866. *Phone:* 714-997-6711. *Toll-free phone:* 888-CUAPPLY. *Fax:* 714-997-6713. *E-mail:* admit@chapman.edu.

Charles R. Drew University of Medicine and Science

Los Angeles, California

http://www.cdrewu.edu/

- **Independent** comprehensive, founded 1966
- **Urban** 11-acre campus with easy access to Los Angeles
- **Endowment** $90.0 million
- **Coed**
- **Moderately difficult** entrance level

FACULTY

Student/faculty ratio: 10:1.

ACADEMICS

Calendar: semesters. *Degrees:* associate, bachelor's, master's, doctoral, post-master's, and postbachelor's certificates.
Library: Health Sciences Library. *Books:* 6,436 (physical), 3,500 (digital/electronic); *Serial titles:* 596 (physical), 11,765 (digital/electronic); *Databases:* 38. Weekly public service hours: 91; students can reserve study rooms.

STUDENT LIFE

Housing options: Campus housing is provided by a third party.

Activities and organizations: Student Government, Critical Exploration of Academic Literature (CEAL), Charles R. Drew University Alumni Association, Pre-Health Society, Pre-Dental Society.

Campus security: 24-hour emergency response devices, late-night transport/escort service.

Student services: personal/psychological counseling.

COSTS & FINANCIAL AID

Costs (2018–19) *One-time required fee:* $100. *Comprehensive fee:* $27,166 includes full-time tuition ($13,872) and room and board ($13,294). Full-time tuition and fees vary according to course load, degree level, and program. Part-time tuition: $578 per unit. Part-time tuition and fees vary according to course load, degree level, and program.

Financial Aid *Financial aid deadline:* 7/31.

APPLYING

Standardized Tests *Required for some:* SAT or ACT (for admission).

Options: electronic application, early admission, early decision, early action, deferred entrance.

Application fee: $35.

Required: essay or personal statement, high school transcript, minimum 2.0 GPA. *Required for some:* pre-admission assessment exams.

CONTACT

Charles R. Drew University of Medicine and Science, 1731 East 120th Street, Los Angeles, CA 90059.

Claremont McKenna College

Claremont, California

http://www.cmc.edu/

- **Independent** comprehensive, founded 1946
- **Suburban** 69-acre campus with easy access to Los Angeles
- **Endowment** $835.3 million
- **Coed** 1,324 undergraduate students, 100% full-time, 48% women, 52% men
- **Most difficult** entrance level, 9% of applicants were admitted

UNDERGRAD STUDENTS

1,321 full-time, 3 part-time. Students come from 49 states and territories; 43 other countries; 54% are from out of state; 4% Black or African American, non-Hispanic/Latino; 15% Hispanic/Latino; 11% Asian, non-Hispanic/Latino; 0.1% Native Hawaiian or other Pacific Islander, non-Hispanic/Latino; 6% Two or more races, non-Hispanic/Latino; 6% Race/ethnicity unknown; 16% international; 0.8% transferred in; 96% live on campus.

Freshmen:

Admission: 6,272 applied, 584 admitted, 325 enrolled. *Test scores:* SAT evidence-based reading and writing scores over 500: 100%; SAT math scores over 500: 100%; ACT scores over 18: 100%; SAT evidence-based reading and writing scores over 600: 99%; SAT math scores over 600: 97%; ACT scores over 24: 99%; SAT evidence-based reading and writing scores over 700: 57%; SAT math scores over 700: 64%; ACT scores over 30: 90%.

Retention: 96% of full-time freshmen returned.

FACULTY

Total: 179, 88% full-time, 98% with terminal degrees.

Student/faculty ratio: 8:1.

ACADEMICS

Calendar: semesters. *Degrees:* bachelor's and master's.

Special study options: advanced placement credit, double majors, honors programs, independent study, internships, off-campus study, services for LD students, student-designed majors, study abroad. *ROTC:* Army (b), Air Force (c).

Unusual degree programs: 3-2 engineering with Columbia University, Harvey Mudd College.

Computers: 220 computers/terminals are available on campus for general student use. Students can access the following: campus intranet, computer help desk, free student e-mail accounts, online (class) grades, online (class) registration, online (class) schedules. Campuswide network is available. 100% of college-owned or -operated housing units are wired for high-speed Internet access. Wireless service is available via entire campus.

Library: Claremont Colleges Library plus 2 others. *Books:* 1.0 million (physical), 2.2 million (digital/electronic); *Serial titles:* 28,182 (physical),

81,005 (digital/electronic); *Databases:* 490. Weekly public service hours: 111; students can reserve study rooms.

STUDENT LIFE

Housing options: on-campus residence required for freshman year; coed. Campus housing is university owned. Freshman campus housing is guaranteed.

Activities and organizations: drama/theater group, student-run newspaper, radio station, choral group, Associated Students of Claremont McKenna College, College Programming Board, Asian Pacific American Mentoring Program (APAM).

Athletics Member NCAA. All Division III. *Intercollegiate sports:* archery M(c)/W(c), badminton M(c)/W(c), baseball M, basketball M/W, cross-country running M/W, equestrian sports M(c)/W(c), fencing M(c)/W(c), field hockey M(c)/W(c), football M, golf M/W, ice hockey M(c)/W(c), lacrosse M(c)/W, racquetball M(c)/W(c), rock climbing M(c)/W(c), rugby M(c)/W(c), sand volleyball M(c)/W(c), skiing (downhill) M(c)/W(c), soccer M/W, softball W, squash M(c)/W(c), swimming and diving M/W, tennis M/W, track and field M/W, ultimate Frisbee M(c)/W(c), volleyball M(c)/W, water polo M/W. *Intramural sports:* badminton M/W, basketball M/W, football M/W, sand volleyball M/W, soccer M/W, table tennis M/W, tennis M(c)/W(c), ultimate Frisbee M/W, volleyball M/W, water polo M/W.

Campus security: 24-hour emergency response devices and patrols, student patrols, late-night transport/escort service, controlled dormitory access.

Student services: health clinic, personal/psychological counseling.

COSTS & FINANCIAL AID

Costs (2019–20) *Comprehensive fee:* $73,775 includes full-time tuition ($56,190), mandatory fees ($285), and room and board ($17,300). Part-time tuition: $9365 per course. *College room only:* $9300.

Financial Aid Of all full-time matriculated undergraduates who enrolled in 2018, 574 applied for aid, 532 were judged to have need, 529 had their need fully met. In 2018, 86 non-need-based awards were made. *Average percent of need met:* 100. *Average financial aid package:* $52,467. *Average need-based loan:* $4060. *Average need-based gift aid:* $48,754. *Average non-need-based aid:* $18,788. *Average indebtedness upon graduation:* $19,355. *Financial aid deadline:* 2/1.

APPLYING

Standardized Tests *Required:* SAT or ACT (for admission). *Required for some:* SAT Subject Tests (for admission), TOEFL or IELTS for students for whom English is not their first language and the primary language of instruction in high school was not English.

Options: electronic application, early decision, deferred entrance.

Application fee: $70.

Required: essay or personal statement, high school transcript, 3 letters of recommendation. *Recommended:* interview.

Early decision deadline: 11/1 (for plan 1), 1/5 (for plan 2).

Notification: 4/1 (freshmen), 12/15 (early decision plan 1), 2/15 (early decision plan 2).

CONTACT

Ms. Jennifer Sandoval-Dancs, Director of Admission, Claremont McKenna College, Office of Admission and Financial Aid, 888 Columbia Avenue, Claremont, CA 91711. *Phone:* 909-621-8088. *Fax:* 909-621-8516. *E-mail:* jennifer.sandoval@cmc.edu.

Cogswell Polytechnical College

San Jose, California

http://www.cogswell.edu/

- **Proprietary** comprehensive, founded 1887
- **Suburban** 2-acre campus with easy access to San Francisco, San Jose
- **Coed**
- **Moderately difficult** entrance level

FACULTY

Student/faculty ratio: 13:1.

ACADEMICS

Calendar: semesters. *Degrees:* bachelor's and master's.

Library: Cogswell College Library. *Books:* 5,007 (physical); *Serial titles:* 920 (physical); *Databases:* 14.

STUDENT LIFE
Housing options: coed. Campus housing is provided by a third party. Freshman applicants given priority for college housing.

Activities and organizations: choral group, ASB, Game Development club, Audio Production and Engineering club, Comic Club, E-Sports.

Campus security: 24-hour emergency response devices.

Student services: personal/psychological counseling.

COSTS & FINANCIAL AID
Costs (2018–19) *Tuition:* $19,056 full-time, $794 per credit part-time. Full-time tuition and fees vary according to course load. Part-time tuition and fees vary according to course load. *Required fees:* $1000 full-time, $500 per term part-time. *Room only:* $11,000. Room and board charges vary according to housing facility.

Financial Aid Of all full-time matriculated undergraduates who enrolled in 2015, 17 Federal Work-Study jobs (averaging $2328).

APPLYING
Standardized Tests *Recommended:* SAT or ACT (for admission).

Options: electronic application, deferred entrance.

Required: essay or personal statement, high school transcript, minimum 2.0 GPA. *Required for some:* letters of recommendation, portfolio for Digital Art and Animation, Digital Audio Technology and Game Design Art majors. *Recommended:* minimum 2.7 GPA, interview.

CONTACT
Richard Henson, Director of Admissions, Cogswell Polytechnical College, 191 Baypointe Parkway, San Jose, CA 95134. *Phone:* 408-498-5103 Ext. 103. *Toll-free phone:* 800-264-7955. *Fax:* 408-747-0764. *E-mail:* rhenson@cogswell.edu.

The Colburn School Conservatory of Music
Los Angeles, California
http://www.colburnschool.edu/

CONTACT
Ms. Jessica Cameron, Manager of Admissions, The Colburn School Conservatory of Music, 200 South Grand Avenue, Los Angeles, CA 90012. *Phone:* 213-621-4534. *Fax:* 213-625-0371. *E-mail:* admissions@ colburnschool.edu.

Columbia College Hollywood
Tarzana, California
http://www.columbiacollege.edu/

CONTACT
Carmen Munoz, Admissions Director, Columbia College Hollywood, 18618 Oxnard Street, Tarzana, CA 91356. *Phone:* 818-345-8414 Ext. 203. *Toll-free phone:* 800-785-0585. *Fax:* 818-345-9053. *E-mail:* admissions@columbiacollege.edu.

Concordia University Irvine
Irvine, California
http://www.cui.edu/
- **Independent** comprehensive, founded 1972, affiliated with Lutheran Church–Missouri Synod, part of The Concordia University System
- **Suburban** 70-acre campus with easy access to Los Angeles
- **Endowment** $35.1 million
- **Coed** 1,808 undergraduate students, 93% full-time, 62% women, 38% men
- **Moderately difficult** entrance level, 62% of applicants were admitted

UNDERGRAD STUDENTS
1,680 full-time, 128 part-time. Students come from 40 states and territories; 32 other countries; 18% are from out of state; 5% Black or African American, non-Hispanic/Latino; 24% Hispanic/Latino; 8% Asian, non-Hispanic/Latino; 0.4% Native Hawaiian or other Pacific Islander, non-Hispanic/Latino; 0.4% American Indian or Alaska Native, non-Hispanic/Latino; 8% Two or more races, non-Hispanic/Latino; 0.4% Race/ethnicity unknown; 5% international; 8% transferred in; 47% live on campus.

Freshmen:
Admission: 3,995 applied, 2,468 admitted, 319 enrolled. *Average high school GPA:* 3.5. *Test scores:* SAT evidence-based reading and writing scores over 500: 84%; SAT math scores over 500: 80%; ACT scores over 18: 90%; SAT evidence-based reading and writing scores over 600: 34%; SAT math scores over 600: 27%; ACT scores over 24: 44%; SAT evidence-based reading and writing scores over 700: 7%; SAT math scores over 700: 3%; ACT scores over 30: 14%.

Retention: 78% of full-time freshmen returned.

FACULTY
Total: 458, 24% full-time, 36% with terminal degrees.

Student/faculty ratio: 17:1.

ACADEMICS
Calendar: semesters. *Degrees:* associate, bachelor's, master's, doctoral, and postbachelor's certificates (associate's degree for international students only).

Special study options: academic remediation for entering students, accelerated degree program, adult/continuing education programs, advanced placement credit, distance learning, double majors, honors programs, independent study, internships, off-campus study, part-time degree program, services for LD students, study abroad, summer session for credit. *ROTC:* Army (c).

Computers: 64 computers/terminals are available on campus for general student use. Students can access the following: computer help desk, free student e-mail accounts, online (class) grades, online (class) registration, online (class) schedules. Campuswide network is available. 100% of college-owned or -operated housing units are wired for high-speed Internet access. Wireless service is available via entire campus.

Library: Concordia University Library. *Books:* 72,408 (physical), 196,626 (digital/electronic); *Serial titles:* 42 (physical), 22,390 (digital/electronic); *Databases:* 40. Weekly public service hours: 89.

STUDENT LIFE
Housing options: on-campus residence required for freshman year; coed, women-only, special housing for students with disabilities. Campus housing is university owned. Freshman campus housing is guaranteed.

Activities and organizations: drama/theater group, student-run newspaper, choral group, intramurals, Screaming Eagles, Lacrosse, Abbey West, LEAD Student Activities.

Athletics Member NCAA. All Division II. *Intercollegiate sports:* baseball M(s), basketball M(s)/W(s), cross-country running M(s)/W(s), lacrosse M(s)(c)/W(s)(c), sand volleyball W(s), soccer M(s)/W(s), softball W(s), swimming and diving M(s)/W(s), tennis M(s)/W(s), track and field M(s)/W(s), volleyball M(s)/W(s), water polo M(s)/W(s). *Intramural sports:* basketball M/W, bowling M/W, cheerleading M(c)/W(c), football M/W, soccer M/W, softball M/W, track and field M/W, ultimate Frisbee M/W, volleyball M/W.

Campus security: 24-hour emergency response devices and patrols, student patrols, late-night transport/escort service.

Student services: health clinic, personal/psychological counseling.

COSTS & FINANCIAL AID
Costs (2019–20) *Comprehensive fee:* $48,610 includes full-time tuition ($35,990), mandatory fees ($750), and room and board ($11,870). Part-time tuition: $1056 per credit. *College room only:* $6840.

Financial Aid Of all full-time matriculated undergraduates who enrolled in 2018, 1,304 applied for aid, 1,144 were judged to have need, 161 had their need fully met. 76 Federal Work-Study jobs (averaging $2582). In 2018, 328 non-need-based awards were made. *Average percent of need met:* 63. *Average financial aid package:* $23,749. *Average need-based loan:* $4541. *Average need-based gift aid:* $21,116. *Average non-need-based aid:* $11,757. *Average indebtedness upon graduation:* $31,516. *Financial aid deadline:* 3/2.

APPLYING
Standardized Tests *Required:* SAT or ACT (for admission).

Options: electronic application, early action, deferred entrance.

Application fee: $50.

Required: high school transcript. *Recommended:* essay or personal statement, minimum 2.8 GPA, 1 letter of recommendation, interview.

Application deadlines: 7/27 (freshmen), 7/27 (out-of-state freshmen), 7/27 (transfers), 2/15 (early action).

Notification: continuous (freshmen), continuous (out-of-state freshmen), continuous (transfers), 3/1 (early action).

CONTACT
Ms. Susan Park, Director of Undergraduate Admissions, Concordia University Irvine, 1530 Concordia West, Irvine, CA 92612-3299. *Phone:* 800-229-1200. *Toll-free phone:* 800-229-1200. *Fax:* 949-214-3520. *E-mail:* admission@cui.edu.

Design Institute of San Diego
San Diego, California
http://www.disd.edu/

- **Proprietary** 4-year, founded 1977
- **Urban** campus with easy access to San Diego
- **Coed**
- 50% of applicants were admitted

FACULTY
Student/faculty ratio: 9:1.

ACADEMICS
Calendar: semesters. *Degree:* bachelor's.
Library: DISD Library. *Books:* 6,179 (physical); *Serial titles:* 84 (physical). Weekly public service hours: 56.

STUDENT LIFE
Housing options: college housing not available.
Activities and organizations: ASID Student Chapter, IIDA Student Chapter, Student Mentor Program, Student Ambassador.
Campus security: security guard patrols during the semester from 5:30 - 10:30 pm Monday through Thursday, no classes on Friday past 5:00 pm.
Student services: veterans affairs office.

COSTS
Costs (2018–19) *One-time required fee:* $139. *Tuition:* $23,850 full-time, $994 per unit part-time. Full-time tuition and fees vary according to class time, course load, and program. Part-time tuition and fees vary according to class time, course load, and program. *Required fees:* $10 full-time, $10 per year part-time. *Payment plans:* installment, deferred payment.

APPLYING
Options: electronic application, early decision.
Required: essay or personal statement, high school transcript, 2 letters of recommendation. *Required for some:* official transcripts from all colleges attended. *Recommended:* minimum 2.0 GPA, interview.

CONTACT
Mr. Christopher Pfeil, Admissions, Design Institute of San Diego, 8555 Commerce Avenue, San Diego, CA 92121. *Phone:* 858-566-1200 Ext. 1025. *Toll-free phone:* 800-619-4337. *Fax:* 858-566-2711. *E-mail:* admissions@disd.edu.

DeVry University–Folsom Campus
Folsom, California
http://www.devry.edu/

CONTACT
DeVry University–Folsom Campus, 950 Iron Point Road, Folsom, CA 95630. *Toll-free phone:* 866-338-7934.

DeVry University–Fremont Campus
Fremont, California
http://www.devry.edu/

CONTACT
Admissions Office, DeVry University–Fremont Campus, 6600 Dumbarton Circle, Fremont, CA 94555. *Phone:* 510-574-1200. *Toll-free phone:* 866-338-7934.

DeVry University–Long Beach Campus
Long Beach, California
http://www.devry.edu/

CONTACT
Admissions Office, DeVry University–Long Beach Campus, 3880 Kilroy Airport Way, Long Beach, CA 90806. *Phone:* 562-427-0861. *Toll-free phone:* 866-338-7934.

DeVry University–Pomona Campus
Pomona, California
http://www.devry.edu/

CONTACT
DeVry University–Pomona Campus, 901 Corporate Center Drive, Pomona, CA 91768. *Phone:* 909-622-8866. *Toll-free phone:* 866-338-7934.

DeVry University–San Diego Campus
San Diego, California
http://www.devry.edu/

CONTACT
Admissions Office, DeVry University–San Diego Campus, 2655 Camino Del Rio North, Suite 350, San Diego, CA 92108-1633. *Phone:* 619-683-2446. *Toll-free phone:* 866-338-7934.

DeVry University–Sherman Oaks Campus
Sherman Oaks, California
http://www.devry.edu/

CONTACT
Admissions Office, DeVry University–Sherman Oaks Campus, 15301 Ventura Boulevard, D-100, Sherman Oaks, CA 91403. *Phone:* 818-713-8111. *Toll-free phone:* 866-338-7934.

Dominican University of California
San Rafael, California
http://www.dominican.edu/

- **Independent** comprehensive, founded 1890, affiliated with Roman Catholic Church
- **Suburban** 85-acre campus with easy access to San Francisco
- **Endowment** $28.3 million
- **Coed**
- **Moderately difficult** entrance level

FACULTY
Student/faculty ratio: 9:1.

ACADEMICS
Calendar: semesters. *Degrees:* bachelor's and master's.
Library: Archbishop Alemany Library. *Books:* 110,523 (physical); *Databases:* 84.

STUDENT LIFE
Housing options: coed, special housing for students with disabilities. Campus housing is university owned. Freshman applicants given priority for college housing.
Activities and organizations: drama/theater group, student-run newspaper, radio station, choral group, Filipino Cultural Club, BSU, Perceptions, Global Ambassadors, Intramural Club/Programming.
Athletics Member NCAA. All Division II.
Campus security: 24-hour patrols, late-night transport/escort service, controlled dormitory access.
Student services: health clinic, personal/psychological counseling.

COSTS & FINANCIAL AID

Costs (2018–19) *Comprehensive fee:* $59,340 includes full-time tuition ($44,240), mandatory fees ($450), and room and board ($14,650). Full-time tuition and fees vary according to course load. Part-time tuition: $1850 per credit hour. Part-time tuition and fees vary according to course load. *Required fees:* $150 per term part-time. *College room only:* $8280. Room and board charges vary according to board plan.

Financial Aid Of all full-time matriculated undergraduates who enrolled in 2017, 1,105 applied for aid, 896 were judged to have need, 104 had their need fully met. 188 Federal Work-Study jobs (averaging $1878). 15 state and other part-time jobs (averaging $13,234). In 2017, 204 non-need-based awards were made. *Average percent of need met:* 67. *Average financial aid package:* $32,182. *Average need-based loan:* $4606. *Average need-based gift aid:* $25,688. *Average non-need-based aid:* $18,548. *Average indebtedness upon graduation:* $52,559.

APPLYING

Standardized Tests *Required:* SAT or ACT (for admission).

Options: electronic application, deferred entrance.

Required: essay or personal statement, high school transcript, minimum 2.0 GPA, 1 letter of recommendation. *Recommended:* interview.

CONTACT

Mr. Rich Toledo, Assistant Vice President, Undergraduate Admissions, Dominican University of California, 50 Acacia Avenue, San Rafael, CA 94901-2298. *Phone:* 415-485-3206. *Toll-free phone:* 888-323-6763. *Fax:* 415-485-3287. *E-mail:* rich.toledo@dominican.edu.

Epic Bible College
Sacramento, California
http://epic.edu/

CONTACT

Ms. Sheila Knoll, Assistant Director of Records, Epic Bible College, 4330 Auburn Boulevard, Sacramento, CA 95841. *Phone:* 916-348-4689. *E-mail:* kclarke@tlbc.edu.

Feather River College
Quincy, California
http://www.frc.edu/

- **District-supported** primarily 2-year, founded 1968, part of California Community College System
- **Rural** 420-acre campus
- **Endowment** $48,167
- **Coed**
- **Noncompetitive** entrance level

FACULTY
Student/faculty ratio: 21:1.

ACADEMICS
Calendar: semesters plus summer and winter terms. *Degrees:* certificates, diplomas, associate, and bachelor's.
Library: Feather River College Library. *Books:* 24,291 (physical), 350,000 (digital/electronic); *Serial titles:* 98 (physical), 28,376 (digital/electronic); *Databases:* 35. Weekly public service hours: 61; students can reserve study rooms.

STUDENT LIFE
Housing options: coed. Campus housing is provided by a third party.

Activities and organizations: drama/theater group, choral group, Phi Theta Kappa Honor Society, International and Cultural Club, Horse Show Team, Student Environmental Association, Student Alliance for Equity.

Campus security: student patrols, part-time private security company patrols.

Student services: health clinic, personal/psychological counseling.

COSTS & FINANCIAL AID
Costs (2018–19) *Tuition:* state resident $1380 full-time, $46 per credit part-time; nonresident $8430 full-time, $281 per credit part-time. Full-time tuition and fees vary according to course load. Part-time tuition and fees vary according to course load. *Required fees:* $81 full-time, $2 per credit part-time, $18 per term part-time. *Room only:* $5350. Room and board charges vary according to housing facility.

Financial Aid Of all full-time matriculated undergraduates who enrolled in 2017, 22 Federal Work-Study jobs (averaging $750). 103 state and other part-time jobs (averaging $1504).

APPLYING
Standardized Tests *Recommended:* ACCUPLACER.

Options: electronic application.

CONTACT
Mrs. Leslie Mikesell, Director of Admissions and Records, Feather River College, 570 Golden Eagle Avenue, Quincy, CA 95971. *Phone:* 530-283-0202 Ext. 285. *Toll-free phone:* 800-442-9799. *E-mail:* info@frc.edu.

FIDM/Fashion Institute of Design & Merchandising, Los Angeles Campus
Los Angeles, California
http://www.fidm.edu/

- **Proprietary** 4-year, founded 1969, part of FIDM/Fashion Institute of Design & Merchandising
- **Urban** campus with easy access to Los Angeles
- **Coed** 2,154 undergraduate students, 99% full-time, 90% women, 10% men
- **Moderately difficult** entrance level, 53% of applicants were admitted

UNDERGRAD STUDENTS
2,140 full-time, 14 part-time. 50% are from out of state.

Freshmen:
Admission: 1,728 applied, 915 admitted, 546 enrolled.

FACULTY
Student/faculty ratio: 13:1.

ACADEMICS
Calendar: quarters. *Degrees:* associate and bachelor's (also includes Orange County Campus).

Special study options: academic remediation for entering students, accelerated degree program, adult/continuing education programs, advanced placement credit, cooperative education, distance learning, English as a second language, independent study, internships, off-campus study, part-time degree program, services for LD students, study abroad, summer session for credit.

Computers: 433 computers/terminals and 20 ports are available on campus for general student use. Students can access the following: campus intranet, computer help desk, free student e-mail accounts, online (class) grades, online (class) registration, online (class) schedules. Campuswide network is available. Wireless service is available via classrooms, computer centers, computer labs, learning centers, libraries, student centers.
Library: FIDM Los Angeles Campus Library. *Books:* 48,534 (physical), 2,778 (digital/electronic); *Serial titles:* 548 (physical); *Databases:* 39. Students can reserve study rooms.

STUDENT LIFE
Housing options: college housing not available.

Activities and organizations: Cross-Cultural Student Alliance, Fashion Industry Club, Phi Theta Kappa Honor Society, Student Council, FIDM MODE Magazine.

Campus security: 24-hour emergency response devices and patrols, late-night transport/escort service.

Student services: personal/psychological counseling, veterans affairs office.

COSTS
Costs (2019–20) *Tuition:* $31,015 full-time. *Required fees:* $1295 full-time.

APPLYING
Standardized Tests *Recommended:* SAT and SAT Subject Tests or ACT (for admission).

Options: electronic application, deferred entrance.

Application fee: $25.

Required: essay or personal statement, high school transcript, minimum 2.5 GPA, 3 letters of recommendation, interview, major-determined project.

Application deadlines: rolling (freshmen), rolling (out-of-state freshmen), rolling (transfers).

Notification: continuous (freshmen), continuous (out-of-state freshmen), continuous (transfers).

CONTACT
Ms. Susan Aronson, Executive Director of Admissions, FIDM/Fashion Institute of Design & Merchandising, Los Angeles Campus, 919 South Grand Avenue, Los Angeles, CA 90015. *Phone:* 213-624-1200 Ext. 5400. *Toll-free phone:* 800-624-1200. *E-mail:* saronson@fidm.edu.

FIDM/Fashion Institute of Design & Merchandising, San Francisco Campus

San Francisco, California
http://www.fidm.edu/

- **Proprietary** 4-year, founded 1973, part of FIDM/Fashion Institute of Design & Merchandising
- **Urban** campus with easy access to San Francisco
- **Coed**
- **Moderately difficult** entrance level

FACULTY
Student/faculty ratio: 7:1.

ACADEMICS
Calendar: quarters. *Degrees:* associate and bachelor's.
Library: FIDM San Francisco Library. Students can reserve study rooms.

STUDENT LIFE
Housing options: college housing not available.
Activities and organizations: Cross-Cultural Student Alliance, Fashion Industry Club, Phi Theta Kappa- National Honor Society, Student Council, FIDM MODE Magazine.
Campus security: 24-hour emergency response devices and patrols, security escorts.
Student services: personal/psychological counseling, veterans affairs office.

COSTS
Costs (2018–19) *Tuition:* $32,075 full-time, $685 per credit hour part-time. Full-time tuition and fees vary according to degree level and program. Part-time tuition and fees vary according to degree level and program. *Required fees:* $1152 full-time.

APPLYING
Standardized Tests *Recommended:* SAT or ACT (for admission).
Options: electronic application, deferred entrance.
Application fee: $225.
Required: essay or personal statement, high school transcript, minimum 2.5 GPA, 3 letters of recommendation, interview, major-determined project.

CONTACT
Ms. Sheryl Badalamenti, Director of Admissions, FIDM/Fashion Institute of Design & Merchandising, San Francisco Campus, 55 Stockton Street, San Francisco, CA 94108-5829. *Phone:* 415-433-6691 Ext. 1550. *Toll-free phone:* 800-422-3436. *E-mail:* sbadalamenti@fidm.edu.

Fremont College

Cerritos, California
http://www.fremont.edu/

CONTACT
Natasha Dawson, Director of Admissions, Fremont College, 18000 Studebaker Road, Suite 900A, Cerritos, CA 90703. *Phone:* 562-809-5100. *Toll-free phone:* 800-373-6668. *Fax:* 562-809-5100. *E-mail:* info@fremont.edu.

Fresno Pacific University

Fresno, California
http://www.fresno.edu/

CONTACT
Andy Johnson, Director of Undergraduate Admissions, Fresno Pacific University, 1717 South Chestnut Avenue, Fresno, CA 93727. *Phone:* 559-453-2000. *Toll-free phone:* 800-660-6089. *Fax:* 559-453-2007. *E-mail:* andy.johnson@fresno.edu.

Gnomon School of Visual Effects

Hollywood, California
http://www.gnomon.edu/

CONTACT
Gnomon School of Visual Effects, 1015 N. Cahuenga Boulevard, Suite 54301, Hollywood, CA 90038.

Golden Gate University

San Francisco, California
http://www.ggu.edu/

- **Independent** university, founded 1901
- **Urban** campus with easy access to San Francisco Bay Area
- **Endowment** $29.8 million
- **Coed**
- **Moderately difficult** entrance level

FACULTY
Student/faculty ratio: 16:1.

ACADEMICS
Calendar: trimesters. *Degrees:* certificates, associate, bachelor's, master's, doctoral, and postbachelor's certificates.
Library: Golden Gate University Library plus 1 other. *Books:* 43,127 (physical), 15,700 (digital/electronic); *Serial titles:* 55,000 (digital/electronic); *Databases:* 116. Weekly public service hours: 90; students can reserve study rooms.

STUDENT LIFE
Housing options: college housing not available.
Activities and organizations: student-run newspaper, American Marketing Association, Korean Student Association, Japanese Student Association, Thai Student Association, Computing Society.
Campus security: late-night transport/escort service.
Student services: personal/psychological counseling.

FINANCIAL AID
Financial Aid Of all full-time matriculated undergraduates who enrolled in 2013, 299 applied for aid, 239 were judged to have need, 49 had their need fully met. 18 Federal Work-Study jobs (averaging $5000). In 2013, 49 non-need-based awards were made. *Average percent of need met:* 20. *Average financial aid package:* $10,350. *Average need-based loan:* $5500. *Average need-based gift aid:* $3750. *Average non-need-based aid:* $3750.

APPLYING
Options: electronic application, deferred entrance.
Application fee: $55.
Required: high school transcript, minimum 2.0 GPA. *Required for some:* minimum 3.2 GPA, interview. *Recommended:* essay or personal statement, minimum 3.0 GPA.

CONTACT
Mr. Louis D. Riccardi Jr., Director of Enrollment Services, Golden Gate University, 536 Mission Street, San Francisco, CA 94105-2968. *Phone:* 415-442-7800. *Toll-free phone:* 800-448-3381. *Fax:* 415-442-7807. *E-mail:* info@ggu.edu.

Grace Mission University

Fullerton, California

http://www.gm.edu/

CONTACT
Grace Mission University, 1645 West Valencia Drive, Fullerton, CA 92833.

Gurnick Academy of Medical Arts

San Mateo, California

http://www.gurnick.edu/

- **Proprietary** primarily 2-year
- **Coed**

ACADEMICS
Degrees: certificates, diplomas, associate, and bachelor's.

CONTACT
Gurnick Academy of Medical Arts, 2121 South El Camino Real, Building C 2000, San Mateo, CA 94403.

Harvey Mudd College

Claremont, California

http://www.hmc.edu/

- **Independent** 4-year, founded 1955, part of The Claremont Colleges
- **Suburban** 33-acre campus with easy access to Los Angeles
- **Endowment** $298.9 million
- **Coed**
- **Most difficult** entrance level

FACULTY
Student/faculty ratio: 8:1.

ACADEMICS
Calendar: semesters. *Degree:* bachelor's.
Library: Claremont Colleges Library plus 1 other.

STUDENT LIFE
Housing options: on-campus residence required for freshman year; coed. Campus housing is university owned. Freshman campus housing is guaranteed.
Activities and organizations: drama/theater group, student-run newspaper, radio station, choral group, Claremont Colleges Ballroom Dance Company, Science Bus, Society of Women Engineers (SWE), Intervarsity Christian Fellowship, Gonzo Unicycle Madness (Unicycle Club).
Athletics Member NCAA. All Division III.
Campus security: 24-hour emergency response devices and patrols, late-night transport/escort service, controlled dormitory access.
Student services: health clinic, personal/psychological counseling, women's center.

COSTS & FINANCIAL AID
Costs (2018–19) *One-time required fee:* $250. *Comprehensive fee:* $74,753 includes full-time tuition ($56,331), mandatory fees ($295), and room and board ($18,127). Part-time tuition: $1760 per unit. Part-time tuition and fees vary according to course load. *College room only:* $9888. Room and board charges vary according to board plan.
Financial Aid Of all full-time matriculated undergraduates who enrolled in 2017, 485 applied for aid, 411 were judged to have need, 411 had their need fully met. In 2017, 158 non-need-based awards were made. *Average percent of need met:* 100. *Average financial aid package:* $45,484. *Average need-based loan:* $5605. *Average need-based gift aid:* $42,182. *Average non-need-based aid:* $15,800. *Average indebtedness upon graduation:* $31,594. *Financial aid deadline:* 2/1.

APPLYING
Standardized Tests *Required:* SAT or ACT (for admission), SAT Subject Tests (for admission).
Options: electronic application, early admission, early decision, deferred entrance.
Application fee: $70.

Required: essay or personal statement, high school transcript, 3 letters of recommendation. *Recommended:* interview.

CONTACT
Harvey Mudd College, 301 Platt Boulevard, Claremont, CA 91711-5994.

Holy Names University

Oakland, California

http://www.hnu.edu/

- **Independent Roman Catholic** comprehensive, founded 1868
- **Urban** 60-acre campus with easy access to San Francisco
- **Coed**
- **Moderately difficult** entrance level

FACULTY
Student/faculty ratio: 8:1.

ACADEMICS
Calendar: semesters. *Degrees:* certificates, bachelor's, master's, post-master's, and postbachelor's certificates.
Library: Cushing Library. *Books:* 41,811 (physical), 137,046 (digital/electronic); *Databases:* 49. Students can reserve study rooms.

STUDENT LIFE
Housing options: coed. Campus housing is university owned. Freshman campus housing is guaranteed.
Activities and organizations: drama/theater group, choral group, Drama Club, Latinos Unidos, Black Student Union, Biology Club, Hiking Club.
Athletics Member NCAA. All Division II.
Campus security: 24-hour emergency response devices, late-night transport/escort service, controlled dormitory access, 24-hour security main gate.
Student services: personal/psychological counseling.

COSTS & FINANCIAL AID
Costs (2018–19) *Comprehensive fee:* $52,506 includes full-time tuition ($38,800), mandatory fees ($516), and room and board ($13,190). Full-time tuition and fees vary according to course level, course load, degree level, program, and reciprocity agreements. Part-time tuition: $1331 per unit. Part-time tuition and fees vary according to course level, course load, degree level, program, and reciprocity agreements. *Required fees:* $258 per term part-time. *College room only:* $6812. Room and board charges vary according to board plan and housing facility.
Financial Aid Of all full-time matriculated undergraduates who enrolled in 2006, 373 applied for aid, 247 were judged to have need, 58 had their need fully met. 50 Federal Work-Study jobs (averaging $1699). 53 state and other part-time jobs (averaging $1750). In 2006, 77 non-need-based awards were made. *Average percent of need met:* 43. *Average financial aid package:* $15,554. *Average need-based loan:* $4154. *Average need-based gift aid:* $13,258. *Average non-need-based aid:* $10,557. *Average indebtedness upon graduation:* $10,500. *Financial aid deadline:* 6/30.

APPLYING
Standardized Tests *Required:* SAT or ACT (for admission).
Options: electronic application, deferred entrance.
Application fee: $20.
Required: essay or personal statement, high school transcript, 1 letter of recommendation, minimum 1 recommendation. *Required for some:* interview.

CONTACT
Holy Names University, 3500 Mountain Boulevard, Oakland, CA 94619. *Phone:* 510-436-1351. *Toll-free phone:* 800-430-1321. *Fax:* 510-436-1325. *E-mail:* admissions@hnu.edu.

See next page for display ad and page 1024 for the College Close-Up.

Homestead Schools

Torrance, California

http://www.homesteadschools.com/

CONTACT
Homestead Schools, 23844 Hawthorne Boulevard, Suite 200, Torrance, CA 90505.

Hope International University

Fullerton, California

http://www.hiu.edu/

- **Independent** comprehensive, founded 1928, affiliated with Christian Churches and Churches of Christ
- **Suburban** 16-acre campus with easy access to Los Angeles
- **Coed**
- **Moderately difficult** entrance level

FACULTY
Student/faculty ratio: 9:1.

ACADEMICS
Calendar: 4-1-4. *Degrees:* certificates, associate, bachelor's, master's, and postbachelor's certificates.
Library: Darling Library.

STUDENT LIFE
Housing options: on-campus residence required through sophomore year; men-only, women-only. Campus housing is university owned. Freshman campus housing is guaranteed.

Activities and organizations: drama/theater group, student-run newspaper, choral group, Campus Ministries, International Student Organization, Musical Theater, Student Government, Student Publications.

Athletics Member NAIA, NCCAA.

Campus security: 24-hour emergency response devices and patrols, late-night transport/escort service, controlled dormitory access.

Student services: personal/psychological counseling.

COSTS & FINANCIAL AID
Costs (2018–19) *Comprehensive fee:* $43,890 includes full-time tuition ($32,250), mandatory fees ($1150), and room and board ($10,490). Full-time tuition and fees vary according to course level, course load, degree level, location, program, and reciprocity agreements. Part-time tuition: $1465 per credit hour. Part-time tuition and fees vary according to course level, course load, degree level, location, program, and reciprocity

agreements. *College room only:* $5000. Room and board charges vary according to board plan.
Financial Aid Of all full-time matriculated undergraduates who enrolled in 2017, 325 applied for aid, 310 were judged to have need, 7 had their need fully met. In 2017, 15 non-need-based awards were made. *Average percent of need met:* 30. *Average financial aid package:* $28,415. *Average need-based loan:* $2863. *Average need-based gift aid:* $10,971. *Average non-need-based aid:* $4747. *Average indebtedness upon graduation:* $33,016.

APPLYING
Standardized Tests *Required:* SAT or ACT (for admission).
Options: electronic application.
Application fee: $40.
Required: essay or personal statement, high school transcript, minimum 2.5 GPA, 2 letters of recommendation, rank in upper 50% of high school class. *Required for some:* interview.

CONTACT
Hope International University, 2500 East Nutwood Avenue, Fullerton, CA 92831-3138. *Toll-free phone:* 866-722-HOPE.

Humboldt State University

Arcata, California

http://www.humboldt.edu/

- **State-supported** comprehensive, founded 1913, part of California State University System
- **Rural** 161-acre campus
- **Coed** 7,195 undergraduate students, 93% full-time, 57% women, 43% men
- **Minimally difficult** entrance level, 75% of applicants were admitted

UNDERGRAD STUDENTS
6,700 full-time, 495 part-time. Students come from 51 states and territories; 33 other countries; 6% are from out of state; 4% Black or African American, non-Hispanic/Latino; 35% Hispanic/Latino; 3% Asian, non-Hispanic/Latino; 0.3% Native Hawaiian or other Pacific Islander, non-Hispanic/Latino; 1% American Indian or Alaska Native, non-

Hispanic/Latino; 7% Two or more races, non-Hispanic/Latino; 6% Race/ethnicity unknown; 1% international; 14% transferred in; 26% live on campus.

Freshmen:
Admission: 10,957 applied, 8,230 admitted, 1,051 enrolled. *Average high school GPA:* 3.3. *Test scores:* SAT evidence-based reading and writing scores over 500: 70%; SAT math scores over 500: 68%; ACT scores over 18: 76%; SAT evidence-based reading and writing scores over 600: 28%; SAT math scores over 600: 16%; ACT scores over 24: 29%; SAT evidence-based reading and writing scores over 700: 3%; SAT math scores over 700: 2%; ACT scores over 30: 3%.
Retention: 71% of full-time freshmen returned.

FACULTY
Total: 548, 44% full-time, 57% with terminal degrees.
Student/faculty ratio: 22:1.

ACADEMICS
Calendar: semesters. *Degrees:* bachelor's, master's, post-master's, and postbachelor's certificates.
Special study options: academic remediation for entering students, adult/continuing education programs, advanced placement credit, cooperative education, distance learning, double majors, English as a second language, honors programs, independent study, internships, off-campus study, part-time degree program, services for LD students, student-designed majors, study abroad, summer session for credit.
Computers: 1,098 computers/terminals are available on campus for general student use. Students can access the following: campus intranet, computer help desk, free student e-mail accounts, online (class) grades, online (class) registration, online (class) schedules. Campuswide network is available. 100% of college-owned or -operated housing units are wired for high-speed Internet access. Wireless service is available via entire campus.
Library: Humbolot State University Library. *Books:* 487,338 (physical), 165,816 (digital/electronic); *Serial titles:* 34,235 (physical), 190 (digital/electronic); *Databases:* 89. Weekly public service hours: 100; students can reserve study rooms.

STUDENT LIFE
Housing options: coed. Campus housing is university owned. Freshman campus housing is guaranteed.
Activities and organizations: drama/theater group, student-run newspaper, radio station, choral group, marching band, Bicycle Learning Center, Campus Center for Appropriate Technology (CCAT), Youth Educational Services, HOLA, MECHA, national fraternities, national sororities.
Athletics Member NCAA. All Division II. *Intercollegiate sports:* basketball M(s)/W(s), cheerleading M(c)/W(c), crew M(c)/W, cross-country running M(s)/W(s), lacrosse M(c)/W(c), soccer M(s)/W(s), softball W(s), track and field M(s)/W(s), volleyball W(s). *Intramural sports:* archery M(c)/W(c), baseball M(c), basketball M/W, fencing M(c), field hockey W(c), rugby M(c)/W(c), soccer M/W, ultimate Frisbee M(c)/W(c), volleyball M(c), water polo M(c).
Campus security: 24-hour emergency response devices and patrols, late-night transport/escort service, controlled dormitory access.
Student services: health clinic, personal/psychological counseling, women's center, veterans affairs office.

COSTS & FINANCIAL AID
Costs (2019–20) Tuition: state resident $5742 full-time, $3330 per term part-time; nonresident $17,622 full-time, $396 per credit part-time.
Required fees: $1934 full-time, $1492 part-time. *Room and board:* $13,562; room only: $6216.
Financial Aid Of all full-time matriculated undergraduates who enrolled in 2017, 6,381 applied for aid, 5,747 were judged to have need, 407 had their need fully met. In 2017, 331 non-need-based awards were made. *Average percent of need met:* 67. *Average financial aid package:* $13,985. *Average need-based loan:* $7072. *Average need-based gift aid:* $9147. *Average non-need-based aid:* $933. *Average indebtedness upon graduation:* $23,368.

APPLYING
Standardized Tests *Required for some:* SAT or ACT (for admission).
Options: electronic application, deferred entrance.

Application fee: $55.
Required: high school transcript, minimum 2.0 GPA.
Notification: continuous (freshmen), continuous (transfers).
CONTACT
Mr. Steven Ladwig, Associate Director of Admissions, Humboldt State University, 1 Harpst Street, Arcata, CA 95521. *Phone:* 707-826-4402. *Toll-free phone:* 866-850-9556. *Fax:* 707-826-6190. *E-mail:* hsuinfo@humboldt.edu.

Humphreys University
Stockton, California
http://www.humphreys.edu/
CONTACT
Humphreys University, 6650 Inglewood Avenue, Stockton, CA 95207-3896. *Phone:* 209-235-2901.

Interior Designers Institute
Newport Beach, California
http://www.idi.edu/
CONTACT
Interior Designers Institute, 1061 Camelback Road, Newport Beach, CA 92660.

John F. Kennedy University
Pleasant Hill, California
http://www.jfku.edu/
CONTACT
Ms. Jen Miller-Hogg, Director of Admissions, John F. Kennedy University, 100 Ellinwood Way, Pleasant Hill, CA 94523-4817. *Phone:* 925-969-3584. *Toll-free phone:* 800-696-JFKU. *E-mail:* jmhogg@jfku.edu.

John Paul the Great Catholic University
Escondido, California
http://www.jpcatholic.edu/
- **Independent** comprehensive, founded 2006, affiliated with Roman Catholic Church
- **Urban** 3-acre campus with easy access to San Diego
- **Coed** 286 undergraduate students, 94% full-time, 43% women, 57% men
- **Moderately difficult** entrance level, 90% of applicants were admitted

UNDERGRAD STUDENTS
268 full-time, 18 part-time. Students come from 35 states and territories; 4 other countries; 48% are from out of state; 2% Black or African American, non-Hispanic/Latino; 26% Hispanic/Latino; 3% Asian, non-Hispanic/Latino; 0.7% Native Hawaiian or other Pacific Islander, non-Hispanic/Latino; 4% Two or more races, non-Hispanic/Latino; 14% Race/ethnicity unknown; 3% international; 9% transferred in; 77% live on campus.

Freshmen:
Admission: 220 applied, 199 admitted, 85 enrolled. *Average high school GPA:* 3.4. *Test scores:* SAT evidence-based reading and writing scores over 500: 74%; SAT math scores over 500: 63%; ACT scores over 18: 92%; SAT evidence-based reading and writing scores over 600: 50%; SAT math scores over 600: 26%; ACT scores over 24: 50%; SAT evidence-based reading and writing scores over 700: 8%; SAT math scores over 700: 3%; ACT scores over 30: 17%.
Retention: 80% of full-time freshmen returned.

FACULTY
Total: 41, 20% full-time, 22% with terminal degrees.
Student/faculty ratio: 15:1.

ACADEMICS
Calendar: quarters. *Degrees:* bachelor's and master's.

Special study options: advanced placement credit, distance learning, double majors, independent study, internships, part-time degree program, study abroad, summer session for credit.

Computers: 35 computers/terminals are available on campus for general student use. Students can access the following: computer help desk. Campuswide network is available. 100% of college-owned or -operated housing units are wired for high-speed Internet access. Wireless service is available via entire campus.

Library: John Paul the Great Catholic University Library. *Books:* 21,325 (physical).

STUDENT LIFE

Housing options: on-campus residence required through senior year; men-only, women-only. Campus housing is leased by the school. Freshman campus housing is guaranteed.

Activities and organizations: drama/theater group, student-run newspaper, choral group, Student government, Knights of Columbus, Flag football, Swing dance club, Gaming club.

Campus security: student patrols.

Student services: personal/psychological counseling.

COSTS & FINANCIAL AID

Costs (2019–20) *Tuition:* $26,100 full-time, $700 per credit part-time. No tuition increase for student's term of enrollment. *Required fees:* $900 full-time. *Room only:* $7710.

Financial Aid Of all full-time matriculated undergraduates who enrolled in 2017, 200 applied for aid, 178 were judged to have need, 13 had their need fully met. In 2017, 65 non-need-based awards were made. *Average percent of need met:* 46. *Average financial aid package:* $18,249. *Average need-based loan:* $4227. *Average need-based gift aid:* $14,829. *Average non-need-based aid:* $8447.

APPLYING

Standardized Tests *Required for some:* SAT or ACT (for admission).

Options: electronic application, deferred entrance.

Application fee: $50.

Required: essay or personal statement, high school transcript, minimum 2.6 GPA. *Recommended:* interview.

Application deadlines: rolling (freshmen), rolling (transfers).

Notification: continuous (freshmen), continuous (transfers).

CONTACT

Mr. Martin Harold, Vice President of Admissions, John Paul the Great Catholic University, 220 W. Grand Avenue, Escondido, CA 92025. *Phone:* 858-653-6740 Ext. 1101. *Fax:* 858-653-3791. *E-mail:* mharold@jpcatholic.com.

Laguna College of Art & Design

Laguna Beach, California

http://www.lcad.edu/

- **Independent** comprehensive, founded 1962
- **Small-town** 9-acre campus with easy access to Los Angeles
- **Endowment** $1.7 million
- **Coed**
- **Very difficult** entrance level

FACULTY

Student/faculty ratio: 12:1.

ACADEMICS

Calendar: semesters. *Degrees:* certificates, bachelor's, master's, and postbachelor's certificates.

Library: Dennis and Leslie Power Library plus 1 other. Weekly public service hours: 54.

STUDENT LIFE

Housing options: coed. Campus housing is leased by the school. Freshman applicants given priority for college housing.

Campus security: 24-hour patrols, late-night transport/escort service.

Student services: personal/psychological counseling.

COSTS & FINANCIAL AID

Costs (2018–19) *Tuition:* $30,700 full-time, $1267 per unit part-time. Full-time tuition and fees vary according to course load and degree level.

Part-time tuition and fees vary according to course load and degree level. *Room only:* $10,000.

Financial Aid Of all full-time matriculated undergraduates who enrolled in 2018, 636 applied for aid, 636 were judged to have need. 30 Federal Work-Study jobs (averaging $1666). *Average indebtedness upon graduation:* $38,000.

APPLYING

Standardized Tests *Recommended:* SAT or ACT (for admission).

Options: early admission, deferred entrance.

Application fee: $45.

Required: essay or personal statement, high school transcript, minimum 2.5 GPA, portfolio. *Required for some:* 2 letters of recommendation, interview.

CONTACT

Madison Keyes, Admissions Coordinator, Laguna College of Art & Design, 2222 Laguna Canyon Road, Laguna Beach, CA 92651. *Phone:* 949-376-6000 Ext. 248. *Toll-free phone:* 800-255-0762. *E-mail:* mkeyes@lcad.edu.

La Sierra University

Riverside, California

http://www.lasierra.edu/

- **Independent Seventh-day Adventist** comprehensive, founded 1922, part of Seventh-Day Adventist Education System
- **Suburban** 150-acre campus with easy access to Los Angeles
- **Endowment** $17.2 million
- **Coed** 1,842 undergraduate students, 89% full-time, 60% women, 40% men
- **Minimally difficult** entrance level, 49% of applicants were admitted

UNDERGRAD STUDENTS

1,647 full-time, 195 part-time. Students come from 48 states and territories; 138 other countries; 11% are from out of state; 7% Black or African American, non-Hispanic/Latino; 47% Hispanic/Latino; 17% Asian, non-Hispanic/Latino; 1% Native Hawaiian or other Pacific Islander, non-Hispanic/Latino; 0.3% American Indian or Alaska Native, non-Hispanic/Latino; 4% Two or more races, non-Hispanic/Latino; 0.1% Race/ethnicity unknown; 11% international; 8% transferred in; 25% live on campus.

Freshmen:

Admission: 4,688 applied, 2,306 admitted, 399 enrolled. *Average high school GPA:* 3.3.

Retention: 89% of full-time freshmen returned.

FACULTY

Total: 118, 80% full-time, 85% with terminal degrees.

Student/faculty ratio: 15:1.

ACADEMICS

Calendar: quarters. *Degrees:* certificates, bachelor's, master's, doctoral, post-master's, and postbachelor's certificates.

Special study options: academic remediation for entering students, accelerated degree program, adult/continuing education programs, advanced placement credit, distance learning, double majors, English as a second language, honors programs, independent study, internships, off-campus study, part-time degree program, services for LD students, student-designed majors, study abroad, summer session for credit.

Unusual degree programs: 3-2 business administration; criminal justice.

Computers: 300 computers/terminals are available on campus for general student use. Students can access the following: computer help desk, free student e-mail accounts, online (class) grades, online (class) registration, online (class) schedules, student portals. Campuswide network is available. Wireless service is available via entire campus.

Library: University Library plus 1 other. *Books:* 246,563 (physical), 155,250 (digital/electronic); *Serial titles:* 610 (physical); *Databases:* 121. Weekly public service hours: 76; students can reserve study rooms.

STUDENT LIFE

Housing options: coed, men-only, women-only, cooperative, special housing for students with disabilities. Campus housing is university owned. Freshman campus housing is guaranteed.

Activities and organizations: drama/theater group, student-run newspaper, choral group, Pre Dentistry, Pre Med, Enactus (SIFE), International Club, Black Student Association.

Athletics Member NAIA. *Intercollegiate sports:* basketball M/W, golf M, soccer M, softball W, volleyball W. *Intramural sports:* baseball M, basketball M/W, soccer M, softball W, volleyball W.

Campus security: 24-hour emergency response devices and patrols, student patrols, late-night transport/escort service, controlled dormitory access.

Student services: health clinic, personal/psychological counseling, women's center.

COSTS & FINANCIAL AID
Costs (2019–20) *Comprehensive fee:* $41,985 includes full-time tuition ($32,580), mandatory fees ($990), and room and board ($8415). Part-time tuition: $905 per quarter hour. *College room only:* $4628.

Financial Aid *Financial aid deadline:* 8/15.

APPLYING
Standardized Tests *Required:* SAT or ACT (for admission).

Options: electronic application, deferred entrance.

Required: high school transcript, minimum 2.0 GPA, Eligibility Index Table (combination of GPA and test scores). *Required for some:* essay or personal statement, 1 letter of recommendation, interview. *Recommended:* minimum 2.0 GPA.

Application deadlines: 2/1 (freshmen), 7/1 (transfers).

Notification: continuous (freshmen), continuous (transfers).

CONTACT
Ms. Ivy Teheda, Associate Director of Admissions, La Sierra University, 4500 Riverwalk Parkway, Riverside, CA 92505. *Phone:* 951-785-2957. *Toll-free phone:* 800-874-5587. *Fax:* 951-785-2447. *E-mail:* iteheda@ lasierra.edu.

Life Pacific College
San Dimas, California
http://www.lifepacific.edu/

CONTACT
Ms. Dorienne Elston, Director of Admissions, Life Pacific College, 1100 Covina Boulevard, San Dimas, CA 91773-3298. *Phone:* 909-599-5433 Ext. 314. *Toll-free phone:* 877-886-5433 Ext. 314. *Fax:* 909-706-3070. *E-mail:* adm@lifepacific.edu.

Lincoln University
Oakland, California
http://www.lincolnuca.edu/
- **Independent** comprehensive, founded 1919
- **Urban** campus
- **Coed**
- **Minimally difficult** entrance level

FACULTY
Student/faculty ratio: 17:1.

ACADEMICS
Calendar: semesters. *Degrees:* bachelor's, master's, and doctoral.
Library: Lincoln University Library. *Books:* 14,400 (physical), 128,000 (digital/electronic); *Serial titles:* 350 (physical), 5,050 (digital/electronic); *Databases:* 19.

STUDENT LIFE
Housing options: college housing not available.

Campus security: 24-hour emergency response devices.

Student services: personal/psychological counseling.

APPLYING
Options: electronic application, deferred entrance.

Application fee: $75.

Required: essay or personal statement, high school transcript, minimum 2.0 GPA. *Required for some:* letters of recommendation, interview.

CONTACT
Mr. Sunny Saggi, Admissions Officer, Lincoln University, 401 15th Street, Oakland, CA 94612. *Phone:* 510-628-8010 Ext. 8011. *Toll-free phone:* 888-810-9998. *Fax:* 510-628-8012. *E-mail:* admissions@ lincolnuca.edu.

Loma Linda University
Loma Linda, California
http://www.llu.edu/

CONTACT
Admissions Office, Loma Linda University, 11139 Anderson Street, Loma Linda, CA 92350. *Phone:* 909-558-1000. *Toll-free phone:* 800-422-4558.

Los Angeles Academy of Figurative Art
Van Nuys, California
http://www.laafa.edu/

CONTACT
Los Angeles Academy of Figurative Art, 16926 Saticoy Street, Van Nuys, CA 91406.

★ Los Angeles Film School
Hollywood, California
http://www.lafilm.edu/

CONTACT
Los Angeles Film School, 6363 Sunset Boulevard, Hollywood, CA 90028. *Toll-free phone:* 877-952-3456.

See next page for display ad and page 1032 for the College Close-Up.

Loyola Marymount University
Los Angeles, California
http://www.lmu.edu/
- **Independent Roman Catholic** comprehensive, founded 1911
- **Suburban** 142-acre campus with easy access to Los Angeles
- **Endowment** $477.6 million
- **Coed** 6,700 undergraduate students, 97% full-time, 55% women, 45% men
- **47% of applicants were admitted**

UNDERGRAD STUDENTS
6,466 full-time, 234 part-time. Students come from 93 other countries; 32% are from out of state; 7% Black or African American, non-Hispanic/Latino; 22% Hispanic/Latino; 10% Asian, non-Hispanic/Latino; 0.2% Native Hawaiian or other Pacific Islander, non-Hispanic/Latino; 7% Two or more races, non-Hispanic/Latino; 10% international; 7% transferred in; 50% live on campus.

Freshmen:
Admission: 17,846 applied, 8,411 admitted, 1,512 enrolled. *Average high school GPA:* 3.8. *Test scores:* SAT evidence-based reading and writing scores over 500: 99%; SAT math scores over 500: 100%; ACT scores over 18: 100%; SAT evidence-based reading and writing scores over 600: 83%; SAT math scores over 600: 76%; ACT scores over 24: 96%; SAT evidence-based reading and writing scores over 700: 20%; SAT math scores over 700: 27%; ACT scores over 30: 43%.

Retention: 90% of full-time freshmen returned.

FACULTY
Student/faculty ratio: 10:1.

ACADEMICS
Calendar: semesters. *Degrees:* bachelor's, master's, doctoral, post-master's, and postbachelor's certificates.

Special study options: accelerated degree program, advanced placement credit, distance learning, double majors, English as a second language, honors programs, independent study, internships, part-time degree program, student-designed majors, study abroad. *ROTC:* Army (c), Air Force (b).

Unusual degree programs: 3-2 Mechanical Engineering, Healthcare Systems Engineering, Educational Studies.

Computers: 820 computers/terminals are available on campus for general student use. Students can access the following: campus intranet, computer help desk, free student e-mail accounts, online (class) grades, online (class) registration, online (class) schedules. Campuswide network is available. 100% of college-owned or -operated housing units are wired for high-speed Internet access. Wireless service is available via entire campus.

Library: William H. Hannon Library. Study areas open 24 hours, 5–7 days a week; students can reserve study rooms.

STUDENT LIFE

Housing options: coed, men-only, women-only, special housing for students with disabilities. Campus housing is university owned. Freshman applicants given priority for college housing.

Activities and organizations: drama/theater group, student-run newspaper, radio and television station, choral group, national fraternities, national sororities.

Athletics Member NCAA. All Division I. *Intercollegiate sports:* baseball M(s), basketball M(s)/W(s), cheerleading M/W, crew M/W(s), cross-country running M(s)/W(s), golf M(s), soccer M(s)/W(s), softball W(s), swimming and diving W(s), tennis M(s)/W(s), track and field M/W, volleyball W(s), water polo M(s)/W(s). *Intramural sports:* baseball M(c), basketball M/W(c), football M/W, ice hockey M(c), lacrosse M(c)/W(c), rugby M(c), sand volleyball M/W, skiing (downhill) M(c)/W(c), soccer M(c)/W(c), table tennis M/W, tennis M(c)/W(c), volleyball M(c)/W(c).

Campus security: 24-hour emergency response devices and patrols, late-night transport/escort service.

Student services: health clinic, personal/psychological counseling, veterans affairs office.

COSTS & FINANCIAL AID

Costs (2018–19) *One-time required fee:* $350. *Comprehensive fee:* $63,357 includes full-time tuition ($47,470), mandatory fees ($702), and room and board ($15,185). Full-time tuition and fees vary according to reciprocity agreements. Part-time tuition: $1981 per credit hour. Part-time tuition and fees vary according to course load. *Required fees:* $8 per credit hour part-time, $65 per term part-time. *College room only:* $10,785. Room and board charges vary according to board plan and housing facility. *Payment plan:* installment. *Waivers:* employees or children of employees.

Financial Aid Of all full-time matriculated undergraduates who enrolled in 2017, 4,310 applied for aid, 3,242 were judged to have need, 730 had their need fully met. 1,306 Federal Work-Study jobs (averaging $1932). 2,123 state and other part-time jobs (averaging $1986). In 2017, 1689 non-need-based awards were made. *Average percent of need met:* 66. *Average financial aid package:* $30,544. *Average need-based loan:* $6223. *Average need-based gift aid:* $22,088. *Average non-need-based aid:* $10,282. *Average indebtedness upon graduation:* $32,262.

APPLYING

Standardized Tests *Required:* SAT or ACT (for admission).

Options: electronic application, early admission, early decision, early action, deferred entrance.

Application fee: $60.

Required: essay or personal statement, high school transcript, 1 letter of recommendation. *Required for some:* portfolio or audition required for animation, dance, music, and theatre arts programs, portfolio optional for production (film and television) and studio arts programs. *Recommended:* portfolio or audition required for animation, dance, music, and theatre arts programs, portfolio optional for production (film and television) and studio arts programs.

Application deadlines: 1/15 (freshmen), 3/15 (transfers), 11/1 (early action).

Early decision deadline: 11/1.

Notification: continuous (freshmen), continuous (transfers), 12/1 (early decision), 12/20 (early action).

CONTACT

Mr. Matthew X. Fissinger, Assistant Vice Provost for Undergraduate Admission, Loyola Marymount University, 1 LMU Drive, Los Angeles, CA 90045. *Phone:* 310-338-2750. *Toll-free phone:* 800-LMU-INFO. *E-mail:* admission@lmu.edu.

Marymount California University

Rancho Palos Verdes, California

http://www.marymountcalifornia.edu/

- **Independent Roman Catholic** comprehensive, founded 1932
- **Suburban** 26-acre campus with easy access to Los Angeles
- **Endowment** $10.7 million
- **Coed** 735 undergraduate students, 98% full-time, 49% women, 51% men
- **Minimally difficult** entrance level, 85% of applicants were admitted

UNDERGRAD STUDENTS

721 full-time, 14 part-time. 11% are from out of state; 7% Black or African American, non-Hispanic/Latino; 40% Hispanic/Latino; 5% Asian, non-Hispanic/Latino; 0.4% Native Hawaiian or other Pacific Islander, non-Hispanic/Latino; 0.3% American Indian or Alaska Native, non-Hispanic/Latino; 3% Two or more races, non-Hispanic/Latino; 4% Race/ethnicity unknown; 18% international; 11% transferred in; 34% live on campus.

Freshmen:

Admission: 1,621 applied, 1,378 admitted, 151 enrolled. *Average high school GPA:* 3.0. *Test scores:* SAT evidence-based reading and writing scores over 500: 69%; SAT math scores over 500: 64%; ACT scores over 18: 73%; SAT evidence-based reading and writing scores over 600: 26%; SAT math scores over 600: 25%; ACT scores over 24: 32%; SAT math scores over 700: 6%; ACT scores over 30: 5%.

Retention: 53% of full-time freshmen returned.

FACULTY

Total: 61, 56% full-time, 51% with terminal degrees.

Student/faculty ratio: 16:1.

ACADEMICS

Calendar: semesters. *Degrees:* associate, bachelor's, and master's.

Special study options: academic remediation for entering students, accelerated degree program, adult/continuing education programs, advanced placement credit, cooperative education, distance learning, English as a second language, honors programs, independent study, internships, off-campus study, part-time degree program, services for LD students, study abroad, summer session for credit.

Unusual degree programs: 3-2 business administration.

Computers: 210 computers/terminals are available on campus for general student use. Students can access the following: campus intranet, computer help desk, free student e-mail accounts, online (class) grades, online (class) registration, online (class) schedules. Campuswide network is available. 100% of college-owned or -operated housing units are wired for high-speed Internet access. Wireless service is available via entire campus.

Library: College Library plus 1 other. *Books:* 23,246 (physical), 135,971 (digital/electronic); *Serial titles:* 255 (physical), 30,329 (digital/electronic); *Databases:* 51. Weekly public service hours: 60; students can reserve study rooms.

STUDENT LIFE

Housing options: coed, special housing for students with disabilities. Campus housing is university owned. Freshman applicants given priority for college housing.

Activities and organizations: drama/theater group, choral group, Latinos Unidos, Student Veterans Organization, Marymount Pride, Black Student Union, Society for Advancement of Management (SAM).

Athletics Member NAIA. *Intercollegiate sports:* baseball M(s), golf M(s), lacrosse M(s)/W(s), soccer M(s)/W(s), track and field M(s). *Intramural sports:* basketball M/W, golf M/W, lacrosse M/W, soccer M/W, softball M/W, swimming and diving M/W, track and field M/W, volleyball M/W.

Campus security: 24-hour emergency response devices and patrols, late-night transport/escort service, controlled dormitory access.

Student services: health clinic, personal/psychological counseling, veterans affairs office.

COSTS & FINANCIAL AID

Costs (2018–19) *One-time required fee:* $300. *Comprehensive fee:* $50,800 includes full-time tuition ($34,134), mandatory fees ($2000), and room and board ($14,666). Part-time tuition: $1475 per credit hour. *Required fees:* $700 per year part-time. *College room only:* $9250. Room

and board charges vary according to board plan and housing facility. *Payment plan:* installment. *Waivers:* senior citizens and employees or children of employees.

Financial Aid Of all full-time matriculated undergraduates who enrolled in 2018, 575 applied for aid, 569 were judged to have need, 126 had their need fully met. In 2018, 33 non-need-based awards were made. *Average percent of need met:* 65. *Average financial aid package:* $32,169. *Average need-based loan:* $3385. *Average need-based gift aid:* $23,540. *Average non-need-based aid:* $11,015. *Average indebtedness upon graduation:* $25,905. *Financial aid deadline:* 2/15.

APPLYING

Standardized Tests *Recommended:* SAT or ACT (for admission).

Options: electronic application, early admission, deferred entrance.

Application fee: $50.

Required: high school transcript. *Required for some:* essay or personal statement, interview. *Recommended:* minimum 2.0 GPA.

Notification: continuous until 9/1 (freshmen), continuous until 9/1 (transfers).

CONTACT

Meshach Puerto, Assistant Director of Admissions, Marymount California University, 30800 Palos Verdes Drive East, Rancho Palos Verdes, CA 90275. *Phone:* 310-377-5501 Ext. 7378. *Fax:* 310-303-7698. *E-mail:* mpuerto@marymountcalifornia.edu.

The Master's University

Santa Clarita, California

http://www.masters.edu/

- **Independent nondenominational** comprehensive, founded 1927
- **Suburban** 110-acre campus with easy access to Los Angeles
- **Endowment** $15.4 million
- **Coed**
- **Moderately difficult** entrance level

FACULTY

Student/faculty ratio: 12:1.

ACADEMICS

Calendar: semesters. *Degrees:* bachelor's, master's, and doctoral.
Library: Robert L. Powell Library plus 1 other. *Books:* 98,047 (physical), 210,005 (digital/electronic); *Serial titles:* 657 (physical), 18,615 (digital/electronic); *Databases:* 33. Weekly public service hours: 74.

STUDENT LIFE

Housing options: on-campus residence required through junior year; men-only, women-only. Campus housing is university owned. Freshman campus housing is guaranteed.

Activities and organizations: drama/theater group, choral group, University Singers Choir, Summer Missions, Intramural Sports, Church Ministries, Theatre Arts Group.

Athletics Member NAIA.

Campus security: 24-hour patrols.

Student services: health clinic, personal/psychological counseling, veterans affairs office.

COSTS & FINANCIAL AID

Costs (2018–19) *Comprehensive fee:* $36,590 includes full-time tuition ($24,950), mandatory fees ($440), and room and board ($11,200). Full-time tuition and fees vary according to class time, course load, location, and program. Part-time tuition: $1050 per credit hour. Part-time tuition and fees vary according to class time, course load, location, and program. *Room and board:* Room and board charges vary according to board plan.

Financial Aid Of all full-time matriculated undergraduates who enrolled in 2015, 878 applied for aid, 758 were judged to have need, 101 had their need fully met. 60 Federal Work-Study jobs (averaging $2577). 174 state and other part-time jobs (averaging $1904). In 2015, 143 non-need-based awards were made. *Average percent of need met:* 66. *Average financial aid package:* $22,088. *Average need-based loan:* $4249. *Average need-based gift aid:* $18,112. *Average non-need-based aid:* $9865. *Average indebtedness upon graduation:* $29,133.

APPLYING

Standardized Tests *Required:* SAT or ACT (for admission).

Options: electronic application, early admission, early action, deferred entrance.

Application fee: $40.

Required: essay or personal statement, high school transcript, minimum 2.8 GPA, 2 letters of recommendation. *Recommended:* interview.

CONTACT
Mr. Dariu Dumitru, Director of Admissions, The Master's University, 21726 Placerita Canyon Road, Santa Clarita, CA 91321. *Phone:* 661-362-2363. *Toll-free phone:* 800-568-6248. *Fax:* 661-362-2718. *E-mail:* admissions@masters.edu.

Menlo College
Atherton, California
http://www.menlo.edu/

CONTACT
Priscila DeSouza, Associate Dean of Enrollment Management, Menlo College, 1000 El Camino Real, Atherton, CA 94027. *Phone:* 650-543-3786. *Toll-free phone:* 800-556-3656. *Fax:* 650-543-4496. *E-mail:* admissions@menlo.edu.

★ Mills College
Oakland, California
http://www.mills.edu/

- **Independent** comprehensive, founded 1852
- **Urban** 135-acre campus with easy access to San Francisco
- **Endowment** $184.9 million
- **Undergraduate: women only; graduate: coed** 761 undergraduate students, 97% full-time, 100% women
- **Moderately difficult** entrance level, 87% of applicants were admitted

UNDERGRAD STUDENTS
739 full-time, 22 part-time. Students come from 37 states and territories; 4 other countries; 19% are from out of state; 9% Black or African American, non-Hispanic/Latino; 28% Hispanic/Latino; 10% Asian, non-Hispanic/Latino; 0.1% Native Hawaiian or other Pacific Islander, non-Hispanic/Latino; 0.4% American Indian or Alaska Native, non-Hispanic/Latino; 9% Two or more races, non-Hispanic/Latino; 0.5% Race/ethnicity unknown; 0.9% international; 11% transferred in; 64% live on campus.

Freshmen:
Admission: 965 applied, 837 admitted, 174 enrolled. *Average high school GPA:* 3.5.
Retention: 77% of full-time freshmen returned.

FACULTY
Total: 174, 47% full-time, 72% with terminal degrees.
Student/faculty ratio: 10:1.

ACADEMICS
Calendar: semesters. *Degrees:* certificates, bachelor's, master's, doctoral, and postbachelor's certificates.

Special study options: accelerated degree program, adult/continuing education programs, advanced placement credit, cooperative education, double majors, independent study, internships, off-campus study, part-time degree program, services for LD students, student-designed majors, study abroad, summer session for credit. *ROTC:* Army (c).

Unusual degree programs: 3-2 engineering with University of Southern California; education, public policy, infant mental health, mathematics.

Computers: 335 computers/terminals and 3,000 ports are available on campus for general student use. Students can access the following: campus intranet, computer help desk, free student e-mail accounts, online (class) grades, online (class) registration, online (class) schedules, online degree audit. Campuswide network is available. 100% of college-owned or -operated housing units are wired for high-speed Internet access. Wireless service is available via entire campus.

Library: F. W. Olin Library. *Books:* 190,417 (physical), 156,636 (digital/electronic); *Serial titles:* 153 (physical), 51,607 (digital/electronic); *Databases:* 39. Weekly public service hours: 89; students can reserve study rooms.

STUDENT LIFE
Housing options: coed, women-only, cooperative, special housing for students with disabilities. Campus housing is university owned. Freshman campus housing is guaranteed.

Activities and organizations: drama/theater group, student-run newspaper, choral group, Associated Students of Mills College, The Campanil, The Mills Choir, Mujeres Unidas, Asian Pacific Islander Student Association.

Athletics Member NCAA. All Division III. *Intercollegiate sports:* crew W, cross-country running W, rowing W, soccer W, swimming and diving W, tennis W, volleyball W. *Intramural sports:* basketball W, cheerleading W(c), soccer W, softball W(c), track and field W(c), volleyball W.

Campus security: 24-hour emergency response devices and patrols, late-night transport/escort service, controlled dormitory access.

Student services: health clinic, personal/psychological counseling, women's center.

COSTS & FINANCIAL AID
Costs (2018–19) *Comprehensive fee:* $43,705 includes full-time tuition ($28,765), mandatory fees ($1492), and room and board ($13,448). Full-time tuition and fees vary according to course load. Part-time tuition: $1199 per semester hour. Part-time tuition and fees vary according to course load. *Required fees:* $1492 per year part-time. *College room only:* $7064. Room and board charges vary according to board plan and housing facility. *Payment plan:* installment. *Waivers:* employees or children of employees.

Financial Aid Of all full-time matriculated undergraduates who enrolled in 2018, 664 applied for aid, 610 were judged to have need, 60 had their need fully met. In 2018, 35 non-need-based awards were made. *Average percent of need met:* 70. *Average financial aid package:* $28,449. *Average need-based loan:* $6729. *Average need-based gift aid:* $22,495. *Average non-need-based aid:* $7233. *Average indebtedness upon graduation:* $29,693.

APPLYING
Options: electronic application, early admission, early action, deferred entrance.

Application fee: $50.

Required: essay or personal statement, high school transcript, 1 letter of recommendation, college transcripts. *Recommended:* interview.

Application deadlines: 1/15 (freshmen), 3/1 (transfers), 11/15 (early action).

Notification: 3/30 (freshmen), 4/1 (transfers).

CONTACT
Mrs. Robynne Royster, Director of Undergraduate Admissions, Mills College, 5000 MacArthur Boulevard, Oakland, CA 94613-1301. *Phone:* 510-430-2135. *Toll-free phone:* 800-87-MILLS. *Fax:* 510-430-3314. *E-mail:* admission@mills.edu.

Mount Saint Mary's University
Los Angeles, California
http://www.msmu.edu/

- **Independent Roman Catholic** comprehensive, founded 1925
- **Urban** 56-acre campus with easy access to Los Angeles
- **Endowment** $138.5 million
- **Coed, primarily women**
- **81% of applicants were admitted**

FACULTY
Student/faculty ratio: 11:1.

ACADEMICS
Calendar: semesters. *Degrees:* associate, bachelor's, master's, doctoral, and post-master's certificates.
Library: Charles Willard Coe Library plus 1 other. *Books:* 88,758 (physical), 396,855 (digital/electronic); *Serial titles:* 168 (physical), 39,316 (digital/electronic); *Databases:* 215. Weekly public service hours: 91; study areas open 24 hours, 5–7 days a week.

STUDENT LIFE
Housing options: men-only, women-only. Campus housing is university owned. Freshman applicants given priority for college housing.

Activities and organizations: drama/theater group, student-run newspaper, choral group, Sakura Society, Pangkat Pilipino, MSMU Women in Film, Athenian Print, Na Pua O Ka'Aina (NPOKA), national sororities.

Campus security: 24-hour emergency response devices and patrols, late-night transport/escort service, controlled dormitory access.

Student services: health clinic, personal/psychological counseling, women's center, veterans affairs office.

COSTS & FINANCIAL AID
Costs (2018–19) *Comprehensive fee:* $53,405 includes full-time tuition ($40,018), mandatory fees ($1152), and room and board ($12,235). Full-time tuition and fees vary according to course load, degree level, and program. Part-time tuition and fees vary according to course load, degree level, and program. *Room and board:* Room and board charges vary according to board plan and housing facility.

Financial Aid Of all full-time matriculated undergraduates who enrolled in 2018, 1,716 applied for aid, 1,678 were judged to have need, 54 had their need fully met. In 2018, 108 non-need-based awards were made. *Average percent of need met:* 70. *Average financial aid package:* $39,155. *Average need-based loan:* $3511. *Average need-based gift aid:* $24,749. *Average non-need-based aid:* $16,228. *Average indebtedness upon graduation:* $30,120.

APPLYING
Standardized Tests *Required for some:* SAT or ACT (for admission).

Options: electronic application, early admission, early action.

Required: essay or personal statement, high school transcript, minimum 2.5 GPA, 1 letter of recommendation. *Recommended:* 2 letters of recommendation, interview.

CONTACT
Erika Yamasaki, Director of Admissions, Mount Saint Mary's University, 12001 Chalon Road, Los Angeles, CA 90049-1599. *Phone:* 800-999-9893. *Toll-free phone:* 800-999-9893. *Fax:* 310-954-4259. *E-mail:* admissions@msmu.edu.

Mt. Sierra College
Monrovia, California
http://www.mtsierra.edu/

CONTACT
Mt. Sierra College, 800 Royal Oaks Drive, Suite 101, Monrovia, CA 91016. *Phone:* 888-486-9818. *Toll-free phone:* 888-828-8800.

Musicians Institute
Hollywood, California
http://www.mi.edu/

CONTACT
Musicians Institute, 1655 North McCadden Place, Hollywood, CA 90028. *Phone:* 323-860-4345. *Toll-free phone:* 800-255-PLAY.

National University
La Jolla, California
http://www.nu.edu/
- **Independent** comprehensive, founded 1971, part of National University System
- **Urban** campus with easy access to San Diego
- **Coed** 7,735 undergraduate students, 37% full-time, 57% women, 43% men
- **Noncompetitive** entrance level

UNDERGRAD STUDENTS
2,884 full-time, 4,851 part-time. Students come from 52 states and territories; 75 other countries; 11% are from out of state; 10% Black or African American, non-Hispanic/Latino; 26% Hispanic/Latino; 9% Asian, non-Hispanic/Latino; 1% Native Hawaiian or other Pacific Islander, non-Hispanic/Latino; 0.5% American Indian or Alaska Native, non-Hispanic/Latino; 6% Two or more races, non-Hispanic/Latino; 12% Race/ethnicity unknown; 2% international; 43% transferred in.

Freshmen:
Admission: 20 enrolled.
Retention: 50% of full-time freshmen returned.
FACULTY
Total: 1,390, 19% full-time, 41% with terminal degrees.
Student/faculty ratio: 17:1.

ACADEMICS
Calendar: continuous. *Degrees:* certificates, associate, bachelor's, master's, doctoral, post-master's, and postbachelor's certificates.

Special study options: academic remediation for entering students, accelerated degree program, adult/continuing education programs, advanced placement credit, cooperative education, distance learning, double majors, English as a second language, independent study, internships, off-campus study, part-time degree program, services for LD students, study abroad, summer session for credit. *ROTC:* Army (c), Air Force (c).

Computers: 2,800 computers/terminals are available on campus for general student use. Students can access the following: computer help desk, free student e-mail accounts, online (class) grades, online (class) registration, online (class) schedules. Campuswide network is available. Wireless service is available via entire campus.
Library: National University Library. *Books:* 201,123 (physical), 368,486 (digital/electronic); *Serial titles:* 3,050 (physical), 95,256 (digital/electronic); *Databases:* 190. Weekly public service hours: 72; students can reserve study rooms.

STUDENT LIFE
Housing options: college housing not available.
Campus security: 24-hour emergency response devices and patrols, late-night transport/escort service.
Student services: veterans affairs office.

COSTS & FINANCIAL AID
Costs (2019–20) *Tuition:* $13,320 full-time, $370 per unit part-time.
Financial Aid *Average indebtedness upon graduation:* $52,986.

APPLYING
Options: electronic application, deferred entrance.
Required: high school transcript, minimum 2.0 GPA. *Required for some:* essay or personal statement.
Application deadlines: rolling (freshmen), rolling (transfers).
Notification: continuous (freshmen), continuous (transfers).

CONTACT
Dr. Brandon Jouganatos, Enrollment Management, National University, 11255 North Torrey Pines Road, La Jolla, CA 92037-1011. *Toll-free phone:* 800-628-8648.

NewSchool of Architecture and Design
San Diego, California
http://www.newschoolarch.edu/

CONTACT
Kirk Nielson, Director of Enrollment and Field Recruitment, NewSchool of Architecture and Design, 1249 F Street, San Diego, CA 92101. *Phone:* 619-684-8841. *Toll-free phone:* 800-490-7081. *E-mail:* knielson@newschoolarch.edu.

New York Film Academy
Burbank, California
http://www.nyfa.edu/

CONTACT
Admissions Office, New York Film Academy, 3300 Riverside Drive, Burbank, CA 91505. *Phone:* 818-333-3558. *Fax:* 818-333-3557. *E-mail:* studios@nyfa.edu.

Northcentral University

San Diego, California

http://www.ncu.edu/

- **Proprietary** upper-level
- **Coed**
- **Minimally difficult** entrance level

ACADEMICS

Calendar: continuous. *Degrees:* bachelor's, master's, doctoral, post-master's, and postbachelor's certificates (offers only distance learning programs).
Library: Northcentral University Library (Virtual). *Databases:* 123. Weekly public service hours: 79.

STUDENT LIFE

Student services: veterans affairs office.

APPLYING

Options: electronic application.

CONTACT

Northcentral University, 2488 Historic Decatur Road, Suite 100, San Diego, CA 92106. *Phone:* 866-776-0331. *Toll-free phone:* 866-776-0331.

Northwestern Polytechnic University

Fremont, California

http://www.npu.edu/

CONTACT

Mr. Michael Tang, Admission Officer, Northwestern Polytechnic University, 47671 Westinghouse Drive, Fremont, CA 94539. *Phone:* 510-592-9688 Ext. 15. *Fax:* 510-657-8975. *E-mail:* admission@npu.edu.

Notre Dame de Namur University

Belmont, California

http://www.ndnu.edu/

- **Independent Roman Catholic** comprehensive, founded 1851
- **Suburban** 50-acre campus with easy access to San Francisco
- **Endowment** $22.5 million
- **Coed**
- **Moderately difficult** entrance level

FACULTY

Student/faculty ratio: 11:1.

ACADEMICS

Calendar: semesters. *Degrees:* bachelor's, master's, doctoral, and postbachelor's certificates.
Library: The Carl Gellert and Celia Berta Gellert Library plus 1 other. *Books:* 88,990 (physical), 194,534 (digital/electronic); *Databases:* 50.

STUDENT LIFE

Housing options: on-campus residence required through sophomore year; coed. Campus housing is university owned. Freshman campus housing is guaranteed.
Activities and organizations: drama/theater group, student-run newspaper, choral group.
Athletics Member NCAA. All Division II.
Campus security: 24-hour emergency response devices and patrols, late-night transport/escort service, controlled dormitory access.
Student services: health clinic, personal/psychological counseling.

COSTS & FINANCIAL AID

Costs (2018–19) *Comprehensive fee:* $49,844 includes full-time tuition ($34,910), mandatory fees ($440), and room and board ($14,494). Part-time tuition: $1126 per credit hour. Part-time tuition and fees vary according to course load and program. *Required fees:* $50 per term part-time. *College room only:* $9312. Room and board charges vary according to board plan and housing facility.
Financial Aid Of all full-time matriculated undergraduates who enrolled in 2017, 597 applied for aid, 565 were judged to have need, 24 had their need fully met. In 2017, 96 non-need-based awards were made. *Average percent of need met:* 61. *Average financial aid package:* $28,073. *Average need-based loan:* $4193. *Average need-based gift aid:* $23,487.

Average non-need-based aid: $10,876. *Average indebtedness upon graduation:* $27,403.

APPLYING

Standardized Tests *Required:* SAT or ACT (for admission).
Options: electronic application, early admission, early action, deferred entrance.
Application fee: $50.
Required: essay or personal statement, high school transcript. *Required for some:* interview, audition for music programs.

CONTACT

Notre Dame de Namur University, 1500 Ralston Avenue, Belmont, CA 94002-1908. *Phone:* 650-508-3600. *Toll-free phone:* 800-263-0545.

Occidental College

Los Angeles, California

http://www.oxy.edu/

- **Independent** comprehensive, founded 1887
- **Urban** 120-acre campus with easy access to Los Angeles
- **Endowment** $413.4 million
- **Coed** 2,055 undergraduate students, 99% full-time, 58% women, 42% men
- **Very difficult** entrance level, 42% of applicants were admitted

UNDERGRAD STUDENTS

2,035 full-time, 20 part-time. Students come from 47 states and territories; 58 other countries; 51% are from out of state; 5% Black or African American, non-Hispanic/Latino; 14% Hispanic/Latino; 13% Asian, non-Hispanic/Latino; 0.2% Native Hawaiian or other Pacific Islander, non-Hispanic/Latino; 8% Two or more races, non-Hispanic/Latino; 2% Race/ethnicity unknown; 7% international; 2% transferred in; 81% live on campus.

Freshmen:
Admission: 6,775 applied, 2,831 admitted, 564 enrolled. *Average high school GPA:* 3.6. *Test scores:* SAT evidence-based reading and writing scores over 500: 100%; SAT math scores over 500: 100%; ACT scores over 18: 100%; SAT evidence-based reading and writing scores over 600: 96%; SAT math scores over 600: 90%; ACT scores over 24: 98%; SAT evidence-based reading and writing scores over 700: 46%; SAT math scores over 700: 39%; ACT scores over 30: 51%.
Retention: 91% of full-time freshmen returned.

FACULTY

Total: 277, 68% full-time.
Student/faculty ratio: 9:1.

ACADEMICS

Calendar: semesters. *Degrees:* diplomas, bachelor's, and master's.
Special study options: advanced placement credit, double majors, honors programs, independent study, internships, off-campus study, services for LD students, student-designed majors, study abroad. *ROTC:* Army (c), Air Force (c).
Unusual degree programs: 3-2 engineering with California Institute of Technology, Columbia University; law with Columbia University, biotechnology with Keck Graduate Institute.
Computers: 200 computers/terminals are available on campus for general student use. Students can access the following: campus intranet, computer help desk, free student e-mail accounts, online (class) grades, online (class) registration, online (class) schedules. Campuswide network is available. 98% of college-owned or -operated housing units are wired for high-speed Internet access. Wireless service is available via entire campus.
Library: Mary Norton Clapp Library and Academic Commons plus 2 others. Study areas open 24 hours, 5–7 days a week; students can reserve study rooms.

STUDENT LIFE

Housing options: on-campus residence required through junior year; coed, women-only. Campus housing is university owned. Freshman campus housing is guaranteed.
Activities and organizations: drama/theater group, student-run newspaper, radio station, choral group, Dance Production, Outdoor Club,

Hawai'i Club, Ski & Snowboard Club, Pulse, national fraternities, national sororities.

Athletics Member NCAA. All Division III. *Intercollegiate sports:* baseball M, basketball M/W, cross-country running M/W, football M, golf M/W, lacrosse M(c)/W, rugby M(c)/W(c), soccer M/W, softball W, swimming and diving M/W, tennis M/W, track and field M/W, ultimate Frisbee M(c)/W(c), volleyball W, water polo M/W. *Intramural sports:* basketball M/W, cheerleading W(c), soccer M/W.

Campus security: 24-hour emergency response devices and patrols, late-night transport/escort service, controlled dormitory access, Surveillance cameras; emergency notification system; blue light phones.

Student services: health clinic, personal/psychological counseling, women's center.

COSTS & FINANCIAL AID
Costs (2019–20) *Comprehensive fee:* $72,610 includes full-time tuition ($55,980), mandatory fees ($596), and room and board ($16,034). Part-time tuition: $2333 per unit. *College room only:* $9124. *Payment plan:* tuition prepayment.

Financial Aid Of all full-time matriculated undergraduates who enrolled in 2017, 1,354 applied for aid, 1,166 were judged to have need, 1,162 had their need fully met. 813 Federal Work-Study jobs (averaging $2819). 130 state and other part-time jobs (averaging $1454). In 2017, 252 non-need-based awards were made. *Average percent of need met:* 100. *Average financial aid package:* $48,977. *Average need-based loan:* $5856. *Average need-based gift aid:* $40,877. *Average non-need-based aid:* $11,988. *Average indebtedness upon graduation:* $32,055. *Financial aid deadline:* 1/15.

APPLYING
Standardized Tests *Required:* SAT or ACT (for admission). *Recommended:* SAT Subject Tests (for admission).

Options: electronic application, early admission, early decision, deferred entrance.

Application fee: $65.

Required: essay or personal statement, high school transcript, 2 letters of recommendation. *Recommended:* interview.

Application deadlines: 1/15 (freshmen), 4/1 (transfers).

Early decision deadline: 11/15 (for plan 1), 1/1 (for plan 2).

Notification: 3/25 (freshmen), 5/1 (transfers), 12/15 (early decision).

CONTACT
Mr. Vince Cuseo, Vice President of Enrollment and Dean of the College, Occidental College, 1600 Campus Road, Los Angeles, CA 90041. *Phone:* 323-259-2700. *Toll-free phone:* 800-825-5262. *Fax:* 323-341-4875. *E-mail:* admission@oxy.edu.

Otis College of Art and Design
Los Angeles, California
http://www.otis.edu/

CONTACT
Otis College of Art and Design, 9045 Lincoln Boulevard, Los Angeles, CA 90045-9785. *Phone:* 310-665-2577. *Toll-free phone:* 800-527-OTIS.

Pacific College
Costa Mesa, California
http://www.pacific-college.edu/

CONTACT
Pacific College, 3160 Red Hill Avenue, Costa Mesa, CA 92626.

Pacific Oaks College
Pasadena, California
http://www.pacificoaks.edu/

CONTACT
Ms. Augusta Pickens, Office of Admissions, Pacific Oaks College, 5 Westmoreland Place, Pasadena, CA 91103. *Phone:* 626-397-1349. *Toll-free phone:* 877-314-2380. *Fax:* 626-666-1220. *E-mail:* admissions@pacificoaks.edu.

Pacific States University
Los Angeles, California
http://www.psuca.edu/

CONTACT
Mr. Maawiya Ayeva, Director of Admissions, Pacific States University, 3424 Wilshire Boulevard, 12th Floor, Los Angeles, CA 90010. *Phone:* 323-731-2383 Ext. 202. *Toll-free phone:* 888-200-0383. *Fax:* 323-731-7276. *E-mail:* admissions@psuca.edu.

Pacific Union College
Angwin, California
http://www.puc.edu/

CONTACT
Mr. Craig Philpott, Associate Director, Admissions, Pacific Union College, Enrollment Services, One Angwin Avenue, Angwin, CA 94508. *Phone:* 800-862-7080. *Toll-free phone:* 800-862-7080. *Fax:* 707-965-6671. *E-mail:* enroll@puc.edu.

Palo Alto University
Palo Alto, California
http://www.paloaltou.edu/
- **Independent** upper-level
- **Rural** campus with easy access to San Francisco Bay Area/Silicon Valley
- **Endowment** $2.4 million
- **Coed**

FACULTY
Student/faculty ratio: 12:1.

ACADEMICS
Calendar: quarters. *Degrees:* bachelor's, master's, and doctoral.
Library: Omar Seddiqui Research Library. *Books:* 1,771 (physical), 257,269 (digital/electronic); *Serial titles:* 2 (physical), 221,448 (digital/electronic); *Databases:* 53. Weekly public service hours: 71; students can reserve study rooms.

STUDENT LIFE
Housing options: college housing not available.

Student services: personal/psychological counseling, veterans affairs office.

COSTS
Costs (2018–19) *Tuition:* $17,451 full-time. Full-time tuition and fees vary according to class time. No tuition increase for student's term of enrollment. *Required fees:* $5301 full-time.

APPLYING
Options: electronic application, deferred entrance.

CONTACT
Mr. Lenard Wilson, Assistant Director of Undergraduate Admissions, Palo Alto University, 1791 Arastradero Road, Palo Alto, CA 94304. *Phone:* 650-417-2050. *Toll-free phone:* 800-818-6136. *E-mail:* undergrad@paloaltou.edu.

Pepperdine University
Malibu, California
http://www.pepperdine.edu/
- **Independent** university, founded 1937, affiliated with Church of Christ
- **Suburban** 830-acre campus with easy access to Los Angeles
- **Endowment** $861.6 million
- **Coed** 3,627 undergraduate students, 92% full-time, 59% women, 41% men
- **Very difficult** entrance level, 40% of applicants were admitted

UNDERGRAD STUDENTS
3,336 full-time, 291 part-time. Students come from 54 states and territories; 71 other countries; 45% are from out of state; 5% Black or African American, non-Hispanic/Latino; 14% Hispanic/Latino; 10% Asian, non-Hispanic/Latino; 0.2% Native Hawaiian or other Pacific Islander, non-Hispanic/Latino; 0.4% American Indian or Alaska Native,

non-Hispanic/Latino; 6% Two or more races, non-Hispanic/Latino; 2% Race/ethnicity unknown; 13% international; 2% transferred in; 57% live on campus.

Freshmen:

Admission: 11,704 applied, 4,664 admitted, 803 enrolled. *Average high school GPA:* 3.7. *Test scores:* SAT evidence-based reading and writing scores over 500: 99%; SAT math scores over 500: 99%; ACT scores over 18: 100%; SAT evidence-based reading and writing scores over 600: 82%; SAT math scores over 600: 80%; ACT scores over 24: 92%; SAT evidence-based reading and writing scores over 700: 24%; SAT math scores over 700: 37%; ACT scores over 30: 47%.

Retention: 91% of full-time freshmen returned.

FACULTY

Total: 694, 57% full-time, 75% with terminal degrees.
Student/faculty ratio: 13:1.

ACADEMICS

Calendar: semesters. *Degrees:* bachelor's, master's, doctoral, and postbachelor's certificates.

Special study options: adult/continuing education programs, advanced placement credit, distance learning, double majors, honors programs, independent study, internships, part-time degree program, services for LD students, student-designed majors, study abroad, summer session for credit. *ROTC:* Army (c), Air Force (c).

Unusual degree programs: 3-2 engineering with University of Southern California, Washington University in St. Louis.

Computers: 240 computers/terminals are available on campus for general student use. Students can access the following: campus intranet, computer help desk, free student e-mail accounts, online (class) grades, online (class) registration, online (class) schedules. Campuswide network is available. 100% of college-owned or -operated housing units are wired for high-speed Internet access. Wireless service is available via entire campus.

Library: Payson Library plus 5 others. *Books:* 311,392 (physical), 356,075 (digital/electronic); *Serial titles:* 312 (physical), 66,464 (digital/electronic); *Databases:* 128. Weekly public service hours: 112; students can reserve study rooms.

STUDENT LIFE

Housing options: on-campus residence required through sophomore year; men-only, women-only, special housing for students with disabilities. Campus housing is university owned. Freshman campus housing is guaranteed.

Activities and organizations: drama/theater group, student-run newspaper, radio and television station, choral group, Latino Student Association, Black Student Union, Interfraternity Council, International Justice Mission, national fraternities, national sororities.

Athletics Member NCAA. All Division I. *Intercollegiate sports:* baseball M(s), basketball M(s)/W(s), cross-country running M(s)/W(s), golf M(s)/W(s), soccer W(s), swimming and diving W(s), tennis M(s)/W(s), track and field M(s)/W(s), volleyball M(s)/W(s), water polo M(s). *Intramural sports:* basketball M/W, football M/W, golf M(c)/W(c), lacrosse W(c), rugby M(c), soccer M/W, tennis M(c)/W(c), ultimate Frisbee M(c)/W(c), volleyball M/W.

Campus security: 24-hour emergency response devices and patrols, student patrols, late-night transport/escort service, controlled dormitory access, front gate security, 24-hour security in residence halls, controlled access, crime prevention programs.

Student services: health clinic, personal/psychological counseling.

COSTS & FINANCIAL AID

Costs (2018–19) *Comprehensive fee:* $69,252 includes full-time tuition ($53,680), mandatory fees ($252), and room and board ($15,320). Part-time tuition: $1685 per credit hour. *Room and board:* Room and board charges vary according to board plan and housing facility. *Payment plan:* installment. *Waivers:* employees or children of employees.

Financial Aid Of all full-time matriculated undergraduates who enrolled in 2017, 3,236 applied for aid, 1,690 were judged to have need, 293 had their need fully met. In 2017, 932 non-need-based awards were made. *Average percent of need met:* 74. *Average financial aid package:* $40,510. *Average need-based loan:* $5867. *Average need-based gift aid:* $36,718. *Average non-need-based aid:* $17,846. *Average indebtedness upon graduation:* $31,410.

APPLYING

Standardized Tests *Required:* SAT or ACT (for admission).

Options: electronic application.

Application fee: $65.

Required: essay or personal statement, high school transcript, 2 letters of recommendation.

Application deadlines: 1/5 (freshmen), 1/5 (transfers).

Notification: 4/1 (freshmen), 4/1 (transfers).

CONTACT

Mr. Falone Serna, Director of Admission, Enrollment Management, Pepperdine University, 24255 Pacific Coast Highway, Malibu, CA 90263. *Phone:* 310-506-4392. *E-mail:* falone.serna@pepperdine.edu.

See previous page for display ad and page 1074 for the College Close-Up.

Pima Medical Institute

Chula Vista, California

http://www.pmi.edu/

CONTACT

Admissions Office, Pima Medical Institute, 780 Bay Boulevard, Chula Vista, CA 91910. *Phone:* 619-425-3200. *Toll-free phone:* 800-477-PIMA.

Pitzer College

Claremont, California

http://www.pitzer.edu/

- **Independent** 4-year, founded 1963, part of The Claremont Colleges
- **Suburban** 35-acre campus with easy access to Los Angeles
- **Endowment** $141.5 million
- **Coed** 1,106 undergraduate students, 98% full-time, 56% women, 44% men
- **Very difficult** entrance level, 13% of applicants were admitted

UNDERGRAD STUDENTS

1,083 full-time, 23 part-time. Students come from 46 states and territories; 33 other countries; 56% are from out of state; 6% Black or African American, non-Hispanic/Latino; 14% Hispanic/Latino; 10% Asian, non-Hispanic/Latino; 0.3% Native Hawaiian or other Pacific Islander, non-Hispanic/Latino; 0.3% American Indian or Alaska Native, non-Hispanic/Latino; 7% Two or more races, non-Hispanic/Latino; 6% Race/ethnicity unknown; 12% international; 2% transferred in; 73% live on campus.

Freshmen:

Admission: 4,358 applied, 581 admitted, 273 enrolled. *Average high school GPA:* 3.9. *Test scores:* SAT evidence-based reading and writing scores over 500: 100%; SAT math scores over 500: 100%; ACT scores over 18: 100%; SAT evidence-based reading and writing scores over 600: 98%; SAT math scores over 600: 94%; ACT scores over 24: 100%; SAT evidence-based reading and writing scores over 700: 54%; SAT math scores over 700: 58%; ACT scores over 30: 80%.

Retention: 91% of full-time freshmen returned.

FACULTY

Total: 108, 76% full-time, 95% with terminal degrees.

Student/faculty ratio: 11:1.

ACADEMICS

Calendar: semesters. *Degree:* bachelor's.

Special study options: adult/continuing education programs, advanced placement credit, cooperative education, double majors, English as a second language, honors programs, independent study, internships, off-campus study, part-time degree program, services for LD students, student-designed majors, study abroad, summer session for credit. *ROTC:* Army (c), Air Force (c).

Unusual degree programs: 3-2 business administration with Claremont Graduate University; Economics, Information Systems and Technology, Psychology, Public Policy, Education, Mathematics, Cultural Studies,

English, History, Music, Philosophy, Religion, Women's Studies, Teacher Education with Claremont Graduate University; BA/DO linkage pr.

Computers: Students can access the following: campus intranet, computer help desk, free student e-mail accounts, online (class) grades, online (class) registration, online (class) schedules. Campuswide network is available. 100% of college-owned or -operated housing units are wired for high-speed Internet access. Wireless service is available via entire campus.

Library: Honnold Library plus 3 others. *Books:* 1.0 million (physical), 2.2 million (digital/electronic); *Serial titles:* 28,182 (physical), 81,005 (digital/electronic); *Databases:* 490. Weekly public service hours: 107; students can reserve study rooms.

STUDENT LIFE

Housing options: on-campus residence required for freshman year; coed, cooperative, special housing for students with disabilities. Campus housing is university owned. Freshman campus housing is guaranteed.

Activities and organizations: drama/theater group, student-run newspaper, radio station, choral group, Pitzer Outdoor Adventure, Live Your Best Life Records, Latino Student Union, Pitzer International Student Association, Asian Pacific American Coalition.

Athletics Member NCAA. All Division III except golf (Division II). *Intercollegiate sports:* baseball M, basketball M/W, cross-country running M/W, football M, golf M/W, lacrosse W, soccer M/W, softball W, swimming and diving M/W, tennis M/W, track and field M/W, volleyball W, water polo M/W. *Intramural sports:* badminton M(c)/W(c), basketball M/W, equestrian sports M(c)/W(c), fencing M(c)/W(c), field hockey M(c)/W(c), football M, ice hockey M(c)/W(c), lacrosse M(c), rugby M(c)/W(c), soccer M/W(c), tennis M(c)/W(c), ultimate Frisbee M(c)/W(c), volleyball M(c)/W(c).

Campus security: 24-hour emergency response devices and patrols, late-night transport/escort service, controlled dormitory access.

Student services: health clinic, personal/psychological counseling, women's center.

COSTS & FINANCIAL AID

Costs (2018–19) *Comprehensive fee:* $70,900 includes full-time tuition ($53,776), mandatory fees ($280), and room and board ($16,844). Part-time tuition: $6722 per course. Part-time tuition and fees vary according to course load. *Required fees:* $280 per year part-time. *College room only:* $9720. Room and board charges vary according to board plan and housing facility. *Payment plans:* installment, deferred payment. *Waivers:* employees or children of employees.

Financial Aid Of all full-time matriculated undergraduates who enrolled in 2018, 517 applied for aid, 431 were judged to have need, 423 had their need fully met. 335 Federal Work-Study jobs (averaging $2462). 18 state and other part-time jobs (averaging $1850). In 2018, 17 non-need-based awards were made. *Average percent of need met:* 100. *Average financial aid package:* $48,350. *Average need-based loan:* $4465. *Average need-based gift aid:* $43,813. *Average non-need-based aid:* $6334. *Average indebtedness upon graduation:* $17,848. *Financial aid deadline:* 1/1.

APPLYING

Standardized Tests *Required for some:* SAT or ACT (for admission).

Options: electronic application, early decision, deferred entrance.

Application fee: $70.

Required: essay or personal statement, high school transcript, minimum 2.0 GPA, 3 letters of recommendation. *Recommended:* interview.

Application deadlines: 1/1 (freshmen), 1/1 (out-of-state freshmen), 4/1 (transfers).

Early decision deadline: 11/15 (for plan 1), 1/1 (for plan 2).

Notification: 4/1 (freshmen), 4/1 (out-of-state freshmen), 5/15 (transfers), 12/18 (early decision plan 1), 2/15 (early decision plan 2).

CONTACT

Ms. Yvonne Berumen, Vice President for Admission and Financial Aid, Pitzer College, 1050 North Mills Avenue, Claremont, CA 91711-6101. *Phone:* 909-621-8129. *Toll-free phone:* 800-748-9371. *Fax:* 909-621-8770. *E-mail:* admission@pitzer.edu.

Platt College

Alhambra, California
http://www.plattcollege.edu/

CONTACT
Mr. Detroit Whiteside, Director of Admissions, Platt College, 1000 South Fremont A9W, Alhambra, CA 91803. *Phone:* 323-258-8050. *Toll-free phone:* 888-866-6697 (in-state); 888-80-PLATT (out-of-state).

Platt College

Ontario, California
http://www.plattcollege.edu/

CONTACT
Ms. Jennifer Abandonato, Director of Admissions, Platt College, 3700 Inland Empire Boulevard, Ontario, CA 91764. *Phone:* 909-941-9410. *Toll-free phone:* 888-80-PLATT.

Platt College

Riverside, California
http://www.plattcollege.edu/

CONTACT
Platt College, 6465 Sycamore Canyon Boulevard, Suite 100, Riverside, CA 92507. *Toll-free phone:* 888-807-5288.

Platt College San Diego

San Diego, California
http://www.platt.edu/

CONTACT
Mr. Steve Gallup, Director of Admissions, Platt College San Diego, 6250 El Cajon Boulevard, San Diego, CA 92115-3919. *Phone:* 619-265-0107. *Toll-free phone:* 866-752-8826. *Fax:* 619-265-8655. *E-mail:* sgallup@platt.edu.

Point Loma Nazarene University

San Diego, California
http://www.pointloma.edu/

- **Independent Nazarene** comprehensive, founded 1902
- **Suburban** 93-acre campus with easy access to San Diego
- **Coed** 3,196 undergraduate students, 83% full-time, 65% women, 35% men
- **Moderately difficult** entrance level, 69% of applicants were admitted

UNDERGRAD STUDENTS
2,656 full-time, 540 part-time. Students come from 42 states and territories; 19 other countries; 17% are from out of state; 2% Black or African American, non-Hispanic/Latino; 27% Hispanic/Latino; 7% Asian, non-Hispanic/Latino; 0.9% Native Hawaiian or other Pacific Islander, non-Hispanic/Latino; 0.4% American Indian or Alaska Native, non-Hispanic/Latino; 8% Two or more races, non-Hispanic/Latino; 2% Race/ethnicity unknown; 1% international; 12% transferred in; 56% live on campus.

Freshmen:
Admission: 3,473 applied, 2,394 admitted, 657 enrolled. *Average high school GPA:* 3.9. *Test scores:* SAT evidence-based reading and writing scores over 500: 98%; SAT math scores over 500: 97%; ACT scores over 18: 100%; SAT evidence-based reading and writing scores over 600: 63%; SAT math scores over 600: 51%; ACT scores over 24: 80%; SAT evidence-based reading and writing scores over 700: 8%; SAT math scores over 700: 9%; ACT scores over 30: 19%.
Retention: 85% of full-time freshmen returned.

FACULTY
Total: 490, 30% full-time, 48% with terminal degrees.

Student/faculty ratio: 14:1.

ACADEMICS
Calendar: semesters. *Degrees:* certificates, bachelor's, master's, doctoral, and post-master's certificates.

Special study options: academic remediation for entering students, accelerated degree program, adult/continuing education programs, advanced placement credit, distance learning, double majors, external degree program, honors programs, independent study, internships, off-campus study, part-time degree program, services for LD students, study abroad, summer session for credit. *ROTC:* Army (c), Navy (c), Air Force (c).

Computers: 346 computers/terminals and 5,320 ports are available on campus for general student use. Students can access the following: campus intranet, computer help desk, free student e-mail accounts, online (class) grades, online (class) registration, online (class) schedules. Campuswide network is available. 100% of college-owned or -operated housing units are wired for high-speed Internet access. Wireless service is available via entire campus.
Library: Ryan Library.

STUDENT LIFE
Housing options: on-campus residence required through sophomore year; men-only, women-only, special housing for students with disabilities. Campus housing is university owned. Freshman campus housing is guaranteed.

Activities and organizations: drama/theater group, student-run newspaper, radio and television station, choral group.

Athletics Member NCAA. All Division II. *Intercollegiate sports:* baseball M(s), basketball M(s)/W(s), cross-country running W(s), soccer M(s)/W(s), tennis M(s)/W(s), track and field W(s), volleyball W(s). *Intramural sports:* basketball M/W, cheerleading M(c)/W(c), football M/W, rugby M(c)/W(c), soccer M/W, softball M/W, tennis M/W, ultimate Frisbee M/W, volleyball M/W.

Campus security: 24-hour patrols, student patrols, late-night transport/escort service.

Student services: health clinic, personal/psychological counseling, women's center, veterans affairs office.

COSTS & FINANCIAL AID
Costs (2018–19) *Comprehensive fee:* $46,150 includes full-time tuition ($35,100), mandatory fees ($600), and room and board ($10,450). Full-time tuition and fees vary according to course load and program. Part-time tuition: $1465 per credit hour. Part-time tuition and fees vary according to course load and program. *Room and board:* Room and board charges vary according to board plan. *Payment plan:* installment. *Waivers:* senior citizens and employees or children of employees.

Financial Aid Of all full-time matriculated undergraduates who enrolled in 2017, 2,076 applied for aid, 1,739 were judged to have need, 282 had their need fully met. In 2017, 529 non-need-based awards were made. *Average percent of need met:* 64. *Average financial aid package:* $24,518. *Average need-based loan:* $4892. *Average need-based gift aid:* $18,676. *Average non-need-based aid:* $11,041. *Average indebtedness upon graduation:* $34,653.

APPLYING
Standardized Tests *Required:* SAT or ACT (for admission). *Recommended:* SAT (for admission), ACT (for admission).

Options: electronic application, early action.

Application fee: $55.

Required: essay or personal statement, high school transcript, minimum 2.8 GPA, 2 letters of recommendation.

Application deadlines: 2/15 (freshmen), 11/15 (early action).
Notification: 4/1 (freshmen).

CONTACT
Shannon Hutchison, Director of Undergraduate Admissions, Point Loma Nazarene University, 3900 Lomaland Drive, San Diego, CA 92106. *Phone:* 619-849-2541. *Toll-free phone:* 800-733-7770. *Fax:* 619-849-2601. *E-mail:* admissions@pointloma.edu.

Pomona College
Claremont, California
http://www.pomona.edu/

- **Independent** 4-year, founded 1887
- **Suburban** 140-acre campus with easy access to Los Angeles
- **Endowment** $2.2 billion
- **Coed**
- **Most difficult** entrance level

FACULTY
Student/faculty ratio: 8:1.

ACADEMICS
Calendar: semesters. *Degree:* bachelor's.
Library: Honnold/Mudd Library plus 4 others.

STUDENT LIFE
Housing options: on-campus residence required for freshman year; coed. Campus housing is university owned. Freshman campus housing is guaranteed.

Activities and organizations: drama/theater group, student-run newspaper, radio station, choral group, Student Government, music/choral organizations, service organizations, intramural sports, outdoor activities club.

Athletics Member NCAA. All Division III.

Campus security: 24-hour emergency response devices and patrols, late-night transport/escort service, controlled dormitory access.

Student services: health clinic, personal/psychological counseling, women's center.

COSTS & FINANCIAL AID
Costs (2018–19) *Comprehensive fee:* $69,496 includes full-time tuition ($52,412), mandatory fees ($368), and room and board ($16,716). *Room and board:* Room and board charges vary according to board plan.

Financial Aid Of all full-time matriculated undergraduates who enrolled in 2017, 1,121 applied for aid, 953 were judged to have need, 953 had their need fully met. In 2017, 3 non-need-based awards were made. *Average percent of need met:* 100. *Average financial aid package:* $55,390. *Average need-based gift aid:* $53,123. *Average non-need-based aid:* $5000. *Average indebtedness upon graduation:* $17,303. *Financial aid deadline:* 1/15.

APPLYING
Standardized Tests *Required:* SAT or ACT (for admission).
Options: electronic application, early admission, early decision, deferred entrance.
Application fee: $70.
Required: essay or personal statement, high school transcript, 2 letters of recommendation. *Recommended:* supplemental forms for visual and performing arts and science research.

CONTACT
Pomona College, 333 North College Way, Claremont, CA 91711.

Providence Christian College
Pasadena, California
http://www.providencecc.edu/

CONTACT
Providence Christian College, 1539 East Howard Street, Pasadena, CA 91124.

SAE Expression College
Emeryville, California
http://www.sae.edu/

CONTACT
SAE Expression College, 6601 Shellmound Street, Emeryville, CA 94608. *Toll-free phone:* 877-833-8800.

Saint Mary's College of California
Moraga, California
http://www.stmarys-ca.edu/

- **Independent Roman Catholic** upper-level, founded 1863
- **Suburban** 420-acre campus with easy access to San Francisco
- **Endowment** $178.6 million
- **Coed**
- **Moderately difficult** entrance level

FACULTY
Student/faculty ratio: 11:1.

ACADEMICS
Calendar: 4-1-4. *Degrees:* bachelor's, master's, and doctoral.
Library: St. Albert Hall Library. *Books:* 179,912 (physical), 179,777 (digital/electronic); *Serial titles:* 926 (physical), 150,000 (digital/electronic); *Databases:* 219. Weekly public service hours: 102; study areas open 24 hours, 5–7 days a week; students can reserve study rooms.

STUDENT LIFE
Housing options: coed, men-only, special housing for students with disabilities. Campus housing is university owned. Freshman campus housing is guaranteed.

Activities and organizations: drama/theater group, student-run newspaper, radio station, choral group, Gael Force, Campus Activities Board, LASA-Latin American Student Association-Black Student Union, La Hermandad, Asian Pacific American Student Association.

Athletics Member NCAA. All Division I.

Campus security: 24-hour emergency response devices and patrols, late-night transport/escort service.

Student services: health clinic, personal/psychological counseling, women's center.

COSTS & FINANCIAL AID
Costs (2018–19) *Comprehensive fee:* $62,650 includes full-time tuition ($47,130), mandatory fees ($150), and room and board ($15,370). Part-time tuition: $5906 per course. *Required fees:* $75 per term part-time. *Room and board:* Room and board charges vary according to board plan and housing facility.

Financial Aid Of all full-time matriculated undergraduates who enrolled in 2018, 1,967 applied for aid, 1,740 were judged to have need, 8 had their need fully met. 396 Federal Work-Study jobs (averaging $2405). In 2018, 800 non-need-based awards were made. *Average percent of need met:* 66. *Average financial aid package:* $34,296. *Average need-based loan:* $4281. *Average need-based gift aid:* $21,484. *Average non-need-based aid:* $17,385. *Average indebtedness upon graduation:* $30,583.

APPLYING
Standardized Tests *Required:* SAT or ACT (for admission).
Options: electronic application, early action, deferred entrance.
Application fee: $60.

CONTACT
Dr. Angelica Moore, Dean of Admissions, Saint Mary's College of California, 1928 St. Mary's Road, P.M.B. 4800, Moraga, CA 94575. *Phone:* 925-631-4553. *Toll-free phone:* 800-800-4SMC. *Fax:* 925-376-7193. *E-mail:* smcadmit@stmarys-ca.edu.

Samuel Merritt University
Oakland, California
http://www.samuelmerritt.edu/

- **Independent** upper-level, founded 1909
- **Urban** 1-acre campus with easy access to San Francisco
- **Endowment** $47.1 million
- **Coed, primarily women**

FACULTY
Student/faculty ratio: 10:1.

ACADEMICS
Calendar: trimesters. *Degrees:* bachelor's, master's, doctoral, and post-master's certificates (bachelor's degree offered jointly with Saint Mary's College of California).

Library: John A. Graziano Memorial Library. *Books:* 8,453 (physical), 337 (digital/electronic); *Serial titles:* 714 (physical), 19,832 (digital/electronic); *Databases:* 22. Weekly public service hours: 86; students can reserve study rooms.

STUDENT LIFE
Housing options: college housing not available.

Activities and organizations: Student Body Association, California Podiatric Medical Students'; Association (CPMSA), International Healthcare Club, Community Service Honor Society, Scholars in Service.

Campus security: 24-hour emergency response devices and patrols, late-night transport/escort service, 24-hour controlled access.

Student services: health clinic, personal/psychological counseling, veterans affairs office.

FINANCIAL AID
Financial Aid Of all full-time matriculated undergraduates who enrolled in 2016, 678 applied for aid, 663 were judged to have need. 138 Federal Work-Study jobs (averaging $1903). *Average percent of need met:* 19. *Average financial aid package:* $11,861. *Average need-based loan:* $6110. *Average need-based gift aid:* $13,002.

APPLYING
Options: electronic application.

Application fee: $45.

CONTACT
Samuel Merritt University, 3100 Telegraph Avenue, Oakland, CA 94609-3108. *Phone:* 510-869-1508. *Toll-free phone:* 800-607-6377.

San Diego Christian College
Santee, California
http://www.sdcc.edu/

CONTACT
Christine Roberts, Admissions Director, San Diego Christian College, 200 Riverview Parkway, Santee, CA 92017. *Phone:* 619-201-8760. *Toll-free phone:* 800-676-2242. *Fax:* 619-201-8749. *E-mail:* christine.roberts@sdcc.edu.

San Diego State University
San Diego, California
http://www.sdsu.edu/

- **State-supported** university, founded 1897, part of California State University System
- **Urban** 288-acre campus with easy access to San Diego
- **Endowment** $305.8 million
- **Coed** 30,393 undergraduate students, 90% full-time, 55% women, 45% men
- **Very difficult** entrance level, 34% of applicants were admitted

UNDERGRAD STUDENTS
27,398 full-time, 2,995 part-time. Students come from 54 states and territories; 114 other countries; 11% are from out of state; 4% Black or African American, non-Hispanic/Latino; 31% Hispanic/Latino; 13% Asian, non-Hispanic/Latino; 0.2% Native Hawaiian or other Pacific Islander, non-Hispanic/Latino; 0.3% American Indian or Alaska Native, non-Hispanic/Latino; 7% Two or more races, non-Hispanic/Latino; 4% Race/ethnicity unknown; 7% international; 11% transferred in; 19% live on campus.

Freshmen:
Admission: 69,043 applied, 23,766 admitted, 5,750 enrolled. *Average high school GPA:* 3.7. *Test scores:* SAT evidence-based reading and writing scores over 500: 94%; SAT math scores over 500: 94%; ACT scores over 18: 96%; SAT evidence-based reading and writing scores over 600: 57%; SAT math scores over 600: 51%; ACT scores over 24: 65%; SAT evidence-based reading and writing scores over 700: 7%; SAT math scores over 700: 13%; ACT scores over 30: 17%.

Retention: 89% of full-time freshmen returned.

FACULTY
Total: 1,888, 49% full-time, 62% with terminal degrees.

Student/faculty ratio: 27:1.

ACADEMICS
Calendar: semesters. *Degrees:* bachelor's, master's, doctoral, and postbachelor's certificates.

Special study options: advanced placement credit, distance learning, double majors, English as a second language, external degree program, freshman honors college, honors programs, independent study, internships, off-campus study, part-time degree program, services for LD students, student-designed majors, study abroad, summer session for credit. *ROTC:* Army (b), Navy (c), Air Force (b).

Computers: 2,000 computers/terminals and 1,500 ports are available on campus for general student use. Students can access the following: computer help desk, free student e-mail accounts, online (class) grades, online (class) registration, online (class) schedules, learning management system. Campuswide network is available. 100% of college-owned or -operated housing units are wired for high-speed Internet access. Wireless service is available via entire campus.

Library: Malcolm A. Love Library. *Books:* 1.3 million (physical), 1.0 million (digital/electronic); *Serial titles:* 45,107 (physical), 92,142 (digital/electronic); *Databases:* 317. Weekly public service hours: 168; study areas open 24 hours, 5–7 days a week; students can reserve study rooms.

STUDENT LIFE
Housing options: on-campus residence required through sophomore year; coed, special housing for students with disabilities. Campus housing is university owned. Freshman applicants given priority for college housing.

Activities and organizations: drama/theater group, student-run newspaper, radio and television station, choral group, marching band, AB Samahan, Asian Pacific Student Alliance, Enviro-Business Society, M.E.Ch.A de SDSU, Social fraternities and sororities, including both general and culturally based organizations, national fraternities, national sororities.

Athletics Member NCAA. All Division I. *Intercollegiate sports:* baseball M(s), basketball M(s)/W(s), cross-country running W(s), football M(s), golf M(s)/W(s)(c), lacrosse W(s), rowing W(s), soccer M(s)/W(s), softball W(s), swimming and diving W(s), tennis M(s)/W(s), track and field W(s), volleyball W(s), water polo W(s). *Intramural sports:* basketball M/W, bowling M/W, football M/W, ice hockey M(c), lacrosse M(c)/W(c), rowing M(c)/W(c), rugby M(c), skiing (downhill) M(c)/W(c), soccer M(c)/W(c), softball M/W, tennis M(c)/W(c), triathlon M(c)/W(c), ultimate Frisbee M(c)/W(c), volleyball M(c)/W(c), water polo M(c)/W(c).

Campus security: 24-hour emergency response devices and patrols, student patrols, late-night transport/escort service, controlled dormitory access.

Student services: health clinic, personal/psychological counseling, women's center, veterans affairs office.

COSTS & FINANCIAL AID
Costs (2019–20) *Tuition:* area resident $5742 full-time; state resident $5742 full-time; nonresident $17,622 full-time. *Required fees:* $1768 full-time. *Room and board:* $17,752.

Financial Aid Of all full-time matriculated undergraduates who enrolled in 2018, 17,800 applied for aid, 14,500 were judged to have need, 3,400 had their need fully met. 690 Federal Work-Study jobs (averaging $2190). In 2018, 1643 non-need-based awards were made. *Average percent of need met:* 68. *Average financial aid package:* $10,100. *Average need-based loan:* $4100. *Average need-based gift aid:* $9800. *Average non-need-based aid:* $2200. *Average indebtedness upon graduation:* $21,327. *Financial aid deadline:* 3/2.

APPLYING
Standardized Tests *Required:* SAT or ACT (for admission).

Options: electronic application.

Application fee: $55.

Required: high school transcript.

CONTACT
Sabrina Cortell, Director of Admissions, San Diego State University, 5500 Campanile Drive, San Diego, CA 92182. *Phone:* 619-594-6336. *Toll-free phone:* 855-594-6336 (in-state); 855-594-3983 (out-of-state). *E-mail:* admissions@sdsu.edu.

San Diego State University–Imperial Valley Campus
Calexico, California
http://www.ivcampus.sdsu.edu/

CONTACT
Aracely Bororquez, Admissions Department, San Diego State University–Imperial Valley Campus, 720 Heber Avenue, Calexico, CA 92231. *Phone:* 760-768-5506. *Fax:* 760-768-5589. *E-mail:* transfer@mail.sdsu.edu.

San Francisco Art Institute
San Francisco, California
http://www.sfai.edu/
- **Independent** comprehensive, founded 1871
- **Urban** 4-acre campus with easy access to San Francisco
- **Endowment** $10.3 million
- **Coed**
- **Moderately difficult** entrance level

FACULTY
Student/faculty ratio: 9:1.

ACADEMICS
Calendar: semesters. *Degrees:* bachelor's, master's, and postbachelor's certificates.
Library: Anne Bremer Memorial Library plus 1 other. *Books:* 32,775 (physical); *Serial titles:* 126 (physical), 791 (digital/electronic); *Databases:* 6. Weekly public service hours: 59.

STUDENT LIFE
Housing options: on-campus residence required for freshman year; coed. Campus housing is leased by the school and is provided by a third party. Freshman applicants given priority for college housing.
Activities and organizations: student-run newspaper, radio station, Student Union, LOGS (Legion of Graduate Students), Film Club, Photo Club, SFAeye.
Campus security: 24-hour patrols, security cameras.
Student services: personal/psychological counseling.

COSTS & FINANCIAL AID
Costs (2018–19) *One-time required fee:* $200. *Comprehensive fee:* $62,243 includes full-time tuition ($45,664), mandatory fees ($870), and room and board ($15,709). Full-time tuition and fees vary according to degree level. Part-time tuition: $2000 per credit. Part-time tuition and fees vary according to degree level. *College room only:* $11,650. Room and board charges vary according to housing facility.
Financial Aid Of all full-time matriculated undergraduates who enrolled in 2018, 163 applied for aid, 146 were judged to have need, 9 had their need fully met. In 2018, 118 non-need-based awards were made. *Average percent of need met:* 47. *Average financial aid package:* $17,954. *Average need-based loan:* $2290. *Average need-based gift aid:* $5808. *Average non-need-based aid:* $7320. *Average indebtedness upon graduation:* $27,630.

APPLYING
Standardized Tests *Recommended:* SAT or ACT (for admission).
Options: electronic application, early action, deferred entrance.
Application fee: $75.
Required: essay or personal statement, high school transcript, 1 letter of recommendation, portfolio and artist statement for BFA applicants, critical essay for BA applicants. *Recommended:* minimum 2.5 GPA, interview.

CONTACT
Office of Admissions, San Francisco Art Institute, 800 Chestnut Street, San Francisco, CA 94133. *Phone:* 415-749-4500. *Toll-free phone:* 800-345-SFAI. *Fax:* 415-749-4592. *E-mail:* admissions@sfai.edu.

San Francisco Conservatory of Music
San Francisco, California
http://www.sfcm.edu/
- **Independent** comprehensive, founded 1917
- **Urban** 2-acre campus with easy access to San Francisco Bay Area
- **Endowment** $41.3 million
- **Coed**
- **Very difficult** entrance level

FACULTY
Student/faculty ratio: 7:1.

ACADEMICS
Calendar: semesters. *Degrees:* diplomas, bachelor's, master's, post-master's, and postbachelor's certificates.
Library: San Francisco Conservatory of Music Library. *Books:* 24,129 (physical), 31,094 (digital/electronic); *Serial titles:* 64 (physical), 448 (digital/electronic); *Databases:* 11. Weekly public service hours: 72.

STUDENT LIFE
Housing options: on-campus residence required through sophomore year; coed. Campus housing is leased by the school and is provided by a third party. Freshman campus housing is guaranteed.
Activities and organizations: drama/theater group, choral group, Yoga Group, Student Counsel.
Campus security: 24-hour emergency response devices and patrols, controlled dormitory access, resident assistant on-call for residential hall residents, after hours on-call mental health counseling.
Student services: personal/psychological counseling.

COSTS & FINANCIAL AID
Costs (2018–19) *Comprehensive fee:* $62,625 includes full-time tuition ($45,000), mandatory fees ($1110), and room and board ($16,515). Part-time tuition: $1980 per credit. *Required fees:* $1110 per year part-time. *College room only:* $12,710.
Financial Aid Of all full-time matriculated undergraduates who enrolled in 2017, 182 applied for aid, 170 were judged to have need, 16 had their need fully met. 23 Federal Work-Study jobs (averaging $2500). In 2017, 21 non-need-based awards were made. *Average percent of need met:* 75. *Average financial aid package:* $35,000. *Average need-based loan:* $7500. *Average need-based gift aid:* $23,000. *Average non-need-based aid:* $18,300. *Average indebtedness upon graduation:* $42,000. *Financial aid deadline:* 3/1.

APPLYING
Options: electronic application, deferred entrance.
Application fee: $110.
Required: essay or personal statement, high school transcript, minimum 2.5 GPA, 2 letters of recommendation, audition, pre-screen recording in select areas. *Required for some:* interview.

CONTACT
Ms. Melissa Cocco-Mitten, Director of Admissions, San Francisco Conservatory of Music, 50 Oak Street, San Francisco, CA 94102. *Phone:* 415-503-6231. *Fax:* 415-503-6299. *E-mail:* admit@sfcm.edu.

San Francisco State University
San Francisco, California
http://www.sfsu.edu/
- **State-supported** university, founded 1899, part of California State University System
- **Urban** 142-acre campus
- **Endowment** $83.7 million
- **Coed** 26,498 undergraduate students, 84% full-time, 56% women, 44% men
- **Moderately difficult** entrance level, 72% of applicants were admitted

UNDERGRAD STUDENTS
22,159 full-time, 4,339 part-time. 1% are from out of state; 6% Black or African American, non-Hispanic/Latino; 34% Hispanic/Latino; 26% Asian, non-Hispanic/Latino; 0.4% Native Hawaiian or other Pacific Islander, non-Hispanic/Latino; 0.1% American Indian or Alaska Native, non-Hispanic/Latino; 6% Two or more races, non-Hispanic/Latino; 4%

Race/ethnicity unknown; 7% international; 13% transferred in; 15% live on campus.

Freshmen:
Admission: 35,606 applied, 25,550 admitted, 4,287 enrolled. *Average high school GPA:* 3.3. *Test scores:* SAT evidence-based reading and writing scores over 500: 68%; SAT math scores over 500: 67%; ACT scores over 18: 72%; SAT evidence-based reading and writing scores over 600: 21%; SAT math scores over 600: 18%; ACT scores over 24: 23%; SAT evidence-based reading and writing scores over 700: 1%; SAT math scores over 700: 2%; ACT scores over 30: 3%.

Retention: 79% of full-time freshmen returned.

FACULTY
Total: 1,764, 43% full-time, 47% with terminal degrees.

ACADEMICS
Calendar: semesters. *Degrees:* certificates, bachelor's, master's, doctoral, post-master's, and postbachelor's certificates.

Special study options: academic remediation for entering students, accelerated degree program, adult/continuing education programs, advanced placement credit, cooperative education, distance learning, double majors, English as a second language, honors programs, independent study, internships, off-campus study, part-time degree program, services for LD students, student-designed majors, study abroad, summer session for credit. *ROTC:* Army (c), Air Force (c).

Computers: 2,000 computers/terminals and 800 ports are available on campus for general student use. Students can access the following: campus intranet, computer help desk, free student e-mail accounts, online (class) grades, online (class) registration, online (class) schedules. Campuswide network is available. 100% of college-owned or -operated housing units are wired for high-speed Internet access. Wireless service is available via entire campus.
Library: J. Paul Leonard Library. Study areas open 24 hours, 5–7 days a week; students can reserve study rooms.

STUDENT LIFE
Housing options: coed, women-only, special housing for students with disabilities. Campus housing is university owned. Freshman applicants given priority for college housing.

Activities and organizations: drama/theater group, student-run newspaper, radio and television station, choral group, national fraternities, national sororities.

Athletics Member NCAA. All Division II. *Intercollegiate sports:* baseball M(s), basketball M(s)/W(s), cross-country running M(s)/W(s), soccer M(s)/W(s), softball W(s), track and field W(s), volleyball W(s), wrestling M(s). *Intramural sports:* basketball M/W, cheerleading M(c)/W(c), ice hockey M(c)/W(c), rugby M(c)/W(c), soccer M/W, tennis M/W, volleyball M/W, water polo M(c)/W(c).

Campus security: 24-hour emergency response devices and patrols, student patrols, late-night transport/escort service, controlled dormitory access.

Student services: health clinic, personal/psychological counseling, women's center, legal services, veterans affairs office.

COSTS & FINANCIAL AID
Costs (2019–20) *Tuition:* area resident $5742 full-time; state resident $5742 full-time; nonresident $17,622 full-time. *Required fees:* $1518 full-time. *Room and board:* $13,462.
Financial Aid Of all full-time matriculated undergraduates who enrolled in 2018, 17,392 applied for aid, 15,632 were judged to have need, 3,364 had their need fully met. In 2018, 395 non-need-based awards were made. *Average percent of need met:* 65. *Average financial aid package:* $14,770. *Average need-based loan:* $4336. *Average need-based gift aid:* $9300. *Average non-need-based aid:* $2656. *Average indebtedness upon graduation:* $6069.

APPLYING
Standardized Tests *Required:* SAT or ACT (for admission).
Options: electronic application.
Application fee: $55.
Required: high school transcript.
Notification: 12/1 (freshmen), 12/1 (transfers).

CONTACT
Mr. Edward Carrigan, Director, Undergraduate Admissions, San Francisco State University, 1600 Holloway Avenue, San Francisco, CA 94132-1722. *Phone:* 415-338-7211. *E-mail:* edwardc@sfsu.edu.

San Jose State University
San Jose, California
http://www.sjsu.edu/
- **State-supported** comprehensive, founded 1857, part of California State University System
- **Urban** 152-acre campus
- **Coed** 27,327 undergraduate students, 85% full-time, 49% women, 51% men
- **Very difficult** entrance level, 55% of applicants were admitted

UNDERGRAD STUDENTS
23,099 full-time, 4,228 part-time. Students come from 42 states and territories; 122 other countries; 1% are from out of state; 3% Black or African American, non-Hispanic/Latino; 28% Hispanic/Latino; 36% Asian, non-Hispanic/Latino; 0.5% Native Hawaiian or other Pacific Islander, non-Hispanic/Latino; 0.1% American Indian or Alaska Native, non-Hispanic/Latino; 5% Two or more races, non-Hispanic/Latino; 4% Race/ethnicity unknown; 8% international; 14% transferred in; 14% live on campus.

Freshmen:
Admission: 36,243 applied, 19,811 admitted, 3,774 enrolled. *Average high school GPA:* 3.5. *Test scores:* SAT evidence-based reading and writing scores over 500: 84%; SAT math scores over 500: 87%; ACT scores over 18: 85%; SAT evidence-based reading and writing scores over 600: 37%; SAT math scores over 600: 44%; ACT scores over 24: 41%; SAT evidence-based reading and writing scores over 700: 5%; SAT math scores over 700: 12%; ACT scores over 30: 8%.

Retention: 83% of full-time freshmen returned.

FACULTY
Total: 1,858, 39% full-time.
Student/faculty ratio: 28:1.

ACADEMICS
Calendar: semesters. *Degrees:* certificates, bachelor's, master's, and doctoral.

Special study options: academic remediation for entering students, adult/continuing education programs, advanced placement credit, distance learning, double majors, honors programs, independent study, internships, off-campus study, part-time degree program, services for LD students, student-designed majors, study abroad, summer session for credit. *ROTC:* Army (c), Air Force (b).

Computers: Students can access the following: computer help desk, free student e-mail accounts, online (class) grades, online (class) registration, online (class) schedules. Campuswide network is available. Wireless service is available via entire campus.
Library: Dr. Martin Luther King Jr. Library plus 1 other. *Books:* 1.2 million (physical), 801,700 (digital/electronic); *Serial titles:* 1.3 million (physical), 1.3 million (digital/electronic); *Databases:* 408. Weekly public service hours: 139.

STUDENT LIFE
Housing options: on-campus residence required for freshman year; coed, men-only, women-only. Freshman applicants given priority for college housing.

Activities and organizations: drama/theater group, student-run newspaper, radio and television station, choral group, marching band, national fraternities, national sororities.

Athletics Member NCAA. All Division I except football (Division I-A). *Intercollegiate sports:* baseball M(s), basketball M(s)/W(s), cheerleading M/W, cross-country running M(s)/W(s), golf M(s)/W(s), gymnastics W(s), soccer M(s)/W(s), softball W(s), swimming and diving W(s), tennis W(s), track and field M(s), volleyball W(s), water polo M(s)/W(s). *Intramural sports:* archery M(c)/W(c), badminton M(c)/W(c), baseball M(c)/W(c), basketball M(c)/W(c), bowling M(c)/W(c), fencing M(c)/W(c), gymnastics M(c)/W(c), ice hockey M(c)/W(c), lacrosse M(c)/W(c), rugby M(c)/W(c), soccer M(c)/W(c), swimming and diving

M(c)/W(c), tennis M(c)/W(c), triathlon M(c)/W(c), ultimate Frisbee M(c)/W(c), volleyball M(c)/W(c), water polo M(c)/W(c), wrestling M(c).

Campus security: 24-hour emergency response devices and patrols, student patrols, late-night transport/escort service.

Student services: health clinic, personal/psychological counseling, women's center.

COSTS & FINANCIAL AID

Costs (2018–19) *Tuition:* state resident $5742 full-time, $1665 per term part-time; nonresident $15,246 full-time, $4041 per term part-time. *Required fees:* $1946 full-time, $1946 per year part-time. *Room and board:* $16,442; room only: $11,642. Room and board charges vary according to board plan, housing facility, and location. *Payment plans:* installment, deferred payment. *Waivers:* employees or children of employees.

Financial Aid Of all full-time matriculated undergraduates who enrolled in 2017, 16,121 applied for aid, 15,217 were judged to have need, 10,409 had their need fully met. In 2017, 31 non-need-based awards were made. *Average percent of need met:* 86. *Average financial aid package:* $18,759. *Average need-based loan:* $4380. *Average need-based gift aid:* $11,567. *Average non-need-based aid:* $1803. *Average indebtedness upon graduation:* $18,925. *Financial aid deadline:* 4/26.

APPLYING

Standardized Tests *Required:* SAT or ACT (for admission).

Options: electronic application.

Application fee: $55.

Required: high school transcript.

Application deadlines: 12/15 (freshmen), 12/15 (transfers).

Notification: continuous until 12/15 (freshmen), continuous until 12/15 (transfers).

CONTACT

Ms. Deanna Gonzales, Director of Undergraduate Admissions & Outreach, San Jose State University, One Washington Square, San Jose, CA 95192-0001. *Phone:* 408-283-7500. *Fax:* 408-924-2050. *E-mail:* admissions@sjsu.edu.

Santa Barbara Business College
Bakersfield, California
http://www.sbbcollege.edu/

CONTACT
Santa Barbara Business College, 5300 California Avenue, Bakersfield, CA 93309.

Santa Barbara Business College
Santa Maria, California
http://www.sbbcollege.edu/

CONTACT
Santa Barbara Business College, 303 East Plaza Drive, Santa Maria, CA 93454.

Santa Barbara Business College
Ventura, California
http://www.sbbcollege.edu/

CONTACT
Santa Barbara Business College, 4839 Market Street, Ventura, CA 93003.

Santa Clara University
Santa Clara, California
http://www.scu.edu/

- **Independent Roman Catholic (Jesuit)** university, founded 1851
- **Suburban** 106-acre campus with easy access to San Francisco, San Jose
- **Endowment** $905.9 million
- **Coed**
- **Very difficult** entrance level

FACULTY
Student/faculty ratio: 11:1.

ACADEMICS

Calendar: quarters. *Degrees:* bachelor's, master's, doctoral, and postbachelor's certificates.

Library: University Library plus 1 other. *Books:* 606,483 (physical), 658,072 (digital/electronic); *Serial titles:* 14,096 (physical), 84,245 (digital/electronic); *Databases:* 356. Weekly public service hours: 121; students can reserve study rooms.

STUDENT LIFE

Housing options: coed, special housing for students with disabilities. Campus housing is university owned. Freshman applicants given priority for college housing.

Activities and organizations: drama/theater group, student-run newspaper, radio station, choral group, marching band.

Athletics Member NCAA. All Division I.

Campus security: 24-hour emergency response devices and patrols, late-night transport/escort service, controlled dormitory access.

Student services: health clinic, personal/psychological counseling, veterans affairs office.

COSTS & FINANCIAL AID

Costs (2018–19) *Comprehensive fee:* $66,621 includes full-time tuition ($51,081), mandatory fees ($630), and room and board ($14,910). Part-time tuition: $1419 per unit. Part-time tuition and fees vary according to course load. *Room and board:* Room and board charges vary according to board plan and housing facility.

Financial Aid Of all full-time matriculated undergraduates who enrolled in 2018, 3,174 applied for aid, 2,419 were judged to have need, 683 had their need fully met. 234 Federal Work-Study jobs (averaging $3372). In 2018, 1530 non-need-based awards were made. *Average percent of need met:* 76. *Average financial aid package:* $37,858. *Average need-based loan:* $4415. *Average need-based gift aid:* $30,817. *Average non-need-based aid:* $16,948. *Average indebtedness upon graduation:* $28,808.

APPLYING

Standardized Tests *Required:* SAT or ACT (for admission).

Options: electronic application, early admission, early decision, early action, deferred entrance.

Application fee: $60.

Required: essay or personal statement, high school transcript, 1 letter of recommendation.

CONTACT

Mrs. Eva Blanco Masias, Dean of Undergraduate Admissions, Santa Clara University, 500 El Camino Real, Santa Clara, CA 95053. *Phone:* 408-554-4700. *Fax:* 408-554-5255. *E-mail:* admission@scu.edu.

Scripps College
Claremont, California
http://www.scrippscollege.edu/

- **Independent** 4-year, founded 1926
- **Suburban** 35-acre campus with easy access to Los Angeles
- **Women only** 1,048 undergraduate students, 99% full-time
- **Very difficult** entrance level, 24% of applicants were admitted

UNDERGRAD STUDENTS

1,042 full-time, 6 part-time. 55% are from out of state; 4% Black or African American, non-Hispanic/Latino; 14% Hispanic/Latino; 17% Asian, non-Hispanic/Latino; 0.2% Native Hawaiian or other Pacific Islander, non-Hispanic/Latino; 5% Two or more races, non-Hispanic/Latino; 3% Race/ethnicity unknown; 5% international; 1% transferred in; 94% live on campus.

Freshmen:
Admission: 3,160 applied, 766 admitted, 252 enrolled. *Average high school GPA:* 4.1. *Test scores:* SAT evidence-based reading and writing scores over 500: 100%; SAT math scores over 500: 100%; ACT scores over 18: 100%; SAT evidence-based reading and writing scores over 600: 97%; SAT math scores over 600: 90%; ACT scores over 24: 98%; SAT evidence-based reading and writing scores over 700: 54%; SAT math scores over 700: 45%; ACT scores over 30: 80%.

Retention: 92% of full-time freshmen returned.

FACULTY

Total: 126, 77% full-time, 95% with terminal degrees.

Student/faculty ratio: 10:1.

ACADEMICS

Calendar: semesters. *Degrees:* bachelor's and postbachelor's certificates.

Special study options: accelerated degree program, advanced placement credit, cooperative education, double majors, independent study, internships, off-campus study, services for LD students, student-designed majors, study abroad. *ROTC:* Army (c), Air Force (c).

Unusual degree programs: 3-2 business administration with Claremont Graduate University; engineering with Harvey Mudd College; American politics, economics, philosophy, public policy, international studies, religion with Claremont Graduate University.

Computers: Students can access the following: campus intranet, computer help desk, free student e-mail accounts, online (class) grades, online (class) registration, online (class) schedules, 2 ports per dorm room. Campuswide network is available. 100% of college-owned or -operated housing units are wired for high-speed Internet access. Wireless service is available via entire campus.

Library: Honnold/Mudd Library plus 2 others. Students can reserve study rooms.

STUDENT LIFE

Housing options: on-campus residence required for freshman year; women-only, special housing for students with disabilities. Campus housing is university owned. Freshman campus housing is guaranteed.

Activities and organizations: drama/theater group, student-run newspaper, radio station, choral group, Scripps Associated Students.

Athletics Member NCAA. All Division III except golf (Division II). *Intercollegiate sports:* basketball W, cross-country running W, equestrian sports W(c), fencing W(c), golf W, lacrosse W, rugby W(c), skiing (downhill) W(c), soccer W, softball W, swimming and diving W, tennis W, track and field W, ultimate Frisbee W(c), volleyball W, water polo W. *Intramural sports:* basketball W, soccer W, softball W, volleyball W, water polo W.

Campus security: 24-hour emergency response devices and patrols, late-night transport/escort service, controlled dormitory access.

Student services: health clinic, personal/psychological counseling, women's center.

COSTS & FINANCIAL AID

Costs (2018–19) *Comprehensive fee:* $71,956 includes full-time tuition ($54,806), mandatory fees ($218), and room and board ($16,932). Full-time tuition and fees vary according to course load and degree level. Part-time tuition: $6851 per course. Part-time tuition and fees vary according to course load and degree level. *College room only:* $9220. Room and board charges vary according to board plan. *Payment plans:* tuition prepayment, installment. *Waivers:* employees or children of employees.

Financial Aid Of all full-time matriculated undergraduates who enrolled in 2017, 509 applied for aid, 398 were judged to have need, 398 had their need fully met. In 2017, 150 non-need-based awards were made. *Average percent of need met:* 100. *Average financial aid package:* $44,090. *Average need-based loan:* $3806. *Average need-based gift aid:* $39,239. *Average non-need-based aid:* $20,435. *Average indebtedness upon graduation:* $17,756. *Financial aid deadline:* 2/1.

APPLYING

Standardized Tests *Required:* SAT or ACT (for admission).

Options: electronic application, early admission, early decision, deferred entrance.

Application fee: $60.

Required: essay or personal statement, high school transcript, 2 letters of recommendation, school report completed by the student's secondary school counselor. *Recommended:* minimum 3.0 GPA.

Early decision deadline: 11/15 (for plan 1), 1/4 (for plan 2).

Notification: 4/1 (freshmen), 12/15 (early decision plan 1), 2/15 (early decision plan 2).

CONTACT

Laura Stratton, Director of Admission, Scripps College, 1030 Columbia Avenue, Claremont, CA 91711. *Phone:* 909-621-8149. *Toll-free phone:* 800-770-1333. *Fax:* 909-607-7508. *E-mail:* admission@scrippscollege.edu.

Shasta Bible College

Redding, California

http://www.shasta.edu/

CONTACT

Connie Barton, Registrar, Shasta Bible College, 2951 Goodwater Avenue, Redding, CA 96002. *Phone:* 530-221-4275 Ext. 26. *Toll-free phone:* 800-800-4SBC. *Fax:* 530-221-6929. *E-mail:* registrar@shasta.edu.

Simpson University

Redding, California

http://www.simpsonu.edu/

CONTACT

Mr. Molly McKeever, Director of Undergraduate Admissions, Simpson University, 2211 College View Drive, Redding, CA 96003-8606. *Phone:* 530-226-5600. *Toll-free phone:* 888-9-SIMPSON. *Fax:* 530-226-4861. *E-mail:* admissions@simpsonu.edu.

Soka University of America

Aliso Viejo, California

http://www.soka.edu/

- **Independent** comprehensive, founded 1987
- **Suburban** 103-acre campus with easy access to Los Angeles, San Diego
- **Endowment** $1.2 billion
- **Coed** 428 undergraduate students, 100% full-time, 66% women, 34% men
- **Most difficult** entrance level, 39% of applicants were admitted

UNDERGRAD STUDENTS

428 full-time. Students come from 30 states and territories; 31 other countries; 57% are from out of state; 4% Black or African American, non-Hispanic/Latino; 12% Hispanic/Latino; 13% Asian, non-Hispanic/Latino; 0.5% Native Hawaiian or other Pacific Islander, non-Hispanic/Latino; 6% Two or more races, non-Hispanic/Latino; 2% Race/ethnicity unknown; 44% international; 99% live on campus.

Freshmen:
Admission: 462 applied, 180 admitted, 111 enrolled. *Average high school GPA:* 3.9. *Test scores:* SAT evidence-based reading and writing scores over 500: 100%; SAT math scores over 500: 100%; ACT scores over 18: 100%; SAT evidence-based reading and writing scores over 600: 67%; SAT math scores over 600: 79%; ACT scores over 24: 86%; SAT evidence-based reading and writing scores over 700: 16%; SAT math scores over 700: 51%; ACT scores over 30: 31%.

Retention: 92% of full-time freshmen returned.

FACULTY

Total: 73, 63% full-time, 82% with terminal degrees.

Student/faculty ratio: 8:1.

ACADEMICS

Calendar: semesters. *Degrees:* bachelor's and master's.

Special study options: cooperative education, independent study, internships, off-campus study, services for LD students, study abroad.

Computers: 100 computers/terminals and 100 ports are available on campus for general student use. Students can access the following: campus intranet, computer help desk, free student e-mail accounts, online (class) grades, online (class) registration, online (class) schedules, course and administrative applications. Campuswide network is available. 100% of college-owned or -operated housing units are wired for high-speed Internet access. Wireless service is available via entire campus.

Library: Daisaku and Kaneko Ikeda Library. *Books:* 95,080 (physical), 261,022 (digital/electronic); *Serial titles:* 96 (physical), 7,563 (digital/electronic); *Databases:* 170. Study areas open 24 hours, 5–7 days a week; students can reserve study rooms.

STUDENT LIFE

Housing options: on-campus residence required through senior year; coed, men-only, women-only, cooperative, special housing for students with disabilities. Campus housing is university owned. Freshman campus housing is guaranteed.

Activities and organizations: choral group, Josho Daiko (Japanese Drum Club), Rhythmission (Hip Hop Dance Club), Sualseros (Salsa Dance Club), Ka Pilina Ho'olokahi (Hawaiian Dance Club), Soul Wings (Choir).

Athletics Member NAIA. *Intercollegiate sports:* cross-country running M(s)/W(s), golf W(s), soccer M(s)/W(s), swimming and diving M(s)/W(s), track and field M(s)/W(s). *Intramural sports:* archery M(c)/W(c), baseball M(c), basketball M(c)/W(c), cheerleading M(c)/W(c), tennis M(c)/W(c), volleyball M(c)/W(c).

Campus security: 24-hour emergency response devices and patrols, student patrols, late-night transport/escort service, controlled dormitory access.

Student services: health clinic, personal/psychological counseling.

COSTS & FINANCIAL AID
Costs (2019–20) *Comprehensive fee:* $47,014 includes full-time tuition ($32,250), mandatory fees ($1732), and room and board ($13,032). Part-time tuition: $1344 per credit hour.

Financial Aid Of all full-time matriculated undergraduates who enrolled in 2017, 411 applied for aid, 350 were judged to have need, 249 had their need fully met. 34 Federal Work-Study jobs (averaging $1969). In 2017, 22 non-need-based awards were made. *Average percent of need met:* 88. *Average financial aid package:* $36,220. *Average need-based loan:* $4092. *Average need-based gift aid:* $24,414. *Average non-need-based aid:* $11,409. *Average indebtedness upon graduation:* $23,441. *Financial aid deadline:* 3/2.

APPLYING
Standardized Tests *Required:* SAT or ACT (for admission).

Options: electronic application, early admission, early action, deferred entrance.

Application fee: $45.

Required: essay or personal statement, high school transcript, 2 letters of recommendation, IERF evaluation for course work completed abroad. *Recommended:* interview.

Application deadlines: 1/15 (freshmen), 11/1 (early action).

Notification: 3/1 (freshmen), 12/1 (early action).

CONTACT
Erica Espejo, Admission Operations Coordinator, Soka University of America, Enrollment Services, 1 University Drive, Aliso Viejo, CA 92656. *Phone:* 949-480-4151 Ext. 4151. *Toll-free phone:* 888-600-SOKA. *Fax:* 949-480-4151. *E-mail:* eespejo@soka.edu.

Sonoma State University
Rohnert Park, California
http://www.sonoma.edu/

- **State-supported** comprehensive, founded 1960, part of California State University System
- **Small-town** 280-acre campus with easy access to San Francisco
- **Endowment** $47.1 million
- **Coed** 8,565 undergraduate students, 92% full-time, 61% women, 39% men
- **Moderately difficult** entrance level, 92% of applicants were admitted

UNDERGRAD STUDENTS
7,855 full-time, 710 part-time. 2% Black or African American, non-Hispanic/Latino; 34% Hispanic/Latino; 5% Asian, non-Hispanic/Latino; 0.3% Native Hawaiian or other Pacific Islander, non-Hispanic/Latino; 0.4% American Indian or Alaska Native, non-Hispanic/Latino; 6% Two or more races, non-Hispanic/Latino; 6% Race/ethnicity unknown; 3% international; 9% transferred in; 32% live on campus.

Freshmen:
Admission: 14,129 applied, 13,036 admitted, 1,740 enrolled. *Average high school GPA:* 3.2. *Test scores:* SAT evidence-based reading and writing scores over 500: 76%; SAT math scores over 500: 70%; ACT scores over 18: 83%; SAT evidence-based reading and writing scores over 600: 22%; SAT math scores over 600: 17%; ACT scores over 24: 28%; SAT evidence-based reading and writing scores over 700: 1%; SAT math scores over 700: 1%; ACT scores over 30: 2%.

Retention: 80% of full-time freshmen returned.

FACULTY
Total: 597, 42% full-time, 61% with terminal degrees.

Student/faculty ratio: 23:1.

ACADEMICS
Calendar: semesters. *Degrees:* bachelor's and master's.

Special study options: academic remediation for entering students, accelerated degree program, adult/continuing education programs, advanced placement credit, cooperative education, distance learning, double majors, English as a second language, honors programs, independent study, internships, off-campus study, part-time degree program, services for LD students, student-designed majors, study abroad, summer session for credit. *ROTC:* Army (c), Air Force (c).

Computers: Students can access the following: computer help desk, free student e-mail accounts, online (class) grades, online (class) registration, online (class) schedules. Campuswide network is available. 100% of college-owned or -operated housing units are wired for high-speed Internet access. Wireless service is available via entire campus.

Library: Jean and Charles Schultz Information Center plus 1 other. Students can reserve study rooms.

STUDENT LIFE
Housing options: coed, special housing for students with disabilities. Campus housing is university owned. Freshman applicants given priority for college housing.

Activities and organizations: drama/theater group, student-run newspaper, radio station, choral group, national fraternities, national sororities.

Athletics Member NCAA. All Division II. *Intercollegiate sports:* baseball M(s), basketball M(s)/W(s), cross-country running W, golf M, soccer M(s)/W(s), softball W(s), tennis M(s)/W(s), track and field W, volleyball W(s), water polo W. *Intramural sports:* archery M(c)/W(c), basketball M/W, cheerleading M/W, crew M/W, cross-country running M, fencing M, field hockey W, football M/W, lacrosse M(c)/W(c), rock climbing M/W, rowing M/W, soccer M/W, ultimate Frisbee M(c)/W(c), volleyball M(c)/W(c).

Campus security: 24-hour emergency response devices and patrols, student patrols, late-night transport/escort service, controlled dormitory access.

Student services: health clinic, personal/psychological counseling, women's center, legal services, veterans affairs office.

FINANCIAL AID
Financial Aid Of all full-time matriculated undergraduates who enrolled in 2018, 5,755 applied for aid, 4,706 were judged to have need, 64 had their need fully met. In 2018, 28 non-need-based awards were made. *Average percent of need met:* 58. *Average financial aid package:* $10,653. *Average need-based loan:* $2332. *Average need-based gift aid:* $8321. *Average non-need-based aid:* $2910. *Average indebtedness upon graduation:* $46,917.

APPLYING
Standardized Tests *Required:* SAT or ACT (for admission).

Options: electronic application, early admission.

Application fee: $55.

Required: high school transcript.

Application deadlines: rolling (freshmen), rolling (transfers).

Notification: continuous (freshmen), continuous (transfers).

CONTACT
Ms. Natalie Kalogiannis, Director of Admissions, Sonoma State University, 1801 East Cotati Avenue, Rohnert Park, CA 94928-3609. *Phone:* 707-664-2874. *E-mail:* natalie.kalogiannis@sonoma.edu.

Southern California Institute of Architecture
Los Angeles, California
http://www.sciarc.edu/

CONTACT
Jamie Black, Admissions Counselor, Southern California Institute of Architecture, 960 East Third Street, Los Angeles, CA 90013. *Phone:* 213-356-5320. *Fax:* 213-613-2260. *E-mail:* admissions@sciarc.edu.

Southern California Institute of Technology

Anaheim, California

http://www.scitech.edu/

CONTACT
Mrs. Sam Rokni, Southern California Institute of Technology, 525 N. Muller Street, Anaheim, CA 92801. *Phone:* 714-300-0300 Ext. 227. *Fax:* 714-300-0311. *E-mail:* admissions@scitech.edu.

Southern California Seminary

El Cajon, California

http://www.socalsem.edu/

CONTACT
Southern California Seminary, 2075 East Madison Avenue, El Cajon, CA 92019. *Phone:* 619-201-8959. *Toll-free phone:* 888-389-7244.

Southern States University

San Diego, California

http://www.ssu.edu/

CONTACT
Southern States University, 1094 Cudahy Place, Suite 120, San Diego, CA 92110.

Stanbridge University

Irvine, California

http://www.stanbridge.edu/

CONTACT
Stanbridge University, 2041 Business Center Drive, Irvine, CA 92612.

Stanford University

Stanford, California

http://www.stanford.edu/

- **Independent** university, founded 1891
- **Suburban** 8180-acre campus with easy access to San Francisco, San Jose
- **Coed**
- **Most difficult** entrance level

FACULTY
Student/faculty ratio: 4:1.

ACADEMICS
Calendar: quarters. *Degrees:* bachelor's, master's, doctoral, and postbachelor's certificates.
Library: Green Library plus 20 others. *Books:* 9.5 million (physical), 1.5 million (digital/electronic); *Serial titles:* 77,000 (physical). Study areas open 24 hours, 5–7 days a week; students can reserve study rooms.

STUDENT LIFE
Housing options: on-campus residence required for freshman year; coed, women-only, cooperative, special housing for students with disabilities. Campus housing is university owned. Freshman campus housing is guaranteed.

Activities and organizations: drama/theater group, student-run newspaper, radio and television station, choral group, marching band, Ram's Head (theatre club), Axe Committee (athletic support), Business Association of Stanford Entrepreneurial Students, Asian-American Student Association, Stanford Daily, national fraternities, national sororities.

Athletics Member NCAA, NAIA. All NCAA Division I.

Campus security: 24-hour emergency response devices and patrols, late-night transport/escort service, controlled dormitory access.

Student services: health clinic, personal/psychological counseling, women's center, legal services, veterans affairs office.

COSTS & FINANCIAL AID
Costs (2018–19) *Comprehensive fee:* $67,117 includes full-time tuition ($50,703), mandatory fees ($651), and room and board ($15,763). *Room and board:* Room and board charges vary according to board plan.

Financial Aid Of all full-time matriculated undergraduates who enrolled in 2017, 3,762 applied for aid, 3,434 were judged to have need, 3,097 had their need fully met. 548 Federal Work-Study jobs (averaging $2405). 1,837 state and other part-time jobs (averaging $2271). In 2017, 17 non-need-based awards were made. *Average percent of need met:* 100. *Average financial aid package:* $54,210. *Average need-based loan:* $3190. *Average need-based gift aid:* $50,542. *Average non-need-based aid:* $13,252. *Average indebtedness upon graduation:* $21,348.

APPLYING
Standardized Tests *Required:* SAT or ACT (for admission). *Recommended:* SAT Subject Tests (for admission).

Options: electronic application, early action, deferred entrance.

Application fee: $90.

Required: essay or personal statement, high school transcript, 2 letters of recommendation.

CONTACT
Stanford University, 450 Serra Mall, Stanford, CA 94305-2004.

Studio School

Los Angeles, California

http://www.studioschool.org/

CONTACT
Studio School, 1201 West 5th Street, Los Angeles, CA 90017.

SUM Bible College & Theological Seminary

Oakland, California

http://www.sum.edu/

CONTACT
Admissions, SUM Bible College & Theological Seminary, 735 105th Avenue, Oakland, CA 94603. *Phone:* 510-567-6174. *Toll-free phone:* 888-567-6174. *Fax:* 510-568-1024.

Thomas Aquinas College

Santa Paula, California

http://www.thomasaquinas.edu/

- **Independent Roman Catholic** 4-year, founded 1971
- **Rural** 131-acre campus with easy access to Los Angeles
- **Endowment** $22.5 million
- **Coed**
- **Very difficult** entrance level

FACULTY
Student/faculty ratio: 11:1.

ACADEMICS
Calendar: semesters. *Degree:* bachelor's.
Library: St. Bernardine Library. *Books:* 62,852 (physical); *Serial titles:* 78 (physical). Students can reserve study rooms.

STUDENT LIFE
Housing options: on-campus residence required through senior year; men-only, women-only. Campus housing is university owned. Freshman campus housing is guaranteed.

Activities and organizations: drama/theater group, choral group, Musical Groups (Choir, Chamber Orchestra), Theatre Groups, Language Clubs, Pro-Life Ministry, Religious groups.

Campus security: daily security patrol.

Student services: personal/psychological counseling.

COSTS & FINANCIAL AID
Costs (2018–19) *Comprehensive fee:* $33,400 includes full-time tuition ($25,000) and room and board ($8400).

Financial Aid Of all full-time matriculated undergraduates who enrolled in 2018, 297 applied for aid, 288 were judged to have need, 288 had their need fully met. 260 state and other part-time jobs (averaging $5238). *Average percent of need met:* 100. *Average financial aid package:* $21,064. *Average need-based loan:* $4361. *Average need-based gift aid:* $14,552. *Average indebtedness upon graduation:* $18,317. *Financial aid deadline:* 3/2.

APPLYING
Standardized Tests *Required:* SAT or ACT (for admission).

Options: electronic application.

Required: essay or personal statement, high school transcript, 3 letters of recommendation. *Required for some:* interview. *Recommended:* minimum 3.0 GPA.

CONTACT
Mr. Jonathan P. Daly, Director of Admissions, Thomas Aquinas College, 10000 Ojai Road, Santa Paula, CA 93060-9621. *Phone:* 805-525-4417 Ext. 5901. *Toll-free phone:* 800-634-9797. *Fax:* 805-421-5905. *E-mail:* admissions@thomasaquinas.edu.

Touro College Los Angeles
West Hollywood, California
http://www.touro.edu/losangeles/
- **Independent** 4-year, founded 2005
- **Coed**

ACADEMICS
Calendar: semesters. *Degree:* bachelor's.

COSTS
Costs (2018–19) *Tuition:* $16,940 full-time, $710 per credit hour part-time. Full-time tuition and fees vary according to program. Part-time tuition and fees vary according to program. No tuition increase for student's term of enrollment. *Required fees:* $300 full-time, $150 per term part-time.

CONTACT
Touro College Los Angeles, 1317 North Crescent Heights Boulevard, West Hollywood, CA 90046.

Touro University Worldwide
Los Alamitos, California
http://www.tuw.edu/
- **Independent** comprehensive
- **Coed**

FACULTY
Student/faculty ratio: 22:1.

ACADEMICS
Degrees: associate, bachelor's, master's, and doctoral.

COSTS
Costs (2018–19) *Tuition:* $10,800 full-time, $400 per credit hour part-time. Full-time tuition and fees vary according to program. Part-time tuition and fees vary according to program. No tuition increase for student's term of enrollment. *Payment plans:* tuition prepayment, installment.

APPLYING
Options: electronic application.

CONTACT
Touro University Worldwide, 10601 Calle Lee, Suite 179, Los Alamitos, CA 90720.

Trident University International
Cypress, California
http://www.trident.edu/

CONTACT
Trident University International, 5757 Plaza Drive, Suite 100, Cypress, CA 90630. *Phone:* 800-579-3197.

United States University
San Diego, California
http://www.usuniversity.edu/

CONTACT
Admissions, United States University, 7675 Mission Valley Road, San Diego, CA 92108. *Phone:* 619-477-6310. *Toll-free phone:* 888-422-3381. *Fax:* 619-477-7340.

University of Antelope Valley
Lancaster, California
http://www.uav.edu/

CONTACT
University of Antelope Valley, 44055 North Sierra Highway, Lancaster, CA 93534.

University of California, Berkeley
Berkeley, California
http://www.berkeley.edu/
- **State-supported** university, founded 1868, part of University of California System
- **Urban** 1232-acre campus with easy access to San Francisco
- **Coed**
- 17% of applicants were admitted

FACULTY
Student/faculty ratio: 18:1.

ACADEMICS
Calendar: semesters. *Degrees:* bachelor's, master's, doctoral, and postbachelor's certificates.
Library: Doe Library.

STUDENT LIFE
Housing options: coed, men-only, women-only, cooperative, special housing for students with disabilities. Campus housing is university owned and is provided by a third party. Freshman campus housing is guaranteed.

Activities and organizations: drama/theater group, student-run newspaper, radio and television station, choral group, marching band, national fraternities, national sororities.

Athletics Member NCAA. All Division I.

Campus security: 24-hour emergency response devices and patrols, late-night transport/escort service, controlled dormitory access, Office of Emergency Preparedness.

Student services: health clinic, personal/psychological counseling, women's center, legal services.

COSTS & FINANCIAL AID
Costs (2018–19) *Tuition:* state resident $11,442 full-time; nonresident $40,434 full-time. *Required fees:* $2742 full-time. *Room and board:* $16,160. Room and board charges vary according to board plan and housing facility.

Financial Aid Of all full-time matriculated undergraduates who enrolled in 2018, 17,130 applied for aid, 13,802 were judged to have need, 4,209 had their need fully met. In 2018, 1800 non-need-based awards were made. *Average percent of need met:* 83. *Average financial aid package:* $25,566. *Average need-based loan:* $6991. *Average need-based gift aid:* $21,662. *Average non-need-based aid:* $8335. *Average indebtedness upon graduation:* $18,225. *Financial aid deadline:* 3/2.

APPLYING
Standardized Tests *Required:* SAT or ACT (for admission). *Recommended:* SAT Subject Tests (for admission).

Options: electronic application.

Application fee: $70.

Required: essay or personal statement.

CONTACT
University of California, Berkeley, Berkeley, CA 94720.

University of California, Davis
Davis, California
http://www.ucdavis.edu/

- **State-supported** university, founded 1908, part of University of California System
- **Suburban** 5300-acre campus with easy access to San Francisco
- **Coed** 30,810 undergraduate students, 98% full-time, 61% women, 39% men
- **Very difficult** entrance level, 41% of applicants were admitted

UNDERGRAD STUDENTS
30,058 full-time, 752 part-time. 5% are from out of state; 2% Black or African American, non-Hispanic/Latino; 22% Hispanic/Latino; 27% Asian, non-Hispanic/Latino; 0.4% Native Hawaiian or other Pacific Islander, non-Hispanic/Latino; 0.2% American Indian or Alaska Native, non-Hispanic/Latino; 5% Two or more races, non-Hispanic/Latino; 2% Race/ethnicity unknown; 17% international; 10% transferred in; 25% live on campus.

Freshmen:
Admission: 76,377 applied, 31,564 admitted, 6,405 enrolled. *Average high school GPA:* 4.0. *Test scores:* SAT evidence-based reading and writing scores over 500: 94%; SAT math scores over 500: 95%; ACT scores over 18: 98%; SAT evidence-based reading and writing scores over 600: 63%; SAT math scores over 600: 70%; ACT scores over 24: 82%; SAT evidence-based reading and writing scores over 700: 16%; SAT math scores over 700: 39%; ACT scores over 30: 41%.

Retention: 92% of full-time freshmen returned.

FACULTY
Total: 2,133, 74% full-time, 91% with terminal degrees.

ACADEMICS
Calendar: quarters. *Degrees:* bachelor's, master's, doctoral, post-master's, and postbachelor's certificates.

Special study options: academic remediation for entering students, adult/continuing education programs, advanced placement credit, double majors, English as a second language, freshman honors college, honors programs, independent study, internships, part-time degree program, services for LD students, student-designed majors, study abroad, summer session for credit. *ROTC:* Army (b), Navy (c), Air Force (c).

Computers: Students can access the following: campus intranet, computer help desk, free student e-mail accounts, online (class) grades, online (class) registration, online (class) schedules, software packages. Campuswide network is available. 100% of college-owned or -operated housing units are wired for high-speed Internet access. Wireless service is available via classrooms, libraries.

Library: Peter J. Shields Library plus 6 others. *Books:* 4.9 million (physical), 1.3 million (digital/electronic); *Serial titles:* 106,593 (physical).

STUDENT LIFE
Housing options: coed, women-only, cooperative, special housing for students with disabilities. Campus housing is university owned, leased by the school and is provided by a third party. Freshman campus housing is guaranteed.

Activities and organizations: drama/theater group, student-run newspaper, radio and television station, choral group, marching band, national fraternities, national sororities.

Athletics Member NCAA. All Division I except football (Division I-AA). *Intercollegiate sports:* baseball M(s), basketball M(s)/W(s), cross-country running M(s)/W(s), field hockey W(s), golf M(s)/W(s)(c), gymnastics W(s), lacrosse W(s), soccer M(s)/W(s), softball W(s), swimming and diving W(s), tennis M(s)/W(s), track and field M(s)/W(s), volleyball W(s), water polo M(s)/W(s). *Intramural sports:* archery M(c)/W(c), badminton M(c)/W(c), basketball M/W, crew M(c)/W(c), equestrian sports M(c)/W(c), fencing M(c), field hockey W(c), football M/W, golf M/W, gymnastics M(c), ice hockey M(c)/W, lacrosse M(c)/W(c), racquetball M(c)/W(c), riflery M(c)/W(c), rugby M(c), sailing M(c)/W(c), skiing (cross-country) M(c)/W(c), skiing (downhill) M(c)/W(c), soccer M/W, softball M/W, swimming and diving W(c), table tennis M/W, tennis M/W, volleyball M(c)/W, water polo W(c).

Campus security: 24-hour emergency response devices and patrols, student patrols, late-night transport/escort service, controlled dormitory access, Campus Violence Prevention Program (CVPP).

Student services: health clinic, personal/psychological counseling, women's center, legal services, veterans affairs office.

COSTS & FINANCIAL AID
Costs (2018–19) *Tuition:* state resident $11,502 full-time; nonresident $40,497 full-time. *Required fees:* $2961 full-time. *Room and board:* $15,765. Room and board charges vary according to board plan.

Financial Aid Of all full-time matriculated undergraduates who enrolled in 2018, 20,587 applied for aid, 17,573 were judged to have need, 3,871 had their need fully met. In 2018, 1103 non-need-based awards were made. *Average percent of need met:* 81. *Average financial aid package:* $22,044. *Average need-based loan:* $5993. *Average need-based gift aid:* $19,236. *Average non-need-based aid:* $6833. *Average indebtedness upon graduation:* $18,575.

APPLYING
Standardized Tests *Required:* SAT or ACT (for admission).

Options: electronic application.

Application fee: $70.

Required: essay or personal statement, high school transcript, high school subject requirements.

Notification: 3/15 (freshmen), continuous until 3/15 (transfers).

CONTACT
Ebony Lewis, Executive Director, Admissions, University of California, Davis, One Shields Avenue, Davis, CA 95616. *Phone:* 530-754-0707. *E-mail:* ucdlewis@ucdavis.edu.

University of California, Irvine
Irvine, California
http://www.uci.edu/

- **State-supported** university, founded 1965, part of University of California System
- **Suburban** 1477-acre campus with easy access to Los Angeles
- **Coed** 29,736 undergraduate students, 98% full-time, 51% women, 49% men
- **Very difficult** entrance level, 29% of applicants were admitted

UNDERGRAD STUDENTS
29,250 full-time, 486 part-time. Students come from 46 states and territories; 78 other countries; 3% are from out of state; 2% Black or African American, non-Hispanic/Latino; 26% Hispanic/Latino; 36% Asian, non-Hispanic/Latino; 0.3% Native Hawaiian or other Pacific Islander, non-Hispanic/Latino; 0.1% American Indian or Alaska Native, non-Hispanic/Latino; 4% Two or more races, non-Hispanic/Latino; 1% Race/ethnicity unknown; 17% international; 9% transferred in; 38% live on campus.

Freshmen:
Admission: 95,065 applied, 27,339 admitted, 5,794 enrolled. *Average high school GPA:* 4.0. *Test scores:* SAT evidence-based reading and writing scores over 500: 97%; SAT math scores over 500: 97%; SAT evidence-based reading and writing scores over 600: 68%; SAT math scores over 600: 77%; SAT evidence-based reading and writing scores over 700: 23%; SAT math scores over 700: 45%.

Retention: 93% of full-time freshmen returned.

FACULTY
Total: 1,702, 80% full-time, 98% with terminal degrees.

Student/faculty ratio: 18:1.

ACADEMICS
Calendar: quarters. *Degrees:* bachelor's, master's, doctoral, and postbachelor's certificates.

Special study options: accelerated degree program, advanced placement credit, distance learning, double majors, English as a second language, honors programs, independent study, internships, off-campus study, services for LD students, study abroad, summer session for credit. *ROTC:* Army (b), Air Force (c).

Computers: 1,500 computers/terminals are available on campus for general student use. Students can access the following: campus intranet, computer help desk, free student e-mail accounts, online (class) grades, online (class) registration, online (class) schedules. Campuswide network is available. 100% of college-owned or -operated housing units are wired for high-speed Internet access. Wireless service is available via entire campus.

Library: Langson Library plus 4 others. *Books:* 2.0 million (physical), 1.3 million (digital/electronic); *Serial titles:* 4,309 (physical), 177,370 (digital/electronic); *Databases:* 1,652. Study areas open 24 hours, 5–7 days a week; students can reserve study rooms.

STUDENT LIFE
Housing options: coed, men-only, women-only, special housing for students with disabilities. Campus housing is university owned and is provided by a third party. Freshman campus housing is guaranteed.

Activities and organizations: drama/theater group, student-run newspaper, radio station, choral group, marching band, national fraternities, national sororities.

Athletics Member NCAA. All Division I. *Intercollegiate sports:* archery M(c)/W(c), badminton M(c)/W(c), baseball M(s), basketball M(s)/W(s), crew M(c)/W(c), cross-country running M(s)/W(s), fencing M(c)/W(c), golf M(s)/W(s)(c), lacrosse M(c)/W(c), rugby M(c)/W(c), sailing M(c)/W(c), soccer M(s)/W(s), table tennis M(c)/W(c), tennis M(s)/W(s), track and field M(s)/W(s), ultimate Frisbee M(c)/W(c), volleyball M(s)/W(s), water polo M(s)/W(s), wrestling M(c)/W(c). *Intramural sports:* basketball M/W, bowling M/W, football M/W, racquetball M/W, soccer M/W, softball M/W, swimming and diving M/W, table tennis M/W, tennis M/W, track and field M/W, ultimate Frisbee M/W, volleyball M/W, water polo M/W, wrestling M/W.

Campus security: 24-hour emergency response devices and patrols, student patrols, late-night transport/escort service, controlled dormitory access.

Student services: health clinic, personal/psychological counseling, veterans affairs office.

COSTS & FINANCIAL AID
Costs (2018–19) *Tuition:* state resident $11,442 full-time; nonresident $40,434 full-time. *Required fees:* $4172 full-time. *Room and board:* $15,263. Room and board charges vary according to board plan and housing facility. *Payment plan:* installment. *Waivers:* employees or children of employees.

Financial Aid Of all full-time matriculated undergraduates who enrolled in 2018, 20,425 applied for aid, 1,790 were judged to have need, 3,128 had their need fully met. In 2018, 635 non-need-based awards were made. *Average percent of need met:* 79. *Average financial aid package:* $23,096. *Average need-based loan:* $7215. *Average need-based gift aid:* $19,488. *Average non-need-based aid:* $8013. *Average indebtedness upon graduation:* $19,039. *Financial aid deadline:* 6/26.

APPLYING
Standardized Tests *Required:* SAT or ACT (for admission).

Options: electronic application.

Application fee: $70.

Required: essay or personal statement, high school transcript.

Application deadlines: 11/30 (freshmen), 11/30 (transfers).

Notification: 3/31 (freshmen), 4/30 (transfers).

CONTACT
Patricia Morales, Director, Admission and Relations with Schools, University of California, Irvine, Irvine, CA 92697. *Phone:* 949-824-6701. *Fax:* 949-824-7708. *E-mail:* patricia.morales@uci.edu.

University of California, Los Angeles
Los Angeles, California
http://www.ucla.edu/

- **State-supported** university, founded 1919, part of University of California System
- **Urban** 419-acre campus with easy access to Los Angeles
- **Endowment** $3.6 billion
- **Coed** 31,577 undergraduate students, 98% full-time, 58% women, 42% men
- **Very difficult** entrance level, 14% of applicants were admitted

UNDERGRAD STUDENTS
31,009 full-time, 568 part-time. 13% are from out of state; 3% Black or African American, non-Hispanic/Latino; 22% Hispanic/Latino; 28% Asian, non-Hispanic/Latino; 0.3% Native Hawaiian or other Pacific Islander, non-Hispanic/Latino; 0.2% American Indian or Alaska Native, non-Hispanic/Latino; 6% Two or more races, non-Hispanic/Latino; 2% Race/ethnicity unknown; 12% international; 11% transferred in; 48% live on campus.

Freshmen:
Admission: 113,761 applied, 15,970 admitted, 6,240 enrolled. *Average high school GPA:* 3.9. *Test scores:* SAT evidence-based reading and writing scores over 500: 99%; SAT math scores over 500: 98%; ACT scores over 18: 100%; SAT evidence-based reading and writing scores over 600: 87%; SAT math scores over 600: 82%; ACT scores over 24: 90%; SAT evidence-based reading and writing scores over 700: 51%; SAT math scores over 700: 59%; ACT scores over 30: 70%.

Retention: 97% of full-time freshmen returned.

FACULTY
Total: 3,180, 71% full-time, 98% with terminal degrees.
Student/faculty ratio: 17:1.

ACADEMICS
Calendar: quarters. *Degrees:* bachelor's, master's, and doctoral.

Special study options: accelerated degree program, advanced placement credit, double majors, freshman honors college, independent study, internships, off-campus study, services for LD students, student-designed majors, study abroad, summer session for credit. *ROTC:* Army (b), Navy (b), Air Force (b).

Computers: 4,000 computers/terminals are available on campus for general student use. Students can access the following: campus intranet, computer help desk, free student e-mail accounts, online (class) grades, online (class) registration, online (class) schedules, 24/7 Chat with a Librarian. Campuswide network is available. 100% of college-owned or -operated housing units are wired for high-speed Internet access. Wireless service is available via entire campus.

Library: Charles E. Young Research Library plus 13 others. *Books:* 13.8 million (physical), 2.1 million (digital/electronic); *Serial titles:* 9,543 (physical), 99,598 (digital/electronic); *Databases:* 1,794. Weekly public service hours: 104; study areas open 24 hours, 5–7 days a week; students can reserve study rooms.

STUDENT LIFE
Housing options: coed, cooperative, special housing for students with disabilities. Campus housing is university owned. Freshman campus housing is guaranteed.

Activities and organizations: drama/theater group, student-run newspaper, radio and television station, choral group, marching band, national fraternities, national sororities.

Athletics Member NCAA. All Division I except football (Division I-A). *Intercollegiate sports:* baseball M(s), basketball M(s)/W(s), crew W(s), cross-country running M(s)/W(s), golf M(s)/W(s)(c), gymnastics W(s), soccer M(s)/W(s), softball W(s), swimming and diving W(s), tennis M(s)/W(s), track and field M(s)/W(s), volleyball M(s)/W(s), water polo M(s)/W(s). *Intramural sports:* archery M/W, badminton M/W, basketball M/W, bowling M/W, crew M/W, cross-country running M/W, fencing M/W, field hockey W, football M/W, golf M/W, gymnastics M/W, ice hockey M/W, lacrosse M/W, racquetball M/W, riflery M/W, rugby M/W, sailing M/W, skiing (cross-country) M/W, skiing (downhill) M/W, soccer M/W, softball M/W, squash M/W, swimming and diving M/W, table tennis M/W, tennis M/W, track and field M/W, ultimate Frisbee M/W, volleyball M/W, water polo M/W.

Campus security: 24-hour emergency response devices and patrols, student patrols, late-night transport/escort service, controlled dormitory access.

Student services: health clinic, personal/psychological counseling, women's center, legal services, veterans affairs office.

COSTS & FINANCIAL AID
Costs (2018–19) *One-time required fee:* $165. *Tuition:* state resident $11,442 full-time; nonresident $40,434 full-time. *Required fees:* $2108 full-time. *Room and board:* $15,816. Room and board charges vary according to board plan and housing facility.

Financial Aid Of all full-time matriculated undergraduates who enrolled in 2018, 17,722 applied for aid, 16,060 were judged to have need, 3,855 had their need fully met. 2,441 Federal Work-Study jobs (averaging $2130). 24 state and other part-time jobs (averaging $3114). In 2018, 1012 non-need-based awards were made. *Average percent of need met:* 82. *Average financial aid package:* $23,990. *Average need-based loan:* $7365. *Average need-based gift aid:* $20,775. *Average non-need-based aid:* $6036. *Average indebtedness upon graduation:* $22,390.

APPLYING
Standardized Tests *Required:* SAT or ACT (for admission).
Options: electronic application.
Application fee: $70.
Required: essay or personal statement, high school transcript.
Application deadlines: 11/30 (freshmen), 11/30 (transfers).
Notification: 3/31 (freshmen), 4/30 (transfers).

CONTACT
Gary Clark, Director of Undergraduate Admissions, University of California, Los Angeles, 405 Hilgard Avenue, Los Angeles, CA 90095. *Phone:* 310-825-3101. *E-mail:* ugadm@saonet.ucla.edu.

University of California, Merced
Merced, California
http://www.ucmerced.edu/

- **State-supported** university, part of University of California System
- **Small-town** 815-acre campus with easy access to Fresno
- **Endowment** $38,592
- **Coed** 211,253 undergraduate students, 100% full-time, 2% women, 98% men
- **Moderately difficult** entrance level, 66% of applicants were admitted

UNDERGRAD STUDENTS
211,185 full-time, 68 part-time. Students come from 13 states and territories; 13 other countries; 5% Black or African American, non-Hispanic/Latino; 55% Hispanic/Latino; 19% Asian, non-Hispanic/Latino; 0.6% Native Hawaiian or other Pacific Islander, non-Hispanic/Latino; 0.1% American Indian or Alaska Native, non-Hispanic/Latino; 3% Two or more races, non-Hispanic/Latino; 0.5% Race/ethnicity unknown; 7% international; 0.1% transferred in; 38% live on campus.

Freshmen:
Admission: 25,121 applied, 16,624 admitted, 2,217 enrolled. *Average high school GPA:* 3.6. *Test scores:* SAT evidence-based reading and writing scores over 500: 60%; SAT math scores over 500: 58%; ACT scores over 18: 79%; SAT evidence-based reading and writing scores over 600: 15%; SAT math scores over 600: 21%; ACT scores over 24: 25%; SAT evidence-based reading and writing scores over 700: 4%; SAT math scores over 700: 3%; ACT scores over 30: 3%.
Retention: 86% of full-time freshmen returned.

FACULTY
Total: 407, 91% full-time, 86% with terminal degrees.
Student/faculty ratio: 18:1.

ACADEMICS
Degrees: bachelor's, master's, and doctoral.
Special study options: academic remediation for entering students, advanced placement credit, double majors, independent study, internships, off-campus study, part-time degree program, services for LD students, study abroad, summer session for credit.
Computers: 220 computers/terminals are available on campus for general student use. Students can access the following: campus intranet, computer help desk, free student e-mail accounts, online (class) grades, online (class) registration, online (class) schedules, student calendar, 10Gb online cloud storage, free office software. Campuswide network is available. 100% of college-owned or -operated housing units are wired for high-speed Internet access. Wireless service is available via entire campus.
Library: Kolligian Library. *Books:* 140,278 (physical), 1.7 million (digital/electronic); *Serial titles:* 100,836 (physical). Weekly public service hours: 97; students can reserve study rooms.

STUDENT LIFE
Housing options: coed, special housing for students with disabilities. Campus housing is university owned. Freshman campus housing is guaranteed.
Activities and organizations: drama/theater group, student-run newspaper, radio station, choral group, marching band, Philipino American Alliance, Vietnamese Student Association, Intervarsity Christian Fellowship, Latino Associated Students, Hip Hop Movement, national fraternities, national sororities.
Athletics Member NAIA. *Intercollegiate sports:* basketball M(s)/W(s), cross-country running M(s)/W(s), golf M(c), soccer M(s)/W(s), volleyball M(s)/W(s). *Intramural sports:* archery M/W, baseball M(c), basketball M/W, cheerleading M(c)/W(c), football M/W, lacrosse M(c)/W(c), soccer M/W, softball M(c)/W(c), table tennis M(c)/W(c), ultimate Frisbee M/W, volleyball M/W, weight lifting M(c)/W(c), wrestling M(c)/W(c).
Campus security: 24-hour emergency response devices and patrols, student patrols, late-night transport/escort service, controlled dormitory access.
Student services: health clinic, personal/psychological counseling, women's center, legal services.

COSTS & FINANCIAL AID
Costs (2018–19) *Tuition:* state resident $11,502 full-time, $2875 per term part-time; nonresident $39,516 full-time, $9879 per term part-time. Full-time tuition and fees vary according to course load. Part-time tuition and fees vary according to course load. *Required fees:* $2125 full-time, $2125 per year part-time. *Room and board:* $16,454. Room and board charges vary according to board plan. *Payment plan:* deferred payment. *Waivers:* employees or children of employees.
Financial Aid In 2018, 250 non-need-based awards were made. *Average financial aid package:* $16,539. *Average need-based loan:* $11,831. *Average need-based gift aid:* $17,735. *Average non-need-based aid:* $5716. *Average indebtedness upon graduation:* $19,551.

APPLYING
Standardized Tests *Required:* SAT or ACT (for admission).
Options: electronic application.
Application fee: $70.
Required: essay or personal statement, high school transcript, minimum 3.0 high school GPA for California residents.
Notification: 3/1 (freshmen), 3/1 (transfers).

CONTACT
Mr. Ruben Lubers, Assistant Director, Admissions and Outreach, University of California, Merced, 5200 North Lake Road, Merced, CA 95343. *Phone:* 209-228-4241. *E-mail:* admissions@ucmerced.edu.

University of California, Riverside
Riverside, California
http://www.ucr.edu/

- **State-supported** university, founded 1954, part of University of California System
- **Suburban** 1200-acre campus with easy access to Los Angeles
- **Endowment** $252.5 million
- **Coed** 20,581 undergraduate students, 98% full-time, 55% women, 45% men
- **Very difficult** entrance level, 51% of applicants were admitted

UNDERGRAD STUDENTS
20,210 full-time, 371 part-time. Students come from 23 states and territories; 95 other countries; 0.6% are from out of state; 3% Black or African American, non-Hispanic/Latino; 42% Hispanic/Latino; 34% Asian, non-Hispanic/Latino; 0.2% Native Hawaiian or other Pacific Islander, non-Hispanic/Latino; 0.1% American Indian or Alaska Native, non-Hispanic/Latino; 6% Two or more races, non-Hispanic/Latino; 1% Race/ethnicity unknown; 3% international; 9% transferred in; 30% live on campus.

Freshmen:
Admission: 49,082 applied, 25,259 admitted, 4,530 enrolled. *Average high school GPA:* 3.8. *Test scores:* SAT evidence-based reading and writing scores over 500: 95%; SAT math scores over 500: 94%; ACT scores over 18: 99%; SAT evidence-based reading and writing scores over

600: 55%; SAT math scores over 600: 55%; ACT scores over 24: 73%; SAT evidence-based reading and writing scores over 700: 7%; SAT math scores over 700: 18%; ACT scores over 30: 23%.

Retention: 89% of full-time freshmen returned.

FACULTY
Total: 1,173, 75% full-time, 98% with terminal degrees.
Student/faculty ratio: 22:1.

ACADEMICS
Calendar: quarters. *Degrees:* bachelor's, master's, and doctoral.

Special study options: accelerated degree program, adult/continuing education programs, advanced placement credit, distance learning, double majors, honors programs, independent study, internships, off-campus study, part-time degree program, services for LD students, study abroad, summer session for credit. *ROTC:* Army (c), Air Force (c).

Unusual degree programs: 3-2 engineering.

Computers: 556 computers/terminals are available on campus for general student use. Students can access the following: campus intranet, computer help desk, free student e-mail accounts, online (class) grades, online (class) registration, online (class) schedules, online viewing of financial information. Campuswide network is available. 100% of college-owned or -operated housing units are wired for high-speed Internet access. Wireless service is available via entire campus.

Library: Tomas Rivera Library plus 4 others. *Books:* 3.0 million (physical), 938,175 (digital/electronic); *Serial titles:* 71,249 (physical); *Databases:* 1,713. Weekly public service hours: 96; study areas open 24 hours, 5–7 days a week; students can reserve study rooms.

STUDENT LIFE
Housing options: coed, special housing for students with disabilities. Campus housing is university owned and is provided by a third party. Freshman campus housing is guaranteed.

Activities and organizations: drama/theater group, student-run newspaper, radio station, choral group, American Red Cross at University of California Riverside, American Medical Student Association, Running Club At UCR, Katipunan Pilipino Student Organization, Circle K International, national fraternities, national sororities.

Athletics Member NCAA. All Division I. *Intercollegiate sports:* baseball M(s), basketball M(s)/W(s), cross-country running M(s)/W(s), golf M(s)/W(s), soccer M(s)/W(s), softball W(s), swimming and diving M(s)/W(s), tennis M(s)/W(s), track and field M(s)/W(s), volleyball W(s). *Intramural sports:* badminton M/W, basketball M/W, racquetball M/W, rugby M(c)/W(c), soccer M/W, softball M/W, swimming and diving M/W, table tennis M(c)/W(c), tennis M/W, track and field M/W, volleyball M/W, wrestling M(c).

Campus security: 24-hour emergency response devices and patrols, student patrols, late-night transport/escort service, controlled dormitory access.

Student services: health clinic, personal/psychological counseling, women's center, legal services, veterans affairs office.

COSTS & FINANCIAL AID
Costs (2018–19) *Tuition:* state resident $11,442 full-time, $5721 per year part-time; nonresident $40,434 full-time, $20,217 per year part-time. Full-time tuition and fees vary according to course load. Part-time tuition and fees vary according to course load. *Required fees:* $4191 full-time, $1397 per term part-time. *Room and board:* $17,475. Room and board charges vary according to board plan and housing facility. *Payment plan:* deferred payment.

Financial Aid Of all full-time matriculated undergraduates who enrolled in 2018, 17,365 applied for aid, 15,802 were judged to have need, 2,588 had their need fully met. In 2018, 599 non-need-based awards were made. *Average percent of need met:* 83. *Average financial aid package:* $22,268. *Average need-based loan:* $5730. *Average need-based gift aid:* $18,195. *Average non-need-based aid:* $9842. *Average indebtedness upon graduation:* $21,126. *Financial aid deadline:* 6/1.

APPLYING
Standardized Tests *Required:* SAT or ACT (for admission).
Options: electronic application.

Application fee: $70.

Required: essay or personal statement, high school transcript, minimum 3.0 GPA.

Application deadlines: 11/30 (freshmen), 11/30 (out-of-state freshmen), 11/30 (transfers).

Notification: continuous until 3/1 (freshmen), continuous until 3/1 (out-of-state freshmen), continuous until 3/1 (transfers).

CONTACT
Ms. Emily D. Engelschall, Director, Undergraduate Admissions, University of California, Riverside, 3221 Student Services, 900 University Avenue, Riverside, CA 92521. *Phone:* 951-827-3986. *Fax:* 951-827-6346. *E-mail:* discover@ucr.edu.

★ University of California, San Diego
La Jolla, California
http://www.ucsd.edu/
- **State-supported** university, founded 1959, part of University of California System
- **Suburban** 1976-acre campus with easy access to San Diego
- **Coed**
- **Very difficult** entrance level

FACULTY
Student/faculty ratio: 19:1.

ACADEMICS
Calendar: quarters. *Degrees:* bachelor's, master's, and doctoral.
Library: Geisel Library plus 1 other. *Books:* 3.5 million (physical), 958,000 (digital/electronic). Study areas open 24 hours, 5–7 days a week; students can reserve study rooms.

STUDENT LIFE
Housing options: coed, special housing for students with disabilities. Campus housing is university owned. Freshman campus housing is guaranteed.

Activities and organizations: drama/theater group, student-run newspaper, radio and television station, choral group, marching band, national fraternities, national sororities.

Athletics Member NCAA. All Division II.

Campus security: 24-hour emergency response devices and patrols, student patrols, late-night transport/escort service, crime prevention programs.

Student services: health clinic, personal/psychological counseling, women's center, legal services, veterans affairs office.

FINANCIAL AID
Financial Aid Of all full-time matriculated undergraduates who enrolled in 2018, 19,315 applied for aid, 16,650 were judged to have need, 4,209 had their need fully met. In 2018, 601 non-need-based awards were made. *Average percent of need met:* 83. *Average financial aid package:* $23,550. *Average need-based loan:* $6433. *Average need-based gift aid:* $19,496. *Average non-need-based aid:* $11,201. *Average indebtedness upon graduation:* $21,061.

APPLYING
Standardized Tests *Required:* SAT and SAT Subject Tests or ACT (for admission), ACT Assessment with Writing or SAT Reasoning Test, plus two SAT Subject Tests (for admission).

Options: electronic application.

Application fee: $70.

Required: essay or personal statement, high school transcript, minimum 2.8 GPA. *Required for some:* minimum 3.4 GPA.

CONTACT
Ms. Adele Brumfield, Assistant Vice Chancellor, Enrollment Management, University of California, San Diego, 9500 Gilman Drive, 0021, La Jolla, CA 92093-0021. *Phone:* 858-534-3156. *E-mail:* admissionsreply@ucsd.edu.

See next page for display ad and page 1130 for the College Close-Up.

University of California, Santa Barbara

Santa Barbara, California

http://www.ucsb.edu/

- **State-supported** university, founded 1909, part of University of California System
- **Suburban** 989-acre campus
- **Endowment** $155.0 million
- **Coed**
- **Very difficult** entrance level

FACULTY
Student/faculty ratio: 17:1.

ACADEMICS
Calendar: quarters plus 6-week summer term. *Degrees:* bachelor's, master's, doctoral, post-master's, and postbachelor's certificates.
Library: Davidson Library plus 1 other. Weekly public service hours: 96; study areas open 24 hours, 5–7 days a week; students can reserve study rooms.

STUDENT LIFE
Housing options: coed, cooperative. Campus housing is university owned and is provided by a third party. Freshman applicants given priority for college housing.

Activities and organizations: drama/theater group, student-run newspaper, radio and television station, choral group, national fraternities, national sororities.

Athletics Member NCAA. All Division I.

Campus security: 24-hour emergency response devices and patrols, student patrols, late-night transport/escort service, controlled dormitory access.

Student services: health clinic, personal/psychological counseling, women's center, legal services.

COSTS & FINANCIAL AID
Costs (2018–19) *Tuition:* state resident $12,570 full-time; nonresident $41,562 full-time. *Required fees:* $1854 full-time. *Room and board:* $15,273. Room and board charges vary according to board plan and housing facility.

Financial Aid Of all full-time matriculated undergraduates who enrolled in 2018, 15,046 applied for aid, 12,836 were judged to have need, 2,185 had their need fully met. In 2018, 511 non-need-based awards were made. *Average percent of need met:* 80. *Average financial aid package:* $23,998. *Average need-based loan:* $6564. *Average need-based gift aid:* $20,707. *Average non-need-based aid:* $8089. *Average indebtedness upon graduation:* $20,004. *Financial aid deadline:* 5/31.

APPLYING
Standardized Tests *Required:* SAT or ACT (for admission). *Recommended:* SAT Subject Tests (for admission).

Options: electronic application.

Application fee: $70.

Required: essay or personal statement, high school transcript. *Required for some:* interview.

CONTACT
Office of Admissions, University of California, Santa Barbara, 1210 Cheadle Hall, Santa Barbara, CA 93106-2014. *Phone:* 805-893-2881. *Fax:* 805-893-2676. *E-mail:* admissions@sa.ucsb.edu.

University of California, Santa Cruz

Santa Cruz, California

http://www.ucsc.edu/

- **State-supported** university, founded 1965, part of University of California System
- **Small-town** 2000-acre campus with easy access to San Francisco, San Jose
- **Endowment** $207.1 million
- **Coed** 17,792 undergraduate students, 97% full-time, 48% women, 52% men
- **Very difficult** entrance level, 47% of applicants were admitted

UNDERGRAD STUDENTS

17,255 full-time, 537 part-time. Students come from 47 states and territories; 50 other countries; 4% are from out of state; 2% Black or African American, non-Hispanic/Latino; 28% Hispanic/Latino; 22% Asian, non-Hispanic/Latino; 0.2% Native Hawaiian or other Pacific Islander, non-Hispanic/Latino; 0.1% American Indian or Alaska Native, non-Hispanic/Latino; 8% Two or more races, non-Hispanic/Latino; 2% Race/ethnicity unknown; 8% international; 10% transferred in; 51% live on campus.

Freshmen:

Admission: 55,355 applied, 26,224 admitted, 3,695 enrolled. *Average high school GPA:* 3.6. *Test scores:* SAT evidence-based reading and writing scores over 500: 97%; SAT math scores over 500: 98%; ACT scores over 18: 99%; SAT evidence-based reading and writing scores over 600: 70%; SAT math scores over 600: 73%; ACT scores over 24: 80%; SAT evidence-based reading and writing scores over 700: 20%; SAT math scores over 700: 35%; ACT scores over 30: 37%.

Retention: 88% of full-time freshmen returned.

FACULTY

Total: 839, 73% full-time, 98% with terminal degrees.

Student/faculty ratio: 19:1.

ACADEMICS

Calendar: quarters. *Degrees:* bachelor's, master's, doctoral, and postbachelor's certificates.

Special study options: accelerated degree program, advanced placement credit, cooperative education, double majors, freshman honors college, honors programs, independent study, internships, off-campus study, services for LD students, student-designed majors, study abroad, summer session for credit. *ROTC:* Army (c), Navy (c), Air Force (c).

Computers: Students can access the following: campus intranet, computer help desk, free student e-mail accounts, online (class) grades, online (class) registration, online (class) schedules. Campuswide network is available. 100% of college-owned or -operated housing units are wired for high-speed Internet access. Wireless service is available via entire campus.

Library: UCSC Library. *Books:* 1.1 million (physical), 1.1 million (digital/electronic); *Serial titles:* 44,167 (physical), 72,348 (digital/electronic); *Databases:* 538. Weekly public service hours: 94; students can reserve study rooms.

STUDENT LIFE

Housing options: coed, men-only, women-only, cooperative. Campus housing is university owned. Freshman campus housing is guaranteed.

Activities and organizations: drama/theater group, student-run newspaper, radio and television station, choral group, marching band, Bayanihan, â??Chinese Student Association, â??City on a Hill Press, â??College Panhellenic & Inter-Greek Council, â??Indian Student Association, national fraternities, national sororities.

Athletics Member NCAA. All Division III. *Intercollegiate sports:* badminton M(c)/W(c), basketball M/W, cheerleading M(c)/W(c), cross-country running M/W, equestrian sports M(c)/W(c), fencing M(c)/W(c), golf W, lacrosse M(c)/W(c), racquetball M(c)/W(c), rugby M(c)/W(c), sailing M(c)/W(c), soccer M/W, softball W(c), swimming and diving M/W, tennis M/W, track and field M/W, triathlon M(c)/W(c), ultimate Frisbee M(c)/W(c), volleyball M/W, water polo M(c)/W(c). *Intramural sports:* basketball M/W, soccer M/W, softball M/W, ultimate Frisbee M/W, volleyball M/W, water polo M/W.

Campus security: 24-hour emergency response devices and patrols, late-night transport/escort service, controlled dormitory access.

Student services: health clinic, personal/psychological counseling, women's center.

COSTS & FINANCIAL AID

Costs (2018–19) *Tuition:* state resident $11,502 full-time; nonresident $39,516 full-time. Part-time tuition and fees vary according to course load. *Required fees:* $2507 full-time. *Room and board:* $16,407. Room and board charges vary according to board plan and housing facility. *Payment plan:* installment.

Financial Aid Of all full-time matriculated undergraduates who enrolled in 2018, 11,932 applied for aid, 10,129 were judged to have need, 2,414 had their need fully met. 1,241 Federal Work-Study jobs (averaging

$2685). In 2018, 1658 non-need-based awards were made. *Average percent of need met:* 84. *Average financial aid package:* $25,395. *Average need-based loan:* $6600. *Average need-based gift aid:* $21,020. *Average non-need-based aid:* $5657. *Average indebtedness upon graduation:* $22,092. *Financial aid deadline:* 3/2.

APPLYING

Standardized Tests *Required:* SAT or ACT (for admission).

Options: electronic application.

Application fee: $70.

Required: essay or personal statement, high school transcript, minimum 3.0 GPA, minimum high school GPA of 3.0 for California residents, 3.4 for non-residents. *Required for some:* minimum 3.4 GPA.

Application deadlines: 11/30 (freshmen), 11/30 (transfers).

Notification: 3/31 (freshmen), 4/30 (transfers).

CONTACT

Blia Yang, Director, Admissions, University of California, Santa Cruz, 1156 High Street, Santa Cruz, CA 95064. *Phone:* 831-459-4008. *Fax:* 831-459-4452. *E-mail:* admissions@ucsc.edu.

University of La Verne

La Verne, California

http://www.laverne.edu/

- **Independent** university, founded 1891
- **Suburban** 66-acre campus with easy access to Los Angeles
- **Coed** 2,798 undergraduate students, 97% full-time, 58% women, 42% men
- **Moderately difficult** entrance level, 51% of applicants were admitted

UNDERGRAD STUDENTS

2,721 full-time, 77 part-time. Students come from 22 states and territories; 36 other countries; 4% are from out of state; 5% Black or African American, non-Hispanic/Latino; 57% Hispanic/Latino; 5% Asian, non-Hispanic/Latino; 0.5% Native Hawaiian or other Pacific Islander, non-Hispanic/Latino; 0.1% American Indian or Alaska Native, non-Hispanic/Latino; 5% Two or more races, non-Hispanic/Latino; 2% Race/ethnicity unknown; 7% international; 7% transferred in; 30% live on campus.

Freshmen:

Admission: 7,276 applied, 3,703 admitted, 673 enrolled. *Average high school GPA:* 3.5. *Test scores:* SAT evidence-based reading and writing scores over 500: 85%; SAT math scores over 500: 84%; ACT scores over 18: 87%; SAT evidence-based reading and writing scores over 600: 28%; SAT math scores over 600: 29%; ACT scores over 24: 38%; SAT evidence-based reading and writing scores over 700: 2%; SAT math scores over 700: 5%; ACT scores over 30: 6%.

Retention: 83% of full-time freshmen returned.

FACULTY

Total: 534, 44% full-time.

Student/faculty ratio: 12:1.

ACADEMICS

Calendar: 4-1-4. *Degrees:* certificates, bachelor's, master's, and doctoral (also offers continuing education program with significant enrollment not reflected in profile).

Special study options: academic remediation for entering students, adult/continuing education programs, advanced placement credit, distance learning, double majors, English as a second language, freshman honors college, honors programs, independent study, internships, off-campus study, part-time degree program, services for LD students, student-designed majors, study abroad, summer session for credit. *ROTC:* Army (c).

Computers: Students can access the following: computer help desk, free student e-mail accounts, online (class) grades, online (class) registration, online (class) schedules, MyLaVerne (online). Campuswide network is available. 100% of college-owned or -operated housing units are wired for high-speed Internet access. Wireless service is available via entire campus.

Library: Wilson Library. Students can reserve study rooms.

STUDENT LIFE

Housing options: coed, men-only, women-only. Campus housing is university owned.

Activities and organizations: drama/theater group, student-run newspaper, radio and television station, choral group, Associated Students of La Verne, Latino Student Forum, Black Student Union, Psi Chi, Voices in Action, national fraternities, national sororities.

Athletics Member NCAA. All Division III. *Intercollegiate sports:* baseball M, basketball M/W, cross-country running M/W, football M, golf M, soccer M/W, softball W, swimming and diving M/W, tennis M/W, track and field M/W, volleyball W, water polo M/W.

Campus security: 24-hour emergency response devices and patrols, late-night transport/escort service, controlled dormitory access.

Student services: health clinic, personal/psychological counseling, veterans affairs office.

COSTS & FINANCIAL AID

Costs (2019–20) *Comprehensive fee:* $57,690 includes full-time tuition ($43,004), mandatory fees ($1496), and room and board ($13,190). Part-time tuition: $1260 per semester hour.

Financial Aid Of all full-time matriculated undergraduates who enrolled in 2018, 2,385 applied for aid, 2,268 were judged to have need, 436 had their need fully met. In 2018, 359 non-need-based awards were made. *Average percent of need met:* 61. *Average financial aid package:* $29,047. *Average need-based loan:* $4207. *Average need-based gift aid:* $16,680. *Average non-need-based aid:* $12,916. *Average indebtedness upon graduation:* $33,384.

APPLYING

Standardized Tests *Required:* SAT or ACT (for admission).

Options: electronic application, deferred entrance.

Application fee: $50.

Required: essay or personal statement, high school transcript, 2 letters of recommendation.

Application deadlines: 2/1 (freshmen), 4/1 (transfers).

Notification: continuous (freshmen), continuous (transfers).

CONTACT

Mr. Erasmo Fuentes, Director, Admission, University of La Verne, 1950 Third Street, La Verne, CA 91750. *Phone:* 800-876-4858. *Toll-free phone:* 800-876-4858. *Fax:* 909-392-2714. *E-mail:* admissions@ulv.edu.

University of Phoenix–Bay Area Campus

San Jose, California
http://www.phoenix.edu/

CONTACT

Marc Booker, Senior Director, Office of Admissions and Evaluation, University of Phoenix–Bay Area Campus, 4035 South Riverpoint Parkway, Mail Stop CF-L101, Phoenix, AZ 85040-1958. *Phone:* 602-557-4609. *Toll-free phone:* 866-766-0766. *Fax:* 480-643-1156.

University of Phoenix–Central Valley Campus

Fresno, California
http://www.phoenix.edu/

CONTACT

Marc Booker, Senior Director, Office of Admissions and Evaluation, University of Phoenix–Central Valley Campus, 4035 South Riverpoint Parkway, Mail Stop CF-L101, Phoenix, AZ 85040. *Phone:* 602-557-4609. *Toll-free phone:* 866-766-0766. *Fax:* 480-643-1156.

University of Phoenix–Sacramento Valley Campus

Sacramento, California
http://www.phoenix.edu/

CONTACT

Marc Booker, Senior Director, Office of Admissions and Evaluation, University of Phoenix–Sacramento Valley Campus, 4035 South Riverpoint Parkway, Mail Stop CF-L101, Phoenix, AZ 85040. *Phone:* 602-557-4609. *Toll-free phone:* 866-766-0766. *Fax:* 480-643-1156.

University of Phoenix–San Diego Campus

San Diego, California
http://www.phoenix.edu/

CONTACT

Marc Booker, Senior Director, Office of Admissions and Evaluation, University of Phoenix–San Diego Campus, 4035 South Riverpoint Parkway, Mail Stop CF-L101, Phoenix, AZ 85040. *Phone:* 602-557-4609. *Toll-free phone:* 866-766-0766. *Fax:* 480-643-1156.

University of Redlands

Redlands, California
http://www.redlands.edu/

CONTACT

Ms. Belinda Sandoval Zazueta, Director of Undergraduate Admission, University of Redlands, 1200 East Colton Avenue, PO Box 3080, Redlands, CA 92373-0999. *Phone:* 909-748-8074. *Toll-free phone:* 800-455-5064. *Fax:* 909-335-4089. *E-mail:* belinda_sandoval@redlands.edu.

University of Saint Katherine

San Marcos, California
http://www.usk.edu/

CONTACT

Dean Marina Karavokiris, Dean of Admissions and Registrar, University of Saint Katherine, 1637 Capalina Road, San Marcos, CA 92069. *Phone:* 760-471-1316 Ext. 307. *Fax:* 760-471-1314. *E-mail:* admissions@stkath.org.

University of San Diego

San Diego, California
http://www.sandiego.edu/

- **Independent Roman Catholic** university, founded 1949
- **Urban** 180-acre campus with easy access to San Diego
- **Endowment** $530.0 million
- **Coed** 5,855 undergraduate students, 97% full-time, 55% women, 45% men
- **Very difficult** entrance level, 53% of applicants were admitted

UNDERGRAD STUDENTS

5,678 full-time, 177 part-time. Students come from 48 states and territories; 64 other countries; 56% are from out of state; 4% Black or African American, non-Hispanic/Latino; 20% Hispanic/Latino; 7% Asian, non-Hispanic/Latino; 0.3% Native Hawaiian or other Pacific Islander, non-Hispanic/Latino; 0.3% American Indian or Alaska Native, non-Hispanic/Latino; 6% Two or more races, non-Hispanic/Latino; 3% Race/ethnicity unknown; 10% international; 5% transferred in; 46% live on campus.

Freshmen:
Admission: 13,287 applied, 7,031 admitted, 1,310 enrolled. *Average high school GPA:* 3.9. *Test scores:* SAT evidence-based reading and writing scores over 500: 99%; SAT math scores over 500: 98%; ACT scores over 18: 100%; SAT evidence-based reading and writing scores over 600: 76%; SAT math scores over 600: 74%; ACT scores over 24: 89%; SAT evidence-based reading and writing scores over 700: 15%; SAT math scores over 700: 22%; ACT scores over 30: 34%.

Retention: 90% of full-time freshmen returned.

FACULTY
Total: 998, 48% full-time, 76% with terminal degrees.
Student/faculty ratio: 14:1.

ACADEMICS
Calendar: 4-1-4. *Degrees:* bachelor's, master's, doctoral, and postbachelor's certificates.

Special study options: advanced placement credit, double majors, English as a second language, honors programs, independent study, internships, part-time degree program, services for LD students, study abroad, summer session for credit. *ROTC:* Army (c), Navy (b), Air Force (c).

Computers: 1,066 computers/terminals and 4,250 ports are available on campus for general student use. Students can access the following: campus intranet, computer help desk, free student e-mail accounts, online (class) grades, online (class) registration, online (class) schedules. Campuswide network is available. 100% of college-owned or -operated housing units are wired for high-speed Internet access. Wireless service is available via entire campus.
Library: Helen K. and James S. Copley Library plus 1 other. *Books:* 455,753 (physical), 870,474 (digital/electronic); *Serial titles:* 10,446 (physical), 146,831 (digital/electronic); *Databases:* 391. Weekly public service hours: 116; students can reserve study rooms.

STUDENT LIFE
Housing options: on-campus residence required through sophomore year; coed, men-only, women-only, special housing for students with disabilities. Campus housing is university owned. Freshman campus housing is guaranteed.

Activities and organizations: drama/theater group, student-run newspaper, radio and television station, choral group, marching band, American Marketing Association - USD Chapter, Student Vegans United, Be Blue - Go Green, Asian Student Organization, International Student Organization, national fraternities, national sororities.

Athletics Member NCAA. All Division I except football (Division I-AA). *Intercollegiate sports:* baseball M(s), basketball M(s)/W(s), crew M/W(s), cross-country running M(s)/W(s), equestrian sports M(c)/W(c), golf M(s), lacrosse M(c)/W(c), rock climbing M(c)/W(c), rugby M(c), soccer M(s)/W(s), softball W(s), swimming and diving W(s), tennis M(s)/W(s), track and field W(s), ultimate Frisbee M(c)/W(c), volleyball M(c)/W(c). *Intramural sports:* baseball M(c), basketball M/W, cross-country running M(c)/W(c), football M/W, golf M(c), ice hockey M(c), soccer M(c)/W(c), softball M/W, tennis M(c)/W(c), ultimate Frisbee M/W, volleyball M/W(c), water polo M(c).

Campus security: 24-hour emergency response devices and patrols, late-night transport/escort service, controlled dormitory access.

Student services: health clinic, personal/psychological counseling, women's center, legal services.

COSTS & FINANCIAL AID
Costs (2019–20) *Comprehensive fee:* $65,312 includes full-time tuition ($50,450), mandatory fees ($736), and room and board ($14,126). Part-time tuition: $1740 per credit. *Required fees:* $376 per year part-time.

Financial Aid Of all full-time matriculated undergraduates who enrolled in 2017, 3,291 applied for aid, 2,864 were judged to have need, 356 had their need fully met. 522 Federal Work-Study jobs (averaging $2297). In 2017, 1105 non-need-based awards were made. *Average percent of need met:* 71. *Average financial aid package:* $35,359. *Average need-based loan:* $7377. *Average need-based gift aid:* $28,712. *Average non-need-based aid:* $16,574. *Average indebtedness upon graduation:* $31,264.

APPLYING
Standardized Tests *Required:* SAT or ACT (for admission).
Options: electronic application, deferred entrance.
Application fee: $55.
Required: essay or personal statement, high school transcript, 1 letter of recommendation.
Application deadlines: 12/15 (freshmen), 12/15 (out-of-state freshmen), 3/1 (transfers).
Notification: 2/20 (freshmen), continuous until 2/20 (out-of-state freshmen), continuous until 6/30 (transfers).

CONTACT
Ms. Minh-Ha Hoang, Director of Admissions, University of San Diego, 5998 Alcala Park, San Diego, CA 92110. *Phone:* 619-260-4506. *Toll-free phone:* 800-248-4873. *Fax:* 619-260-6836. *E-mail:* admissions@sandiego.edu.

⭐ University of San Francisco
San Francisco, California
http://www.usfca.edu/
- **Independent Roman Catholic (Jesuit)** university, founded 1855
- **Urban** 55-acre campus with easy access to San Francisco Bay Area
- **Endowment** $345.5 million
- **Coed** 6,704 undergraduate students, 96% full-time, 63% women, 37% men
- **Moderately difficult** entrance level, 65% of applicants were admitted

UNDERGRAD STUDENTS
6,435 full-time, 269 part-time. Students come from 54 states and territories; 83 other countries; 17% are from out of state; 4% Black or African American, non-Hispanic/Latino; 21% Hispanic/Latino; 24% Asian, non-Hispanic/Latino; 0.6% Native Hawaiian or other Pacific Islander, non-Hispanic/Latino; 0.2% American Indian or Alaska Native, non-Hispanic/Latino; 8% Two or more races, non-Hispanic/Latino; 2% Race/ethnicity unknown; 14% international; 6% transferred in; 36% live on campus.

Freshmen:
Admission: 18,411 applied, 11,885 admitted, 1,542 enrolled. *Average high school GPA:* 3.5. *Test scores:* SAT evidence-based reading and writing scores over 500: 96%; SAT math scores over 500: 97%; ACT scores over 18: 99%; SAT evidence-based reading and writing scores over 600: 61%; SAT math scores over 600: 56%; ACT scores over 24: 71%; SAT evidence-based reading and writing scores over 700: 9%; SAT math scores over 700: 15%; ACT scores over 30: 19%.
Retention: 83% of full-time freshmen returned.

FACULTY
Total: 1,179, 41% full-time, 65% with terminal degrees.
Student/faculty ratio: 14:1.

ACADEMICS
Calendar: 4-1-4. *Degrees:* certificates, bachelor's, master's, doctoral, post-master's, and postbachelor's certificates.

Special study options: accelerated degree program, adult/continuing education programs, advanced placement credit, cooperative education, distance learning, double majors, English as a second language, external degree program, freshman honors college, honors programs, independent study, internships, off-campus study, part-time degree program, services for LD students, student-designed majors, study abroad, summer session for credit. *ROTC:* Army (b), Air Force (c).

Unusual degree programs: 3-2 engineering with University of Southern California.

Computers: 257 computers/terminals are available on campus for general student use. Students can access the following: campus intranet, computer help desk, free student e-mail accounts, online (class) grades, online (class) registration, online (class) schedules. Campuswide network is available. 100% of college-owned or -operated housing units are wired for high-speed Internet access. Wireless service is available via entire campus.
Library: Gleeson Library|Geschke Center plus 1 other. *Books:* 580,130 (physical), 664,362 (digital/electronic); *Serial titles:* 7,960 (physical), 135,406 (digital/electronic); *Databases:* 348. Weekly public service hours: 136; study areas open 24 hours, 5–7 days a week; students can reserve study rooms.

STUDENT LIFE
Housing options: on-campus residence required for freshman year; coed, women-only. Campus housing is university owned and leased by the school. Freshman campus housing is guaranteed.

Activities and organizations: drama/theater group, student-run newspaper, radio and television station, choral group, marching band, national fraternities, national sororities.

Athletics Member NCAA. All Division I. *Intercollegiate sports:* baseball M(s), basketball M(s)/W(s), cross-country running M(s)/W(s), golf

M(s)/W(s), soccer M(s)/W(s), softball M(c)/W(c), tennis M(s)/W(s), track and field M(s)/W(s), volleyball M(c)/W(s). *Intramural sports:* badminton M(c)/W(c), basketball M/W, equestrian sports M(c)/W(c), fencing M(c)/W(c), football M/W, golf M(c)/W(c), lacrosse M(c), rock climbing M/W, rugby M(c)/W(c), sailing M(c)/W(c), skiing (cross-country) M(c)/W(c), soccer M/W, softball M/W, swimming and diving M/W, table tennis M/W, tennis M(c)/W(c), ultimate Frisbee M(c)/W(c), volleyball M/W, water polo M(c)/W(c).

Campus security: 24-hour emergency response devices and patrols, student patrols, late-night transport/escort service, controlled dormitory access.

Student services: health clinic, personal/psychological counseling, women's center.

COSTS & FINANCIAL AID

Costs (2019–20) *Comprehensive fee:* $65,692 includes full-time tuition ($49,740), mandatory fees ($542), and room and board ($15,410). Part-time tuition: $1770 per credit hour. *Required fees:* $271 per term part-time. *College room only:* $10,470.

Financial Aid Of all full-time matriculated undergraduates who enrolled in 2018, 4,270 applied for aid, 3,839 were judged to have need, 291 had their need fully met. 1,071 Federal Work-Study jobs (averaging $4682). 740 state and other part-time jobs (averaging $4628). In 2018, 1367 non-need-based awards were made. *Average percent of need met:* 68. *Average financial aid package:* $35,749. *Average need-based loan:* $4037. *Average need-based gift aid:* $30,051. *Average non-need-based aid:* $18,006. *Average indebtedness upon graduation:* $33,475. *Financial aid deadline:* 1/15.

APPLYING

Standardized Tests *Required:* SAT or ACT (for admission). *Required for some:* TOEFL, IELTS or PTE Academic if English is not the student's native language.

Options: electronic application, early admission, early decision, early action, deferred entrance.

Application fee: $70.

Required: essay or personal statement, high school transcript, 1 letter of recommendation. *Recommended:* minimum 2.5 GPA.

Application deadlines: 1/15 (freshmen), rolling (transfers), 11/1 (early action).

Early decision deadline: 11/1.

Notification: continuous until 3/15 (freshmen), continuous until 4/1 (transfers), 12/1 (early decision), 12/14 (early action).

CONTACT
April Crabtree, Assistant Vice Provost, Undergraduate Admission, University of San Francisco, 2130 Fulton Street, San Francisco, CA 94117-1080. *Phone:* 415-422-5287. *Toll-free phone:* 800-CALL-USF. *E-mail:* admissions@usfca.edu.

See below for display ad and page 1146 for the College Close-Up.

University of Southern California
Los Angeles, California
http://www.usc.edu/

- **Independent** university, founded 1880
- **Urban** 229-acre campus with easy access to Los Angeles
- **Endowment** $4.6 billion
- **Coed**
- **Most difficult** entrance level

FACULTY
Student/faculty ratio: 8:1.

ACADEMICS
Calendar: semesters. *Degrees:* bachelor's, master's, doctoral, post-master's, and postbachelor's certificates.
Library: Doheny Memorial Library plus 23 others.

STUDENT LIFE
Housing options: coed, special housing for students with disabilities. Campus housing is university owned and is provided by a third party. Freshman campus housing is guaranteed.

Activities and organizations: drama/theater group, student-run newspaper, radio and television station, choral group, marching band, national fraternities, national sororities.

Athletics Member NCAA. All Division I except football (Division I-A).

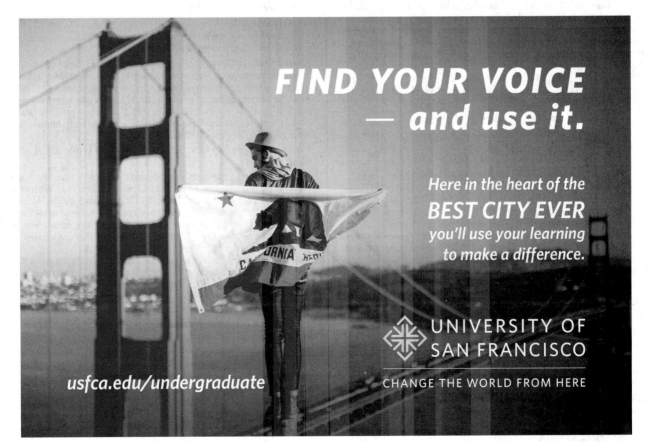

Campus security: 24-hour emergency response devices and patrols, student patrols, late-night transport/escort service, controlled dormitory access.

Student services: health clinic, personal/psychological counseling, women's center, legal services.

COSTS & FINANCIAL AID
Costs (2018–19) *One-time required fee:* $350. *Comprehensive fee:* $69,208 includes full-time tuition ($53,448), mandatory fees ($875), and room and board ($14,885). Full-time tuition and fees vary according to program. Part-time tuition: $1800 per credit hour. Part-time tuition and fees vary according to course load and program. *College room only:* $8985. Room and board charges vary according to board plan and housing facility. *Payment plans:* tuition prepayment, installment.

Financial Aid Of all full-time matriculated undergraduates who enrolled in 2017, 9,101 applied for aid, 6,944 were judged to have need, 5,870 had their need fully met. In 2017, 3884 non-need-based awards were made. *Average percent of need met:* 100. *Average financial aid package:* $51,884. *Average need-based loan:* $6203. *Average need-based gift aid:* $38,603. *Average non-need-based aid:* $18,846. *Average indebtedness upon graduation:* $28,228.

APPLYING
Standardized Tests *Required:* SAT or ACT (for admission).
Options: electronic application, deferred entrance.
Application fee: $85.
Required: essay or personal statement, high school transcript.

CONTACT
Timothy Brunold, Dean of Admission, University of Southern California, University Park Campus, Los Angeles, CA 90089. *Phone:* 213-740-1111. *Fax:* 213-821-0200. *E-mail:* admitusc@usc.edu.

University of the Pacific
Stockton, California
http://www.pacific.edu/
- **Independent** university, founded 1851
- **Suburban** 175-acre campus with easy access to Sacramento
- **Coed**
- **Moderately difficult** entrance level

FACULTY
Student/faculty ratio: 13:1.

ACADEMICS
Calendar: semesters. *Degrees:* bachelor's, master's, and doctoral.
Library: University of the Pacific Library plus 1 other.

STUDENT LIFE
Housing options: on-campus residence required through sophomore year; coed, cooperative. Campus housing is university owned. Freshman campus housing is guaranteed.

Activities and organizations: drama/theater group, student-run newspaper, radio station, choral group, national fraternities, national sororities.

Athletics Member NCAA. All Division I.

Campus security: 24-hour emergency response devices and patrols, late-night transport/escort service, controlled dormitory access.

Student services: health clinic, personal/psychological counseling, legal services.

COSTS & FINANCIAL AID
Costs (2018–19) *Comprehensive fee:* $61,690 includes full-time tuition ($47,480), mandatory fees ($560), and room and board ($13,650). Part-time tuition: $1638 per credit hour. Part-time tuition and fees vary according to course load. *Room and board:* Room and board charges vary according to board plan and housing facility.

Financial Aid Of all full-time matriculated undergraduates who enrolled in 2018, 2,798 applied for aid, 2,577 were judged to have need, 268 had their need fully met. In 2018, 514 non-need-based awards were made. *Average percent of need met:* 59. *Average financial aid package:* $36,515. *Average need-based loan:* $6789. *Average need-based gift aid:* $30,999. *Average non-need-based aid:* $16,244. *Average indebtedness upon graduation:* $30,586.

APPLYING
Standardized Tests *Required:* SAT or ACT (for admission).
Recommended: SAT and SAT Subject Tests or ACT (for admission).
Options: electronic application, early action.
Application fee: $35.
Required: essay or personal statement, high school transcript.

CONTACT
Mr. Rich Toledo, Director of Admissions, University of the Pacific, 3601 Pacific Avenue, Stockton, CA 95211-0197. *Phone:* 209-946-2211. *Fax:* 209-946-2413. *E-mail:* admissions@pacific.edu.

University of the People
Pasadena, California
http://www.uopeople.edu/

CONTACT
University of the People, 225 South Lake Avenue, Suite 300, Pasadena, CA 91101.

University of the West
Rosemead, California
http://www.uwest.edu/

CONTACT
University of the West, 1409 Walnut Grove Avenue, Rosemead, CA 91770. *Phone:* 626-571-8811 Ext. 311.

Vanguard University of Southern California
Costa Mesa, California
http://www.vanguard.edu/
- **Independent** comprehensive, founded 1920, affiliated with Assemblies of God
- **Suburban** 38-acre campus with easy access to Los Angeles
- **Coed** 1,848 undergraduate students, 86% full-time, 67% women, 33% men
- **Moderately difficult** entrance level, 40% of applicants were admitted

UNDERGRAD STUDENTS
1,588 full-time, 260 part-time. 10% are from out of state; 5% Black or African American, non-Hispanic/Latino; 42% Hispanic/Latino; 4% Asian, non-Hispanic/Latino; 1% Native Hawaiian or other Pacific Islander, non-Hispanic/Latino; 0.3% American Indian or Alaska Native, non-Hispanic/Latino; 3% Two or more races, non-Hispanic/Latino; 4% Race/ethnicity unknown; 2% international; 5% transferred in; 50% live on campus.

Freshmen:
Admission: 4,414 applied, 1,773 admitted, 461 enrolled. *Average high school GPA:* 3.3. *Test scores:* SAT evidence-based reading and writing scores over 500: 68%; SAT math scores over 500: 62%; ACT scores over 18: 73%; SAT evidence-based reading and writing scores over 600: 16%; SAT math scores over 600: 13%; ACT scores over 24: 23%; SAT evidence-based reading and writing scores over 700: 1%; ACT scores over 30: 3%.

Retention: 75% of full-time freshmen returned.

FACULTY
Total: 240, 29% full-time, 47% with terminal degrees.
Student/faculty ratio: 14:1.

ACADEMICS
Calendar: semesters. *Degrees:* certificates, associate, bachelor's, master's, and postbachelor's certificates.

Special study options: accelerated degree program, adult/continuing education programs, advanced placement credit, distance learning, double majors, independent study, internships, off-campus study, part-time degree program, services for LD students, study abroad, summer session for credit. *ROTC:* Army (c), Air Force (c).

Computers: 100 computers/terminals and 50 ports are available on campus for general student use. Students can access the following:

computer help desk, free student e-mail accounts, online (class) grades, online (class) registration, online (class) schedules. Campuswide network is available. 100% of college-owned or -operated housing units are wired for high-speed Internet access. Wireless service is available via entire campus.
Library: O. Cope Budge Library. Students can reserve study rooms.

STUDENT LIFE
Housing options: coed, men-only, women-only, special housing for students with disabilities. Campus housing is university owned. Freshman campus housing is guaranteed.

Activities and organizations: drama/theater group, student-run newspaper, choral group, local outreach, Global Missions, student organizations/clubs, choral groups.

Athletics Member NAIA. *Intercollegiate sports:* baseball M(s), basketball M(s)/W(s), cross-country running M(s)/W(s), soccer M(s)/W(s), softball W(s), track and field M(s)/W(s), volleyball W(s). *Intramural sports:* basketball M/W, football M/W, soccer M/W, softball M/W, volleyball M/W.

Campus security: 24-hour emergency response devices and patrols, student patrols, late-night transport/escort service, controlled dormitory access.

Student services: health clinic, personal/psychological counseling, women's center, veterans affairs office.

COSTS & FINANCIAL AID
Costs (2019–20) *Comprehensive fee:* $45,050 includes full-time tuition ($34,500), mandatory fees ($600), and room and board ($9950). *College room only:* $6000.

Financial Aid Of all full-time matriculated undergraduates who enrolled in 2018, 1,410 applied for aid, 1,406 were judged to have need, 1,406 had their need fully met. In 2018, 1491 non-need-based awards were made. *Average financial aid package:* $15,670. *Average need-based gift aid:* $8020. *Average non-need-based aid:* $8521. *Average indebtedness upon graduation:* $24,840.

APPLYING
Standardized Tests *Required:* SAT or ACT (for admission).

Options: electronic application, early admission, early action, deferred entrance.

Application fee: $45.

Required: essay or personal statement, high school transcript, minimum 2.8 GPA, 2 letters of recommendation. *Required for some:* interview.

Notification: 5/1 (freshmen), continuous (transfers).

CONTACT
Kristi Pruett, Undergraduate Admissions, Vanguard University of Southern California, 55 Fair Drive, Costa Mesa, CA 92626. *Phone:* 800-722-6279 Ext. 4107. *Toll-free phone:* 800-722-6279. *Fax:* 714-966-5471. *E-mail:* admissions@vanguard.edu.

Westcliff University
Irvine, California
http://www.westcliff.edu/

CONTACT
Westcliff University, 16715 Von Karman Avenue, Irvine, CA 92606.

West Coast Ultrasound Institute
Beverly Hills, California
http://wcui.edu/

CONTACT
West Coast Ultrasound Institute, 291 S. La Cienega Boulevard, Suite 500, Beverly Hills, CA 90211.

West Coast University
Anaheim, California
http://westcoastuniversity.edu/

CONTACT
West Coast University, 1477 S. Manchester Avenue, Anaheim, CA 92802.

West Coast University
North Hollywood, California
http://www.westcoastuniversity.edu/

CONTACT
Mr. Roger A. Miller, Dean of Admissions and Registrar, West Coast University, 12215 Victory Boulevard, North Hollywood, CA 91606. *Phone:* 213-427-4400. *Toll-free phone:* 866-508-2684. *E-mail:* info@katz.wcula.edu.

West Coast University
Ontario, California
http://westcoastuniversity.edu/

CONTACT
West Coast University, 2855 E. Guasti Road, Ontario, CA 91761.

Westmont College
Santa Barbara, California
http://www.westmont.edu/

- **Independent nondenominational** 4-year, founded 1937
- **Suburban** 111-acre campus with easy access to Los Angeles
- **Endowment** $84.0 million
- **Coed** 1,277 undergraduate students, 99% full-time, 61% women, 39% men
- **Moderately difficult** entrance level, 62% of applicants were admitted

UNDERGRAD STUDENTS
1,266 full-time, 11 part-time. Students come from 41 states and territories; 20 other countries; 27% are from out of state; 2% Black or African American, non-Hispanic/Latino; 18% Hispanic/Latino; 8% Asian, non-Hispanic/Latino; 0.6% Native Hawaiian or other Pacific Islander, non-Hispanic/Latino; 0.2% American Indian or Alaska Native, non-Hispanic/Latino; 6% Two or more races, non-Hispanic/Latino; 6% Race/ethnicity unknown; 2% international; 4% transferred in; 95% live on campus.

Freshmen:
Admission: 2,937 applied, 1,833 admitted, 345 enrolled. *Average high school GPA:* 3.8. *Test scores:* SAT evidence-based reading and writing scores over 500: 96%; SAT math scores over 500: 95%; ACT scores over 18: 100%; SAT evidence-based reading and writing scores over 600: 65%; SAT math scores over 600: 54%; ACT scores over 24: 73%; SAT evidence-based reading and writing scores over 700: 23%; SAT math scores over 700: 19%; ACT scores over 30: 30%.

Retention: 82% of full-time freshmen returned.

FACULTY
Total: 154, 62% full-time, 69% with terminal degrees.
Student/faculty ratio: 11:1.

ACADEMICS
Calendar: semesters. *Degree:* bachelor's.

Special study options: academic remediation for entering students, accelerated degree program, advanced placement credit, double majors, honors programs, internships, off-campus study, services for LD students, student-designed majors, study abroad, summer session for credit. *ROTC:* Army (c), Air Force (c).

Unusual degree programs: 3-2 engineering with Washington University in St. Louis; Boston University; University of Southern California; University of California, Berkeley, Los Angeles, and Santa Barbara; California Polytechnic State University; Stanford University.

Computers: 100 computers/terminals and 100 ports are available on campus for general student use. Students can access the following: campus intranet, computer help desk, free student e-mail accounts, online (class) grades, online (class) registration, online (class) schedules. Campuswide network is available. 100% of college-owned or -operated housing units are wired for high-speed Internet access. Wireless service is available via entire campus.
Library: Roger John Voskuyl Library. *Books:* 129,978 (physical), 186,115 (digital/electronic); *Serial titles:* 418 (physical), 70,790 (digital/electronic); *Databases:* 68. Weekly public service hours: 102;

study areas open 24 hours, 5–7 days a week; students can reserve study rooms.

STUDENT LIFE

Housing options: on-campus residence required through senior year; coed, cooperative, special housing for students with disabilities. Campus housing is university owned. Freshman campus housing is guaranteed.

Activities and organizations: drama/theater group, student-run newspaper, choral group, Student Ministries, Student Government, Competitive Athletics, Music, Art and Theater ensembles, Intramural Sports.

Athletics Member NAIA. *Intercollegiate sports:* baseball M(s), basketball M(s)/W(s), cross-country running M(s)/W(s), rugby M(c), soccer M(s)/W(s), tennis M(s)/W(s), track and field M(s)/W(s), volleyball M(c)/W(s). *Intramural sports:* basketball M/W, cheerleading W(c), football M/W, rugby M(c), sailing M(c)/W(c), soccer M/W, ultimate Frisbee M(c), volleyball M/W, water polo M(c)/W(c).

Campus security: 24-hour emergency response devices and patrols, late-night transport/escort service, controlled dormitory access.

Student services: health clinic, personal/psychological counseling, women's center.

COSTS & FINANCIAL AID

Costs (2019–20) *Comprehensive fee:* $61,240 includes full-time tuition ($45,410), mandatory fees ($1184), and room and board ($14,646). Part-time tuition: $2120 per unit. *College room only:* $8996.

Financial Aid Of all full-time matriculated undergraduates who enrolled in 2018, 982 applied for aid, 854 were judged to have need, 218 had their need fully met. 313 Federal Work-Study jobs (averaging $1883). In 2018, 325 non-need-based awards were made. *Average percent of need met:* 83. *Average financial aid package:* $36,098. *Average need-based loan:* $5780. *Average need-based gift aid:* $27,357. *Average non-need-based aid:* $20,517. *Average indebtedness upon graduation:* $35,362.

APPLYING

Standardized Tests *Required:* SAT or ACT (for admission).

Options: electronic application, early action.

Required: essay or personal statement, high school transcript, 1 letter of recommendation. *Required for some:* interview. *Recommended:* interview.

Application deadlines: rolling (freshmen), rolling (transfers), 11/15 (early action).

Notification: continuous (freshmen), continuous (transfers), 12/1 (early action).

CONTACT

Irene Neller, Vice President for Enrollment, Marketing and Communications, Westmont College, 955 La Paz Road, Santa Barbara, CA 93108-1099. *Phone:* 805-565-6016. *Toll-free phone:* 800-777-9011. *E-mail:* ineller@westmont.edu.

See below for display ad and page 1154 for the College Close-Up.

★ Whittier College
Whittier, California
http://www.whittier.edu/

- **Independent** comprehensive, founded 1887
- **Suburban** 95-acre campus with easy access to Los Angeles
- **Endowment** $117.0 million
- **Coed** 1,732 undergraduate students, 98% full-time, 58% women, 42% men
- **Moderately difficult** entrance level, 76% of applicants were admitted

UNDERGRAD STUDENTS

1,699 full-time, 33 part-time. Students come from 32 states and territories; 27 other countries; 23% are from out of state; 5% Black or African American, non-Hispanic/Latino; 51% Hispanic/Latino; 7% Asian, non-Hispanic/Latino; 0.3% Native Hawaiian or other Pacific Islander, non-Hispanic/Latino; 0.5% American Indian or Alaska Native, non-Hispanic/Latino; 7% Two or more races, non-Hispanic/Latino; 1% Race/ethnicity unknown; 3% international; 5% transferred in; 45% live on campus.

Freshmen:

Admission: 6,220 applied, 4,724 admitted, 512 enrolled. *Average high school GPA:* 3.6. *Test scores:* SAT evidence-based reading and writing scores over 500: 86%; SAT math scores over 500: 83%; ACT scores over 18: 93%; SAT evidence-based reading and writing scores over 600: 35%; SAT math scores over 600: 28%; ACT scores over 24: 38%; SAT evidence-based reading and writing scores over 700: 3%; SAT math scores over 700: 4%; ACT scores over 30: 6%.

Retention: 76% of full-time freshmen returned.

FACULTY

Total: 162, 72% full-time, 78% with terminal degrees.

Student/faculty ratio: 12:1.

ACADEMICS

Calendar: 4-1-4. *Degrees:* bachelor's, master's, and doctoral.

Special study options: academic remediation for entering students, accelerated degree program, adult/continuing education programs, advanced placement credit, distance learning, double majors, independent study, internships, off-campus study, services for LD students, student-designed majors, study abroad, summer session for credit. *ROTC:* Army (c).

Unusual degree programs: 3-2 engineering with University of Southern California, University of Minnesota.

Computers: 175 computers/terminals and 175 ports are available on campus for general student use. Students can access the following: campus intranet, computer help desk, free student e-mail accounts, online (class) grades, online (class) registration, online (class) schedules. Campuswide network is available. 100% of college-owned or -operated housing units are wired for high-speed Internet access. Wireless service is available via entire campus.

Library: Bonnie Bell Wardman Library plus 1 other. *Books:* 180,054 (physical), 178,258 (digital/electronic); *Serial titles:* 2,730 (physical), 222,633 (digital/electronic); *Databases:* 67. Study areas open 24 hours, 5–7 days a week; students can reserve study rooms.

STUDENT LIFE

Housing options: on-campus residence required through junior year; coed, special housing for students with disabilities. Campus housing is university owned. Freshman campus housing is guaranteed.

Activities and organizations: drama/theater group, student-run newspaper, radio and television station, choral group, Hispanic Students Association, Hawaiian Islander Club, Black Student Union, Asian Students Association, Environment & Sustainability - Raising Awareness for the Environment / Urban Agriculture / Food Recovery Network.

Athletics Member NCAA. All Division III. *Intercollegiate sports:* baseball M, basketball M/W, cross-country running M/W, football M, golf M/W, lacrosse M/W, soccer M/W, softball W, swimming and diving M/W, tennis M/W, track and field M/W, volleyball W, water polo M/W. *Intramural sports:* basketball M/W, softball M/W, volleyball M/W.

Campus security: 24-hour emergency response devices and patrols, late-night transport/escort service, controlled dormitory access.

Student services: health clinic, personal/psychological counseling, veterans affairs office.

COSTS & FINANCIAL AID

Costs (2018–19) *Comprehensive fee:* $61,856 includes full-time tuition ($47,496), mandatory fees ($390), and room and board ($13,970). Full-time tuition and fees vary according to course load. Part-time tuition: $1979 per semester hour. Part-time tuition and fees vary according to course load. *College room only:* $7666. Room and board charges vary according to board plan. *Payment plan:* installment. *Waivers:* employees or children of employees.

Financial Aid Of all full-time matriculated undergraduates who enrolled in 2018, 1,406 applied for aid, 1,298 were judged to have need, 201 had their need fully met. 119 Federal Work-Study jobs (averaging $2231). 740 state and other part-time jobs (averaging $2473). In 2018, 355 non-need-based awards were made. *Average percent of need met:* 77. *Average financial aid package:* $38,799. *Average need-based loan:* $5182. *Average need-based gift aid:* $36,009. *Average non-need-based aid:* $23,963. *Average indebtedness upon graduation:* $32,167. *Financial aid deadline:* 6/30.

APPLYING
Standardized Tests *Required for some:* SAT or ACT (for admission). *Recommended:* SAT Subject Tests (for admission).

Options: electronic application, early action, deferred entrance.

Application fee: $50.

Required: essay or personal statement, high school transcript, minimum 2.5 GPA, 2 letters of recommendation. *Required for some:* minimum 3.0 GPA. *Recommended:* minimum 2.5 GPA, interview.

Application deadlines: rolling (freshmen), rolling (out-of-state freshmen), rolling (transfers), 11/15 (early action).

Notification: continuous (freshmen), continuous (out-of-state freshmen), 3/1 (transfers).

CONTACT
Ms. Janine Bissic, Director of Admission, Whittier College, Office of Admission, 13406 East Philadelphia Street, Whittier, CA 90608-0634. *Phone:* 562-907-4238. *Fax:* 562-907-4870. *E-mail:* admission@whittier.edu.

See previous page for display ad and page 1160 for the College Close-Up.

William Jessup University
Rocklin, California
http://www.jessup.edu/

CONTACT
Traditional Undergraduate Admission, William Jessup University, 2121 University Avenue, Rocklin, CA 95765. *Phone:* 916-577-2222. *Fax:* 916-577-2220. *E-mail:* admissions@jessup.edu.

★ Woodbury University
Burbank, California
http://www.woodbury.edu/

- **Independent** comprehensive, founded 1884
- **Suburban** 22-acre campus with easy access to Los Angeles
- **Coed** 1,059 undergraduate students, 94% full-time, 51% women, 49% men
- **Moderately difficult** entrance level, 66% of applicants were admitted

UNDERGRAD STUDENTS
993 full-time, 66 part-time. 15% are from out of state; 3% Black or African American, non-Hispanic/Latino; 35% Hispanic/Latino; 9% Asian, non-Hispanic/Latino; 0.4% Native Hawaiian or other Pacific Islander, non-Hispanic/Latino; 0.1% American Indian or Alaska Native, non-Hispanic/Latino; 3% Two or more races, non-Hispanic/Latino; 0.1% Race/ethnicity unknown; 15% international; 15% transferred in; 21% live on campus.

Freshmen:
Admission: 2,120 applied, 1,392 admitted, 178 enrolled. *Average high school GPA:* 3.3. *Test scores:* SAT evidence-based reading and writing scores over 500: 71%; SAT math scores over 500: 73%; ACT scores over 18: 85%; SAT evidence-based reading and writing scores over 600: 14%; SAT math scores over 600: 14%; ACT scores over 24: 35%; SAT evidence-based reading and writing scores over 700: 4%; ACT scores over 30: 4%.

Retention: 77% of full-time freshmen returned.

FACULTY
Total: 217, 29% full-time, 61% with terminal degrees.

Student/faculty ratio: 9:1.

ACADEMICS
Calendar: semesters. *Degrees:* bachelor's and master's.

Special study options: academic remediation for entering students, advanced placement credit, double majors, independent study, internships, part-time degree program, services for LD students, student-designed majors, study abroad, summer session for credit.

Computers: Students can access the following: campus intranet, computer help desk, free student e-mail accounts, online (class) grades, online (class) registration, online (class) schedules. Campuswide network is available. 100% of college-owned or -operated housing units are wired

for high-speed Internet access. Wireless service is available via classrooms, computer centers, computer labs, learning centers, libraries, student centers.

Library: Los Angeles Times Library. *Books:* 57,193 (physical), 80,142 (digital/electronic); *Serial titles:* 322 (physical), 53,689 (digital/electronic); *Databases:* 44.

STUDENT LIFE
Housing options: coed. Campus housing is university owned and is provided by a third party. Freshman applicants given priority for college housing.

Activities and organizations: national fraternities, national sororities.

Campus security: 24-hour patrols, late-night transport/escort service, controlled dormitory access.

Student services: health clinic, personal/psychological counseling.

COSTS & FINANCIAL AID
Costs (2019–20) *Comprehensive fee:* $53,250 includes full-time tuition ($39,712), mandatory fees ($1470), and room and board ($12,068). Part-time tuition: $1293 per credit hour. *Required fees:* $1293 per credit part-time, $735 per term part-time. *College room only:* $7508.

Financial Aid Of all full-time matriculated undergraduates who enrolled in 2018, 747 applied for aid, 710 were judged to have need, 22 had their need fully met. In 2018, 126 non-need-based awards were made. *Average percent of need met:* 65. *Average financial aid package:* $32,188. *Average need-based loan:* $9343. *Average need-based gift aid:* $24,257. *Average non-need-based aid:* $11,926. *Average indebtedness upon graduation:* $34,285.

APPLYING
Options: electronic application, deferred entrance.

Application fee: $75.

Required: high school transcript, minimum 2.5 GPA. *Recommended:* essay or personal statement, 1 letter of recommendation.

Application deadlines: rolling (freshmen), rolling (transfers).

Notification: continuous (freshmen), continuous (transfers).

CONTACT
Sabrina Taylor, Associate Vice President, Admissions, Woodbury University, 7500 North Glenoaks Boulevard, Burbank, CA 91504-1052. *Phone:* 818-252-5225. *Toll-free phone:* 800-784-WOOD. *E-mail:* sabrina.taylor@woodbury.edu.

World Mission University
Los Angeles, California
http://www.wmu.edu/

CONTACT
World Mission University, 500 Shatto Place, Suite 600, Los Angeles, CA 90020.

Yeshiva Ohr Elchonon Chabad/West Coast Talmudical Seminary
Los Angeles, California
http://www.yoec.edu/

CONTACT
Rabbi Ezra Binyomin Schochet, Dean, Yeshiva Ohr Elchonon Chabad/West Coast Talmudical Seminary, 7215 Waring Avenue, Los Angeles, CA 90046-7660. *Phone:* 323-937-3763. *E-mail:* roshyeshiva@yoec.edu.

Zaytuna College
Berkeley, California
http://www.zaytuna.edu/

CONTACT
Yusuf Samara, Admissions, Zaytuna College, 2401 Le Conte Avenue, Berkeley, CA 94709. *Phone:* 510-900-3156. *E-mail:* admissions@zaytuna.org.

COLORADO

Adams State University
Alamosa, Colorado
http://www.adams.edu/

- **State-supported** comprehensive, founded 1921
- **Small-town** 90-acre campus with easy access to Pueblo
- **Endowment** $64,882
- **Coed** 1,991 undergraduate students, 74% full-time, 44% women, 56% men
- **Moderately difficult** entrance level, 99% of applicants were admitted

UNDERGRAD STUDENTS
1,481 full-time, 510 part-time. 39% are from out of state; 8% Black or African American, non-Hispanic/Latino; 35% Hispanic/Latino; 0.7% Asian, non-Hispanic/Latino; 0.5% Native Hawaiian or other Pacific Islander, non-Hispanic/Latino; 1% American Indian or Alaska Native, non-Hispanic/Latino; 3% Two or more races, non-Hispanic/Latino; 10% Race/ethnicity unknown; 0.6% international; 12% transferred in; 45% live on campus.

Freshmen:
Admission: 1,698 applied, 1,675 admitted, 460 enrolled. *Average high school GPA:* 3.2. *Test scores:* SAT evidence-based reading and writing scores over 500: 47%; SAT math scores over 500: 51%; ACT scores over 18: 65%; SAT evidence-based reading and writing scores over 600: 11%; SAT math scores over 600: 9%; ACT scores over 24: 13%; SAT math scores over 700: 1%; ACT scores over 30: 2%.
Retention: 54% of full-time freshmen returned.

FACULTY
Total: 221, 44% full-time, 38% with terminal degrees.
Student/faculty ratio: 15:1.

ACADEMICS
Calendar: semesters. *Degrees:* associate, bachelor's, master's, and doctoral.
Special study options: academic remediation for entering students, accelerated degree program, adult/continuing education programs, advanced placement credit, cooperative education, distance learning, double majors, external degree program, independent study, internships, off-campus study, part-time degree program, services for LD students, student-designed majors, study abroad, summer session for credit.
Computers: 322 computers/terminals are available on campus for general student use. Students can access the following: campus intranet, computer help desk, free student e-mail accounts, online (class) grades, online (class) registration, online (class) schedules. Campuswide network is available. 100% of college-owned or -operated housing units are wired for high-speed Internet access. Wireless service is available via entire campus.
Library: Nielsen Library. *Books:* 252 (physical), 891 (digital/electronic); *Serial titles:* 102 (physical), 372 (digital/electronic); *Databases:* 60. Weekly public service hours: 84.

STUDENT LIFE
Housing options: on-campus residence required through sophomore year; coed, men-only, women-only. Campus housing is university owned. Freshman campus housing is guaranteed.
Activities and organizations: drama/theater group, student-run newspaper, radio station, choral group, marching band, Student Programming Board, Student government, Semillas de la Tierra, Newman Club, Fellowship of Christian Athletes.
Athletics Member NCAA. All Division II except golf (Division I). *Intercollegiate sports:* baseball M(s), basketball M(s)/W(s), cross-country running M(s)/W(s), football M(s)/W(s), golf M(s)/W(s), lacrosse M(s)/W(s), soccer M(s)/W(s), softball W(s), swimming and diving M(s)/W(s), track and field M(s)/W(s), volleyball W(s), wrestling M(s). *Intramural sports:* basketball M/W, bowling M/W, cheerleading M(c)/W(c), football M/W, golf M(c)/W(c), racquetball M/W, rock climbing M/W, rugby M(c)/W(c), skiing (cross-country) M/W, skiing (downhill) M/W, soccer M/W, softball M/W, swimming and diving M/W, volleyball M/W, water polo M/W.

Campus security: 24-hour emergency response devices and patrols, student patrols, late-night transport/escort service, controlled dormitory access.
Student services: personal/psychological counseling, veterans affairs office.

COSTS & FINANCIAL AID
Costs (2018–19) *Tuition:* state resident $5736 full-time, $239 per credit hour part-time; nonresident $16,752 full-time, $698 per credit hour part-time. Full-time tuition and fees vary according to course load and location. Part-time tuition and fees vary according to course load and location. No tuition increase for student's term of enrollment. *Required fees:* $3704 full-time, $151 per credit hour part-time. *Room and board:* $8782; room only: $4222. Room and board charges vary according to board plan and housing facility. *Payment plans:* installment, deferred payment. *Waivers:* senior citizens and employees or children of employees.
Financial Aid Of all full-time matriculated undergraduates who enrolled in 2017, 1,472 applied for aid, 1,126 were judged to have need, 72 had their need fully met. *Average percent of need met:* 67. *Average financial aid package:* $14,467. *Average need-based loan:* $4017. *Average need-based gift aid:* $9728. *Average indebtedness upon graduation:* $22,822.

APPLYING
Standardized Tests *Required:* SAT (for admission). *Recommended:* ACT (for admission), SAT or ACT (for admission).
Options: electronic application, early admission, deferred entrance.
Application fee: $30.
Required: high school transcript, minimum 2.0 GPA. *Required for some:* essay or personal statement, audition for music majors, portfolio for art majors.
Application deadlines: rolling (freshmen), rolling (transfers).
Notification: continuous (freshmen), continuous (transfers).

CONTACT
Ms. Karla Hardesty, Director of Enrollment Management, Adams State University, 208 Edgemont Boulevard, Alamosa, CO 81101. *Phone:* 719-587-8124. *Toll-free phone:* 800-824-6494. *Fax:* 719-587-7522. *E-mail:* karla_hardesty@adams.edu.

American Sentinel University
Aurora, Colorado
http://www.americansentinel.edu/

CONTACT
Natalie Nixon, Vice President of Admission, American Sentinel University, 2260 South Xanadu Way, Suite 310, Aurora, CO 80014. *Phone:* 800-729-2427. *Toll-free phone:* 800-729-2427. *Fax:* 866-505-2450. *E-mail:* natalie.nixon@americansentinel.edu.

Arapahoe Community College
Littleton, Colorado
http://www.arapahoe.edu/

- **State-supported** primarily 2-year, founded 1965, part of Colorado Community College and Occupational Education System
- **Suburban** 52-acre campus with easy access to Denver
- **Coed** 10,697 undergraduate students, 17% full-time, 59% women, 41% men
- **Noncompetitive** entrance level, 100% of applicants were admitted

UNDERGRAD STUDENTS
1,860 full-time, 8,837 part-time. Students come from 47 states and territories; 2 other countries; 15% are from out of state; 2% Black or African American, non-Hispanic/Latino; 14% Hispanic/Latino; 4% Asian, non-Hispanic/Latino; 0.3% Native Hawaiian or other Pacific Islander, non-Hispanic/Latino; 0.4% American Indian or Alaska Native, non-Hispanic/Latino; 4% Two or more races, non-Hispanic/Latino; 9% Race/ethnicity unknown; 1% international; 5% transferred in.

Freshmen:
Admission: 3,851 applied, 3,851 admitted, 997 enrolled.

FACULTY
Total: 489, 21% full-time.
Student/faculty ratio: 23:1.

ACADEMICS
Calendar: semesters. *Degrees:* certificates, diplomas, associate, and bachelor's.

Special study options: academic remediation for entering students, accelerated degree program, adult/continuing education programs, advanced placement credit, cooperative education, distance learning, double majors, English as a second language, external degree program, independent study, internships, off-campus study, part-time degree program, services for LD students, study abroad, summer session for credit. *ROTC:* Army (c), Air Force (c).

Computers: Students can access the following: campus intranet, computer help desk, free student e-mail accounts, online (class) grades, online (class) registration, online (class) schedules. Campuswide network is available. Wireless service is available via entire campus.
Library: Weber Center for Learning Resources plus 1 other. *Books:* 28,076 (physical), 442 (digital/electronic).

STUDENT LIFE
Housing options: college housing not available.

Activities and organizations: drama/theater group, student-run newspaper, choral group, American Society of Interior Designers, National Society of Leadership and Success, Phi Theta Kappa, Student Veterans of America, Transfer Club.

Campus security: 24-hour emergency response devices and patrols, late-night transport/escort service.

Student services: personal/psychological counseling, veterans affairs office.

COSTS
Costs (2018–19) *Tuition:* state resident $4467 full-time, $149 per credit hour part-time; nonresident $18,327 full-time, $611 per credit hour part-time. Full-time tuition and fees vary according to program and reciprocity agreements. Part-time tuition and fees vary according to program and reciprocity agreements. *Required fees:* $344 full-time. *Payment plan:* installment. *Waivers:* employees or children of employees.

APPLYING
Options: electronic application, early admission, deferred entrance.
Application deadlines: rolling (freshmen), rolling (out-of-state freshmen), rolling (transfers).
Notification: continuous (freshmen), continuous (out-of-state freshmen), continuous (transfers).

CONTACT
Darcy Briggs, Director of Enrollment Services, Arapahoe Community College, 5900 South Santa Fe Drive, PO Box 9002, Littleton, CO 80160-9002. *Phone:* 303-797-5623. *E-mail:* darcy.briggs@arapahoe.edu.

Aspen University
Denver, Colorado
http://www.aspen.edu/

CONTACT
Aspen University, 720 South Colorado Boulevard, Suite 1150N, Denver, CO 80246-1930. *Phone:* 303-333-4224. *Toll-free phone:* 800-441-4746.

CollegeAmerica–Colorado Springs
Colorado Springs, Colorado
http://www.collegeamerica.edu/

CONTACT
CollegeAmerica–Colorado Springs, 2020 North Academy Boulevard, Colorado Springs, CO 80909. *Phone:* 719-637-0600. *Toll-free phone:* 800-622-2894.

CollegeAmerica–Fort Collins
Fort Collins, Colorado
http://www.collegeamerica.edu/

CONTACT
CollegeAmerica–Fort Collins, 4601 South Mason Street, Fort Collins, CO 80525. *Phone:* 970-223-6060 Ext. 8002. *Toll-free phone:* 800-622-2894.

Colorado Christian University
Lakewood, Colorado
http://www.ccu.edu/
- **Independent interdenominational** comprehensive, founded 1914
- **Suburban** 26-acre campus with easy access to Denver
- **Coed**
- **Moderately difficult** entrance level

FACULTY
Student/faculty ratio: 15:1.

ACADEMICS
Calendar: semesters. *Degrees:* associate, bachelor's, and master's.
Library: Clifton Fowler Library.

STUDENT LIFE
Housing options: on-campus residence required through sophomore year; men-only, women-only, special housing for students with disabilities. Campus housing is university owned and leased by the school. Freshman campus housing is guaranteed.

Activities and organizations: drama/theater group, choral group.

Athletics Member NCAA. All Division II.

Campus security: 24-hour emergency response devices and patrols, student patrols.

Student services: health clinic, personal/psychological counseling, women's center.

COSTS & FINANCIAL AID
Costs (2018–19) *Comprehensive fee:* $40,886 includes full-time tuition ($29,870), mandatory fees ($500), and room and board ($10,516). Full-time tuition and fees vary according to course load. Part-time tuition and fees vary according to course load. *College room only:* $2915. Room and board charges vary according to board plan and housing facility.

Financial Aid Of all full-time matriculated undergraduates who enrolled in 2004, 750 applied for aid, 615 were judged to have need, 55 had their need fully met. 16 Federal Work-Study jobs (averaging $2000). In 2004, 252 non-need-based awards were made. *Average percent of need met:* 54. *Average financial aid package:* $8931. *Average need-based loan:* $3946. *Average need-based gift aid:* $6056. *Average non-need-based aid:* $12,655. *Average indebtedness upon graduation:* $18,633.

APPLYING
Standardized Tests *Required:* SAT or ACT (for admission).
Options: electronic application, early admission, deferred entrance.
Application fee: $30.
Required: essay or personal statement, high school transcript, 2 letters of recommendation, interview, Spiritual Recommendation. *Required for some:* minimum 2.8 GPA, 3 letters of recommendation, interview.

CONTACT
Jo Leda Martin, Director of Admissions, Colorado Christian University, 8787 West Alameda Avenue, Lakewood, CO 80226. *Phone:* 303-963-3206. *Toll-free phone:* 800-44-FAITH. *Fax:* 303-963-3201. *E-mail:* jomartin@ccu.edu.

The Colorado College
Colorado Springs, Colorado
http://www.coloradocollege.edu/
- **Independent** comprehensive, founded 1874
- **Urban** 90-acre campus with easy access to Denver
- **Endowment** $765.2 million
- **Coed** 2,114 undergraduate students, 99% full-time, 55% women, 45% men
- **Very difficult** entrance level, 15% of applicants were admitted

UNDERGRAD STUDENTS

2,098 full-time, 16 part-time. Students come from 49 states and territories; 46 other countries; 83% are from out of state; 2% Black or African American, non-Hispanic/Latino; 9% Hispanic/Latino; 5% Asian, non-Hispanic/Latino; 0.1% Native Hawaiian or other Pacific Islander, non-Hispanic/Latino; 0.6% American Indian or Alaska Native, non-Hispanic/Latino; 8% Two or more races, non-Hispanic/Latino; 1% Race/ethnicity unknown; 9% international; 2% transferred in; 80% live on campus.

Freshmen:

Admission: 8,546 applied, 1,283 admitted, 544 enrolled. *Test scores:* SAT evidence-based reading and writing scores over 500: 100%; SAT math scores over 500: 100%; ACT scores over 18: 100%; SAT evidence-based reading and writing scores over 600: 95%; SAT math scores over 600: 91%; ACT scores over 24: 100%; SAT evidence-based reading and writing scores over 700: 47%; SAT math scores over 700: 50%; ACT scores over 30: 74%.

Retention: 96% of full-time freshmen returned.

FACULTY

Total: 235, 86% full-time, 95% with terminal degrees.
Student/faculty ratio: 10:1.

ACADEMICS

Calendar: 8 blocks of 3 1/2 week courses. *Degrees:* bachelor's and master's (master's degree in education only).

Special study options: advanced placement credit, double majors, English as a second language, independent study, internships, off-campus study, services for LD students, student-designed majors, study abroad, summer session for credit. *ROTC:* Army (c).

Unusual degree programs: 3-2 engineering with Rensselaer Polytechnic Institute, Washington University in St. Louis, University of Southern California, Columbia University.

Computers: 400 computers/terminals are available on campus for general student use. Students can access the following: campus intranet, computer help desk, free student e-mail accounts, online (class) grades, online (class) registration, online (class) schedules. Campuswide network is available. 100% of college-owned or -operated housing units are wired for high-speed Internet access. Wireless service is available via entire campus.

Library: Tutt Library plus 1 other. *Books:* 392,705 (physical), 319,616 (digital/electronic); *Serial titles:* 4,239 (physical), 80,330 (digital/electronic); *Databases:* 324. Weekly public service hours: 114; students can reserve study rooms.

STUDENT LIFE

Housing options: on-campus residence required through junior year; coed, men-only, women-only. Campus housing is university owned. Freshman campus housing is guaranteed.

Activities and organizations: drama/theater group, student-run newspaper, choral group, national fraternities, national sororities.

Athletics Member NCAA. All Division III except ice hockey (Division I), soccer (Division I). *Intercollegiate sports:* baseball M(c), basketball M/W, cross-country running M/W, equestrian sports M(c)/W(c), ice hockey M(s)/W(c), lacrosse M/W, rugby M(c)/W(c), skiing (downhill) W(c), soccer M/W(s), softball W(c), swimming and diving M/W, tennis M/W, track and field M/W, ultimate Frisbee M(c)/W(c), volleyball W, water polo W(c). *Intramural sports:* basketball M/W, football M, ice hockey M/W, racquetball M/W, soccer M/W, softball M/W, table tennis M/W, ultimate Frisbee M/W, volleyball M/W.

Campus security: 24-hour emergency response devices and patrols, late-night transport/escort service, controlled dormitory access.

Student services: health clinic, personal/psychological counseling.

COSTS & FINANCIAL AID

Costs (2019–20) *One-time required fee:* $250. *Comprehensive fee:* $71,042 includes full-time tuition ($57,612), mandatory fees ($474), and room and board ($12,956). Part-time tuition: $9681 per course. *College room only:* $7756.

Financial Aid Of all full-time matriculated undergraduates who enrolled in 2018, 820 applied for aid, 708 were judged to have need, 708 had their need fully met. In 2018, 178 non-need-based awards were made. *Average percent of need met:* 100. *Average financial aid package:* $51,054.

Average need-based loan: $3909. *Average need-based gift aid:* $49,251. *Average non-need-based aid:* $8982. *Average indebtedness upon graduation:* $23,714. *Financial aid deadline:* 1/15.

APPLYING

Standardized Tests *Required for some:* SAT or ACT (for admission).

Options: electronic application, early decision, early action, deferred entrance.

Application fee: $60.

Required: essay or personal statement, high school transcript, 2 letters of recommendation. *Recommended:* interview.

Application deadlines: 1/15 (freshmen), 3/1 (transfers), 11/10 (early action).

Early decision deadline: 11/10 (for plan 1), 1/15 (for plan 2).

Notification: 4/1 (freshmen), 5/1 (transfers), 12/15 (early decision), 12/19 (early action).

CONTACT

Mr. Carlos Jiminez, Director of Admission, Outreach and Recruitment, The Colorado College, 14 East Cache La Poudre Street, Colorado Springs, CO 80903-3294. *Phone:* 719-389-6344. *Toll-free phone:* 800-542-7214. *Fax:* 719-389-6816. *E-mail:* admission@coloradocollege.edu.

Colorado Mesa University

Grand Junction, Colorado

http://www.coloradomesa.edu/

- **State-supported** comprehensive, founded 1925
- **Suburban** 90-acre campus
- **Endowment** $27.7 million
- **Coed**
- **Minimally difficult** entrance level

FACULTY

Student/faculty ratio: 21:1.

ACADEMICS

Calendar: semesters. *Degrees:* certificates, associate, bachelor's, master's, doctoral, and postbachelor's certificates.
Library: John U. Tomlinson Library. *Books:* 202,919 (physical), 162,000 (digital/electronic); *Databases:* 116. Weekly public service hours: 94; study areas open 24 hours, 5–7 days a week; students can reserve study rooms.

STUDENT LIFE

Housing options: on-campus residence required through junior year; coed, special housing for students with disabilities. Campus housing is university owned. Freshman applicants given priority for college housing.

Activities and organizations: drama/theater group, student-run newspaper, radio and television station, choral group, marching band, Environmental Club, Student Body Association, KMSA radio station, Rodeo Club, Campus Residents Association, national fraternities, national sororities.

Athletics Member NCAA. All Division II.

Campus security: 24-hour emergency response devices and patrols, late-night transport/escort service, controlled dormitory access.

Student services: health clinic, personal/psychological counseling, legal services, veterans affairs office.

COSTS & FINANCIAL AID

Costs (2018–19) *Tuition:* state resident $8343 full-time, $278 per credit hour part-time; nonresident $21,540 full-time, $718 per credit hour part-time. Full-time tuition and fees vary according to course load. Part-time tuition and fees vary according to course load. *Required fees:* $900 full-time, $30 per credit hour part-time. *Room and board:* $10,925; room only: $6000. Room and board charges vary according to board plan and housing facility.

Financial Aid Of all full-time matriculated undergraduates who enrolled in 2017, 5,740 applied for aid, 4,522 were judged to have need, 797 had their need fully met. In 2017, 518 non-need-based awards were made. *Average percent of need met:* 63. *Average financial aid package:* $9757. *Average need-based loan:* $3805. *Average need-based gift aid:* $7313. *Average non-need-based aid:* $3619. *Average indebtedness upon graduation:* $27,481.

APPLYING

Standardized Tests *Required:* SAT or ACT (for admission).

Options: electronic application, deferred entrance.

Application fee: $30.

Required: high school transcript. *Recommended:* 2 letters of recommendation.

CONTACT

Admissions, Colorado Mesa University, 1100 North Avenue, Grand Junction, CO 81501. *Phone:* 970-248-1875. *Toll-free phone:* 800-982-MESA. *Fax:* 970-248-1973. *E-mail:* admissions@coloradomeas.edu.

Colorado Mountain College
Glenwood Springs, Colorado
http://www.coloradomtn.edu/

CONTACT

Vicky Butler, Admissions Assistant, Colorado Mountain College, 3000 CR 114, Glenwood Springs, CO 81601. *Phone:* 970-947-8276. *Toll-free phone:* 800-621-8559. *E-mail:* vvalentine@coloradomtn.edu.

Colorado Mountain College
Leadville, Colorado
http://www.coloradomtn.edu/

CONTACT

Ms. Mary Laing, Admissions Assistant, Colorado Mountain College, 901South Highway 24, Leadville, CO 80461. *Phone:* 719-486-4292. *Toll-free phone:* 800-621-8559. *E-mail:* joinus@coloradomtn.edu.

Colorado Mountain College
Steamboat Springs, Colorado
http://www.coloradomtn.edu/

CONTACT

Ms. Jackie Brazill, Admissions Assistant, Colorado Mountain College, 1275 Crawford Avenue, Steamboat Springs, CO 80487. *Phone:* 970-870-4417 Ext. 4417. *Toll-free phone:* 800-621-8559. *E-mail:* jbrazill@coloradomtn.edu.

Colorado School of Mines
Golden, Colorado
http://www.mines.edu/

- **State-supported** university, founded 1874
- **Small-town** 499-acre campus with easy access to Denver
- **Endowment** $246.1 million
- **Coed** 4,954 undergraduate students, 95% full-time, 30% women, 70% men
- **Very difficult** entrance level, 49% of applicants were admitted

UNDERGRAD STUDENTS

4,707 full-time, 247 part-time. Students come from 51 states and territories; 43 other countries; 41% are from out of state; 1% Black or African American, non-Hispanic/Latino; 9% Hispanic/Latino; 4% Asian, non-Hispanic/Latino; 0.1% Native Hawaiian or other Pacific Islander, non-Hispanic/Latino; 0.4% American Indian or Alaska Native, non-Hispanic/Latino; 6% Two or more races, non-Hispanic/Latino; 2% Race/ethnicity unknown; 6% international; 3% transferred in; 30% live on campus.

Freshmen:

Admission: 12,661 applied, 6,228 admitted, 1,199 enrolled. *Average high school GPA:* 3.8. *Test scores:* SAT evidence-based reading and writing scores over 500: 98%; SAT math scores over 500: 100%; ACT scores over 18: 100%; SAT evidence-based reading and writing scores over 600: 87%; SAT math scores over 600: 97%; ACT scores over 24: 98%; SAT evidence-based reading and writing scores over 700: 34%; SAT math scores over 700: 57%; ACT scores over 30: 64%.

Retention: 92% of full-time freshmen returned.

FACULTY

Total: 572, 53% full-time, 58% with terminal degrees.

Student/faculty ratio: 15:1.

ACADEMICS

Calendar: semesters. *Degrees:* bachelor's, master's, doctoral, and post-master's certificates.

Special study options: accelerated degree program, advanced placement credit, cooperative education, double majors, honors programs, independent study, internships, off-campus study, services for LD students, study abroad, summer session for credit. *ROTC:* Army (b), Air Force (b).

Computers: 1,000 computers/terminals are available on campus for general student use. Students can access the following: campus intranet, computer help desk, free student e-mail accounts, online (class) grades, online (class) registration, online (class) schedules. Campuswide network is available. 100% of college-owned or -operated housing units are wired for high-speed Internet access. Wireless service is available via entire campus.

Library: Arthur Lakes Library. *Books:* 369,304 (physical), 732,071 (digital/electronic); *Serial titles:* 527 (physical), 197,641 (digital/electronic); *Databases:* 162. Weekly public service hours: 107; students can reserve study rooms.

STUDENT LIFE

Housing options: on-campus residence required for freshman year; coed. Campus housing is university owned and is provided by a third party. Freshman campus housing is guaranteed.

Activities and organizations: drama/theater group, student-run newspaper, radio station, choral group, marching band, Society of Women Engineers, Residence Hall Association, Associated Students of Colorado School of Mines, Student Professional Societies/ and/ Religious Organizations, Multicultural Engineering Program, national fraternities, national sororities.

Athletics Member NCAA. All Division II. *Intercollegiate sports:* baseball M(s), basketball M(s)/W(s), bowling M(c)/W(c), cross-country running M(s)/W(s), football M(s), golf M(s), ice hockey M(c), lacrosse M(c)/W(c), rugby M(c)/W(c), skiing (downhill) M(c)/W(c), soccer M(s)/W(s), softball W(s), swimming and diving M(s)/W(s), tennis M(c)/W(c), track and field M(s)/W(s), triathlon M(c)/W(c), ultimate Frisbee M(c)/W(c), volleyball M(c)/W(s), water polo M(c)/W(c), wrestling M(s). *Intramural sports:* badminton M/W, basketball M/W, bowling M/W, cross-country running M/W, field hockey M/W, football M/W, golf M/W, lacrosse M/W, racquetball M/W, rugby M, skiing (downhill) M/W, soccer M/W, softball M/W, swimming and diving M/W, table tennis M/W, tennis M/W, track and field M/W, ultimate Frisbee M/W, volleyball M/W, water polo M/W, wrestling M.

Campus security: 24-hour emergency response devices and patrols, late-night transport/escort service, controlled dormitory access, campus policy department.

Student services: health clinic, personal/psychological counseling, women's center.

COSTS & FINANCIAL AID

Costs (2019–20) *Tuition:* state resident $16,650 full-time; nonresident $36,270 full-time.

Financial Aid Of all full-time matriculated undergraduates who enrolled in 2017, 3,018 applied for aid, 2,134 were judged to have need, 463 had their need fully met. 275 Federal Work-Study jobs (averaging $1414). 1,857 state and other part-time jobs (averaging $1980). In 2017, 1454 non-need-based awards were made. *Average percent of need met:* 59. *Average financial aid package:* $15,736. *Average need-based loan:* $4670. *Average need-based gift aid:* $6309. *Average non-need-based aid:* $8348. *Average indebtedness upon graduation:* $32,482.

APPLYING

Standardized Tests *Required:* SAT or ACT (for admission).

Options: electronic application, deferred entrance.

Application fee: $45.

Required: high school transcript. *Required for some:* essay or personal statement, interview. *Recommended:* minimum 3.8 GPA, rank in upper quartile of high school class.

Notification: continuous until 10/1 (freshmen), continuous until 10/1 (transfers).

CONTACT
Mrs. Kim Medina, Director of Undergraduate Admissions, Colorado School of Mines, Admissions Office, Starzer Welcome Center, 1812 Illinois Street, Golden, CO 80401. *Phone:* 303-273-3220. *Toll-free phone:* 800-446-9488 Ext. 3220. *Fax:* 303-273-3509. *E-mail:* admissions@mines.edu.

Colorado State University

Fort Collins, Colorado
http://www.colostate.edu/

- **State-supported** university, founded 1870, part of Colorado State University System
- **Urban** 4773-acre campus with easy access to Denver
- **Endowment** $356.0 million
- **Coed** 26,400 undergraduate students, 85% full-time, 52% women, 48% men
- **Moderately difficult** entrance level, 84% of applicants were admitted

UNDERGRAD STUDENTS
22,310 full-time, 4,090 part-time. Students come from 55 states and territories; 76 other countries; 26% are from out of state; 2% Black or African American, non-Hispanic/Latino; 14% Hispanic/Latino; 3% Asian, non-Hispanic/Latino; 0.2% Native Hawaiian or other Pacific Islander, non-Hispanic/Latino; 0.4% American Indian or Alaska Native, non-Hispanic/Latino; 4% Two or more races, non-Hispanic/Latino; 1% Race/ethnicity unknown; 4% international; 7% transferred in; 30% live on campus.

Freshmen:
Admission: 24,496 applied, 20,508 admitted, 5,337 enrolled. *Average high school GPA:* 3.6. *Test scores:* SAT evidence-based reading and writing scores over 500: 92%; SAT math scores over 500: 91%; ACT scores over 18: 98%; SAT evidence-based reading and writing scores over 600: 51%; SAT math scores over 600: 43%; ACT scores over 24: 68%; SAT evidence-based reading and writing scores over 700: 8%; SAT math scores over 700: 8%; ACT scores over 30: 18%.

Retention: 84% of full-time freshmen returned.

FACULTY
Total: 1,692, 62% full-time.
Student/faculty ratio: 18:1.

ACADEMICS
Calendar: semesters. *Degrees:* bachelor's, master's, doctoral, and postbachelor's certificates.

Special study options: accelerated degree program, adult/continuing education programs, advanced placement credit, cooperative education, distance learning, double majors, English as a second language, honors programs, independent study, internships, off-campus study, part-time degree program, services for LD students, study abroad, summer session for credit. *ROTC:* Army (b), Air Force (b).

Unusual degree programs: 3-2 engineering.

Computers: 1,700 computers/terminals and 3,000 ports are available on campus for general student use. Students can access the following: campus intranet, computer help desk, free student e-mail accounts, online (class) grades, online (class) registration, online (class) schedules, personalized portal services including transcripts and financials (billing, financial aid). Campuswide network is available. 100% of college-owned or -operated housing units are wired for high-speed Internet access. Wireless service is available via classrooms, computer centers, computer labs, dorm rooms, learning centers, libraries, student centers.

Library: William E. Morgan Library plus 1 other. *Books:* 1.2 million (physical), 1.1 million (digital/electronic); *Serial titles:* 45,581 (physical), 104,097 (digital/electronic); *Databases:* 345. Weekly public service hours: 108; study areas open 24 hours, 5–7 days a week; students can reserve study rooms.

STUDENT LIFE
Housing options: on-campus residence required for freshman year; coed, special housing for students with disabilities. Campus housing is university owned. Freshman campus housing is guaranteed.

Activities and organizations: drama/theater group, student-run newspaper, radio and television station, choral group, marching band, Photography at Colorado State University, Outdoor Club at CSU, Biomedical Student Association, Criminal Justice Organization, Colorado State University Zoology Club, national fraternities, national sororities.

Athletics Member NCAA. All Division I except football (Division I-A). *Intercollegiate sports:* baseball M(c), basketball M(s)/W(s), crew M(c)/W(c), cross-country running M(s)/W(s), field hockey M(c)/W(c), golf M(s)/W(s)(c), ice hockey M(c)/W(c), lacrosse M(c)/W(c), riflery M(c)/W(c), rock climbing M(c)/W(c), rowing M(c)/W(c), rugby M(c)/W(c), skiing (downhill) W(c), soccer M(c)/W(s), softball W(s), swimming and diving M(c)/W(s), table tennis M(c)/W(c), tennis M(c)/W(s), track and field M(s)/W(s), triathlon M(c)/W(c), ultimate Frisbee M(c)/W(c), volleyball M(c)/W(c), water polo M(c)/W(c), wrestling M(c)/W(c). *Intramural sports:* badminton M/W, basketball M/W, bowling M/W, golf M/W, racquetball M/W, sand volleyball M/W, soccer M/W, softball M/W, table tennis M/W, tennis M/W, track and field M/W, ultimate Frisbee M/W, volleyball M/W, water polo M/W.

Campus security: 24-hour emergency response devices and patrols, student patrols, late-night transport/escort service, controlled dormitory access.

Student services: health clinic, personal/psychological counseling, women's center, legal services, veterans affairs office.

COSTS & FINANCIAL AID
Costs (2019–20) *Tuition:* state resident $9426 full-time, $428 per credit hour part-time; nonresident $27,327 full-time, $1366 per credit hour part-time. *Required fees:* $2405 full-time, $59 per credit hour part-time, $296 per term part-time. *Room and board:* $11,964; room only: $5746.

Financial Aid Of all full-time matriculated undergraduates who enrolled in 2017, 15,962 applied for aid, 11,347 were judged to have need, 2,097 had their need fully met. In 2017, 3317 non-need-based awards were made. *Average percent of need met:* 63. *Average financial aid package:* $11,511. *Average need-based loan:* $6494. *Average need-based gift aid:* $8484. *Average non-need-based aid:* $5199. *Average indebtedness upon graduation:* $25,391.

APPLYING
Standardized Tests *Required:* SAT or ACT (for admission).

Options: electronic application, early action, deferred entrance.

Application fee: $50.

Required: essay or personal statement, high school transcript, 1 letter of recommendation.

Application deadlines: 7/1 (freshmen), 6/1 (transfers).

Notification: continuous until 9/15 (freshmen), continuous (transfers), rolling (early action).

CONTACT
Kelly Nolin, Associate Director of Admission, Recruitment and Outreach, Colorado State University, Ammons Hall (1062), Fort Collins, CO 80523-1062. *Phone:* 970-491-6909. *Fax:* 970-491-7799. *E-mail:* admissions@colostate.edu.

Colorado State University–Global Campus

Greenwood Village, Colorado
http://csuglobal.edu/

CONTACT
Colorado State University–Global Campus, 8000 E. Maplewood Avenue, Greenwood Village, CO 80111. *Toll-free phone:* 800-920-6723.

Colorado State University–Pueblo

Pueblo, Colorado
http://www.csupueblo.edu/

- **State-supported** comprehensive, founded 1933, part of Colorado State University System
- **Small-town** 279-acre campus with easy access to Colorado Springs
- **Endowment** $18.2 million
- **Coed** 4,385 undergraduate students, 71% full-time, 52% women, 48% men
- **Minimally difficult** entrance level, 95% of applicants were admitted

UNDERGRAD STUDENTS

3,134 full-time, 1,251 part-time. Students come from 40 states and territories; 37 other countries; 14% are from out of state; 6% Black or African American, non-Hispanic/Latino; 33% Hispanic/Latino; 1% Asian, non-Hispanic/Latino; 0.3% Native Hawaiian or other Pacific Islander, non-Hispanic/Latino; 0.6% American Indian or Alaska Native, non-Hispanic/Latino; 5% Two or more races, non-Hispanic/Latino; 5% Race/ethnicity unknown; 2% international; 9% transferred in; 16% live on campus.

Freshmen:

Admission: 2,435 applied, 2,318 admitted, 699 enrolled. *Average high school GPA:* 3.3. *Test scores:* SAT evidence-based reading and writing scores over 500: 61%; SAT math scores over 500: 61%; ACT scores over 18: 80%; SAT evidence-based reading and writing scores over 600: 15%; SAT math scores over 600: 10%; ACT scores over 24: 27%; SAT evidence-based reading and writing scores over 700: 1%; SAT math scores over 700: 1%; ACT scores over 30: 1%.

Retention: 68% of full-time freshmen returned.

FACULTY

Total: 349, 50% full-time.

Student/faculty ratio: 14:1.

ACADEMICS

Calendar: semesters. *Degrees:* bachelor's, master's, and doctoral.

Special study options: academic remediation for entering students, accelerated degree program, advanced placement credit, cooperative education, distance learning, double majors, English as a second language, external degree program, honors programs, independent study, internships, off-campus study, part-time degree program, services for LD students, study abroad, summer session for credit. *ROTC:* Army (b).

Unusual degree programs: 3-2 business administration; biochemistry, biology, and chemistry programs; combined M.B.A. computer information systems, construction management, and management programs.

Computers: 870 computers/terminals are available on campus for general student use. Students can access the following: campus intranet, computer help desk, free student e-mail accounts, online (class) grades, online (class) registration, online (class) schedules. Campuswide network is available. 100% of college-owned or -operated housing units are wired for high-speed Internet access. Wireless service is available via classrooms, computer centers, computer labs, dorm rooms, learning centers, libraries, student centers.

Library: CSU-Pueblo University Library. *Books:* 183,220 (physical), 227,551 (digital/electronic); *Serial titles:* 2,882 (physical), 157,848 (digital/electronic); *Databases:* 426. Weekly public service hours: 93; students can reserve study rooms.

STUDENT LIFE

Housing options: on-campus residence required through sophomore year; coed. Campus housing is university owned. Freshman campus housing is guaranteed.

Activities and organizations: student-run newspaper, radio and television station, choral group, marching band, Fellowship of Christian Athletes, Black Student Union, Latinx Student Union, National Society of Leadership and Success, Southern Colorado Assoc. of Nursing Students (SCANS), national fraternities, national sororities.

Athletics Member NCAA. All Division II. *Intercollegiate sports:* baseball M(s), basketball M(s)/W(s), cheerleading M/W, cross-country running M(s)/W(s), football M(s), golf M(s)/W(s), lacrosse M(s)/W(s), racquetball M/W, soccer M(s)/W(s), softball M/W(s), squash M, swimming and diving W(s), tennis M(s)/W(s), track and field M(s)/W(s), volleyball W(s), wrestling M(s). *Intramural sports:* baseball M(c), basketball M/W, rock climbing M(c)/W(c), rugby M(c), soccer M(c)/W, softball M/W, volleyball M/W.

Campus security: 24-hour emergency response devices and patrols, student patrols, late-night transport/escort service, controlled dormitory access.

Student services: health clinic, personal/psychological counseling, veterans affairs office.

COSTS & FINANCIAL AID

Costs (2019–20) *Tuition:* area resident $8174 full-time, $272 per credit hour part-time; state resident $8174 full-time, $272 per credit hour part-time; nonresident $24,573 full-time, $819 per credit hour part-time. *Required fees:* $2472 full-time, $82 per credit hour part-time, $1236 per term part-time. *Room and board:* $10,784; room only: $6140.

Financial Aid Of all full-time matriculated undergraduates who enrolled in 2015, 2,933 applied for aid, 2,521 were judged to have need, 168 had their need fully met. 686 Federal Work-Study jobs (averaging $3000). 1,109 state and other part-time jobs (averaging $3000). In 2015, 333 non-need-based awards were made. *Average percent of need met:* 51. *Average financial aid package:* $9865. *Average need-based loan:* $3723. *Average need-based gift aid:* $7340. *Average non-need-based aid:* $3361. *Average indebtedness upon graduation:* $28,914.

APPLYING

Standardized Tests *Required:* SAT or ACT (for admission).

Options: electronic application, deferred entrance.

Application fee: $25.

Required: minimum 2.0 GPA. *Required for some:* essay or personal statement, interview.

Application deadlines: 8/1 (freshmen), 8/1 (out-of-state freshmen), 8/1 (transfers).

Notification: continuous until 9/15 (freshmen), continuous until 9/15 (out-of-state freshmen), continuous (transfers).

CONTACT

Tiffany Kingrey, Director of Admissions, Colorado State University–Pueblo, 2200 Bonforte Boulevard, Pueblo, CO 81001-4901. *Phone:* 719-549-2462. *Fax:* 719-549-2419. *E-mail:* info@csupueblo.edu.

Colorado Technical University Aurora
Aurora, Colorado
http://www.coloradotech.edu/

CONTACT
Rosaland Giboney, Associate Director of Admissions, Colorado Technical University Aurora, 3151 South Vaughn Way, Aurora, CO 80014. *Phone:* 888-404-7555. *Toll-free phone:* 888-309-6555. *E-mail:* rgiboney@coloradotech.edu.

Colorado Technical University Colorado Springs
Colorado Springs, Colorado
http://www.coloradotech.edu/

CONTACT
Beth Braaten, Vice President of Admissions, Colorado Technical University Colorado Springs, 4435 North Chestnut Street, Colorado Springs, CO 80907. *Phone:* 888-404-7555. *Toll-free phone:* 866-942-6555. *E-mail:* bbraaten@coloradotech.edu.

Colorado Technical University Online
Colorado Springs, Colorado
http://www.coloradotech.edu/

CONTACT
William Beckley, Chief Admission Officer, Colorado Technical University Online, 4435 North Chestnut Street, Colorado Springs, CO 80907. *Phone:* 888-404-7555. *Toll-free phone:* 866-813-1836.

Denver College of Nursing
Denver, Colorado
http://www.denvercollegeofnursing.edu/

CONTACT
Denver College of Nursing, 1401 19th Street, Denver, CO 80202. *Toll-free phone:* 888-479-5550.

DeVry University–Westminster Campus

Westminster, Colorado

http://www.devry.edu/

CONTACT
Admissions Office, DeVry University–Westminster Campus, 1870 West 122nd Avenue, Westminster, CO 80234-2010. *Phone:* 303-280-7400. *Toll-free phone:* 866-338-7934.

★ Fort Lewis College

Durango, Colorado

http://www.fortlewis.edu/

- **State-supported** comprehensive, founded 1911
- **Small-town** 350-acre campus
- **Endowment** $9.0 million
- **Coed** 3,267 undergraduate students, 88% full-time, 52% women, 48% men
- **Moderately difficult** entrance level, 91% of applicants were admitted

UNDERGRAD STUDENTS
2,879 full-time, 388 part-time. 55% are from out of state; 1% Black or African American, non-Hispanic/Latino; 11% Hispanic/Latino; 0.6% Asian, non-Hispanic/Latino; 0.2% Native Hawaiian or other Pacific Islander, non-Hispanic/Latino; 27% American Indian or Alaska Native, non-Hispanic/Latino; 11% Two or more races, non-Hispanic/Latino; 3% Race/ethnicity unknown; 0.8% international; 10% transferred in; 42% live on campus.

Freshmen:
Admission: 4,198 applied, 3,817 admitted, 753 enrolled. *Average high school GPA:* 3.2. *Test scores:* SAT evidence-based reading and writing scores over 500: 81%; SAT math scores over 500: 77%; ACT scores over 18: 82%; SAT evidence-based reading and writing scores over 600: 31%; SAT math scores over 600: 22%; ACT scores over 24: 25%; SAT evidence-based reading and writing scores over 700: 2%; SAT math scores over 700: 1%; ACT scores over 30: 1%.
Retention: 62% of full-time freshmen returned.

FACULTY
Total: 241, 71% full-time, 72% with terminal degrees.
Student/faculty ratio: 15:1.

ACADEMICS
Calendar: semesters modified trimesters. *Degrees:* certificates, bachelor's, master's, and postbachelor's certificates.
Special study options: academic remediation for entering students, advanced placement credit, double majors, honors programs, independent study, internships, services for LD students, student-designed majors, study abroad, summer session for credit.
Unusual degree programs: 3-2 social work with University of Denver.
Computers: 825 computers/terminals are available on campus for general student use. Students can access the following: campus intranet, computer help desk, free student e-mail accounts, online (class) grades, online (class) registration, online (class) schedules. Campuswide network is available. 100% of college-owned or -operated housing units are wired for high-speed Internet access. Wireless service is available via entire campus.
Library: John F. Reed Library plus 1 other. *Books:* 138,839 (physical), 213,585 (digital/electronic); *Serial titles:* 4 (physical), 170,201 (digital/electronic); *Databases:* 74. Weekly public service hours: 80; study areas open 24 hours, 5–7 days a week; students can reserve study rooms.

STUDENT LIFE
Housing options: on-campus residence required for freshman year; coed, special housing for students with disabilities. Campus housing is university owned. Freshman applicants given priority for college housing.
Activities and organizations: drama/theater group, student-run newspaper, radio station, KDUR - Campus/community radio, Environmental Center, Student Union Productions, Dance Co-Motion, Master Plan Ministries.

Athletics Member NCAA. All Division II. *Intercollegiate sports:* baseball M(c), basketball M(s)/W(s), cheerleading M(c)/W(c), cross-country running M(s)/W(s), fencing M(c)/W(c), football M(s), golf M(s)/W(s), ice hockey M(c), lacrosse M(c)/W(s), rock climbing M(c)/W(c), rugby M(c)/W(c), skiing (cross-country) M(c)/W(c), skiing (downhill) W(c), soccer M(s)/W(s), softball W(s), tennis M(c)/W(c), track and field M(s)/W(s), ultimate Frisbee M(c)/W(c), volleyball W(s), wrestling M(c)/W(c). *Intramural sports:* badminton M/W, basketball M/W, football M/W, golf M/W, racquetball M/W, soccer M/W, softball M/W, ultimate Frisbee M/W, volleyball M/W.

Campus security: 24-hour emergency response devices and patrols, late-night transport/escort service, controlled dormitory access.
Student services: health clinic, personal/psychological counseling, legal services.

COSTS & FINANCIAL AID
Costs (2018–19) *Tuition:* state resident $7056 full-time, $294 per credit hour part-time; nonresident $17,712 full-time, $738 per credit hour part-time. Full-time tuition and fees vary according to course load and reciprocity agreements. Part-time tuition and fees vary according to course load and reciprocity agreements. *Required fees:* $1984 full-time, $67 per credit hour part-time. *Room and board:* $9878; room only: $4796. Room and board charges vary according to board plan and housing facility. *Payment plan:* installment. *Waivers:* minority students, senior citizens, and employees or children of employees.
Financial Aid Of all full-time matriculated undergraduates who enrolled in 2017, 1,953 applied for aid, 1,646 were judged to have need, 282 had their need fully met. 150 Federal Work-Study jobs (averaging $1926). 278 state and other part-time jobs (averaging $1882). In 2017, 436 non-need-based awards were made. *Average percent of need met:* 91. *Average financial aid package:* $17,649. *Average need-based loan:* $4109. *Average need-based gift aid:* $5226. *Average non-need-based aid:* $4728. *Average indebtedness upon graduation:* $20,379.

APPLYING
Standardized Tests *Required:* SAT or ACT (for admission).
Options: electronic application, deferred entrance.
Application fee: $40.
Required: high school transcript. *Required for some:* interview.
Recommended: essay or personal statement, 2 letters of recommendation.
Application deadlines: 8/1 (out-of-state freshmen), 8/1 (transfers), 11/15 (early action).
Notification: continuous (out-of-state freshmen), continuous (transfers), 12/31 (early action).

CONTACT
Jess Savage, Director of Admissions, Fort Lewis College, 1000 Rim Drive, Admissions, Durango, CO 81301. *Phone:* 877-352-2656. *Toll-free phone:* 877-FLC-COLO. *Fax:* 970-247-7147. *E-mail:* admission@fortlewis.edu.

Johnson & Wales University

Denver, Colorado

http://www.jwu.edu/denver/

CONTACT
Kim Medina, Director of Admissions, Johnson & Wales University, 7150 Montview Boulevard, Denver, CO 80220. *Phone:* 303-256-9300. *Toll-free phone:* 877-598-3368. *Fax:* 303-598-3368. *E-mail:* den@admissions.jwu.edu.

Metropolitan State University of Denver

Denver, Colorado

http://www.msudenver.edu/

- **State-supported** comprehensive, founded 1963
- **Urban** 175-acre campus with easy access to Denver
- **Endowment** $7.1 million
- **Coed**
- **Minimally difficult** entrance level

FACULTY
Student/faculty ratio: 17:1.

ACADEMICS
Calendar: semesters. *Degrees:* certificates, bachelor's, master's, and postbachelor's certificates.
Library: Auraria Library.

STUDENT LIFE
Housing options: college housing not available.

Activities and organizations: drama/theater group, student-run newspaper, radio and television station, choral group, national fraternities, national sororities.

Athletics Member NCAA. All Division II.

Campus security: 24-hour emergency response devices and patrols, late-night transport/escort service.

Student services: health clinic, personal/psychological counseling, women's center, legal services, veterans affairs office.

COSTS & FINANCIAL AID
Costs (2018–19) *Tuition:* state resident $6245 full-time, $345 per credit hour part-time; nonresident $19,426 full-time, $809 per credit hour part-time. Full-time tuition and fees vary according to course load and location. Part-time tuition and fees vary according to course load and location. *Required fees:* $1421 full-time, $23 per credit hour part-time, $361 per term part-time. *Payment plans:* installment, deferred payment.

Financial Aid Of all full-time matriculated undergraduates who enrolled in 2016, 9,539 applied for aid, 8,141 were judged to have need, 459 had their need fully met. 157 Federal Work-Study jobs (averaging $3585). 698 state and other part-time jobs (averaging $3555). In 2016, 626 non-need-based awards were made. *Average percent of need met:* 56. *Average financial aid package:* $9130. *Average need-based loan:* $4089. *Average need-based gift aid:* $6697. *Average non-need-based aid:* $1779. *Average indebtedness upon graduation:* $25,805.

APPLYING
Standardized Tests *Required:* SAT or ACT (for admission). *Required for some:* SAT (for admission), ACT (for admission).

Options: electronic application, deferred entrance.

Application fee: $25.

Required: high school transcript. *Recommended:* minimum 2.0 GPA.

CONTACT
Associate Director of Admissions, Metropolitan State University of Denver, 890 Auraria Parkway, Denver, CO 80204. *Phone:* 303-556-2615.

Naropa University
Boulder, Colorado
http://www.naropa.edu/

- **Independent** comprehensive, founded 1974
- **Urban** 12-acre campus with easy access to Denver
- **Endowment** $7.6 million
- **Coed**
- **Moderately difficult** entrance level

FACULTY
Student/faculty ratio: 9:1.

ACADEMICS
Calendar: semesters. *Degrees:* bachelor's and master's.
Library: Allen Ginsberg Library plus 2 others. *Books:* 36,333 (physical), 177,800 (digital/electronic); *Serial titles:* 335 (physical), 33,467 (digital/electronic); *Databases:* 47. Weekly public service hours: 69.

STUDENT LIFE
Housing options: on-campus residence required for freshman year; men-only, women-only. Campus housing is university owned. Freshman campus housing is guaranteed.

Activities and organizations: drama/theater group, choral group, Student Union of Naropa, ROOT: Reconnecting on Outdoor Terrain, Team Tapas (yoga club), Community of Color and Allies, Naropa Zazen.

Campus security: late-night transport/escort service, controlled dormitory access, foot and vehicle patrol 4:30 pm to midnight, 24 hour on-call Safety and Security Manager.

Student services: personal/psychological counseling.

COSTS & FINANCIAL AID
Costs (2018–19) *Comprehensive fee:* $45,139 includes full-time tuition ($31,620), mandatory fees ($670), and room and board ($12,849). Part-time tuition: $995 per credit. Part-time tuition and fees vary according to course load. *Required fees:* $310 per term part-time. *Room and board:* Room and board charges vary according to housing facility.

Financial Aid Of all full-time matriculated undergraduates who enrolled in 2015, 272 applied for aid, 251 were judged to have need, 1 had their need fully met. 168 Federal Work-Study jobs (averaging $3077). 11 state and other part-time jobs (averaging $2455). In 2015, 15 non-need-based awards were made. *Average percent of need met:* 90. *Average financial aid package:* $37,077. *Average need-based loan:* $11,519. *Average need-based gift aid:* $24,862. *Average non-need-based aid:* $6858. *Average indebtedness upon graduation:* $38,199.

APPLYING
Options: electronic application, deferred entrance.

Application fee: $50.

Required: high school transcript. *Required for some:* essay or personal statement, 1 letter of recommendation, interview.

CONTACT
Ms. Karen Wills, Assistant Dean of Undergraduate Admissions, Naropa University, 2130 Arapahoe Avenue, Boulder, CO 80302. *Phone:* 303-245-4693. *Toll-free phone:* 800-772-6951. *Fax:* 303-546-3536. *E-mail:* kwills@naropa.edu.

National American University
Centennial, Colorado
http://www.national.edu/

CONTACT
National American University, 8242 South University Boulevard, Suite 100, Centennial, CO 80122. *Toll-free phone:* 877-628-5211.

National American University
Colorado Springs, Colorado
http://www.national.edu/

CONTACT
National American University, 1079 Space Center Drive, Suite 140, Colorado Springs, CO 80915. *Toll-free phone:* 855-369-9397.

National American University
Colorado Springs, Colorado
http://www.national.edu/

CONTACT
Director of Admissions, National American University, 1915 Jamboree Drive, Suite 185, Colorado Springs, CO 80920. *Phone:* 719-590-8300. *Toll-free phone:* 855-369-9397. *E-mail:* csadmissions@national.edu.

Nazarene Bible College
Colorado Springs, Colorado
http://www.nbc.edu/

CONTACT
Scott McConnaughey, Director of Admissions/Admissions Counselor, Nazarene Bible College, 1111 Academy Park Loop, Colorado Springs, CO 80910-3704. *Phone:* 719-884-5062. *Toll-free phone:* 800-873-3873. *Fax:* 719-884-5039. *E-mail:* semcconnaughey@nbc.edu.

Pima Medical Institute
Denver, Colorado
http://www.pmi.edu/

CONTACT
Admissions Office, Pima Medical Institute, 7475 Dakin Street, Denver, CO 80221. *Phone:* 303-426-1800. *Toll-free phone:* 800-477-PIMA.

Platt College

Aurora, Colorado

http://www.plattcolorado.edu/

CONTACT
Admissions Office, Platt College, 3100 South Parker Road, Suite 200, Aurora, CO 80014-3141. *Phone:* 303-369-5151.

Pueblo Community College

Pueblo, Colorado

http://www.pueblocc.edu/

- **State-supported** primarily 2-year, founded 1933, part of Colorado Community College System
- **Urban** 35-acre campus
- **Endowment** $1.1 million
- **Coed** 5,650 undergraduate students, 31% full-time, 55% women, 45% men
- **Noncompetitive** entrance level, 100% of applicants were admitted

UNDERGRAD STUDENTS
1,770 full-time, 3,880 part-time. Students come from 23 states and territories; 0.8% are from out of state; 5% Black or African American, non-Hispanic/Latino; 32% Hispanic/Latino; 5% Asian, non-Hispanic/Latino; 0.2% Native Hawaiian or other Pacific Islander, non-Hispanic/Latino; 2% American Indian or Alaska Native, non-Hispanic/Latino; 3% Two or more races, non-Hispanic/Latino; 3% Race/ethnicity unknown; 0.6% international; 9% transferred in.

Freshmen:
Admission: 1,186 applied, 1,186 admitted, 470 enrolled.
Retention: 10% of full-time freshmen returned.

FACULTY
Total: 349, 28% full-time.
Student/faculty ratio: 16:1.

ACADEMICS
Calendar: semesters. *Degrees:* certificates, associate, and bachelor's.
Special study options: academic remediation for entering students, accelerated degree program, advanced placement credit, cooperative education, distance learning, double majors, English as a second language, honors programs, independent study, internships, part-time degree program, services for LD students, summer session for credit.
Computers: 1,180 computers/terminals are available on campus for general student use. Students can access the following: campus intranet, computer help desk, free student e-mail accounts, online (class) grades, online (class) registration, online (class) schedules. Campuswide network is available. Wireless service is available via classrooms, computer centers, computer labs, learning centers, libraries, student centers.
Library: PCC Library. *Books:* 19,162 (physical), 33,004 (digital/electronic); *Serial titles:* 695 (physical), 7,707 (digital/electronic); *Databases:* 12. Weekly public service hours: 60.

STUDENT LIFE
Housing options: college housing not available.
Activities and organizations: drama/theater group, choral group, Phi Theta Kappa, Welding Club, Culinary Arts Club, Performing Arts Club, Art Club.
Campus security: 24-hour emergency response devices and patrols, late-night transport/escort service.
Student services: health clinic, personal/psychological counseling, veterans affairs office.

COSTS
Costs (2019–20) *Tuition:* state resident $4300 full-time, $180 per credit hour part-time; nonresident $15,060 full-time, $628 per credit hour part-time. *Required fees:* $750 full-time, $21 per credit hour part-time, $58 per term part-time.

APPLYING
Options: electronic application, early admission, deferred entrance.
Application deadlines: rolling (freshmen), rolling (transfers).
Notification: continuous until 9/1 (freshmen), continuous until 9/1 (transfers).

CONTACT
Mrs. Barbara Benedict, Director of Admissions and Records, Pueblo Community College, 900 West Orman Avenue, Pueblo, CO 81004. *Phone:* 719-549-3039. *Toll-free phone:* 888-642-6017. *Fax:* 719-549-3012. *E-mail:* barbara.benedict@pueblocc.edu.

Regis University

Denver, Colorado

http://www.regis.edu/

- **Independent Roman Catholic (Jesuit)** comprehensive, founded 1877
- **Urban** 90-acre campus with easy access to Denver, Colorado
- **Endowment** $65.1 million
- **Coed** 3,961 undergraduate students, 60% full-time, 60% women, 40% men
- **Moderately difficult** entrance level, 60% of applicants were admitted

UNDERGRAD STUDENTS
2,373 full-time, 1,588 part-time. Students come from 53 states and territories; 11 other countries; 40% are from out of state; 4% Black or African American, non-Hispanic/Latino; 19% Hispanic/Latino; 4% Asian, non-Hispanic/Latino; 0.3% Native Hawaiian or other Pacific Islander, non-Hispanic/Latino; 0.4% American Indian or Alaska Native, non-Hispanic/Latino; 4% Two or more races, non-Hispanic/Latino; 13% Race/ethnicity unknown; 6% international; 7% transferred in; 22% live on campus.

Freshmen:
Admission: 7,282 applied, 4,399 admitted, 508 enrolled. *Average high school GPA:* 3.6. *Test scores:* SAT evidence-based reading and writing scores over 500: 89%; SAT math scores over 500: 83%; ACT scores over 18: 97%; SAT evidence-based reading and writing scores over 600: 40%; SAT math scores over 600: 30%; ACT scores over 24: 55%; SAT evidence-based reading and writing scores over 700: 5%; SAT math scores over 700: 5%; ACT scores over 30: 9%.
Retention: 79% of full-time freshmen returned.

FACULTY
Total: 704, 44% full-time, 56% with terminal degrees.
Student/faculty ratio: 13:1.

ACADEMICS
Calendar: semesters. *Degrees:* certificates, bachelor's, master's, doctoral, post-master's, and postbachelor's certificates.
Special study options: academic remediation for entering students, accelerated degree program, adult/continuing education programs, advanced placement credit, cooperative education, distance learning, double majors, freshman honors college, honors programs, independent study, internships, off-campus study, part-time degree program, services for LD students, student-designed majors, study abroad, summer session for credit. *ROTC:* Army (c), Navy (c), Air Force (c).
Unusual degree programs: 3-2 engineering with Washington University in St. Louis.
Computers: 600 computers/terminals and 24 ports are available on campus for general student use. Students can access the following: campus intranet, computer help desk, free student e-mail accounts, online (class) grades, online (class) registration, online (class) schedules. Campuswide network is available. Wireless service is available via entire campus.
Library: Dayton Memorial Library. *Books:* 247,545 (physical), 182,210 (digital/electronic); *Serial titles:* 1,558 (physical), 112,666 (digital/electronic); *Databases:* 260. Students can reserve study rooms.

STUDENT LIFE
Housing options: on-campus residence required for freshman year; coed, special housing for students with disabilities. Campus housing is university owned. Freshman applicants given priority for college housing.
Activities and organizations: drama/theater group, student-run newspaper, radio station, choral group.
Athletics Member NCAA. All Division II except golf (Division I). *Intercollegiate sports:* baseball M(s), basketball M(s)/W(s), cross-country running M(s)/W(s), golf M(s)/W(s), lacrosse W(s), soccer M(s)/W(s), softball W(s), volleyball W(s). *Intramural sports:* lacrosse M, rugby M/W, soccer M/W, tennis M/W, volleyball M/W.

Campus security: 24-hour emergency response devices and patrols, student patrols, late-night transport/escort service, controlled dormitory access.

Student services: health clinic, personal/psychological counseling.

COSTS & FINANCIAL AID

Costs (2018–19) *Comprehensive fee:* $48,370 includes full-time tuition ($36,460), mandatory fees ($350), and room and board ($11,560). Full-time tuition and fees vary according to class time, course level, course load, degree level, location, program, reciprocity agreements, and student level. Part-time tuition: $1139 per semester hour. Part-time tuition and fees vary according to class time, course level, course load, degree level, location, program, reciprocity agreements, and student level. *College room only:* $6600. Room and board charges vary according to board plan and housing facility. *Payment plans:* installment, deferred payment. *Waivers:* employees or children of employees.

Financial Aid Of all full-time matriculated undergraduates who enrolled in 2017, 1,861 applied for aid, 1,636 were judged to have need, 208 had their need fully met. 343 Federal Work-Study jobs (averaging $2222). 522 state and other part-time jobs (averaging $2314). In 2017, 511 non-need-based awards were made. *Average percent of need met:* 78. *Average financial aid package:* $29,824. *Average need-based loan:* $4469. *Average need-based gift aid:* $20,657. *Average non-need-based aid:* $16,121. *Average indebtedness upon graduation:* $24,531. *Financial aid deadline:* 8/15.

APPLYING

Standardized Tests *Required:* SAT or ACT (for admission).

Options: electronic application, deferred entrance.

Required: essay or personal statement, high school transcript. *Required for some:* 1 letter of recommendation, interview.

Notification: continuous (transfers).

CONTACT

Ms. Sarah Engel, Director of Admissions, Regis University, 3333 Regis Boulevard, Mail Code A-12, Denver, CO 80221. *Phone:* 303-458-4938. *Toll-free phone:* 800-388-2366 Ext. 4900. *Fax:* 303-964-5534. *E-mail:* sengel@regis.edu.

Rocky Mountain College of Art + Design
Lakewood, Colorado
http://www.rmcad.edu/

CONTACT
Mr. Marc Abraham, Director of Admissions, Rocky Mountain College of Art + Design, 1600 Pierce Street, Lakewood, CO 80214. *Phone:* 321-256-9223. *Toll-free phone:* 800-888-ARTS. *E-mail:* mabraham@rmcad.edu.

United States Air Force Academy
Colorado Springs, Colorado
http://www.usafa.edu/

CONTACT
Dr. Phillip Prosseda, CHIEF, Selections Division, United States Air Force Academy, HQ USAFA/RRS, 2304 Cadet Drive, Suite 2400, USAF Academy, CO 80840-5025. *Phone:* 800-443-9266. *Toll-free phone:* 800-443-9266. *Fax:* 719-333-3012.

★ University of Colorado Boulder
Boulder, Colorado
http://www.colorado.edu/

- **State-supported** university, founded 1876, part of University of Colorado System
- **Suburban** 600-acre campus with easy access to Denver
- **Endowment** $596.0 million
- **Coed**
- **Moderately difficult** entrance level

ACADEMICS
Calendar: semesters. *Degrees:* bachelor's, master's, doctoral, and post-master's certificates.
Library: Norlin Library plus 5 others. *Books:* 664,601 (physical), 984,952 (digital/electronic); *Databases:* 594. Students can reserve study rooms.

Be here.

Be Boulder.
University of Colorado **Boulder**

www.colorado.edu/admissions

18:1 student to faculty ratio

3,900+

#1 college town in America
(American Institue for Economic Research, 2017)

300+

STUDENT LIFE

Housing options: on-campus residence required for freshman year; coed, special housing for students with disabilities. Campus housing is university owned and is provided by a third party. Freshman campus housing is guaranteed.

Activities and organizations: drama/theater group, student-run newspaper, radio and television station, choral group, marching band, Student Government, CU Gaming, Boulder Freeride, Neuroscience Club, Association of Holistic Wellness, national fraternities, national sororities.

Athletics Member NCAA. All Division I except football (Division I-A).

Campus security: 24-hour patrols, student patrols, late-night transport/escort service, controlled dormitory access, University police department, LifeLine Response app connecting to police dispatch center.

Student services: health clinic, personal/psychological counseling, women's center, legal services, veterans affairs office.

COSTS & FINANCIAL AID

Costs (2018–19) *One-time required fee:* $232. *Tuition:* state resident $10,728 full-time; nonresident $35,482 full-time. Full-time tuition and fees vary according to program. Part-time tuition and fees vary according to course load and program. No tuition increase for student's term of enrollment. *Required fees:* $1804 full-time. *Room and board:* $14,418. Room and board charges vary according to board plan, housing facility, and location.

Financial Aid Of all full-time matriculated undergraduates who enrolled in 2018, 14,577 applied for aid, 10,142 were judged to have need, 4,006 had their need fully met. 801 Federal Work-Study jobs (averaging $1624). 913 state and other part-time jobs (averaging $2908). In 2018, 8029 non-need-based awards were made. *Average percent of need met:* 79. *Average financial aid package:* $16,972. *Average need-based loan:* $6269. *Average need-based gift aid:* $11,228. *Average non-need-based aid:* $9313. *Average indebtedness upon graduation:* $23,207.

APPLYING

Standardized Tests *Required:* SAT or ACT (for admission).

Options: electronic application, early action, deferred entrance.

Application fee: $50.

Required: essay or personal statement, high school transcript, 1 letter of recommendation. *Required for some:* audition for music program. *Recommended:* minimum 3.0 GPA.

CONTACT

Admissions Office, University of Colorado Boulder, Regent Administrative Center 125, 552 UCB, Boulder, CO 80309. *Phone:* 303-492-6301. *Fax:* 303-735-2501. *E-mail:* apply@colorado.edu.

See previous page for display ad and page 1132 for the College Close-Up.

University of Colorado Colorado Springs

Colorado Springs, Colorado

http://www.uccs.edu/

- **State-supported** university, founded 1965, part of University of Colorado System
- **Urban** 532-acre campus with easy access to Colorado Springs
- **Coed**
- **Moderately difficult** entrance level

FACULTY

Student/faculty ratio: 19:1.

ACADEMICS

Calendar: semesters. *Degrees:* bachelor's, master's, doctoral, post-master's, and postbachelor's certificates.

Library: Kraemer Family Library. *Books:* 337,790 (physical), 168,770 (digital/electronic); *Serial titles:* 3,020 (physical); *Databases:* 154. Students can reserve study rooms.

STUDENT LIFE

Housing options: on-campus residence required for freshman year; coed. Campus housing is university owned. Freshman applicants given priority for college housing.

Activities and organizations: drama/theater group, student-run newspaper, radio and television station, choral group, Fans Initiating

Growth Honor and Tradition (spirit club), Pi Beta Phi, Sustainability Club, Gamers (computing), El Circulo, national fraternities, national sororities.

Athletics Member NCAA. All Division II.

Campus security: 24-hour emergency response devices and patrols, late-night transport/escort service, controlled dormitory access, emergency text messaging, state-authorized campus police and public safety department.

Student services: health clinic, personal/psychological counseling, veterans affairs office.

COSTS & FINANCIAL AID

Costs (2018–19) *One-time required fee:* $140. *Tuition:* state resident $8850 full-time, $295 per credit hour part-time; nonresident $23,280 full-time, $776 per credit hour part-time. Full-time tuition and fees vary according to course load, degree level, location, program, reciprocity agreements, and student level. Part-time tuition and fees vary according to course load, degree level, location, program, reciprocity agreements, and student level. *Required fees:* $1613 full-time. *Room and board:* $10,500. Room and board charges vary according to board plan, housing facility, and student level.

Financial Aid Of all full-time matriculated undergraduates who enrolled in 2017, 6,190 applied for aid, 5,040 were judged to have need, 272 had their need fully met. 124 Federal Work-Study jobs (averaging $1972). 182 state and other part-time jobs (averaging $2130). In 2017, 677 non-need-based awards were made. *Average percent of need met:* 43. *Average financial aid package:* $8722. *Average need-based loan:* $4048. *Average need-based gift aid:* $3962. *Average non-need-based aid:* $3057. *Average indebtedness upon graduation:* $25,205.

APPLYING

Standardized Tests *Required:* SAT or ACT (for admission).

Options: electronic application, deferred entrance.

Application fee: $50.

Required: high school transcript.

CONTACT

Mr. Chris Beiswanger, Director of Admissions Services, University of Colorado Colorado Springs, 1420 Austin Bluffs Parkway, Colorado Springs, CO 80918. *Phone:* 719-255-3088. *Toll-free phone:* 800-990-8227 Ext. 3383. *E-mail:* cbeiswan@uccs.edu.

University of Colorado Denver

Denver, Colorado

http://www.ucdenver.edu/

- **State-supported** university, founded 1912, part of University of Colorado System
- **Urban** 171-acre campus with easy access to Denver, CO
- **Endowment** $564.7 million
- **Coed** 16,443 undergraduate students, 55% full-time, 55% women, 45% men
- **Moderately difficult** entrance level, 64% of applicants were admitted

UNDERGRAD STUDENTS

8,980 full-time, 7,463 part-time. 9% are from out of state; 5% Black or African American, non-Hispanic/Latino; 24% Hispanic/Latino; 10% Asian, non-Hispanic/Latino; 0.1% Native Hawaiian or other Pacific Islander, non-Hispanic/Latino; 0.3% American Indian or Alaska Native, non-Hispanic/Latino; 6% Two or more races, non-Hispanic/Latino; 1% Race/ethnicity unknown; 8% international; 9% transferred in.

Freshmen:

Admission: 11,315 applied, 7,200 admitted, 1,743 enrolled. *Average high school GPA:* 3.5. *Test scores:* SAT evidence-based reading and writing scores over 500: 79%; SAT math scores over 500: 79%; ACT scores over 18: 93%; SAT evidence-based reading and writing scores over 600: 33%; SAT math scores over 600: 27%; ACT scores over 24: 48%; SAT evidence-based reading and writing scores over 700: 4%; SAT math scores over 700: 5%; ACT scores over 30: 11%.

Retention: 72% of full-time freshmen returned.

FACULTY

Total: 4,825, 83% full-time, 60% with terminal degrees.

Student/faculty ratio: 15:1.

ACADEMICS

Calendar: semesters. *Degrees:* bachelor's, master's, doctoral, post-master's, and postbachelor's certificates.

Special study options: accelerated degree program, advanced placement credit, cooperative education, distance learning, double majors, English as a second language, honors programs, independent study, internships, off-campus study, part-time degree program, services for LD students, student-designed majors, study abroad, summer session for credit. *ROTC:* Army (c), Air Force (c).

Unusual degree programs: 3-2 criminal justice.

Computers: 750 computers/terminals are available on campus for general student use. Students can access the following: campus intranet, computer help desk, free student e-mail accounts, online (class) grades, online (class) registration, online (class) schedules. Campuswide network is available. 100% of college-owned or -operated housing units are wired for high-speed Internet access. Wireless service is available via entire campus.

Library: Auraria Library plus 1 other. *Books:* 573,818 (physical), 325,936 (digital/electronic); *Serial titles:* 5,780 (physical), 92,591 (digital/electronic); *Databases:* 308. Weekly public service hours: 85; students can reserve study rooms.

STUDENT LIFE

Housing options: college housing not availableCampus housing is provided by a third party.

Activities and organizations: drama/theater group, student-run newspaper, choral group, Veterans Student Organization (Service), Golden Key Honor Society (Academic), Minority Association for Pre-Health Students (Health), Future Doctors of Denver, Intercultural Club Beijing (Cultural and Social).

Athletics *Intramural sports:* basketball M(c)/W(c), cheerleading M(c)/W(c), cross-country running M(c)/W(c), golf M(c)/W(c), ice hockey M(c), lacrosse M(c)/W(c), soccer M(c)/W(c), tennis M(c)/W(c), ultimate Frisbee M(c)/W(c), volleyball W(c).

Campus security: 24-hour emergency response devices and patrols, student patrols, late-night transport/escort service.

Student services: health clinic, personal/psychological counseling, women's center, veterans affairs office.

COSTS & FINANCIAL AID

Costs (2018–19) *Tuition:* state resident $9900 full-time, $330 per credit hour part-time; nonresident $30,510 full-time, $1017 per credit hour part-time. Full-time tuition and fees vary according to course level, course load, degree level, location, program, reciprocity agreements, and student level. Part-time tuition and fees vary according to course level, course load, degree level, location, program, reciprocity agreements, and student level. *Required fees:* $1495 full-time, $1098 per year part-time. *Room and board:* $12,620; room only: $8800. Room and board charges vary according to board plan. *Payment plans:* installment, deferred payment. *Waivers:* employees or children of employees.

Financial Aid Of all full-time matriculated undergraduates who enrolled in 2017, 6,218 applied for aid, 5,272 were judged to have need, 49 had their need fully met. 320 Federal Work-Study jobs (averaging $5083). 257 state and other part-time jobs (averaging $5351). In 2017, 549 non-need-based awards were made. *Average percent of need met: 49. Average financial aid package:* $10,213. *Average need-based loan:* $3905. *Average need-based gift aid:* $7973. *Average non-need-based aid:* $2409. *Average indebtedness upon graduation:* $20,975.

APPLYING

Standardized Tests *Required:* SAT or ACT (for admission).

Options: electronic application, deferred entrance.

Application fee: $50.

Required: minimum 2.5 GPA. *Required for some:* minimum 3.0 GPA, audition, portfolio, entrance exam.

Application deadlines: rolling (out-of-state freshmen), 8/1 (transfers).

Notification: continuous (freshmen), continuous (out-of-state freshmen), continuous (transfers).

CONTACT

Catherine Wilson, Director of Undergraduate Admissions, University of Colorado Denver, PO Box 173364, Campus Box 167, Denver, CO 80217. *Phone:* 303-315-2601. *E-mail:* admissions@ucdenver.edu.

University of Denver
Denver, Colorado
http://www.du.edu/

- **Independent** university, founded 1864
- **Urban** 125-acre campus with easy access to Denver
- **Endowment** $711.3 million
- **Coed**
- **Moderately difficult** entrance level

FACULTY
Student/faculty ratio: 11:1.

ACADEMICS

Calendar: quarters semesters for law school. *Degrees:* certificates, bachelor's, master's, doctoral, post-master's, and postbachelor's certificates.

Library: Anderson Academic Commons plus 1 other. *Books:* 1.7 million (physical), 2.3 million (digital/electronic); *Serial titles:* 594,063 (physical), 218,954 (digital/electronic); *Databases:* 1,306. Weekly public service hours: 145; study areas open 24 hours, 5–7 days a week; students can reserve study rooms.

STUDENT LIFE

Housing options: on-campus residence required through sophomore year; coed, cooperative. Campus housing is university owned. Freshman campus housing is guaranteed.

Activities and organizations: drama/theater group, student-run newspaper, radio station, choral group, Club Sports Council, Alpine Club, DU Programs Board, Greek Life Council, Residence Hall Association, national fraternities, national sororities.

Athletics Member NCAA. All Division I.

Campus security: 24-hour emergency response devices and patrols, late-night transport/escort service, controlled dormitory access, 24-hour locked residence hall entrances.

Student services: health clinic, personal/psychological counseling, women's center, veterans affairs office.

COSTS & FINANCIAL AID

Costs (2018–19) *Comprehensive fee:* $63,561 includes full-time tuition ($49,392), mandatory fees ($1164), and room and board ($13,005). Full-time tuition and fees vary according to course load and program. Part-time tuition: $1372 per credit hour. Part-time tuition and fees vary according to course load and program. *College room only:* $8100. Room and board charges vary according to board plan and housing facility. *Payment plans:* installment, deferred payment.

Financial Aid Of all full-time matriculated undergraduates who enrolled in 2017, 3,010 applied for aid, 2,333 were judged to have need, 782 had their need fully met. 471 Federal Work-Study jobs (averaging $2825). 195 state and other part-time jobs (averaging $3128). In 2017, 2197 non-need-based awards were made. *Average percent of need met: 86. Average financial aid package:* $40,587. *Average need-based loan:* $4291. *Average need-based gift aid:* $34,077. *Average non-need-based aid:* $18,280. *Average indebtedness upon graduation:* $31,526.

APPLYING

Standardized Tests *Required:* SAT or ACT (for admission).

Options: electronic application, early admission, early decision, early action, deferred entrance.

Application fee: $65.

Required: essay or personal statement, high school transcript, 1 letter of recommendation. *Recommended:* 2 letters of recommendation.

CONTACT

Mr. Todd Rinehart, Vice Chancellor for Enrollment, University of Denver, 2197 South University Boulevard, Denver, CO 80208. *Phone:* 303-871-3125. *Toll-free phone:* 800-525-9495. *Fax:* 303-871-3301. *E-mail:* admission@du.edu.

See next page for display ad and page 1134 for the College Close-Up.

A ⭐ *indicates that the school has detailed information with a Premium Profile on Petersons.com.*

University of Northern Colorado

Greeley, Colorado

http://www.unco.edu/

- **State-supported** university, founded 1890
- **Suburban** 237-acre campus with easy access to Denver
- **Endowment** $87.6 million
- **Coed** 9,876 undergraduate students, 81% full-time, 65% women, 35% men
- **Moderately difficult** entrance level, 91% of applicants were admitted

UNDERGRAD STUDENTS

8,047 full-time, 1,829 part-time. Students come from 49 states and territories; 39 other countries; 14% are from out of state; 4% Black or African American, non-Hispanic/Latino; 22% Hispanic/Latino; 2% Asian, non-Hispanic/Latino; 0.2% Native Hawaiian or other Pacific Islander, non-Hispanic/Latino; 0.4% American Indian or Alaska Native, non-Hispanic/Latino; 4% Two or more races, non-Hispanic/Latino; 2% Race/ethnicity unknown; 1% international; 7% transferred in; 34% live on campus.

Freshmen:
Admission: 8,294 applied, 7,527 admitted, 1,858 enrolled. *Average high school GPA:* 3.4. *Test scores:* SAT evidence-based reading and writing scores over 500: 76%; SAT math scores over 500: 73%; ACT scores over 18: 88%; SAT evidence-based reading and writing scores over 600: 29%; SAT math scores over 600: 19%; ACT scores over 24: 36%; SAT evidence-based reading and writing scores over 700: 3%; SAT math scores over 700: 2%; ACT scores over 30: 6%.

Retention: 72% of full-time freshmen returned.

FACULTY

Total: 872, 59% full-time, 68% with terminal degrees.

Student/faculty ratio: 18:1.

ACADEMICS

Calendar: semesters. *Degrees:* bachelor's, master's, and doctoral.

Special study options: accelerated degree program, adult/continuing education programs, advanced placement credit, cooperative education, distance learning, double majors, English as a second language, external degree program, honors programs, independent study, internships, off-campus study, part-time degree program, services for LD students, student-designed majors, study abroad, summer session for credit. *ROTC:* Army (b), Air Force (b).

Computers: 1,723 computers/terminals and 825 ports are available on campus for general student use. Students can access the following: computer help desk, free student e-mail accounts, online (class) grades, online (class) registration, online (class) schedules. Campuswide network is available. 100% of college-owned or -operated housing units are wired for high-speed Internet access. Wireless service is available via entire campus.

Library: James A. Michener Library plus 2 others. *Books:* 1.3 million (physical), 473,007 (digital/electronic); *Serial titles:* 19,480 (physical), 85,939 (digital/electronic); *Databases:* 210. Weekly public service hours: 97; students can reserve study rooms.

STUDENT LIFE

Housing options: on-campus residence required for freshman year; coed, women-only, special housing for students with disabilities. Campus housing is university owned. Freshman campus housing is guaranteed.

Activities and organizations: drama/theater group, student-run newspaper, choral group, marching band, Fraternities and Sororities, Club Sports, Campus Religious/Spiritual Organizations, Academic Clubs, Services Clubs, national fraternities, national sororities.

Athletics Member NCAA. All Division I. *Intercollegiate sports:* baseball M(s), basketball M(s)/W(s), cross-country running M(s)/W(s), football M(s), golf M(s)/W(s), soccer W(s), softball W(s), swimming and diving W(s), tennis M(s)/W(s), track and field M(s)/W(s), volleyball W(s), wrestling M(s). *Intramural sports:* basketball M/W, cross-country running M(c)/W(c), fencing M(c)/W(c), football M/W, golf M/W, ice hockey M(c), lacrosse M(c)/W(c), rugby M(c)/W(c), soccer M/W, softball M/W, swimming and diving M(c)/W(c), tennis M/W, ultimate Frisbee M(c)/W(c), volleyball M/W, water polo M/W, weight lifting M(c)/W(c).

Campus security: 24-hour emergency response devices and patrols, student patrols, late-night transport/escort service, controlled dormitory access.

Student services: health clinic, personal/psychological counseling, women's center, legal services, veterans affairs office.

COSTS & FINANCIAL AID

Costs (2019–20) *One-time required fee:* $250. *Tuition:* area resident $7830 full-time, $295 per credit hour part-time; state resident $7830 full-time, $295 per credit hour part-time; nonresident $19,518 full-time, $755 per credit hour part-time. *Required fees:* $2358 full-time, $111 per credit hour part-time. *Room and board:* $11,204; room only: $5304.

Financial Aid Of all full-time matriculated undergraduates who enrolled in 2017, 6,890 applied for aid, 5,357 were judged to have need, 1,272 had their need fully met. 186 Federal Work-Study jobs (averaging $2538). 508 state and other part-time jobs (averaging $2574). In 2017, 1556 non-need-based awards were made. *Average percent of need met:* 72. *Average financial aid package:* $15,428. *Average need-based loan:* $4673. *Average need-based gift aid:* $7867. *Average non-need-based aid:* $3288. *Average indebtedness upon graduation:* $24,149.

APPLYING

Standardized Tests *Required:* SAT or ACT (for admission).

Options: electronic application, deferred entrance.

Application fee: $50.

Required: high school transcript. *Required for some:* essay or personal statement.

Application deadlines: 8/1 (freshmen), 8/1 (out-of-state freshmen), 8/1 (transfers).

Notification: continuous (freshmen), 9/1 (out-of-state freshmen), continuous (transfers).

CONTACT

Sean Broghammer, Director of Admissions, University of Northern Colorado, Campus Box 10, Carter Hall 3006, Greeley, CO 80639. *Phone:* 970-351-2881. *Toll-free phone:* 888-700-4UNC. *Fax:* 970-351-2984. *E-mail:* admissions@unco.edu.

Western State Colorado University

Gunnison, Colorado

http://www.western.edu/

- **State-supported** comprehensive, founded 1901
- **Rural** 381-acre campus
- **Coed** 2,612 undergraduate students, 72% full-time, 44% women, 56% men
- **Moderately difficult** entrance level, 89% of applicants were admitted

UNDERGRAD STUDENTS

1,883 full-time, 729 part-time. 29% are from out of state; 3% Black or African American, non-Hispanic/Latino; 11% Hispanic/Latino; 0.8% Asian, non-Hispanic/Latino; 0.2% Native Hawaiian or other Pacific Islander, non-Hispanic/Latino; 0.6% American Indian or Alaska Native, non-Hispanic/Latino; 4% Two or more races, non-Hispanic/Latino; 9% Race/ethnicity unknown; 0.5% international; 5% transferred in; 47% live on campus.

Freshmen:

Admission: 1,972 applied, 1,755 admitted, 509 enrolled. *Average high school GPA:* 3.3. *Test scores:* SAT evidence-based reading and writing scores over 500: 78%; SAT math scores over 500: 73%; ACT scores over 18: 89%; SAT evidence-based reading and writing scores over 600: 24%; SAT math scores over 600: 18%; ACT scores over 24: 37%; SAT evidence-based reading and writing scores over 700: 2%; SAT math scores over 700: 1%; ACT scores over 30: 4%.

Retention: 69% of full-time freshmen returned.

FACULTY

Total: 166, 72% full-time, 77% with terminal degrees.
Student/faculty ratio: 18:1.

ACADEMICS

Calendar: semesters. *Degrees:* bachelor's, master's, and postbachelor's certificates.

Special study options: academic remediation for entering students, adult/continuing education programs, advanced placement credit, double majors, honors programs, independent study, internships, off-campus study, part-time degree program, services for LD students, study abroad, summer session for credit.

Computers: 215 computers/terminals are available on campus for general student use. Students can access the following: computer help desk, free student e-mail accounts, online (class) grades, online (class) registration, online (class) schedules. Campuswide network is available. 100% of college-owned or -operated housing units are wired for high-speed Internet access. Wireless service is available via entire campus.
Library: Leslie J. Savage Library plus 1 other. Weekly public service hours: 101; students can reserve study rooms.

STUDENT LIFE

Housing options: on-campus residence required through sophomore year; coed, special housing for students with disabilities. Campus housing is university owned. Freshman campus housing is guaranteed.

Activities and organizations: drama/theater group, student-run newspaper, radio and television station, choral group, Mountain Search and Rescue Team, Student Government Association, Rodeo Club, wilderness pursuits, Peak Productions.

Athletics Member NCAA. All Division II. *Intercollegiate sports:* baseball M(c), basketball M(s)/W(s), cheerleading M(c)/W(c), cross-country running M(s)/W(s), football M(s), ice hockey M(c), lacrosse M(c)/W(c), rock climbing M(c)/W(c), rugby M(c)/W(c), skiing (cross-country) M(c)/W(c), skiing (downhill) W(c), soccer M(c)/W(s), swimming and diving W(s), track and field M(s)/W(s), volleyball M(c)/W(s), wrestling M(s)/W(c). *Intramural sports:* badminton M/W, basketball M/W, field hockey M/W, football M/W, golf M/W, soccer M/W, softball M/W, table tennis M/W, tennis M/W, ultimate Frisbee M/W, volleyball M/W.

Campus security: 24-hour emergency response devices and patrols, student patrols, late-night transport/escort service, controlled dormitory access.

Student services: health clinic, personal/psychological counseling.

COSTS & FINANCIAL AID

Costs (2019–20) *Tuition:* state resident $6624 full-time, $276 per credit hour part-time; nonresident $18,096 full-time, $754 per credit hour part-time. *Required fees:* $3812 full-time. *Room and board:* $9704; room only: $5030.

Financial Aid Of all full-time matriculated undergraduates who enrolled in 2018, 1,684 applied for aid, 1,077 were judged to have need, 29 had their need fully met. In 2018, 485 non-need-based awards were made. *Average percent of need met:* 67. *Average financial aid package:* $11,482. *Average need-based loan:* $4207. *Average need-based gift aid:* $8913. *Average non-need-based aid:* $5070. *Average indebtedness upon graduation:* $28,036.

APPLYING

Standardized Tests *Required:* SAT or ACT (for admission).

Options: electronic application, deferred entrance.

Application fee: $30.

Required: essay or personal statement, high school transcript. *Recommended:* minimum 2.5 GPA.

Application deadlines: rolling (freshmen), rolling (transfers).

Notification: continuous until 10/1 (freshmen), continuous (transfers).

CONTACT

Ms. Lauren Shondeck, Director of Admissions, Western State Colorado University, 600 North Adams Street, Gunnison, CO 81231. *Phone:* 970-943-2243. *Toll-free phone:* 800-876-5309. *E-mail:* lshondeck@ western.edu.

CONNECTICUT

Albertus Magnus College
New Haven, Connecticut
http://www.albertus.edu/

CONTACT
Anthony Reich, Director of Admission, Albertus Magnus College, 700 Prospect Street, New Haven, CT 06511-1189. *Phone:* 203-773-5032 Ext. 5032. *Toll-free phone:* 800-578-9160. *E-mail:* admissions@albertus.edu.

Bais Binyomin Academy
Stamford, Connecticut

CONTACT
Director of Admissions, Bais Binyomin Academy, 132 Prospect Street, Stamford, CT 06901-1202. *Phone:* 203-325-4351.

Central Connecticut State University
New Britain, Connecticut
http://www.ccsu.edu/
- **State-supported** comprehensive, founded 1849, part of Connecticut State Colleges & Universities (CSCU)
- **Suburban** 314-acre campus
- **Endowment** $72.7 million
- **Coed** 9,546 undergraduate students, 79% full-time, 47% women, 53% men
- **Moderately difficult** entrance level, 67% of applicants were admitted

UNDERGRAD STUDENTS
7,576 full-time, 1,970 part-time. Students come from 30 states and territories; 25 other countries; 4% are from out of state; 12% Black or African American, non-Hispanic/Latino; 16% Hispanic/Latino; 5% Asian, non-Hispanic/Latino; 0.1% Native Hawaiian or other Pacific Islander, non-Hispanic/Latino; 0.1% American Indian or Alaska Native, non-Hispanic/Latino; 3% Two or more races, non-Hispanic/Latino; 3% Race/ethnicity unknown; 1% international; 11% transferred in; 25% live on campus.

Freshmen:
Admission: 7,903 applied, 5,314 admitted, 1,464 enrolled. *Average high school GPA:* 3.1. *Test scores:* SAT evidence-based reading and writing scores over 500: 77%; SAT math scores over 500: 69%; ACT scores over 18: 85%; SAT evidence-based reading and writing scores over 600: 23%; SAT math scores over 600: 17%; ACT scores over 24: 33%; SAT evidence-based reading and writing scores over 700: 1%; SAT math scores over 700: 2%; ACT scores over 30: 1%.
Retention: 74% of full-time freshmen returned.

FACULTY
Total: 977, 46% full-time, 53% with terminal degrees.
Student/faculty ratio: 16:1.

ACADEMICS
Calendar: semesters. *Degrees:* bachelor's, master's, doctoral, post-master's, and postbachelor's certificates.

Special study options: academic remediation for entering students, adult/continuing education programs, advanced placement credit, cooperative education, distance learning, double majors, English as a second language, honors programs, independent study, internships, off-campus study, part-time degree program, services for LD students, student-designed majors, study abroad, summer session for credit. *ROTC:* Army (c), Air Force (c).

Computers: 450 computers/terminals and 2,200 ports are available on campus for general student use. Students can access the following: campus intranet, computer help desk, free student e-mail accounts, online (class) grades, online (class) registration, online (class) schedules. Campuswide network is available. 100% of college-owned or -operated housing units are wired for high-speed Internet access. Wireless service is available via entire campus.

Library: Elihu Burritt Library plus 1 other. *Books:* 449,293 (physical), 199,200 (digital/electronic); *Serial titles:* 6,833 (physical), 89,498 (digital/electronic); *Databases:* 151. Weekly public service hours: 84.

STUDENT LIFE
Housing options: coed, women-only, special housing for students with disabilities. Campus housing is university owned.

Activities and organizations: drama/theater group, student-run newspaper, radio and television station, choral group, Inter-Residence Council, student radio station, Program Board (C.A.N.), Student Government Association, A Cappella Society, national fraternities, national sororities.

Athletics Member NCAA. All Division I except football (Division I-AA). *Intercollegiate sports:* baseball M(s), basketball M(s)/W(s), cross-country running M(s)/W(s), lacrosse W(s), soccer M(s)/W(s), softball W(s), swimming and diving W(s), track and field M(s)/W(s), volleyball W(s). *Intramural sports:* baseball M(c), basketball M/W, cheerleading M(c)/W(c), cross-country running M(c)/W(c), equestrian sports M(c)/W(c), fencing M(c)/W(c), football M/W, golf M(c), ice hockey M(c), lacrosse M(c), rugby M(c)/W(c), skiing (downhill) M(c)/W(c), soccer M/W, softball M/W, tennis M(c), ultimate Frisbee M(c), volleyball M/W.

Campus security: 24-hour emergency response devices and patrols, student patrols, late-night transport/escort service, controlled dormitory access.

Student services: health clinic, personal/psychological counseling, women's center, veterans affairs office.

COSTS & FINANCIAL AID
Costs (2019–20) Comprehensive fee: includes mandatory fees ($5144) and room and board ($12,528). *Required fees:* $298 per credit part-time, $78 per term part-time. *College room only:* $7130.

Financial Aid Of all full-time matriculated undergraduates who enrolled in 2018, 6,929 applied for aid, 6,016 were judged to have need, 523 had their need fully met. In 2018, 165 non-need-based awards were made. *Average percent of need met:* 63. *Average financial aid package:* $8824. *Average need-based loan:* $4365. *Average need-based gift aid:* $6309. *Average non-need-based aid:* $2779. *Average indebtedness upon graduation:* $29,728.

APPLYING
Standardized Tests *Required:* SAT or ACT (for admission).
Options: electronic application.
Application fee: $50.
Required: high school transcript, minimum 2.0 GPA, 2 letters of recommendation. *Required for some:* essay or personal statement, interview, high school class rank.
Notification: continuous until 10/15 (freshmen), continuous until 10/15 (transfers).

CONTACT
Lawrence Hall, Central Connecticut State University, 1615 Stanley Street, New Britain, CT 06050. *Phone:* 860-832-2285. *Toll-free phone:* 888-733-2278. *Fax:* 860-832-2522. *E-mail:* admissions@ccsu.edu.

Charter Oak State College
New Britain, Connecticut
http://www.charteroak.edu/
- **State-supported** comprehensive, founded 1973, part of Connecticut State Colleges & Universities (CSCU)
- **Suburban** campus with easy access to Hartford, CT
- **Coed**
- **Noncompetitive** entrance level

FACULTY
Student/faculty ratio: 12:1.

ACADEMICS
Calendar: semesters. *Degrees:* certificates, associate, bachelor's, and master's (offers only external degree programs).

STUDENT LIFE
Housing options: college housing not available.

COSTS

Costs (2018–19) *Tuition:* state resident $9300 full-time, $310 per credit part-time; nonresident $12,240 full-time, $408 per credit part-time. Full-time tuition and fees vary according to course load. Part-time tuition and fees vary according to course load. *Required fees:* $861 full-time, $287 per term part-time.

APPLYING

Options: electronic application, deferred entrance.

Application fee: $75.

Required: 9 college-level credits, minimum 16 years of age.

CONTACT

Charter Oak State College, CT. *Phone:* 860-515-3858.

Connecticut College

New London, Connecticut
http://www.conncoll.edu/

- **Independent** 4-year, founded 1911
- **Small-town** 750-acre campus with easy access to Providence, RI
- **Endowment** $318.3 million
- **Coed** 1,844 undergraduate students, 98% full-time, 61% women, 39% men
- **Very difficult** entrance level, 38% of applicants were admitted

UNDERGRAD STUDENTS

1,798 full-time, 46 part-time. Students come from 40 states and territories; 41 other countries; 83% are from out of state; 4% Black or African American, non-Hispanic/Latino; 9% Hispanic/Latino; 5% Asian, non-Hispanic/Latino; 0.1% Native Hawaiian or other Pacific Islander, non-Hispanic/Latino; 0.1% American Indian or Alaska Native, non-Hispanic/Latino; 4% Two or more races, non-Hispanic/Latino; 2% Race/ethnicity unknown; 7% international; 2% transferred in; 99% live on campus.

Freshmen:

Admission: 6,433 applied, 2,429 admitted, 508 enrolled. *Test scores:* SAT evidence-based reading and writing scores over 500: 100%; SAT math scores over 500: 100%; ACT scores over 18: 100%; SAT evidence-based reading and writing scores over 600: 95%; SAT math scores over 600: 88%; ACT scores over 24: 99%; SAT evidence-based reading and writing scores over 700: 38%; SAT math scores over 700: 42%; ACT scores over 30: 69%.

Retention: 91% of full-time freshmen returned.

FACULTY

Total: 233, 74% full-time, 88% with terminal degrees.

Student/faculty ratio: 9:1.

ACADEMICS

Calendar: semesters. *Degree:* bachelor's.

Special study options: accelerated degree program, adult/continuing education programs, advanced placement credit, double majors, independent study, internships, off-campus study, part-time degree program, services for LD students, student-designed majors, study abroad.

Unusual degree programs: 3-2 engineering with Washington University in St. Louis; Worcester Polytechnic Institute (environmental engineering).

Computers: Students can access the following: campus intranet, computer help desk, free student e-mail accounts, online (class) grades, online (class) registration, online (class) schedules, learning management system. Campuswide network is available. 100% of college-owned or -operated housing units are wired for high-speed Internet access. Wireless service is available via classrooms, computer centers, computer labs, dorm rooms, learning centers, libraries, student centers.

Library: Charles Shain Library plus 1 other. Weekly public service hours: 115.

STUDENT LIFE

Housing options: on-campus residence required through junior year; coed. Campus housing is university owned. Freshman campus housing is guaranteed.

Activities and organizations: drama/theater group, student-run newspaper, radio station, choral group.

Athletics Member NCAA. All Division III. *Intercollegiate sports:* basketball M/W, cross-country running M/W, field hockey W, ice hockey M/W, lacrosse M/W, rowing M/W, sailing M/W, soccer M/W, squash M/W, swimming and diving M/W, tennis M/W, track and field M/W, volleyball W, water polo M/W. *Intramural sports:* baseball M(c), basketball M/W, equestrian sports M(c)/W(c), ice hockey M(c), lacrosse M(c), rugby M(c)/W(c), skiing (downhill) M(c)/W(c), soccer M(c)/W(c), softball M/W, squash M/W, tennis M/W, ultimate Frisbee M(c)/W(c), volleyball M(c)/W(c).

Campus security: 24-hour emergency response devices and patrols, late-night transport/escort service, controlled dormitory access.

Student services: health clinic, personal/psychological counseling, women's center.

COSTS & FINANCIAL AID

Costs (2018–19) *Comprehensive fee:* $69,970 includes full-time tuition ($54,500), mandatory fees ($320), and room and board ($15,150). Part-time tuition: $1622 per credit hour. *College room only:* $8750. *Payment plan:* installment. *Waivers:* employees or children of employees.

Financial Aid Of all full-time matriculated undergraduates who enrolled in 2018, 1,161 applied for aid, 1,032 were judged to have need, 1,032 had their need fully met. In 2018, 275 non-need-based awards were made. *Average percent of need met:* 100. *Average financial aid package:* $45,149. *Average need-based loan:* $4469. *Average need-based gift aid:* $41,921. *Average non-need-based aid:* $14,049. *Average indebtedness upon graduation:* $33,608.

APPLYING

Options: electronic application, early decision, deferred entrance.

Required: essay or personal statement, high school transcript, 2 letters of recommendation. *Recommended:* interview.

Application deadlines: 1/1 (freshmen), 4/1 (transfers).

Early decision deadline: 11/15.

Notification: 3/31 (freshmen), 5/15 (transfers), 12/15 (early decision).

CONTACT

Andrew Strickler, Dean of Admission and Financial Aid, Connecticut College, 270 Mohegan Avenue, New London, CT 06320. *Phone:* 860-439-2200. *E-mail:* admission@conncoll.edu.

Eastern Connecticut State University

Willimantic, Connecticut
http://www.easternct.edu/

CONTACT

Eastern Connecticut State University, CT. *Phone:* 860-465-4381.

Fairfield University

Fairfield, Connecticut
http://www.fairfield.edu/

- **Independent Roman Catholic (Jesuit)** comprehensive, founded 1942
- **Suburban** 200-acre campus with easy access to New York City
- **Endowment** $361.5 million
- **Coed** 4,177 undergraduate students, 95% full-time, 60% women, 40% men
- **Very difficult** entrance level, 60% of applicants were admitted

UNDERGRAD STUDENTS

3,989 full-time, 188 part-time. Students come from 35 states and territories; 49 other countries; 72% are from out of state; 2% Black or African American, non-Hispanic/Latino; 7% Hispanic/Latino; 3% Asian, non-Hispanic/Latino; 0.1% American Indian or Alaska Native, non-Hispanic/Latino; 2% Two or more races, non-Hispanic/Latino; 5% Race/ethnicity unknown; 4% international; 0.9% transferred in; 73% live on campus.

Freshmen:

Admission: 11,361 applied, 6,851 admitted, 1,091 enrolled. *Average high school GPA:* 3.7. *Test scores:* SAT evidence-based reading and writing scores over 500: 99%; SAT math scores over 500: 99%; ACT scores over 18: 100%; SAT evidence-based reading and writing scores over 600: 78%; SAT math scores over 600: 74%; ACT scores over 24: 95%; SAT evidence-based reading and writing scores over 700: 10%; SAT math scores over 700: 16%; ACT scores over 30: 35%.

Retention: 90% of full-time freshmen returned.

FACULTY
Total: 622, 45% full-time, 67% with terminal degrees.
Student/faculty ratio: 12:1.

ACADEMICS
Calendar: semesters. *Degrees:* bachelor's, master's, doctoral, post-master's, and postbachelor's certificates.

Special study options: accelerated degree program, adult/continuing education programs, advanced placement credit, distance learning, double majors, honors programs, independent study, internships, off-campus study, part-time degree program, services for LD students, student-designed majors, study abroad, summer session for credit. *ROTC:* Army (c), Air Force (c).

Computers: 150 computers/terminals are available on campus for general student use. Students can access the following: campus intranet, computer help desk, free student e-mail accounts, online (class) grades, online (class) registration, online (class) schedules. Campuswide network is available. 100% of college-owned or -operated housing units are wired for high-speed Internet access. Wireless service is available via entire campus.

Library: DiMenna-Nyselius Library. *Books:* 373,440 (physical), 924,527 (digital/electronic); *Serial titles:* 1,843 (physical), 52,268 (digital/electronic); *Databases:* 209. Weekly public service hours: 104; study areas open 24 hours, 5–7 days a week; students can reserve study rooms.

STUDENT LIFE
Housing options: coed, special housing for students with disabilities. Campus housing is university owned. Freshman campus housing is guaranteed.

Activities and organizations: drama/theater group, student-run newspaper, radio and television station, choral group, Fairfield University Student Association (FUSA), Inter-Residential Housing Associations (IRHA), Commuter Student Association (CSA), Play Like a Girl (PLAG), Intramural/Club Sports.

Athletics Member NCAA. All Division I. *Intercollegiate sports:* baseball M(s), basketball M(s)/W(s), crew M(s)/W(s), cross-country running M(s)/W(s), field hockey W(s), golf M(s)/W(s)(c), lacrosse M(s)/W(s), rowing M(s)/W(s), soccer M(s)/W(s), softball W(s), swimming and diving M(s)/W(s), tennis M(s)/W(s), volleyball W(s). *Intramural sports:* badminton M/W, baseball M(c), basketball M(c)/W(c), cheerleading M(c)/W(c), cross-country running M(c)/W(c), equestrian sports M(c)/W(c), field hockey M(c)/W(c), golf M(c)/W(c), ice hockey M(c), lacrosse M(c)/W(c), rugby M(c)/W(c), sailing M(c)/W(c), skiing (downhill) M(c)/W(c), soccer M(c)/W(c), softball M/W, swimming and diving M(c)/W(c), table tennis M/W, tennis M(c)/W(c), ultimate Frisbee M(c)/W(c), volleyball M(c)/W(c), wrestling M(c).

Campus security: 24-hour emergency response devices and patrols, late-night transport/escort service, controlled dormitory access.

Student services: health clinic, personal/psychological counseling.

COSTS & FINANCIAL AID
Costs (2018–19) *One-time required fee:* $300. *Comprehensive fee:* $63,060 includes full-time tuition ($47,650), mandatory fees ($700), and room and board ($14,710). Full-time tuition and fees vary according to class time, course level, course load, degree level, and program. Part-time tuition: $725 per credit hour. Part-time tuition and fees vary according to class time, course level, course load, degree level, and program. *Required fees:* $60 per term part-time. *Room and board:* Room and board charges vary according to board plan and housing facility. *Payment plan:* installment. *Waivers:* employees or children of employees.

Financial Aid Of all full-time matriculated undergraduates who enrolled in 2018, 2,024 applied for aid, 1,732 were judged to have need, 431 had their need fully met. 568 Federal Work-Study jobs (averaging $1620). In 2018, 2073 non-need-based awards were made. *Average percent of need met:* 81. *Average financial aid package:* $33,281. *Average need-based loan:* $4340. *Average need-based gift aid:* $17,505. *Average non-need-based aid:* $12,207. *Average indebtedness upon graduation:* $38,596. *Financial aid deadline:* 1/15.

APPLYING
Options: electronic application, early admission, early decision, early action, deferred entrance.

Application fee: $60.

Required: essay or personal statement, high school transcript, 1 letter of recommendation. *Recommended:* interview.

Application deadlines: 1/15 (freshmen), 4/1 (transfers), 11/1 (early action).

Early decision deadline: 11/15 (for plan 1), 1/15 (for plan 2).

Notification: 4/1 (freshmen), continuous (transfers), 12/15 (early decision plan 1), 2/15 (early decision plan 2), 12/20 (early action).

CONTACT
Alison Hildenbrand, Director of Admission, Fairfield University, 1073 North Benson Road, Fairfield, CT 06824. *Phone:* 203-254-4100. *Fax:* 203-254-4199. *E-mail:* admis@fairfield.edu.

Goodwin College
East Hartford, Connecticut
http://www.goodwin.edu/

CONTACT
Mr. Nicholas Lentino, Assistant Vice President for Admissions, Goodwin College, One Riverside Drive, East Hartford, CT 06118. *Phone:* 860-727-6765. *Toll-free phone:* 800-889-3282. *Fax:* 860-291-9550. *E-mail:* nlentino@goodwin.edu.

Holy Apostles College and Seminary
Cromwell, Connecticut
http://www.holyapostles.edu/
- **Independent Roman Catholic** comprehensive, founded 1956
- **Suburban** 17-acre campus with easy access to Hartford, New Haven
- **Coed** 166 undergraduate students, 36% full-time, 51% women, 49% men
- **Noncompetitive** entrance level, 100% of applicants were admitted

UNDERGRAD STUDENTS
60 full-time, 106 part-time. Students come from 33 states and territories; 4 other countries; 48% are from out of state; 0.7% Black or African American, non-Hispanic/Latino; 14% Hispanic/Latino; 6% Asian, non-Hispanic/Latino; 5% Two or more races, non-Hispanic/Latino; 1% Race/ethnicity unknown; 29% international; 7% transferred in.

Freshmen:
Admission: 10 applied, 10 admitted, 11 enrolled.

FACULTY
Total: 83, 19% full-time, 63% with terminal degrees.
Student/faculty ratio: 2:1.

ACADEMICS
Calendar: semesters. *Degrees:* certificates, associate, bachelor's, master's, post-master's, and postbachelor's certificates.

Special study options: academic remediation for entering students, adult/continuing education programs, English as a second language, external degree program, independent study, part-time degree program, services for LD students, summer session for credit.

Computers: 10 computers/terminals are available on campus for general student use. Students can access the following: free student e-mail accounts, online (class) grades, online (class) registration, online (class) schedules. Campuswide network is available. 100% of college-owned or -operated housing units are wired for high-speed Internet access. Wireless service is available via libraries.

Library: Holy Apostles College and Seminary Library. *Books:* 60,000 (physical); *Serial titles:* 145 (physical), 32 (digital/electronic); *Databases:* 5. Weekly public service hours: 70.

STUDENT LIFE
Housing options: college housing not available.

Activities and organizations: Pro-Life Organization.

APPLYING
Standardized Tests *Required:* SAT or ACT (for admission). *Recommended:* SAT (for admission), ACT (for admission).

Options: deferred entrance.

Application fee: $50.

Required: high school transcript, 2 letters of recommendation. *Required for some:* interview.

Application deadlines: rolling (freshmen), rolling (out-of-state freshmen), rolling (transfers).

CONTACT
Fr. Peter Samuel Kucer, Academic Dean, Holy Apostles College and Seminary, Holy Apostles College and Seminary, 33 Prospect Hill Road, Cromwell, CT 06416. *Phone:* 860-632-3063. *Fax:* 860-632-3030. *E-mail:* pkucer@holyapostles.edu.

Mitchell College
New London, Connecticut
http://www.mitchell.edu/

CONTACT
Mr. Bob Martin, Director of Admissions, Mitchell College, 437 Pequot Avenue, New London, CT 06320. *Phone:* 860-701-5178. *Toll-free phone:* 800-443-2811. *Fax:* 860-444-1209. *E-mail:* admissions@mitchell.edu.

Paier College of Art, Inc.
Hamden, Connecticut
http://www.paiercollegeofart.edu/
- **Proprietary** 4-year, founded 1946
- **Suburban** 3-acre campus with easy access to New York City
- **Coed**
- 75% of applicants were admitted

FACULTY
Student/faculty ratio: 3:1.

ACADEMICS
Calendar: semesters plus 1 summer session. *Degree:* certificates, diplomas, and bachelor's.
Library: Adele K. Paier Memorial Library. *Books:* 14,300 (physical), 167 (digital/electronic); *Serial titles:* 80 (physical).

STUDENT LIFE
Housing options: college housing not available.
Activities and organizations: student-run newspaper, Student Council, School Newspaper.
Student services: veterans affairs office.

COSTS & FINANCIAL AID
Costs (2018–19) *Tuition:* $17,100 full-time, $570 per credit hour part-time. Part-time tuition and fees vary according to course load. *Required fees:* $470 full-time, $190 per term part-time.
Financial Aid Of all full-time matriculated undergraduates who enrolled in 2017, 51 applied for aid, 49 were judged to have need, 1 had their need fully met. *Average percent of need met:* 48. *Average financial aid package:* $7816. *Average need-based loan:* $4350. *Average need-based gift aid:* $6220. *Average indebtedness upon graduation:* $13,536.

APPLYING
Standardized Tests *Required:* SAT or ACT (for admission).
Options: early admission.
Application fee: $25.
Required: high school transcript, minimum 2.0 GPA, 2 letters of recommendation, interview, portfolio, interview. *Recommended:* essay or personal statement.

CONTACT
Mrs. Lynn Pascale, Admissions Secretary, Paier College of Art, Inc., 20 Gorham Avenue, Hamden, CT 06514. *Phone:* 203-287-3031. *Fax:* 203-287-3021. *E-mail:* paier.admission@snet.net.

Post University
Waterbury, Connecticut
http://www.post.edu/
- **Independent** comprehensive, founded 1890
- **Suburban** 70-acre campus with easy access to Hartford
- **Coed**
- **Moderately difficult** entrance level

FACULTY
Student/faculty ratio: 20:1.

ACADEMICS
Calendar: semesters. *Degrees:* certificates, associate, bachelor's, master's, post-master's, and postbachelor's certificates.
Library: Trauriq Library and Resource Center. *Books:* 10,320 (physical), 160,000 (digital/electronic); *Serial titles:* 250 (physical), 36,199 (digital/electronic); *Databases:* 43. Weekly public service hours: 75; students can reserve study rooms.

STUDENT LIFE
Housing options: coed, special housing for students with disabilities. Campus housing is university owned.
Activities and organizations: drama/theater group, choral group, Equine Club, Newman Club, GSA, Accounting Club, Choir.
Athletics Member NCAA. All Division II.
Campus security: 24-hour emergency response devices and patrols, late-night transport/escort service, controlled dormitory access, annual and semi-annual emergency preparedness training for students and staff.
Student services: health clinic, personal/psychological counseling.

COSTS & FINANCIAL AID
Costs (2018–19) *Comprehensive fee:* $40,150 includes full-time tuition ($28,250), mandatory fees ($1300), and room and board ($10,600). Full-time tuition and fees vary according to class time, course level, course load, degree level, location, program, and student level. Part-time tuition: $945 per credit hour. Part-time tuition and fees vary according to class time, course level, course load, degree level, location, program, and student level. *Room and board:* Room and board charges vary according to housing facility. *Payment plans:* tuition prepayment, installment.
Financial Aid *Average indebtedness upon graduation:* $20,246.

APPLYING
Standardized Tests *Required:* SAT or ACT (for admission).
Options: electronic application, deferred entrance.
Required: high school transcript, minimum 2.0 GPA, 1 letter of recommendation. *Recommended:* essay or personal statement, interview.

CONTACT
Post University, 800 Country Club Road, Waterbury, CT 06723-2540. *Toll-free phone:* 800-345-2562.

★ Quinnipiac University
Hamden, Connecticut
http://www.qu.edu/
- **Independent** comprehensive, founded 1929
- **Suburban** 600-acre campus with easy access to New Haven, Hartford
- **Endowment** $481.6 million
- **Coed**
- **Moderately difficult** entrance level

FACULTY
Student/faculty ratio: 16:1.

ACADEMICS
Calendar: semesters. *Degrees:* bachelor's, master's, doctoral, post-master's, and postbachelor's certificates.
Library: Arnold Bernhard Library plus 3 others. *Books:* 135,000 (physical), 500,000 (digital/electronic); *Databases:* 190. Weekly public service hours: 93; study areas open 24 hours, 5–7 days a week; students can reserve study rooms.

STUDENT LIFE
Housing options: coed. Campus housing is university owned. Freshman campus housing is guaranteed.

Activities and organizations: drama/theater group, student-run newspaper, radio and television station, choral group, Student Government, Social Programming Board, Drama Club, Chronicle (student newspaper), dance company, national fraternities, national sororities.

Athletics Member NCAA. All Division I.

Campus security: 24-hour emergency response devices and patrols, late-night transport/escort service, controlled dormitory access, text message emergency notification system.

Student services: health clinic, personal/psychological counseling, women's center, veterans affairs office.

COSTS & FINANCIAL AID

Costs (2018–19) *Comprehensive fee:* $62,950 includes full-time tuition ($45,540), mandatory fees ($2420), and room and board ($14,990). Part-time tuition: $1045 per credit hour. Part-time tuition and fees vary according to class time and course load. *Required fees:* $45 per credit hour part-time. *Room and board:* Room and board charges vary according to board plan and housing facility.

Financial Aid Of all full-time matriculated undergraduates who enrolled in 2018, 5,242 applied for aid, 4,468 were judged to have need, 736 had their need fully met. 1,767 Federal Work-Study jobs (averaging $2117). In 2018, 1991 non-need-based awards were made. *Average percent of need met:* 65. *Average financial aid package:* $29,097. *Average need-based loan:* $4477. *Average need-based gift aid:* $23,028. *Average non-need-based aid:* $17,552. *Average indebtedness upon graduation:* $48,544.

APPLYING

Standardized Tests *Required for some:* SAT or ACT (for admission).

Options: electronic application, early decision, deferred entrance.

Application fee: $65.

Required: essay or personal statement, high school transcript, 1 letter of recommendation. *Required for some:* minimum 3.0 GPA. *Recommended:* minimum 3.0 GPA, interview.

CONTACT

Mr. Greg Eichhorn, Vice President for Admissions and Financial Aid, Quinnipiac University, 275 Mount Carmel Avenue, Hamden, CT 06518. *Phone:* 203-582-8600. *Toll-free phone:* 800-462-1944. *Fax:* 203-582-8906. *E-mail:* admissions@qu.edu.

Sacred Heart University

Fairfield, Connecticut

http://www.sacredheart.edu/

- **Independent Roman Catholic** comprehensive, founded 1963
- **Suburban** 350-acre campus with easy access to New York City
- **Endowment** $167.6 million
- **Coed** 5,974 undergraduate students, 86% full-time, 65% women, 35% men
- **Moderately difficult** entrance level, 60% of applicants were admitted

UNDERGRAD STUDENTS

5,130 full-time, 844 part-time. Students come from 39 states and territories; 30 other countries; 62% are from out of state; 5% Black or African American, non-Hispanic/Latino; 12% Hispanic/Latino; 2% Asian, non-Hispanic/Latino; 0.1% Native Hawaiian or other Pacific Islander, non-Hispanic/Latino; 0.2% American Indian or Alaska Native, non-Hispanic/Latino; 2% Two or more races, non-Hispanic/Latino; 6% Race/ethnicity unknown; 1% international; 4% transferred in; 52% live on campus.

Freshmen:

Admission: 10,740 applied, 6,493 admitted, 1,465 enrolled. *Average high school GPA:* 3.5. *Test scores:* SAT evidence-based reading and writing scores over 500: 96%; SAT math scores over 500: 97%; ACT scores over 18: 100%; SAT evidence-based reading and writing scores over 600: 40%; SAT math scores over 600: 38%; ACT scores over 24: 69%; SAT evidence-based reading and writing scores over 700: 2%; SAT math scores over 700: 3%; ACT scores over 30: 4%.

Retention: 83% of full-time freshmen returned.

FACULTY

Total: 954, 33% full-time, 45% with terminal degrees.

Student/faculty ratio: 14:1.

ACADEMICS

Calendar: semesters. *Degrees:* bachelor's, master's, doctoral, and post-master's certificates (also offers part-time program with significant enrollment not reflected in profile).

Special study options: academic remediation for entering students, accelerated degree program, adult/continuing education programs, advanced placement credit, cooperative education, distance learning, double majors, English as a second language, honors programs, independent study, internships, part-time degree program, services for LD students, student-designed majors, study abroad, summer session for credit. *ROTC:* Air Force (c).

Unusual degree programs: 3-2 engineering with Columbia University, Rensselaer Polytechnic Institute; health professions and a law program with Seton Hall University, pre-pharmacy with University of St. Joseph's.

Computers: 499 computers/terminals are available on campus for general student use. Students can access the following: computer help desk, free student e-mail accounts, online (class) grades, online (class) registration. Campuswide network is available. 100% of college-owned or -operated housing units are wired for high-speed Internet access. Wireless service is available via entire campus.

Library: Ryan Matura Library plus 1 other. *Books:* 89,846 (physical), 228,647 (digital/electronic); *Serial titles:* 412 (physical), 62,191 (digital/electronic); *Databases:* 140. Weekly public service hours: 119; students can reserve study rooms.

STUDENT LIFE

Housing options: on-campus residence required through sophomore year; coed, special housing for students with disabilities. Campus housing is university owned and leased by the school. Freshman campus housing is guaranteed.

Activities and organizations: drama/theater group, student-run newspaper, radio and television station, choral group, marching band, Alpha Sigma Lambda Honor Society, Inter Resident Council, Student Nursing Association, Habitat for Humanity, Pre-PT Club, national fraternities, national sororities.

Athletics Member NCAA. All Division I except football (Division I-AA). *Intercollegiate sports:* baseball M(s), basketball M(s)/W(s), bowling W(s), cheerleading W(c), crew W(s), cross-country running M(s)/W(s), equestrian sports W(s), fencing M(s)/W(s), field hockey W(s), golf M(s)/W(s)(c), ice hockey M(s)/W(s), lacrosse M(s)/W(s), rowing W(s), rugby W(s), soccer M(s)/W(s), softball W(s), swimming and diving W(s), tennis M(s)/W(s), track and field M(s)/W(s), volleyball M(s)/W(s), wrestling M(s). *Intramural sports:* baseball M(c), basketball M(c)/W(c), bowling M(c)/W(c), cross-country running M(c)/W(c), fencing W(c), football M(c), golf M(c)/W(c), gymnastics M(c)/W(c), ice hockey M(c), lacrosse M(c)/W(c), rugby M(c), sailing M(c)/W(c), soccer M(c)/W(c), softball M(c)/W(c), swimming and diving W(c), tennis M(c)/W(c), ultimate Frisbee M(c), volleyball M(c)/W(c), weight lifting M(c)/W(c), wrestling M(c).

Campus security: 24-hour emergency response devices and patrols, late-night transport/escort service, controlled dormitory access, Bystander Intervention, Personal Safety Escort Program, Silent Witness Program, crime prevention announcements, SHU Safe App.

Student services: health clinic, personal/psychological counseling, veterans affairs office.

COSTS & FINANCIAL AID

Costs (2018–19) *Comprehensive fee:* $56,730 includes full-time tuition ($41,150), mandatory fees ($270), and room and board ($15,310). Part-time tuition: $625 per credit hour. Part-time tuition and fees vary according to course load. *Required fees:* $115 per term part-time. *College room only:* $10,500. Room and board charges vary according to board plan and housing facility. *Payment plan:* installment. *Waivers:* employees or children of employees.

Financial Aid Of all full-time matriculated undergraduates who enrolled in 2018, 4,003 applied for aid, 3,319 were judged to have need, 548 had their need fully met. 1,398 Federal Work-Study jobs (averaging $1756). 809 state and other part-time jobs (averaging $1418). In 2018, 1658 non-need-based awards were made. *Average percent of need met:* 57. *Average financial aid package:* $21,553. *Average need-based loan:* $4858. *Average need-based gift aid:* $17,261. *Average non-need-based aid:* $13,125. *Average indebtedness upon graduation:* $42,712.

APPLYING

Options: electronic application, early admission, early decision, early action, deferred entrance.

Application fee: $50.

Required: high school transcript, 1 letter of recommendation. *Required for some:* interview, interview for Early Decision candidates. *Recommended:* essay or personal statement.

Early decision deadline: 12/1.

Notification: continuous (freshmen), continuous (transfers), 12/15 (early decision).

CONTACT

Mr. Kevin O'Sullivan, Executive Director of Undergraduate Admissions, Sacred Heart University, 5151 Park Avenue, Fairfield, CT 06825. *Phone:* 203-371-7880. *Fax:* 203-365-7607. *E-mail:* osullivank6@ sacredheart.edu.

Southern Connecticut State University

New Haven, Connecticut
http://www.southernct.edu/

CONTACT

Mrs. Alexis S. Haakonsen, Director of Admissions, Southern Connecticut State University, Admissions House, 131 Farnham Avenue, New Haven, CT 06515-1202. *Phone:* 203-392-5652. *Fax:* 203-392-5727. *E-mail:* haakonsena1@southernct.edu.

Trinity College

Hartford, Connecticut
http://www.trincoll.edu/

CONTACT

Trinity College, 300 Summit Street, Hartford, CT 06106-3100. *Phone:* 860-297-2180.

United States Coast Guard Academy

New London, Connecticut
http://www.uscga.edu/

- **Federally supported** 4-year, founded 1876
- **Suburban** 103-acre campus with easy access to Providence, Hartford
- **Coed**
- **Very difficult** entrance level

FACULTY
Student/faculty ratio: 7:1.

ACADEMICS
Calendar: semesters. *Degree:* bachelor's.
Library: USCG Academy Library. Students can reserve study rooms.

STUDENT LIFE
Housing options: on-campus residence required through senior year; coed. Campus housing is university owned. Freshman campus housing is guaranteed.

Activities and organizations: drama/theater group, choral group, marching band, Club Sports, Musical activities, Multicultural Club, Officers Christian Fellowship, International Dance Club.

Athletics Member NCAA. All Division III.

Campus security: 24-hour patrols, late-night transport/escort service, controlled dormitory access, cadets staff a 24-hour Watch Office.

Student services: health clinic, personal/psychological counseling, legal services, veterans affairs office.

COSTS
Costs (2018–19) *Comprehensive fee:* Tuition, room and board, and medical and dental care are provided by the US government. Each cadet receives a salary from which to pay for uniforms, supplies, and personal expenses.

APPLYING
Standardized Tests *Required:* SAT or ACT (for admission).

Options: electronic application, early action, deferred entrance.

Required: essay or personal statement, high school transcript, 3 letters of recommendation, medical examination, physical fitness examination. *Recommended:* interview.

CONTACT

Mr. Daniel V. Pinch, Associate Director of Admissions for Outreach, United States Coast Guard Academy, 31 Mohegan Avenue, New London, CT 06320-4195. *Phone:* 860-701-6327. *Toll-free phone:* 800-883-8724. *Fax:* 860-701-6700. *E-mail:* daniel.v.pinch@uscga.edu.

University of Bridgeport

Bridgeport, Connecticut
http://www.bridgeport.edu/

- **Independent** comprehensive, founded 1927
- **Urban** 86-acre campus with easy access to New York City
- **Endowment** $38.0 million
- **Coed**
- **Moderately difficult** entrance level

FACULTY
Student/faculty ratio: 16:1.

ACADEMICS
Calendar: semesters. *Degrees:* certificates, associate, bachelor's, master's, doctoral, post-master's, and postbachelor's certificates.
Library: Wahlstrom Library. *Books:* 144,829 (physical), 210,775 (digital/electronic); *Serial titles:* 957 (physical), 68,477 (digital/electronic); *Databases:* 81. Weekly public service hours: 90.

STUDENT LIFE
Housing options: on-campus residence required through sophomore year; coed. Campus housing is university owned. Freshman campus housing is guaranteed.

Activities and organizations: student-run newspaper, choral group, Student Congress, International Relations Club, Black Students Alliance, Latin America Club, Martial Arts Club, national fraternities, national sororities.

Athletics Member NCAA. All Division II.

Campus security: 24-hour emergency response devices and patrols, student patrols, late-night transport/escort service, controlled dormitory access.

Student services: health clinic, personal/psychological counseling, veterans affairs office.

COSTS & FINANCIAL AID
Costs (2018–19) *Tuition:* $30,750 full-time, $1025 per credit hour part-time. Full-time tuition and fees vary according to course load and program. Part-time tuition and fees vary according to course load and program. *Required fees:* $2110 full-time, $220 per term part-time. *Room only:* Room and board charges vary according to board plan and housing facility. *Payment plans:* installment, deferred payment.

Financial Aid Of all full-time matriculated undergraduates who enrolled in 2016, 2,185 applied for aid, 1,886 were judged to have need, 219 had their need fully met. In 2016, 299 non-need-based awards were made. *Average percent of need met:* 60. *Average financial aid package:* $28,677. *Average need-based loan:* $7000. *Average need-based gift aid:* $14,193. *Average non-need-based aid:* $14,220. *Average indebtedness upon graduation:* $21,200.

APPLYING
Standardized Tests *Required:* SAT or ACT (for admission).

Options: electronic application, early admission, deferred entrance.

Application fee: $25.

Required: essay or personal statement, high school transcript, minimum 2.0 GPA. *Required for some:* 2 letters of recommendation, interview, portfolio, audition. *Recommended:* 1 letter of recommendation, interview.

CONTACT

Ms. Jessica N. Crowley Goddu, Director of Undergraduate Admissions, University of Bridgeport, 126 Park Avenue, Bridgeport, CT 06604. *Phone:* 203-576-4812. *Toll-free phone:* 800-EXCEL-UB. *Fax:* 203-576-4941. *E-mail:* admit@bridgeport.edu.

University of Connecticut

Storrs, Connecticut
http://www.uconn.edu/

CONTACT

Nathan Fuerst, Director of Undergraduate Admissions, University of Connecticut, 2131 Hillside Road, U-88, Storrs, CT 06269. *Phone:* 860-486-3137. *Fax:* 860-486-1476. *E-mail:* beahusky@uconn.edu.

★ University of Hartford

West Hartford, Connecticut
http://www.hartford.edu/

- **Independent** comprehensive, founded 1877
- **Suburban** 320-acre campus with easy access to Hartford
- **Endowment** $164.5 million
- **Coed**
- **Moderately difficult** entrance level

FACULTY

Student/faculty ratio: 9:1.

ACADEMICS

Calendar: semesters. *Degrees:* certificates, diplomas, associate, bachelor's, master's, doctoral, post-master's, and postbachelor's certificates.

Library: Mortensen Library plus 1 other. *Books:* 287,556 (physical), 2,540 (digital/electronic); *Serial titles:* 1,479 (physical), 56,360 (digital/electronic); *Databases:* 229. Weekly public service hours: 104.

STUDENT LIFE

Housing options: coed, women-only, special housing for students with disabilities. Campus housing is university owned and leased by the school. Freshman campus housing is guaranteed.

Activities and organizations: drama/theater group, student-run newspaper, radio and television station, choral group, Program Council, Brothers and Sisters United, Hillel, Student Government Association, Residence Hall Association, national fraternities, national sororities.

Athletics Member NCAA. All Division I.

Campus security: 24-hour emergency response devices and patrols, late-night transport/escort service, controlled dormitory access, bicycle patrols.

Student services: health clinic, personal/psychological counseling, women's center, legal services.

COSTS & FINANCIAL AID

Costs (2018–19) *Comprehensive fee:* $53,170 includes full-time tuition ($37,802), mandatory fees ($2892), and room and board ($12,476). Full-time tuition and fees vary according to program. Part-time tuition: $550 per credit hour. Part-time tuition and fees vary according to course load and program. *College room only:* $8008. Room and board charges vary according to board plan and housing facility. *Payment plans:* tuition prepayment, installment.

Financial Aid Of all full-time matriculated undergraduates who enrolled in 2018, 3,556 applied for aid, 3,266 were judged to have need, 455 had their need fully met. 546 Federal Work-Study jobs (averaging $1894). In 2018, 887 non-need-based awards were made. *Average percent of need met:* 69. *Average financial aid package:* $29,084. *Average need-based loan:* $4356. *Average need-based gift aid:* $23,538. *Average non-need-based aid:* $17,837.

APPLYING

Standardized Tests *Required:* SAT or ACT (for admission).

Options: electronic application, early admission, early action, deferred entrance.

Application fee: $35.

Required: high school transcript. *Recommended:* essay or personal statement, 2 letters of recommendation, interview.

CONTACT

Mr. Richard Zeiser, Dean of Admissions, University of Hartford, 200 Bloomfield Avenue, West Hartford, CT 06117. *Phone:* 860-768-4296. *Toll-free phone:* 800-947-4303. *Fax:* 860-768-4961. *E-mail:* admissions@hartford.edu.

★ University of New Haven

West Haven, Connecticut
http://www.newhaven.edu/

- **Independent** comprehensive, founded 1920
- **Suburban** 82-acre campus with easy access to New Haven
- **Coed** 5,092 undergraduate students, 94% full-time, 54% women, 46% men
- **Moderately difficult** entrance level, 84% of applicants were admitted

UNDERGRAD STUDENTS

4,768 full-time, 324 part-time. Students come from 44 states and territories; 32 other countries; 55% are from out of state; 12% Black or African American, non-Hispanic/Latino; 12% Hispanic/Latino; 3% Asian, non-Hispanic/Latino; 0.1% Native Hawaiian or other Pacific Islander, non-Hispanic/Latino; 0.4% American Indian or Alaska Native, non-Hispanic/Latino; 0.7% Two or more races, non-Hispanic/Latino; 5% Race/ethnicity unknown; 4% international; 4% transferred in; 53% live on campus.

Freshmen:
Admission: 10,426 applied, 8,744 admitted, 1,338 enrolled. *Average high school GPA:* 3.4. *Test scores:* SAT evidence-based reading and writing scores over 500: 87%; SAT math scores over 500: 83%; ACT scores over 18: 91%; SAT evidence-based reading and writing scores over 600: 36%; SAT math scores over 600: 28%; ACT scores over 24: 44%; SAT evidence-based reading and writing scores over 700: 4%; SAT math scores over 700: 5%; ACT scores over 30: 8%.

Retention: 76% of full-time freshmen returned.

FACULTY

Total: 662, 39% full-time, 60% with terminal degrees.

Student/faculty ratio: 16:1.

ACADEMICS

Calendar: 4-1-4. *Degrees:* certificates, associate, bachelor's, master's, doctoral, post-master's, and postbachelor's certificates.

Special study options: academic remediation for entering students, accelerated degree program, adult/continuing education programs, advanced placement credit, cooperative education, distance learning, double majors, English as a second language, honors programs, independent study, internships, off-campus study, part-time degree program, services for LD students, study abroad, summer session for credit. *ROTC:* Army (b), Air Force (c).

Computers: Students can access the following: campus intranet, computer help desk, free student e-mail accounts, online (class) grades, online (class) registration, online (class) schedules, computer repair services. Campuswide network is available. Wireless service is available via entire campus.

Library: Marvin K. Peterson Library.

STUDENT LIFE

Housing options: coed, special housing for students with disabilities. Campus housing is university owned and leased by the school. Freshman campus housing is guaranteed.

Activities and organizations: drama/theater group, student-run newspaper, radio station, marching band, national fraternities, national sororities.

Athletics Member NCAA. All Division II. *Intercollegiate sports:* baseball M(s), basketball M(s)/W(s), cross-country running M(s)/W(s), field hockey W(s), football M(s), ice hockey M(c), lacrosse M(c)/W(s), rugby M(c), soccer M(s)/W(s), softball W(s), tennis W(s), track and field M(s)/W(s), ultimate Frisbee M(c)/W(c), volleyball M(c)/W(s), wrestling M(c). *Intramural sports:* basketball M/W, cheerleading M/W, racquetball M/W, soccer M/W, softball M/W, tennis M/W, volleyball M/W.

Campus security: 24-hour emergency response devices and patrols, student patrols, late-night transport/escort service, controlled dormitory access.

Student services: health clinic, personal/psychological counseling, veterans affairs office.

COSTS & FINANCIAL AID

Costs (2018–19) *Comprehensive fee:* $55,170 includes full-time tuition ($37,870), mandatory fees ($1400), and room and board ($15,900). Full-time tuition and fees vary according to course load and program. Part-time tuition: $1260 per credit hour. Part-time tuition and fees vary according to class time, course load, and program. *Required fees:* $105 per term part-time. *College room only:* $10,150. Room and board charges vary according to board plan and housing facility. *Payment plan:* installment. *Waivers:* senior citizens and employees or children of employees.

Financial Aid Of all full-time matriculated undergraduates who enrolled in 2018, 4,006 applied for aid, 3,690 were judged to have need, 570 had their need fully met. In 2018, 735 non-need-based awards were made. *Average percent of need met:* 59. *Average financial aid package:* $23,954. *Average need-based loan:* $4228. *Average need-based gift aid:* $20,685. *Average non-need-based aid:* $17,025. *Average indebtedness upon graduation:* $48,673.

APPLYING

Standardized Tests *Required:* SAT or ACT (for admission).

Options: electronic application, early decision, early action.

Application fee: $50.

Required: essay or personal statement, high school transcript. *Recommended:* interview.

Application deadlines: rolling (freshmen), rolling (out-of-state freshmen), rolling (transfers), 12/15 (early action).

Early decision deadline: 12/1.

Notification: continuous (freshmen), continuous (out-of-state freshmen), continuous (transfers), 12/15 (early decision), 1/15 (early action).

CONTACT

Mr. Jason Riendeau, Director of Undergraduate Admissions, University of New Haven, Bayer Hall, 300 Boston Post Road, West Haven, CT 06516. *Phone:* 203-932-2920. *Toll-free phone:* 800-342-5864. *E-mail:* jriendeau@newhaven.edu.

See below for display ad and page 1142 for the College Close-Up.

University of Saint Joseph
West Hartford, Connecticut
http://www.usj.edu/

- **Independent Roman Catholic** comprehensive, founded 1932
- **Suburban** 90-acre campus with easy access to Hartford
- **Coed, primarily women**
- **Moderately difficult** entrance level

FACULTY
Student/faculty ratio: 9:1.

ACADEMICS
Calendar: semesters. *Degrees:* certificates, bachelor's, master's, doctoral, post-master's, and postbachelor's certificates.
Library: Pope Pius XII Library.

STUDENT LIFE
Housing options: coed, women-only, special housing for students with disabilities. Campus housing is university owned.

Activities and organizations: drama/theater group, choral group.

Athletics Member NCAA. All Division III.

Campus security: 24-hour emergency response devices and patrols, late-night transport/escort service, controlled dormitory access.

Student services: health clinic, personal/psychological counseling.

COSTS & FINANCIAL AID
Costs (2018–19) *Comprehensive fee:* $50,601 includes full-time tuition ($37,361), mandatory fees ($1812), and room and board ($11,428). Full-time tuition and fees vary according to course load, degree level, location, program, and student level. Part-time tuition: $843 per credit hour. Part-time tuition and fees vary according to course load, degree level, location, program, and student level. *Required fees:* $60 per credit hour part-time. *College room only:* $6438. Room and board charges vary according to board plan and housing facility.

Financial Aid Of all full-time matriculated undergraduates who enrolled in 2017, 598 applied for aid, 572 were judged to have need, 81 had their need fully met. 166 Federal Work-Study jobs (averaging $1711). 121 state and other part-time jobs (averaging $1792). In 2017, 45 non-need-based

awards were made. *Average percent of need met:* 73. *Average financial aid package:* $27,986. *Average need-based loan:* $5814. *Average need-based gift aid:* $22,970. *Average non-need-based aid:* $15,954. *Average indebtedness upon graduation:* $38,916.

APPLYING
Standardized Tests *Required for some:* SAT or ACT (for admission).

Options: electronic application, deferred entrance.

Application fee: $50.

Required: high school transcript, 1 letter of recommendation. *Recommended:* essay or personal statement, interview.

CONTACT
University of Saint Joseph, 1678 Asylum Avenue, West Hartford, CT 06117-2700. *Toll-free phone:* 866-442-8752.

Wesleyan University
Middletown, Connecticut
http://www.wesleyan.edu/
- **Independent** university, founded 1831
- **Suburban** 316-acre campus with easy access to Hartford, CT; New Haven, CT; Springfield, MA
- **Endowment** $1.1 billion
- **Coed** 3,009 undergraduate students, 97% full-time, 55% women, 45% men
- **Most difficult** entrance level, 17% of applicants were admitted

UNDERGRAD STUDENTS
2,928 full-time, 81 part-time. Students come from 50 states and territories; 54 other countries; 93% are from out of state; 6% Black or African American, non-Hispanic/Latino; 12% Hispanic/Latino; 7% Asian, non-Hispanic/Latino; 6% Two or more races, non-Hispanic/Latino; 3% Race/ethnicity unknown; 12% international; 1% transferred in; 99% live on campus.

Freshmen:
Admission: 12,706 applied, 2,218 admitted, 803 enrolled. *Test scores:* SAT evidence-based reading and writing scores over 500: 100%; SAT math scores over 500: 99%; ACT scores over 18: 100%; SAT evidence-based reading and writing scores over 600: 93%; SAT math scores over 600: 90%; ACT scores over 24: 98%; SAT evidence-based reading and writing scores over 700: 58%; SAT math scores over 700: 56%; ACT scores over 30: 80%.

Retention: 96% of full-time freshmen returned.

FACULTY
Total: 438, 84% full-time, 87% with terminal degrees.

Student/faculty ratio: 8:1.

ACADEMICS
Calendar: semesters. *Degrees:* bachelor's, master's, doctoral, and post-master's certificates.

Special study options: accelerated degree program, advanced placement credit, double majors, honors programs, independent study, internships, off-campus study, services for LD students, student-designed majors, study abroad, summer session for credit. *ROTC:* Air Force (c).

Unusual degree programs: 3-2 engineering with Columbia University, California Institute of Technology, Dartmouth College.

Computers: 118 computers/terminals and 7,200 ports are available on campus for general student use. Students can access the following: campus intranet, computer help desk, free student e-mail accounts, online (class) registration, online (class) schedules, electronic portfolio, course drop/add, learning management system, software training. Campuswide network is available. 100% of college-owned or -operated housing units are wired for high-speed Internet access. Wireless service is available via entire campus.

Library: Olin Memorial Library plus 1 other. *Books:* 1.2 million (physical), 502,915 (digital/electronic); *Serial titles:* 7,507 (physical), 86,968 (digital/electronic); *Databases:* 332. Weekly public service hours: 113.

STUDENT LIFE
Housing options: on-campus residence required through senior year; coed, men-only, women-only, special housing for students with disabilities. Campus housing is university owned. Freshman campus housing is guaranteed.

Activities and organizations: drama/theater group, student-run newspaper, radio station, choral group, Mock Trial, Athletic Clubs, Spectrum, Burlesque, Espwesso, national fraternities, national sororities.

Athletics Member NCAA. All Division III. *Intercollegiate sports:* badminton M(c)/W(c), baseball M, basketball M/W, crew M/W, cross-country running M/W, equestrian sports M(c)/W(c), fencing M(c)/W(c), field hockey W, football M, golf M, ice hockey M/W, lacrosse M/W, rugby M(c)/W(c), sailing M(c)/W(c), soccer M/W, softball W, squash M/W, swimming and diving M/W, tennis M/W, track and field M/W, ultimate Frisbee M(c)/W(c), volleyball W, water polo M(c)/W(c), wrestling M. *Intramural sports:* basketball M/W, ice hockey M/W, soccer M/W, softball M/W, squash M/W, ultimate Frisbee M/W, water polo M/W.

Campus security: 24-hour emergency response devices and patrols, late-night transport/escort service, controlled dormitory access, Self-defense classes offered by certified instructors.

Student services: health clinic, personal/psychological counseling, veterans affairs office.

COSTS & FINANCIAL AID
Costs (2019–20) *Comprehensive fee:* $72,728 includes full-time tuition ($56,704), mandatory fees ($300), and room and board ($15,724).

Financial Aid Of all full-time matriculated undergraduates who enrolled in 2018, 1,299 applied for aid, 1,232 were judged to have need, 1,232 had their need fully met. 1,187 Federal Work-Study jobs (averaging $2524). 252 state and other part-time jobs (averaging $2498). In 2018, 22 non-need-based awards were made. *Average percent of need met:* 100. *Average financial aid package:* $56,471. *Average need-based loan:* $4314. *Average need-based gift aid:* $50,051. *Average non-need-based aid:* $38,615. *Average indebtedness upon graduation:* $23,454. *Financial aid deadline:* 2/15.

APPLYING
Standardized Tests *Required for some:* SAT and SAT Subject Tests or ACT (for admission).

Options: electronic application, early admission, early decision, deferred entrance.

Application fee: $55.

Required: essay or personal statement, high school transcript, 2 letters of recommendation. *Recommended:* interview.

Application deadlines: 1/1 (freshmen), 3/15 (transfers).

Early decision deadline: 11/15.

Notification: 4/1 (freshmen), 5/15 (transfers), 12/15 (early decision).

CONTACT
Ms. Nancy Hargrave Meislahn, Vice President and Dean of Admission and Financial Aid, Wesleyan University, Stewart M. Reid House, Admission Office, 70 Wyllys Avenue, Middletown, CT 06459. *Phone:* 860-685-3000. *Fax:* 860-685-3001. *E-mail:* admission@wesleyan.edu.

Western Connecticut State University
Danbury, Connecticut
http://www.wcsu.edu/
- **State-supported** comprehensive, founded 1903, part of Connecticut State Colleges & Universities (CSCU)
- **Urban** 340-acre campus with easy access to New York City
- **Endowment** $19.1 million
- **Coed** 5,028 undergraduate students, 82% full-time, 52% women, 48% men
- **Moderately difficult** entrance level, 79% of applicants were admitted

UNDERGRAD STUDENTS
4,128 full-time, 900 part-time. Students come from 13 states and territories; 2 other countries; 15% are from out of state; 10% Black or African American, non-Hispanic/Latino; 19% Hispanic/Latino; 4% Asian, non-Hispanic/Latino; 0.1% Native Hawaiian or other Pacific Islander, non-Hispanic/Latino; 0.2% American Indian or Alaska Native, non-Hispanic/Latino; 3% Two or more races, non-Hispanic/Latino; 3% Race/ethnicity unknown; 10% transferred in; 30% live on campus.

Freshmen:

Admission: 5,375 applied, 4,259 admitted, 899 enrolled. *Average high school GPA:* 3.1. *Test scores:* SAT evidence-based reading and writing scores over 500: 85%; SAT math scores over 500: 80%; ACT scores over 18: 96%; SAT evidence-based reading and writing scores over 600: 31%; SAT math scores over 600: 21%; ACT scores over 24: 39%; SAT evidence-based reading and writing scores over 700: 4%; SAT math scores over 700: 2%; ACT scores over 30: 8%.

Retention: 74% of full-time freshmen returned.

FACULTY
Total: 614, 36% full-time, 33% with terminal degrees.
Student/faculty ratio: 13:1.

ACADEMICS
Calendar: semesters. *Degrees:* associate, bachelor's, master's, doctoral, and post-master's certificates.

Special study options: advanced placement credit, cooperative education, distance learning, honors programs, independent study, internships, part-time degree program, services for LD students, student-designed majors, study abroad, summer session for credit. *ROTC:* Army (c), Air Force (c).

Computers: 1,034 computers/terminals and 1,065 ports are available on campus for general student use. Students can access the following: computer help desk, free student e-mail accounts, online (class) grades, online (class) registration, online (class) schedules, online payment. Campuswide network is available. 100% of college-owned or -operated housing units are wired for high-speed Internet access. Wireless service is available via entire campus.
Library: Ruth Haas Library plus 2 others. *Books:* 204,701 (physical), 240,140 (digital/electronic); *Serial titles:* 302 (physical), 67,162 (digital/electronic); *Databases:* 188. Weekly public service hours: 144; students can reserve study rooms.

STUDENT LIFE
Housing options: coed. Campus housing is university owned.

Activities and organizations: drama/theater group, student-run newspaper, radio station, choral group, National Society of Collegiate Scholars, Criminology Club, Jazz Club, American Marketing Club, Meteorology, national fraternities, national sororities.

Athletics Member NCAA. All Division III. *Intercollegiate sports:* baseball M, basketball M/W, cheerleading W(c), cross-country running M/W, field hockey W, football M, golf M, lacrosse M/W, soccer M/W, softball W, swimming and diving M/W, tennis M/W, volleyball W. *Intramural sports:* basketball M/W, football M, ice hockey M(c), rock climbing M(c)/W(c), soccer M/W, softball W.

Campus security: 24-hour emergency response devices and patrols, student patrols, late-night transport/escort service, controlled dormitory access.

Student services: health clinic, personal/psychological counseling, women's center, veterans affairs office.

COSTS & FINANCIAL AID
Costs (2019–20) *Tuition:* state resident $5924 full-time, $247 per credit hour part-time; nonresident $17,726 full-time, $247 per credit hour part-time. *Required fees:* $5420 full-time, $291 per credit part-time, $60 per term part-time. *Room and board:* $13,452; room only: $7794.

Financial Aid Of all full-time matriculated undergraduates who enrolled in 2017, 3,466 applied for aid, 2,638 were judged to have need, 385 had their need fully met. 126 Federal Work-Study jobs (averaging $2526). In 2017, 126 non-need-based awards were made. *Average percent of need met:* 42. *Average financial aid package:* $9666. *Average need-based loan:* $4288. *Average need-based gift aid:* $3822. *Average non-need-based aid:* $3973. *Average indebtedness upon graduation:* $35,177. *Financial aid deadline:* 3/10.

APPLYING
Standardized Tests *Recommended:* SAT (for admission), SAT or ACT (for admission).

Options: electronic application, deferred entrance.
Application fee: $50.
Required: high school transcript. *Required for some:* essay or personal statement, interview.
Application deadlines: rolling (freshmen), rolling (transfers).
Notification: continuous (freshmen), continuous (transfers).

CONTACT
Mr. Jay E. Murray, Associate Vice President for Enrollment Services, Western Connecticut State University, 181 White Street, Danbury, CT 06810-6885. *Phone:* 203-837-8000. *Toll-free phone:* 877-837-WCSU. *Fax:* 203-837-8011. *E-mail:* murrayj@wcsu.edu.

Yale University
New Haven, Connecticut
http://www.yale.edu/
- **Independent** university, founded 1701
- **Urban** 342-acre campus with easy access to New York City
- **Endowment** $25.6 billion
- **Coed**
- **Most difficult** entrance level

FACULTY
Student/faculty ratio: 6:1.

ACADEMICS
Calendar: semesters. *Degrees:* bachelor's, master's, doctoral, and post-master's certificates.
Library: Sterling Memorial Library plus 15 others. *Books:* 13.8 million (physical), 1.8 million (digital/electronic). Weekly public service hours: 93; students can reserve study rooms.

STUDENT LIFE
Housing options: on-campus residence required through sophomore year; coed, special housing for students with disabilities. Campus housing is university owned. Freshman campus housing is guaranteed.

Activities and organizations: drama/theater group, student-run newspaper, radio and television station, choral group, marching band, national fraternities, national sororities.

Athletics Member NCAA. All Division I except football (Division I-AA).

Campus security: 24-hour emergency response devices and patrols, late-night transport/escort service, controlled dormitory access.

Student services: health clinic, personal/psychological counseling, women's center.

COSTS & FINANCIAL AID
Costs (2018–19) *Comprehensive fee:* $69,430 includes full-time tuition ($53,430) and room and board ($16,000). *College room only:* $9000. Room and board charges vary according to board plan.

Financial Aid Of all full-time matriculated undergraduates who enrolled in 2018, 3,440 applied for aid, 3,127 were judged to have need, 3,127 had their need fully met. *Average percent of need met:* 100. *Average financial aid package:* $59,070. *Average need-based loan:* $3164. *Average need-based gift aid:* $56,602. *Average indebtedness upon graduation:* $14,575. *Financial aid deadline:* 3/1.

APPLYING
Standardized Tests *Required:* SAT or ACT (for admission). *Recommended:* SAT Subject Tests (for admission).
Options: electronic application, early action, deferred entrance.
Application fee: $80.
Required: essay or personal statement, high school transcript, 3 letters of recommendation. *Recommended:* interview.

CONTACT
Undergraduate Admissions, Yale University, PO Box 208234, New Haven, CT 06520. *Phone:* 203-432-9300. *E-mail:* student.questions@yale.edu.

DELAWARE

Delaware State University

Dover, Delaware
http://www.desu.edu/

- **State-supported** university, founded 1891, part of Delaware Higher Education Commission
- **Small-town** 400-acre campus
- **Coed**
- **Moderately difficult** entrance level

ACADEMICS
Calendar: semesters. *Degrees:* certificates, bachelor's, master's, and doctoral.
Library: William C. Jason Library.

STUDENT LIFE
Housing options: coed, men-only, women-only. Campus housing is university owned. Freshman applicants given priority for college housing.

Activities and organizations: drama/theater group, student-run newspaper, radio and television station, choral group, marching band, SGA, NPHC, Women's Senate, RHA, Men's Council, national fraternities, national sororities.

Athletics Member NCAA. All Division I except football (Division I-AA).

Campus security: 24-hour emergency response devices and patrols, student patrols, late-night transport/escort service, controlled dormitory access.

Student services: health clinic, personal/psychological counseling, women's center.

FINANCIAL AID
Financial Aid Of all full-time matriculated undergraduates who enrolled in 2016, 3,301 applied for aid, 2,971 were judged to have need, 467 had their need fully met. In 2016, 91 non-need-based awards were made. *Average percent of need met:* 77. *Average financial aid package:* $11,234. *Average need-based loan:* $3883. *Average need-based gift aid:* $5250. *Average non-need-based aid:* $4530. *Average indebtedness upon graduation:* $36,812.

APPLYING
Options: electronic application, early admission.
Application fee: $35.
Required: high school transcript, minimum 2.0 GPA.

CONTACT
Mrs. Erin Hill, Executive Director for Admissions, Delaware State University, 1200 North DuPont Highway, Dover, DE 19901-2277. *Phone:* 302-857-6351. *Toll-free phone:* 800-845-2544. *Fax:* 302-857-6352. *E-mail:* ehill@desu.edu.

Goldey-Beacom College

Wilmington, Delaware
http://www.gbc.edu/

CONTACT
Mr. Larry Eby, Director of Admissions, Goldey-Beacom College, 4701 Limestone Road, Wilmington, DE 19808. *Phone:* 302-225-6289. *Toll-free phone:* 800-833-4877. *Fax:* 302-996-5408. *E-mail:* admissions@gbc.edu.

University of Delaware

Newark, Delaware
http://www.udel.edu/

- **State-related** university, founded 1743
- **Small-town** 1000-acre campus with easy access to Philadelphia, Baltimore
- **Coed**
- **Moderately difficult** entrance level

FACULTY
Student/faculty ratio: 13:1.

ACADEMICS
Calendar: 4-1-4. *Degrees:* associate, bachelor's, master's, and doctoral.
Library: Hugh Morris Library.

STUDENT LIFE
Housing options: on-campus residence required for freshman year; coed, women-only, special housing for students with disabilities. Campus housing is university owned. Freshman campus housing is guaranteed.

Activities and organizations: drama/theater group, student-run newspaper, radio station, choral group, marching band, national fraternities, national sororities.

Athletics Member NCAA. All Division I except football (Division I-AA).

Campus security: 24-hour emergency response devices and patrols, student patrols, late-night transport/escort service, controlled dormitory access.

Student services: health clinic, personal/psychological counseling, women's center.

COSTS & FINANCIAL AID
Costs (2018–19) *Tuition:* state resident $12,250 full-time, $510 per credit hour part-time; nonresident $32,880 full-time, $1370 per credit hour part-time. *Required fees:* $1430 full-time. *Room and board:* $12,862; room only: $7798. Room and board charges vary according to board plan and housing facility.

Financial Aid *Average indebtedness upon graduation:* $34,144. *Financial aid deadline:* 3/15.

APPLYING
Standardized Tests *Required:* SAT or ACT (for admission). *Required for some:* SAT Subject Tests (for admission). *Recommended:* SAT Subject Tests (for admission).

Options: electronic application, early admission, deferred entrance.

Application fee: $75.

Required: essay or personal statement, high school transcript, 1 letter of recommendation.

CONTACT
Dr. Douglas Zander, Director of Admissions, University of Delaware, 122 University Visitors Center, Newark, DE 19716. *Phone:* 302-831-8123. *Fax:* 302-831-6905. *E-mail:* admissions@udel.edu.

Wesley College

Dover, Delaware
http://www.wesley.edu/

CONTACT
Mr. Christopher Jester, Assistant Director of Undergraduate Admissions, Wesley College, 120 North State Street, Dover, DE 19901-3875. *Phone:* 302-736-2468. *Toll-free phone:* 800-937-5398. *E-mail:* christopher.jester@wesley.edu.

Wilmington University

New Castle, Delaware
http://www.wilmu.edu/

- **Independent** university, founded 1967
- **Suburban** 17-acre campus with easy access to Philadelphia
- **Endowment** $73.9 million
- **Coed**
- **Noncompetitive** entrance level

FACULTY
Student/faculty ratio: 17:1.

ACADEMICS
Calendar: semesters. *Degrees:* certificates, associate, bachelor's, master's, doctoral, post-master's, and postbachelor's certificates.
Library: Robert C. and Dorothy M. Peoples Library plus 1 other. *Books:* 104,530 (physical), 179,000 (digital/electronic); *Serial titles:* 50 (physical), 98,000 (digital/electronic).

STUDENT LIFE
Housing options: college housing not available.

Activities and organizations: Student Government Association, Green Team, Photography Club, WU Student United Way, Wildcat Cheerleaders.

Athletics Member NCAA. All Division II.

Campus security: 24-hour emergency response devices and patrols, late-night transport/escort service.

COSTS & FINANCIAL AID

Costs (2018–19) *Tuition:* $8928 full-time, $372 per credit part-time. Full-time tuition and fees vary according to degree level and location. Part-time tuition and fees vary according to degree level and location. *Required fees:* $50 full-time, $25 per term part-time.

Financial Aid Of all full-time matriculated undergraduates who enrolled in 2004, 1,217 applied for aid, 900 were judged to have need. 25 Federal Work-Study jobs (averaging $2000). In 2004, 74 non-need-based awards were made. *Average percent of need met:* 48. *Average financial aid package:* $5770. *Average need-based loan:* $3889. *Average need-based gift aid:* $2464. *Average non-need-based aid:* $1100. *Average indebtedness upon graduation:* $17,486.

APPLYING

Options: electronic application, early admission, deferred entrance.

Application fee: $25.

Required: high school transcript. *Recommended:* interview.

CONTACT

Ms. Laura Morris, Director of Admissions, Wilmington University, 320 North DuPont Highway, New Castle, DE 19720-6491. *Phone:* 302-295-1179. *Toll-free phone:* 877-967-5464. *E-mail:* undergradadmissions@wilmu.edu.

DISTRICT OF COLUMBIA

American University
Washington, District of Columbia
http://www.american.edu/

- **Independent Methodist** university, founded 1893
- **Suburban** 84-acre campus with easy access to Washington, DC
- **Endowment** $676.4 million
- **Coed** 8,287 undergraduate students, 96% full-time, 62% women, 38% men
- **Very difficult** entrance level, 32% of applicants were admitted

UNDERGRAD STUDENTS

7,952 full-time, 335 part-time. Students come from 55 states and territories; 123 other countries; 83% are from out of state; 7% Black or African American, non-Hispanic/Latino; 12% Hispanic/Latino; 7% Asian, non-Hispanic/Latino; 0.1% Native Hawaiian or other Pacific Islander, non-Hispanic/Latino; 0.1% American Indian or Alaska Native, non-Hispanic/Latino; 4% Two or more races, non-Hispanic/Latino; 4% Race/ethnicity unknown; 13% international; 4% transferred in.

Freshmen:

Admission: 18,984 applied, 5,986 admitted, 1,757 enrolled. *Average high school GPA:* 3.7. *Test scores:* SAT evidence-based reading and writing scores over 500: 99%; SAT math scores over 500: 99%; ACT scores over 18: 100%; SAT evidence-based reading and writing scores over 600: 88%; SAT math scores over 600: 71%; ACT scores over 24: 94%; SAT evidence-based reading and writing scores over 700: 29%; SAT math scores over 700: 17%; ACT scores over 30: 43%.

Retention: 88% of full-time freshmen returned.

FACULTY

Total: 1,517, 54% full-time, 51% with terminal degrees.

Student/faculty ratio: 11:1.

ACADEMICS

Calendar: semesters. *Degrees:* certificates, associate, bachelor's, master's, doctoral, and postbachelor's certificates.

Special study options: accelerated degree program, advanced placement credit, cooperative education, distance learning, double majors, English as a second language, honors programs, independent study, internships, off-campus study, part-time degree program, services for LD students, student-designed majors, study abroad, summer session for credit. *ROTC:* Army (c), Air Force (c).

Unusual degree programs: 3-2 engineering with University of Maryland, College Park.

Computers: 700 computers/terminals and 7,000 ports are available on campus for general student use. Students can access the following: campus intranet, computer help desk, free student e-mail accounts, online (class) grades, online (class) registration, online (class) schedules, online e-support through learning management system. Campuswide network is available. 100% of college-owned or -operated housing units are wired for high-speed Internet access. Wireless service is available via entire campus.

Library: Bender Library plus 1 other. *Books:* 700,000 (physical), 800,000 (digital/electronic); *Serial titles:* 650 (physical), 145,000 (digital/electronic); *Databases:* 500. Study areas open 24 hours, 5–7 days a week; students can reserve study rooms.

STUDENT LIFE

Housing options: coed, special housing for students with disabilities. Campus housing is university owned and leased by the school. Freshman campus housing is guaranteed.

Activities and organizations: drama/theater group, student-run newspaper, radio and television station, choral group, Kennedy Political Union, Habitat for Humanity, Student government, Amnesty International, Multiple Ethnic and religious organizations, national fraternities, national sororities.

Athletics Member NCAA. All Division I. *Intercollegiate sports:* basketball M(s)/W(s), cross-country running M(s)/W(s), field hockey W(s), lacrosse W(s), soccer M(s)/W(s), swimming and diving M/W, track and field M(s)/W(s), volleyball W(s), wrestling M(s). *Intramural sports:* baseball M(c)/W(c), basketball M/W, crew M(c)/W(c), equestrian sports M(c)/W(c), fencing W(c), field hockey M(c), football M/W, golf M(c)/W(c), gymnastics M(c)/W(c), ice hockey M(c)/W(c), lacrosse M(c)/W(c), rugby M(c)/W(c), sailing M(c)/W(c), soccer M/W, table tennis M/W, tennis M/W, track and field M/W, ultimate Frisbee M(c)/W(c), volleyball M/W, water polo M/W, weight lifting M.

Campus security: 24-hour emergency response devices and patrols, late-night transport/escort service, controlled dormitory access.

Student services: health clinic, personal/psychological counseling, women's center, veterans affairs office.

COSTS & FINANCIAL AID

Costs (2019–20) *Comprehensive fee:* $64,769 includes full-time tuition ($49,070), mandatory fees ($819), and room and board ($14,880). Part-time tuition: $1635 per credit hour. *Required fees:* $170 part-time. *College room only:* $9996. *Payment plan:* tuition prepayment.

Financial Aid Of all full-time matriculated undergraduates who enrolled in 2018, 4,517 applied for aid, 3,655 were judged to have need, 422 had their need fully met. In 2018, 594 non-need-based awards were made. *Average percent of need met:* 71. *Average financial aid package:* $33,952. *Average need-based loan:* $4390. *Average need-based gift aid:* $27,651. *Average non-need-based aid:* $14,410. *Average indebtedness upon graduation:* $35,122. *Financial aid deadline:* 1/15.

APPLYING

Options: electronic application, early admission, early decision, deferred entrance.

Application fee: $70.

Required: essay or personal statement, high school transcript. *Recommended:* 2 letters of recommendation.

Application deadlines: 11/15 (freshmen), 5/1 (transfers).

Early decision deadline: 11/15.

Notification: 4/1 (freshmen), continuous (transfers), 12/31 (early decision).

CONTACT

Dr. Andrea Felder, Assistant Vice Provost, Undergraduate Admissions, American University, 4400 Massachusetts Avenue, NW, Washington, DC 20016-8001. *Phone:* 202-885-6000. *E-mail:* admissions@american.edu.

A ★ *indicates that the school has detailed information with a Premium Profile on Petersons.com.*

The Catholic University of America
Washington, District of Columbia
http://www.catholic.edu/

- **Independent** university, founded 1887, affiliated with Roman Catholic Church
- **Urban** 176-acre campus with easy access to Washington DC
- **Coed** 3,332 undergraduate students, 96% full-time, 53% women, 47% men
- **Moderately difficult** entrance level, 84% of applicants were admitted

UNDERGRAD STUDENTS
3,198 full-time, 134 part-time. Students come from 49 states and territories; 31 other countries; 96% are from out of state; 4% Black or African American, non-Hispanic/Latino; 14% Hispanic/Latino; 4% Asian, non-Hispanic/Latino; 0.1% Native Hawaiian or other Pacific Islander, non-Hispanic/Latino; 0.2% American Indian or Alaska Native, non-Hispanic/Latino; 5% Two or more races, non-Hispanic/Latino; 2% Race/ethnicity unknown; 6% international; 3% transferred in; 58% live on campus.

Freshmen:
Admission: 6,096 applied, 5,101 admitted, 834 enrolled. *Average high school GPA:* 3.5. *Test scores:* SAT evidence-based reading and writing scores over 500: 98%; SAT math scores over 500: 94%; ACT scores over 18: 99%; SAT evidence-based reading and writing scores over 600: 68%; SAT math scores over 600: 54%; ACT scores over 24: 80%; SAT evidence-based reading and writing scores over 700: 13%; SAT math scores over 700: 13%; ACT scores over 30: 30%.

Retention: 87% of full-time freshmen returned.

FACULTY
Total: 793, 48% full-time, 42% with terminal degrees.
Student/faculty ratio: 7:1.

ACADEMICS
Calendar: semesters. *Degrees:* certificates, bachelor's, master's, doctoral, post-master's, and postbachelor's certificates.

Special study options: accelerated degree program, adult/continuing education programs, advanced placement credit, cooperative education, distance learning, double majors, English as a second language, external degree program, honors programs, independent study, internships, off-campus study, part-time degree program, services for LD students, study abroad, summer session for credit. *ROTC:* Army (c), Navy (c), Air Force (c).

Unusual degree programs: 3-2 business administration; engineering; nursing; social work; architecture, accounting, education, psychology.

Computers: 542 computers/terminals and 13,403 ports are available on campus for general student use. Students can access the following: campus intranet, computer help desk, free student e-mail accounts, online (class) grades, online (class) registration, online (class) schedules. Campuswide network is available. 100% of college-owned or -operated housing units are wired for high-speed Internet access. Wireless service is available via entire campus.

Library: Mullen Library plus 1 other. *Books:* 734,247 (physical), 390,119 (digital/electronic); *Serial titles:* 342,482 (physical), 135,001 (digital/electronic); *Databases:* 482. Weekly public service hours: 102.

STUDENT LIFE
Housing options: on-campus residence required through sophomore year; men-only, women-only. Campus housing is university owned. Freshman campus housing is guaranteed.

Activities and organizations: drama/theater group, student-run newspaper, radio station, choral group, College Republicans, Habitat for Humanity, Student Nurse's Association, Cardinals for Life, College Democrats, national fraternities, national sororities.

Athletics Member NCAA. All Division III. *Intercollegiate sports:* baseball M, basketball M/W, crew M/W, cross-country running M/W, field hockey W, football M, golf M/W, lacrosse M/W, soccer M/W, softball W, swimming and diving M/W, tennis M/W, track and field M/W, volleyball W. *Intramural sports:* badminton M/W, basketball M/W, cheerleading M(c)/W(c), football M, ice hockey M(c), lacrosse M(c), racquetball M/W, rowing M(c)/W(c), rugby M(c)/W(c), sailing M(c)/W(c), soccer M/W, softball M/W, tennis M/W, track and field M/W, ultimate Frisbee M(c)/W(c), volleyball M/W.

Campus security: 24-hour emergency response devices and patrols, late-night transport/escort service, controlled dormitory access, controlled access of academic buildings.

Student services: health clinic, personal/psychological counseling, legal services.

COSTS & FINANCIAL AID
Costs (2019–20) *Comprehensive fee:* $63,006 includes full-time tuition ($46,950), mandatory fees ($796), and room and board ($15,260). *Required fees:* $1860 per credit hour part-time.

Financial Aid Of all full-time matriculated undergraduates who enrolled in 2018, 2,075 applied for aid, 1,757 were judged to have need, 725 had their need fully met. 215 Federal Work-Study jobs (averaging $2000). In 2018, 1082 non-need-based awards were made. *Average percent of need met:* 79. *Average financial aid package:* $31,789. *Average need-based loan:* $4424. *Average need-based gift aid:* $28,429. *Average non-need-based aid:* $21,461. *Average indebtedness upon graduation:* $46,437. *Financial aid deadline:* 4/1.

APPLYING
Options: electronic application, early decision, early action, deferred entrance.

Application fee: $55.

Required: essay or personal statement, high school transcript, 1 letter of recommendation. *Recommended:* minimum 3.0 GPA, interview.

Application deadlines: 1/15 (freshmen), 6/1 (transfers), 11/1 (early action).

Early decision deadline: 11/15 (for plan 1), 1/15 (for plan 2).

Notification: 3/15 (freshmen), 12/20 (early decision plan 1), 2/15 (early decision plan 2), 12/20 (early action).

CONTACT
James Dewey-Rosenfeld, Dean of Undergraduate Admission, The Catholic University of America, 102 Father Oâ??Connell Hall, 620 Michigan Avenue, NE, Washington, DC 20064. *Phone:* 202-319-5305. *Toll-free phone:* 800-673-2772. *Fax:* 202-319-6533. *E-mail:* cua-admissions@cua.edu.

Gallaudet University
Washington, District of Columbia
http://www.gallaudet.edu/

CONTACT
Gallaudet University, 800 Florida Avenue, NE, Washington, DC 20002-3625. *Phone:* 202-651-5750. *Toll-free phone:* 800-995-0550.

Georgetown University
Washington, District of Columbia
http://www.georgetown.edu/

- **Independent Roman Catholic (Jesuit)** university, founded 1789
- **Urban** 104-acre campus with easy access to Washington, DC
- **Coed**
- **Most difficult** entrance level

FACULTY
Student/faculty ratio: 11:1.

ACADEMICS
Calendar: semesters. *Degrees:* certificates, bachelor's, master's, doctoral, post-master's, and postbachelor's certificates.
Library: Joseph Mark Lauinger Memorial Library plus 6 others. *Books:* 2.4 million (physical), 1.9 million (digital/electronic); *Serial titles:* 52,479 (physical), 275,836 (digital/electronic); *Databases:* 1,556. Weekly public service hours: 100; study areas open 24 hours, 5–7 days a week; students can reserve study rooms.

STUDENT LIFE
Housing options: on-campus residence required through sophomore year; coed, special housing for students with disabilities. Campus housing is university owned. Freshman campus housing is guaranteed.

Activities and organizations: drama/theater group, student-run newspaper, radio and television station, choral group, Georgetown University Student Association (Student Government), International

Relations Club, College Democrats, Georgetown University Grilling Society, Black Student Alliance.

Athletics Member NCAA. All Division I except football (Division I-AA).

Campus security: 24-hour emergency response devices and patrols, late-night transport/escort service, controlled dormitory access, student guards at residence halls and academic facilities.

Student services: health clinic, personal/psychological counseling, women's center, veterans affairs office.

COSTS & FINANCIAL AID

Costs (2018–19) *Comprehensive fee:* $71,181 includes full-time tuition ($53,520), mandatory fees ($584), and room and board ($17,077). Full-time tuition and fees vary according to course load and program. Part-time tuition: $2230 per credit hour. Part-time tuition and fees vary according to course load and program. *College room only:* $11,180. Room and board charges vary according to board plan and housing facility.

Financial Aid Of all full-time matriculated undergraduates who enrolled in 2018, 3,257 applied for aid, 2,670 were judged to have need, 2,670 had their need fully met. 2,545 Federal Work-Study jobs (averaging $2883). *Average percent of need met:* 100. *Average financial aid package:* $48,279. *Average need-based loan:* $4087. *Average need-based gift aid:* $45,585. *Average indebtedness upon graduation:* $25,726. *Financial aid deadline:* 2/1.

APPLYING

Standardized Tests *Required:* SAT or ACT (for admission). *Recommended:* SAT Subject Tests (for admission).

Options: electronic application, early action, deferred entrance.

Application fee: $75.

Required: essay or personal statement, high school transcript, 2 letters of recommendation, interview.

CONTACT

Dean Charles A. Deacon, Dean of Undergraduate Admissions, Georgetown University, 37th and O Street, NW, Washington, DC 20057. *Phone:* 202-687-3600. *Fax:* 202-687-5084.

The George Washington University
Washington, District of Columbia
http://www.gwu.edu/

- **Independent** university, founded 1821
- **Urban** 36-acre campus
- **Coed**
- **Most difficult** entrance level

ACADEMICS

Calendar: semesters. *Degrees:* certificates, associate, bachelor's, master's, doctoral, post-master's, and postbachelor's certificates.

Library: Gelman Library.

STUDENT LIFE

Housing options: on-campus residence required through sophomore year; coed, women-only. Campus housing is university owned. Freshman campus housing is guaranteed.

Activities and organizations: drama/theater group, student-run newspaper, radio and television station, choral group, marching band, Program Board, Student Association, Residence Hall Association, College Democrats, College Republicans, national fraternities, national sororities.

Athletics Member NCAA. All Division I.

Campus security: 24-hour emergency response devices and patrols, late-night transport/escort service, controlled dormitory access.

Student services: health clinic, personal/psychological counseling, legal services.

FINANCIAL AID

Financial Aid Of all full-time matriculated undergraduates who enrolled in 2018, 6,476 applied for aid, 5,373 were judged to have need, 2,027 had their need fully met. In 2018, 3196 non-need-based awards were made. *Average percent of need met:* 84. *Average financial aid package:* $47,368. *Average need-based loan:* $7098. *Average need-based gift aid:* $32,089. *Average non-need-based aid:* $20,455. *Average indebtedness upon graduation:* $33,305. *Financial aid deadline:* 2/1.

APPLYING

Standardized Tests *Required for some:* SAT and SAT Subject Tests or ACT (for admission).

Options: electronic application, early admission, early decision, deferred entrance.

Application fee: $75.

Required: essay or personal statement, high school transcript, 2 letters of recommendation.

CONTACT

The George Washington University, 2121 I Street, NW, Washington, DC 20052. *Phone:* 202-994-6040.

Howard University
Washington, District of Columbia
http://www.howard.edu/

CONTACT

Tammy McCants, Associate Director of Admissions, Howard University, 2400 Sixth Street N.W., Suite 111, Washington, DC 20059. *Phone:* 202-806-2763. *Toll-free phone:* 800-822-6363. *Fax:* 202-806-4465. *E-mail:* admission@howard.edu.

National Intelligence University
Washington, District of Columbia
http://www.ni-u.edu/

CONTACT

National Intelligence University, Washington, DC 20340-5100.

Strayer University–Takoma Park Campus
Washington, District of Columbia
http://www.strayer.edu/district-columbia/takoma-park/

CONTACT

Strayer University–Takoma Park Campus, 6830 Laurel Street, NW, Washington, DC 20012. *Toll-free phone:* 888-311-0355.

Strayer University–Washington Campus
Washington, District of Columbia
http://www.strayer.edu/district-columbia/washington/

CONTACT

Strayer University–Washington Campus, 1133 15th Street, NW, Washington, DC 20025. *Toll-free phone:* 888-311-0355.

Trinity Washington University
Washington, District of Columbia
http://www.trinitydc.edu/

CONTACT

Director of Admissions, Trinity Washington University, 125 Michigan Avenue, NE, Washington, DC 20017-1094. *Phone:* 800-492-6882. *Toll-free phone:* 800-IWANTTC. *E-mail:* admissions@trinitydc.edu.

University of the District of Columbia
Washington, District of Columbia
http://www.udc.edu/

CONTACT

Ms. Nicole L. Daniels, Director of Undergraduate Recruitment and Admissions, University of the District of Columbia, 4200 Connecticut Avenue NW, Washington, DC 20008. *Phone:* 202-274-6430. *Fax:* 202-274-5553. *E-mail:* nicole.daniels@udc.edu.

University of the Potomac
Washington, District of Columbia
http://www.potomac.edu/

- **Proprietary** comprehensive, founded 1991
- **Urban** campus with easy access to Washington DC; Tysons, VA
- **Coed**
- **Noncompetitive** entrance level

FACULTY
Student/faculty ratio: 5:1.

ACADEMICS
Calendar: 6 8-week terms. *Degrees:* certificates, associate, bachelor's, and master's.
Library: Learning Resource Center - Washington Campus plus 1 other. *Books:* 4,500 (physical); *Serial titles:* 20 (physical), 5 (digital/electronic); *Databases:* 5. Weekly public service hours: 35.

STUDENT LIFE
Housing options: college housing not available.
Campus security: late-night transport/escort service.
Student services: veterans affairs office.

APPLYING
Options: electronic application.
Required: interview.

CONTACT
Gina Rice-Holland, Director of Admissions, University of the Potomac, 1401 H Street NW, Suite 100, Washington, DC 20005. *Phone:* 202-274-2338. *Toll-free phone:* 888-686-0876. *E-mail:* gina.riceholland@potomac.edu.

FLORIDA

AdventHealth University
Orlando, Florida
http://www.ahu.edu/

- **Independent** comprehensive, founded 1992
- **Urban** 9-acre campus with easy access to Orlando
- **Endowment** $8.0 million
- **Coed** 1,341 undergraduate students, 39% full-time, 79% women, 21% men
- **Minimally difficult** entrance level, 87% of applicants were admitted

UNDERGRAD STUDENTS
528 full-time, 813 part-time. Students come from 40 states and territories; 11 other countries; 23% are from out of state; 19% Black or African American, non-Hispanic/Latino; 32% Hispanic/Latino; 5% Asian, non-Hispanic/Latino; 0.6% Native Hawaiian or other Pacific Islander, non-Hispanic/Latino; 0.2% American Indian or Alaska Native, non-Hispanic/Latino; 4% Two or more races, non-Hispanic/Latino; 3% Race/ethnicity unknown; 2% international; 11% transferred in; 11% live on campus.

Freshmen:
Admission: 267 applied, 232 admitted, 94 enrolled. *Test scores:* SAT evidence-based reading and writing scores over 500: 58%; SAT math scores over 500: 43%; ACT scores over 18: 63%; SAT evidence-based reading and writing scores over 600: 17%; SAT math scores over 600: 7%; ACT scores over 24: 15%.
Retention: 66% of full-time freshmen returned.

FACULTY
Total: 256, 36% full-time, 35% with terminal degrees.
Student/faculty ratio: 8:1.

ACADEMICS
Calendar: trimesters. *Degrees:* certificates, associate, bachelor's, master's, doctoral, and postbachelor's certificates.

Special study options: academic remediation for entering students, distance learning, double majors, freshman honors college, independent study, internships, services for LD students, summer session for credit.
Computers: 51 computers/terminals are available on campus for general student use. Students can access the following: campus intranet, computer help desk, free student e-mail accounts, online (class) grades, online (class) registration, online (class) schedules, Online Registration. Campuswide network is available. Wireless service is available via entire campus.
Library: R. A. Williams Library. *Books:* 11,979 (physical), 19,173 (digital/electronic); *Serial titles:* 25 (physical), 28,121 (digital/electronic); *Databases:* 120. Weekly public service hours: 65; students can reserve study rooms.

STUDENT LIFE
Housing options: coed. Campus housing is leased by the school.
Activities and organizations: drama/theater group, choral group, Student Nursing Association, Student Occupational Therapy Association, Pre Physician Assistant, Pre PT/OT, Campus Ministries.
Campus security: 24-hour emergency response devices and patrols, controlled dormitory access.
Student services: personal/psychological counseling, veterans affairs office.

COSTS & FINANCIAL AID
Costs (2019–20) *Tuition:* $15,300 full-time, $510 per credit hour part-time. *Required fees:* $600 full-time, $300 per term part-time. *Room only:* $4200.
Financial Aid Of all full-time matriculated undergraduates who enrolled in 2018, 498 applied for aid, 451 were judged to have need, 16 had their need fully met. In 2018, 19 non-need-based awards were made. *Average percent of need met:* 30. *Average financial aid package:* $9634. *Average need-based loan:* $3592. *Average need-based gift aid:* $7319. *Average non-need-based aid:* $2564. *Average indebtedness upon graduation:* $38,990. *Financial aid deadline:* 7/15.

APPLYING
Standardized Tests *Required for some:* SAT or ACT (for admission), TOEFL for non-native English Speakers.
Options: electronic application, early admission, early action, deferred entrance.
Application fee: $20.
Required: high school transcript, minimum 2.5 GPA.
Application deadlines: 7/1 (freshmen), 7/1 (out-of-state freshmen), 7/1 (transfers), 5/1 (early action).
Notification: 7/15 (freshmen), 7/15 (out-of-state freshmen), 7/15 (transfers).

CONTACT
Mrs. Lillian Garrido, Director of Admissions, AdventHealth University, 671 Winyah Drive, Orlando, FL 32803. *Phone:* 407-303-7742. *Toll-free phone:* 800-500-7747. *Fax:* 407-303-0753. *E-mail:* lillian.garrido@ahu.edu.

Albizu University, Miami Campus
Miami, Florida
http://www.albizu.edu/

CONTACT
Ms. Maria Elena Torres, Admissions Officer, Albizu University, Miami Campus, 2173 NW 99 Avenue, Miami, FL 33172. *Phone:* 305-593-1223 Ext. 3134. *Toll-free phone:* 888-GO-TO-CAU (in-state); 800-GO-TO-CAU (out-of-state). *Fax:* 305-593-1854. *E-mail:* matorres@albizu.edu.

Altierus Career College
Tampa, Florida
http://www.altierus.edu/

CONTACT
Altierus Career College, 3319 West Hillsborough Avenue, Tampa, FL 33614. *Phone:* 813-879-6000 Ext. 129.

American College for Medical Careers
Orlando, Florida
http://www.acmc.edu/

CONTACT
American College for Medical Careers, 5959 Lake Ellenor Drive, Orlando, FL 32809. *Toll-free phone:* 888-599-7887.

Argosy University, Tampa
Tampa, Florida
http://www.argosy.edu/locations/tampa/

CONTACT
Argosy University, Tampa, 1403 North Howard Avenue, Tampa, FL 33607. *Phone:* 813-393-5290. *Toll-free phone:* 800-850-6488.

The Art Institute of Tampa, a branch of Miami International University of Art & Design
Tampa, Florida
http://www.artinstitutes.edu/tampa/

CONTACT
The Art Institute of Tampa, a branch of Miami International University of Art & Design, Parkside at Tampa Bay Park, 4401 North Himes Avenue, Suite 150, Tampa, FL 33614. *Phone:* 813-873-2112. *Toll-free phone:* 866-703-3277.

Atlantis University
Miami, Florida
http://www.atlantisuniversity.edu/

CONTACT
Atlantis University, 1442 Biscayne Boulevard, Miami, FL 33132.

Ave Maria University
Ave Maria, Florida
http://www.avemaria.edu/

CONTACT
Ave Maria University, 5050 Ave Maria Boulevard, Ave Maria, FL 34142. *Phone:* 239-280-2487. *Toll-free phone:* 877-283-8648. *Fax:* 239-280-2559.

The Baptist College of Florida
Graceville, Florida
http://www.baptistcollege.edu/
- **Independent Southern Baptist** comprehensive, founded 1943
- **Small-town** 250-acre campus
- **Endowment** $7.8 million
- **Coed**
- **Noncompetitive** entrance level

FACULTY
Student/faculty ratio: 9:1.

ACADEMICS
Calendar: semesters. *Degrees:* associate, bachelor's, and master's.
Library: Ida J. MacMillan Library plus 1 other. *Books:* 90,006 (physical), 88,931 (digital/electronic); *Serial titles:* 5,602 (physical), 5,602 (digital/electronic); *Databases:* 16. Weekly public service hours: 66.

STUDENT LIFE
Housing options: on-campus residence required through sophomore year; men-only, women-only, special housing for students with disabilities. Campus housing is university owned. Freshman campus housing is guaranteed.
Activities and organizations: drama/theater group, choral group, Baptist Collegiate Ministry, College Choir, AACC.

Campus security: student patrols, patrols by police officers 11 pm to 7 am.
Student services: personal/psychological counseling, veterans affairs office.

COSTS & FINANCIAL AID
Costs (2018–19) *Comprehensive fee:* $16,012 includes full-time tuition ($10,500), mandatory fees ($900), and room and board ($4612). Part-time tuition: $350 per credit hour. *Required fees:* $30 per credit hour part-time. *Room and board:* Room and board charges vary according to board plan and housing facility.

Financial Aid Of all full-time matriculated undergraduates who enrolled in 2018, 326 applied for aid, 290 were judged to have need, 12 had their need fully met. 24 Federal Work-Study jobs (averaging $1958). In 2018, 16 non-need-based awards were made. *Average percent of need met:* 34. *Average financial aid package:* $8989. *Average need-based loan:* $3448. *Average need-based gift aid:* $6816. *Average non-need-based aid:* $2073. *Average indebtedness upon graduation:* $24,444.

APPLYING
Standardized Tests *Required:* SAT or ACT (for admission).
Options: electronic application, deferred entrance.
Application fee: $25.
Required: essay or personal statement, high school transcript, minimum 2.5 GPA, 2 letters of recommendation, Christian/church member for 1 year minimum. *Recommended:* interview.

CONTACT
The Baptist College of Florida, 5400 College Drive, Graceville, FL 32440. *Phone:* 850-263-3261 Ext. 460. *Toll-free phone:* 800-328-2660 Ext. 460.

Barry University
Miami Shores, Florida
http://www.barry.edu/
- **Independent Roman Catholic** university, founded 1940
- **Suburban** 122-acre campus with easy access to Miami
- **Coed**
- **Moderately difficult** entrance level

FACULTY
Student/faculty ratio: 13:1.

ACADEMICS
Calendar: semesters. *Degrees:* certificates, bachelor's, master's, doctoral, post-master's, and postbachelor's certificates.
Library: Monsignor William Barry Memorial Library plus 1 other.

STUDENT LIFE
Housing options: on-campus residence required for freshman year; coed, men-only, women-only, special housing for students with disabilities. Campus housing is university owned.
Activities and organizations: drama/theater group, student-run newspaper, radio and television station, choral group, Student Government Association, Campus Activities Board, SCUBA Society, Caribbean Students Association, Jamaican Association, national fraternities, national sororities.
Athletics Member NCAA. All Division II.
Campus security: 24-hour emergency response devices and patrols, late-night transport/escort service.
Student services: health clinic, personal/psychological counseling.

COSTS & FINANCIAL AID
Costs (2018–19) *Comprehensive fee:* $40,800 includes full-time tuition ($29,700) and room and board ($11,100). Part-time tuition: $925 per credit hour. Part-time tuition and fees vary according to course load. *Room and board:* Room and board charges vary according to housing facility. *Payment plans:* installment, deferred payment.

Financial Aid Of all full-time matriculated undergraduates who enrolled in 2018, 2,356 applied for aid, 2,259 were judged to have need, 114 had their need fully met. In 2018, 255 non-need-based awards were made. *Average percent of need met:* 58. *Average financial aid package:* $22,982. *Average need-based loan:* $4231. *Average need-based gift aid:*

$9354. *Average non-need-based aid:* $9849. *Average indebtedness upon graduation:* $41,293.

APPLYING

Standardized Tests *Required:* SAT or ACT (for admission).

Options: electronic application, early admission, deferred entrance.

Application fee: $30.

Required: high school transcript, minimum 2.0 GPA. *Required for some:* essay or personal statement. *Recommended:* interview.

CONTACT

Barry University, 11300 Northeast Second Avenue, Miami Shores, FL 33161-6695. *Phone:* 305-899-3394. *Toll-free phone:* 800-695-2279.

Beacon College

Leesburg, Florida

http://www.beaconcollege.edu/

- **Independent** 4-year, founded 1989
- **Small-town** 19-acre campus with easy access to Orlando
- **Endowment** $83,990
- **Coed**
- **Moderately difficult** entrance level

FACULTY

Student/faculty ratio: 11:1.

ACADEMICS

Calendar: semesters. *Degree:* bachelor's.

Library: Beacon College Library. *Books:* 11,113 (physical), 346,154 (digital/electronic); *Serial titles:* 40 (physical); *Databases:* 15. Weekly public service hours: 76; students can reserve study rooms.

STUDENT LIFE

Housing options: coed. Campus housing is university owned and leased by the school. Freshman campus housing is guaranteed.

Activities and organizations: drama/theater group, student-run radio station, Gamma Beta Phi, Performance Club, Psychology & Human Services Club, Nerd Culture Club, Equine Club, national fraternities, national sororities.

Campus security: 24-hour emergency response devices and patrols, student patrols, late-night transport/escort service.

Student services: health clinic, personal/psychological counseling.

COSTS & FINANCIAL AID

Costs (2018–19) *Comprehensive fee:* $50,406 includes full-time tuition ($39,016) and room and board ($11,390). Full-time tuition and fees vary according to course load. Part-time tuition: $1300 per credit hour. Part-time tuition and fees vary according to course load. *College room only:* $7216. Room and board charges vary according to housing facility.

Financial Aid Of all full-time matriculated undergraduates who enrolled in 2015, 137 applied for aid, 118 were judged to have need. In 2015, 67 non-need-based awards were made. *Average financial aid package:* $12,366. *Average need-based loan:* $3438. *Average need-based gift aid:* $18,625. *Average non-need-based aid:* $4470. *Average indebtedness upon graduation:* $27,000.

APPLYING

Options: electronic application, early admission, deferred entrance.

Application fee: $50.

Required: high school transcript, 3 letters of recommendation, psycho-educational evaluation showing diagnosed learning disability or ADHD. *Recommended:* minimum 2.0 GPA, interview.

CONTACT

Ms. Dale Herold, Vice President of Admissions and Enrollment Management, Beacon College, 105 East Main Street, Leesburg, FL 34748. *Phone:* 352-638-9778. *Fax:* 352-787-0796. *E-mail:* dherold@ beaconcollege.edu.

Belhaven University

Orlando, Florida

http://orlando.belhaven.edu/

CONTACT

Jeremy Couch, Director of Admission, Belhaven University, 5200 Vineland Road, Suite 100, Orlando, FL 32811. *Phone:* 407-804-1424. *Toll-free phone:* 877-804-1424. *Fax:* 407-661-1732. *E-mail:* orlando@ belhaven.edu.

Bethune-Cookman University

Daytona Beach, Florida

http://www.cookman.edu/

- **Independent Methodist** comprehensive, founded 1904
- **Urban** 60-acre campus with easy access to Orlando
- **Endowment** $47.9 million
- **Coed**
- **Minimally difficult** entrance level

FACULTY

Student/faculty ratio: 16:1.

ACADEMICS

Calendar: semesters. *Degrees:* bachelor's and master's.

Library: Carl S. Swisher Library plus 1 other. *Books:* 83,794 (physical), 269,009 (digital/electronic); *Serial titles:* 20 (physical), 36,000 (digital/electronic); *Databases:* 34. Weekly public service hours: 92; study areas open 24 hours, 5–7 days a week; students can reserve study rooms.

STUDENT LIFE

Housing options: on-campus residence required through sophomore year; coed, men-only, women-only. Campus housing is university owned. Freshman campus housing is guaranteed.

Activities and organizations: drama/theater group, student-run newspaper, radio station, choral group, marching band, National Council of Negro Women, Gamma Sigma Sigma Sorority, Phenomenal Woman Think Tank, What's Next Dance Company, NAACP, national fraternities, national sororities.

Athletics Member NCAA, NAIA. All NCAA Division I except football (Division I-AA).

Campus security: 24-hour emergency response devices and patrols, student patrols, late-night transport/escort service.

Student services: health clinic, personal/psychological counseling, veterans affairs office.

COSTS & FINANCIAL AID

Costs (2018–19) *One-time required fee:* $300. *Comprehensive fee:* $24,226 includes full-time tuition ($13,844), mandatory fees ($970), and room and board ($9412). Full-time tuition and fees vary according to degree level. Part-time tuition: $577 per credit hour. Part-time tuition and fees vary according to course load and degree level. *Required fees:* $50 per credit hour part-time. *Room and board:* Room and board charges vary according to housing facility.

Financial Aid Of all full-time matriculated undergraduates who enrolled in 2018, 3,216 applied for aid, 3,117 were judged to have need, 140 had their need fully met. 200 Federal Work-Study jobs (averaging $2500). 100 state and other part-time jobs (averaging $2000). In 2018, 52 non-need-based awards were made. *Average percent of need met:* 53. *Average financial aid package:* $15,089. *Average need-based loan:* $4312. *Average need-based gift aid:* $11,337. *Average non-need-based aid:* $11,118. *Average indebtedness upon graduation:* $38,728.

APPLYING

Standardized Tests *Required:* SAT or ACT (for admission).

Options: electronic application, early admission, deferred entrance.

Application fee: $25.

Required: high school transcript, minimum 2.3 GPA, 1 letter of recommendation, medical history. *Required for some:* interview. *Recommended:* essay or personal statement.

CONTACT

Treran Porter, Director of Recruitment, Bethune-Cookman University, FL. *Phone:* 386-481-2603. *Toll-free phone:* 800-448-0228. *E-mail:* portert@ cookman.edu.

Broward College
Fort Lauderdale, Florida
http://www.broward.edu/

CONTACT
Mr. Willie J. Alexander, Associate Vice President for Student Affairs/College Registrar, Broward College, 225 East Las Olas Boulevard, Fort Lauderdale, FL 33301. *Phone:* 954-201-7471. *Fax:* 954-201-7466. *E-mail:* walexand@broward.edu.

Chamberlain College of Nursing
Jacksonville, Florida
http://www.chamberlain.edu/

CONTACT
Admissions, Chamberlain College of Nursing, 5200 Belfort Road, Jacksonville, FL 32256. *Phone:* 904-251-8100. *Toll-free phone:* 877-751-5783.

Chamberlain College of Nursing
Miramar, Florida
http://www.chamberlain.edu/

CONTACT
Director of Recruitment, Chamberlain College of Nursing, 2300 SW 145th Avenue, Miramar, FL 33027. *Phone:* 954-885-3510. *Toll-free phone:* 877-751-5783.

Chipola College
Marianna, Florida
http://www.chipola.edu/
- **State-supported** primarily 2-year, founded 1947
- **Rural** 105-acre campus
- **Coed**
- **Noncompetitive** entrance level

FACULTY
Student/faculty ratio: 24:1.

ACADEMICS
Calendar: semesters. *Degrees:* certificates, associate, and bachelor's.
Library: Chipola Library. *Books:* 30,000 (physical), 67,000 (digital/electronic); *Serial titles:* 150 (physical); *Databases:* 100. Weekly public service hours: 60; students can reserve study rooms.

STUDENT LIFE
Housing options: college housing not available.
Activities and organizations: drama/theater group, student-run newspaper, choral group.
Athletics Member NJCAA.
Campus security: night security personnel.
Student services: veterans affairs office.

COSTS
Costs (2018–19) *Tuition:* state resident $104 per credit hour part-time; nonresident $298 per credit hour part-time. Full-time tuition and fees vary according to degree level. Part-time tuition and fees vary according to degree level.

APPLYING
Options: early admission.
Required: high school transcript.

CONTACT
Mrs. Kathy L. Rehberg, Registrar, Chipola College, 3094 Indian Circle, Marianna, FL 32446-3065. *Phone:* 850-718-2233. *Fax:* 850-718-2287. *E-mail:* rehbergk@chipola.edu.

City College
Altamonte Springs, Florida
http://www.citycollege.edu/

CONTACT
Ms. Kimberly Bowden, Director of Admissions, City College, 177 Montgomery Road, Altamonte Springs, FL 32714. *Phone:* 352-335-4000. *Fax:* 352-335-4303. *E-mail:* kbowden@citycollege.edu.

City College
Fort Lauderdale, Florida
http://www.citycollege.edu/

CONTACT
City College, 2000 West Commercial Boulevard, Suite 200, Fort Lauderdale, FL 33309. *Phone:* 954-492-5353. *Toll-free phone:* 866-314-5681.

City College
Gainesville, Florida
http://www.citycollege.edu/

CONTACT
Admissions Office, City College, 7001 Northwest 4th Boulevard, Gainesville, FL 32607. *Phone:* 352-335-4000.

City College
Hollywood, Florida
http://www.citycollege.edu/

CONTACT
City College, 6565 Taft Street, Hollywood, FL 33024. *Toll-free phone:* 866-314-5681.

City College
Miami, Florida
http://www.citycollege.edu/

CONTACT
Admissions Office, City College, 9300 South Dadeland Boulevard, Suite PH, Miami, FL 33156. *Phone:* 305-666-9242. *Fax:* 305-666-9243.

College of Business and Technology– Main Campus
Miami, Florida
http://www.cbt.edu/
- **Proprietary** primarily 2-year, founded 1988
- **Urban** campus
- **Coed**
- **Minimally difficult** entrance level

FACULTY
Student/faculty ratio: 10:1.

ACADEMICS
Calendar: semesters. *Degrees:* certificates, diplomas, associate, and bachelor's.
Library: CBT College-Miami Branch Library (Use Flagler). *Books:* 590 (physical); *Serial titles:* 8 (physical); *Databases:* 50.

STUDENT LIFE
Housing options: college housing not available.
Campus security: security guard posted at main entrance, local police department.

COSTS
Costs (2018–19) *Tuition:* $11,952 full-time. *Required fees:* $1500 full-time.

APPLYING
Application fee: $25.

Required: high school transcript, interview.

CONTACT
College of Business and Technology–Main Campus, 8700 West Flagler Street, Suite 420, Miami, FL 33174. *Phone:* 305-273-4499 Ext. 1100.

College of Business and Technology–Miami Gardens
Miami Gardens, Florida
http://www.cbt.edu/
- **Proprietary** primarily 2-year, founded 2012
- **Urban** campus with easy access to Miami
- **Coed**
- **Minimally difficult** entrance level

FACULTY
Student/faculty ratio: 15:1.

ACADEMICS
Calendar: semesters. *Degrees:* certificates, diplomas, associate, and bachelor's.
Library: CBT College–Miami Gardens Library. *Books:* 1,085 (physical); *Serial titles:* 18 (physical); *Databases:* 50.

STUDENT LIFE
Housing options: college housing not available.
Campus security: local police department.

COSTS
Costs (2018–19) *Tuition:* $11,952 full-time. *Required fees:* $1500 full-time.

APPLYING
Application fee: $25.
Required: high school transcript, interview.

CONTACT
College of Business and Technology–Miami Gardens, 5190 NW 167 Street, Miami Gardens, FL 33014. *Phone:* 305-273-4499 Ext. 1100.

College of Central Florida
Ocala, Florida
http://www.cf.edu/
- **State and locally supported** primarily 2-year, founded 1957, part of Florida College System
- **Small-town** 139-acre campus
- **Endowment** $65.4 million
- **Coed** 6,820 undergraduate students, 44% full-time, 62% women, 38% men
- **Noncompetitive** entrance level, 39% of applicants were admitted

UNDERGRAD STUDENTS
3,016 full-time, 3,804 part-time. 3% are from out of state; 14% Black or African American, non-Hispanic/Latino; 15% Hispanic/Latino; 2% Asian, non-Hispanic/Latino; 0.5% Native Hawaiian or other Pacific Islander, non-Hispanic/Latino; 0.4% American Indian or Alaska Native, non-Hispanic/Latino; 5% Two or more races, non-Hispanic/Latino; 1% Race/ethnicity unknown; 2% international; 6% transferred in.

Freshmen:
Admission: 4,090 applied, 1,593 admitted, 1,334 enrolled.

ACADEMICS
Calendar: semesters. *Degrees:* certificates, diplomas, associate, and bachelor's.
Special study options: academic remediation for entering students, adult/continuing education programs, advanced placement credit, cooperative education, distance learning, English as a second language, freshman honors college, honors programs, independent study, internships, part-time degree program, services for LD students, summer session for credit.
Computers: 2,500 computers/terminals are available on campus for general student use. Students can access the following: campus intranet, computer help desk, online (class) grades, online (class) registration, online (class) schedules. Campuswide network is available. Wireless service is available via classrooms, computer centers, computer labs, learning centers, libraries, student centers.
Library: Clifford B. Stearns Learning Resources Center. *Books:* 75,935 (physical), 43,910 (digital/electronic); *Databases:* 152. Students can reserve study rooms.

STUDENT LIFE
Housing options: college housing not available.
Activities and organizations: drama/theater group, student-run newspaper, choral group, Inspirational Choir, Model United Nations, Performing Arts, Phi Theta Kappa (PTK), Student Nurses Association.
Athletics Member NJCAA. *Intercollegiate sports:* baseball M(s), basketball M(s)/W(s), softball W(s), volleyball W(s). *Intramural sports:* bowling M/W.
Campus security: 24-hour emergency response devices and patrols, student patrols, late-night transport/escort service.
Student services: personal/psychological counseling.

COSTS & FINANCIAL AID
Costs (2019–20) *Tuition:* $107 per credit hour part-time; state resident $107 per credit part-time; nonresident $422 per credit hour part-time.
Financial Aid Of all full-time matriculated undergraduates who enrolled in 2017, 1,184 applied for aid, 753 were judged to have need, 23 had their need fully met. In 2017, 38 non-need-based awards were made. *Average percent of need met:* 55. *Average financial aid package:* $1744. *Average need-based loan:* $2164. *Average need-based gift aid:* $1731. *Average non-need-based aid:* $889.

APPLYING
Options: electronic application, early admission.
Application fee: $30.
Required: high school transcript.
Application deadlines: rolling (freshmen), rolling (transfers).
Notification: continuous (freshmen), continuous (transfers).

CONTACT
Mr. Alton Austin, Director of Enrollment Services/Registrar, College of Central Florida, 3001 SW College Road, Ocala, FL 34474. *Phone:* 352-237-2111 Ext. 1751. *Fax:* 352-873-5882. *E-mail:* austina@cf.edu.

Daytona State College
Daytona Beach, Florida
http://www.daytonastate.edu/
- **State-supported** primarily 2-year, founded 1957, part of Florida College System
- **Suburban** 100-acre campus with easy access to Orlando
- **Endowment** $13.4 million
- **Coed** 19,530 undergraduate students, 40% full-time, 62% women, 38% men
- **Noncompetitive** entrance level

UNDERGRAD STUDENTS
7,848 full-time, 11,682 part-time. Students come from 26 other countries; 2% are from out of state; 13% Black or African American, non-Hispanic/Latino; 17% Hispanic/Latino; 2% Asian, non-Hispanic/Latino; 0.1% Native Hawaiian or other Pacific Islander, non-Hispanic/Latino; 0.2% American Indian or Alaska Native, non-Hispanic/Latino; 4% Two or more races, non-Hispanic/Latino; 2% Race/ethnicity unknown; 0.2% international.

Freshmen:
Admission: 1,417 enrolled.

FACULTY
Total: 913, 29% full-time, 17% with terminal degrees.
Student/faculty ratio: 16:1.

ACADEMICS
Calendar: semesters. *Degrees:* certificates, diplomas, associate, bachelor's, and postbachelor's certificates.
Special study options: academic remediation for entering students, adult/continuing education programs, advanced placement credit, cooperative education, distance learning, English as a second language, external degree program, freshman honors college, honors programs,

independent study, internships, off-campus study, part-time degree program, services for LD students, study abroad, summer session for credit. *ROTC:* Army (c), Air Force (c).

Computers: 3,200 computers/terminals are available on campus for general student use. Students can access the following: campus intranet, computer help desk, free student e-mail accounts, online (class) grades, online (class) registration, online (class) schedules. Campuswide network is available. Wireless service is available via entire campus.

Library: Mary Karl Memorial Learning Resources Center plus 1 other. *Books:* 36,000 (physical), 175,000 (digital/electronic); *Serial titles:* 164 (physical); *Databases:* 100. Weekly public service hours: 68; students can reserve study rooms.

STUDENT LIFE
Housing options: college housing not available.

Activities and organizations: drama/theater group, student-run newspaper, choral group, Phi Theta Kappa International Honors Society, Student Government Association, Student Respiratory Therapy Club, Business Club, Student Paralegal Club, national fraternities, national sororities.

Athletics Member NJCAA. *Intercollegiate sports:* baseball M(s), basketball M(s)/W(s), cross-country running M(s)/W(s), soccer M(s)/W(s), softball W(s), volleyball W(s). *Intramural sports:* basketball M/W, football M/W, golf W, soccer M/W, table tennis M/W, volleyball M/W.

Campus security: 24-hour emergency response devices and patrols, late-night transport/escort service, emergency alert system capable of delivering text messages, voice calls, and email messages to college email accounts.

Student services: personal/psychological counseling, women's center, veterans affairs office.

COSTS & FINANCIAL AID
Costs (2018–19) *Tuition:* state resident $3071 full-time, $102 per credit hour part-time; nonresident $11,960 full-time, $399 per credit hour part-time. Full-time tuition and fees vary according to course level and course load. Part-time tuition and fees vary according to course level and course load. *Required fees:* $33 full-time, $1 per credit hour part-time. *Payment plan:* installment. *Waivers:* employees or children of employees.

Financial Aid Of all full-time matriculated undergraduates who enrolled in 2017, 2,424 applied for aid, 2,418 were judged to have need. 118 Federal Work-Study jobs (averaging $1585). In 2017, 82 non-need-based awards were made. *Average need-based loan:* $1517. *Average need-based gift aid:* $1815. *Average non-need-based aid:* $1878. *Average indebtedness upon graduation:* $2483.

APPLYING
Options: electronic application, early admission, deferred entrance.
Required: high school transcript.
Application deadlines: rolling (freshmen), rolling (transfers).
Notification: continuous (freshmen), continuous (transfers).

CONTACT
Dr. Karen Sanders, Director of Admissions and Recruitment, Daytona State College, 1200 International Speedway Boulevard, Daytona Beach, FL 32114. *Phone:* 386-506-3050. *E-mail:* karen.sanders@daytonastate.edu.

DeVry University–Jacksonville Campus
Jacksonville, Florida
http://www.devry.edu/

CONTACT
Admissions Office, DeVry University–Jacksonville Campus, 5200 Belfort Road, Suite 175, Jacksonville, FL 32256-6040. *Phone:* 904-367-4942. *Toll-free phone:* 866-338-7934.

DeVry University–Miramar Campus
Miramar, Florida
http://www.devry.edu/

CONTACT
DeVry University–Miramar Campus, 2300 Southwest 145th Avenue, Miramar, FL 33027. *Phone:* 954-499-9775. *Toll-free phone:* 866-338-7934.

DeVry University–Orlando Campus
Orlando, Florida
http://www.devry.edu/

CONTACT
DeVry University–Orlando Campus, 7352 Greenbriar Parkway, Orlando, FL 32819. *Phone:* 407-345-2800. *Toll-free phone:* 866-338-7934.

Eastern Florida State College
Cocoa, Florida
http://www.easternflorida.edu/

CONTACT
Ms. Stephanie Burnette, Registrar, Eastern Florida State College, 1519 Clearlake Road, Cocoa, FL 32922-6597. *Phone:* 321-433-7271. *Fax:* 321-433-7172. *E-mail:* cocoaadmissions@brevardcc.edu.

Eckerd College
St. Petersburg, Florida
http://www.eckerd.edu/
- **Independent Presbyterian** 4-year, founded 1958
- **Suburban** 188-acre campus with easy access to Tampa
- **Endowment** $58.3 million
- **Coed** 2,000 undergraduate students, 97% full-time, 66% women, 34% men
- **Moderately difficult** entrance level, 68% of applicants were admitted

UNDERGRAD STUDENTS
1,940 full-time, 60 part-time. Students come from 46 states and territories; 42 other countries; 79% are from out of state; 3% Black or African American, non-Hispanic/Latino; 8% Hispanic/Latino; 3% Asian, non-Hispanic/Latino; 0.2% Native Hawaiian or other Pacific Islander, non-Hispanic/Latino; 0.4% American Indian or Alaska Native, non-Hispanic/Latino; 4% Two or more races, non-Hispanic/Latino; 0.6% Race/ethnicity unknown; 4% international; 2% transferred in; 88% live on campus.

Freshmen:
Admission: 4,830 applied, 3,268 admitted, 581 enrolled. *Average high school GPA:* 3.5. *Test scores:* SAT evidence-based reading and writing scores over 500: 94%; SAT math scores over 500: 89%; ACT scores over 18: 99%; SAT evidence-based reading and writing scores over 600: 58%; SAT math scores over 600: 40%; ACT scores over 24: 70%; SAT evidence-based reading and writing scores over 700: 10%; SAT math scores over 700: 9%; ACT scores over 30: 20%.

Retention: 81% of full-time freshmen returned.

FACULTY
Total: 180, 84% full-time, 83% with terminal degrees.
Student/faculty ratio: 12:1.

ACADEMICS
Calendar: 4-1-4. *Degree:* bachelor's.

Special study options: accelerated degree program, adult/continuing education programs, advanced placement credit, double majors, external degree program, honors programs, independent study, internships, off-campus study, part-time degree program, services for LD students, student-designed majors, study abroad, summer session for credit. *ROTC:* Army (c), Air Force (c).

Unusual degree programs: 3-2 engineering with Columbia University.

Computers: 300 computers/terminals and 2,000 ports are available on campus for general student use. Students can access the following: campus intranet, computer help desk, free student e-mail accounts, online

(class) grades, online (class) registration, online (class) schedules, free computer repair shop. Campuswide network is available. 100% of college-owned or -operated housing units are wired for high-speed Internet access. Wireless service is available via entire campus.
Library: Peter Armacost Library. *Books:* 156,516 (physical), 168,633 (digital/electronic); *Serial titles:* 773 (physical), 182,151 (digital/electronic); *Databases:* 201.

STUDENT LIFE
Housing options: on-campus residence required for freshman year; coed, women-only. Campus housing is university owned. Freshman campus housing is guaranteed.

Activities and organizations: drama/theater group, student-run newspaper, radio and television station, choral group, Marine Science Club, Water Search and Rescue Team, The Current (student newspaper), A cappella Vocal Group, Organization of Students.

Athletics Member NCAA. All Division II except golf (Division I). *Intercollegiate sports:* baseball M(s), basketball M(s)/W(s), golf M(s)/W(s), sailing M/W, sand volleyball M, soccer M(s)/W(s), softball W(s), tennis M(s)/W(s), volleyball W(s). *Intramural sports:* baseball M, basketball M/W, bowling M/W, cheerleading M(c)/W(c), equestrian sports M(c)/W(c), fencing W(c), field hockey M(c)/W(c), football M(c)/W(c), golf M(c)/W(c), lacrosse M(c)/W(c), rugby M(c)/W(c), sailing M/W, soccer M(c)/W(c), softball M/W, swimming and diving M(c)/W(c), table tennis M/W, tennis M(c)/W(c), ultimate Frisbee M(c)/W(c), volleyball M/W.

Campus security: 24-hour emergency response devices and patrols, student patrols, late-night transport/escort service, controlled dormitory access.

Student services: health clinic, personal/psychological counseling, women's center.

COSTS & FINANCIAL AID
Costs (2018–19) *Comprehensive fee:* $55,206 includes full-time tuition ($42,428), mandatory fees ($616), and room and board ($12,162). *College room only:* $6362. Room and board charges vary according to board plan and housing facility. *Payment plan:* installment. *Waivers:* employees or children of employees.

Financial Aid Of all full-time matriculated undergraduates who enrolled in 2018, 1,347 applied for aid, 1,164 were judged to have need, 219 had their need fully met. 956 Federal Work-Study jobs (averaging $2000). In 2018, 763 non-need-based awards were made. *Average percent of need met:* 87. *Average financial aid package:* $38,458. *Average need-based loan:* $3764. *Average need-based gift aid:* $26,850. *Average non-need-based aid:* $17,765. *Average indebtedness upon graduation:* $37,896.

APPLYING
Standardized Tests *Required:* SAT or ACT (for admission). *Recommended:* SAT Subject Tests (for admission).

Options: electronic application, early action, deferred entrance.

Application fee: $40.

Required: essay or personal statement, high school transcript. *Recommended:* interview.

Application deadlines: rolling (freshmen), rolling (transfers), 11/15 (early action).

Notification: continuous (freshmen), continuous (transfers).

CONTACT
Ms. Lucille Lopez, Campus Visit Coordinator, Eckerd College, 4200 54th Avenue South, St. Petersburg, FL 33711. *Phone:* 727-864-8331. *Toll-free phone:* 800-456-9009. *Fax:* 727-866-2304. *E-mail:* admissions@eckerd.edu.

Edward Waters College
Jacksonville, Florida
http://www.ewc.edu/

CONTACT
Edward Waters College, 1658 Kings Road, Jacksonville, FL 32209-6199. *Phone:* 904-470-8202. *Toll-free phone:* 888-898-3191.

Embry-Riddle Aeronautical University–Daytona
Daytona Beach, Florida
http://www.daytonabeach.erau.edu/
- **Independent** university, founded 1926
- **Suburban** 289-acre campus with easy access to Orlando
- **Endowment** $90.4 million
- **Coed** 5,984 undergraduate students, 94% full-time, 23% women, 77% men
- **Moderately difficult** entrance level, 65% of applicants were admitted

UNDERGRAD STUDENTS
5,601 full-time, 383 part-time. Students come from 52 states and territories; 97 other countries; 63% are from out of state; 5% Black or African American, non-Hispanic/Latino; 14% Hispanic/Latino; 5% Asian, non-Hispanic/Latino; 0.2% Native Hawaiian or other Pacific Islander, non-Hispanic/Latino; 0.2% American Indian or Alaska Native, non-Hispanic/Latino; 4% Two or more races, non-Hispanic/Latino; 3% Race/ethnicity unknown; 13% international; 3% transferred in; 39% live on campus.

Freshmen:
Admission: 6,017 applied, 3,941 admitted, 1,418 enrolled. *Average high school GPA:* 3.8. *Test scores:* SAT evidence-based reading and writing scores over 500: 93%; SAT math scores over 500: 94%; ACT scores over 18: 96%; SAT evidence-based reading and writing scores over 600: 54%; SAT math scores over 600: 56%; ACT scores over 24: 64%; SAT evidence-based reading and writing scores over 700: 9%; SAT math scores over 700: 17%; ACT scores over 30: 20%.

Retention: 82% of full-time freshmen returned.

ACADEMICS
Calendar: semesters. *Degrees:* associate, bachelor's, master's, doctoral, and postbachelor's certificates.

Special study options: academic remediation for entering students, accelerated degree program, advanced placement credit, cooperative education, double majors, English as a second language, honors programs, internships, part-time degree program, services for LD students, study abroad, summer session for credit. *ROTC:* Army (b), Navy (b), Air Force (b).

Computers: 355 computers/terminals are available on campus for general student use. Students can access the following: campus intranet, computer help desk, free student e-mail accounts, online (class) grades, online (class) registration, online (class) schedules. Campuswide network is available. 100% of college-owned or -operated housing units are wired for high-speed Internet access. Wireless service is available via entire campus.

Library: Jack R. Hunt Memorial Library. *Books:* 53,116 (physical), 122,788 (digital/electronic); *Serial titles:* 456 (physical), 78,964 (digital/electronic); *Databases:* 172. Students can reserve study rooms.

STUDENT LIFE
Housing options: on-campus residence required for freshman year; coed. Campus housing is university owned. Freshman campus housing is guaranteed.

Activities and organizations: drama/theater group, student-run newspaper, radio station, choral group, Eagle Wing, Future Professional Pilots Association, African Student Association, Caribbean Student Association, Sigma Gamma Tau, national fraternities, national sororities.

Athletics Member NCAA, NAIA. All NCAA Division II except men's and women's golf (Division I). *Intercollegiate sports:* baseball M(s), basketball M(s)/W(s), cheerleading M/W, cross-country running M(s)/W(s), golf M(s)/W(s), lacrosse M(s)/W(s), rowing M(s)/W(s), soccer M(s)/W(s), softball W(s), tennis M(s)/W(s), track and field M(s)/W(s), volleyball W(s). *Intramural sports:* archery M(c)/W(c), basketball M(c)/W(c), equestrian sports M(c)/W(c), football M/W, golf M/W, ice hockey M(c), lacrosse M(c), racquetball M(c)/W(c), rowing M(c)/W(c), rugby M(c), soccer M/W, softball M/W, swimming and diving M(c)/W(c), table tennis M/W, tennis M/W, ultimate Frisbee M(c)/W(c), volleyball M/W.

Campus security: 24-hour emergency response devices and patrols, student patrols, late-night transport/escort service, controlled dormitory access.

Student services: health clinic, personal/psychological counseling, women's center, veterans affairs office.

COSTS & FINANCIAL AID
Costs (2019–20) *One-time required fee:* $150. *Comprehensive fee:* $48,614 includes full-time tuition ($35,424), mandatory fees ($1444), and room and board ($11,746). Part-time tuition: $1476 per credit hour. *Required fees:* $722 per term part-time. *College room only:* $7080.

Financial Aid Of all full-time matriculated undergraduates who enrolled in 2018, 3,868 applied for aid, 3,392 were judged to have need. In 2018, 1267 non-need-based awards were made. *Average financial aid package:* $18,528. *Average need-based loan:* $4229. *Average need-based gift aid:* $14,779. *Average non-need-based aid:* $11,104.

APPLYING
Standardized Tests *Recommended:* SAT or ACT (for admission).
Options: electronic application, deferred entrance.
Application fee: $50.
Required: high school transcript, minimum 2.0 GPA. *Required for some:* medical examination for flight students. *Recommended:* essay or personal statement, 2 letters of recommendation.
Application deadlines: rolling (freshmen), rolling (transfers).
Notification: continuous (freshmen), continuous (transfers).

CONTACT
Mr. Pablo A Alvarez, Director, Daytona Beach Admissions, Embry-Riddle Aeronautical University–Daytona, 600 South Clyde Morris Boulevard, Daytona Beach, FL 32114-3900. *Phone:* 386-226-6100. *Toll-free phone:* 800-862-2416. *Fax:* 386-226-7070. *E-mail:* dbadmit@erau.edu.

Embry-Riddle Aeronautical University–Worldwide
Daytona Beach, Florida
http://www.worldwide.erau.edu/
- **Independent** comprehensive, founded 1970
- **Endowment** $3.6 million
- **Coed** 11,671 undergraduate students, 25% full-time, 13% women, 87% men
- **Minimally difficult** entrance level, 59% of applicants were admitted

UNDERGRAD STUDENTS
2,872 full-time, 8,799 part-time. 8% Black or African American, non-Hispanic/Latino; 15% Hispanic/Latino; 5% Asian, non-Hispanic/Latino; 0.9% Native Hawaiian or other Pacific Islander, non-Hispanic/Latino; 0.5% American Indian or Alaska Native, non-Hispanic/Latino; 3% Two or more races, non-Hispanic/Latino; 9% Race/ethnicity unknown; 3% international; 12% transferred in.

Freshmen:
Admission: 1,264 applied, 740 admitted, 653 enrolled.

ACADEMICS
Calendar: 5 9-week terms with monthly starts. *Degrees:* certificates, associate, bachelor's, master's, doctoral, and postbachelor's certificates (programs offered at 100 military bases worldwide).
Special study options: accelerated degree program, advanced placement credit, cooperative education, distance learning, double majors, external degree program, independent study, off-campus study, part-time degree program, services for LD students, study abroad, summer session for credit. *ROTC:* Army (b), Navy (b), Air Force (b).
Computers: Students can access the following: free student e-mail accounts, online (class) grades, online (class) registration, online (class) schedules, ERAU Worldwide does not have a physical campus; courses are offered online and at military bases worldwide. Worldwide students may use residential campus facilities.
Library: Jack R. Hunt Memorial Library located in Daytona Beach. *Books:* 53,116 (physical), 122,788 (digital/electronic); *Serial titles:* 456 (physical), 78,964 (digital/electronic); *Databases:* 172.

STUDENT LIFE
Student services: veterans affairs office.

COSTS & FINANCIAL AID
Costs (2019–20) *Tuition:* $413 per credit hour part-time.
Financial Aid Of all full-time matriculated undergraduates who enrolled in 2017, 1,166 applied for aid, 1,116 were judged to have need. *Average financial aid package:* $5326. *Average need-based loan:* $4402. *Average need-based gift aid:* $4534.

APPLYING
Standardized Tests *Required for some:* SAT or ACT (for admission).
Options: electronic application, deferred entrance.
Application fee: $50.
Required: minimum 2.0 GPA. *Required for some:* high school transcript, 2 letters of recommendation.
Application deadlines: rolling (freshmen), rolling (transfers).
Notification: continuous (freshmen), continuous (transfers).

CONTACT
Ms. Valerie Kisseloff, Director of Admissions, Embry-Riddle Aeronautical University–Worldwide, 600 South Clyde Morris Boulevard, Daytona Beach, FL 32114-3900. *Phone:* 800-522-6787. *Toll-free phone:* 800-522-6787. *Fax:* 386-226-6984. *E-mail:* worldwide@erau.edu.

Everglades University
Boca Raton, Florida
http://www.evergladesuniversity.edu/
CONTACT
Everglades University, 5002 T-Rex Avenue, Suite 100, Boca Raton, FL 33431. *Phone:* 561-912-1211. *Toll-free phone:* 888-772-6077.

Everglades University
Maitland, Florida
http://www.evergladesuniversity.edu/
CONTACT
Everglades University, 850 Trafalgar Court, Suite 100, Maitland, FL 32751. *Phone:* 407-277-0311. *Toll-free phone:* 866-289-1078.

Everglades University
Sarasota, Florida
http://www.evergladesuniversity.edu/
CONTACT
Everglades University, 6001 Lake Osprey Drive #110, Sarasota, FL 34240. *Phone:* 866-289-1078. *Toll-free phone:* 888-854-8308.

Flagler College
St. Augustine, Florida
http://www.flagler.edu/
- **Independent** comprehensive, founded 1968
- **Small-town** 49-acre campus with easy access to Jacksonville
- **Endowment** $49.0 million
- **Coed**
- 57% of applicants were admitted

FACULTY
Student/faculty ratio: 16:1.

ACADEMICS
Calendar: semesters. *Degrees:* bachelor's and master's.
Library: Proctor Library. *Books:* 102,047 (physical), 212,689 (digital/electronic); *Serial titles:* 630 (physical), 44,000 (digital/electronic); *Databases:* 60. Weekly public service hours: 100; students can reserve study rooms.

STUDENT LIFE
Housing options: men-only, women-only. Campus housing is university owned. Freshman campus housing is guaranteed.
Activities and organizations: drama/theater group, student-run newspaper, radio station, choral group, Student Government Association, Inter-Varsity, International Student Club, Flagler College Volunteers, Phi Alpha Omega (women's service club).

Athletics Member NCAA. All Division II.

Campus security: 24-hour emergency response devices and patrols, student patrols, late-night transport/escort service, controlled dormitory access, transport/escort service is provided from 6:00 pm until 6:00 am daily.

Student services: health clinic, personal/psychological counseling.

COSTS & FINANCIAL AID

Costs (2018–19) *Comprehensive fee:* $30,290 includes full-time tuition ($18,850), mandatory fees ($100), and room and board ($11,340). Full-time tuition and fees vary according to location. Part-time tuition: $645 per credit hour. Part-time tuition and fees vary according to location. *College room only:* $5800. Room and board charges vary according to board plan and housing facility.

Financial Aid Of all full-time matriculated undergraduates who enrolled in 2017, 2,074 applied for aid, 1,679 were judged to have need, 233 had their need fully met. In 2017, 551 non-need-based awards were made. *Average percent of need met:* 59. *Average financial aid package:* $13,564. *Average need-based loan:* $4316. *Average need-based gift aid:* $9579. *Average non-need-based aid:* $2785. *Average indebtedness upon graduation:* $29,705.

APPLYING

Standardized Tests *Required:* SAT or ACT (for admission).

Options: electronic application, early admission, early decision, deferred entrance.

Application fee: $50.

Required: essay or personal statement, high school transcript, letters of recommendation. *Required for some:* interview, interview for early admission.

CONTACT

Ms. Rachel Branch, Director of Admissions, Flagler College, 74 King Street, St. Augustine, FL 32085. *Phone:* 904-819-6294. *Toll-free phone:* 800-304-4208. *Fax:* 904-819-6466. *E-mail:* rbranch@flagler.edu.

Flagler College–Tallahassee

Tallahassee, Florida
http://www.flagler.edu/

CONTACT
Flagler College–Tallahassee, 444 Appleyard Drive, Tallahassee, FL 32304.

Florida Agricultural and Mechanical University

Tallahassee, Florida
http://www.famu.edu/

- **State-supported** university, founded 1887, part of State University System of Florida
- **Urban** 419-acre campus with easy access to Jacksonville
- **Endowment** $96.4 million
- **Coed** 8,137 undergraduate students, 86% full-time, 65% women, 35% men
- **Moderately difficult** entrance level, 39% of applicants were admitted

UNDERGRAD STUDENTS

6,958 full-time, 1,179 part-time. Students come from 42 states and territories; 43 other countries; 14% are from out of state; 85% Black or African American, non-Hispanic/Latino; 4% Hispanic/Latino; 0.6% Asian, non-Hispanic/Latino; 4% Two or more races, non-Hispanic/Latino; 0.5% international; 6% transferred in; 30% live on campus.

Freshmen:
Admission: 8,976 applied, 3,488 admitted, 1,430 enrolled. *Average high school GPA:* 3.4. *Test scores:* SAT evidence-based reading and writing scores over 500: 95%; SAT math scores over 500: 87%; ACT scores over 18: 88%; SAT evidence-based reading and writing scores over 600: 25%; SAT math scores over 600: 17%; ACT scores over 24: 21%; SAT evidence-based reading and writing scores over 700: 1%; SAT math scores over 700: 1%; ACT scores over 30: 1%.

Retention: 81% of full-time freshmen returned.

FACULTY
Total: 682, 79% full-time, 57% with terminal degrees.
Student/faculty ratio: 16:1.

ACADEMICS
Calendar: semesters. *Degrees:* associate, bachelor's, master's, doctoral, and post-master's certificates.

Special study options: academic remediation for entering students, accelerated degree program, adult/continuing education programs, advanced placement credit, cooperative education, distance learning, double majors, honors programs, independent study, internships, off-campus study, part-time degree program, services for LD students, study abroad, summer session for credit. *ROTC:* Army (b), Navy (b), Air Force (c).

Unusual degree programs: 3-2 business administration; occupational therapy, architecture.

Computers: 4,000 computers/terminals and 8,000 ports are available on campus for general student use. Students can access the following: campus intranet, computer help desk, free student e-mail accounts, online (class) grades, online (class) registration, online (class) schedules. Campuswide network is available. 100% of college-owned or -operated housing units are wired for high-speed Internet access. Wireless service is available via classrooms, computer centers, computer labs, dorm rooms, learning centers, libraries, student centers.

Library: Samuel H. Coleman Memorial Library plus 4 others. *Books:* 1.1 million (physical), 468,561 (digital/electronic); *Serial titles:* 17,167 (physical), 240,002 (digital/electronic); *Databases:* 314. Weekly public service hours: 135; study areas open 24 hours, 5–7 days a week; students can reserve study rooms.

STUDENT LIFE
Housing options: on-campus residence required for freshman year; coed, men-only, women-only, special housing for students with disabilities. Campus housing is university owned. Freshman applicants given priority for college housing.

Activities and organizations: drama/theater group, student-run newspaper, radio and television station, choral group, marching band, National Council of Negro Women, FAMU Chapter, American Society of Mechanical Engineers, Psi Chi International Honor Society, Caribbean Student Association, Academy of Student Pharmacists/Student National Pharmaceutical Association, national fraternities, national sororities.

Athletics Member NCAA. All Division I except football (Division I-AA). *Intercollegiate sports:* baseball M(s), basketball M(s)/W(s), bowling W(s), cheerleading M/W, cross-country running M(s)/W(s), golf M(s)/W(s)(c), softball W(s), swimming and diving M(s)/W(s), tennis M(s)/W(s), track and field M(s)/W(s), volleyball W(s). *Intramural sports:* badminton M/W, basketball M/W, bowling M/W, cheerleading W, football M, golf M/W, gymnastics M/W, racquetball M/W, skiing (downhill) M/W, soccer M/W, softball M/W, swimming and diving M/W, table tennis M/W, tennis M/W, track and field M/W, ultimate Frisbee M/W, volleyball M/W, weight lifting M/W, wrestling M/W.

Campus security: 24-hour emergency response devices and patrols, late-night transport/escort service, controlled dormitory access.

Student services: health clinic, personal/psychological counseling.

COSTS & FINANCIAL AID
Costs (2019–20) *Tuition:* state resident $5645 full-time, $188 per credit hour part-time; nonresident $17,585 full-time. *Required fees:* $140 full-time. *Room and board:* $10,838; room only: $6012. *Payment plan:* tuition prepayment.

Financial Aid Of all full-time matriculated undergraduates who enrolled in 2016, 6,306 applied for aid, 5,593 were judged to have need, 613 had their need fully met. 240 Federal Work-Study jobs (averaging $1913). In 2016, 163 non-need-based awards were made. *Average percent of need met:* 62. *Average financial aid package:* $13,408. *Average need-based loan:* $4036. *Average need-based gift aid:* $5899. *Average non-need-based aid:* $10,014. *Average indebtedness upon graduation:* $7454.

APPLYING
Standardized Tests *Required:* SAT or ACT (for admission).
Options: electronic application, early admission.
Application fee: $30.

Required: essay or personal statement, high school transcript, minimum 2.5 GPA, 3 letters of recommendation. *Required for some:* interview, audition for music major applicants. *Recommended:* minimum 3.0 GPA.

Notification: continuous (freshmen), continuous (transfers).

CONTACT
Ms. Chestr Hood, Director, Admissions, Florida Agricultural and Mechanical University, Office of Admissions, Tallahassee, FL 32307. *Phone:* 850-599-3796. *Toll-free phone:* 866-642-1198. *Fax:* 850-599-3069. *E-mail:* ugrdadmissions@famu.edu.

Florida Atlantic University
Boca Raton, Florida
http://www.fau.edu/
- **State-supported** university, founded 1961, part of State University System of Florida
- **Suburban** 850-acre campus with easy access to Miami, Fort Lauderdale, West Palm Beach
- **Endowment** $299.3 million
- **Coed** 24,569 undergraduate students, 67% full-time, 56% women, 44% men
- **Moderately difficult** entrance level, 59% of applicants were admitted

UNDERGRAD STUDENTS
16,443 full-time, 8,126 part-time. Students come from 47 states and territories; 119 other countries; 6% are from out of state; 20% Black or African American, non-Hispanic/Latino; 28% Hispanic/Latino; 4% Asian, non-Hispanic/Latino; 0.1% Native Hawaiian or other Pacific Islander, non-Hispanic/Latino; 0.2% American Indian or Alaska Native, non-Hispanic/Latino; 4% Two or more races, non-Hispanic/Latino; 0.9% Race/ethnicity unknown; 3% international; 9% transferred in; 19% live on campus.

Freshmen:
Admission: 17,120 applied, 10,156 admitted, 3,152 enrolled. *Average high school GPA:* 4.0. *Test scores:* SAT evidence-based reading and writing scores over 500: 96%; SAT math scores over 500: 92%; ACT scores over 18: 99%; SAT evidence-based reading and writing scores over 600: 42%; SAT math scores over 600: 31%; ACT scores over 24: 44%; SAT evidence-based reading and writing scores over 700: 4%; SAT math scores over 700: 4%; ACT scores over 30: 7%.

Retention: 82% of full-time freshmen returned.

FACULTY
Total: 1,473, 62% full-time, 69% with terminal degrees.
Student/faculty ratio: 24:1.

ACADEMICS
Calendar: semesters. *Degrees:* certificates, associate, bachelor's, master's, doctoral, and post-master's certificates.

Special study options: accelerated degree program, adult/continuing education programs, advanced placement credit, cooperative education, distance learning, double majors, English as a second language, freshman honors college, honors programs, independent study, internships, off-campus study, part-time degree program, services for LD students, study abroad, summer session for credit. *ROTC:* Army (b), Air Force (c).

Unusual degree programs: 3-2 business administration; engineering; nursing; architecture, mathematics.

Computers: 1,350 computers/terminals are available on campus for general student use. Students can access the following: campus intranet, computer help desk, free student e-mail accounts, online (class) grades, online (class) registration, online (class) schedules. Campuswide network is available. 100% of college-owned or -operated housing units are wired for high-speed Internet access. Wireless service is available via entire campus.
Library: S. E. Wimberly Library plus 2 others. *Books:* 907,932 (physical), 1.3 million (digital/electronic); *Serial titles:* 31,489 (physical), 194,584 (digital/electronic); *Databases:* 628. Study areas open 24 hours, 5–7 days a week.

STUDENT LIFE
Housing options: on-campus residence required for freshman year; coed. Campus housing is university owned. Freshman campus housing is guaranteed.

Activities and organizations: drama/theater group, student-run newspaper, radio and television station, choral group, marching band, American Society of Civil Engineers, Dive Club, Pre-Law Society, Submarine Club, American Criminal Justice Society, national fraternities, national sororities.

Athletics Member NCAA. All Division I. *Intercollegiate sports:* baseball M(s), basketball M(s)/W(s), cheerleading M/W, cross-country running M/W, football M(s), golf M(s)/W(s)(c), soccer M/W, softball W(s), swimming and diving M/W, tennis M/W, track and field W, volleyball W(s). *Intramural sports:* baseball M/W, bowling M/W, football M, ice hockey M(c)/W(c), lacrosse M(c), rock climbing M(c)/W(c), rugby M(c)/W(c), sailing M(c)/W(c), soccer M/W, softball W, table tennis M/W, ultimate Frisbee M/W, volleyball M/W, weight lifting M(c), wrestling M(c).

Campus security: 24-hour emergency response devices and patrols, student patrols, late-night transport/escort service, controlled dormitory access.

Student services: health clinic, personal/psychological counseling, women's center, veterans affairs office.

COSTS & FINANCIAL AID
Costs (2019–20) *Tuition:* state resident $6039 full-time, $105 per credit hour part-time; nonresident $21,595 full-time, $599 per credit hour part-time. *Required fees:* $96 part-time. *Room and board:* $11,950; room only: $8238.

Financial Aid Of all full-time matriculated undergraduates who enrolled in 2018, 11,737 applied for aid, 9,722 were judged to have need, 1,099 had their need fully met. 324 Federal Work-Study jobs (averaging $2346). 6 state and other part-time jobs (averaging $2256). In 2018, 177 non-need-based awards were made. *Average percent of need met:* 62. *Average financial aid package:* $13,887. *Average need-based loan:* $6918. *Average need-based gift aid:* $7714. *Average non-need-based aid:* $3678. *Average indebtedness upon graduation:* $23,454.

APPLYING
Standardized Tests *Required:* SAT or ACT (for admission).
Options: electronic application, early admission, deferred entrance.
Application fee: $30.
Required: high school transcript.
Notification: continuous (freshmen), continuous (transfers).

CONTACT
Ms. Maura Flaschner, Executive Director, Undergraduate Admissions, Florida Atlantic University, 777 Glades Road, Boca Raton, FL 33431-0991. *Phone:* 561-297-3040. *Fax:* 561-297-2758. *E-mail:* admissions@fau.edu.

Florida College
Temple Terrace, Florida
http://www.floridacollege.edu/
- **Independent** 4-year, founded 1944
- **Suburban** 95-acre campus with easy access to Tampa
- **Endowment** $16.5 million
- **Coed** 516 undergraduate students, 96% full-time, 53% women, 47% men
- **Moderately difficult** entrance level, 74% of applicants were admitted

UNDERGRAD STUDENTS
494 full-time, 22 part-time. Students come from 34 states and territories; 6 other countries; 7% Black or African American, non-Hispanic/Latino; 7% Hispanic/Latino; 1% Asian, non-Hispanic/Latino; 0.8% American Indian or Alaska Native, non-Hispanic/Latino; 5% Two or more races, non-Hispanic/Latino; 0.4% Race/ethnicity unknown; 2% international; 81% live on campus.

Freshmen:
Admission: 331 applied, 244 admitted, 204 enrolled. *Test scores:* SAT evidence-based reading and writing scores over 500: 57%; SAT math scores over 500: 57%; ACT scores over 18: 83%; SAT evidence-based reading and writing scores over 600: 33%; SAT math scores over 600: 19%; ACT scores over 24: 48%; SAT evidence-based reading and writing scores over 700: 14%; SAT math scores over 700: 5%; ACT scores over 30: 10%.

FACULTY
Total: 52, 65% full-time, 44% with terminal degrees.
Student/faculty ratio: 13:1.

ACADEMICS
Calendar: semesters. *Degrees:* associate and bachelor's.
Special study options: academic remediation for entering students, advanced placement credit, independent study, summer session for credit.
ROTC: Army (c), Air Force (c).
Computers: 85 computers/terminals are available on campus for general student use. Students can access the following: campus intranet, computer help desk, free student e-mail accounts, online (class) grades, online (class) schedules. Campuswide network is available. 100% of college-owned or -operated housing units are wired for high-speed Internet access. Wireless service is available via classrooms, computer centers, computer labs, dorm rooms, libraries, student centers.
Library: Chatlos Library.

STUDENT LIFE
Housing options: on-campus residence required through sophomore year; men-only, women-only. Campus housing is university owned. Freshman campus housing is guaranteed.
Activities and organizations: drama/theater group, choral group, Co-ed Societies, ROTARACT CLUB, NAFME, SBGA, Footlighters.
Athletics Member NAIA, USCAA. *Intercollegiate sports:* basketball M(s)/W, cheerleading W, cross-country running M/W, soccer M(s)/W(s), volleyball W(s). *Intramural sports:* basketball M/W, football M/W, soccer M/W, softball M/W, ultimate Frisbee M/W, volleyball M/W.
Campus security: controlled dormitory access.
Student services: health clinic, personal/psychological counseling.

FINANCIAL AID
Financial Aid Of all full-time matriculated undergraduates who enrolled in 2015, 434 applied for aid, 372 were judged to have need, 41 had their need fully met. 35 Federal Work-Study jobs (averaging $665). In 2015, 75 non-need-based awards were made. *Average percent of need met:* 56. *Average financial aid package:* $10,644. *Average need-based loan:* $4113. *Average need-based gift aid:* $7068. *Average non-need-based aid:* $4048.

APPLYING
Standardized Tests *Required:* SAT or ACT (for admission).
Options: electronic application.
Application fee: $40.
Required: high school transcript, minimum 2.0 GPA, 2 letters of recommendation. *Required for some:* essay for international students.
Notification: continuous (freshmen), continuous (transfers).

CONTACT
Mrs. Colleen Engel, Assistant Director of Admissions, Florida College, 119 North Glen Arven Avenue, Temple Terrace, FL 33617. *Phone:* 813-988-5131 Ext. 152. *Fax:* 813-899-1799. *E-mail:* admissions@floridacollege.edu.

Florida Gateway College
Lake City, Florida
http://www.fgc.edu/

CONTACT
Admissions, Florida Gateway College, 149 SE College Place, Lake City, FL 32025-8703. *Phone:* 386-755-4236. *E-mail:* admissions@fgc.edu.

Florida Gulf Coast University
Fort Myers, Florida
http://www.fgcu.edu/
- **State-supported** comprehensive, founded 1991, part of State University System of Florida
- **Suburban** 760-acre campus
- **Endowment** $72.9 million
- **Coed**
- **Moderately difficult** entrance level

FACULTY
Student/faculty ratio: 22:1.

ACADEMICS
Calendar: semesters. *Degrees:* certificates, associate, bachelor's, master's, doctoral, and post-master's certificates.
Library: Library Services plus 1 other. *Books:* 242,131 (physical), 73,000 (digital/electronic); *Serial titles:* 128,865 (digital/electronic); *Databases:* 389. Students can reserve study rooms.

STUDENT LIFE
Housing options: coed. Campus housing is university owned.
Activities and organizations: drama/theater group, student-run newspaper, Student Government, Ignite (Religious Organization), International Club, Martial Arts Club, Physical Therapy Association, national fraternities, national sororities.
Athletics Member NCAA. All Division I.
Campus security: 24-hour emergency response devices and patrols, late-night transport/escort service.
Student services: health clinic, personal/psychological counseling.

COSTS & FINANCIAL AID
Costs (2018–19) *Tuition:* state resident $4191 full-time; nonresident $22,328 full-time. Full-time tuition and fees vary according to course load. Part-time tuition and fees vary according to course load. *Required fees:* $1927 full-time. *Room and board:* $8620; room only: $4820. Room and board charges vary according to board plan.
Financial Aid Of all full-time matriculated undergraduates who enrolled in 2017, 7,481 applied for aid, 4,735 were judged to have need, 507 had their need fully met. 245 Federal Work-Study jobs (averaging $1658). 9 state and other part-time jobs (averaging $2030). In 2017, 530 non-need-based awards were made. *Average percent of need met:* 64. *Average financial aid package:* $10,693. *Average need-based loan:* $7179. *Average need-based gift aid:* $7021. *Average non-need-based aid:* $2661. *Average indebtedness upon graduation:* $26,488. *Financial aid deadline:* 6/30.

APPLYING
Standardized Tests *Required:* SAT or ACT (for admission).
Options: electronic application, deferred entrance.
Application fee: $30.
Required: high school transcript, minimum 2.5 GPA.

CONTACT
Florida Gulf Coast University, 10501 FGCU Boulevard South, Fort Myers, FL 33965-6565. *Phone:* 239-590-7878. *Toll-free phone:* 888-889-1095.

Florida Institute of Technology
Melbourne, Florida
http://www.fit.edu/
- **Independent** university, founded 1958
- **Suburban** 130-acre campus with easy access to Orlando
- **Coed**
- **Moderately difficult** entrance level

FACULTY
Student/faculty ratio: 15:1.

ACADEMICS
Calendar: semesters. *Degrees:* bachelor's, master's, doctoral, and post-master's certificates.
Library: Evans Library. *Books:* 131,564 (physical), 728,454 (digital/electronic); *Serial titles:* 1,605 (physical), 56,994 (digital/electronic); *Databases:* 161. Weekly public service hours: 96; students can reserve study rooms.

STUDENT LIFE
Housing options: on-campus residence required through sophomore year; coed. Campus housing is university owned. Freshman campus housing is guaranteed.
Activities and organizations: drama/theater group, student-run newspaper, radio and television station, choral group, Florida Institute of Technology Society for Science Fiction and Fantasy (FITSSFF), International Student Services Organization (ISSO), Student Government

Association (SGA), Surf Club, Campus Activities Board, national fraternities, national sororities.

Athletics Member NCAA. All Division II.

Campus security: 24-hour emergency response devices and patrols, late-night transport/escort service, controlled dormitory access.

Student services: health clinic, personal/psychological counseling, women's center, veterans affairs office.

COSTS & FINANCIAL AID

Costs (2018–19) *Comprehensive fee:* $54,730 includes full-time tuition ($41,100), mandatory fees ($750), and room and board ($12,880). Full-time tuition and fees vary according to course load and program. Part-time tuition: $1170 per credit hour. *College room only:* $7000. Room and board charges vary according to board plan and housing facility.

Financial Aid Of all full-time matriculated undergraduates who enrolled in 2018, 2,006 applied for aid, 1,800 were judged to have need, 575 had their need fully met. 488 Federal Work-Study jobs (averaging $2500). 415 state and other part-time jobs (averaging $2000). In 2018, 921 non-need-based awards were made. *Average percent of need met:* 85. *Average financial aid package:* $39,736. *Average need-based loan:* $3827. *Average need-based gift aid:* $27,526. *Average non-need-based aid:* $14,908. *Average indebtedness upon graduation:* $33,511.

APPLYING

Standardized Tests *Required:* SAT or ACT (for admission).

Options: electronic application, deferred entrance.

Required: essay or personal statement, high school transcript, minimum 2.6 GPA, 1 letter of recommendation. *Recommended:* minimum 3.3 GPA, interview.

CONTACT

Florida Institute of Technology, 150 West University Boulevard, Melbourne, FL 32901-6975. *Toll-free phone:* 800-888-4348.

Florida International University
Miami, Florida
http://www.fiu.edu/

- **State-supported** university, founded 1965, part of State University System of Florida
- **Urban** 576-acre campus with easy access to Miami
- **Endowment** $196.3 million
- **Coed**
- **Moderately difficult** entrance level

FACULTY
Student/faculty ratio: 25:1.

ACADEMICS
Calendar: semesters. *Degrees:* bachelor's, master's, doctoral, and postbachelor's certificates.
Library: Steven and Dorothea Green Library plus 4 others. *Books:* 1.5 million (physical), 443,863 (digital/electronic); *Serial titles:* 63,945 (physical), 111,662 (digital/electronic); *Databases:* 808. Weekly public service hours: 112; students can reserve study rooms.

STUDENT LIFE
Housing options: coed. Campus housing is university owned.

Activities and organizations: drama/theater group, student-run newspaper, radio station, choral group, marching band, Students for Community Service, Black Student Leadership Council, Hospitality Management Student Club, Hispanic Students Association, Haitian Students Organization, national fraternities, national sororities.

Athletics Member NCAA. All Division I.

Campus security: 24-hour emergency response devices and patrols, late-night transport/escort service, controlled dormitory access.

Student services: health clinic, personal/psychological counseling, women's center.

COSTS & FINANCIAL AID
Costs (2018–19) *Tuition:* state resident $6168 full-time, $205 per credit hour part-time; nonresident $18,566 full-time, $619 per credit hour part-time. *Required fees:* $390 full-time. *Room and board:* $10,882; room only: $6984. Room and board charges vary according to board plan and housing facility.

Financial Aid Of all full-time matriculated undergraduates who enrolled in 2017, 18,765 applied for aid, 18,522 were judged to have need, 1,845 had their need fully met. In 2017, 1096 non-need-based awards were made. *Average percent of need met:* 28. *Average financial aid package:* $9512. *Average need-based loan:* $4539. *Average need-based gift aid:* $6896. *Average non-need-based aid:* $2247. *Average indebtedness upon graduation:* $19,923. *Financial aid deadline:* 5/15.

APPLYING
Standardized Tests *Required:* SAT or ACT (for admission). *Required for some:* TOEFL for applicants whose native language is not English.

Options: electronic application.

Application fee: $30.

Required: high school transcript. *Required for some:* portfolio or audition.

CONTACT
Ms. Jody Glassman, Director of Admissions, Florida International University, 11200 SW Eighth Street, PC 140, Miami, FL 33199. *Phone:* 305-348-3662. *E-mail:* admiss@fiu.edu.

Florida Keys Community College
Key West, Florida
http://www.fkcc.edu/

- **State-supported** primarily 2-year, founded 1965, part of Florida College System
- **Small-town** 20-acre campus
- **Coed**
- **Noncompetitive** entrance level

FACULTY
Student/faculty ratio: 12:1.

ACADEMICS
Calendar: semesters. *Degrees:* certificates, associate, and bachelor's.
Library: Florida Keys Community College Library. Students can reserve study rooms.

STUDENT LIFE
Housing options: coed. Campus housing is university owned.

Activities and organizations: choral group.

Campus security: 24-hour patrols.

Student services: personal/psychological counseling, veterans affairs office.

COSTS & FINANCIAL AID
Costs (2018–19) *Tuition:* state resident $2483 full-time, $109 per credit hour part-time; nonresident $9933 full-time, $439 per credit hour part-time. Full-time tuition and fees vary according to degree level. Part-time tuition and fees vary according to degree level. *Required fees:* $793 full-time. *Room only:* $10,508. Room and board charges vary according to board plan.

Financial Aid Of all full-time matriculated undergraduates who enrolled in 2017, 30 Federal Work-Study jobs (averaging $2000).

APPLYING
Options: electronic application, early admission, deferred entrance.
Application fee: $30.

Required for some: essay or personal statement, high school transcript, letters of recommendation.

CONTACT
Florida Keys Community College, 5901 College Road, Key West, FL 33040-4397. *Phone:* 305-296-9081 Ext. 237.

Florida Memorial University
Miami-Dade, Florida
http://www.fmuniv.edu/

CONTACT
Mrs. Peggy Murray Martin, Director of Admissions and International Student Advisor, Florida Memorial University, 15800 NW 42nd Avenue, Miami-Dade, FL 33054. *Phone:* 305-626-3147. *Toll-free phone:* 800-822-1362.

Florida National University

Hialeah, Florida
http://www.fnu.edu/
- **Proprietary** comprehensive, founded 1982
- **Urban** 4-acre campus with easy access to Miami
- **Coed**
- **Moderately difficult** entrance level

FACULTY
Student/faculty ratio: 31:1.

ACADEMICS
Calendar: semesters. *Degrees:* certificates, diplomas, associate, bachelor's, master's, post-master's, and postbachelor's certificates. **Library:** Hialeah Campus Library plus 1 other. *Books:* 21,521 (physical), 144,218 (digital/electronic); *Serial titles:* 55 (physical), 196,357 (digital/electronic); *Databases:* 32. Weekly public service hours: 69; students can reserve study rooms.

STUDENT LIFE
Housing options: college housing not available.

Activities and organizations: student-run newspaper, Student Government Association, Bible Club, Salsa Club, W.I.C.S (Women Community Service), Criminal Justice Society, national fraternities.

Athletics Member USCAA.

Campus security: 24-hour emergency response devices.

COSTS & FINANCIAL AID
Costs (2018–19) *Tuition:* $13,200 full-time, $550 per credit hour part-time. No tuition increase for student's term of enrollment. *Required fees:* $488 full-time. *Payment plans:* tuition prepayment, installment.

Financial Aid Of all full-time matriculated undergraduates who enrolled in 2017, 2,475 applied for aid, 2,351 were judged to have need. 25 Federal Work-Study jobs (averaging $3700). *Average indebtedness upon graduation:* $11,083.

APPLYING
Standardized Tests *Required:* SAT or ACT (for admission).

Options: electronic application, deferred entrance.

Required: high school transcript, interview.

CONTACT
Mr. Robert Lopez, Director of Admissions, Florida National University, 4425 W. Jose Regueiro (20th) Avenue, Hialeah, FL 33012. *Phone:* 305-821-3333. *Fax:* 305-362-0595. *E-mail:* rlopez@fnu.edu.

Florida Polytechnic University

Lakeland, Florida
http://www.floridapoly.edu/

CONTACT
Florida Polytechnic University, 4700 Research Way, Lakeland, FL 33805.

Florida Southern College

Lakeland, Florida
http://www.flsouthern.edu/
- **Independent** comprehensive, founded 1885, affiliated with United Methodist Church
- **Suburban** 113-acre campus with easy access to Tampa, Orlando
- **Endowment** $91.4 million
- **Coed** 2,723 undergraduate students, 92% full-time, 65% women, 35% men
- **Moderately difficult** entrance level, 50% of applicants were admitted

UNDERGRAD STUDENTS
2,502 full-time, 221 part-time. Students come from 48 states and territories; 46 other countries; 35% are from out of state; 6% Black or African American, non-Hispanic/Latino; 12% Hispanic/Latino; 3% Asian, non-Hispanic/Latino; 0.1% Native Hawaiian or other Pacific Islander, non-Hispanic/Latino; 1% American Indian or Alaska Native, non-Hispanic/Latino; 0.6% Two or more races, non-Hispanic/Latino; 2% Race/ethnicity unknown; 3% international; 3% transferred in; 79% live on campus.

Freshmen:
Admission: 7,254 applied, 3,644 admitted, 707 enrolled. *Average high school GPA:* 3.8. *Test scores:* SAT evidence-based reading and writing scores over 500: 99%; SAT math scores over 500: 98%; ACT scores over 18: 100%; SAT evidence-based reading and writing scores over 600: 60%; SAT math scores over 600: 47%; ACT scores over 24: 72%; SAT evidence-based reading and writing scores over 700: 9%; SAT math scores over 700: 7%; ACT scores over 30: 14%.

Retention: 82% of full-time freshmen returned.

FACULTY
Total: 317, 47% full-time, 59% with terminal degrees.
Student/faculty ratio: 15:1.

ACADEMICS
Calendar: semesters. *Degrees:* bachelor's, master's, doctoral, and post-master's certificates.

Special study options: accelerated degree program, adult/continuing education programs, advanced placement credit, distance learning, double majors, external degree program, honors programs, independent study, internships, off-campus study, part-time degree program, student-designed majors, study abroad, summer session for credit. *ROTC:* Army (b), Air Force (c).

Unusual degree programs: 3-2 business administration; engineering with Washington University in St. Louis; environmental science with Duke University, accounting/accountancy with Florida Southern College, medicine with Lake Erie College of Osteopathic Medicine.

Computers: 490 computers/terminals and 65 ports are available on campus for general student use. Students can access the following: campus intranet, computer help desk, free student e-mail accounts, online (class) grades, online (class) registration, online (class) schedules, campus portal. Campuswide network is available. 100% of college-owned or -operated housing units are wired for high-speed Internet access. Wireless service is available via entire campus.

Library: Roux Library plus 1 other. *Books:* 160,667 (physical), 167,731 (digital/electronic); *Serial titles:* 22 (physical), 97,772 (digital/electronic); *Databases:* 118. Weekly public service hours: 104; students can reserve study rooms.

STUDENT LIFE
Housing options: on-campus residence required through senior year; coed, men-only, women-only, special housing for students with disabilities. Campus housing is university owned. Freshman campus housing is guaranteed.

Activities and organizations: drama/theater group, student-run newspaper, television station, choral group, Astronomy Club, FLoSoCo, Beyond (Campus Ministry), ACE, Garden Club, national fraternities, national sororities.

Athletics Member NCAA. All Division II except golf (Division I), sand volleyball (Division I). *Intercollegiate sports:* baseball M(s), basketball M(s)/W(s), cheerleading W(c), cross-country running M(s)/W(s), equestrian sports W(c), golf M(s)/W(s), ice hockey M(c), lacrosse M(s)/W(s), sand volleyball W(s), soccer M(s)/W(s), softball W(s), swimming and diving M(s)/W(s), tennis M(s)/W(s), track and field M/W, volleyball W(s). *Intramural sports:* basketball M/W, bowling M/W, football M/W, soccer M/W, softball M/W, swimming and diving M/W, tennis M/W, ultimate Frisbee M/W, volleyball M/W, water polo M/W.

Campus security: 24-hour emergency response devices and patrols, student patrols, late-night transport/escort service, controlled dormitory access.

Student services: health clinic, personal/psychological counseling.

COSTS & FINANCIAL AID
Costs (2018–19) *One-time required fee:* $100. *Comprehensive fee:* $48,018 includes full-time tuition ($35,600), mandatory fees ($748), and room and board ($11,670). Part-time tuition: $998 per credit hour. Part-time tuition and fees vary according to class time and course load. *College room only:* $7070. Room and board charges vary according to board plan and housing facility. *Payment plan:* installment. *Waivers:* children of alumni and employees or children of employees.

Financial Aid Of all full-time matriculated undergraduates who enrolled in 2018, 1,920 applied for aid, 1,653 were judged to have need, 455 had their need fully met. 172 Federal Work-Study jobs (averaging $2260). In 2018, 771 non-need-based awards were made. *Average percent of need* *met:* 77. *Average financial aid package:* $31,099. *Average need-based loan:* $5293. *Average need-based gift aid:* $24,633. *Average non-need-based aid:* $24,106. *Average indebtedness upon graduation:* $28,974. *Financial aid deadline:* 7/1.

APPLYING
Standardized Tests *Required:* SAT or ACT (for admission).

Options: electronic application, early admission, early decision, deferred entrance.

Required: high school transcript, minimum 2.0 GPA, 1 letter of recommendation. *Recommended:* essay or personal statement, interview.

Application deadlines: 5/1 (freshmen), 5/1 (out-of-state freshmen), rolling (transfers).

Early decision deadline: 11/1.

Notification: continuous (freshmen), continuous (out-of-state freshmen), continuous (transfers), 12/1 (early decision).

CONTACT
Ms. Arden Mitchell, Director of Admissions, Florida Southern College, 111 Lake Hollingsworth Drive, Lakeland, FL 33801-5698. *Phone:* 863-680-4131. *Toll-free phone:* 800-274-4131. *Fax:* 863-680-4120. *E-mail:* amitchell@flsouthern.edu.

Florida SouthWestern State College

Fort Myers, Florida
http://www.fsw.edu/

CONTACT
FSW Admissions, Florida SouthWestern State College, 8099 College Parkway, Fort Myers, FL 33919. *Phone:* 239-489-9054. *Fax:* 239-489-9094. *E-mail:* admissions@fsw.edu.

Florida State College at Jacksonville

Jacksonville, Florida
http://www.fscj.edu/

CONTACT
Dr. Peter Biegel, Registrar, Florida State College at Jacksonville, 501 West State Street, Jacksonville, FL 32202. *Phone:* 904-632-5112. *Toll-free phone:* 888-873-1145. *E-mail:* pbiegel@fscj.edu.

Florida State University

Tallahassee, Florida
http://www.fsu.edu/
- **State-supported** university, founded 1851, part of State University System of Florida
- **Suburban** 477-acre campus
- **Endowment** $639.4 million
- **Coed**
- **Very difficult** entrance level

FACULTY
Student/faculty ratio: 22:1.

ACADEMICS
Calendar: semesters. *Degrees:* certificates, associate, bachelor's, master's, doctoral, post-master's, and postbachelor's certificates.
Library: Robert Manning Strozier Library plus 8 others. *Books:* 2.3 million (physical), 1.6 million (digital/electronic); *Serial titles:* 125,007 (digital/electronic); *Databases:* 1,144. Weekly public service hours: 134; study areas open 24 hours, 5–7 days a week; students can reserve study rooms.

STUDENT LIFE
Housing options: coed, special housing for students with disabilities. Campus housing is university owned. Freshman applicants given priority for college housing.

Activities and organizations: drama/theater group, student-run newspaper, radio and television station, choral group, marching band, Student Government, Honors Program, Golden Key Honor Society, Marching Chiefs, Intramural Sports, national fraternities, national sororities.

Athletics Member NCAA. All Division I except football (Division I-A).
Campus security: 24-hour emergency response devices and patrols, late-night transport/escort service, controlled dormitory access.
Student services: health clinic, personal/psychological counseling, women's center, legal services, veterans affairs office.

COSTS & FINANCIAL AID
Costs (2018–19) *Tuition:* state resident $4640 full-time, $216 per credit hour part-time; nonresident $19,806 full-time, $721 per credit hour part-time. Full-time tuition and fees vary according to course load, degree level, and location. Part-time tuition and fees vary according to course load, degree level, and location. *Required fees:* $1867 full-time. *Room and board:* $10,458; room only: $6380. Room and board charges vary according to board plan and housing facility. *Payment plans:* tuition prepayment, installment.

Financial Aid Of all full-time matriculated undergraduates who enrolled in 2016, 20,291 applied for aid, 14,299 were judged to have need, 1,545 had their need fully met. 855 Federal Work-Study jobs (averaging $2400). 21 state and other part-time jobs (averaging $2400). In 2016, 4466 non-need-based awards were made. *Average percent of need met:* 65. *Average financial aid package:* $13,013. *Average need-based loan:* $4450. *Average need-based gift aid:* $10,859. *Average non-need-based aid:* $4987. *Average indebtedness upon graduation:* $23,679.

APPLYING
Standardized Tests *Required:* SAT or ACT (for admission).
Options: electronic application, early admission, deferred entrance.
Application fee: $30.
Required: high school transcript. *Recommended:* essay or personal statement.

CONTACT
Florida State University, 600 West College Avenue, Tallahassee, FL 32306. *Phone:* 850-644-1389.

Fortis College

Cutler Bay, Florida
http://www.fortis.edu/

CONTACT
Fortis College, 19600 South Dixie Highway, Suite B, Cutler Bay, FL 33157. *Toll-free phone:* 855-4-FORTIS.

★ Full Sail University

Winter Park, Florida
http://www.fullsail.edu/

CONTACT
Ms. Mary Beth Plank, Director of Admissions, Full Sail University, 3300 University Boulevard, Winter Park, FL 32792-7437. *Phone:* 407-679-6333. *Toll-free phone:* 800-226-7625. *E-mail:* admissions@fullsail.com.

Gulf Coast State College

Panama City, Florida
http://www.gulfcoast.edu/
- **State-supported** primarily 2-year, founded 1957, part of Florida College System
- **Urban** 80-acre campus
- **Endowment** $30.5 million
- **Coed**
- **Noncompetitive** entrance level

FACULTY
Student/faculty ratio: 19:1.

ACADEMICS
Calendar: semesters. *Degrees:* certificates, associate, and bachelor's.
Library: Gulf Coast State College Library. *Books:* 32,529 (physical), 57,578 (digital/electronic); *Serial titles:* 43 (physical), 55,302 (digital/electronic); *Databases:* 176.

STUDENT LIFE
Housing options: college housing not available.

Activities and organizations: drama/theater group, student-run newspaper, radio and television station, choral group, Student Government Association.

Athletics Member NJCAA.

Campus security: 24-hour patrols, late-night transport/escort service, patrols by trained security personnel during campus hours.

Student services: personal/psychological counseling, veterans affairs office.

COSTS & FINANCIAL AID

Costs (2018–19) *Tuition:* state resident $2370 full-time, $99 per credit hour part-time; nonresident $8633 full-time, $360 per credit hour part-time. Full-time tuition and fees vary according to degree level. Part-time tuition and fees vary according to degree level. *Required fees:* $620 full-time, $26 per credit hour part-time.

Financial Aid Of all full-time matriculated undergraduates who enrolled in 2017, 145 Federal Work-Study jobs (averaging $3200). 60 state and other part-time jobs (averaging $2600).

APPLYING

Options: electronic application, early admission, deferred entrance.

Application fee: $20.

Required: high school transcript.

CONTACT

Mrs. Sam Wagner, Application Process Specialist, Gulf Coast State College, 5230 West U.S. Highway 98, Panama City, FL 32401. *Phone:* 850-769-1551 Ext. 2936. *Fax:* 850-913-3308. *E-mail:* swagner1@gulfcoast.edu.

Herzing University
Winter Park, Florida
http://www.herzing.edu/orlando

CONTACT

Herzing University, 1865 SR 436, Winter Park, FL 32792. *Toll-free phone:* 800-596-0724.

Hobe Sound Bible College
Hobe Sound, Florida
http://www.hsbc.edu/

- **Independent nondenominational** 4-year, founded 1960
- **Small-town** 84-acre campus
- **Endowment** $755,758
- **Coed**
- **Noncompetitive** entrance level

FACULTY
Student/faculty ratio: 13:1.

ACADEMICS
Calendar: semesters. *Degrees:* certificates, associate, and bachelor's.
Library: College Library.

STUDENT LIFE
Housing options: on-campus residence required through senior year; men-only, women-only.

Activities and organizations: choral group.

Campus security: student patrols, late-night transport/escort service, controlled dormitory access.

COSTS & FINANCIAL AID

Costs (2018–19) *Comprehensive fee:* $12,710 includes full-time tuition ($5600), mandatory fees ($940), and room and board ($6170). Part-time tuition: $325 per credit hour. Part-time tuition and fees vary according to course load. *Required fees:* $940 per year part-time. *College room only:* $2370. *Payment plans:* installment, deferred payment.

Financial Aid *Average financial aid package:* $3550. *Average indebtedness upon graduation:* $7000.

APPLYING

Standardized Tests *Required:* SAT or ACT (for admission).

Options: early admission.

Application fee: $25.

Required: essay or personal statement, high school transcript, 3 letters of recommendation, photograph, medical report.

CONTACT

Mrs. Elizabeth McMillan, Director of Admissions, Hobe Sound Bible College, PO Box 1065, Hobe Sound, FL 33475-1065. *Phone:* 772-545-1400 Ext. 1019. *E-mail:* elizabethmcmillan@hsbc.edu.

Hodges University
Naples, Florida
http://www.hodges.edu/

CONTACT

Hodges University, 2655 Northbrooke Drive, Naples, FL 34119. *Phone:* 239-513-1122 Ext. 6104. *Toll-free phone:* 800-466-8017.

Indian River State College
Fort Pierce, Florida
http://www.irsc.edu/

CONTACT

Mr. Eileen Storck, Dean of Educational Services, Indian River State College, 3209 Virginia Avenue, Fort Pierce, FL 34981-5596. *Phone:* 772-462-7361. *Toll-free phone:* 866-792-4772. *E-mail:* estrock@irsc.edu.

Jacksonville University
Jacksonville, Florida
http://www.ju.edu/

- **Independent** comprehensive, founded 1934
- **Suburban** 260-acre campus with easy access to Jacksonville, Saint Augustine
- **Endowment** $44.7 million
- **Coed** 2,920 undergraduate students, 78% full-time, 61% women, 39% men
- **Moderately difficult** entrance level, 90% of applicants were admitted

UNDERGRAD STUDENTS

2,292 full-time, 628 part-time. Students come from 52 states and territories; 49 other countries; 35% are from out of state; 21% Black or African American, non-Hispanic/Latino; 12% Hispanic/Latino; 3% Asian, non-Hispanic/Latino; 0.4% Native Hawaiian or other Pacific Islander, non-Hispanic/Latino; 0.3% American Indian or Alaska Native, non-Hispanic/Latino; 3% Two or more races, non-Hispanic/Latino; 7% international; 8% transferred in; 47% live on campus.

Freshmen:
Admission: 4,298 applied, 3,865 admitted, 624 enrolled. *Average high school GPA:* 3.3. *Test scores:* SAT evidence-based reading and writing scores over 500: 80%; SAT math scores over 500: 72%; ACT scores over 18: 91%; SAT evidence-based reading and writing scores over 600: 40%; SAT math scores over 600: 43%; ACT scores over 24: 49%; SAT evidence-based reading and writing scores over 700: 20%; SAT math scores over 700: 14%; ACT scores over 30: 7%.

Retention: 77% of full-time freshmen returned.

FACULTY
Total: 429, 56% full-time, 56% with terminal degrees.
Student/faculty ratio: 11:1.

ACADEMICS
Calendar: semesters. *Degrees:* bachelor's, master's, doctoral, post-master's, and postbachelor's certificates.

Special study options: academic remediation for entering students, accelerated degree program, adult/continuing education programs, advanced placement credit, cooperative education, distance learning, double majors, English as a second language, freshman honors college, honors programs, independent study, internships, off-campus study, part-time degree program, services for LD students, student-designed majors, study abroad, summer session for credit. *ROTC:* Army (b), Navy (b).

Unusual degree programs: 3-2 business administration; engineering; nursing; mathematics.

Computers: 400 computers/terminals and 1,205 ports are available on campus for general student use. Students can access the following:

campus intranet, computer help desk, free student e-mail accounts, online (class) grades, online (class) registration, online (class) schedules, learning management systems. Campuswide network is available. 100% of college-owned or -operated housing units are wired for high-speed Internet access. Wireless service is available via entire campus.
Library: Carl S. Swisher Library. *Books:* 187,294 (physical), 268,187 (digital/electronic); *Serial titles:* 7,434 (physical), 55,516 (digital/electronic); *Databases:* 69. Weekly public service hours: 88; students can reserve study rooms.

STUDENT LIFE

Housing options: on-campus residence required through junior year; coed, men-only, women-only, special housing for students with disabilities. Campus housing is university owned. Freshman campus housing is guaranteed.

Activities and organizations: drama/theater group, student-run newspaper, radio and television station, choral group, marching band, Honor Student Association - Academic, Campus Connection 838 - Religious - Social, International Students Association - Social, Alpha Delta Pi - Sorority, Student Veterans of America - Special Interest, national fraternities, national sororities.

Athletics Member NCAA. All Division I except football (Division I-AA). *Intercollegiate sports:* baseball M(s), basketball M(s)/W(s), crew M(s)/W(s), cross-country running M/W(s), golf M(s)/W(s)(c), lacrosse M(s)/W(s), sand volleyball W, soccer M(s)/W(s), softball W(s), track and field W(s), volleyball W(s). *Intramural sports:* basketball M/W, cheerleading M(c)/W(c), football M/W, riflery M(c)/W(c), sailing M(c)/W(c), sand volleyball M/W, soccer M/W, softball M/W, ultimate Frisbee M/W, volleyball M/W.

Campus security: 24-hour emergency response devices and patrols, student patrols, late-night transport/escort service, controlled dormitory access, trained security patrols during evening hours.

Student services: health clinic, personal/psychological counseling, veterans affairs office.

COSTS & FINANCIAL AID

Costs (2019–20) *Comprehensive fee:* $52,470 includes full-time tuition ($38,140) and room and board ($14,330). Part-time tuition: $1275 per credit hour. *Required fees:* $625 per credit hour part-time. *College room only:* $9200.

Financial Aid Of all full-time matriculated undergraduates who enrolled in 2018, 2,275 applied for aid, 1,690 were judged to have need, 474 had their need fully met. 232 Federal Work-Study jobs (averaging $733). 99 state and other part-time jobs (averaging $1058). In 2018, 293 non-need-based awards were made. *Average percent of need met:* 74. *Average financial aid package:* $28,599. *Average need-based loan:* $3275. *Average need-based gift aid:* $21,450. *Average non-need-based aid:* $17,574.

APPLYING

Options: electronic application, early admission, deferred entrance.
Application fee: $30.

Required: high school transcript, minimum 2.0 GPA. *Required for some:* essay or personal statement, 2 letters of recommendation, audition for music, dance, and theater majors; portfolio for art, computer art, and design majors; interview for the Honors Program. *Recommended:* interview.

Application deadlines: rolling (freshmen), rolling (transfers).
Notification: continuous (freshmen), continuous (transfers).

CONTACT

Mr. Robert Stewart, Senior Vice President, Enrollment Management, Jacksonville University, 2800 University Boulevard North, Jacksonville, FL 32211. *Phone:* 904-256-7005. *Toll-free phone:* 800-225-2027. *Fax:* 904-256-7012. *E-mail:* rstewar6@ju.edu.

Johnson & Wales University
North Miami, Florida
http://www.jwu.edu/northmiami/

CONTACT

Jeff Greenip, Director of Admissions, Johnson & Wales University, 1701 Northeast 127th Street, North Miami, FL 33181. *Phone:* 305-892-7600. *Toll-free phone:* 866-598-3567. *Fax:* 305-892-7020. *E-mail:* mia@admissions.jwu.edu.

Johnson University Florida
Kissimmee, Florida
http://www.johnsonu.edu/
- **Independent** comprehensive, founded 1976, affiliated with Christian Churches and Churches of Christ
- **Small-town** 40-acre campus with easy access to Orlando
- **Coed** 201 undergraduate students, 93% full-time, 39% women, 61% men
- **Minimally difficult** entrance level, 65% of applicants were admitted

UNDERGRAD STUDENTS

187 full-time, 14 part-time. Students come from 16 states and territories; 3 other countries; 15% are from out of state; 16% Black or African American, non-Hispanic/Latino; 20% Hispanic/Latino; 0.5% Asian, non-Hispanic/Latino; 0.5% Native Hawaiian or other Pacific Islander, non-Hispanic/Latino; 3% Two or more races, non-Hispanic/Latino; 5% Race/ethnicity unknown; 4% international; 29% transferred in; 74% live on campus.

Freshmen:

Admission: 133 applied, 87 admitted, 70 enrolled. *Average high school GPA:* 3.1. *Test scores:* SAT evidence-based reading and writing scores over 500: 58%; SAT math scores over 500: 55%; ACT scores over 18: 53%; SAT evidence-based reading and writing scores over 600: 18%; SAT math scores over 600: 12%; ACT scores over 24: 9%; SAT evidence-based reading and writing scores over 700: 3%.

Retention: 67% of full-time freshmen returned.

FACULTY

Total: 33, 30% full-time, 55% with terminal degrees.
Student/faculty ratio: 10:1.

ACADEMICS

Calendar: semesters. *Degrees:* certificates, associate, bachelor's, and master's.

Special study options: adult/continuing education programs, advanced placement credit, distance learning, double majors, independent study, internships, part-time degree program, study abroad, summer session for credit.

Computers: 16 computers/terminals are available on campus for general student use. Students can access the following: campus intranet, computer help desk, free student e-mail accounts, online (class) grades, online (class) registration, online (class) schedules. Campuswide network is available. 100% of college-owned or -operated housing units are wired for high-speed Internet access. Wireless service is available via entire campus.

Library: Library. *Books:* 35,023 (physical), 345,536 (digital/electronic); *Serial titles:* 120 (physical), 44,275 (digital/electronic); *Databases:* 2,145.

STUDENT LIFE

Housing options: men-only, women-only. Campus housing is university owned.

Activities and organizations: choral group, Student Government Association, Harvesters (Missions), Timothy club (preachers), Ultimate Frisbee.

Athletics Member NCCAA. *Intercollegiate sports:* basketball M/W, soccer M, volleyball W. *Intramural sports:* sand volleyball M/W, ultimate Frisbee M.

Campus security: controlled dormitory access.

Student services: personal/psychological counseling.

COSTS & FINANCIAL AID

Costs (2019–20) *Comprehensive fee:* $24,378 includes full-time tuition ($15,480), mandatory fees ($1440), and room and board ($7458). Part-time tuition: $500 per credit hour.

Financial Aid Of all full-time matriculated undergraduates who enrolled in 2017, 162 applied for aid, 151 were judged to have need, 19 had their need fully met. In 2017, 11 non-need-based awards were made. *Average percent of need met:* 66. *Average financial aid package:* $12,008. *Average need-based loan:* $3660. *Average need-based gift aid:* $9040. *Average non-need-based aid:* $4961. *Average indebtedness upon graduation:* $28,906.

APPLYING

Standardized Tests *Required:* SAT or ACT (for admission).

Options: electronic application, early admission, deferred entrance.
Application fee: $35.

Required: essay or personal statement, high school transcript, minimum 2.5 GPA, 3 letters of recommendation. *Required for some:* interview.

Application deadlines: 7/15 (freshmen), 7/15 (out-of-state freshmen), 7/15 (transfers).

Notification: continuous until 8/15 (freshmen), continuous until 8/15 (transfers).

CONTACT
Mr. Doug Johnson, Director of Admissions, Johnson University Florida, 1011 Bill Beck Boulevard, Kissimmee, FL 34744. *Phone:* 407-569-1380. *Toll-free phone:* 888-468-6322. *Fax:* 321-206-2007. *E-mail:* djohnson@johnsonu.edu.

Jose Maria Vargas University
Pembroke Pines, Florida
http://www.jmvu.edu/

CONTACT
Jose Maria Vargas University, 10131 Pines Boulevard, Pembroke Pines, FL 33026.

Keiser University
Fort Lauderdale, Florida
http://www.keiseruniversity.edu/
- **Independent** university, founded 1977
- **Urban** campus
- **Coed**

FACULTY
Student/faculty ratio: 12:1.

ACADEMICS
Calendar: 3 semesters per year. *Degrees:* associate, bachelor's, master's, doctoral, and post-master's certificates (profile includes data from campuses located in Daytona Beach, Fort Lauderdale, Fort Myers, Jacksonville, Lakeland, Melbourne, Miami, Orlando, Pembroke Pines, Port St. Lucie, Sarasota, Tallahassee, Tampa, and West Palm Beach; not all programs offered at all locations, but many classes offered 100% online).
Library: Keiser University Library. *Books:* 150,394 (physical), 145,000 (digital/electronic); *Serial titles:* 188 (physical), 29 (digital/electronic); *Databases:* 257.

STUDENT LIFE
Housing options: college housing not available.

Activities and organizations: Student Government Association, Phi Theta Kappa, Sigma Beta Delta International Honor Society, Alpha Phi Sigma National Honor Society, Student Nurses Association.

Athletics Member NAIA.

Campus security: 24-hour patrols, late-night transport/escort service, AlertNow Rapid Communications Service, Campus Response Teams.

Student services: veterans affairs office.

COSTS & FINANCIAL AID
Costs (2018–19) *Tuition:* $28,320 full-time, $1180 per credit hour part-time. *Required fees:* $1760 full-time. *Room only:* $6224.

Financial Aid Of all full-time matriculated undergraduates who enrolled in 2017, 14,502 applied for aid, 14,502 were judged to have need, 14,502 had their need fully met. 35 Federal Work-Study jobs (averaging $2876). In 2017, 5500 non-need-based awards were made. *Average percent of need met:* 82. *Average financial aid package:* $7409. *Average need-based loan:* $10,562. *Average need-based gift aid:* $7409. *Average non-need-based aid:* $1134.

APPLYING
Standardized Tests *Required:* SAT or ACT or Wonderlic aptitude test (for admission).

Options: electronic application.

Application fee: $55.
Required: high school transcript.

CONTACT
Keiser University, 1500 NW 49th Street, Fort Lauderdale, FL 33309. *Phone:* 954-439-2720. *Toll-free phone:* 888-534-7379.

Lynn University
Boca Raton, Florida
http://www.lynn.edu/
- **Independent** comprehensive, founded 1962
- **Suburban** 123-acre campus with easy access to Fort Lauderdale
- **Coed**
- **Moderately difficult** entrance level

FACULTY
Student/faculty ratio: 17:1.

ACADEMICS
Calendar: semesters plus 3 summer sessions. *Degrees:* associate, bachelor's, master's, doctoral, post-master's, and postbachelor's certificates.
Library: Eugene M. and Christine E. Lynn Library. *Books:* 58,952 (physical), 239,257 (digital/electronic); *Serial titles:* 401 (physical), 43,029 (digital/electronic); *Databases:* 118. Weekly public service hours: 96.

STUDENT LIFE
Housing options: on-campus residence required through sophomore year; coed, special housing for students with disabilities. Campus housing is university owned. Freshman campus housing is guaranteed.

Activities and organizations: drama/theater group, student-run newspaper, radio and television station, Knights of the Round Table, intramural groups, student newspaper, Student Activities Board, Greek Life, national fraternities, national sororities.

Athletics Member NCAA. All Division II.

Campus security: 24-hour emergency response devices and patrols, late-night transport/escort service, controlled dormitory access, video monitor at residence entrances.

Student services: health clinic, personal/psychological counseling, women's center.

COSTS & FINANCIAL AID
Costs (2018–19) *One-time required fee:* $1000. *Comprehensive fee:* $50,380 includes full-time tuition ($35,960), mandatory fees ($2250), and room and board ($12,170). Full-time tuition and fees vary according to program. Part-time tuition: $1040 per credit hour. Part-time tuition and fees vary according to course load and program. *Room and board:* Room and board charges vary according to board plan and housing facility. *Payment plans:* installment, deferred payment.

Financial Aid Of all full-time matriculated undergraduates who enrolled in 2017, 1,550 applied for aid, 756 were judged to have need, 752 had their need fully met. 224 Federal Work-Study jobs (averaging $2055). 35 state and other part-time jobs (averaging $8516). In 2017, 523 non-need-based awards were made. *Average percent of need met:* 52. *Average financial aid package:* $22,741. *Average need-based loan:* $4751. *Average need-based gift aid:* $10,401. *Average non-need-based aid:* $10,810. *Average indebtedness upon graduation:* $32,533.

APPLYING
Standardized Tests *Recommended:* SAT or ACT (for admission).

Options: electronic application, early admission, early action, deferred entrance.

Application fee: $45.

Required: essay or personal statement, high school transcript. *Required for some:* audition for Conservatory of Music. *Recommended:* interview.

CONTACT
Stefano Papaleo, Director of Undergraduate Admission, Lynn University, Admission, 3601 North Military Trail, Boca Raton, FL 33431. *Phone:* 561-237-7831. *Toll-free phone:* 800-888-5966. *Fax:* 561-237-7100. *E-mail:* spapaleo@lynn.edu.

Marconi International University
Miami, Florida
http://www.miuniversity.edu/

CONTACT
Admissions, Marconi International University, 111 NE 1st Street, 6th floor, Miami, FL 33132. *Phone:* 954-374-4701. *E-mail:* info@marconiinternational.org.

Miami Dade College
Miami, Florida
http://www.mdc.edu/

- **State and locally supported** primarily 2-year, founded 1960, part of Florida College System
- **Urban** campus
- **Endowment** $137.1 million
- **Coed**
- **Noncompetitive** entrance level

FACULTY
Student/faculty ratio: 26:1.

ACADEMICS
Calendar: 16-16-6-6. *Degrees:* certificates, associate, bachelor's, and postbachelor's certificates.
Library: Miami Dade College Learning Resources plus 9 others. *Books:* 185,820 (physical), 60,221 (digital/electronic); *Serial titles:* 708 (physical), 46,482 (digital/electronic); *Databases:* 126. Weekly public service hours: 69; students can reserve study rooms.

STUDENT LIFE
Housing options: college housing not available.
Activities and organizations: drama/theater group, student-run newspaper, radio and television station, choral group, Student Government Association, Phi Theta Kappa, Phi Beta Lambda (business), Future Educators of America Professional, Kappa Delta Pi Honor Society (education).
Athletics Member NCAA, NJCAA. All NCAA Division I.
Campus security: 24-hour emergency response devices and patrols, student patrols, late-night transport/escort service, Emergency Mass Notification System (EMNS), campus public address systems, LiveSafe mobile safety App for students/employees.
Student services: health clinic, personal/psychological counseling, veterans affairs office.

COSTS & FINANCIAL AID
Costs (2018–19) *One-time required fee:* $30. *Tuition:* state resident $1987 full-time, $83 per credit hour part-time; nonresident $7947 full-time, $331 per credit hour part-time. Full-time tuition and fees vary according to course load, degree level, and program. Part-time tuition and fees vary according to course load, degree level, and program. *Required fees:* $851 full-time, $35 per credit hour part-time.
Financial Aid Of all full-time matriculated undergraduates who enrolled in 2017, 800 Federal Work-Study jobs (averaging $5000). 125 state and other part-time jobs (averaging $5000).

APPLYING
Options: electronic application, early admission.
Application fee: $30.
Required: high school transcript.

CONTACT
Ms. Elisabet Vizoso, Interim College Registrar, Miami Dade College, 11011 SW 104th Street, Miami, FL 33176. *Phone:* 305-237-2206. *Fax:* 305-237-2532. *E-mail:* evizoso@mdc.edu.

Miami International University of Art & Design
Miami, Florida
http://www.artinstitutes.edu/miami/

CONTACT
Miami International University of Art & Design, 1501 Biscayne Boulevard, Suite 100, Miami, FL 33132-1418. *Phone:* 305-428-5700. *Toll-free phone:* 800-225-9023.

Miami Regional University
Miami Springs, Florida
http://www.mru.edu/

CONTACT
Miami Regional University, 700 South Royal Poinciana Boulevard, Miami Springs, FL 33166.

Millennia Atlantic University
Doral, Florida
http://www.maufl.edu/

CONTACT
Millennia Atlantic University, 3801 NW 97th Avenue, Doral, FL 33178.

New College of Florida
Sarasota, Florida
http://www.ncf.edu/

- **State-supported** comprehensive, founded 1960, part of State University System of Florida
- **Suburban** 110-acre campus with easy access to Tampa-St. Petersburg
- **Endowment** $41.5 million
- **Coed** 808 undergraduate students, 100% full-time, 62% women, 38% men
- **Very difficult** entrance level, 77% of applicants were admitted

UNDERGRAD STUDENTS
808 full-time. Students come from 40 states and territories; 20 other countries; 17% are from out of state; 3% Black or African American, non-Hispanic/Latino; 17% Hispanic/Latino; 3% Asian, non-Hispanic/Latino; 3% Two or more races, non-Hispanic/Latino; 1% Race/ethnicity unknown; 2% international; 4% transferred in; 79% live on campus.

Freshmen:
Admission: 1,340 applied, 1,029 admitted, 192 enrolled. *Average high school GPA:* 4.0. *Test scores:* SAT evidence-based reading and writing scores over 500: 100%; SAT math scores over 500: 99%; ACT scores over 18: 100%; SAT evidence-based reading and writing scores over 600: 88%; SAT math scores over 600: 71%; ACT scores over 24: 93%; SAT evidence-based reading and writing scores over 700: 39%; SAT math scores over 700: 27%; ACT scores over 30: 48%.
Retention: 76% of full-time freshmen returned.

FACULTY
Total: 122, 72% full-time, 92% with terminal degrees.
Student/faculty ratio: 10:1.

ACADEMICS
Calendar: 4-1-4. *Degrees:* bachelor's and master's.
Special study options: accelerated degree program, double majors, freshman honors college, honors programs, independent study, internships, off-campus study, services for LD students, student-designed majors, study abroad, summer session for credit.
Computers: 105 computers/terminals and 1,356 ports are available on campus for general student use. Students can access the following: campus intranet, computer help desk, free student e-mail accounts, online (class) grades, online (class) registration, online (class) schedules. Campuswide network is available. 100% of college-owned or -operated housing units are wired for high-speed Internet access. Wireless service is available via classrooms, computer labs, dorm rooms, learning centers, libraries, student centers.

Library: Jane Bancroft Cook Library. *Books:* 226,520 (physical), 26,632 (digital/electronic); *Serial titles:* 1,411 (physical), 1,899 (digital/electronic); *Databases:* 210. Weekly public service hours: 96.

STUDENT LIFE

Housing options: on-campus residence required through senior year; coed, special housing for students with disabilities. Campus housing is university owned. Freshman campus housing is guaranteed.

Activities and organizations: drama/theater group, student-run newspaper, radio station, choral group, Dance Collective, Queery, New College Student Alliance, Generation Action, Bullsharks Dive Club.

Athletics *Intercollegiate sports:* sailing M/W. *Intramural sports:* basketball M(c)/W(c), golf M(c)/W(c), racquetball M(c)/W(c), sailing M(c)/W(c), sand volleyball M(c)/W(c), soccer M(c)/W(c), softball M(c)/W(c), swimming and diving M(c)/W(c), table tennis M(c)/W(c), tennis M(c)/W(c), ultimate Frisbee M(c)/W(c), weight lifting M(c)/W(c).

Campus security: 24-hour emergency response devices and patrols, student patrols, late-night transport/escort service, controlled dormitory access, campus police are state certified police officers and available 24/7.

Student services: health clinic, personal/psychological counseling.

COSTS & FINANCIAL AID

Costs (2019–20) *Tuition:* state resident $6916 full-time; nonresident $29,944 full-time.

Financial Aid Of all full-time matriculated undergraduates who enrolled in 2018, 623 applied for aid, 430 were judged to have need, 119 had their need fully met. 33 Federal Work-Study jobs (averaging $910). In 2018, 298 non-need-based awards were made. *Average percent of need met:* 88. *Average financial aid package:* $14,877. *Average need-based loan:* $3692. *Average need-based gift aid:* $9987. *Average non-need-based aid:* $2557. *Average indebtedness upon graduation:* $17,466.

APPLYING

Standardized Tests *Required:* SAT or ACT (for admission).

Options: electronic application, early admission, early decision, deferred entrance.

Application fee: $30.

Required: essay or personal statement, high school transcript, 1 letter of recommendation. *Recommended:* minimum 3.0 GPA.

Application deadlines: 4/15 (freshmen), 7/1 (transfers).

Notification: 4/25 (freshmen), 7/31 (transfers).

CONTACT

Joy Hamm, Dean of Admissions and Financial Aid, New College of Florida, 5800 Bay Shore Road, Sarasota, FL 34243. *Phone:* 941-487-5000. *Fax:* 941-487-5010. *E-mail:* admissions@ncf.edu.

See below for display ad and page 1056 for the College Close-Up.

New World School of the Arts
Miami, Florida

http://www.mdc.edu/nwsa/

- **State-supported** 4-year, founded 1984
- **Urban** 5-acre campus with easy access to Miami-Dade, Broward, Palm Beach Counties
- **Endowment** $8.3 million
- **Coed**
- **Noncompetitive** entrance level

FACULTY

Student/faculty ratio: 5:1.

ACADEMICS

Calendar: semesters. *Degrees:* associate and bachelor's.
Library: Miami Dade Community College Library (Wolfson Campus) plus 1 other. Students can reserve study rooms.

STUDENT LIFE

Housing options: college housing not available.

Activities and organizations: Student Government.

Campus security: 24-hour emergency response devices and patrols.

Student services: personal/psychological counseling.

APPLYING

Standardized Tests *Recommended:* SAT or ACT (for admission).

Options: electronic application, early decision.

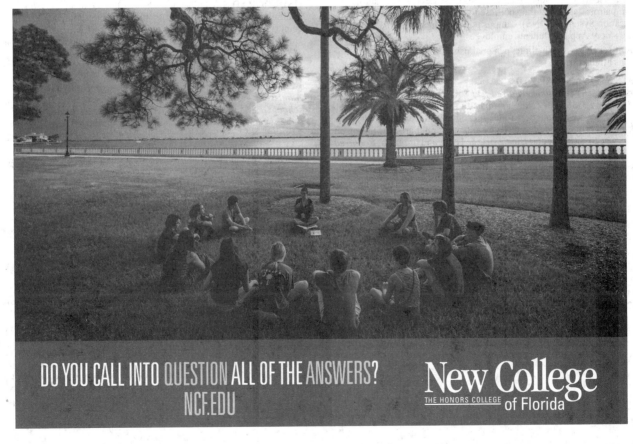

DO YOU CALL INTO QUESTION ALL OF THE ANSWERS?
NCF.EDU

New College
THE HONORS COLLEGE of Florida

Required: essay or personal statement, high school transcript, 2 letters of recommendation, interview, audition or portfolio submission.

CONTACT
Eloisa Ferrer, Recruitment and Admissions Coordinator, New World School of the Arts, 300 NE 2nd Avenue, Miami, FL 33132. *Phone:* 305-237-7408. *Fax:* 305-237-3794. *E-mail:* eferrer2@mdc.edu.

Northwest Florida State College
Niceville, Florida
http://www.nwfsc.edu/

CONTACT
Ms. Karen Cooper, Director of Admissions, Northwest Florida State College, 100 College Boulevard, Niceville, FL 32578. *Phone:* 850-729-4901. *Fax:* 850-729-5206. *E-mail:* cooperk@nwfsc.edu.

Nova Southeastern University
Fort Lauderdale, Florida
http://www.nova.edu/
- **Independent** university, founded 1964
- **Suburban** 314-acre campus
- **Endowment** $117.8 million
- **Coed**
- **Moderately difficult** entrance level

FACULTY
Student/faculty ratio: 17:1.

ACADEMICS
Calendar: trimesters. *Degrees:* certificates, associate, bachelor's, master's, doctoral, post-master's, and postbachelor's certificates.
Library: Alvin Sherman Library, Research, and Information Technology Center plus 4 others. *Books:* 498,823 (physical), 379,928 (digital/electronic); *Serial titles:* 6,035 (physical), 20,738 (digital/electronic); *Databases:* 577. Study areas open 24 hours, 5–7 days a week; students can reserve study rooms.

STUDENT LIFE
Housing options: on-campus residence required through sophomore year; coed, special housing for students with disabilities. Campus housing is university owned. Freshman campus housing is guaranteed.

Activities and organizations: drama/theater group, student-run newspaper, radio and television station, choral group, HOSA: Future Health Professionals, Make-a Meal Service Organization, Student Government Association, Delta Epsilon Iota, Pre-Med, national fraternities, national sororities.

Athletics Member NCAA. All Division II.

Campus security: 24-hour emergency response devices and patrols, late-night transport/escort service, controlled dormitory access, shuttle bus service.

Student services: health clinic, personal/psychological counseling, veterans affairs office.

COSTS & FINANCIAL AID
Costs (2018–19) *Tuition:* $29,940 full-time, $998 per credit hour part-time. Full-time tuition and fees vary according to program. Part-time tuition and fees vary according to course load and program. *Required fees:* $960 full-time. *Room only:* $9938. Room and board charges vary according to board plan and housing facility. *Payment plans:* installment, deferred payment.

Financial Aid Of all full-time matriculated undergraduates who enrolled in 2018, 3,008 applied for aid, 2,670 were judged to have need, 395 had their need fully met. 1,427 Federal Work-Study jobs (averaging $4912). 538 state and other part-time jobs (averaging $1260). In 2018, 856 non-need-based awards were made. *Average percent of need met:* 77. *Average financial aid package:* $32,151. *Average need-based loan:* $2936. *Average need-based gift aid:* $20,726. *Average non-need-based aid:* $13,369. *Average indebtedness upon graduation:* $31,438.

APPLYING
Standardized Tests *Required:* SAT or ACT (for admission).
Options: electronic application, early admission, early decision, early action, deferred entrance.

Application fee: $50.
Required: minimum 3.0 GPA. *Required for some:* essay or personal statement, high school transcript.

CONTACT
Nova Southeastern University, 3301 College Avenue, Fort Lauderdale, FL 33314-7796. *Phone:* 954-262-8000. *Toll-free phone:* 800-541-NOVA.

Palm Beach Atlantic University
West Palm Beach, Florida
http://www.pba.edu/
- **Independent nondenominational** comprehensive, founded 1968
- **Urban** 100-acre campus with easy access to Miami-Dade County
- **Endowment** $81.2 million
- **Coed** 2,855 undergraduate students, 79% full-time, 63% women, 37% men
- **Moderately difficult** entrance level, 95% of applicants were admitted

UNDERGRAD STUDENTS
2,269 full-time, 586 part-time. 36% are from out of state; 9% Black or African American, non-Hispanic/Latino; 16% Hispanic/Latino; 2% Asian, non-Hispanic/Latino; 0.3% Native Hawaiian or other Pacific Islander, non-Hispanic/Latino; 0.2% American Indian or Alaska Native, non-Hispanic/Latino; 3% Two or more races, non-Hispanic/Latino; 2% Race/ethnicity unknown; 5% international; 8% transferred in; 48% live on campus.

Freshmen:
Admission: 1,444 applied, 1,376 admitted, 526 enrolled. *Test scores:* SAT evidence-based reading and writing scores over 500: 70%; SAT math scores over 500: 73%; ACT scores over 18: 92%; SAT evidence-based reading and writing scores over 600: 39%; SAT math scores over 600: 23%; ACT scores over 24: 48%; SAT evidence-based reading and writing scores over 700: 7%; SAT math scores over 700: 3%; ACT scores over 30: 7%.
Retention: 75% of full-time freshmen returned.

FACULTY
Total: 373, 48% full-time, 65% with terminal degrees.
Student/faculty ratio: 12:1.

ACADEMICS
Calendar: semesters. *Degrees:* bachelor's, master's, and doctoral.
Special study options: academic remediation for entering students, accelerated degree program, adult/continuing education programs, advanced placement credit, distance learning, double majors, honors programs, independent study, internships, off-campus study, part-time degree program, services for LD students, student-designed majors, study abroad, summer session for credit. *ROTC:* Army (c).

Unusual degree programs: 3-2 divinity.

Computers: 350 computers/terminals are available on campus for general student use. Students can access the following: campus intranet, computer help desk, free student e-mail accounts, online (class) grades, online (class) registration, online (class) schedules. Campuswide network is available. 100% of college-owned or -operated housing units are wired for high-speed Internet access. Wireless service is available via entire campus.
Library: Warren Library plus 1 other. *Books:* 143,334 (physical), 126,921 (digital/electronic); *Serial titles:* 114 (physical), 121,795 (digital/electronic); *Databases:* 143. Weekly public service hours: 100; students can reserve study rooms.

STUDENT LIFE
Housing options: on-campus residence required through senior year; coed, men-only, women-only. Campus housing is university owned and leased by the school. Freshman campus housing is guaranteed.

Activities and organizations: drama/theater group, student-run newspaper, choral group, Impact Leadership Team, Nursing Student Association, Nurses Christian Fellowship, Student Government, Sigma Alpha Omega.

Athletics Member NCAA. All Division II except golf (Division I). *Intercollegiate sports:* baseball M(s), basketball M(s)/W(s), cheerleading M(c)/W(c), crew M(c)/W(c), cross-country running M(s)/W(s), golf M(s)/W(s), lacrosse M(s)/W(s), soccer M(s)/W(s), softball W(s), tennis

M(s)/W(s), track and field M(s)/W(s), volleyball W(s). *Intramural sports:* basketball M/W, sand volleyball M/W, soccer M(c)/W, softball M/W, ultimate Frisbee M/W, volleyball M/W.

Campus security: 24-hour emergency response devices and patrols, late-night transport/escort service, controlled dormitory access.

Student services: health clinic, personal/psychological counseling.

COSTS & FINANCIAL AID

Costs (2019–20) *Tuition:* $31,920 full-time, $767 per credit hour part-time. *Required fees:* $580 full-time. *Room only:* $5530.

Financial Aid Of all full-time matriculated undergraduates who enrolled in 2018, 1,907 applied for aid, 1,667 were judged to have need, 279 had their need fully met. In 2018, 543 non-need-based awards were made. *Average percent of need met:* 63. *Average financial aid package:* $22,570. *Average need-based loan:* $3712. *Average need-based gift aid:* $19,894. *Average non-need-based aid:* $12,987. *Average indebtedness upon graduation:* $27,441.

APPLYING

Standardized Tests *Required:* SAT or ACT (for admission).

Options: electronic application, early admission, early action, deferred entrance.

Application fee: $50.

Required: essay or personal statement, high school transcript. *Required for some:* interview.

Application deadlines: rolling (freshmen), rolling (transfers).

Notification: continuous (freshmen), continuous (transfers).

CONTACT

Mr. Joseph Bryan, Assistant Vice President for Admissions, Palm Beach Atlantic University, 901 South Flagler Drive, PO Box 24708, West Palm Beach, FL 33416-4708. *Phone:* 561-803-2102. *Toll-free phone:* 888-GO-TO-PBA. *Fax:* 561-803-2115. *E-mail:* joseph_bryan@pba.edu.

Palm Beach State College

Lake Worth, Florida

http://www.palmbeachstate.edu/

- **State-supported** 4-year, founded 1933, part of Florida College System
- **Urban** 114-acre campus with easy access to West Palm Beach
- **Endowment** $18.3 million
- **Coed**
- **Noncompetitive** entrance level

FACULTY
Student/faculty ratio: 23:1.

ACADEMICS
Calendar: semesters. *Degrees:* certificates, diplomas, associate, and bachelor's.
Library: Harold C. Manor Library plus 5 others. Weekly public service hours: 72; students can reserve study rooms.

STUDENT LIFE
Housing options: college housing not available.

Activities and organizations: drama/theater group, student-run newspaper, choral group, Student Government, Phi Theta Kappa, Students for International Understanding, Black Student Union, Drama Club, national fraternities.

Athletics Member NJCAA.

Campus security: 24-hour emergency response devices and patrols.

Student services: health clinic, personal/psychological counseling, women's center, veterans affairs office.

COSTS
Costs (2018–19) *One-time required fee:* $40. *Tuition:* state resident $3050 full-time, $101 per credit hour part-time; nonresident $11,740 full-time, $363 per credit hour part-time. Full-time tuition and fees vary according to degree level. Part-time tuition and fees vary according to degree level. *Required fees:* $20 full-time.

APPLYING
Standardized Tests *Recommended:* SAT and SAT Subject Tests or ACT (for admission).

Options: electronic application, early admission, deferred entrance.

Application fee: $40.

Required: high school transcript.

CONTACT
Palm Beach State College, 4200 Congress Avenue, Lake Worth, FL 33461-4796.

Pasco-Hernando State College

New Port Richey, Florida

http://www.phsc.edu/

CONTACT
Ms. Estela Carrion, Director of Admissions and Student Records, Pasco-Hernando State College, 10230 Ridge Road, New Port Richey, FL 34654-5199. *Phone:* 727-816-3261. *Toll-free phone:* 877-TRY-PHSC. *Fax:* 727-816-3389. *E-mail:* carrioe@phsc.edu.

Pensacola Christian College

Pensacola, Florida

http://www.pcci.edu/

CONTACT
Pensacola Christian College, 250 Brent Lane, Pensacola, FL 32503-2267. *Toll-free phone:* 800-722-4636.

Pensacola State College

Pensacola, Florida

http://www.pensacolastate.edu/

- **State-supported** primarily 2-year, founded 1948, part of Florida College System
- **Urban** 130-acre campus with easy access to Mobile, Alabama
- **Endowment** $11.3 million
- **Coed**
- **Noncompetitive** entrance level

FACULTY
Student/faculty ratio: 19:1.

ACADEMICS
Calendar: semesters. *Degrees:* certificates, diplomas, associate, and bachelor's.
Library: Edward M. Chadbourne Library plus 3 others. Students can reserve study rooms.

STUDENT LIFE
Housing options: college housing not available.

Activities and organizations: drama/theater group, student-run newspaper, choral group, Student Government Association, Health Occupations Students of America (HOSA), SkillsUSA, African-American Student Association, Forestry Club.

Athletics Member NJCAA.

Campus security: 24-hour emergency response devices and patrols, late-night transport/escort service.

Student services: personal/psychological counseling, veterans affairs office.

COSTS & FINANCIAL AID
Costs (2018–19) *One-time required fee:* $30. *Tuition:* state resident $2510 full-time, $105 per credit hour part-time; nonresident $10,074 full-time, $420 per credit hour part-time. Full-time tuition and fees vary according to course level and degree level. Part-time tuition and fees vary according to course level and degree level.

Financial Aid Of all full-time matriculated undergraduates who enrolled in 2017, 120 Federal Work-Study jobs (averaging $3000).

APPLYING
Options: electronic application, early admission.

Application fee: $30.

Required: high school transcript.

CONTACT
Ms. Kathy Dutremble, Registrar, Pensacola State College, 1000 College Boulevard, Pensacola, FL 32504. *Phone:* 850-484-2076. *Fax:* 850-484-1020. *E-mail:* kdutremble@pensacolastate.edu.

Polk State College
Winter Haven, Florida
http://www.polk.edu/

- **State-supported** 4-year, founded 1964, part of Florida College System
- **Suburban** 98-acre campus with easy access to Orlando, Tampa
- **Coed**
- **Noncompetitive** entrance level

FACULTY
Student/faculty ratio: 25:1.

ACADEMICS
Calendar: semesters 16-16-6-6. *Degrees:* certificates, diplomas, associate, and bachelor's.
Library: Polk State College Libraries plus 1 other. *Books:* 82,640 (physical), 110,114 (digital/electronic).

STUDENT LIFE
Housing options: college housing not available.
Activities and organizations: drama/theater group, choral group, Florida Student Nursing Association, Honors Program Student Council, Phi Theta Kappa (PTK), Student Government Association, SALO (Student Activities and Leadership Office).
Athletics Member NJCAA.
Campus security: 24-hour emergency response devices and patrols.
Student services: personal/psychological counseling, legal services, veterans affairs office.

COSTS
Costs (2018–19) *Tuition:* state resident $3367 full-time, $112 per credit hour part-time; nonresident $12,272 full-time, $409 per credit hour part-time. Full-time tuition and fees vary according to course level, course load, and degree level. Part-time tuition and fees vary according to course level, course load, and degree level.

APPLYING
Options: electronic application, early admission, deferred entrance.
Required: high school transcript.

CONTACT
Polk State College, 999 Avenue H, NE, Winter Haven, FL 33881-4299. *Phone:* 863-297-1021.

Polytechnic University of Puerto Rico, Miami Campus
Miami, Florida
http://www.pupr.edu/miami/

- **Independent** comprehensive
- **Urban** campus with easy access to Miami-Dade
- **Coed**

FACULTY
Student/faculty ratio: 10:1.

ACADEMICS
Degrees: bachelor's and master's.

STUDENT LIFE
Housing options: college housing not available.

APPLYING
Options: electronic application.
Application fee: $30.

CONTACT
Polytechnic University of Puerto Rico, Miami Campus, 8180 Northwest 36th Street, Suite 401, Miami, FL 33166. *Phone:* 305-418-8000. *Toll-free phone:* 888-729-7659.

Polytechnic University of Puerto Rico, Orlando Campus
Orlando, Florida
http://www.pupr.edu/orlando/

CONTACT
Teresa Cardona, Director of Recruitment and Admission, Polytechnic University of Puerto Rico, Orlando Campus, 550 North Econlockhatchee Trail, Orlando, FL 32825. *Phone:* 407-677-7000. *Toll-free phone:* 888-577-POLY. *Fax:* 407-677-5082.

Rasmussen College Fort Myers
Fort Myers, Florida
http://www.rasmussen.edu/

CONTACT
Ms. Susan Hammerstrom, Director of Admissions, Rasmussen College Fort Myers, 9160 Forum Corporate Parkway, Suite 100, Fort Myers, FL 33905. *Phone:* 239-477-2100. *Toll-free phone:* 888-549-6755. *E-mail:* susan.hammerstrom@rasmussen.edu.

Rasmussen College Land O' Lakes
Land O' Lakes, Florida
http://www.rasmussen.edu/

CONTACT
Ms. Susan Hammerstrom, Director of Admissions, Rasmussen College Land O' Lakes, 18600 Fernview Street, Land O' Lakes, FL 34638. *Phone:* 813-435-3601. *Toll-free phone:* 888-549-6755. *E-mail:* susan.hammerstrom@rasmussen.edu.

Rasmussen College New Port Richey
New Port Richey, Florida
http://www.rasmussen.edu/

- **Proprietary** 4-year, part of Rasmussen College System
- **Suburban** campus
- **Coed**
- **Minimally difficult** entrance level

FACULTY
Student/faculty ratio: 22:1.

ACADEMICS
Calendar: quarters. *Degrees:* certificates, diplomas, associate, bachelor's, and postbachelor's certificates.
Library: Rasmussen College Library - New Port Richey.

STUDENT LIFE
Housing options: college housing not available.

FINANCIAL AID
Financial Aid Of all full-time matriculated undergraduates who enrolled in 2017, 6 Federal Work-Study jobs.

APPLYING
Standardized Tests *Required:* institutional exam (for admission).
Options: electronic application, early admission, deferred entrance.
Required: high school transcript, minimum 2.0 GPA. ***Required for some:*** interview.

CONTACT
Dwayne Bertotto, Vice President of Admissions and Student Experience, Rasmussen College New Port Richey, 8300 Norman Center Drive, Suite 300, Bloomington, MN 55437. *Phone:* 952-806-3958. *Toll-free phone:* 888-549-6755. *E-mail:* dwayne.bertotto@rasmussen.edu.

Rasmussen College Ocala

Ocala, Florida

http://www.rasmussen.edu/

- **Proprietary** 4-year, founded 1984, part of Rasmussen College System
- **Suburban** campus with easy access to Orlando
- **Coed**
- **Minimally difficult** entrance level

FACULTY
Student/faculty ratio: 22:1.

ACADEMICS
Calendar: quarters. *Degrees:* certificates, diplomas, associate, and bachelor's.
Library: Rasmussen College Library - Ocala.

STUDENT LIFE
Housing options: college housing not available.

APPLYING
Standardized Tests *Required:* institutional exam (for admission).
Options: electronic application, early admission, deferred entrance.
Required: high school transcript, minimum 2.0 GPA. *Required for some:* interview.

CONTACT
Dwayne Bertotto, Vice President of Admissions and Student Experience, Rasmussen College Ocala, 8300 Norman Center Drive, Suite 300, Bloomington, MN 55437. *Phone:* 952-806-3958. *Toll-free phone:* 888-549-6755. *E-mail:* dwayne.bertotto@rasmussen.edu.

Rasmussen College Ocala School of Nursing

Ocala, Florida

http://www.rasmussen.edu/

CONTACT
Ms. Susan Hammerstrom, Director of Admissions, Rasmussen College Ocala School of Nursing, 2100 SW 22nd Place, Ocala, FL 34471. *Phone:* 352-291-8560. *Toll-free phone:* 888-549-6755. *E-mail:* susan.hammerstrom@rasmussen.edu.

Rasmussen College Tampa/Brandon

Tampa, Florida

http://www.rasmussen.edu/

CONTACT
Ms. Susan Hammerstrom, Director of Admissions, Rasmussen College Tampa/Brandon, 4042 Park Oaks Boulevard, Suite 100, Tampa, FL 33610. *Phone:* 813-246-7600. *Toll-free phone:* 888-549-6755. *E-mail:* susan.hammerstrom@rasmussen.edu.

Ringling College of Art and Design

Sarasota, Florida

http://www.ringling.edu/

- **Independent** 4-year, founded 1931
- **Urban** 49-acre campus with easy access to Tampa-St. Petersburg
- **Endowment** $47.5 million
- **Coed**
- **Moderately difficult** entrance level

FACULTY
Student/faculty ratio: 11:1.

ACADEMICS
Calendar: semesters. *Degree:* bachelor's.
Library: Alfred R. Goldstein Library. *Books:* 51,891 (physical), 133,879 (digital/electronic); *Serial titles:* 12,169 (physical); *Databases:* 28. Weekly public service hours: 84; study areas open 24 hours, 5–7 days a week; students can reserve study rooms.

STUDENT LIFE
Housing options: coed, men-only, women-only. Campus housing is university owned. Freshman applicants given priority for college housing.
Activities and organizations: drama/theater group, student-run television station, choral group, Student Government Association, Digital Painting Sketch Club, Resident Student Association, MOSAIC, Quidditch Team.
Campus security: 24-hour emergency response devices and patrols, late-night transport/escort service, controlled dormitory access, lighted campus.
Student services: health clinic, personal/psychological counseling, legal services.

COSTS & FINANCIAL AID
Costs (2018–19) *Comprehensive fee:* $61,090 includes full-time tuition ($42,330), mandatory fees ($4090), and room and board ($14,670). Full-time tuition and fees vary according to course load, program, and student level. Part-time tuition: $1972 per credit hour. Part-time tuition and fees vary according to program and student level. *Room and board:* Room and board charges vary according to board plan and housing facility.
Financial Aid Of all full-time matriculated undergraduates who enrolled in 2018, 1,126 applied for aid, 1,007 were judged to have need, 52 had their need fully met. In 2018, 470 non-need-based awards were made. *Average percent of need met:* 50. *Average financial aid package:* $27,112. *Average need-based loan:* $8405. *Average need-based gift aid:* $17,826. *Average non-need-based aid:* $11,336. *Average indebtedness upon graduation:* $41,746.

APPLYING
Options: electronic application, early action, deferred entrance.
Application fee: $70.
Required: essay or personal statement, high school transcript, minimum 2.0 GPA, 2 letters of recommendation, portfolio, resume. *Recommended:* interview.

CONTACT
Ringling College of Art and Design, 2700 North Tamiami Trail, Sarasota, FL 34234-5895. *Phone:* 941-359-7523. *Toll-free phone:* 800-255-7695. *E-mail:* admissions@ringling.edu.

Rollins College

Winter Park, Florida

http://www.rollins.edu/

- **Independent** comprehensive, founded 1885
- **Suburban** 80-acre campus with easy access to Orlando
- **Endowment** $354.8 million
- **Coed** 2,034 undergraduate students, 100% full-time, 60% women, 40% men
- **Moderately difficult** entrance level, 72% of applicants were admitted

UNDERGRAD STUDENTS
2,027 full-time, 7 part-time. Students come from 41 states and territories; 57 other countries; 45% are from out of state; 4% Black or African American, non-Hispanic/Latino; 18% Hispanic/Latino; 3% Asian, non-Hispanic/Latino; 0.1% American Indian or Alaska Native, non-Hispanic/Latino; 5% Two or more races, non-Hispanic/Latino; 3% Race/ethnicity unknown; 9% international; 4% transferred in; 62% live on campus.

Freshmen:
Admission: 5,055 applied, 3,635 admitted, 549 enrolled. *Average high school GPA:* 3.3. *Test scores:* SAT evidence-based reading and writing scores over 500: 98%; SAT math scores over 500: 96%; ACT scores over 18: 100%; SAT evidence-based reading and writing scores over 600: 71%; SAT math scores over 600: 57%; ACT scores over 24: 80%; SAT evidence-based reading and writing scores over 700: 16%; SAT math scores over 700: 14%; ACT scores over 30: 26%.
Retention: 86% of full-time freshmen returned.

FACULTY
Total: 231, 100% full-time, 92% with terminal degrees.
Student/faculty ratio: 10:1.

ACADEMICS
Calendar: semesters. *Degrees:* bachelor's, master's, and doctoral.

Special study options: academic remediation for entering students, accelerated degree program, adult/continuing education programs, advanced placement credit, double majors, honors programs, independent study, internships, off-campus study, part-time degree program, services for LD students, student-designed majors, study abroad, summer session for credit.

Unusual degree programs: 3-2 business administration with Rollins College; engineering with Columbia University, Washington University in St. Louis, Auburn University; Environmental management with Duke University.

Computers: 254 computers/terminals are available on campus for general student use. Students can access the following: campus intranet, computer help desk, free student e-mail accounts, online (class) grades, online (class) registration, online (class) schedules. Campuswide network is available. 100% of college-owned or -operated housing units are wired for high-speed Internet access. Wireless service is available via entire campus.

Library: Olin Library. *Books:* 204,677 (physical), 236,421 (digital/electronic); *Serial titles:* 117 (physical), 104,688 (digital/electronic); *Databases:* 107. Weekly public service hours: 96; study areas open 24 hours, 5–7 days a week; students can reserve study rooms.

STUDENT LIFE

Housing options: on-campus residence required through sophomore year; coed, men-only, women-only, special housing for students with disabilities. Campus housing is university owned. Freshman campus housing is guaranteed.

Activities and organizations: drama/theater group, student-run newspaper, radio and television station, choral group, Black Student Union, Student Government Association, Eco-Rollins, Spectrum, WPRK 91.5, national fraternities, national sororities.

Athletics Member NCAA. All Division II except golf (Division I). *Intercollegiate sports:* baseball M(s), basketball M(s)/W(s), crew M/W, cross-country running M/W, golf M(s)/W(s), lacrosse M/W, sailing M/W, skiing (downhill) W, soccer M(s)/W(s), softball W(s), swimming and diving M/W, tennis M(s)/W(s), volleyball W(s). *Intramural sports:* baseball M, basketball M/W, bowling M/W, equestrian sports W(c), ice hockey M(c), soccer M/W, softball M/W, table tennis M/W, tennis M/W, ultimate Frisbee M/W, volleyball M/W.

Campus security: 24-hour emergency response devices and patrols, late-night transport/escort service, controlled dormitory access.

Student services: health clinic, personal/psychological counseling, women's center.

COSTS & FINANCIAL AID

Costs (2018–19) *Comprehensive fee:* $64,230 includes full-time tuition ($49,760) and room and board ($14,470). *College room only:* $8720. Room and board charges vary according to housing facility. *Payment plan:* installment. *Waivers:* employees or children of employees.

Financial Aid Of all full-time matriculated undergraduates who enrolled in 2018, 1,245 applied for aid, 1,097 were judged to have need, 188 had their need fully met. In 2018, 631 non-need-based awards were made. *Average percent of need met:* 84. *Average financial aid package:* $40,450. *Average need-based loan:* $4053. *Average need-based gift aid:* $35,036. *Average non-need-based aid:* $22,478. *Average indebtedness upon graduation:* $31,459.

APPLYING

Standardized Tests *Required:* Selection of Test Score Waived Option (TSWO) or official SAT/ACT scores (for admission).

Options: electronic application, early admission, early decision, deferred entrance.

Application fee: $50.

Required: essay or personal statement, high school transcript, 1 letter of recommendation. *Recommended:* minimum 2.0 GPA, interview.

Application deadlines: 2/1 (freshmen), 4/15 (transfers).

Early decision deadline: 11/15.

Notification: 4/1 (freshmen), continuous (transfers).

CONTACT

Dr. Faye Tydlaska, Vice President of Enrollment Management and Marketing, Rollins College, 1000 Holt Avenue, Campus Box 2720, Winter Park, FL 32789. *Phone:* 407-646-2000 Ext. 2161. *E-mail:* admissions@rollins.edu.

St. John Vianney College Seminary
Miami, Florida
http://www.sjvcs.edu/

CONTACT
Br. Edward Van Merrienboer, Academic Dean, St. John Vianney College Seminary, 2900 Southwest 87th Avenue, Miami, FL 33165-3244. *Phone:* 305-223-4561 Ext. 13.

Saint Leo University
Saint Leo, Florida
http://www.saintleo.edu/

- **Independent Roman Catholic** comprehensive, founded 1889
- **Rural** 280-acre campus with easy access to Tampa, Orlando
- **Endowment** $67.6 million
- **Coed** 2,086 undergraduate students, 97% full-time, 56% women, 44% men
- **Moderately difficult** entrance level, 84% of applicants were admitted

UNDERGRAD STUDENTS
2,022 full-time, 64 part-time. Students come from 46 states and territories; 66 other countries; 26% are from out of state; 14% Black or African American, non-Hispanic/Latino; 21% Hispanic/Latino; 2% Asian, non-Hispanic/Latino; 0.5% American Indian or Alaska Native, non-Hispanic/Latino; 2% Two or more races, non-Hispanic/Latino; 9% Race/ethnicity unknown; 12% international; 6% transferred in; 67% live on campus.

Freshmen:
Admission: 3,507 applied, 2,950 admitted, 561 enrolled. *Average high school GPA:* 3.5.

Retention: 72% of full-time freshmen returned.

FACULTY
Total: 194, 61% full-time, 60% with terminal degrees.

Student/faculty ratio: 14:1.

ACADEMICS
Calendar: semesters. *Degrees:* certificates, associate, bachelor's, master's, doctoral, and postbachelor's certificates.

Special study options: academic remediation for entering students, accelerated degree program, adult/continuing education programs, advanced placement credit, distance learning, double majors, English as a second language, honors programs, independent study, internships, part-time degree program, services for LD students, study abroad, summer session for credit. *ROTC:* Army (b), Air Force (b).

Computers: 150 computers/terminals are available on campus for general student use. Students can access the following: campus intranet, computer help desk, free student e-mail accounts, online (class) grades, online (class) registration, online (class) schedules. Campuswide network is available. 100% of college-owned or -operated housing units are wired for high-speed Internet access. Wireless service is available via classrooms, computer centers, computer labs, dorm rooms, learning centers, libraries, student centers.

Library: Cannon Memorial Library plus 1 other. *Books:* 86,985 (physical), 363,788 (digital/electronic); *Serial titles:* 1,430 (physical), 100,630 (digital/electronic); *Databases:* 121. Weekly public service hours: 112.

STUDENT LIFE
Housing options: on-campus residence required through junior year; coed, men-only, women-only, special housing for students with disabilities. Campus housing is university owned. Freshman applicants given priority for college housing.

Activities and organizations: drama/theater group, student-run newspaper, choral group, Caribbean Student Association, Alpha Phi Omega, Intercultural Student Association, Opus Fides, Pacioli Accounting Club, national fraternities, national sororities.

Athletics Member NCAA. All Division II except golf (Division I). *Intercollegiate sports:* baseball M(s), basketball M(s)/W(s), cross-country running M(s)/W(s), golf M(s)/W(s), lacrosse M(s)/W(s), soccer M(s)/W(s), softball W(s), swimming and diving M(s)/W(s), tennis M(s)/W(s), track and field M(s)/W(s), volleyball W(s). *Intramural* *sports:* basketball M/W, bowling M/W, fencing W, field hockey M, football M/W, sand volleyball M/W, soccer M/W, ultimate Frisbee M/W.

Campus security: 24-hour emergency response devices and patrols, late-night transport/escort service, controlled dormitory access.

Student services: health clinic, personal/psychological counseling, veterans affairs office.

COSTS & FINANCIAL AID
Costs (2019–20) *Comprehensive fee:* $35,000 includes full-time tuition ($23,100), mandatory fees ($650), and room and board ($11,250). *College room only:* $6000.

Financial Aid Of all full-time matriculated undergraduates who enrolled in 2018, 1,672 applied for aid, 1,480 were judged to have need, 334 had their need fully met. 689 Federal Work-Study jobs (averaging $4381). 7 state and other part-time jobs (averaging $3782). In 2018, 501 non-need-based awards were made. *Average percent of need met:* 78. *Average financial aid package:* $24,320. *Average need-based loan:* $3946. *Average need-based gift aid:* $18,310. *Average non-need-based aid:* $8533. *Average indebtedness upon graduation:* $26,447.

APPLYING
Options: electronic application, early admission, deferred entrance.

Required: high school transcript, 1 letter of recommendation. *Recommended:* interview.

Application deadlines: rolling (freshmen), rolling (transfers).

Notification: continuous (freshmen), continuous (transfers).

CONTACT
Mr. Nicholas Macchio, Saint Leo University, MC 2008, PO Box 6665, Saint Leo, FL 33574-6665. *Phone:* 800-334-5532. *Toll-free phone:* 800-334-5532. *Fax:* 352-588-8257. *E-mail:* admissions@saintleo.edu.

St. Petersburg College
St. Petersburg, Florida
http://www.spcollege.edu/

CONTACT
Ms. Eva Christensen, Director of Admissions and Records, St. Petersburg College, PO Box 13489, St. Petersburg, FL 33733-3489. *Phone:* 727-341-3166. *E-mail:* information@spcollege.edu.

St. Thomas University
Miami Gardens, Florida
http://www.stu.edu/
- **Independent Roman Catholic** university, founded 1961
- **Suburban** 140-acre campus with easy access to Miami, FL
- **Endowment** $25.6 million
- **Coed**
- **Moderately difficult** entrance level

FACULTY
Student/faculty ratio: 11:1.

ACADEMICS
Calendar: semesters. *Degrees:* certificates, bachelor's, master's, doctoral, post-master's, and postbachelor's certificates.
Library: St. Thomas University Library plus 1 other. *Books:* 555,242 (physical), 479,232 (digital/electronic); *Serial titles:* 146,423 (physical), 146,423 (digital/electronic); *Databases:* 410. Weekly public service hours: 101; students can reserve study rooms.

STUDENT LIFE
Housing options: coed. Campus housing is university owned.

Activities and organizations: choral group, marching band, Psychology Club, Nursing Students Association, Criminal Justice, Caribbean Students Association, Future Teachers of America.

Athletics Member NAIA.

Campus security: 24-hour emergency response devices and patrols, late-night transport/escort service, controlled dormitory access.

Student services: health clinic, personal/psychological counseling.

COSTS
Costs (2018–19) *Comprehensive fee:* $42,780 includes full-time tuition ($30,900), mandatory fees ($180), and room and board ($11,700). Full-time tuition and fees vary according to course load and program. Part-time tuition: $1030 per credit hour. Part-time tuition and fees vary according to course load and program. *Required fees:* $75 per course part-time, $120 per term part-time. *College room only:* $7200. Room and board charges vary according to board plan and housing facility. *Payment plans:* installment, deferred payment.

APPLYING
Standardized Tests *Recommended:* SAT or ACT (for admission).

Options: electronic application.

Application fee: $40.

Required: high school transcript, minimum 2.5 GPA. *Required for some:* interview. *Recommended:* essay or personal statement, 1 letter of recommendation.

CONTACT
Mr. Anthony Noriega, Associate Director of Admissions, St. Thomas University, 16401 Northwest 37th Avenue, Miami Gardens, FL 33054-6459. *Phone:* 305-628-6617. *Toll-free phone:* 800-367-9010. *E-mail:* ajnoriega@stu.edu.

San Ignacio University
Doral, Florida
http://www.sanignaciouniversity.edu/

CONTACT
San Ignacio University, 10395 NW 41st Street, Suite 125, Doral, FL 33178.

Santa Fe College
Gainesville, Florida
http://www.sfcollege.edu/

CONTACT
Santa Fe College, 3000 Northwest 83rd Street, Gainesville, FL 32606. *Phone:* 352-395-4177.

Schiller International University
Largo, Florida
http://www.schiller.edu/

CONTACT
Admissions Officer, Schiller International University, Largo, FL 33770. *Toll-free phone:* 800-261-9571 (in-state); 800-261-9751 (out-of-state). *Fax:* 727-738-6376. *E-mail:* admissions@schiller.edu.

Seminole State College of Florida
Sanford, Florida
http://www.seminolestate.edu/
- **State and locally supported** primarily 2-year, founded 1966, part of Florida College System
- **Small-town** 200-acre campus with easy access to Orlando
- **Endowment** $24.6 million
- **Coed**
- **Noncompetitive** entrance level

FACULTY
Student/faculty ratio: 26:1.

ACADEMICS
Calendar: semesters. *Degrees:* certificates, diplomas, associate, bachelor's, and postbachelor's certificates.
Library: Seminole State Library at Sanford Lake Mary plus 3 others. *Books:* 67,023 (physical), 145,374 (digital/electronic); *Serial titles:* 520 (physical), 18,003 (digital/electronic); *Databases:* 130. Weekly public service hours: 60; students can reserve study rooms.

STUDENT LIFE
Housing options: college housing not available.

Activities and organizations: drama/theater group, student-run newspaper, choral group, Phi Beta Lambda, Phi Theta Kappa, Student Government Association, Sigma Phi Gamma, Hispanic Student Association.

Athletics Member NJCAA.

Campus security: 24-hour emergency response devices and patrols, late-night transport/escort service.

Student services: personal/psychological counseling, veterans affairs office.

COSTS

Costs (2018–19) *Tuition:* state resident $3131 full-time, $104 per credit hour part-time; nonresident $12,739 full-time, $382 per credit hour part-time. Full-time tuition and fees vary according to degree level. Part-time tuition and fees vary according to degree level.

APPLYING

Options: electronic application, early admission, deferred entrance.

Required: high school transcript, minimum 2.0 GPA.

CONTACT

Seminole State College of Florida, 100 Weldon Boulevard, Sanford, FL 32773-6199.

Southeastern University

Lakeland, Florida

http://www.seu.edu/

- **Independent** comprehensive, founded 1935, affiliated with Assemblies of God
- **Suburban** 87-acre campus with easy access to Tampa, Orlando
- **Endowment** $9.3 million
- **Coed** 7,708 undergraduate students, 64% full-time, 57% women, 43% men
- **Minimally difficult** entrance level, 48% of applicants were admitted

UNDERGRAD STUDENTS

4,909 full-time, 2,799 part-time. 49% are from out of state; 14% Black or African American, non-Hispanic/Latino; 21% Hispanic/Latino; 1% Asian, non-Hispanic/Latino; 0.5% Native Hawaiian or other Pacific Islander, non-Hispanic/Latino; 0.5% American Indian or Alaska Native, non-Hispanic/Latino; 0.9% Two or more races, non-Hispanic/Latino; 1% Race/ethnicity unknown; 1% international; 12% transferred in; 31% live on campus.

Freshmen:

Admission: 4,996 applied, 2,405 admitted, 1,460 enrolled. *Average high school GPA:* 3.5. *Test scores:* SAT evidence-based reading and writing scores over 500: 72%; SAT math scores over 500: 61%; ACT scores over 18: 76%; SAT evidence-based reading and writing scores over 600: 27%; SAT math scores over 600: 15%; ACT scores over 24: 27%; SAT evidence-based reading and writing scores over 700: 2%; SAT math scores over 700: 2%; ACT scores over 30: 3%.

Retention: 68% of full-time freshmen returned.

FACULTY

Total: 613, 26% full-time, 38% with terminal degrees.

Student/faculty ratio: 20:1.

ACADEMICS

Calendar: semesters. *Degrees:* certificates, associate, bachelor's, master's, doctoral, post-master's, and postbachelor's certificates.

Special study options: academic remediation for entering students, adult/continuing education programs, advanced placement credit, cooperative education, distance learning, double majors, honors programs, independent study, internships, off-campus study, part-time degree program, services for LD students, study abroad, summer session for credit. *ROTC:* Army (c).

Computers: 220 computers/terminals are available on campus for general student use. Students can access the following: campus intranet, computer help desk, free student e-mail accounts, online (class) grades, online (class) registration, online (class) schedules, network programs. Campuswide network is available. 100% of college-owned or -operated housing units are wired for high-speed Internet access. Wireless service is available via entire campus.

Library: Steelman Library. *Books:* 79,844 (physical), 215,769 (digital/electronic).

STUDENT LIFE

Housing options: on-campus residence required through sophomore year; men-only, women-only. Campus housing is university owned. Freshman campus housing is guaranteed.

Activities and organizations: drama/theater group, student-run newspaper, radio and television station, choral group.

Athletics Member NAIA. *Intercollegiate sports:* baseball M(s), basketball M(s)/W(s), cheerleading M/W, cross-country running M(s)/W(s), football M(s), golf M(s), soccer M(s)/W(s), softball W(s), tennis M(s)/W(s), volleyball W(s), wrestling M(s). *Intramural sports:* basketball M/W, football M/W, soccer M/W, softball M/W, ultimate Frisbee M/W, volleyball M/W.

Campus security: 24-hour emergency response devices and patrols, late-night transport/escort service, controlled dormitory access.

Student services: health clinic, personal/psychological counseling.

COSTS & FINANCIAL AID

Costs (2019–20) *Comprehensive fee:* $35,702 includes full-time tuition ($24,870), mandatory fees ($1000), and room and board ($9832). Part-time tuition: $1036 per credit hour.

Financial Aid Of all full-time matriculated undergraduates who enrolled in 2018, 4,196 applied for aid, 3,691 were judged to have need, 430 had their need fully met. 96 Federal Work-Study jobs (averaging $2062). In 2018, 991 non-need-based awards were made. *Average percent of need met:* 62. *Average financial aid package:* $15,641. *Average need-based loan:* $4043. *Average need-based gift aid:* $5967. *Average non-need-based aid:* $9225. *Average indebtedness upon graduation:* $30,254.

APPLYING

Standardized Tests *Required:* SAT or ACT (for admission).

Options: electronic application, early admission, deferred entrance.

Application fee: $40.

Required: essay or personal statement, high school transcript, 1 letter of recommendation. *Required for some:* interview.

Notification: 6/1 (freshmen), continuous (transfers).

CONTACT

Ms. Sarah Clark, Executive Director of Admission, Southeastern University, 1000 Longfellow Boulevard, Lakeland, FL 33801. *Phone:* 863-667-5018. *Toll-free phone:* 800-500-8760. *E-mail:* admission@seu.edu.

Southern Technical College

Fort Myers, Florida

http://www.southerntech.edu/locations/ft-myers/

CONTACT

Ms. Tiffany Quinlan, Director of Admissions, Southern Technical College, 1685 Medical Lane, Fort Myers, FL 33907. *Phone:* 239-939-4766. *Toll-free phone:* 877-347-5492. *Fax:* 239-936-4040. *E-mail:* tquinlan@southerntech.edu.

Southern Technical College

Tampa, Florida

http://www.southerntech.edu/locations/tampa/

CONTACT

Admissions, Southern Technical College, 3910 Riga Boulevard, Tampa, FL 33619. *Phone:* 813-630-4401. *Toll-free phone:* 877-347-5492.

South Florida Bible College and Theological Seminary

Deerfield Beach, Florida

http://www.sfbc.edu/

CONTACT

South Florida Bible College and Theological Seminary, 2200 SW 10th Street, Deerfield Beach, FL 33442.

South Florida State College

Avon Park, Florida

http://www.southflorida.edu/

- **State-supported** primarily 2-year, founded 1965, part of Florida State College System
- **Rural** 228-acre campus with easy access to Tampa, St. Petersburg, Orlando
- **Endowment** $6.2 million
- **Coed**
- **Noncompetitive** entrance level

FACULTY
Student/faculty ratio: 16:1.

ACADEMICS
Calendar: semesters. *Degrees:* certificates, diplomas, associate, and bachelor's.
Library: Library Services.

STUDENT LIFE
Housing options: Campus housing is provided by a third party.
Activities and organizations: Phi Theta Kappa, Phi Beta Lambda, Art Club, Anime and Gaming Club, Basketball Club.
Athletics Member NJCAA.
Campus security: 24-hour emergency response devices and patrols, late-night transport/escort service.
Student services: personal/psychological counseling.

COSTS & FINANCIAL AID
Costs (2018–19) *One-time required fee:* $15. *Tuition:* state resident $2593 full-time, $105 per credit hour part-time; nonresident $9722 full-time, $394 per credit hour part-time. Full-time tuition and fees vary according to course level, course load, degree level, and program. Part-time tuition and fees vary according to course level, course load, degree level, and program. *Room and board:* $6040; room only: $2040.
Financial Aid *Average need-based gift aid:* $4666. *Average indebtedness upon graduation:* $3083.

APPLYING
Options: electronic application, early admission, deferred entrance.
Application fee: $15.
Required: high school transcript.

CONTACT
Ms. Brenda Desantiago, Admissions, South Florida State College, 600 West College Drive, Avon Park, FL 33825. *Phone:* 863-784-7416.

South University

Royal Palm Beach, Florida

http://www.southuniversity.edu/west-palm-beach/

CONTACT
South University, University Centre, 9801 Belvedere Road, Royal Palm Beach, FL 33411. *Phone:* 561-273-6500. *Toll-free phone:* 866-629-2902.

South University

Tampa, Florida

http://www.southuniversity.edu/tampa/

CONTACT
South University, 4401 North Himes Avenue, Suite 175, Tampa, FL 33614. *Phone:* 813-393-3800. *Toll-free phone:* 800-846-1472.

State College of Florida Manatee-Sarasota

Bradenton, Florida

http://www.scf.edu/

CONTACT
Ms. MariLynn Lewy, Assistant Vice President of Student Services, State College of Florida Manatee-Sarasota, Bradenton, FL 34206. *Phone:* 941-752-5384. *Fax:* 941-727-6380. *E-mail:* lewym@scf.edu.

Stetson University

DeLand, Florida

http://www.stetson.edu/

- **Independent** comprehensive, founded 1883
- **Small-town** 159-acre campus with easy access to Orlando
- **Endowment** $242.9 million
- **Coed** 3,150 undergraduate students, 99% full-time, 56% women, 44% men
- **Moderately difficult** entrance level, 68% of applicants were admitted

UNDERGRAD STUDENTS
3,111 full-time, 39 part-time. Students come from 43 states and territories; 64 other countries; 26% are from out of state; 8% Black or African American, non-Hispanic/Latino; 17% Hispanic/Latino; 2% Asian, non-Hispanic/Latino; 0.1% Native Hawaiian or other Pacific Islander, non-Hispanic/Latino; 0.1% American Indian or Alaska Native, non-Hispanic/Latino; 5% Two or more races, non-Hispanic/Latino; 1% Race/ethnicity unknown; 6% international; 4% transferred in; 64% live on campus.

Freshmen:
Admission: 13,330 applied, 9,121 admitted, 895 enrolled. *Average high school GPA:* 3.8. *Test scores:* SAT evidence-based reading and writing scores over 500: 98%; SAT math scores over 500: 95%; ACT scores over 18: 98%; SAT evidence-based reading and writing scores over 600: 65%; SAT math scores over 600: 46%; ACT scores over 24: 72%; SAT evidence-based reading and writing scores over 700: 12%; SAT math scores over 700: 8%; ACT scores over 30: 23%.
Retention: 76% of full-time freshmen returned.

FACULTY
Total: 432, 62% full-time, 81% with terminal degrees.
Student/faculty ratio: 13:1.

ACADEMICS
Calendar: semesters. *Degrees:* bachelor's, master's, doctoral, and post-master's certificates.
Special study options: accelerated degree program, advanced placement credit, distance learning, double majors, honors programs, independent study, internships, off-campus study, part-time degree program, services for LD students, student-designed majors, study abroad, summer session for credit. *ROTC:* Army (c), Air Force (c).
Unusual degree programs: 3-2 engineering; forestry with Duke University; environmental management with Duke University, public administration with American University.
Computers: 600 computers/terminals are available on campus for general student use. Students can access the following: campus intranet, computer help desk, free student e-mail accounts, online (class) grades, online (class) registration, online (class) schedules. Campuswide network is available. 100% of college-owned or -operated housing units are wired for high-speed Internet access. Wireless service is available via entire campus.
Library: duPont-Ball Library plus 1 other. *Books:* 230,712 (physical), 194,199 (digital/electronic); *Serial titles:* 227 (physical), 159,553 (digital/electronic); *Databases:* 134. Weekly public service hours: 104; students can reserve study rooms.

STUDENT LIFE
Housing options: on-campus residence required through junior year; coed, men-only, women-only. Campus housing is university owned and leased by the school. Freshman campus housing is guaranteed.
Activities and organizations: drama/theater group, student-run newspaper, radio station, choral group, Caribbean Student Association, Fellowship of Christian Athletes, Kaleidoscope (promotes inclusivity), Black Student Association, Hatter Productions, national fraternities, national sororities.
Athletics Member NCAA. All Division I. *Intercollegiate sports:* baseball M(s), basketball M(s)/W(s), crew M(s)/W(s), cross-country running M(s)/W(s), football M, golf M(s)/W(s)(c), lacrosse W(s), soccer M(s)/W(s), softball W(s), tennis M(s)/W(s), volleyball W(s). *Intramural sports:* baseball M(c), basketball M/W(c), equestrian sports M(c)/W(c), golf M(c)/W(c), ice hockey M(c)/W(c), lacrosse M(c)/W(c), riflery M(c)/W(c), sand volleyball M/W, soccer M(c)/W(c), softball M/W(c), tennis M/W, ultimate Frisbee M(c)/W(c), volleyball M/W(c).

Campus security: 24-hour emergency response devices and patrols, student patrols, late-night transport/escort service, controlled dormitory access.

Student services: health clinic, personal/psychological counseling, veterans affairs office.

COSTS & FINANCIAL AID
Costs (2019–20) *Comprehensive fee:* $61,498 includes full-time tuition ($47,270), mandatory fees ($360), and room and board ($13,868). Part-time tuition: $1190 per credit hour. *College room only:* $8142.

Financial Aid Of all full-time matriculated undergraduates who enrolled in 2018, 2,302 applied for aid, 2,095 were judged to have need, 444 had their need fully met. 478 Federal Work-Study jobs (averaging $2430). 68 state and other part-time jobs (averaging $3925). In 2018, 814 non-need-based awards were made. *Average percent of need met:* 77. *Average financial aid package:* $38,914. *Average need-based loan:* $4387. *Average need-based gift aid:* $32,490. *Average non-need-based aid:* $25,352. *Average indebtedness upon graduation:* $35,399.

APPLYING
Standardized Tests *Required for some:* SAT or ACT (for admission).
Options: electronic application, early action, deferred entrance.
Application fee: $50.
Required: essay or personal statement, high school transcript, 1 letter of recommendation. *Recommended:* interview.
Application deadlines: rolling (freshmen), rolling (transfers).
Notification: continuous (freshmen), continuous (transfers).

CONTACT
Ms. Dana Simmons, Director of Enrollment Operations and Communications, Stetson University, 421 N. Woodland Boulevard, Unit 8378, DeLand, FL 32723. *Phone:* 386-822-7100. *Toll-free phone:* 800-688-0101. *Fax:* 386-822-7112. *E-mail:* admissions@stetson.edu.

Strayer University–Baymeadows Campus
Jacksonville, Florida
http://www.strayer.edu/florida/baymeadows/

CONTACT
Strayer University–Baymeadows Campus, 8375 Dix Ellis Trail, Suite 200, Jacksonville, FL 32256. *Toll-free phone:* 888-311-0355.

Strayer University–Fort Lauderdale Campus
Fort Lauderdale, Florida
http://www.strayer.edu/florida/fort-lauderdale/

CONTACT
Strayer University–Fort Lauderdale Campus, 2307 West Broward Boulevard, Suite 100, Fort Lauderdale, FL 33312. *Toll-free phone:* 888-311-0355.

Strayer University–Maitland Campus
Maitland, Florida
http://www.strayer.edu/florida/maitland/

CONTACT
Strayer University–Maitland Campus, 901 North Lake Destiny Road, Suite 370, Maitland, FL 32751. *Toll-free phone:* 888-311-0355.

Strayer University–Miramar Campus
Hollywood, Florida
http://www.strayer.edu/florida/miramar/

CONTACT
Strayer University–Miramar Campus, 15620 Southwest 29th Street, Hollywood, FL 33027. *Toll-free phone:* 888-311-0355.

Strayer University–Orlando East Campus
Orlando, Florida
http://www.strayer.edu/florida/orlando-east/

CONTACT
Strayer University–Orlando East Campus, 2200 North Alafaya Trail, Suite 500, Orlando, FL 32826. *Toll-free phone:* 888-311-0355.

Strayer University–Palm Beach Gardens Campus
West Palm Beach, Florida
http://www.strayer.edu/florida/palm-beach-gardens/

CONTACT
Strayer University–Palm Beach Gardens Campus, 11025 RCA Center Drive, Suite 200, West Palm Beach, FL 33410. *Toll-free phone:* 888-311-0355.

Strayer University–Sand Lake Campus
Orlando, Florida
http://www.strayer.edu/florida/sand-lake/

CONTACT
Strayer University–Sand Lake Campus, 8529 South Park Circle, Orlando, FL 32819. *Toll-free phone:* 888-311-0355.

Strayer University–Tampa East Campus
Tampa, Florida
http://www.strayer.edu/florida/tampa-east/

CONTACT
Strayer University–Tampa East Campus, 5650 Breckenridge Park Drive, Suite 300, Tampa, FL 33610. *Toll-free phone:* 888-311-0355.

Tallahassee Community College
Tallahassee, Florida
http://www.tcc.fl.edu/
- **State and locally supported** primarily 2-year, founded 1966, part of Florida College System
- **Suburban** 214-acre campus
- **Endowment** $9.3 million
- **Coed**
- **Noncompetitive** entrance level

FACULTY
Student/faculty ratio: 22:1.

ACADEMICS
Calendar: semesters. *Degrees:* certificates, associate, and bachelor's.
Library: Tallahassee Community College Library. *Books:* 82,774 (physical), 53,129 (digital/electronic); *Serial titles:* 59 (physical), 42,687 (digital/electronic); *Databases:* 105. Weekly public service hours: 68; students can reserve study rooms.

STUDENT LIFE
Housing options: college housing not available.
Activities and organizations: drama/theater group, student-run newspaper, choral group, Student Government Association, International Student Organization, Phi Theta Kappa, Model United Nations, Honors Council.
Athletics Member NJCAA.
Campus security: 24-hour emergency response devices and patrols, late-night transport/escort service.
Student services: personal/psychological counseling, veterans affairs office.

COSTS & FINANCIAL AID

Costs (2018–19) *Tuition:* state resident $2002 full-time, $101 per credit hour part-time; nonresident $7982 full-time, $387 per credit hour part-time. *Required fees:* $24 full-time.

Financial Aid Of all full-time matriculated undergraduates who enrolled in 2017, 3,844 applied for aid, 2,633 were judged to have need. 107 Federal Work-Study jobs (averaging $1802). *Average financial aid package:* $3977. *Average need-based gift aid:* $3775.

APPLYING

Options: electronic application, early admission, deferred entrance.

Required: high school transcript.

CONTACT

Student Success Center, Tallahassee Community College, 444 Appleyard Drive, Tallahassee, FL 32304-2895. *Phone:* 850-201-8555. *E-mail:* admissions@tcc.fl.edu.

Talmudic University

Miami Beach, Florida

http://www.talmudicu.edu/

CONTACT

Rabbi Yeshaya Greenberg, Dean of Students, Talmudic University, 4000 Alton Road, Miami Beach, FL 33140. *Phone:* 305-534-7050. *Fax:* 305-534-8444. *E-mail:* yandtg@gmail.com.

Trinity Baptist College

Jacksonville, Florida

http://www.tbc.edu/

CONTACT

Melissa Gibson, Trinity Baptist College, 800 Hammond Boulevard, Jacksonville, FL 32219. *Phone:* 904-596-2307. *Toll-free phone:* 800-786-2206. *E-mail:* mgibson@tbc.edu.

Trinity College of Florida

Trinity, Florida

http://www.trinitycollege.edu/

- **Independent nondenominational** 4-year, founded 1932
- **Small-town** 40-acre campus with easy access to Tampa
- **Endowment** $726,911
- **Coed**
- **Noncompetitive** entrance level

FACULTY

Student/faculty ratio: 9:1.

ACADEMICS

Calendar: semesters. *Degrees:* certificates, associate, and bachelor's. **Library:** Raymond H. Center, M.D. Library. *Books:* 33,116 (physical), 165,300 (digital/electronic); *Serial titles:* 38 (physical); *Databases:* 9. Weekly public service hours: 60.

STUDENT LIFE

Housing options: men-only, women-only, special housing for students with disabilities. Campus housing is university owned and leased by the school. Freshman campus housing is guaranteed.

Activities and organizations: choral group, Student Government Association, Great Commission Missionary Fellowship, Prayer Group, Trinity Against Trafficking.

Athletics Member NCCAA.

Campus security: student patrols, security cameras.

Student services: personal/psychological counseling.

COSTS & FINANCIAL AID

Costs (2018–19) *Comprehensive fee:* $23,315 includes full-time tuition ($15,300), mandatory fees ($1040), and room and board ($6975). Full-time tuition and fees vary according to course load and program. Part-time tuition: $510 per credit hour. Part-time tuition and fees vary according to course load and program. *Required fees:* $520 per term part-time.

Financial Aid Of all full-time matriculated undergraduates who enrolled in 2018, 167 applied for aid, 149 were judged to have need, 31 had their

need fully met. 20 Federal Work-Study jobs (averaging $2830). 1 state and other part-time job (averaging $3853). In 2018, 16 non-need-based awards were made. *Average percent of need met:* 70. *Average financial aid package:* $13,365. *Average need-based loan:* $6787. *Average need-based gift aid:* $7574. *Average non-need-based aid:* $4554. *Average indebtedness upon graduation:* $38,898.

APPLYING

Standardized Tests *Required:* SAT or ACT (for admission).

Options: electronic application, deferred entrance.

Application fee: $35.

Required: essay or personal statement, high school transcript, 2 letters of recommendation. *Required for some:* interview. *Recommended:* minimum 2.2 GPA.

CONTACT

Mr. Alton Shady, Admissions Representative, Trinity College of Florida, 2430 Welbilt Boulevard, Trinity, FL 34655. *Phone:* 727-376-6911 Ext. 309. *Toll-free phone:* 800-388-0869. *Fax:* 727-569-1410. *E-mail:* ashady@trinitycollege.edu.

Unilatina International College

Miramar, Florida

http://www.unilatina.edu/

CONTACT

Unilatina International College, 3130 Commerce Parkway, Miramar, FL 33025.

University of Central Florida

Orlando, Florida

http://www.ucf.edu/

- **State-supported** university, founded 1963, part of State University System of Florida
- **Suburban** 1415-acre campus with easy access to Orlando
- **Endowment** $161.6 million
- **Coed** 58,913 undergraduate students, 71% full-time, 54% women, 46% men
- **Moderately difficult** entrance level, 43% of applicants were admitted

UNDERGRAD STUDENTS

41,852 full-time, 17,061 part-time. Students come from 50 states and territories; 132 other countries; 7% are from out of state; 11% Black or African American, non-Hispanic/Latino; 28% Hispanic/Latino; 6% Asian, non-Hispanic/Latino; 0.2% Native Hawaiian or other Pacific Islander, non-Hispanic/Latino; 0.2% American Indian or Alaska Native, non-Hispanic/Latino; 4% Two or more races, non-Hispanic/Latino; 0.8% Race/ethnicity unknown; 2% international; 12% transferred in; 17% live on campus.

Freshmen:

Admission: 41,816 applied, 17,786 admitted, 7,234 enrolled. *Average high school GPA:* 4.0. *Test scores:* SAT evidence-based reading and writing scores over 500: 99%; SAT math scores over 500: 99%; ACT scores over 18: 100%; SAT evidence-based reading and writing scores over 600: 72%; SAT math scores over 600: 63%; ACT scores over 24: 84%; SAT evidence-based reading and writing scores over 700: 13%; SAT math scores over 700: 15%; ACT scores over 30: 23%.

Retention: 90% of full-time freshmen returned.

FACULTY

Total: 2,123, 76% full-time, 74% with terminal degrees.

Student/faculty ratio: 30:1.

ACADEMICS

Calendar: semesters. *Degrees:* certificates, associate, bachelor's, master's, doctoral, post-master's, and postbachelor's certificates.

Special study options: accelerated degree program, adult/continuing education programs, advanced placement credit, cooperative education, distance learning, double majors, English as a second language, freshman honors college, honors programs, independent study, internships, off-campus study, part-time degree program, services for LD students, study abroad, summer session for credit. *ROTC:* Army (b), Air Force (b).

Unusual degree programs: 3-2 engineering; nursing; history, communicative sciences and disorders, computer science, law.

Computers: 4,113 computers/terminals and 500 ports are available on campus for general student use. Students can access the following: campus intranet, computer help desk, free student e-mail accounts, online (class) grades, online (class) registration, online (class) schedules. Campuswide network is available. 100% of college-owned or -operated housing units are wired for high-speed Internet access. Wireless service is available via entire campus.

Library: University Libraries plus 3 others. *Books:* 1.6 million (physical), 181,480 (digital/electronic); *Serial titles:* 737 (physical), 68,194 (digital/electronic); *Databases:* 481. Weekly public service hours: 105; students can reserve study rooms.

STUDENT LIFE

Housing options: coed. Campus housing is university owned and is provided by a third party. Freshman applicants given priority for college housing.

Activities and organizations: drama/theater group, student-run radio and television station, choral group, marching band, Volunteer UCF, RWC Intramural Sports, Fraternity and Sorority Life, Multicultural Student Center and Organizations, Knight-thon Dance Marathon, national fraternities, national sororities.

Athletics Member NCAA. All Division I except football (Division I-A). *Intercollegiate sports:* baseball M(s), basketball M(s)/W(s), cheerleading W(s), crew W(s), cross-country running W(s), golf M(s)/W(s)(c), soccer M(s)/W(s), softball W(s), tennis M(s)/W(s), track and field W(s), volleyball W(s). *Intramural sports:* badminton M/W, baseball M, basketball M/W, bowling M(c)/W(c), crew M(c)/W, equestrian sports M(c)/W(c), fencing M(c), golf M/W, ice hockey M(c), lacrosse M(c)/W(c), racquetball M/W, rock climbing M(c)/W(c), rugby M(c)/W(c), soccer M/W, softball W(c), swimming and diving M(c)/W(c), table tennis M(c)/W(c), tennis M/W, triathlon M(c)/W(c), ultimate Frisbee M(c)/W(c), volleyball M/W, water polo M(c)/W(c), wrestling M(c)/W(c).

Campus security: 24-hour emergency response devices and patrols, late-night transport/escort service, controlled dormitory access.

Student services: health clinic, personal/psychological counseling, women's center, legal services, veterans affairs office.

COSTS & FINANCIAL AID

Costs (2018–19) *Tuition:* state resident $6368 full-time, $212 per credit hour part-time; nonresident $22,467 full-time, $749 per credit hour part-time. Full-time tuition and fees vary according to course load. Part-time tuition and fees vary according to course load. *Room and board:* $9617; room only: $5400. Room and board charges vary according to board plan and housing facility. *Payment plans:* tuition prepayment, deferred payment. *Waivers:* senior citizens and employees or children of employees.

Financial Aid Of all full-time matriculated undergraduates who enrolled in 2017, 31,774 applied for aid, 24,728 were judged to have need, 2,804 had their need fully met. 863 Federal Work-Study jobs (averaging $3778). In 2017, 1959 non-need-based awards were made. *Average percent of need met:* 61. *Average financial aid package:* $9982. *Average need-based loan:* $4673. *Average need-based gift aid:* $6831. *Average non-need-based aid:* $3932. *Average indebtedness upon graduation:* $22,722. *Financial aid deadline:* 6/30.

APPLYING

Standardized Tests *Required:* SAT or ACT (for admission).

Options: electronic application, early admission.

Application fee: $30.

Required: minimum 2.5 GPA. *Required for some:* high school transcript. *Recommended:* essay or personal statement.

Application deadlines: 5/1 (freshmen), 7/1 (transfers).

Notification: continuous (freshmen), continuous (transfers).

CONTACT

Dr. Gordon Chavis Jr., Associate Vice President, Undergraduate Admissions, Student Financial Assistance and Outreach Programs, University of Central Florida, PO Box 160111, Orlando, FL 32816-0111. *Phone:* 407-823-3000. *Fax:* 407-823-5625. *E-mail:* admission@ucf.edu.

University of Florida
Gainesville, Florida
http://www.ufl.edu/

- **State-supported** university, founded 1853, part of Board of Trustees
- **Suburban** 2000-acre campus with easy access to Jacksonville
- **Endowment** $1.7 million
- **Coed** 35,491 undergraduate students, 91% full-time, 56% women, 44% men
- **Very difficult** entrance level, 39% of applicants were admitted

UNDERGRAD STUDENTS

32,209 full-time, 3,282 part-time. Students come from 51 states and territories; 140 other countries; 7% are from out of state; 6% Black or African American, non-Hispanic/Latino; 22% Hispanic/Latino; 9% Asian, non-Hispanic/Latino; 0.4% Native Hawaiian or other Pacific Islander, non-Hispanic/Latino; 0.2% American Indian or Alaska Native, non-Hispanic/Latino; 4% Two or more races, non-Hispanic/Latino; 3% Race/ethnicity unknown; 3% international; 6% transferred in; 22% live on campus.

Freshmen:

Admission: 38,905 applied, 15,077 admitted, 6,792 enrolled. *Average high school GPA:* 4.4. *Test scores:* SAT evidence-based reading and writing scores over 500: 99%; SAT math scores over 500: 98%; ACT scores over 18: 100%; SAT evidence-based reading and writing scores over 600: 90%; SAT math scores over 600: 87%; ACT scores over 24: 93%; SAT evidence-based reading and writing scores over 700: 35%; SAT math scores over 700: 43%; ACT scores over 30: 51%.

ACADEMICS

Calendar: semesters. *Degrees:* certificates, associate, bachelor's, master's, doctoral, post-master's, and postbachelor's certificates.

Special study options: accelerated degree program, adult/continuing education programs, advanced placement credit, cooperative education, distance learning, double majors, English as a second language, external degree program, honors programs, independent study, internships, off-campus study, part-time degree program, services for LD students, student-designed majors, study abroad, summer session for credit. *ROTC:* Army (b), Navy (b), Air Force (b).

Unusual degree programs: 3-2 business administration; engineering with The University of the Virgin Islands; forestry.

Computers: 1,327 computers/terminals and 245 ports are available on campus for general student use. Students can access the following: campus intranet, computer help desk, free student e-mail accounts, online (class) grades, online (class) registration, online (class) schedules, course management system; virtual labs/applications. Campuswide network is available. 100% of college-owned or -operated housing units are wired for high-speed Internet access. Wireless service is available via entire campus.

Library: George A. Smathers Libraries plus 7 others. *Books:* 5.8 million (physical), 1.5 million (digital/electronic); *Serial titles:* 2,716 (physical), 125,667 (digital/electronic); *Databases:* 1,092. Weekly public service hours: 168; study areas open 24 hours, 5–7 days a week; students can reserve study rooms.

STUDENT LIFE

Housing options: coed, special housing for students with disabilities. Campus housing is university owned and is provided by a third party.

Activities and organizations: drama/theater group, student-run newspaper, radio and television station, choral group, marching band, Student Government, Hispanic Student Association, Black Student Union, Inter-Residence Hall Association, Asian American Student Union, national fraternities, national sororities.

Athletics Member NCAA. All Division I. *Intercollegiate sports:* baseball M(s), basketball M(s)/W(s), bowling M(c)/W(c), cheerleading M(s)/W(s), cross-country running M(s)/W(s), football M(s), golf M(s), gymnastics W(s), lacrosse W(s), racquetball M(c)/W(c), soccer M/W(s), softball W(s), swimming and diving M(s)/W(s), table tennis M(c)/W(c), tennis M(s)/W(s), track and field M(s)/W(s), ultimate Frisbee M(c)/W(c), volleyball M/W(s). *Intramural sports:* archery M(c)/W(c), badminton M(c)/W(c), baseball M(c), basketball M/W, bowling M/W, cheerleading W(c), crew M(c)/W(c), cross-country running M(c)/W(c), equestrian sports M(c)/W(c), fencing M(c)/W(c), field hockey M(c)/W(c), football M/W, golf M(c)/W(c), gymnastics W(c), ice hockey M(c), lacrosse

M(c)/W(c), racquetball M/W, rock climbing M(c)/W(c), rugby M(c)/W(c), sailing M(c)/W(c), sand volleyball M/W, soccer M/W, softball M/W, swimming and diving M/W, table tennis M/W, tennis M/W, track and field M/W, ultimate Frisbee M/W, volleyball M/W, water polo M(c)/W(c), weight lifting M(c)/W(c), wrestling M(c)/W(c).

Campus security: 24-hour emergency response devices and patrols, student patrols, late-night transport/escort service, controlled dormitory access, crime and rape prevention programs.

Student services: health clinic, personal/psychological counseling, women's center, legal services, veterans affairs office.

FINANCIAL AID
Financial Aid Of all full-time matriculated undergraduates who enrolled in 2017, 22,536 applied for aid, 16,548 were judged to have need, 3,960 had their need fully met. 1,066 Federal Work-Study jobs (averaging $2283). 5,369 state and other part-time jobs (averaging $3545). In 2017, 1929 non-need-based awards were made. *Average percent of need met:* 98. *Average financial aid package:* $14,611. *Average need-based loan:* $4397. *Average need-based gift aid:* $8476. *Average non-need-based aid:* $2814. *Average indebtedness upon graduation:* $21,800.

APPLYING
Standardized Tests *Required:* SAT or ACT (for admission). *Required for some:* SAT Subject Tests (for admission).

Options: electronic application.

Application fee: $30.

Required: essay or personal statement. *Required for some:* high school transcript.

Application deadlines: 3/1 (freshmen), rolling (transfers).

Notification: 2/9 (freshmen), continuous (transfers).

CONTACT
Dr. Zina Evans, Vice President for Enrollment Management and Associate Provost, University of Florida, Gainesville, FL 32611. *Phone:* 352-392-1365. *E-mail:* zevans@ufl.edu.

University of Fort Lauderdale
Lauderhill, Florida
http://uftl.edu/

CONTACT
University of Fort Lauderdale, 4093 NW 16th Street, Lauderhill, FL 33313.

University of Miami
Coral Gables, Florida
http://www.miami.edu/
- **Independent** university, founded 1925
- **Suburban** 239-acre campus with easy access to Miami
- **Endowment** $948.6 million
- **Coed**
- **Very difficult** entrance level

FACULTY
Student/faculty ratio: 12:1.

ACADEMICS
Calendar: semesters. *Degrees:* certificates, bachelor's, master's, doctoral, post-master's, and postbachelor's certificates.
Library: Otto G. Richter Library plus 6 others. *Books:* 2.8 million (physical), 1.0 million (digital/electronic); *Serial titles:* 1,216 (physical), 113,585 (digital/electronic); *Databases:* 677. Weekly public service hours: 118; students can reserve study rooms.

STUDENT LIFE
Housing options: on-campus residence required for freshman year; coed, special housing for students with disabilities. Campus housing is university owned. Freshman campus housing is guaranteed.

Activities and organizations: drama/theater group, student-run newspaper, radio and television station, choral group, marching band, Hurricane Productions, Federation of Club Sports, Association of Greek Letter Organizations, Panhellenic Council, Scuba Club, national fraternities, national sororities.

Athletics Member NCAA. All Division I except football (Division I-A).
Campus security: 24-hour emergency response devices and patrols, student patrols, late-night transport/escort service, controlled dormitory access, programs, seminars, activities, classes and publications are available to students, faculty, staff, parents and friends.

Student services: health clinic, personal/psychological counseling, veterans affairs office.

COSTS & FINANCIAL AID
Costs (2018–19) *Comprehensive fee:* $64,334 includes full-time tuition ($48,720), mandatory fees ($1506), and room and board ($14,108). Full-time tuition and fees vary according to course load. Part-time tuition: $2030 per credit hour. Part-time tuition and fees vary according to course load and program. *Required fees:* $260 per term part-time. *College room only:* $8120. Room and board charges vary according to board plan and housing facility.

Financial Aid Of all full-time matriculated undergraduates who enrolled in 2018, 5,183 applied for aid, 4,251 were judged to have need, 3,780 had their need fully met. 2,007 Federal Work-Study jobs (averaging $2962). 195 state and other part-time jobs (averaging $2936). In 2018, 3033 non-need-based awards were made. *Average percent of need met:* 93. *Average financial aid package:* $40,813. *Average need-based loan:* $4273. *Average need-based gift aid:* $33,923. *Average non-need-based aid:* $21,088. *Average indebtedness upon graduation:* $22,000. *Financial aid deadline:* 4/15.

APPLYING
Standardized Tests *Required:* SAT or ACT (for admission). *Required for some:* SAT and SAT Subject Tests or ACT (for admission).

Options: electronic application, early admission, early decision, early action, deferred entrance.

Application fee: $70.

Required: essay or personal statement, high school transcript, 1 letter of recommendation. *Required for some:* college transcript(s) and statement of good standing from prior institution(s), auditions for selected academic programs.

CONTACT
Mr. Mark Reid, Executive Director of Admission, University of Miami, PO Box 248025, Coral Gables, FL 33124. *Phone:* 305-284-4323. *Fax:* 305-284-6605. *E-mail:* mreid@miami.edu.

University of North Florida
Jacksonville, Florida
http://www.unf.edu/
- **State-supported** comprehensive, founded 1965, part of State University System of Florida
- **Urban** 1300-acre campus with easy access to Jacksonville, FL
- **Endowment** $107.1 million
- **Coed** 14,494 undergraduate students, 72% full-time, 56% women, 44% men
- **Moderately difficult** entrance level, 61% of applicants were admitted

UNDERGRAD STUDENTS
10,457 full-time, 4,037 part-time. Students come from 48 states and territories; 65 other countries; 4% are from out of state; 9% Black or African American, non-Hispanic/Latino; 13% Hispanic/Latino; 5% Asian, non-Hispanic/Latino; 0.1% Native Hawaiian or other Pacific Islander, non-Hispanic/Latino; 0.2% American Indian or Alaska Native, non-Hispanic/Latino; 5% Two or more races, non-Hispanic/Latino; 0.6% Race/ethnicity unknown; 2% international; 10% transferred in; 22% live on campus.

Freshmen:
Admission: 14,330 applied, 8,753 admitted, 2,472 enrolled. *Average high school GPA:* 3.9. *Test scores:* SAT evidence-based reading and writing scores over 500: 99%; SAT math scores over 500: 97%; ACT scores over 18: 100%; SAT evidence-based reading and writing scores over 600: 60%; SAT math scores over 600: 44%; ACT scores over 24: 54%; SAT evidence-based reading and writing scores over 700: 8%; SAT math scores over 700: 6%; ACT scores over 30: 9%.

Retention: 81% of full-time freshmen returned.

FACULTY
Total: 977, 58% full-time, 60% with terminal degrees.
Student/faculty ratio: 18:1.

ACADEMICS
Calendar: semesters. *Degrees:* associate, bachelor's, master's, doctoral, post-master's, and postbachelor's certificates (doctoral degree in education only).

Special study options: accelerated degree program, adult/continuing education programs, advanced placement credit, cooperative education, distance learning, double majors, English as a second language, honors programs, independent study, internships, off-campus study, part-time degree program, services for LD students, study abroad, summer session for credit. *ROTC:* Army (b), Navy (c).

Unusual degree programs: 3-2 computer science.

Computers: 700 computers/terminals are available on campus for general student use. Students can access the following: campus intranet, computer help desk, free student e-mail accounts, online (class) grades, online (class) registration, online (class) schedules, reduced prices for students on certain business and design software. Campuswide network is available. 100% of college-owned or -operated housing units are wired for high-speed Internet access. Wireless service is available via entire campus.

Library: Thomas G. Carpenter Library. *Books:* 568,299 (physical), 543,121 (digital/electronic); *Serial titles:* 12,479 (physical), 211,959 (digital/electronic); *Databases:* 284. Students can reserve study rooms.

STUDENT LIFE
Housing options: coed, special housing for students with disabilities. Campus housing is university owned. Freshman campus housing is guaranteed.

Activities and organizations: drama/theater group, student-run newspaper, radio and television station, choral group, Student Government Association, African American Student Association, International Student Association, Filipino Student Association, National Education Association, national fraternities, national sororities.

Athletics Member NCAA. All Division I. *Intercollegiate sports:* baseball M(s), basketball M(s)/W(s), cross-country running M(s)/W(s), golf M(s)/W(c), soccer M(s)/W(s), softball W(s), swimming and diving W(s), tennis M(s)/W(s), track and field M(s)/W(s), volleyball W(s). *Intramural sports:* badminton M/W, basketball M/W, bowling M/W, fencing M(c), field hockey W(c), football M/W, golf M/W, lacrosse M(c)/W(c), racquetball M(c)/W(c), rugby M(c), sailing M(c)/W(c), soccer M/W, swimming and diving M/W, table tennis M/W, track and field M/W, ultimate Frisbee M(c)/W(c), volleyball M(c)/W(c).

Campus security: 24-hour emergency response devices and patrols, late-night transport/escort service, controlled dormitory access, electronic parking lot security.

Student services: health clinic, personal/psychological counseling, women's center.

COSTS & FINANCIAL AID
Costs (2018–19) *Tuition:* state resident $4281 full-time, $143 per credit hour part-time; nonresident $17,999 full-time, $600 per credit hour part-time. Full-time tuition and fees vary according to course load. Part-time tuition and fees vary according to course load. *Required fees:* $2113 full-time, $70 per credit hour part-time. *Room and board:* $9846; room only: $5772. Room and board charges vary according to board plan and housing facility. *Payment plan:* installment. *Waivers:* senior citizens and employees or children of employees.

Financial Aid Of all full-time matriculated undergraduates who enrolled in 2018, 7,220 applied for aid, 5,403 were judged to have need, 391 had their need fully met. 163 Federal Work-Study jobs (averaging $2916). In 2018, 1259 non-need-based awards were made. *Average percent of need met:* 90. *Average financial aid package:* $10,079. *Average need-based loan:* $4132. *Average need-based gift aid:* $7436. *Average non-need-based aid:* $3024. *Average indebtedness upon graduation:* $19,290.

APPLYING
Standardized Tests *Required:* SAT or ACT (for admission).

Options: electronic application, deferred entrance.

Application fee: $30.

Required: high school transcript, minimum 2.5 GPA. *Required for some:* essay or personal statement. *Recommended:* minimum 3.0 GPA.

Application deadlines: rolling (freshmen), 5/10 (transfers).
Notification: continuous (freshmen), continuous (transfers).

CONTACT
Ms. Karen Lucas, Director of Admissions, University of North Florida, 1 UNF Drive, Jacksonville, FL 32224. *Phone:* 904-620-5252. *Fax:* 904-620-2014. *E-mail:* admissions@unf.edu.

University of South Florida
Tampa, Florida
http://www.usf.edu/

- **State-supported** university, founded 1956, part of State University System of Florida
- **Urban** 1562-acre campus
- **Endowment** $480.4 million
- **Coed** 32,238 undergraduate students, 77% full-time, 55% women, 45% men
- 47% of applicants were admitted

UNDERGRAD STUDENTS
24,833 full-time, 7,405 part-time. Students come from 145 other countries; 6% are from out of state; 10% Black or African American, non-Hispanic/Latino; 21% Hispanic/Latino; 7% Asian, non-Hispanic/Latino; 0.2% Native Hawaiian or other Pacific Islander, non-Hispanic/Latino; 0.2% American Indian or Alaska Native, non-Hispanic/Latino; 4% Two or more races, non-Hispanic/Latino; 3% Race/ethnicity unknown; 7% international; 12% transferred in; 18% live on campus.

Freshmen:
Admission: 28,623 applied, 13,349 admitted, 4,422 enrolled. *Average high school GPA:* 4.0. *Test scores:* SAT evidence-based reading and writing scores over 500: 100%; SAT math scores over 500: 99%; ACT scores over 18: 100%; SAT evidence-based reading and writing scores over 600: 73%; SAT math scores over 600: 64%; ACT scores over 24: 88%; SAT evidence-based reading and writing scores over 700: 11%; SAT math scores over 700: 14%; ACT scores over 30: 26%.
Retention: 91% of full-time freshmen returned.

FACULTY
Total: 2,028, 64% full-time, 68% with terminal degrees.
Student/faculty ratio: 24:1.

ACADEMICS
Calendar: semesters. *Degrees:* associate, bachelor's, master's, and doctoral.

Special study options: academic remediation for entering students, accelerated degree program, adult/continuing education programs, advanced placement credit, cooperative education, distance learning, double majors, freshman honors college, honors programs, internships, off-campus study, part-time degree program, services for LD students, study abroad, summer session for credit. *ROTC:* Army (b), Navy (b), Air Force (b).

Computers: 825 computers/terminals and 2,000 ports are available on campus for general student use. Students can access the following: campus intranet, computer help desk, free student e-mail accounts, online (class) grades, online (class) registration, online (class) schedules. Campuswide network is available. 100% of college-owned or -operated housing units are wired for high-speed Internet access. Wireless service is available via entire campus.

Library: Tampa Campus Library plus 5 others. *Books:* 1.8 million (physical), 652,513 (digital/electronic); *Serial titles:* 537 (physical), 58,975 (digital/electronic); *Databases:* 939. Weekly public service hours: 116; study areas open 24 hours, 5–7 days a week; students can reserve study rooms.

STUDENT LIFE
Housing options: coed. Campus housing is university owned.

Activities and organizations: drama/theater group, student-run newspaper, radio and television station, choral group, marching band, Student Government, Campus Activities Board, USF Ambassadors, Student Admissions Representatives, national fraternities, national sororities.

Athletics Member NCAA. All Division I except football (Division I-A). *Intercollegiate sports:* badminton M(c)/W(c), baseball M(s), basketball

W(s), bowling M(c)/W(c), crew M(c)/W(c), cross-country running M(s)/W(s), fencing M(c)/W(c), golf M(s)/W(s)(c), gymnastics M(c)/W(c), rugby M(c)/W(c), soccer M(s)/W(s), softball W(s), tennis M(s)/W(s), track and field M(s)/W(s), volleyball M(c)/W(s). *Intramural sports:* badminton M/W, basketball M/W, bowling M/W, football M, golf M/W, racquetball M/W, soccer M/W, swimming and diving M/W, tennis M/W, track and field M/W, volleyball M/W, weight lifting M.

Campus security: 24-hour emergency response devices and patrols, student patrols, late-night transport/escort service, controlled dormitory access.

Student services: health clinic, personal/psychological counseling, women's center, legal services.

COSTS & FINANCIAL AID
Costs (2019–20) *Tuition:* area resident $4559 full-time, $152 per credit hour part-time; nonresident $15,473 full-time, $516 per credit hour part-time. *Required fees:* $1851 full-time. *Room and board:* $11,610; room only: $7752.

Financial Aid Of all full-time matriculated undergraduates who enrolled in 2017, 21,401 applied for aid, 17,917 were judged to have need, 1,986 had their need fully met. 791 Federal Work-Study jobs (averaging $3126). 294 state and other part-time jobs (averaging $1592). In 2017, 2508 non-need-based awards were made. *Average percent of need met:* 63. *Average financial aid package:* $12,536. *Average need-based loan:* $6337. *Average need-based gift aid:* $9093. *Average non-need-based aid:* $2955. *Average indebtedness upon graduation:* $21,565.

APPLYING
Standardized Tests *Required:* SAT or ACT (for admission).

Options: electronic application, early admission, deferred entrance.

Application fee: $30.

Recommended: high school transcript.

Notification: continuous (freshmen), continuous (transfers).

CONTACT
Mr. Glen Besterfield, Dean for Undergraduate Admissions, University of South Florida, 4202 East Fowler Avenue, Tampa, FL 33620-9951. *Phone:* 813-974-3350. *Fax:* 813-974-9689. *E-mail:* besterfi@usf.edu.

University of South Florida, St. Petersburg
St. Petersburg, Florida
http://www.usfsp.edu/
- **State-supported** comprehensive, founded 1965, part of University of South Florida System
- **Urban** 48-acre campus with easy access to Tampa
- **Endowment** $19.1 million
- **Coed**
- 40% of applicants were admitted

FACULTY
Student/faculty ratio: 16:1.

ACADEMICS
Calendar: semesters. *Degrees:* certificates, bachelor's, and master's.
Library: Nelson Poynter Memorial Library. *Books:* 212,904 (physical), 693,313 (digital/electronic); *Serial titles:* 7,817 (physical), 64,928 (digital/electronic); *Databases:* 939. Weekly public service hours: 79; students can reserve study rooms.

STUDENT LIFE
Housing options: on-campus residence required for freshman year; coed. Campus housing is university owned and is provided by a third party. Freshman applicants given priority for college housing.

Activities and organizations: drama/theater group, student-run newspaper, radio station, Student Government, Harborside Activities Board, Delta Sigma Pi, Multicultural Activities Council, HERD Step Team.

Campus security: 24-hour emergency response devices and patrols, late-night transport/escort service, controlled dormitory access.

Student services: health clinic, personal/psychological counseling, veterans affairs office.

COSTS
Costs (2018–19) *Tuition:* state resident $4206 full-time, $140 per credit hour part-time; nonresident $15,120 full-time, $504 per credit hour part-time. *Required fees:* $1615 full-time, $54 per credit hour part-time. *Room and board:* $11,160. Room and board charges vary according to board plan and housing facility.

APPLYING
Standardized Tests *Required:* SAT or ACT (for admission).

Options: early admission, early action.

Application fee: $30.

Required: high school transcript, minimum 2.5 GPA.

CONTACT
University of South Florida, St. Petersburg, 140 Seventh Avenue South, St. Petersburg, FL 33701. *Phone:* 727-873-4142. *Fax:* 727-873-4525. *E-mail:* admissions@usfsp.edu.

University of South Florida Sarasota-Manatee
Sarasota, Florida
http://www.usfsm.edu/
- **State-supported** comprehensive, founded 1956, part of University of South Florida System
- **Urban** 31-acre campus with easy access to Tampa
- **Endowment** $10.8 million
- **Coed** 1,917 undergraduate students, 53% full-time, 61% women, 39% men
- **Moderately difficult** entrance level, 32% of applicants were admitted

UNDERGRAD STUDENTS
1,008 full-time, 909 part-time. 3% are from out of state; 5% Black or African American, non-Hispanic/Latino; 16% Hispanic/Latino; 2% Asian, non-Hispanic/Latino; 0.4% American Indian or Alaska Native, non-Hispanic/Latino; 3% Two or more races, non-Hispanic/Latino; 3% Race/ethnicity unknown; 3% international; 18% transferred in.

Freshmen:
Admission: 771 applied, 250 admitted, 113 enrolled. *Average high school GPA:* 3.9. *Test scores:* SAT evidence-based reading and writing scores over 500: 100%; SAT math scores over 500: 100%; ACT scores over 18: 100%; SAT evidence-based reading and writing scores over 600: 65%; SAT math scores over 600: 47%; ACT scores over 24: 77%; SAT evidence-based reading and writing scores over 700: 3%; SAT math scores over 700: 8%; ACT scores over 30: 11%.

Retention: 89% of full-time freshmen returned.

FACULTY
Total: 160, 57% full-time, 69% with terminal degrees.
Student/faculty ratio: 14:1.

ACADEMICS
Calendar: semesters. *Degrees:* certificates, associate, bachelor's, master's, and post-master's certificates.

Special study options: advanced placement credit, distance learning, double majors, honors programs, independent study, internships, part-time degree program, services for LD students, study abroad, summer session for credit. *ROTC:* Army (c), Navy (c), Air Force (c).

Computers: 61 computers/terminals and 450 ports are available on campus for general student use. Students can access the following: campus intranet, computer help desk, free student e-mail accounts, online (class) grades, online (class) registration, online (class) schedules. Campuswide network is available. Wireless service is available via entire campus.

Library: USF Libraries. *Books:* 1,231 (physical), 721,020 (digital/electronic); *Serial titles:* 65,050 (digital/electronic); *Databases:* 941. Weekly public service hours: 96; students can reserve study rooms.

STUDENT LIFE
Housing options: college housing not available.

Activities and organizations: Box Office Bulls, The Adventure Club, Gamers' Club, Student Veteran Society, The Criminology Club.

Campus security: 24-hour emergency response devices and patrols, late-night transport/escort service.

Student services: health clinic, personal/psychological counseling, veterans affairs office.

COSTS

Costs (2018–19) *Tuition:* state resident $4206 full-time, $140 per credit hour part-time; nonresident $15,120 full-time, $504 per credit hour part-time. Full-time tuition and fees vary according to course load and program. Part-time tuition and fees vary according to course load and program. *Required fees:* $1381 full-time, $46 per credit hour part-time, $10 per term part-time. *Waivers:* employees or children of employees.

APPLYING

Standardized Tests *Required:* SAT or ACT (for admission). *Recommended:* SAT Subject Tests (for admission).

Options: electronic application, deferred entrance.

Application fee: $30.

Required: high school transcript, minimum 3.3 GPA. *Required for some:* minimum 3.3 GPA, interview. *Recommended:* essay or personal statement, minimum 3.3 GPA, 2 letters of recommendation.

Notification: continuous (freshmen), continuous (out-of-state freshmen), continuous (transfers).

CONTACT

Mr. Brandon Avery, Interim Director, Admissions, University of South Florida Sarasota-Manatee, 8350 N. Tamiami Trail, C107, Sarasota, FL 34232. *Phone:* 941-359-4330. *Fax:* 941-359-4264. *E-mail:* bavery@sar.usf.edu.

The University of Tampa

Tampa, Florida

http://www.ut.edu/

- **Independent** comprehensive, founded 1931
- **Urban** 110-acre campus with easy access to Tampa-St. Petersburg, Clearwater
- **Coed** 8,443 undergraduate students, 96% full-time, 58% women, 42% men
- **Moderately difficult** entrance level, 49% of applicants were admitted

UNDERGRAD STUDENTS

8,146 full-time, 297 part-time. Students come from 50 states and territories; 140 other countries; 71% are from out of state; 5% Black or African American, non-Hispanic/Latino; 13% Hispanic/Latino; 2% Asian, non-Hispanic/Latino; 0.2% Native Hawaiian or other Pacific Islander, non-Hispanic/Latino; 0.1% American Indian or Alaska Native, non-Hispanic/Latino; 3% Two or more races, non-Hispanic/Latino; 6% Race/ethnicity unknown; 9% international; 6% transferred in; 51% live on campus.

Freshmen:

Admission: 22,310 applied, 10,862 admitted, 2,164 enrolled. *Average high school GPA:* 3.4. *Test scores:* SAT evidence-based reading and writing scores over 500: 96%; SAT math scores over 500: 94%; ACT scores over 18: 99%; SAT evidence-based reading and writing scores over 600: 47%; SAT math scores over 600: 36%; ACT scores over 24: 61%; SAT evidence-based reading and writing scores over 700: 3%; SAT math scores over 700: 4%; ACT scores over 30: 9%.

Retention: 76% of full-time freshmen returned.

FACULTY

Total: 795, 47% full-time, 59% with terminal degrees.

Student/faculty ratio: 17:1.

ACADEMICS

Calendar: semesters. *Degrees:* certificates, bachelor's, master's, and post-master's certificates.

Special study options: academic remediation for entering students, adult/continuing education programs, advanced placement credit, cooperative education, double majors, English as a second language, honors programs, independent study, internships, part-time degree program, services for LD students, study abroad, summer session for credit. *ROTC:* Army (b), Navy (c), Air Force (c).

Unusual degree programs: 3-2 chemistry/business administration.

Computers: 791 computers/terminals and 8,000 ports are available on campus for general student use. Students can access the following: campus intranet, computer help desk, free student e-mail accounts, online (class) grades, online (class) registration, online (class) schedules. Campuswide network is available. 100% of college-owned or -operated housing units are wired for high-speed Internet access. Wireless service is available via entire campus.

Library: Macdonald Kelce Library. *Books:* 195,067 (physical), 145,016 (digital/electronic); *Serial titles:* 1,214 (physical), 190,560 (digital/electronic); *Databases:* 214. Weekly public service hours: 100; students can reserve study rooms.

STUDENT LIFE

Housing options: coed, special housing for students with disabilities. Campus housing is university owned and leased by the school. Freshman applicants given priority for college housing.

Activities and organizations: drama/theater group, student-run newspaper, radio and television station, choral group, Greek Life, student government, PEACE (volunteer organization), Student Productions, Minaret, national fraternities, national sororities.

Athletics Member NCAA. All Division II except golf (Division I), lacrosse (Division I), track and field (Division I). *Intercollegiate sports:* baseball M(s), basketball M(s)/W(s), crew W(s), cross-country running M(s)/W(s), golf M(s)/W(s), lacrosse M(s)/W(s), soccer M(s)/W(s), softball W(s), swimming and diving M(s)/W(s), tennis W(s), track and field M(s)/W(s), volleyball W(s). *Intramural sports:* basketball M/W, cheerleading W(c), crew M(c), equestrian sports W(c), fencing W(c), field hockey M(c), football M/W, golf M/W, ice hockey M(c), soccer M/W, softball M/W, swimming and diving M/W, tennis M(c)/W(c), ultimate Frisbee M/W, volleyball M/W.

Campus security: 24-hour emergency response devices and patrols, student patrols, late-night transport/escort service, controlled dormitory access.

Student services: health clinic, personal/psychological counseling, women's center.

COSTS & FINANCIAL AID

Costs (2018–19) *Comprehensive fee:* $40,018 includes full-time tuition ($27,206), mandatory fees ($2002), and room and board ($10,810). Full-time tuition and fees vary according to class time, course load, and program. Part-time tuition: $579 per credit hour. Part-time tuition and fees vary according to class time, course load, and program. *Required fees:* $40 per term part-time. *Room and board:* Room and board charges vary according to board plan and housing facility. *Payment plan:* installment. *Waivers:* employees or children of employees.

Financial Aid Of all full-time matriculated undergraduates who enrolled in 2018, 5,728 applied for aid, 4,765 were judged to have need, 420 had their need fully met. 533 Federal Work-Study jobs (averaging $2000). 167 state and other part-time jobs (averaging $2000). In 2018, 2529 non-need-based awards were made. *Average percent of need met:* 60. *Average financial aid package:* $17,834. *Average need-based loan:* $4315. *Average need-based gift aid:* $14,076. *Average non-need-based aid:* $8347. *Average indebtedness upon graduation:* $32,727.

APPLYING

Standardized Tests *Required:* SAT or ACT (for admission).

Options: electronic application, early admission, early action, deferred entrance.

Application fee: $40.

Required: essay or personal statement, high school transcript, minimum 2.0 GPA. *Required for some:* 1 letter of recommendation. *Recommended:* interview.

Application deadlines: rolling (freshmen), rolling (transfers), 11/15 (early action).

Notification: continuous until 10/1 (freshmen), continuous (transfers).

CONTACT

Mr. Dennis Nostrand, Vice President for Enrollment, The University of Tampa, 401 West Kennedy Boulevard, Tampa, FL 33606-1480. *Phone:* 813-257-1808. *Toll-free phone:* 888-646-2738 (in-state); 888-MINARET (out-of-state). *Fax:* 813-258-7398. *E-mail:* admissions@ut.edu.

University of West Florida

Pensacola, Florida

http://www.uwf.edu/

CONTACT
Katie Condon, Director of Admissions, University of West Florida, Admissions, 11000 University Parkway, Pensacola, FL 32514. *Phone:* 850-474-2230. *Toll-free phone:* 800-263-1074. *Fax:* 850-474-3460. *E-mail:* admissions@uwf.edu.

Valencia College

Orlando, Florida

http://valenciacollege.edu/

- **State-supported** 4-year, founded 1967, part of Florida College System
- **Urban** 654-acre campus with easy access to Orlando
- **Endowment** $70.3 million
- **Coed**
- 98% of applicants were admitted

FACULTY
Student/faculty ratio: 23:1.

ACADEMICS
Calendar: semesters. *Degrees:* certificates, diplomas, associate, and bachelor's.
Library: Library plus 4 others. *Books:* 153,869 (physical), 180,848 (digital/electronic); *Serial titles:* 261 (physical), 52,262 (digital/electronic); *Databases:* 188. Weekly public service hours: 87; students can reserve study rooms.

STUDENT LIFE
Housing options: college housing not available.

Activities and organizations: drama/theater group, student-run newspaper, choral group, National Society for Leadership and Success, PTK, Honors, Gay-Straight Alliance, Valencia Hospitality.

Campus security: 24-hour emergency response devices and patrols, late-night transport/escort service, video monitoring for certain areas.

Student services: personal/psychological counseling, veterans affairs office.

COSTS & FINANCIAL AID
Costs (2018–19) *Tuition:* state resident $2473 full-time; nonresident $9383 full-time. Full-time tuition and fees vary according to degree level. Part-time tuition and fees vary according to degree level.

Financial Aid Of all full-time matriculated undergraduates who enrolled in 2017, 10,723 applied for aid, 9,098 were judged to have need, 88 had their need fully met. 244 Federal Work-Study jobs (averaging $3019). 114 state and other part-time jobs (averaging $4275). In 2017, 126 non-need-based awards were made. *Average percent of need met:* 41. *Average financial aid package:* $6373. *Average need-based loan:* $2810. *Average need-based gift aid:* $5687. *Average non-need-based aid:* $1486. *Average indebtedness upon graduation:* $20,951.

APPLYING
Options: electronic application, early admission, deferred entrance.

Application fee: $35.

Required for some: high school transcript, professional license for some allied health bachelors programs. *Recommended:* high school transcript.

CONTACT
Dr. Linda K. Herlocker, Assistant Vice President of Admissions and Records, Valencia College, West Campus, MC 4-8, 1800 S. Kirkman Road, SSB 104-D, Orlando, FL 32811-2302. *Phone:* 407-582-1511. *Fax:* 407-582-1866. *E-mail:* lherlocker@valenciacollege.edu.

Warner University

Lake Wales, Florida

http://www.warner.edu/

CONTACT
Mr. Jason Roe, Director of Admissions, Warner University, Warner Southern Center, 13895 Highway 27, Lake Wales, FL 33859. *Phone:* 863-638-7212 Ext. 7213. *Toll-free phone:* 800-309-9563. *Fax:* 863-638-1472. *E-mail:* admissions@warner.edu.

Webber International University

Babson Park, Florida

http://www.webber.edu/

- **Independent** comprehensive, founded 1927
- **Small-town** 110-acre campus with easy access to Orlando
- **Coed**
- **Moderately difficult** entrance level

FACULTY
Student/faculty ratio: 21:1.

ACADEMICS
Calendar: semesters. *Degrees:* associate, bachelor's, and master's.
Library: Grace and Roger Babson Library. *Books:* 1,041 (physical); *Databases:* 127. Weekly public service hours: 70; students can reserve study rooms.

STUDENT LIFE
Housing options: on-campus residence required through sophomore year; men-only, women-only. Campus housing is university owned. Freshman campus housing is guaranteed.

Activities and organizations: student-run newspaper, Student Leadership Association, Phi Beta Lambda, Society of International Students, Fellowship of Christian Athletes, Rotaract.

Athletics Member NAIA.

Campus security: 24-hour emergency response devices and patrols, late-night transport/escort service.

Student services: health clinic, personal/psychological counseling, veterans affairs office.

COSTS & FINANCIAL AID
Costs (2018–19) *Comprehensive fee:* $35,410 includes full-time tuition ($23,380), mandatory fees ($2736), and room and board ($9294). Full-time tuition and fees vary according to class time, course load, and program. Part-time tuition: $366 per credit hour. Part-time tuition and fees vary according to class time, course load, and program. *Room and board:* Room and board charges vary according to board plan, gender, and housing facility.

Financial Aid Of all full-time matriculated undergraduates who enrolled in 2018, 463 applied for aid, 440 were judged to have need, 31 had their need fully met. 42 Federal Work-Study jobs (averaging $811). 38 state and other part-time jobs (averaging $1013). In 2018, 113 non-need-based awards were made. *Average percent of need met:* 60. *Average financial aid package:* $21,206. *Average need-based loan:* $4035. *Average need-based gift aid:* $17,696. *Average non-need-based aid:* $6693. *Average indebtedness upon graduation:* $27,296. *Financial aid deadline:* 8/1.

APPLYING
Standardized Tests *Required for some:* SAT or ACT (for admission).

Options: electronic application.

Required: high school transcript, minimum 2.0 GPA. *Required for some:* letters of recommendation, interview. *Recommended:* essay or personal statement.

CONTACT
Office of Admissions, Webber International University, PO Box 96, Babson Park, FL 33827. *Phone:* 863-638-2910. *Toll-free phone:* 800-741-1844. *Fax:* 863-638-1591. *E-mail:* admissions@webber.edu.

West Coast University

Doral, Florida

http://westcoastuniversity.edu/

CONTACT
West Coast University, 9250 NW 36th Street, Doral, FL 33178.

Yeshiva Gedolah Rabbinical College

Miami Beach, Florida

CONTACT
Yeshiva Gedolah Rabbinical College, 1140 Alton Road, Miami Beach, FL 33139.

GEORGIA

Abraham Baldwin Agricultural College
Tifton, Georgia
http://www.abac.edu/

CONTACT
Mrs. Donna Webb, Director of Enrollment Services, Abraham Baldwin Agricultural College, Box 4, 2802 Moore Highway, Tifton, GA 31793-2601. *Phone:* 229-391-5004. *Toll-free phone:* 800-733-3653. *Fax:* 229-391-5002. *E-mail:* dwebb@abac.edu.

Agnes Scott College
Decatur, Georgia
http://www.agnesscott.edu/
- **Independent** comprehensive, founded 1889, affiliated with Presbyterian Church (U.S.A.)
- **Urban** 100-acre campus with easy access to Atlanta
- **Endowment** $229.4 million
- **Women only** 996 undergraduate students, 99% full-time
- **Moderately difficult** entrance level, 70% of applicants were admitted

UNDERGRAD STUDENTS
985 full-time, 11 part-time. Students come from 41 states and territories; 28 other countries; 42% are from out of state; 31% Black or African American, non-Hispanic/Latino; 13% Hispanic/Latino; 8% Asian, non-Hispanic/Latino; 0.1% Native Hawaiian or other Pacific Islander, non-Hispanic/Latino; 0.2% American Indian or Alaska Native, non-Hispanic/Latino; 6% Two or more races, non-Hispanic/Latino; 3% Race/ethnicity unknown; 7% international; 0.8% transferred in; 84% live on campus.

Freshmen:
Admission: 1,625 applied, 1,144 admitted, 324 enrolled. *Average high school GPA:* 3.8. *Test scores:* SAT evidence-based reading and writing scores over 500: 98%; SAT math scores over 500: 88%; ACT scores over 18: 99%; SAT evidence-based reading and writing scores over 600: 65%; SAT math scores over 600: 40%; ACT scores over 24: 74%; SAT evidence-based reading and writing scores over 700: 19%; SAT math scores over 700: 8%; ACT scores over 30: 20%.
Retention: 79% of full-time freshmen returned.

FACULTY
Total: 133, 61% full-time, 89% with terminal degrees.
Student/faculty ratio: 10:1.

ACADEMICS
Calendar: semesters. *Degrees:* bachelor's, master's, and postbachelor's certificates.
Special study options: accelerated degree program, adult/continuing education programs, advanced placement credit, distance learning, double majors, independent study, internships, off-campus study, part-time degree program, services for LD students, student-designed majors, study abroad, summer session for credit. *ROTC:* Army (c), Air Force (c).
Unusual degree programs: 3-2 engineering with Georgia Institute of Technology; nursing with Emory University; computer science with Emory University.
Computers: 450 computers/terminals are available on campus for general student use. Students can access the following: campus intranet, computer help desk, free student e-mail accounts, online (class) grades, online (class) registration, online (class) schedules. Campuswide network is available. 100% of college-owned or -operated housing units are wired for high-speed Internet access. Wireless service is available via entire campus.
Library: McCain Library. *Books:* 240,240 (physical), 57,182 (digital/electronic); *Databases:* 474. Study areas open 24 hours, 5–7 days a week.

STUDENT LIFE
Housing options: on-campus residence required through senior year; women-only. Campus housing is university owned. Freshman campus housing is guaranteed.
Activities and organizations: drama/theater group, student-run newspaper, radio station, choral group, marching band.
Athletics Member NCAA. All Division III. *Intercollegiate sports:* basketball W, cross-country running W, soccer W, softball W, tennis W, volleyball W. *Intramural sports:* archery W, badminton W, cheerleading W(c), lacrosse W(c), swimming and diving W(c), tennis W.
Campus security: 24-hour emergency response devices and patrols, late-night transport/escort service, controlled dormitory access.
Student services: health clinic, personal/psychological counseling.

COSTS & FINANCIAL AID
Costs (2019–20) *Comprehensive fee:* $55,360 includes full-time tuition ($42,360), mandatory fees ($330), and room and board ($12,670). Part-time tuition: $1765 per credit hour.
Financial Aid Of all full-time matriculated undergraduates who enrolled in 2018, 812 applied for aid, 736 were judged to have need, 150 had their need fully met. In 2018, 223 non-need-based awards were made. *Average percent of need met:* 84. *Average financial aid package:* $37,199. *Average need-based loan:* $4223. *Average need-based gift aid:* $31,236. *Average non-need-based aid:* $28,676. *Average indebtedness upon graduation:* $30,850. *Financial aid deadline:* 5/1.

APPLYING
Standardized Tests *Required for some:* SAT and SAT Subject Tests or ACT (for admission).
Options: electronic application, early admission, early decision, early action, deferred entrance.
Required: essay or personal statement, high school transcript. *Recommended:* interview.
Application deadlines: 6/1 (transfers), 11/15 (early action).
Early decision deadline: 11/1.
Notification: 4/15 (freshmen), continuous (transfers), 12/1 (early decision), 1/15 (early action).

CONTACT
Ms. Aimee S. Kahn-Foss, Director of Admission, Agnes Scott College, 141 East College Avenue, Decatur, GA 30030-3797. *Phone:* 404-471-6285. *Toll-free phone:* 800-868-8602. *Fax:* 404-471-6414. *E-mail:* admission@agnesscott.edu.

Albany State University
Albany, Georgia
http://www.asurams.edu/

CONTACT
Interim Director, Enrollment Services, Albany State University, 504 College Drive, Albany, GA 31705-2717. *Phone:* 229-430-4646. *Toll-free phone:* 800-822-7267. *Fax:* 229-430-4105. *E-mail:* enrollmentservices@asurams.edu.

American InterContinental University Atlanta
Atlanta, Georgia
http://www.aiuniv.edu/

CONTACT
American InterContinental University Atlanta, 6600 Peachtree-Dunwoody Road, 500 Embassy Row, Atlanta, GA 30328. *Phone:* 877-564-6248. *Toll-free phone:* 800-353-1744. *Fax:* 877-564-6248.

Argosy University, Atlanta
Atlanta, Georgia
http://www.argosy.edu/locations/atlanta/

CONTACT
Argosy University, Atlanta, 980 Hammond Drive, Suite 100, Atlanta, GA 30328. *Phone:* 770-671-1200. *Toll-free phone:* 888-671-4777.

A ★ indicates that the school has detailed information with a Premium Profile on Petersons.com.

www.petersons.com 207

The Art Institute of Atlanta
Atlanta, Georgia
http://www.artinstitutes.edu/atlanta/

CONTACT
The Art Institute of Atlanta, 6600 Peachtree Dunwoody Road, NE, 100 Embassy Row, Atlanta, GA 30328. *Phone:* 770-394-8300. *Toll-free phone:* 800-275-4242.

Ashworth College
Norcross, Georgia
http://www.ashworthcollege.edu/

CONTACT
Mr. Eric Ryall, Registrar, Ashworth College, 6625 The Corners Parkway, Suite 500, Norcross, GA 30092. *Phone:* 770-729-8400 Ext. 5297. *Toll-free phone:* 800-957-5412.

Augusta University
Augusta, Georgia
http://www.augusta.edu/

CONTACT
Augusta University, 1120 15th Street, Augusta, GA 30912. *Phone:* 706-737-1632. *Toll-free phone:* 800-519-3388.

Berry College
Mount Berry, Georgia
http://www.berry.edu/

- **Independent interdenominational** comprehensive, founded 1902
- **Suburban** 27,000-acre campus with easy access to Atlanta
- **Endowment** $968.5 million
- **Coed**
- **Moderately difficult** entrance level

FACULTY
Student/faculty ratio: 11:1.

ACADEMICS
Calendar: semesters. *Degrees:* bachelor's and master's.
Library: Memorial Library plus 1 other. *Books:* 246,222 (physical), 664,520 (digital/electronic); *Serial titles:* 7,978 (physical), 44,764 (digital/electronic); *Databases:* 224. Weekly public service hours: 106; students can reserve study rooms.

STUDENT LIFE
Housing options: on-campus residence required through senior year; coed, men-only, women-only. Campus housing is university owned. Freshman campus housing is guaranteed.

Activities and organizations: drama/theater group, student-run newspaper, choral group, Student Government Association, Campus Outreach, Block-n-Bridle, Allied Health, Athletes Bettering the Community.

Athletics Member NCAA. All Division III.

Campus security: 24-hour emergency response devices and patrols, controlled dormitory access, lighted pathways, gated campus, mobile police patrols, identification of valuables, limited access to campus, on-campus police officers.

Student services: health clinic, personal/psychological counseling.

COSTS & FINANCIAL AID
Costs (2018–19) *Comprehensive fee:* $49,326 includes full-time tuition ($36,330), mandatory fees ($226), and room and board ($12,770). Part-time tuition: $1211 per credit hour. *College room only:* $7220. Room and board charges vary according to board plan and housing facility.

Financial Aid Of all full-time matriculated undergraduates who enrolled in 2018, 1,673 applied for aid, 1,351 were judged to have need, 350 had their need fully met. 334 Federal Work-Study jobs (averaging $2290). 183 state and other part-time jobs (averaging $4772). In 2018, 540 non-need-based awards were made. *Average percent of need met:* 84. *Average*

financial aid package: $31,114. *Average need-based loan:* $5149. *Average need-based gift aid:* $26,094. *Average non-need-based aid:* $16,354. *Average indebtedness upon graduation:* $26,858.

APPLYING
Standardized Tests *Required:* SAT or ACT (for admission).

Options: electronic application, early admission, early decision, early action.

Required: essay or personal statement, high school transcript, 1 letter of recommendation. *Required for some:* 2 letters of recommendation. *Recommended:* interview.

CONTACT
Mr. Timothy Tarpley, Director of Operations, Enrollment Management, Berry College, PO Box 490159, 2277 Martha Berry Highway, NW, Mount Berry, GA 30149-0159. *Phone:* 706-236-2215. *Toll-free phone:* 800-237-7942. *E-mail:* admissions@berry.edu.

Beulah Heights University
Atlanta, Georgia
http://www.beulah.edu/

- **Independent Pentecostal** comprehensive, founded 1918
- **Urban** 10-acre campus with easy access to Atlanta
- **Coed**
- **Noncompetitive** entrance level

FACULTY
Student/faculty ratio: 5:1.

ACADEMICS
Calendar: semesters. *Degrees:* associate, bachelor's, master's, and doctoral.
Library: Barth Memorial Library. *Books:* 51,672 (physical). Weekly public service hours: 57.

STUDENT LIFE
Housing options: men-only, women-only. Campus housing is university owned.

Activities and organizations: student-run newspaper, choral group, Chapel Choir, Student Government Association, Club Give.

Campus security: 24-hour emergency response devices and patrols.

Student services: personal/psychological counseling, veterans affairs office.

COSTS & FINANCIAL AID
Costs (2018–19) *Tuition:* $10,440 full-time, $318 per credit hour part-time. Full-time tuition and fees vary according to course load. *Required fees:* $610 full-time, $310 per term part-time. *Room only:* $6750. Room and board charges vary according to housing facility. *Payment plans:* installment, deferred payment.

Financial Aid Of all full-time matriculated undergraduates who enrolled in 2009, 113 applied for aid, 113 were judged to have need. 13 Federal Work-Study jobs (averaging $4335). *Average percent of need met:* 75. *Average financial aid package:* $5619. *Average need-based loan:* $2250. *Average need-based gift aid:* $3500. *Average indebtedness upon graduation:* $40,000.

APPLYING
Standardized Tests *Required for some:* TOEFL for international students. *Recommended:* SAT or ACT (for admission).

Options: electronic application, early admission.

Application fee: $50.

Required: essay or personal statement, high school transcript, minimum 2.0 GPA, 2 letters of recommendation, Statement of Faith. *Recommended:* interview.

CONTACT
Mrs. Bianca Phillips, Admissions Coordinator, Beulah Heights University, 892 Berne Street, SE, Atlanta, GA 30316. *Phone:* 404-627-2681 Ext. 117. *Toll-free phone:* 888-777-BHBC. *E-mail:* bianca.phillips@beulah.edu.

Brenau University

Gainesville, Georgia
http://www.brenau.edu/

- **Independent** comprehensive, founded 1878
- **Suburban** 57-acre campus with easy access to Atlanta
- **Endowment** $47.9 million
- **Coed, primarily women** 1,754 undergraduate students, 62% full-time, 90% women, 10% men
- **Moderately difficult** entrance level, 65% of applicants were admitted

UNDERGRAD STUDENTS
1,090 full-time, 664 part-time. Students come from 27 states and territories; 15 other countries; 7% are from out of state; 29% Black or African American, non-Hispanic/Latino; 10% Hispanic/Latino; 2% Asian, non-Hispanic/Latino; 0.1% Native Hawaiian or other Pacific Islander, non-Hispanic/Latino; 0.4% American Indian or Alaska Native, non-Hispanic/Latino; 2% Two or more races, non-Hispanic/Latino; 4% Race/ethnicity unknown; 5% international; 16% transferred in; 23% live on campus.

Freshmen:
Admission: 1,902 applied, 1,231 admitted, 190 enrolled. *Average high school GPA:* 3.5.
Retention: 50% of full-time freshmen returned.

FACULTY
Total: 97, 68% full-time, 61% with terminal degrees.
Student/faculty ratio: 11:1.

ACADEMICS
Calendar: semesters. *Degrees:* certificates, associate, bachelor's, master's, doctoral, post-master's, and postbachelor's certificates (also offers coed evening and weekend programs with significant enrollment not reflected in profile).

Special study options: academic remediation for entering students, accelerated degree program, advanced placement credit, distance learning, double majors, honors programs, independent study, internships, part-time degree program, services for LD students, study abroad, summer session for credit.

Computers: 157 computers/terminals and 190 ports are available on campus for general student use. Students can access the following: campus intranet, computer help desk, free student e-mail accounts, online (class) grades, online (class) registration, online (class) schedules. Campuswide network is available. 100% of college-owned or -operated housing units are wired for high-speed Internet access. Wireless service is available via entire campus.
Library: Brenau Trustee Library. *Books:* 83,560 (physical), 431,102 (digital/electronic); *Serial titles:* 190 (physical), 64,642 (digital/electronic); *Databases:* 155. Weekly public service hours: 76; students can reserve study rooms.

STUDENT LIFE
Housing options: on-campus residence required through junior year; men-only, women-only, special housing for students with disabilities. Campus housing is university owned. Freshman campus housing is guaranteed.

Activities and organizations: drama/theater group, student-run newspaper, radio station, choral group, Student Activities Board, Student Government Association, Black Student Association, International Student Association, Her Campus, national sororities.

Athletics Member NAIA. *Intercollegiate sports:* basketball W(s), cheerleading W(s), crew W(c), cross-country running W(s), golf W(s), lacrosse W(s), soccer W(s), softball W(s), swimming and diving W(s), tennis W(s), track and field W(s), volleyball W(s).

Campus security: 24-hour emergency response devices and patrols, late-night transport/escort service.

Student services: health clinic, personal/psychological counseling, women's center, veterans affairs office.

COSTS & FINANCIAL AID
Costs (2019–20) *Comprehensive fee:* $43,290 includes full-time tuition ($29,370), mandatory fees ($1420), and room and board ($12,500). Part-time tuition: $979 per semester hour. *Required fees:* $210 part-time.

Financial Aid Of all full-time matriculated undergraduates who enrolled in 2017, 958 applied for aid, 904 were judged to have need, 94 had their need fully met. 115 Federal Work-Study jobs (averaging $1854). 107 state and other part-time jobs (averaging $1303). In 2017, 33 non-need-based awards were made. *Average percent of need met:* 57. *Average financial aid package:* $19,551. *Average need-based loan:* $5136. *Average need-based gift aid:* $14,503. *Average non-need-based aid:* $11,907. *Average indebtedness upon graduation:* $35,719.

APPLYING
Options: electronic application, deferred entrance.

Required for some: essay or personal statement, high school transcript, minimum 2.0 GPA, interview.

Application deadlines: rolling (freshmen), rolling (out-of-state freshmen), rolling (transfers).

Notification: continuous (freshmen), continuous (out-of-state freshmen), continuous (transfers).

CONTACT
Ray Lian, Brenau University, Admissions, 500 Washington Street, SE, Gainesville, GA 30501. *Phone:* 770-534-6171. *Toll-free phone:* 800-252-5119. *Fax:* 770-538-4701. *E-mail:* rlian@brenau.edu.

Brewton-Parker College

Mt. Vernon, Georgia
http://www.bpc.edu/

- **Independent Southern Baptist** 4-year, founded 1904
- **Rural** 280-acre campus
- **Coed**
- **Minimally difficult** entrance level

FACULTY
Student/faculty ratio: 13:1.

ACADEMICS
Calendar: semesters. *Degrees:* associate, bachelor's, and postbachelor's certificates.
Library: Fountain-New Library. *Books:* 88,734 (physical); *Serial titles:* 6,729 (physical); *Databases:* 290. Weekly public service hours: 78; students can reserve study rooms.

STUDENT LIFE
Housing options: on-campus residence required through junior year; men-only, women-only. Campus housing is university owned. Freshman campus housing is guaranteed.

Activities and organizations: drama/theater group, student-run newspaper, choral group, Council of Intramural Activities, Student Activities Council, Student Government Association, Circle K, Baptist Student Union.

Athletics Member NAIA.

Campus security: 24-hour emergency response devices, controlled dormitory access, campus security is provided from 6 pm to 6 am.

Student services: personal/psychological counseling, veterans affairs office.

COSTS & FINANCIAL AID
Costs (2018–19) *One-time required fee:* $200. *Comprehensive fee:* $26,620 includes full-time tuition ($16,940), mandatory fees ($1300), and room and board ($8380). Full-time tuition and fees vary according to course load, location, and program. Part-time tuition: $500 per credit hour. Part-time tuition and fees vary according to course load, location, and program. *Required fees:* $700 per year part-time. *College room only:* $3300. Room and board charges vary according to board plan and housing facility.

Financial Aid Of all full-time matriculated undergraduates who enrolled in 2009, 819 applied for aid, 736 were judged to have need, 118 had their need fully met. 170 Federal Work-Study jobs (averaging $676). 114 state and other part-time jobs (averaging $466). In 2009, 96 non-need-based awards were made. *Average percent of need met:* 71. *Average financial aid package:* $11,736. *Average need-based loan:* $3436. *Average need-based gift aid:* $9011. *Average non-need-based aid:* $3915. *Average indebtedness upon graduation:* $28,231. *Financial aid deadline:* 5/1.

APPLYING
Standardized Tests *Required:* SAT or ACT (for admission).

Options: electronic application.

Application fee: $35.

Required: high school transcript, minimum 2.0 GPA.

CONTACT
Ms. Tiffany Quarterman, Admissions Office Manager, Brewton-Parker College, PO Box 197, Mount Vernon, GA 30445. *Phone:* 912-583-3250. *Toll-free phone:* 800-342-1087. *Fax:* 912-583-3598. *E-mail:* admissions@bpc.edu.

Carver College
Atlanta, Georgia
http://www.carver.edu/

CONTACT
Bertha Mack, Admissions Officer, Carver College, 3870 Cascade Road SW, Atlanta, GA 30331. *Phone:* 404-527-4520 Ext. 209. *Fax:* 404-527-4524. *E-mail:* info@carver.edu.

Chamberlain College of Nursing
Atlanta, Georgia
http://www.chamberlain.edu/

CONTACT
Chamberlain College of Nursing, 5775 Peachtree Dunwoody Road NE, Suite A-100, Atlanta, GA 30342. *Toll-free phone:* 877-751-5783.

Clark Atlanta University
Atlanta, Georgia
http://www.cau.edu/

- **Independent United Methodist** university, founded 1865
- **Urban** 126-acre campus
- **Endowment** $68.5 million
- **Coed**
- **Moderately difficult** entrance level

FACULTY
Student/faculty ratio: 20:1.

ACADEMICS
Calendar: semesters. *Degrees:* bachelor's, master's, doctoral, post-master's, and postbachelor's certificates.
Library: Robert W. Woodruff Library.

STUDENT LIFE
Housing options: on-campus residence required through sophomore year; coed, men-only, women-only. Campus housing is university owned and is provided by a third party. Freshman applicants given priority for college housing.

Activities and organizations: drama/theater group, student-run newspaper, radio and television station, choral group, marching band, Spirit Boosters, Pre-Alumni Council, Campus Activities Board, Orientation Guides, National Association for the Advancement of Colored People, national fraternities, national sororities.

Athletics Member NCAA. All Division II.

Campus security: 24-hour emergency response devices and patrols, late-night transport/escort service, controlled dormitory access.

Student services: health clinic, personal/psychological counseling.

COSTS & FINANCIAL AID
Costs (2018–19) *Comprehensive fee:* $31,710 includes full-time tuition ($20,680), mandatory fees ($1506), and room and board ($9524). Part-time tuition: $862 per credit hour. *Room and board:* Room and board charges vary according to board plan and housing facility.

Financial Aid Of all full-time matriculated undergraduates who enrolled in 2016, 2,780 applied for aid, 2,638 were judged to have need, 1,261 had their need fully met. 201 Federal Work-Study jobs (averaging $1740). *Average percent of need met:* 45. *Average financial aid package:* $7324. *Average need-based loan:* $2453. *Average need-based gift aid:* $5425. *Average indebtedness upon graduation:* $40,393.

APPLYING
Standardized Tests *Required:* SAT or ACT (for admission).

Options: electronic application, early admission, deferred entrance.

Application fee: $35.

Required: essay or personal statement, high school transcript, minimum 2.5 GPA, 2 letters of recommendation. *Required for some:* interview.

CONTACT
Ms. Lorri Rice, Director of Recruitment and Admissions, Clark Atlanta University, 223 James P. Brawley Drive, SW, Atlanta, GA 30314. *Phone:* 404-880-8043. *Toll-free phone:* 800-688-3228. *Fax:* 404-880-6174. *E-mail:* cauadmissions@cau.edu.

Clayton State University
Morrow, Georgia
http://www.clayton.edu/

- **State-supported** comprehensive, founded 1969, part of University System of Georgia
- **Suburban** 163-acre campus with easy access to Atlanta
- **Coed**
- **Minimally difficult** entrance level

FACULTY
Student/faculty ratio: 17:1.

ACADEMICS
Calendar: semesters. *Degrees:* certificates, associate, bachelor's, and master's.
Library: Clayton State University Library.

STUDENT LIFE
Housing options: on-campus residence required for freshman year; coed. Campus housing is university owned. Freshman applicants given priority for college housing.

Activities and organizations: drama/theater group, student-run newspaper, radio station, choral group, national fraternities, national sororities.

Athletics Member NCAA. All Division II.

Campus security: 24-hour emergency response devices and patrols, late-night transport/escort service, controlled dormitory access, lighted pathways.

Student services: health clinic, personal/psychological counseling, veterans affairs office.

COSTS & FINANCIAL AID
Costs (2018–19) *Tuition:* state resident $4956 full-time, $165 per credit hour part-time; nonresident $18,032 full-time, $601 per credit hour part-time. Full-time tuition and fees vary according to course load. Part-time tuition and fees vary according to course load. *Required fees:* $1454 full-time. *Room and board:* $10,180; room only: $6400. Room and board charges vary according to board plan and housing facility.

Financial Aid Of all full-time matriculated undergraduates who enrolled in 2017, 3,251 applied for aid, 3,029 were judged to have need, 86 had their need fully met. 67 Federal Work-Study jobs (averaging $4556). In 2017, 25 non-need-based awards were made. *Average percent of need met:* 47. *Average financial aid package:* $10,024. *Average need-based loan:* $4067. *Average need-based gift aid:* $7108. *Average non-need-based aid:* $2045. *Average indebtedness upon graduation:* $30,423.

APPLYING
Standardized Tests *Required:* SAT or ACT (for admission).

Options: electronic application, early admission, deferred entrance.

Application fee: $40.

Required: high school transcript, proof of immunization.

CONTACT
Admissions, Clayton State University, 2000 Clayton State Boulevard, Morrow, GA 30260-0285. *Phone:* 678-466-4115. *Fax:* 678-466-4149. *E-mail:* csc-info@clayton.edu.

College of Coastal Georgia
Brunswick, Georgia
http://www.ccga.edu/
- **State-supported** 4-year, founded 1961, part of University System of Georgia
- **Small-town** 193-acre campus with easy access to Jacksonville
- **Endowment** $8.8 million
- **Coed** 3,546 undergraduate students, 59% full-time, 68% women, 32% men
- **Minimally difficult** entrance level, 93% of applicants were admitted

UNDERGRAD STUDENTS
2,078 full-time, 1,468 part-time. Students come from 27 states and territories; 44 other countries; 5% are from out of state; 19% Black or African American, non-Hispanic/Latino; 6% Hispanic/Latino; 2% Asian, non-Hispanic/Latino; 0.1% Native Hawaiian or other Pacific Islander, non-Hispanic/Latino; 0.3% American Indian or Alaska Native, non-Hispanic/Latino; 4% Two or more races, non-Hispanic/Latino; 2% Race/ethnicity unknown; 1% international; 6% transferred in; 18% live on campus.

Freshmen:
Admission: 1,611 applied, 1,494 admitted, 795 enrolled. *Average high school GPA:* 3.0. *Test scores:* SAT evidence-based reading and writing scores over 500: 59%; SAT math scores over 500: 49%; ACT scores over 18: 64%; SAT evidence-based reading and writing scores over 600: 17%; SAT math scores over 600: 7%; ACT scores over 24: 13%; SAT evidence-based reading and writing scores over 700: 1%; SAT math scores over 700: 1%; ACT scores over 30: 1%.
Retention: 59% of full-time freshmen returned.

FACULTY
Total: 190, 56% full-time.
Student/faculty ratio: 19:1.

ACADEMICS
Calendar: semesters. *Degrees:* associate and bachelor's.
Special study options: academic remediation for entering students, advanced placement credit, distance learning, double majors, honors programs, internships, part-time degree program, services for LD students, study abroad, summer session for credit.
Computers: 395 computers/terminals and 300 ports are available on campus for general student use. Students can access the following: computer help desk, free student e-mail accounts, online (class) grades, online (class) registration, online (class) schedules. Campuswide network is available. 100% of college-owned or -operated housing units are wired for high-speed Internet access. Wireless service is available via entire campus.
Library: Clara Wood Gould Memorial Library. *Books:* 54,662 (physical), 150,476 (digital/electronic); *Serial titles:* 109 (physical), 168,333 (digital/electronic); *Databases:* 338. Weekly public service hours: 77; students can reserve study rooms.

STUDENT LIFE
Housing options: on-campus residence required for freshman year; coed. Campus housing is university owned, leased by the school and is provided by a third party. Freshman campus housing is guaranteed.
Activities and organizations: student-run newspaper, International Association, Coastal Georgia Association of Nursing Students, Urban Gaming Club, Association of Coastal Educators, CCGA Biology Club.
Athletics Member NAIA. *Intercollegiate sports:* basketball M(s)/W(s), golf M(s), softball W(s), tennis M(s)/W(s), volleyball W(s). *Intramural sports:* baseball M(c), basketball M/W, bowling M, cheerleading W(c), cross-country running M(c)/W(c), football M/W, golf M/W, lacrosse W(c), rugby M(c), sailing M(c)/W(c), soccer M/W, softball M/W, ultimate Frisbee M/W, wrestling M(c).
Campus security: 24-hour emergency response devices and patrols, late-night transport/escort service, controlled dormitory access.
Student services: health clinic, personal/psychological counseling, veterans affairs office.

COSTS & FINANCIAL AID
Costs (2018–19) *One-time required fee:* $25. *Tuition:* state resident $3126 full-time, $104 per credit hour part-time; nonresident $11,548 full-time, $385 per credit hour part-time. Full-time tuition and fees vary according to course load. Part-time tuition and fees vary according to course load. *Required fees:* $1570 full-time, $455 per term part-time. *Room and board:* $10,036; room only: $6416. Room and board charges vary according to board plan, housing facility, and location. *Payment plan:* installment. *Waivers:* senior citizens and employees or children of employees.

Financial Aid Of all full-time matriculated undergraduates who enrolled in 2017, 1,716 applied for aid, 1,267 were judged to have need, 44 had their need fully met. 8 Federal Work-Study jobs (averaging $363). In 2017, 100 non-need-based awards were made. *Average percent of need met:* 61. *Average financial aid package:* $10,843. *Average need-based loan:* $3443. *Average need-based gift aid:* $6428. *Average non-need-based aid:* $1883. *Average indebtedness upon graduation:* $19,554. *Financial aid deadline:* 6/1.

APPLYING
Standardized Tests *Required:* SAT or ACT (for admission).
Options: electronic application, early admission, deferred entrance.
Application fee: $25.
Required: high school transcript, minimum 2.0 GPA, immunization records, proof of residency.
Application deadlines: 8/5 (freshmen), 8/5 (out-of-state freshmen), 8/5 (transfers).
Notification: continuous (freshmen), continuous (transfers).

CONTACT
Dr. Amy Clines, AVP Recruitment and Admissions, College of Coastal Georgia, One College Drive, Brunswick, GA 31520. *Phone:* 912-279-5775. *Toll-free phone:* 800-675-7235. *Fax:* 912-262-3072. *E-mail:* admiss@ccga.edu.

Columbus State University
Columbus, Georgia
http://www.columbusstate.edu/
- **State-supported** comprehensive, founded 1958, part of University System of Georgia
- **Suburban** 132-acre campus with easy access to Atlanta
- **Coed**
- **Minimally difficult** entrance level

FACULTY
Student/faculty ratio: 17:1.

ACADEMICS
Calendar: semesters. *Degrees:* certificates, associate, bachelor's, master's, doctoral, post-master's, and postbachelor's certificates.
Library: Simon Schwob Memorial Library plus 1 other. *Books:* 379,660 (physical); *Serial titles:* 1,103 (physical).

STUDENT LIFE
Housing options: on-campus residence required for freshman year; coed, men-only, women-only, special housing for students with disabilities. Campus housing is university owned. Freshman applicants given priority for college housing.
Activities and organizations: drama/theater group, student-run newspaper, choral group, Student Government Association, Student Activities Council, Campus Ministry Association, African Students Association, SABER Student Newspaper, national fraternities, national sororities.
Athletics Member NCAA. All Division II.
Campus security: 24-hour emergency response devices and patrols, late-night transport/escort service, controlled dormitory access.
Student services: health clinic, personal/psychological counseling, veterans affairs office.

COSTS & FINANCIAL AID
Costs (2018–19) *Tuition:* state resident $5330 full-time, $178 per credit hour part-time; nonresident $18,812 full-time, $627 per credit hour part-time. Full-time tuition and fees vary according to course load, degree level, and program. Part-time tuition and fees vary according to course load, degree level, and program. *Required fees:* $1870 full-time, $935 per term part-time. *Room and board:* $10,762; room only: $6712. Room and board charges vary according to board plan and housing facility.

Financial Aid Of all full-time matriculated undergraduates who enrolled in 2018, 4,077 applied for aid, 3,336 were judged to have need, 548 had their need fully met. In 2018, 191 non-need-based awards were made. *Average percent of need met:* 71. *Average financial aid package:* $9881. *Average need-based loan:* $4260. *Average need-based gift aid:* $5127. *Average non-need-based aid:* $1453. *Average indebtedness upon graduation:* $30,597.

APPLYING
Standardized Tests *Required:* SAT or ACT (for admission).

Options: electronic application, early admission, deferred entrance.

Application fee: $40.

Required: high school transcript, minimum 2.5 GPA, proof of immunization.

CONTACT
Columbus State University, 4225 University Avenue, Columbus, GA 31907-5645. *Phone:* 706-507-8827. *Toll-free phone:* 866-264-2035.

Covenant College

Lookout Mountain, Georgia
http://www.covenant.edu/

- **Independent** comprehensive, founded 1955, affiliated with Presbyterian Church in America
- **Suburban** 350-acre campus
- **Coed** 1,002 undergraduate students, 97% full-time, 52% women, 48% men
- **Moderately difficult** entrance level, 97% of applicants were admitted

UNDERGRAD STUDENTS
969 full-time, 33 part-time. 70% are from out of state; 3% Black or African American, non-Hispanic/Latino; 2% Hispanic/Latino; 1% Asian, non-Hispanic/Latino; 0.3% American Indian or Alaska Native, non-Hispanic/Latino; 5% Two or more races, non-Hispanic/Latino; 0.1% Race/ethnicity unknown; 4% international; 3% transferred in; 83% live on campus.

Freshmen:
Admission: 672 applied, 653 admitted, 249 enrolled. *Average high school GPA:* 3.7. *Test scores:* SAT evidence-based reading and writing scores over 500: 96%; SAT math scores over 500: 91%; ACT scores over 18: 100%; SAT evidence-based reading and writing scores over 600: 71%; SAT math scores over 600: 50%; ACT scores over 24: 74%; SAT evidence-based reading and writing scores over 700: 23%; SAT math scores over 700: 14%; ACT scores over 30: 30%.

Retention: 86% of full-time freshmen returned.

FACULTY
Total: 102, 61% full-time, 70% with terminal degrees.

Student/faculty ratio: 13:1.

ACADEMICS
Calendar: semesters. *Degrees:* bachelor's and master's (master's degree in education only).

Special study options: academic remediation for entering students, adult/continuing education programs, advanced placement credit, double majors, English as a second language, independent study, internships, off-campus study, part-time degree program, services for LD students, student-designed majors, study abroad, summer session for credit. *ROTC:* Army (c).

Computers: Students can access the following: computer help desk, free student e-mail accounts, online (class) registration, online student information system. Campuswide network is available. 100% of college-owned or -operated housing units are wired for high-speed Internet access. Wireless service is available via classrooms, computer labs, dorm rooms, libraries.

Library: Kresge Memorial Library.

STUDENT LIFE
Housing options: on-campus residence required through junior year; coed. Campus housing is university owned. Freshman campus housing is guaranteed.

Activities and organizations: drama/theater group, student-run newspaper, radio station, choral group.

Athletics Member NCAA, NAIA, NCCAA. All NCAA Division III. *Intercollegiate sports:* baseball M, basketball M/W, cross-country running M/W, golf M, soccer M/W, softball W, tennis M/W, volleyball W. *Intramural sports:* badminton M/W, basketball M/W, football M, soccer M/W, volleyball M/W.

Campus security: controlled dormitory access, night security guards.

Student services: health clinic, personal/psychological counseling, women's center.

COSTS & FINANCIAL AID
Costs (2019–20) *Comprehensive fee:* $46,300 includes full-time tuition ($34,660), mandatory fees ($980), and room and board ($10,660). Part-time tuition: $1490 per credit hour.

Financial Aid Of all full-time matriculated undergraduates who enrolled in 2017, 772 applied for aid, 673 were judged to have need, 220 had their need fully met. In 2017, 288 non-need-based awards were made. *Average percent of need met:* 81. *Average financial aid package:* $28,920. *Average need-based loan:* $6817. *Average need-based gift aid:* $22,940. *Average non-need-based aid:* $16,181. *Average indebtedness upon graduation:* $25,007.

APPLYING
Standardized Tests *Required:* SAT or ACT (for admission).

Options: electronic application, early admission, early action, deferred entrance.

Application fee: $35.

Required: essay or personal statement, high school transcript, minimum 2.5 GPA, 2 letters of recommendation, interview.

CONTACT
Mr. Philip Howlett, Assistant Director of Admissions, Covenant College, 14049 Scenic Highway, Lookout Mountain, GA 30750. *Phone:* 706-419-1145. *Toll-free phone:* 888-451-2683. *Fax:* 706-820-0893. *E-mail:* admissions@covenant.edu.

Dalton State College

Dalton, Georgia
http://www.daltonstate.edu/

CONTACT
Katherine Logan, Director of Admissions, Dalton State College, 650 College Drive, Dalton, GA 30720-3797. *Phone:* 706-272-4524. *Toll-free phone:* 800-829-4436. *Fax:* 706-272-2530. *E-mail:* klogan@daltonstate.edu.

DeVry University–Alpharetta Campus

Alpharetta, Georgia
http://www.devry.edu/

CONTACT
Admissions Office, DeVry University–Alpharetta Campus, 2555 Northwinds Parkway, Alpharetta, GA 30009. *Phone:* 770-619-3600. *Toll-free phone:* 866-338-7934.

DeVry University–Decatur Campus

Decatur, Georgia
http://www.devry.edu/

CONTACT
DeVry University–Decatur Campus, 1 West Court Square, Suite 100, Decatur, GA 30030. *Phone:* 404-270-2700. *Toll-free phone:* 866-338-7934.

East Georgia State College

Swainsboro, Georgia
http://www.ega.edu/

CONTACT
East Georgia State College, 131 College Circle, Swainsboro, GA 30401-2699. *Phone:* 478-289-2112.

Emmanuel College

Franklin Springs, Georgia

http://www.ec.edu/

- **Independent** 4-year, founded 1919, affiliated with Pentecostal Holiness Church
- **Rural** 90-acre campus with easy access to Atlanta, GA
- **Endowment** $5.2 million
- **Coed** 920 undergraduate students, 88% full-time, 50% women, 50% men
- **Minimally difficult** entrance level, 42% of applicants were admitted

UNDERGRAD STUDENTS

811 full-time, 109 part-time. Students come from 30 states and territories; 20 other countries; 31% are from out of state; 14% Black or African American, non-Hispanic/Latino; 6% Hispanic/Latino; 0.8% Asian, non-Hispanic/Latino; 0.8% Native Hawaiian or other Pacific Islander, non-Hispanic/Latino; 0.3% American Indian or Alaska Native, non-Hispanic/Latino; 3% Two or more races, non-Hispanic/Latino; 8% international; 6% transferred in; 60% live on campus.

Freshmen:

Admission: 1,089 applied, 457 admitted, 247 enrolled. *Average high school GPA:* 3.4.

Retention: 58% of full-time freshmen returned.

FACULTY

Total: 88, 55% full-time, 48% with terminal degrees.

Student/faculty ratio: 15:1.

ACADEMICS

Calendar: semesters. *Degrees:* associate and bachelor's.

Special study options: advanced placement credit, distance learning, honors programs, independent study, internships, part-time degree program, services for LD students, study abroad, summer session for credit.

Unusual degree programs: 3-2 psychology with Richmont University.

Computers: 80 computers/terminals are available on campus for general student use. Students can access the following: campus intranet, computer help desk, free student e-mail accounts, online (class) grades, online (class) registration, online (class) schedules. Campuswide network is available. 100% of college-owned or -operated housing units are wired for high-speed Internet access. Wireless service is available via entire campus.

Library: Shaw-Leslie Library plus 1 other. *Books:* 41,206 (physical), 50,364 (digital/electronic); *Serial titles:* 99 (physical); *Databases:* 124. Weekly public service hours: 84; students can reserve study rooms.

STUDENT LIFE

Housing options: on-campus residence required through sophomore year; men-only, women-only. Campus housing is university owned. Freshman campus housing is guaranteed.

Activities and organizations: drama/theater group, choral group, Students in Free Enterprise (SIFE), Fellowship of Christian Athletes, SOS, BSU, International Students Club.

Athletics Member NCAA, NCCAA. All NCAA Division II. *Intercollegiate sports:* archery M(s)/W(s), baseball M(s), basketball M(s)/W(s), bowling M(s)/W(s), cross-country running M(s)/W(s), golf M(s), lacrosse M(s)/W(s), riflery M(s)/W(s), soccer M(s)/W(s), softball W(s), swimming and diving M(s)/W(s), tennis M(s)/W(s), track and field M(s)/W(s), volleyball M(s)/W(s), wrestling M(s)/W(s). *Intramural sports:* basketball M/W, football M/W, golf M/W, soccer M/W, tennis M/W, track and field M/W, volleyball M/W, weight lifting M/W.

Campus security: 24-hour patrols.

Student services: personal/psychological counseling, veterans affairs office.

COSTS & FINANCIAL AID

Costs (2019–20) *Comprehensive fee:* $28,612 includes full-time tuition ($20,352), mandatory fees ($360), and room and board ($7900). Part-time tuition: $856 per credit hour.

Financial Aid Of all full-time matriculated undergraduates who enrolled in 2018, 651 applied for aid, 576 were judged to have need, 90 had their need fully met. 87 Federal Work-Study jobs (averaging $1117). 117 state and other part-time jobs (averaging $1078). In 2018, 117 non-need-based awards were made. *Average percent of need met:* 67. *Average financial aid package:* $16,800. *Average need-based loan:* $3781. *Average need-based gift aid:* $12,965. *Average non-need-based aid:* $4706. *Average indebtedness upon graduation:* $9033. *Financial aid deadline:* 6/15.

APPLYING

Standardized Tests *Required:* SAT or ACT (for admission).

Options: electronic application, early admission, deferred entrance.

Application fee: $25.

Required: essay or personal statement, high school transcript. *Required for some:* interview.

Notification: continuous until 8/1 (freshmen), continuous until 8/1 (transfers).

CONTACT

Ms. Kelley Garrett, Director of Admissions, Emmanuel College, PO Box 129, 181 Spring Street, Franklin Springs, GA 30639-0129. *Phone:* 706-245-7226 Ext. 2814. *Toll-free phone:* 800-860-8800. *E-mail:* admissions@ec.edu.

Emory University

Atlanta, Georgia

http://www.emory.edu/

- **Independent Methodist** university, founded 1836
- **Suburban** 631-acre campus with easy access to Atlanta
- **Endowment** $6.9 billion
- **Coed**
- **Most difficult** entrance level

FACULTY

Student/faculty ratio: 9:1.

ACADEMICS

Calendar: semesters. *Degrees:* bachelor's, master's, doctoral, post-master's, and postbachelor's certificates (enrollment figures include Emory University, Oxford College; application data for main campus only).

Library: Robert W. Woodruff Library plus 8 others. *Books:* 2.3 million (physical), 943,697 (digital/electronic); *Serial titles:* 78,038 (physical), 156,766 (digital/electronic); *Databases:* 892.

STUDENT LIFE

Housing options: on-campus residence required through sophomore year; coed. Campus housing is university owned. Freshman campus housing is guaranteed.

Activities and organizations: drama/theater group, student-run newspaper, radio and television station, choral group, Volunteer Emory, music/theater, Student Government, Outdoor Emory, Hillel, national fraternities, national sororities.

Athletics Member NCAA. All Division III.

Campus security: 24-hour emergency response devices and patrols, student patrols, late-night transport/escort service, controlled dormitory access.

Student services: health clinic, personal/psychological counseling, women's center, legal services, veterans affairs office.

COSTS & FINANCIAL AID

Costs (2018–19) *Comprehensive fee:* $65,762 includes full-time tuition ($50,590), mandatory fees ($716), and room and board ($14,456). Part-time tuition: $2108 per credit hour. *College room only:* $8306. Room and board charges vary according to board plan and housing facility.

Financial Aid Of all full-time matriculated undergraduates who enrolled in 2018, 3,666 applied for aid, 3,223 were judged to have need, 3,159 had their need fully met. In 2018, 347 non-need-based awards were made. *Average percent of need met:* 100. *Average financial aid package:* $44,968. *Average need-based loan:* $6018. *Average need-based gift aid:* $41,583. *Average non-need-based aid:* $29,383. *Average indebtedness upon graduation:* $29,658. *Financial aid deadline:* 3/1.

APPLYING

Standardized Tests *Required:* SAT or ACT (for admission).

Options: electronic application, early admission, early decision, deferred entrance.

Application fee: $75.

Required: essay or personal statement, high school transcript, 2 letters of recommendation.

CONTACT
Dr. John Latting, Dean of Admission, Emory University, 1390 Oxford Road NE, 3rd Floor, Atlanta, GA 30322-1100. *Phone:* 404-727-6036. *Toll-free phone:* 800-727-6036. *Fax:* 404-727-4303. *E-mail:* admiss@emory.edu.

Fort Valley State University
Fort Valley, Georgia
http://www.fvsu.edu/

CONTACT
Mr. Donald Moore, Director of Admissions and Recruitment, Fort Valley State University, 1005 State University Drive, Fort Valley, GA 31030. *Phone:* 478-825-6307. *Toll-free phone:* 877-462-3878. *Fax:* 478-825-6169. *E-mail:* admissap@fvsu.edu.

Georgia College & State University
Milledgeville, Georgia
http://www.gcsu.edu/

- **State-supported** comprehensive, founded 1889, part of University System of Georgia
- **Small-town** 680-acre campus
- **Endowment** $44.0 million
- **Coed** 5,958 undergraduate students, 91% full-time, 63% women, 37% men
- **Moderately difficult** entrance level, 78% of applicants were admitted

UNDERGRAD STUDENTS
5,410 full-time, 548 part-time. Students come from 20 states and territories; 27 other countries; 1% are from out of state; 5% Black or African American, non-Hispanic/Latino; 6% Hispanic/Latino; 1% Asian, non-Hispanic/Latino; 0.1% American Indian or Alaska Native, non-Hispanic/Latino; 3% Two or more races, non-Hispanic/Latino; 0.3% Race/ethnicity unknown; 0.5% international; 4% transferred in; 36% live on campus.

Freshmen:
Admission: 4,329 applied, 3,367 admitted, 1,483 enrolled. *Average high school GPA:* 3.5. *Test scores:* SAT evidence-based reading and writing scores over 500: 98%; SAT math scores over 500: 96%; ACT scores over 18: 100%; SAT evidence-based reading and writing scores over 600: 57%; SAT math scores over 600: 41%; ACT scores over 24: 66%; SAT evidence-based reading and writing scores over 700: 7%; SAT math scores over 700: 4%; ACT scores over 30: 9%.
Retention: 85% of full-time freshmen returned.

FACULTY
Total: 416, 80% full-time, 72% with terminal degrees.
Student/faculty ratio: 17:1.

ACADEMICS
Calendar: semesters. *Degrees:* certificates, bachelor's, master's, doctoral, and post-master's certificates.
Special study options: accelerated degree program, advanced placement credit, distance learning, double majors, English as a second language, external degree program, freshman honors college, honors programs, independent study, internships, part-time degree program, services for LD students, student-designed majors, study abroad, summer session for credit. *ROTC:* Army (c).
Unusual degree programs: 3-2 engineering with Georgia Institute of Technology.
Computers: 900 computers/terminals and 6,295 ports are available on campus for general student use. Students can access the following: campus intranet, computer help desk, free student e-mail accounts, online (class) grades, online (class) registration, online (class) schedules. Campuswide network is available. 100% of college-owned or -operated housing units are wired for high-speed Internet access. Wireless service is available via entire campus.
Library: Ina Dillard Russell Library plus 1 other. *Books:* 168,202 (physical), 490,414 (digital/electronic); *Serial titles:* 4,160 (physical),

159,746 (digital/electronic); *Databases:* 374. Weekly public service hours: 102; students can reserve study rooms.

STUDENT LIFE
Housing options: on-campus residence required for freshman year; coed, cooperative, special housing for students with disabilities. Campus housing is university owned and leased by the school. Freshman campus housing is guaranteed.
Activities and organizations: drama/theater group, student-run newspaper, radio station, choral group, Alpha Lambda Delta, Circle K, Gamma Beta Phi, Swipe out Hunger, Wesley Foundation of Campus Ministries, national fraternities, national sororities.
Athletics Member NCAA. All Division II. *Intercollegiate sports:* baseball M(s), basketball M(s)/W(s), cheerleading M/W, cross-country running M(s)/W(s), golf M(s), soccer W(s), softball W(s), tennis M(s)/W(s), volleyball W(s). *Intramural sports:* baseball M(c), basketball M/W, equestrian sports W(c), football M/W, golf M(c), ice hockey M(c), lacrosse M(c)/W(c), rugby M(c)/W(c), soccer M(c)/W(c), softball M(c)/W(c), swimming and diving W(c), tennis M(c)/W(c), ultimate Frisbee M(c)/W(c), volleyball M/W(c), water polo M(c)/W(c).
Campus security: 24-hour emergency response devices and patrols, student patrols, late-night transport/escort service, controlled dormitory access.
Student services: health clinic, personal/psychological counseling, women's center, veterans affairs office.

COSTS & FINANCIAL AID
Costs (2018–19) *Tuition:* state resident $7324 full-time; nonresident $26,038 full-time. Full-time tuition and fees vary according to course load, location, and program. Part-time tuition and fees vary according to course load, location, and program. *Required fees:* $2022 full-time. *Room and board:* $12,964; room only: $7208. Room and board charges vary according to board plan, housing facility, and location. *Payment plan:* installment. *Waivers:* senior citizens and employees or children of employees.
Financial Aid Of all full-time matriculated undergraduates who enrolled in 2018, 4,220 applied for aid, 2,759 were judged to have need, 555 had their need fully met. In 2018, 213 non-need-based awards were made. *Average percent of need met:* 60. *Average financial aid package:* $11,058. *Average need-based loan:* $4737. *Average need-based gift aid:* $4765. *Average non-need-based aid:* $2098. *Average indebtedness upon graduation:* $31,402.

APPLYING
Standardized Tests *Required:* SAT or ACT (for admission). *Required for some:* SAT Subject Tests (for admission).
Options: electronic application, early admission, early action, deferred entrance.
Application fee: $40.
Required: proof of immunization. *Required for some:* essay or personal statement, high school transcript.
Application deadlines: rolling (out-of-state freshmen), 7/1 (transfers).
Notification: continuous (freshmen), continuous (out-of-state freshmen), continuous (transfers).

CONTACT
Mr. Ramon Blakley, Director of Admissions, Undergraduate, Georgia College & State University, CPO Box 023, Milledgeville, GA 31061. *Phone:* 478-445-1283. *Toll-free phone:* 800-342-0471. *Fax:* 478-445-3653. *E-mail:* admissions@gcsu.edu.

Georgia Gwinnett College
Lawrenceville, Georgia
http://www.ggc.edu/

- **State-supported** 4-year, part of University System of Georgia
- **Suburban** 260-acre campus with easy access to Atlanta
- **Coed**
- **Noncompetitive** entrance level

FACULTY
Student/faculty ratio: 18:1.

ACADEMICS
Calendar: semesters. *Degrees:* associate and bachelor's.

Library: Daniel J. Kaufman Library and Learning Center. *Books:* 76,355 (physical), 118,119 (digital/electronic); *Serial titles:* 141 (physical), 5,119 (digital/electronic); *Databases:* 112. Weekly public service hours: 79; students can reserve study rooms.

STUDENT LIFE

Housing options: coed. Campus housing is university owned. Freshman campus housing is guaranteed.

Athletics Member NAIA.

Campus security: 24-hour emergency response devices and patrols, student patrols, late-night transport/escort service, controlled dormitory access.

Student services: health clinic, personal/psychological counseling, veterans affairs office.

COSTS

Costs (2018–19) *Tuition:* state resident $3920 full-time, $131 per credit hour part-time; nonresident $14,634 full-time, $488 per credit hour part-time. Full-time tuition and fees vary according to course load. Part-time tuition and fees vary according to course load. *Required fees:* $1714 full-time, $480 per term part-time. *Room and board:* $13,086; room only: $9838. Room and board charges vary according to board plan and housing facility. *Payment plans:* installment, deferred payment.

APPLYING

Standardized Tests *Required:* SAT or ACT (for admission).

Options: electronic application, deferred entrance.

Application fee: $20.

Required: high school transcript, minimum 2.0 GPA.

CONTACT

Admissions Office, Georgia Gwinnett College, 1000 University Center Lane, Lawrenceville, GA 30043. *Phone:* 678-407-5313. *Toll-free phone:* 877-704-4422. *E-mail:* ggcadmissions@ggc.edu.

Georgia Highlands College

Rome, Georgia

http://www.highlands.edu/

- **State-supported** primarily 2-year, founded 1970, part of University System of Georgia
- **Suburban** 226-acre campus with easy access to Atlanta
- **Endowment** $40,227
- **Coed** 6,184 undergraduate students, 47% full-time, 62% women, 38% men
- **Noncompetitive** entrance level

UNDERGRAD STUDENTS

2,885 full-time, 3,299 part-time. Students come from 23 states and territories; 1% are from out of state; 16% Black or African American, non-Hispanic/Latino; 15% Hispanic/Latino; 2% Asian, non-Hispanic/Latino; 0.1% Native Hawaiian or other Pacific Islander, non-Hispanic/Latino; 0.2% American Indian or Alaska Native, non-Hispanic/Latino; 4% Two or more races, non-Hispanic/Latino; 0.4% Race/ethnicity unknown; 6% transferred in.

Freshmen:
Admission: 1,308 enrolled. *Average high school GPA:* 3.0.
Retention: 67% of full-time freshmen returned.

FACULTY

Total: 277, 47% full-time, 25% with terminal degrees.
Student/faculty ratio: 21:1.

ACADEMICS

Calendar: semesters. *Degrees:* associate and bachelor's.

Special study options: academic remediation for entering students, advanced placement credit, cooperative education, distance learning, double majors, honors programs, independent study, part-time degree program, services for LD students, study abroad, summer session for credit.

Computers: 867 computers/terminals are available on campus for general student use. Students can access the following: campus intranet, free student e-mail accounts, online (class) grades, online (class) registration, online (class) schedules. Campuswide network is available. Wireless service is available via entire campus.

Library: Georgia Highlands College Library–Floyd Campus plus 4 others. *Books:* 79,592 (physical), 178,561 (digital/electronic); *Serial titles:* 48 (physical), 4,380 (digital/electronic); *Databases:* 382. Weekly public service hours: 58; students can reserve study rooms.

STUDENT LIFE

Housing options: college housing not available.

Activities and organizations: student-run newspaper, Association of Nursing Students, Green Highlands, Brother 2 Brother, Student Government Association, Phi Theta Kappa.

Athletics Member NJCAA. *Intercollegiate sports:* baseball M(s), basketball M(s)/W(s), softball W(s). *Intramural sports:* basketball M/W, cheerleading M/W, football M/W, golf M/W, skiing (downhill) M/W, table tennis M/W, tennis M/W, ultimate Frisbee M/W, volleyball M/W, weight lifting M/W.

Campus security: 24-hour emergency response devices and patrols, emergency phone/email alert system.

Student services: personal/psychological counseling, veterans affairs office.

COSTS & FINANCIAL AID

Costs (2018–19) *One-time required fee:* $30. *Tuition:* state resident $2224 full-time, $93 per credit hour part-time; nonresident $8421 full-time, $351 per credit hour part-time. Full-time tuition and fees vary according to course load and location. Part-time tuition and fees vary according to course load and location. *Required fees:* $1064 full-time, $412 per term part-time. *Payment plan:* installment. *Waivers:* senior citizens.

Financial Aid Of all full-time matriculated undergraduates who enrolled in 2017, 50 Federal Work-Study jobs (averaging $3500).

APPLYING

Standardized Tests *Required for some:* COMPASS. *Recommended:* SAT or ACT (for admission).

Options: electronic application, deferred entrance.

Application fee: $30.

Required: high school transcript, minimum 2.0 GPA.

Notification: continuous (freshmen), continuous (transfers).

CONTACT

Charlene Graham, Assistant Director of Admissions, Georgia Highlands College, 3175 Cedartown Highway, Rome, GA 30161. *Phone:* 706-295-6339. *Toll-free phone:* 800-332-2406. *Fax:* 706-295-6341. *E-mail:* cgraham@highlands.edu.

Georgia Institute of Technology

Atlanta, Georgia

http://www.gatech.edu/

- **State-supported** university, founded 1885, part of University System of Georgia
- **Urban** 400-acre campus
- **Endowment** $2.0 billion
- **Coed**
- 23% of applicants were admitted

FACULTY

Student/faculty ratio: 22:1.

ACADEMICS

Calendar: semesters. *Degrees:* bachelor's, master's, and doctoral.
Library: Georgia Institute of Technology Library plus 1 other. *Books:* 909,730 (physical), 1.0 million (digital/electronic); *Serial titles:* 12,999 (physical), 29,621 (digital/electronic); *Databases:* 336. Weekly public service hours: 168; study areas open 24 hours, 5–7 days a week; students can reserve study rooms.

STUDENT LIFE

Housing options: coed, men-only, women-only, special housing for students with disabilities. Campus housing is university owned. Freshman campus housing is guaranteed.

Activities and organizations: drama/theater group, student-run newspaper, radio and television station, choral group, marching band, national fraternities, national sororities.

Athletics Member NCAA. All Division I.

Campus security: 24-hour emergency response devices and patrols, late-night transport/escort service, controlled dormitory access, lighted pathways/sidewalks, emergency notification system, self-defense education, emergency telephones, shuttle buses, video cameras.

Student services: health clinic, personal/psychological counseling, women's center, legal services, veterans affairs office.

COSTS & FINANCIAL AID

Costs (2018–19) *Tuition:* state resident $10,008 full-time, $2974 per term part-time; nonresident $30,604 full-time, $9081 per term part-time. Part-time tuition and fees vary according to course load. *Required fees:* $2410 full-time, $1205 per term part-time. *Room and board:* $14,126; room only: $9286. Room and board charges vary according to board plan, housing facility, and student level.

Financial Aid Of all full-time matriculated undergraduates who enrolled in 2017, 9,165 applied for aid, 5,850 were judged to have need, 1,403 had their need fully met. In 2017, 3867 non-need-based awards were made. *Average percent of need met:* 57. *Average financial aid package:* $14,422. *Average need-based loan:* $4882. *Average need-based gift aid:* $12,581. *Average non-need-based aid:* $10,185. *Average indebtedness upon graduation:* $32,760. *Financial aid deadline:* 1/31.

APPLYING

Standardized Tests *Required:* SAT or ACT (for admission).

Options: electronic application, early admission, early action, deferred entrance.

Application fee: $75.

Required: essay or personal statement, high school transcript.

CONTACT

Mr. Rick A. Clark Jr., Director of Undergraduate Admissions, Georgia Institute of Technology, Office of Undergraduate Admission, Atlanta, GA 30332-0320. *Phone:* 404-894-4154. *Fax:* 404-894-9511. *E-mail:* admission@gatech.edu.

Georgia Military College

Milledgeville, Georgia

http://www.gmc.edu/

- **Public** primarily 2-year, founded 1879
- **Small-town** campus
- **Endowment** $1.5 million
- **Coed**
- **Noncompetitive** entrance level

FACULTY

Student/faculty ratio: 15:1.

ACADEMICS

Calendar: quarters. *Degrees:* associate and bachelor's.

Library: Sibley Cone Library plus 1 other. *Books:* 38,125 (physical), 57,769 (digital/electronic); *Serial titles:* 52 (physical); *Databases:* 331. Weekly public service hours: 68.

STUDENT LIFE

Housing options: on-campus residence required through sophomore year; coed. Campus housing is university owned. Freshman campus housing is guaranteed.

Activities and organizations: drama/theater group, student-run newspaper, choral group, Student Government Association, Alpha Phi Omega National Service Fraternity, Phi Theta Kappa, Drama Club, Biology Club.

Athletics Member NJCAA.

Campus security: 24-hour emergency response devices and patrols, controlled dormitory access.

Student services: health clinic, veterans affairs office.

COSTS & FINANCIAL AID

Costs (2018–19) *Tuition:* state resident $5445 full-time, $121 per credit hour part-time; nonresident $5445 full-time, $121 per credit hour part-time. Full-time tuition and fees vary according to location. Part-time

tuition and fees vary according to location. *Required fees:* $679 full-time, $15 per credit hour part-time. *Room and board:* $7500; room only: $3150. Room and board charges vary according to location.

Financial Aid Of all full-time matriculated undergraduates who enrolled in 2017, 5,060 applied for aid, 4,319 were judged to have need, 975 had their need fully met. In 2017, 685 non-need-based awards were made. *Average percent of need met:* 20. *Average financial aid package:* $10,096. *Average need-based loan:* $2253. *Average need-based gift aid:* $3845. *Average non-need-based aid:* $2222.

APPLYING

Options: electronic application, early admission, deferred entrance.

Application fee: $35.

Required for some: high school transcript, interview.

CONTACT

Georgia Military College, 201 East Greene Street, Old Capitol Building, Milledgeville, GA 31061-3398. *Phone:* 478-387-4890. *Toll-free phone:* 800-342-0413.

Georgia Southern University

Statesboro, Georgia

http://www.georgiasouthern.edu/

- **State-supported** university, founded 1906, part of University System of Georgia
- **Small-town** 900-acre campus
- **Endowment** $47.7 million
- **Coed** 23,134 undergraduate students, 84% full-time, 55% women, 45% men
- **Moderately difficult** entrance level, 68% of applicants were admitted

UNDERGRAD STUDENTS

19,483 full-time, 3,651 part-time. Students come from 50 states and territories; 86 other countries; 6% are from out of state; 25% Black or African American, non-Hispanic/Latino; 7% Hispanic/Latino; 2% Asian, non-Hispanic/Latino; 0.1% Native Hawaiian or other Pacific Islander, non-Hispanic/Latino; 0.4% American Indian or Alaska Native, non-Hispanic/Latino; 4% Two or more races, non-Hispanic/Latino; 0.5% Race/ethnicity unknown; 1% international; 6% transferred in; 26% live on campus.

Freshmen:
Admission: 11,522 applied, 7,797 admitted, 4,347 enrolled. *Average high school GPA:* 3.4. *Test scores:* SAT evidence-based reading and writing scores over 500: 96%; SAT math scores over 500: 90%; ACT scores over 18: 41%; SAT evidence-based reading and writing scores over 600: 37%; SAT math scores over 600: 24%; ACT scores over 24: 9%; SAT evidence-based reading and writing scores over 700: 3%; SAT math scores over 700: 2%; ACT scores over 30: 4%.

Retention: 78% of full-time freshmen returned.

FACULTY

Total: 1,387, 80% full-time, 70% with terminal degrees.

Student/faculty ratio: 22:1.

ACADEMICS

Calendar: semesters. *Degrees:* certificates, bachelor's, master's, doctoral, post-master's, and postbachelor's certificates.

Special study options: academic remediation for entering students, accelerated degree program, adult/continuing education programs, advanced placement credit, cooperative education, distance learning, double majors, English as a second language, honors programs, independent study, internships, off-campus study, part-time degree program, services for LD students, student-designed majors, study abroad, summer session for credit. *ROTC:* Army (b).

Unusual degree programs: 3-2 engineering with Georgia Institute of Technology; nursing.

Computers: 3,743 computers/terminals and 5,200 ports are available on campus for general student use. Students can access the following: campus intranet, computer help desk, free student e-mail accounts, online (class) grades, online (class) registration, online (class) schedules, online degree audit, online career services, and online healthcare. Campuswide network is available. 100% of college-owned or -operated housing units are wired for high-speed Internet access. Wireless service is available via entire campus.

Library: Henderson Library. *Books:* 649,104 (physical), 656,518 (digital/electronic); *Serial titles:* 15,006 (physical), 104,711 (digital/electronic); *Databases:* 325. Weekly public service hours: 143; study areas open 24 hours, 5–7 days a week; students can reserve study rooms.

STUDENT LIFE

Housing options: on-campus residence required for freshman year; coed, special housing for students with disabilities. Campus housing is university owned. Freshman applicants given priority for college housing.

Activities and organizations: drama/theater group, student-run newspaper, radio station, choral group, marching band, Residence Hall Association, Campus Religious Ministries, Student Government Association, Club Sports and Recreation, Greek Life, national fraternities, national sororities.

Athletics Member NCAA. All Division I. *Intercollegiate sports:* baseball M(s), basketball M(s)/W(s), cheerleading M/W, cross-country running W(s), football M(s), golf M(s)/W(s)(c), riflery W(s), soccer M(s)/W(s), softball W(s), swimming and diving W(s), tennis M(s)/W(s), track and field W(s), volleyball W(s). *Intramural sports:* archery M/W, baseball M(c), basketball M/W, bowling M/W, cheerleading M(c)/W(c), cross-country running M(c)/W(c), equestrian sports M(c)/W(c), fencing M(c), field hockey W(c), football M/W, golf M/W, lacrosse M(c)/W(c), riflery M(c)/W(c), rugby M(c)/W(c), soccer M/W, softball M/W, swimming and diving M(c)/W(c), tennis M/W, track and field M(c)/W(c), ultimate Frisbee M/W, volleyball M/W, water polo M(c)/W(c), wrestling M(c).

Campus security: 24-hour emergency response devices and patrols, student patrols, late-night transport/escort service, controlled dormitory access.

Student services: health clinic, personal/psychological counseling, women's center, legal services, veterans affairs office.

COSTS & FINANCIAL AID

Costs (2018–19) *Tuition:* state resident $5330 full-time, $178 per credit hour part-time; nonresident $18,812 full-time, $627 per credit hour part-time. Full-time tuition and fees vary according to course load, degree level, location, and program. Part-time tuition and fees vary according to course load, degree level, location, and program. *Required fees:* $2092 full-time, $1046 per term part-time. *Room and board:* $10,070; room only: $6320. Room and board charges vary according to board plan, housing facility, and location. *Payment plan:* installment. *Waivers:* senior citizens and employees or children of employees.

Financial Aid Of all full-time matriculated undergraduates who enrolled in 2017, 14,174 applied for aid, 10,074 were judged to have need, 1,205 had their need fully met. 214 Federal Work-Study jobs (averaging $1650). In 2017, 423 non-need-based awards were made. *Average percent of need met:* 57. *Average financial aid package:* $10,873. *Average need-based loan:* $5435. *Average need-based gift aid:* $7680. *Average non-need-based aid:* $1907. *Average indebtedness upon graduation:* $29,030.

APPLYING

Standardized Tests *Required:* SAT or ACT (for admission).

Options: electronic application, early admission, deferred entrance.

Application fee: $30.

Required: minimum 2.5 GPA. *Required for some:* high school transcript.

Application deadlines: 5/1 (freshmen), 5/1 (out-of-state freshmen), 8/1 (transfers).

Notification: continuous (freshmen), continuous (out-of-state freshmen), continuous (transfers).

CONTACT

Mrs. Christy Rikard, Interim Director, Georgia Southern University, PO Box 8024, Statesboro, GA 30460. *Phone:* 912-478-5391. *Fax:* 912-478-7240. *E-mail:* admissions@georgiasouthern.edu.

Georgia Southern University–Armstrong Campus
Savannah, Georgia
http://www.georgiasouthern.edu/

- **State-supported** comprehensive, founded 1935, part of University System of Georgia
- **Suburban** 267-acre campus
- **Endowment** $12.2 million
- **Coed**
- 78% of applicants were admitted

FACULTY
Student/faculty ratio: 16:1.

ACADEMICS
Calendar: semesters. *Degrees:* certificates, associate, bachelor's, master's, doctoral, post-master's, and postbachelor's certificates.
Library: Lane Library plus 1 other. *Books:* 207,421 (physical), 215,400 (digital/electronic); *Serial titles:* 500 (physical), 2,000 (digital/electronic); *Databases:* 300. Weekly public service hours: 108; students can reserve study rooms.

STUDENT LIFE
Housing options: on-campus residence required for freshman year; coed. Campus housing is leased by the school and is provided by a third party. Freshman applicants given priority for college housing.

Activities and organizations: drama/theater group, student-run newspaper, choral group, Hispanic Outreach and Leadership at Armstrong (HOLA), Student Government Association, Campus Union Board, Gay Straight Alliance, Collegiate 100, national fraternities, national sororities.

Campus security: 24-hour emergency response devices and patrols, student patrols, late-night transport/escort service, controlled dormitory access, personal safety app.

Student services: health clinic, personal/psychological counseling, veterans affairs office.

COSTS & FINANCIAL AID
Costs (2018–19) *Tuition:* state resident $5330 full-time, $178 per credit hour part-time; nonresident $18,812 full-time, $627 per credit hour part-time. Full-time tuition and fees vary according to course load, location, and program. Part-time tuition and fees vary according to course load, location, and program. *Required fees:* $1054 full-time, $527 per term part-time. *Room and board:* $10,630. Room and board charges vary according to board plan and housing facility.

Financial Aid Of all full-time matriculated undergraduates who enrolled in 2017, 14,174 applied for aid, 10,074 were judged to have need, 1,205 had their need fully met. In 2017, 423 non-need-based awards were made. *Average percent of need met:* 57. *Average financial aid package:* $10,873. *Average need-based loan:* $5469. *Average need-based gift aid:* $7680. *Average non-need-based aid:* $1907. *Average indebtedness upon graduation:* $29,030.

APPLYING
Standardized Tests *Required:* SAT or ACT (for admission). *Required for some:* SAT Subject Tests (for admission).

Options: electronic application.

Application fee: $30.

Required: high school transcript, minimum 2.5 GPA.

CONTACT
Amy Smither, Director of Admissions, Georgia Southern University–Armstrong Campus, 11935 Abercorn Street, Savannah, GA 31419. *Phone:* 912-478-5391. *Toll-free phone:* 800-633-2349. *Fax:* 912-344-3417. *E-mail:* amysmith@georgiasouthern.com.

★ Georgia Southwestern State University

Americus, Georgia

http://www.gsw.edu/

- **State-supported** comprehensive, founded 1906, part of University System of Georgia
- **Small-town** 250-acre campus
- **Endowment** $35.6 million
- **Coed**
- **Moderately difficult** entrance level

FACULTY

Student/faculty ratio: 18:1.

ACADEMICS

Calendar: semesters. *Degrees:* bachelor's, master's, post-master's, and postbachelor's certificates.

Library: James Earl Carter Library. *Books:* 207,635 (physical), 68,397 (digital/electronic); *Serial titles:* 76 (physical), 81 (digital/electronic); *Databases:* 277. Weekly public service hours: 72; students can reserve study rooms.

STUDENT LIFE

Housing options: on-campus residence required through sophomore year; coed. Campus housing is university owned. Freshman applicants given priority for college housing.

Activities and organizations: drama/theater group, student-run newspaper, choral group, National sororities and fraternities, African Student Association, Enactus, Outdoor Club, International Student Association, national fraternities, national sororities.

Athletics Member NCAA. All Division II.

Campus security: 24-hour emergency response devices and patrols, late-night transport/escort service, controlled dormitory access.

Student services: health clinic, personal/psychological counseling.

COSTS & FINANCIAL AID

Costs (2018–19) *Tuition:* state resident $4956 full-time, $165 per credit hour part-time; nonresident $18,032 full-time, $601 per credit hour part-time. Full-time tuition and fees vary according to course load, location, and program. Part-time tuition and fees vary according to course load, location, and program. *Required fees:* $1380 full-time, $448 per term part-time. *Room and board:* $8120; room only: $4070. Room and board charges vary according to board plan and housing facility.

Financial Aid Of all full-time matriculated undergraduates who enrolled in 2017, 1,571 applied for aid, 1,281 were judged to have need, 157 had their need fully met. 115 Federal Work-Study jobs (averaging $1868). In 2017, 114 non-need-based awards were made. *Average percent of need met:* 67. *Average financial aid package:* $9680. *Average need-based loan:* $3886. *Average need-based gift aid:* $4700. *Average non-need-based aid:* $2083. *Average indebtedness upon graduation:* $25,775. *Financial aid deadline:* 6/15.

APPLYING

Standardized Tests *Required:* SAT or ACT (for admission).

Options: electronic application, early admission, deferred entrance.

Application fee: $25.

Required: high school transcript, minimum 2.0 GPA, college preparatory curriculum. *Recommended:* interview.

CONTACT

Mr. David Jenkins, Assistant Director of Admissions, Georgia Southwestern State University, Americus, GA 31709. *Phone:* 229-928-1273. *Toll-free phone:* 800-338-0082. *Fax:* 229-931-2983. *E-mail:* admissions@gsw.edu.

Georgia State University

Atlanta, Georgia

http://www.gsu.edu/

- **State-supported** university, founded 1913, part of University System of Georgia
- **Urban** 109-acre campus with easy access to Atlanta
- **Endowment** $167.1 million
- **Coed** 27,190 undergraduate students, 77% full-time, 59% women, 41% men
- **Moderately difficult** entrance level, 57% of applicants were admitted

UNDERGRAD STUDENTS

21,041 full-time, 6,149 part-time. Students come from 53 states and territories; 129 other countries; 4% are from out of state; 41% Black or African American, non-Hispanic/Latino; 12% Hispanic/Latino; 14% Asian, non-Hispanic/Latino; 0.0% Native Hawaiian or other Pacific Islander, non-Hispanic/Latino; 0.1% American Indian or Alaska Native, non-Hispanic/Latino; 6% Two or more races, non-Hispanic/Latino; 0.8% Race/ethnicity unknown; 3% international; 6% transferred in; 21% live on campus.

Freshmen:

Admission: 19,838 applied, 11,393 admitted, 5,001 enrolled. *Average high school GPA:* 3.5. *Test scores:* SAT evidence-based reading and writing scores over 500: 81%; SAT math scores over 500: 69%; ACT scores over 18: 96%; SAT evidence-based reading and writing scores over 600: 20%; SAT math scores over 600: 27%; ACT scores over 24: 46%; SAT evidence-based reading and writing scores over 700: 3%; SAT math scores over 700: 4%; ACT scores over 30: 10%.

Retention: 83% of full-time freshmen returned.

FACULTY

Total: 1,581, 73% full-time, 84% with terminal degrees.

Student/faculty ratio: 23:1.

ACADEMICS

Calendar: semesters. *Degrees:* certificates, associate, bachelor's, master's, doctoral, post-master's, and postbachelor's certificates.

Special study options: advanced placement credit, cooperative education, distance learning, double majors, English as a second language, honors programs, independent study, internships, part-time degree program, services for LD students, study abroad, summer session for credit. *ROTC:* Army (b), Navy (c), Air Force (c).

Computers: 2,040 computers/terminals and 28,816 ports are available on campus for general student use. Students can access the following: computer help desk, free student e-mail accounts, online (class) grades, online (class) registration, online (class) schedules. Campuswide network is available. 100% of college-owned or -operated housing units are wired for high-speed Internet access. Wireless service is available via entire campus.

Library: University Library plus 6 others. *Books:* 1.9 million (physical), 686,132 (digital/electronic); *Serial titles:* 21,654 (digital/electronic). Students can reserve study rooms.

STUDENT LIFE

Housing options: coed, special housing for students with disabilities. Campus housing is university owned and leased by the school. Freshman applicants given priority for college housing.

Activities and organizations: drama/theater group, student-run newspaper, radio and television station, choral group, marching band, Spotlight Programs Board, Fraternities/Sororities, Service Organizations, Academic Organizations, Sports Clubs, national fraternities, national sororities.

Athletics Member NCAA. All Division I. *Intercollegiate sports:* baseball M(s), basketball M(s)/W(s), cross-country running W(s), football M(s), golf M(s)/W(s)(c), rugby M(c), soccer M(s)/W(s), softball W(s), squash M(c)/W(c), swimming and diving M(c)/W(c), table tennis M(c)/W(c), tennis M(s)/W(s), track and field W(s), ultimate Frisbee M(c)/W(c), volleyball W(s). *Intramural sports:* badminton M(c)/W(c), basketball M/W, bowling M/W, crew M(c)/W(c), equestrian sports M(c)/W(c), fencing M(c)/W(c), football M/W, golf M/W, lacrosse M(c)/W(c), racquetball M/W, rock climbing M(c)/W(c), rowing M(c)/W(c), rugby M(c), soccer M/W, table tennis M/W, tennis M(c)/W(c), ultimate Frisbee M/W, volleyball M/W, wrestling M(c)/W(c).

Campus security: 24-hour emergency response devices and patrols, late-night transport/escort service, controlled dormitory access.

Student services: health clinic, personal/psychological counseling.

COSTS & FINANCIAL AID

Costs (2018–19) *Tuition:* state resident $8730 full-time, $291 per credit hour part-time; nonresident $27,304 full-time, $910 per credit hour part-time. Part-time tuition and fees vary according to course load. *Required fees:* $2128 full-time, $1064 per term part-time. *Room and board:* $14,692; room only: $10,824. Room and board charges vary according to board plan and housing facility. *Waivers:* senior citizens and employees or children of employees.

Financial Aid Of all full-time matriculated undergraduates who enrolled in 2017, 23,271 applied for aid, 20,031 were judged to have need, 796 had their need fully met. *Average percent of need met:* 51. *Average financial aid package:* $10,739. *Average need-based gift aid:* $5626. *Average indebtedness upon graduation:* $29,584.

APPLYING

Standardized Tests *Required:* SAT or ACT (for admission).

Options: electronic application, early admission, early action, deferred entrance.

Application fee: $60.

Required: high school transcript, minimum 2.8 GPA, college preparatory curriculum as specified by the University System of Georgia Board of Regents, combined SAT of 830, minimum Freshman Index of 2500. *Recommended:* essay or personal statement, 1 letter of recommendation.

Application deadlines: 3/1 (freshmen), 3/1 (out-of-state freshmen), 8/1 (transfers), 11/15 (early action).

Notification: 4/15 (freshmen), 4/15 (out-of-state freshmen), continuous (transfers), 12/15 (early action).

CONTACT

Scott Burke, Assistant Vice President for Undergraduate Admissions, Georgia State University, PO Box 4009, Atlanta, GA 30302-4009. *Phone:* 404-413-2500. *Fax:* 404-413-2002. *E-mail:* onestopshop@gsu.edu.

Gordon State College

Barnesville, Georgia
http://www.gordonstate.edu/

- **State-supported** primarily 2-year, founded 1852, part of University System of Georgia
- **Small-town** 235-acre campus with easy access to Atlanta
- **Coed**
- **83%** of applicants were admitted

FACULTY
Student/faculty ratio: 21:1.

ACADEMICS
Calendar: semesters. *Degrees:* associate and bachelor's.
Library: Dorothy W. Hightower Collaborative Learning Center and Library. *Books:* 103,423 (physical), 35,999 (digital/electronic); *Serial titles:* 401 (physical), 87,985 (digital/electronic); *Databases:* 325. Weekly public service hours: 73.

STUDENT LIFE
Housing options: on-campus residence required for freshman year; coed. Campus housing is university owned. Freshman applicants given priority for college housing.

Activities and organizations: drama/theater group, student-run newspaper, choral group, Campus Activity Board, Student Government Association, Earth Wind Fire (science club), Student African American Brotherhood (SAAB), Swazi Step Team.

Athletics Member NJCAA.

Campus security: 24-hour emergency response devices and patrols, student patrols, controlled dormitory access, Resident Assistants and Resident Directors in housing, parking patrol.

Student services: health clinic, personal/psychological counseling, veterans affairs office.

COSTS & FINANCIAL AID
Costs (2018–19) *Tuition:* state resident $3126 full-time, $104 per credit hour part-time; nonresident $11,548 full-time, $385 per credit hour part-

time. *Required fees:* $1166 full-time, $550 per term part-time. *Room and board:* $8408. Room and board charges vary according to board plan and housing facility.

Financial Aid Of all full-time matriculated undergraduates who enrolled in 2017, 75 Federal Work-Study jobs (averaging $1850).

APPLYING
Standardized Tests *Required:* SAT or ACT (for admission).

Options: electronic application, early admission.

Application fee: $30.

Required: high school transcript.

CONTACT
Gordon State College, 419 College Drive, Barnesville, GA 30204-1762. *Phone:* 678-359-5021. *Toll-free phone:* 800-282-6504.

Herzing University

Atlanta, Georgia
http://www.herzing.edu/atlanta/

CONTACT
Herzing University, 3393 Peachtree Road, NE, Suite 1003, Atlanta, GA 30326. *Toll-free phone:* 800-596-0724.

Kennesaw State University

Kennesaw, Georgia
http://www.kennesaw.edu/

- **State-supported** comprehensive, founded 1963, part of University System of Georgia
- **Suburban** 602-acre campus with easy access to Atlanta
- **Endowment** $40.3 million
- **Coed** 32,274 undergraduate students, 75% full-time, 48% women, 52% men
- **Moderately difficult** entrance level, 58% of applicants were admitted

UNDERGRAD STUDENTS
24,150 full-time, 8,124 part-time. Students come from 54 states and territories; 129 other countries; 13% are from out of state; 21% Black or African American, non-Hispanic/Latino; 10% Hispanic/Latino; 5% Asian, non-Hispanic/Latino; 0.1% Native Hawaiian or other Pacific Islander, non-Hispanic/Latino; 0.2% American Indian or Alaska Native, non-Hispanic/Latino; 5% Two or more races, non-Hispanic/Latino; 2% Race/ethnicity unknown; 2% international; 7% transferred in; 16% live on campus.

Freshmen:
Admission: 13,427 applied, 7,779 admitted, 4,784 enrolled. *Average high school GPA:* 3.4.
Retention: 79% of full-time freshmen returned.

FACULTY
Total: 1,941, 61% full-time, 64% with terminal degrees.
Student/faculty ratio: 20:1.

ACADEMICS
Calendar: semesters. *Degrees:* certificates, bachelor's, master's, doctoral, post-master's, and postbachelor's certificates.

Special study options: adult/continuing education programs, advanced placement credit, cooperative education, distance learning, double majors, English as a second language, freshman honors college, honors programs, internships, off-campus study, part-time degree program, services for LD students, study abroad, summer session for credit. *ROTC:* Army (c), Navy (c), Air Force (c).

Computers: 4,500 computers/terminals and 38,000 ports are available on campus for general student use. Students can access the following: campus intranet, computer help desk, free student e-mail accounts, online (class) grades, online (class) registration, online (class) schedules. Campuswide network is available. 100% of college-owned or -operated housing units are wired for high-speed Internet access. Wireless service is available via classrooms, computer centers, computer labs, dorm rooms, learning centers, libraries, student centers.
Library: Kennesaw State University Library System plus 2 others. *Books:* 378,276 (physical), 656,005 (digital/electronic); *Serial titles:*

1,273 (physical), 115,672 (digital/electronic); *Databases:* 476. Students can reserve study rooms.

STUDENT LIFE

Housing options: coed, special housing for students with disabilities. Campus housing is provided by a third party. Freshman applicants given priority for college housing.

Activities and organizations: drama/theater group, student-run newspaper, radio station, choral group, marching band, Kennesaw Activities Board, African American Student Alliance, International Student Association, KSU eSports Organization, IEEE Computer Society, national fraternities, national sororities.

Athletics Member NCAA. All Division I. *Intercollegiate sports:* baseball M(s), basketball M(s)/W(s), cross-country running M(s)/W(s), football M(s), golf M(s)/W(s), lacrosse W(s), soccer W(s), softball W(s), tennis M(s)/W(s), track and field M(s)/W(s), volleyball W(s). *Intramural sports:* archery M(c)/W(c), badminton M, baseball M(c), basketball M/W, bowling M/W, cross-country running M(c)/W(c), equestrian sports W(c), fencing M(c)/W(c), field hockey W(c), football M/W, golf M/W, gymnastics M(c)/W(c), ice hockey M(c), lacrosse M(c)/W(c), racquetball M/W, rugby M(c)/W(c), sand volleyball M/W, soccer M/W, softball M/W, swimming and diving M(c)/W(c), table tennis M(c)/W(c), tennis M/W, ultimate Frisbee M(c)/W(c), volleyball M(c)/W(c), water polo M(c)/W(c).

Campus security: 24-hour emergency response devices and patrols, student patrols, late-night transport/escort service, controlled dormitory access.

Student services: health clinic, personal/psychological counseling, veterans affairs office.

COSTS & FINANCIAL AID

Costs (2018–19) *Tuition:* state resident $5426 full-time, $181 per credit hour part-time; nonresident $19,152 full-time, $638 per credit hour part-time. Full-time tuition and fees vary according to course load, degree level, location, program, and student level. Part-time tuition and fees vary according to course load, degree level, location, program, and student level. *Required fees:* $2006 full-time, $1003 per term part-time. *Room and board:* $11,467. Room and board charges vary according to board plan, housing facility, and student level. *Payment plans:* installment, deferred payment. *Waivers:* senior citizens and employees or children of employees.

Financial Aid Of all full-time matriculated undergraduates who enrolled in 2018, 20,172 applied for aid, 17,165 were judged to have need, 940 had their need fully met. In 2018, 167 non-need-based awards were made. *Average percent of need met:* 43. *Average financial aid package:* $11,593. *Average need-based loan:* $5085. *Average need-based gift aid:* $7094. *Average non-need-based aid:* $1122. *Average indebtedness upon graduation:* $25,525. *Financial aid deadline:* 6/1.

APPLYING

Standardized Tests *Required:* (for admission).

Options: electronic application, early admission, early action.

Application fee: $40.

Required: high school transcript, minimum 2.5 GPA.

Application deadlines: 5/3 (freshmen), 5/3 (out-of-state freshmen), 6/14 (transfers), 11/1 (early action).

Notification: continuous until 12/1 (freshmen), 12/1 (out-of-state freshmen), 12/8 (early action).

CONTACT

Ms. Jackie Quiroga, Interim Senior Director of Admissions, Kennesaw State University, 1000 Chastain Road, Kennesaw, GA 30144. *Phone:* 770-578-2548. *Fax:* 470-578-9169. *E-mail:* ksuadmit@kennesaw.edu.

LaGrange College
LaGrange, Georgia
http://www.lagrange.edu/

- **Independent United Methodist** comprehensive, founded 1831
- **Small-town** 120-acre campus with easy access to Atlanta
- **Endowment** $56.4 million
- **Coed** 877 undergraduate students, 95% full-time, 52% women, 48% men
- **Moderately difficult** entrance level, 48% of applicants were admitted

UNDERGRAD STUDENTS

831 full-time, 46 part-time. Students come from 19 states and territories; 7 other countries; 16% are from out of state; 19% Black or African American, non-Hispanic/Latino; 1% Hispanic/Latino; 1% Asian, non-Hispanic/Latino; 0.6% American Indian or Alaska Native, non-Hispanic/Latino; 2% Two or more races, non-Hispanic/Latino; 0.1% Race/ethnicity unknown; 1% international; 13% transferred in; 58% live on campus.

Freshmen:

Admission: 1,511 applied, 728 admitted, 211 enrolled. *Average high school GPA:* 3.5. *Test scores:* SAT evidence-based reading and writing scores over 500: 81%; SAT math scores over 500: 81%; ACT scores over 18: 96%; SAT evidence-based reading and writing scores over 600: 28%; SAT math scores over 600: 14%; ACT scores over 24: 24%; SAT evidence-based reading and writing scores over 700: 1%; SAT math scores over 700: 2%; ACT scores over 30: 2%.

Retention: 60% of full-time freshmen returned.

FACULTY

Total: 113, 67% full-time, 65% with terminal degrees.

Student/faculty ratio: 11:1.

ACADEMICS

Calendar: 4-1-4. *Degrees:* bachelor's and master's.

Special study options: accelerated degree program, adult/continuing education programs, advanced placement credit, distance learning, double majors, independent study, internships, part-time degree program, services for LD students, student-designed majors, study abroad, summer session for credit.

Unusual degree programs: 3-2 engineering with Georgia Institute of Technology, Auburn University.

Computers: 116 computers/terminals and 960 ports are available on campus for general student use. Students can access the following: campus intranet, free student e-mail accounts, online (class) grades, online (class) registration, online (class) schedules. Campuswide network is available. 100% of college-owned or -operated housing units are wired for high-speed Internet access. Wireless service is available via entire campus.

Library: Frank and Laura Lewis Library. *Books:* 83,082 (physical), 351,244 (digital/electronic); *Serial titles:* 23 (physical), 21 (digital/electronic); *Databases:* 192. Weekly public service hours: 84; study areas open 24 hours, 5–7 days a week; students can reserve study rooms.

STUDENT LIFE

Housing options: on-campus residence required through senior year; coed, men-only, women-only, special housing for students with disabilities. Campus housing is university owned. Freshman campus housing is guaranteed.

Activities and organizations: drama/theater group, student-run newspaper, choral group, marching band, Campus Circle, LC Miracle, Panhellenic (Sorority Leadership), Black Student Union, Student Government, national fraternities, national sororities.

Athletics Member NCAA. All Division III. *Intercollegiate sports:* baseball M, basketball M/W, cheerleading W, cross-country running M/W, football M, golf M, lacrosse W, soccer M/W, softball W, swimming and diving M/W, tennis M/W, volleyball W. *Intramural sports:* basketball M/W, softball M/W, table tennis M/W, water polo M/W.

Campus security: 24-hour patrols, controlled dormitory access, mass notification system (e2Campus) to send emergency messages to students and employees.

Student services: health clinic, personal/psychological counseling.

COSTS & FINANCIAL AID

Costs (2018–19) *One-time required fee:* $150. *Comprehensive fee:* $42,130 includes full-time tuition ($30,170), mandatory fees ($330), and room and board ($11,630). Full-time tuition and fees vary according to class time, course load, degree level, and program. Part-time tuition: $1240 per semester hour. Part-time tuition and fees vary according to class time, course load, degree level, and program. *College room only:* $6430. Room and board charges vary according to board plan and housing facility. *Payment plan:* installment. *Waivers:* senior citizens and employees or children of employees.

Financial Aid Of all full-time matriculated undergraduates who enrolled in 2017, 833 applied for aid, 773 were judged to have need, 137 had their need fully met. In 2017, 87 non-need-based awards were made. *Average percent of need met:* 74. *Average financial aid package:* $26,065. *Average need-based loan:* $3934. *Average need-based gift aid:* $6979. *Average non-need-based aid:* $12,224. *Average indebtedness upon graduation:* $35,094. *Financial aid deadline:* 5/1.

APPLYING
Standardized Tests *Required:* SAT or ACT (for admission). *Required for some:* SAT (for admission), ACT (for admission).

Options: electronic application, deferred entrance.

Required: essay or personal statement, high school transcript. **Required for some:** minimum 2.5 GPA, 3 letters of recommendation, interview.

Application deadlines: rolling (freshmen), rolling (transfers).

Notification: continuous (freshmen), continuous (transfers).

CONTACT
Ms. Holly Phillips, Administrative Coordinator, LaGrange College, 601 Broad Street, LaGrange, GA 30240-2999. *Phone:* 706-880-8005. *Toll-free phone:* 800-593-2885. *Fax:* 706-880-8010. *E-mail:* hphillips@lagrange.edu.

Life University
Marietta, Georgia
http://www.life.edu/
- **Independent** comprehensive, founded 1974
- **Suburban** 96-acre campus with easy access to Atlanta Metro
- **Coed** 898 undergraduate students, 81% full-time, 55% women, 45% men
- **Minimally difficult** entrance level, 37% of applicants were admitted

UNDERGRAD STUDENTS
727 full-time, 171 part-time. Students come from 54 states and territories; 46 other countries; 43% are from out of state; 25% Black or African American, non-Hispanic/Latino; 24% Hispanic/Latino; 3% Asian, non-Hispanic/Latino; 1% American Indian or Alaska Native, non-Hispanic/Latino; 3% Race/ethnicity unknown; 2% international; 13% transferred in; 10% live on campus.

Freshmen:
Admission: 701 applied, 257 admitted, 163 enrolled. *Average high school GPA:* 2.9. *Test scores:* ACT scores over 18: 73%; ACT scores over 24: 9%.

Retention: 62% of full-time freshmen returned.

FACULTY
Total: 183, 70% full-time, 80% with terminal degrees.
Student/faculty ratio: 12:1.

ACADEMICS
Calendar: quarters. *Degrees:* certificates, associate, bachelor's, master's, and doctoral.

Special study options: academic remediation for entering students, accelerated degree program, advanced placement credit, cooperative education, distance learning, double majors, English as a second language, independent study, internships, off-campus study, part-time degree program, services for LD students, student-designed majors, study abroad, summer session for credit.

Computers: Students can access the following: campus intranet, computer help desk, free student e-mail accounts, online (class) grades, online (class) registration. Campuswide network is available. 100% of college-owned or -operated housing units are wired for high-speed Internet access. Wireless service is available via entire campus.

Library: Library & Learning Services. *Books:* 33,771 (physical), 39,225 (digital/electronic); *Serial titles:* 66 (physical), 31,104 (digital/electronic); *Databases:* 25. Weekly public service hours: 98; students can reserve study rooms.

STUDENT LIFE
Housing options: coed. Campus housing is university owned.

Activities and organizations: student-run newspaper, Student Ambassadors, Campus Activities Board, League of Chiropractic Women, Functional Neurology Club, Hispanic Club.

Athletics Member NAIA. *Intercollegiate sports:* basketball M(s)/W(s), bowling M(s)/W, cheerleading M/W, cross-country running W(s), ice hockey M(s), lacrosse W(s), rugby M(s)/W(s), soccer M(s)/W(s), swimming and diving W(s), track and field W(s), volleyball W(s), wrestling M(s)/W(s). *Intramural sports:* basketball M/W, cross-country running M/W, rugby M/W, soccer M, softball M/W, table tennis M, tennis M/W, volleyball M/W, weight lifting M/W.

Campus security: 24-hour emergency response devices and patrols, controlled dormitory access.

Student services: health clinic, personal/psychological counseling.

COSTS & FINANCIAL AID
Costs (2018–19) *Tuition:* $11,703 full-time, $249 per credit hour part-time. Full-time tuition and fees vary according to course load. *Required fees:* $1491 full-time. *Room only:* Room and board charges vary according to housing facility. *Payment plan:* installment. *Waivers:* employees or children of employees.

Financial Aid Of all full-time matriculated undergraduates who enrolled in 2018, 617 applied for aid, 563 were judged to have need, 13 had their need fully met. 143 Federal Work-Study jobs (averaging $340,000). In 2018, 4 non-need-based awards were made. *Average percent of need met:* 34. *Average financial aid package:* $11,700. *Average need-based loan:* $4300. *Average need-based gift aid:* $5500. *Average non-need-based aid:* $300. *Average indebtedness upon graduation:* $45,000.

APPLYING
Standardized Tests *Required:* SAT or ACT (for admission).

Options: electronic application.

Application fee: $50.

Required: high school transcript, minimum 2.0 GPA.

Notification: continuous (freshmen), continuous (transfers).

CONTACT
Cynthia Boyd, Vice President Enrollment Management and Marketing, Life University, 1269 Barclay Circle, Marietta, GA 30060. *Phone:* 770-426-2756. *Toll-free phone:* 800-543-3202. *Fax:* 770-426-2895.

Luther Rice College & Seminary
Lithonia, Georgia
http://www.lutherrice.edu/
- **Independent Baptist** comprehensive, founded 1962
- **Suburban** 5-acre campus with easy access to Atlanta
- **Endowment** $556,351
- **Coed**
- **Noncompetitive** entrance level

FACULTY
Student/faculty ratio: 24:1.

ACADEMICS
Calendar: semesters. *Degrees:* bachelor's, master's, and doctoral.
Library: Smith Library. Weekly public service hours: 41.

STUDENT LIFE
Housing options: college housing not available.

Activities and organizations: SGA - Student Government Association.

Campus security: 24-hour emergency response devices.

Student services: personal/psychological counseling, veterans affairs office.

COSTS
Costs (2018–19) *One-time required fee:* $175. *Tuition:* $8520 full-time, $274 per credit hour part-time. Full-time tuition and fees vary according to degree level and location. *Required fees:* $1000 full-time, $100 per course part-time. *Room only:* $13,496. Room and board charges vary according to location.

APPLYING
Options: electronic application.

Application fee: $50.

Required: essay or personal statement, high school transcript, letters of recommendation, Bible exam.

CONTACT
Laura Powell, Admissions Associate, Luther Rice College & Seminary, 3038 Evans Mill Road, Lithonia, GA 30038. *Phone:* 770-484-1204 Ext. 5278. *Toll-free phone:* 800-442-1577. *Fax:* 770-484-1155. *E-mail:* admissions@lutherrice.edu.

Mercer University
Macon, Georgia
http://www.mercer.edu/

- **Independent Baptist** university, founded 1833
- **Urban** 150-acre campus
- **Coed** 3,372 undergraduate students, 98% full-time, 54% women, 46% men
- **Moderately difficult** entrance level, 73% of applicants were admitted

UNDERGRAD STUDENTS
3,310 full-time, 62 part-time. Students come from 39 states and territories; 39 other countries; 16% are from out of state; 19% Black or African American, non-Hispanic/Latino; 6% Hispanic/Latino; 9% Asian, non-Hispanic/Latino; 0.1% Native Hawaiian or other Pacific Islander, non-Hispanic/Latino; 0.2% American Indian or Alaska Native, non-Hispanic/Latino; 5% Two or more races, non-Hispanic/Latino; 3% Race/ethnicity unknown; 3% international; 2% transferred in; 76% live on campus.

Freshmen:
Admission: 4,749 applied, 3,479 admitted, 973 enrolled. *Average high school GPA:* 3.9. *Test scores:* SAT evidence-based reading and writing scores over 500: 98%; SAT math scores over 500: 99%; ACT scores over 18: 100%; SAT evidence-based reading and writing scores over 600: 78%; SAT math scores over 600: 64%; ACT scores over 24: 85%; SAT evidence-based reading and writing scores over 700: 13%; SAT math scores over 700: 15%; ACT scores over 30: 29%.

Retention: 89% of full-time freshmen returned.

FACULTY
Total: 755, 52% full-time, 75% with terminal degrees.
Student/faculty ratio: 13:1.

ACADEMICS
Calendar: semesters. *Degrees:* certificates, bachelor's, master's, doctoral, post-master's, and postbachelor's certificates.
Special study options: accelerated degree program, adult/continuing education programs, advanced placement credit, cooperative education, distance learning, double majors, English as a second language, honors programs, independent study, internships, off-campus study, part-time degree program, services for LD students, student-designed majors, study abroad, summer session for credit. *ROTC:* Army (b).
Unusual degree programs: 3-2 engineering; nursing; pharmacy, physical therapy, physicians assistant.
Computers: Students can access the following: campus intranet, computer help desk, free student e-mail accounts, online (class) grades, online (class) registration, online (class) schedules. Campuswide network is available. 100% of college-owned or -operated housing units are wired for high-speed Internet access. Wireless service is available via entire campus.
Library: Jack Tarver Library plus 3 others. Study areas open 24 hours, 5–7 days a week; students can reserve study rooms.

STUDENT LIFE
Housing options: on-campus residence required through junior year; coed, men-only, women-only, special housing for students with disabilities. Campus housing is university owned and is provided by a third party. Freshman campus housing is guaranteed.
Activities and organizations: drama/theater group, student-run newspaper, radio station, choral group, marching band, national fraternities, national sororities.
Athletics Member NCAA. All Division I. *Intercollegiate sports:* baseball M(s), basketball M(s)/W(s), cross-country running M(s)/W(s), football M(s), golf M(s)/W(s), lacrosse M(s)/W(s), sand volleyball W(s), soccer M(s)/W(s), softball W(s), tennis M(s)/W(s), track and field W(s), volleyball W(s). *Intramural sports:* basketball M/W, cheerleading M/W, equestrian sports M/W, fencing M(c), field hockey W(c), golf M/W, lacrosse M(c), soccer M(c)/W(c), swimming and diving M(c)/W(c), table tennis M/W, tennis M/W, volleyball M/W, wrestling M(c).

Campus security: 24-hour emergency response devices and patrols, student patrols, late-night transport/escort service, controlled dormitory access.

Student services: health clinic, personal/psychological counseling.

COSTS & FINANCIAL AID
Costs (2018–19) *Comprehensive fee:* $49,416 includes full-time tuition ($36,594), mandatory fees ($300), and room and board ($12,522). Full-time tuition and fees vary according to location. Part-time tuition: $1220 per credit hour. Part-time tuition and fees vary according to course load and location. *Required fees:* $10 per credit hour part-time. *College room only:* $6364. Room and board charges vary according to board plan, housing facility, location, and student level. *Payment plan:* installment. *Waivers:* employees or children of employees.

Financial Aid Of all full-time matriculated undergraduates who enrolled in 2018, 2,784 applied for aid, 2,323 were judged to have need, 994 had their need fully met. In 2018, 907 non-need-based awards were made. *Average percent of need met:* 86. *Average financial aid package:* $36,740. *Average need-based loan:* $10,424. *Average need-based gift aid:* $25,812. *Average non-need-based aid:* $19,778. *Average indebtedness upon graduation:* $24,748.

APPLYING
Standardized Tests *Required:* SAT or ACT (for admission).
Options: electronic application, early action, deferred entrance.
Application fee: $50.
Required: essay or personal statement, high school transcript, minimum 3.3 GPA, 1 letter of recommendation. *Recommended:* interview.
Application deadlines: 7/1 (freshmen), rolling (transfers), 3/1 (early action).
Notification: continuous (freshmen), continuous (transfers), rolling (early action).

CONTACT
Mr. Stephen P. Karafa, Director of Freshman Admissions, Mercer University, 1501 Mercer University Drive, Macon, GA 31207-0003. *Phone:* 478-301-2373. *Toll-free phone:* 800-MERCER-U. *Fax:* 478-301-2828. *E-mail:* karafa_sp@mercer.edu.

Middle Georgia State University
Macon, Georgia
http://www.mga.edu/

- **State-supported** comprehensive, founded 2015, part of University System of Georgia
- **Urban** 419-acre campus with easy access to Atlanta
- **Endowment** $874,853
- **Coed**
- **Minimally difficult** entrance level

FACULTY
Student/faculty ratio: 19:1.

ACADEMICS
Calendar: semesters. *Degrees:* certificates, associate, bachelor's, master's, and postbachelor's certificates.
Library: Macon State University Library. *Books:* 125,996 (physical), 246,646 (digital/electronic); *Serial titles:* 85 (physical), 51,575 (digital/electronic); *Databases:* 138. Weekly public service hours: 23; students can reserve study rooms.

STUDENT LIFE
Housing options: on-campus residence required for freshman year; coed. Campus housing is university owned.

Activities and organizations: drama/theater group, student-run newspaper, television station, choral group, marching band, Brothers of Leadership and Distinction (BOLD), Middle Georgia State Association of Nursing Students (MGSANS), Black Student Unification (BSU), Student Government Association (SGA), International Students and Studies Association (ISSA), national fraternities, national sororities.

Athletics Member NAIA.

Campus security: 24-hour emergency response devices and patrols, late-night transport/escort service.

Student services: health clinic, personal/psychological counseling, veterans affairs office.

COSTS

Costs (2018–19) *Tuition:* state resident $3326 full-time, $111 per credit hour part-time; nonresident $12,286 full-time, $410 per credit hour part-time. Full-time tuition and fees vary according to program. Part-time tuition and fees vary according to program. *Required fees:* $1282 full-time. *Room and board:* $7614; room only: $5390. Room and board charges vary according to board plan, housing facility, and location.

APPLYING

Standardized Tests *Required:* SAT or ACT (for admission).

Options: electronic application, early admission.

Application fee: $30.

Required: high school transcript, minimum 2.0 GPA.

CONTACT

Middle Georgia State University, 100 University Parkway, Macon, GA 31206. *Toll-free phone:* 877-238-8664.

Morehouse College

Atlanta, Georgia

http://www.morehouse.edu/

- **Independent** 4-year, founded 1867
- **Urban** 66-acre campus with easy access to Atlanta, Georgia
- **Men only**
- **Moderately difficult** entrance level

FACULTY

Student/faculty ratio: 12:1.

ACADEMICS

Calendar: semesters. *Degree:* bachelor's.

Library: Atlanta University Center Robert R. Woodruff Library. Students can reserve study rooms.

STUDENT LIFE

Housing options: on-campus residence required through junior year; men-only. Campus housing is university owned. Freshman campus housing is guaranteed.

Activities and organizations: drama/theater group, student-run newspaper, choral group, marching band, Morehouse College Glee Club, Morehouse Business Association, SGA, Morehouse Public Health Association, Pre-Law Society, national fraternities.

Athletics Member NCAA. All Division II.

Campus security: 24-hour patrols, late-night transport/escort service, controlled dormitory access, emergency call boxes, safety tips and awareness training.

Student services: health clinic, personal/psychological counseling.

COSTS & FINANCIAL AID

Costs (2018–19) *Comprehensive fee:* $41,012 includes full-time tuition ($25,368), mandatory fees ($2206), and room and board ($13,438). Full-time tuition and fees vary according to course load. Part-time tuition: $1046 per credit hour. Part-time tuition and fees vary according to course load. *College room only:* $7510. Room and board charges vary according to board plan and housing facility.

Financial Aid Of all full-time matriculated undergraduates who enrolled in 2017, 1,956 applied for aid, 1,712 were judged to have need. In 2017, 24 non-need-based awards were made. *Average financial aid package:* $23,565. *Average need-based loan:* $4349. *Average need-based gift aid:* $20,851. *Average non-need-based aid:* $28,810. *Average indebtedness upon graduation:* $31,833. *Financial aid deadline:* 4/1.

APPLYING

Standardized Tests *Required:* SAT or ACT (for admission). *Recommended:* SAT and SAT Subject Tests or ACT (for admission).

Options: electronic application, early admission, early decision, early action, deferred entrance.

Application fee: $50.

Required: essay or personal statement, high school transcript, interview. *Recommended:* minimum 3.0 GPA.

CONTACT

Morehouse College, 830 Westview Drive, SW, Atlanta, GA 30314. *Phone:* 470-639-0391. *Toll-free phone:* 800-851-1254.

Oglethorpe University

Atlanta, Georgia

http://www.oglethorpe.edu/

- **Independent** 4-year, founded 1835
- **Suburban** 102-acre campus with easy access to Atlanta
- **Endowment** $33.9 million
- **Coed** 1,264 undergraduate students, 96% full-time, 57% women, 43% men
- **Very difficult** entrance level, 62% of applicants were admitted

UNDERGRAD STUDENTS

1,212 full-time, 52 part-time. Students come from 34 states and territories; 28 other countries; 21% are from out of state; 24% Black or African American, non-Hispanic/Latino; 11% Hispanic/Latino; 5% Asian, non-Hispanic/Latino; 0.1% Native Hawaiian or other Pacific Islander, non-Hispanic/Latino; 0.8% American Indian or Alaska Native, non-Hispanic/Latino; 1% Two or more races, non-Hispanic/Latino; 8% Race/ethnicity unknown; 9% international; 53% live on campus.

Freshmen:

Admission: 2,203 applied, 1,358 admitted, 334 enrolled. *Average high school GPA:* 3.6. *Test scores:* SAT evidence-based reading and writing scores over 500: 95%; SAT math scores over 500: 96%; ACT scores over 18: 100%; SAT evidence-based reading and writing scores over 600: 61%; SAT math scores over 600: 40%; ACT scores over 24: 53%; SAT evidence-based reading and writing scores over 700: 10%; SAT math scores over 700: 6%; ACT scores over 30: 9%.

Retention: 80% of full-time freshmen returned.

FACULTY

Total: 115, 57% full-time, 83% with terminal degrees.

ACADEMICS

Calendar: semesters. *Degree:* bachelor's.

Special study options: accelerated degree program, adult/continuing education programs, advanced placement credit, cooperative education, double majors, honors programs, independent study, internships, off-campus study, part-time degree program, services for LD students, student-designed majors, study abroad, summer session for credit. *ROTC:* Army (c), Navy (c), Air Force (c).

Unusual degree programs: 3-2 engineering.

Computers: 65 computers/terminals and 500 ports are available on campus for general student use. Students can access the following: campus intranet, computer help desk, free student e-mail accounts, online (class) grades, online (class) registration, online (class) schedules. Campuswide network is available. Wireless service is available via entire campus.

Library: Philip Weltner Library. *Books:* 129,876 (physical), 936,821 (digital/electronic); *Serial titles:* 278 (physical), 27,589 (digital/electronic); *Databases:* 308. Weekly public service hours: 81; study areas open 24 hours, 5–7 days a week.

STUDENT LIFE

Housing options: on-campus residence required through sophomore year; coed. Campus housing is university owned. Freshman campus housing is guaranteed.

Activities and organizations: drama/theater group, student-run newspaper, choral group, SGA, Oglethorpe South Asian Club (OSAC), Historical Martial Arts (HMA), Oglethorpe Latinx Organization ((H)OLA), mOUthing Off Improv, national fraternities, national sororities.

Athletics Member NCAA. All Division III. *Intercollegiate sports:* baseball M, basketball M/W, cross-country running M/W, golf M/W, lacrosse M/W, soccer M/W, tennis M/W, track and field M/W, volleyball W. *Intramural sports:* badminton M/W, basketball M/W, football M/W, lacrosse M/W, softball M/W, table tennis M/W, tennis M/W, volleyball M/W.

Campus security: 24-hour emergency response devices and patrols, late-night transport/escort service, controlled dormitory access.

Student services: health clinic, personal/psychological counseling.

COSTS & FINANCIAL AID

Costs (2019–20) *Comprehensive fee:* $53,510 includes full-time tuition ($39,580), mandatory fees ($530), and room and board ($13,400). Part-time tuition: $1647 per credit hour. *Payment plan:* tuition prepayment.

Financial Aid Of all full-time matriculated undergraduates who enrolled in 2017, 955 applied for aid, 873 were judged to have need, 136 had their need fully met. 122 Federal Work-Study jobs (averaging $1652). In 2017, 339 non-need-based awards were made. *Average percent of need met:* 71. *Average financial aid package:* $30,835. *Average need-based loan:* $4118. *Average need-based gift aid:* $26,008. *Average non-need-based aid:* $20,022. *Average indebtedness upon graduation:* $32,739.

APPLYING

Standardized Tests *Required:* SAT or ACT (for admission).

Options: electronic application, early admission, early action, deferred entrance.

Application fee: $50.

Required: essay or personal statement, high school transcript, 1 letter of recommendation. *Recommended:* minimum 2.5 GPA, interview.

Application deadlines: rolling (freshmen), rolling (out-of-state freshmen), rolling (transfers).

Notification: continuous (freshmen), continuous (transfers).

CONTACT

Lucy Leusch, Vice President for Enrollment and Financial Aid, Oglethorpe University, 4484 Peachtree Road NE, Atlanta, GA 30319. *Phone:* 404-3648309. *Toll-free phone:* 800-428-4484. *E-mail:* lleusch@oglethorpe.edu.

Paine College

Augusta, Georgia
http://www.paine.edu/

CONTACT

Mr. R. Wayne Woodson, Dean of Students, Paine College, 1235 15th Street, Augusta, GA 30901-3182. *Phone:* 706-821-8320. *Toll-free phone:* 800-476-7703. *Fax:* 706-821-8691. *E-mail:* rwoodson@paine.edu.

Piedmont College

Demorest, Georgia
http://www.piedmont.edu/

- **Independent** comprehensive, founded 1897, affiliated with United Church of Christ
- **Rural** 186-acre campus with easy access to Atlanta
- **Endowment** $53.0 million
- **Coed** 1,262 undergraduate students, 91% full-time, 65% women, 35% men
- **Moderately difficult** entrance level, 60% of applicants were admitted

UNDERGRAD STUDENTS

1,153 full-time, 109 part-time. Students come from 24 states and territories; 8 other countries; 7% are from out of state; 11% Black or African American, non-Hispanic/Latino; 6% Hispanic/Latino; 1% Asian, non-Hispanic/Latino; 0.1% Native Hawaiian or other Pacific Islander, non-Hispanic/Latino; 0.4% American Indian or Alaska Native, non-Hispanic/Latino; 0.2% Two or more races, non-Hispanic/Latino; 11% Race/ethnicity unknown; 0.8% international; 9% transferred in; 74% live on campus.

Freshmen:

Admission: 1,379 applied, 822 admitted, 256 enrolled. *Average high school GPA:* 3.4. *Test scores:* SAT evidence-based reading and writing scores over 500: 78%; SAT math scores over 500: 67%; ACT scores over 18: 86%; SAT evidence-based reading and writing scores over 600: 26%; SAT math scores over 600: 13%; ACT scores over 24: 33%; SAT evidence-based reading and writing scores over 700: 1%; SAT math scores over 700: 1%; ACT scores over 30: 2%.

Retention: 61% of full-time freshmen returned.

FACULTY

Total: 293, 46% full-time, 78% with terminal degrees.

Student/faculty ratio: 10:1.

ACADEMICS

Calendar: semesters. *Degrees:* certificates, bachelor's, master's, doctoral, and post-master's certificates.

Special study options: accelerated degree program, adult/continuing education programs, advanced placement credit, cooperative education, distance learning, double majors, honors programs, independent study, internships, off-campus study, part-time degree program, services for LD students, student-designed majors, study abroad, summer session for credit.

Unusual degree programs: 3-2 engineering with Georgia Institute of Technology; Athletic Training.

Computers: 225 computers/terminals are available on campus for general student use. Students can access the following: campus intranet, computer help desk, free student e-mail accounts, online (class) grades, online (class) registration, online (class) schedules. Campuswide network is available. Wireless service is available via classrooms, computer centers, computer labs, dorm rooms, learning centers, libraries, student centers. **Library:** Arrendale Library plus 2 others. *Books:* 85,631 (physical), 766,654 (digital/electronic); *Serial titles:* 76 (physical); *Databases:* 197. Students can reserve study rooms.

STUDENT LIFE

Housing options: on-campus residence required through sophomore year; coed, men-only, women-only, special housing for students with disabilities. Campus housing is university owned. Freshman campus housing is guaranteed.

Activities and organizations: drama/theater group, student-run newspaper, radio and television station, choral group, Campus Activity Board, Student Government Association, Team Piedmont, National Society of Leadership and Success, American Marketing Association-Piedmont Chapter.

Athletics Member NCAA. All Division III. *Intercollegiate sports:* baseball M, basketball M/W, cross-country running M/W, golf M/W, lacrosse M/W, soccer M/W, softball W, tennis M/W, track and field M/W, volleyball W. *Intramural sports:* cheerleading W.

Campus security: 24-hour emergency response devices and patrols, late-night transport/escort service.

Student services: personal/psychological counseling, veterans affairs office.

COSTS & FINANCIAL AID

Costs (2019–20) *Comprehensive fee:* $37,216 includes full-time tuition ($26,492), mandatory fees ($200), and room and board ($10,524). Part-time tuition: $1011 per credit hour. *Required fees:* $100 per term part-time.

Financial Aid Of all full-time matriculated undergraduates who enrolled in 2018, 1,062 applied for aid, 943 were judged to have need, 152 had their need fully met. 98 Federal Work-Study jobs (averaging $2544). 139 state and other part-time jobs (averaging $2768). In 2018, 179 non-need-based awards were made. *Average percent of need met:* 68. *Average financial aid package:* $20,870. *Average need-based loan:* $4429. *Average need-based gift aid:* $17,008. *Average non-need-based aid:* $14,468. *Average indebtedness upon graduation:* $30,780.

APPLYING

Standardized Tests *Required:* SAT or ACT (for admission).

Options: electronic application, early admission, deferred entrance.

Required: high school transcript. *Required for some:* interview. *Recommended:* essay or personal statement.

CONTACT

Ms. Brenda Boonstra, Director of Undergraduate Admissions, Piedmont College, PO Box 10, 165 Central Avenue, Demorest, GA 30535. *Phone:* 706-776-0103 Ext. 1188. *Toll-free phone:* 800-277-7020. *Fax:* 706-776-6635. *E-mail:* bboonstra@piedmont.edu.

Point University
West Point, Georgia
http://point.edu/

- **Independent Christian** comprehensive, founded 1937
- **Small-town** campus with easy access to Atlanta, GA and Montgomery, AL
- **Coed** 2,213 undergraduate students, 50% full-time, 55% women, 45% men
- **Moderately difficult** entrance level, 53% of applicants were admitted

UNDERGRAD STUDENTS
1,108 full-time, 1,105 part-time. Students come from 29 states and territories; 19 other countries; 28% are from out of state; 26% Black or African American, non-Hispanic/Latino; 5% Hispanic/Latino; 2% Asian, non-Hispanic/Latino; 0.2% Native Hawaiian or other Pacific Islander, non-Hispanic/Latino; 0.5% American Indian or Alaska Native, non-Hispanic/Latino; 7% Two or more races, non-Hispanic/Latino; 16% Race/ethnicity unknown; 2% international; 6% transferred in; 56% live on campus.

Freshmen:
Admission: 1,228 applied, 653 admitted, 247 enrolled. *Average high school GPA:* 3.3.

Retention: 50% of full-time freshmen returned.

FACULTY
Total: 183, 25% full-time, 39% with terminal degrees.

Student/faculty ratio: 15:1.

ACADEMICS
Calendar: semesters. *Degrees:* certificates, associate, bachelor's, and master's.

Special study options: accelerated degree program, adult/continuing education programs, advanced placement credit, distance learning, double majors, independent study, part-time degree program, services for LD students, summer session for credit.

Computers: 115 computers/terminals and 50 ports are available on campus for general student use. Students can access the following: campus intranet, computer help desk, free student e-mail accounts, online (class) grades, online (class) registration, online (class) schedules. Campuswide network is available. 100% of college-owned or -operated housing units are wired for high-speed Internet access. Wireless service is available via entire campus.

Library: Point University Library plus 1 other.

STUDENT LIFE
Housing options: on-campus residence required through sophomore year; men-only, women-only. Campus housing is leased by the school. Freshman campus housing is guaranteed.

Activities and organizations: choral group, marching band, Student Government Association, Community Concert Band, Campus Life Ministers, Campus Activities Board, Fellowship of Christian Athletes (FCA).

Athletics Member NAIA. *Intercollegiate sports:* baseball M(s), basketball M(s)/W(s), cheerleading M(s)/W(s), cross-country running M(s)/W(s), football M(s), golf M(s)/W(s), lacrosse M(s)/W(s), soccer M(s)/W(s), softball W(s), swimming and diving M(s)/W(s), tennis M(s)/W(s), volleyball W(s). *Intramural sports:* basketball M/W, football M/W, sand volleyball M/W, softball M/W, table tennis M/W, ultimate Frisbee M/W, volleyball M/W.

Campus security: 24-hour patrols.

Student services: personal/psychological counseling.

COSTS
Costs (2019–20) *Comprehensive fee:* $29,285 includes full-time tuition ($20,085), mandatory fees ($1200), and room and board ($8000). Part-time tuition: $650 per credit hour. *College room only:* $4000.

APPLYING
Options: electronic application, deferred entrance.

Required: high school transcript, minimum 2.0 GPA, 1 letter of recommendation. *Required for some:* essay or personal statement, college transcript if applicable.

Notification: continuous (freshmen), continuous (transfers).

CONTACT
Rusty Hassell, Executive Director of Enrollment, Point University, 507 West 10th Street, West Point, GA 31833. *Phone:* 706-385-1000. *Toll-free phone:* 855-37-POINT. *Fax:* 706-645-9473. *E-mail:* admissions@point.edu.

Reformed University
Lawrenceville, Georgia

CONTACT
Reformed University, 1724 Atkinson Road, Lawrenceville, GA 30043.

Reinhardt University
Waleska, Georgia
http://www.reinhardt.edu/

- **Independent** comprehensive, founded 1883, affiliated with United Methodist Church
- **Rural** 600-acre campus with easy access to Atlanta
- **Coed** 1,473 undergraduate students, 89% full-time, 49% women, 51% men
- **Moderately difficult** entrance level, 90% of applicants were admitted

UNDERGRAD STUDENTS
1,307 full-time, 166 part-time. 7% are from out of state; 18% Black or African American, non-Hispanic/Latino; 8% Hispanic/Latino; 1% Asian, non-Hispanic/Latino; 0.1% Native Hawaiian or other Pacific Islander, non-Hispanic/Latino; 0.4% American Indian or Alaska Native, non-Hispanic/Latino; 3% Two or more races, non-Hispanic/Latino; 6% Race/ethnicity unknown; 0.1% international; 7% transferred in; 47% live on campus.

Freshmen:
Admission: 1,172 applied, 1,055 admitted, 351 enrolled. *Average high school GPA:* 3.3. *Test scores:* SAT evidence-based reading and writing scores over 500: 79%; SAT math scores over 500: 73%; ACT scores over 18: 80%; SAT evidence-based reading and writing scores over 600: 28%; SAT math scores over 600: 19%; ACT scores over 24: 24%; SAT math scores over 700: 3%; ACT scores over 30: 2%.

Retention: 60% of full-time freshmen returned.

FACULTY
Total: 83.

Student/faculty ratio: 12:1.

ACADEMICS
Calendar: semesters. *Degrees:* associate, bachelor's, and master's.

Special study options: academic remediation for entering students, adult/continuing education programs, advanced placement credit, cooperative education, distance learning, double majors, freshman honors college, honors programs, independent study, internships, off-campus study, part-time degree program, services for LD students, student-designed majors, study abroad, summer session for credit.

Computers: Students can access the following: campus intranet, computer help desk, free student e-mail accounts, online (class) grades, online (class) registration, online (class) schedules. Campuswide network is available. 100% of college-owned or -operated housing units are wired for high-speed Internet access. Wireless service is available via classrooms, computer centers, computer labs, dorm rooms, learning centers, libraries, student centers.

Library: Hill Freeman Library/Spruill Learning Center plus 1 other. *Books:* 61,496 (physical), 183,453 (digital/electronic); *Serial titles:* 52 (physical), 27,855 (digital/electronic); *Databases:* 167.

STUDENT LIFE
Housing options: on-campus residence required for freshman year; men-only, women-only, special housing for students with disabilities. Campus housing is university owned. Freshman campus housing is guaranteed.

Activities and organizations: drama/theater group, student-run newspaper, television station, choral group.

Athletics Member NAIA. *Intercollegiate sports:* baseball M(s), basketball M(s)/W(s), cheerleading M(s)/W(s), cross-country running M(s)/W(s), football M(s), golf M(s)/W(s), lacrosse M(s)/W(s), soccer M(s)/W(s), softball W(s), tennis M(s)/W(s), track and field M(s)/W(s), volleyball W(s), wrestling M(s). *Intramural sports:* basketball M/W, bowling M/W, football M, ultimate Frisbee W.

Campus security: 24-hour emergency response devices and patrols, late-night transport/escort service, controlled dormitory access.

Student services: health clinic, personal/psychological counseling.

COSTS & FINANCIAL AID

Costs (2019–20) *Comprehensive fee:* $34,800 includes full-time tuition ($23,300), mandatory fees ($1000), and room and board ($10,500). Part-time tuition: $792 per credit hour.

Financial Aid Of all full-time matriculated undergraduates who enrolled in 2017, 1,110 applied for aid, 984 were judged to have need, 133 had their need fully met. 122 Federal Work-Study jobs (averaging $613). 162 state and other part-time jobs (averaging $513). In 2017, 182 non-need-based awards were made. *Average percent of need met:* 61. *Average financial aid package:* $15,618. *Average need-based loan:* $4064. *Average need-based gift aid:* $12,576. *Average non-need-based aid:* $6376. *Average indebtedness upon graduation:* $27,532.

APPLYING

Standardized Tests *Required:* SAT or ACT (for admission).

Options: electronic application, early admission, deferred entrance.

Required: high school transcript, minimum 2.0 GPA.

CONTACT

Ms. Lacey L. Satterfield, Director of Admissions, Reinhardt University, 7300 Reinhardt Circle, Waleska, GA 30183-0128. *Phone:* 770-720-5620. *E-mail:* lls@reinhardt.edu.

Savannah College of Art and Design
Savannah, Georgia
http://www.scad.edu/

- **Independent** comprehensive, founded 1978
- **Urban** campus
- **Coed** 12,217 undergraduate students, 84% full-time, 68% women, 32% men
- **Moderately difficult** entrance level, 72% of applicants were admitted

UNDERGRAD STUDENTS

10,305 full-time, 1,912 part-time. Students come from 53 states and territories; 111 other countries; 80% are from out of state; 10% Black or African American, non-Hispanic/Latino; 7% Hispanic/Latino; 5% Asian, non-Hispanic/Latino; 0.5% Native Hawaiian or other Pacific Islander, non-Hispanic/Latino; 0.6% American Indian or Alaska Native, non-Hispanic/Latino; 3% Race/ethnicity unknown; 22% international; 5% transferred in; 44% live on campus.

Freshmen:

Admission: 14,797 applied, 10,605 admitted, 2,878 enrolled. *Test scores:* SAT evidence-based reading and writing scores over 500: 89%; SAT math scores over 500: 79%; ACT scores over 18: 93%; SAT evidence-based reading and writing scores over 600: 47%; SAT math scores over 600: 28%; ACT scores over 24: 53%; SAT evidence-based reading and writing scores over 700: 7%; SAT math scores over 700: 5%; ACT scores over 30: 14%.

Retention: 85% of full-time freshmen returned.

FACULTY

Total: 726, 80% full-time, 81% with terminal degrees.

Student/faculty ratio: 20:1.

ACADEMICS

Calendar: quarters. *Degrees:* certificates, bachelor's, and master's.

Special study options: accelerated degree program, advanced placement credit, cooperative education, distance learning, double majors, English as a second language, independent study, internships, off-campus study, part-time degree program, services for LD students, study abroad, summer session for credit.

Computers: 3,464 computers/terminals are available on campus for general student use. Students can access the following: campus intranet, computer help desk, free student e-mail accounts, online (class) grades, online (class) registration, online (class) schedules. Campuswide network is available. 100% of college-owned or -operated housing units are wired for high-speed Internet access. Wireless service is available via entire campus.

Library: Jen Library plus 4 others. *Books:* 264,695 (physical), 215,544 (digital/electronic); *Serial titles:* 901 (physical), 50,630 (digital/electronic); *Databases:* 81. Weekly public service hours: 106; students can reserve study rooms.

STUDENT LIFE

Housing options: coed, special housing for students with disabilities. Campus housing is university owned and leased by the school. Freshman applicants given priority for college housing.

Activities and organizations: drama/theater group, student-run newspaper, radio station, choral group.

Athletics Member NAIA. *Intercollegiate sports:* bowling M(s)/W(s), cross-country running M(s)/W(s), equestrian sports M(s)/W(s), golf M(s)/W(s), lacrosse M(s)/W(s), soccer M(s)/W(s), swimming and diving M(s)/W(s), tennis M(s)/W(s), track and field M(s)/W(s). *Intramural sports:* basketball M/W, sand volleyball M/W, soccer M/W, table tennis M/W, volleyball M/W.

Campus security: 24-hour emergency response devices and patrols, late-night transport/escort service, controlled dormitory access.

Student services: health clinic, personal/psychological counseling.

COSTS & FINANCIAL AID

Costs (2019–20) *One-time required fee:* $500. *Comprehensive fee:* $52,737 includes full-time tuition ($37,575) and room and board ($15,162). Part-time tuition: $4175 per course. *College room only:* $10,224.

Financial Aid Of all full-time matriculated undergraduates who enrolled in 2017, 5,574 applied for aid, 4,721 were judged to have need, 332 had their need fully met. 395 Federal Work-Study jobs (averaging $1186). 770 state and other part-time jobs (averaging $1279). In 2017, 4067 non-need-based awards were made. *Average percent of need met:* 41. *Average financial aid package:* $16,982. *Average need-based loan:* $4144. *Average need-based gift aid:* $13,217. *Average non-need-based aid:* $10,093. *Average indebtedness upon graduation:* $39,328.

APPLYING

Standardized Tests *Required:* SAT or ACT (for admission), TOEFL scores are required for International students (for admission).

Options: electronic application, early admission, deferred entrance.

Application fee: $40.

Required for some: essay or personal statement, high school transcript, interview, portfolio/audition for performing arts, riding, writing, or visual arts. *Recommended:* essay or personal statement, interview.

Application deadlines: rolling (freshmen), rolling (transfers).

Notification: continuous (freshmen), continuous (transfers).

CONTACT

Ms. Jenny Jaquillard, Executive Director of Admissions Recruitment, Savannah College of Art and Design, 342 Bull Street, PO Box 3146, Savannah, GA 31402-3146. *Phone:* 912-525-5100. *Toll-free phone:* 800-869-7223. *E-mail:* admission@scad.edu.

Savannah State University
Savannah, Georgia
http://www.savannahstate.edu/

CONTACT

Mr. Descatur Potier, Assistant Vice President of Academic Affairs for Enrollment Services/Director of Admission, Savannah State University, PO Box 20209, 3219 College Street, Savannah, GA 31404. *Phone:* 912-358-4014. *Toll-free phone:* 800-788-0478. *Fax:* 912-650-8009. *E-mail:* potierd@savannahstate.edu.

Shorter University
Rome, Georgia
http://www.shorter.edu/

- **Independent Baptist** comprehensive, founded 1873
- **Small-town** 155-acre campus with easy access to Atlanta
- **Endowment** $14.8 million
- **Coed**
- **Moderately difficult** entrance level

ACADEMICS
Calendar: semesters. *Degrees:* associate, bachelor's, and master's.
Library: Livingston Library. *Books:* 118,322 (physical), 575,620 (digital/electronic); *Serial titles:* 1,183 (physical), 117,578 (digital/electronic); *Databases:* 233. Students can reserve study rooms.

STUDENT LIFE
Housing options: men-only, women-only. Campus housing is university owned. Freshman applicants given priority for college housing.

Activities and organizations: drama/theater group, student-run newspaper, radio and television station, choral group, marching band, Baptist Collegiate Ministries, Student Government Association, Fellowship of Christian Athletes, Habitat for Humanity, SAVE (Students Advocating Volunteer Efforts), national fraternities, national sororities.

Athletics Member NCAA. All Division II.

Campus security: 24-hour emergency response devices and patrols.

Student services: health clinic, personal/psychological counseling.

COSTS & FINANCIAL AID
Costs (2018–19) *Comprehensive fee:* $31,770 includes full-time tuition ($21,940), mandatory fees ($430), and room and board ($9400). Full-time tuition and fees vary according to course load, location, and program. Part-time tuition: $550 per credit hour. Part-time tuition and fees vary according to location and program. *Required fees:* $8 per credit hour part-time. *College room only:* $5000. Room and board charges vary according to board plan and housing facility.

Financial Aid Of all full-time matriculated undergraduates who enrolled in 2012, 1,198 applied for aid, 1,078 were judged to have need, 197 had their need fully met. In 2012, 124 non-need-based awards were made. *Average percent of need met:* 61. *Average financial aid package:* $16,335. *Average need-based loan:* $4164. *Average need-based gift aid:* $12,863. *Average non-need-based aid:* $5371.

APPLYING
Standardized Tests *Required:* SAT or ACT (for admission).

Options: electronic application, early admission, deferred entrance.

Application fee: $25.

Required: essay or personal statement, high school transcript. *Required for some:* interview, audition for music and theater programs. *Recommended:* minimum 2.0 GPA, 1 letter of recommendation, interview.

CONTACT
Shorter University, 315 Shorter Avenue, Rome, GA 30165. *Phone:* 706-233-7342. *Toll-free phone:* 800-868-6980.

South Georgia State College
Douglas, Georgia
http://www.sgc.edu/

CONTACT
South Georgia State College, 100 West College Park Drive, Douglas, GA 31533-5098. *Phone:* 912-260-4409. *Toll-free phone:* 800-342-6364.

South University
Savannah, Georgia
http://www.southuniversity.edu/savannah/

CONTACT
South University, 709 Mall Boulevard, Savannah, GA 31406. *Phone:* 912-201-8000. *Toll-free phone:* 866-629-2901.

Spelman College
Atlanta, Georgia
http://www.spelman.edu/

- **Independent** 4-year, founded 1881
- **Urban** 39-acre campus with easy access to Atlanta
- **Endowment** $367.9 million
- **Women only**
- **Very difficult** entrance level

FACULTY
Student/faculty ratio: 11:1.

ACADEMICS
Calendar: semesters. *Degree:* bachelor's.
Library: Robert Woodruff Library plus 1 other. *Books:* 489,081 (physical), 139,636 (digital/electronic); *Serial titles:* 987 (physical), 122,146 (digital/electronic); *Databases:* 317. Weekly public service hours: 95; students can reserve study rooms.

STUDENT LIFE
Housing options: on-campus residence required through sophomore year; women-only. Campus housing is university owned and leased by the school. Freshman applicants given priority for college housing.

Activities and organizations: drama/theater group, student-run newspaper, choral group, Glee Club, Theater Program, Student Government, Honors Program, Religious Groups, national sororities.

Campus security: 24-hour emergency response devices and patrols, late-night transport/escort service, controlled dormitory access, lighted pathways/sidewalks.

Student services: health clinic, personal/psychological counseling, women's center.

COSTS & FINANCIAL AID
Costs (2018–19) *One-time required fee:* $250. *Comprehensive fee:* $42,929 includes full-time tuition ($25,151), mandatory fees ($3913), and room and board ($13,865). Part-time tuition: $1040 per credit hour. *Required fees:* $1457 per term part-time. *College room only:* $8128.

Financial Aid Of all full-time matriculated undergraduates who enrolled in 2018, 1,902 applied for aid, 1,726 were judged to have need, 823 had their need fully met. In 2018, 20 non-need-based awards were made. *Average percent of need met:* 34. *Average financial aid package:* $17,630. *Average need-based loan:* $4812. *Average need-based gift aid:* $14,611. *Average non-need-based aid:* $16,426. *Average indebtedness upon graduation:* $35,582.

APPLYING
Standardized Tests *Required:* SAT or ACT (for admission). *Required for some:* SAT and SAT Subject Tests or ACT (for admission).

Options: electronic application, early admission, early decision, early action, deferred entrance.

Application fee: $40.

Required: essay or personal statement, high school transcript, minimum 2.0 GPA, 2 letters of recommendation.

CONTACT
Ms. Tiffany Nelson, Director of Admissions, Spelman College, 350 Spelman Lane, SW, Atlanta, GA 30314-4399. *Phone:* 800-982-2411. *Toll-free phone:* 800-982-2411. *Fax:* 404-270-5201. *E-mail:* admiss@spelman.edu.

Strayer University–Augusta Campus
Augusta, Georgia
http://www.strayer.edu/georgia/augusta/

CONTACT
Strayer University–Augusta Campus, 1330 Augusta West Parkway, Augusta, GA 30909. *Toll-free phone:* 888-311-0355.

Strayer University–Chamblee Campus
Atlanta, Georgia
http://www.strayer.edu/georgia/chamblee/

CONTACT
Strayer University–Chamblee Campus, 3355 Northeast Expressway, Suite 100, Atlanta, GA 30341. *Toll-free phone:* 888-311-0355.

Strayer University–Cobb County Campus
Atlanta, Georgia
http://www.strayer.edu/georgia/cobb-county/

CONTACT
Strayer University–Cobb County Campus, 3101 Towercreek Parkway, SE, Suite 700, Atlanta, GA 30339. *Toll-free phone:* 888-311-0355.

Strayer University–Columbus Campus
Columbus, Georgia
http://www.strayer.edu/georgia/columbus/

CONTACT
Strayer University–Columbus Campus, 408 12th Street, Suite 102, Columbus, GA 31901. *Toll-free phone:* 888-311-0355.

Strayer University–Douglasville Campus
Douglasville, Georgia
http://www.strayer.edu/georgia/douglasville/

CONTACT
Strayer University–Douglasville Campus, 4655 Timber Ridge Drive, Douglasville, GA 30135. *Toll-free phone:* 888-311-0355.

Strayer University–Lithonia Campus
Lithonia, Georgia
http://www.strayer.edu/georgia/lithonia/

CONTACT
Strayer University–Lithonia Campus, 3120 Stonecrest Boulevard, Suite 200, Lithonia, GA 30038. *Toll-free phone:* 888-311-0355.

Strayer University–Morrow Campus
Morrow, Georgia
http://www.strayer.edu/georgia/morrow/

CONTACT
Strayer University–Morrow Campus, 3000 Corporate Center Drive, Suite 100, Morrow, GA 30260. *Toll-free phone:* 888-311-0355.

Strayer University–Savannah Campus
Savannah, Georgia
http://www.strayer.edu/georgia/savannah/

CONTACT
Strayer University–Savannah Campus, 8001 Chatham Center Drive, Suite 300, Savannah, GA 31405. *Toll-free phone:* 888-311-0355.

Thomas University
Thomasville, Georgia
http://www.thomasu.edu/
- **Independent** comprehensive, founded 1950
- **Small-town** 24-acre campus
- **Endowment** $4.2 million
- **Coed**
- **Minimally difficult** entrance level

FACULTY
Student/faculty ratio: 6:1.

ACADEMICS
Calendar: semesters. *Degrees:* associate, bachelor's, master's, post-master's, and postbachelor's certificates.
Library: Thomas University Library plus 1 other. Weekly public service hours: 60.

STUDENT LIFE
Housing options: on-campus residence required through sophomore year; coed. Campus housing is university owned. Freshman applicants given priority for college housing.
Activities and organizations: drama/theater group, student-run newspaper, choral group, Student Government Association, Professional Management Association, National Society for Leadership and Success.
Athletics Member NAIA.
Campus security: late-night transport/escort service, controlled dormitory access, evening security guards.
Student services: personal/psychological counseling.

COSTS & FINANCIAL AID
Costs (2018–19) *Comprehensive fee:* $23,980 includes full-time tuition ($15,940), mandatory fees ($1000), and room and board ($7040). Part-time tuition: $630 per credit hour. *Required fees:* $550 per year part-time. *College room only:* $6000. Room and board charges vary according to housing facility.
Financial Aid Of all full-time matriculated undergraduates who enrolled in 2016, 101 applied for aid. 41 Federal Work-Study jobs (averaging $1584).

APPLYING
Options: electronic application, early admission, deferred entrance.
Application fee: $25.
Required: high school transcript.

CONTACT
Mrs. Rita Gagliano, Office of Admission, Thomas University, 1501 Millpond Road, Thomasville, GA 31792. *Phone:* 229-227-6942. *Toll-free phone:* 800-538-9784. *Fax:* 229-227-6919. *E-mail:* rgagliano@thomasu.edu.

Toccoa Falls College
Toccoa Falls, Georgia
http://www.tfc.edu/
- **Independent interdenominational** 4-year, founded 1907
- **Small-town** 1100-acre campus with easy access to Atlanta, GA metro area
- **Endowment** $2.8 million
- **Coed** 1,656 undergraduate students, 54% full-time, 57% women, 43% men
- **Moderately difficult** entrance level, 59% of applicants were admitted

UNDERGRAD STUDENTS
890 full-time, 766 part-time. Students come from 33 states and territories; 8 other countries; 35% are from out of state; 11% Black or African American, non-Hispanic/Latino; 5% Hispanic/Latino; 5% Asian, non-Hispanic/Latino; 0.1% Native Hawaiian or other Pacific Islander, non-Hispanic/Latino; 0.2% American Indian or Alaska Native, non-Hispanic/Latino; 2% Two or more races, non-Hispanic/Latino; 2% Race/ethnicity unknown; 0.5% international; 3% transferred in; 51% live on campus.

Freshmen:

Admission: 962 applied, 565 admitted, 218 enrolled. *Average high school GPA:* 3.4. *Test scores:* SAT evidence-based reading and writing scores over 500: 72%; SAT math scores over 500: 62%; ACT scores over 18: 81%; SAT evidence-based reading and writing scores over 600: 26%; SAT math scores over 600: 14%; ACT scores over 24: 28%; SAT evidence-based reading and writing scores over 700: 4%; SAT math scores over 700: 1%; ACT scores over 30: 1%.

Retention: 60% of full-time freshmen returned.

FACULTY
Total: 138, 34% full-time, 39% with terminal degrees.
Student/faculty ratio: 15:1.

ACADEMICS
Calendar: 4-1-4. *Degrees:* certificates, associate, and bachelor's.
Special study options: advanced placement credit, distance learning, double majors, independent study, internships, part-time degree program, services for LD students, study abroad, summer session for credit.
Computers: 47 computers/terminals are available on campus for general student use. Students can access the following: campus intranet, computer help desk, free student e-mail accounts, online (class) grades, online (class) registration, online (class) schedules. Campuswide network is available. 95% of college-owned or -operated housing units are wired for high-speed Internet access. Wireless service is available via entire campus.
Library: Seby Jones Library plus 1 other. *Books:* 52,639 (physical), 719,908 (digital/electronic); *Serial titles:* 33 (physical), 73,000 (digital/electronic); *Databases:* 279. Weekly public service hours: 83; students can reserve study rooms.

STUDENT LIFE
Housing options: on-campus residence required through junior year; men-only, women-only. Campus housing is university owned. Freshman campus housing is guaranteed.
Activities and organizations: drama/theater group, student-run newspaper, radio station, choral group, Outdoor Club, Hmong Student Fellowship, The Justice Campaign, Toccoa Falls for Life, Theatrical Society.
Athletics Member NCCAA. *Intercollegiate sports:* baseball M, basketball M/W, soccer M/W, volleyball W. *Intramural sports:* basketball M/W, cross-country running M(c)/W(c), football M/W, soccer M/W, softball M/W, ultimate Frisbee M/W, volleyball M/W.
Campus security: student patrols.
Student services: health clinic, personal/psychological counseling.

COSTS & FINANCIAL AID
Costs (2019–20) *Comprehensive fee:* $31,680 includes full-time tuition ($22,414), mandatory fees ($770), and room and board ($8496). Part-time tuition: $934. *Required fees:* $770 per year part-time.
Financial Aid Of all full-time matriculated undergraduates who enrolled in 2018, 641 applied for aid, 600 were judged to have need, 84 had their need fully met. In 2018, 58 non-need-based awards were made. *Average percent of need met:* 67. *Average financial aid package:* $19,651. *Average need-based loan:* $3692. *Average need-based gift aid:* $15,594. *Average non-need-based aid:* $10,301.

APPLYING
Standardized Tests *Required:* SAT or ACT (for admission).
Options: electronic application, early admission, deferred entrance.
Application fee: $30.
Required: essay or personal statement, high school transcript, minimum 2.0 GPA, 1 letter of recommendation. *Required for some:* interview.
Application deadlines: rolling (freshmen), rolling (transfers).
Notification: continuous (freshmen), continuous (transfers).

CONTACT
Mr. Ronnie Stewart, Toccoa Falls College, 107 Kincaid Drive, MSC 899, Toccoa Falls, GA 30598. *Phone:* 706-886-6831 Ext. 5378. *Toll-free phone:* 888-785-5624. *Fax:* 706-282-6012. *E-mail:* rstewart@tfc.edu.

Truett McConnell University
Cleveland, Georgia
http://www.truett.edu/
- **Independent Baptist** comprehensive, founded 1946
- **Rural** 200-acre campus with easy access to Atlanta
- **Coed**
- **Minimally difficult** entrance level

FACULTY
Student/faculty ratio: 15:1.

ACADEMICS
Calendar: semesters. *Degrees:* bachelor's and master's.
Library: Cofer Library.

STUDENT LIFE
Housing options: on-campus residence required through senior year; men-only, women-only. Campus housing is university owned.
Activities and organizations: choral group.
Athletics Member NAIA.
Campus security: 24-hour weekday patrols, 10-hour weekend patrols by trained security personnel.

COSTS & FINANCIAL AID
Costs (2018–19) *Comprehensive fee:* $27,780 includes full-time tuition ($19,320), mandatory fees ($910), and room and board ($7550). Full-time tuition and fees vary according to course load, degree level, location, and program. Part-time tuition: $805 per credit hour. Part-time tuition and fees vary according to course load, degree level, location, and program. *Required fees:* $455 per term part-time. *Room and board:* Room and board charges vary according to housing facility.
Financial Aid Of all full-time matriculated undergraduates who enrolled in 2018, 724 applied for aid, 626 were judged to have need, 142 had their need fully met. 25 Federal Work-Study jobs (averaging $2018). In 2018, 141 non-need-based awards were made. *Average percent of need met:* 70. *Average financial aid package:* $16,398. *Average need-based loan:* $4537. *Average need-based gift aid:* $13,220. *Average non-need-based aid:* $7671. *Average indebtedness upon graduation:* $27,331.

APPLYING
Standardized Tests *Required:* SAT or ACT (for admission).
Options: electronic application, early admission, deferred entrance.
Required: high school transcript, minimum 2.0 GPA. *Required for some:* essay or personal statement, 1 letter of recommendation, interview.

CONTACT
Truett McConnell University, 100 Alumni Drive, Cleveland, GA 30528. *Phone:* 706-865-2134 Ext. 4301. *Toll-free phone:* 800-226-8621.

University of Georgia
Athens, Georgia
http://www.uga.edu/
- **State-supported** university, founded 1785, part of University System of Georgia
- **Suburban** 767-acre campus with easy access to Atlanta
- **Endowment** $1.3 billion
- **Coed** 29,611 undergraduate students, 94% full-time, 57% women, 43% men
- **Moderately difficult** entrance level, 49% of applicants were admitted

UNDERGRAD STUDENTS
27,947 full-time, 1,664 part-time. Students come from 52 states and territories; 124 other countries; 11% are from out of state; 8% Black or African American, non-Hispanic/Latino; 6% Hispanic/Latino; 10% Asian, non-Hispanic/Latino; 0.1% Native Hawaiian or other Pacific Islander, non-Hispanic/Latino; 0.1% American Indian or Alaska Native, non-Hispanic/Latino; 4% Two or more races, non-Hispanic/Latino; 1% Race/ethnicity unknown; 1% international; 5% transferred in; 34% live on campus.

Freshmen:
Admission: 26,027 applied, 12,659 admitted, 5,727 enrolled. *Average high school GPA:* 4.0. *Test scores:* SAT evidence-based reading and writing scores over 500: 100%; SAT math scores over 500: 99%; ACT

scores over 18: 100%; SAT evidence-based reading and writing scores over 600: 89%; SAT math scores over 600: 83%; ACT scores over 24: 93%; SAT evidence-based reading and writing scores over 700: 28%; SAT math scores over 700: 33%; ACT scores over 30: 48%.

Retention: 95% of full-time freshmen returned.

FACULTY
Total: 2,371, 88% full-time, 91% with terminal degrees.
Student/faculty ratio: 17:1.

ACADEMICS
Calendar: semesters. *Degrees:* certificates, bachelor's, master's, doctoral, post-master's, and postbachelor's certificates.

Special study options: academic remediation for entering students, accelerated degree program, adult/continuing education programs, advanced placement credit, cooperative education, distance learning, double majors, external degree program, honors programs, independent study, internships, off-campus study, part-time degree program, services for LD students, student-designed majors, study abroad, summer session for credit. *ROTC:* Army (b), Air Force (b).

Computers: Students can access the following: campus intranet, computer help desk, free student e-mail accounts, online (class) grades, online (class) registration, online (class) schedules. Campuswide network is available. 100% of college-owned or -operated housing units are wired for high-speed Internet access. Wireless service is available via entire campus.

Library: Ilah Dunlap Little Memorial Library plus 4 others. *Books:* 5.3 million (digital/electronic). Students can reserve study rooms.

STUDENT LIFE
Housing options: on-campus residence required for freshman year; coed, women-only, special housing for students with disabilities. Campus housing is university owned. Freshman campus housing is guaranteed.

Activities and organizations: drama/theater group, student-run newspaper, radio station, choral group, marching band, Intramural Sports, Recreational sports program, Tate Movie Screening, University Union, Red Coat Band, national fraternities, national sororities.

Athletics Member NCAA. All Division I except football (Division I-A). *Intercollegiate sports:* archery M(c)/W(c), badminton M(c)/W(c), baseball M(s), basketball M(s)/W(s), cheerleading M(c)/W(c), crew M(c)/W(c), cross-country running M(s)/W(s), equestrian sports M(c)/W(s), fencing M(c)/W(c), golf M(s)/W(s)(c), gymnastics M(c)/W(s), ice hockey M(c), lacrosse M(c)/W(c), rugby M(c)/W(c), sailing M(c)/W(c), soccer M(c)/W(s), softball W(s), swimming and diving M(s)/W(s), tennis M(s)/W(s), track and field M(s)/W(s), ultimate Frisbee M(c)/W(c), volleyball M(c)/W(s), water polo M(c)/W(c), wrestling M(c). *Intramural sports:* badminton M/W, basketball M/W, football M/W, golf M/W, racquetball M/W, soccer M/W, softball M/W, tennis M/W, ultimate Frisbee M/W, volleyball M/W, water polo M/W.

Campus security: 24-hour emergency response devices and patrols, late-night transport/escort service, controlled dormitory access.

Student services: health clinic, personal/psychological counseling, women's center, legal services, veterans affairs office.

COSTS & FINANCIAL AID
Costs (2018–19) *Tuition:* state resident $9552 full-time; nonresident $28,126 full-time. Full-time tuition and fees vary according to course load, location, and program. Part-time tuition and fees vary according to course load, location, and program. *Required fees:* $2278 full-time. *Room and board:* $10,038; room only: $6042. Room and board charges vary according to board plan and housing facility. *Waivers:* senior citizens.

Financial Aid Of all full-time matriculated undergraduates who enrolled in 2018, 19,865 applied for aid, 11,948 were judged to have need, 3,051 had their need fully met. 374 Federal Work-Study jobs (averaging $2439). In 2018, 1000 non-need-based awards were made. *Average percent of need met:* 73. *Average financial aid package:* $12,562. *Average need-based loan:* $4257. *Average need-based gift aid:* $9776. *Average non-need-based aid:* $3121. *Average indebtedness upon graduation:* $22,872.

APPLYING
Standardized Tests *Required:* SAT or ACT (for admission).

Options: electronic application, early admission, early action, deferred entrance.

Application fee: $70.

Required: high school transcript, counselor evaluation. *Recommended:* essay or personal statement, minimum 2.0 GPA.

Application deadlines: 1/8 (freshmen), 4/1 (transfers), 10/15 (early action).

Notification: 4/1 (freshmen), continuous (transfers), 12/1 (early action).

CONTACT
Mr. Charles Carabello, Associate Director for Enrollment Management, University of Georgia, Terrell Hall, Athens, GA 30602. *Phone:* 706-542-8776. *Fax:* 706-542-1466. *E-mail:* admproc@uga.edu.

University of North Georgia
Dahlonega, Georgia
http://www.ung.edu/
- **State-supported** comprehensive, founded 1873, part of University System of Georgia
- **Small-town** 1077-acre campus with easy access to Atlanta
- **Endowment** $58.4 million
- **Coed**
- **Moderately difficult** entrance level

FACULTY
Student/faculty ratio: 19:1.

ACADEMICS
Calendar: semesters. *Degrees:* certificates, associate, bachelor's, master's, doctoral, post-master's, and postbachelor's certificates.
Library: Library Technology Center plus 4 others. *Books:* 195,525 (physical), 433,929 (digital/electronic); *Serial titles:* 168 (physical); *Databases:* 298. Weekly public service hours: 94; students can reserve study rooms.

STUDENT LIFE
Housing options: on-campus residence required through sophomore year; coed, men-only, women-only, special housing for students with disabilities. Campus housing is university owned. Freshman applicants given priority for college housing.

Activities and organizations: drama/theater group, student-run newspaper, radio station, choral group, marching band, Student Government Association, Commuter Council, Graduate Student Senate, Student Activities Board, Greek organizations, national fraternities, national sororities.

Athletics Member NCAA. All Division II.

Campus security: 24-hour emergency response devices and patrols, late-night transport/escort service, controlled dormitory access.

Student services: health clinic, personal/psychological counseling, veterans affairs office.

COSTS & FINANCIAL AID
Costs (2018–19) *Tuition:* state resident $5460 full-time, $182 per credit hour part-time; nonresident $19,272 full-time, $642 per credit hour part-time. Full-time tuition and fees vary according to course load, degree level, and location. Part-time tuition and fees vary according to course load, degree level, and location. *Required fees:* $1876 full-time. *Room and board:* $10,800; room only: $5726. Room and board charges vary according to board plan and housing facility.

Financial Aid Of all full-time matriculated undergraduates who enrolled in 2017, 9,980 applied for aid, 7,603 were judged to have need, 4,401 had their need fully met. 178 Federal Work-Study jobs (averaging $1195). In 2017, 562 non-need-based awards were made. *Average percent of need met:* 63. *Average financial aid package:* $14,234. *Average need-based loan:* $5230. *Average need-based gift aid:* $5948. *Average non-need-based aid:* $1349. *Average indebtedness upon graduation:* $12,345.

APPLYING
Standardized Tests *Required:* SAT or ACT (for admission).

Options: electronic application, early admission.

Application fee: $30.

Required: high school transcript, minimum 2.0 GPA, proof of immunization.

CONTACT
Molly Potts, Director of Admissions, University of North Georgia, Admissions Center, 3820 Mundy Mill Road, Oakwood, GA 30566. *Phone:* 678-717-3849. *Toll-free phone:* 800-498-9581. *E-mail:* molly.potts@ung.edu.

University of West Georgia
Carrollton, Georgia
http://www.westga.edu/

- **State-supported** comprehensive, founded 1933, part of University System of Georgia
- **Rural** 645-acre campus with easy access to Atlanta
- **Endowment** $32.6 million
- **Coed** 11,135 undergraduate students, 78% full-time, 63% women, 37% men
- **Moderately difficult** entrance level, 59% of applicants were admitted

UNDERGRAD STUDENTS
8,728 full-time, 2,407 part-time. Students come from 38 states and territories; 72 other countries; 7% are from out of state; 37% Black or African American, non-Hispanic/Latino; 8% Hispanic/Latino; 1% Asian, non-Hispanic/Latino; 0.2% Native Hawaiian or other Pacific Islander, non-Hispanic/Latino; 0.1% American Indian or Alaska Native, non-Hispanic/Latino; 4% Two or more races, non-Hispanic/Latino; 1% Race/ethnicity unknown; 1% international; 6% transferred in; 28% live on campus.

Freshmen:
Admission: 7,924 applied, 4,642 admitted, 2,289 enrolled. *Average high school GPA:* 3.2. *Test scores:* SAT math scores over 500: 37%; ACT scores over 18: 81%; SAT math scores over 600: 6%; ACT scores over 24: 17%; ACT scores over 30: 1%.
Retention: 69% of full-time freshmen returned.

FACULTY
Total: 737, 62% full-time, 64% with terminal degrees.
Student/faculty ratio: 20:1.

ACADEMICS
Calendar: semesters. *Degrees:* bachelor's, master's, doctoral, post-master's, and postbachelor's certificates.

Special study options: accelerated degree program, advanced placement credit, cooperative education, distance learning, double majors, external degree program, freshman honors college, honors programs, independent study, internships, off-campus study, part-time degree program, services for LD students, study abroad, summer session for credit. *ROTC:* Air Force (c).

Unusual degree programs: 3-2 engineering with USG Regentâ??s Engineering Transfer Program (RETP) (Mercer University, Georgia Tech, UGA, Kennesaw State, and Georgia Southern).

Computers: 1,200 computers/terminals are available on campus for general student use. Students can access the following: campus intranet, computer help desk, free student e-mail accounts, online (class) grades, online (class) registration, online (class) schedules. Campuswide network is available. 100% of college-owned or -operated housing units are wired for high-speed Internet access. Wireless service is available via entire campus.
Library: Irvine Sullivan Ingram Library plus 1 other. Weekly public service hours: 109; study areas open 24 hours, 5–7 days a week; students can reserve study rooms.

STUDENT LIFE
Housing options: on-campus residence required for freshman year; coed, women-only, special housing for students with disabilities. Campus housing is university owned and leased by the school. Freshman campus housing is guaranteed.

Activities and organizations: drama/theater group, student-run newspaper, radio and television station, choral group, marching band, Black Student Alliance, Student Activities Council, Baptist Collegiate Ministries, Campus Outreach, United Voices Gospel Choir, national fraternities, national sororities.

Athletics Member NCAA. All Division II. *Intercollegiate sports:* baseball M(s), basketball M(s)/W(s), cheerleading W(s), cross-country running M(s)/W(s), football M(s), golf M(s)/W(s), soccer W(s), softball W(s), tennis W(s), track and field W(s), volleyball W(s). *Intramural sports:* baseball M(c), basketball M(c)/W(c), equestrian sports W(c), golf M/W, lacrosse M(c), rock climbing M(c)/W(c), soccer M(c), ultimate Frisbee M/W, weight lifting M/W, wrestling M(c).

Campus security: 24-hour emergency response devices and patrols, student patrols, late-night transport/escort service, controlled dormitory access.

Student services: health clinic, personal/psychological counseling, veterans affairs office.

COSTS & FINANCIAL AID
Costs (2019–20) *Tuition:* state resident $5330 full-time, $178 per semester hour part-time; nonresident $18,812 full-time, $627 per semester hour part-time. *Required fees:* $2024 full-time. *Room and board:* $10,488; room only: $5600.

Financial Aid Of all full-time matriculated undergraduates who enrolled in 2018, 7,450 applied for aid, 5,978 were judged to have need, 3,745 had their need fully met. In 2018, 387 non-need-based awards were made. *Average percent of need met:* 53. *Average financial aid package:* $8610. *Average need-based loan:* $3972. *Average need-based gift aid:* $5017. *Average non-need-based aid:* $2568. *Average indebtedness upon graduation:* $29,413. *Financial aid deadline:* 7/1.

APPLYING
Standardized Tests *Required:* SAT or ACT (for admission).
Options: electronic application, early admission, deferred entrance.
Application fee: $40.
Required: minimum 2.5 GPA, proof of immunization. *Required for some:* high school transcript.
Application deadlines: rolling (freshmen), rolling (transfers).
Notification: continuous (freshmen), continuous (transfers).

CONTACT
Mr. Justin Barlow, Director of Admissions, University of West Georgia, 1601 Maple Street, Carrollton, GA 30118. *Phone:* 678-839-5600. *Fax:* 678-839-4747. *E-mail:* admiss@westga.edu.

Valdosta State University
Valdosta, Georgia
http://www.valdosta.edu/

- **State-supported** university, founded 1906, part of University System of Georgia
- **Small-town** 180-acre campus
- **Endowment** $7.5 million
- **Coed**
- **Moderately difficult** entrance level

FACULTY
Student/faculty ratio: 20:1.

ACADEMICS
Calendar: semesters. *Degrees:* certificates, associate, bachelor's, master's, doctoral, post-master's, and postbachelor's certificates.
Library: Odum Library. *Books:* 579,774 (physical), 408,139 (digital/electronic); *Serial titles:* 10,877 (physical), 39,852 (digital/electronic); *Databases:* 237. Students can reserve study rooms.

STUDENT LIFE
Housing options: on-campus residence required for freshman year; coed, special housing for students with disabilities. Campus housing is university owned. Freshman applicants given priority for college housing.

Activities and organizations: drama/theater group, student-run newspaper, radio and television station, choral group, marching band, Black Student League, Enactus, Psychology Club, Collegiate women of VSU, College Republican Society, national fraternities, national sororities.

Athletics Member NCAA. All Division II.

Campus security: 24-hour emergency response devices and patrols, late-night transport/escort service, controlled dormitory access, bicycle patrols, security cameras, mobile security app.

Student services: health clinic, personal/psychological counseling, veterans affairs office.

COSTS & FINANCIAL AID

Costs (2018–19) *Tuition:* state resident $4264 full-time, $178 per credit hour part-time; nonresident $15,050 full-time, $627 per credit hour part-time. Full-time tuition and fees vary according to course load, location, program, and reciprocity agreements. Part-time tuition and fees vary according to course load, location, program, and reciprocity agreements. *Required fees:* $2146 full-time, $1073 per term part-time. *Room and board:* $7900; room only: $4060. Room and board charges vary according to board plan and housing facility.

Financial Aid Of all full-time matriculated undergraduates who enrolled in 2017, 6,202 applied for aid, 5,481 were judged to have need, 620 had their need fully met. In 2017, 135 non-need-based awards were made. *Average percent of need met: 89. Average financial aid package:* $16,121. *Average need-based loan: $4006. Average need-based gift aid:* $6419. *Average non-need-based aid: $2368. Average indebtedness upon graduation:* $27,233.

APPLYING

Standardized Tests *Required:* SAT or ACT (for admission).

Options: electronic application, deferred entrance.

Application fee: $40.

Required: high school transcript.

CONTACT

Mr. Ryan M. Hogan, Director of Admissions, Valdosta State University, Office of Admissions, 1500 North Patterson Street, Valdosta, GA 31698. *Phone:* 229-333-5791. *Toll-free phone:* 800-618-1878. *Fax:* 229-333-5482. *E-mail:* admissions@valdosta.edu.

Wesleyan College

Macon, Georgia

http://www.wesleyancollege.edu/

- **Independent United Methodist** comprehensive, founded 1836
- **Suburban** 200-acre campus with easy access to Atlanta
- **Endowment** $60.0 million
- **Undergraduate: women only; graduate: coed** 725 undergraduate students, 68% full-time, 92% women, 8% men
- **Moderately difficult** entrance level, 48% of applicants were admitted

UNDERGRAD STUDENTS

490 full-time, 235 part-time. Students come from 15 states and territories; 17 other countries; 9% are from out of state; 34% Black or African American, non-Hispanic/Latino; 6% Hispanic/Latino; 2% Asian, non-Hispanic/Latino; 0.2% American Indian or Alaska Native, non-Hispanic/Latino; 4% Two or more races, non-Hispanic/Latino; 2% Race/ethnicity unknown; 9% international; 7% transferred in; 60% live on campus.

Freshmen:

Admission: 890 applied, 426 admitted, 158 enrolled. *Average high school GPA:* 3.4. *Test scores:* SAT evidence-based reading and writing scores over 500: 73%; SAT math scores over 500: 50%; ACT scores over 18: 80%; SAT evidence-based reading and writing scores over 600: 19%; SAT math scores over 600: 9%; ACT scores over 24: 15%; SAT evidence-based reading and writing scores over 700: 3%; SAT math scores over 700: 3%; ACT scores over 30: 2%.

Retention: 78% of full-time freshmen returned.

FACULTY

Total: 104, 54% full-time, 47% with terminal degrees.

Student/faculty ratio: 15:1.

ACADEMICS

Calendar: semesters. *Degrees:* bachelor's and master's.

Special study options: adult/continuing education programs, advanced placement credit, cooperative education, distance learning, double majors, honors programs, independent study, internships, off-campus study, part-time degree program, services for LD students, student-designed majors, study abroad, summer session for credit. *ROTC:* Army (c).

Unusual degree programs: 3-2 engineering with Georgia Institute of Technology, Auburn University, Mercer University; Dual-degree J.D. program with Mercer University.

Computers: 63 computers/terminals are available on campus for general student use. Students can access the following: campus intranet, computer help desk, free student e-mail accounts, online (class) grades, online (class) registration, online (class) schedules, online payment. Campuswide network is available. 100% of college-owned or -operated housing units are wired for high-speed Internet access. Wireless service is available via entire campus.

Library: Willet Memorial Library. *Books:* 88,108 (physical), 260,161 (digital/electronic); *Serial titles:* 646 (physical), 24,701 (digital/electronic); *Databases:* 294. Study areas open 24 hours, 5–7 days a week; students can reserve study rooms.

STUDENT LIFE

Housing options: women-only, special housing for students with disabilities. Campus housing is university owned. Freshman campus housing is guaranteed.

Activities and organizations: drama/theater group, student-run newspaper, choral group, Student Government Association (SGA), Black Student Alliance (BSA), A.X.I.S. (Association of eXemplary International Students), GLBAL (Gay, Lesbian, Bi-sexual Alliance), Campus Activities Board (CAB).

Athletics Member NCAA. All Division III. *Intercollegiate sports:* basketball W, equestrian sports W, soccer W, softball W, tennis W, volleyball W.

Campus security: 24-hour emergency response devices and patrols, late-night transport/escort service, controlled dormitory access.

Student services: health clinic, personal/psychological counseling, women's center.

COSTS & FINANCIAL AID

Costs (2019–20) *One-time required fee:* $200. *Comprehensive fee:* $33,830 includes full-time tuition ($22,770), mandatory fees ($1000), and room and board ($10,060). Part-time tuition: $540 per semester hour. *Required fees:* $40 per semester hour part-time.

Financial Aid Of all full-time matriculated undergraduates who enrolled in 2018, 401 applied for aid, 366 were judged to have need, 73 had their need fully met. 32 Federal Work-Study jobs (averaging $1296). 75 state and other part-time jobs (averaging $1224). In 2018, 73 non-need-based awards were made. *Average percent of need met: 68. Average financial aid package:* $22,184. *Average need-based loan: $4647. Average need-based gift aid:* $18,761. *Average non-need-based aid: $13,041. Average indebtedness upon graduation:* $33,345.

APPLYING

Standardized Tests *Required:* SAT or ACT (for admission).

Options: electronic application, early admission, deferred entrance.

Application fee: $30.

Required: high school transcript, minimum 2.0 GPA. *Required for some:* interview. *Recommended:* essay or personal statement, 2 letters of recommendation.

Application deadlines: rolling (freshmen), rolling (out-of-state freshmen), rolling (transfers).

Early decision deadline: 11/15.

Notification: continuous (freshmen), continuous (out-of-state freshmen), continuous (transfers).

CONTACT

Clint Hobbs, Vice President of Enrollment, Wesleyan College, 4760 Forsyth Road, Macon, GA 31210-4462. *Phone:* 478-757-5206. *Toll-free phone:* 800-447-6610. *Fax:* 478-757-4030. *E-mail:* admissions@wesleyancollege.edu.

Young Harris College

Young Harris, Georgia

http://www.yhc.edu/

CONTACT

Mr. Clinton G. Hobbs, Vice President for Enrollment Management, Young Harris College, PO Box 116, Young Harris, GA 30582-0098. *Phone:* 706-379-3111. *Toll-free phone:* 800-241-3754. *Fax:* 706-379-3108. *E-mail:* admissions@yhc.edu.

HAWAII

Argosy University, Hawai`i

Honolulu, Hawaii
http://www.argosy.edu/locations/hawaii/

CONTACT
Argosy University, Hawai`i, 1001 Bishop Street, Suite 400, Honolulu, HI 96813. *Phone:* 808-536-5555. *Toll-free phone:* 888-323-2777.

Brigham Young University–Hawaii

Laie, Hawaii
http://www.byuh.edu/

CONTACT
Mr. Arapata P. Meha, Brigham Young University–Hawaii, 55-220 Kulanui Street, Laie, HI 96762-1294. *Phone:* 808-675-3731. *Fax:* 808-675-3741. *E-mail:* admissions@byuh.edu.

Chaminade University of Honolulu

Honolulu, Hawaii
http://www.chaminade.edu/

- **Independent Roman Catholic** comprehensive, founded 1955
- **Urban** 62-acre campus with easy access to Honolulu
- **Endowment** $19.1 million
- **Coed**
- **Moderately difficult** entrance level

FACULTY
Student/faculty ratio: 11:1.

ACADEMICS
Calendar: semesters. *Degrees:* associate, bachelor's, master's, post-master's, and postbachelor's certificates.
Library: Sullivan Library. *Books:* 47,508 (physical), 133,757 (digital/electronic); *Serial titles:* 142 (physical), 36,441 (digital/electronic); *Databases:* 99.

STUDENT LIFE
Housing options: coed, women-only, special housing for students with disabilities. Campus housing is university owned and leased by the school.

Activities and organizations: drama/theater group, student-run newspaper, radio station, choral group, Lumana O Samoa (Samoan Club), Kaimi Lalakea (Hawaiian Club), Rotaract, Residence Hall Association, Chaminade Student Government Association.

Athletics Member NCAA. All Division II.

Campus security: 24-hour emergency response devices and patrols, late-night transport/escort service, controlled dormitory access.

Student services: personal/psychological counseling.

COSTS & FINANCIAL AID
Costs (2018–19) *One-time required fee:* $180. *Comprehensive fee:* $39,004 includes full-time tuition ($25,260), mandatory fees ($114), and room and board ($13,630). Full-time tuition and fees vary according to course load, location, and program. Part-time tuition: $842 per credit. Part-time tuition and fees vary according to course load, location, and program. *Room and board:* Room and board charges vary according to board plan and housing facility.

Financial Aid Of all full-time matriculated undergraduates who enrolled in 2017, 910 applied for aid, 761 were judged to have need, 98 had their need fully met. In 2017, 336 non-need-based awards were made. *Average percent of need met:* 67. *Average financial aid package:* $20,566. *Average need-based loan:* $4259. *Average need-based gift aid:* $4621. *Average non-need-based aid:* $12,104. *Average indebtedness upon graduation:* $23,933.

APPLYING
Standardized Tests *Required:* SAT or ACT (for admission), TOEFL for international students (for admission).

Options: electronic application, deferred entrance.

Application fee: $50.
Required: essay or personal statement, high school transcript, minimum 2.5 GPA. *Required for some:* minimum 2.8 GPA, 2 letters of recommendation, interview. *Recommended:* minimum 3.0 GPA.

CONTACT
Office of Admissions, Chaminade University of Honolulu, 3140 Waialae Avenue, Honolulu, HI 96816-1578. *Phone:* 808-735-8340. *Toll-free phone:* 800-735-3733. *Fax:* 808-739-4647. *E-mail:* admissions@chaminade.edu.

Hawai`i Pacific University

Honolulu, Hawaii
http://www.hpu.edu/

- **Independent** comprehensive, founded 1965
- **Urban** 140-acre campus
- **Endowment** $44.4 million
- **Coed**
- **Moderately difficult** entrance level

FACULTY
Student/faculty ratio: 12:1.

ACADEMICS
Calendar: semesters. *Degrees:* certificates, associate, bachelor's, master's, doctoral, post-master's, and postbachelor's certificates.
Library: Meader Library plus 2 others. *Books:* 103,021 (physical), 191,075 (digital/electronic); *Serial titles:* 64 (physical), 4,520 (digital/electronic); *Databases:* 101. Students can reserve study rooms.

STUDENT LIFE
Housing options: coed. Campus housing is university owned. Freshman applicants given priority for college housing.

Activities and organizations: drama/theater group, student-run newspaper, choral group, Student Government Association, Campus Activities Board, Student Nurses Association, Travel Industry Management Student Organization, Christian Student Organization.

Athletics Member NCAA. All Division II.

Campus security: 24-hour emergency response devices and patrols, late-night transport/escort service, controlled dormitory access, emergency notification, patrol system and emergency exit alarms in residence halls.

Student services: health clinic, personal/psychological counseling, veterans affairs office.

COSTS & FINANCIAL AID
Costs (2018–19) *Comprehensive fee:* $40,780 includes full-time tuition ($25,630), mandatory fees ($350), and room and board ($14,800). Full-time tuition and fees vary according to course level, course load, degree level, location, program, and student level. Part-time tuition: $855 per credit. Part-time tuition and fees vary according to course level, course load, degree level, location, program, and student level. *Required fees:* $25 per term part-time. *Room and board:* Room and board charges vary according to board plan, housing facility, and location.

Financial Aid Of all full-time matriculated undergraduates who enrolled in 2017, 1,537 applied for aid, 1,406 were judged to have need, 101 had their need fully met. 604 Federal Work-Study jobs (averaging $2765). In 2017, 634 non-need-based awards were made. *Average percent of need met:* 56. *Average financial aid package:* $14,367. *Average need-based loan:* $5662. *Average need-based gift aid:* $3072. *Average non-need-based aid:* $6936. *Average indebtedness upon graduation:* $27,481.

APPLYING
Standardized Tests *Required:* SAT or ACT (for admission). *Required for some:* TOEFL or IELTS.

Options: electronic application, early action, deferred entrance.

Application fee: $50.
Required: high school transcript, minimum 2.5 GPA. *Required for some:* interview. *Recommended:* essay or personal statement, 2 letters of recommendation.

CONTACT
Marissa Bratton, Director of Admissions, Hawai`i Pacific University, 1 Aloha Tower Drive, Honolulu, HI 96813. *Phone:* 808-544-0238. *Toll-free phone:* 866-225-5478. *Fax:* 808-544-1136. *E-mail:* admissions@hpu.edu.

Pacific Rim Christian University

Honolulu, Hawaii

http://www.pacrim.edu/

CONTACT
Pacific Rim Christian University, 2223 Ho'one'e Place, Honolulu, HI 96819.

Remington College–Honolulu Campus

Honolulu, Hawaii

http://www.remingtoncollege.edu/

CONTACT
Louis LaMair, Director of Recruitment, Remington College–Honolulu Campus, 1111 Bishop Street, Suite 400, Honolulu, HI 96813. *Phone:* 808-942-1000. *Toll-free phone:* 800-323-8122. *Fax:* 808-533-3064. *E-mail:* louis.lamair@remingtoncollege.edu.

University of Hawaii at Hilo

Hilo, Hawaii

http://hilo.hawaii.edu/

CONTACT
University of Hawaii at Hilo, Admissions, 200 W. Kawili Street, Hilo, HI 96720. *Phone:* 808-932-7446. *Toll-free phone:* 800-897-4456. *Fax:* 808-932-7459. *E-mail:* uhhadm@hawaii.edu.

University of Hawaii at Manoa

Honolulu, Hawaii

http://manoa.hawaii.edu/

- **State-supported** university, founded 1907, part of University of Hawaii System
- **Urban** 320-acre campus with easy access to Honolulu
- **Coed** 12,968 undergraduate students, 83% full-time, 57% women, 43% men
- **Moderately difficult** entrance level, 83% of applicants were admitted

UNDERGRAD STUDENTS
10,739 full-time, 2,229 part-time. Students come from 51 states and territories; 64 other countries; 28% are from out of state; 2% Black or African American, non-Hispanic/Latino; 2% Hispanic/Latino; 40% Asian, non-Hispanic/Latino; 17% Native Hawaiian or other Pacific Islander, non-Hispanic/Latino; 0.4% American Indian or Alaska Native, non-Hispanic/Latino; 16% Two or more races, non-Hispanic/Latino; 0.2% Race/ethnicity unknown; 3% international; 12% transferred in; 23% live on campus.

Freshmen:
Admission: 9,350 applied, 7,805 admitted, 2,209 enrolled. *Average high school GPA:* 3.6. *Test scores:* SAT evidence-based reading and writing scores over 500: 90%; SAT math scores over 500: 89%; ACT scores over 18: 96%; SAT evidence-based reading and writing scores over 600: 39%; SAT math scores over 600: 35%; ACT scores over 24: 48%; SAT evidence-based reading and writing scores over 700: 4%; SAT math scores over 700: 6%; ACT scores over 30: 8%.
Retention: 79% of full-time freshmen returned.

FACULTY
Total: 1,416, 81% full-time, 88% with terminal degrees.
Student/faculty ratio: 10:1.

ACADEMICS
Calendar: semesters. *Degrees:* bachelor's, master's, doctoral, and postbachelor's certificates.
Special study options: advanced placement credit, cooperative education, distance learning, double majors, English as a second language, honors programs, independent study, internships, off-campus study, part-time degree program, services for LD students, student-designed majors, study abroad, summer session for credit. *ROTC:* Army (b), Air Force (b).

Computers: 117 computers/terminals and 6 ports are available on campus for general student use. Students can access the following: campus intranet, computer help desk, free student e-mail accounts, online (class) grades, online (class) registration, online (class) schedules. Campuswide network is available. 100% of college-owned or -operated housing units are wired for high-speed Internet access. Wireless service is available via entire campus.
Library: Hamilton Library plus 6 others. *Books:* 2.3 million (physical), 261,550 (digital/electronic); *Serial titles:* 25,284 (physical), 65,122 (digital/electronic); *Databases:* 395. Weekly public service hours: 89; study areas open 24 hours, 5–7 days a week; students can reserve study rooms.

STUDENT LIFE
Housing options: coed, special housing for students with disabilities. Campus housing is university owned. Freshman applicants given priority for college housing.

Activities and organizations: drama/theater group, student-run newspaper, radio station, choral group, marching band, Biology Club, Pre-Medical Association, International Student Association, Katipunan, Timpuyog, national fraternities, national sororities.

Athletics Member NCAA. All Division I except football (Division I-A). *Intercollegiate sports:* archery M, baseball M(s), basketball M(s)/W(s), cheerleading M(s)/W(s), cross-country running W(s), golf M(s)/W(s)(c), sailing M/W, soccer W(s), softball W(s), swimming and diving M(s)/W(s), tennis M(s)/W(s), track and field W(s), volleyball M(s)/W(s), water polo W(s). *Intramural sports:* badminton M/W, basketball M/W, crew M/W, cross-country running M/W, golf M/W, rugby M, sailing M/W, soccer M, softball M, swimming and diving M/W, table tennis M/W, tennis M/W, track and field M/W, ultimate Frisbee M/W, volleyball M/W, weight lifting M/W, wrestling M/W.

Campus security: 24-hour emergency response devices and patrols, student patrols, late-night transport/escort service, controlled dormitory access.

Student services: health clinic, personal/psychological counseling, women's center.

COSTS & FINANCIAL AID
Costs (2019–20) *Tuition:* $462 part-time; state resident $11,088 full-time, $462 per credit hour part-time; nonresident $33,120 full-time, $1380 per credit hour part-time. *Required fees:* $882 full-time, $436 per term part-time. *Room and board:* $12,686; room only: $7110.

Financial Aid Of all full-time matriculated undergraduates who enrolled in 2018, 8,581 applied for aid, 5,795 were judged to have need, 1,675 had their need fully met. 363 Federal Work-Study jobs (averaging $2898). In 2018, 2587 non-need-based awards were made. *Average percent of need met:* 70. *Average financial aid package:* $14,899. *Average need-based loan:* $4472. *Average need-based gift aid:* $10,157. *Average non-need-based aid:* $13,430. *Average indebtedness upon graduation:* $24,593.

APPLYING
Standardized Tests *Required:* SAT or ACT (for admission). *Recommended:* SAT (for admission), ACT (for admission).
Options: electronic application.
Application fee: $70.
Required: high school transcript, minimum 2.8 GPA.
Notification: continuous (freshmen), continuous (transfers).

CONTACT
Ms. Lisa Buto, Student Services Specialist, University of Hawaii at Manoa, 2600 Campus Road, Room 001, Honolulu, HI 96822. *Phone:* 808-956-8975. *Toll-free phone:* 800-823-9771. *Fax:* 808-956-4148. *E-mail:* uhmanoa.admissions@hawaii.edu.

University of Hawaii Maui College

Kahului, Hawaii

http://maui.hawaii.edu/

CONTACT
Mr. Stephen Kameda, Director of Admissions and Records, University of Hawaii Maui College, 310 Kaahumanu Avenue, Kahului, HI 96732. *Phone:* 808-984-3267. *Toll-free phone:* 800-479-6692. *Fax:* 808-984-3872. *E-mail:* skameda@hawaii.edu.

University of Hawaii–West Oahu

Kapolei, Hawaii

http://www.uhwo.hawaii.edu/

CONTACT

Mr. Craig Morimoto, University of Hawaii–West Oahu, HI. *Phone:* 808-689-2916. *Toll-free phone:* 866-299-8656. *E-mail:* uhwoadm@hawaii.edu.

University of Phoenix–Hawaii Campus

Honolulu, Hawaii

http://www.phoenix.edu/

CONTACT

Marc Booker, Senior Director, Office of Admissions and Evaluation, University of Phoenix–Hawaii Campus, 4035 South Riverpoint Parkway, Mail Stop CF-L101, Phoenix, AZ 85040. *Phone:* 602-557-4609. *Toll-free phone:* 866-766-0766. *Fax:* 480-643-1156.

IDAHO

Boise Bible College

Boise, Idaho

http://www.boisebible.edu/

CONTACT

Russell Grove, Director of Admissions, Boise Bible College, 8695 West Marigold Street, Boise, ID 83714-1220. *Phone:* 208-376-7731. *Toll-free phone:* 800-893-7755. *Fax:* 208-376-7743. *E-mail:* rgrove@boisebible.edu.

Boise State University

Boise, Idaho

http://www.boisestate.edu/

- **State-supported** university, founded 1932, part of Idaho System of Higher Education
- **Urban** 287-acre campus
- **Coed**
- **Moderately difficult** entrance level

ACADEMICS

Calendar: semesters. *Degrees:* associate, bachelor's, master's, doctoral, and postbachelor's certificates.

Library: Albertson's Library plus 1 other. *Books:* 644,899 (physical), 60,977 (digital/electronic); *Serial titles:* 112,213 (digital/electronic); *Databases:* 303. Weekly public service hours: 115; study areas open 24 hours, 5–7 days a week; students can reserve study rooms.

STUDENT LIFE

Housing options: coed, men-only, women-only. Campus housing is university owned. Freshman applicants given priority for college housing.

Activities and organizations: drama/theater group, student-run newspaper, radio station, choral group, marching band, national fraternities, national sororities.

Athletics Member NCAA. All Division I except football (Division I-A).

Campus security: 24-hour emergency response devices and patrols, late-night transport/escort service, controlled dormitory access.

Student services: health clinic, personal/psychological counseling, women's center, legal services, veterans affairs office.

COSTS & FINANCIAL AID

Costs (2018–19) *Tuition:* state resident $5259 full-time, $350 per credit hour part-time; nonresident $21,341 full-time, $689 per credit hour part-time. Full-time tuition and fees vary according to course load and reciprocity agreements. Part-time tuition and fees vary according to course load. *Required fees:* $2435 full-time, $111 per term part-time. *Room and board:* $8994. Room and board charges vary according to board plan and housing facility.

Financial Aid Of all full-time matriculated undergraduates who enrolled in 2017, 7,389 applied for aid, 7,298 were judged to have need, 912 had their need fully met. 250 Federal Work-Study jobs (averaging $2460). 156 state and other part-time jobs (averaging $2646). In 2017, 209 non-need-based awards were made. *Average percent of need met:* 57. *Average financial aid package:* $10,213. *Average need-based loan:* $4063. *Average need-based gift aid:* $6047. *Average non-need-based aid:* $3222. *Average indebtedness upon graduation:* $27,870. *Financial aid deadline:* 6/30.

APPLYING

Standardized Tests *Required for some:* SAT or ACT (for admission).

Options: electronic application.

Application fee: $50.

Required for some: high school transcript.

CONTACT

Ms. Kelly Talbert, Director/Admissions, Boise State University, 1910 University Drive, Boise, ID 83725. *Phone:* 208-426-3844. *Toll-free phone:* 800-824-7017. *E-mail:* bsuinfo@boisestate.edu.

Brigham Young University–Idaho

Rexburg, Idaho

http://www.byui.edu/

- **Independent** 4-year, founded 1888, affiliated with The Church of Jesus Christ of Latter-day Saints
- **Small-town** 255-acre campus
- **Coed**
- **Moderately difficult** entrance level

FACULTY

Student/faculty ratio: 25:1.

ACADEMICS

Calendar: semesters. *Degrees:* associate and bachelor's.

Library: David O. McKay Library. Students can reserve study rooms.

STUDENT LIFE

Housing options: men-only, women-only. Campus housing is university owned.

Activities and organizations: drama/theater group, student-run newspaper, radio station, choral group, national fraternities, national sororities.

Campus security: 24-hour emergency response devices and patrols, late-night transport/escort service.

Student services: health clinic, personal/psychological counseling, legal services.

FINANCIAL AID

Financial Aid Of all full-time matriculated undergraduates who enrolled in 2017, 2,400 state and other part-time jobs.

APPLYING

Standardized Tests *Required:* SAT or ACT (for admission).

Options: electronic application.

Application fee: $35.

Required: essay or personal statement, high school transcript, interview.

CONTACT

Brigham Young University–Idaho, 525 South Center Street, Rexburg, ID 83460. *Phone:* 208-496-1310.

The College of Idaho

Caldwell, Idaho

http://www.collegeofidaho.edu/

- **Independent** comprehensive, founded 1891
- **Suburban** 50-acre campus
- **Coed** 946 undergraduate students, 97% full-time, 52% women, 48% men
- **Moderately difficult** entrance level, 49% of applicants were admitted

UNDERGRAD STUDENTS

919 full-time, 27 part-time. 36% are from out of state; 2% Black or African American, non-Hispanic/Latino; 14% Hispanic/Latino; 2% Asian, non-Hispanic/Latino; 1% Native Hawaiian or other Pacific Islander, non-

Hispanic/Latino; 0.3% American Indian or Alaska Native, non-Hispanic/Latino; 5% Two or more races, non-Hispanic/Latino; 2% Race/ethnicity unknown; 13% international; 5% transferred in; 68% live on campus.

Freshmen:
Admission: 2,754 applied, 1,355 admitted, 286 enrolled. *Average high school GPA:* 3.7. *Test scores:* SAT evidence-based reading and writing scores over 500: 83%; SAT math scores over 500: 82%; ACT scores over 18: 93%; SAT evidence-based reading and writing scores over 600: 36%; SAT math scores over 600: 27%; ACT scores over 24: 47%; SAT evidence-based reading and writing scores over 700: 6%; SAT math scores over 700: 2%; ACT scores over 30: 11%.

Retention: 79% of full-time freshmen returned.

FACULTY
Total: 139, 58% full-time, 58% with terminal degrees.
Student/faculty ratio: 9:1.

ACADEMICS
Calendar: 12-6-12 week calendar. *Degrees:* bachelor's and master's.

Special study options: academic remediation for entering students, advanced placement credit, cooperative education, double majors, English as a second language, honors programs, independent study, internships, off-campus study, part-time degree program, services for LD students, study abroad, summer session for credit. *ROTC:* Army (c).

Unusual degree programs: 3-2 engineering with Washington University in St. Louis, Columbia University; nursing with Idaho State University.

Computers: 100 computers/terminals are available on campus for general student use. Students can access the following: campus intranet, computer help desk, free student e-mail accounts, online (class) grades, online (class) registration, online (class) schedules, online course syllabi, course assignments, course discussion. Campuswide network is available. 100% of college-owned or -operated housing units are wired for high-speed Internet access. Wireless service is available via entire campus.
Library: Cruzen-Murray.

STUDENT LIFE
Housing options: on-campus residence required through junior year; coed, special housing for students with disabilities. Campus housing is university owned. Freshman campus housing is guaranteed.

Activities and organizations: drama/theater group, student-run newspaper, choral group, marching band, national fraternities, national sororities.

Athletics Member NAIA. *Intercollegiate sports:* baseball M(s), basketball M(s)/W(s), cross-country running M(s)/W(s), golf M(s), lacrosse M(c)/W(c), skiing (cross-country) M/W, skiing (downhill) W(s), soccer M(s)/W(s), softball W(s), swimming and diving M(s)/W(s), tennis W(s), track and field M(s)/W(s), volleyball W(s). *Intramural sports:* badminton M/W, basketball M/W, football M/W, soccer M/W, softball M/W, ultimate Frisbee M/W, volleyball M/W.

Campus security: 24-hour emergency response devices and patrols, student patrols, late-night transport/escort service, controlled dormitory access.

Student services: health clinic, personal/psychological counseling, women's center, veterans affairs office.

COSTS & FINANCIAL AID
Costs (2019–20) *Comprehensive fee:* $41,543 includes full-time tuition ($31,000), mandatory fees ($755), and room and board ($9788). Part-time tuition: $1285 per credit.

Financial Aid Of all full-time matriculated undergraduates who enrolled in 2018, 655 applied for aid, 578 were judged to have need, 145 had their need fully met. In 2018, 330 non-need-based awards were made. *Average percent of need met:* 44. *Average financial aid package:* $29,430. *Average need-based loan:* $4228. *Average need-based gift aid:* $5543. *Average non-need-based aid:* $22,108. *Average indebtedness upon graduation:* $30,422.

APPLYING
Standardized Tests *Required for some:* SAT or ACT (for admission).
Options: electronic application, early admission, early action, deferred entrance.

Required: essay or personal statement, high school transcript, 1 letter of recommendation. *Recommended:* interview, class rank, extracurricular resumé.

Application deadlines: 2/16 (freshmen), 8/1 (transfers).
Notification: continuous (freshmen), continuous (transfers).

CONTACT
Brian Bava, Vice President of Enrollment Management, The College of Idaho, 2112 Cleveland Boulevard, Caldwell, ID 83605-4432. *Phone:* 208-459-5319. *Toll-free phone:* 800-244-3246. *E-mail:* admission@collegeofidaho.edu.

Idaho State University
Pocatello, Idaho
http://www.isu.edu/
- **State-supported** university, founded 1901
- **Urban** 1100-acre campus
- **Coed** 10,416 undergraduate students, 59% full-time, 56% women, 44% men
- **Minimally difficult** entrance level, 100% of applicants were admitted

UNDERGRAD STUDENTS
6,137 full-time, 4,279 part-time. Students come from 40 states and territories; 49 other countries; 9% are from out of state; 1% Black or African American, non-Hispanic/Latino; 13% Hispanic/Latino; 1% Asian, non-Hispanic/Latino; 0.3% Native Hawaiian or other Pacific Islander, non-Hispanic/Latino; 2% American Indian or Alaska Native, non-Hispanic/Latino; 3% Two or more races, non-Hispanic/Latino; 2% Race/ethnicity unknown; 5% international; 4% transferred in; 16% live on campus.

Freshmen:
Admission: 3,253 applied, 3,249 admitted, 1,297 enrolled. *Average high school GPA:* 3.3. *Test scores:* SAT evidence-based reading and writing scores over 500: 62%; SAT math scores over 500: 57%; ACT scores over 18: 80%; SAT evidence-based reading and writing scores over 600: 22%; SAT math scores over 600: 17%; ACT scores over 24: 33%; SAT evidence-based reading and writing scores over 700: 3%; SAT math scores over 700: 2%; ACT scores over 30: 7%.

Retention: 64% of full-time freshmen returned.

FACULTY
Total: 806, 77% full-time.
Student/faculty ratio: 14:1.

ACADEMICS
Calendar: semesters. *Degrees:* certificates, bachelor's, master's, doctoral, post-master's, and postbachelor's certificates.

Special study options: academic remediation for entering students, accelerated degree program, adult/continuing education programs, advanced placement credit, cooperative education, distance learning, double majors, English as a second language, honors programs, independent study, internships, off-campus study, part-time degree program, services for LD students, student-designed majors, study abroad, summer session for credit. *ROTC:* Army (b).

Computers: 155 computers/terminals are available on campus for general student use. Students can access the following: campus intranet, computer help desk, free student e-mail accounts, online (class) grades, online (class) registration, online (class) schedules. Campuswide network is available. 100% of college-owned or -operated housing units are wired for high-speed Internet access. Wireless service is available via entire campus.
Library: Eli M. Oboler Library. *Books:* 620,925 (physical), 211,589 (digital/electronic); *Serial titles:* 150,874 (physical), 15,214 (digital/electronic); *Databases:* 173. Weekly public service hours: 103; students can reserve study rooms.

STUDENT LIFE
Housing options: coed, men-only, women-only, special housing for students with disabilities. Campus housing is university owned.

Activities and organizations: drama/theater group, student-run newspaper, radio and television station, choral group, marching band, national fraternities, national sororities.

Athletics Member NCAA. All Division I except football (Division I-AA). *Intercollegiate sports:* basketball M(s)/W(s), cross-country running M(s)/W(s), soccer W(s), softball W(s), tennis M(s)/W(s), track and field M(s)/W(s), volleyball W(s). *Intramural sports:* basketball M/W, cross-country running M/W, football M, golf W, rock climbing M(c)/W(c), soccer M/W, softball M/W, tennis M/W, track and field M/W, volleyball M/W.

Campus security: 24-hour emergency response devices and patrols, late-night transport/escort service, controlled dormitory access.

Student services: health clinic, personal/psychological counseling, women's center, veterans affairs office.

FINANCIAL AID

Financial Aid Of all full-time matriculated undergraduates who enrolled in 2017, 4,931 applied for aid, 4,278 were judged to have need, 209 had their need fully met. In 2017, 568 non-need-based awards were made. *Average percent of need met:* 47. *Average financial aid package:* $9000. *Average need-based loan:* $3785. *Average need-based gift aid:* $5097. *Average non-need-based aid:* $2450. *Average indebtedness upon graduation:* $29,167.

APPLYING

Standardized Tests *Required:* SAT or ACT (for admission). *Recommended:* ACT (for admission).

Options: electronic application, early admission, deferred entrance.

Application fee: $50.

Required: high school transcript, minimum 2.0 GPA.

Application deadlines: rolling (freshmen), rolling (out-of-state freshmen), rolling (transfers).

Notification: continuous (freshmen), continuous (out-of-state freshmen), continuous (transfers).

CONTACT

Ms. Nicole Joseph, Director of Admissions, Idaho State University, 921 South 8th Avenue, Pocatello, ID 83209. *Phone:* 208-282-2475. *Fax:* 208-282-4511. *E-mail:* admiss@isu.edu.

Lewis-Clark State College

Lewiston, Idaho
http://www.lcsc.edu/

CONTACT

Soo Lee Bruce-Smith, Coordinator of New Student Recruitment, Lewis-Clark State College, 500 Eighth Avenue, Lewiston, ID 83501-2698. *Phone:* 208-792-2210. *Toll-free phone:* 800-933-5272. *Fax:* 208-792-2876. *E-mail:* admissions@lcsc.edu.

New Saint Andrews College

Moscow, Idaho
http://www.nsa.edu/

- **Independent Christian** comprehensive, founded 1993
- **Small-town** campus
- **Coed**
- **Moderately difficult** entrance level

FACULTY
Student/faculty ratio: 12:1.

ACADEMICS
Calendar: 4 8-week terms. *Degrees:* associate, bachelor's, master's, and postbachelor's certificates.
Library: Tyndale Library plus 1 other. Students can reserve study rooms.

STUDENT LIFE
Housing options: college housing not available.

Activities and organizations: drama/theater group, choral group, Students for the Relief of the Oppressed, Nursing Home Visits and Elderly Assistance (snow and leaf removal, firewood distribution), Blood Drives, Fall Carnival, St. Andrews Day Food Bank Drive.

Campus security: 24-hour emergency response devices.

Student services: personal/psychological counseling.

COSTS
Costs (2018–19) *Tuition:* $475 per credit hour part-time. Full-time tuition and fees vary according to course load and program. Part-time tuition and fees vary according to program.

APPLYING
Standardized Tests *Required:* SAT or ACT (for admission).

Options: electronic application, deferred entrance.

Application fee: $40.

Required: essay or personal statement, high school transcript, 2 letters of recommendation. *Required for some:* interview.

CONTACT
Mr. John Sawyer, Director of Student Recruitment, New Saint Andrews College, PO Box 9025, Moscow, ID 83843. *Phone:* 208-882-1566 Ext. 100. *Fax:* 208-882-4293. *E-mail:* info@nsa.edu.

Northwest Nazarene University

Nampa, Idaho
http://www.nnu.edu/

- **Independent** comprehensive, founded 1913, affiliated with Church of the Nazarene
- **Small-town** 85-acre campus with easy access to Boise
- **Coed**
- **Moderately difficult** entrance level

FACULTY
Student/faculty ratio: 16:1.

ACADEMICS
Calendar: semesters. *Degrees:* associate, bachelor's, master's, doctoral, post-master's, and postbachelor's certificates.
Library: John E. Riley Library.

STUDENT LIFE
Housing options: on-campus residence required through sophomore year; men-only, women-only, special housing for students with disabilities. Campus housing is university owned. Freshman campus housing is guaranteed.

Activities and organizations: drama/theater group, student-run newspaper, choral group, Students in Free Enterprise (SIFE), Student Government Association, Fellowship of Christian Athletes, The Crusader newspaper, The Oasis yearbook.

Athletics Member NCAA. All Division II.

Campus security: 24-hour emergency response devices and patrols, student patrols, late-night transport/escort service, controlled dormitory access, residence hall check-in system, on-campus police hub.

Student services: health clinic, personal/psychological counseling.

COSTS & FINANCIAL AID
Costs (2018–19) *Comprehensive fee:* $37,200 includes full-time tuition ($29,300), mandatory fees ($500), and room and board ($7400). Full-time tuition and fees vary according to class time, course load, degree level, location, program, and reciprocity agreements. Part-time tuition: $1200 per credit hour. Part-time tuition and fees vary according to class time, location, and program. *Required fees:* $250 per term part-time. *College room only:* $3550. Room and board charges vary according to board plan.

Financial Aid Of all full-time matriculated undergraduates who enrolled in 2018, 944 applied for aid, 840 were judged to have need, 423 had their need fully met. In 2018, 250 non-need-based awards were made. *Average percent of need met:* 28. *Average financial aid package:* $25,613. *Average need-based loan:* $4324. *Average need-based gift aid:* $7271. *Average non-need-based aid:* $12,651. *Average indebtedness upon graduation:* $33,518.

APPLYING
Standardized Tests *Required:* SAT or ACT (for admission).

Options: electronic application, early action, deferred entrance.

Required: essay or personal statement, high school transcript, minimum 2.5 GPA, 2 letters of recommendation. *Required for some:* interview.

CONTACT
Northwest Nazarene University, 623 S. University Boulevard, Nampa, ID 83686-5897. *Phone:* 208-467-8950. *Toll-free phone:* 877-668-4968.

Stevens-Henager College

Boise, Idaho

http://www.stevenshenager.edu/

CONTACT
David Breck, Director of Admission, Stevens-Henager College, 1444 South Entertainment Avenue, Boise, ID 83709. *Phone:* 208-383-4540. *Toll-free phone:* 800-622-2640. *Fax:* 208-345-6999.

Stevens-Henager College

Idaho Falls, Idaho

http://www.stevenshenager.edu/

CONTACT
Stevens-Henager College, 901 Pier View Drive, Suite 105, Idaho Falls, ID 83402. *Toll-free phone:* 800-622-2640.

University of Idaho

Moscow, Idaho

http://www.uidaho.edu/

- **State-supported** university, founded 1889
- **Small-town** 810-acre campus
- **Endowment** $279.9 million
- **Coed** 9,568 undergraduate students, 74% full-time, 50% women, 50% men
- **Moderately difficult** entrance level, 77% of applicants were admitted

UNDERGRAD STUDENTS
7,039 full-time, 2,529 part-time. Students come from 51 states and territories; 45 other countries; 22% are from out of state; 1% Black or African American, non-Hispanic/Latino; 10% Hispanic/Latino; 1% Asian, non-Hispanic/Latino; 0.4% Native Hawaiian or other Pacific Islander, non-Hispanic/Latino; 0.9% American Indian or Alaska Native, non-Hispanic/Latino; 4% Two or more races, non-Hispanic/Latino; 8% Race/ethnicity unknown; 4% international; 6% transferred in; 37% live on campus.

Freshmen:
Admission: 7,938 applied, 6,132 admitted, 1,434 enrolled. *Average high school GPA:* 3.4. *Test scores:* SAT evidence-based reading and writing scores over 500: 81%; SAT math scores over 500: 76%; ACT scores over 18: 88%; SAT evidence-based reading and writing scores over 600: 36%; SAT math scores over 600: 28%; ACT scores over 24: 45%; SAT evidence-based reading and writing scores over 700: 5%; SAT math scores over 700: 4%; ACT scores over 30: 9%.
Retention: 81% of full-time freshmen returned.

FACULTY
Total: 715, 84% full-time, 75% with terminal degrees.
Student/faculty ratio: 14:1.

ACADEMICS
Calendar: semesters. *Degrees:* certificates, bachelor's, master's, doctoral, post-master's, and postbachelor's certificates.

Special study options: academic remediation for entering students, accelerated degree program, adult/continuing education programs, advanced placement credit, cooperative education, distance learning, double majors, English as a second language, honors programs, independent study, internships, off-campus study, part-time degree program, services for LD students, study abroad, summer session for credit. *ROTC:* Army (b), Navy (b), Air Force (c).

Computers: 510 computers/terminals are available on campus for general student use. Students can access the following: campus intranet, computer help desk, free student e-mail accounts, online (class) grades, online (class) registration, online (class) schedules. Campuswide network is available. 100% of college-owned or -operated housing units are wired for high-speed Internet access. Wireless service is available via entire campus.
Library: University of Idaho Library plus 1 other. *Books:* 1.5 million (physical), 1.3 million (digital/electronic); *Serial titles:* 109,553 (physical), 177,970 (digital/electronic).

STUDENT LIFE
Housing options: on-campus residence required for freshman year; coed, men-only, women-only, cooperative, special housing for students with disabilities. Campus housing is university owned. Freshman campus housing is guaranteed.

Activities and organizations: drama/theater group, student-run newspaper, radio and television station, choral group, marching band, Student Alumni Relations Board (SARB), Associate Students University of Idaho (ASUI), Vandal Volunteers Club, Earth Club, Gender and Sexuality Alliance, national fraternities, national sororities.

Athletics Member NCAA. All Division I except football (Division I-A). *Intercollegiate sports:* basketball M(s)/W(s), cross-country running M(s)/W(s), golf M(s)/W(s), soccer W(s), swimming and diving W(s), tennis M(s)/W(s), track and field M(s)/W(s), volleyball W(s). *Intramural sports:* badminton M/W, baseball M, basketball M/W, cheerleading M, equestrian sports M(c)/W(c), football M, golf M/W, ice hockey M(c)/W(c), lacrosse M(c)/W(c), racquetball M/W, rock climbing M(c)/W(c), rugby M(c)/W(c), sand volleyball M/W, skiing (cross-country) M/W, skiing (downhill) M(c)/W(c), soccer M/W, softball M/W, swimming and diving M/W, table tennis M/W, tennis M/W, track and field M/W, ultimate Frisbee M/W, volleyball M/W, water polo M(c)/W(c), weight lifting M/W, wrestling M.

Campus security: 24-hour emergency response devices and patrols, late-night transport/escort service, controlled dormitory access.

Student services: health clinic, personal/psychological counseling, women's center, veterans affairs office.

COSTS & FINANCIAL AID
Costs (2018–19) *Tuition:* state resident $5778 full-time, $348 per credit hour part-time; nonresident $23,414 full-time, $1230 per credit hour part-time. Full-time tuition and fees vary according to course load, program, and reciprocity agreements. Part-time tuition and fees vary according to program and reciprocity agreements. *Required fees:* $2086 full-time, $46 per credit hour part-time. *Room and board:* $8880. Room and board charges vary according to board plan and housing facility. *Payment plan:* installment. *Waivers:* employees or children of employees.

Financial Aid Of all full-time matriculated undergraduates who enrolled in 2017, 6,110 applied for aid, 4,972 were judged to have need, 1,536 had their need fully met. 514 Federal Work-Study jobs (averaging $1304). 143 state and other part-time jobs (averaging $1528). In 2017, 1640 non-need-based awards were made. *Average percent of need met:* 78. *Average financial aid package:* $14,071. *Average need-based loan:* $6837. *Average need-based gift aid:* $4914. *Average non-need-based aid:* $5307. *Average indebtedness upon graduation:* $24,764.

APPLYING
Standardized Tests *Required:* SAT or ACT (for admission). *Required for some:* SAT and SAT Subject Tests or ACT (for admission).

Options: electronic application, deferred entrance.

Application fee: $60.

Required: high school transcript, minimum 2.2 GPA. *Required for some:* essay or personal statement.

Application deadlines: 8/1 (freshmen), rolling (transfers).

Notification: continuous (freshmen), continuous (transfers).

CONTACT
Ms. Melissa Goodwin, Associate Director, Admissions, University of Idaho, 875 Perimeter Drive, MS 4264, Moscow, ID 83844-4264. *Phone:* 208-885-9030. *Toll-free phone:* 888-884-3246. *Fax:* 208-885-9119. *E-mail:* admissions@uidaho.edu.

ILLINOIS

Ambria College of Nursing

Hoffman Estates, Illinois

http://www.ambria.edu/

CONTACT
Ambria College of Nursing, 5210 Trillium Boulevard, Hoffman Estates, IL 60192.

American Academy of Art

Chicago, Illinois

http://www.aaart.edu/

- **Independent** 4-year, founded 1923
- **Urban** campus with easy access to Chicago
- **Coed**
- **Moderately difficult** entrance level

FACULTY
Student/faculty ratio: 14:1.

ACADEMICS
Calendar: semesters. *Degree:* bachelor's.
Library: Irving Shapiro Library.

STUDENT LIFE
Housing options: Campus housing is leased by the school.
Campus security: 24-hour emergency response devices.

COSTS & FINANCIAL AID
Costs (2018–19) *Tuition:* $33,800 full-time. Full-time tuition and fees vary according to course load. Part-time tuition and fees vary according to course load. *Required fees:* $720 full-time.
Financial Aid *Average percent of need met:* 70.

APPLYING
Options: electronic application.
Application fee: $25.
Required: high school transcript, interview.

CONTACT
Mr. Stuart Rosenbloom, Director of Admissions, American Academy of Art, 332 South Michigan Avenue, Suite 300, Chicago, IL 60604-4302. *Phone:* 312-461-0600 Ext. 129. *Toll-free phone:* 888-461-0600. *E-mail:* srosenbloom@aaart.edu.

American InterContinental University Online

Schaumburg, Illinois

http://www.aiuniv.edu/

CONTACT
Jennifer Ziegenmier, Senior Vice President of Admissions and Marketing, American InterContinental University Online, 231 N. Martingale Road, 6th Floor, Schaumburg, IL 60173. *Phone:* 877-564-6248. *Toll-free phone:* 877-701-3800. *E-mail:* jziegenmier@aiuonline.edu.

Argosy University, Chicago

Chicago, Illinois

http://www.argosy.edu/chicago-illinois/default.aspx

CONTACT
Argosy University, Chicago, 225 North Michigan Avenue, Suite 1300, Chicago, IL 60601. *Phone:* 312-777-7600. *Toll-free phone:* 800-626-4123.

Augustana College

Rock Island, Illinois

http://www.augustana.edu/

- **Independent** 4-year, founded 1860, affiliated with Evangelical Lutheran Church in America
- **Suburban** 115-acre campus
- **Endowment** $168.8 million
- **Coed**
- **Moderately difficult** entrance level

FACULTY
Student/faculty ratio: 12:1.

ACADEMICS
Calendar: quarters. *Degree:* bachelor's.
Library: Thomas Tredway Library plus 1 other. *Books:* 128,238 (physical), 4,470 (digital/electronic); *Serial titles:* 233 (physical), 120,219 (digital/electronic); *Databases:* 106. Weekly public service hours: 100.

STUDENT LIFE
Housing options: on-campus residence required through junior year; coed. Campus housing is university owned. Freshman campus housing is guaranteed.
Activities and organizations: drama/theater group, student-run newspaper, radio station, choral group, College Union Board of Managers, Student Government Association, student newspaper, student radio station, service organizations (APO, Dance Marathon committee).
Athletics Member NCAA. All Division III.
Campus security: 24-hour emergency response devices and patrols, late-night transport/escort service, controlled dormitory access.
Student services: personal/psychological counseling.

COSTS & FINANCIAL AID
Costs (2018–19) *Comprehensive fee:* $52,707 includes full-time tuition ($42,135) and room and board ($10,572). Part-time tuition: $1808 per credit. Part-time tuition and fees vary according to course load. *College room only:* $5079. Room and board charges vary according to board plan and housing facility. *Payment plans:* tuition prepayment, installment.
Financial Aid Of all full-time matriculated undergraduates who enrolled in 2016, 2,265 applied for aid, 1,928 were judged to have need, 426 had their need fully met. 1,313 Federal Work-Study jobs (averaging $2339). In 2016, 570 non-need-based awards were made. *Average percent of need met:* 86. *Average financial aid package:* $30,840. *Average need-based loan:* $4825. *Average need-based gift aid:* $24,787. *Average non-need-based aid:* $21,096. *Average indebtedness upon graduation:* $34,964.

APPLYING
Options: electronic application, early admission, early decision, early action, deferred entrance.
Required: high school transcript. *Required for some:* essay or personal statement, interview. *Recommended:* essay or personal statement, 1 letter of recommendation, interview.

CONTACT
W. Kent Barnds, Vice President of Enrollment Management, Augustana College, 639 38th Street, Rock Island, IL 61201. *Phone:* 309-794-7662. *Toll-free phone:* 800-798-8100. *Fax:* 309-794-8797. *E-mail:* admissions@augustana.edu.

Aurora University

Aurora, Illinois

http://www.aurora.edu/

- **Independent** comprehensive, founded 1893
- **Suburban** 70-acre campus with easy access to Chicago
- **Endowment** $41.2 million
- **Coed** 4,020 undergraduate students, 88% full-time, 65% women, 35% men
- **Moderately difficult** entrance level, 81% of applicants were admitted

UNDERGRAD STUDENTS
3,537 full-time, 483 part-time. Students come from 38 states and territories; 3 other countries; 11% are from out of state; 7% Black or African American, non-Hispanic/Latino; 31% Hispanic/Latino; 2% Asian, non-Hispanic/Latino; 0.1% Native Hawaiian or other Pacific Islander, non-Hispanic/Latino; 0.2% American Indian or Alaska Native, non-Hispanic/Latino; 3% Two or more races, non-Hispanic/Latino; 7% Race/ethnicity unknown; 0.3% international; 14% transferred in; 16% live on campus.

Freshmen:
Admission: 3,296 applied, 2,675 admitted, 762 enrolled. *Average high school GPA:* 3.4. *Test scores:* SAT evidence-based reading and writing scores over 500: 71%; SAT math scores over 500: 68%; ACT scores over 18: 90%; SAT evidence-based reading and writing scores over 600: 19%; SAT math scores over 600: 13%; ACT scores over 24: 24%; SAT evidence-based reading and writing scores over 700: 1%; SAT math scores over 700: 1%; ACT scores over 30: 2%.
Retention: 75% of full-time freshmen returned.

FACULTY
Total: 447, 31% full-time.
Student/faculty ratio: 18:1.

ACADEMICS
Calendar: semesters. *Degrees:* bachelor's, master's, doctoral, and post-master's certificates.

Special study options: academic remediation for entering students, accelerated degree program, adult/continuing education programs, advanced placement credit, distance learning, double majors, independent study, internships, off-campus study, part-time degree program, services for LD students, student-designed majors, study abroad, summer session for credit. *ROTC:* Army (c).

Unusual degree programs: Exercise Science/Athletic Training.

Computers: 193 computers/terminals are available on campus for general student use. Students can access the following: campus intranet, computer help desk, free student e-mail accounts, online (class) grades, online (class) registration, online (class) schedules, learning management system. Campuswide network is available. 100% of college-owned or -operated housing units are wired for high-speed Internet access. Wireless service is available via classrooms, computer labs, dorm rooms, learning centers, libraries, student centers.

Library: Charles B. Phillips Library plus 1 other. *Books:* 24,587 (physical), 178,780 (digital/electronic); *Serial titles:* 2 (physical), 71,529 (digital/electronic); *Databases:* 63. Weekly public service hours: 96; students can reserve study rooms.

STUDENT LIFE
Housing options: coed. Campus housing is university owned. Freshman applicants given priority for college housing.

Activities and organizations: drama/theater group, student-run newspaper, radio and television station, choral group, Latin American Student Organization, American Marketing Association, Student Nursing Association, Phi Eta Sigma, Spartan Athletic Training Student Organization, national fraternities, national sororities.

Athletics Member NCAA. All Division III. *Intercollegiate sports:* baseball M, basketball M/W, bowling W, cross-country running M/W, football M, golf M/W, ice hockey M/W, lacrosse M/W, soccer M/W, softball W, tennis M/W, track and field M/W, volleyball M/W. *Intramural sports:* badminton M/W, basketball M/W, cheerleading M(c)/W(c), football M/W, ice hockey M(c), soccer M/W, softball M/W, ultimate Frisbee M/W, volleyball M/W.

Campus security: 24-hour emergency response devices and patrols, late-night transport/escort service, controlled dormitory access.

Student services: health clinic, personal/psychological counseling.

COSTS & FINANCIAL AID
Costs (2019–20) *Comprehensive fee:* $36,760 includes full-time tuition ($24,800), mandatory fees ($260), and room and board ($11,700). Part-time tuition: $710 per semester hour. *College room only:* $6500.

Financial Aid Of all full-time matriculated undergraduates who enrolled in 2018, 3,092 applied for aid, 2,858 were judged to have need, 309 had their need fully met. 2,139 Federal Work-Study jobs (averaging $1894). 33 state and other part-time jobs (averaging $10,245). In 2018, 586 non-need-based awards were made. *Average percent of need met:* 79. *Average financial aid package:* $21,396. *Average need-based loan:* $3360. *Average need-based gift aid:* $15,624. *Average non-need-based aid:* $10,511. *Average indebtedness upon graduation:* $28,373.

APPLYING
Standardized Tests *Required:* SAT or ACT (for admission).

Options: electronic application, deferred entrance.

Required: high school transcript, minimum 2.0 GPA. *Required for some:* essay or personal statement, 2 letters of recommendation, interview.

Application deadlines: rolling (freshmen), rolling (transfers).

Notification: continuous (freshmen), continuous (transfers).

CONTACT
Mr. James Lancaster, Vice President for Enrollment, Aurora University, 347 South Gladstone Avenue, Aurora, IL 60506-4892. *Phone:* 630-844-5533. *Toll-free phone:* 800-742-5281. *Fax:* 630-844-5535. *E-mail:* admission@aurora.edu.

Benedictine University
Lisle, Illinois
http://www.ben.edu/
- **Independent Roman Catholic** comprehensive, founded 1887
- **Suburban** 108-acre campus with easy access to Chicago
- **Endowment** $36.4 million
- **Coed** 2,718 undergraduate students, 87% full-time, 54% women, 46% men
- **Moderately difficult** entrance level, 65% of applicants were admitted

UNDERGRAD STUDENTS
2,372 full-time, 346 part-time. Students come from 49 states and territories; 11 other countries; 10% are from out of state; 8% Black or African American, non-Hispanic/Latino; 17% Hispanic/Latino; 14% Asian, non-Hispanic/Latino; 0.4% Native Hawaiian or other Pacific Islander, non-Hispanic/Latino; 0.7% American Indian or Alaska Native, non-Hispanic/Latino; 15% Race/ethnicity unknown; 1% international; 11% transferred in; 22% live on campus.

Freshmen:
Admission: 5,257 applied, 3,435 admitted, 455 enrolled. *Average high school GPA:* 3.4. *Test scores:* SAT evidence-based reading and writing scores over 500: 73%; SAT math scores over 500: 75%; ACT scores over 18: 90%; SAT evidence-based reading and writing scores over 600: 28%; SAT math scores over 600: 22%; ACT scores over 24: 36%; SAT evidence-based reading and writing scores over 700: 2%; SAT math scores over 700: 4%; ACT scores over 30: 4%.

Retention: 72% of full-time freshmen returned.

FACULTY
Total: 436, 35% full-time, 54% with terminal degrees.
Student/faculty ratio: 12:1.

ACADEMICS
Calendar: semesters. *Degrees:* certificates, diplomas, bachelor's, master's, doctoral, and postbachelor's certificates.

Special study options: academic remediation for entering students, accelerated degree program, adult/continuing education programs, advanced placement credit, distance learning, double majors, English as a second language, honors programs, independent study, internships, off-campus study, part-time degree program, services for LD students, study abroad, summer session for credit. *ROTC:* Army (c).

Unusual degree programs: 3-2 engineering with Illinois Institute of Technology; nursing.

Computers: 275 computers/terminals and 275 ports are available on campus for general student use. Students can access the following: computer help desk, free student e-mail accounts, online (class) grades, online (class) registration, online (class) schedules. Campuswide network is available. 100% of college-owned or -operated housing units are wired for high-speed Internet access. Wireless service is available via entire campus.

Library: Benedictine Library. *Books:* 90,762 (physical), 187,960 (digital/electronic); *Serial titles:* 1,498 (physical), 51,758 (digital/electronic); *Databases:* 61. Students can reserve study rooms.

STUDENT LIFE
Housing options: coed, men-only, women-only, special housing for students with disabilities. Campus housing is university owned. Freshman campus housing is guaranteed.

Activities and organizations: student-run newspaper, radio and television station, choral group, Student Senate, MSA-Muslim Student Association, AMSA-American Medical Student Association, The Candor-Student Newspaper, Programming Board.

Athletics Member NCAA, NAIA. All NCAA Division III except golf (Division II). *Intercollegiate sports:* baseball M, basketball M/W, cross-country running M/W, football M, golf M/W, lacrosse M/W, soccer M/W, softball W, track and field M/W, volleyball M/W. *Intramural sports:* basketball M/W, bowling M/W, cheerleading W(c), football M, lacrosse M(c), softball M/W, table tennis M/W, volleyball M/W.

Campus security: 24-hour emergency response devices and patrols, late-night transport/escort service, controlled dormitory access.

Student services: health clinic, personal/psychological counseling.

COSTS & FINANCIAL AID

Costs (2019–20) *Tuition:* $34,290 full-time, $1090 per credit hour part-time. *Required fees:* $1590 full-time, $60 per credit hour part-time.

Financial Aid Of all full-time matriculated undergraduates who enrolled in 2018, 1,985 applied for aid, 1,859 were judged to have need. In 2018, 414 non-need-based awards were made. *Average financial aid package:* $24,713. *Average need-based loan:* $4370. *Average need-based gift aid:* $8567. *Average non-need-based aid:* $13,566. *Average indebtedness upon graduation:* $33,295.

APPLYING

Standardized Tests *Required:* SAT or ACT (for admission).

Options: electronic application, deferred entrance.

Application fee: $40.

Required: essay or personal statement, high school transcript. *Required for some:* interview. *Recommended:* rank in upper 50% of high school class.

Application deadlines: rolling (freshmen), rolling (transfers).

Notification: continuous (freshmen), continuous (transfers).

CONTACT

Ms. Karen Campana, Chief Retention Officer, Benedictine University, 5700 College Road, Lisle, IL 60532-0900. *Toll-free phone:* 888-829-6363. *E-mail:* admissions@ben.edu.

Blackburn College

Carlinville, Illinois
http://www.blackburn.edu/

- **Independent Presbyterian** 4-year, founded 1837
- **Small-town** 80-acre campus with easy access to St. Louis
- **Endowment** $23.4 million
- **Coed** 566 undergraduate students, 97% full-time, 60% women, 40% men
- **Moderately difficult** entrance level, 54% of applicants were admitted

UNDERGRAD STUDENTS

548 full-time, 18 part-time. Students come from 20 states and territories; 8 other countries; 10% are from out of state; 12% Black or African American, non-Hispanic/Latino; 4% Hispanic/Latino; 1% Asian, non-Hispanic/Latino; 0.2% Native Hawaiian or other Pacific Islander, non-Hispanic/Latino; 2% Two or more races, non-Hispanic/Latino; 2% Race/ethnicity unknown; 2% international; 5% transferred in; 69% live on campus.

Freshmen:

Admission: 869 applied, 466 admitted, 168 enrolled. *Average high school GPA:* 3.4. *Test scores:* SAT evidence-based reading and writing scores over 500: 68%; SAT math scores over 500: 63%; SAT evidence-based reading and writing scores over 600: 16%; SAT math scores over 600: 10%; SAT evidence-based reading and writing scores over 700: 1%; SAT math scores over 700: 2%.

Retention: 70% of full-time freshmen returned.

FACULTY

Total: 75, 51% full-time, 51% with terminal degrees.

Student/faculty ratio: 13:1.

ACADEMICS

Calendar: semesters. *Degree:* bachelor's.

Special study options: advanced placement credit, cooperative education, double majors, honors programs, independent study, internships, off-campus study, services for LD students, student-designed majors, study abroad, summer session for credit.

Unusual degree programs: 3-2 nursing with St. John's College (Springfield).

Computers: 202 computers/terminals are available on campus for general student use. Students can access the following: computer help desk, free student e-mail accounts, online (class) grades, online (class) registration, online (class) schedules. Campuswide network is available. 100% of college-owned or -operated housing units are wired for high-speed Internet access. Wireless service is available via entire campus.

Library: Lumpkin Learning Commons. *Books:* 62,000 (physical); *Serial titles:* 40 (physical); *Databases:* 21. Weekly public service hours: 80; students can reserve study rooms.

STUDENT LIFE

Housing options: on-campus residence required through junior year; coed, men-only, women-only. Campus housing is university owned. Freshman campus housing is guaranteed.

Activities and organizations: drama/theater group, student-run newspaper, radio station, choral group, Habitat for Humanity, Pre-Health Professions, Running Club, Trading Card Games, Spectrum.

Athletics Member NCAA. All Division III. *Intercollegiate sports:* baseball M, basketball M/W, cross-country running M/W, golf M/W, soccer M/W, softball W, tennis M/W, volleyball W. *Intramural sports:* badminton M/W, basketball M/W, football M/W, golf M/W, racquetball M/W, soccer M/W, softball M/W, table tennis M/W, tennis M/W, ultimate Frisbee M/W, volleyball M/W.

Campus security: student patrols, late-night transport/escort service.

Student services: personal/psychological counseling.

COSTS & FINANCIAL AID

Costs (2019–20) *Comprehensive fee:* $31,610 includes full-time tuition ($23,510) and room and board ($8100). Part-time tuition: $765 per credit hour. *College room only:* $4800.

Financial Aid Of all full-time matriculated undergraduates who enrolled in 2018, 532 applied for aid, 495 were judged to have need, 432 had their need fully met. In 2018, 39 non-need-based awards were made. *Average percent of need met:* 87. *Average financial aid package:* $19,123. *Average need-based loan:* $3677. *Average need-based gift aid:* $19,123. *Average non-need-based aid:* $4607. *Average indebtedness upon graduation:* $30,677.

APPLYING

Standardized Tests *Required:* SAT or ACT (for admission).

Options: electronic application, deferred entrance.

Required: high school transcript, minimum 2.0 GPA. *Required for some:* essay or personal statement, 3 letters of recommendation, interview. *Recommended:* minimum 2.5 GPA.

Application deadlines: rolling (freshmen), rolling (out-of-state freshmen), rolling (transfers).

Notification: continuous (freshmen), continuous (out-of-state freshmen), continuous (transfers).

CONTACT

Mr. Justin Norwood, Director of Admissions, Blackburn College, 700 College Avenue, Carlinville, IL 62626. *Phone:* 217-854-5559. *Toll-free phone:* 800-233-3550. *E-mail:* justin.norwood@blackburn.edu.

Blessing-Rieman College of Nursing & Health Sciences

Quincy, Illinois
http://www.brcn.edu/

CONTACT

Ms. Heather Mutter, Admissions Counselor, Blessing-Rieman College of Nursing & Health Sciences, Broadway at 11th Street, POB 7005, Quincy, IL 62305-7005. *Phone:* 217-228-5520 Ext. 6979. *Toll-free phone:* 800-877-9140. *Fax:* 217-223-4661. *E-mail:* admissions@brcn.edu.

⭐ Bradley University

Peoria, Illinois
http://www.bradley.edu/

- **Independent** comprehensive, founded 1897
- **Suburban** 85-acre campus
- **Endowment** $312.5 million
- **Coed** 4,606 undergraduate students, 97% full-time, 51% women, 49% men
- **Moderately difficult** entrance level, 67% of applicants were admitted

UNDERGRAD STUDENTS

4,462 full-time, 144 part-time. Students come from 47 states and territories; 42 other countries; 18% are from out of state; 7% Black or African American, non-Hispanic/Latino; 10% Hispanic/Latino; 3% Asian, non-Hispanic/Latino; 3% Two or more races, non-Hispanic/Latino; 2% Race/ethnicity unknown; 2% international; 4% transferred in; 67% live on campus.

Freshmen:

Admission: 11,209 applied, 7,489 admitted, 1,090 enrolled. *Average high school GPA:* 3.8. *Test scores:* SAT evidence-based reading and writing scores over 500: 93%; SAT math scores over 500: 91%; ACT scores over 18: 100%; SAT evidence-based reading and writing scores over 600: 50%; SAT math scores over 600: 42%; ACT scores over 24: 71%; SAT evidence-based reading and writing scores over 700: 6%; SAT math scores over 700: 11%; ACT scores over 30: 15%.

Retention: 82% of full-time freshmen returned.

FACULTY
Total: 589, 60% full-time, 48% with terminal degrees.

Student/faculty ratio: 12:1.

ACADEMICS
Calendar: semesters. *Degrees:* bachelor's, master's, doctoral, post-master's, and postbachelor's certificates.

Special study options: accelerated degree program, advanced placement credit, cooperative education, distance learning, double majors, honors programs, independent study, internships, off-campus study, part-time degree program, services for LD students, student-designed majors, study abroad, summer session for credit. *ROTC:* Army (b).

Computers: 80 computers/terminals and 3,123 ports are available on campus for general student use. Students can access the following: campus intranet, computer help desk, free student e-mail accounts, online (class) grades, online (class) registration, online (class) schedules, Online directory, catalog, library materials and other resources. Campuswide network is available. 100% of college-owned or -operated housing units are wired for high-speed Internet access. Wireless service is available via entire campus.

Library: Cullom-Davis Library. *Books:* 545,721 (physical), 5,632 (digital/electronic); *Serial titles:* 1,557 (physical), 54,082 (digital/electronic); *Databases:* 54. Weekly public service hours: 129; students can reserve study rooms.

STUDENT LIFE
Housing options: on-campus residence required through sophomore year; coed. Campus housing is university owned, leased by the school and is provided by a third party. Freshman campus housing is guaranteed.

Activities and organizations: drama/theater group, student-run newspaper, radio and television station, choral group, Activities Council of Bradley University, CRU (Campus Christian group), Fraternity/Sorority Life, Service on Saturday, Alpha Phi Omega (Coed Service), national fraternities, national sororities.

Athletics Member NCAA. All Division I. *Intercollegiate sports:* baseball M(s), basketball M(s)/W(s), cheerleading M/W, cross-country running M(s)/W(s), golf M(s)/W(s)(c), soccer M(s), softball W(s), table tennis M(c), tennis W(s), track and field M(s)/W(s), volleyball M(c)/W(s), wrestling M(c). *Intramural sports:* badminton M/W, baseball M(c), basketball M/W, bowling M/W, fencing M(c), field hockey W(c), football M/W, golf M/W, ice hockey M(c), lacrosse M(c)/W(c), racquetball M/W, rock climbing M(c)/W(c), soccer M(c)/W(c), softball M/W(c), swimming and diving M/W, table tennis M/W, tennis M/W, triathlon M(c)/W(c), ultimate Frisbee M(c)/W(c), volleyball M/W, water polo M(c)/W(c), wrestling M/W.

Campus security: 24-hour emergency response devices and patrols, student patrols, late-night transport/escort service, controlled dormitory access, emergency text messaging, mass notification/emergency communication system in 20 academic buildings.

Student services: health clinic, personal/psychological counseling.

COSTS & FINANCIAL AID
Costs (2018–19) *One-time required fee:* $200. *Comprehensive fee:* $44,380 includes full-time tuition ($33,360), mandatory fees ($400), and room and board ($10,620). Full-time tuition and fees vary according to course load and program. Part-time tuition: $890 per credit hour. Part-time tuition and fees vary according to course load and program. *Required fees:* $400 per year part-time. *College room only:* $6140. Room and board charges vary according to board plan and housing facility. *Payment plans:* installment, deferred payment. *Waivers:* senior citizens and employees or children of employees.

Financial Aid Of all full-time matriculated undergraduates who enrolled in 2018, 3,835 applied for aid, 3,246 were judged to have need, 503 had their need fully met. 307 Federal Work-Study jobs (averaging $1914). In 2018, 1163 non-need-based awards were made. *Average percent of need met:* 72. *Average financial aid package:* $24,915. *Average need-based loan:* $6132. *Average need-based gift aid:* $19,993. *Average non-need-based aid:* $12,719. *Average indebtedness upon graduation:* $29,233.

APPLYING
Standardized Tests *Required:* SAT or ACT (for admission).

Options: electronic application, deferred entrance.

Required: essay or personal statement, high school transcript. *Required for some:* audition required of music majors and recommended for theatre majors, portfolio recommended for art majors. *Recommended:* minimum 2.8 GPA, 1 letter of recommendation, interview.

Application deadlines: rolling (freshmen), rolling (transfers).

Notification: continuous (freshmen), continuous (transfers).

CONTACT
Dr. Justin Ball, Vice President for Enrollment Management, Bradley University, 1501 W. Bradley Avenue, Peoria, IL 61625. *Phone:* 309-677-1000. *Toll-free phone:* 800-447-6460. *Fax:* 309-677-2797. *E-mail:* admissions@bradley.edu.

Chamberlain College of Nursing
Addison, Illinois
http://www.chamberlain.edu/

CONTACT
Admissions, Chamberlain College of Nursing, 1221 North Swift Road, Addison, IL 60101. *Phone:* 630-953-3680. *Toll-free phone:* 877-751-5783.

Chamberlain College of Nursing
Chicago, Illinois
http://www.chamberlain.edu/

CONTACT
Admissions, Chamberlain College of Nursing, 3300 North Campbell Avenue, Chicago, IL 60618. *Phone:* 773-961-3000. *Toll-free phone:* 877-751-5783.

Chamberlain College of Nursing
Tinley Park, Illinois
http://www.chamberlain.edu/

CONTACT
Chamberlain College of Nursing, 18624 West Creek Drive, Tinley Park, IL 60477. *Toll-free phone:* 877-751-5783.

Chicago State University
Chicago, Illinois
http://www.csu.edu/

CONTACT
Mr. John Martinez, Associate Director of Admissions, Chicago State University, 95th Street at King Drive, ADM 200, Chicago, IL 60628. *Phone:* 773-995-3578. *Fax:* 773-995-3820. *E-mail:* jmarti21@csu.edu.

Columbia College Chicago
Chicago, Illinois
http://www.colum.edu/
- **Independent** comprehensive, founded 1890
- **Urban** campus with easy access to Chicago
- **Coed** 6,568 undergraduate students, 92% full-time, 58% women, 42% men
- **Minimally difficult** entrance level, 87% of applicants were admitted

UNDERGRAD STUDENTS
6,073 full-time, 495 part-time. Students come from 58 states and territories; 28 other countries; 44% are from out of state; 13% Black or African American, non-Hispanic/Latino; 16% Hispanic/Latino; 4% Asian, non-Hispanic/Latino; 0.1% Native Hawaiian or other Pacific Islander, non-Hispanic/Latino; 0.2% American Indian or Alaska Native, non-

Hispanic/Latino; 5% Two or more races, non-Hispanic/Latino; 3% Race/ethnicity unknown; 5% international; 11% transferred in; 34% live on campus.

Freshmen:
Admission: 8,088 applied, 7,041 admitted, 1,305 enrolled. *Average high school GPA:* 3.3. *Test scores:* SAT evidence-based reading and writing scores over 500: 82%; SAT math scores over 500: 72%; ACT scores over 18: 88%; SAT evidence-based reading and writing scores over 600: 44%; SAT math scores over 600: 22%; ACT scores over 24: 43%; SAT evidence-based reading and writing scores over 700: 7%; SAT math scores over 700: 4%; ACT scores over 30: 7%.

Retention: 68% of full-time freshmen returned.

FACULTY
Total: 926, 30% full-time.
Student/faculty ratio: 14:1.

ACADEMICS
Calendar: semesters. *Degrees:* bachelor's, master's, and postbachelor's certificates.

Special study options: academic remediation for entering students, adult/continuing education programs, advanced placement credit, cooperative education, distance learning, double majors, English as a second language, honors programs, independent study, internships, off-campus study, part-time degree program, services for LD students, study abroad, summer session for credit.

Computers: Students can access the following: campus intranet, computer help desk, free student e-mail accounts, online (class) grades, online (class) registration, online (class) schedules. Campuswide network is available. 100% of college-owned or -operated housing units are wired for high-speed Internet access.
Library: Columbia College Chicago Library. *Books:* 295,362 (physical), 61,291 (digital/electronic); *Serial titles:* 553 (physical); *Databases:* 180. Students can reserve study rooms.

STUDENT LIFE
Housing options: coed, special housing for students with disabilities. Campus housing is university owned and leased by the school.

Activities and organizations: drama/theater group, student-run newspaper, radio and television station, choral group, Black Student Union, Columbia Pride, Muggles Association of Columbia, Improv Club, Student Athletics Association.

Athletics *Intercollegiate sports:* basketball M(c)/W(c). *Intramural sports:* soccer M(c)/W(c), volleyball M(c)/W(c).

Campus security: 24-hour emergency response devices and patrols, late-night transport/escort service, controlled dormitory access.

Student services: health clinic, personal/psychological counseling, veterans affairs office.

COSTS & FINANCIAL AID
Costs (2019–20) *Tuition:* $26,610 full-time, $919 per credit hour part-time.
Financial Aid Of all full-time matriculated undergraduates who enrolled in 2017, 5,356 applied for aid, 4,244 were judged to have need, 1,262 had their need fully met. 190 Federal Work-Study jobs (averaging $3900). In 2017, 55 non-need-based awards were made. *Average percent of need met:* 50. *Average financial aid package:* $14,142. *Average need-based loan:* $4265. *Average need-based gift aid:* $10,976. *Average non-need-based aid:* $18,096. *Financial aid deadline:* 6/30.

APPLYING
Options: electronic application, deferred entrance.
Application fee: $50.
Required: high school transcript. *Recommended:* minimum 2.0 GPA, Work samples aren't required for admission, but we do invite you to upload any creative work you feel strengthens your application. Portfolios may also be submitted for scholarship and award consideration. Guidelines for portfolio submission by field of study can be found on our website..
Application deadlines: 8/15 (freshmen), rolling (transfers).
Notification: continuous until 11/1 (freshmen), continuous (transfers).

CONTACT
Derek Brinkley, Senior Director of Admissions and Recruitment, Columbia College Chicago, 600 South Michigan Avenue, Chicago, IL 60605-1996. *Phone:* 312-369-7493. *E-mail:* dbrinkley@colum.edu.

Concordia University Chicago
River Forest, Illinois
http://www.cuchicago.edu/
- **Independent** comprehensive, founded 1864, affiliated with Lutheran Church–Missouri Synod, part of Concordia University System
- **Suburban** 40-acre campus with easy access to Chicago
- **Coed** 1,477 undergraduate students, 92% full-time, 59% women, 41% men
- **Moderately difficult** entrance level, 76% of applicants were admitted

UNDERGRAD STUDENTS
1,366 full-time, 111 part-time. 27% are from out of state; 13% Black or African American, non-Hispanic/Latino; 32% Hispanic/Latino; 2% Asian, non-Hispanic/Latino; 0.2% Native Hawaiian or other Pacific Islander, non-Hispanic/Latino; 0.1% American Indian or Alaska Native, non-Hispanic/Latino; 3% Two or more races, non-Hispanic/Latino; 1% Race/ethnicity unknown; 3% international; 9% transferred in; 38% live on campus.

Freshmen:
Admission: 5,024 applied, 3,818 admitted, 394 enrolled. *Average high school GPA:* 3.0. *Test scores:* SAT evidence-based reading and writing scores over 500: 73%; SAT math scores over 500: 75%; ACT scores over 18: 94%; SAT evidence-based reading and writing scores over 600: 24%; SAT math scores over 600: 19%; ACT scores over 24: 35%; SAT evidence-based reading and writing scores over 700: 3%; SAT math scores over 700: 2%; ACT scores over 30: 8%.

Retention: 73% of full-time freshmen returned.

FACULTY
Total: 529, 36% full-time, 58% with terminal degrees.
Student/faculty ratio: 10:1.

ACADEMICS
Calendar: semesters. *Degrees:* certificates, associate, bachelor's, master's, doctoral, and post-master's certificates.

Special study options: accelerated degree program, adult/continuing education programs, distance learning, double majors, honors programs, independent study, internships, part-time degree program, student-designed majors, study abroad.

Computers: Students can access the following: campus intranet, computer help desk, free student e-mail accounts, online (class) grades, online (class) registration, online (class) schedules. Campuswide network is available. 100% of college-owned or -operated housing units are wired for high-speed Internet access. Wireless service is available via entire campus.
Library: Klinck Memorial Library. *Books:* 160,000 (physical); *Databases:* 80. Weekly public service hours: 89; students can reserve study rooms.

STUDENT LIFE
Housing options: coed. Campus housing is university owned. Freshman campus housing is guaranteed.

Activities and organizations: drama/theater group, student-run newspaper, radio and television station, choral group, Campus Ministry, College Life, Student Government Association, Campus Activities Board, Art·Club.

Athletics Member NCAA. All Division III. *Intercollegiate sports:* basketball M/W, cheerleading W, cross-country running M/W, football M, lacrosse M/W, soccer M/W, tennis M/W, track and field M/W, volleyball W. *Intramural sports:* baseball M(c), basketball M(c)/W(c), soccer M(c)/W(c), softball W(c), ultimate Frisbee M(c)/W(c), volleyball M(c)/W(c).

Campus security: 24-hour emergency response devices and patrols, student patrols, late-night transport/escort service, controlled dormitory access, emergency call boxes.

Student services: health clinic, personal/psychological counseling.

COSTS & FINANCIAL AID

Costs (2019–20) *Comprehensive fee:* $42,876 includes full-time tuition ($31,926), mandatory fees ($954), and room and board ($9996). Part-time tuition: $956 per credit hour. *College room only:* $6280.

Financial Aid Of all full-time matriculated undergraduates who enrolled in 2017, 1,193 applied for aid, 1,113 were judged to have need, 152 had their need fully met. In 2017, 160 non-need-based awards were made. *Average percent of need met:* 76. *Average financial aid package:* $23,201. *Average need-based loan:* $4138. *Average need-based gift aid:* $19,232. *Average non-need-based aid:* $14,830. *Average indebtedness upon graduation:* $28,280. *Financial aid deadline:* 6/1.

APPLYING

Standardized Tests *Required:* SAT or ACT (for admission).

Options: electronic application, early admission, deferred entrance.

Required: high school transcript, minimum 2.0 GPA, 1 letter of recommendation, general college preparatory program for degree seeking students. *Required for some:* essay or personal statement, interview.

Application deadlines: rolling (freshmen), rolling (transfers).

CONTACT

Ms. Gwen Kanelos, Director of Admission, Concordia University Chicago, 7400 Augusta Street, River Forest, IL 60305. *Phone:* 708-209-3101. *Toll-free phone:* 800-285-2668. *Fax:* 708-209-3473. *E-mail:* gwen.kanelos@cuchicago.edu.

DePaul University

Chicago, Illinois

http://www.depaul.edu/

- **Independent Roman Catholic** university, founded 1898
- **Urban** 38-acre campus with easy access to Chicago
- **Endowment** $593.4 million
- **Coed** 14,507 undergraduate students, 88% full-time, 53% women, 47% men
- **Moderately difficult** entrance level, 68% of applicants were admitted

UNDERGRAD STUDENTS

12,795 full-time, 1,712 part-time. Students come from 51 states and territories; 113 other countries; 25% are from out of state; 8% Black or African American, non-Hispanic/Latino; 19% Hispanic/Latino; 10% Asian, non-Hispanic/Latino; 0.2% Native Hawaiian or other Pacific Islander, non-Hispanic/Latino; 0.2% American Indian or Alaska Native, non-Hispanic/Latino; 5% Two or more races, non-Hispanic/Latino; 3% Race/ethnicity unknown; 3% international; 9% transferred in; 19% live on campus.

Freshmen:

Admission: 26,169 applied, 17,673 admitted, 2,575 enrolled. *Average high school GPA:* 3.7. *Test scores:* SAT evidence-based reading and writing scores over 500: 92%; SAT math scores over 500: 89%; SAT evidence-based reading and writing scores over 600: 53%; SAT math scores over 600: 43%; SAT evidence-based reading and writing scores over 700: 9%; SAT math scores over 700: 9%.

Retention: 86% of full-time freshmen returned.

FACULTY

Total: 1,850, 49% full-time, 58% with terminal degrees.

Student/faculty ratio: 16:1.

ACADEMICS

Calendar: quarters College of Law on semester system. *Degrees:* certificates, bachelor's, master's, doctoral, post-master's, and postbachelor's certificates.

ROTC: Army (b).

Unusual degree programs: 3-2 engineering with Chemical Engineering combined degree program with the Illinois Institute of Technology (IIT); Visit DePaul's website for combined degree programs: https://www.depaul.edu/academics/undergraduate/Pages/combined-degrees.aspx.

Computers: 1,500 computers/terminals are available on campus for general student use. Students can access the following: campus intranet, computer help desk, free student e-mail accounts, online (class) grades, online (class) registration, online (class) schedules, tuition payments, degree progress, financial aid, transcript requests, housing services, student employment information. Campuswide network is available. 100% of college-owned or -operated housing units are wired for high-speed Internet access. Wireless service is available via entire campus.

Library: John T. Richardson Library plus 2 others. *Books:* 572,086 (physical), 550,015 (digital/electronic); *Serial titles:* 20,100 (physical), 79,967 (digital/electronic). Students can reserve study rooms.

STUDENT LIFE

Housing options: coed, special housing for students with disabilities. Campus housing is university owned, leased by the school and is provided by a third party. Freshman campus housing is guaranteed.

Activities and organizations: drama/theater group, student-run newspaper, radio station, choral group, DePaul Community Service Association (DCSA), Black Student Union, DemonTHON, Panhellenic Council, DePaul Activities Board, national fraternities, national sororities.

Athletics Member NCAA. All Division I. *Intercollegiate sports:* basketball M(s)/W(s), cross-country running M(s)/W(s), golf M(s), soccer M(s)/W(s), softball W(s), tennis M(s)/W(s), track and field M(s)/W(s), volleyball W(s). *Intramural sports:* badminton M(c)/W(c), baseball M(c)/W(c), basketball M/W(c), crew M(c)/W(c), fencing M(c)/W(c), football M/W, golf M(c)/W(c), ice hockey M(c)/W(c), lacrosse M(c)/W(c), racquetball M/W, rock climbing M(c)/W(c), rowing M(c)/W(c), rugby M(c)/W(c), sailing M(c)/W(c), skiing (downhill) M(c)/W(c), soccer M(c)/W(c), softball M/W, swimming and diving M(c)/W(c), table tennis M/W, tennis M(c)/W(c), ultimate Frisbee M(c)/W(c), volleyball M(c)/W(c), water polo M(c)/W(c).

Campus security: 24-hour emergency response devices and patrols, late-night transport/escort service, controlled dormitory access.

Student services: health clinic, personal/psychological counseling, women's center, legal services, veterans affairs office.

COSTS & FINANCIAL AID

Costs (2018–19) *Comprehensive fee:* $54,210 includes full-time tuition ($39,369), mandatory fees ($606), and room and board ($14,235). Full-time tuition and fees vary according to course load, program, and student level. Part-time tuition: $630 per credit hour. Part-time tuition and fees vary according to course load, program, and student level. *College room only:* $10,224. Room and board charges vary according to board plan, housing facility, and location. *Payment plans:* installment, deferred payment. *Waivers:* employees or children of employees.

Financial Aid Of all full-time matriculated undergraduates who enrolled in 2017, 10,255 applied for aid, 9,072 were judged to have need, 762 had their need fully met. 606 Federal Work-Study jobs (averaging $4170). In 2017, 2401 non-need-based awards were made. *Average percent of need met:* 64. *Average financial aid package:* $24,524. *Average need-based loan:* $4307. *Average need-based gift aid:* $20,719. *Average non-need-based aid:* $13,937. *Average indebtedness upon graduation:* $29,542.

APPLYING

Standardized Tests *Recommended:* SAT or ACT (for admission).

Options: electronic application, early action, deferred entrance.

Required: high school transcript, minimum 2.3 GPA, 1 letter of recommendation. *Required for some:* minimum 3.0 GPA, interview, Audition/Interviews required for the School of Music and Theatre School applicants. Animation majors must submit portfolio and creative statement.. *Recommended:* essay or personal statement, minimum 2.8 GPA.

Application deadlines: 2/1 (freshmen), rolling (transfers), 11/15 (early action).

Notification: 3/15 (freshmen), continuous (transfers), 1/15 (early action).

CONTACT

Carlene Klaas, Dean of Undergraduate Admission, DePaul University, 1 East Jackson Boulevard, Suite 900, Chicago, IL 60604. *Phone:* 312-362-8300. *Toll-free phone:* 800-4DE-PAUL. *E-mail:* admission@depaul.edu.

DeVry University–Addison Campus

Addison, Illinois

http://www.devry.edu/

CONTACT

Admissions Office, DeVry University–Addison Campus, 1221 North Swift Road, Addison, IL 60101-6106. *Phone:* 630-953-1300. *Toll-free phone:* 866-338-7934.

DeVry University–Chicago Campus

Chicago, Illinois
http://www.devry.edu/

CONTACT
DeVry University–Chicago Campus, 3300 North Campbell Avenue, Chicago, IL 60618. *Phone:* 773-929-8500. *Toll-free phone:* 866-338-7934.

DeVry University Online

Addison, Illinois
http://www.devry.edu/

CONTACT
DeVry University Online, 1221 North Swift Road, Addison, IL 60101. *Phone:* 877-496-9050. *Toll-free phone:* 866-338-7934.

DeVry University–Tinley Park Campus

Tinley Park, Illinois
http://www.devry.edu/

CONTACT
Admissions Office, DeVry University–Tinley Park Campus, 18624 West Creek Drive, Tinley Park, IL 60477 . *Phone:* 708-342-3300. *Toll-free phone:* 866-338-7934.

Dominican University

River Forest, Illinois
http://www.dom.edu/

- **Independent Roman Catholic** comprehensive, founded 1901
- **Suburban** 30-acre campus with easy access to Chicago
- **Endowment** $35.3 million
- **Coed** 2,106 undergraduate students, 94% full-time, 68% women, 32% men
- **Moderately difficult** entrance level, 64% of applicants were admitted

UNDERGRAD STUDENTS
1,974 full-time, 132 part-time. Students come from 30 states and territories; 9 other countries; 7% are from out of state; 6% Black or African American, non-Hispanic/Latino; 79% Hispanic/Latino; 3% Asian, non-Hispanic/Latino; 0.1% Native Hawaiian or other Pacific Islander, non-Hispanic/Latino; 0.3% American Indian or Alaska Native, non-Hispanic/Latino; 1% Two or more races, non-Hispanic/Latino; 2% Race/ethnicity unknown; 2% international; 8% transferred in; 26% live on campus.

Freshmen:
Admission: 4,813 applied, 3,070 admitted, 447 enrolled. *Average high school GPA:* 3.7. *Test scores:* SAT evidence-based reading and writing scores over 500: 70%; SAT math scores over 500: 62%; ACT scores over 18: 89%; SAT evidence-based reading and writing scores over 600: 19%; SAT math scores over 600: 12%; ACT scores over 24: 30%; SAT evidence-based reading and writing scores over 700: 1%; SAT math scores over 700: 2%; ACT scores over 30: 2%.

Retention: 83% of full-time freshmen returned.

FACULTY
Total: 394, 40% full-time, 63% with terminal degrees.
Student/faculty ratio: 11:1.

ACADEMICS
Calendar: semesters. *Degrees:* bachelor's, master's, doctoral, post-master's, and postbachelor's certificates.

Special study options: academic remediation for entering students, accelerated degree program, adult/continuing education programs, advanced placement credit, distance learning, double majors, English as a second language, honors programs, independent study, internships, off-campus study, part-time degree program, services for LD students, student-designed majors, study abroad, summer session for credit.

Unusual degree programs: 3-2 business administration; engineering with Illinois Institute of Technology; nursing; social work; library science, pharmacy with Midwestern University.

Computers: 550 computers/terminals and 4,000 ports are available on campus for general student use. Students can access the following: campus intranet, computer help desk, free student e-mail accounts, online (class) grades, online (class) registration, online (class) schedules. Campuswide network is available. 100% of college-owned or -operated housing units are wired for high-speed Internet access. Wireless service is available via entire campus.
Library: Rebecca Crown Library. *Books:* 247,967 (physical), 9,389 (digital/electronic); *Serial titles:* 280 (physical), 53,047 (digital/electronic); *Databases:* 114. Weekly public service hours: 100; students can reserve study rooms.

STUDENT LIFE
Housing options: coed, women-only, special housing for students with disabilities. Campus housing is university owned and leased by the school. Freshman applicants given priority for college housing.

Activities and organizations: drama/theater group, student-run newspaper, choral group, Polish Club, Commuter Student Association, Nutrition Club, Organization of Latin American Students, Fashion Club.

Athletics Member NCAA. All Division III. *Intercollegiate sports:* baseball M, basketball M/W, cross-country running M/W, golf M, soccer M/W, softball W, tennis M/W, volleyball M/W. *Intramural sports:* basketball M/W, bowling M/W, football M/W, racquetball M/W, soccer M/W, ultimate Frisbee M/W, volleyball M/W.

Campus security: 24-hour emergency response devices and patrols, student patrols, late-night transport/escort service, controlled dormitory access.

Student services: health clinic, personal/psychological counseling.

COSTS & FINANCIAL AID
Costs (2019–20) *One-time required fee:* $150. *Comprehensive fee:* $44,969 includes full-time tuition ($33,950), mandatory fees ($470), and room and board ($10,549). Part-time tuition: $1133 per credit hour. *Required fees:* $90 per term part-time.

Financial Aid Of all full-time matriculated undergraduates who enrolled in 2018, 1,680 applied for aid, 1,605 were judged to have need, 144 had their need fully met. In 2018, 278 non-need-based awards were made. *Average percent of need met:* 73. *Average financial aid package:* $26,129. *Average need-based loan:* $4392. *Average need-based gift aid:* $21,905. *Average non-need-based aid:* $18,782. *Average indebtedness upon graduation:* $28,387.

APPLYING
Standardized Tests *Required:* SAT or ACT (for admission).

Options: electronic application, deferred entrance.

Application fee: $25.

Required: high school transcript. *Required for some:* interview. *Recommended:* essay or personal statement, minimum 2.5 GPA.

Application deadlines: rolling (freshmen), rolling (out-of-state freshmen), rolling (transfers).

Notification: continuous (freshmen), continuous (out-of-state freshmen), continuous (transfers).

CONTACT
Mr. Glenn Hamilton, Assistant Vice President, Enrollment Management, Dominican University, 7900 West Division Street, River Forest, IL 60305. *Phone:* 708-524-6800. *Toll-free phone:* 800-828-8475. *Fax:* 708-524-6864. *E-mail:* domadmis@dom.edu.

Eastern Illinois University

Charleston, Illinois
http://www.eiu.edu/

- **State-supported** comprehensive, founded 1895
- **Small-town** 320-acre campus
- **Endowment** $88.6 million
- **Coed** 6,012 undergraduate students, 68% full-time, 57% women, 43% men
- **Moderately difficult** entrance level, 47% of applicants were admitted

UNDERGRAD STUDENTS
4,091 full-time, 1,921 part-time. Students come from 34 states and territories; 38 other countries; 7% are from out of state; 17% Black or African American, non-Hispanic/Latino; 12% Hispanic/Latino; 2% Asian,

non-Hispanic/Latino; 0.1% Native Hawaiian or other Pacific Islander, non-Hispanic/Latino; 0.2% American Indian or Alaska Native, non-Hispanic/Latino; 2% Two or more races, non-Hispanic/Latino; 3% Race/ethnicity unknown; 2% international; 32% transferred in; 30% live on campus.

Freshmen:
Admission: 8,420 applied, 3,947 admitted, 798 enrolled. *Average high school GPA:* 3.2. *Test scores:* SAT evidence-based reading and writing scores over 500: 61%; SAT math scores over 500: 52%; ACT scores over 18: 78%; SAT evidence-based reading and writing scores over 600: 19%; SAT math scores over 600: 11%; ACT scores over 24: 22%; SAT evidence-based reading and writing scores over 700: 2%; SAT math scores over 700: 2%; ACT scores over 30: 5%.
Retention: 70% of full-time freshmen returned.

FACULTY
Total: 506, 75% full-time, 55% with terminal degrees.
Student/faculty ratio: 14:1.

ACADEMICS
Calendar: semesters. *Degrees:* bachelor's, master's, post-master's, and postbachelor's certificates.
Special study options: academic remediation for entering students, accelerated degree program, adult/continuing education programs, advanced placement credit, distance learning, double majors, English as a second language, freshman honors college, honors programs, independent study, internships, off-campus study, part-time degree program, services for LD students, study abroad, summer session for credit. *ROTC:* Army (b).
Unusual degree programs: 3-2 engineering with University of Illinois at Urbana–Champaign, Southern Illinois University at Carbondale.
Computers: 900 computers/terminals and 10,000 ports are available on campus for general student use. Students can access the following: computer help desk, free student e-mail accounts, online (class) grades, online (class) registration, online (class) schedules. Campuswide network is available. 100% of college-owned or -operated housing units are wired for high-speed Internet access. Wireless service is available via classrooms, computer centers, computer labs, dorm rooms, learning centers, libraries, student centers.
Library: Booth Library. *Books:* 1.0 million (physical), 1.3 million (digital/electronic); *Serial titles:* 55 (physical), 55,520 (digital/electronic); *Databases:* 217. Weekly public service hours: 98.

STUDENT LIFE
Housing options: on-campus residence required for freshman year; coed, men-only, women-only. Campus housing is university owned. Freshman campus housing is guaranteed.
Activities and organizations: drama/theater group, student-run newspaper, radio and television station, choral group, marching band, Greek Organizations, Religious Student Organizations, Intramural Sports, University Board, Civic Engagement & Volunteerism, national fraternities, national sororities.
Athletics Member NCAA. All Division I except football (Division I-AA). *Intercollegiate sports:* baseball M(s), basketball M(s)/W(s), cross-country running M(s)/W(s), golf M(s)/W(s), ice hockey M(c), racquetball M(c)/W(c), soccer M(s)/W(s), softball W(s), swimming and diving M(s)/W(s), tennis M(s)/W(s), track and field M(s)/W(s), ultimate Frisbee M(c)/W(c), volleyball W(s). *Intramural sports:* badminton M/W, baseball M(c), basketball M/W, bowling M/W, equestrian sports M(c)/W(c), racquetball M/W, rugby M(c), soccer M/W, softball M/W, table tennis M/W, tennis M/W, volleyball M/W.
Campus security: 24-hour emergency response devices and patrols, student patrols, controlled dormitory access.
Student services: health clinic, personal/psychological counseling, women's center, legal services, veterans affairs office.

COSTS & FINANCIAL AID
Costs (2018–19) *Tuition:* state resident $8880 full-time, $296 per credit hour part-time; nonresident $11,100 full-time, $370 per credit hour part-time. Full-time tuition and fees vary according to course load and student level. Part-time tuition and fees vary according to course load and student level. No tuition increase for student's term of enrollment. *Required fees:* $2923 full-time, $111 per credit hour part-time. *Room and board:* $9882. Room and board charges vary according to board plan and housing

facility. *Payment plan:* installment. *Waivers:* senior citizens and employees or children of employees.
Financial Aid Of all full-time matriculated undergraduates who enrolled in 2018, 3,558 applied for aid, 2,992 were judged to have need, 220 had their need fully met. 171 Federal Work-Study jobs (averaging $808). 1,139 state and other part-time jobs (averaging $1138). In 2018, 476 non-need-based awards were made. *Average percent of need met:* 56. *Average financial aid package:* $13,272. *Average need-based loan:* $4205. *Average need-based gift aid:* $8835. *Average non-need-based aid:* $3942. *Average indebtedness upon graduation:* $28,213.

APPLYING
Standardized Tests *Required:* SAT or ACT (for admission).
Options: electronic application, deferred entrance.
Application fee: $30.
Required: high school transcript, minimum 2.3 GPA. *Required for some:* essay or personal statement, 1 letter of recommendation, audition for music program.
Application deadlines: rolling (freshmen), rolling (transfers).
Notification: continuous (freshmen), continuous (transfers).

CONTACT
Denise Lee, Interim Associate Director of Admissions, Eastern Illinois University, 600 Lincoln Avenue, Charleston, IL 61920. *Phone:* 217-581-7975. *Toll-free phone:* 877-581-2348. *Fax:* 217-581-7060. *E-mail:* dalee@eiu.edu.

East-West University
Chicago, Illinois
http://www.eastwest.edu/

CONTACT
Bryan Lambert, Director of Enrollment, East-West University, 816 South Michigan Avenue, Chicago, IL 60605-2103. *Phone:* 312-939-0112 Ext. 1701.

★ Elmhurst College
Elmhurst, Illinois
http://www.elmhurst.edu/

- **Independent** comprehensive, founded 1871, affiliated with United Church of Christ
- **Suburban** 38-acre campus with easy access to Chicago
- **Endowment** $94.8 million
- **Coed**
- **Moderately difficult** entrance level

FACULTY
Student/faculty ratio: 14:1.

ACADEMICS
Calendar: 4-1-4. *Degrees:* bachelor's and master's.
Library: Buehler Library.

STUDENT LIFE
Housing options: coed. Campus housing is university owned, leased by the school and is provided by a third party. Freshman applicants given priority for college housing.
Activities and organizations: drama/theater group, student-run newspaper, radio station, choral group, Programming Board and Student Government, theater and music groups, Black Student Union, residence life groups, Hablamos, national fraternities, national sororities.
Athletics Member NCAA. All Division III except golf (Division II).
Campus security: 24-hour emergency response devices and patrols, late-night transport/escort service, controlled dormitory access.
Student services: health clinic, personal/psychological counseling.

COSTS & FINANCIAL AID
Costs (2018–19) *Comprehensive fee:* $47,421 includes full-time tuition ($36,755), mandatory fees ($300), and room and board ($10,366). Part-time tuition: $1045 per semester hour. Part-time tuition and fees vary according to course load. *College room only:* $6244. Room and board charges vary according to board plan and housing facility.

Financial Aid Of all full-time matriculated undergraduates who enrolled in 2018, 2,313 applied for aid, 2,144 were judged to have need, 370 had their need fully met. In 2018, 203 non-need-based awards were made. *Average percent of need met:* 82. *Average financial aid package:* $28,465. *Average need-based loan:* $4220. *Average need-based gift aid:* $23,108. *Average non-need-based aid:* $14,863. *Average indebtedness upon graduation:* $29,432.

APPLYING

Standardized Tests *Required:* SAT or ACT (for admission).

Options: electronic application, early action, deferred entrance.

Required: high school transcript. *Required for some:* essay or personal statement, interview. *Recommended:* essay or personal statement, interview.

CONTACT

Mrs. Stephanie Levenson, Executive Director of Admission, Elmhurst College, Admission Office, 190 South Prospect Avenue, Elmhurst, IL 60126-3296. *Phone:* 630-617-3400. *Toll-free phone:* 800-697-1871. *Fax:* 630-617-5501. *E-mail:* admit@elmhurst.edu.

See below for display ad and page 1006 for the College Close-Up.

Eureka College

Eureka, Illinois

http://www.eureka.edu/

CONTACT

Mr. Mike Murtagh, Vice President of Institutional Advancement, Eureka College, 300 East College Avenue, Eureka, IL 61530. *Phone:* 309-467-6315. *Toll-free phone:* 888-4-EUREKA. *E-mail:* mmurtagh@eureka.edu.

Governors State University

University Park, Illinois

http://www.govst.edu/

- **State-supported** university, founded 1969
- **Suburban** 742-acre campus with easy access to Chicago
- **Endowment** $2.1 million
- **Coed**
- **Moderately difficult** entrance level

ACADEMICS

Calendar: semesters. *Degrees:* certificates, bachelor's, master's, doctoral, post-master's, and postbachelor's certificates.
Library: University Library. *Books:* 284,377 (physical), 339,176 (digital/electronic); *Serial titles:* 2,438 (physical), 11,484 (digital/electronic); *Databases:* 176. Weekly public service hours: 75; students can reserve study rooms.

STUDENT LIFE

Housing options: coed. Campus housing is university owned.

Activities and organizations: student-run newspaper, choral group.

Athletics Member NAIA.

Campus security: 24-hour emergency response devices and patrols, late-night transport/escort service, controlled dormitory access.

Student services: health clinic, personal/psychological counseling, veterans affairs office.

COSTS & FINANCIAL AID

Costs (2018–19) *Tuition:* state resident $9390 full-time, $313 per credit hour part-time; nonresident $18,780 full-time, $626 per credit hour part-time. Full-time tuition and fees vary according to course load and reciprocity agreements. Part-time tuition and fees vary according to course load and reciprocity agreements. No tuition increase for student's term of enrollment. *Required fees:* $2806 full-time, $91 per credit hour part-time, $38 per term part-time. *Room and board:* $9945; room only: $7945. Room and board charges vary according to board plan and housing facility.

Financial Aid Of all full-time matriculated undergraduates who enrolled in 2017, 1,652 applied for aid, 1,559 were judged to have need, 676 had their need fully met. 112 Federal Work-Study jobs (averaging $2178). In 2017, 21 non-need-based awards were made. *Average percent of need met:* 79. *Average financial aid package:* $11,439. *Average need-based loan:* $3335. *Average need-based gift aid:* $9065. *Average non-need-based aid:* $9016. *Financial aid deadline:* 10/1.

APPLYING
Standardized Tests *Required:* SAT and SAT Subject Tests or ACT (for admission).

Options: electronic application, early admission, early decision, deferred entrance.

Application fee: $25.

Required: high school transcript, minimum 2.8 GPA. *Required for some:* essay or personal statement, interview.

CONTACT
Mr. Paul McGuinness, Director, Admissions, Governors State University, One University Parkway, University Park, IL 60484. *Phone:* 708-235-7308 Ext. 7308. *Toll-free phone:* 800-478-8478. *E-mail:* pmcguinness@govst.edu.

Greenville University
Greenville, Illinois
http://www.greenville.edu/

- **Independent Free Methodist** comprehensive, founded 1892
- **Small-town** 50-acre campus with easy access to St. Louis
- **Endowment** $16.3 million
- **Coed** 964 undergraduate students, 90% full-time, 47% women, 53% men
- **Moderately difficult** entrance level, 48% of applicants were admitted

UNDERGRAD STUDENTS
872 full-time, 92 part-time. Students come from 37 states and territories; 19 other countries; 33% are from out of state; 15% Black or African American, non-Hispanic/Latino; 6% Hispanic/Latino; 0.5% Asian, non-Hispanic/Latino; 2% Two or more races, non-Hispanic/Latino; 4% Race/ethnicity unknown; 6% international; 9% transferred in; 69% live on campus.

Freshmen:
Admission: 2,245 applied, 1,069 admitted, 221 enrolled. *Test scores:* SAT evidence-based reading and writing scores over 500: 61%; SAT math scores over 500: 59%; ACT scores over 18: 77%; SAT evidence-based reading and writing scores over 600: 25%; SAT math scores over 600: 19%; ACT scores over 24: 25%; SAT evidence-based reading and writing scores over 700: 1%; SAT math scores over 700: 1%; ACT scores over 30: 4%.

Retention: 70% of full-time freshmen returned.

FACULTY
Total: 165, 35% full-time, 39% with terminal degrees.
Student/faculty ratio: 13:1.

ACADEMICS
Calendar: 4-1-4. *Degrees:* bachelor's and master's.

Special study options: academic remediation for entering students, accelerated degree program, adult/continuing education programs, advanced placement credit, cooperative education, distance learning, double majors, external degree program, honors programs, independent study, internships, off-campus study, part-time degree program, student-designed majors, study abroad, summer session for credit.

Unusual degree programs: 3-2 engineering with University of Illinois at Urbana–Champaign, Washington University in St. Louis; nursing with St. John's College, Southern Illinois University Edwardsville, Mennonite College of Nursing; chiropractic with Logan College of Chiropractic.

Computers: 50 computers/terminals are available on campus for general student use. Students can access the following: campus intranet, computer help desk, free student e-mail accounts, online (class) grades, online (class) registration, online (class) schedules. Campuswide network is available. 100% of college-owned or -operated housing units are wired for high-speed Internet access. Wireless service is available via entire campus.

Library: Ruby E. Dare Library. *Books:* 131,047 (physical), 7,408 (digital/electronic). Students can reserve study rooms.

STUDENT LIFE
Housing options: on-campus residence required through senior year; men-only, women-only. Campus housing is university owned. Freshman campus housing is guaranteed.

Activities and organizations: drama/theater group, student-run newspaper, radio station, choral group, marching band, Campus Activity Board, Panther Corps Marching Band, Greenville College Student Association, Habitat for Humanity, Music and Entertainment Industry Student Association.

Athletics Member NCAA, NCCAA. All NCAA Division III. *Intercollegiate sports:* baseball M, basketball M/W, cross-country running M/W, football M, golf M/W, soccer M/W, softball W, tennis M/W, track and field M/W, volleyball M/W. *Intramural sports:* basketball M/W, cheerleading W, football M/W, softball M/W, ultimate Frisbee M/W, volleyball M/W.

Campus security: 24-hour emergency response devices and patrols, late-night transport/escort service, controlled dormitory access.

Student services: personal/psychological counseling.

COSTS & FINANCIAL AID
Costs (2019–20) *Comprehensive fee:* $37,502 includes full-time tuition ($27,580), mandatory fees ($374), and room and board ($9548). Part-time tuition: $434 per credit hour. *College room only:* $4698.

Financial Aid Of all full-time matriculated undergraduates who enrolled in 2018, 675 applied for aid, 630 were judged to have need, 86 had their need fully met. 122 Federal Work-Study jobs (averaging $1586). In 2018, 142 non-need-based awards were made. *Average percent of need met:* 74. *Average financial aid package:* $23,812. *Average need-based loan:* $4083. *Average need-based gift aid:* $19,979. *Average non-need-based aid:* $14,183. *Average indebtedness upon graduation:* $32,956.

APPLYING
Standardized Tests *Required:* SAT or ACT (for admission).

Options: electronic application, early admission, deferred entrance.

Required: essay or personal statement, high school transcript, minimum 2.3 GPA, agreement to lifestyle statement. *Required for some:* interview.

Application deadlines: rolling (freshmen), rolling (transfers).

Notification: continuous (freshmen), continuous (transfers).

CONTACT
Mr. Colin McLaughlin, Director of Traditional Admissions, Greenville University, 315 East College Avenue, Greenville, IL 62246. *Phone:* 618-664-7100. *Toll-free phone:* 800-345-4440. *Fax:* 618-664-9841. *E-mail:* admissions@greenville.edu.

Hebrew Theological College
Skokie, Illinois
http://www.htc.edu/

CONTACT
Rabbi Berish Cardash, Hebrew Theological College, 7135 North Carpenter Road, Skokie, IL 60077-3263. *Phone:* 847-982-2500.

Illinois College
Jacksonville, Illinois
http://www.ic.edu/

- **Independent interdenominational** comprehensive, founded 1829
- **Small-town** 62-acre campus with easy access to St. Louis
- **Coed** 983 undergraduate students, 99% full-time, 51% women, 49% men
- **Moderately difficult** entrance level, 76% of applicants were admitted

UNDERGRAD STUDENTS
976 full-time, 7 part-time. 12% are from out of state; 10% Black or African American, non-Hispanic/Latino; 7% Hispanic/Latino; 0.5% Asian, non-Hispanic/Latino; 0.1% Native Hawaiian or other Pacific Islander, non-Hispanic/Latino; 0.3% American Indian or Alaska Native, non-Hispanic/Latino; 4% Two or more races, non-Hispanic/Latino; 0.1% Race/ethnicity unknown; 6% international; 3% transferred in; 84% live on campus.

Freshmen:

Admission: 3,378 applied, 2,565 admitted, 294 enrolled. *Average high school GPA:* 3.5. *Test scores:* SAT evidence-based reading and writing scores over 500: 70%; SAT math scores over 500: 76%; ACT scores over 18: 93%; SAT evidence-based reading and writing scores over 600: 24%; SAT math scores over 600: 16%; ACT scores over 24: 41%; SAT evidence-based reading and writing scores over 700: 2%; SAT math scores over 700: 2%; ACT scores over 30: 5%.

Retention: 77% of full-time freshmen returned.

FACULTY

Total: 90, 73% full-time, 66% with terminal degrees.

Student/faculty ratio: 12:1.

ACADEMICS

Calendar: semesters. *Degrees:* bachelor's and master's.

Computers: Students can access the following: computer help desk, free student e-mail accounts, online (class) grades, online (class) registration, online (class) schedules. Campuswide network is available. Wireless service is available via entire campus.

Library: Schewe Library.

STUDENT LIFE

Housing options: on-campus residence required through junior year; coed, men-only, women-only. Campus housing is university owned. Freshman campus housing is guaranteed.

Athletics Member NCAA. All Division III except golf (Division II). *Intercollegiate sports:* baseball M, cheerleading W, cross-country running M/W, football M, golf M/W, soccer M/W, softball W, swimming and diving M/W, tennis M/W, track and field M/W, volleyball W. *Intramural sports:* badminton M/W, basketball M/W, fencing M, field hockey W, football M, racquetball M/W, softball M/W, swimming and diving M/W, volleyball M/W, water polo M/W, weight lifting M/W.

Campus security: 24-hour emergency response devices and patrols, late-night transport/escort service, controlled dormitory access.

COSTS & FINANCIAL AID

Costs (2018–19) *Comprehensive fee:* $42,370 includes full-time tuition ($32,540), mandatory fees ($550), and room and board ($9280). Part-time tuition: $1015 per credit hour. Part-time tuition and fees vary according to course load. *Required fees:* $138 per term part-time. *Room and board:* Room and board charges vary according to board plan and housing facility. *Payment plan:* installment. *Waivers:* employees or children of employees.

Financial Aid Of all full-time matriculated undergraduates who enrolled in 2017, 851 applied for aid, 795 were judged to have need, 205 had their need fully met. In 2017, 147 non-need-based awards were made. *Average percent of need met:* 88. *Average financial aid package:* $28,676. *Average need-based loan:* $4756. *Average need-based gift aid:* $23,775. *Average non-need-based aid:* $18,733. *Average indebtedness upon graduation:* $32,156.

APPLYING

Options: electronic application, early admission, deferred entrance.

Required: essay or personal statement, high school transcript. *Required for some:* essay or personal statement, 1 letter of recommendation. *Recommended:* minimum 2.5 GPA.

Notification: continuous until 9/1 (freshmen), continuous until 9/1 (out-of-state freshmen), continuous until 9/1 (transfers).

CONTACT

Mr. Rick Bystry, Associate Director of Admission, Illinois College, 1101 West College, Jacksonville, IL 62650. *Phone:* 217-245-3030. *Toll-free phone:* 866-464-5265. *Fax:* 217-245-3034. *E-mail:* admissions@ic.edu.

Illinois Institute of Technology

Chicago, Illinois

http://www.iit.edu/

CONTACT

Ms. Toni Riley, Director, Undergraduate Admissions Office, Illinois Institute of Technology, Office of Undergraduate Admission, Perlstein 101, 10 West 33rd Street, Chicago, IL 60616. *Phone:* 312-567-5239. *Toll-free phone:* 800-448-2329. *E-mail:* admission@iit.edu.

Illinois State University

Normal, Illinois

http://www.illinoisstate.edu/

- **State-supported** university, founded 1857
- **Suburban** 1111-acre campus
- **Endowment** $112.7 million
- **Coed**
- **Minimally difficult** entrance level

FACULTY

Student/faculty ratio: 17:1.

ACADEMICS

Calendar: semesters. *Degrees:* certificates, bachelor's, master's, doctoral, post-master's, and postbachelor's certificates.

Library: Milner Library. *Books:* 1.4 million (physical), 190,817 (digital/electronic); *Serial titles:* 97,570 (digital/electronic); *Databases:* 251. Students can reserve study rooms.

STUDENT LIFE

Housing options: on-campus residence required through sophomore year; coed, women-only, special housing for students with disabilities. Campus housing is university owned. Freshman campus housing is guaranteed.

Activities and organizations: drama/theater group, student-run newspaper, radio and television station, choral group, marching band, national fraternities, national sororities.

Athletics Member NCAA. All Division I except football (Division I-AA).

Campus security: 24-hour emergency response devices and patrols, student patrols, late-night transport/escort service, controlled dormitory access.

Student services: health clinic, personal/psychological counseling, women's center, legal services, veterans affairs office.

COSTS & FINANCIAL AID

Costs (2018–19) *Tuition:* state resident $11,524 full-time, $384 per credit hour part-time; nonresident $23,048 full-time, $768 per credit hour part-time. Full-time tuition and fees vary according to degree level. Part-time tuition and fees vary according to degree level. No tuition increase for student's term of enrollment. *Required fees:* $2992 full-time, $82 per credit hour part-time. *Room and board:* $9850; room only: $5334. Room and board charges vary according to board plan and housing facility.

Financial Aid Of all full-time matriculated undergraduates who enrolled in 2017, 13,602 applied for aid, 10,739 were judged to have need, 1,365 had their need fully met. 476 Federal Work-Study jobs (averaging $1728). In 2017, 913 non-need-based awards were made. *Average percent of need met:* 46. *Average financial aid package:* $11,506. *Average need-based loan:* $4302. *Average need-based gift aid:* $9646. *Average non-need-based aid:* $3398. *Average indebtedness upon graduation:* $30,240.

APPLYING

Standardized Tests *Required:* SAT or ACT (for admission).

Options: electronic application.

Application fee: $50.

Required for some: interview. *Recommended:* essay or personal statement, high school transcript.

CONTACT

Mr. Jeff Mavros, Director of Admissions, Illinois State University, Campus Box 2200, Normal, IL 61790-2200. *Phone:* 309-438-2181. *Toll-free phone:* 800-366-2478. *Fax:* 309-438-3932. *E-mail:* admissions@ilstu.edu.

Illinois Wesleyan University

Bloomington, Illinois

http://www.iwu.edu/

- **Independent** 4-year, founded 1850
- **Suburban** 85-acre campus
- **Endowment** $206.7 million
- **Coed**
- **Very difficult** entrance level

FACULTY

Student/faculty ratio: 10:1.

ACADEMICS

Calendar: 4-4-1. *Degree:* bachelor's.

Library: The Ames Library. *Books:* 193,789 (physical), 35,089 (digital/electronic); *Serial titles:* 2,056 (physical), 80,933 (digital/electronic); *Databases:* 181. Students can reserve study rooms.

STUDENT LIFE

Housing options: on-campus residence required through junior year; coed, special housing for students with disabilities. Campus housing is university owned. Freshman campus housing is guaranteed.

Activities and organizations: drama/theater group, student-run newspaper, radio and television station, choral group, national fraternities, national sororities.

Athletics Member NCAA. All Division III.

Campus security: 24-hour emergency response devices and patrols, late-night transport/escort service, controlled dormitory access, emergency response team.

Student services: health clinic, personal/psychological counseling.

COSTS & FINANCIAL AID

Costs (2018–19) *Comprehensive fee:* $58,620 includes full-time tuition ($47,434), mandatory fees ($202), and room and board ($10,984). Part-time tuition: $1482 per credit hour. *College room only:* $6878. Room and board charges vary according to housing facility.

Financial Aid Of all full-time matriculated undergraduates who enrolled in 2018, 1,386 applied for aid, 1,175 were judged to have need, 213 had their need fully met. In 2018, 496 non-need-based awards were made. *Average percent of need met:* 84. *Average financial aid package:* $36,743. *Average need-based loan:* $5481. *Average need-based gift aid:* $30,077. *Average non-need-based aid:* $21,432. *Average indebtedness upon graduation:* $35,077.

APPLYING

Standardized Tests *Required:* SAT or ACT (for admission).

Options: electronic application, early admission, early action, deferred entrance.

Required: essay or personal statement, high school transcript, minimum 2.0 GPA, 1 letter of recommendation. *Recommended:* minimum 3.0 GPA, 2 letters of recommendation, interview.

CONTACT

Mr. Greg King, Associate Vice President for Enrollment Management, Illinois Wesleyan University, PO Box 2900, Bloomington, IL 61702-2900. *Phone:* 309-556-3031. *Toll-free phone:* 800-332-2498. *Fax:* 309-556-3820. *E-mail:* iwuadmit@iwu.edu.

Judson University

Elgin, Illinois

http://www.judsonu.edu/

- **Independent Baptist** comprehensive, founded 1963
- **Suburban** 90-acre campus with easy access to Chicago
- **Endowment** $11.2 million
- **Coed** 1,034 undergraduate students, 66% full-time, 59% women, 41% men
- **Moderately difficult** entrance level, 75% of applicants were admitted

UNDERGRAD STUDENTS

679 full-time, 355 part-time. Students come from 35 states and territories; 33 other countries; 14% are from out of state; 12% Black or African American, non-Hispanic/Latino; 21% Hispanic/Latino; 2% Asian, non-Hispanic/Latino; 0.3% Native Hawaiian or other Pacific Islander, non-Hispanic/Latino; 2% Two or more races, non-Hispanic/Latino; 10% Race/ethnicity unknown; 5% international; 17% transferred in; 60% live on campus.

Freshmen:
Admission: 512 applied, 385 admitted, 168 enrolled. *Average high school GPA:* 3.4. *Test scores:* SAT evidence-based reading and writing scores over 500: 63%; SAT math scores over 500: 67%; ACT scores over 18: 85%; SAT evidence-based reading and writing scores over 600: 24%; SAT math scores over 600: 22%; ACT scores over 24: 37%; SAT evidence-based reading and writing scores over 700: 3%; SAT math scores over 700: 2%; ACT scores over 30: 6%.

Retention: 69% of full-time freshmen returned.

FACULTY

Total: 194, 30% full-time, 29% with terminal degrees.

Student/faculty ratio: 10:1.

ACADEMICS

Calendar: semesters. *Degrees:* certificates, associate, bachelor's, master's, doctoral, and postbachelor's certificates.

Special study options: academic remediation for entering students, accelerated degree program, adult/continuing education programs, advanced placement credit, distance learning, double majors, honors programs, independent study, internships, off-campus study, part-time degree program, services for LD students, student-designed majors, study abroad, summer session for credit. *ROTC:* Army (c).

Computers: 140 computers/terminals are available on campus for general student use. Students can access the following: campus intranet, computer help desk, free student e-mail accounts, online (class) grades, online (class) registration, online (class) schedules. Campuswide network is available. 100% of college-owned or -operated housing units are wired for high-speed Internet access. Wireless service is available via entire campus.

Library: Benjamin P. Browne Library. *Books:* 120,765 (physical), 6,280 (digital/electronic); *Serial titles:* 158 (physical), 48,401 (digital/electronic); *Databases:* 53. Weekly public service hours: 76; students can reserve study rooms.

STUDENT LIFE

Housing options: on-campus residence required through senior year; coed, men-only, women-only, special housing for students with disabilities. Campus housing is university owned. Freshman campus housing is guaranteed.

Activities and organizations: drama/theater group, choral group, Judson Student Organization, University Ministries, Judson Choir, Fellowship of Christian Athletes, Judson Business Society.

Athletics Member NAIA, NCCAA. *Intercollegiate sports:* baseball M(s), basketball M(s)/W(s), bowling M(s)/W(s), cheerleading M(s)/W(s), cross-country running M(s)/W(s), football M, golf M(s)/W(s), soccer M(s)/W(s), softball W(s), tennis M(s)/W(s), track and field M(s)/W(s), volleyball M(s)/W(s). *Intramural sports:* basketball M/W, soccer M/W, volleyball M/W.

Campus security: 24-hour emergency response devices and patrols, controlled dormitory access.

Student services: health clinic, personal/psychological counseling.

COSTS & FINANCIAL AID

Costs (2019–20) *One-time required fee:* $100. *Comprehensive fee:* $40,160 includes full-time tuition ($28,840), mandatory fees ($1030), and room and board ($10,290). Part-time tuition: $1185 per credit hour.

Financial Aid Of all full-time matriculated undergraduates who enrolled in 2017, 552 applied for aid, 505 were judged to have need, 133 had their need fully met. 230 Federal Work-Study jobs (averaging $1536). In 2017, 159 non-need-based awards were made. *Average percent of need met:* 60. *Average financial aid package:* $20,982. *Average need-based loan:* $4153. *Average need-based gift aid:* $8328. *Average non-need-based aid:* $17,564. *Average indebtedness upon graduation:* $39,724. *Financial aid deadline:* 8/1.

APPLYING

Standardized Tests *Required:* SAT or ACT (for admission).

Options: electronic application.

Application fee: $50.

Required: high school transcript, minimum 2.0 GPA, minimum ACT score of 21, lifestyle statement. *Required for some:* essay or personal statement. *Recommended:* essay or personal statement.

Application deadlines: rolling (freshmen), rolling (out-of-state freshmen), rolling (transfers).

Notification: continuous (freshmen), continuous (out-of-state freshmen), continuous (transfers).

CONTACT

Mrs. Molly Smith, Director of Admissions, Judson University, 1151 North State Street, Elgin, IL 60123. *Phone:* 847-628-2521. *Toll-free phone:* 800-879-5376. *Fax:* 847-628-2526. *E-mail:* molly.smith@judsonu.edu.

Kendall College at National Louis University

Chicago, Illinois

http://www.kendall.edu/

CONTACT

Ms. Angela Batchelor, Manager of Enrollment, Kendall College at National Louis University, 900 North Branch Street, Chicago, IL 60642. *Toll-free phone:* 888-90-KENDALL. *E-mail:* info@kendall.edu.

Knox College

Galesburg, Illinois

http://www.knox.edu/

- **Independent** 4-year, founded 1837
- **Small-town** 82-acre campus with easy access to Peoria, Quad Cities
- **Endowment** $160.1 million
- **Coed** 1,333 undergraduate students, 98% full-time, 57% women, 43% men
- **Very difficult** entrance level, 74% of applicants were admitted

UNDERGRAD STUDENTS

1,310 full-time, 23 part-time. Students come from 43 states and territories; 48 other countries; 45% are from out of state; 8% Black or African American, non-Hispanic/Latino; 15% Hispanic/Latino; 5% Asian, non-Hispanic/Latino; 0.2% Native Hawaiian or other Pacific Islander, non-Hispanic/Latino; 5% Two or more races, non-Hispanic/Latino; 2% Race/ethnicity unknown; 17% international; 3% transferred in; 86% live on campus.

Freshmen:

Admission: 2,738 applied, 2,032 admitted, 345 enrolled. *Average high school GPA:* 3.6. *Test scores:* SAT evidence-based reading and writing scores over 500: 92%; SAT math scores over 500: 92%; ACT scores over 18: 99%; SAT evidence-based reading and writing scores over 600: 61%; SAT math scores over 600: 53%; ACT scores over 24: 74%; SAT evidence-based reading and writing scores over 700: 16%; SAT math scores over 700: 21%; ACT scores over 30: 35%.

Retention: 81% of full-time freshmen returned.

FACULTY

Total: 136, 82% full-time, 83% with terminal degrees.

Student/faculty ratio: 11:1.

ACADEMICS

Calendar: trimesters. *Degree:* bachelor's.

Special study options: advanced placement credit, double majors, English as a second language, honors programs, independent study, internships, off-campus study, part-time degree program, services for LD students, student-designed majors, study abroad.

Unusual degree programs: 3-2 engineering with University of Illinois at Urbana–Champaign, Washington University in St. Louis, Columbia University, Rensselaer Polytechnic Institute; forestry with Duke University; nursing with Rush University.

Computers: 275 computers/terminals are available on campus for general student use. Students can access the following: campus intranet, computer help desk, free student e-mail accounts, online (class) grades, online (class) registration, online (class) schedules, transcripts, learning management system, streaming video, print billing. Campuswide network is available. 100% of college-owned or -operated housing units are wired for high-speed Internet access. Wireless service is available via entire campus.

Library: Henry M. Seymour Library plus 1 other. *Books:* 331,297 (physical), 15,164 (digital/electronic); *Serial titles:* 152 (physical), 87,337 (digital/electronic); *Databases:* 200. Weekly public service hours: 106; students can reserve study rooms.

STUDENT LIFE

Housing options: on-campus residence required through junior year; coed, men-only, women-only, special housing for students with disabilities. Campus housing is university owned. Freshman campus housing is guaranteed.

Activities and organizations: drama/theater group, student-run newspaper, radio station, choral group, International Club, Best Buddies (Assistance and Friendship for Individuals with Intellectual Disabilities), Blessings in a Backpack, Alpha Phi Omega (APO, Co-ed Service Fraternity), Improv Club, national fraternities, national sororities.

Athletics Member NCAA. All Division III except golf (Division II). *Intercollegiate sports:* baseball M, basketball M/W, cross-country running M/W, football M, golf M/W, soccer M/W, softball W, swimming and diving M/W, tennis M/W, track and field M/W, volleyball W. *Intramural sports:* basketball M/W, equestrian sports M(c)/W(c), soccer M/W, ultimate Frisbee M(c)/W(c), volleyball M/W, water polo M(c)/W(c).

Campus security: 24-hour emergency response devices and patrols, late-night transport/escort service.

Student services: health clinic, personal/psychological counseling.

COSTS & FINANCIAL AID

Costs (2019–20) *Comprehensive fee:* $58,236 includes full-time tuition ($47,385), mandatory fees ($783), and room and board ($10,068). *College room only:* $5040.

Financial Aid Of all full-time matriculated undergraduates who enrolled in 2018, 1,147 applied for aid, 947 were judged to have need, 216 had their need fully met. 648 Federal Work-Study jobs (averaging $2200). In 2018, 320 non-need-based awards were made. *Average percent of need met:* 89. *Average financial aid package:* $38,817. *Average need-based loan:* $3604. *Average need-based gift aid:* $31,428. *Average non-need-based aid:* $22,708. *Average indebtedness upon graduation:* $32,212.

APPLYING

Standardized Tests *Required for some:* SAT or ACT (for admission).

Options: electronic application, early admission, early decision, early action, deferred entrance.

Application fee: $50.

Required: essay or personal statement, high school transcript, 2 letters of recommendation. *Recommended:* interview.

Application deadlines: 4/1 (transfers), 12/1 (early action).

Early decision deadline: 11/1.

Notification: 3/15 (freshmen), 5/1 (transfers), 11/15 (early decision), 1/15 (early action).

CONTACT

Mr. Paul Steenis, Vice President for Enrollment & Dean of Admission, Knox College, 2 East South Street, Campus Box148, Galesburg, IL 61401. *Phone:* 309-341-7100. *Toll-free phone:* 800-678-KNOX. *Fax:* 309-341-7070. *E-mail:* admission@knox.edu.

Lake Forest College

Lake Forest, Illinois

http://www.lakeforest.edu/

- **Independent** comprehensive, founded 1857
- **Suburban** 107-acre campus with easy access to Chicago
- **Endowment** $90.6 million
- **Coed** 1,492 undergraduate students, 99% full-time, 57% women, 43% men
- **Moderately difficult** entrance level, 58% of applicants were admitted

UNDERGRAD STUDENTS

1,472 full-time, 20 part-time. Students come from 41 states and territories; 77 other countries; 38% are from out of state; 5% Black or African American, non-Hispanic/Latino; 14% Hispanic/Latino; 5% Asian, non-Hispanic/Latino; 0.1% Native Hawaiian or other Pacific Islander, non-Hispanic/Latino; 0.3% American Indian or Alaska Native, non-Hispanic/Latino; 4% Two or more races, non-Hispanic/Latino; 4% Race/ethnicity unknown; 11% international; 5% transferred in; 78% live on campus.

Freshmen:

Admission: 4,147 applied, 2,402 admitted, 392 enrolled. *Average high school GPA:* 3.6. *Test scores:* SAT evidence-based reading and writing scores over 500: 98%; SAT math scores over 500: 94%; ACT scores over 18: 100%; SAT evidence-based reading and writing scores over 600: 55%; SAT math scores over 600: 54%; ACT scores over 24: 71%; SAT evidence-based reading and writing scores over 700: 9%; SAT math scores over 700: 15%; ACT scores over 30: 21%.

Retention: 83% of full-time freshmen returned.

FACULTY

Total: 178, 57% full-time, 73% with terminal degrees.

Student/faculty ratio: 12:1.

ACADEMICS

Calendar: semesters. *Degrees:* bachelor's, master's, and postbachelor's certificates.

Special study options: accelerated degree program, advanced placement credit, double majors, honors programs, independent study, internships, off-campus study, part-time degree program, services for LD students, student-designed majors, study abroad, summer session for credit.

Unusual degree programs: 3-2 engineering with Washington University in St. Louis.

Computers: 400 computers/terminals and 2,000 ports are available on campus for general student use. Students can access the following: campus intranet, computer help desk, free student e-mail accounts, online (class) grades, online (class) registration, online (class) schedules, file storage. Campuswide network is available. 100% of college-owned or -operated housing units are wired for high-speed Internet access. Wireless service is available via entire campus.

Library: Donnelley and Lee Library. Study areas open 24 hours, 5–7 days a week; students can reserve study rooms.

STUDENT LIFE

Housing options: on-campus residence required through junior year; coed. Campus housing is university owned. Freshman applicants given priority for college housing.

Activities and organizations: drama/theater group, student-run newspaper, radio station, choral group, Athletic Council, Student Government, United Black Association, PRIDE, Alpha Tau Omega, national fraternities, national sororities.

Athletics Member NCAA. All Division III. *Intercollegiate sports:* archery M(c)/W(c), basketball M/W, cheerleading M(c)/W(c), cross-country running M/W, equestrian sports M(c)/W(c), fencing M(c)/W(c), football M, golf M/W, ice hockey M/W, lacrosse M(c)/W(c), rugby M(c)/W(c), sailing M(c)/W(c), soccer M/W, softball W, swimming and diving M/W, tennis M/W, track and field M/W, ultimate Frisbee M(c)/W(c), volleyball W, water polo M(c)/W(c). *Intramural sports:* badminton M/W, basketball M/W, ice hockey M/W, soccer M/W, table tennis M/W, volleyball M/W.

Campus security: 24-hour emergency response devices and patrols, student patrols, late-night transport/escort service, controlled dormitory access.

Student services: health clinic, personal/psychological counseling.

COSTS & FINANCIAL AID

Costs (2019–20) *Comprehensive fee:* $59,100 includes full-time tuition ($47,680), mandatory fees ($744), and room and board ($10,676). *College room only:* $5140.

Financial Aid *Financial aid deadline:* 5/1.

APPLYING

Standardized Tests *Recommended:* SAT or ACT (for admission).

Options: electronic application, early decision, early action, deferred entrance.

Required: essay or personal statement, high school transcript, 1 letter of recommendation. *Recommended:* interview.

Application deadlines: 2/15 (freshmen), 1/1 (transfers), 11/15 (early action).

Early decision deadline: 11/15.

Notification: continuous until 3/10 (freshmen), 12/15 (early decision).

CONTACT

Christopher Ellertson, Vice President for Enrollment, Lake Forest College, 555 North Sheridan Road, Lake Forest, IL 60045-2338. *Phone:* 847-735-5000. *Toll-free phone:* 800-828-4751. *Fax:* 847-735-6271. *E-mail:* admissions@lakeforest.edu.

Lakeview College of Nursing

Danville, Illinois

http://www.lakeviewcol.edu/

CONTACT
Admissions Office, Lakeview College of Nursing, 903 North Logan Avenue, Danville, IL 61832. *Phone:* 217-709-0920. *Fax:* 217-709-0953. *E-mail:* admission@lakeviewcol.edu.

Lewis University

Romeoville, Illinois

http://www.lewisu.edu/

- **Independent** comprehensive, founded 1932, affiliated with Roman Catholic Church
- **Suburban** 410-acre campus with easy access to Chicago
- **Coed**
- **Moderately difficult** entrance level

FACULTY

Student/faculty ratio: 13:1.

ACADEMICS

Calendar: semesters. *Degrees:* certificates, associate, bachelor's, master's, doctoral, post-master's, and postbachelor's certificates.

Library: Lewis University Library. *Books:* 120,468 (physical), 527,534 (digital/electronic); *Serial titles:* 1,622 (physical), 151,185 (digital/electronic); *Databases:* 115. Weekly public service hours: 102; students can reserve study rooms.

STUDENT LIFE

Housing options: coed. Campus housing is university owned. Freshman campus housing is guaranteed.

Activities and organizations: drama/theater group, student-run newspaper, radio and television station, choral group, Student Governing Board, Student Nurses Association, Latin American Student Organization, Theta Kappa Pi Sorority, Delta Sigma Pi (business fraternity), national fraternities, national sororities.

Athletics Member NCAA. All Division II except volleyball (Division I).

Campus security: 24-hour emergency response devices and patrols, late-night transport/escort service, controlled dormitory access, Emergency notification system.

Student services: health clinic, personal/psychological counseling, veterans affairs office.

COSTS & FINANCIAL AID

Costs (2018–19) *Comprehensive fee:* $43,028 includes full-time tuition ($32,300), mandatory fees ($150), and room and board ($10,578). Full-time tuition and fees vary according to course load, location, and program. Part-time tuition: $948 per credit hour. Part-time tuition and fees vary according to course load, location, and program. *Required fees:* $75 per term part-time. *Room and board:* Room and board charges vary according to board plan and housing facility.

Financial Aid Of all full-time matriculated undergraduates who enrolled in 2018, 3,032 applied for aid, 2,686 were judged to have need, 557 had their need fully met. In 2018, 641 non-need-based awards were made. *Average percent of need met:* 88. *Average financial aid package:* $27,329. *Average need-based loan:* $4493. *Average need-based gift aid:* $17,636. *Average non-need-based aid:* $12,692. *Average indebtedness upon graduation:* $35,284. *Financial aid deadline:* 5/1.

APPLYING

Standardized Tests *Required:* SAT or ACT (for admission).

Options: electronic application, deferred entrance.

Application fee: $40.

Required: high school transcript, minimum 2.0 GPA. *Required for some:* interview.

CONTACT

Mr. Ryan Cockerill, Director of Admission, Lewis University, Unit #297, One University Parkway, Romeoville, IL 60446. *Phone:* 815-836-5237. *Toll-free phone:* 800-897-9000. *Fax:* 815-836-5002. *E-mail:* cockerry@lewisu.edu.

Lincoln Christian University

Lincoln, Illinois

http://www.lincolnchristian.edu/

- **Independent** comprehensive, founded 1944, affiliated with Christian Churches and Churches of Christ
- **Small-town** 100-acre campus
- **Endowment** $5.2 million
- **Coed** 415 undergraduate students, 81% full-time, 50% women, 50% men
- **Moderately difficult** entrance level, 62% of applicants were admitted

UNDERGRAD STUDENTS

337 full-time, 78 part-time. Students come from 27 states and territories; 2 other countries; 26% are from out of state; 7% Black or African American, non-Hispanic/Latino; 1% Hispanic/Latino; 0.7% Asian, non-Hispanic/Latino; 0.2% Native Hawaiian or other Pacific Islander, non-Hispanic/Latino; 1% Two or more races, non-Hispanic/Latino; 0.7% Race/ethnicity unknown; 5% international; 5% transferred in; 22% live on campus.

Freshmen:

Admission: 301 applied, 187 admitted, 64 enrolled. *Average high school GPA:* 3.4.

Retention: 82% of full-time freshmen returned.

FACULTY

Total: 69, 48% full-time, 62% with terminal degrees.

Student/faculty ratio: 12:1.

ACADEMICS

Calendar: semesters. *Degrees:* associate, bachelor's, master's, and doctoral.

Special study options: academic remediation for entering students, adult/continuing education programs, advanced placement credit, cooperative education, distance learning, double majors, external degree program, honors programs, independent study, internships, off-campus study, part-time degree program, services for LD students, study abroad, summer session for credit.

Computers: 51 computers/terminals are available on campus for general student use. Students can access the following: campus intranet, computer help desk, free student e-mail accounts, online (class) grades, online (class) registration, online (class) schedules. Campuswide network is available. 100% of college-owned or -operated housing units are wired for high-speed Internet access. Wireless service is available via entire campus.

Library: Jessie Eury Library. *Books:* 92,813 (physical), 55,082 (digital/electronic); *Serial titles:* 719 (physical), 15,442 (digital/electronic); *Databases:* 52. Weekly public service hours: 82; students can reserve study rooms.

STUDENT LIFE

Housing options: on-campus residence required through senior year; men-only, women-only. Campus housing is university owned. Freshman campus housing is guaranteed.

Activities and organizations: drama/theater group, choral group, Chorale, Student Cabinet, American Association of Christian Counselors (AACC) - Student Chapter, Cheerleading.

Athletics Member NAIA, NCCAA. *Intercollegiate sports:* baseball M(s), basketball M(s)/W(s), soccer M(s)/W(s), volleyball W(s). *Intramural sports:* badminton M/W, basketball M/W, sand volleyball M/W, soccer M/W, ultimate Frisbee M/W, volleyball M/W.

Campus security: 24-hour emergency response devices, student patrols, controlled dormitory access.

Student services: personal/psychological counseling, veterans affairs office.

COSTS & FINANCIAL AID

Costs (2018–19) *Comprehensive fee:* $20,764 includes full-time tuition ($13,200) and room and board ($7564). Part-time tuition: $440 per credit hour. *College room only:* $3600. Room and board charges vary according to housing facility. *Payment plan:* installment. *Waivers:* senior citizens and employees or children of employees.

Financial Aid Of all full-time matriculated undergraduates who enrolled in 2017, 348 applied for aid, 289 were judged to have need, 18 had their need fully met. In 2017, 53 non-need-based awards were made. *Average percent of need met:* 56. *Average financial aid package:* $13,404. *Average need-based loan:* $3881. *Average need-based gift aid:* $7987. *Average non-need-based aid:* $2600. *Average indebtedness upon graduation:* $26,654.

APPLYING

Standardized Tests *Required:* SAT or ACT (for admission).

Options: electronic application, deferred entrance.

Required: essay or personal statement, 3 letters of recommendation. *Required for some:* high school transcript, interview.

Application deadlines: rolling (freshmen), rolling (transfers).

Notification: continuous (freshmen), continuous (transfers).

CONTACT

Mrs. Mary K. Davis, Admissions Office Manager, Lincoln Christian University, 100 Campus View Drive, Lincoln, IL 62656. *Phone:* 217-732-3168 Ext. 2251. *Toll-free phone:* 888-522-5228. *Fax:* 217-732-4199. *E-mail:* enroll@lincolnchristian.edu.

Lincoln College

Lincoln, Illinois

http://www.lincolncollege.edu/

- **Independent** 4-year, founded 1865
- **Small-town** 42-acre campus
- **Endowment** $20.5 million
- **Coed**
- **Minimally difficult** entrance level

FACULTY

Student/faculty ratio: 14:1.

ACADEMICS

Calendar: semesters. *Degrees:* associate and bachelor's.

Library: McKinstry Library. *Books:* 23,449 (physical), 182,420 (digital/electronic); *Serial titles:* 3 (physical); *Databases:* 38. Students can reserve study rooms.

STUDENT LIFE

Housing options: on-campus residence required through sophomore year; men-only, women-only. Campus housing is university owned. Freshman campus housing is guaranteed.

Activities and organizations: drama/theater group, student-run radio and television station, choral group, Black Student Union, Phi Theta Kappa, Purple Pulse, Student Activities Board, Woment of Worth.

Athletics Member NJCAA.

Campus security: 24-hour emergency response devices and patrols, controlled dormitory access.

Student services: health clinic, personal/psychological counseling, veterans affairs office.

COSTS & FINANCIAL AID

Costs (2018–19) *One-time required fee:* $50. *Comprehensive fee:* $26,300 includes full-time tuition ($17,500), mandatory fees ($1100), and room and board ($7700). Part-time tuition: $310 per credit hour. No tuition increase for student's term of enrollment. *College room only:* $3000. Room and board charges vary according to housing facility. *Payment plans:* tuition prepayment, installment.

Financial Aid Of all full-time matriculated undergraduates who enrolled in 2017, 200 Federal Work-Study jobs (averaging $900).

APPLYING

Standardized Tests *Required:* SAT or ACT (for admission).

Options: electronic application, early admission, deferred entrance.

Required: high school transcript, minimum 2.0 GPA. *Required for some:* essay or personal statement, 2 letters of recommendation, interview.

CONTACT

Lincoln College, 300 Keokuk Street, Lincoln, IL 62656-1699. *Phone:* 217-735-7251 Ext. 7251. *Toll-free phone:* 800-569-0558.

Loyola University Chicago

Chicago, Illinois

http://www.luc.edu/

- **Independent Roman Catholic (Jesuit)** university, founded 1870
- **Urban** 105-acre campus
- **Endowment** $640.3 million
- **Coed** 11,919 undergraduate students, 94% full-time, 67% women, 33% men
- **Moderately difficult** entrance level, 68% of applicants were admitted

UNDERGRAD STUDENTS

11,189 full-time, 730 part-time. Students come from 52 states and territories; 106 other countries; 37% are from out of state; 5% Black or African American, non-Hispanic/Latino; 16% Hispanic/Latino; 13% Asian, non-Hispanic/Latino; 0.3% Native Hawaiian or other Pacific Islander, non-Hispanic/Latino; 0.1% American Indian or Alaska Native, non-Hispanic/Latino; 4% Two or more races, non-Hispanic/Latino; 1% Race/ethnicity unknown; 5% international; 4% transferred in; 40% live on campus.

Freshmen:

Admission: 25,122 applied, 17,064 admitted, 2,770 enrolled. *Average high school GPA:* 3.7. *Test scores:* SAT evidence-based reading and writing scores over 500: 97%; SAT math scores over 500: 95%; ACT scores over 18: 100%; SAT evidence-based reading and writing scores over 600: 61%; SAT math scores over 600: 50%; ACT scores over 24: 85%; SAT evidence-based reading and writing scores over 700: 10%; SAT math scores over 700: 12%; ACT scores over 30: 29%.

Retention: 85% of full-time freshmen returned.

FACULTY

Total: 1,682, 50% full-time, 47% with terminal degrees.

Student/faculty ratio: 14:1.

ACADEMICS

Calendar: semesters. *Degrees:* certificates, associate, bachelor's, master's, doctoral, post-master's, and postbachelor's certificates (also offers adult part-time program with significant enrollment not reflected in profile).

Special study options: accelerated degree program, adult/continuing education programs, advanced placement credit, cooperative education, distance learning, double majors, English as a second language, freshman honors college, honors programs, independent study, internships, off-campus study, part-time degree program, services for LD students, study abroad, summer session for credit. *ROTC:* Army (b), Navy (c), Air Force (c).

Unusual degree programs: 3-2 business administration; engineering; social work; political science, sociology, psychology/applied social psychology, computers, biology, accounting, information technology, criminal justice and criminology.

Computers: 1,300 computers/terminals are available on campus for general student use. Students can access the following: campus intranet, computer help desk, free student e-mail accounts, online (class) grades, online (class) registration, online (class) schedules. Campuswide network is available. 100% of college-owned or -operated housing units are wired for high-speed Internet access. Wireless service is available via entire campus.

Library: Cudahy Library plus 7 others. *Books:* 1.9 million (physical), 568,720 (digital/electronic); *Serial titles:* 2,245 (physical), 58,389 (digital/electronic); *Databases:* 545. Weekly public service hours: 144; study areas open 24 hours, 5–7 days a week; students can reserve study rooms.

STUDENT LIFE

Housing options: on-campus residence required through sophomore year; coed, special housing for students with disabilities. Campus housing is university owned. Freshman campus housing is guaranteed.

Activities and organizations: drama/theater group, student-run newspaper, radio station, choral group, Panhellenic Council, National Society of Collegiate Scholars, Vegetarian and Vegan Society, Interfraternity Council, American Medical Student Association, national fraternities, national sororities.

Athletics Member NCAA. All Division I. *Intercollegiate sports:* basketball M(s)/W(s), cross-country running M(s)/W(s), golf M(s)/W(s)(c), soccer M(s)/W(s), softball W(s), track and field M(s)/W(s), volleyball M(s)/W(s). *Intramural sports:* baseball M(c), basketball M/W, cross-country running M(c)/W(c), field hockey M(c)/W(c), football M(c)/W(c), golf M(c)/W(c), ice hockey M(c)/W(c), lacrosse M(c)/W(c), racquetball M/W, rugby M(c)/W(c), soccer M(c)/W(c), softball W(c), swimming and diving M(c)/W(c), table tennis M/W, tennis M(c)/W(c), ultimate Frisbee M(c)/W(c), volleyball M(c)/W(c), water polo M(c)/W(c).

Campus security: 24-hour emergency response devices, late-night transport/escort service, controlled dormitory access.

Student services: health clinic, personal/psychological counseling, women's center, veterans affairs office.

COSTS & FINANCIAL AID

Costs (2019–20) *Comprehensive fee:* $60,323 includes full-time tuition ($44,105), mandatory fees ($1438), and room and board ($14,780). Part-time tuition: $814 per credit hour. *Required fees:* $230 per year part-time. *College room only:* $9260.

Financial Aid Of all full-time matriculated undergraduates who enrolled in 2018, 8,262 applied for aid, 7,156 were judged to have need, 1,060 had their need fully met. 5,087 Federal Work-Study jobs (averaging $2797). In 2018, 3398 non-need-based awards were made. *Average percent of need met:* 83. *Average financial aid package:* $35,671. *Average need-based loan:* $4263. *Average need-based gift aid:* $22,358. *Average non-need-based aid:* $17,532. *Average indebtedness upon graduation:* $35,509.

APPLYING

Standardized Tests *Required:* SAT or ACT (for admission).

Options: electronic application.

CONTACT

Ms. Erin Moriarty, Director of Undergraduate Admissions, Loyola University Chicago, 1032 West Sheridan Road, Chicago, IL 60660. *Phone:* 773-508-3079. *Toll-free phone:* 800-262-2373. *E-mail:* admission@luc.edu.

MacMurray College

Jacksonville, Illinois

http://www.mac.edu/

CONTACT

Kristen Chenoweth, Associate Director of Admissions, MacMurray College, 447 East College Avenue, Jacksonville, IL 62650. *Phone:* 217-479-7063. *Toll-free phone:* 800-252-7485. *Fax:* 217-291-0702. *E-mail:* kristen.chenoweth@mac.edu.

McKendree University

Lebanon, Illinois

http://www.mckendree.edu/

- **Independent** university, founded 1828, affiliated with United Methodist Church
- **Suburban** 235-acre campus with easy access to St. Louis, MO; Belleville, IL
- **Coed**
- **Moderately difficult** entrance level

FACULTY

Student/faculty ratio: 14:1.

ACADEMICS

Calendar: semesters. *Degrees:* associate, bachelor's, master's, doctoral, and post-master's certificates.

Library: Holman Library. *Books:* 76,806 (physical), 11,853 (digital/electronic); *Serial titles:* 5,099 (physical), 7,229 (digital/electronic); *Databases:* 59. Students can reserve study rooms.

STUDENT LIFE

Housing options: on-campus residence required through junior year; coed, special housing for students with disabilities. Campus housing is university owned and leased by the school. Freshman campus housing is guaranteed.

Activities and organizations: drama/theater group, student-run newspaper, radio station, choral group, marching band, Center for Public Service, Wonders of Wellness, Campus Ministries, APO, Debate, national fraternities, national sororities.

Athletics Member NCAA. All Division II except volleyball (Division I).

Campus security: 24-hour emergency response devices and patrols, student patrols, late-night transport/escort service, controlled dormitory access.

Student services: health clinic, personal/psychological counseling.

COSTS & FINANCIAL AID
Costs (2018–19) *Comprehensive fee:* $40,440 includes full-time tuition ($29,420), mandatory fees ($1100), and room and board ($9920). Full-time tuition and fees vary according to course load, degree level, and location. Part-time tuition: $960 per credit hour. Part-time tuition and fees vary according to course load, degree level, and location. *College room only:* $5120. Room and board charges vary according to board plan and housing facility. *Payment plans:* installment, deferred payment.

Financial Aid Of all full-time matriculated undergraduates who enrolled in 2017, 1,419 applied for aid, 1,295 were judged to have need, 246 had their need fully met. 331 Federal Work-Study jobs (averaging $930). 91 state and other part-time jobs (averaging $1158). In 2017, 278 non-need-based awards were made. *Average percent of need met:* 73. *Average financial aid package:* $21,635. *Average need-based loan:* $4450. *Average need-based gift aid:* $18,616. *Average non-need-based aid:* $12,212. *Average indebtedness upon graduation:* $27,535.

APPLYING
Standardized Tests *Required:* SAT or ACT (for admission).

Options: electronic application, deferred entrance.

Required: essay or personal statement, high school transcript, minimum 2.5 GPA, 1 letter of recommendation, rank in upper 50% of high school class, minimum ACT score of 20. *Required for some:* interview.

CONTACT
Mrs. Josie Blasdel, Director of Undergraduate Admission, McKendree University, 701 College Road, Lebanon, IL 62254. *Phone:* 618-537-6836. *Toll-free phone:* 800-232-7228. *E-mail:* jlblasdel@mckendree.edu.

Methodist College
Peoria, Illinois
http://www.methodistcol.edu/

CONTACT
Methodist College, 415 St. Mark Court, Peoria, IL 61603.

Midstate College
Peoria, Illinois
http://www.midstate.edu/

CONTACT
Ms. Jessica Hancock, Director of Admissions, Midstate College, 411 West Northmoor Road, Peoria, IL 61614. *Phone:* 309-692-4092. *Toll-free phone:* 800-251-4299. *Fax:* 309-692-3893. *E-mail:* jhancock2@midstate.edu.

Millikin University
Decatur, Illinois
http://www.millikin.edu/
- **Independent** comprehensive, founded 1901, affiliated with Presbyterian Church (U.S.A.)
- **Suburban** 75-acre campus
- **Endowment** $110.5 million
- **Coed** 1,985 undergraduate students, 95% full-time, 57% women, 43% men
- **Moderately difficult** entrance level, 61% of applicants were admitted

UNDERGRAD STUDENTS
1,894 full-time, 91 part-time. Students come from 37 states and territories; 30 other countries; 19% are from out of state; 14% Black or African American, non-Hispanic/Latino; 7% Hispanic/Latino; 1% Asian, non-Hispanic/Latino; 0.1% Native Hawaiian or other Pacific Islander, non-Hispanic/Latino; 0.2% American Indian or Alaska Native, non-Hispanic/Latino; 5% Two or more races, non-Hispanic/Latino; 2% Race/ethnicity unknown; 5% international; 5% transferred in; 58% live on campus.

Freshmen:
Admission: 4,512 applied, 2,764 admitted, 468 enrolled. *Average high school GPA:* 3.4. *Test scores:* SAT evidence-based reading and writing scores over 500: 72%; SAT math scores over 500: 70%; ACT scores over 18: 92%; SAT evidence-based reading and writing scores over 600: 33%; SAT math scores over 600: 21%; ACT scores over 24: 46%; SAT evidence-based reading and writing scores over 700: 4%; SAT math scores over 700: 2%; ACT scores over 30: 10%.

Retention: 78% of full-time freshmen returned.

FACULTY
Total: 292, 52% full-time, 49% with terminal degrees.

Student/faculty ratio: 10:1.

ACADEMICS
Calendar: semesters. *Degrees:* certificates, bachelor's, master's, doctoral, and postbachelor's certificates.

Special study options: academic remediation for entering students, accelerated degree program, adult/continuing education programs, advanced placement credit, distance learning, double majors, English as a second language, honors programs, independent study, internships, off-campus study, part-time degree program, services for LD students, student-designed majors, study abroad, summer session for credit.

Unusual degree programs: 3-2 engineering with Washington University in St. Louis, University of Missouri–Kansas City; occupational therapy with Washington University, pharmacy with Midwestern University.

Computers: 135 computers/terminals and 300 ports are available on campus for general student use. Students can access the following: computer help desk, free student e-mail accounts, online (class) grades, online (class) registration, online (class) schedules, online degree audit, online financials (view and pay bills, financial aid). Campuswide network is available. 100% of college-owned or -operated housing units are wired for high-speed Internet access. Wireless service is available via classrooms, computer centers, computer labs, dorm rooms, learning centers, libraries, student centers.

Library: Staley Library. *Books:* 122,725 (physical), 23,745 (digital/electronic); *Serial titles:* 543 (physical), 49 (digital/electronic); *Databases:* 49. Weekly public service hours: 113; students can reserve study rooms.

STUDENT LIFE
Housing options: on-campus residence required through junior year; coed, special housing for students with disabilities. Campus housing is university owned, leased by the school and is provided by a third party. Freshman campus housing is guaranteed.

Activities and organizations: drama/theater group, student-run newspaper, radio station, choral group, University Center Board, Multicultural Student Council, Student Housing Council, Panhellenic Council, Interfraternity Council, national fraternities, national sororities.

Athletics Member NCAA. All Division III except golf (Division II). *Intercollegiate sports:* baseball M, basketball M/W, cross-country running M/W, football M, golf M/W, soccer M/W, softball W, swimming and diving M/W, tennis M/W, track and field M/W, triathlon W, volleyball M/W, wrestling M. *Intramural sports:* basketball M/W, cheerleading M(c)/W(c), football M/W, soccer M/W, softball M/W, ultimate Frisbee M/W, volleyball M/W.

Campus security: 24-hour emergency response devices and patrols, late-night transport/escort service, controlled dormitory access.

Student services: health clinic, personal/psychological counseling, women's center.

COSTS & FINANCIAL AID
Costs (2019–20) *Comprehensive fee:* $48,848 includes full-time tuition ($36,262), mandatory fees ($792), and room and board ($11,794). Part-time tuition: $511 per credit hour. *Required fees:* $22 per credit hour part-time. *College room only:* $9038.

Financial Aid Of all full-time matriculated undergraduates who enrolled in 2017, 1,653 applied for aid, 1,508 were judged to have need, 559 had their need fully met. 463 Federal Work-Study jobs (averaging $1024). 435 state and other part-time jobs (averaging $808). In 2017, 136 non-need-based awards were made. *Average percent of need met:* 85. *Average financial aid package:* $26,207. *Average need-based loan:* $4691. *Average need-based gift aid:* $8961. *Average non-need-based aid:* $16,945. *Average indebtedness upon graduation:* $34,378.

APPLYING

Standardized Tests *Required:* SAT or ACT (for admission).

Options: electronic application, deferred entrance.

Required: high school transcript, minimum 2.0 GPA, 2 letters of recommendation. *Required for some:* audition for music/theatre, art portfolio review. *Recommended:* interview.

Application deadlines: rolling (freshmen), rolling (transfers).

Notification: continuous (freshmen), continuous (transfers).

CONTACT

Mr. Kyle Taylor, Director of Admission, Millikin University, 1184 West Main Street, Decatur, IL 62522-2084. *Phone:* 217-424-6210. *Toll-free phone:* 800-373-7733. *Fax:* 217-425-4669. *E-mail:* admis@millikin.edu.

Monmouth College

Monmouth, Illinois

http://www.monmouthcollege.edu/

- **Independent** 4-year, founded 1853, affiliated with Presbyterian Church
- **Small-town** 112-acre campus
- **Endowment** $113.8 million
- **Coed**
- **Moderately difficult** entrance level

FACULTY
Student/faculty ratio: 11:1.

ACADEMICS
Calendar: semesters. *Degree:* bachelor's.
Library: Hewes Library. *Books:* 206,954 (physical), 33,996 (digital/electronic); *Serial titles:* 3,400 (physical), 28,190 (digital/electronic); *Databases:* 115. Weekly public service hours: 96; students can reserve study rooms.

STUDENT LIFE
Housing options: on-campus residence required through senior year; coed, men-only, women-only, special housing for students with disabilities. Campus housing is university owned. Freshman campus housing is guaranteed.

Activities and organizations: drama/theater group, student-run newspaper, radio and television station, choral group, marching band, Fighting Scots Marching Band and Jazz Band, Associated Students of Monmouth College, Crimson Masque (theatre), Alternative Spring Break, Coalition for Ethnic Awareness, national fraternities, national sororities.

Athletics Member NCAA. All Division III.

Campus security: 24-hour emergency response devices and patrols, late-night transport/escort service, controlled dormitory access, full-time Director of Campus Security.

Student services: personal/psychological counseling.

COSTS & FINANCIAL AID
Costs (2018–19) *One-time required fee:* $195. *Comprehensive fee:* $46,640 includes full-time tuition ($37,674) and room and board ($8966). Part-time tuition: $4709 per course. *College room only:* $5054. Room and board charges vary according to housing facility.

Financial Aid Of all full-time matriculated undergraduates who enrolled in 2018, 811 applied for aid, 772 were judged to have need, 201 had their need fully met. 386 Federal Work-Study jobs (averaging $1516). In 2018, 122 non-need-based awards were made. *Average percent of need met:* 89. *Average financial aid package:* $34,502. *Average need-based loan:* $4138. *Average need-based gift aid:* $28,908. *Average non-need-based aid:* $23,050. *Average indebtedness upon graduation:* $30,252.

APPLYING
Standardized Tests *Required:* SAT or ACT (for admission).

Options: electronic application, deferred entrance.

Required: high school transcript. *Required for some:* interview. *Recommended:* essay or personal statement, minimum 2.7 GPA, letters of recommendation, interview.

CONTACT
Mr. Trent Gilbert, Vice President for Enrollment Management, Monmouth College, 700 East Broadway, Monmouth, IL 61462-1988. *Phone:* 309-457-2131. *Toll-free phone:* 800-747-2687. *Fax:* 309-457-2141. *E-mail:* admissions@monmouthcollege.edu.

Moody Bible Institute

Chicago, Illinois

http://www.moody.edu/

CONTACT
Ms. Jacqueline Holman, Admissions Office, Moody Bible Institute, 820 North LaSalle Boulevard, Chicago, IL 60610. *Phone:* 312-329-4307. *Toll-free phone:* 800-967-4MBI. *Fax:* 312-329-8987. *E-mail:* admissions@moody.edu.

National Louis University

Chicago, Illinois

http://www.nl.edu/

- **Independent** university, founded 1886
- **Urban** 12-acre campus
- **Coed**
- **Moderately difficult** entrance level

FACULTY
Student/faculty ratio: 17:1.

ACADEMICS
Calendar: quarters. *Degrees:* bachelor's, master's, doctoral, post-master's, and postbachelor's certificates.
Library: NLU Library.

STUDENT LIFE
Housing options: college housing not available.

Campus security: 24-hour emergency response devices and patrols.

Student services: personal/psychological counseling, veterans affairs office.

FINANCIAL AID
Financial Aid Of all full-time matriculated undergraduates who enrolled in 2011, 772 applied for aid, 736 were judged to have need, 10 had their need fully met. 66 Federal Work-Study jobs (averaging $3890). In 2011, 52 non-need-based awards were made. *Average percent of need met:* 43. *Average financial aid package:* $12,225. *Average need-based loan:* $4426. *Average need-based gift aid:* $8302. *Average non-need-based aid:* $5605. *Average indebtedness upon graduation:* $29,900.

APPLYING
Standardized Tests *Recommended:* SAT or ACT (for admission).

Options: electronic application, deferred entrance.

Required: high school transcript, minimum 2.0 GPA. *Recommended:* interview.

CONTACT
National Louis University, 1000 Capitol Drive, Wheeling, IL 60090. *Phone:* 888-NLU-TODAY. *Toll-free phone:* 888-658-8632.

North Central College

Naperville, Illinois

http://www.northcentralcollege.edu/

- **Independent United Methodist** comprehensive, founded 1861
- **Suburban** 68-acre campus with easy access to Chicago
- **Endowment** $110.0 million
- **Coed**
- **Moderately difficult** entrance level

FACULTY
Student/faculty ratio: 14:1.

ACADEMICS
Calendar: quarters. *Degrees:* bachelor's, master's, and postbachelor's certificates.
Library: Oesterle Library. *Books:* 135,388 (physical), 74,330 (digital/electronic); *Databases:* 137.

STUDENT LIFE
Housing options: on-campus residence required through sophomore year; coed, men-only, women-only, special housing for students with disabilities. Campus housing is university owned. Freshman applicants given priority for college housing.

Activities and organizations: drama/theater group, student-run newspaper, radio station, choral group, marching band, College Union Activities Board, WONC (student radio station), Cardinals in Action (service group), ENACTUS (Students in Free Enterprise SIFE), Residence Hall Association.

Athletics Member NCAA. All Division III.

Campus security: 24-hour emergency response devices and patrols, late-night transport/escort service, controlled dormitory access.

Student services: health clinic, personal/psychological counseling, veterans affairs office.

COSTS & FINANCIAL AID
Costs (2018–19) *Comprehensive fee:* $49,899 includes full-time tuition ($38,700), mandatory fees ($180), and room and board ($11,019). Part-time tuition: $1075 per credit hour. Part-time tuition and fees vary according to course load. *Room and board:* Room and board charges vary according to housing facility.

Financial Aid Of all full-time matriculated undergraduates who enrolled in 2017, 2,266 applied for aid, 2,042 were judged to have need, 383 had their need fully met. 1,527 Federal Work-Study jobs (averaging $233). In 2017, 566 non-need-based awards were made. *Average percent of need met:* 79. *Average financial aid package:* $27,601. *Average need-based loan:* $4564. *Average need-based gift aid:* $22,447. *Average non-need-based aid:* $18,225. *Average indebtedness upon graduation:* $38,267.

APPLYING
Standardized Tests *Required:* SAT or ACT (for admission). *Recommended:* ACT (for admission).

Options: electronic application, deferred entrance.

Application fee: $25.

Required: high school transcript, minimum 2.5 GPA. *Required for some:* interview. *Recommended:* essay or personal statement, 1 letter of recommendation.

CONTACT
Ms. Martha Stolze, Dean of Admission, North Central College, 30 North Brainard Street, PO Box 3063, Naperville, IL 60566-7063. *Phone:* 630-637-5800. *Toll-free phone:* 800-411-1861. *Fax:* 630-637-5819. *E-mail:* admissions@noctrl.edu.

Northeastern Illinois University
Chicago, Illinois
http://www.neiu.edu/

CONTACT
Ms. Zarrin Kerwell, Admissions Counselor, Northeastern Illinois University, 5500 North St. Louis Avenue, Chicago, IL 60625. *Phone:* 773-442-4026. *Fax:* 773-794-6243. *E-mail:* admrec@neiu.edu.

Northern Illinois University
De Kalb, Illinois
http://www.niu.edu/

- **State-supported** university, founded 1895
- **Small-town** 650-acre campus with easy access to Chicago
- **Endowment** $6.5 million
- **Coed** 12,788 undergraduate students, 88% full-time, 50% women, 50% men
- **Moderately difficult** entrance level, 54% of applicants were admitted

UNDERGRAD STUDENTS
11,190 full-time, 1,598 part-time. Students come from 47 states and territories; 47 other countries; 3% are from out of state; 17% Black or African American, non-Hispanic/Latino; 19% Hispanic/Latino; 6% Asian, non-Hispanic/Latino; 0.1% Native Hawaiian or other Pacific Islander, non-Hispanic/Latino; 0.1% American Indian or Alaska Native, non-Hispanic/Latino; 4% Two or more races, non-Hispanic/Latino; 0.3% Race/ethnicity unknown; 2% international; 12% transferred in; 28% live on campus.

Freshmen:
Admission: 14,154 applied, 7,698 admitted, 1,856 enrolled. *Average high school GPA:* 3.3. *Test scores:* ACT scores over 18: 85%; ACT scores over 24: 36%; ACT scores over 30: 6%.

Retention: 73% of full-time freshmen returned.

FACULTY
Total: 1,090, 76% full-time, 74% with terminal degrees.
Student/faculty ratio: 14:1.

ACADEMICS
Calendar: semesters. *Degrees:* bachelor's, master's, and doctoral.

Special study options: accelerated degree program, adult/continuing education programs, advanced placement credit, cooperative education, double majors, honors programs, independent study, internships, off-campus study, part-time degree program, services for LD students, student-designed majors, study abroad, summer session for credit. *ROTC:* Army (b), Air Force (c).

Computers: 1,500 computers/terminals are available on campus for general student use. Students can access the following: computer help desk, free student e-mail accounts, online (class) grades, online (class) registration, online (class) schedules. Campuswide network is available. 100% of college-owned or -operated housing units are wired for high-speed Internet access. Wireless service is available via entire campus.
Library: Founders Memorial Library plus 4 others. *Books:* 1.8 million (physical), 595,551 (digital/electronic); *Serial titles:* 1,206 (physical), 82,960 (digital/electronic); *Databases:* 311. Weekly public service hours: 100; students can reserve study rooms.

STUDENT LIFE
Housing options: on-campus residence required through senior year; coed. Campus housing is university owned. Freshman applicants given priority for college housing.

Activities and organizations: drama/theater group, student-run newspaper, radio station, choral group, marching band, American Marketing Association, Delta Sigma Pi, Pi Sigma Epsilon, Black Choir, Student Volunteer Choir, national fraternities, national sororities.

Athletics Member NCAA. All Division I except football (Division I-A). *Intercollegiate sports:* baseball M(s), basketball M(s)/W(s), cross-country running W, golf M(s)/W(s)(c), gymnastics W(s), soccer M(s)/W(s), softball W(s), swimming and diving M(s)/W(s), tennis M(s)/W(s), volleyball W(s), wrestling M(s). *Intramural sports:* archery M(c)/W(c), badminton M/W, basketball M/W, bowling M(c)/W(c), cross-country running W, football M/W, golf M/W, ice hockey M(c)/W(c), lacrosse M(c)/W(c), racquetball M/W, rugby M(c)/W(c), skiing (downhill) M(c)/W(c), soccer M/W, softball M/W, table tennis M/W, tennis M/W, track and field M(c)/W(c), volleyball M/W, water polo M(c)/W(c), weight lifting M(c)/W(c).

Campus security: 24-hour emergency response devices and patrols, student patrols, late-night transport/escort service, controlled dormitory access.

Student services: health clinic, personal/psychological counseling, women's center, legal services.

FINANCIAL AID
Financial Aid Of all full-time matriculated undergraduates who enrolled in 2017, 10,252 applied for aid, 9,057 were judged to have need, 642 had their need fully met. 879 Federal Work-Study jobs (averaging $2676). In 2017, 1145 non-need-based awards were made. *Average percent of need met:* 58. *Average financial aid package:* $11,829. *Average need-based loan:* $4557. *Average need-based gift aid:* $8496. *Average non-need-based aid:* $4176. *Average indebtedness upon graduation:* $33,912.

APPLYING
Standardized Tests *Required:* SAT or ACT (for admission).

Options: electronic application.

Application fee: $40.

Required: high school transcript, high school class rank.

Notification: continuous (freshmen), continuous (transfers).

CONTACT
Quinten Clay, Director of Admissions, Northern Illinois University, Student Affairs & Enrollment Management, DeKalb, IL 60115-2857. *Phone:* 815-753-0446. *Toll-free phone:* 800-892-3050. *E-mail:* admissions@niu.edu.

North Park University

Chicago, Illinois
http://www.northpark.edu/

CONTACT
Office of Admissions, North Park University, 3225 West Foster Avenue, Chicago, IL 60625-4895. *Phone:* 773-244-5500. *Toll-free phone:* 800-888-NPC8. *Fax:* 773-583-0858. *E-mail:* afao@northpark.edu.

Northwestern University

Evanston, Illinois
http://www.northwestern.edu/
- **Independent** university, founded 1851
- **Suburban** 250-acre campus with easy access to Chicago
- **Coed** 8,256 undergraduate students, 98% full-time, 51% women, 49% men
- **Most difficult** entrance level, 8% of applicants were admitted

UNDERGRAD STUDENTS
8,077 full-time, 179 part-time. Students come from 75 other countries; 68% are from out of state; 6% Black or African American, non-Hispanic/Latino; 13% Hispanic/Latino; 18% Asian, non-Hispanic/Latino; 0.1% American Indian or Alaska Native, non-Hispanic/Latino; 6% Two or more races, non-Hispanic/Latino; 4% Race/ethnicity unknown; 9% international; 2% transferred in; 60% live on campus.

Freshmen:
Admission: 40,425 applied, 3,422 admitted, 1,931 enrolled. *Test scores:* SAT evidence-based reading and writing scores over 500: 99%; SAT math scores over 500: 100%; ACT scores over 18: 100%; SAT evidence-based reading and writing scores over 600: 97%; SAT math scores over 600: 98%; ACT scores over 24: 99%; SAT evidence-based reading and writing scores over 700: 75%; SAT math scores over 700: 86%; ACT scores over 30: 93%.

Retention: 98% of full-time freshmen returned.

FACULTY
Total: 1,772, 86% full-time, 100% with terminal degrees.
Student/faculty ratio: 7:1.

ACADEMICS
Calendar: quarters. *Degrees:* certificates, bachelor's, master's, doctoral, and post-master's certificates.

Special study options: accelerated degree program, adult/continuing education programs, advanced placement credit, cooperative education, double majors, honors programs, independent study, internships, part-time degree program, services for LD students, student-designed majors, study abroad, summer session for credit. *ROTC:* Army (c), Navy (b), Air Force (c).

Computers: Students can access the following: campus intranet, computer help desk, free student e-mail accounts, online (class) grades, online (class) registration, online (class) schedules. Campuswide network is available. 100% of college-owned or -operated housing units are wired for high-speed Internet access. Wireless service is available via entire campus.
Library: University Library plus 6 others.

STUDENT LIFE
Housing options: coed, men-only, women-only. Campus housing is university owned. Freshman campus housing is guaranteed.

Activities and organizations: drama/theater group, student-run newspaper, radio and television station, choral group, marching band, national fraternities, national sororities.

Athletics Member NCAA. All Division I.

Campus security: 24-hour emergency response devices and patrols, late-night transport/escort service, controlled dormitory access.

Student services: health clinic, personal/psychological counseling, women's center, veterans affairs office.

COSTS & FINANCIAL AID
Costs (2018–19) *Comprehensive fee:* $71,193 includes full-time tuition ($54,120), mandatory fees ($447), and room and board ($16,626). *Room*

and board: Room and board charges vary according to board plan and housing facility. *Payment plan:* installment.

Financial Aid *Average indebtedness upon graduation:* $19,718. *Financial aid deadline:* 3/5.

APPLYING
Standardized Tests *Required:* SAT or ACT (for admission). *Required for some:* SAT Subject Tests (for admission).

Options: electronic application, early admission, early decision, deferred entrance.

Application fee: $75.

Required: essay or personal statement, high school transcript, 1 letter of recommendation. *Required for some:* audition for music program.

Application deadlines: 1/1 (freshmen), 3/15 (transfers).

Early decision deadline: 11/1.

Notification: 4/1 (freshmen), continuous (transfers), 12/15 (early decision).

CONTACT
Mr. Christopher Watson, Dean of Undergraduate Enrollment and Assistant Vice President for Student Outreach, Northwestern University, 1801 Hinman Avenue, PO Box 3060, Evanston, IL 60208. *Phone:* 847-491-7271. *E-mail:* ug-admission@northwestern.edu.

★ Olivet Nazarene University

Bourbonnais, Illinois
http://www.olivet.edu/
- **Independent** comprehensive, founded 1907, affiliated with Church of the Nazarene
- **Small-town** 275-acre campus with easy access to Chicago
- **Endowment** $33.2 million
- **Coed**
- **Moderately difficult** entrance level

FACULTY
Student/faculty ratio: 19:1.

ACADEMICS
Calendar: semesters. *Degrees:* bachelor's, master's, and doctoral.
Library: Benner Library. *Books:* 127,535 (physical), 215,890 (digital/electronic); *Serial titles:* 627 (physical), 65,313 (digital/electronic); *Databases:* 263. Students can reserve study rooms.

STUDENT LIFE
Housing options: on-campus residence required through senior year; men-only, women-only. Campus housing is university owned. Freshman campus housing is guaranteed.

Activities and organizations: drama/theater group, student-run newspaper, radio station, choral group, marching band, Fellowship of Christian Athletes, C.A.U.S.E. (College and University Serving and Enabling), Diakonia, Student Education Association, Women's Residence Association.

Athletics Member NAIA, NCCAA.

Campus security: 24-hour patrols, late-night transport/escort service.

Student services: health clinic, personal/psychological counseling.

COSTS & FINANCIAL AID
Costs (2018–19) *Comprehensive fee:* $43,970 includes full-time tuition ($35,080), mandatory fees ($990), and room and board ($7900). Part-time tuition: $1462 per semester hour. Part-time tuition and fees vary according to course load. *Room and board:* Room and board charges vary according to board plan.

Financial Aid Of all full-time matriculated undergraduates who enrolled in 2018, 2,518 applied for aid, 2,309 were judged to have need, 569 had their need fully met. In 2018, 493 non-need-based awards were made. *Average percent of need met:* 85. *Average financial aid package:* $29,996. *Average need-based loan:* $4306. *Average need-based gift aid:* $23,825. *Average non-need-based aid:* $16,719. *Average indebtedness upon graduation:* $32,205.

APPLYING
Standardized Tests *Required:* SAT or ACT (for admission).
Options: electronic application, deferred entrance.

Application fee: $25.

Required: high school transcript, minimum 2.0 GPA. *Required for some:* 2 letters of recommendation. *Recommended:* essay or personal statement, interview.

CONTACT
Mr. Jordan Gerstenberger, Director of Recruitment, Olivet Nazarene University, One University Avenue, Bourbonnais, IL 60914. *Phone:* 815-928-5595. *Toll-free phone:* 800-648-1463.

Principia College
Elsah, Illinois
http://www.principiacollege.edu/

- **Independent Christian Science** 4-year, founded 1910
- **Rural** 2600-acre campus with easy access to St. Louis
- **Endowment** $377.5 million
- **Coed**
- **Moderately difficult** entrance level

FACULTY
Student/faculty ratio: 6:1.

ACADEMICS
Calendar: semesters. *Degree:* bachelor's.
Library: Marshall Brooks Library plus 1 other. *Books:* 168,085 (physical), 338,122 (digital/electronic); *Serial titles:* 237 (physical), 99,238 (digital/electronic); *Databases:* 96. Weekly public service hours: 90; students can reserve study rooms.

STUDENT LIFE
Housing options: on-campus residence required through senior year; coed, men-only, women-only. Campus housing is university owned. Freshman campus housing is guaranteed.

Activities and organizations: drama/theater group, student-run newspaper, radio and television station, choral group, Christian Science Organization, Community Service Team, Solidarity (Multi-club group), Rugby Club, Student Government.

Athletics Member NCAA. All Division III.

Campus security: 24-hour emergency response devices and patrols, controlled dormitory access.

Student services: health clinic.

COSTS & FINANCIAL AID
Costs (2018–19) *Comprehensive fee:* $41,080 includes full-time tuition ($28,770), mandatory fees ($700), and room and board ($11,610). Full-time tuition and fees vary according to course load. Part-time tuition: $959 per credit hour. Part-time tuition and fees vary according to course load. *College room only:* $5510. Room and board charges vary according to board plan.

Financial Aid Of all full-time matriculated undergraduates who enrolled in 2018, 322 applied for aid, 308 were judged to have need. In 2018, 94 non-need-based awards were made. *Average percent of need met:* 77. *Average financial aid package:* $32,875. *Average need-based loan:* $5642. *Average need-based gift aid:* $29,065. *Average non-need-based aid:* $20,576. *Average indebtedness upon graduation:* $21,509.

APPLYING
Standardized Tests *Required:* SAT or ACT (for admission).

Options: electronic application, deferred entrance.

Required: essay or personal statement, high school transcript, minimum 2.4 GPA, 3 letters of recommendation, Christian Science commitment. *Required for some:* interview. *Recommended:* interview.

CONTACT
Ms. Tami Gavaletz, Director of Admissions and Financial Aid, Principia College, 1 Maybeck Place, Elsah, IL 62028. *Phone:* 618-374-5187. *Toll-free phone:* 800-277-4648 Ext. 2804.

Quincy University
Quincy, Illinois
http://www.quincy.edu/

CONTACT
Ms. Abby Wayman, Associate Director, Admissions, Quincy University, Admissions Office, 1800 College Avenue, Quincy, IL 62301-2699. *Phone:* 217-228-5432 Ext. 3414. *Toll-free phone:* 800-688-4295. *E-mail:* admissions@quincy.edu.

Rasmussen College Aurora
Aurora, Illinois
http://www.rasmussen.edu/

CONTACT
Ms. Susan Hammerstrom, Director of Admissions, Rasmussen College Aurora, 2363 Sequoia Drive, Aurora, IL 60506. *Phone:* 630-888-3500. *Toll-free phone:* 888-549-6755. *E-mail:* susan.hammerstrom@rasmussen.edu.

Rasmussen College Mokena/Tinley Park
Mokena, Illinois
http://www.rasmussen.edu/

CONTACT
Ms. Susan Hammerstrom, Director of Admissions, Rasmussen College Mokena/Tinley Park, 8650 West Spring Lake Road, Mokena, IL 60448. *Phone:* 815-534-3300. *Toll-free phone:* 888-549-6755.

Rasmussen College Rockford
Rockford, Illinois
http://www.rasmussen.edu/

- **Proprietary** 4-year, part of Rasmussen College System
- **Suburban** campus
- **Coed**
- **Minimally difficult** entrance level

FACULTY
Student/faculty ratio: 22:1.

ACADEMICS
Calendar: quarters. *Degrees:* certificates, diplomas, associate, and bachelor's.
Library: Rasmussen College Library - Rockford.

STUDENT LIFE
Housing options: college housing not available.

APPLYING
Standardized Tests *Required:* institutional exam (for admission).

Options: electronic application, early admission, deferred entrance.

Required: high school transcript, minimum 2.0 GPA. *Required for some:* interview.

CONTACT
Dwayne Bertotto, Vice President of Admissions and Student Experience, Rasmussen College Rockford, 8300 Norman Center Drive, Suite 300, Bloomington, MN 55437. *Phone:* 952-806-3958. *Toll-free phone:* 888-549-6755. *E-mail:* dwayne.bertotto@rasmussen.edu.

Rasmussen College Romeoville/Joliet
Romeoville, Illinois
http://www.rasmussen.edu/

CONTACT
Ms. Susan Hammerstrom, Director of Admissions, Rasmussen College Romeoville/Joliet, 1400 West Normantown Road, Romeoville, IL 60446. *Phone:* 815-306-2600. *Toll-free phone:* 888-549-6755. *E-mail:* susan.hammerstrom@rasmussen.edu.

Resurrection University

Chicago, Illinois
http://www.resu.edu/

- **Independent** upper-level, founded 1982
- **Urban** 10-acre campus with easy access to Chicago
- **Endowment** $1.5 million
- **Coed**
- **Moderately difficult** entrance level

FACULTY
Student/faculty ratio: 7:1.

ACADEMICS
Calendar: semesters. *Degrees:* certificates, bachelor's, master's, doctoral, and postbachelor's certificates.
Library: Resurrection University Library.

STUDENT LIFE
Housing options: college housing not available.
Campus security: 24-hour emergency response devices and patrols, late-night transport/escort service.
Student services: personal/psychological counseling.

COSTS & FINANCIAL AID
Costs (2018–19) *One-time required fee:* $150. *Tuition:* $37,578 full-time. Full-time tuition and fees vary according to course load, degree level, and program. Part-time tuition and fees vary according to course load, degree level, and program. *Required fees:* $870 full-time.
Financial Aid Of all full-time matriculated undergraduates who enrolled in 2017, 459 applied for aid, 459 were judged to have need. In 2017, 10 non-need-based awards were made. *Average percent of need met:* 30. *Average financial aid package:* $23,000. *Average need-based loan:* $5500. *Average need-based gift aid:* $5960. *Average non-need-based aid:* $2000.

APPLYING
Standardized Tests *Required for some:* TEAS.
Options: electronic application, deferred entrance.
Application fee: $50.

CONTACT
Resurrection University, 1431 N. Claremont Avenue, Chicago, IL 60622. *Phone:* 773-252-5307.

Robert Morris University Illinois

Chicago, Illinois
http://www.robertmorris.edu/

- **Independent** comprehensive, founded 1913
- **Urban** campus with easy access to Chicago
- **Endowment** $17.9 million
- **Coed**
- **Minimally difficult** entrance level

FACULTY
Student/faculty ratio: 21:1.

ACADEMICS
Calendar: 5 10-week academic sessions per year. *Degrees:* associate, bachelor's, and master's.
Library: Information Technology Library. *Books:* 165,268 (physical), 58,182 (digital/electronic); *Databases:* 37. Weekly public service hours: 74; students can reserve study rooms.

STUDENT LIFE
Housing options: coed. Campus housing is leased by the school. Freshman applicants given priority for college housing.
Activities and organizations: drama/theater group, student-run newspaper, choral group, marching band, UNA-USA, Eagles United for a Cause, Eagles Soaring for a Change, Cooks for a Cause, Eagle Newspaper.
Athletics Member NAIA, USCAA.
Campus security: late-night transport/escort service, controlled dormitory access, Urban campus has multiple security officers at all times who are off-duty Chicago police officers.

Student services: personal/psychological counseling, veterans affairs office.

COSTS & FINANCIAL AID
Costs (2018–19) *Comprehensive fee:* $43,338 includes full-time tuition ($28,050), mandatory fees ($480), and room and board ($14,808). Part-time tuition: $775 per quarter hour. Part-time tuition and fees vary according to course load.
Financial Aid Of all full-time matriculated undergraduates who enrolled in 2016, 2,653 applied for aid, 2,586 were judged to have need, 119 had their need fully met. 146 Federal Work-Study jobs (averaging $2239). In 2016, 93 non-need-based awards were made. *Average percent of need met:* 56. *Average financial aid package:* $17,114. *Average need-based loan:* $4198. *Average need-based gift aid:* $13,866. *Average non-need-based aid:* $18,623. *Average indebtedness upon graduation:* $34,382.

APPLYING
Standardized Tests *Required for some:* SAT or ACT (for admission), ACT for nursing and surgical technology programs.
Options: electronic application, deferred entrance.
Application fee: $20.
Required for some: high school transcript. *Recommended:* interview.

CONTACT
Admissions Office, Robert Morris University Illinois, 401 South State Street, Chicago, IL 60605. *Phone:* 800-762-5960. *Toll-free phone:* 800-762-5960. *Fax:* 312-935-4440. *E-mail:* enroll@robertmorris.edu.

Rockford University

Rockford, Illinois
http://www.rockford.edu/

- **Independent** comprehensive, founded 1847
- **Suburban** 150-acre campus with easy access to Chicago
- **Coed** 1,002 undergraduate students, 89% full-time, 55% women, 45% men
- **Minimally difficult** entrance level, 49% of applicants were admitted

UNDERGRAD STUDENTS
888 full-time, 114 part-time. 15% are from out of state; 10% Black or African American, non-Hispanic/Latino; 17% Hispanic/Latino; 2% Asian, non-Hispanic/Latino; 0.2% American Indian or Alaska Native, non-Hispanic/Latino; 3% Two or more races, non-Hispanic/Latino; 0.6% Race/ethnicity unknown; 7% international; 15% transferred in; 35% live on campus.

Freshmen:
Admission: 2,682 applied, 1,315 admitted, 161 enrolled. *Average high school GPA:* 3.3. *Test scores:* SAT evidence-based reading and writing scores over 500: 76%; SAT math scores over 500: 74%; ACT scores over 18: 93%; SAT evidence-based reading and writing scores over 600: 26%; SAT math scores over 600: 23%; ACT scores over 24: 25%; SAT evidence-based reading and writing scores over 700: 4%; SAT math scores over 700: 4%; ACT scores over 30: 5%.
Retention: 66% of full-time freshmen returned.

FACULTY
Total: 156, 49% full-time, 42% with terminal degrees.
Student/faculty ratio: 10:1.

ACADEMICS
Calendar: semesters. *Degrees:* bachelor's, master's, and postbachelor's certificates.
Special study options: academic remediation for entering students, accelerated degree program, adult/continuing education programs, advanced placement credit, distance learning, double majors, English as a second language, honors programs, independent study, internships, off-campus study, part-time degree program, services for LD students, study abroad, summer session for credit.
Computers: 94 computers/terminals and 4 ports are available on campus for general student use. Students can access the following: campus intranet, computer help desk, free student e-mail accounts, online (class) grades, online (class) registration, online (class) schedules, online bill payment. Campuswide network is available. 100% of college-owned or -

operated housing units are wired for high-speed Internet access. Wireless service is available via entire campus.

Library: Howard Colman Library. *Books:* 134,831 (physical), 140,140 (digital/electronic); *Serial titles:* 157 (physical), 23,000 (digital/electronic); *Databases:* 27. Weekly public service hours: 85; students can reserve study rooms.

STUDENT LIFE
Housing options: coed, special housing for students with disabilities. Campus housing is university owned.

Activities and organizations: drama/theater group, student-run newspaper, radio station, choral group, Campus Activities Board, Multicultural Club, Student Government Association, Nursing Student Organization, Alpha Helix.

Athletics Member NCAA. All Division III. *Intercollegiate sports:* baseball M, basketball M/W, cross-country running M/W, football M, soccer M/W, softball W, track and field M/W, volleyball W. *Intramural sports:* basketball M/W, football M/W, volleyball W.

Campus security: 24-hour emergency response devices and patrols, student patrols, late-night transport/escort service, controlled dormitory access.

Student services: health clinic, personal/psychological counseling.

COSTS & FINANCIAL AID
Costs (2018–19) *Comprehensive fee:* $39,590 includes full-time tuition ($30,800), mandatory fees ($130), and room and board ($8660). Full-time tuition and fees vary according to course load. Part-time tuition: $795 per credit hour. Part-time tuition and fees vary according to course load. *College room only:* $4700. Room and board charges vary according to board plan and housing facility. *Payment plan:* installment. *Waivers:* employees or children of employees.

Financial Aid Of all full-time matriculated undergraduates who enrolled in 2017, 799 applied for aid, 768 were judged to have need, 77 had their need fully met. 139 Federal Work-Study jobs (averaging $718). 185 state and other part-time jobs (averaging $828). In 2017, 79 non-need-based awards were made. *Average percent of need met:* 65. *Average financial aid package:* $20,584. *Average need-based loan:* $4927. *Average need-based gift aid:* $15,822. *Average non-need-based aid:* $11,139. *Average indebtedness upon graduation:* $35,489.

APPLYING
Standardized Tests *Required:* SAT or ACT (for admission).

Options: electronic application, early admission.

Required: high school transcript. *Required for some:* essay or personal statement, minimum 2.7 GPA, 2 letters of recommendation. *Recommended:* minimum 2.7 GPA.

Notification: continuous (freshmen), continuous (out-of-state freshmen), continuous (transfers).

CONTACT
Ms. Jennifer Nordstrom, Associate Vice President for Undergraduate Admission, Rockford University, 5050 East State Street, Rockford, IL 61108-2393. *Phone:* 815-226-4050. *Toll-free phone:* 800-892-2984. *Fax:* 815-226-2822. *E-mail:* admissions@rockford.edu.

Roosevelt University
Chicago, Illinois
http://www.roosevelt.edu/
- **Independent** comprehensive, founded 1945
- **Urban** campus with easy access to Chicago
- **Endowment** $109.6 million
- **Coed**
- **Moderately difficult** entrance level

FACULTY
Student/faculty ratio: 10:1.

ACADEMICS
Calendar: semesters. *Degrees:* bachelor's, master's, doctoral, and postbachelor's certificates.

Library: Murray-Green Library plus 4 others. *Books:* 152,557 (physical), 43,963 (digital/electronic); *Serial titles:* 174 (physical), 41,406 (digital/electronic); *Databases:* 198.

STUDENT LIFE
Housing options: on-campus residence required through sophomore year; coed. Campus housing is university owned, leased by the school and is provided by a third party. Freshman campus housing is guaranteed.

Activities and organizations: student-run newspaper, radio station, SPEED Programming Board, Student Government Association, Roosevelt Black Student Union, Alpha Phi Omega Co-ed Service Fraternity, Alpha Gamma Delta Sorority Inc, national fraternities, national sororities.

Athletics Member NAIA.

Campus security: 24-hour emergency response devices and patrols, late-night transport/escort service, controlled dormitory access.

Student services: personal/psychological counseling.

COSTS & FINANCIAL AID
Costs (2018–19) *Comprehensive fee:* $43,055 includes full-time tuition ($29,832) and room and board ($13,223). Full-time tuition and fees vary according to program. Part-time tuition: $797 per credit hour. Part-time tuition and fees vary according to program. *Required fees:* $303 per term part-time. *College room only:* $9412. Room and board charges vary according to board plan and housing facility.

Financial Aid Of all full-time matriculated undergraduates who enrolled in 2014, 2,812 applied for aid, 2,397 were judged to have need, 169 had their need fully met. In 2014, 500 non-need-based awards were made. *Average percent of need met:* 75. *Average financial aid package:* $22,318. *Average need-based loan:* $8800. *Average need-based gift aid:* $9000. *Average non-need-based aid:* $7000.

APPLYING
Standardized Tests *Required:* SAT or ACT (for admission).

Options: electronic application, deferred entrance.

Application fee: $25.

Required: high school transcript, minimum 2.5 GPA, audition for music and theater programs. *Required for some:* essay or personal statement, interview. *Recommended:* essay or personal statement.

CONTACT
Mr. Al Nunez, Director of Admission, Roosevelt University, 430 S. Michigan Avenue, Chicago, IL 60605. *Phone:* 312-341-2187. *Toll-free phone:* 877-APPLYRU. *E-mail:* anunez13@roosevelt.edu.

Rush University
Chicago, Illinois
http://www.rushu.rush.edu/

CONTACT
Rush University, 600 South Paulina, Chicago, IL 60612-3832. *Phone:* 312-942-7100.

Saint Anthony College of Nursing
Rockford, Illinois
http://www.sacn.edu/

CONTACT
Ms. April Lipnitzky, Enrollment Management Coordinator, Saint Anthony College of Nursing, 5658 East State Street, Rockford, IL 61108-2468. *Phone:* 815-227-2141. *Fax:* 815-227-2730. *E-mail:* admissions@sacn.edu.

St. Augustine College
Chicago, Illinois
http://www.staugustine.edu/

CONTACT
Ms. Gloria Quiroz, Director of Admissions, St. Augustine College, 1333-1345 West Argyle, Chicago, IL 60640-3501. *Phone:* 773-878-3256. *Fax:* 773-878-0937. *E-mail:* info@staugustine.edu.

Saint Francis Medical Center College of Nursing

Peoria, Illinois

http://www.sfmccon.edu/

- **Independent Roman Catholic** upper-level, founded 1986
- **Urban** campus
- **Coed, primarily women**
- **84% of applicants were admitted**

FACULTY

Student/faculty ratio: 10:1.

ACADEMICS

Calendar: semesters. *Degrees:* bachelor's, master's, doctoral, and post-master's certificates.

Library: Sister Mary Ludgera Pieperbeck Learning and Resource Center plus 1 other. *Books:* 4,054 (physical), 298 (digital/electronic); *Serial titles:* 126 (physical); *Databases:* 57. Students can reserve study rooms.

STUDENT LIFE

Housing options: coed. Campus housing is university owned.

Activities and organizations: Student Senate, SNAI, Minority Student Association, Tau Omicron.

Campus security: 24-hour emergency response devices and patrols, late-night transport/escort service, controlled dormitory access.

Student services: health clinic, personal/psychological counseling.

COSTS & FINANCIAL AID

Costs (2018–19) *Tuition:* $20,020 full-time, $616 per semester hour part-time. Full-time tuition and fees vary according to course load, degree level, program, and student level. Part-time tuition and fees vary according to course load, degree level, program, and student level. *Required fees:* $1037 full-time, $215 per term part-time. *Room only:* $1850.

Financial Aid Of all full-time matriculated undergraduates who enrolled in 2018, 265 applied for aid, 219 were judged to have need, 9 had their need fully met. In 2018, 26 non-need-based awards were made. *Average percent of need met:* 45. *Average financial aid package:* $11,243. *Average need-based loan:* $5491. *Average need-based gift aid:* $7470. *Average non-need-based aid:* $2715.

APPLYING

Options: deferred entrance.

Application fee: $50.

CONTACT

Saint Francis Medical Center College of Nursing, 511 Northeast Greenleaf Street, Peoria, IL 61603-3783. *Phone:* 309-624-8980.

St. John's College

Springfield, Illinois

http://www.sjcs.edu/

CONTACT

St. John's College, 729 East Carpenter Street, Springfield, IL 62702. *Phone:* 217-525-5628.

Saint Xavier University

Chicago, Illinois

http://www.sxu.edu/

CONTACT

Dr. Kathleen Carlson, Vice President, Saint Xavier University, 3700 West 103rd Street, Chicago, IL 60655-3105. *Phone:* 773-298-3305. *Toll-free phone:* 800-462-9288. *E-mail:* carlson@sxu.edu.

School of the Art Institute of Chicago

Chicago, Illinois

http://www.saic.edu/

CONTACT

Ms. Asia Mitchell, Director, Undergraduate Admissions, School of the Art Institute of Chicago, 36 South Wabash, Chicago, IL 60603. *Phone:* 312-629-6100. *Toll-free phone:* 800-232-SAIC. *Fax:* 312-629-6101. *E-mail:* ugadmiss@saic.edu.

Southern Illinois University Carbondale

Carbondale, Illinois

http://www.siu.edu/

- **State-supported** university, founded 1869, part of Southern Illinois University
- **Rural** 1136-acre campus with easy access to St. Louis
- **Coed** 9,512 undergraduate students, 85% full-time, 46% women, 54% men
- **Moderately difficult** entrance level, 72% of applicants were admitted

UNDERGRAD STUDENTS

8,070 full-time, 1,442 part-time. 20% are from out of state; 15% Black or African American, non-Hispanic/Latino; 9% Hispanic/Latino; 2% Asian, non-Hispanic/Latino; 0.1% Native Hawaiian or other Pacific Islander, non-Hispanic/Latino; 0.3% American Indian or Alaska Native, non-Hispanic/Latino; 3% Two or more races, non-Hispanic/Latino; 0.1% Race/ethnicity unknown; 4% international; 13% transferred in; 22% live on campus.

Freshmen:

Admission: 6,219 applied, 4,475 admitted, 1,133 enrolled. *Average high school GPA:* 3.2. *Test scores:* SAT evidence-based reading and writing scores over 500: 79%; SAT math scores over 500: 77%; ACT scores over 18: 92%; SAT evidence-based reading and writing scores over 600: 34%; SAT math scores over 600: 26%; ACT scores over 24: 50%; SAT evidence-based reading and writing scores over 700: 4%; SAT math scores over 700: 5%; ACT scores over 30: 11%.

Retention: 71% of full-time freshmen returned.

FACULTY

Total: 940, 83% full-time, 70% with terminal degrees.

Student/faculty ratio: 14:1.

ACADEMICS

Calendar: semesters plus 8-week summer session. *Degrees:* certificates, associate, bachelor's, master's, doctoral, and postbachelor's certificates.

Special study options: academic remediation for entering students, accelerated degree program, adult/continuing education programs, advanced placement credit, cooperative education, distance learning, double majors, English as a second language, honors programs, independent study, internships, off-campus study, part-time degree program, services for LD students, student-designed majors, study abroad, summer session for credit. *ROTC:* Army (b), Air Force (b).

Computers: 1,900 computers/terminals are available on campus for general student use. Students can access the following: computer help desk, free student e-mail accounts, online (class) grades, online (class) registration, online (class) schedules. Campuswide network is available. 100% of college-owned or -operated housing units are wired for high-speed Internet access. Wireless service is available via classrooms, computer centers, computer labs, dorm rooms, learning centers, libraries, student centers.

Library: Morris Library plus 1 other. *Books:* 2.6 million (physical), 243,170 (digital/electronic); *Serial titles:* 286 (physical), 65,075 (digital/electronic); *Databases:* 175. Weekly public service hours: 100; students can reserve study rooms.

STUDENT LIFE

Housing options: on-campus residence required for freshman year; coed, men-only, women-only, special housing for students with disabilities. Campus housing is university owned. Freshman campus housing is guaranteed.

Activities and organizations: drama/theater group, student-run newspaper, radio and television station, choral group, marching band, Undergraduate Student Government, Greek Councils, International Student Council, Black Affairs Council, Dawg Pound, national fraternities, national sororities.

Athletics Member NCAA. All Division I except football (Division I-AA). *Intercollegiate sports:* baseball M(s), basketball M(s)/W(s), cheerleading M/W, cross-country running M(s)/W(s), golf M(s)/W(s), soccer M(c)/W(s), softball W(s), swimming and diving M(s)/W(s), track and field M(s)/W(s), volleyball W(s). *Intramural sports:* archery M(c)/W(c), badminton M(c)/W(c), baseball M(c), basketball M/W, bowling M(c)/W(c), equestrian sports M(c)/W(c), fencing M(c), field hockey W(c), gymnastics M(c)/W(c), lacrosse M(c), racquetball M/W, rock climbing M(c)/W(c), rugby M(c)/W(c), sailing M(c)/W(c), soccer M(c)/W(c), softball W(c), swimming and diving W, table tennis M(c)/W(c), tennis M(c)/W(c), triathlon M(c)/W(c), ultimate Frisbee M(c)/W(c), volleyball M(c)/W(c), water polo M(c)/W(c), weight lifting M(c)/W(c), wrestling M(c)/W(c).

Campus security: 24-hour emergency response devices and patrols, student patrols, late-night transport/escort service, controlled dormitory access, well-lit pathways, night safety vans, student transit system and extensive video security camera system.

Student services: health clinic, personal/psychological counseling, women's center, legal services, veterans affairs office.

COSTS & FINANCIAL AID

Costs (2018–19) *Tuition:* state resident $9638 full-time, $321 per credit hour part-time; nonresident $9638 full-time, $803 per credit hour part-time. Full-time tuition and fees vary according to course load, location, program, reciprocity agreements, and student level. Part-time tuition and fees vary according to course load, location, program, reciprocity agreements, and student level. No tuition increase for student's term of enrollment. Part time fees are based on a student taking 6 credit hours per semester. *Required fees:* $5066 full-time, $2960 per year part-time. *Room and board:* $10,622. Room and board charges vary according to board plan and housing facility. *Payment plan:* installment. *Waivers:* children of alumni, senior citizens, and employees or children of employees.

Financial Aid Of all full-time matriculated undergraduates who enrolled in 2018, 6,413 applied for aid, 5,586 were judged to have need, 505 had their need fully met. 2,561 Federal Work-Study jobs (averaging $2827). In 2018, 427 non-need-based awards were made. *Average percent of need met:* 57. *Average financial aid package:* $15,514. *Average need-based loan:* $4559. *Average need-based gift aid:* $8112. *Average non-need-based aid:* $7225. *Average indebtedness upon graduation:* $30,326.

APPLYING

Standardized Tests *Required:* SAT or ACT (for admission).

Options: electronic application, deferred entrance.

Application fee: $40.

Required: high school transcript.

Application deadlines: rolling (freshmen), rolling (transfers).

Notification: continuous (freshmen), continuous (transfers).

CONTACT

Tamora Workman, Director of the Registrar's Office, Southern Illinois University Carbondale, Office of Registrar, 1263 Lincoln Drive, MC 4701, Carbondale, IL 62901. *Phone:* 618-453-2963. *Fax:* 618-453-2915. *E-mail:* regstrar@siu.edu.

Southern Illinois University Edwardsville

Edwardsville, Illinois

http://www.siue.edu/

- **State-supported** university, founded 1957, part of Southern Illinois University
- **Suburban** 2660-acre campus with easy access to St. Louis
- **Endowment** $23.1 million
- **Coed** 10,833 undergraduate students, 83% full-time, 53% women, 47% men
- **Moderately difficult** entrance level, 87% of applicants were admitted

UNDERGRAD STUDENTS

8,979 full-time, 1,854 part-time. Students come from 52 states and territories; 34 other countries; 14% are from out of state; 13% Black or African American, non-Hispanic/Latino; 5% Hispanic/Latino; 2% Asian, non-Hispanic/Latino; 0.1% Native Hawaiian or other Pacific Islander, non-Hispanic/Latino; 0.3% American Indian or Alaska Native, non-Hispanic/Latino; 4% Two or more races, non-Hispanic/Latino; 1% Race/ethnicity unknown; 1% international; 11% transferred in; 25% live on campus.

Freshmen:

Admission: 6,410 applied, 5,605 admitted, 1,706 enrolled. *Average high school GPA:* 3.6. *Test scores:* SAT evidence-based reading and writing scores over 500: 81%; SAT math scores over 500: 77%; ACT scores over 18: 95%; SAT evidence-based reading and writing scores over 600: 34%; SAT math scores over 600: 29%; ACT scores over 24: 52%; SAT evidence-based reading and writing scores over 700: 2%; SAT math scores over 700: 4%; ACT scores over 30: 9%.

Retention: 75% of full-time freshmen returned.

FACULTY

Total: 862, 71% full-time, 67% with terminal degrees.

Student/faculty ratio: 19:1.

ACADEMICS

Calendar: semesters. *Degrees:* bachelor's, master's, doctoral, post-master's, and postbachelor's certificates.

Special study options: academic remediation for entering students, accelerated degree program, advanced placement credit, cooperative education, distance learning, double majors, English as a second language, external degree program, honors programs, independent study, internships, off-campus study, part-time degree program, services for LD students, student-designed majors, study abroad, summer session for credit. *ROTC:* Army (b), Air Force (c).

Unusual degree programs: 3-2 engineering.

Computers: 315 computers/terminals are available on campus for general student use. Students can access the following: campus intranet, computer help desk, free student e-mail accounts, online (class) grades, online (class) registration, online (class) schedules, online job finder. Campuswide network is available. 100% of college-owned or -operated housing units are wired for high-speed Internet access. Wireless service is available via entire campus.

Library: Lovejoy Library. *Books:* 522,502 (physical), 91,353 (digital/electronic); *Serial titles:* 35,778 (physical), 35,637 (digital/electronic). Students can reserve study rooms.

STUDENT LIFE

Housing options: coed, special housing for students with disabilities. Campus housing is university owned. Freshman applicants given priority for college housing.

Activities and organizations: drama/theater group, student-run newspaper, radio station, choral group, Fraternity and Sorority Life, Campus Activities Board, Sports Clubs/Intramurals, Dance Marathon, Student Government, national fraternities, national sororities.

Athletics Member NCAA. All Division I. *Intercollegiate sports:* baseball M(s), basketball M(s)/W(s), cross-country running M(s)/W(s), golf M(s), soccer M(s)/W(s), softball W(s), tennis W(s), track and field M(s)/W(s), volleyball W(s), wrestling M(s). *Intramural sports:* archery M(c)/W(c), badminton M/W, baseball M(c), basketball M/W, bowling M/W, cheerleading M(c)/W(c), cross-country running M(c)/W(c), equestrian sports M(c)/W(c), fencing M(c)/W(c), football M(c), golf M(c)/W(c), ice hockey M(c), racquetball M/W, rock climbing M(c)/W(c), sand volleyball M/W, soccer M/W, softball M/W, swimming and diving M(c)/W(c), table tennis M/W, tennis M/W, ultimate Frisbee M(c)/W(c), volleyball M(c)/W(c), wrestling M(c).

Campus security: 24-hour emergency response devices and patrols, late-night transport/escort service, controlled dormitory access.

Student services: health clinic, personal/psychological counseling, veterans affairs office.

COSTS & FINANCIAL AID

Costs (2019–20) *Tuition:* state resident $9123 full-time; nonresident $9123 full-time. No tuition increase for student's term of enrollment. *Required fees:* $3096 full-time. *Room and board:* $10,701; room only: $7110.

Financial Aid Of all full-time matriculated undergraduates who enrolled in 2015, 8,167 applied for aid, 6,499 were judged to have need, 2,442 had their need fully met. In 2015, 521 non-need-based awards were made. *Average percent of need met:* 60. *Average financial aid package:* $11,223. *Average need-based loan:* $4496. *Average need-based gift aid:* $7760. *Average non-need-based aid:* $5113. *Average indebtedness upon graduation:* $22,277.

APPLYING

Standardized Tests *Required:* SAT or ACT (for admission).

Options: electronic application, early admission, deferred entrance.

Application fee: $40.

Required: high school transcript, minimum 2.0 GPA, college transcript(s). *Required for some:* essay or personal statement.

Application deadlines: 5/1 (freshmen), rolling (transfers).

Notification: continuous (freshmen), continuous (transfers).

CONTACT

Mr. Todd Burrell, Director of Undergraduate Admissions, Southern Illinois University Edwardsville, Campus Box 1600, Rendleman Hall, Edwardsville, IL 62026-1600. *Phone:* 618-650-3705. *Toll-free phone:* 800-447-SIUE. *Fax:* 618-650-5013. *E-mail:* admissions@siue.edu.

Telshe Yeshiva–Chicago

Chicago, Illinois

CONTACT

Rosh Hayeshiva, Telshe Yeshiva–Chicago, 3535 West Foster Avenue, Chicago, IL 60625-5598. *Phone:* 773-463-7738.

Trinity Christian College

Palos Heights, Illinois

http://www.trnty.edu/

- **Independent Christian Reformed** comprehensive, founded 1959, part of n/a
- **Suburban** 53-acre campus with easy access to Chicago
- **Endowment** $10.8 million
- **Coed** 1,063 undergraduate students, 83% full-time, 67% women, 33% men
- **Moderately difficult** entrance level, 80% of applicants were admitted

UNDERGRAD STUDENTS

883 full-time, 180 part-time. Students come from 29 states and territories; 10 other countries; 33% are from out of state; 8% Black or African American, non-Hispanic/Latino; 12% Hispanic/Latino; 1% Asian, non-Hispanic/Latino; 0.1% Native Hawaiian or other Pacific Islander, non-Hispanic/Latino; 0.2% American Indian or Alaska Native, non-Hispanic/Latino; 1% Two or more races, non-Hispanic/Latino; 4% Race/ethnicity unknown; 12% international; 8% transferred in; 42% live on campus.

Freshmen:

Admission: 768 applied, 616 admitted, 153 enrolled. *Average high school GPA:* 3.3. *Test scores:* SAT evidence-based reading and writing scores over 500: 64%; SAT math scores over 500: 66%; ACT scores over 18: 87%; SAT evidence-based reading and writing scores over 600: 18%; SAT math scores over 600: 15%; ACT scores over 24: 39%; SAT evidence-based reading and writing scores over 700: 5%; SAT math scores over 700: 2%; ACT scores over 30: 11%.

Retention: 80% of full-time freshmen returned.

FACULTY

Total: 142, 49% full-time, 49% with terminal degrees.

Student/faculty ratio: 10:1.

ACADEMICS

Calendar: semesters plus 2 week interim term. *Degrees:* bachelor's and master's.

Special study options: academic remediation for entering students, accelerated degree program, adult/continuing education programs, advanced placement credit, cooperative education, distance learning, double majors, English as a second language, honors programs, independent study, internships, off-campus study, part-time degree program, services for LD students, study abroad, summer session for credit.

Computers: 170 computers/terminals are available on campus for general student use. Students can access the following: campus intranet, computer help desk, free student e-mail accounts, online (class) grades, online (class) registration, online (class) schedules. Campuswide network is available. 100% of college-owned or -operated housing units are wired for high-speed Internet access. Wireless service is available via entire campus.

Library: Jennie Huizenga Memorial Library plus 1 other. *Books:* 60,951 (physical), 6,449 (digital/electronic); *Serial titles:* 20 (physical), 45,797 (digital/electronic); *Databases:* 61. Weekly public service hours: 84; students can reserve study rooms.

STUDENT LIFE

Housing options: coed. Campus housing is university owned. Freshman campus housing is guaranteed.

Activities and organizations: drama/theater group, student-run newspaper, choral group, Student Association, Student ministries, Campus newspaper, Pro-Life Task Force, PACE (prison tutoring program).

Athletics Member NAIA, NCCAA. *Intercollegiate sports:* baseball M(s), basketball M(s)/W(s), cross-country running M(s)/W(s), golf M(s), soccer M(s)/W(s), softball W(s), track and field M(s)/W(s), volleyball M/W(s). *Intramural sports:* basketball M/W, soccer M/W, volleyball M/W.

Campus security: 24-hour emergency response devices and patrols, student patrols, late-night transport/escort service, controlled dormitory access, security cameras, Code Blue Emergency Phones.

Student services: personal/psychological counseling.

COSTS & FINANCIAL AID

Costs (2019–20) *One-time required fee:* $225. *Comprehensive fee:* $40,900 includes full-time tuition ($30,700), mandatory fees ($250), and room and board ($9950). Part-time tuition: $992 per credit hour.

Financial Aid Of all full-time matriculated undergraduates who enrolled in 2017, 770 applied for aid, 697 were judged to have need, 115 had their need fully met. In 2017, 99 non-need-based awards were made. *Average percent of need met:* 73. *Average financial aid package:* $20,865. *Average need-based loan:* $4589. *Average need-based gift aid:* $16,760. *Average non-need-based aid:* $10,560. *Average indebtedness upon graduation:* $29,978.

APPLYING

Standardized Tests *Required:* SAT or ACT (for admission).

Options: electronic application, deferred entrance.

Required: essay or personal statement, high school transcript, minimum 2.5 GPA, interview. *Required for some:* 1 letter of recommendation, ACT Composite score of 19 or combined SAT score of 980.

Application deadlines: rolling (freshmen), rolling (transfers).

Notification: continuous (freshmen), continuous (transfers).

CONTACT

Brittany Minnesma, Assistant Director of Admissions, Trinity Christian College, 6601 West College Drive, Palos Heights, IL 60463. *Phone:* 708-239-4808. *Toll-free phone:* 866-TRIN-4-ME. *Fax:* 708-239-4826. *E-mail:* brittany.minnesma@trnty.edu.

Trinity College of Nursing and Health Sciences

Rock Island, Illinois

http://www.trinitycollegeqc.edu/

CONTACT

Ms. Lori Perez, Admissions Representative, Trinity College of Nursing and Health Sciences, 2122 25th Avenue, Rock Island, IL 61201. *Phone:* 309-779-7700. *Fax:* 309-779-7748. *E-mail:* perezlj@ihs.org.

Trinity International University

Deerfield, Illinois

http://www.tiu.edu/

CONTACT

Mr. Aaron Mahl, Director of Undergraduate Admissions, Trinity International University, 2065 Half Day Road, Deerfield, IL 60015-1284. *Phone:* 847-317-7000. *Toll-free phone:* 800-822-3225. *Fax:* 847-317-8097. *E-mail:* tcadmissions@tiu.edu.

University of Chicago

Chicago, Illinois

http://www.uchicago.edu/

- **Independent** university, founded 1890
- **Urban** 217-acre campus with easy access to Chicago
- **Coed** 6,552 undergraduate students, 100% full-time, 49% women, 51% men
- **Most difficult** entrance level, 7% of applicants were admitted

UNDERGRAD STUDENTS

6,551 full-time, 1 part-time. Students come from 52 states and territories; 77 other countries; 81% are from out of state; 5% Black or African American, non-Hispanic/Latino; 14% Hispanic/Latino; 19% Asian, non-Hispanic/Latino; 0.1% American Indian or Alaska Native, non-Hispanic/Latino; 6% Two or more races, non-Hispanic/Latino; 2% Race/ethnicity unknown; 14% international; 0.5% transferred in; 55% live on campus.

Freshmen:

Admission: 32,283 applied, 2,345 admitted, 1,809 enrolled. *Average high school GPA:* 4.5. *Test scores:* SAT evidence-based reading and writing scores over 500: 100%; SAT math scores over 500: 100%; ACT scores over 18: 100%; SAT evidence-based reading and writing scores over 600: 100%; SAT math scores over 600: 99%; ACT scores over 24: 100%; SAT evidence-based reading and writing scores over 700: 88%; SAT math scores over 700: 93%; ACT scores over 30: 97%.

Retention: 99% of full-time freshmen returned.

FACULTY

Total: 1,720, 85% full-time, 100% with terminal degrees.

Student/faculty ratio: 5:1.

ACADEMICS

Calendar: quarters. *Degrees:* bachelor's, master's, doctoral, and postbachelor's certificates.

Special study options: accelerated degree program, advanced placement credit, double majors, English as a second language, independent study, internships, off-campus study, services for LD students, student-designed majors, study abroad, summer session for credit. *ROTC:* Army (c), Air Force (c).

Unusual degree programs: 3-2 social work; public policy, social sciences, humanities, international relations, computer science.

Computers: Students can access the following: campus intranet, computer help desk, free student e-mail accounts, online (class) grades, online (class) registration, online (class) schedules. Campuswide network is available. Wireless service is available via entire campus.

Library: Joseph Regenstein Library plus 5 others. Students can reserve study rooms.

STUDENT LIFE

Housing options: on-campus residence required for freshman year; coed, special housing for students with disabilities. Campus housing is university owned. Freshman campus housing is guaranteed.

Activities and organizations: drama/theater group, student-run newspaper, radio station, choral group, University Theatre, Model United Nations, Council on University Programming, South Asian Students Association, Splash, national fraternities, national sororities.

Athletics Member NCAA. All Division III. *Intercollegiate sports:* baseball M, basketball M/W, cross-country running M/W, football M, lacrosse W, soccer M/W, softball W, swimming and diving M/W, tennis M/W, track and field M/W, volleyball W, wrestling M. *Intramural sports:* badminton M/W, basketball M/W, bowling M/W, cheerleading M(c)/W(c), crew M(c)/W(c), fencing M(c)/W(c), golf M(c)/W(c),

gymnastics M(c)/W(c), ice hockey W(c), racquetball M/W, rugby M(c)/W(c), sailing M(c)/W(c), soccer M/W, softball M/W, squash M(c)/W(c), swimming and diving M/W, table tennis M/W, tennis M/W, track and field M/W, triathlon M(c)/W(c), ultimate Frisbee M/W, volleyball M/W, water polo M(c)/W(c).

Campus security: 24-hour emergency response devices and patrols, student patrols, late-night transport/escort service, controlled dormitory access.

Student services: health clinic, personal/psychological counseling, women's center.

COSTS & FINANCIAL AID

Costs (2018–19) *One-time required fee:* $1224. *Comprehensive fee:* $73,356 includes full-time tuition ($55,425), mandatory fees ($1581), and room and board ($16,350). *College room only:* $9819. Room and board charges vary according to board plan, housing facility, and student level. *Payment plan:* installment. *Waivers:* employees or children of employees.

Financial Aid Of all full-time matriculated undergraduates who enrolled in 2018, 3,234 applied for aid, 2,721 were judged to have need, 2,721 had their need fully met. *Average percent of need met:* 100. *Average financial aid package:* $57,011. *Average need-based loan:* $3359. *Average need-based gift aid:* $50,697. *Average indebtedness upon graduation:* $19,817.

APPLYING

Options: electronic application, early admission, early decision, early action, deferred entrance.

Application fee: $75.

Required: essay or personal statement, high school transcript, 2 letters of recommendation.

Application deadlines: 1/1 (freshmen), 3/1 (transfers).

Notification: 4/1 (freshmen), 5/9 (transfers).

CONTACT

Mr. James G. Nondorf, Vice President for Enrollment and Student Advancement and Dean of Admissions and Financial Aid, University of Chicago, Rosenwald Hall, 1101 East 58th Street, Suite 105, Chicago, IL 60637. *Phone:* 773-702-8650. *Fax:* 773-702-4199. *E-mail:* collegeadmissions@uchicago.edu.

University of Illinois at Chicago

Chicago, Illinois

http://www.uic.edu/

- **State-supported** university, founded 1946, part of University of Illinois System
- **Urban** 240-acre campus with easy access to Chicago
- **Endowment** $321.6 million
- **Coed**
- **Moderately difficult** entrance level

FACULTY

Student/faculty ratio: 17:1.

ACADEMICS

Calendar: semesters. *Degrees:* bachelor's, master's, doctoral, post-master's, and postbachelor's certificates.

Library: Richard J. Daley Library plus 2 others. *Books:* 1.6 million (physical), 617,614 (digital/electronic); *Serial titles:* 61,000 (digital/electronic); *Databases:* 100. Weekly public service hours: 140; study areas open 24 hours, 5–7 days a week; students can reserve study rooms.

STUDENT LIFE

Housing options: coed. Campus housing is university owned.

Activities and organizations: drama/theater group, student-run newspaper, radio station, choral group, Muslim Student Association, Alternative Spring Break, Filipinos in Alliance, Society of Future Physicians, Ski and Snowboard Club, national fraternities, national sororities.

Athletics Member NCAA. All Division I.

Campus security: 24-hour emergency response devices and patrols, student patrols, late-night transport/escort service, controlled dormitory access, housing ID stickers, guest escort policy, 24-hour closed circuit videos for exits and entrances, security screen for first floor.

COLLEGES AT-A-GLANCE

Student services: health clinic, personal/psychological counseling, women's center, legal services, veterans affairs office.

COSTS & FINANCIAL AID
Costs (2018–19) *Tuition:* state resident $10,584 full-time, $394 per credit hour part-time; nonresident $23,440 full-time, $803 per credit hour part-time. Full-time tuition and fees vary according to degree level and program. Part-time tuition and fees vary according to course load, degree level, and program. No tuition increase for student's term of enrollment. *Required fees:* $3030 full-time. *Room and board:* $10,960; room only: $7930. Room and board charges vary according to board plan and housing facility.

Financial Aid Of all full-time matriculated undergraduates who enrolled in 2017, 14,861 applied for aid, 13,489 were judged to have need, 935 had their need fully met. 848 Federal Work-Study jobs (averaging $3000). 3,225 state and other part-time jobs (averaging $2500). In 2017, 563 non-need-based awards were made. *Average percent of need met:* 59. *Average financial aid package:* $14,401. *Average need-based loan:* $4288. *Average need-based gift aid:* $13,102. *Average non-need-based aid:* $5313. *Average indebtedness upon graduation:* $27,668.

APPLYING
Standardized Tests *Required:* SAT or ACT (for admission).
Options: electronic application, early admission, early action.
Application fee: $50.
Required: essay or personal statement, high school transcript. *Required for some:* audition for music and theater majors, portfolio for art majors.

CONTACT
Ms. Maureen Woods, Associate Director, Admissions Undergraduate, University of Illinois at Chicago, Chicago. *Phone:* 312-996-4111. *Fax:* 312-413-7628. *E-mail:* uic.admit@uic.edu.

University of Illinois at Springfield
Springfield, Illinois
http://www.uis.edu/
- **State-supported** comprehensive, founded 1969, part of University of Illinois System
- **Suburban** 746-acre campus
- **Endowment** $19.2 million
- **Coed** 2,814 undergraduate students, 64% full-time, 50% women, 50% men
- **Moderately difficult** entrance level, 53% of applicants were admitted

UNDERGRAD STUDENTS
1,799 full-time, 1,015 part-time. Students come from 47 states and territories; 34 other countries; 12% are from out of state; 14% Black or African American, non-Hispanic/Latino; 9% Hispanic/Latino; 3% Asian, non-Hispanic/Latino; 0.2% American Indian or Alaska Native, non-Hispanic/Latino; 3% Two or more races, non-Hispanic/Latino; 0.9% Race/ethnicity unknown; 3% international; 17% transferred in; 31% live on campus.

Freshmen:
Admission: 2,374 applied, 1,254 admitted, 316 enrolled. *Average high school GPA:* 3.6. *Test scores:* SAT evidence-based reading and writing scores over 500: 76%; SAT math scores over 500: 73%; ACT scores over 18: 91%; SAT evidence-based reading and writing scores over 600: 31%; SAT math scores over 600: 28%; ACT scores over 24: 55%; SAT evidence-based reading and writing scores over 700: 6%; SAT math scores over 700: 7%; ACT scores over 30: 17%.
Retention: 77% of full-time freshmen returned.

FACULTY
Total: 372, 57% full-time, 63% with terminal degrees.
Student/faculty ratio: 13:1.

ACADEMICS
Calendar: semesters. *Degrees:* bachelor's, master's, doctoral, post-master's, and postbachelor's certificates.
Special study options: academic remediation for entering students, advanced placement credit, cooperative education, distance learning, English as a second language, honors programs, independent study, internships, off-campus study, part-time degree program, services for LD students, study abroad, summer session for credit.

Computers: 560 computers/terminals and 63 ports are available on campus for general student use. Students can access the following: campus intranet, computer help desk, free student e-mail accounts, online (class) grades, online (class) registration, online (class) schedules. Campuswide network is available. 100% of college-owned or -operated housing units are wired for high-speed Internet access. Wireless service is available via entire campus.
Library: Norris L Brookens Library plus 1 other. *Books:* 352,668 (physical), 215,723 (digital/electronic); *Serial titles:* 9,513 (physical), 14,928 (digital/electronic); *Databases:* 176. Weekly public service hours: 90; students can reserve study rooms.

STUDENT LIFE
Housing options: on-campus residence required for freshman year; coed, special housing for students with disabilities. Campus housing is university owned. Freshman campus housing is guaranteed.

Activities and organizations: drama/theater group, student-run newspaper, radio station, choral group, Christian Student Fellowship, Sigma Sigma Sigma, Delta Kappa Epsilon, International Student Organization, Alternative Spring Break, national fraternities, national sororities.

Athletics Member NCAA. All Division II. *Intercollegiate sports:* baseball M(s), basketball M(s)/W(s), cheerleading M(s)/W(s), cross-country running M(s)/W(s), golf M(s)/W(s), soccer M(s)/W(s), softball W(s), tennis M(s)/W(s), track and field M(s)/W(s), volleyball W(s). *Intramural sports:* badminton M/W, basketball M/W, football M/W, racquetball M/W, sailing M(c)/W(c), sand volleyball M/W, soccer M(c)/W, softball M/W, table tennis M/W, tennis M/W, volleyball M(c)/W(c).

Campus security: 24-hour emergency response devices and patrols, late-night transport/escort service, controlled dormitory access.

Student services: health clinic, personal/psychological counseling, women's center, veterans affairs office.

COSTS & FINANCIAL AID
Costs (2019–20) *Tuition:* state resident $9405 full-time, $314 per credit hour part-time; nonresident $18,930 full-time, $631 per credit hour part-time. *Required fees:* $2408 full-time. *Room and board:* $11,660; room only: $7460.

Financial Aid Of all full-time matriculated undergraduates who enrolled in 2017, 1,550 applied for aid, 1,292 were judged to have need, 186 had their need fully met. In 2017, 299 non-need-based awards were made. *Average percent of need met:* 71. *Average financial aid package:* $13,798. *Average need-based loan:* $4133. *Average need-based gift aid:* $11,303. *Average non-need-based aid:* $8067. *Average indebtedness upon graduation:* $22,248. *Financial aid deadline:* 11/15.

APPLYING
Standardized Tests *Required:* SAT or ACT (for admission).
Recommended: SAT and SAT Subject Tests or ACT (for admission).
Options: electronic application, deferred entrance.
Application fee: $50.
Required: high school transcript.
Application deadlines: rolling (freshmen), rolling (transfers).
Notification: continuous (transfers).

CONTACT
Fernando Planas, Director of Admissions, University of Illinois at Springfield, One University Plaza, MS UHB 1080, Springfield, IL 62703-5407. *Phone:* 217-206-4847. *Toll-free phone:* 888-977-4847. *E-mail:* admissions@uis.edu.

University of Illinois at Urbana–Champaign
Champaign, Illinois
http://www.illinois.edu/

CONTACT
Stacey Kostell, Director of Admissions, University of Illinois at Urbana–Champaign, 901 West Illinois, Urbana, IL 61801. *Phone:* 217-333-0302. *Fax:* 217-244-4614. *E-mail:* ugradadmissions@uiuc.edu.

University of St. Francis
Joliet, Illinois
http://www.stfrancis.edu/
- **Independent Roman Catholic** comprehensive, founded 1920
- **Suburban** 18-acre campus with easy access to Chicago
- **Endowment** $16.5 million
- **Coed**
- **Moderately difficult** entrance level

FACULTY
Student/faculty ratio: 12:1.

ACADEMICS
Calendar: semesters. *Degrees:* certificates, bachelor's, master's, doctoral, post-master's, and postbachelor's certificates.
Library: Brown Library. *Books:* 113,077 (physical), 4,118 (digital/electronic); *Serial titles:* 605 (physical), 113 (digital/electronic); *Databases:* 76. Weekly public service hours: 74; students can reserve study rooms.

STUDENT LIFE
Housing options: coed, special housing for students with disabilities. Campus housing is university owned. Freshman campus housing is guaranteed.

Activities and organizations: drama/theater group, student-run newspaper, radio and television station, choral group, Student Nurses Association, Student Business Association, Justice League, Student Athletic Advisory Committee, Unidos Vamos a Alcanzar (UVA), national sororities.

Athletics Member NAIA.

Campus security: 24-hour emergency response devices and patrols, student patrols, late-night transport/escort service, controlled dormitory access, First Response trained security personnel.

Student services: health clinic, personal/psychological counseling.

COSTS & FINANCIAL AID
Costs (2018–19) *Comprehensive fee:* $42,250 includes full-time tuition ($32,000), mandatory fees ($320), and room and board ($9930). Full-time tuition and fees vary according to degree level, location, and program. Part-time tuition: $825 per credit hour. Part-time tuition and fees vary according to degree level and program. *Required fees:* $75 per term part-time. *Room and board:* Room and board charges vary according to housing facility. *Payment plans:* installment, deferred payment.

Financial Aid Of all full-time matriculated undergraduates who enrolled in 2018, 1,196 applied for aid, 1,101 were judged to have need, 237 had their need fully met. 158 Federal Work-Study jobs (averaging $2772). 300 state and other part-time jobs (averaging $2500). In 2018, 208 non-need-based awards were made. *Average percent of need met:* 80. *Average financial aid package:* $25,288. *Average need-based loan:* $4405. *Average need-based gift aid:* $21,054. *Average non-need-based aid:* $12,744. *Average indebtedness upon graduation:* $30,851.

APPLYING
Standardized Tests *Required:* SAT or ACT (for admission).
Options: electronic application, deferred entrance.
Required: high school transcript, minimum 2.5 GPA. *Required for some:* essay or personal statement, 2 letters of recommendation, interview.

CONTACT
Mr. Eric Ruiz, Director of Freshman Admissions, University of St. Francis, 500 North Wilcox Street, Joliet, IL 60435-6188. *Phone:* 800-735-7500. *Toll-free phone:* 800-735-7500. *Fax:* 815-740-5070. *E-mail:* eruiz@stfrancis.edu.

VanderCook College of Music
Chicago, Illinois
http://www.vandercook.edu/
- **Independent** comprehensive, founded 1909
- **Urban** 1-acre campus with easy access to Chicago
- **Endowment** $514,572
- **Coed**
- **Moderately difficult** entrance level

FACULTY
Student/faculty ratio: 3:1.

ACADEMICS
Calendar: semesters. *Degrees:* bachelor's and master's.
Library: Harry Ruppel Memorial Library plus 1 other. *Books:* 16,985 (physical), 6,827 (digital/electronic); *Serial titles:* 200 (physical), 100 (digital/electronic); *Databases:* 28. Weekly public service hours: 54; students can reserve study rooms.

STUDENT LIFE
Housing options: coed, special housing for students with disabilities. Campus housing is provided by a third party.

Activities and organizations: student-run radio station, choral group, NAfME (National Association for Music Education), ACDA (American Choral Directors Association), NBA (National Band Association), ASTA (American String Teachers Association), national fraternities, national sororities.

Campus security: 24-hour emergency response devices and patrols, late-night transport/escort service, controlled dormitory access.

Student services: health clinic, personal/psychological counseling.

COSTS & FINANCIAL AID
Costs (2018–19) *Comprehensive fee:* $40,508 includes full-time tuition ($26,548), mandatory fees ($1886), and room and board ($12,074). Full-time tuition and fees vary according to course level, course load, and program. Part-time tuition: $1115 per semester hour. Part-time tuition and fees vary according to course level, course load, and program. *College room only:* $6150.

Financial Aid Of all full-time matriculated undergraduates who enrolled in 2018, 84 applied for aid, 66 were judged to have need. 21 Federal Work-Study jobs (averaging $799). 5 state and other part-time jobs (averaging $531). In 2018, 15 non-need-based awards were made. *Average financial aid package:* $16,149. *Average need-based loan:* $4438. *Average need-based gift aid:* $11,089. *Average non-need-based aid:* $9299. *Average indebtedness upon graduation:* $35,559.

APPLYING
Standardized Tests *Required:* SAT or ACT (for admission).
Options: electronic application, early admission.
Application fee: $35.
Required: essay or personal statement, high school transcript, 3 letters of recommendation, interview, audition on the applicant's primary instrument or voice. *Required for some:* minimum 3.0 GPA. *Recommended:* minimum 3.0 GPA.

CONTACT
Mrs. LeeAnn L. Meyer, Director of Admissions and Retention, VanderCook College of Music, 3140 South Federal Street, Chicago, IL 60616. *Phone:* 312-788-1120 Ext. 230. *Fax:* 312-225-5211. *E-mail:* admissions@vandercook.edu.

Western Illinois University
Macomb, Illinois
http://www.wiu.edu/
- **State-supported** comprehensive, founded 1899
- **Small-town** 1050-acre campus with easy access to Quad Cities; Peoria, IL; Springfield, IL
- **Endowment** $55.8 million
- **Coed** 6,754 undergraduate students, 88% full-time, 52% women, 48% men
- **Moderately difficult** entrance level, 59% of applicants were admitted

UNDERGRAD STUDENTS
5,949 full-time, 805 part-time. Students come from 43 states and territories; 61 other countries; 11% are from out of state; 21% Black or African American, non-Hispanic/Latino; 13% Hispanic/Latino; 1% Asian, non-Hispanic/Latino; 0.1% American Indian or Alaska Native, non-Hispanic/Latino; 3% Two or more races, non-Hispanic/Latino; 2% Race/ethnicity unknown; 1% international; 11% transferred in; 42% live on campus.

Freshmen:
Admission: 9,151 applied, 5,379 admitted, 934 enrolled. *Average high school GPA:* 3.3. *Test scores:* SAT evidence-based reading and writing

scores over 500: 60%; SAT math scores over 500: 56%; ACT scores over 18: 83%; SAT evidence-based reading and writing scores over 600: 15%; SAT math scores over 600: 11%; ACT scores over 24: 24%; SAT evidence-based reading and writing scores over 700: 2%; SAT math scores over 700: 2%; ACT scores over 30: 7%.

Retention: 65% of full-time freshmen returned.

FACULTY
Total: 587, 90% full-time, 70% with terminal degrees.
Student/faculty ratio: 14:1.

ACADEMICS
Calendar: semesters. *Degrees:* bachelor's, master's, doctoral, post-master's, and postbachelor's certificates.

Special study options: academic remediation for entering students, adult/continuing education programs, advanced placement credit, distance learning, double majors, English as a second language, external degree program, freshman honors college, honors programs, independent study, internships, off-campus study, part-time degree program, services for LD students, student-designed majors, study abroad, summer session for credit. *ROTC:* Army (b).

Unusual degree programs: 3-2 engineering with University of Iowa, University of Illinois; arts and sciences/clinical laboratory science; general studies/chiropractic with Palmer College of Chiropractic.

Computers: 632 computers/terminals and 1,012 ports are available on campus for general student use. Students can access the following: computer help desk, free student e-mail accounts, online (class) grades, online (class) registration, online (class) schedules. Campuswide network is available. 100% of college-owned or -operated housing units are wired for high-speed Internet access. Wireless service is available via entire campus.

Library: Leslie Malpass Library plus 4 others. *Books:* 765,987 (physical), 149,419 (digital/electronic); *Serial titles:* 154,171 (physical), 77,503 (digital/electronic); *Databases:* 116.

STUDENT LIFE
Housing options: on-campus residence required through sophomore year; coed, men-only, women-only, special housing for students with disabilities. Campus housing is university owned. Freshman campus housing is guaranteed.

Activities and organizations: drama/theater group, student-run newspaper, radio and television station, choral group, marching band, Student Government Association, Black Student Association, University Union Board, Western's All Volunteer Effort (WAVE), Inter Hall Council, national fraternities, national sororities.

Athletics Member NCAA. All Division I except football (Division I-AA). *Intercollegiate sports:* baseball M(s), basketball M(s)/W(s), cross-country running M(s)/W(s), golf M(s)/W(c), soccer M(s)/W(s), softball W(s), swimming and diving M(s)/W(s), tennis W(s), track and field M(s)/W(s), volleyball W(s). *Intramural sports:* badminton M(c)/W(c), baseball M(c), basketball M/W, bowling M(c), cheerleading M/W, cross-country running M/W, equestrian sports M(c)/W(c), fencing M(c), field hockey W(c), football M/W, golf M/W, ice hockey M(c), lacrosse M(c), racquetball M/W, rugby M/W, sand volleyball M/W, soccer M/W, softball M/W, swimming and diving M/W, table tennis M/W, tennis M/W, ultimate Frisbee M(c)/W(c), volleyball M/W, water polo M/W, wrestling M.

Campus security: 24-hour emergency response devices and patrols, student patrols, late-night transport/escort service, controlled dormitory access.

Student services: health clinic, personal/psychological counseling, women's center, legal services, veterans affairs office.

COSTS & FINANCIAL AID
Costs (2018–19) *One-time required fee:* $200. *Tuition:* state resident $8541 full-time, $285 per credit hour part-time; nonresident $8541 full-time, $285 per credit hour part-time. Full-time tuition and fees vary according to course load, location, and student level. Part-time tuition and fees vary according to course load, location, and student level. No tuition increase for student's term of enrollment. Student Health Insurance $1684/year for students with 9 or more credit hours. Can be waived. *Required fees:* $2726 full-time, $91 per credit hour part-time. *Room and board:* $9630; room only: $5880. Room and board charges vary according to board plan, housing facility, and student level. *Payment plan:*

installment. *Waivers:* senior citizens and employees or children of employees.

Financial Aid Of all full-time matriculated undergraduates who enrolled in 2018, 5,146 applied for aid, 4,591 were judged to have need, 1,201 had their need fully met. 193 Federal Work-Study jobs (averaging $2665). 1,279 state and other part-time jobs (averaging $1561). In 2018, 456 non-need-based awards were made. *Average percent of need met:* 64. *Average financial aid package:* $12,684. *Average need-based loan:* $4264. *Average need-based gift aid:* $9832. *Average non-need-based aid:* $3560. *Average indebtedness upon graduation:* $31,326.

APPLYING
Standardized Tests *Required:* SAT or ACT (for admission).
Options: electronic application, deferred entrance.
Application fee: $30.
Required: high school transcript, minimum 2.5 GPA.
Application deadlines: rolling (freshmen), rolling (out-of-state freshmen), rolling (transfers).
Notification: continuous (freshmen), continuous (out-of-state freshmen), continuous (transfers).

CONTACT
Ms. Kassandra Daly, Interim Director of Admissions, Western Illinois University, 1 University Circle, Macomb, IL 61455-1390. *Phone:* 309-298-3157. *Toll-free phone:* 877-742-5948. *Fax:* 309-298-3111. *E-mail:* kj-daly@wiu.edu.

Wheaton College
Wheaton, Illinois
http://www.wheaton.edu/
- **Independent nondenominational** comprehensive, founded 1860
- **Suburban** 80-acre campus with easy access to Chicago
- **Endowment** $489.1 million
- **Coed** 2,401 undergraduate students, 97% full-time, 55% women, 45% men
- **Very difficult** entrance level, 83% of applicants were admitted

UNDERGRAD STUDENTS
2,326 full-time, 75 part-time. Students come from 51 states and territories; 43 other countries; 73% are from out of state; 3% Black or African American, non-Hispanic/Latino; 6% Hispanic/Latino; 9% Asian, non-Hispanic/Latino; 0.1% American Indian or Alaska Native, non-Hispanic/Latino; 5% Two or more races, non-Hispanic/Latino; 0.4% Race/ethnicity unknown; 3% international; 2% transferred in; 89% live on campus.

Freshmen:
Admission: 1,850 applied, 1,529 admitted, 610 enrolled. *Average high school GPA:* 3.7. *Test scores:* SAT evidence-based reading and writing scores over 500: 99%; SAT math scores over 500: 98%; ACT scores over 18: 100%; SAT evidence-based reading and writing scores over 600: 84%; SAT math scores over 600: 72%; ACT scores over 24: 94%; SAT evidence-based reading and writing scores over 700: 32%; SAT math scores over 700: 35%; ACT scores over 30: 52%.
Retention: 92% of full-time freshmen returned.

FACULTY
Total: 352, 63% full-time, 73% with terminal degrees.
Student/faculty ratio: 11:1.

ACADEMICS
Calendar: semesters. *Degrees:* bachelor's, master's, doctoral, and postbachelor's certificates.

Special study options: advanced placement credit, double majors, independent study, internships, off-campus study, services for LD students, student-designed majors, study abroad, summer session for credit. *ROTC:* Army (b), Air Force (c).

Unusual degree programs: 3-2 engineering with Illinois Institute of Technology; nursing with Emory University, Indiana Wesleyan University.

Computers: 325 computers/terminals and 3,500 ports are available on campus for general student use. Students can access the following: campus intranet, computer help desk, free student e-mail accounts, online (class) grades, online (class) registration, online (class) schedules, financial information, degree requirements evaluation. Campuswide network is available. 100% of college-owned or -operated housing units are wired for high-speed Internet access. Wireless service is available via entire campus.

Library: Buswell Memorial Library. *Books:* 357,263 (physical), 162,503 (digital/electronic); *Serial titles:* 371 (physical), 6,140 (digital/electronic); *Databases:* 214. Weekly public service hours: 94; students can reserve study rooms.

STUDENT LIFE

Housing options: on-campus residence required through senior year; coed, men-only, women-only, cooperative, special housing for students with disabilities. Campus housing is university owned. Freshman campus housing is guaranteed.

Activities and organizations: drama/theater group, student-run newspaper, choral group, Discipleship small groups, intramurals, Club Sports, Christian Service Council, New Student Orientation.

Athletics Member NCAA. All Division III except golf (Division II). *Intercollegiate sports:* baseball M, basketball M/W, cheerleading W(c), crew M(c)/W(c), cross-country running M/W, football M, golf M/W, ice hockey M(c), lacrosse M(c)/W(c), rowing M(c)/W, soccer M/W, softball W, swimming and diving M/W, tennis M/W, track and field M/W, volleyball W, wrestling M. *Intramural sports:* badminton M/W, basketball M/W, football M, golf M/W, soccer M/W, softball M, ultimate Frisbee M/W, volleyball M/W.

Campus security: 24-hour emergency response devices and patrols, student patrols, late-night transport/escort service, controlled dormitory access.

Student services: health clinic, personal/psychological counseling.

COSTS & FINANCIAL AID

Costs (2019–20) *Comprehensive fee:* $48,330 includes full-time tuition ($37,700) and room and board ($10,630). Part-time tuition: $1571 per credit hour. *College room only:* $6300.

Financial Aid Of all full-time matriculated undergraduates who enrolled in 2018, 1,684 applied for aid, 1,362 were judged to have need, 218 had their need fully met. 200 Federal Work-Study jobs (averaging $1237). In 2018, 535 non-need-based awards were made. *Average percent of need met:* 78. *Average financial aid package:* $24,887. *Average need-based loan:* $4550. *Average need-based gift aid:* $21,693. *Average non-need-based aid:* $8754. *Average indebtedness upon graduation:* $27,661.

APPLYING

Standardized Tests *Required:* SAT or ACT (for admission).

Options: electronic application, early action, deferred entrance.

Application fee: $50.

Required: essay or personal statement, high school transcript, 2 letters of recommendation. *Recommended:* interview.

Application deadlines: 1/10 (freshmen), 3/1 (transfers), 11/1 (early action).

Notification: 4/1 (freshmen), continuous until 3/1 (transfers), 12/31 (early action).

CONTACT

Jason Kircher, Director of Admissions, Wheaton College, 501 College Avenue, Wheaton, IL 60187-5593. *Phone:* 630-752-5011. *Toll-free phone:* 800-222-2419. *Fax:* 630-752-5285. *E-mail:* admissions@wheaton.edu.

See below for display ad and page 1158 for the College Close-Up.

INDIANA

Anderson University
Anderson, Indiana
http://www.anderson.edu/

- **Independent** comprehensive, founded 1917, affiliated with Church of God
- **Suburban** 163-acre campus with easy access to Indianapolis
- **Endowment** $33.7 million
- **Coed**
- **Moderately difficult** entrance level

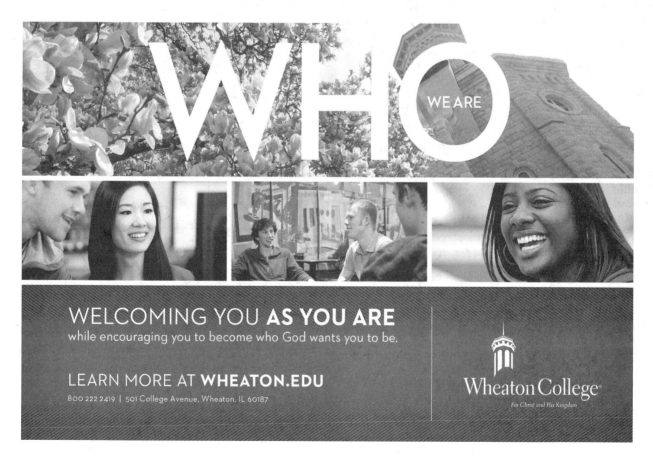

FACULTY
Student/faculty ratio: 10:1.

ACADEMICS
Calendar: semesters. *Degrees:* associate, bachelor's, master's, and doctoral.
Library: Robert A. Nicholson Library. *Books:* 318,141 (physical), 261,900 (digital/electronic); *Serial titles:* 7,348 (physical), 53,279 (digital/electronic); *Databases:* 136. Weekly public service hours: 95; study areas open 24 hours, 5–7 days a week; students can reserve study rooms.

STUDENT LIFE
Housing options: on-campus residence required through junior year; men-only, women-only. Campus housing is university owned. Freshman campus housing is guaranteed.

Activities and organizations: drama/theater group, student-run newspaper, radio station, choral group, Adult and Continuing Education Students Association, Multicultural Student Union, Campus Ministries.

Athletics Member NCAA. All Division III.

Campus security: 24-hour emergency response devices and patrols, student patrols, late-night transport/escort service, controlled dormitory access, 24-hour crime line.

Student services: health clinic, personal/psychological counseling.

COSTS & FINANCIAL AID
Costs (2018–19) *Comprehensive fee:* $40,340 includes full-time tuition ($29,950), mandatory fees ($500), and room and board ($9890). Part-time tuition: $1249 per semester hour. Part-time tuition and fees vary according to course load. *College room only:* $6180. Room and board charges vary according to board plan and housing facility.

Financial Aid Of all full-time matriculated undergraduates who enrolled in 2014, 1,549 applied for aid, 1,410 were judged to have need, 604 had their need fully met. In 2014, 307 non-need-based awards were made. *Average percent of need met:* 88. *Average financial aid package:* $23,905. *Average need-based loan:* $10,011. *Average need-based gift aid:* $15,932. *Average non-need-based aid:* $14,313.

APPLYING
Standardized Tests *Required:* SAT or ACT (for admission).

Options: electronic application, deferred entrance.

Application fee: $25.

Required: high school transcript, minimum 2.0 GPA, 2 letters of recommendation, lifestyle statement. *Required for some:* interview. *Recommended:* essay or personal statement.

CONTACT
Ms. Kynan Simison, Director of Admissions, Anderson University, 1100 East 5th Street, Anderson, IN 46012-3495. *Phone:* 765-641-4076. *Toll-free phone:* 800-428-6414. *Fax:* 765-641-3851. *E-mail:* info@anderson.edu.

Ball State University

Muncie, Indiana
http://www.bsu.edu/

- **State-supported** university, founded 1918
- **Suburban** 1140-acre campus with easy access to Indianapolis
- **Endowment** $201.8 million
- **Coed**
- 62% of applicants were admitted

FACULTY
Student/faculty ratio: 17:1.

ACADEMICS
Calendar: semesters. *Degrees:* certificates, bachelor's, master's, doctoral, post-master's, and postbachelor's certificates.
Library: Bracken Library plus 2 others. *Books:* 822,983 (physical), 15,244 (digital/electronic); *Serial titles:* 13,599 (physical), 103,640 (digital/electronic); *Databases:* 296. Weekly public service hours: 123; students can reserve study rooms.

STUDENT LIFE
Housing options: on-campus residence required for freshman year; coed, men-only, women-only, special housing for students with disabilities.

Campus housing is university owned. Freshman campus housing is guaranteed.

Activities and organizations: drama/theater group, student-run newspaper, radio and television station, choral group, marching band, Student Voluntary Services, National Society of Collegiate Scholars, Dance Marathon, Cardinal Catholic, National Society of Leadership and Success, national fraternities, national sororities.

Athletics Member NCAA. All Division I except football (Division I-A).

Campus security: 24-hour emergency response devices and patrols, late-night transport/escort service, controlled dormitory access.

Student services: health clinic, personal/psychological counseling, women's center, legal services, veterans affairs office.

COSTS & FINANCIAL AID
Costs (2018–19) *Tuition:* state resident $9234 full-time, $304 per credit hour part-time; nonresident $25,806 full-time, $1023 per credit hour part-time. Full-time tuition and fees vary according to program and reciprocity agreements. Part-time tuition and fees vary according to course load, program, and reciprocity agreements. *Required fees:* $662 full-time. *Room and board:* $10,234. Room and board charges vary according to board plan and housing facility.

Financial Aid Of all full-time matriculated undergraduates who enrolled in 2018, 12,693 applied for aid, 10,084 were judged to have need, 4,064 had their need fully met. In 2018, 2112 non-need-based awards were made. *Average percent of need met:* 66. *Average financial aid package:* $13,785. *Average need-based loan:* $4152. *Average need-based gift aid:* $6490. *Average non-need-based aid:* $8175. *Average indebtedness upon graduation:* $28,275.

APPLYING
Standardized Tests *Required for some:* SAT or ACT (for admission).

Options: electronic application.

Application fee: $55.

Required: high school transcript. *Required for some:* essay or personal statement.

CONTACT
Ball State University, 2000 West University Avenue, Muncie, IN 47306. *Phone:* 765-285-8300. *Toll-free phone:* 800-482-4BSU.

★ Bethel College

Mishawaka, Indiana
http://www.bethelcollege.edu/

- **Independent** comprehensive, founded 1947, affiliated with Missionary Church
- **Suburban** 80-acre campus
- **Endowment** $9.3 million
- **Coed**
- **Minimally difficult** entrance level

FACULTY
Student/faculty ratio: 12:1.

ACADEMICS
Calendar: semesters. *Degrees:* associate, bachelor's, and master's.
Library: Otis and Elizabeth Bowen Library. *Books:* 80,904 (physical), 174,107 (digital/electronic); *Serial titles:* 473 (physical), 58,644 (digital/electronic); *Databases:* 89. Weekly public service hours: 79.

STUDENT LIFE
Housing options: on-campus residence required through sophomore year; men-only, women-only. Campus housing is university owned.

Activities and organizations: drama/theater group, student-run newspaper, radio station, choral group, Student Government, Psychology Club, America Sign Language Club.

Athletics Member NAIA, NCCAA.

Campus security: 24-hour emergency response devices and patrols, late-night transport/escort service, controlled dormitory access.

Student services: health clinic, personal/psychological counseling.

COSTS & FINANCIAL AID
Costs (2018–19) *Comprehensive fee:* $37,590 includes full-time tuition ($28,140), mandatory fees ($450), and room and board ($9000). Full-time tuition and fees vary according to program. Part-time tuition: $895 per

credit hour. Part-time tuition and fees vary according to course load and program. *Required fees:* $250 per year part-time. *College room only:* $4280. Room and board charges vary according to board plan and housing facility.

Financial Aid Of all full-time matriculated undergraduates who enrolled in 2018, 110 Federal Work-Study jobs (averaging $1). In 2018, 145 non-need-based awards were made. *Average non-need-based aid:* $13,653. *Average indebtedness upon graduation:* $33,565. *Financial aid deadline:* 4/15.

APPLYING
Standardized Tests *Required:* SAT or ACT (for admission).
Options: electronic application, early admission, deferred entrance.
Required: high school transcript, minimum 2.0 GPA. *Recommended:* essay or personal statement, minimum 2.5 GPA, interview.

CONTACT
Stephanie Hochstetler, Director of Admission, Bethel College, 1001 Bethel Circle, Mishawaka, IN 46545. *Phone:* 574-807-7600. *Toll-free phone:* 800-422-4101. *Fax:* 574-807-7650. *E-mail:* admissions@bethelcollege.edu.

Butler University
Indianapolis, Indiana
http://www.butler.edu/
- **Independent** comprehensive, founded 1855
- **Suburban** 295-acre campus with easy access to Indianapolis
- **Endowment** $216.1 million
- **Coed** 4,698 undergraduate students, 96% full-time, 60% women, 40% men
- **Moderately difficult** entrance level, 68% of applicants were admitted

UNDERGRAD STUDENTS
4,520 full-time, 178 part-time. Students come from 48 states and territories; 42 other countries; 55% are from out of state; 4% Black or African American, non-Hispanic/Latino; 4% Hispanic/Latino; 3% Asian, non-Hispanic/Latino; 0.2% American Indian or Alaska Native, non-Hispanic/Latino; 3% Two or more races, non-Hispanic/Latino; 2% Race/ethnicity unknown; 1% international; 2% transferred in; 67% live on campus.

Freshmen:
Admission: 16,418 applied, 11,127 admitted, 1,326 enrolled. *Average high school GPA:* 3.9. *Test scores:* SAT evidence-based reading and writing scores over 500: 100%; SAT math scores over 500: 99%; ACT scores over 18: 99%; SAT evidence-based reading and writing scores over 600: 70%; SAT math scores over 600: 63%; ACT scores over 24: 84%; SAT evidence-based reading and writing scores over 700: 10%; SAT math scores over 700: 15%; ACT scores over 30: 30%.

Retention: 89% of full-time freshmen returned.

FACULTY
Total: 595, 63% full-time.
Student/faculty ratio: 11:1.

ACADEMICS
Calendar: semesters. *Degrees:* bachelor's, master's, doctoral, and postbachelor's certificates.
Special study options: accelerated degree program, advanced placement credit, cooperative education, distance learning, double majors, honors programs, independent study, internships, off-campus study, services for LD students, student-designed majors, study abroad, summer session for credit. *ROTC:* Army (c), Air Force (c).
Unusual degree programs: 3-2 engineering with Indiana University–Purdue University Indianapolis.
Computers: 490 computers/terminals are available on campus for general student use. Students can access the following: campus intranet, computer help desk, free student e-mail accounts, online (class) grades, online (class) registration, online (class) schedules. Campuswide network is available. 100% of college-owned or -operated housing units are wired for high-speed Internet access. Wireless service is available via entire campus.
Library: Irwin Library plus 2 others. *Books:* 195,698 (physical), 821,771 (digital/electronic); *Serial titles:* 13,168 (physical), 99,038

(digital/electronic); *Databases:* 323. Weekly public service hours: 106; students can reserve study rooms.

STUDENT LIFE
Housing options: on-campus residence required through junior year; coed, women-only. Campus housing is university owned. Freshman campus housing is guaranteed.
Activities and organizations: drama/theater group, student-run newspaper, radio and television station, choral group, marching band, Pre-Pharmacy Club, American Chemical Society Students Affiliate, Answers for Autism (Butler University Chapter), Delta Delta Delta, Kappa Psi Pharmaceutical Fraternity, national fraternities, national sororities.
Athletics Member NCAA. All Division I except football (Division I-AA). *Intercollegiate sports:* baseball M(s), basketball M(s)/W(s), crew M(c)/W(c), cross-country running M(s)/W(s), equestrian sports W(c), golf M(s)/W(s)(c), ice hockey M(c), lacrosse M(c)/W(s), rugby M(c), soccer M(s)/W(s), softball W(s), swimming and diving M(c)/W, tennis M(s)/W(s), track and field M(s)/W(s), ultimate Frisbee M(c)/W(c), volleyball M(c)/W(s). *Intramural sports:* badminton M/W, baseball M, basketball M/W, bowling M/W, football M, soccer M/W, softball M/W, swimming and diving M/W, table tennis M/W, tennis M/W, track and field M/W, volleyball M/W, weight lifting M/W.
Campus security: 24-hour emergency response devices and patrols, late-night transport/escort service, controlled dormitory access.
Student services: health clinic, personal/psychological counseling.

COSTS & FINANCIAL AID
Costs (2019–20) *Comprehensive fee:* $57,900 includes full-time tuition ($41,370), mandatory fees ($990), and room and board ($15,540). Part-time tuition: $1720 per credit hour. *College room only:* $8300.
Financial Aid Of all full-time matriculated undergraduates who enrolled in 2018, 4,525 applied for aid, 2,743 were judged to have need, 320 had their need fully met. 338 Federal Work-Study jobs (averaging $782). In 2018, 1756 non-need-based awards were made. *Average percent of need met:* 66. *Average financial aid package:* $26,085. *Average need-based loan:* $4477. *Average need-based gift aid:* $21,842. *Average non-need-based aid:* $15,937. *Average indebtedness upon graduation:* $38,191.

APPLYING
Standardized Tests *Required:* SAT or ACT (for admission).
Options: electronic application, early action, deferred entrance.
Application deadlines: 2/1 (freshmen), 8/15 (transfers).
Notification: continuous (freshmen), continuous (transfers).

CONTACT
Mr. Delorean Menifee, Director of Admission, Butler University, 4600 Sunset Avenue, Indianapolis, IN 46208-3485. *Phone:* 317-940-8100. *Toll-free phone:* 888-940-8100. *Fax:* 317-940-8150. *E-mail:* admission@butler.edu.

Calumet College of Saint Joseph
Whiting, Indiana
http://www.ccsj.edu/
- **Independent Roman Catholic** comprehensive, founded 1951
- **Urban** 25-acre campus with easy access to Chicago
- **Endowment** $4.3 million
- **Coed** 584 undergraduate students, 49% full-time, 42% women, 58% men
- **Noncompetitive** entrance level, 22% of applicants were admitted

UNDERGRAD STUDENTS
285 full-time, 299 part-time. Students come from 15 states and territories; 15 other countries; 50% are from out of state; 21% Black or African American, non-Hispanic/Latino; 25% Hispanic/Latino; 0.9% Asian, non-Hispanic/Latino; 0.2% Native Hawaiian or other Pacific Islander, non-Hispanic/Latino; 0.2% American Indian or Alaska Native, non-Hispanic/Latino; 3% Two or more races, non-Hispanic/Latino; 21% Race/ethnicity unknown; 3% transferred in.

Freshmen:
Admission: 655 applied, 141 admitted, 116 enrolled. *Average high school GPA:* 2.7. *Test scores:* ACT scores over 18: 12%; ACT scores over 24: 4%.
Retention: 54% of full-time freshmen returned.

FACULTY
Total: 85, 33% full-time, 45% with terminal degrees.
Student/faculty ratio: 10:1.

ACADEMICS
Calendar: semesters. *Degrees:* certificates, associate, bachelor's, and master's.

Special study options: academic remediation for entering students, accelerated degree program, adult/continuing education programs, advanced placement credit, cooperative education, distance learning, double majors, external degree program, honors programs, independent study, internships, part-time degree program, services for LD students, summer session for credit.

Computers: 241 computers/terminals are available on campus for general student use. Students can access the following: computer help desk, free student e-mail accounts, online (class) grades, online (class) schedules. Campuswide network is available. Wireless service is available via entire campus.
Library: Mary Gorman Specker Memorial Library. *Books:* 10,000 (physical), 7,128 (digital/electronic); *Serial titles:* 2 (physical); *Databases:* 62. Weekly public service hours: 59.

STUDENT LIFE
Housing options: college housing not available.

Activities and organizations: drama/theater group, student-run newspaper, Student Government, Los Amigos Hispanic Club, Criminal Justice Club, Drama Club, GIVE.

Athletics Member NAIA. *Intercollegiate sports:* baseball M(s), basketball M(s)/W(s), bowling M(s)/W(s), cheerleading W(s), cross-country running M(s)/W(s), golf M(s), soccer M(s)/W(s), softball W(s), tennis M(s)/W(s), track and field M(s)/W(s), volleyball M(s)/W(s), wrestling M(s).

Student services: personal/psychological counseling, veterans affairs office.

COSTS & FINANCIAL AID
Costs (2019–20) *Tuition:* $19,400 full-time, $620 per credit hour part-time. No tuition increase for student's term of enrollment. *Required fees:* $970 full-time, $135 per term part-time.

Financial Aid Of all full-time matriculated undergraduates who enrolled in 2017, 384 applied for aid, 349 were judged to have need, 43 had their need fully met. 22 Federal Work-Study jobs (averaging $809). In 2017, 14 non-need-based awards were made. *Average percent of need met:* 48. *Average financial aid package:* $13,997. *Average need-based loan:* $3820. *Average need-based gift aid:* $9634. *Average non-need-based aid:* $2427. *Average indebtedness upon graduation:* $24,431.

APPLYING
Standardized Tests *Required:* ACCUPLACER (for admission). *Recommended:* SAT or ACT (for admission).

Options: electronic application, deferred entrance.

Required: high school transcript. *Required for some:* essay or personal statement, 1 letter of recommendation. *Recommended:* minimum 2.0 GPA, interview.

Application deadlines: rolling (freshmen), rolling (transfers).
Notification: continuous (freshmen), continuous (transfers).

CONTACT
Mr. Andy Marks, Director of Enrollment, Calumet College of Saint Joseph, 2400 New York Avenue, Whiting, IN 46394. *Phone:* 219-473-4295. *Toll-free phone:* 877-700-9100. *Fax:* 219-473-4336. *E-mail:* admissions@ccsj.edu.

Chamberlain College of Nursing
Indianapolis, Indiana
http://www.chamberlain.edu/

CONTACT
Chamberlain College of Nursing, 9100 Keystone Crossing, Indianapolis, IN 46240. *Toll-free phone:* 877-751-5783.

Crossroads Bible College
Indianapolis, Indiana
http://www.crossroads.edu/

CONTACT
Michael Garrison, Admissions Counselor, Crossroads Bible College, 601 North Shortridge Road, Indianapolis, IN 46219. *Phone:* 317-789-8266. *Toll-free phone:* 800-822-3119. *E-mail:* admissions@crossroads.edu.

DePauw University
Greencastle, Indiana
http://www.depauw.edu/

- **Independent** 4-year, founded 1837, affiliated with United Methodist Church
- **Small-town** 655-acre campus with easy access to Indianapolis
- **Endowment** $614.6 million
- **Coed**
- **Moderately difficult** entrance level

FACULTY
Student/faculty ratio: 9:1.

ACADEMICS
Calendar: 4-1-4. *Degree:* bachelor's.
Library: Roy O. West Library plus 2 others. Study areas open 24 hours, 5–7 days a week; students can reserve study rooms.

STUDENT LIFE
Housing options: on-campus residence required through senior year; coed, special housing for students with disabilities. Campus housing is university owned. Freshman campus housing is guaranteed.

Activities and organizations: drama/theater group, student-run newspaper, radio and television station, choral group, national fraternities, national sororities.

Athletics Member NCAA. All Division III.

Campus security: 24-hour emergency response devices and patrols, student patrols, late-night transport/escort service, controlled dormitory access.

Student services: health clinic, personal/psychological counseling, women's center.

COSTS & FINANCIAL AID
Costs (2018–19) *Comprehensive fee:* $62,724 includes full-time tuition ($48,860), mandatory fees ($844), and room and board ($13,020). *Room and board:* Room and board charges vary according to board plan.

Financial Aid Of all full-time matriculated undergraduates who enrolled in 2018, 1,446 applied for aid, 1,249 were judged to have need, 323 had their need fully met. In 2018, 843 non-need-based awards were made. *Average percent of need met:* 90. *Average financial aid package:* $43,827. *Average need-based loan:* $4426. *Average need-based gift aid:* $39,150. *Average non-need-based aid:* $22,798. *Average indebtedness upon graduation:* $25,813. *Financial aid deadline:* 2/1.

APPLYING
Standardized Tests *Required:* SAT or ACT (for admission).

Options: electronic application, early admission, early decision, early action, deferred entrance.

Required: essay or personal statement, high school transcript, 1 letter of recommendation. *Recommended:* interview.

CONTACT
Ms. Rachel Schmidtke, Director of Recruitment, DePauw University, 204 East Seminary Street, Greencastle, IN 46135. *Phone:* 765-658-4104. *Toll-free phone:* 800-447-2495. *Fax:* 765-658-4007. *E-mail:* rachelschmidtke@depauw.edu.

★ Earlham College
Richmond, Indiana
http://www.earlham.edu/

- **Independent** comprehensive, founded 1847, affiliated with Society of Friends
- **Small-town** 800-acre campus with easy access to Cincinnati, Indianapolis, Dayton
- **Endowment** $425.4 million
- **Coed** 1,050 undergraduate students, 99% full-time, 54% women, 46% men
- **Very difficult** entrance level, 52% of applicants were admitted

UNDERGRAD STUDENTS

1,043 full-time, 7 part-time. Students come from 47 states and territories; 72 other countries; 90% are from out of state; 9% Black or African American, non-Hispanic/Latino; 7% Hispanic/Latino; 4% Asian, non-Hispanic/Latino; 0.1% Native Hawaiian or other Pacific Islander, non-Hispanic/Latino; 0.4% American Indian or Alaska Native, non-Hispanic/Latino; 2% Two or more races, non-Hispanic/Latino; 5% Race/ethnicity unknown; 21% international; 1% transferred in; 95% live on campus.

Freshmen:

Admission: 2,799 applied, 1,452 admitted, 271 enrolled. *Average high school GPA:* 3.7. *Test scores:* SAT evidence-based reading and writing scores over 500: 98%; SAT math scores over 500: 97%; ACT scores over 18: 100%; SAT evidence-based reading and writing scores over 600: 63%; SAT math scores over 600: 68%; ACT scores over 24: 85%; SAT evidence-based reading and writing scores over 700: 22%; SAT math scores over 700: 23%; ACT scores over 30: 39%.

Retention: 82% of full-time freshmen returned.

FACULTY

Total: 115, 93% full-time, 91% with terminal degrees.
Student/faculty ratio: 10:1.

ACADEMICS

Calendar: semesters. *Degrees:* bachelor's, master's, and postbachelor's certificates.

Special study options: cooperative education, double majors, English as a second language, honors programs, independent study, internships, off-campus study, services for LD students, student-designed majors, study abroad.

Unusual degree programs: 3-2 engineering with Columbia University, University of Minnesota, Rensselaer Polytechnic Institute.

Computers: 266 computers/terminals are available on campus for general student use. Students can access the following: campus intranet, computer help desk, free student e-mail accounts, online (class) grades, online (class) registration, online (class) schedules. Campuswide network is available. 100% of college-owned or -operated housing units are wired for high-speed Internet access. Wireless service is available via entire campus.

Library: Lilly Library plus 1 other. *Books:* 329,649 (physical), 1.9 million (digital/electronic); *Databases:* 169. Students can reserve study rooms.

STUDENT LIFE

Housing options: on-campus residence required through senior year; coed, men-only, women-only, special housing for students with disabilities. Campus housing is university owned. Freshman campus housing is guaranteed.

Activities and organizations: drama/theater group, student-run newspaper, radio station, choral group, Gospel Revelations Chorus, Dance Alloy, club sports, Student Government, Black Student Union.

Athletics Member NCAA, NAIA. All NCAA Division III. *Intercollegiate sports:* baseball M, basketball M/W, cheerleading M(c)/W(c), cross-country running M/W, equestrian sports M(c)/W(c), field hockey W, golf M, lacrosse M(c)/W(c), rugby M(c)/W(c), soccer M/W, tennis M/W, track and field M/W, ultimate Frisbee M(c)/W(c). *Intramural sports:* basketball M/W, bowling M/W, racquetball M/W, rock climbing M/W, soccer M/W, ultimate Frisbee M/W.

Campus security: 24-hour emergency response devices and patrols, student patrols, late-night transport/escort service, controlled dormitory access.

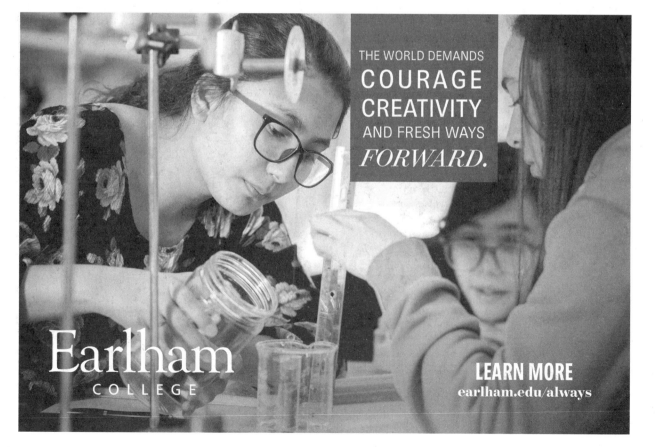

A ★ *indicates that the school has detailed information with a Premium Profile on Petersons.com.*

Student services: health clinic, personal/psychological counseling, women's center.

COSTS & FINANCIAL AID

Costs (2019–20) *Comprehensive fee:* $58,265 includes full-time tuition ($46,410), mandatory fees ($970), and room and board ($10,885). Part-time tuition: $1547 per credit hour. *College room only:* $5775.

Financial Aid Of all full-time matriculated undergraduates who enrolled in 2017, 936 applied for aid, 916 were judged to have need, 582 had their need fully met. 650 Federal Work-Study jobs (averaging $2200). In 2017, 118 non-need-based awards were made. *Average percent of need met:* 94. *Average financial aid package:* $40,345. *Average need-based loan:* $3123. *Average need-based gift aid:* $36,021. *Average non-need-based aid:* $22,958. *Average indebtedness upon graduation:* $30,133. *Financial aid deadline:* 3/1.

APPLYING

Standardized Tests *Required for some:* SAT or ACT (for admission).

Options: electronic application, early admission, early decision, early action, deferred entrance.

Required: essay or personal statement, high school transcript, 2 letters of recommendation. *Recommended:* minimum 3.0 GPA, interview.

Application deadlines: 2/15 (freshmen), 4/1 (transfers), 12/1 (early action).

Early decision deadline: 11/15.

Notification: 4/1 (freshmen), continuous until 5/1 (transfers), 12/15 (early decision), 1/15 (early action).

CONTACT

Susan Hillmann de Castaneda, Director of Admissions, Earlham College, 801 National Road West, Richmond, IN 47374. *Phone:* 765-983-1600. *Toll-free phone:* 800-327-5426. *Fax:* 765-983-1560. *E-mail:* admission@earlham.edu.

See previous page for display ad and page 1002 for the College Close-Up.

★ Franklin College
Franklin, Indiana
http://www.franklincollege.edu/

- **Independent** comprehensive, founded 1834, affiliated with American Baptist Churches in the U.S.A.
- **Suburban** 207-acre campus with easy access to Indianapolis
- **Endowment** $84.6 million
- **Coed**
- **Moderately difficult** entrance level

FACULTY
Student/faculty ratio: 11:1.

ACADEMICS
Calendar: 4-1-4. *Degrees:* bachelor's and master's. **Library:** Hamilton Library. *Books:* 104,767 (physical), 1.5 million (digital/electronic); *Serial titles:* 33,498 (physical), 136,773 (digital/electronic); *Databases:* 78. Weekly public service hours: 83; students can reserve study rooms.

STUDENT LIFE
Housing options: on-campus residence required through junior year; coed, men-only, women-only, special housing for students with disabilities. Campus housing is university owned. Freshman campus housing is guaranteed.

Activities and organizations: drama/theater group, student-run newspaper, radio station, choral group, Student Entertainment Board, Student Congress, FC Volunteers, national fraternities, national sororities.

Athletics Member NCAA. All Division III.

Campus security: 24-hour emergency response devices and patrols, student patrols, late-night transport/escort service, controlled dormitory access.

Student services: health clinic, personal/psychological counseling.

COSTS & FINANCIAL AID
Costs (2018–19) *Comprehensive fee:* $41,529 includes full-time tuition ($31,810), mandatory fees ($200), and room and board ($9519). Full-time tuition and fees vary according to course load and degree level. Part-time

It's not about what you know.
IT'S ABOUT WHO YOU BECOME.

RANKED #1 LIBERAL ARTS COLLEGE IN INDIANA
—WASHINGTON MONTHLY

FRANKLIN COLLEGE

tuition: $460 per credit hour. Part-time tuition and fees vary according to course load and degree level. *Required fees:* $7 per credit hour part-time. *College room only:* $5682. Room and board charges vary according to board plan.

Financial Aid Of all full-time matriculated undergraduates who enrolled in 2017, 913 applied for aid, 822 were judged to have need, 114 had their need fully met. In 2017, 141 non-need-based awards were made. *Average percent of need met:* 72. *Average financial aid package:* $23,559. *Average need-based loan:* $4221. *Average need-based gift aid:* $20,245. *Average non-need-based aid:* $13,847. *Average indebtedness upon graduation:* $36,154.

APPLYING
Standardized Tests *Required:* SAT or ACT (for admission).

Options: electronic application, deferred entrance.

Application fee: $40.

Required: high school transcript. *Required for some:* interview. *Recommended:* essay or personal statement.

CONTACT
Ms. Tara Evans, Director of Admissions, Franklin College, 101 Branigin Boulevard, Franklin, IN 46131-2623. *Phone:* 317-738-8075. *Toll-free phone:* 800-852-0232. *Fax:* 317-738-8075. *E-mail:* admissions@ franklincollege.edu.

See previous page for display ad and page 1012 for the College Close-Up.

Goshen College
Goshen, Indiana
http://www.goshen.edu/
- **Independent Mennonite** comprehensive, founded 1894
- **Small-town** 135-acre campus
- **Endowment** $112.2 million
- **Coed** 845 undergraduate students, 94% full-time, 62% women, 38% men
- **Moderately difficult** entrance level, 68% of applicants were admitted

UNDERGRAD STUDENTS
798 full-time, 47 part-time. Students come from 37 states and territories; 27 other countries; 41% are from out of state; 4% Black or African American, non-Hispanic/Latino; 23% Hispanic/Latino; 2% Asian, non-Hispanic/Latino; 0.1% Native Hawaiian or other Pacific Islander, non-Hispanic/Latino; 0.1% American Indian or Alaska Native, non-Hispanic/Latino; 2% Two or more races, non-Hispanic/Latino; 0.7% Race/ethnicity unknown; 8% international; 9% transferred in; 57% live on campus.

Freshmen:
Admission: 1,219 applied, 825 admitted, 200 enrolled. *Average high school GPA:* 3.5. *Test scores:* SAT evidence-based reading and writing scores over 500: 72%; SAT math scores over 500: 77%; ACT scores over 18: 89%; SAT evidence-based reading and writing scores over 600: 31%; SAT math scores over 600: 23%; ACT scores over 24: 48%; SAT evidence-based reading and writing scores over 700: 8%; SAT math scores over 700: 5%; ACT scores over 30: 17%.

Retention: 73% of full-time freshmen returned.

FACULTY
Total: 100, 62% full-time, 55% with terminal degrees.

Student/faculty ratio: 11:1.

ACADEMICS
Calendar: semesters. *Degrees:* bachelor's, master's, and doctoral.

Special study options: academic remediation for entering students, accelerated degree program, adult/continuing education programs, advanced placement credit, distance learning, double majors, independent study, internships, off-campus study, part-time degree program, services for LD students, student-designed majors, study abroad, summer session for credit.

Unusual degree programs: 3-2 engineering with Case Western Reserve University, University of Illinois at Urbana–Champaign, University of Notre Dame, Washington University in St. Louis.

Computers: 160 computers/terminals and 2,000 ports are available on campus for general student use. Students can access the following: campus intranet, computer help desk, free student e-mail accounts, online (class) grades, online (class) registration, online (class) schedules. Campuswide network is available. 100% of college-owned or -operated housing units are wired for high-speed Internet access. Wireless service is available via entire campus.

Library: The Harold and Wilma Good Library plus 1 other. *Books:* 189,524 (physical), 201,282 (digital/electronic); *Serial titles:* 3,203 (physical), 21,953 (digital/electronic); *Databases:* 72. Weekly public service hours: 89; students can reserve study rooms.

STUDENT LIFE
Housing options: on-campus residence required through junior year; coed, men-only, women-only, special housing for students with disabilities. Campus housing is university owned. Freshman campus housing is guaranteed.

Activities and organizations: drama/theater group, student-run newspaper, radio and television station, choral group, International Student Club, Latino Student Union, PAX - Peace Club, Goshen Student Women's Organization, Business Club.

Athletics Member NAIA. *Intercollegiate sports:* baseball M(s), basketball M(s)/W(s), cross-country running M(s)/W(s), golf M(s), soccer M(s)/W(s), softball W(s), tennis M(s)/W(s), track and field M(s)/W(s), volleyball M(s)/W(s). *Intramural sports:* badminton M/W, basketball M/W, racquetball M/W, soccer M/W, softball W, table tennis M/W, tennis M/W, ultimate Frisbee M/W, volleyball M/W.

Campus security: 24-hour emergency response devices and patrols, late-night transport/escort service, controlled dormitory access.

Student services: health clinic, personal/psychological counseling.

COSTS & FINANCIAL AID
Costs (2019–20) Comprehensive fee: $45,300 includes full-time tuition ($34,540) and room and board ($10,760). Part-time tuition: $1425 per credit hour. *College room only:* $5810.

Financial Aid Of all full-time matriculated undergraduates who enrolled in 2018, 660 applied for aid, 610 were judged to have need, 135 had their need fully met. 364 Federal Work-Study jobs (averaging $1109). 52 state and other part-time jobs (averaging $1842). In 2018, 174 non-need-based awards were made. *Average percent of need met:* 83. *Average financial aid package:* $28,162. *Average need-based loan:* $4842. *Average need-based gift aid:* $23,986. *Average non-need-based aid:* $15,724. *Average indebtedness upon graduation:* $27,062.

APPLYING
Standardized Tests *Required:* SAT or ACT (for admission).

Options: electronic application, deferred entrance.

Application fee: $25.

Required: minimum 2.0 GPA. *Required for some:* essay or personal statement, high school transcript. *Recommended:* minimum 2.8 GPA, 1 letter of recommendation, interview, rank in upper 50% of high school class.

Application deadlines: 7/15 (freshmen), 8/15 (transfers).

Notification: continuous (freshmen), continuous (transfers).

CONTACT
Ms. Linda VandenBosch, Director of Admissions, Goshen College, 1700 S Main St, Goshen, IN 46526. *Phone:* 574-5357535. *Toll-free phone:* 800-348-7422. *E-mail:* admissions@goshen.edu.

Grace College
Winona Lake, Indiana
http://www.grace.edu/

CONTACT
Mrs. Nikki Sproul, Admissions Office, Grace College, 200 Seminary Drive, Winona Lake, IN 46590. *Phone:* 574-372-5100 Ext. 6008. *Toll-free phone:* 800-54-GRACE. *Fax:* 574-372-5120. *E-mail:* enroll@grace.edu.

Hanover College

Hanover, Indiana
http://www.hanover.edu/

- **Independent Presbyterian** 4-year, founded 1827
- **Rural** 630-acre campus with easy access to Louisville
- **Endowment** $136.2 million
- **Coed** 1,104 undergraduate students, 99% full-time, 55% women, 45% men
- **Moderately difficult** entrance level, 79% of applicants were admitted

UNDERGRAD STUDENTS
1,097 full-time, 7 part-time. Students come from 22 states and territories; 18 other countries; 33% are from out of state; 6% Black or African American, non-Hispanic/Latino; 3% Hispanic/Latino; 0.7% Asian, non-Hispanic/Latino; 0.3% Native Hawaiian or other Pacific Islander, non-Hispanic/Latino; 0.3% American Indian or Alaska Native, non-Hispanic/Latino; 2% Two or more races, non-Hispanic/Latino; 11% Race/ethnicity unknown; 3% international; 1% transferred in; 93% live on campus.

Freshmen:
Admission: 3,229 applied, 2,562 admitted, 356 enrolled. *Average high school GPA:* 3.7. *Test scores:* SAT evidence-based reading and writing scores over 500: 85%; SAT math scores over 500: 84%; ACT scores over 18: 96%; SAT evidence-based reading and writing scores over 600: 34%; SAT math scores over 600: 29%; ACT scores over 24: 69%; SAT evidence-based reading and writing scores over 700: 9%; SAT math scores over 700: 4%; ACT scores over 30: 9%.

Retention: 75% of full-time freshmen returned.

FACULTY
Total: 100, 84% full-time, 89% with terminal degrees.

Student/faculty ratio: 12:1.

ACADEMICS
Calendar: 4-4-1. *Degree:* bachelor's.

Special study options: advanced placement credit, cooperative education, distance learning, double majors, independent study, internships, off-campus study, services for LD students, student-designed majors, study abroad, summer session for credit.

Unusual degree programs: nursing.

Computers: 120 computers/terminals and 1,550 ports are available on campus for general student use. Students can access the following: campus intranet, computer help desk, free student e-mail accounts, online (class) grades, online (class) registration, online (class) schedules. Campuswide network is available. 100% of college-owned or -operated housing units are wired for high-speed Internet access. Wireless service is available via entire campus.

Library: Duggan Library. *Books:* 196,284 (physical), 213,376 (digital/electronic); *Serial titles:* 6,584 (physical), 183,744 (digital/electronic); *Databases:* 117. Students can reserve study rooms.

STUDENT LIFE
Housing options: on-campus residence required through senior year; coed, men-only, women-only. Campus housing is university owned and leased by the school. Freshman campus housing is guaranteed.

Activities and organizations: drama/theater group, student-run newspaper, radio and television station, choral group, marching band, Delight Ministries, Alpha Lambda Delta, Love Out Loud, Art Club, International Club, national fraternities, national sororities.

Athletics Member NCAA. All Division III except golf (Division II). *Intercollegiate sports:* baseball M, basketball M/W, cross-country running M/W, football M, golf M/W, lacrosse M/W, soccer M/W, softball W, swimming and diving M/W, tennis M/W, track and field M/W, volleyball W. *Intramural sports:* archery W(c), basketball M/W, football M/W, rugby M(c)/W(c), soccer M/W, softball M/W, ultimate Frisbee M(c), volleyball M/W.

Campus security: 24-hour emergency response devices and patrols, late-night transport/escort service, controlled dormitory access.

Student services: health clinic, personal/psychological counseling.

COSTS & FINANCIAL AID
Costs (2019–20) *One-time required fee:* $350. *Comprehensive fee:* $50,700 includes full-time tuition ($37,980), mandatory fees ($770), and room and board ($11,950). Part-time tuition: $1055 per unit. *College room only:* $5950.

Financial Aid Of all full-time matriculated undergraduates who enrolled in 2017, 941 applied for aid, 855 were judged to have need, 260 had their need fully met. 363 Federal Work-Study jobs (averaging $1561). In 2017, 221 non-need-based awards were made. *Average percent of need met:* 84. *Average financial aid package:* $31,586. *Average need-based loan:* $4426. *Average need-based gift aid:* $27,477. *Average non-need-based aid:* $22,467. *Average indebtedness upon graduation:* $30,665.

APPLYING
Standardized Tests *Recommended:* SAT or ACT (for admission).

Options: electronic application, early admission, early action, deferred entrance.

Required: essay or personal statement, high school transcript, 1 letter of recommendation. *Recommended:* interview.

Application deadlines: rolling (freshmen), rolling (transfers).

Notification: continuous until 9/1 (freshmen), continuous (transfers).

CONTACT
Ms. Angela Jackinowski, Application Specialist, Hanover College, 517 Ball Drive, Hanover, IN 47243. *Phone:* 812-866-7023. *Toll-free phone:* 800-213-2178. *Fax:* 812-866-7098. *E-mail:* admission@hanover.edu.

Holy Cross College

Notre Dame, Indiana
http://www.hcc-nd.edu/

CONTACT
Holy Cross College, 54515 SR 933 N., PO Box 308, Notre Dame, IN 46556. *Phone:* 574-239-8338. *E-mail:* admissions@hcc-nd.edu.

Horizon University

Indianapolis, Indiana
http://www.horizonuniversity.edu/

- **Independent** 4-year, founded 1993
- **Suburban** 100-acre campus with easy access to Indianapolis, IN
- **Coed**
- **Noncompetitive** entrance level

FACULTY
Student/faculty ratio: 2:1.

ACADEMICS
Calendar: semesters. *Degrees:* certificates, associate, and bachelor's.

STUDENT LIFE
Housing options: college housing not available.

COSTS
Costs (2018–19) *Tuition:* $9000 full-time, $250 per semester hour part-time. *Required fees:* $300 full-time, $100 per term part-time.

APPLYING
Options: electronic application.

Required: essay or personal statement, high school transcript, minimum 2.0 GPA, 2 letters of recommendation, interview.

CONTACT
Horizon University, 7700 Indian Lake Road, Indianapolis, IN 46236. *Toll-free phone:* 800-553-HORIZON.

Huntington University

Huntington, Indiana
http://www.huntington.edu/

CONTACT
Huntington University, 2303 College Avenue, Huntington, IN 46750-1299. *Phone:* 260-356-6000. *Toll-free phone:* 800-642-6493.

Indiana State University

Terre Haute, Indiana
http://www.indstate.edu/

- **State-supported** university, founded 1865
- **Small-town** 435-acre campus with easy access to Indianapolis
- **Endowment** $48.0 million
- **Coed** 11,050 undergraduate students, 80% full-time, 56% women, 44% men
- **Moderately difficult** entrance level, 90% of applicants were admitted

UNDERGRAD STUDENTS
8,891 full-time, 2,159 part-time. Students come from 51 states and territories; 62 other countries; 25% are from out of state; 18% Black or African American, non-Hispanic/Latino; 5% Hispanic/Latino; 1% Asian, non-Hispanic/Latino; 0.1% Native Hawaiian or other Pacific Islander, non-Hispanic/Latino; 0.4% American Indian or Alaska Native, non-Hispanic/Latino; 4% Two or more races, non-Hispanic/Latino; 3% Race/ethnicity unknown; 3% international; 7% transferred in; 32% live on campus.

Freshmen:
Admission: 12,861 applied, 11,563 admitted, 2,402 enrolled. *Average high school GPA:* 3.2. *Test scores:* SAT evidence-based reading and writing scores over 500: 59%; SAT math scores over 500: 57%; ACT scores over 18: 64%; SAT evidence-based reading and writing scores over 600: 16%; SAT math scores over 600: 13%; ACT scores over 24: 23%; SAT evidence-based reading and writing scores over 700: 1%; SAT math scores over 700: 1%; ACT scores over 30: 3%.
Retention: 62% of full-time freshmen returned.

FACULTY
Total: 703, 66% full-time, 57% with terminal degrees.
Student/faculty ratio: 21:1.

ACADEMICS
Calendar: semesters. *Degrees:* certificates, bachelor's, master's, doctoral, post-master's, and postbachelor's certificates.
Special study options: academic remediation for entering students, accelerated degree program, adult/continuing education programs, advanced placement credit, cooperative education, distance learning, double majors, English as a second language, freshman honors college, honors programs, independent study, internships, off-campus study, part-time degree program, services for LD students, study abroad, summer session for credit. *ROTC:* Army (b), Air Force (b).
Computers: 170 computers/terminals are available on campus for general student use. Students can access the following: campus intranet, computer help desk, free student e-mail accounts, online (class) grades, online (class) registration, online (class) schedules. Campuswide network is available. 100% of college-owned or -operated housing units are wired for high-speed Internet access. Wireless service is available via entire campus.
Library: Cunningham Memorial Library plus 1 other. *Books:* 952,660 (physical), 825,318 (digital/electronic); *Serial titles:* 64,989 (physical), 83,801 (digital/electronic); *Databases:* 357. Weekly public service hours: 132; study areas open 24 hours, 5–7 days a week; students can reserve study rooms.

STUDENT LIFE
Housing options: on-campus residence required for freshman year; coed, men-only, women-only, special housing for students with disabilities. Campus housing is university owned. Freshman campus housing is guaranteed.
Activities and organizations: drama/theater group, student-run newspaper, radio station, choral group, marching band, Union Board, Student Government Association, Panhellenic Council (sororities), Interfraternity Council (fraternities), Residence Hall Association, national fraternities, national sororities.
Athletics Member NCAA. All Division I except football (Division I-AA). *Intercollegiate sports:* baseball M(s), basketball M(s)/W(s), cross-country running M(s)/W(s), golf W(s), soccer W(s), softball W(s), swimming and diving W(s), track and field M(s)/W(s), volleyball W(s). *Intramural sports:* badminton M/W, basketball M/W, bowling M(c)/W(c), rugby M(c), sand volleyball M/W, soccer M/W, softball M/W, swimming and diving M/W, tennis M/W, track and field M/W, ultimate Frisbee M(c)/W(c), volleyball M/W, wrestling M(c).
Campus security: 24-hour emergency response devices and patrols, student patrols, late-night transport/escort service, RAVE Campus Alert Emails/Texts; Workshops and Video Training; Motorist Assistance; Other Education Opportunities;.
Student services: health clinic, personal/psychological counseling, women's center, veterans affairs office.

COSTS & FINANCIAL AID
Costs (2018–19) *Tuition:* state resident $8890 full-time, $322 per credit hour part-time; nonresident $19,636 full-time, $695 per credit hour part-time. Full-time tuition and fees vary according to reciprocity agreements. Part-time tuition and fees vary according to course load and reciprocity agreements. *Required fees:* $200 full-time, $100 per term part-time. *Room and board:* $10,590; room only: $6706. Room and board charges vary according to board plan, housing facility, and student level. *Payment plans:* installment, deferred payment. *Waivers:* senior citizens and employees or children of employees.
Financial Aid Of all full-time matriculated undergraduates who enrolled in 2017, 8,230 applied for aid, 6,996 were judged to have need, 614 had their need fully met. In 2017, 793 non-need-based awards were made. *Average percent of need met:* 80. *Average financial aid package:* $10,930. *Average need-based loan:* $3842. *Average need-based gift aid:* $6354. *Average non-need-based aid:* $5274. *Average indebtedness upon graduation:* $26,833. *Financial aid deadline:* 7/1.

APPLYING
Standardized Tests *Required:* SAT or ACT (for admission).
Options: electronic application, deferred entrance.
Application fee: $25.
Required: high school transcript. *Required for some:* interview. *Recommended:* minimum 2.5 GPA.
Notification: continuous (freshmen), continuous (transfers).

CONTACT
Mr. Richard Toomey, Assistant Vice President of Enrollment Management, Indiana State University, 318 North Sixth Street, John W. Moore Welcome Center, Terre Haute, IN 47809-9989. *Phone:* 812-237-2121. *Toll-free phone:* 800-468-6478. *Fax:* 812-237-8023. *E-mail:* admissions@indstate.edu.

Indiana Tech

Fort Wayne, Indiana
http://www.indianatech.edu/

- **Independent** comprehensive, founded 1930
- **Urban** 42-acre campus
- **Endowment** $123.2 million
- **Coed**
- **Moderately difficult** entrance level

FACULTY
Student/faculty ratio: 20:1.

ACADEMICS
Calendar: semesters. *Degrees:* associate, bachelor's, master's, and doctoral.
Library: McMillen Library. *Books:* 15,633 (physical), 60,903 (digital/electronic); *Serial titles:* 182 (physical), 500,000 (digital/electronic); *Databases:* 10. Weekly public service hours: 72; students can reserve study rooms.

STUDENT LIFE
Housing options: on-campus residence required through sophomore year; coed. Campus housing is university owned.
Activities and organizations: Multicultural Club, NSBE, Indiana Tech Gaming Society, Tech LOL, Cyber Defense Club of Indiana Tech, national fraternities.
Athletics Member NAIA.
Campus security: 24-hour emergency response devices and patrols, student patrols, late-night transport/escort service, controlled dormitory access.
Student services: personal/psychological counseling.

COSTS & FINANCIAL AID

Costs (2018–19) *Comprehensive fee:* $36,920 includes full-time tuition ($26,460), mandatory fees ($440), and room and board ($10,020). Full-time tuition and fees vary according to course load and program. Part-time tuition: $520 per credit hour. Part-time tuition and fees vary according to course load and program. No tuition increase for student's term of enrollment. *Required fees:* $165 per term part-time. *Room and board:* Room and board charges vary according to board plan and housing facility.

Financial Aid Of all full-time matriculated undergraduates who enrolled in 2017, 1,200 applied for aid, 1,117 were judged to have need, 215 had their need fully met. 68 Federal Work-Study jobs (averaging $1025). In 2017, 22 non-need-based awards were made. *Average percent of need met:* 72. *Average financial aid package:* $21,823. *Average need-based loan:* $4550. *Average need-based gift aid:* $18,159. *Average non-need-based aid:* $10,915. *Average indebtedness upon graduation:* $41,844.

APPLYING

Standardized Tests *Required:* SAT or ACT (for admission). *Recommended:* AP Exam Results.

Options: electronic application.

Required: high school transcript, minimum 2.0 GPA. *Required for some:* essay or personal statement, minimum 3.0 GPA, 2 letters of recommendation, interview, interview.

CONTACT

Mr. Robert Confer, Director of Admissions, Indiana Tech, 1600 East Washington Boulevard, Fort Wayne, IN 46803. *Phone:* 260-422-5561 Ext. 2424. *Toll-free phone:* 800-937-2448. *Fax:* 260-422-7696. *E-mail:* admissions@indianatech.edu.

Indiana University Bloomington

Bloomington, Indiana

http://www.iub.edu/

- **State-supported** university, founded 1820, part of Indiana University System
- **Small-town** 1939-acre campus with easy access to Indianapolis
- **Endowment** $1.3 billion
- **Coed** 33,301 undergraduate students, 96% full-time, 50% women, 50% men
- **Moderately difficult** entrance level, 77% of applicants were admitted

UNDERGRAD STUDENTS

32,109 full-time, 1,192 part-time. Students come from 52 states and territories; 115 other countries; 35% are from out of state; 5% Black or African American, non-Hispanic/Latino; 6% Hispanic/Latino; 6% Asian, non-Hispanic/Latino; 0.1% American Indian or Alaska Native, non-Hispanic/Latino; 4% Two or more races, non-Hispanic/Latino; 0.2% Race/ethnicity unknown; 9% international; 2% transferred in; 37% live on campus.

Freshmen:

Admission: 44,169 applied, 33,970 admitted, 8,097 enrolled. *Average high school GPA:* 3.7. *Test scores:* SAT evidence-based reading and writing scores over 500: 96%; SAT math scores over 500: 97%; ACT scores over 18: 99%; SAT evidence-based reading and writing scores over 600: 65%; SAT math scores over 600: 62%; ACT scores over 24: 81%; SAT evidence-based reading and writing scores over 700: 14%; SAT math scores over 700: 22%; ACT scores over 30: 37%. *Retention:* 91% of full-time freshmen returned.

FACULTY

Total: 2,495, 86% full-time, 81% with terminal degrees. **Student/faculty ratio:** 17:1.

ACADEMICS

Calendar: semesters plus summer sessions. *Degrees:* certificates, diplomas, associate, bachelor's, master's, doctoral, post-master's, and postbachelor's certificates.

Special study options: academic remediation for entering students, accelerated degree program, adult/continuing education programs, advanced placement credit, cooperative education, distance learning, double majors, English as a second language, external degree program, freshman honors college, honors programs, independent study, internships, off-campus study, part-time degree program, services for LD students, student-designed majors, study abroad, summer session for credit. *ROTC:* Army (b), Air Force (b).

Unusual degree programs: 3-2 business administration.

Computers: 2,150 computers/terminals are available on campus for general student use. Students can access the following: campus intranet, computer help desk, free student e-mail accounts, online (class) grades, online (class) registration, online (class) schedules. Campuswide network is available. 95% of college-owned or -operated housing units are wired for high-speed Internet access. Wireless service is available via entire campus.

Library: Indiana University Library plus 16 others. *Books:* 4.6 million (physical), 1.6 million (digital/electronic); *Serial titles:* 153,297 (physical), 111,600 (digital/electronic); *Databases:* 2,011. Study areas open 24 hours, 5–7 days a week; students can reserve study rooms.

STUDENT LIFE

Housing options: on-campus residence required for freshman year; coed, men-only, women-only, cooperative, special housing for students with disabilities. Campus housing is university owned. Freshman campus housing is guaranteed.

Activities and organizations: drama/theater group, student-run newspaper, radio and television station, choral group, marching band, Union Board, Student Association, Student Foundation, Habitat for Humanity, Student Athletic Board, national fraternities, national sororities.

Athletics Member NCAA. All Division I. *Intercollegiate sports:* baseball M(s), basketball M(s)/W(s), cross-country running M(s)/W(s), field hockey W, football M(s), golf M(s)/W(s), rowing W(s), soccer M(s)/W(s), softball W(s), swimming and diving M(s)/W(s), tennis M(s)/W(s), track and field M(s)/W(s), volleyball W(s), water polo W(s), wrestling M(s). *Intramural sports:* badminton M(c)/W(c), baseball M(c)/W(c), basketball M/W, equestrian sports M(c)/W(c), fencing M(c)/W(c), field hockey M(c)/W(c), gymnastics M(c)/W(c), ice hockey M(c)/W(c), lacrosse M(c)/W(c), racquetball M/W, rugby M(c)/W(c), sailing M(c)/W(c), soccer M/W, softball M/W, swimming and diving M(c)/W(c), table tennis M/W, tennis M/W, track and field M/W, ultimate Frisbee M/W, volleyball M/W, water polo M(c).

Campus security: 24-hour emergency response devices and patrols, late-night transport/escort service.

Student services: health clinic, personal/psychological counseling, women's center, legal services, veterans affairs office.

COSTS & FINANCIAL AID

Costs (2018–19) *Tuition:* state resident $9342 full-time, $292 per credit hour part-time; nonresident $34,117 full-time, $1066 per credit hour part-time. Full-time tuition and fees vary according to program. Part-time tuition and fees vary according to course load and program. *Required fees:* $1339 full-time. *Room and board:* $10,466. Room and board charges vary according to board plan and housing facility. *Payment plans:* installment, deferred payment. *Waivers:* senior citizens and employees or children of employees.

Financial Aid Of all full-time matriculated undergraduates who enrolled in 2017, 19,193 applied for aid, 13,225 were judged to have need, 3,623 had their need fully met. 453 Federal Work-Study jobs (averaging $1934). In 2017, 9031 non-need-based awards were made. *Average percent of need met:* 71. *Average financial aid package:* $13,948. *Average need-based loan:* $4289. *Average need-based gift aid:* $12,180. *Average non-need-based aid:* $6683. *Average indebtedness upon graduation:* $28,352.

APPLYING

Standardized Tests *Required:* SAT or ACT (for admission). *Recommended:* SAT Subject Tests (for admission).

Options: electronic application, early action, deferred entrance.

Application fee: $65.

Required: essay or personal statement, high school transcript.

Application deadlines: rolling (freshmen), rolling (transfers), 11/1 (early action).

Notification: continuous (transfers), 1/15 (early action).

CONTACT
Ms. Sacha Thieme, Executive Director of Admissions, Indiana University Bloomington, 940 E. Seventh Street, Bloomington, IN 47405. *Phone:* 812-855-0661. *Fax:* 812-855-5102. *E-mail:* iuadmit@indiana.edu.

Indiana University East
Richmond, Indiana
http://www.iue.edu/
- **State-supported** comprehensive, founded 1971, part of Indiana University System
- **Small-town** 182-acre campus with easy access to Indianapolis
- **Endowment** $5.6 million
- **Coed** 3,379 undergraduate students, 59% full-time, 64% women, 36% men
- **Moderately difficult** entrance level, 65% of applicants were admitted

UNDERGRAD STUDENTS
1,986 full-time, 1,393 part-time. Students come from 46 states and territories; 51 other countries; 27% are from out of state; 5% Black or African American, non-Hispanic/Latino; 4% Hispanic/Latino; 1% Asian, non-Hispanic/Latino; 0.3% American Indian or Alaska Native, non-Hispanic/Latino; 3% Two or more races, non-Hispanic/Latino; 6% Race/ethnicity unknown; 2% international; 12% transferred in.

Freshmen:
Admission: 1,979 applied, 1,284 admitted, 455 enrolled. *Average high school GPA:* 3.2. *Test scores:* SAT evidence-based reading and writing scores over 500: 63%; SAT math scores over 500: 58%; ACT scores over 18: 73%; SAT evidence-based reading and writing scores over 600: 15%; SAT math scores over 600: 11%; ACT scores over 24: 28%; SAT evidence-based reading and writing scores over 700: 1%; SAT math scores over 700: 2%; ACT scores over 30: 4%.

Retention: 65% of full-time freshmen returned.

FACULTY
Total: 274, 42% full-time, 46% with terminal degrees.
Student/faculty ratio: 14:1.

ACADEMICS
Calendar: semesters. *Degrees:* certificates, bachelor's, master's, and postbachelor's certificates.

Special study options: academic remediation for entering students, accelerated degree program, adult/continuing education programs, advanced placement credit, cooperative education, distance learning, double majors, external degree program, honors programs, independent study, internships, off-campus study, part-time degree program, services for LD students, study abroad, summer session for credit.

Computers: 196 computers/terminals are available on campus for general student use. Students can access the following: computer help desk, free student e-mail accounts, online (class) grades, online (class) registration, online (class) schedules. Campuswide network is available. Wireless service is available via entire campus.
Library: IU East Campus Library. *Books:* 21,911 (physical), 185,438 (digital/electronic); *Serial titles:* 2 (physical), 94,601 (digital/electronic); *Databases:* 524. Students can reserve study rooms.

STUDENT LIFE
Housing options: college housing not available.

Activities and organizations: drama/theater group, student-run newspaper, television station, choral group, Student Government Association.

Athletics Member NAIA. *Intercollegiate sports:* basketball M/W, cross-country running M/W, golf M/W, soccer M/W, tennis M/W, track and field M/W, volleyball W.

Campus security: 24-hour emergency response devices, late-night transport/escort service.

Student services: personal/psychological counseling, veterans affairs office.

COSTS & FINANCIAL AID
Costs (2018–19) *Tuition:* state resident $6727 full-time, $224 per credit hour part-time; nonresident $18,783 full-time, $626 per credit hour part-time. Full-time tuition and fees vary according to program and reciprocity agreements. Part-time tuition and fees vary according to course load, program, and reciprocity agreements. *Required fees:* $617 full-time. *Payment plans:* installment, deferred payment. *Waivers:* senior citizens and employees or children of employees.

Financial Aid Of all full-time matriculated undergraduates who enrolled in 2017, 1,676 applied for aid, 1,416 were judged to have need, 279 had their need fully met. 39 Federal Work-Study jobs (averaging $2473). In 2017, 146 non-need-based awards were made. *Average percent of need met:* 69. *Average financial aid package:* $9093. *Average need-based loan:* $3742. *Average need-based gift aid:* $7537. *Average non-need-based aid:* $2131. *Average indebtedness upon graduation:* $22,790.

APPLYING
Standardized Tests *Required for some:* SAT or ACT (for admission).

Options: electronic application, early admission, deferred entrance.

Application fee: $35.

Required: high school transcript. *Required for some:* 1 letter of recommendation.

Application deadlines: rolling (freshmen), rolling (transfers).

Notification: continuous (freshmen), continuous (transfers).

CONTACT
Ms. Molly Vanderpool, Executive Director, Recruitment and Transitions, Admissions, Indiana University East, 2325 Chester Boulevard, Whitewater Hall 151, Richmond, IN 47374-1289. *Phone:* 765-973-8208. *Toll-free phone:* 800-959-EAST. *Fax:* 765-973-8209. *E-mail:* applynow@iue.edu.

Indiana University Kokomo
Kokomo, Indiana
http://www.iuk.edu/
- **State-supported** comprehensive, founded 1945, part of Indiana University System
- **Small-town** 51-acre campus with easy access to Indianapolis
- **Endowment** $6.6 million
- **Coed** 2,912 undergraduate students, 78% full-time, 64% women, 36% men
- **Minimally difficult** entrance level, 80% of applicants were admitted

UNDERGRAD STUDENTS
2,259 full-time, 653 part-time. Students come from 17 states and territories; 25 other countries; 2% are from out of state; 4% Black or African American, non-Hispanic/Latino; 5% Hispanic/Latino; 1% Asian, non-Hispanic/Latino; 0.4% American Indian or Alaska Native, non-Hispanic/Latino; 3% Two or more races, non-Hispanic/Latino; 3% Race/ethnicity unknown; 1% international; 9% transferred in.

Freshmen:
Admission: 2,499 applied, 1,999 admitted, 639 enrolled. *Average high school GPA:* 3.3. *Test scores:* SAT evidence-based reading and writing scores over 500: 67%; SAT math scores over 500: 65%; ACT scores over 18: 85%; SAT evidence-based reading and writing scores over 600: 16%; SAT math scores over 600: 11%; ACT scores over 24: 24%; SAT evidence-based reading and writing scores over 700: 1%; ACT scores over 30: 1%.

Retention: 60% of full-time freshmen returned.

FACULTY
Total: 265, 50% full-time, 39% with terminal degrees.
Student/faculty ratio: 16:1.

ACADEMICS
Calendar: semesters. *Degrees:* certificates, associate, bachelor's, master's, and postbachelor's certificates.

Special study options: academic remediation for entering students, accelerated degree program, adult/continuing education programs, advanced placement credit, distance learning, double majors, English as a second language, external degree program, freshman honors college, honors programs, independent study, internships, part-time degree program, services for LD students, study abroad, summer session for credit.

Computers: 325 computers/terminals are available on campus for general student use. Students can access the following: campus intranet, computer help desk, free student e-mail accounts, online (class) grades, online (class) registration, online (class) schedules. Campuswide network is available. Wireless service is available via entire campus.

Library: IU Kokomo Library. *Books:* 92,259 (physical), 1.4 million (digital/electronic); *Serial titles:* 1,849 (physical), 116,559 (digital/electronic); *Databases:* 393. Students can reserve study rooms.

STUDENT LIFE

Housing options: college housing not available.

Activities and organizations: drama/theater group, student-run newspaper, choral group, national sororities.

Athletics Member NAIA. *Intercollegiate sports:* baseball M, basketball M/W, cross-country running M/W, golf M/W, soccer W, tennis W, track and field M/W, volleyball W.

Campus security: late-night transport/escort service.

Student services: personal/psychological counseling.

COSTS & FINANCIAL AID

Costs (2018–19) *Tuition:* state resident $6727 full-time, $224 per credit hour part-time; nonresident $18,783 full-time, $626 per credit hour part-time. Full-time tuition and fees vary according to program and reciprocity agreements. Part-time tuition and fees vary according to course load, program, and reciprocity agreements. *Required fees:* $617 full-time. *Payment plans:* installment, deferred payment. *Waivers:* senior citizens and employees or children of employees.

Financial Aid Of all full-time matriculated undergraduates who enrolled in 2017, 1,926 applied for aid, 1,503 were judged to have need, 214 had their need fully met. 72 Federal Work-Study jobs (averaging $1687). In 2017, 145 non-need-based awards were made. *Average percent of need met:* 67. *Average financial aid package:* $8910. *Average need-based loan:* $3546. *Average need-based gift aid:* $7796. *Average non-need-based aid:* $2331. *Average indebtedness upon graduation:* $23,454. *Financial aid deadline:* 6/30.

APPLYING

Standardized Tests *Required for some:* SAT or ACT (for admission).

Options: electronic application, deferred entrance.

Application fee: $35.

Required: high school transcript.

Notification: continuous (freshmen), continuous (transfers).

CONTACT

Ms. Angie Siders, Director of Admissions, Indiana University Kokomo, Kelley Student Center, Room 230, 2300 South Washington Street, Kokomo, IN 46904-9003. *Phone:* 765-455-9217. *Toll-free phone:* 888-875-4485. *Fax:* 765-455-9537. *E-mail:* iuadmis@iuk.edu.

Indiana University Northwest

Gary, Indiana

http://www.iun.edu/

- **State-supported** comprehensive, founded 1959, part of Indiana University System
- **Suburban** 43-acre campus with easy access to Chicago
- **Endowment** $10.3 million
- **Coed** 3,534 undergraduate students, 71% full-time, 70% women, 30% men
- **Minimally difficult** entrance level, 80% of applicants were admitted

UNDERGRAD STUDENTS

2,515 full-time, 1,019 part-time. Students come from 12 states and territories; 34 other countries; 3% are from out of state; 16% Black or African American, non-Hispanic/Latino; 24% Hispanic/Latino; 3% Asian, non-Hispanic/Latino; 0.2% American Indian or Alaska Native, non-Hispanic/Latino; 3% Two or more races, non-Hispanic/Latino; 2% Race/ethnicity unknown; 0.5% international; 8% transferred in.

Freshmen:

Admission: 2,182 applied, 1,737 admitted, 674 enrolled. *Average high school GPA:* 3.0. *Test scores:* SAT evidence-based reading and writing scores over 500: 56%; SAT math scores over 500: 54%; ACT scores over 18: 76%; SAT evidence-based reading and writing scores over 600: 13%; SAT math scores over 600: 9%; ACT scores over 24: 24%; ACT scores over 30: 2%.

Retention: 66% of full-time freshmen returned.

FACULTY

Total: 346, 49% full-time, 49% with terminal degrees.

Student/faculty ratio: 14:1.

ACADEMICS

Calendar: semesters. *Degrees:* certificates, associate, bachelor's, master's, and postbachelor's certificates.

Special study options: academic remediation for entering students, accelerated degree program, adult/continuing education programs, advanced placement credit, cooperative education, distance learning, double majors, external degree program, honors programs, independent study, internships, off-campus study, part-time degree program, services for LD students, student-designed majors, study abroad, summer session for credit. *ROTC:* Army (b).

Computers: 682 computers/terminals are available on campus for general student use. Students can access the following: campus intranet, computer help desk, free student e-mail accounts, online (class) grades, online (class) registration, online (class) schedules. Campuswide network is available. Wireless service is available via entire campus.

Library: John W. Anderson Library. *Books:* 252,605 (physical), 837,493 (digital/electronic); *Serial titles:* 2,342 (physical), 136,256 (digital/electronic); *Databases:* 539. Students can reserve study rooms.

STUDENT LIFE

Housing options: college housing not available.

Activities and organizations: drama/theater group, student-run newspaper, radio station, Student Government Association, Student Ambassadors, Art Club, Modern Languages Club, national fraternities, national sororities.

Athletics Member NAIA. *Intercollegiate sports:* basketball M(s)/W(s), cross-country running M(s)/W(s), golf M(s)/W(s), soccer M, tennis M/W, volleyball W(s). *Intramural sports:* basketball M/W, cheerleading M(c)/W(c), cross-country running M(c)/W(c), football M(c)/W(c), ice hockey M(c)/W(c), soccer M(c)/W(c), softball M(c)/W(c), volleyball M/W.

Campus security: 24-hour emergency response devices and patrols, late-night transport/escort service.

Student services: health clinic, personal/psychological counseling, veterans affairs office.

COSTS & FINANCIAL AID

Costs (2018–19) *Tuition:* state resident $6727 full-time, $224 per credit hour part-time; nonresident $18,783 full-time, $626 per credit hour part-time. Full-time tuition and fees vary according to program and reciprocity agreements. Part-time tuition and fees vary according to course load, program, and reciprocity agreements. *Required fees:* $617 full-time. *Payment plans:* installment, deferred payment. *Waivers:* senior citizens and employees or children of employees.

Financial Aid Of all full-time matriculated undergraduates who enrolled in 2017, 2,269 applied for aid, 1,818 were judged to have need, 250 had their need fully met. 84 Federal Work-Study jobs (averaging $1840). In 2017, 164 non-need-based awards were made. *Average percent of need met:* 68. *Average financial aid package:* $8928. *Average need-based loan:* $3639. *Average need-based gift aid:* $7838. *Average non-need-based aid:* $3818. *Average indebtedness upon graduation:* $27,466.

APPLYING

Standardized Tests *Required:* SAT or ACT (for admission).

Options: electronic application, deferred entrance.

Application fee: $35.

Required: high school transcript, minimum 2.0 GPA.

Application deadlines: rolling (freshmen), rolling (transfers).

Notification: continuous (freshmen), continuous (transfers).

CONTACT

Dorothy Frink, Director of Admissions and Strategic Recruitment, Indiana University Northwest, 3400 Broadway, Gary, IN 46408-1197. *Phone:* 219-980-6994. *Toll-free phone:* 800-968-7486. *Fax:* 219-981-4219. *E-mail:* defrink@iun.edu.

Indiana University–Purdue University Indianapolis

Indianapolis, Indiana
http://www.iupui.edu/

- **State-supported** university, founded 1969, part of Indiana University System
- **Urban** 536-acre campus with easy access to Indianapolis
- **Endowment** $1.0 billion
- **Coed** 21,246 undergraduate students, 83% full-time, 58% women, 42% men
- **Moderately difficult** entrance level, 81% of applicants were admitted

UNDERGRAD STUDENTS
17,555 full-time, 3,691 part-time. Students come from 46 states and territories; 135 other countries; 5% are from out of state; 9% Black or African American, non-Hispanic/Latino; 8% Hispanic/Latino; 5% Asian, non-Hispanic/Latino; 0.1% American Indian or Alaska Native, non-Hispanic/Latino; 5% Two or more races, non-Hispanic/Latino; 0.5% Race/ethnicity unknown; 4% international; 6% transferred in; 12% live on campus.

Freshmen:
Admission: 13,339 applied, 10,820 admitted, 4,103 enrolled. *Average high school GPA:* 3.5. *Test scores:* SAT evidence-based reading and writing scores over 500: 78%; SAT math scores over 500: 77%; ACT scores over 18: 86%; SAT evidence-based reading and writing scores over 600: 29%; SAT math scores over 600: 24%; ACT scores over 24: 39%; SAT evidence-based reading and writing scores over 700: 3%; SAT math scores over 700: 4%; ACT scores over 30: 8%.

Retention: 72% of full-time freshmen returned.

FACULTY
Total: 3,687, 68% full-time, 68% with terminal degrees.
Student/faculty ratio: 17:1.

ACADEMICS
Calendar: semesters. *Degrees:* certificates, associate, bachelor's, master's, doctoral, post-master's, and postbachelor's certificates.

Special study options: academic remediation for entering students, accelerated degree program, adult/continuing education programs, advanced placement credit, cooperative education, distance learning, double majors, English as a second language, external degree program, freshman honors college, honors programs, independent study, internships, off-campus study, part-time degree program, services for LD students, student-designed majors, study abroad, summer session for credit. *ROTC:* Army (b), Air Force (c).

Computers: 1,158 computers/terminals are available on campus for general student use. Students can access the following: campus intranet, computer help desk, free student e-mail accounts, online (class) grades, online (class) registration, online (class) schedules. Campuswide network is available. 100% of college-owned or -operated housing units are wired for high-speed Internet access. Wireless service is available via entire campus.
Library: University Library plus 4 others. *Books:* 1.6 million (physical), 613,573 (digital/electronic); *Serial titles:* 10,792 (physical), 282,617 (digital/electronic); *Databases:* 902. Study areas open 24 hours, 5–7 days a week; students can reserve study rooms.

STUDENT LIFE
Housing options: coed, special housing for students with disabilities. Campus housing is university owned.

Activities and organizations: drama/theater group, student-run newspaper, choral group, national fraternities, national sororities.

Athletics Member NCAA. All Division I. *Intercollegiate sports:* basketball M(s)/W(s), cheerleading M/W, cross-country running M(s)/W(s), golf M(s)/W(s), soccer M(s)/W(s), softball W(s), swimming and diving M(s)/W(s), tennis M(s)/W(s), track and field M(s)/W(s), volleyball W(s). *Intramural sports:* badminton M(c)/W(c), baseball M(c)/W(c), basketball M/W, cross-country running M(c)/W(c), equestrian sports M(c)/W(c), fencing M(c)/W(c), football M/W, golf M(c)/W(c), ice hockey M(c)/W(c), rowing M(c)/W(c), rugby M(c)/W(c), soccer M/W, tennis M(c)/W(c), track and field M(c)/W(c), ultimate Frisbee M/W, volleyball M/W.

Campus security: 24-hour emergency response devices and patrols, late-night transport/escort service, controlled dormitory access.
Student services: health clinic, personal/psychological counseling, women's center, veterans affairs office.

COSTS & FINANCIAL AID
Costs (2018–19) *Tuition:* state resident $8371 full-time, $279 per credit hour part-time; nonresident $28,727 full-time, $958 per credit hour part-time. Full-time tuition and fees vary according to location, program, and reciprocity agreements. Part-time tuition and fees vary according to course load, location, program, and reciprocity agreements. *Required fees:* $1094 full-time. *Room and board:* $9730. Room and board charges vary according to board plan and housing facility. *Payment plans:* installment, deferred payment. *Waivers:* senior citizens and employees or children of employees.

Financial Aid Of all full-time matriculated undergraduates who enrolled in 2017, 14,352 applied for aid, 11,707 were judged to have need, 2,319 had their need fully met. 471 Federal Work-Study jobs (averaging $2237). In 2017, 1817 non-need-based awards were made. *Average percent of need met:* 69. *Average financial aid package:* $11,727. *Average need-based loan:* $4075. *Average need-based gift aid:* $10,290. *Average non-need-based aid:* $6311. *Average indebtedness upon graduation:* $27,155.

APPLYING
Standardized Tests *Required:* SAT or ACT (for admission).
Options: electronic application.
Application fee: $65.
Required: essay or personal statement, high school transcript. *Required for some:* portfolio for art program.
Notification: continuous (freshmen), continuous (transfers).

CONTACT
Indiana University–Purdue University Indianapolis, 420 University Boulevard, Indianapolis, IN 46202.

Indiana University South Bend

South Bend, Indiana
http://www.iusb.edu/

- **State-supported** comprehensive, founded 1922, part of Indiana University System
- **Suburban** 105-acre campus with easy access to Chicago
- **Endowment** $19.1 million
- **Coed** 4,707 undergraduate students, 77% full-time, 63% women, 37% men
- **Moderately difficult** entrance level, 82% of applicants were admitted

UNDERGRAD STUDENTS
3,614 full-time, 1,093 part-time. Students come from 16 states and territories; 26 other countries; 5% are from out of state; 8% Black or African American, non-Hispanic/Latino; 12% Hispanic/Latino; 2% Asian, non-Hispanic/Latino; 0.1% Native Hawaiian or other Pacific Islander, non-Hispanic/Latino; 0.2% American Indian or Alaska Native, non-Hispanic/Latino; 5% Two or more races, non-Hispanic/Latino; 0.9% Race/ethnicity unknown; 3% international; 7% transferred in; 8% live on campus.

Freshmen:
Admission: 3,011 applied, 2,466 admitted, 929 enrolled. *Average high school GPA:* 3.2. *Test scores:* SAT evidence-based reading and writing scores over 500: 65%; SAT math scores over 500: 61%; ACT scores over 18: 69%; SAT evidence-based reading and writing scores over 600: 17%; SAT math scores over 600: 12%; ACT scores over 24: 23%; SAT evidence-based reading and writing scores over 700: 1%; SAT math scores over 700: 1%; ACT scores over 30: 1%.

Retention: 63% of full-time freshmen returned.

FACULTY
Total: 439, 57% full-time, 54% with terminal degrees.
Student/faculty ratio: 13:1.

ACADEMICS
Calendar: semesters. *Degrees:* certificates, diplomas, associate, bachelor's, master's, and postbachelor's certificates.

Special study options: accelerated degree program, adult/continuing education programs, advanced placement credit, distance learning, double majors, English as a second language, external degree program, freshman honors college, honors programs, independent study, internships, off-campus study, part-time degree program, services for LD students, study abroad, summer session for credit. *ROTC:* Army (c), Air Force (c).

Computers: 730 computers/terminals are available on campus for general student use. Students can access the following: computer help desk, free student e-mail accounts, online (class) grades, online (class) registration, online (class) schedules. Campuswide network is available. 100% of college-owned or -operated housing units are wired for high-speed Internet access. Wireless service is available via entire campus.

Library: Franklin D. Schurz Library plus 1 other. *Books:* 356,495 (physical), 942,808 (digital/electronic); *Serial titles:* 7,253 (physical), 112,145 (digital/electronic); *Databases:* 408. Students can reserve study rooms.

STUDENT LIFE

Housing options: coed. Campus housing is university owned.

Activities and organizations: drama/theater group, student-run newspaper, choral group, national fraternities, national sororities.

Athletics Member NAIA. *Intercollegiate sports:* baseball M(s), basketball M(s)/W(s), cross-country running M(s)/W(s), golf M(s)/W(s), soccer W(s), softball W(s), tennis M(s)/W(s), volleyball W(s). *Intramural sports:* cheerleading M(c)/W(c), equestrian sports M(c)/W(c), golf M(c)/W(c), soccer M(c), volleyball W(c).

Campus security: 24-hour emergency response devices and patrols, late-night transport/escort service.

Student services: health clinic, personal/psychological counseling, women's center, veterans affairs office.

COSTS & FINANCIAL AID

Costs (2018–19) *Tuition:* state resident $6727 full-time, $224 per credit hour part-time; nonresident $18,783 full-time, $626 per credit hour part-time. Full-time tuition and fees vary according to program and reciprocity agreements. Part-time tuition and fees vary according to course load, program, and reciprocity agreements. *Required fees:* $617 full-time. *Room only:* $9034. Room and board charges vary according to housing facility. *Payment plans:* installment, deferred payment. *Waivers:* senior citizens and employees or children of employees.

Financial Aid Of all full-time matriculated undergraduates who enrolled in 2017, 3,251 applied for aid, 2,764 were judged to have need, 289 had their need fully met. 231 Federal Work-Study jobs (averaging $1862). In 2017, 277 non-need-based awards were made. *Average percent of need met:* 67. *Average financial aid package:* $9320. *Average need-based loan:* $3529. *Average need-based gift aid:* $7836. *Average non-need-based aid:* $2516. *Average indebtedness upon graduation:* $25,293.

APPLYING

Standardized Tests *Required:* SAT or ACT (for admission).

Options: electronic application, deferred entrance.

Application fee: $35.

Required: high school transcript, minimum 2.0 GPA.

Application deadlines: rolling (freshmen), rolling (transfers).

Notification: continuous (freshmen), continuous (transfers).

CONTACT

Ms. Constance Peterson-Miller, Director of Admissions and International Student Services, Indiana University South Bend, 1700 Mishawaka Avenue, PO Box 7111, South Bend, IN 46634-7111. *Phone:* 574-520-4839. *Toll-free phone:* 877-GO-2-IUSB. *Fax:* 574-520-4834. *E-mail:* admissions@iusb.edu.

Indiana University Southeast

New Albany, Indiana

http://www.ius.edu/

- **State-supported** comprehensive, founded 1941, part of Indiana University System
- **Suburban** 179-acre campus with easy access to Louisville
- **Endowment** $15.0 million
- **Coed** 4,659 undergraduate students, 69% full-time, 61% women, 39% men
- **Minimally difficult** entrance level, 85% of applicants were admitted

UNDERGRAD STUDENTS

3,204 full-time, 1,455 part-time. Students come from 23 states and territories; 43 other countries; 30% are from out of state; 7% Black or African American, non-Hispanic/Latino; 5% Hispanic/Latino; 2% Asian, non-Hispanic/Latino; 0.1% American Indian or Alaska Native, non-Hispanic/Latino; 4% Two or more races, non-Hispanic/Latino; 0.7% Race/ethnicity unknown; 0.7% international; 7% transferred in; 8% live on campus.

Freshmen:
Admission: 2,794 applied, 2,377 admitted, 1,012 enrolled. *Average high school GPA:* 3.3. *Test scores:* SAT evidence-based reading and writing scores over 500: 68%; SAT math scores over 500: 63%; ACT scores over 18: 72%; SAT evidence-based reading and writing scores over 600: 22%; SAT math scores over 600: 14%; ACT scores over 24: 22%; SAT evidence-based reading and writing scores over 700: 2%; SAT math scores over 700: 1%; ACT scores over 30: 3%.

Retention: 59% of full-time freshmen returned.

FACULTY
Total: 431, 48% full-time, 51% with terminal degrees.

Student/faculty ratio: 14:1.

ACADEMICS
Calendar: semesters. *Degrees:* certificates, bachelor's, master's, and postbachelor's certificates.

Special study options: academic remediation for entering students, accelerated degree program, adult/continuing education programs, advanced placement credit, distance learning, double majors, English as a second language, external degree program, honors programs, independent study, internships, off-campus study, part-time degree program, services for LD students, student-designed majors, study abroad, summer session for credit. *ROTC:* Army (c), Air Force (c).

Computers: 890 computers/terminals are available on campus for general student use. Students can access the following: computer help desk, free student e-mail accounts, online (class) grades, online (class) registration, online (class) schedules. Campuswide network is available. 100% of college-owned or -operated housing units are wired for high-speed Internet access. Wireless service is available via entire campus.

Library: IU Southeast Library. *Books:* 350,569 (physical), 948,599 (digital/electronic); *Serial titles:* 199 (physical), 184,000 (digital/electronic); *Databases:* 338. Students can reserve study rooms.

STUDENT LIFE
Housing options: Campus housing is university owned.

Activities and organizations: drama/theater group, student-run newspaper, choral group, national fraternities, national sororities.

Athletics Member NAIA. *Intercollegiate sports:* baseball M(s), basketball M(s)/W(s), softball W(s), tennis M(s)/W(s), volleyball W(s).

Campus security: 24-hour emergency response devices and patrols, late-night transport/escort service.

Student services: personal/psychological counseling, veterans affairs office.

COSTS & FINANCIAL AID
Costs (2018–19) *Tuition:* state resident $6727 full-time, $224 per credit hour part-time; nonresident $18,783 full-time, $626 per credit hour part-time. Full-time tuition and fees vary according to program and reciprocity agreements. Part-time tuition and fees vary according to course load, program, and reciprocity agreements. *Required fees:* $617 full-time. *Room only:* $9906. Room and board charges vary according to board plan and housing facility. *Payment plans:* installment, deferred payment. *Waivers:* senior citizens and employees or children of employees.

Financial Aid Of all full-time matriculated undergraduates who enrolled in 2017, 2,692 applied for aid, 2,150 were judged to have need, 260 had their need fully met. 100 Federal Work-Study jobs (averaging $1663). In 2017, 228 non-need-based awards were made. *Average percent of need met:* 66. *Average financial aid package:* $8744. *Average need-based loan:* $3795. *Average need-based gift aid:* $7291. *Average non-need-based aid:* $1966. *Average indebtedness upon graduation:* $21,910.

APPLYING
Standardized Tests *Required:* SAT or ACT (for admission).

Options: electronic application, early admission, deferred entrance.

Application fee: $35.

Required: high school transcript.

Application deadlines: rolling (freshmen), rolling (transfers).

Notification: continuous (freshmen), continuous (transfers).

CONTACT
Mr. Christopher Crews, Director of Recruitment and Admission, Indiana University Southeast, University Center South Room 102, 4201 Grant Line Road, New Albany, IN 47150-6405. *Phone:* 812-941-2212. *Toll-free phone:* 800-852-8835. *Fax:* 812-941-2595. *E-mail:* admissions@ius.edu.

Indiana Wesleyan University

Marion, Indiana
http://www.indwes.edu/

- **Independent Wesleyan** comprehensive, founded 1920
- **Small-town** 300-acre campus with easy access to Indianapolis
- **Coed**
- **Moderately difficult** entrance level

FACULTY
Student/faculty ratio: 13:1.

ACADEMICS
Calendar: semesters. *Degrees:* associate, bachelor's, master's, doctoral, post-master's, and postbachelor's certificates (also offers adult program with significant enrollment not reflected in profile).
Library: Lewis A. Jackson Library. Students can reserve study rooms.

STUDENT LIFE
Housing options: on-campus residence required through junior year; men-only, women-only. Campus housing is university owned. Freshman campus housing is guaranteed.

Activities and organizations: drama/theater group, student-run newspaper, radio and television station, choral group, Student Government Organization, Student Activities Council, University Players, World Christian Fellowship, Sixth Man Club.

Athletics Member NAIA, NCCAA.

Campus security: 24-hour emergency response devices and patrols, late-night transport/escort service, controlled dormitory access.

Student services: health clinic, personal/psychological counseling.

COSTS & FINANCIAL AID
Costs (2018–19) *Comprehensive fee:* $34,292 includes full-time tuition ($25,980) and room and board ($8312). Full-time tuition and fees vary according to course load and degree level. Part-time tuition: $555 per credit hour. Part-time tuition and fees vary according to course load and degree level. *College room only:* $4154. Room and board charges vary according to board plan. *Payment plans:* installment, deferred payment.

Financial Aid Of all full-time matriculated undergraduates who enrolled in 2017, 2,323 applied for aid, 2,051 were judged to have need, 1,198 had their need fully met. In 2017, 271 non-need-based awards were made. *Average percent of need met:* 92. *Average financial aid package:* $29,681. *Average need-based loan:* $4009. *Average need-based gift aid:* $3548. *Average non-need-based aid:* $9802. *Average indebtedness upon graduation:* $30,355.

APPLYING
Standardized Tests *Required:* SAT or ACT (for admission). *Required for some:* TOEFL for non-English speaking and some non-resident alien students.

Options: electronic application, deferred entrance.

Required: essay or personal statement, high school transcript, minimum 2.5 GPA, 2 letters of recommendation.

CONTACT
Mr. Adam Farmer, Director of Admissions, Indiana Wesleyan University, 4201 South Washington Street, Marion, IN 46953. *Phone:* 866-468-6498 Ext. 2138. *Toll-free phone:* 866-468-6498. *E-mail:* admissions@indwes.edu.

International Business College

Fort Wayne, Indiana
http://www.ibcfortwayne.edu/

CONTACT
Admissions Office, International Business College, 5699 Coventry Lane, Fort Wayne, IN 46804. *Phone:* 260-459-4500. *Toll-free phone:* 800-589-6363.

Manchester University

North Manchester, Indiana
http://www.manchester.edu/

- **Independent** comprehensive, founded 1889, affiliated with Church of the Brethren
- **Small-town** 125-acre campus
- **Endowment** $60.2 million
- **Coed** 1,191 undergraduate students, 99% full-time, 53% women, 47% men
- **Moderately difficult** entrance level, 59% of applicants were admitted

UNDERGRAD STUDENTS
1,176 full-time, 15 part-time. Students come from 26 states and territories; 20 other countries; 17% are from out of state; 8% Black or African American, non-Hispanic/Latino; 7% Hispanic/Latino; 1% Asian, non-Hispanic/Latino; 0.1% American Indian or Alaska Native, non-Hispanic/Latino; 4% Two or more races, non-Hispanic/Latino; 3% Race/ethnicity unknown; 4% international; 2% transferred in; 74% live on campus.

Freshmen:
Admission: 4,253 applied, 2,523 admitted, 408 enrolled. *Average high school GPA:* 3.4.
Retention: 60% of full-time freshmen returned.

FACULTY
Total: 140, 52% full-time, 49% with terminal degrees.
Student/faculty ratio: 14:1.

ACADEMICS
Calendar: 4-1-4. *Degrees:* associate, bachelor's, master's, and doctoral.
Special study options: accelerated degree program, advanced placement credit, distance learning, double majors, honors programs, independent study, internships, off-campus study, part-time degree program, services for LD students, student-designed majors, study abroad, summer session for credit.

Unusual degree programs: 3-2 engineering with Washington University in St. Louis, Purdue University, Ohio State University, Columbia University.

Computers: 226 computers/terminals are available on campus for general student use. Students can access the following: campus intranet, computer help desk, free student e-mail accounts, online (class) grades, online (class) registration, online (class) schedules. Campuswide network is available. 100% of college-owned or -operated housing units are wired for high-speed Internet access. Wireless service is available via classrooms, computer centers, computer labs, dorm rooms, learning centers, libraries, student centers.
Library: Funderburg Library. Study areas open 24 hours, 5–7 days a week.

STUDENT LIFE
Housing options: on-campus residence required through junior year; coed, special housing for students with disabilities. Campus housing is university owned. Freshman campus housing is guaranteed.

Activities and organizations: drama/theater group, student-run newspaper, radio station, choral group, College of Business Club, Fellowship of Christian Athletes, Student Education Association, African Student Association, Asian Awareness Association.

Athletics Member NCAA. All Division III except golf (Division II). *Intercollegiate sports:* baseball M, basketball M/W, cheerleading W, cross-country running M/W, football M, golf M/W, soccer M/W, softball W, swimming and diving M/W, tennis M/W, track and field M/W, volleyball W, wrestling M. *Intramural sports:* basketball M/W, football M/W, soccer M/W, softball M/W, volleyball M/W.

Campus security: 24-hour patrols, student patrols, late-night transport/escort service.

Student services: health clinic, personal/psychological counseling.

COSTS & FINANCIAL AID

Costs (2019–20) *One-time required fee:* $250. *Comprehensive fee:* $43,674 includes full-time tuition ($32,366), mandatory fees ($1258), and room and board ($10,050). Part-time tuition: $745 per credit hour. *Required fees:* $35 per credit hour part-time. *College room only:* $5350.

Financial Aid Of all full-time matriculated undergraduates who enrolled in 2018, 1,078 applied for aid, 981 were judged to have need, 220 had their need fully met. In 2018, 168 non-need-based awards were made. *Average percent of need met:* 85. *Average financial aid package:* $30,801. *Average need-based loan:* $4084. *Average need-based gift aid:* $25,397. *Average non-need-based aid:* $19,168. *Average indebtedness upon graduation:* $33,838.

APPLYING

Options: electronic application, deferred entrance.

Application fee: $25.

Required: high school transcript, 1 letter of recommendation, rank in upper 50% of high school class. *Required for some:* minimum 3.0 GPA. *Recommended:* minimum 2.3 GPA.

Application deadlines: rolling (freshmen), rolling (transfers).

Notification: continuous (freshmen), continuous (transfers).

CONTACT

Ms. Brandi Chauncey, Director of Admissions, Manchester University, 604 East College Avenue, North Manchester, IN 46962. *Phone:* 260-982-5232. *Toll-free phone:* 800-852-3648. *E-mail:* bcchauncey@manchester.edu.

Marian University

Indianapolis, Indiana
http://www.marian.edu/

- **Independent Roman Catholic** comprehensive, founded 1851
- **Suburban** 114-acre campus with easy access to Indianapolis
- **Endowment** $63.7 million
- **Coed** 2,428 undergraduate students, 82% full-time, 63% women, 37% men
- **Moderately difficult** entrance level, 61% of applicants were admitted

UNDERGRAD STUDENTS

1,995 full-time, 433 part-time. Students come from 35 states and territories; 34 other countries; 23% are from out of state; 11% Black or African American, non-Hispanic/Latino; 6% Hispanic/Latino; 3% Asian, non-Hispanic/Latino; 0.1% Native Hawaiian or other Pacific Islander, non-Hispanic/Latino; 3% Two or more races, non-Hispanic/Latino; 3% Race/ethnicity unknown; 1% international; 2% transferred in; 49% live on campus.

Freshmen:
Admission: 2,325 applied, 1,427 admitted, 425 enrolled. *Average high school GPA:* 3.5. *Test scores:* SAT evidence-based reading and writing scores over 500: 80%; SAT math scores over 500: 84%; ACT scores over 18: 88%; SAT evidence-based reading and writing scores over 600: 29%; SAT math scores over 600: 27%; ACT scores over 24: 44%; SAT evidence-based reading and writing scores over 700: 2%; SAT math scores over 700: 3%; ACT scores over 30: 8%.
Retention: 77% of full-time freshmen returned.

FACULTY

Total: 316, 49% full-time, 47% with terminal degrees.

Student/faculty ratio: 14:1.

ACADEMICS

Calendar: semesters. *Degrees:* associate, bachelor's, master's, and doctoral.

Special study options: academic remediation for entering students, accelerated degree program, adult/continuing education programs, advanced placement credit, cooperative education, distance learning, double majors, honors programs, independent study, internships, off-campus study, part-time degree program, services for LD students, study abroad, summer session for credit. *ROTC:* Army (c).

Computers: 201 computers/terminals are available on campus for general student use. Students can access the following: computer help desk, free student e-mail accounts, online (class) grades, online (class) registration, online (class) schedules. Campuswide network is available. 100% of college-owned or -operated housing units are wired for high-speed Internet access. Wireless service is available via entire campus.

Library: Mother Theresa Hackelmeier Memorial Library. *Books:* 80,118 (physical); *Serial titles:* 150 (physical), 44,749 (digital/electronic). Weekly public service hours: 95.

STUDENT LIFE

Housing options: on-campus residence required through junior year; coed. Campus housing is university owned. Freshman campus housing is guaranteed.

Activities and organizations: drama/theater group, student-run newspaper, choral group, marching band, Student Government Association, College Mentors for Kids, Best Buddies, Knight Nation, Sophia Club.

Athletics Member NAIA. *Intercollegiate sports:* baseball M(s), basketball M(s)/W(s), bowling M(s)/W(s), cheerleading M(s)(c)/W(s)(c), cross-country running M(s)/W(s), football M(s), golf M(s)/W(s), lacrosse W(s), soccer M(s)/W(s), softball W(s), tennis M(s)/W(s), track and field M(s)/W(s), volleyball W(s), weight lifting M(s)/W(s), wrestling M(s). *Intramural sports:* basketball M/W, cheerleading M/W, football M/W, ultimate Frisbee M/W, volleyball M/W.

Campus security: 24-hour emergency response devices and patrols, student patrols, late-night transport/escort service, controlled dormitory access.

Student services: health clinic, personal/psychological counseling.

COSTS & FINANCIAL AID

Costs (2019–20) *Comprehensive fee:* $14,460 includes full-time tuition ($3500) and room and board ($10,960). Part-time tuition: $1500 per credit hour.

Financial Aid Of all full-time matriculated undergraduates who enrolled in 2017, 1,418 applied for aid, 1,154 were judged to have need, 201 had their need fully met. 148 Federal Work-Study jobs (averaging $1500). In 2017, 227 non-need-based awards were made. *Average percent of need met:* 77. *Average financial aid package:* $27,762. *Average need-based loan:* $4194. *Average need-based gift aid:* $24,294. *Average non-need-based aid:* $13,310. *Average indebtedness upon graduation:* $34,435.

APPLYING

Standardized Tests *Required:* SAT or ACT (for admission).

Options: electronic application, deferred entrance.

Required: high school transcript, college transcripts for transfer students. *Required for some:* essay or personal statement, 1 letter of recommendation, interview.

Notification: continuous (freshmen), continuous (transfers).

CONTACT

Ms. Luann Brames, Director of Freshmen Admission, Marian University, 3200 Cold Spring Road, Indianapolis, IN 46222. *Phone:* 317-955-6300. *Toll-free phone:* 800-772-7264. *Fax:* 317-955-6401. *E-mail:* admissions@marian.edu.

Martin University

Indianapolis, Indiana
http://www.martin.edu/

CONTACT

Ms. Brenda Shaheed, Director of Enrollment Management, Martin University, 2171 Avondale Place, PO Box 18567, Indianapolis, IN 46218-3867. *Phone:* 317-543-3237. *Fax:* 317-543-4790.

Mid-America College of Funeral Service

Jeffersonville, Indiana
http://www.mid-america.edu/

CONTACT

Mr. Richard Nelson, Dean of Students, Mid-America College of Funeral Service, 3111 Hamburg Pike, Jeffersonville, IN 47130-9630. *Phone:* 812-288-8878. *Toll-free phone:* 800-221-6158. *Fax:* 812-288-5942. *E-mail:* macfs@mindspring.com.

National American University

Indianapolis, Indiana

http://www.national.edu/

CONTACT

Dr. Rhonda Parker, Campus Director, National American University, 3600 Woodview Trace, Suite 200, Indianapolis, IN 46268. *Phone:* 317-578-7353. *Toll-free phone:* 800-609-1430.

Oakland City University

Oakland City, Indiana

http://www.oak.edu/

- **Independent General Baptist** comprehensive, founded 1885
- **Rural** 20-acre campus
- **Endowment** $5.2 million
- **Coed** 1,231 undergraduate students, 48% full-time, 53% women, 47% men
- **Minimally difficult** entrance level, 50% of applicants were admitted

UNDERGRAD STUDENTS

597 full-time, 634 part-time. Students come from 17 states and territories; 12 other countries; 19% are from out of state; 7% Black or African American, non-Hispanic/Latino; 4% Hispanic/Latino; 0.2% Asian, non-Hispanic/Latino; 0.5% American Indian or Alaska Native, non-Hispanic/Latino; 3% Two or more races, non-Hispanic/Latino; 7% Race/ethnicity unknown; 3% international; 5% transferred in; 61% live on campus.

Freshmen:

Admission: 1,010 applied, 502 admitted, 140 enrolled. *Average high school GPA:* 3.3. *Test scores:* SAT evidence-based reading and writing scores over 500: 55%; SAT math scores over 500: 62%; ACT scores over 18: 60%; SAT evidence-based reading and writing scores over 600: 9%; SAT math scores over 600: 8%; ACT scores over 24: 12%; SAT evidence-based reading and writing scores over 700: 4%; ACT scores over 30: 2%.

Retention: 62% of full-time freshmen returned.

FACULTY

Total: 155, 23% full-time.

Student/faculty ratio: 12:1.

ACADEMICS

Calendar: semesters. *Degrees:* certificates, associate, bachelor's, master's, and doctoral.

Special study options: academic remediation for entering students, accelerated degree program, adult/continuing education programs, advanced placement credit, distance learning, external degree program, part-time degree program, services for LD students, summer session for credit.

Computers: 200 computers/terminals are available on campus for general student use. Students can access the following: campus intranet, computer help desk, free student e-mail accounts, online (class) grades, online (class) registration, online (class) schedules. Campuswide network is available. Wireless service is available via entire campus.

Library: Barger-Richardson Library. *Books:* 84,412 (physical), 17,690 (digital/electronic); *Serial titles:* 79 (physical), 50,255 (digital/electronic); *Databases:* 52.

STUDENT LIFE

Housing options: men-only, women-only. Campus housing is university owned. Freshman campus housing is guaranteed.

Activities and organizations: drama/theater group, student-run newspaper, choral group, Student Government Association, Good News Players, Art Guild, FOCUS, intramural sports.

Athletics Member NCAA, NCCAA. All NCAA Division II except golf (Division I). *Intercollegiate sports:* baseball M(s), basketball M(s)/W(s), cheerleading W(s), cross-country running M(s)/W(s), golf M(s)/W(s), soccer M(s)/W(s), softball W(s), tennis M(s)/W(s), volleyball W(s). *Intramural sports:* basketball M/W, bowling M/W, football M/W, softball M/W, table tennis M/W, tennis M/W, volleyball M/W.

Campus security: 24-hour patrols, student patrols.

Student services: personal/psychological counseling.

COSTS & FINANCIAL AID

Costs (2019–20) *Comprehensive fee:* $34,700 includes full-time tuition ($24,300) and room and board ($10,400). Part-time tuition: $810 per credit hour. *College room only:* $3600.

Financial Aid Of all full-time matriculated undergraduates who enrolled in 2017, 411 applied for aid, 411 were judged to have need. *Average percent of need met:* 35. *Average financial aid package:* $13,420. *Average need-based gift aid:* $11,594.

APPLYING

Standardized Tests *Required for some:* SAT or ACT (for admission).

Options: electronic application, early admission, deferred entrance.

Application fee: $35.

Required: high school transcript, minimum 2.0 GPA. *Recommended:* essay or personal statement, interview.

CONTACT

Miss Jennifer Cates, Assistant Director of Admissions, Oakland City University, 138 North Lucretia Street, Oakland City, IN 47660. *Phone:* 812-749-1220. *Toll-free phone:* 800-737-5125. *E-mail:* jcates@oak.edu.

Purdue University

West Lafayette, Indiana

http://www.purdue.edu/

- **State-supported** university, founded 1869, part of Purdue University System
- **Suburban** 2660-acre campus with easy access to Indianapolis
- **Endowment** $2.5 billion
- **Coed** 32,672 undergraduate students, 96% full-time, 43% women, 57% men
- **Moderately difficult** entrance level, 58% of applicants were admitted

UNDERGRAD STUDENTS

31,217 full-time, 1,455 part-time. Students come from 47 states and territories; 111 other countries; 39% are from out of state; 3% Black or African American, non-Hispanic/Latino; 5% Hispanic/Latino; 9% Asian, non-Hispanic/Latino; 0.1% Native Hawaiian or other Pacific Islander, non-Hispanic/Latino; 0.1% American Indian or Alaska Native, non-Hispanic/Latino; 4% Two or more races, non-Hispanic/Latino; 2% Race/ethnicity unknown; 14% international; 2% transferred in; 41% live on campus.

Freshmen:

Admission: 53,439 applied, 30,965 admitted, 8,357 enrolled. *Average high school GPA:* 3.7. *Test scores:* SAT evidence-based reading and writing scores over 500: 98%; SAT math scores over 500: 98%; ACT scores over 18: 100%; SAT evidence-based reading and writing scores over 600: 72%; SAT math scores over 600: 74%; ACT scores over 24: 86%; SAT evidence-based reading and writing scores over 700: 19%; SAT math scores over 700: 38%; ACT scores over 30: 44%.

Retention: 92% of full-time freshmen returned.

FACULTY

Total: 2,700, 87% full-time, 96% with terminal degrees.

Student/faculty ratio: 13:1.

ACADEMICS

Calendar: semesters. *Degrees:* certificates, associate, bachelor's, master's, doctoral, post-master's, and postbachelor's certificates.

Special study options: accelerated degree program, adult/continuing education programs, cooperative education, distance learning, double majors, English as a second language, honors programs, independent study, part-time degree program, services for LD students, study abroad, summer session for credit. *ROTC:* Army (b), Navy (b), Air Force (b).

Unusual degree programs: 3-2 business administration; engineering; forestry; nursing; social work; pharmacy.

Computers: 5,237 computers/terminals and 79,961 ports are available on campus for general student use. Students can access the following: campus intranet, computer help desk, free student e-mail accounts, online (class) grades, online (class) registration, online (class) schedules. Campuswide network is available. 100% of college-owned or -operated housing units are wired for high-speed Internet access. Wireless service is available via entire campus.

A ★ *indicates that the school has detailed information with a Premium Profile on Petersons.com.*

Library: Purdue University Libraries plus 9 others. *Books:* 946,376 (physical), 2.5 million (digital/electronic); *Serial titles:* 44,788 (physical), 136,167 (digital/electronic); *Databases:* 580. Weekly public service hours: 168; study areas open 24 hours, 5–7 days a week; students can reserve study rooms.

STUDENT LIFE

Housing options: coed, men-only, women-only, cooperative, special housing for students with disabilities. Campus housing is university owned. Freshman applicants given priority for college housing.

Activities and organizations: drama/theater group, student-run newspaper, radio station, choral group, marching band, Purdue Student Government, FSCL Councils, RHA, Purdue Engineering Student Council, AG Council, national fraternities, national sororities.

Athletics Member NCAA. All Division I except football (Division I-A). *Intercollegiate sports:* baseball M(s), basketball M(s)/W(s), cross-country running M(s)/W(s), golf M(s)/W(s), soccer W(s), softball W(s), swimming and diving M(s)/W(s), tennis M(s)/W(s), track and field M(s)/W(s), volleyball W(s), wrestling M(s). *Intramural sports:* archery M(c)/W(c), badminton M(c)/W(c), baseball M(c), basketball M(c)/W(c), bowling M(c)/W(c), crew M(c)/W(c), cross-country running M(c)/W(c), equestrian sports M(c)/W(c), fencing M(c), field hockey W(c), gymnastics M(c)/W(c), ice hockey M(c), lacrosse M(c)/W(c), racquetball M(c)/W(c), riflery M(c)/W(c), rock climbing M(c)/W(c), rugby M(c)/W(c), sailing M(c)/W(c), soccer M(c)/W(c), squash M(c)/W(c), swimming and diving M(c)/W(c), table tennis M(c)/W(c), tennis M(c)/W(c), track and field M(c)/W(c), ultimate Frisbee M(c)/W(c), volleyball M(c)/W(c), water polo M(c)/W(c).

Campus security: 24-hour emergency response devices and patrols, student patrols, late-night transport/escort service, controlled dormitory access.

Student services: health clinic, personal/psychological counseling, women's center, legal services, veterans affairs office.

COSTS & FINANCIAL AID

Costs (2019–20) *Tuition:* state resident $9208 full-time, $330 per credit hour part-time; nonresident $28,010 full-time, $930 per credit hour part-time. *Required fees:* $784 full-time, $18 per credit hour part-time, $18 per credit hour part-time. *Room and board:* $10,030; room only: $4860.

Financial Aid Of all full-time matriculated undergraduates who enrolled in 2017, 16,257 applied for aid, 12,232 were judged to have need, 4,243 had their need fully met. In 2017, 4064 non-need-based awards were made. *Average percent of need met:* 78. *Average financial aid package:* $14,138. *Average need-based loan:* $4962. *Average need-based gift aid:* $12,621. *Average non-need-based aid:* $5035. *Average indebtedness upon graduation:* $28,440.

APPLYING

Standardized Tests *Required:* SAT or ACT (for admission).

Options: electronic application, early admission, early action, deferred entrance.

Application fee: $60.

Required: essay or personal statement, high school transcript.

Application deadlines: rolling (freshmen), rolling (transfers).

Notification: 12/12 (freshmen).

CONTACT

Ms. Kristina M. Wong Davis, Vice Provost for Enrollment Management, Purdue University, 475 Stadium Mall Drive, Schleman Hall, West Lafayette, IN 47907-2050. *Phone:* 765-494-9116. *Fax:* 765-494-0544. *E-mail:* admissions@purdue.edu.

Purdue University Fort Wayne

Fort Wayne, Indiana
http://www.pfw.edu/

CONTACT

Angela Morren, Undergraduate Applications Coordinator, Purdue University Fort Wayne, 2101 East Coliseum Boulevard, Fort Wayne, IN 46805-1499. *Phone:* 260-481-6142. *Toll-free phone:* 800-324-4739. *Fax:* 260-481-6880. *E-mail:* morrena@ipfw.edu.

Purdue University Global

Indianapolis, Indiana
http://www.purdueglobal.edu/

CONTACT

Purdue University Global, 9000 Keystone Crossing, Suite 800, Indianapolis, IN 46240.

Purdue University Northwest

Hammond, Indiana
http://www.pnw.edu/

- **State-supported** comprehensive, founded 2016, part of Purdue University System
- **Urban** 454-acre campus with easy access to Chicago
- **Endowment** $25.1 million
- **Coed** 9,573 undergraduate students, 61% full-time, 56% women, 44% men
- **Moderately difficult** entrance level, 97% of applicants were admitted

UNDERGRAD STUDENTS

5,806 full-time, 3,767 part-time. Students come from 29 states and territories; 37 other countries; 10% are from out of state; 10% Black or African American, non-Hispanic/Latino; 20% Hispanic/Latino; 3% Asian, non-Hispanic/Latino; 0.1% Native Hawaiian or other Pacific Islander, non-Hispanic/Latino; 0.3% American Indian or Alaska Native, non-Hispanic/Latino; 3% Two or more races, non-Hispanic/Latino; 1% Race/ethnicity unknown; 3% international; 9% transferred in; 7% live on campus.

Freshmen:
Admission: 1,686 applied, 1,631 admitted, 1,172 enrolled. *Average high school GPA:* 3.1. *Test scores:* SAT evidence-based reading and writing scores over 500: 72%; SAT math scores over 500: 71%; ACT scores over 18: 87%; SAT evidence-based reading and writing scores over 600: 20%; SAT math scores over 600: 16%; ACT scores over 24: 32%; SAT evidence-based reading and writing scores over 700: 1%; SAT math scores over 700: 2%; ACT scores over 30: 2%.

Retention: 69% of full-time freshmen returned.

FACULTY

Total: 699, 53% full-time, 42% with terminal degrees.

Student/faculty ratio: 16:1.

ACADEMICS

Calendar: semesters. *Degrees:* certificates, associate, bachelor's, master's, doctoral, post-master's, and postbachelor's certificates.

Special study options: academic remediation for entering students, accelerated degree program, adult/continuing education programs, advanced placement credit, cooperative education, distance learning, double majors, English as a second language, freshman honors college, honors programs, independent study, internships, part-time degree program, services for LD students, study abroad, summer session for credit. *ROTC:* Army (b).

Computers: 1,700 computers/terminals and 1,700 ports are available on campus for general student use. Students can access the following: campus intranet, computer help desk, free student e-mail accounts, online (class) grades, online (class) registration, online (class) schedules. Campuswide network is available. 100% of college-owned or -operated housing units are wired for high-speed Internet access. Wireless service is available via entire campus.

Library: Purdue University Northwest Libraries plus 2 others. *Books:* 200,372 (physical), 428,023 (digital/electronic); *Serial titles:* 1,735 (physical), 80,832 (digital/electronic); *Databases:* 180. Weekly public service hours: 138.

STUDENT LIFE

Housing options: coed. Campus housing is university owned.

Activities and organizations: drama/theater group, student-run newspaper, choral group, Black Student Union, Women in Business, National Society of Black Engineers, American Sign Language Club, Student Athlete Advisory Committee, national fraternities, national sororities.

Athletics Member NCAA, NAIA. All NCAA Division II. *Intercollegiate sports:* baseball M(s), basketball M(s)/W(s), cross-country running M(s)/W(s), golf M(s), soccer M(s)/W(s), softball W(s), tennis M(s)/W(s), volleyball W(s). *Intramural sports:* basketball M/W, bowling M/W, football M/W, golf M/W, racquetball M/W, sand volleyball M/W, soccer M/W, table tennis M/W, ultimate Frisbee M/W, volleyball M/W.

Campus security: 24-hour emergency response devices and patrols, student patrols, late-night transport/escort service, controlled dormitory access.

Student services: health clinic, personal/psychological counseling, veterans affairs office.

COSTS & FINANCIAL AID
Costs (2018–19) *Tuition:* state resident $7686 full-time, $231 per credit hour part-time; nonresident $17,368 full-time, $554 per credit hour part-time. Full-time tuition and fees vary according to course level and program. Part-time tuition and fees vary according to program. *Required fees:* $753 full-time, $25 per credit hour part-time. *Room and board:* $7640; room only: $2790. Room and board charges vary according to housing facility. *Payment plans:* installment, deferred payment. *Waivers:* senior citizens and employees or children of employees.

Financial Aid Of all full-time matriculated undergraduates who enrolled in 2014, 4,236 applied for aid, 3,567 were judged to have need, 172 had their need fully met. 105 Federal Work-Study jobs (averaging $2322). In 2014, 215 non-need-based awards were made. *Average percent of need met:* 11. *Average financial aid package:* $7768. *Average need-based loan:* $3388. *Average need-based gift aid:* $5782. *Average non-need-based aid:* $3124. *Average indebtedness upon graduation:* $27,902.

APPLYING
Standardized Tests *Required:* SAT or ACT (for admission).

Options: electronic application.

Application fee: $25.

Required: high school transcript, minimum 2.0 GPA.

Application deadlines: 8/1 (freshmen), 8/1 (out-of-state freshmen), 8/1 (transfers).

Notification: continuous (freshmen), continuous (out-of-state freshmen), continuous (transfers).

CONTACT
Mrs. Karen Stachyra, Director of Undergraduate Admissions, Purdue University Northwest, 2200 169th Street, Hammond, IN 46323-2094. *Phone:* 219-989-2768. *Toll-free phone:* 800-447-8738. *E-mail:* kstachyr@pnw.edu.

Radiological Technologies University VT

South Bend, Indiana
http://www.rtuvt.edu/

CONTACT
Radiological Technologies University VT, 100 East Wayne Street, Suite 140, South Bend, IN 46601.

Rose-Hulman Institute of Technology

Terre Haute, Indiana
http://www.rose-hulman.edu/
- **Independent** comprehensive, founded 1874
- **Suburban** 200-acre campus with easy access to Indianapolis
- **Endowment** $206.2 million
- **Coed, primarily men**
- **Very difficult** entrance level

FACULTY
Student/faculty ratio: 11:1.

ACADEMICS
Calendar: quarters. *Degrees:* bachelor's and master's.
Library: John A. Logan Library. *Books:* 29,406 (physical), 301,291 (digital/electronic); *Serial titles:* 42 (physical), 41,278 (digital/electronic); *Databases:* 33. Weekly public service hours: 101; students can reserve study rooms.

STUDENT LIFE
Housing options: on-campus residence required for freshman year; coed, men-only. Campus housing is university owned. Freshman applicants given priority for college housing.

Activities and organizations: drama/theater group, student-run newspaper, radio station, choral group, Residence Hall Association, Student Activities Board, Branam Innovation Center competition teams, Drama Club, Diversity organizations, national fraternities, national sororities.

Athletics Member NCAA. All Division III.

Campus security: 24-hour emergency response devices and patrols, late-night transport/escort service, controlled dormitory access.

Student services: health clinic, personal/psychological counseling.

COSTS & FINANCIAL AID
Costs (2018–19) *One-time required fee:* $2300. *Comprehensive fee:* $62,337 includes full-time tuition ($46,641), mandatory fees ($930), and room and board ($14,766). Full-time tuition and fees vary according to course load. Part-time tuition: $1361 per credit hour. Part-time tuition and fees vary according to course load. *College room only:* $8988. Room and board charges vary according to board plan. *Payment plans:* tuition prepayment, installment.

Financial Aid *Average indebtedness upon graduation:* $45,345.

APPLYING
Standardized Tests *Required:* SAT or ACT (for admission).

Options: electronic application, early action, deferred entrance.

Application fee: $50.

Required: essay or personal statement, high school transcript, 1 letter of recommendation, curricular prerequisites.

CONTACT
Mrs. Lisa Norton, Dean of Admissions, Rose-Hulman Institute of Technology, 5500 Wabash Avenue, CM 1, Terre Haute, IN 47803-3920. *Phone:* 812-877-8213. *Toll-free phone:* 800-248-7448. *Fax:* 812-877-8941. *E-mail:* admissions@rose-hulman.edu.

Saint Mary-of-the-Woods College

Saint Mary of the Woods, Indiana
http://www.smwc.edu/
- **Independent Roman Catholic** comprehensive, founded 1840
- **Rural** 67-acre campus with easy access to Indianapolis
- **Coed, primarily women**
- **Minimally difficult** entrance level

FACULTY
Student/faculty ratio: 7:1.

ACADEMICS
Calendar: semesters. *Degrees:* certificates, associate, bachelor's, master's, and postbachelor's certificates (also offers external degree program with significant enrollment not reflected in profile).
Library: Rooney Library.

STUDENT LIFE
Housing options: on-campus residence required through senior year; coed, special housing for students with disabilities. Campus housing is university owned. Freshman campus housing is guaranteed.

Activities and organizations: drama/theater group, student-run newspaper, choral group.

Athletics Member USCAA.

Campus security: 24-hour emergency response devices and patrols, late-night transport/escort service, Resident Assistants (RAs) patrol the residence hall 3-4 times per night.

Student services: health clinic, personal/psychological counseling.

COSTS & FINANCIAL AID
Costs (2018–19) *Comprehensive fee:* $40,874 includes full-time tuition ($29,510), mandatory fees ($450), and room and board ($10,914). Full-time tuition and fees vary according to location, program, and student level. Part-time tuition: $496 per credit hour. Part-time tuition and fees vary according to course load, location, program, and student level. No tuition increase for student's term of enrollment. *College room only:*

$6614. Room and board charges vary according to board plan and housing facility.

Financial Aid Of all full-time matriculated undergraduates who enrolled in 2017, 481 applied for aid, 481 were judged to have need. *Average financial aid package:* $26,216. *Average need-based loan:* $3844. *Average need-based gift aid:* $21,230. *Financial aid deadline:* 3/10.

APPLYING
Standardized Tests *Required:* SAT or ACT (for admission).

Options: electronic application, early admission, deferred entrance.

Required: high school transcript, minimum 2.0 GPA. *Required for some:* essay or personal statement, minimum 1.0 GPA, official transcripts from all previous institutions for transfers; proof of RN license, valid driver's license, and background check for RN-to-BSN program; background check and Praxis II scores for teacher licensure. *Recommended:* essay or personal statement.

CONTACT
Ryan McDonald, Director of Campus Admissions, Saint Mary-of-the-Woods College, Rooney Library, 1 St. Mary of the Woods College, St Mary of the Woods, IN 47876. *Phone:* 812-535-5106. *Toll-free phone:* 800-926-SMWC. *Fax:* 812-535-5010. *E-mail:* rmcdonald@smwc.edu.

Saint Mary's College
Notre Dame, Indiana
http://www.saintmarys.edu/

CONTACT
Sarah Dvorak, Director of Admission, Saint Mary's College, Notre Dame, IN 46556. *Phone:* 574-284-4587. *Toll-free phone:* 800-551-7621. *Fax:* 574-284-4841. *E-mail:* sdvorak@saintmarys.edu.

See next page for display ad and page 1100 for the College Close-Up.

Taylor University
Upland, Indiana
http://www.taylor.edu/

- **Independent interdenominational** comprehensive, founded 1846
- **Rural** 950-acre campus with easy access to Indianapolis
- **Endowment** $95.9 million
- **Coed** 2,167 undergraduate students, 85% full-time, 55% women, 45% men
- **Moderately difficult** entrance level, 78% of applicants were admitted

UNDERGRAD STUDENTS
1,846 full-time, 321 part-time. Students come from 42 states and territories; 31 other countries; 45% are from out of state; 3% Black or African American, non-Hispanic/Latino; 4% Hispanic/Latino; 3% Asian, non-Hispanic/Latino; 0.3% Native Hawaiian or other Pacific Islander, non-Hispanic/Latino; 0.6% American Indian or Alaska Native, non-Hispanic/Latino; 0.8% Two or more races, non-Hispanic/Latino; 5% international; 2% transferred in; 89% live on campus.

Freshmen:
Admission: 2,165 applied, 1,681 admitted, 532 enrolled. *Average high school GPA:* 3.7. *Test scores:* SAT evidence-based reading and writing scores over 500: 89%; SAT math scores over 500: 89%; ACT scores over 18: 94%; SAT evidence-based reading and writing scores over 600: 54%; SAT math scores over 600: 46%; ACT scores over 24: 61%; SAT evidence-based reading and writing scores over 700: 12%; SAT math scores over 700: 8%; ACT scores over 30: 19%.

Retention: 86% of full-time freshmen returned.

FACULTY
Total: 201, 67% full-time, 70% with terminal degrees.

Student/faculty ratio: 13:1.

ACADEMICS
Calendar: 4-1-4. *Degrees:* diplomas, bachelor's, and master's.

Special study options: academic remediation for entering students, advanced placement credit, cooperative education, distance learning, double majors, English as a second language, honors programs, independent study, internships, off-campus study, part-time degree

program, services for LD students, student-designed majors, study abroad, summer session for credit.

Computers: 375 computers/terminals are available on campus for general student use. Students can access the following: campus intranet, computer help desk, free student e-mail accounts, online (class) grades, online (class) registration, online (class) schedules. Campuswide network is available. 100% of college-owned or -operated housing units are wired for high-speed Internet access. Wireless service is available via entire campus.

Library: Zondervan Library. *Books:* 128,733 (physical), 228,315 (digital/electronic); *Serial titles:* 631 (physical); *Databases:* 115. Weekly public service hours: 96; study areas open 24 hours, 5–7 days a week.

STUDENT LIFE
Housing options: on-campus residence required through junior year; men-only, women-only. Campus housing is university owned and is provided by a third party. Freshman campus housing is guaranteed.

Activities and organizations: drama/theater group, student-run newspaper, radio and television station, choral group, Spring Break Missions, Lighthouse, Alpha Pi Lota, Encounter, Kappa Delta Pi.

Athletics Member NAIA. *Intercollegiate sports:* baseball M(s), basketball M(s)/W(s), cross-country running M(s)/W(s), football M(s), golf M(s), lacrosse M, soccer M(s)/W(s), softball W(s), tennis M(s)/W(s), track and field M(s)/W(s), volleyball W(s). *Intramural sports:* badminton M/W, basketball M/W, equestrian sports W(c), lacrosse M(c)/W(c), racquetball M/W, soccer M/W, softball M/W, tennis M/W, ultimate Frisbee M/W, volleyball M/W.

Campus security: 24-hour patrols, student patrols, late-night transport/escort service, controlled dormitory access.

Student services: health clinic, personal/psychological counseling.

COSTS & FINANCIAL AID
Costs (2019–20) *Comprehensive fee:* $45,255 includes full-time tuition ($35,050), mandatory fees ($255), and room and board ($9950). Part-time tuition: $1235 per credit hour. *Required fees:* $45 per term part-time. *College room only:* $5230.

Financial Aid Of all full-time matriculated undergraduates who enrolled in 2018, 1,352 applied for aid, 1,149 were judged to have need, 335 had their need fully met. 796 Federal Work-Study jobs (averaging $636). In 2018, 530 non-need-based awards were made. *Average percent of need met:* 78. *Average financial aid package:* $24,925. *Average need-based loan:* $4276. *Average need-based gift aid:* $21,020. *Average non-need-based aid:* $14,440. *Average indebtedness upon graduation:* $28,764. *Financial aid deadline:* 4/15.

APPLYING
Standardized Tests *Required:* SAT or ACT (for admission).

Options: electronic application, early action, deferred entrance.

Application fee: $25.

Required: essay or personal statement, high school transcript, 2 letters of recommendation, interview. *Recommended:* minimum 2.8 GPA.

Application deadlines: rolling (freshmen), rolling (transfers).

Notification: continuous (freshmen), continuous (transfers).

CONTACT
Jesslyn Ridge, Visit Coordinator, Taylor University, 236 West Reade Avenue, Upland, IN 46989-1001. *Phone:* 765-998-5511. *Toll-free phone:* 800-882-3456. *Fax:* 765-998-4925. *E-mail:* admissions@taylor.edu.

Trine University
Angola, Indiana
http://www.trine.edu/

- **Independent** comprehensive, founded 1884
- **Small-town** 400-acre campus
- **Endowment** $32.0 million
- **Coed**
- **Moderately difficult** entrance level

FACULTY
Student/faculty ratio: 16:1.

ACADEMICS

Calendar: semesters. *Degrees:* associate, bachelor's, master's, and doctoral.

Library: Sponsel Library plus 1 other. *Books:* 23,523 (physical), 225,584 (digital/electronic); *Serial titles:* 19 (physical), 21,141 (digital/electronic); *Databases:* 87.

STUDENT LIFE

Housing options: on-campus residence required through senior year; coed, men-only, women-only, special housing for students with disabilities. Campus housing is university owned and is provided by a third party. Freshman campus housing is guaranteed.

Activities and organizations: drama/theater group, student-run radio station, choral group, marching band, Campus Christian House, Society of Women Engineers, Multicultural Student Organization, SPEAK, Trine Disc Golf Collective, national fraternities, national sororities.

Athletics Member NCAA. All Division III.

Campus security: 24-hour emergency response devices and patrols, late-night transport/escort service, controlled dormitory access.

Student services: health clinic, personal/psychological counseling.

COSTS & FINANCIAL AID

Costs (2018–19) *Comprehensive fee:* $42,986 includes full-time tuition ($31,700), mandatory fees ($476), and room and board ($10,810). Full-time tuition and fees vary according to course load and program. Part-time tuition: $990 per credit hour. Part-time tuition and fees vary according to course load and program. *College room only:* $6370. Room and board charges vary according to board plan and housing facility.

Financial Aid Of all full-time matriculated undergraduates who enrolled in 2017, 1,885 applied for aid, 169 were judged to have need, 377 had their need fully met. In 2017, 280 non-need-based awards were made. *Average percent of need met:* 81. *Average financial aid package:* $28,164. *Average need-based loan:* $5195. *Average need-based gift aid:* $22,202. *Average non-need-based aid:* $15,176. *Average indebtedness upon graduation:* $36,421. *Financial aid deadline:* 8/1.

APPLYING

Standardized Tests *Required:* SAT or ACT (for admission).

Options: electronic application, deferred entrance.

Required: high school transcript, minimum 2.5 GPA. *Recommended:* essay or personal statement, 2 letters of recommendation, interview.

CONTACT

Ms. Theresa Knight, Admission Coordinator, Trine University, 1 University Avenue, Angola, IN 46703. *Phone:* 260-665-4132. *Toll-free phone:* 800-347-4878. *E-mail:* admit@trine.edu.

See next page for display ad and page 1126 for the College Close-Up.

University of Evansville

Evansville, Indiana

http://www.evansville.edu/

- **Independent** comprehensive, founded 1854, affiliated with United Methodist Church
- **Urban** 75-acre campus
- **Endowment** $127.8 million
- **Coed**
- **Moderately difficult** entrance level

FACULTY

Student/faculty ratio: 11:1.

ACADEMICS

Calendar: semesters. *Degrees:* associate, bachelor's, master's, and doctoral.

Library: University of Evansville Libraries. *Books:* 235,259 (physical), 222,903 (digital/electronic); *Serial titles:* 56,159 (digital/electronic); *Databases:* 128. Weekly public service hours: 97; students can reserve study rooms.

STUDENT LIFE

Housing options: on-campus residence required through sophomore year; coed, men-only, women-only, special housing for students with disabilities. Campus housing is university owned. Freshman campus housing is guaranteed.

Get a great return on investment at Trine University.

Trine graduates are in demand with 99.7% of 2018 grads employed. Plus, Trine is ranked nationally for its graduates having the least amount of debt.

TRINE
UNIVERSITY

TRINE
UNIVERSITY

260-665-4100 or 800-347-4878
ANGOLA, INDIANA

Activities and organizations: drama/theater group, student-run newspaper, radio station, choral group, Resident Students Association, International Club, PT Club, Newman Club, Venturing, national fraternities, national sororities.

Athletics Member NCAA. All Division I.

Campus security: 24-hour emergency response devices and patrols, student patrols, late-night transport/escort service, controlled dormitory access.

Student services: health clinic, personal/psychological counseling, veterans affairs office.

COSTS & FINANCIAL AID

Costs (2018–19) *Comprehensive fee:* $48,876 includes full-time tuition ($35,300), mandatory fees ($1116), and room and board ($12,460). Full-time tuition and fees vary according to location and program. Part-time tuition: $990 per credit hour. Part-time tuition and fees vary according to course load and program. *Required fees:* $148 per term part-time. *College room only:* $6540. Room and board charges vary according to board plan, housing facility, and location.

Financial Aid Of all full-time matriculated undergraduates who enrolled in 2018, 1,467 applied for aid, 1,308 were judged to have need, 369 had their need fully met. 339 Federal Work-Study jobs (averaging $1736). 49 state and other part-time jobs (averaging $2062). In 2018, 505 non-need-based awards were made. *Average percent of need met:* 83. *Average financial aid package:* $31,813. *Average need-based loan:* $4340. *Average need-based gift aid:* $26,182. *Average non-need-based aid:* $21,068. *Average indebtedness upon graduation:* $35,837.

APPLYING

Standardized Tests *Required for some:* SAT or ACT (for admission).

Options: electronic application, early admission, early action, deferred entrance.

Required: high school transcript. *Required for some:* essay or personal statement, interview, SAT and/or ACT scores. *Recommended:* minimum 3.0 GPA, 1 letter of recommendation, interview.

CONTACT

Kenton Hargis, Director of Admission, University of Evansville, 1800 Lincoln Avenue, Evansville, IN 47722. *Phone:* 812-488-2142. *Toll-free phone:* 800-423-8633 Ext. 2468. *E-mail:* kh88@evansville.edu.

University of Indianapolis
Indianapolis, Indiana
http://www.uindy.edu/

CONTACT
Mr. Ronald Wilks, Associate Vice President of Admissions, University of Indianapolis, 1400 East Hanna Avenue, Indianapolis, IN 46227-3697. *Phone:* 317-788-3216. *Toll-free phone:* 800-232-8634 Ext. 3216. *Fax:* 317-788-3300. *E-mail:* admissions@uindy.edu.

University of Notre Dame
Notre Dame, Indiana
http://www.nd.edu/

- **Independent Roman Catholic** university, founded 1842
- **Suburban** 1250-acre campus
- **Endowment** $13.4 billion
- **Coed** 8,617 undergraduate students, 100% full-time, 48% women, 52% men
- **Most difficult** entrance level, 18% of applicants were admitted

UNDERGRAD STUDENTS
8,607 full-time, 10 part-time. Students come from 54 states and territories; 71 other countries; 92% are from out of state; 4% Black or African American, non-Hispanic/Latino; 11% Hispanic/Latino; 5% Asian, non-Hispanic/Latino; 0.2% American Indian or Alaska Native, non-Hispanic/Latino; 5% Two or more races, non-Hispanic/Latino; 0.6% Race/ethnicity unknown; 7% international; 2% transferred in; 78% live on campus.

Freshmen:
Admission: 20,371 applied, 3,601 admitted, 2,070 enrolled. *Test scores:* SAT evidence-based reading and writing scores over 500: 100%; SAT

math scores over 500: 100%; ACT scores over 18: 100%; SAT evidence-based reading and writing scores over 600: 98%; SAT math scores over 600: 98%; ACT scores over 24: 99%; SAT evidence-based reading and writing scores over 700: 72%; SAT math scores over 700: 81%; ACT scores over 30: 92%.

Retention: 98% of full-time freshmen returned.

FACULTY
Total: 1,386, 88% full-time, 87% with terminal degrees.
Student/faculty ratio: 10:1.

ACADEMICS
Calendar: semesters. *Degrees:* bachelor's, master's, and doctoral.

Special study options: advanced placement credit, distance learning, double majors, honors programs, independent study, internships, off-campus study, services for LD students, student-designed majors, study abroad, summer session for credit. *ROTC:* Army (b), Navy (b), Air Force (b).

Computers: 782 computers/terminals and 14,887 ports are available on campus for general student use. Students can access the following: computer help desk, free student e-mail accounts, online (class) grades, online (class) registration, online (class) schedules. Campuswide network is available. Wireless service is available via entire campus.
Library: Hesburgh Library plus 11 others.

STUDENT LIFE
Housing options: on-campus residence required for freshman year; men-only, women-only. Campus housing is university owned. Freshman campus housing is guaranteed.

Activities and organizations: drama/theater group, student-run newspaper, radio station, choral group, marching band, marching band, Circle K, Finance Club, Notre Dame/St. Mary's Right to Life.

Athletics Member NCAA. All Division I except football (Division I-A). *Intercollegiate sports:* baseball M(s), basketball M(s)/W(s), crew W(s), cross-country running M(s)/W(s), fencing M(s)/W(s), golf M(s)/W(s)(c), ice hockey M(s), lacrosse M(s)/W(s), soccer M(s)/W(s), softball W(s), swimming and diving M(s)/W(s), tennis M(s)/W(s), track and field M(s)/W(s), volleyball W(s). *Intramural sports:* badminton M/W, baseball M, basketball M/W, bowling M(c)/W(c), crew M(c), equestrian sports M(c)/W(c), fencing W(c), football M/W, golf M/W, gymnastics M(c)/W(c), ice hockey M/W(c), lacrosse M/W, racquetball M/W, rugby M(c)/W(c), sailing M(c)/W(c), skiing (cross-country) M(c)/W(c), skiing (downhill) M(c)/W(c), soccer M/W, softball M/W, squash M(c)/W(c), table tennis M/W, tennis M/W, ultimate Frisbee M/W, volleyball M(c)/W(c), water polo M(c)/W(c), wrestling M(c).

Campus security: 24-hour emergency response devices and patrols, student patrols, late-night transport/escort service, controlled dormitory access.

Student services: health clinic, personal/psychological counseling, women's center.

COSTS & FINANCIAL AID
Costs (2018–19) *Comprehensive fee:* $68,801 includes full-time tuition ($52,884), mandatory fees ($507), and room and board ($15,410). Part-time tuition: $2201 per credit hour. *Payment plan:* installment. *Waivers:* employees or children of employees.

Financial Aid Of all full-time matriculated undergraduates who enrolled in 2018, 5,012 applied for aid, 4,134 were judged to have need, 4,117 had their need fully met. 1,484 Federal Work-Study jobs (averaging $2650). 3,275 state and other part-time jobs (averaging $3437). In 2018, 420 non-need-based awards were made. *Average percent of need met:* 100. *Average financial aid package:* $51,128. *Average need-based loan:* $5236. *Average need-based gift aid:* $40,175. *Average non-need-based aid:* $13,232. *Average indebtedness upon graduation:* $27,686.

APPLYING
Standardized Tests *Required:* SAT or ACT (for admission). *Required for some:* SAT Subject Tests (for admission).

Options: electronic application, early action, deferred entrance.
Application fee: $75.

Required: essay or personal statement, high school transcript, 1 letter of recommendation.

Application deadlines: 12/1 (freshmen), 3/15 (transfers), 11/1 (early action).

Notification: 4/10 (freshmen).

CONTACT
Mr. Donald Bishop, Assistant Vice President, Undergraduate Enrollment, University of Notre Dame, Notre Dame, IN 46556. *Phone:* 574-631-7505. *Fax:* 574-631-8865. *E-mail:* admissions@nd.edu.

University of Saint Francis
Fort Wayne, Indiana
http://www.sf.edu/
- **Independent Roman Catholic** comprehensive, founded 1890
- **Urban** 100-acre campus
- **Endowment** $34.1 million
- **Coed** 1,778 undergraduate students, 85% full-time, 72% women, 28% men
- **Noncompetitive** entrance level, 93% of applicants were admitted

UNDERGRAD STUDENTS
1,511 full-time, 267 part-time. Students come from 18 states and territories; 6 other countries; 11% are from out of state; 7% Black or African American, non-Hispanic/Latino; 8% Hispanic/Latino; 2% Asian, non-Hispanic/Latino; 0.1% Native Hawaiian or other Pacific Islander, non-Hispanic/Latino; 0.1% American Indian or Alaska Native, non-Hispanic/Latino; 3% Two or more races, non-Hispanic/Latino; 1% Race/ethnicity unknown; 0.9% international; 10% transferred in; 23% live on campus.

Freshmen:
Admission: 1,490 applied, 1,392 admitted, 347 enrolled. *Average high school GPA:* 3.3. *Test scores:* SAT evidence-based reading and writing scores over 500: 66%; SAT math scores over 500: 66%; ACT scores over 18: 83%; SAT evidence-based reading and writing scores over 600: 21%; SAT math scores over 600: 13%; ACT scores over 24: 28%; SAT evidence-based reading and writing scores over 700: 1%; SAT math scores over 700: 1%; ACT scores over 30: 3%.

Retention: 74% of full-time freshmen returned.

FACULTY
Total: 301, 45% full-time, 34% with terminal degrees.
Student/faculty ratio: 10:1.

ACADEMICS
Calendar: semesters. *Degrees:* certificates, associate, bachelor's, master's, doctoral, and post-master's certificates.

Special study options: academic remediation for entering students, advanced placement credit, cooperative education, distance learning, double majors, honors programs, independent study, internships, off-campus study, part-time degree program, services for LD students, student-designed majors, summer session for credit. *ROTC:* Army (c).

Computers: 120 computers/terminals are available on campus for general student use. Students can access the following: campus intranet, computer help desk, free student e-mail accounts, online (class) grades, online (class) registration, online (class) schedules. Campuswide network is available. 100% of college-owned or -operated housing units are wired for high-speed Internet access. Wireless service is available via entire campus.
Library: Lee and Jim Vann Library. *Books:* 64,241 (physical), 163,451 (digital/electronic); *Serial titles:* 798 (physical), 41,820 (digital/electronic); *Databases:* 110. Weekly public service hours: 86; study areas open 24 hours, 5–7 days a week; students can reserve study rooms.

STUDENT LIFE
Housing options: on-campus residence required through junior year; coed, men-only, women-only, special housing for students with disabilities. Campus housing is university owned. Freshman applicants given priority for college housing.

Activities and organizations: drama/theater group, student-run newspaper, choral group, marching band, Student Activities Council, Student Government Association, Intramural Sports, Residence Hall Association, Ultimate Frisbee.

Athletics Member NAIA. *Intercollegiate sports:* baseball M(s), basketball M(s)/W(s), cheerleading M(s)/W(s), cross-country running M(s)/W(s), football M(s), golf M(s)/W(s), soccer M(s)/W(s), softball

W(s), tennis M(s)/W(s), track and field M(s)/W(s), volleyball W(s). *Intramural sports:* basketball M/W, football M/W, skiing (downhill) M/W, ultimate Frisbee M(c)/W(c), volleyball M/W.

Campus security: 24-hour emergency response devices and patrols, late-night transport/escort service, controlled dormitory access.

Student services: personal/psychological counseling.

COSTS & FINANCIAL AID
Costs (2019–20) *One-time required fee:* $100. *Comprehensive fee:* $41,660 includes full-time tuition ($30,380), mandatory fees ($1100), and room and board ($10,180). Part-time tuition: $965 per semester hour. *Required fees:* $30 per semester hour part-time, $155 per term part-time.

Financial Aid Of all full-time matriculated undergraduates who enrolled in 2009, 1,477 applied for aid, 1,316 were judged to have need, 258 had their need fully met. 629 Federal Work-Study jobs (averaging $1411). In 2009, 146 non-need-based awards were made. *Average percent of need met:* 72. *Average financial aid package:* $16,158. *Average need-based loan:* $4028. *Average need-based gift aid:* $12,247. *Average non-need-based aid:* $5446. *Average indebtedness upon graduation:* $28,428. *Financial aid deadline:* 6/30.

APPLYING
Standardized Tests *Required:* SAT or ACT (for admission).

Options: electronic application, deferred entrance.

Required: high school transcript, minimum 2.3 GPA. *Required for some:* essay or personal statement, interview. *Recommended:* essay or personal statement.

Application deadlines: rolling (freshmen), rolling (transfers).

Notification: continuous (freshmen), continuous (transfers).

CONTACT
Mrs. Sarah Heckley, Director of Admissions, University of Saint Francis, 2701 Spring Street, Fort Wayne, IN 46808. *Phone:* 260-399-7700 Ext. 6301. *Toll-free phone:* 800-729-4732. *E-mail:* admis@sf.edu.

University of Southern Indiana

Evansville, Indiana
http://www.usi.edu/

- **State-supported** comprehensive, founded 1965, part of Indiana Commission for Higher Education
- **Suburban** 1400-acre campus
- **Coed** 7,513 undergraduate students, 85% full-time, 62% women, 38% men
- **Moderately difficult** entrance level, 95% of applicants were admitted

UNDERGRAD STUDENTS
6,422 full-time, 1,091 part-time. 15% are from out of state; 4% Black or African American, non-Hispanic/Latino; 4% Hispanic/Latino; 1% Asian, non-Hispanic/Latino; 0.1% Native Hawaiian or other Pacific Islander, non-Hispanic/Latino; 0.2% American Indian or Alaska Native, non-Hispanic/Latino; 2% Two or more races, non-Hispanic/Latino; 0.1% Race/ethnicity unknown; 2% international; 7% transferred in; 32% live on campus.

Freshmen:
Admission: 4,461 applied, 4,220 admitted, 1,656 enrolled. *Average high school GPA:* 3.4. *Test scores:* SAT evidence-based reading and writing scores over 500: 74%; SAT math scores over 500: 73%; ACT scores over 18: 86%; SAT evidence-based reading and writing scores over 600: 25%; SAT math scores over 600: 20%; ACT scores over 24: 36%; SAT evidence-based reading and writing scores over 700: 3%; SAT math scores over 700: 2%; ACT scores over 30: 5%.

Retention: 72% of full-time freshmen returned.

FACULTY
Total: 651, 56% full-time, 51% with terminal degrees.

Student/faculty ratio: 17:1.

ACADEMICS
Calendar: semesters. *Degrees:* certificates, associate, bachelor's, master's, doctoral, post-master's, and postbachelor's certificates.

Special study options: academic remediation for entering students, accelerated degree program, adult/continuing education programs, advanced placement credit, cooperative education, distance learning,

double majors, English as a second language, honors programs, independent study, internships, part-time degree program, services for LD students, study abroad, summer session for credit. *ROTC:* Army (b).

Computers: 1,165 computers/terminals are available on campus for general student use. Students can access the following: campus intranet, computer help desk, free student e-mail accounts, online (class) grades, online (class) registration, online (class) schedules. Campuswide network is available. 100% of college-owned or -operated housing units are wired for high-speed Internet access. Wireless service is available via entire campus.

Library: David L. Rice Library. *Books:* 241,710 (physical), 230,844 (digital/electronic); *Serial titles:* 1,075 (physical), 141,229 (digital/electronic); *Databases:* 168. Weekly public service hours: 114; students can reserve study rooms.

STUDENT LIFE
Housing options: coed, special housing for students with disabilities. Campus housing is university owned.

Activities and organizations: drama/theater group, student-run newspaper, radio and television station, choral group, Sororities, Fraternities, Riley Dance Marathon, Activities Programming Board, Student Government Association, national fraternities, national sororities.

Athletics Member NCAA. All Division II except golf (Division I). *Intercollegiate sports:* baseball M(s), basketball M(s)/W(s), cheerleading M(c)/W(c), cross-country running M(s)/W(s), golf M(s)/W(s), soccer M(s)/W(s), softball W(s), tennis M(s)/W(s), track and field M(s)/W(s), volleyball W(s). *Intramural sports:* badminton M/W, basketball M/W, bowling M/W, football M/W, golf M/W, rugby M(c)/W(c), sand volleyball M/W, soccer M/W, softball M/W, table tennis M/W, tennis M/W, ultimate Frisbee M(c)/W(c), volleyball M/W, wrestling M(c).

Campus security: 24-hour emergency response devices and patrols, student patrols, late-night transport/escort service, controlled dormitory access.

Student services: health clinic, personal/psychological counseling, veterans affairs office.

FINANCIAL AID
Financial Aid Of all full-time matriculated undergraduates who enrolled in 2018, 5,928 applied for aid, 4,195 were judged to have need, 1,147 had their need fully met. In 2018, 1269 non-need-based awards were made. *Average percent of need met:* 87. *Average financial aid package:* $10,566. *Average need-based loan:* $4129. *Average need-based gift aid:* $10,762. *Average non-need-based aid:* $4575. *Average indebtedness upon graduation:* $24,074.

APPLYING
Standardized Tests *Required:* SAT or ACT (for admission).

Options: electronic application.

Application fee: $40.

Required: high school transcript. *Required for some:* interview. *Recommended:* minimum 2.5 GPA.

Notification: continuous (freshmen).

CONTACT
Mr. Rashad Smith, Director of Undergraduate Admissions, University of Southern Indiana, 8600 University Boulevard, Evansville, IN 47712-3590. *Phone:* 812-464-1765. *Toll-free phone:* 800-467-1965. *Fax:* 812-465-7154. *E-mail:* enroll@usi.edu.

Valparaiso University

Valparaiso, Indiana
http://www.valpo.edu/

- **Independent** comprehensive, founded 1859, affiliated with Lutheran Church
- **Small-town** 350-acre campus with easy access to Chicago
- **Endowment** $250.4 million
- **Coed** 3,217 undergraduate students, 98% full-time, 56% women, 44% men
- **Moderately difficult** entrance level, 89% of applicants were admitted

UNDERGRAD STUDENTS
3,138 full-time, 79 part-time. Students come from 44 states and territories; 35 other countries; 54% are from out of state; 5% Black or African

American, non-Hispanic/Latino; 9% Hispanic/Latino; 2% Asian, non-Hispanic/Latino; 0.1% American Indian or Alaska Native, non-Hispanic/Latino; 4% Two or more races, non-Hispanic/Latino; 4% Race/ethnicity unknown; 4% international; 6% transferred in; 62% live on campus.

Freshmen:
Admission: 7,062 applied, 6,307 admitted, 756 enrolled. *Average high school GPA:* 3.7. *Test scores:* SAT evidence-based reading and writing scores over 500: 92%; SAT math scores over 500: 91%; ACT scores over 18: 98%; SAT evidence-based reading and writing scores over 600: 47%; SAT math scores over 600: 43%; ACT scores over 24: 68%; SAT evidence-based reading and writing scores over 700: 7%; SAT math scores over 700: 6%; ACT scores over 30: 18%.

Retention: 80% of full-time freshmen returned.

FACULTY
Total: 414, 74% full-time, 76% with terminal degrees.
Student/faculty ratio: 11:1.

ACADEMICS
Calendar: semesters. *Degrees:* certificates, associate, bachelor's, master's, doctoral, post-master's, and postbachelor's certificates.

Special study options: accelerated degree program, adult/continuing education programs, advanced placement credit, cooperative education, distance learning, double majors, English as a second language, freshman honors college, honors programs, independent study, internships, off-campus study, part-time degree program, services for LD students, student-designed majors, study abroad, summer session for credit. *ROTC:* Army (c), Air Force (c).

Unusual degree programs: 3-2 physician assistant.

Computers: 500 computers/terminals are available on campus for general student use. Students can access the following: campus intranet, computer help desk, free student e-mail accounts, online (class) grades, online (class) registration, online (class) schedules, Web Academic Information, Degree Audit, Online Course Evaluations. Campuswide network is available. 100% of college-owned or -operated housing units are wired for high-speed Internet access. Wireless service is available via entire campus.

Library: Christopher Center for Library and Information Resources plus 1 other. *Books:* 614,267 (physical), 160,863 (digital/electronic); *Serial titles:* 123 (physical), 310,054 (digital/electronic); *Databases:* 200. Weekly public service hours: 113.

STUDENT LIFE
Housing options: on-campus residence required through junior year; coed, women-only. Campus housing is university owned and leased by the school. Freshman campus housing is guaranteed.

Activities and organizations: drama/theater group, student-run newspaper, radio station, choral group, Student Government, Student Volunteer Organization, Chapel Programs, Union Board, national fraternities, national sororities.

Athletics Member NCAA. All Division I except football (Division I-AA). *Intercollegiate sports:* baseball M(s), basketball M(s)/W(s), bowling W(s), cross-country running M(s)/W(s), golf M(s)/W(s), soccer M(s)/W(s), softball W(s), swimming and diving M(s)/W(s), tennis M(s)/W(s), track and field M(s)/W(s), volleyball W(s). *Intramural sports:* badminton M/W, basketball M/W, bowling M/W, cheerleading M/W, football M/W, golf M/W, racquetball M/W, soccer M(c)/W(c), softball M/W, table tennis M/W, tennis M(c)/W(c), triathlon M/W, ultimate Frisbee M(c)/W(c), volleyball M/W.

Campus security: 24-hour emergency response devices and patrols, late-night transport/escort service, controlled dormitory access.

Student services: health clinic, personal/psychological counseling, legal services.

COSTS & FINANCIAL AID
Costs (2019–20) *Comprehensive fee:* $54,080 includes full-time tuition ($40,520), mandatory fees ($1300), and room and board ($12,260). Part-time tuition: $1785 per credit hour. *College room only:* $7580.

Financial Aid Of all full-time matriculated undergraduates who enrolled in 2017, 2,742 applied for aid, 2,487 were judged to have need, 1,103 had their need fully met. 467 Federal Work-Study jobs (averaging $1300). 924 state and other part-time jobs (averaging $2150). In 2017, 594 non-need-based awards were made. *Average percent of need met:* 94. *Average financial aid package:* $32,540. *Average need-based loan:* $5106. *Average need-based gift aid:* $28,084. *Average non-need-based aid:* $19,692. *Average indebtedness upon graduation:* $38,265.

APPLYING
Standardized Tests *Required:* SAT or ACT (for admission).

Options: electronic application, deferred entrance.

Required: essay or personal statement, high school transcript. *Recommended:* 2 letters of recommendation, interview.

Application deadlines: rolling (freshmen), rolling (transfers).

Notification: continuous (freshmen), continuous (transfers).

CONTACT
Mr. Bart Harvey, Director of Freshman Admission and Operations, Valparaiso University, Duesenberg Welcome Center, 1620 Chapel Drive, Valparaiso, IN 46383-6493. *Phone:* 219-464-5011. *Toll-free phone:* 888-GO-VALPO. *Fax:* 219-464-6898. *E-mail:* undergrad.admission@valpo.edu.

Vincennes University
Vincennes, Indiana
http://www.vinu.edu/
- **State-supported** primarily 2-year, founded 1801
- **Small-town** 160-acre campus
- **Coed** 17,481 undergraduate students, 28% full-time, 46% women, 54% men
- **Noncompetitive** entrance level, 77% of applicants were admitted

UNDERGRAD STUDENTS
4,970 full-time, 12,511 part-time. 17% are from out of state; 10% Black or African American, non-Hispanic/Latino; 15% Hispanic/Latino; 2% Asian, non-Hispanic/Latino; 0.2% Native Hawaiian or other Pacific Islander, non-Hispanic/Latino; 0.4% American Indian or Alaska Native, non-Hispanic/Latino; 2% Two or more races, non-Hispanic/Latino; 5% Race/ethnicity unknown; 0.2% international; 0.8% transferred in; 37% live on campus.

Freshmen:
Admission: 4,728 applied, 3,656 admitted, 2,193 enrolled.
Retention: 56% of full-time freshmen returned.

FACULTY
Total: 817, 22% full-time.
Student/faculty ratio: 16:1.

ACADEMICS
Calendar: semesters. *Degrees:* certificates, associate, and bachelor's.

Special study options: academic remediation for entering students, accelerated degree program, adult/continuing education programs, advanced placement credit, distance learning, double majors, English as a second language, external degree program, freshman honors college, honors programs, independent study, internships, off-campus study, part-time degree program, services for LD students, student-designed majors, summer session for credit. *ROTC:* Army (c).

Computers: 1,500 computers/terminals are available on campus for general student use. Campuswide network is available.
Library: Shake Learning Resource Center. *Books:* 85,614 (physical), 104,859 (digital/electronic); *Serial titles:* 1,377 (physical); *Databases:* 99.

STUDENT LIFE
Housing options: on-campus residence required for freshman year; coed, men-only, women-only, special housing for students with disabilities. Campus housing is university owned. Freshman campus housing is guaranteed.

Activities and organizations: drama/theater group, student-run newspaper, radio and television station, choral group, national fraternities, national sororities.

Athletics Member NJCAA. *Intercollegiate sports:* baseball M, basketball M/W, bowling M, cross-country running M/W, golf M, track and field M/W, volleyball W.

Campus security: 24-hour emergency response devices and patrols, student patrols, late-night transport/escort service, controlled dormitory access.

Student services: health clinic, personal/psychological counseling.

APPLYING
Options: electronic application, deferred entrance.

Application fee: $20.

Required: high school transcript. *Required for some:* interview.

Application deadlines: rolling (freshmen), rolling (transfers).

Notification: continuous until 8/1 (freshmen), continuous (transfers).

CONTACT
Heidi M. Whitehead, Director of Admissions, Vincennes University, 1002 North First Street, Vincennes, IN 47591. *Phone:* 812-888-4313. *Toll-free phone:* 800-742-9198. *Fax:* 812-888-5707.

Wabash College
Crawfordsville, Indiana
http://www.wabash.edu/

- **Independent** 4-year, founded 1832
- **Small-town** 94-acre campus with easy access to Indianapolis
- **Endowment** $349.7 million
- **Men only** 882 undergraduate students, 100% full-time
- **Moderately difficult** entrance level, 65% of applicants were admitted

UNDERGRAD STUDENTS
881 full-time, 1 part-time. Students come from 27 states and territories; 17 other countries; 21% are from out of state; 6% Black or African American, non-Hispanic/Latino; 9% Hispanic/Latino; 0.9% Asian, non-Hispanic/Latino; 3% Two or more races, non-Hispanic/Latino; 2% Race/ethnicity unknown; 6% international; 1% transferred in; 98% live on campus.

Freshmen:
Admission: 1,336 applied, 868 admitted, 274 enrolled. *Average high school GPA:* 3.7. *Test scores:* SAT evidence-based reading and writing scores over 500: 94%; SAT math scores over 500: 95%; ACT scores over 18: 98%; SAT evidence-based reading and writing scores over 600: 48%; SAT math scores over 600: 53%; ACT scores over 24: 65%; SAT evidence-based reading and writing scores over 700: 11%; SAT math scores over 700: 16%; ACT scores over 30: 18%.

Retention: 86% of full-time freshmen returned.

FACULTY
Total: 99, 84% full-time, 93% with terminal degrees.

Student/faculty ratio: 10:1.

ACADEMICS
Calendar: semesters. *Degree:* bachelor's.

Special study options: advanced placement credit, double majors, independent study, internships, off-campus study, services for LD students, student-designed majors, study abroad.

Unusual degree programs: 3-2 engineering with Purdue University, Columbia University, Washington University in St. Louis.

Computers: 321 computers/terminals and 2,600 ports are available on campus for general student use. Students can access the following: campus intranet, computer help desk, free student e-mail accounts, online (class) grades, online (class) registration, online (class) schedules, online course management, degree audit, expenses. Campuswide network is available. 100% of college-owned or -operated housing units are wired for high-speed Internet access. Wireless service is available via entire campus.

Library: Lilly Library. *Books:* 254,041 (physical), 351,882 (digital/electronic); *Serial titles:* 81 (physical), 400,768 (digital/electronic); *Databases:* 82. Weekly public service hours: 105.

STUDENT LIFE
Housing options: on-campus residence required through senior year; men-only. Campus housing is university owned. Freshman campus housing is guaranteed.

Activities and organizations: drama/theater group, student-run newspaper, radio station, choral group, Inter-Fraternity Council, Malcolm X Institute for Black Studies, Sphinx Club, Student Government, Independent Men's Association, national fraternities.

Athletics Member NCAA. All Division III. *Intercollegiate sports:* baseball M, basketball M, cross-country running M, football M, golf M, lacrosse M, soccer M, swimming and diving M, tennis M, track and field M, wrestling M. *Intramural sports:* basketball M, bowling M, football M, rugby M, soccer M, softball M, tennis M, ultimate Frisbee M, weight lifting M.

Campus security: 24-hour emergency response devices and patrols.

Student services: health clinic, personal/psychological counseling.

COSTS & FINANCIAL AID
Costs (2019–20) *Comprehensive fee:* $55,220 includes full-time tuition ($43,870), mandatory fees ($850), and room and board ($10,500). Part-time tuition: $1828 per credit hour. *College room only:* $5700. *Payment plan:* tuition prepayment.

Financial Aid Of all full-time matriculated undergraduates who enrolled in 2017, 798 applied for aid, 653 were judged to have need, 526 had their need fully met. 207 Federal Work-Study jobs (averaging $2912). 312 state and other part-time jobs (averaging $2876). In 2017, 206 non-need-based awards were made. *Average percent of need met:* 94. *Average financial aid package:* $37,666. *Average need-based loan:* $4348. *Average need-based gift aid:* $30,123. *Average non-need-based aid:* $22,589. *Average indebtedness upon graduation:* $35,726.

APPLYING
Standardized Tests *Required:* SAT or ACT (for admission).

Options: electronic application, early admission, early decision, early action, deferred entrance.

Application fee: $50.

Required: high school transcript, 1 letter of recommendation, General college-preparatory program. *Required for some:* essay or personal statement, interview.

Application deadlines: rolling (transfers), 12/1 (early action).

Early decision deadline: 11/1.

Notification: continuous until 1/28 (freshmen), continuous until 1/28 (out-of-state freshmen), continuous (transfers), 12/5 (early decision), 12/31 (early action).

CONTACT
Mr. Charles M Timmons, Director of Admissions and Dean for Enrollment Management, Wabash College, PO Box 362, 410 West Wabash Avenue, Crawfordsville, IN 47933-0352. *Phone:* 765-361-6054. *Toll-free phone:* 800-345-5385. *Fax:* 765-361-6437. *E-mail:* timmonsc@wabash.edu.

IOWA

Allen College
Waterloo, Iowa
http://www.allencollege.edu/

- **Independent** comprehensive, founded 1989
- **Suburban** 20-acre campus
- **Endowment** $7.5 million
- **Coed, primarily women** 341 undergraduate students, 89% full-time, 92% women, 8% men
- **Moderately difficult** entrance level

UNDERGRAD STUDENTS
302 full-time, 39 part-time. Students come from 7 states and territories; 2 other countries; 4% are from out of state; 0.9% Black or African American, non-Hispanic/Latino; 1% Hispanic/Latino; 1% Asian, non-Hispanic/Latino; 0.3% American Indian or Alaska Native, non-Hispanic/Latino; 2% Two or more races, non-Hispanic/Latino; 6% Race/ethnicity unknown; 0.6% international; 36% transferred in.

FACULTY
Total: 57, 72% full-time, 58% with terminal degrees.

Student/faculty ratio: 17:1.

ACADEMICS
Calendar: semesters. *Degrees:* certificates, associate, bachelor's, master's, doctoral, and post-master's certificates (liberal arts and general education courses offered at either University of North Iowa or Wartburg College).

Special study options: accelerated degree program, advanced placement credit, cooperative education, distance learning, honors programs, independent study, internships, off-campus study, part-time degree program. *ROTC:* Army (c).

Unusual degree programs: 3-2 nursing with Wartburg College, Loras College, Central College, Simpson College.

Computers: 32 computers/terminals are available on campus for general student use. Students can access the following: campus intranet, computer help desk, free student e-mail accounts, online (class) grades, online (class) schedules, online proctoring exams. Campuswide network is available. 100% of college-owned or -operated housing units are wired for high-speed Internet access. Wireless service is available via entire campus.

Library: Barrett Library plus 1 other. *Books:* 13,280 (physical), 9,138 (digital/electronic); *Serial titles:* 208 (physical), 3,610 (digital/electronic); *Databases:* 47. Weekly public service hours: 50; study areas open 24 hours, 5–7 days a week; students can reserve study rooms.

STUDENT LIFE
Housing options: college housing not availableCampus housing is provided by a third party.

Activities and organizations: choral group, Allen Student Nurses's Association, Nurses'; Christian Fellowship.

Campus security: 24-hour patrols, late-night transport/escort service, controlled dormitory access.

Student services: health clinic, personal/psychological counseling.

COSTS & FINANCIAL AID
Costs (2019–20) *Comprehensive fee:* $26,332 includes full-time tuition ($17,612), mandatory fees ($1440), and room and board ($7280). Part-time tuition: $629 per credit hour. *Required fees:* $86 per credit hour part-time. *College room only:* $3640.

Financial Aid Of all full-time matriculated undergraduates who enrolled in 2017, 311 applied for aid, 272 were judged to have need, 14 had their need fully met. 15 Federal Work-Study jobs (averaging $3000). In 2017, 28 non-need-based awards were made. *Average percent of need met:* 51. *Average financial aid package:* $11,693. *Average need-based loan:* $4797. *Average need-based gift aid:* $5846. *Average non-need-based aid:* $1250.

APPLYING
Standardized Tests *Required for some:* SAT or ACT (for admission), ATI, TEAS for undergraduate pre-licensure students.

Options: electronic application.

Application fee: $50.

Required for some: essay or personal statement, high school transcript, 1 letter of recommendation, interview.

Application deadlines: 2/1 (freshmen), 2/1 (transfers).

Notification: continuous until 3/1 (freshmen), continuous until 3/1 (transfers).

CONTACT
Jamie Jordan, Administrative Assistant, Student Services, Allen College, Barrett Forum, 1825 Logan Avenue, Waterloo, IA 50703. *Phone:* 319-226-2014. *Fax:* 319-226-2010. *E-mail:* admissions@allencollege.edu.

Briar Cliff University
Sioux City, Iowa
http://www.briarcliff.edu/

CONTACT
Mr. Brian Eben, Assistant Vice President for Enrollment Management, Briar Cliff University, 3303 Rebecca Street, Sioux City, IA 51104. *Phone:* 712-279-5200. *Toll-free phone:* 800-662-3303. *Fax:* 712-279-1632. *E-mail:* admissions@briarcliff.edu.

Buena Vista University
Storm Lake, Iowa
http://www.bvu.edu/
- **Independent** comprehensive, founded 1891, affiliated with Presbyterian Church (U.S.A.)
- **Small-town** 60-acre campus
- **Endowment** $138.1 million
- **Coed** 732 undergraduate students, 98% full-time, 49% women, 51% men
- **Moderately difficult** entrance level, 57% of applicants were admitted

UNDERGRAD STUDENTS
719 full-time, 13 part-time. Students come from 25 states and territories; 12 other countries; 29% are from out of state; 6% Black or African American, non-Hispanic/Latino; 9% Hispanic/Latino; 0.6% Asian, non-Hispanic/Latino; 0.1% Native Hawaiian or other Pacific Islander, non-Hispanic/Latino; 0.4% American Indian or Alaska Native, non-Hispanic/Latino; 3% Two or more races, non-Hispanic/Latino; 7% Race/ethnicity unknown; 3% international; 5% transferred in; 90% live on campus.

Freshmen:
Admission: 2,055 applied, 1,174 admitted, 201 enrolled. *Average high school GPA:* 3.4. *Test scores:* ACT scores over 18: 87%; ACT scores over 24: 32%; ACT scores over 30: 6%.

Retention: 60% of full-time freshmen returned.

FACULTY
Total: 101, 81% full-time, 61% with terminal degrees.

Student/faculty ratio: 9:1.

ACADEMICS
Calendar: 4-1-4. *Degrees:* bachelor's and master's.

Special study options: academic remediation for entering students, adult/continuing education programs, advanced placement credit, distance learning, double majors, English as a second language, external degree program, honors programs, independent study, internships, off-campus study, part-time degree program, services for LD students, student-designed majors, study abroad, summer session for credit. *ROTC:* Army (b).

Unusual degree programs: 3-2 engineering with Washington University in St. Louis.

Computers: Students can access the following: campus intranet, computer help desk, free student e-mail accounts, online (class) grades, online (class) registration, online (class) schedules. Campuswide network is available. 100% of college-owned or -operated housing units are wired for high-speed Internet access. Wireless service is available via entire campus.

Library: BVU Library. *Books:* 107,288 (physical), 164,907 (digital/electronic); *Serial titles:* 842 (physical), 23,059 (digital/electronic); *Databases:* 104. Weekly public service hours: 94; students can reserve study rooms.

STUDENT LIFE
Housing options: on-campus residence required through senior year; coed, special housing for students with disabilities. Campus housing is university owned. Freshman campus housing is guaranteed.

Activities and organizations: drama/theater group, student-run newspaper, radio and television station, choral group, Student Activities Board, Orientation Team, Esprit De Corps, Student Senate, Student Mobilizing Outreach and Volunteer Efforts.

Athletics Member NCAA. All Division III except golf (Division II). *Intercollegiate sports:* baseball M, basketball M/W, cross-country running M/W, football M, golf M/W, soccer M/W, softball W, tennis M/W, track and field M/W, volleyball W, wrestling M. *Intramural sports:* basketball M/W, racquetball M/W, softball M/W, table tennis M/W, tennis M/W, volleyball M/W.

Campus security: 24-hour emergency response devices, late-night transport/escort service, controlled dormitory access, night security patrols.

Student services: health clinic, personal/psychological counseling.

COSTS & FINANCIAL AID

Costs (2019–20) *Comprehensive fee:* $45,066 includes full-time tuition ($35,194) and room and board ($9872). Part-time tuition: $1184 per credit hour. *College room only:* $4941.

Financial Aid Of all full-time matriculated undergraduates who enrolled in 2018, 651 applied for aid, 605 were judged to have need, 114 had their need fully met. In 2018, 98 non-need-based awards were made. *Average percent of need met:* 80. *Average financial aid package:* $30,158. *Average need-based loan:* $4713. *Average need-based gift aid:* $25,206. *Average non-need-based aid:* $18,570. *Average indebtedness upon graduation:* $38,938.

APPLYING

Standardized Tests *Required:* SAT or ACT (for admission). *Recommended:* ACT (for admission).

Options: electronic application, deferred entrance.

Required: high school transcript. *Required for some:* essay or personal statement, interview. *Recommended:* minimum 3.0 GPA.

Notification: continuous (freshmen), continuous (transfers).

CONTACT

Nick Boone, Director of Admissions, Buena Vista University, 610 West Fourth Street, Storm Lake, IA 50588. *Phone:* 712-749-2078. *Toll-free phone:* 800-383-9600. *E-mail:* BooneN@bvu.edu.

Central College

Pella, Iowa

http://www.central.edu/

CONTACT

Chevy Freiburger, Director of Admission, Central College, 812 University, Pella, IA 50112. *Phone:* 641-628-7637. *Toll-free phone:* 877-462-3687. *Fax:* 641-628-5983. *E-mail:* freiburgerc@central.edu.

Clarke University

Dubuque, Iowa

http://www.clarke.edu/

- **Independent Roman Catholic** comprehensive, founded 1843
- **Urban** 55-acre campus
- **Endowment** $31.3 million
- **Coed**
- **Moderately difficult** entrance level

FACULTY

Student/faculty ratio: 8:1.

ACADEMICS

Calendar: semesters. *Degrees:* associate, bachelor's, master's, and doctoral.

Library: Nicholas J. Schrupp Library. *Books:* 76,525 (physical), 136,800 (digital/electronic); *Serial titles:* 150 (physical), 53,000 (digital/electronic); *Databases:* 60. Weekly public service hours: 90.

STUDENT LIFE

Housing options: on-campus residence required through sophomore year; coed, men-only, women-only. Campus housing is university owned. Freshman campus housing is guaranteed.

Activities and organizations: drama/theater group, choral group, Admissions Student Team, Student Multicultural Organization, Concert Choir, Campus Ministry, Student Government.

Athletics Member NAIA.

Campus security: 24-hour emergency response devices and patrols, late-night transport/escort service, controlled dormitory access.

Student services: health clinic, personal/psychological counseling.

COSTS & FINANCIAL AID

Costs (2018–19) *Comprehensive fee:* $42,950 includes full-time tuition ($32,300), mandatory fees ($1050), and room and board ($9600). Part-time tuition: $720 per credit hour. *College room only:* $4600. Room and board charges vary according to board plan. *Payment plans:* installment, deferred payment.

Financial Aid *Average indebtedness upon graduation:* $39,907.

APPLYING

Standardized Tests *Required:* SAT or ACT (for admission).

Options: electronic application, deferred entrance.

Application fee: $25.

Required: high school transcript, minimum 2.0 GPA.

CONTACT

Mrs. Alicia Schmitt, Associate Director of Admissions, Clarke University, 1550 Clarke Drive, Dubuque, IA 52001-3198. *Phone:* 563-588-6373. *Toll-free phone:* 800-383-2345. *E-mail:* admissions@clarke.edu.

Coe College

Cedar Rapids, Iowa

http://www.coe.edu/

- **Independent** 4-year, founded 1851, affiliated with Presbyterian Church
- **Urban** 53-acre campus
- **Endowment** $85.6 million
- **Coed**
- **Moderately difficult** entrance level

FACULTY

Student/faculty ratio: 11:1.

ACADEMICS

Calendar: 4-4-1. *Degree:* bachelor's.

Library: Stewart Memorial Library plus 1 other. *Books:* 238,645 (physical), 289,126 (digital/electronic); *Serial titles:* 751 (physical), 3,630 (digital/electronic); *Databases:* 140. Weekly public service hours: 106.

STUDENT LIFE

Housing options: on-campus residence required through senior year; coed, men-only, women-only, special housing for students with disabilities. Campus housing is university owned. Freshman campus housing is guaranteed.

Activities and organizations: drama/theater group, student-run newspaper, radio station, choral group, Multicultural Fusion, Coe Alliance, Student Senate, Habitat for Humanity, International Club, national fraternities, national sororities.

Athletics Member NCAA. All Division III.

Campus security: 24-hour emergency response devices and patrols, late-night transport/escort service, controlled dormitory access.

Student services: health clinic, personal/psychological counseling.

COSTS & FINANCIAL AID

Costs (2018–19) *Comprehensive fee:* $54,480 includes full-time tuition ($44,700), mandatory fees ($300), and room and board ($9480). Part-time tuition: $5587 per course. Part-time tuition and fees vary according to course load. *Room and board:* Room and board charges vary according to board plan and housing facility.

Financial Aid Of all full-time matriculated undergraduates who enrolled in 2018, 1,196 applied for aid, 1,116 were judged to have need, 189 had their need fully met. 662 Federal Work-Study jobs (averaging $1807). 253 state and other part-time jobs (averaging $1550). In 2018, 237 non-need-based awards were made. *Average percent of need met:* 83. *Average financial aid package:* $37,350. *Average need-based loan:* $4283. *Average need-based gift aid:* $32,869. *Average non-need-based aid:* $26,222. *Average indebtedness upon graduation:* $34,769.

APPLYING

Standardized Tests *Required:* SAT or ACT (for admission).

Options: electronic application, early admission, early action, deferred entrance.

Application fee: $30.

Required: essay or personal statement, high school transcript, 1 letter of recommendation. *Recommended:* minimum 3.0 GPA, interview.

CONTACT

Julie Staker, Vice President for Admission and Marketing, Coe College, 1220 1st Avenue NE, Cedar Rapids, IA 52402-5070. *Phone:* 319-399-8500. *Toll-free phone:* 877-225-5263. *Fax:* 319-399-8816. *E-mail:* admission@coe.edu.

Cornell College

Mount Vernon, Iowa

http://www.cornellcollege.edu/

- **Independent Methodist** 4-year, founded 1853
- **Small-town** 129-acre campus
- **Endowment** $77.7 million
- **Coed** 1,025 undergraduate students, 99% full-time, 48% women, 52% men
- **Moderately difficult** entrance level, 61% of applicants were admitted

UNDERGRAD STUDENTS

1,017 full-time, 8 part-time. Students come from 48 states and territories; 19 other countries; 76% are from out of state; 6% Black or African American, non-Hispanic/Latino; 8% Hispanic/Latino; 4% Asian, non-Hispanic/Latino; 0.1% Native Hawaiian or other Pacific Islander, non-Hispanic/Latino; 2% American Indian or Alaska Native, non-Hispanic/Latino; 1% Two or more races, non-Hispanic/Latino; 4% Race/ethnicity unknown; 7% international; 3% transferred in; 88% live on campus.

Freshmen:

Admission: 2,532 applied, 1,545 admitted, 296 enrolled. *Average high school GPA:* 3.5. *Test scores:* SAT evidence-based reading and writing scores over 500: 93%; SAT math scores over 500: 90%; ACT scores over 18: 98%; SAT evidence-based reading and writing scores over 600: 57%; SAT math scores over 600: 47%; ACT scores over 24: 69%; SAT evidence-based reading and writing scores over 700: 16%; SAT math scores over 700: 14%; ACT scores over 30: 31%.

Retention: 82% of full-time freshmen returned.

FACULTY

Total: 114, 65% full-time, 88% with terminal degrees.

Student/faculty ratio: 11:1.

ACADEMICS

Calendar: 8 3.5 week terms. *Degree:* bachelor's.

Special study options: advanced placement credit, double majors, English as a second language, independent study, internships, off-campus study, services for LD students, student-designed majors, study abroad.

Unusual degree programs: 3-2 engineering with University of Minnesota; forestry with Duke University; architecture with Washington University in St. Louis Law with the University of Iowa.

Computers: 259 computers/terminals and 1,200 ports are available on campus for general student use. Students can access the following: campus intranet, computer help desk, free student e-mail accounts, online (class) grades, online (class) registration, online (class) schedules. Campuswide network is available. 100% of college-owned or -operated housing units are wired for high-speed Internet access. Wireless service is available via entire campus.

Library: Cole Library plus 1 other. *Books:* 232,914 (physical); *Serial titles:* 491 (digital/electronic). Weekly public service hours: 70; students can reserve study rooms.

STUDENT LIFE

Housing options: on-campus residence required through senior year; coed, women-only. Campus housing is university owned and leased by the school. Freshman campus housing is guaranteed.

Activities and organizations: drama/theater group, student-run newspaper, radio station, choral group, Student-initiated Living-Learning Community, Chess and Games, Environmental Club, Performing Arts and Activities Council, Alliance.

Athletics Member NCAA. All Division III. *Intercollegiate sports:* baseball M, basketball M/W, cross-country running M/W, football M, lacrosse M/W, soccer M/W, softball W, tennis M/W, track and field M/W, ultimate Frisbee M(c)/W(c), volleyball M(c)/W, wrestling M. *Intramural sports:* badminton M/W, basketball M/W, bowling M/W, cheerleading M/W, fencing M(c), field hockey W(c), football M/W, golf M/W, ice hockey M/W, lacrosse M(c)/W(c), racquetball M/W, soccer M/W, softball M/W, table tennis M/W, tennis M/W, track and field M/W, ultimate Frisbee M/W, volleyball M/W, weight lifting M/W, wrestling M/W.

Campus security: 24-hour emergency response devices and patrols, late-night transport/escort service, controlled dormitory access.

Student services: health clinic, personal/psychological counseling.

COSTS & FINANCIAL AID

Costs (2019–20) *Comprehensive fee:* $53,736 includes full-time tuition ($43,550), mandatory fees ($426), and room and board ($9760). Part-time tuition: $3141 per course. *College room only:* $4500.

Financial Aid Of all full-time matriculated undergraduates who enrolled in 2018, 800 applied for aid, 704 were judged to have need, 162 had their need fully met. In 2018, 302 non-need-based awards were made. *Average percent of need met:* 81. *Average financial aid package:* $32,475. *Average need-based loan:* $4465. *Average need-based gift aid:* $28,494. *Average non-need-based aid:* $22,582. *Average indebtedness upon graduation:* $31,142.

APPLYING

Options: electronic application, early admission, early decision, early action, deferred entrance.

Required: essay or personal statement, high school transcript.

Application deadlines: rolling (out-of-state freshmen), 3/1 (transfers).

Early decision deadline: 11/1.

Notification: 3/20 (freshmen), continuous (out-of-state freshmen), continuous (transfers), rolling (early action).

CONTACT

Ms. Marie Schofer, Director of Admissions, Cornell College, 600 First Street SW, Mount Vernon, IA 52314-1098. *Phone:* 319-895-4159. *Toll-free phone:* 800-747-1112. *Fax:* 319-895-4451. *E-mail:* admission@cornellcollege.edu.

Divine Word College

Epworth, Iowa

http://www.dwci.edu/

CONTACT

Divine Word College, 102 Jacoby Drive SW, Epworth, IA 52045-0380. *Phone:* 563-876-3353. *Toll-free phone:* 800-553-3321.

Dordt College

Sioux Center, Iowa

http://www.dordt.edu/

CONTACT

Mr. Howard Wislon, Vice President for Enrollment, Dordt College, 498 4th Avenue, NE, Sioux Center, IA 51250-1697. *Phone:* 712-722-6080. *Toll-free phone:* 800-343-6738. *Fax:* 712-722-6035. *E-mail:* admissions@dordt.edu.

Drake University

Des Moines, Iowa

http://www.drake.edu/

- **Independent** university, founded 1881
- **Urban** 120-acre campus
- **Endowment** $210.6 million
- **Coed** 3,015 undergraduate students, 94% full-time, 58% women, 42% men
- **Moderately difficult** entrance level, 68% of applicants were admitted

UNDERGRAD STUDENTS

2,834 full-time, 181 part-time. 65% are from out of state; 5% Black or African American, non-Hispanic/Latino; 6% Hispanic/Latino; 4% Asian, non-Hispanic/Latino; 3% Two or more races, non-Hispanic/Latino; 0.3% Race/ethnicity unknown; 4% international; 4% transferred in; 70% live on campus.

Freshmen:

Admission: 6,886 applied, 4,659 admitted, 750 enrolled. *Average high school GPA:* 3.7. *Test scores:* SAT evidence-based reading and writing scores over 500: 93%; SAT math scores over 500: 91%; ACT scores over 18: 99%; SAT evidence-based reading and writing scores over 600: 69%; SAT math scores over 600: 64%; ACT scores over 24: 81%; SAT evidence-based reading and writing scores over 700: 17%; SAT math scores over 700: 18%; ACT scores over 30: 29%.

Retention: 89% of full-time freshmen returned.

FACULTY
Total: 472, 65% full-time, 70% with terminal degrees.

ACADEMICS
Calendar: semesters. *Degrees:* bachelor's, master's, doctoral, post-master's, and postbachelor's certificates.

Special study options: accelerated degree program, advanced placement credit, cooperative education, distance learning, double majors, English as a second language, honors programs, independent study, internships, off-campus study, part-time degree program, services for LD students, student-designed majors, study abroad, summer session for credit. *ROTC:* Army (c), Air Force (c).

Unusual degree programs: 3-2 journalism and law, arts and sciences and law, accounting.

Computers: Students can access the following: campus intranet, computer help desk, free student e-mail accounts, online (class) grades, online (class) registration, online (class) schedules. Campuswide network is available. 100% of college-owned or -operated housing units are wired for high-speed Internet access. Wireless service is available via classrooms, computer centers, computer labs, dorm rooms, libraries, student centers.

Library: Cowles Library plus 1 other. Study areas open 24 hours, 5–7 days a week; students can reserve study rooms.

STUDENT LIFE
Housing options: on-campus residence required through sophomore year; coed, special housing for students with disabilities. Campus housing is university owned and is provided by a third party. Freshman campus housing is guaranteed.

Activities and organizations: drama/theater group, student-run newspaper, radio and television station, choral group, marching band, Student Activities Board, Drake Magazine, Dog Pound Pep Squad, Alpha Phi Omega, Residence Hall Association, national fraternities, national sororities.

Athletics Member NCAA. All Division I except football (Division I-AA). *Intercollegiate sports:* basketball M(s)/W(s), cheerleading M(s)/W(s), crew W, cross-country running M(s)/W(s), golf M(s), soccer M(s)/W(s), softball W(s), tennis M(s)/W(s), track and field M(s)/W(s), volleyball W(s). *Intramural sports:* badminton M/W, basketball M/W, football M/W, golf M/W, racquetball M/W, soccer M(c)/W, softball M/W, swimming and diving M/W, tennis M/W, volleyball M/W(c).

Campus security: 24-hour emergency response devices and patrols, late-night transport/escort service, controlled dormitory access.

Student services: health clinic, personal/psychological counseling, legal services.

COSTS & FINANCIAL AID
Costs (2018–19) *Comprehensive fee:* $51,924 includes full-time tuition ($41,250), mandatory fees ($146), and room and board ($10,528). Full-time tuition and fees vary according to course load, degree level, program, and student level. Part-time tuition: $845 per credit hour. Part-time tuition and fees vary according to class time, degree level, and program. No tuition increase for student's term of enrollment. *College room only:* $4692. Room and board charges vary according to board plan and housing facility. *Payment plan:* installment. *Waivers:* children of alumni, senior citizens, and employees or children of employees.

Financial Aid Of all full-time matriculated undergraduates who enrolled in 2018, 2,083 applied for aid, 1,730 were judged to have need, 484 had their need fully met. 1,397 Federal Work-Study jobs (averaging $1901). In 2018, 894 non-need-based awards were made. *Average percent of need met:* 75. *Average financial aid package:* $29,286. *Average need-based loan:* $3996. *Average need-based gift aid:* $22,489. *Average non-need-based aid:* $18,112. *Average indebtedness upon graduation:* $34,391.

APPLYING
Standardized Tests *Required for some:* SAT or ACT (for admission).

Options: electronic application, early admission, deferred entrance.

Required: high school transcript, . *Recommended:* essay or personal statement, letters of recommendation, interview.

Application deadlines: 3/1 (freshmen), rolling (transfers).

Notification: continuous (freshmen), continuous (transfers).

CONTACT
Ms. Anne Kremer, Dean of Admission, Drake University, 2507 University Avenue, Des Moines, IA 50311-4516. *Phone:* 515-271-3182. *Toll-free phone:* 800-44-DRAKE Ext. 3181. *Fax:* 515-271-2831. *E-mail:* anne.kremer@drake.edu.

Emmaus Bible College
Dubuque, Iowa
http://www.emmaus.edu/
- **Independent nondenominational** 4-year, founded 1941
- **Small-town** 22-acre campus
- **Coed**
- **Noncompetitive** entrance level

FACULTY
Student/faculty ratio: 10:1.

ACADEMICS
Calendar: semesters. *Degrees:* certificates, associate, and bachelor's.
Library: The Emmaus Bible College Library plus 1 other. Weekly public service hours: 130.

STUDENT LIFE
Housing options: on-campus residence required through senior year; men-only, women-only. Campus housing is university owned. Freshman campus housing is guaranteed.

Activities and organizations: choral group.

Athletics Member NCCAA.

Campus security: 24-hour emergency response devices, student patrols, controlled dormitory access.

Student services: personal/psychological counseling, veterans affairs office.

COSTS
Costs (2018–19) *Comprehensive fee:* $26,900 includes full-time tuition ($18,400) and room and board ($8500). Full-time tuition and fees vary according to course load. Part-time tuition: $765 per credit hour.

APPLYING
Standardized Tests *Required:* SAT or ACT (for admission).

Options: electronic application, deferred entrance.

Required: essay or personal statement, high school transcript, minimum 2.0 GPA, 1 letter of recommendation.

CONTACT
Emmaus Bible College, 2570 Asbury Road, Dubuque, IA 52001-3097. *Toll-free phone:* 800-397-2425.

Faith Baptist Bible College and Theological Seminary
Ankeny, Iowa
http://www.faith.edu/

CONTACT
Miss Mary Tubbs, Admissions Coordinator, Faith Baptist Bible College and Theological Seminary, 1900 NW 4th Street, Ankeny, IA 50023. *Phone:* 515-964-0601. *Toll-free phone:* 888-FAITH 4U. *Fax:* 515-964-1638. *E-mail:* admissions@faith.edu.

Graceland University
Lamoni, Iowa
http://www.graceland.edu/
- **Independent Community of Christ** comprehensive, founded 1895
- **Rural** 170-acre campus with easy access to Des Moines
- **Endowment** $53.3 million
- **Coed** 1,180 undergraduate students, 87% full-time, 58% women, 42% men
- **Moderately difficult** entrance level, 58% of applicants were admitted

UNDERGRAD STUDENTS
1,023 full-time, 157 part-time. Students come from 40 states and territories; 20 other countries; 73% are from out of state; 9% Black or

African American, non-Hispanic/Latino; 10% Hispanic/Latino; 1% Asian, non-Hispanic/Latino; 2% Native Hawaiian or other Pacific Islander, non-Hispanic/Latino; 0.5% American Indian or Alaska Native, non-Hispanic/Latino; 4% Two or more races, non-Hispanic/Latino; 8% Race/ethnicity unknown; 5% international; 8% transferred in; 74% live on campus.

Freshmen:

Admission: 3,004 applied, 1,744 admitted, 267 enrolled. *Average high school GPA:* 3.3. *Test scores:* SAT evidence-based reading and writing scores over 500: 62%; SAT math scores over 500: 61%; ACT scores over 18: 81%; SAT evidence-based reading and writing scores over 600: 13%; SAT math scores over 600: 12%; ACT scores over 24: 17%; ACT scores over 30: 4%.

Retention: 59% of full-time freshmen returned.

FACULTY

Total: 156, 43% full-time, 54% with terminal degrees.
Student/faculty ratio: 17:1.

ACADEMICS

Calendar: 4-1-4. *Degrees:* certificates, bachelor's, master's, doctoral, and post-master's certificates.

Special study options: academic remediation for entering students, accelerated degree program, adult/continuing education programs, advanced placement credit, cooperative education, distance learning, double majors, freshman honors college, honors programs, independent study, internships, part-time degree program, services for LD students, student-designed majors, study abroad, summer session for credit.

Computers: 178 computers/terminals are available on campus for general student use. Students can access the following: campus intranet, computer help desk, free student e-mail accounts, online (class) grades, online (class) registration, online (class) schedules. Campuswide network is available. 100% of college-owned or -operated housing units are wired for high-speed Internet access. Wireless service is available via classrooms, computer centers, computer labs, dorm rooms, learning centers, libraries, student centers.

Library: F. M. Smith Library. *Books:* 80,000 (physical), 350,000 (digital/electronic); *Serial titles:* 130 (physical), 60 (digital/electronic); *Databases:* 50. Weekly public service hours: 80; students can reserve study rooms.

STUDENT LIFE

Housing options: on-campus residence required through senior year; men-only, women-only, special housing for students with disabilities. Campus housing is university owned. Freshman campus housing is guaranteed.

Activities and organizations: drama/theater group, student-run newspaper, radio station, choral group, marching band, Black Student Union, Latin Club, Enactus, Social Equality Alliance, Communication Club.

Athletics Member NAIA. *Intercollegiate sports:* baseball M(s), basketball M(s)/W(s), cheerleading M(s)/W(s), cross-country running M(s)/W(s), football M(s), golf M(s)/W(s), soccer M(s)/W(s), softball W(s), track and field M(s)/W(s), volleyball M(s)/W(s), wrestling M(s). *Intramural sports:* basketball M/W, football M/W, soccer M/W, softball M/W, table tennis M/W, ultimate Frisbee M/W, volleyball M/W.

Campus security: 24-hour emergency response devices, controlled dormitory access.

Student services: health clinic, personal/psychological counseling.

COSTS & FINANCIAL AID

Costs (2019–20) *Comprehensive fee:* $39,520 includes full-time tuition ($29,750), mandatory fees ($670), and room and board ($9100). Part-time tuition: $800 per semester hour. *College room only:* $3490.

Financial Aid Of all full-time matriculated undergraduates who enrolled in 2018, 924 applied for aid, 864 were judged to have need, 152 had their need fully met. 275 Federal Work-Study jobs (averaging $1249). 479 state and other part-time jobs (averaging $1353). In 2018, 152 non-need-based awards were made. *Average percent of need met:* 76. *Average financial aid package:* $24,742. *Average need-based loan:* $4440. *Average need-based gift aid:* $20,353. *Average non-need-based aid:* $15,575. *Average indebtedness upon graduation:* $33,934.

APPLYING

Standardized Tests *Required:* SAT or ACT (for admission), TOEFL or IELTS for all students whose first language is not English (for admission).

Options: electronic application.

Required: high school transcript, 2 of the following: minimum high school GPA of 2.5, rank in top half of class, or minimum SAT score of 960/ACT of 21. *Required for some:* essay or personal statement, 2 letters of recommendation, interview.

Application deadlines: rolling (freshmen), rolling (transfers).
Notification: continuous (freshmen), continuous (transfers).

CONTACT

Mr. Kevin Brown, Director of Admissions, Graceland University, 1 University Place, Lamoni, IA 50140. *Phone:* 641-784-5149. *Toll-free phone:* 866-GRACELAND. *Fax:* 641-784-5480. *E-mail:* admissions@graceland.edu.

★ Grand View University
Des Moines, Iowa
http://www.grandview.edu/

- **Independent** comprehensive, founded 1896, affiliated with Evangelical Lutheran Church in America
- **Urban** 25-acre campus
- **Endowment** $22.6 million
- **Coed**
- **Minimally difficult** entrance level

FACULTY

Student/faculty ratio: 13:1.

ACADEMICS

Calendar: semesters. *Degrees:* certificates, bachelor's, master's, and postbachelor's certificates.
Library: Grand View University Library plus 1 other. *Books:* 88,382 (physical), 45,490 (digital/electronic); *Serial titles:* 514 (physical), 75,889 (digital/electronic); *Databases:* 29. Weekly public service hours: 86.

STUDENT LIFE

Housing options: on-campus residence required through junior year; coed. Campus housing is university owned. Freshman applicants given priority for college housing.

Activities and organizations: drama/theater group, student-run newspaper, radio station, choral group, Nursing Student Association, Art Club, Science Club, Education Club, Business Club.

Athletics Member NAIA.

Campus security: 24-hour emergency response devices and patrols, late-night transport/escort service, controlled dormitory access, night security patrols.

Student services: health clinic, personal/psychological counseling, veterans affairs office.

COSTS & FINANCIAL AID

Costs (2018–19) *Comprehensive fee:* $36,786 includes full-time tuition ($26,922), mandatory fees ($686), and room and board ($9178). Full-time tuition and fees vary according to class time and course load. Part-time tuition: $669 per credit hour. Part-time tuition and fees vary according to class time and course load. *Room and board:* Room and board charges vary according to board plan and housing facility.

Financial Aid Of all full-time matriculated undergraduates who enrolled in 2018, 1,401 applied for aid, 1,254 were judged to have need, 288 had their need fully met. In 2018, 279 non-need-based awards were made. *Average percent of need met:* 75. *Average financial aid package:* $21,187. *Average need-based loan:* $4089. *Average need-based gift aid:* $19,036. *Average non-need-based aid:* $10,654. *Average indebtedness upon graduation:* $34,436.

APPLYING

Standardized Tests *Required:* SAT or ACT (for admission).
Options: electronic application.
Required: high school transcript. *Recommended:* minimum 2.0 GPA.

CONTACT

Mr. Ryan Thompson, Director of Admissions, Grand View University, 1200 Grandview Avenue, Des Moines, IA 50316-1599. *Phone:* 515-263-2810. *Toll-free phone:* 800-444-6083. *Fax:* 515-263-2974. *E-mail:* admissions@grandview.edu.

A ★ *indicates that the school has detailed information with a Premium Profile on Petersons.com.*

Grinnell College

Grinnell, Iowa
http://www.grinnell.edu/

- **Independent** 4-year, founded 1846
- **Small-town** 120-acre campus
- **Endowment** $1.9 billion
- **Coed**
- **Very difficult** entrance level

FACULTY
Student/faculty ratio: 9:1.

ACADEMICS
Calendar: semesters. *Degree:* bachelor's.
Library: Burling Library plus 2 others. *Books:* 488,334 (physical), 474,326 (digital/electronic); *Serial titles:* 6,491 (physical), 11,577 (digital/electronic); *Databases:* 346. Weekly public service hours: 109.

STUDENT LIFE
Housing options: on-campus residence required through sophomore year; coed, cooperative, special housing for students with disabilities. Campus housing is university owned. Freshman campus housing is guaranteed.

Activities and organizations: drama/theater group, student-run newspaper, radio station, choral group, Concerned Black Students, International Student Organization, Student Organization of Latinas/Latinos, Campus Democrats, Ultimate Frisbee.

Athletics Member NCAA. All Division III.

Campus security: 24-hour emergency response devices and patrols, student patrols, late-night transport/escort service, controlled dormitory access.

Student services: health clinic, personal/psychological counseling.

COSTS & FINANCIAL AID
Costs (2018–19) *Comprehensive fee:* $65,202 includes full-time tuition ($51,924), mandatory fees ($468), and room and board ($12,810). Part-time tuition: $1571 per credit hour. *College room only:* $6050. Room and board charges vary according to board plan and housing facility.

Financial Aid Of all full-time matriculated undergraduates who enrolled in 2018, 1,212 applied for aid, 1,103 were judged to have need, 1,103 had their need fully met. In 2018, 333 non-need-based awards were made. *Average percent of need met:* 100. *Average financial aid package:* $49,880. *Average need-based loan:* $3862. *Average need-based gift aid:* $43,783. *Average non-need-based aid:* $18,721. *Average indebtedness upon graduation:* $18,694. *Financial aid deadline:* 1/15.

APPLYING
Standardized Tests *Required:* SAT or ACT (for admission).

Options: electronic application, early admission, early decision, deferred entrance.

Required: essay or personal statement, high school transcript, 3 letters of recommendation. *Recommended:* interview.

CONTACT
Ms. Sarah Fischer, Director of Admission, Grinnell College, 1103 Park Street, Grinnell, IA 50112. *Phone:* 641-269-3600. *Toll-free phone:* 800-247-0113. *Fax:* 641-269-4800. *E-mail:* askgrin@grinnell.edu.

Hamilton Technical College

Davenport, Iowa
http://www.hamiltontechcollege.edu/

CONTACT
Hamilton Technical College, 1011 East 53rd Street, Davenport, IA 52807-2653. *Phone:* 563-386-3570. *Toll-free phone:* 866-966-4825.

INSTE Bible College

Ankeny, Iowa
http://www.inste.edu/

CONTACT
Admissions, INSTE Bible College, 2302 SW 3rd Street, Ankeny, IA 50023. *Phone:* 515-289-9200. *Fax:* 515-289-9201. *E-mail:* inste@inste.edu.

Iowa State University of Science and Technology

Ames, Iowa
http://www.iastate.edu/

- **State-supported** university, founded 1858
- **Suburban** 1795-acre campus with easy access to Des Moines
- **Endowment** $838.9 million
- **Coed** 29,621 undergraduate students, 94% full-time, 42% women, 58% men
- **Moderately difficult** entrance level, 91% of applicants were admitted

UNDERGRAD STUDENTS
27,929 full-time, 1,692 part-time. Students come from 52 states and territories; 123 other countries; 37% are from out of state; 3% Black or African American, non-Hispanic/Latino; 6% Hispanic/Latino; 3% Asian, non-Hispanic/Latino; 0.1% Native Hawaiian or other Pacific Islander, non-Hispanic/Latino; 0.2% American Indian or Alaska Native, non-Hispanic/Latino; 2% Two or more races, non-Hispanic/Latino; 5% Race/ethnicity unknown; 6% international; 5% transferred in; 41% live on campus.

Freshmen:
Admission: 18,855 applied, 17,082 admitted, 6,047 enrolled. *Average high school GPA:* 3.6. *Test scores:* SAT evidence-based reading and writing scores over 500: 91%; SAT math scores over 500: 88%; ACT scores over 18: 97%; SAT evidence-based reading and writing scores over 600: 56%; SAT math scores over 600: 52%; ACT scores over 24: 63%; SAT evidence-based reading and writing scores over 700: 20%; SAT math scores over 700: 11%; ACT scores over 30: 17%.
Retention: 88% of full-time freshmen returned.

FACULTY
Total: 1,851, 84% full-time, 88% with terminal degrees.
Student/faculty ratio: 19:1.

ACADEMICS
Calendar: semesters. *Degrees:* bachelor's, master's, doctoral, post-master's, and postbachelor's certificates.

Special study options: academic remediation for entering students, accelerated degree program, adult/continuing education programs, advanced placement credit, cooperative education, distance learning, double majors, English as a second language, external degree program, freshman honors college, honors programs, independent study, internships, off-campus study, part-time degree program, services for LD students, student-designed majors, study abroad, summer session for credit. *ROTC:* Army (b), Navy (b), Air Force (b).

Unusual degree programs: 3-2 engineering with William Penn College.

Computers: 2,557 computers/terminals are available on campus for general student use. Students can access the following: campus intranet, computer help desk, free student e-mail accounts, online (class) grades, online (class) registration, online (class) schedules, network services. Campuswide network is available. 100% of college-owned or -operated housing units are wired for high-speed Internet access. Wireless service is available via entire campus.

Library: Parks Library (University Library) plus 1 other. *Books:* 2.8 million (physical), 460,516 (digital/electronic); *Serial titles:* 32,462 (physical), 110,162 (digital/electronic); *Databases:* 287. Weekly public service hours: 113; students can reserve study rooms.

STUDENT LIFE
Housing options: coed, men-only, women-only, special housing for students with disabilities. Campus housing is university owned.

Activities and organizations: drama/theater group, student-run newspaper, radio and television station, choral group, marching band, Greek Life, Intramural Sports Activities, Club Sports, national fraternities, national sororities.

Athletics Member NCAA. All Division I except football (Division I-A). *Intercollegiate sports:* basketball M(s)/W(s), cross-country running M(s)/W(s), golf M(s)/W(s)(c), gymnastics W(s), soccer W(s), softball W(s), swimming and diving W(s), tennis W(s), track and field M(s)/W(s), volleyball W(s), wrestling M(s). *Intramural sports:* archery M(c)/W(c), badminton M(c)/W(c), baseball M(c)/W(c), basketball M/W, bowling M(c)/W(c), crew M(c)/W(c), equestrian sports M(c)/W(c), fencing

M(c)/W(c), field hockey M(c)/W(c), football M/W, golf M/W, gymnastics W, ice hockey M/W, lacrosse M(c)/W(c), racquetball M(c)/W(c), riflery M(c)/W(c), rock climbing M(c)/W(c), rugby M(c)/W(c), skiing (downhill) M(c)/W(c), soccer M/W, softball W(c), swimming and diving M(c)/W(c), table tennis M(c)/W(c), tennis M/W, track and field M/W, ultimate Frisbee M/W, volleyball M/W, water polo M(c)/W(c), weight lifting M(c)/W(c), wrestling M/W.

Campus security: 24-hour emergency response devices and patrols, late-night transport/escort service, controlled dormitory access.

Student services: health clinic, personal/psychological counseling, women's center, legal services, veterans affairs office.

COSTS & FINANCIAL AID

Costs (2018–19) *Tuition:* state resident $7740 full-time, $323 per credit hour part-time; nonresident $22,144 full-time, $923 per credit hour part-time. Full-time tuition and fees vary according to class time, course level, degree level, program, and student level. Part-time tuition and fees vary according to class time, course level, course load, degree level, program, and student level. *Required fees:* $1248 full-time. *Room and board:* $8720; room only: $4694. Room and board charges vary according to board plan and housing facility. *Payment plans:* installment, deferred payment.

Financial Aid Of all full-time matriculated undergraduates who enrolled in 2017, 21,524 applied for aid, 14,775 were judged to have need, 3,087 had their need fully met. 1,596 Federal Work-Study jobs (averaging $841). 11,694 state and other part-time jobs (averaging $2092). In 2017, 9495 non-need-based awards were made. *Average percent of need met:* 78. *Average financial aid package:* $13,006. *Average need-based loan:* $4362. *Average need-based gift aid:* $8066. *Average non-need-based aid:* $3738. *Average indebtedness upon graduation:* $28,701.

APPLYING

Standardized Tests *Required:* SAT or ACT (for admission).

Options: electronic application, early admission, deferred entrance.

Application fee: $40.

Required: high school transcript, minimum Regent Admission Index (RAI) of 245, high school course requirements.

Application deadlines: rolling (freshmen), rolling (transfers).

Notification: continuous (freshmen), continuous (transfers).

CONTACT

Phillip B. Caffrey, Associate Director for Admissions, Iowa State University of Science and Technology, 100 Enrollment Services, 2433 Union Drive, Ames, IA 50011-2042. *Phone:* 515-294-5836. *Toll-free phone:* 800-262-3810. *Fax:* 515-294-2592. *E-mail:* pbcaffr@iastate.edu.

Iowa Wesleyan University

Mount Pleasant, Iowa

http://www.iw.edu/

CONTACT

Julie Duplessis, Director of Enrollment, Iowa Wesleyan University, 601 N. Main Street, Mount Pleasant, IA 52641. *Phone:* 319-385-6208. *Toll-free phone:* 800-582-2383. *Fax:* 319-385-6240. *E-mail:* julie.duplessis@iw.edu.

Loras College

Dubuque, Iowa

http://www.loras.edu/

- **Independent Roman Catholic** comprehensive, founded 1839
- **Suburban** 64-acre campus
- **Endowment** $39.8 million
- **Coed** 1,393 undergraduate students, 97% full-time, 45% women, 55% men
- **Moderately difficult** entrance level, 93% of applicants were admitted

UNDERGRAD STUDENTS

1,345 full-time, 48 part-time. Students come from 26 states and territories; 10 other countries; 58% are from out of state; 3% Black or African American, non-Hispanic/Latino; 8% Hispanic/Latino; 0.7% Asian, non-Hispanic/Latino; 0.1% Native Hawaiian or other Pacific Islander, non-Hispanic/Latino; 0.1% American Indian or Alaska Native, non-Hispanic/Latino; 2% Two or more races, non-Hispanic/Latino; 4%

Race/ethnicity unknown; 2% international; 4% transferred in; 65% live on campus.

Freshmen:
Admission: 1,312 applied, 1,216 admitted, 362 enrolled. *Average high school GPA:* 3.4. *Test scores:* SAT evidence-based reading and writing scores over 500: 75%; SAT math scores over 500: 79%; ACT scores over 18: 81%; SAT evidence-based reading and writing scores over 600: 20%; SAT math scores over 600: 26%; ACT scores over 24: 35%; SAT evidence-based reading and writing scores over 700: 3%; SAT math scores over 700: 4%; ACT scores over 30: 9%.
Retention: 81% of full-time freshmen returned.

FACULTY
Total: 144, 69% full-time, 66% with terminal degrees.
Student/faculty ratio: 12:1.

ACADEMICS
Calendar: semesters plus January term. *Degrees:* bachelor's, master's, and postbachelor's certificates.

Special study options: academic remediation for entering students, advanced placement credit, cooperative education, distance learning, double majors, honors programs, independent study, internships, off-campus study, part-time degree program, services for LD students, student-designed majors, study abroad, summer session for credit. *ROTC:* Army (c).

Unusual degree programs: 3-2 business administration; nursing with Allen College; athletic training.

Computers: 5 computers/terminals and 991 ports are available on campus for general student use. Students can access the following: campus intranet, computer help desk, free student e-mail accounts, online (class) grades, online (class) registration, online (class) schedules. Campuswide network is available. 100% of college-owned or -operated housing units are wired for high-speed Internet access. Wireless service is available via entire campus.

Library: Loras College Library. *Books:* 212,063 (physical), 357,608 (digital/electronic); *Serial titles:* 37 (physical), 37,834 (digital/electronic); *Databases:* 123. Weekly public service hours: 91; students can reserve study rooms.

STUDENT LIFE
Housing options: on-campus residence required through junior year; coed, men-only, women-only. Campus housing is university owned. Freshman campus housing is guaranteed.

Activities and organizations: drama/theater group, student-run newspaper, radio and television station, choral group, Dance Marathon, Campus Activities Board, DuBuddies, Social Work Club, American Chemical Society, national fraternities, national sororities.

Athletics Member NCAA. All Division III except golf (Division II). *Intercollegiate sports:* baseball M, basketball M/W, cheerleading M(c)/W(c), cross-country running M/W, football M, golf M/W, ice hockey M(c)/W(c), lacrosse M/W, rugby M(c)/W(c), soccer M/W, softball W, swimming and diving M/W, tennis M/W, track and field M/W, ultimate Frisbee M(c)/W(c), volleyball M/W, wrestling M. *Intramural sports:* basketball M/W, racquetball M/W, soccer M/W, softball M/W, volleyball M/W.

Campus security: 24-hour emergency response devices and patrols, late-night transport/escort service, controlled dormitory access.

Student services: health clinic, personal/psychological counseling.

COSTS & FINANCIAL AID
Costs (2019–20) *Comprehensive fee:* $43,643 includes full-time tuition ($33,500), mandatory fees ($1718), and room and board ($8425). Part-time tuition: $750 per credit hour. *Required fees:* $45 per credit hour part-time. *College room only:* $4000.

Financial Aid Of all full-time matriculated undergraduates who enrolled in 2018, 1,199 applied for aid, 1,065 were judged to have need, 284 had their need fully met. 576 Federal Work-Study jobs (averaging $2402). 12 state and other part-time jobs (averaging $1250). In 2018, 270 non-need-based awards were made. *Average percent of need met:* 85. *Average financial aid package:* $27,972. *Average need-based loan:* $4359. *Average need-based gift aid:* $22,145. *Average non-need-based aid:* $18,483. *Average indebtedness upon graduation:* $30,864.

APPLYING

Standardized Tests *Required:* SAT or ACT (for admission).

Options: electronic application, deferred entrance.

Required: high school transcript, minimum 2.5 GPA. *Required for some:* essay or personal statement, 1 letter of recommendation, interview. *Recommended:* 1 letter of recommendation.

Application deadlines: rolling (freshmen), rolling (transfers).

Notification: continuous (freshmen), continuous (transfers).

CONTACT

Mr. Kyle Klapatauskas, Director of Admission Recruitment and Retention, Loras College, 1450 Alta Vista, Dubuque, IA 52004-0178. *Phone:* 563-588-7639. *Toll-free phone:* 800-245-6727. *E-mail:* kyle.klapatauskas@loras.edu.

Luther College

Decorah, Iowa

http://www.luther.edu/

- **Independent** 4-year, founded 1861, affiliated with Evangelical Lutheran Church in America
- **Small-town** 200-acre campus
- **Endowment** $161.8 million
- **Coed**
- **Moderately difficult** entrance level

FACULTY

Student/faculty ratio: 11:1.

ACADEMICS

Calendar: 4-1-4. *Degree:* bachelor's.

Library: Preus Library. *Books:* 202,938 (physical), 292,640 (digital/electronic); *Serial titles:* 17,086 (physical), 17,086 (digital/electronic); *Databases:* 99. Weekly public service hours: 104; students can reserve study rooms.

STUDENT LIFE

Housing options: on-campus residence required through senior year; coed, special housing for students with disabilities. Campus housing is university owned. Freshman campus housing is guaranteed.

Activities and organizations: drama/theater group, student-run newspaper, radio station, choral group, Alpha Phi Omega, college ministries, recreational sports, Student Activities Council, Diversity groups.

Athletics Member NCAA. All Division III.

Campus security: 24-hour emergency response devices and patrols, late-night transport/escort service, controlled dormitory access.

Student services: health clinic, personal/psychological counseling, women's center.

COSTS & FINANCIAL AID

Costs (2018–19) *Comprehensive fee:* $51,750 includes full-time tuition ($41,950), mandatory fees ($340), and room and board ($9460). Full-time tuition and fees vary according to course load. Part-time tuition: $1498 per credit hour. Part-time tuition and fees vary according to course load. *College room only:* $4420. Room and board charges vary according to board plan and housing facility.

Financial Aid Of all full-time matriculated undergraduates who enrolled in 2018, 1,722 applied for aid, 1,520 were judged to have need, 607 had their need fully met. 749 Federal Work-Study jobs (averaging $2099). 71 state and other part-time jobs (averaging $4713). In 2018, 426 non-need-based awards were made. *Average percent of need met:* 90. *Average financial aid package:* $37,623. *Average need-based loan:* $8070. *Average need-based gift aid:* $30,183. *Average non-need-based aid:* $22,783. *Average indebtedness upon graduation:* $35,809.

APPLYING

Standardized Tests *Required:* SAT or ACT (for admission).

Options: electronic application, deferred entrance.

Required: essay or personal statement, high school transcript, 1 letter of recommendation. *Recommended:* interview.

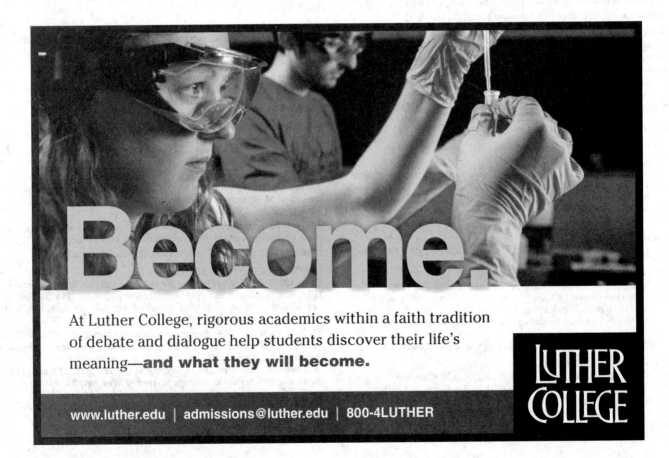

Become.

At Luther College, rigorous academics within a faith tradition of debate and dialogue help students discover their life's meaning—**and what they will become.**

www.luther.edu | admissions@luther.edu | 800-4LUTHER

LUTHER COLLEGE

CONTACT

Mr. Derek Hartl, Associate Vice President and Director of Admissions, Luther College, 700 College Drive, Decorah, IA 52101. *Phone:* 563-387-1433. *Toll-free phone:* 800-458-8437. *Fax:* 563-387-2159. *E-mail:* hartde01@luther.edu.

See previous page for display ad and page 1036 for the College Close-Up.

Maharishi University of Management

Fairfield, Iowa

http://www.mum.edu/

- **Independent** university, founded 1971
- **Small-town** 242-acre campus
- **Coed** 324 undergraduate students, 53% full-time, 63% women, 37% men
- **Moderately difficult** entrance level, 64% of applicants were admitted

UNDERGRAD STUDENTS

173 full-time, 151 part-time. 88% are from out of state; 11% Black or African American, non-Hispanic/Latino; 10% Hispanic/Latino; 2% Asian, non-Hispanic/Latino; 0.8% Native Hawaiian or other Pacific Islander, non-Hispanic/Latino; 0.8% American Indian or Alaska Native, non-Hispanic/Latino; 4% Two or more races, non-Hispanic/Latino; 31% Race/ethnicity unknown; 5% international; 8% transferred in; 58% live on campus.

Freshmen:

Admission: 42 applied, 27 admitted, 20 enrolled.

Retention: 53% of full-time freshmen returned.

FACULTY

Total: 156, 71% full-time, 56% with terminal degrees.

Student/faculty ratio: 9:1.

ACADEMICS

Calendar: semesters. *Degrees:* certificates, bachelor's, master's, doctoral, and postbachelor's certificates.

Special study options: adult/continuing education programs, double majors, English as a second language, independent study, off-campus study, student-designed majors.

Computers: Students can access the following: campus intranet, computer help desk, free student e-mail accounts, online (class) grades, online (class) schedules. Campuswide network is available. 100% of college-owned or -operated housing units are wired for high-speed Internet access. Wireless service is available via entire campus.

Library: Maharishi University of Management Library. Weekly public service hours: 55.

STUDENT LIFE

Housing options: on-campus residence required through senior year; men-only, women-only. Campus housing is university owned. Freshman campus housing is guaranteed.

Athletics *Intercollegiate sports:* soccer M(c)/W(c), ultimate Frisbee M(c)/W(c), volleyball M(c)/W(c). *Intramural sports:* archery M/W, badminton M/W, basketball M/W, football M/W, gymnastics M/W, rock climbing M/W, sailing M/W, soccer M/W, table tennis M/W, tennis M/W, ultimate Frisbee M/W, volleyball M/W.

Campus security: 24-hour emergency response devices and patrols, late-night transport/escort service, controlled dormitory access.

Student services: health clinic, personal/psychological counseling.

COSTS & FINANCIAL AID

Costs (2019–20) *Comprehensive fee:* $23,930 includes full-time tuition ($16,000), mandatory fees ($530), and room and board ($7400). Part-time tuition: $500 per unit.

Financial Aid Of all full-time matriculated undergraduates who enrolled in 2006, 150 applied for aid, 148 were judged to have need, 32 had their need fully met. 120 Federal Work-Study jobs (averaging $1422). 7 state and other part-time jobs (averaging $2729). In 2006, 5 non-need-based awards were made. *Average percent of need met:* 89. *Average financial aid package:* $23,963. *Average need-based loan:* $8281. *Average need-based gift aid:* $14,082. *Average non-need-based aid:* $9300. *Average indebtedness upon graduation:* $22,691.

APPLYING

Options: electronic application, early admission, deferred entrance.

Application fee: $20.

Required: essay or personal statement, high school transcript, minimum 2.5 GPA, 2 letters of recommendation. *Recommended:* interview.

CONTACT

June Humphreys, Lead US Admissions Counselor, Maharishi University of Management, Office of Admissions, Fairfield, IA 52557. *Phone:* 641-472-1110 Ext. 4807. *Toll-free phone:* 800-369-6480. *Fax:* 641-472-1179. *E-mail:* admissions@mum.edu.

Mercy College of Health Sciences

Des Moines, Iowa

http://www.mchs.edu/

CONTACT

Heather Gaumer, Director of Admissions, Mercy College of Health Sciences, 921 Sixth Avenue, Des Moines, IA 50309-1200. *Phone:* 515-643-6604. *Toll-free phone:* 800-637-2994. *Fax:* 515-643-6698. *E-mail:* hgaumer@mercydesmoines.org.

Morningside College

Sioux City, Iowa

http://www.morningside.edu/

- **Independent** comprehensive, founded 1894, affiliated with United Methodist Church
- **Suburban** 69-acre campus with easy access to Omaha, NE
- **Endowment** $47.1 million
- **Coed** 1,281 undergraduate students, 95% full-time, 50% women, 50% men
- **Moderately difficult** entrance level, 58% of applicants were admitted

UNDERGRAD STUDENTS

1,212 full-time, 69 part-time. Students come from 26 states and territories; 19 other countries; 45% are from out of state; 2% Black or African American, non-Hispanic/Latino; 7% Hispanic/Latino; 1% Asian, non-Hispanic/Latino; 0.2% Native Hawaiian or other Pacific Islander, non-Hispanic/Latino; 0.5% American Indian or Alaska Native, non-Hispanic/Latino; 4% Two or more races, non-Hispanic/Latino; 7% Race/ethnicity unknown; 5% international; 4% transferred in; 55% live on campus.

Freshmen:

Admission: 4,385 applied, 2,525 admitted, 345 enrolled. *Average high school GPA:* 3.4. *Test scores:* ACT scores over 18: 92%; ACT scores over 24: 35%; ACT scores over 30: 5%.

Retention: 71% of full-time freshmen returned.

FACULTY

Total: 240, 33% full-time, 49% with terminal degrees.

Student/faculty ratio: 14:1.

ACADEMICS

Calendar: semesters. *Degrees:* bachelor's, master's, post-master's, and postbachelor's certificates.

Special study options: academic remediation for entering students, adult/continuing education programs, advanced placement credit, distance learning, double majors, English as a second language, honors programs, independent study, internships, off-campus study, part-time degree program, services for LD students, student-designed majors, study abroad, summer session for credit. *ROTC:* Army (c).

Computers: Students can access the following: campus intranet, computer help desk, free student e-mail accounts, online (class) grades, online (class) registration, online (class) schedules, academic and financial records. Campuswide network is available. 100% of college-owned or -operated housing units are wired for high-speed Internet access. Wireless service is available via entire campus.

Library: Hickman-Johnson-Furrow Learning Center. *Books:* 40,458 (physical), 325 (digital/electronic); *Serial titles:* 516 (physical), 74 (digital/electronic); *Databases:* 46. Weekly public service hours: 93.

STUDENT LIFE

Housing options: on-campus residence required through junior year; coed. Campus housing is university owned. Freshman campus housing is guaranteed.

Activities and organizations: drama/theater group, student-run newspaper, radio and television station, choral group, marching band, Student Government/Activities Council, Student Ambassadors, Homecoming Committee, national fraternities, national sororities.

Athletics Member NCAA, NAIA. All NCAA Division II. *Intercollegiate sports:* baseball M(s), basketball M(s)/W(s), bowling M/W, cross-country running M(s)/W(s), football M(s), golf M(s), soccer M(s)/W(s), softball W(s), swimming and diving M(s)/W(s), tennis M(s)/W(s), track and field M(s)/W(s), volleyball W(s), wrestling M(s). *Intramural sports:* basketball M/W, bowling M/W, ultimate Frisbee M/W, volleyball M/W.

Campus security: 24-hour emergency response devices and patrols, student patrols, late-night transport/escort service, controlled dormitory access.

Student services: health clinic, personal/psychological counseling, women's center.

COSTS & FINANCIAL AID

Costs (2019–20) *Comprehensive fee:* $42,560 includes full-time tuition ($31,220), mandatory fees ($1500), and room and board ($9840). Part-time tuition: $570 per credit hour. *College room only:* $5320.

Financial Aid Of all full-time matriculated undergraduates who enrolled in 2017, 1,107 applied for aid, 994 were judged to have need, 238 had their need fully met. 542 Federal Work-Study jobs (averaging $1346). 265 state and other part-time jobs (averaging $2000). In 2017, 257 non-need-based awards were made. *Average percent of need met:* 74. *Average financial aid package:* $24,135. *Average need-based loan:* $4635. *Average need-based gift aid:* $6366. *Average non-need-based aid:* $15,529. *Average indebtedness upon graduation:* $36,449.

APPLYING

Standardized Tests *Required:* SAT or ACT (for admission).

Options: electronic application, deferred entrance.

Required: high school transcript, minimum 2.5 GPA, minimum ACT score of 20 or SAT of 1410 and either rank in top half of class or 2.5 GPA. *Recommended:* interview.

Application deadlines: rolling (freshmen), rolling (transfers).

Notification: continuous (freshmen), continuous (transfers).

CONTACT

Mrs. Stephanie Peters, Director of Admissions, Morningside College, 1501 Morningside Avenue, Sioux City, IA 51106. *Phone:* 712-274-5111. *Toll-free phone:* 800-831-0806 Ext. 5111. *Fax:* 712-274-5101. *E-mail:* mscadm@morningside.edu.

Mount Mercy University

Cedar Rapids, Iowa

http://www.mtmercy.edu/

- **Independent Roman Catholic** comprehensive, founded 1928
- **Suburban** 40-acre campus with easy access to Iowa City
- **Endowment** $26.4 million
- **Coed**
- **Moderately difficult** entrance level

FACULTY
Student/faculty ratio: 15:1.

ACADEMICS
Calendar: 4-1-4. *Degrees:* bachelor's, master's, and doctoral.
Library: Busse Library. *Books:* 124,017 (physical), 191,793 (digital/electronic); *Serial titles:* 3,972 (physical). Students can reserve study rooms.

STUDENT LIFE
Housing options: on-campus residence required through sophomore year; coed, men-only, women-only. Campus housing is university owned. Freshman campus housing is guaranteed.

Activities and organizations: drama/theater group, student-run newspaper, choral group, Student Ambassadors, Mount Mercy University Association of Nursing Students, Cheerleaders, Black Student Union, Student Government Association.

Athletics Member NCAA, NAIA. All NCAA Division III.

Campus security: 24-hour emergency response devices and patrols, student patrols, late-night transport/escort service, controlled dormitory

access, Department of Public Safety operational 24-hours a day, 7 days a week.

Student services: health clinic, personal/psychological counseling, veterans affairs office.

COSTS & FINANCIAL AID

Costs (2018–19) *Comprehensive fee:* $41,532 includes full-time tuition ($31,598), mandatory fees ($400), and room and board ($9534). Full-time tuition and fees vary according to course load. Part-time tuition: $958 per credit hour. Part-time tuition and fees vary according to course load. *Required fees:* $180 per year part-time. *Room and board:* Room and board charges vary according to board plan and housing facility.

Financial Aid Of all full-time matriculated undergraduates who enrolled in 2018, 1,017 applied for aid, 928 were judged to have need, 163 had their need fully met. In 2018, 176 non-need-based awards were made. *Average percent of need met:* 74. *Average financial aid package:* $25,140. *Average need-based loan:* $3866. *Average need-based gift aid:* $21,468. *Average non-need-based aid:* $14,102. *Average indebtedness upon graduation:* $25,739.

APPLYING

Standardized Tests *Required:* SAT or ACT (for admission).

Options: electronic application, deferred entrance.

Required: high school transcript, minimum 2.5 GPA. *Required for some:* 1 letter of recommendation.

CONTACT

Dr. Teresa Crumley, Dean of Admission, Mount Mercy University, 1330 Elmhurst Drive, NE, Cedar Rapids, IA 52402. *Phone:* 319-368-6460. *Toll-free phone:* 800-248-4504. *Fax:* 319-363-5270. *E-mail:* tcrumley@mtmercy.edu.

Northwestern College

Orange City, Iowa

http://www.nwciowa.edu/

- **Independent** comprehensive, founded 1882, affiliated with Reformed Church in America
- **Small-town** 100-acre campus
- **Endowment** $49.4 million
- **Coed**
- **Moderately difficult** entrance level

FACULTY
Student/faculty ratio: 11:1.

ACADEMICS
Calendar: semesters. *Degrees:* bachelor's, master's, and postbachelor's certificates.
Library: DeWitt Learning Commons plus 1 other. *Books:* 80,887 (physical), 151,137 (digital/electronic); *Serial titles:* 2,286 (physical), 80,593 (digital/electronic); *Databases:* 65. Weekly public service hours: 98; students can reserve study rooms.

STUDENT LIFE
Housing options: on-campus residence required through senior year; men-only, women-only, special housing for students with disabilities. Campus housing is university owned. Freshman campus housing is guaranteed.

Activities and organizations: drama/theater group, student-run newspaper, choral group, Drama Ministries Ensemble, A cappella Choir, Discipleship Groups, Fellowship of Christian Athletes, International Club.

Athletics Member NAIA.

Campus security: 24-hour emergency response devices, controlled dormitory access.

Student services: health clinic, personal/psychological counseling.

COSTS & FINANCIAL AID
Costs (2018–19) *Comprehensive fee:* $40,300 includes full-time tuition ($30,900), mandatory fees ($200), and room and board ($9200). Part-time tuition: $650 per credit hour. Part-time tuition and fees vary according to course load. *Required fees:* $75 per term part-time. *Room and board:* Room and board charges vary according to board plan and housing facility. *Payment plans:* tuition prepayment, installment.

Financial Aid Of all full-time matriculated undergraduates who enrolled in 2017, 845 applied for aid, 734 were judged to have need, 444 had their need fully met. 144 Federal Work-Study jobs (averaging $1550). 666 state and other part-time jobs (averaging $1089). In 2017, 253 non-need-based awards were made. *Average percent of need met:* 93. *Average financial aid package:* $25,672. *Average need-based loan:* $4947. *Average need-based gift aid:* $7244. *Average non-need-based aid:* $12,162. *Average indebtedness upon graduation:* $32,164.

APPLYING

Standardized Tests *Required:* SAT or ACT (for admission).

Options: electronic application, early admission, deferred entrance.

Required: essay or personal statement, high school transcript, minimum 2.0 GPA. *Recommended:* minimum 2.5 GPA, 1 letter of recommendation, interview.

CONTACT
Mrs. Jackie Davis, Director of Admissions, Northwestern College, 101 7th Street SW, Orange City, IA 51041. *Phone:* 712-737-7114. *Toll-free phone:* 800-747-4757. *Fax:* 712-707-7164. *E-mail:* admissions@ nwciowa.edu.

Palmer College of Chiropractic

Davenport, Iowa
http://www.palmer.edu/

CONTACT
Ms. Lisa Gisel, Undergraduate Admissions Representative, Palmer College of Chiropractic, 1000 Brady Street, Davenport, IA 52803-5287. *Phone:* 563-884-5743. *Toll-free phone:* 800-722-3648. *Fax:* 563-884-5226. *E-mail:* lisa.gisel@palmer.edu.

Purdue University Global

Cedar Falls, Iowa
http://www.purdueglobal.edu/

CONTACT
Purdue University Global, 7009 Nordic Drive, Cedar Falls, IA 50613. *Phone:* 319-277-0220. *Toll-free phone:* 844-PURDUE-G.

Purdue University Global

Cedar Rapids, Iowa
http://www.purdueglobal.edu/

CONTACT
Purdue University Global, 3165 Edgewood Parkway, SW, Cedar Rapids, IA 52404. *Phone:* 319-363-0481. *Toll-free phone:* 844-PURDUE-G.

Purdue University Global

Davenport, Iowa
http://www.purdueglobal.edu/

CONTACT
Purdue University Global, 1801 East Kimberly Road, Suite 1, Davenport, IA 52807. *Phone:* 563-355-3500. *Toll-free phone:* 844-PURDUE-G.

Purdue University Global

Mason City, Iowa
http://www.purdueglobal.edu/

CONTACT
Purdue University Global, 2570 4th Street, SW, Mason City, IA 50401. *Phone:* 641-423-2530. *Toll-free phone:* 844-PURDUE-G.

Purdue University Global

Urbandale, Iowa
http://www.purdueglobal.edu/

CONTACT
Purdue University Global, 4655 121st Street, Urbandale, IA 50323. *Phone:* 515-727-2100. *Toll-free phone:* 844-PURDUE-G.

St. Ambrose University

Davenport, Iowa
http://www.sau.edu/
- **Independent Roman Catholic** comprehensive, founded 1882
- **Urban** 118-acre campus
- **Endowment** $139.8 million
- **Coed**
- **Moderately difficult** entrance level

FACULTY
Student/faculty ratio: 12:1.

ACADEMICS
Calendar: semesters. *Degrees:* bachelor's, master's, doctoral, and post-master's certificates.
Library: SAU Library plus 1 other. *Books:* 172,923 (physical), 13,678 (digital/electronic); *Serial titles:* 502 (physical); *Databases:* 85. Weekly public service hours: 95; students can reserve study rooms.

STUDENT LIFE
Housing options: on-campus residence required through sophomore year; coed, men-only, women-only, special housing for students with disabilities. Campus housing is university owned. Freshman campus housing is guaranteed.

Activities and organizations: drama/theater group, student-run newspaper, radio and television station, choral group, marching band, Dance Marathon, Habitat for Humanity, Biology Club, Ambrosians for Peace and Justice, SPTO - Student Physical Therapy Organization.

Athletics Member NAIA.

Campus security: 24-hour emergency response devices and patrols, student patrols, late-night transport/escort service, controlled dormitory access, off-duty officer available three nights/week for 4.5 hours per night, twelve cameras record various public areas on campus.

Student services: health clinic, personal/psychological counseling, veterans affairs office.

COSTS & FINANCIAL AID
Costs (2018–19) *Comprehensive fee:* $41,364 includes full-time tuition ($30,614), mandatory fees ($280), and room and board ($10,470). Full-time tuition and fees vary according to course load and location. Part-time tuition: $942 per credit hour. Part-time tuition and fees vary according to course load and location. *Required fees:* $280 per term part-time. *College room only:* $6384. Room and board charges vary according to board plan and housing facility. *Payment plans:* installment, deferred payment.

Financial Aid Of all full-time matriculated undergraduates who enrolled in 2018, 1,814 applied for aid, 1,616 were judged to have need, 357 had their need fully met. 558 Federal Work-Study jobs (averaging $1782). 257 state and other part-time jobs (averaging $1770). In 2018, 416 non-need-based awards were made. *Average percent of need met:* 69. *Average financial aid package:* $22,923. *Average need-based loan:* $4279. *Average need-based gift aid:* $18,085. *Average non-need-based aid:* $14,492. *Average indebtedness upon graduation:* $37,593.

APPLYING
Standardized Tests *Required:* SAT or ACT (for admission).

Options: electronic application, deferred entrance.

Required: high school transcript, minimum 2.5 GPA. *Required for some:* interview. *Recommended:* interview.

CONTACT
Ms. Allison Conklin, Associate Director of First Year Admissions, St. Ambrose University, 518 W. Locust Street, Davenport, IA 52803. *Phone:* 563-333-6300. *Toll-free phone:* 800-383-2627. *Fax:* 563-333-6297. *E-mail:* conklinallisonj@sau.edu.

St. Luke's College

Sioux City, Iowa
http://stlukescollege.edu/
- **Independent** primarily 2-year, founded 1967
- **Rural** 3-acre campus with easy access to Omaha
- **Endowment** $1.2 million
- **Coed** 270 undergraduate students, 47% full-time, 91% women, 9% men
- **Minimally difficult** entrance level, 100% of applicants were admitted

UNDERGRAD STUDENTS

127 full-time, 143 part-time. Students come from 15 states and territories; 1 other country; 41% are from out of state; 3% Black or African American, non-Hispanic/Latino; 8% Hispanic/Latino; 3% Asian, non-Hispanic/Latino; 0.4% Native Hawaiian or other Pacific Islander, non-Hispanic/Latino; 2% American Indian or Alaska Native, non-Hispanic/Latino; 3% Two or more races, non-Hispanic/Latino; 0.4% Race/ethnicity unknown; 13% transferred in.

Freshmen:
Admission: 15 applied, 15 admitted, 10 enrolled. ***Average high school GPA:*** 3.5.

Retention: 100% of full-time freshmen returned.

FACULTY
Total: 36, 61% full-time, 14% with terminal degrees.
Student/faculty ratio: 6:1.

ACADEMICS
Calendar: semesters. *Degrees:* certificates, associate, and bachelor's.

Special study options: advanced placement credit, distance learning, internships, services for LD students, summer session for credit.

Computers: 9 computers/terminals are available on campus for general student use. Students can access the following: campus intranet, computer help desk, free student e-mail accounts, online (class) grades, online (class) registration, online (class) schedules. Campuswide network is available. Wireless service is available via entire campus.
Library: St. Luke's College Library. *Books:* 2,205 (physical); *Serial titles:* 63 (physical); *Databases:* 5. Weekly public service hours: 56.

STUDENT LIFE
Housing options: college housing not available.

Campus security: 24-hour emergency response devices and patrols, late-night transport/escort service.

Student services: health clinic, personal/psychological counseling.

COSTS & FINANCIAL AID
Costs (2019–20) *Tuition:* $18,900 full-time, $525 part-time. ***Required fees:*** $1560 full-time, $1560 per year part-time.

Financial Aid Of all full-time matriculated undergraduates who enrolled in 2017, 81 applied for aid, 81 were judged to have need. 5 Federal Work-Study jobs (averaging $900). *Average percent of need met:* 80. *Average financial aid package:* $11,650. *Average need-based loan:* $6938. *Average need-based gift aid:* $4981. *Average indebtedness upon graduation:* $19,465.

APPLYING
Standardized Tests *Required:* SAT or ACT (for admission).

Options: electronic application.

Required: essay or personal statement, high school transcript, minimum 2.5 GPA, interview.

Notification: continuous (freshmen), continuous (out-of-state freshmen), continuous (transfers), rolling (early decision plan 1), rolling (early decision plan 2), rolling (early action).

CONTACT
Ms. Sherry McCarthy, Admissions Coordinator, St. Luke's College, 2720 Stone Park Boulevard, Sioux City, IA 51104. *Phone:* 712-279-3149. *Toll-free phone:* 800-352-4660 Ext. 3149. *Fax:* 712-233-8017. *E-mail:* sherry.mccarthy@stlukescollege.edu.

Shiloh University

Kalona, Iowa
http://www.shilohuniversity.edu/
- **Independent** comprehensive, founded 2007
- **Small-town** 200-acre campus
- **Coed** 14 undergraduate students, 64% women, 36% men
- **Noncompetitive** entrance level, 33% of applicants were admitted

UNDERGRAD STUDENTS
14 part-time. Students come from 16 states and territories; 2 other countries; 88% are from out of state; 7% Black or African American, non-Hispanic/Latino; 7% Hispanic/Latino; 7% Asian, non-Hispanic/Latino; 271% transferred in.

Freshmen:
Admission: 3 applied, 1 admitted.
Retention: 60% of full-time freshmen returned.

FACULTY
Total: 34, 21% full-time, 38% with terminal degrees.
Student/faculty ratio: 1:1.

ACADEMICS
Degrees: certificates, associate, bachelor's, master's, doctoral, and postbachelor's certificates.

Special study options: distance learning, off-campus study, part-time degree program, services for LD students, summer session for credit.

Computers: Students can access the following: online (class) grades, online (class) registration, online (class) schedules.
Library: University e-Library. *Databases:* 2.

COSTS
Costs (2019–20) *Tuition:* $4725 full-time, $175 per credit hour part-time.

APPLYING
Options: electronic application, early admission, deferred entrance.

Required: essay or personal statement, high school transcript, minimum 2.0 GPA. *Required for some:* 1 letter of recommendation.

Application deadlines: 7/5 (freshmen), 7/1 (out-of-state freshmen), 7/5 (transfers).

Notification: 7/19 (freshmen), continuous (out-of-state freshmen), continuous until 7/19 (transfers).

CONTACT
Mr. Jeremy Daniel Richardson, Admissions Coordinator, Shiloh University, 100 Shiloh Drive, Kalona, IA 52247. *Phone:* 319-656-2447. *Fax:* 319-656-2448. *E-mail:* admissions@shilohuniversity.edu.

★ Simpson College

Indianola, Iowa
http://www.simpson.edu/
- **Independent United Methodist** comprehensive, founded 1860
- **Suburban** 85-acre campus with easy access to Des Moines
- **Endowment** $84.6 million
- **Coed**
- **Moderately difficult** entrance level

FACULTY
Student/faculty ratio: 10:1.

ACADEMICS
Calendar: 4-4-1. *Degrees:* bachelor's, master's, and postbachelor's certificates.
Library: Dunn Library. *Books:* 116,870 (physical), 168,359 (digital/electronic); *Serial titles:* 234 (physical), 278,513 (digital/electronic); *Databases:* 38. Weekly public service hours: 95.

STUDENT LIFE
Housing options: on-campus residence required through junior year; coed, men-only, women-only. Campus housing is university owned. Freshman campus housing is guaranteed.

Activities and organizations: drama/theater group, student-run newspaper, radio station, choral group, Religious Life Community, Campus Activities Board, Student Government Association, Residence Hall Association, intramurals, national fraternities, national sororities.

Athletics Member NCAA. All Division III.

Campus security: 24-hour emergency response devices and patrols, student patrols, late-night transport/escort service, controlled dormitory access, SAFE (Simpson Alert for Emergencies) provides phone calls in case of campus security/weather emergencies.

Student services: health clinic, personal/psychological counseling, women's center, veterans affairs office.

COSTS & FINANCIAL AID
Costs (2018–19) *One-time required fee:* $200. *Comprehensive fee:* $47,524 includes full-time tuition ($38,412), mandatory fees ($732), and room and board ($8380). Full-time tuition and fees vary according to class time, course load, degree level, and program. Part-time tuition: $375 per

credit hour. Part-time tuition and fees vary according to class time, course load, degree level, and program. *Required fees:* $6 per credit hour part-time. *College room only:* $4062. Room and board charges vary according to board plan and housing facility.

Financial Aid Of all full-time matriculated undergraduates who enrolled in 2018, 1,117 applied for aid, 1,028 were judged to have need, 199 had their need fully met. 236 Federal Work-Study jobs (averaging $1264). 498 state and other part-time jobs (averaging $1518). In 2018, 176 non-need-based awards were made. *Average percent of need met:* 80. *Average financial aid package:* $31,822. *Average need-based loan:* $4422. *Average need-based gift aid:* $26,929. *Average non-need-based aid:* $21,675. *Average indebtedness upon graduation:* $36,575.

APPLYING
Standardized Tests *Required:* SAT or ACT (for admission).

Options: electronic application, deferred entrance.

Required: high school transcript, guidance counselor recommendation form. *Recommended:* minimum 3.0 GPA, interview.

CONTACT
Simpson College, 701 North C Street, Indianola, IA 50125-1297. *Toll-free phone:* 800-362-2454.

See next page for display ad and page 1110 for the College Close-Up.

★ University of Dubuque
Dubuque, Iowa
http://www.dbq.edu/

- **Independent Presbyterian** comprehensive, founded 1852
- **Suburban** 77-acre campus
- **Endowment** $132.6 million
- **Coed**
- **Moderately difficult** entrance level

FACULTY
Student/faculty ratio: 13:1.

ACADEMICS
Calendar: 4-1-4. *Degrees:* associate, bachelor's, master's, and doctoral.

Library: Charles C. Myers Library. *Books:* 134,278 (physical), 178,036 (digital/electronic); *Serial titles:* 180 (physical), 30,070 (digital/electronic); *Databases:* 58. Weekly public service hours: 109.

STUDENT LIFE
Housing options: on-campus residence required through junior year; coed, special housing for students with disabilities. Campus housing is university owned. Freshman campus housing is guaranteed.

Activities and organizations: drama/theater group, student-run newspaper, choral group, Greek Council, Saudi Student Organization, Student Nurses Association, Accounting Club, ROTC.

Athletics Member NCAA. All Division III except golf (Division II).

Campus security: 24-hour patrols, late-night transport/escort service, controlled dormitory access.

Student services: health clinic, personal/psychological counseling, veterans affairs office.

COSTS & FINANCIAL AID
Costs (2018–19) *Comprehensive fee:* $43,890 includes full-time tuition ($32,670), mandatory fees ($1440), and room and board ($9780). Part-time tuition: $880 per credit hour. *College room only:* $4930. Room and board charges vary according to board plan and housing facility.

Financial Aid Of all full-time matriculated undergraduates who enrolled in 2018, 1,563 applied for aid, 1,460 were judged to have need, 216 had their need fully met. 202 Federal Work-Study jobs (averaging $2000). 185 state and other part-time jobs (averaging $2000). In 2018, 174 non-need-based awards were made. *Average percent of need met:* 70. *Average financial aid package:* $28,896. *Average need-based loan:* $6933. *Average need-based gift aid:* $22,501. *Average non-need-based aid:* $14,940. *Average indebtedness upon graduation:* $26,346.

APPLYING
Standardized Tests *Required:* SAT or ACT (for admission).

Options: electronic application, deferred entrance.

Application fee: $25.

Required: essay or personal statement, high school transcript, 2 letters of recommendation. *Recommended:* interview.

CONTACT
Mr. Bob Broshous, Director of Admissions, University of Dubuque, 2000 University Avenue, Dubuque, IA 52001-5099. *Phone:* 563-589-3199. *Toll-free phone:* 800-722-5583. *Fax:* 563-589-3690. *E-mail:* admissns@dbq.edu.

See previous page for display ad and page 1136 for the College Close-Up.

The University of Iowa
Iowa City, Iowa
http://www.uiowa.edu/

CONTACT
Debra Miller, Senior Associate Director, Undergraduate Evaluation, The University of Iowa, 108 Calvin Hall, Iowa City, IA 52242. *Phone:* 319-335-3847. *Toll-free phone:* 800-553-4692. *Fax:* 319-335-1535. *E-mail:* admissions@uiowa.edu.

University of Northern Iowa
Cedar Falls, Iowa
http://www.uni.edu/

- **State-supported** comprehensive, founded 1876, part of Board of Regents, State of Iowa
- **Suburban** 908-acre campus
- **Endowment** $137.5 million
- **Coed** 9,561 undergraduate students, 91% full-time, 58% women, 42% men
- **Moderately difficult** entrance level, 81% of applicants were admitted

UNDERGRAD STUDENTS
8,745 full-time, 816 part-time. Students come from 32 states and territories; 60 other countries; 6% are from out of state; 3% Black or African American, non-Hispanic/Latino; 4% Hispanic/Latino; 1% Asian, non-Hispanic/Latino; 0.1% Native Hawaiian or other Pacific Islander, non-Hispanic/Latino; 0.4% American Indian or Alaska Native, non-Hispanic/Latino; 2% Two or more races, non-Hispanic/Latino; 4% Race/ethnicity unknown; 3% international; 8% transferred in; 32% live on campus.

Freshmen:
Admission: 5,217 applied, 4,212 admitted, 1,661 enrolled. *Average high school GPA:* 3.6. *Test scores:* ACT scores over 18: 94%; ACT scores over 24: 39%; ACT scores over 30: 6%.
Retention: 84% of full-time freshmen returned.

FACULTY
Total: 655, 76% full-time, 70% with terminal degrees.
Student/faculty ratio: 18:1.

ACADEMICS
Calendar: semesters. *Degrees:* bachelor's, master's, and doctoral.
Special study options: academic remediation for entering students, accelerated degree program, adult/continuing education programs, advanced placement credit, cooperative education, distance learning, double majors, English as a second language, external degree program, honors programs, independent study, internships, off-campus study, part-time degree program, services for LD students, student-designed majors, study abroad, summer session for credit. *ROTC:* Army (b).
Unusual degree programs: 3-2 nursing with Allen College, University of Iowa; medical technology with University of Iowa Medical School, cytotechnology with Mayo School of Health-Related Sciences and Mercy College of Health Sciences, chiropractic with Logan College of Chiropractic and Palmer College of Chiropractic.
Computers: 1,900 computers/terminals are available on campus for general student use. Students can access the following: campus intranet, computer help desk, free student e-mail accounts, online (class) grades, online (class) registration, online (class) schedules, student account, degree audit, program of study. Campuswide network is available. 100% of college-owned or -operated housing units are wired for high-speed Internet access. Wireless service is available via entire campus.
Library: Rod Library plus 1 other. *Books:* 746,500 (physical), 338,651 (digital/electronic); *Serial titles:* 20,207 (physical), 64,588 (digital/electronic); *Databases:* 191. Weekly public service hours: 97; students can reserve study rooms.

STUDENT LIFE

Housing options: coed, men-only, women-only. Campus housing is university owned. Freshman campus housing is guaranteed.

Activities and organizations: drama/theater group, student-run newspaper, radio station, choral group, marching band, Dance Marathon, Colleges Against Cancer/Relay for Life, Accounting Club, Phi Eta Sigma, Students Today Alumni Tomorrow, national fraternities, national sororities.

Athletics Member NCAA. All Division I except football (Division I-AA). *Intercollegiate sports:* basketball M(s)/W(s), cross-country running M(s)/W(s), golf M(s)/W(s)(c), soccer W(s), softball W(s), swimming and diving W(s), tennis W(s), track and field M(s)/W(s), volleyball W(s), wrestling M(s). *Intramural sports:* badminton M/W, baseball M(c), basketball M/W, bowling M(c)/W(c), cheerleading M/W, crew M(c)/W(c), cross-country running M(c)/W(c), football M(c), golf M(c)/W(c), ice hockey M(c), racquetball M(c)/W(c), rugby M(c)/W(c), skiing (downhill) M(c)/W(c), soccer M(c)/W(c), softball M(c)/W(c), swimming and diving M(c)/W(c), table tennis M/W, tennis M(c)/W(c), track and field M(c)/W(c), ultimate Frisbee M(c)/W(c), volleyball M/W(c).

Campus security: 24-hour emergency response devices and patrols, student patrols, late-night transport/escort service, controlled dormitory access.

Student services: health clinic, personal/psychological counseling, veterans affairs office.

COSTS & FINANCIAL AID

Costs (2018–19) *Tuition:* state resident $7665 full-time, $320 per credit hour part-time; nonresident $18,207 full-time, $759 per credit hour part-time. Full-time tuition and fees vary according to course load and program. Part-time tuition and fees vary according to course load and program. *Required fees:* $1273 full-time. *Room and board:* $8948; room only: $4540. Room and board charges vary according to board plan and housing facility. *Payment plan:* installment.

Financial Aid Of all full-time matriculated undergraduates who enrolled in 2017, 7,117 applied for aid, 5,571 were judged to have need, 822 had their need fully met. In 2017, 1136 non-need-based awards were made. *Average percent of need met:* 64. *Average financial aid package:* $8237. *Average need-based loan:* $4385. *Average need-based gift aid:* $5104. *Average non-need-based aid:* $3255. *Average indebtedness upon graduation:* $24,474.

APPLYING

Standardized Tests *Required:* SAT or ACT (for admission). *Recommended:* SAT (for admission), ACT (for admission).

Options: electronic application, deferred entrance.

Application fee: $40.

Required: high school transcript, 4 years of English; 3 years each of math, science and social studies; 2 or more years of electives, which may include foreign language and fine arts. *Required for some:* interview.

Notification: 7/1 (freshmen), 8/1 (transfers).

CONTACT

Amy S. Schipper, Associate Director Operations & Data, University of Northern Iowa, 002 Gilchrist, Cedar Falls, IA 50614. *Phone:* 319-273-2281. *Toll-free phone:* 800-772-2037. *Fax:* 319-273-2885. *E-mail:* admissions@uni.edu.

Upper Iowa University

Fayette, Iowa

http://www.uiu.edu/

- **Independent** comprehensive, founded 1857
- **Rural** 100-acre campus with easy access to Minneapolis-St. Paul, Chicago
- **Endowment** $17.1 million
- **Coed**
- **Moderately difficult** entrance level

FACULTY

Student/faculty ratio: 17:1.

ACADEMICS

Calendar: 6 8-week terms. *Degrees:* certificates, associate, bachelor's, and master's (enrollment figures include extended learning centers and online and distance education programs).

Library: Henderson Wilder Library. *Books:* 68,870 (physical), 7,450 (digital/electronic); *Serial titles:* 211 (physical), 83,993 (digital/electronic); *Databases:* 40. Weekly public service hours: 85.

STUDENT LIFE

Housing options: on-campus residence required through junior year; coed, men-only, women-only. Campus housing is university owned. Freshman campus housing is guaranteed.

Activities and organizations: drama/theater group, student-run newspaper, choral group, Student Athlete Advisory Committee, Peacock Alumni for Student Traditions, UIU Science and Environment Club, Student Government Association, Peacocks for Progress.

Athletics Member NCAA. All Division II.

Campus security: late-night transport/escort service, controlled dormitory access.

Student services: personal/psychological counseling, veterans affairs office.

COSTS & FINANCIAL AID

Costs (2018–19) *Comprehensive fee:* $38,910 includes full-time tuition ($29,700), mandatory fees ($750), and room and board ($8460). Full-time tuition and fees vary according to degree level, location, and program. Part-time tuition: $454 per credit hour. *College room only:* $3900. Room and board charges vary according to board plan, housing facility, and location. *Payment plans:* installment, deferred payment.

Financial Aid Of all full-time matriculated undergraduates who enrolled in 2018, 2,034 applied for aid, 1,919 were judged to have need, 165 had their need fully met. 154 Federal Work-Study jobs (averaging $2362). In 2018, 204 non-need-based awards were made. *Average percent of need met:* 57. *Average financial aid package:* $16,313. *Average need-based loan:* $5543. *Average need-based gift aid:* $12,328. *Average non-need-based aid:* $17,073. *Average indebtedness upon graduation:* $28,927.

APPLYING

Standardized Tests *Required:* SAT or ACT (for admission).

Options: electronic application.

Required: high school transcript, minimum 2.0 GPA.

CONTACT

Ms. Kathy Franken, Vice President of Enrollment Management, Upper Iowa University, 605 Washington Street, Parker Fox Hall, Fayette, IA 52142. *Phone:* 563-425-5868. *Toll-free phone:* 800-553-4150. *Fax:* 563-425-5323. *E-mail:* frankenk@uiu.edu.

Waldorf University

Forest City, Iowa

http://www.waldorf.edu/

- **Independent Lutheran** comprehensive, founded 1903, part of Columbia Southern Education Group
- **Rural** 51-acre campus
- **Coed**
- **Moderately difficult** entrance level

FACULTY

Student/faculty ratio: 19:1.

ACADEMICS

Calendar: semesters. *Degrees:* certificates, associate, bachelor's, and master's.

Library: Luise V. Hanson Library. *Books:* 55,884 (physical), 152,040 (digital/electronic); *Serial titles:* 394 (physical); *Databases:* 87. Weekly public service hours: 97; students can reserve study rooms.

STUDENT LIFE

Housing options: on-campus residence required through junior year; coed, men-only, women-only, cooperative, special housing for students with disabilities. Campus housing is university owned and leased by the school. Freshman campus housing is guaranteed.

Activities and organizations: drama/theater group, student-run newspaper, radio and television station, choral group, Student Activities

Team, Education Club, Campus Ministry groups, intramurals, Radio/TV/Newspaper.

Athletics Member NAIA.

Campus security: 24-hour emergency response devices, student patrols, late-night transport/escort service, controlled dormitory access, evening and night patrols by trained security personnel, camera surveillance system.

Student services: health clinic, personal/psychological counseling.

COSTS & FINANCIAL AID

Costs (2018–19) *Comprehensive fee:* $29,600 includes full-time tuition ($20,934), mandatory fees ($1142), and room and board ($7524). Full-time tuition and fees vary according to class time, course load, and program. Part-time tuition: $295 per credit hour. *Room and board:* Room and board charges vary according to board plan and housing facility. *Payment plans:* installment, deferred payment.

Financial Aid Of all full-time matriculated undergraduates who enrolled in 2015, 1,030 applied for aid, 959 were judged to have need, 98 had their need fully met. In 2015, 111 non-need-based awards were made. *Average percent of need met:* 62. *Average financial aid package:* $13,783. *Average need-based loan:* $4414. *Average need-based gift aid:* $10,658. *Average non-need-based aid:* $7090. *Average indebtedness upon graduation:* $33,494.

APPLYING

Standardized Tests *Required:* SAT or ACT (for admission).

Options: electronic application.

Required: high school transcript. *Required for some:* 1 letter of recommendation, interview. *Recommended:* minimum 2.0 GPA.

CONTACT

Waldorf University, 106 South 6th Street, Forest City, IA 50436. *Toll-free phone:* 800-292-1903.

Wartburg College

Waverly, Iowa

http://www.wartburg.edu/

- **Independent Lutheran** 4-year, founded 1852
- **Small-town** 170-acre campus
- **Endowment** $76.7 million
- **Coed** 1,498 undergraduate students, 97% full-time, 53% women, 47% men
- **Moderately difficult** entrance level, 76% of applicants were admitted

UNDERGRAD STUDENTS

1,456 full-time, 42 part-time. Students come from 35 states and territories; 53 other countries; 31% are from out of state; 4% Black or African American, non-Hispanic/Latino; 5% Hispanic/Latino; 1% Asian, non-Hispanic/Latino; 0.1% Native Hawaiian or other Pacific Islander, non-Hispanic/Latino; 0.1% American Indian or Alaska Native, non-Hispanic/Latino; 3% Two or more races, non-Hispanic/Latino; 3% Race/ethnicity unknown; 7% international; 2% transferred in; 87% live on campus.

Freshmen:

Admission: 4,298 applied, 3,254 admitted, 469 enrolled. *Average high school GPA:* 3.6. *Test scores:* SAT evidence-based reading and writing scores over 500: 78%; SAT math scores over 500: 80%; ACT scores over 18: 92%; SAT evidence-based reading and writing scores over 600: 16%; SAT math scores over 600: 18%; ACT scores over 24: 45%; SAT evidence-based reading and writing scores over 700: 2%; SAT math scores over 700: 2%; ACT scores over 30: 5%.

Retention: 79% of full-time freshmen returned.

FACULTY

Total: 158, 59% full-time, 57% with terminal degrees.

Student/faculty ratio: 11:1.

ACADEMICS

Calendar: 4-4-1. *Degrees:* bachelor's and master's.

Special study options: academic remediation for entering students, accelerated degree program, advanced placement credit, double majors, honors programs, independent study, internships, off-campus study, part-time degree program, services for LD students, student-designed majors, study abroad, summer session for credit.

Unusual degree programs: 3-2 engineering with Iowa State University; nursing with Allen College; pre-seminary with Wartburg Seminary, clinical laboratory science with Mercy College of Health Sciences, pre-Law with The University of Iowa, museum studies with Western Illinois University.

Computers: 349 computers/terminals are available on campus for general student use. Students can access the following: campus intranet, computer help desk, free student e-mail accounts, online (class) grades, online (class) registration, online (class) schedules, billing, satellite. Campuswide network is available. 100% of college-owned or -operated housing units are wired for high-speed Internet access. Wireless service is available via entire campus.

Library: Vogel Library. *Books:* 144,314 (physical), 164,971 (digital/electronic); *Serial titles:* 2,993 (physical), 68,512 (digital/electronic); *Databases:* 176. Weekly public service hours: 91.

STUDENT LIFE

Housing options: on-campus residence required through senior year; coed, men-only, women-only, special housing for students with disabilities. Campus housing is university owned. Freshman campus housing is guaranteed.

Activities and organizations: drama/theater group, student-run newspaper, radio and television station, choral group, Entertainment To Knight (ETK), Student Senate, Wartburg College Dance Marathon (WCDM), Symphonic Band, Wartburg Choir.

Athletics Member NCAA. All Division III except golf (Division II). *Intercollegiate sports:* baseball M, basketball M/W, bowling M/W, cross-country running M/W, football M, golf M/W, lacrosse W, soccer M/W, softball W, tennis M/W, track and field M/W, volleyball W, wrestling M. *Intramural sports:* basketball M/W, bowling M/W, cheerleading W(c), golf M/W, sand volleyball M/W, soccer M/W, softball M/W.

Campus security: 24-hour emergency response devices and patrols, late-night transport/escort service, controlled dormitory access.

Student services: health clinic, personal/psychological counseling.

COSTS & FINANCIAL AID

Costs (2019–20) *Comprehensive fee:* $53,210 includes full-time tuition ($41,830), mandatory fees ($2100), and room and board ($9280). Part-time tuition: $2200 per course. *Required fees:* $125 per term part-time. *College room only:* $5290.

Financial Aid Of all full-time matriculated undergraduates who enrolled in 2017, 1,259 applied for aid, 1,115 were judged to have need, 214 had their need fully met. 534 Federal Work-Study jobs (averaging $1115). 485 state and other part-time jobs (averaging $1829). In 2017, 336 non-need-based awards were made. *Average percent of need met:* 82. *Average financial aid package:* $31,319. *Average need-based loan:* $5507. *Average need-based gift aid:* $26,380. *Average non-need-based aid:* $23,705. *Average indebtedness upon graduation:* $39,559.

APPLYING

Standardized Tests *Required:* SAT or ACT (for admission).

Options: electronic application, early action, deferred entrance.

Required: high school transcript, minimum 2.5 GPA. *Recommended:* secondary school report.

Application deadlines: rolling (freshmen), rolling (transfers).

Notification: continuous (freshmen), continuous (transfers).

CONTACT

Tara Winter, Director of Student Recruitment, Wartburg College, 100 Wartburg Boulevard, PO Box 1003, Waverly, IA 50677-0903. *Phone:* 319-352-8475. *Toll-free phone:* 800-772-2085. *Fax:* 319-352-8579. *E-mail:* admissions@wartburg.edu.

William Penn University

Oskaloosa, Iowa

http://www.wmpenn.edu/

- **Independent** comprehensive, founded 1873, affiliated with Society of Friends
- **Rural** 60-acre campus with easy access to Des Moines
- **Endowment** $4.7 million
- **Coed**
- **Moderately difficult** entrance level

FACULTY
Student/faculty ratio: 18:1.

ACADEMICS
Calendar: semesters. *Degrees:* bachelor's and master's.
Library: Wilcox Library plus 1 other. *Books:* 61,804 (physical), 162,694 (digital/electronic); *Serial titles:* 54 (physical), 48,768 (digital/electronic); *Databases:* 38. Weekly public service hours: 92; students can reserve study rooms.

STUDENT LIFE
Housing options: on-campus residence required through sophomore year; coed, men-only, women-only. Campus housing is university owned. Freshman campus housing is guaranteed.

Activities and organizations: drama/theater group, student-run newspaper, radio and television station, choral group, marching band, Greek Council, Biology Club, Education Club, Student Government Association, Computer Club.

Athletics Member NAIA.

Campus security: 24-hour emergency response devices and patrols, late-night transport/escort service, controlled dormitory access.

Student services: health clinic, personal/psychological counseling.

COSTS & FINANCIAL AID
Costs (2018–19) *Comprehensive fee:* $32,552 includes full-time tuition ($24,870), mandatory fees ($730), and room and board ($6952). Full-time tuition and fees vary according to class time, course load, degree level, location, and program. Part-time tuition: $380 per credit hour. Part-time tuition and fees vary according to class time, course load, degree level, location, and program. *Required fees:* $19 per credit hour part-time. *College room only:* $3102. Room and board charges vary according to housing facility.

Financial Aid Of all full-time matriculated undergraduates who enrolled in 2005, 808 applied for aid, 768 were judged to have need, 238 had their need fully met. 511 Federal Work-Study jobs (averaging $1287). 1 state and other part-time job (averaging $1103). In 2005, 2 non-need-based awards were made. *Average percent of need met:* 82. *Average financial aid package:* $17,782. *Average need-based loan:* $4600. *Average need-based gift aid:* $11,300. *Average non-need-based aid:* $4500. *Average indebtedness upon graduation:* $22,169.

APPLYING
Standardized Tests *Required:* SAT or ACT (for admission).

Options: electronic application, deferred entrance.

Required: high school transcript, minimum 2.0 GPA. *Required for some:* essay or personal statement, letters of recommendation, interview.

CONTACT
Ms. Kerra Strong, Vice President for Enrollment Management, William Penn University, 201 Trueblood Avenue, Oskaloosa, IA 52577-1799. *Phone:* 641-673-1012. *Fax:* 641-673-2113. *E-mail:* admissions@wmpenn.edu.

KANSAS

Baker University

Baldwin City, Kansas

http://www.bakeru.edu/

- **Independent United Methodist** comprehensive, founded 1858
- **Small-town** 26-acre campus with easy access to Kansas City
- **Endowment** $38.6 million
- **Coed** 1,214 undergraduate students, 70% full-time, 50% women, 50% men
- **Moderately difficult** entrance level, 88% of applicants were admitted

UNDERGRAD STUDENTS
850 full-time, 364 part-time. Students come from 27 states and territories; 15 other countries; 28% are from out of state; 9% Black or African American, non-Hispanic/Latino; 9% Hispanic/Latino; 0.9% Asian, non-Hispanic/Latino; 0.6% Native Hawaiian or other Pacific Islander, non-Hispanic/Latino; 0.8% American Indian or Alaska Native, non-Hispanic/Latino; 6% Two or more races, non-Hispanic/Latino; 1% Race/ethnicity unknown; 3% international; 5% transferred in; 83% live on campus.

Freshmen:
Admission: 804 applied, 704 admitted, 244 enrolled. *Average high school GPA:* 3.5. *Test scores:* ACT scores over 18: 134%; ACT scores over 24: 81%; ACT scores over 30: 44%.
Retention: 81% of full-time freshmen returned.

FACULTY
Total: 99, 60% full-time, 65% with terminal degrees.
Student/faculty ratio: 13:1.

ACADEMICS
Calendar: 4-1-4 semesters for nursing program. *Degrees:* bachelor's, master's, and doctoral (profile includes information primarily for undergraduate residential campus in Baldwin City, KS).

Special study options: advanced placement credit, double majors, honors programs, independent study, internships, services for LD students, student-designed majors, study abroad, summer session for credit. *ROTC:* Army (c), Air Force (c).

Unusual degree programs: 3-2 engineering with Washington University in St. Louis, University of Kansas, Kansas State University, University of Missouri–Kansas City.

Computers: 140 computers/terminals are available on campus for general student use. Students can access the following: computer help desk, free student e-mail accounts, online (class) grades, online (class) registration, online (class) schedules. Campuswide network is available. 100% of college-owned or -operated housing units are wired for high-speed Internet access. Wireless service is available via entire campus.
Library: Baker University Library. *Books:* 66,909 (physical), 186,955 (digital/electronic); *Serial titles:* 4,188 (physical), 35,698 (digital/electronic); *Databases:* 50. Weekly public service hours: 73; study areas open 24 hours, 5–7 days a week; students can reserve study rooms.

STUDENT LIFE
Housing options: on-campus residence required through senior year; coed, men-only, women-only, special housing for students with disabilities. Campus housing is university owned. Freshman campus housing is guaranteed.

Activities and organizations: drama/theater group, student-run newspaper, radio and television station, choral group, Exercise Science Student Alliance, Baker University Speech Choir, Mungano, Student Senate, Student Activities Council, national fraternities, national sororities.

Athletics Member NAIA. *Intercollegiate sports:* baseball M(s), basketball M(s)/W(s), bowling M(s)/W(s), cheerleading M(s)/W(s), cross-country running M(s)/W(s), football M(s), golf M(s), soccer M(s)/W(s), softball W(s), tennis M(s)/W(s), track and field M(s)/W(s), volleyball W(s), wrestling M(s)/W(s). *Intramural sports:* basketball M/W, football M/W, sand volleyball M/W, softball M/W, table tennis M/W, ultimate Frisbee M/W, volleyball M/W.

Campus security: 24-hour emergency response devices and patrols, controlled dormitory access.

Student services: health clinic, personal/psychological counseling.

COSTS & FINANCIAL AID
Costs (2019–20) *One-time required fee:* $100. *Comprehensive fee:* $39,130 includes full-time tuition ($29,300), mandatory fees ($580), and room and board ($9250). Part-time tuition: $945 per credit hour. *Required fees:* $200 per year part-time.

Financial Aid Of all full-time matriculated undergraduates who enrolled in 2017, 749 applied for aid, 665 were judged to have need. In 2017, 158 non-need-based awards were made. *Average percent of need met:* 86. *Average financial aid package:* $27,538. *Average need-based loan:* $4817. *Average need-based gift aid:* $6261. *Average non-need-based aid:* $9950. *Average indebtedness upon graduation:* $35,161.

APPLYING
Standardized Tests *Required:* SAT or ACT (for admission).

Options: electronic application, deferred entrance.

Required: high school transcript. *Required for some:* essay or personal statement, 1 letter of recommendation, interview, ACT or SAT scores.

Application deadlines: rolling (freshmen), rolling (transfers).

CONTACT
Mrs. Emma Carter, Director of Admissions, Baker University, PO Box 65, Baldwin City, KS 66006-0065. *Phone:* 785-594-8327. *Toll-free phone:* 800-873-4282. *Fax:* 785-594-8353. *E-mail:* admissions@bakeru.edu.

Barclay College
Haviland, Kansas
http://www.barclaycollege.edu/

- **Independent** comprehensive, founded 1917, affiliated with Society of Friends
- **Rural** 17-acre campus
- **Endowment** $1.5 million
- **Coed**
- **Minimally difficult** entrance level

FACULTY
Student/faculty ratio: 10:1.

ACADEMICS
Calendar: semesters. *Degrees:* certificates, associate, bachelor's, and master's.
Library: Worden Memorial Library. *Books:* 44,420 (physical), 23 (digital/electronic); *Serial titles:* 410 (physical), 4 (digital/electronic); *Databases:* 48. Weekly public service hours: 95.

STUDENT LIFE
Housing options: on-campus residence required through senior year; men-only, women-only. Campus housing is university owned. Freshman campus housing is guaranteed.

Activities and organizations: drama/theater group, choral group.

Athletics Member NCCAA.

Campus security: student patrols.

Student services: personal/psychological counseling.

FINANCIAL AID
Financial Aid Of all full-time matriculated undergraduates who enrolled in 2017, 146 applied for aid, 146 were judged to have need. 53 Federal Work-Study jobs (averaging $1545). 53 state and other part-time jobs (averaging $1545). In 2017, 11 non-need-based awards were made. *Average percent of need met:* 45. *Average financial aid package:* $19,529. *Average need-based loan:* $7685. *Average need-based gift aid:* $11,843. *Average non-need-based aid:* $13,869. *Average indebtedness upon graduation:* $19,926.

APPLYING
Standardized Tests *Required:* SAT or ACT (for admission).

Options: electronic application, early admission, deferred entrance.

Application fee: $15.

Required: essay or personal statement, high school transcript, minimum 2.3 GPA, 2 letters of recommendation, interview.

CONTACT
Mr. Justin Kendall, Admissions Recruiter, Barclay College, 607 North Kingman, Haviland, KS 67059. *Phone:* 620-862-5252 Ext. 21. *Toll-free phone:* 800-862-0226. *Fax:* 620-862-5242. *E-mail:* jkendall@barclaycollege.edu.

Benedictine College
Atchison, Kansas
http://www.benedictine.edu/

- **Independent Roman Catholic** comprehensive, founded 1859
- **Small-town** 225-acre campus with easy access to Kansas City
- **Endowment** $24.3 million
- **Coed**
- **Minimally difficult** entrance level

FACULTY
Student/faculty ratio: 13:1.

ACADEMICS
Calendar: semesters. *Degrees:* certificates, diplomas, associate, bachelor's, master's, and postbachelor's certificates.
Library: Benedictine College Library. *Books:* 198,277 (physical), 139,987 (digital/electronic); *Serial titles:* 45,794 (physical), 400 (digital/electronic); *Databases:* 88. Weekly public service hours: 85.

STUDENT LIFE
Housing options: on-campus residence required through senior year; men-only, women-only. Campus housing is university owned. Freshman campus housing is guaranteed.

Activities and organizations: drama/theater group, student-run newspaper, choral group, marching band, Student Government, ENACTUS, Knights of Columbus, Concert Chorale/Chamber Singers, Ravens Respect Life.

Athletics Member NAIA.

Campus security: 24-hour emergency response devices and patrols, late-night transport/escort service, controlled dormitory access.

Student services: health clinic, personal/psychological counseling.

COSTS & FINANCIAL AID
Costs (2018–19) *Comprehensive fee:* $39,530 includes full-time tuition ($28,730), mandatory fees ($800), and room and board ($10,000). Full-time tuition and fees vary according to course load and degree level. Part-time tuition: $825 per credit hour. Part-time tuition and fees vary according to course load and degree level. *College room only:* $5340. Room and board charges vary according to board plan and housing facility.

Financial Aid Of all full-time matriculated undergraduates who enrolled in 2017, 1,441 applied for aid, 1,228 were judged to have need, 295 had their need fully met. 291 Federal Work-Study jobs (averaging $620). In 2017, 571 non-need-based awards were made. *Average percent of need met:* 80. *Average financial aid package:* $23,698. *Average need-based loan:* $4984. *Average need-based gift aid:* $15,796. *Average non-need-based aid:* $12,748. *Average indebtedness upon graduation:* $29,196.

APPLYING
Standardized Tests *Required:* SAT or ACT (for admission).

Options: electronic application, deferred entrance.

Application fee: $50.

Required: high school transcript, minimum 2.0 GPA, 1 letter of recommendation. *Required for some:* interview.

CONTACT
Mr. Pete Helgesen, Dean of Enrollment Management, Benedictine College, 1020 North 2nd Street, Atchison, KS 66002-1499. *Phone:* 913-367-5340 Ext. 2476. *Toll-free phone:* 800-467-5340. *E-mail:* phelgesen@benedictine.edu.

Bethany College
Lindsborg, Kansas
http://www.bethanylb.edu/

CONTACT
Katie Laier, Dean of Admissions and Financial Aid, Bethany College, 335 East Swensson Avenue, Lindsborg, KS 67456-1895. *Phone:* 785-227-3311 Ext. 8344. *Toll-free phone:* 800-826-2281. *Fax:* 785-227-8993. *E-mail:* admissions@bethanylb.edu.

Bethel College

North Newton, Kansas

http://www.bethelks.edu/

- **Independent** 4-year, founded 1887, affiliated with Mennonite Church USA
- **Small-town** 90-acre campus with easy access to Wichita
- **Endowment** $18.9 million
- **Coed** 444 undergraduate students, 97% full-time, 54% women, 46% men
- **Moderately difficult** entrance level, 44% of applicants were admitted

UNDERGRAD STUDENTS

430 full-time, 14 part-time. Students come from 25 states and territories; 6 other countries; 33% are from out of state; 15% Black or African American, non-Hispanic/Latino; 9% Hispanic/Latino; 2% Asian, non-Hispanic/Latino; 0.9% American Indian or Alaska Native, non-Hispanic/Latino; 2% Two or more races, non-Hispanic/Latino; 2% international; 11% transferred in; 66% live on campus.

Freshmen:

Admission: 1,093 applied, 482 admitted, 107 enrolled. *Average high school GPA:* 3.5. *Test scores:* ACT scores over 18: 81%; ACT scores over 24: 30%; ACT scores over 30: 5%.

Retention: 56% of full-time freshmen returned.

FACULTY

Total: 73, 55% full-time, 44% with terminal degrees.

Student/faculty ratio: 10:1.

ACADEMICS

Calendar: 4-1-4. *Degree:* certificates and bachelor's.

Special study options: adult/continuing education programs, advanced placement credit, cooperative education, double majors, honors programs, independent study, internships, part-time degree program, services for LD students, student-designed majors, study abroad, summer session for credit.

Computers: 47 computers/terminals and 500 ports are available on campus for general student use. Students can access the following: campus intranet, computer help desk, free student e-mail accounts, online (class) grades, online (class) registration, online (class) schedules. Campuswide network is available. 100% of college-owned or -operated housing units are wired for high-speed Internet access. Wireless service is available via entire campus.

Library: Mantz Library plus 1 other. *Books:* 120,875 (physical), 155,552 (digital/electronic); *Serial titles:* 2,990 (physical), 109,552 (digital/electronic); *Databases:* 97. Weekly public service hours: 91; students can reserve study rooms.

STUDENT LIFE

Housing options: on-campus residence required through senior year; coed, special housing for students with disabilities. Campus housing is university owned. Freshman campus housing is guaranteed.

Activities and organizations: drama/theater group, student-run newspaper, radio and television station, choral group, FEMCORE, Fellowship of Christian Athletes, Rock-climbing Club, Social Work Student Organization, We-Belong or Business Club.

Athletics Member NAIA. *Intercollegiate sports:* basketball M(s)/W(s), cheerleading M(s)/W(s), cross-country running M(s)/W(s), football M(s), golf M(s), soccer M(s)/W(s), softball W(s), tennis M(s)/W(s), track and field M(s)/W(s), volleyball W(s). *Intramural sports:* badminton M/W, basketball M/W, soccer M/W, ultimate Frisbee M/W, volleyball M/W.

Campus security: 24-hour emergency response devices and patrols, controlled dormitory access, SMS Alert System.

Student services: health clinic, personal/psychological counseling.

COSTS & FINANCIAL AID

Costs (2019–20) *Comprehensive fee:* $38,370 includes full-time tuition ($29,150), mandatory fees ($240), and room and board ($8980). *College room only:* $4340.

Financial Aid Of all full-time matriculated undergraduates who enrolled in 2018, 424 applied for aid, 386 were judged to have need, 94 had their need fully met. In 2018, 38 non-need-based awards were made. *Average percent of need met:* 83. *Average financial aid package:* $27,796. *Average need-based loan:* $9341. *Average need-based gift aid:* $5583.

Average non-need-based aid: $13,545. *Average indebtedness upon graduation:* $5633.

APPLYING

Standardized Tests *Required:* SAT or ACT (for admission).

Options: electronic application, deferred entrance.

Required: high school transcript. *Required for some:* essay or personal statement, minimum 2.5 GPA, 2 letters of recommendation. *Recommended:* interview.

Application deadlines: rolling (freshmen), rolling (transfers), rolling (early action).

Early decision deadline: rolling (for plan 1), rolling (for plan 2).

Notification: continuous (freshmen), continuous (transfers), rolling (early decision plan 1), rolling (early decision plan 2), rolling (early action).

CONTACT

Mr. Andy Johnson, Vice President for Admissions, Bethel College, 300 East 27th Street, North Newton, KS 67117-0531. *Phone:* 316-284-5230. *Toll-free phone:* 800-522-1887 Ext. 230. *Fax:* 316-284-5870. *E-mail:* admissions@bethelks.edu.

Central Christian College of Kansas

McPherson, Kansas

http://www.centralchristian.edu/

CONTACT

Central Christian College of Kansas, 1200 South Main, PO Box 1403, McPherson, KS 67460-5799. *Phone:* 620-241-0723 Ext. 380. *Toll-free phone:* 800-835-0078.

Cleveland University–Kansas City

Overland Park, Kansas

http://www.cleveland.edu/

CONTACT

Ms. Melissa Denton, Director of Admissions, Cleveland University–Kansas City, 10850 Lowell Avenue, Overland Park, KS 66210. *Phone:* 913-234-0750. *Toll-free phone:* 800-467-2252. *Fax:* 913-234-0906. *E-mail:* kc.admissions@cleveland.edu.

Donnelly College

Kansas City, Kansas

http://www.donnelly.edu/

- **Independent Roman Catholic** primarily 2-year, founded 1949
- **Urban** 4-acre campus
- **Coed**
- **Noncompetitive** entrance level

FACULTY

Student/faculty ratio: 11:1.

ACADEMICS

Calendar: semesters. *Degrees:* certificates, associate, and bachelor's.

Library: Trant Memorial Library plus 1 other.

STUDENT LIFE

Housing options: men-only, women-only. Campus housing is university owned.

Activities and organizations: Organization of Student Leadership, Student Ambassadors, Healthy Student Task Force, Men's Soccer Club, Women's Soccer Club.

Campus security: 24-hour emergency response devices.

Student services: personal/psychological counseling.

COSTS

Costs (2018–19) *Tuition:* $7080 full-time, $295 per credit hour part-time. Full-time tuition and fees vary according to course load, degree level, and program. Part-time tuition and fees vary according to course load, degree level, and program. *Required fees:* $180 full-time, $5 per credit hour part-time, $30 per term part-time.

APPLYING

Options: electronic application, early admission, deferred entrance.

Recommended: high school transcript.

CONTACT
Ms. Kimkisha Stevenson, Director of Admissions, Donnelly College, 608 North 18th Street, Kansas City, KS 66102. *Phone:* 913-621-8762. *Fax:* 913-621-8719. *E-mail:* admissions@donnelly.edu.

Emporia State University

Emporia, Kansas
http://www.emporia.edu/

- **State-supported** comprehensive, founded 1863, part of Kansas State Board of Regents
- **Small-town** 207-acre campus with easy access to Wichita
- **Endowment** $74.4 million
- **Coed**
- **Noncompetitive** entrance level

FACULTY
Student/faculty ratio: 17:1.

ACADEMICS
Calendar: semesters. *Degrees:* bachelor's, master's, doctoral, post-master's, and postbachelor's certificates.
Library: William Allen White Library plus 1 other. *Books:* 389,595 (physical), 153,016 (digital/electronic); *Serial titles:* 35,153 (physical), 278 (digital/electronic); *Databases:* 97. Weekly public service hours: 79; study areas open 24 hours, 5–7 days a week; students can reserve study rooms.

STUDENT LIFE
Housing options: on-campus residence required for freshman year; coed, men-only, women-only, special housing for students with disabilities. Campus housing is university owned. Freshman campus housing is guaranteed.

Activities and organizations: drama/theater group, student-run newspaper, radio station, choral group, marching band, Phi Eta Sigma, Student Chapter of the American Library Association of ESU, TradPlus Student Organization, Arabic Culture Student Organization, Emporia Kansas Association of Nursing Students, national fraternities, national sororities.

Athletics Member NCAA. All Division II.

Campus security: 24-hour emergency response devices and patrols, student patrols, late-night transport/escort service, controlled dormitory access, 24-hour residence hall monitoring, safety and self-awareness programs.

Student services: health clinic, personal/psychological counseling, women's center, legal services.

COSTS & FINANCIAL AID
Costs (2018–19) *Tuition:* state resident $5154 full-time, $172 per credit hour part-time; nonresident $19,071 full-time, $636 per credit hour part-time. Full-time tuition and fees vary according to course load, degree level, and location. Part-time tuition and fees vary according to course load, degree level, and location. *Required fees:* $1604 full-time, $89 per credit hour part-time. *Room and board:* $8912; room only: $5280. Room and board charges vary according to board plan, housing facility, and location. *Payment plans:* installment, deferred payment.

Financial Aid Of all full-time matriculated undergraduates who enrolled in 2018, 2,560 applied for aid, 2,020 were judged to have need, 325 had their need fully met. 196 Federal Work-Study jobs (averaging $2312). 20 state and other part-time jobs (averaging $2111). In 2018, 607 non-need-based awards were made. *Average percent of need met:* 61. *Average financial aid package:* $9377. *Average need-based loan:* $6080. *Average need-based gift aid:* $6077. *Average non-need-based aid:* $3082. *Average indebtedness upon graduation:* $22,878.

APPLYING
Standardized Tests *Required:* SAT or ACT (for admission).
Options: electronic application, early admission, deferred entrance.
Application fee: $30.
Required: high school transcript, minimum ACT score of 21, or rank in the top 1/3 and completed QA core classes with cum 2.0 GPA, 22 Math subscore, or completed 4th year of math. *Recommended:* minimum 2.0 GPA.

CONTACT
Ms. Roxie Pearson, Associate Director of Data Management, Emporia State University, 1 Kellogg Circle, Campus Box 4034, Emporia, KS 66801-5087. *Phone:* 620-341-5465. *Toll-free phone:* 877-GOTOESU (in-state); 877-468-6378 (out-of-state). *Fax:* 620-341-5599. *E-mail:* go2esu@emporia.edu.

Fort Hays State University

Hays, Kansas
http://www.fhsu.edu/

CONTACT
Tricia Cline, Director, Admissions, Fort Hays State University, 600 Park Street, Hays, KS 67601-4099. *Phone:* 785-628-4091. *Toll-free phone:* 800-628-FHSU. *E-mail:* tcline@fhsu.edu.

Friends University

Wichita, Kansas
http://www.friends.edu/

- **Independent** comprehensive, founded 1898, affiliated with Christian non-denominational
- **Urban** 55-acre campus
- **Endowment** $49.1 million
- **Coed**
- **Moderately difficult** entrance level

FACULTY
Student/faculty ratio: 10:1.

ACADEMICS
Calendar: semesters. *Degrees:* bachelor's and master's.
Library: Edmund Stanley Library plus 1 other. *Books:* 88,223 (physical), 141,741 (digital/electronic); *Serial titles:* 202 (physical); *Databases:* 102.

STUDENT LIFE
Housing options: on-campus residence required for freshman year; coed. Campus housing is university owned.

Activities and organizations: drama/theater group, choral group, Concert Choir, Singing Quakers, Zoo Science Club, Psychology Club, Spanish Club.

Athletics Member NAIA.

Campus security: 24-hour emergency response devices and patrols, late-night transport/escort service, controlled dormitory access.

Student services: health clinic, personal/psychological counseling.

COSTS & FINANCIAL AID
Costs (2018–19) *Comprehensive fee:* $36,387 includes full-time tuition ($27,965), mandatory fees ($450), and room and board ($7972). Full-time tuition and fees vary according to class time, course load, degree level, and location. Part-time tuition: $932 per credit hour. Part-time tuition and fees vary according to class time, course load, degree level, and location. *College room only:* $3800. Room and board charges vary according to board plan and housing facility.

Financial Aid Of all full-time matriculated undergraduates who enrolled in 2015, 905 applied for aid, 805 were judged to have need, 283 had their need fully met. 204 Federal Work-Study jobs (averaging $1091). 252 state and other part-time jobs (averaging $1306). In 2015, 100 non-need-based awards were made. *Average percent of need met:* 82. *Average financial aid package:* $16,394. *Average need-based loan:* $4158. *Average need-based gift aid:* $8359. *Average non-need-based aid:* $8975. *Average indebtedness upon graduation:* $28,175.

APPLYING
Standardized Tests *Required for some:* SAT or ACT (for admission). *Recommended:* ACT (for admission), SAT and SAT Subject Tests or ACT (for admission).

Options: electronic application.

Required for some: high school transcript, minimum 2.0 GPA, interview, audition for music, dance and theater programs; portfolio for art program.

CONTACT
Mrs. Miya Williams, Director of Admissions, Friends University, 2100 West University Avenue, Wichita, KS 67213. *Phone:* 316-295-5100. *Toll-free phone:* 800-794-6945. *Fax:* 316-295-5101. *E-mail:* learn@friends.edu.

Grantham University

Lenexa, Kansas
http://www.grantham.edu/

CONTACT
Mr. Les Hyde, Vice President Admissions, Grantham University, 7200 NW 86th Street, Kansas City, MO 64153. *Phone:* 800-955-2527. *Toll-free phone:* 800-955-2527. *Fax:* 816-595-5757. *E-mail:* admissions@ grantham.edu.

Haskell Indian Nations University

Lawrence, Kansas
http://www.haskell.edu/

CONTACT
Ms. Patty Grant, Recruitment Officer, Haskell Indian Nations University, 155 Indian Avenue, #5031, Lawrence, KS 66046-4800. *Phone:* 785-749-8437 Ext. 437.

Hesston College

Hesston, Kansas
http://www.hesston.edu/

- **Independent Mennonite** primarily 2-year, founded 1909
- **Small-town** 50-acre campus with easy access to Wichita
- **Endowment** $12.9 million
- **Coed**
- **Noncompetitive** entrance level

FACULTY
Student/faculty ratio: 8:1.

ACADEMICS
Calendar: semesters. *Degrees:* associate and bachelor's.
Library: Mary Miller Library. Students can reserve study rooms.

STUDENT LIFE
Housing options: on-campus residence required through sophomore year; men-only, women-only. Campus housing is university owned. Freshman campus housing is guaranteed.

Activities and organizations: drama/theater group, student-run newspaper, choral group, Peace and Service Club, Intramural Sports, Ministry Assistants.

Athletics Member NJCAA.

Campus security: 24-hour emergency response devices, controlled dormitory access.

Student services: personal/psychological counseling.

COSTS & FINANCIAL AID
Costs (2018–19) *Comprehensive fee:* $35,700 includes full-time tuition ($26,460), mandatory fees ($440), and room and board ($8800). Full-time tuition and fees vary according to course load and program. Part-time tuition: $1102 per credit hour. Part-time tuition and fees vary according to course load. *Required fees:* $110 per term part-time. *Payment plans:* installment, deferred payment.

Financial Aid Of all full-time matriculated undergraduates who enrolled in 2017, 120 Federal Work-Study jobs (averaging $800).

APPLYING
Standardized Tests *Required:* SAT or ACT (for admission).

Options: electronic application, early admission, deferred entrance.

Required: high school transcript. *Required for some:* 2 letters of recommendation, interview.

CONTACT
Rachel Swartzendruber-Miller, Vice President of Admissions, Hesston College, Hesston, KS 67062. *Phone:* 620-327-8206. *Toll-free phone:* 800-995-2757. *Fax:* 620-327-8300. *E-mail:* admissions@hesston.edu.

Kansas State University

Manhattan, Kansas
http://www.k-state.edu/

- **State-supported** university, founded 1863, part of Kansas Board of Regents
- **Suburban** 668-acre campus
- **Endowment** $506.4 million
- **Coed**
- **Minimally difficult** entrance level

FACULTY
Student/faculty ratio: 18:1.

ACADEMICS
Calendar: semesters. *Degrees:* certificates, associate, bachelor's, master's, doctoral, and postbachelor's certificates.
Library: Hale Library plus 3 others. *Books:* 1.3 million (physical), 1.5 million (digital/electronic); *Serial titles:* 51,881 (physical), 114,285 (digital/electronic); *Databases:* 278. Weekly public service hours: 80; study areas open 24 hours, 5–7 days a week; students can reserve study rooms.

STUDENT LIFE
Housing options: coed, men-only, women-only, cooperative. Campus housing is university owned.

Activities and organizations: drama/theater group, student-run newspaper, radio and television station, choral group, marching band, athletic department groups, marching band, Union Governing Board, theater productions, debate team, national fraternities, national sororities.

Athletics Member NCAA. All Division I except football (Division I-A).

Campus security: 24-hour emergency response devices and patrols, late-night transport/escort service, controlled dormitory access.

Student services: health clinic, personal/psychological counseling, women's center, legal services.

COSTS & FINANCIAL AID
Costs (2018–19) *Tuition:* state resident $9375 full-time; nonresident $24,879 full-time. Full-time tuition and fees vary according to course level, course load, degree level, location, program, and reciprocity agreements. Part-time tuition and fees vary according to course level, course load, degree level, location, program, and reciprocity agreements. *Required fees:* $1008 full-time. *Room and board:* $9680. Room and board charges vary according to board plan, housing facility, and location. *Payment plans:* installment, deferred payment.

Financial Aid Of all full-time matriculated undergraduates who enrolled in 2016, 11,643 applied for aid, 8,771 were judged to have need, 1,667 had their need fully met. In 2016, 1542 non-need-based awards were made. *Average percent of need met:* 78. *Average financial aid package:* $13,182. *Average need-based loan:* $4454. *Average need-based gift aid:* $4299. *Average non-need-based aid:* $4421. *Average indebtedness upon graduation:* $28,318.

APPLYING
Standardized Tests *Required for some:* SAT or ACT (for admission). *Recommended:* SAT or ACT (for admission).

Options: electronic application, early admission.

Application fee: $40.

Required: high school transcript, minimum 2.0 GPA, minimum ACT composite of 21 or top third of high school graduating class.

CONTACT
Ms. Molly McGaughey, Associate Director of Admissions, Kansas State University, 119 Anderson Hall, Manhattan, KS 66506. *Phone:* 785-532-6250. *Toll-free phone:* 800-432-8270. *Fax:* 785-532-6393. *E-mail:* k-state@k-state.edu.

Kansas State University Polytechnic Campus

Salina, Kansas

http://www.polytechnic.k-state.edu/

CONTACT
Kansas State University Polytechnic Campus, 2310 Centennial Road, Salina, KS 67401.

Kansas Wesleyan University

Salina, Kansas

http://www.kwu.edu/

- **Independent United Methodist** comprehensive, founded 1886
- **Small-town** 28-acre campus
- **Endowment** $12.2 million
- **Coed** 668 undergraduate students, 91% full-time, 40% women, 60% men
- **Moderately difficult** entrance level, 47% of applicants were admitted

UNDERGRAD STUDENTS

606 full-time, 62 part-time. Students come from 34 states and territories; 10 other countries; 57% are from out of state; 13% Black or African American, non-Hispanic/Latino; 16% Hispanic/Latino; 0.5% Asian, non-Hispanic/Latino; 0.3% Native Hawaiian or other Pacific Islander, non-Hispanic/Latino; 0.3% American Indian or Alaska Native, non-Hispanic/Latino; 5% Two or more races, non-Hispanic/Latino; 2% Race/ethnicity unknown; 2% international; 12% transferred in; 60% live on campus.

Freshmen:
Admission: 860 applied, 403 admitted, 145 enrolled. *Average high school GPA:* 3.4. *Test scores:* SAT evidence-based reading and writing scores over 500: 70%; SAT math scores over 500: 77%; ACT scores over 18: 87%; SAT evidence-based reading and writing scores over 600: 17%; SAT math scores over 600: 13%; ACT scores over 24: 41%; ACT scores over 30: 5%.
Retention: 58% of full-time freshmen returned.

FACULTY

Total: 87, 54% full-time, 37% with terminal degrees.
Student/faculty ratio: 13:1.

ACADEMICS

Calendar: semesters plus summer term. *Degrees:* associate, bachelor's, and master's.

Special study options: academic remediation for entering students, advanced placement credit, distance learning, double majors, honors programs, independent study, internships, off-campus study, part-time degree program, services for LD students, student-designed majors, study abroad, summer session for credit.

Unusual degree programs: 3-2 engineering with Washington University in St. Louis; Ecospheric Studies with Western Colorado State University Christian Leadership with St. Paul's School of Theology (3+3).

Computers: 195 computers/terminals are available on campus for general student use. Students can access the following: computer help desk, free student e-mail accounts, online (class) grades, online (class) registration, online (class) schedules. Campuswide network is available. 100% of college-owned or -operated housing units are wired for high-speed Internet access. Wireless service is available via entire campus.
Library: Memorial Library. *Books:* 63,237 (physical), 7,273 (digital/electronic); *Serial titles:* 402 (physical); *Databases:* 69. Weekly public service hours: 86; students can reserve study rooms.

STUDENT LIFE

Housing options: on-campus residence required through sophomore year; coed, men-only, women-only. Campus housing is university owned. Freshman campus housing is guaranteed.

Activities and organizations: drama/theater group, student-run newspaper, radio and television station, choral group, Fellowship of Christian Athletes, Student Government, Wesleyan Chorale, Coyote Gaming Club, Coyote Activities Board.

Athletics Member NAIA. *Intercollegiate sports:* baseball M(s), basketball M(s)/W(s), bowling M(s)/W(s), cheerleading M(s)/W(s), cross-country running M(s)/W(s), football M(s), golf M(s)/W(s), soccer M(s)/W(s), softball W(s), tennis M(s)/W(s), track and field M(s)/W(s), volleyball W(s), wrestling M(s). *Intramural sports:* basketball M/W, bowling M/W, football M/W, sand volleyball M/W, softball M/W, table tennis M/W, ultimate Frisbee M/W, volleyball M/W.

Campus security: 24-hour emergency response devices, student patrols, late-night transport/escort service, controlled dormitory access.
Student services: personal/psychological counseling.

COSTS & FINANCIAL AID

Costs (2019–20) *One-time required fee:* $200. *Comprehensive fee:* $39,300 includes full-time tuition ($29,500) and room and board ($9800). Part-time tuition: $3000 per term.
Financial Aid Of all full-time matriculated undergraduates who enrolled in 2016, 657 applied for aid, 559 were judged to have need, 105 had their need fully met. 98 Federal Work-Study jobs (averaging $1488). 31 state and other part-time jobs (averaging $828). In 2016, 82 non-need-based awards were made. *Average percent of need met:* 68. *Average financial aid package:* $21,316. *Average need-based loan:* $4294. *Average need-based gift aid:* $7695. *Average non-need-based aid:* $11,252. *Average indebtedness upon graduation:* $34,526.

APPLYING

Standardized Tests *Required:* SAT or ACT (for admission).
Options: electronic application, deferred entrance.
Application fee: $20.
Required: high school transcript, minimum 2.5 GPA. *Required for some:* essay or personal statement, interview.
Application deadlines: rolling (freshmen), rolling (transfers).
Notification: continuous (freshmen), continuous (transfers).

CONTACT
Mr. Esteban Paredes, Director of Admissions, Kansas Wesleyan University, 100 East Claflin Avenue, Box 20, Salina, KS 67401. *Phone:* 785-833-4307. *Toll-free phone:* 800-874-1154 Ext. 1285. *Fax:* 785-404-1485. *E-mail:* esteban.paredes@kwu.edu.

Manhattan Christian College

Manhattan, Kansas

http://www.mccks.edu/

CONTACT
Ms. Connie Hill, Admissions Office Manager, Manhattan Christian College, 1415 Anderson Avenue, Manhattan, KS 66502. *Phone:* 877-246-4622 Ext. 212. *Toll-free phone:* 877-246-4622. *E-mail:* teka.wilson@mccks.edu.

McPherson College

McPherson, Kansas

http://www.mcpherson.edu/

- **Independent** comprehensive, founded 1887, affiliated with Church of the Brethren
- **Small-town** 26-acre campus
- **Endowment** $39.1 million
- **Coed**
- **Moderately difficult** entrance level

FACULTY

Student/faculty ratio: 13:1.

ACADEMICS

Calendar: 4-1-4. *Degrees:* bachelor's and master's.
Library: Miller Library. *Books:* 42,629 (physical), 164,814 (digital/electronic); *Serial titles:* 681 (physical), 92,937 (digital/electronic); *Databases:* 65. Weekly public service hours: 86; students can reserve study rooms.

STUDENT LIFE

Housing options: coed, men-only, women-only, special housing for students with disabilities. Campus housing is university owned and leased by the school. Freshman campus housing is guaranteed.

Activities and organizations: drama/theater group, student-run newspaper, choral group, Student Activities Board, Student Government

Association, CARS Club, Business Club, Multicultural Student Association.

Athletics Member NAIA.

Campus security: student patrols, controlled dormitory access, Security cameras.

Student services: health clinic, personal/psychological counseling.

COSTS & FINANCIAL AID

Costs (2018–19) *Comprehensive fee:* $37,740 includes full-time tuition ($28,161), mandatory fees ($790), and room and board ($8789). Full-time tuition and fees vary according to course load. Part-time tuition: $430 per credit hour. Part-time tuition and fees vary according to course load. *Required fees:* $50 per term part-time. *Room and board:* Room and board charges vary according to board plan and housing facility.

Financial Aid Of all full-time matriculated undergraduates who enrolled in 2016, 558 applied for aid, 558 were judged to have need, 129 had their need fully met. In 2016, 54 non-need-based awards were made. *Average percent of need met:* 82. *Average financial aid package:* $24,898. *Average need-based loan:* $8592. *Average need-based gift aid:* $5722. *Average non-need-based aid:* $14,626. *Average indebtedness upon graduation:* $28,615.

APPLYING

Standardized Tests *Required:* SAT or ACT (for admission).

Options: electronic application, deferred entrance.

Required: high school transcript, minimum 2.0 GPA.

CONTACT

Ms. Sara Brubaker, Director of Admissions Operations and Financial Aid, McPherson College, 1600 East Euclid, McPherson, KS 67460. *Phone:* 800-365-7402. *Toll-free phone:* 800-365-7402. *E-mail:* admiss@mcpherson.edu.

MidAmerica Nazarene University

Olathe, Kansas

http://www.mnu.edu/

- **Independent** comprehensive, founded 1966, affiliated with Church of the Nazarene
- **Suburban** 105-acre campus with easy access to Kansas City
- **Endowment** $10.6 million
- **Coed**
- **Minimally difficult** entrance level

FACULTY

Student/faculty ratio: 7:1.

ACADEMICS

Calendar: semesters. *Degrees:* associate, bachelor's, master's, post-master's, and postbachelor's certificates.
Library: Mabee Library. *Books:* 88,000 (physical), 249,000 (digital/electronic); *Serial titles:* 397 (physical), 25 (digital/electronic); *Databases:* 35. Weekly public service hours: 81; study areas open 24 hours, 5–7 days a week; students can reserve study rooms.

STUDENT LIFE

Housing options: on-campus residence required through senior year; men-only, women-only, special housing for students with disabilities. Campus housing is university owned. Freshman campus housing is guaranteed.

Activities and organizations: drama/theater group, student-run newspaper, radio and television station, choral group, LOL - Loving on Littles, S.M.I.L.E. - Students Ministering in the Lives of Elderly, Center for Grace, Freedom Fire, Students for Social Justice.

Athletics Member NAIA.

Campus security: 24-hour emergency response devices and patrols, student patrols, late-night transport/escort service, controlled dormitory access.

Student services: personal/psychological counseling, veterans affairs office.

COSTS & FINANCIAL AID

Costs (2018–19) *Comprehensive fee:* $39,444 includes full-time tuition ($29,986), mandatory fees ($750), and room and board ($8708). Full-time tuition and fees vary according to course load, degree level, program, and reciprocity agreements. Part-time tuition: $1119 per credit hour. Part-time tuition and fees vary according to course load, degree level, program, and reciprocity agreements. *College room only:* $4834. Room and board charges vary according to board plan and housing facility.

Financial Aid Of all full-time matriculated undergraduates who enrolled in 2016, 839 applied for aid, 793 were judged to have need, 242 had their need fully met. 100 Federal Work-Study jobs (averaging $1370). In 2016, 146 non-need-based awards were made. *Average percent of need met:* 75. *Average financial aid package:* $25,027. *Average need-based loan:* $7772. *Average need-based gift aid:* $17,239. *Average non-need-based aid:* $17,631. *Average indebtedness upon graduation:* $33,018.

APPLYING

Standardized Tests *Required for some:* SAT or ACT (for admission). *Recommended:* TOEFL for international applicants.

Options: electronic application, deferred entrance.

Required: high school transcript, minimum 2.0 GPA.

CONTACT

Meghan Luoma, MidAmerica Nazarene University, 2030 College Avenue, Olathe, IN 66062. *Phone:* 913-971-3783. *Toll-free phone:* 800-800-8887. *E-mail:* mvluoma@mnu.edu.

National American University

Garden City, Kansas

http://www.national.edu/

CONTACT

National American University, 801 Campus Drive, Garden City, KS 67846.

National American University

Overland Park, Kansas

http://www.national.edu/

CONTACT

Admissions Office, National American University, 10310 Mastin Street, Overland Park, KS 66212. *Toll-free phone:* 866-628-1288.

National American University

Wichita, Kansas

http://www.national.edu/

CONTACT

National American University, 7309 East 21st Street, Suite G40, Wichita, KS 67206. *Toll-free phone:* 877-628-9424.

National American University

Wichita, Kansas

http://www.national.edu/

CONTACT

National American University, 8428 West 13th Street North, Suite 120, Wichita, KS 67212. *Toll-free phone:* 877-628-9424.

Newman University

Wichita, Kansas

http://www.newmanu.edu/

- **Independent Roman Catholic** comprehensive, founded 1933
- **Urban** 61-acre campus with easy access to Sedgwick County
- **Coed**
- **Minimally difficult** entrance level

FACULTY

Student/faculty ratio: 11:1.

ACADEMICS

Calendar: semesters. *Degrees:* associate, bachelor's, and master's.
Library: Dugan Library. Students can reserve study rooms.

STUDENT LIFE

Housing options: on-campus residence required for freshman year; coed. Campus housing is university owned. Freshman campus housing is guaranteed.

Activities and organizations: drama/theater group, student-run newspaper, choral group, Newman University Medical Professionals Club (NUMPC), National Society of Leadership and Success, Student Athlete Advisory Committee, Swing Dance Club, Hispanic American Leadership Organization (HALO).

Athletics Member NCAA. All Division II.

Campus security: 24-hour emergency response devices and patrols, student patrols, late-night transport/escort service, controlled dormitory access.

Student services: personal/psychological counseling.

COSTS & FINANCIAL AID

Costs (2018–19) *Comprehensive fee:* $38,970 includes full-time tuition ($29,260), mandatory fees ($1304), and room and board ($8406). Part-time tuition: $976 per credit hour. Part-time tuition and fees vary according to course load. *College room only:* $4484. Room and board charges vary according to board plan and housing facility.

Financial Aid Of all full-time matriculated undergraduates who enrolled in 2018, 811 applied for aid, 762 were judged to have need, 144 had their need fully met. In 2018, 205 non-need-based awards were made. *Average percent of need met:* 67. *Average financial aid package:* $22,352. *Average need-based loan:* $3967. *Average need-based gift aid:* $19,192. *Average non-need-based aid:* $12,002. *Average indebtedness upon graduation:* $32,133.

APPLYING

Standardized Tests *Required for some:* SAT or ACT (for admission).

Options: electronic application, early admission, deferred entrance.

Required: high school transcript, minimum 2.0 GPA. *Recommended:* interview.

CONTACT

Kristen English, Director of Undergraduate Admissions, Newman University, 3100 McCormick Avenue, Wichita, KS 67213. *Phone:* 316-942-4291 Ext. 2146. *Toll-free phone:* 877-NEWMANU. *Fax:* 316-942-4483. *E-mail:* englishk@newmanu.edu.

Ottawa University

Ottawa, Kansas

http://www.ottawa.edu/

- **Independent American Baptist Churches in the USA** comprehensive, founded 1865
- **Small-town** 64-acre campus with easy access to Kansas City
- **Endowment** $17.6 million
- **Coed** 1,754 undergraduate students, 38% full-time, 60% women, 40% men
- **Moderately difficult** entrance level, 26% of applicants were admitted

UNDERGRAD STUDENTS

673 full-time, 1,081 part-time. Students come from 44 states and territories; 3 other countries; 33% are from out of state; 12% Black or African American, non-Hispanic/Latino; 12% Hispanic/Latino; 2% Asian, non-Hispanic/Latino; 0.3% Native Hawaiian or other Pacific Islander, non-Hispanic/Latino; 3% American Indian or Alaska Native, non-Hispanic/Latino; 4% Two or more races, non-Hispanic/Latino; 6% Race/ethnicity unknown; 80% transferred in; 63% live on campus.

Freshmen:

Admission: 1,168 applied, 302 admitted, 253 enrolled. *Average high school GPA:* 3.1. *Test scores:* SAT evidence-based reading and writing scores over 500: 14%; SAT math scores over 500: 12%; ACT scores over 18: 53%; SAT evidence-based reading and writing scores over 600: 5%; SAT math scores over 600: 3%; ACT scores over 24: 14%; ACT scores over 30: 1%.

Retention: 57% of full-time freshmen returned.

FACULTY

Total: 68, 38% full-time, 26% with terminal degrees.

Student/faculty ratio: 18:1.

ACADEMICS

Calendar: semesters. *Degrees:* certificates, bachelor's, and master's (also offers master's, adult, international and on-line education programs with significant enrollment not reflected in profile).

Special study options: advanced placement credit, distance learning, double majors, independent study, internships, part-time degree program, student-designed majors, study abroad, summer session for credit.

Computers: 40 computers/terminals are available on campus for general student use. Students can access the following: campus intranet, computer help desk, free student e-mail accounts, online (class) grades, online (class) registration, online (class) schedules. Campuswide network is available. 100% of college-owned or -operated housing units are wired for high-speed Internet access. Wireless service is available via entire campus.

Library: Gangwish Library. *Books:* 47,152 (physical), 290,000 (digital/electronic); *Serial titles:* 5 (physical), 424,464 (digital/electronic); *Databases:* 124. Students can reserve study rooms.

STUDENT LIFE

Housing options: on-campus residence required through junior year; coed, women-only. Campus housing is university owned. Freshman campus housing is guaranteed.

Activities and organizations: drama/theater group, student-run newspaper, radio station, choral group, Christian Faith In Action, Student Activities Force, Education Club, Whole Earth Club, Fellowship of Christian Athletes.

Athletics Member NAIA. *Intercollegiate sports:* baseball M(s), basketball M(s)/W(s), bowling M(s)/W(s), cheerleading M(s)/W(s), cross-country running M(s)/W(s), football M(s), golf M(s)/W(s), lacrosse M(s)/W(s), sand volleyball W(s), soccer M(s)/W(s), softball W(s), tennis M(s)/W(s), track and field M(s)/W(s), volleyball M(s)/W(s), weight lifting M(s)/W(s), wrestling M(s)/W(s). *Intramural sports:* basketball M/W, volleyball M/W, weight lifting M/W.

Campus security: 24-hour emergency response devices and patrols, controlled dormitory access.

Student services: health clinic, personal/psychological counseling.

COSTS

Costs (2018–19) *Comprehensive fee:* $35,690 includes full-time tuition ($28,410), mandatory fees ($1280), and room and board ($6000). Full-time tuition and fees vary according to course load and program. Part-time tuition: $1185 per credit hour. Part-time tuition and fees vary according to course load and program. *Required fees:* $531 per year part-time. *College room only:* $5000. Room and board charges vary according to board plan and housing facility. *Payment plan:* installment. *Waivers:* employees or children of employees.

APPLYING

Standardized Tests *Recommended:* SAT or ACT (for admission), SAT and SAT Subject Tests or ACT (for admission).

Options: electronic application.

Application fee: $25.

Required: high school transcript, minimum 2.5 GPA, rank in upper 50% of high school class. *Required for some:* essay or personal statement. *Recommended:* 2 letters of recommendation, interview.

Application deadlines: rolling (freshmen), rolling (transfers).

Notification: continuous (freshmen), continuous (transfers).

CONTACT

Andy J. Stiles, andy.stiles@ottawa.edu, Ottawa University, 1001 S. Cedar St., Ottawa, KS 66067. *Phone:* 785-248-2373. *Toll-free phone:* 800-755-5200. *Fax:* 785-229-1008. *E-mail:* andy.stiles@ottawa.edu.

Pittsburg State University

Pittsburg, Kansas

http://www.pittstate.edu/

- **State-supported** comprehensive, founded 1903, part of Kansas State Board of Regents
- **Small-town** 630-acre campus
- **Coed**
- **Minimally difficult** entrance level

FACULTY
Student/faculty ratio: 18:1.

ACADEMICS
Calendar: semesters. *Degrees:* certificates, associate, bachelor's, master's, doctoral, post-master's, and postbachelor's certificates.
Library: Leonard H. Axe Library plus 2 others.

STUDENT LIFE
Housing options: on-campus residence required for freshman year; coed, special housing for students with disabilities. Campus housing is university owned. Freshman applicants given priority for college housing.

Activities and organizations: drama/theater group, student-run newspaper, radio and television station, choral group, marching band, Student Government Association, student yearbook, student newspaper, Student Activities Council, Students in Free Enterprise (SIFE), national fraternities, national sororities.

Athletics Member NCAA. All Division II.

Campus security: 24-hour emergency response devices and patrols, late-night transport/escort service, controlled dormitory access.

Student services: health clinic, personal/psychological counseling, legal services.

COSTS & FINANCIAL AID
Costs (2018–19) *Tuition:* state resident $5694 full-time, $190 per credit hour part-time; nonresident $17,038 full-time, $568 per credit hour part-time. *Required fees:* $1604 full-time, $72 per credit hour part-time. *Room and board:* $7700. Room and board charges vary according to board plan.

Financial Aid *Average indebtedness upon graduation:* $24,389.

APPLYING
Standardized Tests *Required:* ACT (for admission).

Options: electronic application, deferred entrance.

Application fee: $30.

Required: high school transcript. *Required for some:* minimum 2.0 GPA.

CONTACT
Director of Admission, Pittsburg State University, 1701 South Broadway, Pittsburg, KS 66762. *Phone:* 620-235-4251. *Toll-free phone:* 800-854-7488. *Fax:* 620-235-6003. *E-mail:* psuadmit@pittstate.edu.

Rasmussen College Kansas City/Overland Park
Overland Park, Kansas
http://www.rasmussen.edu/

CONTACT
Ms. Susan Hammerstrom, Director of Admissions, Rasmussen College Kansas City/Overland Park, 11600 College Boulevard, Overland Park, KS 66210. *Phone:* 913-491-7870. *Toll-free phone:* 888-549-6755. *E-mail:* susan.hammerstrom@rasmussen.edu.

Rasmussen College Topeka
Topeka, Kansas
http://www.rasmussen.edu/

CONTACT
Ms. Susan Hammerstrom, Director of Admissions, Rasmussen College Topeka, 620 SW Governor View, Topeka, KS 66606. *Phone:* 785-228-7320. *Toll-free phone:* 888-549-6755. *E-mail:* susan.hammerstrom@rasmussen.edu.

Southwestern College
Winfield, Kansas
http://www.sckans.edu/
- **Independent United Methodist** comprehensive, founded 1885
- **Small-town** 70-acre campus with easy access to Wichita
- **Endowment** $26.5 million
- **Coed**
- **Minimally difficult** entrance level

FACULTY
Student/faculty ratio: 10:1.

ACADEMICS
Calendar: semesters. *Degrees:* certificates, bachelor's, master's, doctoral, and postbachelor's certificates.
Library: Harold and Mary Ellen Deets Library. *Books:* 49,349 (physical), 479,970 (digital/electronic); *Serial titles:* 10 (physical), 21,560 (digital/electronic); *Databases:* 84. Weekly public service hours: 91; students can reserve study rooms.

STUDENT LIFE
Housing options: on-campus residence required through sophomore year; coed, men-only, women-only. Campus housing is university owned. Freshman campus housing is guaranteed.

Activities and organizations: drama/theater group, student-run newspaper, radio and television station, choral group, Discipleship SC, Leadership SC, Student Foundation, Student Government Association, Gaming Club.

Athletics Member NAIA.

Campus security: 24-hour emergency response devices and patrols, late-night transport/escort service, controlled dormitory access.

Student services: personal/psychological counseling, veterans affairs office.

COSTS & FINANCIAL AID
Costs (2018–19) *Comprehensive fee:* $37,910 includes full-time tuition ($30,000), mandatory fees ($150), and room and board ($7760). Full-time tuition and fees vary according to course load, degree level, location, and program. Part-time tuition: $1250 per credit hour. Part-time tuition and fees vary according to course load, degree level, location, and program. *College room only:* $3620. Room and board charges vary according to board plan and housing facility.

Financial Aid Of all full-time matriculated undergraduates who enrolled in 2017, 562 applied for aid, 527 were judged to have need, 45 had their need fully met. 92 Federal Work-Study jobs (averaging $1431). In 2017, 88 non-need-based awards were made. *Average percent of need met:* 69. *Average financial aid package:* $22,374. *Average need-based loan:* $5492. *Average need-based gift aid:* $17,710. *Average non-need-based aid:* $11,949. *Average indebtedness upon graduation:* $36,636.

APPLYING
Standardized Tests *Required:* SAT or ACT (for admission).

Options: electronic application.

Application fee: $25.

Required: high school transcript, minimum 2.6 GPA. *Required for some:* essay or personal statement, 2 letters of recommendation.

CONTACT
Southwestern College, 100 College Street, Winfield, KS 67156-2499. *Phone:* 620-229-6241. *Toll-free phone:* 800-846-1543.

Sterling College
Sterling, Kansas
http://www.sterling.edu/

CONTACT
Marge Jones, Admissions Office Manager, Sterling College, 125 West Cooper, Sterling, KS 67579. *Phone:* 620-278-4275. *Toll-free phone:* 800-346-1017. *Fax:* 620-278-4416. *E-mail:* admissions@sterling.edu.

Tabor College
Hillsboro, Kansas
http://www.tabor.edu/
- **Independent Mennonite Brethren** comprehensive, founded 1908
- **Small-town** 87-acre campus with easy access to Wichita
- **Endowment** $9.4 million
- **Coed** 655 undergraduate students, 83% full-time, 44% women, 56% men
- **Moderately difficult** entrance level, 58% of applicants were admitted

UNDERGRAD STUDENTS
541 full-time, 114 part-time. Students come from 39 states and territories; 14 other countries; 54% are from out of state; 11% Black or African

American, non-Hispanic/Latino; 12% Hispanic/Latino; 0.6% Native Hawaiian or other Pacific Islander, non-Hispanic/Latino; 0.8% American Indian or Alaska Native, non-Hispanic/Latino; 5% Two or more races, non-Hispanic/Latino; 2% Race/ethnicity unknown; 3% international; 9% transferred in; 92% live on campus.

Freshmen:
Admission: 937 applied, 539 admitted, 164 enrolled. *Average high school GPA:* 3.3. *Test scores:* SAT evidence-based reading and writing scores over 500: 68%; SAT math scores over 500: 64%; ACT scores over 18: 87%; SAT evidence-based reading and writing scores over 600: 22%; SAT math scores over 600: 16%; ACT scores over 24: 30%; SAT evidence-based reading and writing scores over 700: 4%; SAT math scores over 700: 4%; ACT scores over 30: 5%.
Retention: 60% of full-time freshmen returned.

FACULTY
Total: 106, 29% full-time, 45% with terminal degrees.
Student/faculty ratio: 10:1.

ACADEMICS
Calendar: 4-1-4 (adult and graduate studies programs run by cohort groups). *Degrees:* associate, bachelor's, and master's.
Special study options: academic remediation for entering students, accelerated degree program, adult/continuing education programs, advanced placement credit, cooperative education, distance learning, double majors, honors programs, independent study, internships, off-campus study, part-time degree program, services for LD students, student-designed majors, study abroad.
Computers: 35 computers/terminals are available on campus for general student use. Students can access the following: computer help desk, free student e-mail accounts, online (class) grades, online (class) schedules, online registration for Hillsboro undergraduate students. Campuswide network is available. 100% of college-owned or -operated housing units are wired for high-speed Internet access. Wireless service is available via entire campus.
Library: Tabor College Library. *Books:* 61,550 (physical), 225,000 (digital/electronic); *Serial titles:* 148 (physical), 5,000 (digital/electronic); *Databases:* 41. Weekly public service hours: 85; students can reserve study rooms.

STUDENT LIFE
Housing options: on-campus residence required through senior year; men-only, women-only, special housing for students with disabilities. Campus housing is university owned.
Activities and organizations: drama/theater group, student-run newspaper, choral group, Student Activities Board, CHUMS (Challenging, Helping and Understanding through Mentorship), Intramurals, WUMP (Wichita Urban Ministries Plunge), Multi-Cultural Student Union.
Athletics Member NAIA. *Intercollegiate sports:* baseball M(s), basketball M(s)/W(s), cheerleading M(s)/W(s), cross-country running M(s)/W(s), football M(s), golf M, soccer M(s)/W(s), softball W(s), swimming and diving M(s)/W(s), tennis M(s)/W(s), track and field M(s)/W(s), volleyball W(s). *Intramural sports:* basketball M/W, soccer M/W, softball M/W, volleyball M/W.
Student services: personal/psychological counseling.

COSTS & FINANCIAL AID
Costs (2019–20) *Comprehensive fee:* $39,350 includes full-time tuition ($28,400), mandatory fees ($975), and room and board ($9975). Part-time tuition: $570 per hour. *Required fees:* $20 per hour part-time.
Financial Aid Of all full-time matriculated undergraduates who enrolled in 2014, 542 applied for aid, 448 were judged to have need, 60 had their need fully met. In 2014, 93 non-need-based awards were made. *Average percent of need met:* 73. *Average financial aid package:* $22,141. *Average need-based loan:* $5417. *Average need-based gift aid:* $5487. *Average non-need-based aid:* $11,390. *Average indebtedness upon graduation:* $47,172. *Financial aid deadline:* 8/15.

APPLYING
Standardized Tests *Required:* SAT or ACT (for admission).
Options: electronic application, deferred entrance.
Application fee: $50.

Required: essay or personal statement, high school transcript, minimum 2.0 GPA, validation of high school graduation date for transfers. *Recommended:* interview.
Application deadlines: rolling (freshmen), rolling (transfers).
Notification: continuous (freshmen), continuous (transfers).

CONTACT
Ms. Kelly Dugger, Assistant Director of Admissions, Tabor College, 400 South Jefferson, Hillsboro, KS 67063. *Phone:* 620-947-3121 Ext. 1724. *Toll-free phone:* 800-822-6799. *Fax:* 620-947-3789. *E-mail:* kellydugger@tabor.edu.

The University of Kansas
Lawrence, Kansas
http://www.ku.edu/

- **State-supported** university, founded 1866, part of Kansas Board of Regents
- **Suburban** 1000-acre campus with easy access to Kansas City
- **Endowment** $1.6 billion
- **Coed**
- **Moderately difficult** entrance level

FACULTY
Student/faculty ratio: 17:1.

ACADEMICS
Calendar: semesters. *Degrees:* certificates, bachelor's, master's, doctoral, post-master's, and postbachelor's certificates (University of Kansas is a single institution with academic programs and facilities at two primary locations: Lawrence and Kansas City).
Library: Watson Library plus 11 others. *Books:* 4.7 million (physical), 1.0 million (digital/electronic). Weekly public service hours: 168; study areas open 24 hours, 5–7 days a week; students can reserve study rooms.

STUDENT LIFE
Housing options: coed, men-only, women-only, cooperative. Campus housing is university owned.
Activities and organizations: drama/theater group, student-run newspaper, radio and television station, choral group, marching band, KU Adventure Club, Panhellenic Association, Center for Community Outreach, Pre-Nursing Club, American Red Cross Club, national fraternities, national sororities.
Athletics Member NCAA. All Division I except football (Division I-A).
Campus security: 24-hour emergency response devices and patrols, late-night transport/escort service, controlled dormitory access, University police department.
Student services: health clinic, personal/psychological counseling, women's center, legal services, veterans affairs office.

COSTS & FINANCIAL AID
Costs (2018–19) *Tuition:* state resident $10,092 full-time, $336 per credit hour part-time; nonresident $26,302 full-time, $877 per credit hour part-time. Full-time tuition and fees vary according to reciprocity agreements. Part-time tuition and fees vary according to reciprocity agreements. *Required fees:* $1056 full-time, $83 per credit hour part-time. *Room and board:* $10,350; room only: $6084. Room and board charges vary according to board plan and housing facility.
Financial Aid Of all full-time matriculated undergraduates who enrolled in 2017, 11,160 applied for aid, 8,134 were judged to have need, 3,148 had their need fully met. 899 Federal Work-Study jobs (averaging $1507). 50 state and other part-time jobs (averaging $4569). In 2017, 3563 non-need-based awards were made. *Average percent of need met:* 76. *Average financial aid package:* $16,486. *Average need-based loan:* $4737. *Average need-based gift aid:* $7918. *Average non-need-based aid:* $6175. *Average indebtedness upon graduation:* $28,112.

APPLYING
Standardized Tests *Required:* SAT or ACT (for admission).
Options: electronic application.
Application fee: $40.
Required: high school transcript, minimum 3.0 GPA, Kansas Qualified Admissions Curriculum with minimum 2.0 GPA for state residents and 2.5 for nonresidents and minimum 3.0 overall GPA and ACT score of

24/SAT of 1160 or minimum 3.25 overall GPA and ACT score of 21/SAT of 1060.

CONTACT
Ms. Lisa Pinamonti Kress, Director of Admissions, The University of Kansas, KU Visitor Center, 1502 Iowa Street, Lawrence, KS 66045-7576. *Phone:* 785-864-3911. *Toll-free phone:* 888-686-7323. *Fax:* 785-864-5017. *E-mail:* adm@ku.edu.

University of Saint Mary
Leavenworth, Kansas
http://www.stmary.edu/

- **Independent Roman Catholic** comprehensive, founded 1923
- **Small-town** 240-acre campus with easy access to Kansas City
- **Endowment** $20.9 million
- **Coed** 732 undergraduate students, 92% full-time, 48% women, 52% men
- **Moderately difficult** entrance level, 61% of applicants were admitted

UNDERGRAD STUDENTS
675 full-time, 57 part-time. Students come from 40 states and territories; 5 other countries; 49% are from out of state; 12% Black or African American, non-Hispanic/Latino; 16% Hispanic/Latino; 1% Asian, non-Hispanic/Latino; 1% Native Hawaiian or other Pacific Islander, non-Hispanic/Latino; 1% American Indian or Alaska Native, non-Hispanic/Latino; 5% Two or more races, non-Hispanic/Latino; 14% Race/ethnicity unknown; 1% international; 16% transferred in; 39% live on campus.

Freshmen:
Admission: 996 applied, 611 admitted, 134 enrolled. *Average high school GPA:* 3.3. *Test scores:* SAT evidence-based reading and writing scores over 500: 71%; SAT math scores over 500: 71%; ACT scores over 18: 93%; SAT evidence-based reading and writing scores over 600: 25%; SAT math scores over 600: 17%; ACT scores over 24: 24%; SAT math scores over 700: 4%; ACT scores over 30: 1%.
Retention: 62% of full-time freshmen returned.

FACULTY
Total: 151, 44% full-time, 66% with terminal degrees.
Student/faculty ratio: 9:1.

ACADEMICS
Calendar: semesters. *Degrees:* associate, bachelor's, master's, and doctoral.

Special study options: academic remediation for entering students, adult/continuing education programs, advanced placement credit, cooperative education, distance learning, double majors, honors programs, independent study, internships, off-campus study, part-time degree program, services for LD students, student-designed majors, study abroad, summer session for credit. *ROTC:* Army (c).

Computers: 30 computers/terminals are available on campus for general student use. Students can access the following: campus intranet, computer help desk, free student e-mail accounts, online (class) grades, online (class) registration, online (class) schedules. Campuswide network is available. 100% of college-owned or -operated housing units are wired for high-speed Internet access. Wireless service is available via entire campus.
Library: Keleher Learning Commons/DePaul Library plus 1 other. *Books:* 75,000 (physical), 10,500 (digital/electronic); *Serial titles:* 15 (physical), 38,459 (digital/electronic); *Databases:* 63. Weekly public service hours: 68; students can reserve study rooms.

STUDENT LIFE
Housing options: on-campus residence required through sophomore year; coed. Campus housing is university owned. Freshman campus housing is guaranteed.

Activities and organizations: drama/theater group, choral group, Student Government Association, BACCHUS, Theatrical Union, campus ministry.

Athletics Member NAIA. *Intercollegiate sports:* baseball M(s), basketball M(s)/W(s), cheerleading M(s)/W(s), cross-country running M(s)/W(s), football M(s), lacrosse M(s)/W(s), soccer M(s)/W(s), softball W(s), swimming and diving M(s)/W(s), track and field M(s)/W(s), volleyball W(s), wrestling M(s)/W(s).

Campus security: 24-hour patrols, late-night transport/escort service, controlled dormitory access.
Student services: personal/psychological counseling.

COSTS & FINANCIAL AID
Costs (2019–20) *Comprehensive fee:* $38,070 includes full-time tuition ($28,860), mandatory fees ($1070), and room and board ($8140). Part-time tuition: $665 per credit hour.
Financial Aid *Average percent of need met:* 82.

APPLYING
Standardized Tests *Required:* SAT or ACT (for admission). *Recommended:* ACT (for admission).
Options: electronic application.
Application fee: $25.
Required: high school transcript, minimum 2.5 GPA.
Application deadlines: rolling (freshmen), rolling (transfers).
Notification: continuous (freshmen), continuous (transfers).

CONTACT
Mr. John Shultz, Vice President of Admissions and Marketing, University of Saint Mary, 4100 South 4th Street, Leavenworth, KS 66048. *Phone:* 913-758-6329. *Toll-free phone:* 800-752-7043. *E-mail:* admiss@stmary.edu.

Washburn University
Topeka, Kansas
http://www.washburn.edu/

CONTACT
Ms. Kris Klima, Director of Admissions, Washburn University, 1700 SW College, MO 114, Topeka, KS 66621. *Phone:* 785-670-1030. *Toll-free phone:* 800-332-0291. *Fax:* 785-670-1113. *E-mail:* admissions@washburn.edu.

Wichita State University
Wichita, Kansas
http://www.wichita.edu/

- **State-supported** university, founded 1895, part of Kansas Board of Regents
- **Urban** 335-acre campus
- **Endowment** $302.0 million
- **Coed**
- **Minimally difficult** entrance level

FACULTY
Student/faculty ratio: 20:1.

ACADEMICS
Calendar: semesters. *Degrees:* certificates, associate, bachelor's, master's, doctoral, post-master's, and postbachelor's certificates.
Library: Ablah Library plus 2 others. *Books:* 1.9 million (physical), 475,186 (digital/electronic); *Serial titles:* 460 (physical), 94,566 (digital/electronic); *Databases:* 269. Study areas open 24 hours, 5–7 days a week; students can reserve study rooms.

STUDENT LIFE
Housing options: on-campus residence required for freshman year; coed, special housing for students with disabilities. Campus housing is university owned. Freshman campus housing is guaranteed.

Activities and organizations: drama/theater group, student-run newspaper, radio station, choral group, national fraternities, national sororities.

Athletics Member NCAA. All Division I.

Campus security: 24-hour emergency response devices and patrols, student patrols, late-night transport/escort service, controlled dormitory access, bicycle patrols by campus security.

Student services: health clinic, personal/psychological counseling, women's center, veterans affairs office.

COSTS & FINANCIAL AID
Costs (2018–19) *Tuition:* state resident $6709 full-time, $224 per credit hour part-time; nonresident $15,890 full-time, $530 per credit hour part-

time. Full-time tuition and fees vary according to course level, course load, degree level, and program. Part-time tuition and fees vary according to course level, course load, degree level, and program. *Required fees:* $1562 full-time, $8 per credit hour part-time, $443 per term part-time. *Room and board:* $11,252. Room and board charges vary according to board plan and housing facility.

Financial Aid Of all full-time matriculated undergraduates who enrolled in 2017, 6,419 applied for aid, 5,207 were judged to have need, 926 had their need fully met. 106 Federal Work-Study jobs (averaging $2696). 83 state and other part-time jobs (averaging $1187). In 2017, 1412 non-need-based awards were made. *Average percent of need met:* 65. *Average financial aid package:* $8068. *Average need-based loan:* $2119. *Average need-based gift aid:* $5107. *Average non-need-based aid:* $1250. *Average indebtedness upon graduation:* $24,630.

APPLYING
Standardized Tests *Required for some:* SAT or ACT (for admission). *Recommended:* SAT or ACT (for admission).

Options: electronic application, deferred entrance.

Application fee: $30.

Required: high school transcript. *Required for some:* minimum 2.5 GPA, rank in upper one-third of high school class or complete the pre-college curriculum with a minimum 2.0 GPA (2.5 GPA for nonresidents).

CONTACT
Wichita State University, 1845 North Fairmount, Wichita, KS 67260. *Phone:* 316-978-3085. *Toll-free phone:* 800-362-2594.

KENTUCKY

Alice Lloyd College
Pippa Passes, Kentucky
http://www.alc.edu/

- **Independent** 4-year, founded 1923
- **Rural** 175-acre campus
- **Endowment** $40.8 million
- **Coed**
- **Minimally difficult** entrance level

FACULTY
Student/faculty ratio: 17:1.

ACADEMICS
Calendar: semesters. *Degree:* bachelor's.
Library: McGaw Library and Learning Center. *Books:* 63,050 (physical), 170,956 (digital/electronic); *Serial titles:* 57 (physical), 23,210 (digital/electronic); *Databases:* 105. Weekly public service hours: 74; students can reserve study rooms.

STUDENT LIFE
Housing options: men-only, women-only. Campus housing is university owned.

Activities and organizations: drama/theater group, student-run newspaper, radio and television station, choral group, Voices of Appalachia, Intramurals, Baptist Collegiate Ministries, Allied Health Sciences Club, Alpha Chi National Honor Society.

Athletics Member NAIA, NCCAA.

Campus security: 24-hour emergency response devices and patrols, late-night transport/escort service, controlled dormitory access, video cameras.

Student services: health clinic, personal/psychological counseling.

COSTS & FINANCIAL AID
Costs (2018–19) *Comprehensive fee:* includes mandatory fees ($2150) and room and board ($6880). The cost of tuition is covered by a combination of scholarships and other financial aid. *Required fees:* $225 per credit part-time. *College room only:* $3300.

Financial Aid Of all full-time matriculated undergraduates who enrolled in 2016, 584 applied for aid, 533 were judged to have need, 68 had their need fully met. 418 Federal Work-Study jobs (averaging $2320). 168 state and other part-time jobs (averaging $2320). In 2016, 57 non-need-based awards were made. *Average percent of need met:* 71. *Average financial*

aid package: $13,681. *Average need-based loan:* $2197. *Average need-based gift aid:* $9872. *Average non-need-based aid:* $5919. *Average indebtedness upon graduation:* $10,141.

APPLYING
Standardized Tests *Required:* SAT or ACT (for admission).

Options: electronic application.

Required: high school transcript, minimum 2.3 GPA, interview. *Required for some:* essay or personal statement, 2 letters of recommendation.

CONTACT
Mr. J. D. Cornett, Director of Admissions, Alice Lloyd College, 100 Purpose Road, Pippa Passes, KY 41844. *Phone:* 606-368-6134. *Toll-free phone:* 888-280-4252. *Fax:* 606-368-6038. *E-mail:* jdcornett@alc.edu.

American National University
Lexington, Kentucky
http://www.an.edu/

CONTACT
Kim Thomasson, Campus Director, American National University, 2376 Sir Barton Way, Lexington, KY 40509. *Phone:* 859-253-0621. *Toll-free phone:* 888-9-JOBREADY.

American National University
Louisville, Kentucky
http://www.an.edu/

CONTACT
Vincent C. Tinebra, Campus Director, American National University, 4205 Dixie Highway, Louisville, KY 40216. *Phone:* 502-447-7634. *Toll-free phone:* 888-9-JOBREADY.

Asbury University
Wilmore, Kentucky
http://www.asbury.edu/

- **Independent nondenominational** comprehensive, founded 1890
- **Small-town** 400-acre campus with easy access to Lexington, KY
- **Endowment** $47.8 million
- **Coed**
- **Moderately difficult** entrance level

FACULTY
Student/faculty ratio: 13:1.

ACADEMICS
Calendar: semesters. *Degrees:* associate, bachelor's, and master's.
Library: Kinlaw Library. *Books:* 157,131 (physical), 168,625 (digital/electronic); *Serial titles:* 442 (physical), 37,780 (digital/electronic); *Databases:* 60. Weekly public service hours: 88; students can reserve study rooms.

STUDENT LIFE
Housing options: on-campus residence required through senior year; men-only, women-only. Campus housing is university owned. Freshman campus housing is guaranteed.

Activities and organizations: drama/theater group, student-run newspaper, radio and television station, choral group, Asbury Student Congress, Spiritual Life Board, Summer Ministry Teams, Asbury Outdoors, WGM Global Cafe.

Athletics Member NAIA, NCCAA.

Campus security: 24-hour emergency response devices, late-night transport/escort service, controlled dormitory access, late night security personnel.

Student services: health clinic, personal/psychological counseling.

COSTS & FINANCIAL AID
Costs (2018–19) *Comprehensive fee:* $37,358 includes full-time tuition ($29,900), mandatory fees ($298), and room and board ($7160). Full-time tuition and fees vary according to course load and program. Part-time tuition: $1150 per credit hour. Part-time tuition and fees vary according to course load and program. *Room and board:* Room and board charges vary according to board plan and housing facility.

Financial Aid Of all full-time matriculated undergraduates who enrolled in 2018, 1,091 applied for aid, 990 were judged to have need, 154 had their need fully met. 818 Federal Work-Study jobs (averaging $1800). In 2018, 92 non-need-based awards were made. *Average percent of need met:* 72. *Average financial aid package:* $21,784. *Average need-based loan:* $3656. *Average need-based gift aid:* $10,539. *Average non-need-based aid:* $10,733. *Average indebtedness upon graduation:* $29,000.

APPLYING

Standardized Tests *Required:* SAT or ACT (for admission).

Options: electronic application, early admission, deferred entrance.

Required: essay or personal statement, high school transcript, minimum 2.5 GPA, 1 letter of recommendation.

CONTACT

Mr. Brandon Combs, Director of Undergraduate Admissions, Asbury University, One Macklem Drive, Wilmore, KY 40390. *Phone:* 800-888-1818. *Toll-free phone:* 800-888-1818. *E-mail:* admissions@asbury.edu.

Beckfield College

Florence, Kentucky
http://www.beckfield.edu/

CONTACT

Mrs. Leah Boerger, Director of Admissions, Beckfield College, 16 Spiral Drive, Florence, KY 41042. *Phone:* 859-371-9393. *E-mail:* lboerger@beckfield.edu.

Bellarmine University

Louisville, Kentucky
http://www.bellarmine.edu/

- **Independent Roman Catholic** comprehensive, founded 1950
- **Suburban** 175-acre campus with easy access to Louisville
- **Endowment** $66.9 million
- **Coed** 2,552 undergraduate students, 94% full-time, 64% women, 36% men
- **Moderately difficult** entrance level, 86% of applicants were admitted

UNDERGRAD STUDENTS

2,401 full-time, 151 part-time. Students come from 41 states and territories; 22 other countries; 29% are from out of state; 5% Black or African American, non-Hispanic/Latino; 4% Hispanic/Latino; 2% Asian, non-Hispanic/Latino; 0.1% Native Hawaiian or other Pacific Islander, non-Hispanic/Latino; 0.2% American Indian or Alaska Native, non-Hispanic/Latino; 4% Two or more races, non-Hispanic/Latino; 4% Race/ethnicity unknown; 1% international; 2% transferred in; 40% live on campus.

Freshmen:

Admission: 5,535 applied, 4,751 admitted, 618 enrolled. *Average high school GPA:* 3.6. *Test scores:* SAT evidence-based reading and writing scores over 500: 93%; SAT math scores over 500: 91%; ACT scores over 18: 100%; SAT evidence-based reading and writing scores over 600: 42%; SAT math scores over 600: 38%; ACT scores over 24: 59%; SAT evidence-based reading and writing scores over 700: 8%; SAT math scores over 700: 7%; ACT scores over 30: 16%.

Retention: 79% of full-time freshmen returned.

FACULTY

Total: 418, 42% full-time, 62% with terminal degrees.

Student/faculty ratio: 12:1.

ACADEMICS

Calendar: semesters. *Degrees:* certificates, bachelor's, master's, doctoral, and postbachelor's certificates.

Special study options: accelerated degree program, adult/continuing education programs, advanced placement credit, cooperative education, distance learning, double majors, freshman honors college, honors programs, independent study, internships, part-time degree program,

services for LD students, student-designed majors, study abroad, summer session for credit. *ROTC:* Army (c), Air Force (c).

Unusual degree programs: 3-2 business administration; Exercise Science-Sport Performance Early Entry-Master of Science in Athletic Training.

Computers: 440 computers/terminals and 440 ports are available on campus for general student use. Students can access the following: campus intranet, computer help desk, free student e-mail accounts, online (class) grades, online (class) registration, online (class) schedules, mobile app. Campuswide network is available. 100% of college-owned or -operated housing units are wired for high-speed Internet access. Wireless service is available via entire campus.

Library: W. L. Lyons Brown Library. *Books:* 130,534 (physical), 288,828 (digital/electronic); *Serial titles:* 189 (physical), 88,144 (digital/electronic); *Databases:* 145. Weekly public service hours: 140; study areas open 24 hours, 5–7 days a week.

STUDENT LIFE

Housing options: on-campus residence required through junior year; coed, men-only, women-only, special housing for students with disabilities. Campus housing is university owned. Freshman campus housing is guaranteed.

Activities and organizations: drama/theater group, student-run newspaper, radio station, choral group, Student Government, Bellarmine Activities Council, Knights Nation, Fellowship of Christian Athletes, Delta Sigma Pi, national fraternities, national sororities.

Athletics Member NCAA. All Division II except lacrosse (Division I). *Intercollegiate sports:* baseball M(s), basketball M(s)/W(s), cheerleading M(s)/W(s), cross-country running M(s)/W(s), field hockey W(s), golf M(s)/W(s), lacrosse M(s), soccer M(s)/W(s), softball W(s), swimming and diving M(s)/W(s), tennis M(s)/W(s), track and field M(s)/W(s), volleyball W(s), wrestling M(s). *Intramural sports:* basketball M/W, bowling M(c)/W(c), football M/W, golf M/W, soccer M/W, softball M/W, swimming and diving M/W, table tennis M/W, tennis M/W, ultimate Frisbee M/W, volleyball M/W.

Campus security: 24-hour emergency response devices and patrols, student patrols, late-night transport/escort service, controlled dormitory access, 24-hour locked residence hall entrances, security cameras.

Student services: health clinic, personal/psychological counseling, veterans affairs office.

COSTS & FINANCIAL AID

Costs (2019–20) *One-time required fee:* $400. *Comprehensive fee:* $51,850 includes full-time tuition ($40,880), mandatory fees ($1550), and room and board ($9420). Part-time tuition: $950 per credit hour. *College room only:* $4800.

Financial Aid Of all full-time matriculated undergraduates who enrolled in 2018, 2,151 applied for aid, 1,896 were judged to have need, 412 had their need fully met. In 2018, 457 non-need-based awards were made. *Average percent of need met:* 77. *Average financial aid package:* $35,031. *Average need-based loan:* $4208. *Average need-based gift aid:* $27,188. *Average non-need-based aid:* $25,049. *Average indebtedness upon graduation:* $29,095.

APPLYING

Standardized Tests *Required:* SAT or ACT (for admission).

Options: electronic application, early admission, early action, deferred entrance.

Application fee: $25.

Required: high school transcript, minimum 2.5 GPA, 1 letter of recommendation. *Required for some:* essay or personal statement. *Recommended:* interview.

Application deadlines: 8/15 (freshmen), rolling (transfers).

Notification: continuous until 9/1 (freshmen), continuous (transfers).

CONTACT

Mr. Timothy A. Sturgeon, Dean of Admission, Bellarmine University, 2001 Newburg Road, Louisville, KY 40205-0671. *Phone:* 502-272-8131. *Toll-free phone:* 800-274-4723 Ext. 8131. *E-mail:* admissions@bellarmine.edu.

Berea College
Berea, Kentucky
http://www.berea.edu/

- **Independent** 4-year, founded 1855
- **Small-town** 140-acre campus
- **Endowment** $1.2 billion
- **Coed** 1,673 undergraduate students, 97% full-time, 58% women, 42% men
- **Moderately difficult** entrance level, 38% of applicants were admitted

UNDERGRAD STUDENTS
1,631 full-time, 42 part-time. Students come from 42 states and territories; 74 other countries; 55% are from out of state; 16% Black or African American, non-Hispanic/Latino; 12% Hispanic/Latino; 3% Asian, non-Hispanic/Latino; 0.1% Native Hawaiian or other Pacific Islander, non-Hispanic/Latino; 0.1% American Indian or Alaska Native, non-Hispanic/Latino; 7% Two or more races, non-Hispanic/Latino; 0.8% Race/ethnicity unknown; 8% international; 3% transferred in; 87% live on campus.

Freshmen:
Admission: 1,575 applied, 602 admitted, 438 enrolled. *Average high school GPA:* 3.5. *Test scores:* SAT evidence-based reading and writing scores over 500: 90%; SAT math scores over 500: 79%; ACT scores over 18: 100%; SAT evidence-based reading and writing scores over 600: 18%; SAT math scores over 600: 35%; ACT scores over 24: 63%; SAT math scores over 700: 7%; ACT scores over 30: 11%.

Retention: 83% of full-time freshmen returned.

FACULTY
Total: 191, 72% full-time, 81% with terminal degrees.

Student/faculty ratio: 10:1.

ACADEMICS
Calendar: semesters. *Degree:* bachelor's.

Special study options: academic remediation for entering students, advanced placement credit, double majors, English as a second language, honors programs, independent study, internships, off-campus study, services for LD students, student-designed majors, study abroad, summer session for credit.

Unusual degree programs: 3-2 engineering with University of Kentucky.

Computers: 7,000 ports are available on campus for general student use. Students can access the following: campus intranet, computer help desk, free student e-mail accounts, online (class) grades, online (class) registration, online (class) schedules. Campuswide network is available. 100% of college-owned or -operated housing units are wired for high-speed Internet access. Wireless service is available via entire campus.

Library: Hutchins Library plus 1 other. *Books:* 325,660 (physical), 242,958 (digital/electronic); *Serial titles:* 99,454 (physical), 8,958 (digital/electronic). Weekly public service hours: 94; students can reserve study rooms.

STUDENT LIFE
Housing options: on-campus residence required through senior year; men-only, women-only. Campus housing is university owned. Freshman campus housing is guaranteed.

Activities and organizations: drama/theater group, student-run newspaper, choral group, Campus Activities Board, Cosmopolitan Club, CELTS (Center for Excellence in Learning through Service), Black Cultural Center, African Student Association.

Athletics Member NCAA. All Division III. *Intercollegiate sports:* baseball M, basketball M/W, cross-country running M/W, golf M, soccer M/W, softball W, tennis M/W, track and field M/W, volleyball W. *Intramural sports:* basketball M/W, football M/W, racquetball M/W, soccer M/W, softball M/W, ultimate Frisbee M/W, volleyball M/W.

Campus security: 24-hour emergency response devices and patrols, late-night transport/escort service, controlled dormitory access.

Student services: health clinic, personal/psychological counseling, women's center.

COSTS & FINANCIAL AID
Costs (2019–20) *Comprehensive fee:* includes mandatory fees ($600) and room and board ($6966).

Financial Aid Of all full-time matriculated undergraduates who enrolled in 2016, 1,612 applied for aid, 1,612 were judged to have need. *Average percent of need met:* 95. *Average financial aid package:* $34,714. *Average need-based loan:* $1781. *Average need-based gift aid:* $32,288. *Average indebtedness upon graduation:* $7468. *Financial aid deadline:* 5/1.

APPLYING
Standardized Tests *Required:* SAT or ACT (for admission).

Options: electronic application.

Required: essay or personal statement, high school transcript. *Recommended:* 2 letters of recommendation, interview.

Application deadlines: 3/31 (freshmen), 3/31 (out-of-state freshmen), 3/31 (transfers).

Notification: continuous until 11/1 (freshmen), continuous until 11/1 (out-of-state freshmen), continuous until 4/15 (transfers).

CONTACT
Mr. Luke Hodson, Director of Admissions, Berea College, CPO 2220, Berea, KY 40404. *Phone:* 859-985-3500. *Toll-free phone:* 800-326-5948. *Fax:* 859-985-3512. *E-mail:* admissions@berea.edu.

Brescia University
Owensboro, Kentucky
http://www.brescia.edu/

- **Independent Roman Catholic** comprehensive, founded 1950
- **Urban** 9-acre campus
- **Endowment** $12.4 million
- **Coed**
- **Moderately difficult** entrance level

FACULTY
Student/faculty ratio: 12:1.

ACADEMICS
Calendar: semesters. *Degrees:* certificates, associate, bachelor's, master's, and postbachelor's certificates.

Library: Fr. Leonard Alvey Library. *Books:* 72,970 (physical), 1,245 (digital/electronic); *Databases:* 75. Students can reserve study rooms.

STUDENT LIFE
Housing options: on-campus residence required through junior year; coed, men-only, women-only. Campus housing is university owned. Freshman applicants given priority for college housing.

Activities and organizations: drama/theater group, student-run newspaper, choral group, Student Government, Alpha Chi, Kentucky Education Association, National Society for Speech Language and Hearing Association, ZEST.

Athletics Member NAIA.

Campus security: 24-hour emergency response devices, late-night transport/escort service, controlled dormitory access.

Student services: personal/psychological counseling, veterans affairs office.

COSTS & FINANCIAL AID
Costs (2018–19) *One-time required fee:* $200. *Comprehensive fee:* $31,450 includes full-time tuition ($21,500), mandatory fees ($600), and room and board ($9350). Full-time tuition and fees vary according to course load, degree level, and location. Part-time tuition: $590 per credit hour. Part-time tuition and fees vary according to course load, degree level, and location. *Room and board:* Room and board charges vary according to board plan and housing facility.

Financial Aid Of all full-time matriculated undergraduates who enrolled in 2015, 925 applied for aid, 899 were judged to have need. 50 Federal Work-Study jobs (averaging $909). 48 state and other part-time jobs (averaging $849). In 2015, 57 non-need-based awards were made. *Average financial aid package:* $25,489. *Average need-based loan:* $3414. *Average need-based gift aid:* $7811. *Average non-need-based aid:* $16,191. *Average indebtedness upon graduation:* $19,060.

APPLYING
Standardized Tests *Required:* SAT or ACT (for admission).

Options: electronic application, deferred entrance.

Application fee: $25.

Required: high school transcript. *Required for some:* essay or personal statement, 1 letter of recommendation, interview.

CONTACT
Brescia University, 717 Frederica Street, Owensboro, KY 42301-3023. *Phone:* 270-686-4241 Ext. 241. *Toll-free phone:* 877-273-7242.

Campbellsville University
Campbellsville, Kentucky
http://www.campbellsville.edu/

- **Independent** comprehensive, founded 1906, affiliated with Kentucky Baptist Convention
- **Small-town** 90-acre campus
- **Endowment** $21.0 million
- **Coed** 5,139 undergraduate students, 44% full-time, 60% women, 40% men
- **Moderately difficult** entrance level, 83% of applicants were admitted

UNDERGRAD STUDENTS
2,263 full-time, 2,876 part-time. Students come from 42 states and territories; 46 other countries; 16% are from out of state; 13% Black or African American, non-Hispanic/Latino; 3% Hispanic/Latino; 0.5% Asian, non-Hispanic/Latino; 0.2% Native Hawaiian or other Pacific Islander, non-Hispanic/Latino; 0.4% American Indian or Alaska Native, non-Hispanic/Latino; 2% Two or more races, non-Hispanic/Latino; 5% Race/ethnicity unknown; 6% international; 5% transferred in; 56% live on campus.

Freshmen:
Admission: 3,542 applied, 2,952 admitted, 661 enrolled. *Average high school GPA:* 3.3. *Test scores:* SAT evidence-based reading and writing scores over 500: 57%; SAT math scores over 500: 71%; ACT scores over 18: 76%; SAT evidence-based reading and writing scores over 600: 14%; SAT math scores over 600: 24%; ACT scores over 24: 25%; SAT evidence-based reading and writing scores over 700: 2%; SAT math scores over 700: 2%; ACT scores over 30: 3%.
Retention: 64% of full-time freshmen returned.

FACULTY
Total: 463, 37% full-time, 36% with terminal degrees.
Student/faculty ratio: 23:1.

ACADEMICS
Calendar: semesters. *Degrees:* certificates, associate, bachelor's, master's, doctoral, post-master's, and postbachelor's certificates.

Special study options: academic remediation for entering students, accelerated degree program, adult/continuing education programs, advanced placement credit, cooperative education, distance learning, double majors, English as a second language, honors programs, independent study, internships, off-campus study, part-time degree program, services for LD students, study abroad, summer session for credit. *ROTC:* Army (c).

Computers: 220 computers/terminals are available on campus for general student use. Students can access the following: campus intranet, computer help desk, free student e-mail accounts, online (class) grades, online (class) registration, online (class) schedules. Campuswide network is available. 100% of college-owned or -operated housing units are wired for high-speed Internet access. Wireless service is available via entire campus.
Library: Montgomery Library. *Books:* 125,057 (physical), 351,230 (digital/electronic); *Serial titles:* 7,762 (digital/electronic); *Databases:* 94. Weekly public service hours: 77; students can reserve study rooms.

STUDENT LIFE
Housing options: on-campus residence required through sophomore year; men-only, women-only. Campus housing is university owned. Freshman campus housing is guaranteed.

Activities and organizations: drama/theater group, student-run newspaper, radio and television station, choral group, marching band, Baptist Campus Ministries, Student Government Association, International Student Association, Black Student Association, KANS (Nursing Society).

Athletics Member NAIA, NCCAA. *Intercollegiate sports:* archery M(s)/W(s), baseball M(s), basketball M(s)/W(s), bowling M(s)/W(s),

cheerleading M(s)/W(s), cross-country running M(s)/W(s), football M(s), golf M(s)/W(s), soccer M(s)/W(s), softball W(s), swimming and diving M(s)/W(s), tennis M(s)/W(s), track and field M(s)/W(s), volleyball M(s)/W(s), wrestling M(s)/W(s). *Intramural sports:* basketball M/W, bowling M/W, football M/W, sand volleyball M/W, soccer M/W, softball M/W, table tennis M/W, tennis M/W, ultimate Frisbee M/W, volleyball M/W.

Campus security: 24-hour emergency response devices and patrols, student patrols, late-night transport/escort service, controlled dormitory access.

Student services: health clinic, personal/psychological counseling.

COSTS & FINANCIAL AID
Costs (2019–20) *Comprehensive fee:* $33,400 includes full-time tuition ($24,900), mandatory fees ($500), and room and board ($8000). Part-time tuition: $1038 per credit hour. *Required fees:* $250 per year part-time.

Financial Aid Of all full-time matriculated undergraduates who enrolled in 2017, 1,805 applied for aid, 1,701 were judged to have need, 247 had their need fully met. In 2017, 120 non-need-based awards were made. *Average percent of need met:* 71. *Average financial aid package:* $19,749. *Average need-based loan:* $3701. *Average need-based gift aid:* $17,217. *Average non-need-based aid:* $12,176. *Average indebtedness upon graduation:* $21,912.

APPLYING
Standardized Tests *Recommended:* SAT or ACT (for admission).
Options: electronic application, deferred entrance.
Application fee: $20.
Required: high school transcript, minimum 2.0 GPA. *Recommended:* essay or personal statement, minimum 3.0 GPA, interview.
Application deadlines: rolling (freshmen), rolling (transfers).
Notification: continuous (freshmen), continuous (transfers).

CONTACT
Mrs. Laura Day, Assistant Director of On-Campus Enrollment, Campbellsville University, 1 University Drive, UPO 782, Campbellsville, KY 42718-2799. *Phone:* 270-789-5526. *Toll-free phone:* 800-264-6014. *Fax:* 270-789-5071. *E-mail:* admissions@campbellsville.edu.

Centre College
Danville, Kentucky
http://www.centre.edu/

- **Independent** 4-year, founded 1819, affiliated with Presbyterian Church (U.S.A.)
- **Small-town** 160-acre campus
- **Endowment** $269.4 million
- **Coed**
- **Very difficult** entrance level

FACULTY
Student/faculty ratio: 10:1.

ACADEMICS
Calendar: 4-1-4. *Degree:* bachelor's.
Library: Doherty Library. *Books:* 231,820 (physical), 33,042 (digital/electronic); *Serial titles:* 536 (physical), 27,570 (digital/electronic); *Databases:* 530. Weekly public service hours: 113; study areas open 24 hours, 5–7 days a week; students can reserve study rooms.

STUDENT LIFE
Housing options: on-campus residence required through senior year; coed, men-only, women-only, special housing for students with disabilities. Campus housing is university owned. Freshman campus housing is guaranteed.

Activities and organizations: drama/theater group, student-run newspaper, radio station, choral group, Student Government Association, Centre Action Reaches Everyone, Student Activities Council, Christian fellowship group, Diversity Student Union, national fraternities, national sororities.

Athletics Member NCAA. All Division III.

Campus security: 24-hour emergency response devices and patrols, late-night transport/escort service, controlled dormitory access.

Student services: health clinic, personal/psychological counseling.

COSTS & FINANCIAL AID

Costs (2018–19) *Comprehensive fee:* $52,180 includes full-time tuition ($41,700) and room and board ($10,480). Part-time tuition: $1489 per credit hour. *College room only:* $5240. Room and board charges vary according to housing facility.

Financial Aid Of all full-time matriculated undergraduates who enrolled in 2018, 1,037 applied for aid, 814 were judged to have need, 260 had their need fully met. 340 Federal Work-Study jobs (averaging $1582). In 2018, 571 non-need-based awards were made. *Average percent of need met:* 86. *Average financial aid package:* $35,122. *Average need-based loan:* $4600. *Average need-based gift aid:* $31,942. *Average non-need-based aid:* $24,713. *Average indebtedness upon graduation:* $26,313.

APPLYING

Standardized Tests *Required:* SAT or ACT (for admission).

Options: electronic application, early admission, early decision, early action, deferred entrance.

Required: essay or personal statement, high school transcript, 1 letter of recommendation. *Recommended:* interview.

CONTACT

Mr. Bob Nesmith, Dean of Admission and Student Financial Aid, Centre College, 600 West Walnut Street, Danville, KY 40422-1394. *Phone:* 859-238-5350. *Toll-free phone:* 800-423-6236. *Fax:* 859-238-5373. *E-mail:* admission@centre.edu.

Clear Creek Baptist Bible College

Pineville, Kentucky

http://www.ccbbc.edu/

CONTACT

Mr. Billy Howell, Director of Admissions, Clear Creek Baptist Bible College, 300 Clear Creek Road, Pineville, KY 40977. *Phone:* 606-337-3196 Ext. 103. *Fax:* 606-337-1631. *E-mail:* bhowell@ccbbc.edu.

Eastern Kentucky University

Richmond, Kentucky

http://www.eku.edu/

CONTACT

Ms. Stephanie Leigh Whaley, Director of Admissions, Eastern Kentucky University, SSB CPO 54, 521 Lancaster Avenue, Richmond, KY 40475-3102. *Phone:* 859-622-2106. *Toll-free phone:* 800-465-9191. *Fax:* 859-622-8024. *E-mail:* admissions@eku.edu.

Galen College of Nursing

Louisville, Kentucky

http://www.galencollege.edu/

CONTACT

Galen College of Nursing, 1031 Zorn Avenue, Suite 400, Louisville, KY 40207. *Toll-free phone:* 877-223-7040.

Georgetown College

Georgetown, Kentucky

http://www.georgetowncollege.edu/

- **Independent** comprehensive, founded 1829, affiliated with Baptist Church
- **Suburban** 104-acre campus with easy access to Cincinnati, OH; Louisville, KY
- **Endowment** $41.7 million
- **Coed** 961 undergraduate students, 95% full-time, 55% women, 45% men
- **Moderately difficult** entrance level, 67% of applicants were admitted

UNDERGRAD STUDENTS

912 full-time, 49 part-time. Students come from 31 states and territories; 9 other countries; 25% are from out of state; 10% Black or African American, non-Hispanic/Latino; 4% Hispanic/Latino; 0.7% Asian, non-Hispanic/Latino; 0.2% American Indian or Alaska Native, non-Hispanic/Latino; 4% Two or more races, non-Hispanic/Latino; 4%

Race/ethnicity unknown; 0.4% international; 6% transferred in; 90% live on campus.

Freshmen:
Admission: 2,498 applied, 1,682 admitted, 262 enrolled. *Average high school GPA:* 3.4. *Test scores:* ACT scores over 18: 97%; ACT scores over 24: 45%; ACT scores over 30: 7%.
Retention: 63% of full-time freshmen returned.

FACULTY

Total: 159, 49% full-time.

Student/faculty ratio: 11:1.

ACADEMICS

Calendar: semesters. *Degrees:* bachelor's and master's.

Special study options: advanced placement credit, cooperative education, distance learning, double majors, English as a second language, honors programs, independent study, internships, off-campus study, part-time degree program, services for LD students, student-designed majors, study abroad, summer session for credit. *ROTC:* Army (c), Air Force (c).

Unusual degree programs: 3-2 engineering with University of Kentucky; nursing with University of Kentucky.

Computers: 120 computers/terminals and 2,000 ports are available on campus for general student use. Students can access the following: campus intranet, computer help desk, free student e-mail accounts, online (class) grades, online (class) registration, online (class) schedules, Library apps for smartphones. Campuswide network is available. 100% of college-owned or -operated housing units are wired for high-speed Internet access. Wireless service is available via entire campus.

Library: Anna Ashcraft Ensor Learning Resource Center. *Books:* 129,442 (physical), 256,326 (digital/electronic); *Serial titles:* 20 (physical), 41,920 (digital/electronic); *Databases:* 133. Weekly public service hours: 92.

STUDENT LIFE

Housing options: on-campus residence required through senior year; men-only, women-only. Campus housing is university owned and leased by the school. Freshman campus housing is guaranteed.

Activities and organizations: drama/theater group, student-run newspaper, radio station, choral group, national fraternities, national sororities.

Athletics Member NAIA. *Intercollegiate sports:* archery M(s)/W(s), baseball M(s), basketball M(s)/W(s), cheerleading M(s)/W(s), cross-country running M(s)/W(s), football M(s), golf M(s)/W(s), lacrosse W(s), soccer M(s)/W(s), softball W(s), tennis M(s)/W(s), track and field M(s)/W(s), volleyball W(s). *Intramural sports:* basketball M/W, football M/W, soccer M/W, softball M/W, tennis M/W, ultimate Frisbee M/W, volleyball M/W.

Campus security: 24-hour patrols, late-night transport/escort service, controlled dormitory access.

Student services: health clinic, personal/psychological counseling, veterans affairs office.

COSTS & FINANCIAL AID

Costs (2019–20) *Comprehensive fee:* $49,970 includes full-time tuition ($39,810) and room and board ($10,160). Part-time tuition: $1230 per credit hour. *College room only:* $4900.

Financial Aid Of all full-time matriculated undergraduates who enrolled in 2018, 842 applied for aid, 792 were judged to have need, 203 had their need fully met. In 2018, 50 non-need-based awards were made. *Average percent of need met:* 84. *Average financial aid package:* $34,952. *Average need-based loan:* $3495. *Average need-based gift aid:* $23,643. *Average non-need-based aid:* $16,266. *Average indebtedness upon graduation:* $31,084.

APPLYING

Standardized Tests *Required:* SAT or ACT (for admission).

Options: electronic application, deferred entrance.

Required: high school transcript, minimum 2.0 GPA. *Required for some:* interview.

Application deadlines: rolling (freshmen), rolling (transfers).

Notification: continuous (freshmen), continuous (transfers).

CONTACT
Mr. Jeremiah Tudor, Dean of Admissions, Georgetown College, 400 East College Street, Georgetown, KY 40324. *Phone:* 502-863-8727. *Toll-free phone:* 800-788-9985. *E-mail:* admissions@georgetowncollege.edu.

Kentucky Christian University
Grayson, Kentucky
http://www.kcu.edu/

CONTACT
Ms. Heather Stacy, Director of Admissions, Kentucky Christian University, 100 Academic Parkway, Grayson, KY 41143. *Phone:* 606-474-3284. *Toll-free phone:* 800-522-3181. *Fax:* 606-474-3155. *E-mail:* sgreer@kcu.edu.

Kentucky Mountain Bible College
Jackson, Kentucky
http://www.kmbc.edu/

- **Independent interdenominational** 4-year, founded 1931
- **Rural** 500-acre campus with easy access to Lexington
- **Coed**
- **Minimally difficult** entrance level

FACULTY
Student/faculty ratio: 13:1.

ACADEMICS
Calendar: semesters. *Degrees:* associate and bachelor's.
Library: Gibson Library plus 1 other. *Books:* 34,770 (physical), 52 (digital/electronic); *Serial titles:* 111 (physical). Weekly public service hours: 70.

STUDENT LIFE
Housing options: on-campus residence required through senior year; men-only, women-only. Campus housing is university owned. Freshman campus housing is guaranteed.

Activities and organizations: drama/theater group, student-run newspaper, choral group, Missionary Involvement, Class Organizations.

Campus security: student patrols.

Student services: personal/psychological counseling.

COSTS & FINANCIAL AID
Costs (2018–19) *One-time required fee:* $640. *Comprehensive fee:* $14,510 includes full-time tuition ($8550), mandatory fees ($910), and room and board ($5050). Full-time tuition and fees vary according to program. Part-time tuition: $285 per credit hour. Part-time tuition and fees vary according to program. *Required fees:* $290 per term part-time. *College room only:* $1900. Room and board charges vary according to housing facility.

Financial Aid Of all full-time matriculated undergraduates who enrolled in 2015, 54 applied for aid, 53 were judged to have need, 5 had their need fully met. In 2015, 7 non-need-based awards were made. *Average percent of need met:* 66. *Average financial aid package:* $9336. *Average need-based loan:* $3707. *Average need-based gift aid:* $5889. *Average non-need-based aid:* $2808. *Average indebtedness upon graduation:* $7370.

APPLYING
Standardized Tests *Required:* ACT (for admission).
Application fee: $25.
Required: essay or personal statement, high school transcript, minimum 2.0 GPA, testimony of Christian belief and practice. *Recommended:* minimum 2.0 GPA, interview.

CONTACT
Mr. David Lorimer, Director of Recruiting, Kentucky Mountain Bible College, PO Box 10, Vancleve, KY 41385. *Phone:* 606-693-5000 Ext. 138. *Toll-free phone:* 800-879-KMBC. *Fax:* 606-693-4884. *E-mail:* dlorimer@kmbc.edu.

Kentucky State University
Frankfort, Kentucky
http://www.kysu.edu/

- **State-related** comprehensive, founded 1886
- **Small-town** 916-acre campus with easy access to Louisville
- **Endowment** $16.6 million
- **Coed**
- 45% of applicants were admitted

FACULTY
Student/faculty ratio: 11:1.

ACADEMICS
Calendar: semesters. *Degrees:* certificates, associate, bachelor's, master's, and doctoral.
Library: Paul G. Blazer Library. *Books:* 170,726 (physical), 23,417 (digital/electronic); *Serial titles:* 1,894 (physical), 38,647 (digital/electronic); *Databases:* 56. Weekly public service hours: 101; study areas open 24 hours, 5–7 days a week.

STUDENT LIFE
Housing options: on-campus residence required through sophomore year; coed, men-only, women-only, special housing for students with disabilities. Campus housing is university owned. Freshman campus housing is guaranteed.

Activities and organizations: drama/theater group, student-run newspaper, choral group, marching band, Collegiate100, Alpha Phi Omega, Drive Our Peer's Education DOPE, Student Ambassador's, Alpha Phi Alpha, national fraternities, national sororities.

Athletics Member NCAA. All Division II.

Campus security: 24-hour emergency response devices and patrols, student patrols, late-night transport/escort service, controlled dormitory access.

Student services: health clinic, personal/psychological counseling, veterans affairs office.

COSTS & FINANCIAL AID
Costs (2018–19) *Tuition:* state resident $7406 full-time, $325 per credit hour part-time; nonresident $18,314 full-time, $802 per credit hour part-time. Full-time tuition and fees vary according to course load. Part-time tuition and fees vary according to course load. *Required fees:* $390 full-time. *Room and board:* $6690; room only: $3340. Room and board charges vary according to board plan and housing facility.

Financial Aid Of all full-time matriculated undergraduates who enrolled in 2018, 1,017 applied for aid, 955 were judged to have need, 98 had their need fully met. 182 Federal Work-Study jobs (averaging $2003). In 2018, 72 non-need-based awards were made. *Average percent of need met:* 72. *Average financial aid package:* $14,443. *Average need-based loan:* $3745. *Average need-based gift aid:* $11,197. *Average non-need-based aid:* $5822. *Average indebtedness upon graduation:* $27,331.

APPLYING
Standardized Tests *Required:* SAT or ACT (for admission).
Required: high school transcript, minimum 2.5 GPA, minimum ACT score of 18.

CONTACT
Kentucky State University, 320 Hill Student Center, 400 East Main Street, Frankfort, KY 40601. *Phone:* 502-597-6813. *Toll-free phone:* 877-367-5978. *Fax:* 502-597-5814. *E-mail:* admissions@kysu.edu.

Kentucky Wesleyan College
Owensboro, Kentucky
http://www.kwc.edu/

CONTACT
Kentucky Wesleyan College, 3000 Frederica Street, Owensboro, KY 42301. *Phone:* 270-852-3120. *Toll-free phone:* 800-999-0592 (in-state); 800-990-0592 (out-of-state).

Lindsey Wilson College
Columbia, Kentucky
http://www.lindsey.edu/
- **Independent United Methodist** comprehensive, founded 1903
- **Rural** 225-acre campus
- **Endowment** $24.3 million
- **Coed**
- **Minimally difficult** entrance level

FACULTY
Student/faculty ratio: 13:1.

ACADEMICS
Calendar: semesters. *Degrees:* associate, bachelor's, master's, and doctoral.
Library: Katie Murrell Library.

STUDENT LIFE
Housing options: on-campus residence required through senior year; men-only, women-only. Campus housing is university owned. Freshman campus housing is guaranteed.
Activities and organizations: drama/theater group, student-run newspaper, choral group, marching band.
Athletics Member NAIA.
Campus security: 24-hour emergency response devices and patrols.
Student services: health clinic, personal/psychological counseling, women's center.

COSTS & FINANCIAL AID
Costs (2018–19) *Comprehensive fee:* $34,235 includes full-time tuition ($24,600), mandatory fees ($250), and room and board ($9385). Full-time tuition and fees vary according to class time, degree level, and location. Part-time tuition: $1025 per credit hour. Part-time tuition and fees vary according to class time, degree level, and location. *Required fees:* $50 per term part-time. *College room only:* $3400.

Financial Aid Of all full-time matriculated undergraduates who enrolled in 2017, 1,893 applied for aid, 1,789 were judged to have need, 413 had their need fully met. 225 Federal Work-Study jobs (averaging $2178). 23 state and other part-time jobs (averaging $2479). *Average need-based loan:* $4183. *Average need-based gift aid:* $19,576. *Average indebtedness upon graduation:* $28,870.

APPLYING
Standardized Tests *Required for some:* SAT or ACT (for admission).
Options: electronic application.
Required: high school transcript. *Recommended:* interview.

CONTACT
Mrs. Charity Ferguson, Assistant Director of Admissions, Lindsey Wilson College, 210 Lindsey Wilson Street, Columbia, KY 42728-1298. *Phone:* 270-384-8100. *Toll-free phone:* 800-264-0138. *Fax:* 270-384-8591.

Midway University
Midway, Kentucky
http://www.midway.edu/

CONTACT
Midway University, 512 East Stephens Street, Midway, KY 40347-1120. *Phone:* 859-846-5799. *Toll-free phone:* 800-755-0031.

Morehead State University
Morehead, Kentucky
http://www.moreheadstate.edu/
- **State-supported** comprehensive, founded 1922
- **Small-town** 1187-acre campus
- **Endowment** $43.0 million
- **Coed**
- **Minimally difficult** entrance level

FACULTY
Student/faculty ratio: 15:1.

ACADEMICS
Calendar: semesters. *Degrees:* certificates, associate, bachelor's, master's, doctoral, post-master's, and postbachelor's certificates.
Library: Camden Carroll Library. *Books:* 339,640 (physical), 121,456 (digital/electronic); *Serial titles:* 29,191 (physical), 72,511 (digital/electronic); *Databases:* 152. Weekly public service hours: 95; students can reserve study rooms.

STUDENT LIFE
Housing options: on-campus residence required through sophomore year; coed, special housing for students with disabilities. Campus housing is university owned. Freshman applicants given priority for college housing.
Activities and organizations: drama/theater group, student-run newspaper, radio and television station, choral group, marching band, Delta Tau Delta Fraternity, Delta Gamma, Phi Sigma Pi (Honors), Baptist Campus Ministries (BCM), Collegiate Future Farmers of America (FFA), national fraternities, national sororities.
Athletics Member NCAA. All Division I except football (Division I-AA).
Campus security: 24-hour emergency response devices and patrols, student patrols, late-night transport/escort service, controlled dormitory access, LiveSafe app—a two-way communication safety app between students and University Police.
Student services: health clinic, personal/psychological counseling, veterans affairs office.

COSTS & FINANCIAL AID
Costs (2018–19) *Tuition:* state resident $8750 full-time, $365 per credit hour part-time; nonresident $13,226 full-time, $552 per credit hour part-time. Full-time tuition and fees vary according to course load, degree level, location, reciprocity agreements, and student level. Part-time tuition and fees vary according to course load, degree level, location, reciprocity agreements, and student level. *Required fees:* $320 full-time, $14 per credit hour part-time. *Room and board:* $9730; room only: $5480. Room and board charges vary according to board plan and housing facility. *Payment plans:* installment, deferred payment.

Financial Aid Of all full-time matriculated undergraduates who enrolled in 2018, 4,870 applied for aid, 4,274 were judged to have need, 875 had their need fully met. 401 Federal Work-Study jobs (averaging $2325). 756 state and other part-time jobs (averaging $2962). In 2018, 737 non-need-based awards were made. *Average percent of need met:* 62. *Average financial aid package:* $12,113. *Average need-based loan:* $3570. *Average need-based gift aid:* $6100. *Average non-need-based aid:* $6600. *Average indebtedness upon graduation:* $29,023.

APPLYING
Standardized Tests *Required:* SAT or ACT (for admission).
Options: electronic application, early admission, deferred entrance.
Application fee: $30.
Required: high school transcript. *Required for some:* essay or personal statement, 1 letter of recommendation, interview.

CONTACT
Mr. Tim Rhodes, Assistant Vice President for Enrollment Services, Morehead State University, 407 Enrollment Services Center, Morehead, KY 40351. *Phone:* 606-783-2000. *Toll-free phone:* 800-585-6781. *Fax:* 606-783-5038. *E-mail:* admissions@moreheadstate.edu.

Murray State University
Murray, Kentucky
http://www.murraystate.edu/
- **State-supported** university, founded 1922
- **Small-town** 261-acre campus
- **Coed** 8,148 undergraduate students, 77% full-time, 60% women, 40% men
- **Moderately difficult** entrance level, 81% of applicants were admitted

UNDERGRAD STUDENTS
6,276 full-time, 1,872 part-time. Students come from 44 states and territories; 39 other countries; 32% are from out of state; 6% Black or African American, non-Hispanic/Latino; 2% Hispanic/Latino; 0.8% Asian, non-Hispanic/Latino; 0.2% American Indian or Alaska Native, non-Hispanic/Latino; 3% Two or more races, non-Hispanic/Latino; 4% Race/ethnicity unknown; 3% international; 7% transferred in; 33% live on campus.

Freshmen:

Admission: 8,256 applied, 6,722 admitted, 1,319 enrolled. *Average high school GPA:* 3.6. *Test scores:* ACT scores over 18: 98%; ACT scores over 24: 55%; SAT math scores over 700: 50%; ACT scores over 30: 12%.

Retention: 79% of full-time freshmen returned.

FACULTY

Total: 593, 75% full-time, 63% with terminal degrees.

Student/faculty ratio: 15:1.

ACADEMICS

Calendar: semesters. *Degrees:* certificates, bachelor's, master's, doctoral, and postbachelor's certificates.

Special study options: academic remediation for entering students, adult/continuing education programs, advanced placement credit, cooperative education, distance learning, double majors, English as a second language, external degree program, freshman honors college, honors programs, independent study, internships, off-campus study, part-time degree program, services for LD students, student-designed majors, study abroad, summer session for credit. *ROTC:* Army (b).

Unusual degree programs: B.S. to J.D.: University of Louisville; BS to M.S. in Occupational Therapy.

Computers: Students can access the following: campus intranet, computer help desk, free student e-mail accounts, online (class) grades, online (class) registration, online (class) schedules, billing accounts, course evaluation forms, receive instant campus alerts, secure on-campus housing, pre-order of food or take-out. Campuswide network is available. 100% of college-owned or -operated housing units are wired for high-speed Internet access. Wireless service is available via entire campus.

Library: Waterfield Library plus 4 others. *Books:* 330,959 (physical), 51,049 (digital/electronic); *Serial titles:* 1,305 (physical), 64,102 (digital/electronic); *Databases:* 127. Weekly public service hours: 107; students can reserve study rooms.

STUDENT LIFE

Housing options: on-campus residence required through sophomore year; coed, women-only, special housing for students with disabilities. Campus housing is university owned. Freshman applicants given priority for college housing.

Activities and organizations: drama/theater group, student-run newspaper, television station, choral group, marching band, Racer Band, Student Government Association, National Panhellenic Council, International Student Organization, MSU Student Ambassadors, national fraternities, national sororities.

Athletics Member NCAA. All Division I except football (Division I-AA). *Intercollegiate sports:* baseball M(s), basketball M(s)/W(s), cheerleading M(c)/W(c), crew M(c)/W(c), cross-country running M/W(s), equestrian sports M(c)/W(c), golf M(s)/W(s)(c), riflery M(s)/W(s), rowing M(c)/W(c), soccer W(s), softball W(s), tennis W(s), track and field W(s), volleyball W(s). *Intramural sports:* archery M(c)/W(c), basketball M/W, bowling M/W, fencing M(c), field hockey W(c), football M/W, golf M/W, racquetball M(c)/W(c), rugby M(c), soccer M/W, softball M/W, swimming and diving M/W, table tennis M/W, tennis M/W, ultimate Frisbee M/W, volleyball M/W, water polo M/W.

Campus security: 24-hour emergency response devices and patrols, student patrols, late-night transport/escort service, controlled dormitory access.

Student services: health clinic, personal/psychological counseling, women's center, veterans affairs office.

COSTS & FINANCIAL AID

Costs (2018–19) *Tuition:* state resident $9084 full-time, $379 per credit hour part-time; nonresident $24,540 full-time, $1023 per credit hour part-time. Full-time tuition and fees vary according to course load and reciprocity agreements. Part-time tuition and fees vary according to reciprocity agreements. *Room and board:* $9190; room only: $5424. Room and board charges vary according to board plan and housing facility. *Payment plan:* installment. *Waivers:* senior citizens and employees or children of employees.

Financial Aid Of all full-time matriculated undergraduates who enrolled in 2018, 5,497 applied for aid, 4,216 were judged to have need, 994 had their need fully met. In 2018, 846 non-need-based awards were made. *Average percent of need met:* 39. *Average financial aid package:* $12,987. *Average need-based loan:* $6243. *Average need-based gift aid:*

$7310. *Average non-need-based aid:* $6576. *Average indebtedness upon graduation:* $28,277.

APPLYING

Standardized Tests *Required:* SAT or ACT (for admission). *Recommended:* ACT (for admission).

Options: electronic application, early admission.

Application fee: $40.

Required: high school transcript, minimum 3.0 GPA, minimum ACT composite score of 18 or SAT score of 870, rank in the top half of high school class or minimum 3.0 GPA; high school curriculum criteria.

Application deadlines: rolling (freshmen), rolling (transfers).

Notification: continuous (freshmen), continuous (transfers).

CONTACT

Ms. Stacy Bell, Assistant Director of Undergraduate Admissions, Murray State University, 102 Curris Center, Murray, KY 42701-0009. *Phone:* 270-809-5044. *Toll-free phone:* 800-272-4678. *E-mail:* msu.admissions@ murraystate.edu.

Northern Kentucky University
Highland Heights, Kentucky
http://www.nku.edu/

- **State-supported** comprehensive, founded 1968
- **Suburban** 428-acre campus with easy access to Cincinnati
- **Endowment** $106.2 million
- **Coed** 11,933 undergraduate students, 72% full-time, 58% women, 42% men
- **Moderately difficult** entrance level, 89% of applicants were admitted

UNDERGRAD STUDENTS

8,570 full-time, 3,363 part-time. Students come from 41 states and territories; 56 other countries; 30% are from out of state; 7% Black or African American, non-Hispanic/Latino; 3% Hispanic/Latino; 1% Asian, non-Hispanic/Latino; 0.1% Native Hawaiian or other Pacific Islander, non-Hispanic/Latino; 0.2% American Indian or Alaska Native, non-Hispanic/Latino; 3% Two or more races, non-Hispanic/Latino; 0.8% Race/ethnicity unknown; 3% international; 7% transferred in; 15% live on campus.

Freshmen:

Admission: 5,995 applied, 5,351 admitted, 1,980 enrolled. *Average high school GPA:* 3.5. *Test scores:* SAT evidence-based reading and writing scores over 500: 83%; SAT math scores over 500: 71%; ACT scores over 18: 96%; SAT evidence-based reading and writing scores over 600: 33%; SAT math scores over 600: 31%; ACT scores over 24: 48%; SAT evidence-based reading and writing scores over 700: 6%; SAT math scores over 700: 11%; ACT scores over 30: 7%.

Retention: 67% of full-time freshmen returned.

FACULTY

Total: 1,004, 56% full-time, 52% with terminal degrees.

ACADEMICS

Calendar: semesters. *Degrees:* certificates, bachelor's, master's, doctoral, post-master's, and postbachelor's certificates.

Special study options: academic remediation for entering students, accelerated degree program, adult/continuing education programs, advanced placement credit, cooperative education, distance learning, double majors, English as a second language, honors programs, independent study, internships, off-campus study, part-time degree program, services for LD students, student-designed majors, study abroad, summer session for credit. *ROTC:* Army (c), Air Force (c).

Unusual degree programs: 3-2 engineering with University of Louisville, University of Kentucky; nursing with Hanover College; Computer Science with Sichuan University in China. Law with Mount St. Joseph, Thomas More, Eastern Kentucky University.

Computers: 200 computers/terminals and 1,500 ports are available on campus for general student use. Students can access the following: campus intranet, computer help desk, free student e-mail accounts, online (class) grades, online (class) registration, online (class) schedules. Campuswide network is available. 100% of college-owned or -operated housing units are wired for high-speed Internet access. Wireless service is available via entire campus.

Library: W. Frank Steely Library plus 1 other. *Books:* 326,648 (physical), 39,448 (digital/electronic); *Serial titles:* 56,176 (digital/electronic); *Databases:* 108. Weekly public service hours: 104; students can reserve study rooms.

STUDENT LIFE

Housing options: on-campus residence required for freshman year; coed, special housing for students with disabilities. Campus housing is university owned. Freshman applicants given priority for college housing.

Activities and organizations: drama/theater group, student-run newspaper, radio and television station, choral group, Sororities, Fraternities, Freshmen Service Leadership Committee, Student Alumni Association, Activities Programming Board, national fraternities, national sororities.

Athletics Member NCAA. All Division I. *Intercollegiate sports:* baseball M(s), basketball M(s)/W(s), cheerleading M(s)/W(s), cross-country running M(s)/W(s), golf M(s)/W(s), soccer M(s)/W(s), softball W(s), tennis M(s)/W(s), track and field M(s)/W(s), volleyball W(s). *Intramural sports:* badminton M(c)/W(c), basketball M/W, bowling M(c)/W(c), cross-country running M(c)/W(c), equestrian sports M(c)/W(c), lacrosse M(c)/W(c), rock climbing M(c)/W(c), skiing (downhill) W(c), soccer M(c)/W(c), tennis M/W, ultimate Frisbee M/W, volleyball M/W, water polo M/W, weight lifting M/W, wrestling M(c).

Campus security: 24-hour emergency response devices and patrols, late-night transport/escort service, controlled dormitory access.

Student services: health clinic, personal/psychological counseling, women's center, legal services, veterans affairs office.

COSTS & FINANCIAL AID

Costs (2018–19) *Tuition:* state resident $9648 full-time, $402 per credit hour part-time; nonresident $19,296 full-time, $804 per credit hour part-time. Full-time tuition and fees vary according to course load, program, and reciprocity agreements. Part-time tuition and fees vary according to course load, program, and reciprocity agreements. *Required fees:* $384 full-time, $16 per credit hour part-time. *Room and board:* $10,022. Room and board charges vary according to board plan and housing facility.

Payment plan: installment. *Waivers:* children of alumni, senior citizens, and employees or children of employees.

Financial Aid Of all full-time matriculated undergraduates who enrolled in 2018, 6,723 applied for aid, 5,464 were judged to have need, 1,167 had their need fully met. In 2018, 1496 non-need-based awards were made. *Average percent of need met:* 68. *Average financial aid package:* $12,149. *Average need-based loan:* $4311. *Average need-based gift aid:* $6099. *Average non-need-based aid:* $6326. *Average indebtedness upon graduation:* $26,502.

APPLYING

Standardized Tests *Required:* SAT or ACT (for admission).

Options: electronic application.

Application fee: $40.

Required: high school transcript, minimum 2.0 GPA. *Required for some:* Some programs require separate applications.

Application deadlines: 8/20 (freshmen), 8/15 (out-of-state freshmen), 8/1 (transfers).

Notification: continuous (freshmen), continuous (out-of-state freshmen), continuous (transfers).

CONTACT

Mrs. Melissa Gorbandt, Office of Admissions, Northern Kentucky University, Lucas Administrative Center, 400 Nunn Drive, Highland Heights, KY 41099. *Phone:* 859-572-5220. *Toll-free phone:* 800-637-9948. *Fax:* 859-572-6665. *E-mail:* beanorse@nku.edu.

See below for display ad and page 1064 for the College Close-Up.

Simmons College of Kentucky
Louisville, Kentucky
http://www.simmonscollegeky.edu/

CONTACT
Simmons College of Kentucky, 1018 South 7th Street, Louisville, KY 40203.

The Southern Baptist Theological Seminary
Louisville, Kentucky
http://www.sbts.edu/

CONTACT
Dr. Daniel DeWitt, The Southern Baptist Theological Seminary, 2825 Lexington Road, Louisville, KY 40280-0004. *Phone:* 502-897-4011 Ext. 4617.

Spalding University
Louisville, Kentucky
http://www.spalding.edu/

CONTACT
Mr. Matt Elder, Director, Undergraduate Admissions, Spalding University, 845 South Third Street, Louisville, KY 40203. *Phone:* 502-873-4177. *Toll-free phone:* 800-896-8941. *Fax:* 502-992-2418. *E-mail:* melder@spalding.edu.

Sullivan University
Louisville, Kentucky
http://www.sullivan.edu/

- **Proprietary** comprehensive, founded 1962, part of The Sullivan University System, Inc.
- **Suburban** 15-acre campus
- **Coed** 2,684 undergraduate students, 62% full-time, 62% women, 38% men
- **Minimally difficult** entrance level, 84% of applicants were admitted

UNDERGRAD STUDENTS
1,652 full-time, 1,032 part-time. Students come from 32 states and territories; 5 other countries; 18% are from out of state; 16% Black or African American, non-Hispanic/Latino; 2% Asian, non-Hispanic/Latino; 0.3% Native Hawaiian or other Pacific Islander, non-Hispanic/Latino; 0.4% American Indian or Alaska Native, non-Hispanic/Latino; 9% Two or more races, non-Hispanic/Latino; 15% Race/ethnicity unknown; 5% transferred in; 6% live on campus.

Freshmen:
Admission: 1,377 applied, 1,158 admitted, 513 enrolled. *Test scores:* SAT evidence-based reading and writing scores over 500: 94%; SAT math scores over 500: 79%; ACT scores over 18: 73%; SAT evidence-based reading and writing scores over 600: 50%; SAT math scores over 600: 26%; ACT scores over 24: 18%; SAT evidence-based reading and writing scores over 700: 6%; SAT math scores over 700: 10%; ACT scores over 30: 1%.

FACULTY
Total: 276, 38% full-time.
Student/faculty ratio: 19:1.

ACADEMICS
Calendar: quarters. *Degrees:* certificates, diplomas, associate, bachelor's, master's, doctoral, and postbachelor's certificates.

Special study options: academic remediation for entering students, accelerated degree program, adult/continuing education programs, cooperative education, distance learning, double majors, independent study, internships, part-time degree program, services for LD students, student-designed majors.

Computers: 93 computers/terminals are available on campus for general student use. Students can access the following: campus intranet, computer help desk, free student e-mail accounts, online (class) grades, online (class) registration, online (class) schedules. Campuswide network is available. 100% of college-owned or -operated housing units are wired for high-speed Internet access. Wireless service is available via entire campus.
Library: Sullivan University Library and Learning Resource Center. *Books:* 31,224 (physical), 67,291 (digital/electronic); *Serial titles:* 29 (physical), 134,525 (digital/electronic); *Databases:* 166. Weekly public service hours: 82.

STUDENT LIFE
Housing options: coed, men-only, women-only, special housing for students with disabilities. Campus housing is university owned. Freshman campus housing is guaranteed.

Activities and organizations: Housing and Residence Life, Student Veterans Association, Sigma Beta Delta, Phi Beta Lambda, Game Club.

Athletics *Intramural sports:* basketball M/W, sand volleyball M/W, soccer M/W, softball M/W, volleyball M/W.

Campus security: 24-hour patrols, late-night transport/escort service, controlled dormitory access.

Student services: personal/psychological counseling.

FINANCIAL AID
Financial Aid Of all full-time matriculated undergraduates who enrolled in 2002, 6,028 applied for aid, 5,247 were judged to have need. 31 Federal Work-Study jobs (averaging $2065). In 2002, 374 non-need-based awards were made. *Average non-need-based aid:* $2000. *Average indebtedness upon graduation:* $15,000.

APPLYING
Standardized Tests *Recommended:* SAT or ACT (for admission).
Options: electronic application, deferred entrance.
Application fee: $30.
Required for some: essay or personal statement, high school transcript, interview, criminal background check and no felony convictions, drug testing, and immunizations.
Application deadlines: rolling (freshmen), rolling (out-of-state freshmen), rolling (transfers).
Notification: continuous (freshmen), continuous (out-of-state freshmen), continuous (transfers).

CONTACT
Ms. Heather Cunningham, Senior Director of Admissions, Sullivan University, 3101 Bardstown Road, Louisville, KY 40205. *Phone:* 502-456-6505. *Toll-free phone:* 800-844-1354. *Fax:* 502-456-0040. *E-mail:* admissions@sullivan.edu.

Thomas More University
Crestview Hills, Kentucky
http://www.thomasmore.edu/

CONTACT
Justin Vogel, Director of Admissions, Thomas More University, 333 Thomas More Parkway, Crestview Hills, KY 41017-3495. *Phone:* 859-344-3307. *Toll-free phone:* 800-825-4557. *Fax:* 859-344-3444. *E-mail:* admissions@thomasmore.edu.

Transylvania University
Lexington, Kentucky
http://www.transy.edu/

- **Independent** 4-year, founded 1780, affiliated with Christian Church (Disciples of Christ)
- **Urban** 40-acre campus with easy access to Cincinnati, Louisville
- **Endowment** $179.2 million
- **Coed**
- **Very difficult** entrance level

FACULTY
Student/faculty ratio: 11:1.

ACADEMICS
Calendar: 4-4-1. *Degree:* bachelor's.
Library: J. Douglas Gay Jr./Frances Carrick Thomas Library. *Books:* 124,199 (physical), 170,342 (digital/electronic); *Serial titles:* 530 (physical), 23,600 (digital/electronic); *Databases:* 70. Weekly public service hours: 102; students can reserve study rooms.

STUDENT LIFE
Housing options: on-campus residence required through junior year; coed, men-only, women-only, special housing for students with disabilities. Campus housing is university owned. Freshman campus housing is guaranteed.

Activities and organizations: drama/theater group, student-run newspaper, radio station, choral group, Student Government Association, Delta Sigma Phi, Phi Mu, Delta Delta Delta, Chi Omega, national fraternities, national sororities.

Athletics Member NCAA. All Division III.

Campus security: 24-hour emergency response devices and patrols, late-night transport/escort service, controlled dormitory access.

Student services: health clinic, personal/psychological counseling.

COSTS & FINANCIAL AID

Costs (2018–19) *Comprehensive fee:* $49,210 includes full-time tuition ($37,170), mandatory fees ($1580), and room and board ($10,460). Part-time tuition: $4130 per course. Part-time tuition and fees vary according to course load. *College room only:* $5920. Room and board charges vary according to board plan and housing facility.

Financial Aid Of all full-time matriculated undergraduates who enrolled in 2018, 806 applied for aid, 692 were judged to have need, 160 had their need fully met. 307 Federal Work-Study jobs (averaging $1651). 27 state and other part-time jobs (averaging $7219). In 2018, 266 non-need-based awards were made. *Average percent of need met:* 78. *Average financial aid package:* $29,205. *Average need-based loan:* $3951. *Average need-based gift aid:* $25,644. *Average non-need-based aid:* $17,749. *Average indebtedness upon graduation:* $33,037.

APPLYING

Options: electronic application, early admission, early action, deferred entrance.

Required: essay or personal statement, high school transcript, minimum 2.8 GPA, 2 letters of recommendation. *Required for some:* interview. *Recommended:* interview.

CONTACT

Dr. Holly Sheilley, Vice President for Enrollment and Student Life, Transylvania University, 300 North Broadway, Lexington, KY 40508-1797. *Phone:* 859-233-8242. *Toll-free phone:* 800-872-6798. *Fax:* 859-281-3649. *E-mail:* admissions@transy.edu/

Union College

Barbourville, Kentucky

http://www.unionky.edu/

- **Independent United Methodist** comprehensive, founded 1879
- **Small-town** 100-acre campus
- **Endowment** $22.7 million
- **Coed** 1,115 undergraduate students, 82% full-time, 52% women, 48% men
- **Moderately difficult** entrance level, 56% of applicants were admitted

UNDERGRAD STUDENTS

912 full-time, 203 part-time. Students come from 34 states and territories; 16 other countries; 29% are from out of state; 14% Black or African American, non-Hispanic/Latino; 2% Hispanic/Latino; 0.2% Asian, non-Hispanic/Latino; 0.2% Native Hawaiian or other Pacific Islander, non-Hispanic/Latino; 0.6% American Indian or Alaska Native, non-Hispanic/Latino; 3% Two or more races, non-Hispanic/Latino; 0.7% Race/ethnicity unknown; 9% international; 9% transferred in; 47% live on campus.

Freshmen:

Admission: 1,539 applied, 867 admitted, 218 enrolled. *Average high school GPA:* 3.2. *Test scores:* ACT scores over 18: 78%; ACT scores over 24: 18%; ACT scores over 30: 1%.

Retention: 65% of full-time freshmen returned.

FACULTY

Total: 131, 40% full-time, 49% with terminal degrees.

Student/faculty ratio: 12:1.

ACADEMICS

Calendar: semesters. *Degrees:* certificates, bachelor's, master's, post-master's, and postbachelor's certificates.

Special study options: academic remediation for entering students, accelerated degree program, advanced placement credit, double majors, English as a second language, honors programs, independent study, off-campus study, part-time degree program, services for LD students, student-designed majors, study abroad, summer session for credit.

Computers: 290 computers/terminals and 550 ports are available on campus for general student use. Students can access the following: campus intranet, computer help desk, free student e-mail accounts, online (class) grades, online (class) registration, online (class) schedules. Campuswide network is available. 100% of college-owned or -operated housing units are wired for high-speed Internet access. Wireless service is available via classrooms, computer centers, computer labs, dorm rooms, learning centers, libraries, student centers.

Library: Weeks-Townsend Memorial Library plus 1 other. *Books:* 121,623 (physical), 386,171 (digital/electronic); *Serial titles:* 42,795 (physical); *Databases:* 124,060.

STUDENT LIFE

Housing options: on-campus residence required through sophomore year; men-only, women-only. Campus housing is university owned. Freshman campus housing is guaranteed.

Activities and organizations: drama/theater group, choral group, Student Ambassadors, Student Government Association, Union Singers, International Club, Spiritual Life Team.

Athletics Member NAIA. *Intercollegiate sports:* archery M(s)/W(s), baseball M(s), basketball M(s)/W(s), bowling M(s)/W(s), cheerleading M(s)/W(s), cross-country running M(s)/W(s), football M(s), golf M(s)/W(s), lacrosse M(s), soccer M(s)/W(s), softball W(s), swimming and diving M(s)/W(s), tennis M(s)/W(s), track and field M(s)/W(s), volleyball W(s). *Intramural sports:* basketball M/W, softball M/W, swimming and diving M/W, table tennis M/W, tennis M/W, volleyball M/W.

Campus security: 24-hour emergency response devices and patrols, late-night transport/escort service, controlled dormitory access.

Student services: health clinic, personal/psychological counseling.

COSTS & FINANCIAL AID

Costs (2019–20) *Comprehensive fee:* $1620 includes full-time tuition ($26,330), mandatory fees ($1620), and room and board ($7500). Part-time tuition: $345 per credit hour. *College room only:* $3300.

Financial Aid Of all full-time matriculated undergraduates who enrolled in 2016, 744 applied for aid, 704 were judged to have need, 84 had their need fully met. 111 Federal Work-Study jobs (averaging $1500). 28 state and other part-time jobs (averaging $1500). In 2016, 73 non-need-based awards were made. *Average percent of need met:* 65. *Average financial aid package:* $23,031. *Average need-based loan:* $4235. *Average need-based gift aid:* $19,313. *Average non-need-based aid:* $16,840. *Average indebtedness upon graduation:* $32,691.

APPLYING

Standardized Tests *Required:* SAT or ACT (for admission).

Options: electronic application, deferred entrance.

Required: high school transcript, minimum 2.0 GPA. *Required for some:* interview, Non-refundable application fee of $100 for international students only..

Application deadlines: rolling (freshmen), rolling (transfers).

Notification: continuous (freshmen), 9/1 (out-of-state freshmen), continuous (transfers).

CONTACT

Mr. Craig Grooms, Vice President for Enrollment and Student Life, Union College, 310 College Street, Barbourville, KY 40906. *Phone:* 606-546-1750. *Toll-free phone:* 800-489-8646. *Fax:* 606-546-1769. *E-mail:* enrollme@unionky.edu.

University of Kentucky

Lexington, Kentucky

http://www.uky.edu/

- **State-supported** university, founded 1865, part of Kentucky does not have a state system.
- **Urban** 813-acre campus with easy access to Cincinnati, Louisville
- **Endowment** $1.3 billion
- **Coed** 22,136 undergraduate students, 93% full-time, 55% women, 45% men
- **Moderately difficult** entrance level, 94% of applicants were admitted

UNDERGRAD STUDENTS
20,484 full-time, 1,652 part-time. Students come from 54 states and territories; 67 other countries; 31% are from out of state; 8% Black or African American, non-Hispanic/Latino; 5% Hispanic/Latino; 3% Asian, non-Hispanic/Latino; 0.1% Native Hawaiian or other Pacific Islander, non-Hispanic/Latino; 0.1% American Indian or Alaska Native, non-Hispanic/Latino; 4% Two or more races, non-Hispanic/Latino; 3% Race/ethnicity unknown; 2% international; 4% transferred in; 31% live on campus.

Freshmen:
Admission: 19,324 applied, 18,258 admitted, 5,077 enrolled. *Average high school GPA:* 3.5. *Test scores:* SAT evidence-based reading and writing scores over 500: 91%; SAT math scores over 500: 90%; ACT scores over 18: 99%; SAT evidence-based reading and writing scores over 600: 52%; SAT math scores over 600: 46%; ACT scores over 24: 68%; SAT evidence-based reading and writing scores over 700: 11%; SAT math scores over 700: 14%; ACT scores over 30: 22%.

Retention: 85% of full-time freshmen returned.

FACULTY
Total: 2,149, 67% full-time, 93% with terminal degrees.

ACADEMICS
Calendar: semesters. *Degrees:* certificates, bachelor's, master's, doctoral, post-master's, and postbachelor's certificates.

Special study options: academic remediation for entering students, accelerated degree program, adult/continuing education programs, advanced placement credit, cooperative education, distance learning, double majors, English as a second language, honors programs, independent study, internships, off-campus study, part-time degree program, services for LD students, student-designed majors, study abroad, summer session for credit. *ROTC:* Army (b), Air Force (b).

Unusual degree programs: 3-2 business administration.

Computers: 1,000 computers/terminals are available on campus for general student use. Students can access the following: campus intranet, computer help desk, free student e-mail accounts, online (class) grades, online (class) registration, online (class) schedules. Campuswide network is available. 100% of college-owned or -operated housing units are wired for high-speed Internet access. Wireless service is available via entire campus.

Library: William T. Young Library plus 10 others. *Books:* 2.5 million (physical), 1.7 million (digital/electronic); *Serial titles:* 56,959 (physical), 175,865 (digital/electronic); *Databases:* 435. Study areas open 24 hours, 5–7 days a week; students can reserve study rooms.

STUDENT LIFE
Housing options: coed, men-only. Campus housing is university owned, leased by the school and is provided by a third party. Freshman applicants given priority for college housing.

Activities and organizations: drama/theater group, student-run newspaper, radio and television station, choral group, marching band, Student Activities Board, Student Government Association, Campus Progressive Coalition, Ski and Snowboard Club, Society of Women Engineers, national fraternities, national sororities.

Athletics Member NCAA. All Division I except football (Division I-A). *Intercollegiate sports:* baseball M(s), basketball M(s)/W(s), cheerleading M/W, cross-country running M(s)/W(s), golf M(s)/W(s), gymnastics W(s), riflery M(s)/W(s), soccer M(s)/W(s), softball W(s), swimming and diving M(s)/W(s), tennis M(s)/W(s), track and field M(s)/W(s), volleyball W(s). *Intramural sports:* archery M/W, badminton M/W, baseball M(c), basketball M/W, bowling M/W, cheerleading M/W, cross-country running M/W, equestrian sports M(c)/W(c), fencing M/W, field hockey W(c), football M/W, golf M(c)/W, gymnastics M, ice hockey M(c), lacrosse M(c)/W, racquetball M/W, rock climbing M/W, rugby M/W(c), skiing (cross-country) M(c)/W(c), skiing (downhill) M(c)/W(c), soccer M/W, softball M/W(c), squash M/W, swimming and diving M/W, table tennis M/W, tennis M/W, track and field M/W, triathlon M(c)/W(c), ultimate Frisbee M(c)/W(c), volleyball M/W, water polo M(c)/W(c), weight lifting M(c)/W(c), wrestling M/W.

Campus security: 24-hour emergency response devices and patrols, late-night transport/escort service, controlled dormitory access.

Student services: health clinic, personal/psychological counseling, women's center, legal services, veterans affairs office.

COSTS & FINANCIAL AID
Costs (2018–19) *Tuition:* state resident $10,896 full-time, $490 per credit hour part-time; nonresident $27,750 full-time, $1189 per credit hour part-time. Full-time tuition and fees vary according to location, program, reciprocity agreements, and student level. Part-time tuition and fees vary according to course load, location, program, reciprocity agreements, and student level. *Required fees:* $1349 full-time, $43 per credit hour part-time. *Room and board:* $12,982; room only: $8832. Room and board charges vary according to board plan and housing facility. *Payment plan:* installment. *Waivers:* employees or children of employees.

Financial Aid Of all full-time matriculated undergraduates who enrolled in 2017, 13,764 applied for aid, 11,025 were judged to have need, 1,741 had their need fully met. In 2017, 5325 non-need-based awards were made. *Average percent of need met:* 54. *Average financial aid package:* $13,391. *Average need-based loan:* $4491. *Average need-based gift aid:* $5900. *Average non-need-based aid:* $9516. *Average indebtedness upon graduation:* $32,437.

APPLYING
Standardized Tests *Required:* SAT or ACT (for admission).

Options: electronic application, early admission, early action, deferred entrance.

Application fee: $50.

Required: essay or personal statement, high school transcript. *Required for some:* Audition required of music and dance majors..

Application deadlines: 2/15 (freshmen), 2/15 (out-of-state freshmen), 8/1 (transfers), 12/1 (early action).

Notification: continuous until 3/15 (freshmen), continuous until 3/15 (out-of-state freshmen), continuous (transfers), rolling (early action).

CONTACT
Scott McDonald, University of Kentucky, 100 W.D. Funkhouser Building, Lexington, KY 40506-0054. *Phone:* 859-257-2000. *Toll-free phone:* 866-900-GO-UK. *Fax:* 859-257-3823. *E-mail:* admission@uky.edu.

University of Louisville
Louisville, Kentucky
http://www.louisville.edu/
- **State-supported** university, founded 1798
- **Urban** 640-acre campus with easy access to Louisville
- **Endowment** $792.2 million
- **Coed** 15,642 undergraduate students, 76% full-time, 52% women, 48% men
- **Moderately difficult** entrance level, 73% of applicants were admitted

UNDERGRAD STUDENTS
11,930 full-time, 3,712 part-time. Students come from 52 states and territories; 63 other countries; 17% are from out of state; 12% Black or African American, non-Hispanic/Latino; 5% Hispanic/Latino; 4% Asian, non-Hispanic/Latino; 0.1% American Indian or Alaska Native, non-Hispanic/Latino; 6% Two or more races, non-Hispanic/Latino; 0.1% Race/ethnicity unknown; 1% international; 6% transferred in; 23% live on campus.

Freshmen:
Admission: 13,570 applied, 9,890 admitted, 2,932 enrolled. *Average high school GPA:* 3.6. *Test scores:* ACT scores over 18: 99%; ACT scores over 24: 64%; ACT scores over 30: 22%.

Retention: 80% of full-time freshmen returned.

FACULTY
Total: 1,511, 61% full-time, 67% with terminal degrees.
Student/faculty ratio: 15:1.

ACADEMICS
Calendar: semesters. *Degrees:* certificates, associate, bachelor's, master's, doctoral, post-master's, and postbachelor's certificates.

Special study options: academic remediation for entering students, accelerated degree program, adult/continuing education programs, advanced placement credit, cooperative education, distance learning, double majors, English as a second language, honors programs, independent study, internships, off-campus study, part-time degree program, services for LD students, study abroad, summer session for credit. *ROTC:* Army (b), Air Force (b).

Unusual degree programs: 3-2 engineering.

Computers: 400 computers/terminals are available on campus for general student use. Students can access the following: computer help desk, free student e-mail accounts, online (class) grades, online (class) registration, online (class) schedules. Campuswide network is available. 100% of college-owned or -operated housing units are wired for high-speed Internet access. Wireless service is available via entire campus.

Library: William F. Ekstrom Library plus 6 others. *Books:* 1.6 million (physical), 367,856 (digital/electronic); *Serial titles:* 2,158 (physical), 90,689 (digital/electronic); *Databases:* 345. Weekly public service hours: 97; study areas open 24 hours, 5–7 days a week; students can reserve study rooms.

STUDENT LIFE

Housing options: on-campus residence required for freshman year; coed, men-only, women-only, special housing for students with disabilities. Campus housing is university owned and leased by the school. Freshman campus housing is guaranteed.

Activities and organizations: drama/theater group, student-run newspaper, choral group, marching band, Baptist Campus Ministry, Society of Porter Scholars, Association of Black Students, Common Ground, Raise Red Dance Marathon, national fraternities, national sororities.

Athletics Member NCAA. All Division I except football (Division I-A). *Intercollegiate sports:* baseball M(s), basketball M(s)/W(s), cheerleading M/W, cross-country running M(s)/W(s), field hockey W(s), golf M(s)/W(s)(c), lacrosse W(s), rowing W(s), soccer M(s)/W(s), softball W(s), swimming and diving M(s)/W(s), tennis M(s)/W(s), track and field M(s)/W(s), volleyball W(s). *Intramural sports:* badminton M/W, basketball M/W, bowling M/W, cross-country running M/W, equestrian sports W(c), fencing M, field hockey W, football M/W, golf M/W, ice hockey M, lacrosse M(c)/W(c), racquetball M/W, rugby M(c), soccer M/W, softball W, swimming and diving M/W, table tennis M/W, tennis M/W, track and field M/W, ultimate Frisbee M/W, volleyball M/W.

Campus security: 24-hour emergency response devices and patrols, late-night transport/escort service, controlled dormitory access.

Student services: health clinic, personal/psychological counseling, women's center, veterans affairs office.

COSTS & FINANCIAL AID

Costs (2019–20) *Tuition:* state resident $11,460 full-time, $478 per credit hour part-time; nonresident $27,082 full-time, $1129 per credit hour part-time. *Required fees:* $196 full-time. *Room and board:* $9058; room only: $5282.

Financial Aid Of all full-time matriculated undergraduates who enrolled in 2018, 9,079 applied for aid, 7,465 were judged to have need, 1,256 had their need fully met. 519 Federal Work-Study jobs (averaging $3574). In 2018, 1727 non-need-based awards were made. *Average percent of need met:* 59. *Average financial aid package:* $12,848. *Average need-based loan:* $4031. *Average need-based gift aid:* $10,272. *Average non-need-based aid:* $8441. *Average indebtedness upon graduation:* $24,631.

APPLYING

Standardized Tests *Required for some:* SAT or ACT (for admission), TOEFL for students whose primary language is not English.

Options: electronic application, deferred entrance.

Application fee: $25.

Required: high school transcript, minimum 2.5 GPA.

Application deadlines: 8/1 (freshmen), rolling (transfers).

Notification: continuous (transfers).

CONTACT

Ms. Jenny L. Sawyer, Executive Director of Admissions, University of Louisville, 2301 South Third Street, Houchens Room 150, Louisville, KY 40292-0001. *Phone:* 502-852-6531. *Toll-free phone:* 800-334-8635. *Fax:* 502-852-4776. *E-mail:* admitme@louisville.edu.

University of Pikeville
Pikeville, Kentucky
http://www.upike.edu/

- **Independent** comprehensive, founded 1889, affiliated with Presbyterian Church (U.S.A.)
- **Small-town** 25-acre campus
- **Endowment** $15.4 million
- **Coed**
- **Noncompetitive** entrance level

FACULTY
Student/faculty ratio: 14:1.

ACADEMICS
Calendar: semesters. *Degrees:* associate, bachelor's, master's, and doctoral.

Library: Allara Library plus 2 others. *Books:* 73,924 (physical), 214,499 (digital/electronic); *Serial titles:* 1,437 (physical), 88,386 (digital/electronic); *Databases:* 73. Weekly public service hours: 105; students can reserve study rooms.

STUDENT LIFE
Housing options: coed, men-only, women-only. Campus housing is university owned.

Activities and organizations: drama/theater group, student-run newspaper, television station, choral group, Student Government, Phi Beta Lambda, Lambda Sigma, Concert Choir, Student Nurses at UPIKE.

Athletics Member NAIA.

Campus security: 24-hour patrols, controlled dormitory access.

Student services: health clinic, veterans affairs office.

COSTS & FINANCIAL AID
Costs (2018–19) *Comprehensive fee:* $28,750 includes full-time tuition ($20,800), mandatory fees ($150), and room and board ($7800). Full-time tuition and fees vary according to course load. Part-time tuition: $867 per semester hour. Part-time tuition and fees vary according to course load. *Room and board:* Room and board charges vary according to housing facility.

Financial Aid Of all full-time matriculated undergraduates who enrolled in 2018, 1,049 applied for aid, 1,045 were judged to have need, 412 had their need fully met. 412 Federal Work-Study jobs (averaging $1683). *Average percent of need met:* 81. *Average financial aid package:* $21,563. *Average need-based loan:* $3889. *Average need-based gift aid:* $15,562. *Average indebtedness upon graduation:* $23,890.

APPLYING
Standardized Tests *Required:* SAT or ACT (for admission).

Options: electronic application, deferred entrance.

Required: high school transcript.

CONTACT
Mr. John Yancey, Director of Admissions, University of Pikeville, 147 Sycamore Street, Pikeville, KY 41501. *Phone:* 606-218-5251. *Toll-free phone:* 866-232-7700. *Fax:* 606-218-5255. *E-mail:* wewantyou@pc.edu.

University of the Cumberlands
Williamsburg, Kentucky
http://www.ucumberlands.edu/

CONTACT
Mrs. Erica Harris, Director of Admissions, University of the Cumberlands, 6178 College Station Drive, Williamsburg, KY 40769. *Phone:* 606-539-4241. *Toll-free phone:* 800-343-1609. *Fax:* 606-539-4303. *E-mail:* admiss@ucumberlands.edu.

Western Kentucky University
Bowling Green, Kentucky
http://www.wku.edu/
- **State-supported** comprehensive, founded 1906
- **Suburban** 235-acre campus with easy access to Nashville
- **Endowment** $163.2 million
- **Coed** 17,030 undergraduate students, 73% full-time, 59% women, 41% men
- **Minimally difficult** entrance level, 97% of applicants were admitted

UNDERGRAD STUDENTS
12,393 full-time, 4,637 part-time. Students come from 47 states and territories; 58 other countries; 22% are from out of state; 8% Black or African American, non-Hispanic/Latino; 4% Hispanic/Latino; 2% Asian, non-Hispanic/Latino; 0.1% Native Hawaiian or other Pacific Islander, non-Hispanic/Latino; 0.3% American Indian or Alaska Native, non-Hispanic/Latino; 3% Two or more races, non-Hispanic/Latino; 0.6% Race/ethnicity unknown; 3% international; 6% transferred in; 35% live on campus.

Freshmen:
Admission: 9,250 applied, 8,992 admitted, 2,934 enrolled. *Average high school GPA:* 3.4. *Test scores:* SAT evidence-based reading and writing scores over 500: 79%; SAT math scores over 500: 68%; ACT scores over 18: 87%; SAT evidence-based reading and writing scores over 600: 26%; SAT math scores over 600: 23%; ACT scores over 24: 47%; SAT evidence-based reading and writing scores over 700: 5%; SAT math scores over 700: 4%; ACT scores over 30: 11%.

Retention: 72% of full-time freshmen returned.

FACULTY
Total: 1,116, 64% full-time, 60% with terminal degrees.
Student/faculty ratio: 18:1.

ACADEMICS
Calendar: semesters. *Degrees:* certificates, associate, bachelor's, master's, doctoral, post-master's, and postbachelor's certificates.

Special study options: academic remediation for entering students, accelerated degree program, adult/continuing education programs, advanced placement credit, cooperative education, distance learning, double majors, English as a second language, freshman honors college, honors programs, independent study, internships, off-campus study, part-time degree program, services for LD students, student-designed majors, study abroad, summer session for credit. *ROTC:* Army (b), Air Force (c).

Unusual degree programs: 3-2 Physics, applied sciences, engineering.

Computers: 312 computers/terminals are available on campus for general student use. Students can access the following: campus intranet, computer help desk, free student e-mail accounts, online (class) grades, online (class) registration, online (class) schedules. Campuswide network is available. 100% of college-owned or -operated housing units are wired for high-speed Internet access. Wireless service is available via entire campus.
Library: Helm-Cravens Library plus 2 others. *Books:* 848,646 (physical), 112,090 (digital/electronic); *Serial titles:* 10,834 (physical), 48,911 (digital/electronic); *Databases:* 48,893. Weekly public service hours: 95; students can reserve study rooms.

STUDENT LIFE
Housing options: on-campus residence required through sophomore year; coed, men-only, women-only. Campus housing is university owned. Freshman applicants given priority for college housing.

Activities and organizations: drama/theater group, student-run newspaper, radio and television station, choral group, marching band, Student Government Association, Campus Activities Board, Campus Crusade for Christ, Campus Ministries, Residence Hall Association, national fraternities, national sororities.

Athletics Member NCAA. All Division I except football (Division I-A). *Intercollegiate sports:* baseball M(s), basketball M(s)/W(s), cross-country running M(s)/W(s), golf M(s)/W(s), soccer W, softball W(s), tennis W(s), track and field M(s)/W(s), volleyball W(s). *Intramural sports:* badminton M(c)/W(c), basketball M/W, fencing M(c)/W(c), football M/W, golf M/W, lacrosse M(c)/W(c), racquetball M/W, rugby M(c)/W(c), soccer M/W, softball M/W, table tennis M/W, tennis M/W, triathlon M(c)/W(c), ultimate Frisbee M/W, volleyball M/W.

Campus security: 24-hour emergency response devices and patrols, student patrols, late-night transport/escort service, controlled dormitory access.
Student services: health clinic, personal/psychological counseling, women's center, legal services, veterans affairs office.

COSTS & FINANCIAL AID
Costs (2018–19) *Tuition:* state resident $10,602 full-time, $442 per credit hour part-time; nonresident $26,496 full-time, $1104 per credit hour part-time. Full-time tuition and fees vary according to reciprocity agreements. Part-time tuition and fees vary according to reciprocity agreements. *Room and board:* $8343; room only: $4768. Room and board charges vary according to board plan and housing facility. *Payment plan:* installment. *Waivers:* senior citizens and employees or children of employees.

Financial Aid Of all full-time matriculated undergraduates who enrolled in 2017, 10,275 applied for aid, 8,243 were judged to have need, 1,353 had their need fully met. 625 Federal Work-Study jobs (averaging $2192). 1,466 state and other part-time jobs (averaging $2558). In 2017, 1739 non-need-based awards were made. *Average percent of need met:* 17. *Average financial aid package:* $14,900. *Average need-based loan:* $3796. *Average need-based gift aid:* $5409. *Average non-need-based aid:* $6482. *Average indebtedness upon graduation:* $27,443.

APPLYING
Standardized Tests *Required:* SAT or ACT (for admission).
Options: electronic application, deferred entrance.
Application fee: $45.
Required: high school transcript, minimum ACT composite score of 20 or greater, SAT combined score of 1020 or greater (940 or greater for tests taken prior to March 2016), unweighted high school GPA of 2.50 or higher, or minimum on Composite Admission Index score.
Notification: continuous (freshmen), continuous (transfers).

CONTACT
Dr. Jace Thomas Lux, Director, Western Kentucky University, 1906 College Heights Boulevard, Bowling Green, KY 42101. *Phone:* 270-745-2551. *Toll-free phone:* 800-495-8463. *E-mail:* jace.lux@wku.edu.

LOUISIANA

★ Centenary College of Louisiana
Shreveport, Louisiana
http://www.centenary.edu/
- **Independent United Methodist** comprehensive, founded 1825
- **Urban** 65-acre campus with easy access to Shreveport
- **Coed** 552 undergraduate students, 98% full-time, 57% women, 43% men
- **Moderately difficult** entrance level, 60% of applicants were admitted

UNDERGRAD STUDENTS
539 full-time, 13 part-time. 14% Black or African American, non-Hispanic/Latino; 10% Hispanic/Latino; 2% Asian, non-Hispanic/Latino; 0.2% Native Hawaiian or other Pacific Islander, non-Hispanic/Latino; 0.5% American Indian or Alaska Native, non-Hispanic/Latino; 6% Two or more races, non-Hispanic/Latino; 3% international.

Freshmen:
Admission: 893 applied, 533 admitted, 169 enrolled. *Average high school GPA:* 3.5. *Test scores:* SAT evidence-based reading and writing scores over 500: 91%; SAT math scores over 500: 88%; ACT scores over 18: 99%; SAT evidence-based reading and writing scores over 600: 32%; SAT math scores over 600: 37%; ACT scores over 24: 58%; SAT evidence-based reading and writing scores over 700: 3%; SAT math scores over 700: 5%; ACT scores over 30: 15%.

Retention: 76% of full-time freshmen returned.

FACULTY
Total: 83, 66% full-time, 75% with terminal degrees.
Student/faculty ratio: 9:1.

ACADEMICS
Calendar: 4-4-1. *Degrees:* bachelor's and master's.

Special study options: advanced placement credit, double majors, honors programs, independent study, internships, off-campus study, part-time degree program, services for LD students, student-designed majors, study abroad, summer session for credit.

Unusual degree programs: 3-2 engineering; speech pathology.

Computers: Students can access the following: free student e-mail accounts, online (class) grades, online (class) schedules. Campuswide network is available. Wireless service is available via classrooms, computer labs, dorm rooms, libraries, student centers.

Library: Magale Library plus 1 other. Students can reserve study rooms.

STUDENT LIFE

Housing options: on-campus residence required through senior year; coed. Campus housing is university owned. Freshman campus housing is guaranteed.

Activities and organizations: drama/theater group, student-run newspaper, radio station, choral group, Intramural sports, Residence Life (Centenary Activities Board), Fellowship of Christian Athletes, Christian Leadership Center, Media Group, national fraternities, national sororities.

Athletics Member NCAA. All Division III. *Intercollegiate sports:* baseball M, basketball M/W, golf M/W, gymnastics W, lacrosse M(c), soccer M/W, softball W, swimming and diving M/W, tennis M/W, volleyball W. *Intramural sports:* basketball M/W, football M/W, soccer M/W, softball M/W, ultimate Frisbee M/W, volleyball M/W.

Campus security: 24-hour emergency response devices and patrols, late-night transport/escort service, controlled dormitory access.

Student services: health clinic, personal/psychological counseling.

COSTS & FINANCIAL AID

Costs (2019–20) *One-time required fee:* $250. *Comprehensive fee:* $50,980 includes full-time tuition ($37,310) and room and board ($13,670). Part-time tuition: $1554 per credit hour.

Financial Aid Of all full-time matriculated undergraduates who enrolled in 2018, 480 applied for aid, 427 were judged to have need, 110 had their need fully met. 185 Federal Work-Study jobs (averaging $2144). 52 state and other part-time jobs (averaging $1738). In 2018, 108 non-need-based awards were made. *Average percent of need met:* 74. *Average financial aid package:* $31,379. *Average need-based loan:* $4215. *Average need-based gift aid:* $27,891. *Average non-need-based aid:* $23,787. *Average indebtedness upon graduation:* $27,359.

APPLYING

Standardized Tests *Required:* SAT or ACT (for admission).

Options: electronic application, early admission, early action, deferred entrance.

Application deadlines: rolling (freshmen), rolling (transfers).

Notification: continuous (freshmen), continuous (transfers).

CONTACT

Ms. Lauren Carlton Hawkins, Associate Director of Admission, Recruitment, Centenary College of Louisiana, Office of Admission, 2911 Centenary Boulevard, Shreveport, LA 71104. *Phone:* 318-869-5131. *Toll-free phone:* 800-234-4448. *Fax:* 318-869-5005. *E-mail:* lcarlton@centenary.edu.

Dillard University

New Orleans, Louisiana
http://www.dillard.edu/

CONTACT

Ms. Monica White, Director for Recruitment, Admissions and Programming, Dillard University, 2601 Gentilly Boulevard, New Orleans, LA 70122-3097. *Phone:* 504-816-4374. *Toll-free phone:* 800-216-8094. *Fax:* 504-816-4895. *E-mail:* acyprian@dillard.edu.

Franciscan Missionaries of Our Lady University

Baton Rouge, Louisiana
http://www.franu.edu/

- **Independent Roman Catholic** comprehensive, founded 1990
- **Urban** 5-acre campus with easy access to New Orleans
- **Coed**
- **Minimally difficult** entrance level

ACADEMICS

Calendar: semesters. *Degrees:* certificates, associate, bachelor's, master's, doctoral, and postbachelor's certificates.

Library: Students can reserve study rooms.

STUDENT LIFE

Housing options: college housing not available.

Activities and organizations: Student Government Association, Cultural Arts Association, Christian Fellowship Association, Mathematics/Science Association.

Campus security: 24-hour patrols.

Student services: health clinic, personal/psychological counseling.

COSTS & FINANCIAL AID

Costs (2018–19) *Tuition:* $12,161 full-time, $507 per credit hour part-time. Full-time tuition and fees vary according to course load, degree level, and program. Part-time tuition and fees vary according to course load, degree level, and program. *Required fees:* $1126 full-time.

Financial Aid Of all full-time matriculated undergraduates who enrolled in 2008, 684 applied for aid, 546 were judged to have need, 10 had their need fully met. *Average financial aid package:* $5175. *Average need-based loan:* $3664. *Average need-based gift aid:* $2486. *Average indebtedness upon graduation:* $12,019.

APPLYING

Standardized Tests *Required:* SAT or ACT (for admission).

Options: electronic application, early admission, deferred entrance.

Application fee: $35.

Required: high school transcript, minimum 2.5 GPA.

CONTACT

Franciscan Missionaries of Our Lady University, LA. *Phone:* 225-768-1718. *E-mail:* admissions@franu.edu.

Grambling State University

Grambling, Louisiana
http://www.gram.edu/

- **State-supported** university, founded 1901, part of University of Louisiana System
- **Small-town** 590-acre campus with easy access to Shreveport
- **Endowment** $6.8 million
- **Coed**
- **Noncompetitive** entrance level

FACULTY

Student/faculty ratio: 26:1.

ACADEMICS

Calendar: semesters. *Degrees:* bachelor's, master's, doctoral, and post-master's certificates.

Library: A. C. Lewis Memorial Library. *Books:* 127,508 (physical), 205,483 (digital/electronic); *Serial titles:* 835 (physical), 51,728 (digital/electronic); *Databases:* 101. Weekly public service hours: 49; students can reserve study rooms.

STUDENT LIFE

Housing options: on-campus residence required through sophomore year; coed, men-only, women-only, special housing for students with disabilities. Campus housing is university owned and leased by the school. Freshman applicants given priority for college housing.

Activities and organizations: drama/theater group, student-run newspaper, radio and television station, choral group, marching band, Tiger Marching Band, Black Dynasty Modeling Troupe, Academic and

Professional Clubs, sororities, fraternities, national fraternities, national sororities.

Athletics Member NCAA. All Division I except football (Division I-AA).

Campus security: 24-hour emergency response devices and patrols, student patrols, late-night transport/escort service, controlled dormitory access.

Student services: health clinic, personal/psychological counseling, veterans affairs office.

COSTS & FINANCIAL AID
Costs (2018–19) *Tuition:* state resident $5140 full-time, $215 per credit hour part-time; nonresident $14,163 full-time, $591 per credit hour part-time. Full-time tuition and fees vary according to program. Part-time tuition and fees vary according to program. *Required fees:* $2295 full-time, $1845 per year part-time. *Room and board:* $10,406; room only: $6728. Room and board charges vary according to housing facility. *Payment plans:* installment, deferred payment.

Financial Aid Of all full-time matriculated undergraduates who enrolled in 2018, 3,786 applied for aid, 3,163 were judged to have need. In 2018, 53 non-need-based awards were made. *Average financial aid package:* $3868. *Average need-based loan:* $3930. *Average need-based gift aid:* $1700. *Average non-need-based aid:* $4005. *Financial aid deadline:* 6/1.

APPLYING
Standardized Tests *Required:* SAT or ACT (for admission).

Options: electronic application, early admission.

Application fee: $20.

Required: high school transcript, minimum 2.0 GPA, 19 units from Required Core 4 Curriculum including no more than one developmental course.

CONTACT
DeVaria Hudson, Director of Admissions and Recruitment, Grambling State University, GSU Box 4200, Grambling, LA 71245. *Phone:* 318-274-6100. *Toll-free phone:* 800-569-4714. *Fax:* 318-274-3292. *E-mail:* hudsond@gram.edu.

Herzing University
Kenner, Louisiana
http://www.herzing.edu/new-orleans

CONTACT
Herzing University, 2500 Williams Boulevard, Kenner, LA 70062. *Toll-free phone:* 800-596-0724.

Louisiana College
Pineville, Louisiana
http://www.lacollege.edu/

- **Independent Southern Baptist** comprehensive, founded 1906
- **Small-town** 81-acre campus
- **Endowment** $37.9 million
- **Coed** 1,004 undergraduate students, 89% full-time, 47% women, 53% men
- **Moderately difficult** entrance level, 78% of applicants were admitted

UNDERGRAD STUDENTS
893 full-time, 111 part-time. Students come from 14 states and territories; 15 other countries; 10% are from out of state; 24% Black or African American, non-Hispanic/Latino; 4% Hispanic/Latino; 1% Asian, non-Hispanic/Latino; 0.2% Native Hawaiian or other Pacific Islander, non-Hispanic/Latino; 0.8% American Indian or Alaska Native, non-Hispanic/Latino; 3% Two or more races, non-Hispanic/Latino; 0.7% Race/ethnicity unknown; 2% international; 7% transferred in; 54% live on campus.

Freshmen:
Admission: 808 applied, 634 admitted, 261 enrolled. *Average high school GPA:* 3.3. *Test scores:* SAT evidence-based reading and writing scores over 500: 50%; SAT math scores over 500: 90%; ACT scores over 18: 91%; SAT evidence-based reading and writing scores over 600: 20%; SAT math scores over 600: 30%; ACT scores over 24: 24%; SAT math scores over 700: 10%; ACT scores over 30: 3%.

Retention: 65% of full-time freshmen returned.

FACULTY
Total: 119, 63% full-time, 55% with terminal degrees.

Student/faculty ratio: 12:1.

ACADEMICS
Calendar: semesters. *Degrees:* certificates, associate, bachelor's, and master's.

Special study options: academic remediation for entering students, accelerated degree program, adult/continuing education programs, advanced placement credit, distance learning, double majors, English as a second language, honors programs, independent study, internships, off-campus study, part-time degree program, services for LD students, student-designed majors, summer session for credit.

Unusual degree programs: 3-2 engineering with Louisiana Tech University.

Computers: 323 computers/terminals are available on campus for general student use. Students can access the following: campus intranet, computer help desk, free student e-mail accounts, online (class) grades, online (class) registration, online (class) schedules. Campuswide network is available. 100% of college-owned or -operated housing units are wired for high-speed Internet access. Wireless service is available via entire campus.

Library: Richard W. Norton Memorial Library. *Books:* 81,432 (physical), 301,231 (digital/electronic); *Serial titles:* 84 (physical), 86,957 (digital/electronic); *Databases:* 138. Weekly public service hours: 70; students can reserve study rooms.

STUDENT LIFE
Housing options: on-campus residence required through sophomore year; men-only, women-only. Campus housing is university owned. Freshman campus housing is guaranteed.

Activities and organizations: drama/theater group, student-run radio and television station, choral group, marching band, Baptist Collegiate Ministry, Delta Xi Omega, Student Government Association, Union Board, Lambda Chi Beta.

Athletics Member NCAA. All Division III. *Intercollegiate sports:* baseball M, basketball M/W, cross-country running M/W, football M, golf M, soccer M/W, softball W, tennis M/W, track and field M/W, volleyball W. *Intramural sports:* badminton M/W, basketball M/W, cheerleading M/W, football M/W, soccer M/W, softball M/W, table tennis M/W, ultimate Frisbee M/W, volleyball M/W.

Campus security: 24-hour emergency response devices and patrols, student patrols, late-night transport/escort service, controlled dormitory access.

Student services: health clinic, personal/psychological counseling.

COSTS & FINANCIAL AID
Costs (2018–19) *Comprehensive fee:* $22,618 includes full-time tuition ($17,000) and room and board ($5618). Full-time tuition and fees vary according to course load, degree level, and student level. Part-time tuition: $531 per credit hour. Part-time tuition and fees vary according to course load, degree level, and student level. *College room only:* $2226. Room and board charges vary according to board plan and housing facility. *Payment plan:* installment. *Waivers:* senior citizens and employees or children of employees.

Financial Aid Of all full-time matriculated undergraduates who enrolled in 2018, 842 applied for aid, 719 were judged to have need, 157 had their need fully met. In 2018, 137 non-need-based awards were made. *Average percent of need met:* 64. *Average financial aid package:* $14,478. *Average need-based loan:* $3441. *Average need-based gift aid:* $12,150. *Average non-need-based aid:* $7780. *Average indebtedness upon graduation:* $25,885.

APPLYING
Standardized Tests *Required:* SAT or ACT (for admission). *Recommended:* ACT (for admission).

Options: electronic application, early action.

Application fee: $25.

Required: high school transcript, minimum 2.0 GPA. *Required for some:* essay or personal statement.

Application deadlines: rolling (freshmen), rolling (transfers).

Notification: continuous (freshmen), continuous (transfers).

CONTACT
Ms. Renee Melder, Director of Admissions, Louisiana College, LC Box 566, Pineville, LA 71359. *Phone:* 318-487-7439. *Toll-free phone:* 800-487-1906. *E-mail:* admissions@lacollege.edu.

Louisiana Culinary Institute
Baton Rouge, Louisiana
http://www.lci.edu/

CONTACT
Louisiana Culinary Institute, 10550 Airline Highway, Baton Rouge, LA 70816. *Toll-free phone:* 877-533-3198.

Louisiana State University and Agricultural & Mechanical College
Baton Rouge, Louisiana
http://www.lsu.edu/

- **State-supported** university, founded 1860, part of Louisiana State University System
- **Urban** 2000-acre campus with easy access to New Orleans
- **Endowment** $457.7 million
- **Coed** 25,361 undergraduate students, 88% full-time, 53% women, 47% men
- **Moderately difficult** entrance level, 74% of applicants were admitted

UNDERGRAD STUDENTS
22,433 full-time, 2,928 part-time. Students come from 52 states and territories; 71 other countries; 18% are from out of state; 13% Black or African American, non-Hispanic/Latino; 7% Hispanic/Latino; 4% Asian, non-Hispanic/Latino; 0.1% Native Hawaiian or other Pacific Islander, non-Hispanic/Latino; 0.4% American Indian or Alaska Native, non-Hispanic/Latino; 2% Two or more races, non-Hispanic/Latino; 1% Race/ethnicity unknown; 2% international; 3% transferred in; 30% live on campus.

Freshmen:
Admission: 24,280 applied, 18,024 admitted, 5,812 enrolled. *Average high school GPA:* 3.4. *Test scores:* SAT evidence-based reading and writing scores over 500: 92%; SAT math scores over 500: 91%; ACT scores over 18: 100%; SAT evidence-based reading and writing scores over 600: 47%; SAT math scores over 600: 45%; ACT scores over 24: 66%; SAT evidence-based reading and writing scores over 700: 8%; SAT math scores over 700: 11%; ACT scores over 30: 19%.

Retention: 84% of full-time freshmen returned.

FACULTY
Total: 1,501, 88% full-time, 82% with terminal degrees.
Student/faculty ratio: 20:1.

ACADEMICS
Calendar: semesters. *Degrees:* certificates, bachelor's, master's, doctoral, post-master's, and postbachelor's certificates.
Special study options: accelerated degree program, adult/continuing education programs, advanced placement credit, cooperative education, distance learning, double majors, English as a second language, freshman honors college, honors programs, independent study, internships, off-campus study, part-time degree program, services for LD students, student-designed majors, study abroad, summer session for credit. *ROTC:* Army (b), Navy (c), Air Force (b).
Computers: 1,314 computers/terminals and 15,000 ports are available on campus for general student use. Students can access the following: computer help desk, free student e-mail accounts, online (class) grades, online (class) registration, online (class) schedules, free software for download, storage, discounts on hardware, virtual computer lab. Campuswide network is available. 100% of college-owned or -operated housing units are wired for high-speed Internet access. Wireless service is available via entire campus.
Library: Troy H. Middleton Library plus 4 others. *Books:* 3.0 million (physical), 601,314 (digital/electronic); *Serial titles:* 627,726 (physical), 336,271 (digital/electronic); *Databases:* 300. Study areas open 24 hours, 5–7 days a week; students can reserve study rooms.

STUDENT LIFE
Housing options: on-campus residence required for freshman year; coed, men-only, women-only, special housing for students with disabilities. Campus housing is university owned. Freshman campus housing is guaranteed.
Activities and organizations: drama/theater group, student-run newspaper, radio and television station, choral group, marching band, intramural athletics, student political organizations, student professional organizations, religious organizations, cultural organizations, national fraternities, national sororities.
Athletics Member NCAA. All Division I except football (Division I-A). *Intercollegiate sports:* baseball M(s), basketball M(s)/W(s), cheerleading M/W, cross-country running M(s)/W(s), golf M(s)/W(s)(c), gymnastics W(s), soccer W(s), softball W(s), swimming and diving M(s)/W(s), tennis M(s)/W(s), track and field M(s)/W(s), volleyball W(s). *Intramural sports:* badminton M/W, baseball M(c), basketball M(c)/W, cross-country running M(c)/W(c), equestrian sports W(c), football M/W, golf M/W, ice hockey M(c)/W(c), lacrosse M(c)/W(c), racquetball M/W, rock climbing M/W, rowing M(c)/W(c), rugby M(c)/W(c), sand volleyball M/W, soccer M(c)/W(c), softball M/W, table tennis M(c)/W(c), tennis M(c)/W(c), triathlon M(c)/W(c), ultimate Frisbee M(c)/W(c), volleyball M(c)/W(c), water polo M(c)/W(c), weight lifting M(c)/W(c).
Campus security: 24-hour emergency response devices and patrols, late-night transport/escort service, controlled dormitory access.
Student services: health clinic, personal/psychological counseling, women's center, legal services, veterans affairs office.

COSTS & FINANCIAL AID
Costs (2018–19) *Tuition:* state resident $8038 full-time; nonresident $24,715 full-time. Full-time tuition and fees vary according to course load. Part-time tuition and fees vary according to course load. *Required fees:* $3912 full-time. *Room and board:* $11,830; room only: $7740. Room and board charges vary according to board plan and housing facility. *Payment plan:* deferred payment. *Waivers:* employees or children of employees.
Financial Aid Of all full-time matriculated undergraduates who enrolled in 2017, 13,393 applied for aid, 10,344 were judged to have need, 1,496 had their need fully met. 1,004 Federal Work-Study jobs (averaging $1963). 4,542 state and other part-time jobs (averaging $2091). In 2017, 3438 non-need-based awards were made. *Average percent of need met:* 60. *Average financial aid package:* $15,296. *Average need-based loan:* $4551. *Average need-based gift aid:* $12,364. *Average non-need-based aid:* $5653. *Average indebtedness upon graduation:* $26,821.

APPLYING
Standardized Tests *Required:* SAT or ACT (for admission).
Options: electronic application, early admission, deferred entrance.
Application fee: $50.
Required: high school transcript, minimum 3.0 GPA, 1 letter of recommendation, ACT Composite score of 22 (18 in English and 19 in Math) or SAT Total Score of 1100 (500 in English and 510 in Math). *Required for some:* essay or personal statement.
Notification: continuous (freshmen), continuous (transfers).

CONTACT
Mr. Emmett Brown, Associate Director, Undergraduate Admissions, Louisiana State University and Agricultural & Mechanical College, 1146 Pleasant Hall, Baton Rouge, LA 70803. *Phone:* 225-578-1175. *Fax:* 225-578-4433. *E-mail:* cbrow63@lsu.edu.

Louisiana State University at Alexandria
Alexandria, Louisiana
http://www.lsua.edu/

CONTACT
Ms. Shelly Kieffer, Director of Enrollment Management, Louisiana State University at Alexandria, 8100 Highway 71 South, Alexandria, LA 71302-9121. *Phone:* 318-473-6424. *Toll-free phone:* 888-473-6417. *Fax:* 318-473-6418. *E-mail:* admissions@lsua.edu.

Louisiana State University Health Sciences Center

New Orleans, Louisiana
http://www.lsuhsc.edu/

- **State-supported** university, founded 1931, part of Louisiana State University System
- **Urban** 80-acre campus with easy access to New Orleans
- **Endowment** $120.1 million
- **Coed**

FACULTY
Student/faculty ratio: 4:1.

ACADEMICS
Calendar: varies by academic program. *Degrees:* associate, bachelor's, master's, and doctoral.
Library: John P. Ische Library plus 2 others. *Books:* 61,199 (physical); *Serial titles:* 4,968 (physical), 3,068 (digital/electronic); *Databases:* 204. Weekly public service hours: 97; study areas open 24 hours, 5–7 days a week.

STUDENT LIFE
Housing options: coed, special housing for students with disabilities. Campus housing is university owned.

Campus security: 24-hour emergency response devices and patrols, late-night transport/escort service, controlled dormitory access.

Student services: health clinic, personal/psychological counseling, veterans affairs office.

COSTS
Costs (2018–19) *Tuition:* state resident $5612 full-time, $357 per semester hour part-time; nonresident $12,394 full-time, $424 per semester hour part-time. Full-time tuition and fees vary according to degree level, program, and reciprocity agreements. Part-time tuition and fees vary according to course load, degree level, program, and reciprocity agreements. *Required fees:* $2696 full-time, $158 per semester hour part-time. *Room only:* $5598. Room and board charges vary according to housing facility.

APPLYING
Options: electronic application.
Application fee: $50.

CONTACT
Louisiana State University Health Sciences Center, 433 Bolivar Street, New Orleans, LA 70112-2223.

Louisiana State University in Shreveport

Shreveport, Louisiana
http://www.lsus.edu/

CONTACT
Louisiana State University in Shreveport, 1 University Place, Shreveport, LA 71115-2399. *Phone:* 318-797-5063. *Toll-free phone:* 800-229-5957.

Louisiana Tech University

Ruston, Louisiana
http://www.latech.edu/

CONTACT
Mrs. Jan B. Albritton, Director of Admissions, Louisiana Tech University, PO Box 3168, Ruston, LA 71272. *Phone:* 318-257-3036. *Toll-free phone:* 800-528-3241. *Fax:* 318-257-2499. *E-mail:* bulldog@latech.edu.

Loyola University New Orleans

New Orleans, Louisiana
http://www.loyno.edu/

- **Independent Roman Catholic (Jesuit)** comprehensive, founded 1912
- **Suburban** 26-acre campus with easy access to New Orleans
- **Endowment** $234.0 million
- **Coed** 2,982 undergraduate students, 90% full-time, 64% women, 36% men
- **Moderately difficult** entrance level, 94% of applicants were admitted

UNDERGRAD STUDENTS
2,691 full-time, 291 part-time. Students come from 50 states and territories; 37 other countries; 57% are from out of state; 17% Black or African American, non-Hispanic/Latino; 18% Hispanic/Latino; 3% Asian, non-Hispanic/Latino; 0.1% Native Hawaiian or other Pacific Islander, non-Hispanic/Latino; 0.5% American Indian or Alaska Native, non-Hispanic/Latino; 4% Two or more races, non-Hispanic/Latino; 8% Race/ethnicity unknown; 2% international; 7% transferred in; 54% live on campus.

Freshmen:
Admission: 4,514 applied, 4,257 admitted, 789 enrolled. *Average high school GPA:* 3.5. *Test scores:* SAT evidence-based reading and writing scores over 500: 93%; SAT math scores over 500: 82%; ACT scores over 18: 97%; SAT evidence-based reading and writing scores over 600: 52%; SAT math scores over 600: 26%; ACT scores over 24: 59%; SAT evidence-based reading and writing scores over 700: 7%; SAT math scores over 700: 4%; ACT scores over 30: 14%.
Retention: 85% of full-time freshmen returned.

FACULTY
Total: 406, 58% full-time, 73% with terminal degrees.
Student/faculty ratio: 11:1.

ACADEMICS
Calendar: semesters. *Degrees:* bachelor's, master's, doctoral, post-master's, and postbachelor's certificates.

Special study options: accelerated degree program, adult/continuing education programs, advanced placement credit, cooperative education, distance learning, double majors, English as a second language, external degree program, honors programs, independent study, internships, off-campus study, part-time degree program, services for LD students, student-designed majors, study abroad, summer session for credit. *ROTC:* Army (c), Navy (c), Air Force (c).

Unusual degree programs: 3-2 engineering with University of New Orleans, The Catholic University of America.

Computers: 525 computers/terminals and 2,500 ports are available on campus for general student use. Students can access the following: campus intranet, computer help desk, free student e-mail accounts, online (class) grades, online (class) registration, online (class) schedules. Campuswide network is available. 100% of college-owned or -operated housing units are wired for high-speed Internet access. Wireless service is available via entire campus.
Library: Monroe Library plus 1 other. *Books:* 353,685 (physical), 42,981 (digital/electronic); *Serial titles:* 1,385 (physical), 250,962 (digital/electronic); *Databases:* 129. Weekly public service hours: 114; students can reserve study rooms.

STUDENT LIFE
Housing options: on-campus residence required through sophomore year; coed, special housing for students with disabilities. Campus housing is university owned. Freshman campus housing is guaranteed.

Activities and organizations: drama/theater group, student-run newspaper, radio station, choral group, Panhellenic Council, Black Student Union, Loyola University Community Action Plan, Quidditch, Interfraternity Council, national fraternities, national sororities.

Athletics Member NAIA. *Intercollegiate sports:* baseball M(s), basketball M(s)/W(s), cheerleading M(s)/W(s), cross-country running M(s)/W(s), golf M(s)/W(s), swimming and diving M(s)/W(s), tennis M(s)/W(s), track and field M(s)/W(s), volleyball W(s). *Intramural sports:* basketball M/W, football M/W, racquetball M/W, rugby M(c), sailing M(c)/W(c), soccer M/W, softball M/W, table tennis M/W, volleyball M/W, water polo M(c)/W(c), weight lifting M/W.

Campus security: 24-hour emergency response devices and patrols, student patrols, late-night transport/escort service, controlled dormitory access.

Student services: health clinic, personal/psychological counseling, women's center.

COSTS & FINANCIAL AID

Costs (2019–20) *One-time required fee:* $250. *Comprehensive fee:* $54,140 includes full-time tuition ($38,926), mandatory fees ($1666), and room and board ($13,548). Part-time tuition: $1094 per credit hour. *Required fees:* $426 part-time. *College room only:* $7430.

Financial Aid Of all full-time matriculated undergraduates who enrolled in 2018, 2,233 applied for aid, 1,954 were judged to have need, 300 had their need fully met. 778 Federal Work-Study jobs (averaging $1580). In 2018, 576 non-need-based awards were made. *Average percent of need met:* 77. *Average financial aid package:* $33,225. *Average need-based loan:* $4026. *Average need-based gift aid:* $29,636. *Average non-need-based aid:* $17,733. *Average indebtedness upon graduation:* $31,341.

APPLYING

Standardized Tests *Required:* SAT or ACT (for admission).

Options: electronic application, early admission, early action.

Required: essay or personal statement, high school transcript, 1 letter of recommendation. *Recommended:* interview.

Application deadlines: rolling (freshmen), rolling (out-of-state freshmen), rolling (transfers).

Notification: continuous (freshmen), continuous (out-of-state freshmen), continuous (transfers).

CONTACT

Mr. Nathan E Ament, Director of Admissions, Loyola University New Orleans, 6363 St. Charles Avenue, Campus Box 18, New Orleans, LA 70118. *Phone:* 504-865-3240. *Toll-free phone:* 800-4-LOYOLA. *Fax:* 504-865-3383. *E-mail:* nament@loyno.edu.

McNeese State University

Lake Charles, Louisiana

http://www.mcneese.edu/

- **State-supported** comprehensive, founded 1939, part of University of Louisiana System
- **Suburban** 766-acre campus
- **Coed** 7,033 undergraduate students, 80% full-time, 59% women, 41% men
- **Moderately difficult** entrance level, 43% of applicants were admitted

UNDERGRAD STUDENTS

5,641 full-time, 1,392 part-time. Students come from 37 states and territories; 54 other countries; 7% are from out of state; 16% Black or African American, non-Hispanic/Latino; 4% Hispanic/Latino; 1% Asian, non-Hispanic/Latino; 0.1% Native Hawaiian or other Pacific Islander, non-Hispanic/Latino; 0.5% American Indian or Alaska Native, non-Hispanic/Latino; 4% Two or more races, non-Hispanic/Latino; 5% international; 5% transferred in.

Freshmen:

Admission: 3,224 applied, 1,373 admitted, 1,373 enrolled. *Average high school GPA:* 3.5.

Retention: 70% of full-time freshmen returned.

FACULTY

Total: 440, 60% full-time.

Student/faculty ratio: 21:1.

ACADEMICS

Calendar: semesters. *Degrees:* associate, bachelor's, master's, post-master's, and postbachelor's certificates.

Special study options: academic remediation for entering students, accelerated degree program, advanced placement credit, cooperative education, distance learning, double majors, English as a second language, freshman honors college, honors programs, independent study,

internships, off-campus study, part-time degree program, services for LD students, study abroad, summer session for credit.

Computers: Students can access the following: computer help desk, free student e-mail accounts, online (class) grades, online (class) registration, online (class) schedules. Campuswide network is available. 100% of college-owned or -operated housing units are wired for high-speed Internet access. Wireless service is available via entire campus.

Library: Frazar Memorial Library plus 1 other.

STUDENT LIFE

Housing options: coed. Campus housing is university owned and leased by the school.

Activities and organizations: drama/theater group, student-run newspaper, choral group, marching band, Student Government Association, International Students Association, Resident Student Association, national fraternities, national sororities.

Athletics Member NCAA. All Division I except football (Division I-AA). *Intercollegiate sports:* baseball M(s), basketball M(s)/W(s), cross-country running M(s)/W(s), golf M(s)/W(s)(c), soccer W(s), softball W(s), tennis W(s), track and field M(s)/W(s), volleyball W(s). *Intramural sports:* badminton M/W, baseball M, basketball M/W, football M/W, golf M/W, racquetball M/W, soccer M/W, softball M/W, swimming and diving M/W, table tennis M/W, tennis M/W, ultimate Frisbee M/W, volleyball M/W, water polo M/W, weight lifting M/W.

Campus security: 24-hour emergency response devices and patrols, late-night transport/escort service, controlled dormitory access.

Student services: health clinic, personal/psychological counseling, women's center.

COSTS & FINANCIAL AID

Costs (2018–19) *Tuition:* state resident $7668 full-time; nonresident $12,667 full-time. Full-time tuition and fees vary according to course load. Part-time tuition and fees vary according to course load. *Required fees:* $2535 full-time. *Room and board:* $7524; room only: $4150. Room and board charges vary according to board plan and housing facility. *Payment plan:* installment. *Waivers:* senior citizens and employees or children of employees.

Financial Aid Of all full-time matriculated undergraduates who enrolled in 2014, 4,704 applied for aid, 3,627 were judged to have need, 408 had their need fully met. *Average percent of need met:* 61. *Average financial aid package:* $9508. *Average need-based loan:* $3711. *Average need-based gift aid:* $4838.

APPLYING

Standardized Tests *Required:* SAT or ACT (for admission).

Options: electronic application, early admission, deferred entrance.

Application fee: $20.

Required: high school transcript, minimum 2.4 GPA, Louisiana Board of Regents high school Core 4 curriculum, no more than one developmental course.

Application deadlines: rolling (freshmen), rolling (transfers).

Notification: continuous (freshmen), continuous (transfers).

CONTACT

Ms. Kourtney Istre, Director of Admissions and Recruiting, McNeese State University, Box 91740, Lake Charles, LA 70609. *Phone:* 337-475-5505. *Toll-free phone:* 800-622-3352. *Fax:* 337-475-5978. *E-mail:* kistre@mcneese.edu.

New Orleans Baptist Theological Seminary

New Orleans, Louisiana

http://www.nobts.edu/

CONTACT

Dr. Paul E. Gregoire Jr., Registrar/Director of Admissions, New Orleans Baptist Theological Seminary, 3939 Gentilly Boulevard, New Orleans, LA 70126-4858. *Phone:* 504-282-4455 Ext. 3337. *Toll-free phone:* 800-662-8701.

Nicholls State University

Thibodaux, Louisiana
http://www.nicholls.edu/

CONTACT
Mrs. Becky L. Durocher, Director of Admissions, Nicholls State University, PO Box 2004-NSU, Thibodaux, LA 70310. *Phone:* 985-448-4507. *Toll-free phone:* 877-NICHOLLS. *Fax:* 985-448-4929. *E-mail:* nicholls@nicholls.edu.

Northwestern State University of Louisiana

Natchitoches, Louisiana
http://www.nsula.edu/
- **State-supported** comprehensive, founded 1884, part of University of Louisiana System
- **Small-town** 916-acre campus
- **Endowment** $15.4 million
- **Coed**
- **Moderately difficult** entrance level

FACULTY
Student/faculty ratio: 19:1.

ACADEMICS
Calendar: semesters. *Degrees:* associate, bachelor's, master's, doctoral, post-master's, and postbachelor's certificates.
Library: Eugene P. Watson Memorial Library plus 1 other. *Books:* 310,849 (physical), 38,166 (digital/electronic); *Serial titles:* 329 (physical), 230 (digital/electronic); *Databases:* 111. Weekly public service hours: 87; students can reserve study rooms.

STUDENT LIFE
Housing options: coed, special housing for students with disabilities. Campus housing is university owned and is provided by a third party. Freshman applicants given priority for college housing.

Activities and organizations: drama/theater group, student-run newspaper, radio and television station, choral group, marching band, Student Activities Board, Student Government Associate, College Panhellenic Council, national fraternities, national sororities.

Athletics Member NCAA. All Division I except football (Division I-AA).

Campus security: 24-hour emergency response devices and patrols, student patrols, late-night transport/escort service, controlled dormitory access.

Student services: health clinic, personal/psychological counseling, veterans affairs office.

COSTS & FINANCIAL AID
Costs (2018–19) *Tuition:* state resident $5180 full-time; nonresident $15,968 full-time. Full-time tuition and fees vary according to course load and location. Part-time tuition and fees vary according to course load and location. *Required fees:* $3400 full-time. *Room and board:* $9230; room only: $5850. Room and board charges vary according to board plan and housing facility.

Financial Aid Of all full-time matriculated undergraduates who enrolled in 2017, 4,866 applied for aid, 4,119 were judged to have need, 433 had their need fully met. In 2017, 365 non-need-based awards were made. *Average percent of need met:* 70. *Average financial aid package:* $15,181. *Average need-based loan:* $7027. *Average need-based gift aid:* $7997. *Average non-need-based aid:* $4322. *Average indebtedness upon graduation:* $27,750.

APPLYING
Standardized Tests *Required:* SAT or ACT (for admission).
Options: electronic application, deferred entrance.
Application fee: $20.
Required: high school transcript, minimum 2.4 GPA, college preparatory curriculum.

CONTACT
Ms. Jana Lucky, Director of University Recruiting, Northwestern State University of Louisiana, 175 Sam Sibley Drive, Recruiting Office, Student Services Center, 1st Floor, Natchitoches, LA 71497. *Phone:* 318-357-4503. *Toll-free phone:* 800-327-1903. *Fax:* 318-357-5567. *E-mail:* recruiting@nsula.edu.

Saint Joseph Seminary College

Saint Benedict, Louisiana
http://www.sjasc.edu/

CONTACT
Saint Joseph Seminary College, 75376 River Road, St. Benedict, LA 70457. *Phone:* 985-867-2273. *Fax:* 985-327-1085. *E-mail:* registrar@sjasc.edu.

Southeastern Louisiana University

Hammond, Louisiana
http://www.southeastern.edu/
- **State-supported** comprehensive, founded 1925, part of University of Louisiana System
- **Small-town** 375-acre campus with easy access to New Orleans
- **Endowment** $52.6 million
- **Coed** 13,360 undergraduate students, 69% full-time, 62% women, 38% men
- **Moderately difficult** entrance level, 90% of applicants were admitted

UNDERGRAD STUDENTS
9,194 full-time, 4,166 part-time. Students come from 44 states and territories; 56 other countries; 4% are from out of state; 20% Black or African American, non-Hispanic/Latino; 7% Hispanic/Latino; 2% Asian, non-Hispanic/Latino; 0.1% Native Hawaiian or other Pacific Islander, non-Hispanic/Latino; 0.3% American Indian or Alaska Native, non-Hispanic/Latino; 4% Two or more races, non-Hispanic/Latino; 4% Race/ethnicity unknown; 1% international; 5% transferred in; 24% live on campus.

Freshmen:
Admission: 4,248 applied, 3,828 admitted, 2,675 enrolled. *Average high school GPA:* 3.3. *Test scores:* ACT scores over 18: 96%; ACT scores over 24: 36%; ACT scores over 30: 2%.
Retention: 67% of full-time freshmen returned.

FACULTY
Total: 611, 82% full-time, 60% with terminal degrees.
Student/faculty ratio: 19:1.

ACADEMICS
Calendar: semesters. *Degrees:* associate, bachelor's, master's, doctoral, post-master's, and postbachelor's certificates.

Special study options: academic remediation for entering students, accelerated degree program, adult/continuing education programs, advanced placement credit, distance learning, double majors, English as a second language, honors programs, independent study, internships, off-campus study, part-time degree program, services for LD students, study abroad, summer session for credit. *ROTC:* Army (b).

Computers: 1,031 computers/terminals and 600 ports are available on campus for general student use. Students can access the following: campus intranet, computer help desk, free student e-mail accounts, online (class) grades, online (class) registration, online (class) schedules, campus Webmail, student newspaper, transcripts, bookstore. Campuswide network is available. 100% of college-owned or -operated housing units are wired for high-speed Internet access. Wireless service is available via classrooms, computer centers, computer labs, dorm rooms, learning centers, libraries, student centers.
Library: Linus A. Sims Memorial Library plus 1 other. *Books:* 1.3 million (physical), 428,672 (digital/electronic); *Serial titles:* 338 (physical), 561 (digital/electronic). Students can reserve study rooms.

STUDENT LIFE
Housing options: coed, women-only, special housing for students with disabilities. Campus housing is university owned.

Activities and organizations: drama/theater group, student-run newspaper, radio and television station, choral group, marching band, Baptist Collegiate Ministry, Catholic Student Association, Gamma Beta Phi, Phi Mu, Alpha Omicron Pi / Sigma Sigma Sigma, national fraternities, national sororities.

Athletics Member NCAA. All Division I except football (Division I-AA). *Intercollegiate sports:* baseball M(s), basketball M(s)/W(s), cross-country running M(s)/W(s), golf M(s), soccer W(s), softball W(s), tennis W(s), track and field M(s)/W(s), volleyball W(s). *Intramural sports:* baseball M/W, basketball M/W, football M/W, racquetball M/W, rugby M(c), soccer M/W, softball M/W, tennis M/W, volleyball M/W, weight lifting M/W.

Campus security: 24-hour emergency response devices and patrols, student patrols, late-night transport/escort service, controlled dormitory access.

Student services: health clinic, personal/psychological counseling.

COSTS & FINANCIAL AID

Costs (2018–19) *Tuition:* state resident $5777 full-time, $340 per credit hour part-time; nonresident $18,255 full-time, $860 per credit hour part-time. Full-time tuition and fees vary according to course load. Part-time tuition and fees vary according to course load. *Required fees:* $2388 full-time. *Room and board:* $8420; room only: $4940. Room and board charges vary according to board plan and housing facility. *Payment plan:* installment. *Waivers:* employees or children of employees.

Financial Aid Of all full-time matriculated undergraduates who enrolled in 2017, 7,289 applied for aid, 5,792 were judged to have need, 608 had their need fully met. 152 Federal Work-Study jobs (averaging $2165). 825 state and other part-time jobs (averaging $1877). In 2017, 613 non-need-based awards were made. *Average need-based loan:* $3635. *Average need-based gift aid:* $5269. *Average non-need-based aid:* $1755. *Average indebtedness upon graduation:* $19,736.

APPLYING

Standardized Tests *Required:* SAT or ACT (for admission).

Options: electronic application, early admission, deferred entrance.

Application fee: $20.

Required: high school transcript, minimum 2.4 GPA, proof of immunization; college transcripts and statement of good standing required for some.

Application deadlines: 8/1 (freshmen), 8/1 (transfers).

Notification: continuous until 10/15 (freshmen), continuous until 10/15 (transfers).

CONTACT

Mr. Anthony Ranatza, Director of Admissions, Southeastern Louisiana University, 548 Ned McGehee Drive, Hammond, LA 70402. *Phone:* 985-549-3329. *Toll-free phone:* 800-222-7358. *Fax:* 985-549-5882. *E-mail:* anthony.ranatza@southeastern.edu.

Southern University and Agricultural and Mechanical College

Baton Rouge, Louisiana

http://www.subr.edu/

- **State-supported** university, founded 1880, part of Southern University System
- **Suburban** 964-acre campus
- **Endowment** $12.9 million
- **Coed** 5,838 undergraduate students, 83% full-time, 64% women, 36% men
- **Moderately difficult** entrance level, 53% of applicants were admitted

UNDERGRAD STUDENTS

4,868 full-time, 970 part-time. Students come from 38 states and territories; 15 other countries; 18% are from out of state; 93% Black or African American, non-Hispanic/Latino; 0.7% Hispanic/Latino; 0.3% Asian, non-Hispanic/Latino; 0.2% American Indian or Alaska Native, non-Hispanic/Latino; 2% Two or more races, non-Hispanic/Latino; 0.8% Race/ethnicity unknown; 0.7% international; 6% transferred in; 31% live on campus.

Freshmen:
Admission: 8,482 applied, 4,489 admitted, 1,342 enrolled. *Average high school GPA:* 3.1. *Test scores:* ACT scores over 18: 58%; ACT scores over 24: 8%.

Retention: 68% of full-time freshmen returned.

FACULTY

Total: 423, 73% full-time, 77% with terminal degrees.

Student/faculty ratio: 16:1.

ACADEMICS

Calendar: semesters. *Degrees:* bachelor's, master's, doctoral, and post-master's certificates.

Special study options: academic remediation for entering students, adult/continuing education programs, advanced placement credit, cooperative education, distance learning, honors programs, internships, off-campus study, part-time degree program, services for LD students, study abroad, summer session for credit. *ROTC:* Army (b), Navy (b), Air Force (c).

Computers: 1,500 computers/terminals and 2,500 ports are available on campus for general student use. Students can access the following: campus intranet, computer help desk, free student e-mail accounts, online (class) grades, online (class) registration, online (class) schedules. Campuswide network is available. 100% of college-owned or -operated housing units are wired for high-speed Internet access. Wireless service is available via classrooms, computer centers, computer labs, learning centers, libraries, student centers.

Library: John B. Cade Library plus 2 others.

STUDENT LIFE

Housing options: on-campus residence required for freshman year; men-only, women-only. Campus housing is university owned. Freshman applicants given priority for college housing.

Activities and organizations: drama/theater group, student-run newspaper, choral group, marching band, Student Government Association, Association for Women Students, Men's Federation, Collegiate 100 Black Men, Southern University Pan Hellenic Council, national fraternities, national sororities.

Athletics Member NCAA. All Division I except football (Division I-AA). *Intercollegiate sports:* baseball M, basketball M(s)/W(s), bowling W(s), cross-country running M(s), golf M(s)/W(s)(c), softball W(s), tennis M(s)/W(s), track and field M(s)/W(s), volleyball W(s). *Intramural sports:* archery M/W, basketball M/W, football M/W, track and field M/W, volleyball M/W, weight lifting M/W.

Campus security: 24-hour emergency response devices and patrols, late-night transport/escort service, controlled dormitory access.

Student services: health clinic, personal/psychological counseling, women's center, legal services.

FINANCIAL AID

Financial Aid Of all full-time matriculated undergraduates who enrolled in 2006, 6,032 applied for aid, 5,642 were judged to have need, 85 had their need fully met. 900 Federal Work-Study jobs (averaging $1800). 300 state and other part-time jobs (averaging $2500). *Average percent of need met:* 85. *Average financial aid package:* $7444. *Average need-based loan:* $3738. *Average need-based gift aid:* $3436. *Average non-need-based aid:* $3151. *Average indebtedness upon graduation:* $23,000.

APPLYING

Standardized Tests *Required:* SAT or ACT (for admission).

Options: electronic application, early admission.

Application fee: $20.

Required: high school transcript, minimum 2.0 GPA, Louisiana Board of Regents Core curriculum of 16.5 units of selected courses.

Notification: continuous (freshmen), continuous (transfers).

CONTACT

Dr. Manicia Finch, Director of Admissions, Southern University and Agricultural and Mechanical College, PO Box 9901, Baton Rouge, LA 70813. *Phone:* 225-771-2430. *Fax:* 225-771-2500. *E-mail:* manicia_finch@subr.edu.

Southern University at New Orleans

New Orleans, Louisiana

http://www.suno.edu/

CONTACT

Southern University at New Orleans, 6400 Press Drive, New Orleans, LA 70126-1009. *Phone:* 504-286-5033.

Southwest University

Kenner, Louisiana

http://www.southwest.edu/

CONTACT
Admissions Office, Southwest University, 2200 Veterans Memorial Boulevard, Kenner, LA 70062. *Phone:* 504-468-2900. *Toll-free phone:* 800-433-5923. *Fax:* 504-468-3213. *E-mail:* admissions@southwest.edu.

Tulane University

New Orleans, Louisiana

http://www.tulane.edu/

- **Independent** university, founded 1834
- **Urban** 110-acre campus
- **Endowment** $1.7 billion
- **Coed** 6,773 undergraduate students, 100% full-time, 60% women, 40% men
- **Very difficult** entrance level, 17% of applicants were admitted

UNDERGRAD STUDENTS
6,747 full-time, 26 part-time. Students come from 53 states and territories; 93 other countries; 79% are from out of state; 4% Black or African American, non-Hispanic/Latino; 7% Hispanic/Latino; 5% Asian, non-Hispanic/Latino; 0.2% Native Hawaiian or other Pacific Islander, non-Hispanic/Latino; 0.1% American Indian or Alaska Native, non-Hispanic/Latino; 4% Two or more races, non-Hispanic/Latino; 1% Race/ethnicity unknown; 5% international; 2% transferred in; 48% live on campus.

Freshmen:
Admission: 38,816 applied, 6,725 admitted, 1,909 enrolled. *Average high school GPA:* 3.6. *Test scores:* SAT evidence-based reading and writing scores over 500: 98%; SAT math scores over 500: 99%; ACT scores over 18: 100%; SAT evidence-based reading and writing scores over 600: 95%; SAT math scores over 600: 94%; ACT scores over 24: 98%; SAT evidence-based reading and writing scores over 700: 56%; SAT math scores over 700: 65%; ACT scores over 30: 86%.

Retention: 94% of full-time freshmen returned.

FACULTY
Total: 1,271, 62% full-time, 78% with terminal degrees.
Student/faculty ratio: 8:1.

ACADEMICS
Calendar: semesters plus 3 summer sessions. *Degrees:* certificates, bachelor's, master's, doctoral, and postbachelor's certificates.
Special study options: accelerated degree program, adult/continuing education programs, advanced placement credit, cooperative education, distance learning, double majors, English as a second language, freshman honors college, honors programs, independent study, internships, off-campus study, part-time degree program, services for LD students, student-designed majors, study abroad, summer session for credit. *ROTC:* Army (b), Navy (b), Air Force (b).
Unusual degree programs: 3-2 business administration; public health tropical medicine, science and engineering.
Computers: 556 computers/terminals are available on campus for general student use. Students can access the following: campus intranet, computer help desk, free student e-mail accounts, online (class) grades, online (class) registration, online (class) schedules. Campuswide network is available. 100% of college-owned or -operated housing units are wired for high-speed Internet access. Wireless service is available via entire campus.
Library: Howard Tilton Memorial Library plus 8 others. *Books:* 4.6 million (physical); *Serial titles:* 77,251 (physical). Study areas open 24 hours, 5–7 days a week.

STUDENT LIFE
Housing options: on-campus residence required through sophomore year; coed, women-only, special housing for students with disabilities. Campus housing is university owned. Freshman campus housing is guaranteed.
Activities and organizations: drama/theater group, student-run newspaper, radio and television station, choral group, marching band, Community Action Council of Tulane Students (CACTUS), Associated Student Body, Tulane University Campus Programming (TUCP), Association of Club Sports (ACS), National Pan-Hellenic Council, national fraternities, national sororities.
Athletics Member NCAA. All Division I except football (Division I-A). *Intercollegiate sports:* baseball M(s), basketball M(s)/W(s), crew M(c)/W(c), cross-country running M(s)/W(s), golf W(s)(c), gymnastics M(c)/W(c), ice hockey M(c)/W(c), lacrosse M(c)/W(c), rugby M(c), sailing M(c)/W(c), soccer M(c)/W(s), swimming and diving M(c)/W(s), tennis M(s)/W(s), track and field M(c)/W(s), volleyball M(c)/W(s), water polo M(c)/W(c). *Intramural sports:* baseball M(c), cheerleading M(c)/W(c), crew M(c)/W(c), cross-country running M(c), fencing M(c)/W(c), field hockey M(c)/W(c), gymnastics M(c)/W(c), ice hockey M(c), lacrosse M(c)/W(c), racquetball M(c)/W(c), rock climbing M(c)/W(c), rugby M(c), sailing M(c)/W(c), soccer M(c)/W(c), swimming and diving M(c)/W(c), tennis M(c)/W(c), track and field M(c)/W, ultimate Frisbee M(c)/W(c), volleyball M(c)/W(c), water polo M(c)/W(c).

Campus security: 24-hour emergency response devices and patrols, student patrols, late-night transport/escort service, controlled dormitory access, on and off-campus shuttle service, crime prevention programs, lighted pathways, TUPD patrols 24 hrs a day 365 days a year, virtual.
Student services: health clinic, personal/psychological counseling, women's center, legal services, veterans affairs office.

COSTS & FINANCIAL AID
Costs (2019–20) *Comprehensive fee:* $73,264 includes full-time tuition ($52,760), mandatory fees ($4040), and room and board ($16,464). *College room only:* $9700. *Payment plan:* tuition prepayment.
Financial Aid Of all full-time matriculated undergraduates who enrolled in 2018, 3,266 applied for aid, 2,308 were judged to have need, 1,246 had their need fully met. 1,413 Federal Work-Study jobs (averaging $3358). 117 state and other part-time jobs (averaging $9293). In 2018, 2926 non-need-based awards were made. *Average percent of need met:* 94. *Average financial aid package:* $47,129. *Average need-based loan:* $4374. *Average need-based gift aid:* $36,085. *Average non-need-based aid:* $25,734. *Average indebtedness upon graduation:* $41,767.

APPLYING
Standardized Tests *Required:* SAT or ACT (for admission).
Options: electronic application, early decision, early action, deferred entrance.
Required: essay or personal statement, high school transcript, 1 letter of recommendation.
Application deadlines: 11/15 (freshmen), 11/15 (early action).
Early decision deadline: 11/1 (for plan 1), 1/7 (for plan 2).
Notification: 4/1 (freshmen), 12/15 (early decision plan 1), 1/28 (early decision plan 2), 1/15 (early action).

CONTACT
Satyajit Dattagupta, Vice President for Enrollment Management and Dean of Admissions, Tulane University, Office of Admissions, 210 Gibson Hall, New Orleans, LA 70118. *Phone:* 504-865-5731. *Toll-free phone:* 800-873-9283. *Fax:* 504-862-8715. *E-mail:* undergrad.admission@tulane.edu.

University of Holy Cross

New Orleans, Louisiana

http://www.uhcno.edu/

CONTACT
Donna Kennedy, Director of Admissions and Financial Aid, University of Holy Cross, 4123 Woodland Drive, New Orleans, LA 70131-7399. *Phone:* 504-398-2175. *Toll-free phone:* 800-259-7744. *E-mail:* dkennedy@olhcc.edu.

University of Louisiana at Lafayette

Lafayette, Louisiana

http://www.louisiana.edu/

CONTACT
Mr. Andy Benoit Jr., Assistant Vice President for Enrollment Management and Director of Enrollment Services and Recruitment, University of Louisiana at Lafayette, PO Drawer 41210, Lafayette, LA 70504. *Phone:* 337-482-6473. *Toll-free phone:* 800-752-6553. *Fax:* 337-482-1317. *E-mail:* admissions@louisiana.edu.

University of Louisiana at Monroe
Monroe, Louisiana
http://www.ulm.edu/

- **State-supported** university, founded 1931, part of University of Louisiana System
- **Urban** 238-acre campus
- **Endowment** $50.6 million
- **Coed**
- **Moderately difficult** entrance level

FACULTY
Student/faculty ratio: 19:1.

ACADEMICS
Calendar: semesters. *Degrees:* associate, bachelor's, master's, doctoral, post-master's, and postbachelor's certificates.
Library: University Library. *Books:* 150,255 (physical), 293,246 (digital/electronic); *Serial titles:* 245 (physical), 93,407 (digital/electronic); *Databases:* 101. Students can reserve study rooms.

STUDENT LIFE
Housing options: coed, men-only, women-only. Campus housing is university owned and leased by the school. Freshman applicants given priority for college housing.
Activities and organizations: drama/theater group, student-run newspaper, radio and television station, choral group, marching band, Maroon Platoon, Alpha Lambda Delta, Louisiana Pharmacist Alliance, Association for Students in Kinesiology, Pre-Pharmacy Organization/Sound of Today, national fraternities, national sororities.
Athletics Member NCAA. All Division I except football (Division I-A).
Campus security: 24-hour emergency response devices and patrols, student patrols, late-night transport/escort service, controlled dormitory access.
Student services: health clinic, personal/psychological counseling.

COSTS & FINANCIAL AID
Costs (2018–19) *Tuition:* state resident $8734 full-time, $686 per credit hour part-time; nonresident $20,834 full-time, $686 per credit hour part-time. Full-time tuition and fees vary according to course load, degree level, and program. Part-time tuition and fees vary according to course load, degree level, and program. *Room and board:* $7868. Room and board charges vary according to board plan and housing facility.
Financial Aid Of all full-time matriculated undergraduates who enrolled in 2017, 4,168 applied for aid, 3,321 were judged to have need, 580 had their need fully met. 398 Federal Work-Study jobs (averaging $1178). In 2017, 1500 non-need-based awards were made. *Average percent of need met:* 72. *Average financial aid package:* $7953. *Average need-based loan:* $2005. *Average need-based gift aid:* $2621. *Average non-need-based aid:* $2710.

APPLYING
Standardized Tests *Required:* SAT or ACT (for admission).
Options: electronic application, early admission.
Application fee: $20.
Required: high school transcript, minimum 2.4 GPA.

CONTACT
Ms. Mary Peterson, Coordinator of Enrollment Services, University of Louisiana at Monroe, Office of Recruitment and Admissions, University Library, 202, Monroe, LA 71209. *Phone:* 318-342-5397. *Toll-free phone:* 800-372-5127. *Fax:* 318-342-1915. *E-mail:* peterson@ulm.edu.

University of New Orleans
New Orleans, Louisiana
http://www.uno.edu/

- **State-supported** university, founded 1958, part of University of Louisiana System
- **Urban** 345-acre campus
- **Coed**
- **57%** of applicants were admitted

FACULTY
Student/faculty ratio: 22:1.

ACADEMICS
Calendar: semesters. *Degrees:* bachelor's, master's, doctoral, and postbachelor's certificates.
Library: Earl K. Long Library. *Books:* 1.0 million (physical), 220,863 (digital/electronic); *Serial titles:* 25,831 (physical), 55,551 (digital/electronic); *Databases:* 154. Students can reserve study rooms.

STUDENT LIFE
Housing options: coed. Campus housing is university owned and is provided by a third party. Freshman applicants given priority for college housing.
Activities and organizations: drama/theater group, student-run newspaper, choral group, Student Activities Council, Student Government, International Student Organization, Vietnamese American Student Association, Greek Life, national fraternities, national sororities.
Athletics Member NCAA. All Division I.
Campus security: 24-hour emergency response devices and patrols, late-night transport/escort service, controlled dormitory access.
Student services: health clinic, personal/psychological counseling, women's center, legal services, veterans affairs office.

COSTS & FINANCIAL AID
Costs (2018–19) *Tuition:* state resident $6090 full-time; nonresident $10,926 full-time. Full-time tuition and fees vary according to course load, degree level, program, and reciprocity agreements. Part-time tuition and fees vary according to course load, degree level, program, and reciprocity agreements. *Required fees:* $2682 full-time. *Room and board:* $10,712. Room and board charges vary according to board plan and housing facility. *Payment plans:* installment, deferred payment.
Financial Aid Of all full-time matriculated undergraduates who enrolled in 2016, 3,680 applied for aid, 3,094 were judged to have need, 386 had their need fully met. In 2016, 325 non-need-based awards were made. *Average percent of need met:* 64. *Average financial aid package:* $9587. *Average need-based loan:* $3813. *Average need-based gift aid:* $5126. *Average non-need-based aid:* $2605. *Average indebtedness upon graduation:* $20,723. *Financial aid deadline:* 6/30.

APPLYING
Standardized Tests *Required:* SAT or ACT (for admission).
Options: electronic application, deferred entrance.
Application fee: $25.
Required: high school transcript.

CONTACT
Mr. Brett Hornsby, Director, Enrollment Operations, University of New Orleans, Privateer Enrollment Center, 105 Earl K. Long Library, New Orleans, LA 70148. *Phone:* 504-280-7394. *Toll-free phone:* 888-514-4275. *Fax:* 504-280-3973. *E-mail:* bjhornsb@uno.edu.

Xavier University of Louisiana
New Orleans, Louisiana
http://www.xula.edu/

- **Independent Roman Catholic** comprehensive, founded 1925
- **Urban** 23-acre campus
- **Coed**
- **Moderately difficult** entrance level

FACULTY
Student/faculty ratio: 14:1.

ACADEMICS
Calendar: semesters. *Degrees:* bachelor's, master's, and doctoral.
Library: Xavier Library.

STUDENT LIFE
Housing options: coed, men-only, women-only, special housing for students with disabilities. Campus housing is university owned. Freshman applicants given priority for college housing.
Activities and organizations: drama/theater group, student-run newspaper, television station, choral group, national fraternities, national sororities.
Athletics Member NAIA.
Campus security: 24-hour emergency response devices and patrols, student patrols, bicycle patrols.

Student services: health clinic, personal/psychological counseling.

COSTS & FINANCIAL AID
Costs (2018–19) *One-time required fee:* $150. *Comprehensive fee:* $33,522 includes full-time tuition ($21,954), mandatory fees ($2465), and room and board ($9103). Part-time tuition: $915 per credit hour. Part-time tuition and fees vary according to course load. *Required fees:* $250 per term part-time. *Room and board:* Room and board charges vary according to housing facility.

Financial Aid Of all full-time matriculated undergraduates who enrolled in 2017, 2,161 applied for aid, 1,734 were judged to have need, 869 had their need fully met. *Average percent of need met:* 72. *Average financial aid package:* $9897. *Average need-based loan:* $1550. *Average need-based gift aid:* $8330. *Average indebtedness upon graduation:* $21,821.

APPLYING
Standardized Tests *Required:* SAT or ACT (for admission).

Options: electronic application, deferred entrance.

Required: high school transcript, minimum 2.0 GPA, 1 letter of recommendation. *Required for some:* interview.

CONTACT
Mr. Winston Brown, Dean of Admissions, Xavier University of Louisiana, 7325 Palmetto Street, New Orleans, LA 70125. *Phone:* 504-520-7388. *Toll-free phone:* 877-XAVIERU. *Fax:* 504-520-7941. *E-mail:* apply@xula.edu.

MAINE

Bates College
Lewiston, Maine
http://www.bates.edu/
- **Independent** 4-year, founded 1855
- **Small-town** 133-acre campus
- **Endowment** $293.8 million
- **Coed**
- **Very difficult** entrance level

FACULTY
Student/faculty ratio: 10:1.

ACADEMICS
Calendar: 4-4-1. *Degree:* bachelor's.
Library: Ladd Library plus 1 other. *Books:* 602,011 (physical), 725,335 (digital/electronic); *Databases:* 371.

STUDENT LIFE
Housing options: on-campus residence required through senior year; coed, men-only, women-only. Campus housing is university owned. Freshman campus housing is guaranteed.

Activities and organizations: drama/theater group, student-run newspaper, radio station, choral group, Outing Club (outdoor recreation), International Club, Chase Hall Committee (student activities planning), Representative Assembly, WRBC (student radio station).

Athletics Member NCAA. All Division III.

Campus security: 24-hour emergency response devices and patrols, student patrols, late-night transport/escort service, controlled dormitory access, emergency contact/notification system.

Student services: health clinic, personal/psychological counseling, women's center.

COSTS & FINANCIAL AID
Costs (2018–19) *Comprehensive fee:* $69,018 includes full-time tuition ($53,794) and room and board ($15,224). *Payment plans:* tuition prepayment, installment.

Financial Aid Of all full-time matriculated undergraduates who enrolled in 2018, 784 applied for aid, 776 were judged to have need, 776 had their need fully met. *Average percent of need met:* 100. *Average financial aid package:* $48,512. *Average need-based loan:* $2953. *Average need-based*

gift aid: $44,590. *Average indebtedness upon graduation:* $21,525. *Financial aid deadline:* 1/1.

APPLYING
Options: electronic application, early admission, early decision, deferred entrance.

Application fee: $60.

Required: essay or personal statement, high school transcript, 3 letters of recommendation. *Recommended:* interview.

CONTACT
Leigh Weisenburger, Dean of Admission and Financial Aid, Bates College, 23 Campus Avenue, Lindholm House, Lewiston, ME 04240-6028. *Phone:* 855-228-3755. *Toll-free phone:* 855-228-3755. *Fax:* 207-786-6025. *E-mail:* admission@bates.edu.

Bowdoin College
Brunswick, Maine
http://www.bowdoin.edu/
- **Independent** 4-year, founded 1794
- **Small-town** 207-acre campus with easy access to Portland
- **Endowment** $1.5 billion
- **Coed**
- **Most difficult** entrance level

FACULTY
Student/faculty ratio: 9:1.

ACADEMICS
Calendar: semesters. *Degree:* bachelor's.
Library: Hawthorne-Longfellow Library plus 3 others. *Books:* 1.2 million (physical), 1.1 million (digital/electronic); *Serial titles:* 7,146 (physical), 80,997 (digital/electronic); *Databases:* 515. Weekly public service hours: 112; students can reserve study rooms.

STUDENT LIFE
Housing options: on-campus residence required through sophomore year; coed, special housing for students with disabilities. Campus housing is university owned. Freshman campus housing is guaranteed.

Activities and organizations: drama/theater group, student-run newspaper, radio station, choral group, Outing Club, Intramural sports, Community Service Volunteer Programs, WBOR 91.1 FM Radio, Bowdoin Orient Student Newspaper.

Athletics Member NCAA. All Division III except men's and women's sailing (Division I), men's and women's skiing (cross-country) (Division I), men's and women's squash (Division I).

Campus security: 24-hour emergency response devices and patrols, late-night transport/escort service, controlled dormitory access, self-defense education, safe ride service, emergency notification system.

Student services: health clinic, personal/psychological counseling, women's center.

COSTS & FINANCIAL AID
Costs (2018–19) *Comprehensive fee:* $68,620 includes full-time tuition ($53,418), mandatory fees ($504), and room and board ($14,698). Part-time tuition: $1043 per credit hour. *College room only:* $6868. Room and board charges vary according to board plan. *Payment plans:* installment, deferred payment.

Financial Aid Of all full-time matriculated undergraduates who enrolled in 2018, 971 applied for aid, 885 were judged to have need, 885 had their need fully met. 585 Federal Work-Study jobs (averaging $1846). 287 state and other part-time jobs (averaging $1833). In 2018, 36 non-need-based awards were made. *Average percent of need met:* 100. *Average financial aid package:* $49,337. *Average need-based gift aid:* $47,522. *Average non-need-based aid:* $1000. *Average indebtedness upon graduation:* $25,482. *Financial aid deadline:* 2/1.

APPLYING
Options: electronic application, early admission, early decision, deferred entrance.

Application fee: $65.

Required: essay or personal statement, high school transcript, 3 letters of recommendation. *Recommended:* interview.

CONTACT
Claudia Marroquin, Director of Admissions, Bowdoin College, 255 Maine Street, Brunswick, ME 04011. *Phone:* 207-725-3100. *Fax:* 207-725-3101. *E-mail:* admissions@bowdoin.edu.

Colby College
Waterville, Maine
http://www.colby.edu/

- **Independent** 4-year, founded 1813
- **Small-town** 714-acre campus with easy access to Portland, ME
- **Endowment** $775.1 million
- **Coed**
- **Most difficult** entrance level

ACADEMICS
Calendar: 4-1-4. *Degree:* bachelor's.
Library: Miller Library plus 3 others. *Books:* 545,763 (physical), 595,720 (digital/electronic); *Serial titles:* 22,931 (physical), 100,911 (digital/electronic); *Databases:* 701. Weekly public service hours: 119; study areas open 24 hours, 5–7 days a week.

STUDENT LIFE
Housing options: on-campus residence required through senior year; coed, cooperative, special housing for students with disabilities. Campus housing is university owned. Freshman campus housing is guaranteed.

Activities and organizations: drama/theater group, student-run newspaper, radio station, choral group, Outing Club, volunteer center, WMHB-FM (College Radio Station), Student Government, Powder and Wig (theater).

Athletics Member NCAA. All Division III except men's and women's skiing (cross-country) (Division I), men's and women's skiing (downhill) (Division I).

Campus security: 24-hour emergency response devices and patrols, student patrols, late-night transport/escort service, controlled dormitory access, campus lighting, student emergency response team, self-defense class, property ID program, party monitors.

Student services: health clinic, personal/psychological counseling, women's center.

COSTS & FINANCIAL AID
Costs (2018–19) *Comprehensive fee:* $69,400 includes full-time tuition ($52,890), mandatory fees ($2320), and room and board ($14,190). Part-time tuition: $2030 per credit hour. Part-time tuition and fees vary according to course load.

Financial Aid Of all full-time matriculated undergraduates who enrolled in 2018, 1,011 applied for aid, 928 were judged to have need, 928 had their need fully met. In 2018, 52 non-need-based awards were made. *Average percent of need met:* 100. *Average financial aid package:* $49,439. *Average need-based gift aid:* $48,637. *Average non-need-based aid:* $1311. *Average indebtedness upon graduation:* $24,437. *Financial aid deadline:* 2/1.

APPLYING
Standardized Tests *Required for some:* SAT or ACT (for admission), SAT and SAT Subject Tests or ACT (for admission).

Options: electronic application, early admission, early decision, deferred entrance.

Required: essay or personal statement, high school transcript, 2 letters of recommendation. *Recommended:* interview.

CONTACT
Denise Walden, Associate Director of Admissions, Colby College, 4000 Mayflower Hill, Waterville, ME 04901-8840. *Phone:* 207-859-4800. *Toll-free phone:* 800-723-3032. *Fax:* 207-859-4828. *E-mail:* admissions@colby.edu.

College of the Atlantic
Bar Harbor, Maine
http://www.coa.edu/

- **Independent** comprehensive, founded 1969
- **Small-town** 35-acre campus
- **Endowment** $53.0 million
- **Coed**
- **Very difficult** entrance level

FACULTY
Student/faculty ratio: 10:1.

ACADEMICS
Calendar: trimesters. *Degrees:* bachelor's and master's.
Library: Thorndike Library. *Books:* 45,700 (physical), 15,500 (digital/electronic); *Serial titles:* 400 (physical), 62,600 (digital/electronic); *Databases:* 76. Weekly public service hours: 101; students can reserve study rooms.

STUDENT LIFE
Housing options: on-campus residence required for freshman year; coed. Campus housing is university owned. Freshman campus housing is guaranteed.

Activities and organizations: drama/theater group, student-run newspaper, choral group, Earth in Brackets [earth], Outing Club, Campus Committee for Sustainability, Spectrum (LGBTQ+), Futbol (soccer) Club.

Campus security: 24-hour emergency response devices and patrols, late-night transport/escort service.

Student services: health clinic, personal/psychological counseling.

COSTS & FINANCIAL AID
Costs (2018–19) *Comprehensive fee:* $53,289 includes full-time tuition ($42,993), mandatory fees ($549), and room and board ($9747). Full-time tuition and fees vary according to course load and degree level. Part-time tuition: $4777 per credit. Part-time tuition and fees vary according to course load and degree level. *Required fees:* $183 per term part-time. *College room only:* $6210. Room and board charges vary according to board plan.

Financial Aid Of all full-time matriculated undergraduates who enrolled in 2018, 284 applied for aid, 263 were judged to have need, 102 had their need fully met. 159 Federal Work-Study jobs (averaging $2875). 85 state and other part-time jobs (averaging $2973). In 2018, 41 non-need-based awards were made. *Average percent of need met:* 94. *Average financial aid package:* $41,564. *Average need-based loan:* $4625. *Average need-based gift aid:* $36,091. *Average non-need-based aid:* $15,100. *Average indebtedness upon graduation:* $24,496. *Financial aid deadline:* 2/1.

APPLYING
Options: electronic application, early admission, early decision, deferred entrance.

Application fee: $50.

Required: essay or personal statement, high school transcript, 3 letters of recommendation. *Recommended:* minimum 3.0 GPA, interview.

CONTACT
Ms. Heather Albert-Knopp, Dean of Admission, College of the Atlantic, 105 Eden Street, Bar Harbor, ME 04609-1198. *Phone:* 207-288-5015. *Toll-free phone:* 800-528-0025. *Fax:* 207-288-4126. *E-mail:* inquiry@coa.edu.

Husson University
Bangor, Maine
http://www.husson.edu/

- **Independent** comprehensive, founded 1898
- **Suburban** 208-acre campus
- **Endowment** $17.3 million
- **Coed**
- **Moderately difficult** entrance level

FACULTY
Student/faculty ratio: 15:1.

ACADEMICS

Calendar: semesters. *Degrees:* certificates, associate, bachelor's, master's, doctoral, post-master's, and postbachelor's certificates.
Library: Sawyer Library. *Books:* 41,659 (physical), 5,539 (digital/electronic); *Serial titles:* 74 (physical), 151 (digital/electronic); *Databases:* 91. Weekly public service hours: 98; study areas open 24 hours, 5–7 days a week; students can reserve study rooms.

STUDENT LIFE

Housing options: on-campus residence required through sophomore year; coed. Campus housing is university owned. Freshman campus housing is guaranteed.

Activities and organizations: drama/theater group, student-run radio station, choral group, Organization of Student Nurses, Organization of Physical Therapy Students, Outdoors Club, International Student Association, Habitat for Humanity, national fraternities, national sororities.

Athletics Member NCAA. All Division III.

Campus security: 24-hour emergency response devices and patrols, late-night transport/escort service, controlled dormitory access.

Student services: health clinic, personal/psychological counseling, veterans affairs office.

COSTS & FINANCIAL AID

Costs (2018–19) *One-time required fee:* $150. *Comprehensive fee:* $27,430 includes full-time tuition ($17,100), mandatory fees ($500), and room and board ($9830). Full-time tuition and fees vary according to class time and location. Part-time tuition: $570 per credit. Part-time tuition and fees vary according to class time, course load, and location. *Required fees:* $120 per year part-time. *College room only:* $4950. Room and board charges vary according to board plan and housing facility. *Payment plans:* tuition prepayment, installment.

Financial Aid Of all full-time matriculated undergraduates who enrolled in 2017, 2,111 applied for aid, 1,901 were judged to have need, 177 had their need fully met. 413 Federal Work-Study jobs (averaging $1600). In 2017, 333 non-need-based awards were made. *Average percent of need met:* 67. *Average financial aid package:* $15,074. *Average need-based loan:* $4287. *Average need-based gift aid:* $8919. *Average non-need-based aid:* $3793. *Average indebtedness upon graduation:* $33,412. *Financial aid deadline:* 4/15.

APPLYING

Standardized Tests *Required:* SAT or ACT (for admission).

Options: electronic application, deferred entrance.

Application fee: $40.

Required: essay or personal statement, high school transcript, 1 letter of recommendation. *Recommended:* minimum 3.0 GPA, interview.

CONTACT

Mr. Adam Smith, Director of Undergraduate Admissions, Husson University, 1 College Circle, Bangor, ME 04401-2999. *Phone:* 207-404-5643. *Toll-free phone:* 800-4-HUSSON. *Fax:* 207-941-7935. *E-mail:* smithad@husson.edu.

Maine College of Art
Portland, Maine
http://www.meca.edu/

CONTACT
Maine College of Art, 522 Congress Street, Portland, ME 04101. *Phone:* 207-699-5023. *Toll-free phone:* 800-699-1509.

Maine College of Health Professions
Lewiston, Maine
http://www.mchp.edu/

- **Independent** primarily 2-year, founded 1891
- **Urban** campus
- **Coed**
- **Moderately difficult** entrance level

FACULTY
Student/faculty ratio: 5:1.

ACADEMICS

Calendar: semesters. *Degrees:* certificates, associate, and bachelor's.
Library: Gerrish True Health Sciences Library plus 1 other. *Books:* 2,816 (physical), 172 (digital/electronic); *Databases:* 17. Study areas open 24 hours, 5–7 days a week.

STUDENT LIFE

Housing options: coed. Campus housing is university owned.

Activities and organizations: Student Government.

Campus security: 24-hour emergency response devices and patrols, late-night transport/escort service, controlled dormitory access.

Student services: health clinic, personal/psychological counseling, veterans affairs office.

COSTS & FINANCIAL AID

Costs (2018–19) *Tuition:* $10,720 full-time, $5360 per year part-time. Full-time tuition and fees vary according to course load and program. Part-time tuition and fees vary according to course load and program. *Required fees:* $1525 full-time. *Room only:* $2350.

Financial Aid Of all full-time matriculated undergraduates who enrolled in 2018, 70 applied for aid, 55 were judged to have need.

APPLYING

Standardized Tests *Required for some:* SAT or ACT (for admission), HESI Entrance Exam for nursing, ACCUPLACER.

Options: electronic application.

Application fee: $50.

Required: essay or personal statement, high school transcript, high school or college-level algebra, second math, biology, chemistry.

CONTACT
Ms. Erica Watson, Admissions Director, Maine College of Health Professions, 70 Middle Street, Lewiston, ME 04240. *Phone:* 207-795-2843. *Fax:* 207-795-2849. *E-mail:* watsoner@mchp.edu.

Maine Maritime Academy
Castine, Maine
http://www.mainemaritime.edu/

CONTACT
Maine Maritime Academy, 1 Pleasant Street, Castine, ME 04420. *Phone:* 207-326-2215. *Toll-free phone:* 800-464-6565 (in-state); 800-227-8465 (out-of-state).

Purdue University Global
Augusta, Maine
http://www.purdueglobal.edu/

CONTACT
Purdue University Global, 14 Marketplace Drive, Augusta, ME 04330. *Toll-free phone:* 844-PURDUE-G.

Purdue University Global
Lewiston, Maine
http://www.purdueglobal.edu/

CONTACT
Purdue University Global, 475 Lisbon Street, Lewiston, ME 04240. *Phone:* 207-333-3300. *Toll-free phone:* 844-PURDUE-G.

Saint Joseph's College of Maine
Standish, Maine
http://www.sjcme.edu/

CONTACT
Kathleen Davis, Vice President for Enrollment Management, Saint Joseph's College of Maine, 278 Whites Bridge Road, Standish, ME 04084-5263. *Phone:* 207-893-7746. *Toll-free phone:* 800-338-7057. *Fax:* 207-893-7862. *E-mail:* admission@sjcme.edu.

Thomas College
Waterville, Maine
http://www.thomas.edu/

CONTACT
Ms. Angela Stinchfield, Director of Admissions, Thomas College, 180 West River Road, Waterville, ME 04901. *Phone:* 207-859-1101. *Toll-free phone:* 800-339-7001. *Fax:* 207-859-1114. *E-mail:* admiss@thomas.edu.

★ Unity College
Unity, Maine
http://www.unity.edu/
- **Independent** comprehensive, founded 1965
- **Rural** 300-acre campus
- **Endowment** $14.0 million
- **Coed**
- **Moderately difficult** entrance level

FACULTY
Student/faculty ratio: 14:1.

ACADEMICS
Calendar: semesters. *Degrees:* bachelor's, master's, and postbachelor's certificates.
Library: Dorothy Webb Quimby Library. *Books:* 52,723 (physical), 15,329 (digital/electronic); *Databases:* 72. Weekly public service hours: 40.

STUDENT LIFE
Housing options: on-campus residence required through sophomore year; coed, men-only, women-only, cooperative, special housing for students with disabilities. Campus housing is university owned. Freshman campus housing is guaranteed.
Activities and organizations: drama/theater group, choral group, Woodsmen Team, Ultimate Frisbee, Outing Club.
Athletics Member USCAA.
Campus security: 24-hour emergency response devices and patrols, security cameras in certain areas.
Student services: health clinic, personal/psychological counseling, veterans affairs office.

COSTS & FINANCIAL AID
Costs (2018–19) *Comprehensive fee:* $39,870 includes full-time tuition ($27,960), mandatory fees ($1200), and room and board ($10,710). Part-time tuition: $1010 per credit. *Room and board:* Room and board charges vary according to board plan and housing facility.
Financial Aid Of all full-time matriculated undergraduates who enrolled in 2017, 641 applied for aid, 584 were judged to have need, 63 had their need fully met. 429 Federal Work-Study jobs (averaging $1429). 16 state and other part-time jobs (averaging $1597). In 2017, 106 non-need-based awards were made. *Average percent of need met:* 72. *Average financial aid package:* $20,848. *Average need-based loan:* $7120. *Average need-based gift aid:* $13,718. *Average non-need-based aid:* $9602.

APPLYING
Standardized Tests *Recommended:* SAT or ACT (for admission).
Options: electronic application, early action, deferred entrance.
Required: essay or personal statement, high school transcript. *Required for some:* interview. *Recommended:* minimum 2.5 GPA, interview.

CONTACT
Mr. Joe Saltalamachia, Director of Admissions, Unity College, 90 Quaker Hill Road, Unity, ME 04988. *Phone:* 207-509-7205. *E-mail:* jsalty@unity.edu.

University of Maine
Orono, Maine
http://www.umaine.edu/
- **State-supported** university, founded 1865, part of University of Maine System
- **Small-town** 660-acre campus
- **Endowment** $323.0 million
- **Coed** 9,365 undergraduate students, 87% full-time, 47% women, 53% men
- **Moderately difficult** entrance level, 92% of applicants were admitted

UNDERGRAD STUDENTS
8,158 full-time, 1,207 part-time. Students come from 50 states and territories; 36 other countries; 37% are from out of state; 2% Black or African American, non-Hispanic/Latino; 4% Hispanic/Latino; 1% Asian, non-Hispanic/Latino; 0.8% American Indian or Alaska Native, non-Hispanic/Latino; 3% Two or more races, non-Hispanic/Latino; 2% Race/ethnicity unknown; 2% international; 4% transferred in; 38% live on campus.

Freshmen:
Admission: 12,457 applied, 11,503 admitted, 2,248 enrolled. *Average high school GPA:* 3.3. *Test scores:* SAT evidence-based reading and writing scores over 500: 90%; SAT math scores over 500: 88%; ACT scores over 18: 97%; SAT evidence-based reading and writing scores over 600: 44%; SAT math scores over 600: 37%; ACT scores over 24: 55%; SAT evidence-based reading and writing scores over 700: 6%; SAT math scores over 700: 7%; ACT scores over 30: 12%.
Retention: 78% of full-time freshmen returned.

FACULTY
Total: 878, 61% full-time, 60% with terminal degrees.
Student/faculty ratio: 16:1.

ACADEMICS
Calendar: semesters. *Degrees:* bachelor's, master's, doctoral, post-master's, and postbachelor's certificates.
Special study options: accelerated degree program, advanced placement credit, distance learning, double majors, English as a second language, freshman honors college, honors programs, independent study, internships, off-campus study, part-time degree program, services for LD students, student-designed majors, study abroad, summer session for credit. *ROTC:* Army (b), Navy (b).
Computers: 600 computers/terminals are available on campus for general student use. Students can access the following: campus intranet, computer help desk, free student e-mail accounts, online (class) grades, online (class) registration, online (class) schedules, online housing and financial aid information. Campuswide network is available. 100% of college-owned or -operated housing units are wired for high-speed Internet access. Wireless service is available via entire campus.
Library: Fogler Library. *Books:* 3.6 million (physical), 1.1 million (digital/electronic); *Serial titles:* 66,214 (physical), 142,082 (digital/electronic); *Databases:* 364. Weekly public service hours: 103; students can reserve study rooms.

STUDENT LIFE
Housing options: on-campus residence required for freshman year; coed, special housing for students with disabilities. Campus housing is university owned. Freshman campus housing is guaranteed.
Activities and organizations: drama/theater group, student-run newspaper, radio station, choral group, marching band, Fraternity and Sorority Life, Alternative Breaks, UMaine Student Government, Campus Activities Board, Wilde Stein, national fraternities, national sororities.
Athletics Member NCAA. All Division I except football (Division I-AA). *Intercollegiate sports:* baseball M(s), basketball M(s)/W(s), cheerleading M(c)/W(c), cross-country running M(s)/W(s), field hockey W(s), ice hockey M(s)/W(s), soccer M(c)/W(s), softball W(s), swimming and diving M/W(s), tennis M(c)/W(s), track and field M(s)/W(s). *Intramural sports:* badminton M/W, baseball M(c), basketball M/W, crew M(c)/W(c), equestrian sports M(c)/W(c), fencing M(c)/W(c), field hockey M(c)/W(c), football M(c), golf M(c)/W(c), ice hockey M(c)/W(c), lacrosse M(c)/W(c), racquetball M/W, rock climbing M(c)/W(c), rugby M(c)/W(c), skiing (cross-country) M/W, skiing (downhill) M(c)/W(c), soccer M/W, softball M/W, swimming and diving M/W, table tennis M/W,

tennis M/W, track and field M/W, ultimate Frisbee M(c)/W(c), volleyball M(c)/W(c), water polo M/W, wrestling M(c).

Campus security: 24-hour emergency response devices and patrols, late-night transport/escort service, controlled dormitory access, area emergency text and email message system.

Student services: health clinic, personal/psychological counseling, women's center, legal services, veterans affairs office.

FINANCIAL AID
Financial Aid Of all full-time matriculated undergraduates who enrolled in 2018, 6,829 applied for aid, 5,486 were judged to have need, 951 had their need fully met. 1,747 Federal Work-Study jobs (averaging $2390). In 2018, 1978 non-need-based awards were made. *Average percent of need met:* 66. *Average financial aid package:* $13,716. *Average need-based loan:* $4159. *Average need-based gift aid:* $8866. *Average non-need-based aid:* $6907. *Average indebtedness upon graduation:* $33,890.

APPLYING
Standardized Tests *Required:* SAT or ACT (for admission).

Options: electronic application, early admission, early action, deferred entrance.

Application fee: $40.

Required: 1 letter of recommendation.

Application deadlines: 2/1 (freshmen), 2/1 (out-of-state freshmen), rolling (transfers), 12/1 (early action).

Notification: continuous (freshmen), continuous (out-of-state freshmen), continuous (transfers), 1/15 (early action).

CONTACT
Lateef O'Connor, Senior Associate Director of Admissions, University of Maine, 5713 Chadbourne Hall, Orono, ME 04469-5713. *Phone:* 207-581-1561. *Toll-free phone:* 877-486-2364. *Fax:* 207-581-1213. *E-mail:* um-admit@maine.edu.

See below for display ad and page 1140 for the College Close-Up.

University of Maine at Augusta
Augusta, Maine
http://www.uma.edu/

CONTACT
Pamela Proulx-Curry, Interim Dean of Enrollment Services, University of Maine at Augusta, 46 University Drive, Robinson Hall, Augusta, ME 04330. *Phone:* 207-621-3465. *Toll-free phone:* 877-862-1234 Ext. 3185 (in-state); 877-862-1234 (out-of-state). *Fax:* 207-621-3333. *E-mail:* umaadm@maine.edu.

University of Maine at Farmington
Farmington, Maine
http://www.umf.maine.edu/

- **State-supported** comprehensive, founded 1863, part of University of Maine System
- **Small-town** 55-acre campus
- **Endowment** $13.1 million
- **Coed** 1,736 undergraduate students, 90% full-time, 66% women, 34% men
- **Moderately difficult** entrance level, 81% of applicants were admitted

UNDERGRAD STUDENTS
1,564 full-time, 172 part-time. 17% are from out of state; 2% Black or African American, non-Hispanic/Latino; 3% Hispanic/Latino; 0.9% Asian, non-Hispanic/Latino; 0.6% American Indian or Alaska Native, non-Hispanic/Latino; 2% Two or more races, non-Hispanic/Latino; 2% Race/ethnicity unknown; 0.4% international; 5% transferred in; 51% live on campus.

Freshmen:
Admission: 1,905 applied, 1,547 admitted, 375 enrolled. *Average high school GPA:* 3.1. *Test scores:* SAT evidence-based reading and writing scores over 500: 76%; SAT math scores over 500: 64%; ACT scores over 18: 100%; SAT evidence-based reading and writing scores over 600: 32%; SAT math scores over 600: 17%; ACT scores over 24: 50%; SAT

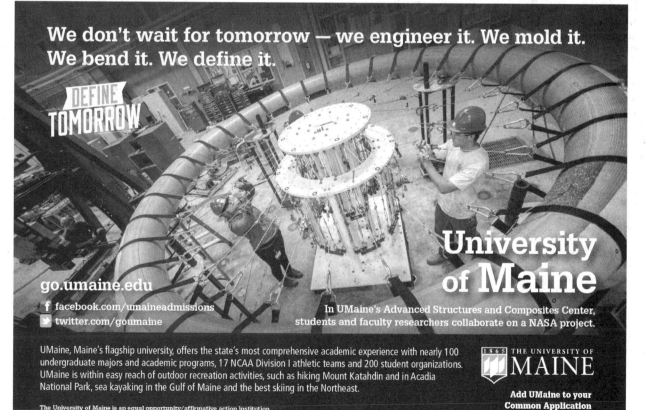

evidence-based reading and writing scores over 700: 5%; SAT math scores over 700: 2%; ACT scores over 30: 8%.

Retention: 71% of full-time freshmen returned.

FACULTY
Total: 195, 61% full-time, 63% with terminal degrees.
Student/faculty ratio: 13:1.

ACADEMICS
Calendar: semesters 3 summer sessions: one of 5 weeks and two of 4 weeks each. *Degrees:* certificates, bachelor's, master's, and postbachelor's certificates.

Special study options: academic remediation for entering students, accelerated degree program, advanced placement credit, distance learning, double majors, honors programs, independent study, internships, off-campus study, part-time degree program, services for LD students, student-designed majors, study abroad, summer session for credit.

Unusual degree programs: 3-2 social work with University of Southern Maine; Logan University.

Computers: 220 computers/terminals and 3,000 ports are available on campus for general student use. Students can access the following: campus intranet, computer help desk, free student e-mail accounts, online (class) grades, online (class) registration, online (class) schedules. Campuswide network is available. 100% of college-owned or -operated housing units are wired for high-speed Internet access. Wireless service is available via entire campus.

Library: Mantor Library plus 1 other. Weekly public service hours: 88; students can reserve study rooms.

STUDENT LIFE
Housing options: on-campus residence required for freshman year; coed, women-only, cooperative, special housing for students with disabilities. Campus housing is university owned. Freshman campus housing is guaranteed.

Activities and organizations: drama/theater group, student-run newspaper, radio station, choral group, Bust-A-Move Beavers, Commuter Council, Intervarsity Christian Fellowship, Student Senate, Campus Residence Council.

Athletics Member NCAA. All Division III. *Intercollegiate sports:* baseball M, basketball M/W, cross-country running M/W, field hockey W, golf M, lacrosse W, skiing (cross-country) M/W, skiing (downhill) W, soccer M/W, softball W, tennis M(c)/W(c), track and field M/W. *Intramural sports:* basketball M/W, cheerleading M(c)/W(c), equestrian sports M(c)/W(c), football M/W, ice hockey M(c)/W(c), rugby M(c)/W(c), skiing (cross-country) M(c)/W(c), skiing (downhill) M(c)/W(c), soccer M/W, softball M/W, swimming and diving M/W, tennis M/W, ultimate Frisbee M(c)/W(c), volleyball M/W.

Campus security: 24-hour emergency response devices and patrols, student patrols, late-night transport/escort service, controlled dormitory access, safety whistles, security cameras.

Student services: health clinic, personal/psychological counseling.

COSTS & FINANCIAL AID
Costs (2018–19) *Tuition:* state resident $9118 full-time, $304 per credit hour part-time; nonresident $18,598 full-time, $620 per credit hour part-time. Full-time tuition and fees vary according to course load and reciprocity agreements. Part-time tuition and fees vary according to course load and reciprocity agreements. *Required fees:* $898 full-time. *Room and board:* $9626; room only: $5180. Room and board charges vary according to board plan and housing facility. *Payment plan:* installment. *Waivers:* minority students, children of alumni, senior citizens, and employees or children of employees.

Financial Aid Of all full-time matriculated undergraduates who enrolled in 2017, 1,508 applied for aid, 1,320 were judged to have need, 549 had their need fully met. In 2017, 106 non-need-based awards were made. *Average percent of need met:* 82. *Average financial aid package:* $14,079. *Average need-based loan:* $6414. *Average need-based gift aid:* $7892. *Average non-need-based aid:* $2594. *Average indebtedness upon graduation:* $31,529.

APPLYING
Options: electronic application, early admission, early action, deferred entrance.

Required: high school transcript, 1 letter of recommendation. *Required for some:* essay or personal statement, Minimum 2.75 GPA for College of Education transfers, 2.5 for Health and Rehabilitation, 2.0 for all others. *Recommended:* interview.

CONTACT
Lisa Ellrich, Associate Director of Admissions, University of Maine at Farmington, 246 Main Street, Farmington, ME 04938-1994. *Phone:* 207-778-7050. *E-mail:* ellrich@maine.edu.

University of Maine at Fort Kent
Fort Kent, Maine
http://www.umfk.maine.edu/

- **State-supported** 4-year, founded 1878, part of University of Maine System
- **Rural** 52-acre campus
- **Endowment** $3.1 million
- **Coed**
- **Minimally difficult** entrance level

FACULTY
Student/faculty ratio: 14:1.

ACADEMICS
Calendar: semesters. *Degrees:* associate and bachelor's.
Library: Waneta Blake Library. *Books:* 44,058 (physical), 9,361 (digital/electronic); *Serial titles:* 92 (physical), 61,183 (digital/electronic); *Databases:* 106. Weekly public service hours: 88; students can reserve study rooms.

STUDENT LIFE
Housing options: on-campus residence required for freshman year; coed. Campus housing is university owned. Freshman applicants given priority for college housing.

Activities and organizations: drama/theater group, Student Nurses Organization, Student Teachers Educational Professional Society, Student Senate, Student Activities Board, Dorm Council, national fraternities, national sororities.

Athletics Member USCAA.

Campus security: controlled dormitory access, night patrols by security personnel 11pm-7am.

Student services: health clinic, personal/psychological counseling.

COSTS & FINANCIAL AID
Costs (2018–19) *Tuition:* state resident $6990 full-time, $233 per credit hour part-time; nonresident $11,190 full-time, $373 per credit hour part-time. *Required fees:* $1125 full-time, $38 per credit hour part-time. *Room and board:* $8220; room only: $4250. Room and board charges vary according to board plan and housing facility.

Financial Aid Of all full-time matriculated undergraduates who enrolled in 2016, 478 applied for aid, 389 were judged to have need, 194 had their need fully met. 98 Federal Work-Study jobs (averaging $1143). In 2016, 28 non-need-based awards were made. *Average percent of need met:* 79. *Average financial aid package:* $11,258. *Average need-based loan:* $6502. *Average need-based gift aid:* $6324. *Average non-need-based aid:* $2813. *Average indebtedness upon graduation:* $24,096.

APPLYING
Standardized Tests *Required for some:* SAT or ACT (for admission).

Options: electronic application, deferred entrance.

Application fee: $40.

Required: essay or personal statement, high school transcript. *Required for some:* interview.

CONTACT
University of Maine at Fort Kent, 23 University Drive, Fort Kent, ME 04743-1292. *Phone:* 207-834-7600. *Toll-free phone:* 888-TRY-UMFK.

University of Maine at Machias
Machias, Maine
http://www.machias.edu/

- **State-supported** 4-year, founded 1909, part of University of Maine System
- **Rural** 42-acre campus
- **Endowment** $2.5 million
- **Coed** 675 undergraduate students, 51% full-time, 71% women, 29% men
- **Moderately difficult** entrance level, 98% of applicants were admitted

UNDERGRAD STUDENTS
345 full-time, 330 part-time. 11% are from out of state; 3% Black or African American, non-Hispanic/Latino; 4% Hispanic/Latino; 0.6% Asian, non-Hispanic/Latino; 0.2% Native Hawaiian or other Pacific Islander, non-Hispanic/Latino; 4% American Indian or Alaska Native, non-Hispanic/Latino; 2% Two or more races, non-Hispanic/Latino; 3% Race/ethnicity unknown; 0.4% international; 5% transferred in; 56% live on campus.

Freshmen:
Admission: 596 applied, 584 admitted, 105 enrolled.
Retention: 55% of full-time freshmen returned.

FACULTY
Total: 66, 42% full-time, 55% with terminal degrees.
Student/faculty ratio: 12:1.

ACADEMICS
Calendar: semesters. *Degrees:* certificates, associate, and bachelor's.

Special study options: academic remediation for entering students, advanced placement credit, cooperative education, distance learning, double majors, independent study, internships, off-campus study, part-time degree program, services for LD students, student-designed majors, study abroad, summer session for credit.

Computers: Students can access the following: campus intranet, computer help desk, free student e-mail accounts, online (class) grades, online (class) schedules.
Library: Merrill Library.

STUDENT LIFE
Housing options: on-campus residence required through sophomore year; coed, special housing for students with disabilities. Campus housing is university owned.

Athletics Member NAIA. *Intercollegiate sports:* basketball M/W, cross-country running M/W, lacrosse M(c)/W(c), soccer M/W, volleyball W. *Intramural sports:* basketball M/W, cheerleading W, fencing M, field hockey W, football M/W, soccer M/W, softball W, water polo M/W.

FINANCIAL AID
Financial Aid Of all full-time matriculated undergraduates who enrolled in 2016, 394 applied for aid, 354 were judged to have need, 217 had their need fully met. In 2016, 2 non-need-based awards were made. *Average percent of need met:* 83. *Average financial aid package:* $14,175. *Average need-based loan:* $6053. *Average need-based gift aid:* $8858. *Average non-need-based aid:* $750. *Average indebtedness upon graduation:* $25,702.

APPLYING
Options: electronic application, early admission, early action, deferred entrance.
Application fee: $40.
Required: essay or personal statement, high school transcript, 1 letter of recommendation. *Required for some:* minimum 2.0 GPA.
Recommended: minimum 2.5 GPA, 2 letters of recommendation, interview.

CONTACT
Lizzie Wahab, Vice President for Enrollment Management, University of Maine at Machias, 116 O'Brien Avenue, Machias, ME 04654. *Phone:* 207-255-1318. *Toll-free phone:* 888-GOTOUMM (in-state); 888-468-6866 (out-of-state). *E-mail:* ummadmissions@maine.edu.

University of Maine at Presque Isle
Presque Isle, Maine
http://www.umpi.edu/

- **State-supported** 4-year, founded 1903, part of University of Maine System
- **Small-town** 150-acre campus
- **Endowment** $1.3 million
- **Coed** 1,554 undergraduate students, 43% full-time, 61% women, 39% men
- **Minimally difficult** entrance level, 92% of applicants were admitted

UNDERGRAD STUDENTS
673 full-time, 881 part-time. Students come from 32 states and territories; 8 other countries; 14% are from out of state; 3% Black or African American, non-Hispanic/Latino; 2% Hispanic/Latino; 0.8% Asian, non-Hispanic/Latino; 0.1% Native Hawaiian or other Pacific Islander, non-Hispanic/Latino; 2% American Indian or Alaska Native, non-Hispanic/Latino; 2% Two or more races, non-Hispanic/Latino; 11% Race/ethnicity unknown; 2% international; 7% transferred in; 34% live on campus.

Freshmen:
Admission: 801 applied, 734 admitted, 168 enrolled. *Average high school GPA:* 3.0. *Test scores:* SAT evidence-based reading and writing scores over 500: 56%; SAT math scores over 500: 53%; ACT scores over 18: 66%; SAT evidence-based reading and writing scores over 600: 19%; SAT math scores over 600: 9%; ACT scores over 24: 22%; SAT math scores over 700: 1%.
Retention: 62% of full-time freshmen returned.

FACULTY
Total: 93, 43% full-time, 41% with terminal degrees.
Student/faculty ratio: 13:1.

ACADEMICS
Calendar: semesters. *Degrees:* certificates, associate, and bachelor's.

Special study options: academic remediation for entering students, accelerated degree program, adult/continuing education programs, advanced placement credit, cooperative education, distance learning, double majors, honors programs, independent study, internships, off-campus study, part-time degree program, services for LD students, student-designed majors, study abroad, summer session for credit.

Computers: Students can access the following: campus intranet, computer help desk, free student e-mail accounts, online (class) grades, online (class) registration, online (class) schedules. Campuswide network is available. 100% of college-owned or -operated housing units are wired for high-speed Internet access. Wireless service is available via entire campus.
Library: Center for Innovative Learning plus 1 other. *Books:* 63,527 (physical), 159,418 (digital/electronic); *Serial titles:* 8 (physical), 75,843 (digital/electronic); *Databases:* 153. Weekly public service hours: 72.

STUDENT LIFE
Housing options: coed, special housing for students with disabilities. Campus housing is university owned. Freshman applicants given priority for college housing.

Activities and organizations: student-run newspaper, radio station, national fraternities, national sororities.

Athletics Member NCAA. All Division III. *Intercollegiate sports:* baseball M, basketball M/W, cross-country running M/W, golf M, skiing (cross-country) M/W, soccer M/W, softball W, volleyball W. *Intramural sports:* basketball M/W, cross-country running M/W, ice hockey M(c)/W(c), skiing (cross-country) M/W, skiing (downhill) M/W, soccer M/W, softball M/W, tennis M, track and field W, volleyball M/W.

Campus security: student patrols, late-night transport/escort service, controlled dormitory access.

Student services: health clinic, personal/psychological counseling, veterans affairs office.

COSTS & FINANCIAL AID
Costs (2019–20) *Tuition:* state resident $7170 full-time, $239 per credit hour part-time; nonresident $11,460 full-time, $382 per credit hour part-time. *Required fees:* $1194 full-time, $25 per credit hour part-time, $54 per term part-time. *Room and board:* $8406; room only: $4850.

Financial Aid Of all full-time matriculated undergraduates who enrolled in 2018, 532 applied for aid, 459 were judged to have need, 287 had their need fully met. In 2018, 26 non-need-based awards were made. *Average percent of need met:* 86. *Average financial aid package:* $12,482. *Average need-based loan:* $5184. *Average need-based gift aid:* $7363. *Average non-need-based aid:* $5624. *Average indebtedness upon graduation:* $20,248.

APPLYING
Options: electronic application, early admission, deferred entrance.
Application fee: $40.
Required: essay or personal statement, high school transcript, 1 letter of recommendation. *Required for some:* interview. *Recommended:* minimum 2.0 GPA.
Application deadlines: rolling (freshmen), rolling (out-of-state freshmen), rolling (transfers), rolling (early action).
Early decision deadline: rolling (for plan 1), rolling (for plan 2).
Notification: continuous (freshmen), continuous (out-of-state freshmen), continuous (transfers), rolling (early decision plan 1), rolling (early decision plan 2), rolling (early action).

CONTACT
Patricia Armstrong, Director of Admission, University of Maine at Presque Isle, 181 Main Street, Presque Isle, ME 04769. *Phone:* 207-768-9533. *E-mail:* patricia.armstrong@umpi.edu.

★ University of New England
Biddeford, Maine
http://www.une.edu/
- **Independent** comprehensive, founded 1831
- **Small-town** 540-acre campus
- **Endowment** $35.5 million
- **Coed**
- **Moderately difficult** entrance level

FACULTY
Student/faculty ratio: 13:1.

ACADEMICS
Calendar: semesters. *Degrees:* bachelor's, master's, doctoral, post-master's, and postbachelor's certificates.
Library: Jack S. Ketchum Library plus 1 other. *Books:* 135,000 (physical), 1.2 million (digital/electronic); *Serial titles:* 140,000 (digital/electronic); *Databases:* 200. Weekly public service hours: 146; study areas open 24 hours, 5–7 days a week; students can reserve study rooms.

STUDENT LIFE
Housing options: on-campus residence required through junior year; coed, women-only, special housing for students with disabilities. Campus housing is university owned. Freshman campus housing is guaranteed.
Activities and organizations: drama/theater group, student-run newspaper, choral group, Student Government, Outing Club, Campus Programming Board, Earth's Eco, Dance Team.
Athletics Member NCAA. All Division III.
Campus security: 24-hour emergency response devices and patrols, late-night transport/escort service, controlled dormitory access.
Student services: health clinic, personal/psychological counseling.

COSTS & FINANCIAL AID
Costs (2018–19) *Comprehensive fee:* $51,610 includes full-time tuition ($36,300), mandatory fees ($1320), and room and board ($13,990). Full-time tuition and fees vary according to course load and program. Part-time tuition: $1280 per credit hour. Part-time tuition and fees vary according to course load and program. *Required fees:* $1320 per year part-time. *Room and board:* Room and board charges vary according to board plan and housing facility.
Financial Aid Of all full-time matriculated undergraduates who enrolled in 2018, 2,055 applied for aid, 1,876 were judged to have need. *Average financial aid package:* $24,047. *Average need-based loan:* $3961. *Average need-based gift aid:* $7290. *Average indebtedness upon graduation:* $40,683.

APPLYING
Standardized Tests *Required:* SAT or ACT (for admission).
Options: electronic application, early admission, early action, deferred entrance.
Application fee: $40.
Required: essay or personal statement, high school transcript.
Recommended: 1 letter of recommendation.

CONTACT
Office of Undergraduate Admissions, University of New England, 11 Hills Beach Road, Biddeford, ME 04005-9526. *Phone:* 800-477-4863. *Toll-free phone:* 800-477-4863. *Fax:* 207-602-5900. *E-mail:* admissions@une.edu.

University of Southern Maine
Portland, Maine
http://www.usm.maine.edu/
- **State-supported** comprehensive, founded 1878, part of University of Maine System
- **Urban** 144-acre campus
- **Endowment** $38.5 million
- **Coed**
- **Moderately difficult** entrance level

FACULTY
Student/faculty ratio: 14:1.

ACADEMICS
Calendar: semesters. *Degrees:* certificates, bachelor's, master's, doctoral, post-master's, and postbachelor's certificates.
Library: Glickman Library plus 3 others.

STUDENT LIFE
Housing options: coed, special housing for students with disabilities. Campus housing is university owned. Freshman applicants given priority for college housing.
Activities and organizations: drama/theater group, student-run newspaper, radio station, choral group, Outing and Ski Clubs, Gorham Events Board, Commuter Student Group, Circle K, national fraternities, national sororities.
Athletics Member NCAA. All Division III except golf (Division II).
Campus security: 24-hour emergency response devices and patrols, late-night transport/escort service, controlled dormitory access, security lighting, preventive programs within residence halls.
Student services: health clinic, personal/psychological counseling, women's center, legal services, veterans affairs office.

COSTS & FINANCIAL AID
Costs (2018–19) *Tuition:* state resident $8130 full-time, $271 per credit hour part-time; nonresident $21,390 full-time, $713 per credit hour part-time. Full-time tuition and fees vary according to course load, degree level, and reciprocity agreements. Part-time tuition and fees vary according to course load, degree level, and reciprocity agreements. *Required fees:* $1390 full-time, $30 per credit hour part-time, $100 per term part-time. *Room and board:* $9450; room only: $5000. Room and board charges vary according to board plan and housing facility.
Financial Aid Of all full-time matriculated undergraduates who enrolled in 2017, 3,328 applied for aid, 2,791 were judged to have need, 1,393 had their need fully met. In 2017, 286 non-need-based awards were made. *Average percent of need met:* 80. *Average financial aid package:* $14,322. *Average need-based loan:* $6777. *Average need-based gift aid:* $8905. *Average non-need-based aid:* $4107.

APPLYING
Standardized Tests *Required:* SAT (for admission).
Options: electronic application, early admission, deferred entrance.
Application fee: $40.
Required: essay or personal statement, high school transcript. *Required for some:* interview, audition for music majors. *Recommended:* 1 letter of recommendation, interview.

CONTACT
Admissions, University of Southern Maine, Portland, ME 04104-9300. *Phone:* 207-780-5670. *Toll-free phone:* 800-800-4USM Ext. 5670. *E-mail:* admitusm@maine.edu.

MARYLAND

Bais HaMedrash and Mesivta of Baltimore
Baltimore, Maryland
http://www.bhmb.edu/

CONTACT
Bais HaMedrash and Mesivta of Baltimore, 6823 Old Pimlico Road, Baltimore, MD 21209.

Bowie State University
Bowie, Maryland
http://www.bowiestate.edu/

- **State-supported** comprehensive, founded 1865, part of University System of Maryland
- **Small-town** 295-acre campus with easy access to Baltimore and Washington, DC
- **Coed**
- **Minimally difficult** entrance level

FACULTY
Student/faculty ratio: 16:1.

ACADEMICS
Calendar: semesters. *Degrees:* certificates, bachelor's, master's, doctoral, and postbachelor's certificates.
Library: Thurgood Marshall Library. Students can reserve study rooms.

STUDENT LIFE
Housing options: coed, men-only, women-only. Campus housing is university owned and is provided by a third party. Freshman applicants given priority for college housing.
Activities and organizations: drama/theater group, student-run newspaper, radio and television station, choral group, marching band, Honda Campus All-Star Challenge, national fraternities, national sororities.
Athletics Member NCAA. All Division II.
Campus security: 24-hour emergency response devices and patrols, student patrols, late-night transport/escort service, controlled dormitory access.
Student services: health clinic, personal/psychological counseling.

COSTS & FINANCIAL AID
Costs (2018–19) *Tuition:* state resident $5536 full-time, $244 per credit hour part-time; nonresident $16,176 full-time, $680 per credit hour part-time. *Required fees:* $2698 full-time, $122 per credit hour part-time. *Room and board:* $10,904. Room and board charges vary according to board plan and housing facility. *Payment plans:* installment, deferred payment.
Financial Aid Of all full-time matriculated undergraduates who enrolled in 2017, 3,177 applied for aid, 3,164 were judged to have need, 485 had their need fully met. In 2017, 49 non-need-based awards were made. *Average percent of need met:* 43. *Average financial aid package:* $8736. *Average need-based loan:* $4017. *Average need-based gift aid:* $7113. *Average non-need-based aid:* $120. *Average indebtedness upon graduation:* $29,433.

APPLYING
Standardized Tests *Required:* SAT or ACT (for admission).
Options: electronic application.
Application fee: $40.
Required: high school transcript, minimum 2.5 GPA.

CONTACT
Mrs. Shirley Holt, Assistant Director of Admissions, Bowie State University, Administration Building, 1st Floor. *Phone:* 301-860-3415. *Toll-free phone:* 877-772-6943. *Fax:* 301-860-3438. *E-mail:* sholt@bowiestate.edu.

Capitol Technology University
Laurel, Maryland
http://www.captechu.edu/

CONTACT
Capitol Technology University, 11301 Springfield Road, Laurel, MD 20708-9759. *Phone:* 301-953-3200 Ext. 3033. *Toll-free phone:* 800-950-1992.

Cecil College
North East, Maryland
http://www.cecil.edu/

- **County-supported** primarily 2-year, founded 1968
- **Small-town** 159-acre campus with easy access to Baltimore
- **Coed**
- **Noncompetitive** entrance level

FACULTY
Student/faculty ratio: 11:1.

ACADEMICS
Calendar: semesters. *Degrees:* certificates, associate, and bachelor's.
Library: Cecil County Veterans Memorial Library.

STUDENT LIFE
Activities and organizations: drama/theater group, Student Government, Non-Traditional Student Organization, Student Nurses Association, national fraternities.
Athletics Member NJCAA.
Campus security: 24-hour emergency response devices, late-night transport/escort service, armed patrols from 6:30 am-7:00 pm.
Student services: personal/psychological counseling, women's center.

COSTS
Costs (2018–19) *Tuition:* area resident $3570 full-time, $119 per credit hour part-time; state resident $6780 full-time, $226 per credit hour part-time; nonresident $8280 full-time, $276 per credit hour part-time. *Required fees:* $735 full-time, $8 per credit hour part-time, $90 per term part-time.

APPLYING
Options: electronic application, early admission, deferred entrance.
Required: high school transcript.

CONTACT
Dr. Christy Dryer, Cecil College, One Seahawk Drive, North East, MD 21901-1999. *Phone:* 410-287-6060. *Fax:* 410-287-1001. *E-mail:* cdryer@cecil.edu.

Coppin State University
Baltimore, Maryland
http://www.coppin.edu/

CONTACT
Ms. Michelle Gross, Director of Admissions, Coppin State University, 2500 West North Avenue, Baltimore, MD 21216-3698. *Phone:* 410-951-3600. *Toll-free phone:* 800-635-3674. *Fax:* 410-523-7351. *E-mail:* mgross@coppin.edu.

Faith Theological Seminary
Baltimore, Maryland
http://www.fts.edu/

CONTACT
Faith Theological Seminary, 529 Walker Avenue, Baltimore, MD 21212. *Phone:* 410-323-6211.

Frostburg State University

Frostburg, Maryland
http://www.frostburg.edu/

- **State-supported** comprehensive, founded 1898, part of University System of Maryland
- **Small-town** 260-acre campus with easy access to Baltimore and Washington, DC
- **Endowment** $25.1 million
- **Coed**
- **Moderately difficult** entrance level

FACULTY
Student/faculty ratio: 15:1.

ACADEMICS
Calendar: semesters. *Degrees:* bachelor's, master's, and doctoral.
Library: Lewis J. Ort Library.

STUDENT LIFE
Housing options: coed, men-only, women-only. Campus housing is university owned and is provided by a third party.

Activities and organizations: drama/theater group, student-run newspaper, radio and television station, choral group, marching band, Student Government Association, Black Student Association, Campus Activities Board, Residence Hall Association, University Programming Council, national fraternities, national sororities.

Athletics Member NCAA. All Division III.

Campus security: 24-hour emergency response devices and patrols, student patrols, late-night transport/escort service, controlled dormitory access, bicycle patrols.

Student services: health clinic, personal/psychological counseling, women's center.

COSTS & FINANCIAL AID
Costs (2018–19) *Tuition:* state resident $6600 full-time, $272 per credit hour part-time; nonresident $20,320 full-time, $570 per credit hour part-time. Full-time tuition and fees vary according to location. Part-time tuition and fees vary according to course load and location. *Required fees:* $2572 full-time, $121 per credit hour part-time, $27 per term part-time. *Room and board:* $9398; room only: $4882. Room and board charges vary according to board plan and housing facility. *Payment plans:* installment, deferred payment.

Financial Aid Of all full-time matriculated undergraduates who enrolled in 2017, 3,480 applied for aid, 2,669 were judged to have need, 386 had their need fully met. 130 Federal Work-Study jobs (averaging $674). In 2017, 853 non-need-based awards were made. *Average percent of need met:* 59. *Average financial aid package:* $9993. *Average need-based loan:* $3932. *Average need-based gift aid:* $7651. *Average non-need-based aid:* $3427. *Average indebtedness upon graduation:* $29,802.

APPLYING
Standardized Tests *Required:* SAT or ACT (for admission).

Options: electronic application, early admission.

Application fee: $30.

Required: high school transcript, minimum 2.0 GPA. *Required for some:* essay or personal statement. *Recommended:* interview.

CONTACT
Frostburg State University, 101 Braddock Road, Frostburg, MD 21532-1099. *Phone:* 301-687-4201.

Goucher College

Baltimore, Maryland
http://www.goucher.edu/

CONTACT
Mr. Carlton E. Surbeck, Director of Admissions, Goucher College, 1021 Dulaney Valley Road, Baltimore, MD 21204. *Phone:* 410-337-6100. *Toll-free phone:* 800-468-2437. *Fax:* 410-337-6354. *E-mail:* admissions@goucher.edu.

Hood College

Frederick, Maryland
http://www.hood.edu/

- **Independent** comprehensive, founded 1893
- **Suburban** 50-acre campus with easy access to Baltimore and Washington, DC
- **Endowment** $99.7 million
- **Coed** 1,092 undergraduate students, 93% full-time, 63% women, 37% men
- **Moderately difficult** entrance level, 71% of applicants were admitted

UNDERGRAD STUDENTS
1,014 full-time, 78 part-time. Students come from 25 states and territories; 14 other countries; 25% are from out of state; 18% Black or African American, non-Hispanic/Latino; 11% Hispanic/Latino; 3% Asian, non-Hispanic/Latino; 0.1% Native Hawaiian or other Pacific Islander, non-Hispanic/Latino; 0.2% American Indian or Alaska Native, non-Hispanic/Latino; 5% Two or more races, non-Hispanic/Latino; 3% Race/ethnicity unknown; 2% international; 10% transferred in; 51% live on campus.

Freshmen:
Admission: 1,562 applied, 1,115 admitted, 239 enrolled. *Average high school GPA:* 3.3.
Retention: 71% of full-time freshmen returned.

FACULTY
Total: 240, 44% full-time, 61% with terminal degrees.
Student/faculty ratio: 10:1.

ACADEMICS
Calendar: semesters. *Degrees:* certificates, bachelor's, master's, doctoral, and postbachelor's certificates (also offers adult program with significant enrollment not reflected in profile).

Special study options: academic remediation for entering students, advanced placement credit, double majors, honors programs, independent study, internships, off-campus study, part-time degree program, services for LD students, student-designed majors, study abroad, summer session for credit. *ROTC:* Army (b).

Unusual degree programs: 3-2 business administration; nursing; social work; communication arts, integrated marketing communications, education, psychology/counseling, environmental science, biology/biomedical science.

Computers: 470 computers/terminals are available on campus for general student use. Students can access the following: campus intranet, computer help desk, free student e-mail accounts, online (class) grades, online (class) registration, online (class) schedules, Virtual Computer Lab (VCL), wireless printing. Campuswide network is available. 100% of college-owned or -operated housing units are wired for high-speed Internet access. Wireless service is available via entire campus.

Library: Beneficial-Hodson Library and Information Technology Center plus 1 other. *Books:* 113,587 (physical), 367,563 (digital/electronic); *Serial titles:* 1,546 (physical), 2,440 (digital/electronic); *Databases:* 148. Students can reserve study rooms.

STUDENT LIFE
Housing options: on-campus residence required through junior year; coed. Campus housing is university owned. Freshman campus housing is guaranteed.

Activities and organizations: drama/theater group, student-run newspaper, radio station, choral group, Black Student Union (BSU), Campus Activities Board (CAB), La Comunidad, Queer Student Union (QSU), Enactus.

Athletics Member NCAA. All Division III. *Intercollegiate sports:* baseball M, basketball M/W, cross-country running M/W, equestrian sports M(c)/W(c), field hockey W, golf M/W, lacrosse M/W, soccer M/W, softball W, swimming and diving M/W, tennis M/W, track and field M/W, volleyball W. *Intramural sports:* cheerleading W(c).

Campus security: 24-hour emergency response devices and patrols, late-night transport/escort service, controlled dormitory access.

Student services: health clinic, personal/psychological counseling.

COSTS & FINANCIAL AID

Costs (2019–20) *Comprehensive fee:* $53,940 includes full-time tuition ($40,460), mandatory fees ($600), and room and board ($12,880). Part-time tuition: $1180 per credit hour. *Required fees:* $195 part-time. *College room only:* $6600.

Financial Aid Of all full-time matriculated undergraduates who enrolled in 2018, 905 applied for aid, 824 were judged to have need, 134 had their need fully met. In 2018, 162 non-need-based awards were made. *Average percent of need met:* 74. *Average financial aid package:* $31,926. *Average need-based loan:* $4095. *Average need-based gift aid:* $28,296. *Average non-need-based aid:* $18,840. *Average indebtedness upon graduation:* $35,237.

APPLYING

Options: electronic application.

Required: essay or personal statement, high school transcript, minimum 2.0 GPA. *Recommended:* 2 letters of recommendation, interview.

Application deadlines: rolling (freshmen), rolling (transfers).

Notification: continuous (freshmen), continuous (transfers).

CONTACT

Mr. William Brown, Vice President for Enrollment Management, Hood College, 401 Rosemont Avenue, Frederick, MD 21701. *Phone:* 301-696-3400. *Toll-free phone:* 800-922-1599. *Fax:* 301-696-3819. *E-mail:* admission@hood.edu.

★ Johns Hopkins University
Baltimore, Maryland
http://www.jhu.edu/

- **Independent** university, founded 1876
- **Urban** 140-acre campus with easy access to Baltimore and Washington, DC
- **Endowment** $4.9 billion
- **Coed** 5,374 undergraduate students, 99% full-time, 52% women, 48% men
- **11%** of applicants were admitted

UNDERGRAD STUDENTS

5,325 full-time, 49 part-time. Students come from 54 states and territories; 51 other countries; 90% are from out of state; 7% Black or African American, non-Hispanic/Latino; 15% Hispanic/Latino; 27% Asian, non-Hispanic/Latino; 0.2% Native Hawaiian or other Pacific Islander, non-Hispanic/Latino; 0.1% American Indian or Alaska Native, non-Hispanic/Latino; 6% Two or more races, non-Hispanic/Latino; 6% Race/ethnicity unknown; 10% international; 1% transferred in; 51% live on campus.

Freshmen:
Admission: 29,129 applied, 3,089 admitted, 1,316 enrolled. *Average high school GPA:* 3.9. *Test scores:* SAT evidence-based reading and writing scores over 500: 100%; SAT math scores over 500: 100%; ACT scores over 18: 101%; SAT evidence-based reading and writing scores over 600: 98%; SAT math scores over 600: 99%; ACT scores over 24: 100%; SAT evidence-based reading and writing scores over 700: 85%; SAT math scores over 700: 93%; ACT scores over 30: 98%.
Retention: 98% of full-time freshmen returned.

FACULTY

Total: 741, 96% full-time, 93% with terminal degrees.
Student/faculty ratio: 8:1.

ACADEMICS

Calendar: 4-1-4. *Degrees:* certificates, diplomas, bachelor's, master's, doctoral, and postbachelor's certificates.

Special study options: advanced placement credit, double majors, independent study, internships, off-campus study, services for LD students, student-designed majors, study abroad, summer session for credit. *ROTC:* Army (b), Air Force (c).

Unusual degree programs: 3-2 engineering; International Studies, Biology, Classics, German, History, Neuroscience, Public Health, Mathematics, Education.

Computers: 200 computers/terminals and 4,000 ports are available on campus for general student use. Students can access the following: campus intranet, computer help desk, free student e-mail accounts, online (class) grades, online (class) registration, online (class) schedules. Campuswide network is available. 100% of college-owned or -operated housing units are wired for high-speed Internet access. Wireless service is available via entire campus.

Library: The Sheridan Libraries plus 2 others. *Books:* 2.4 million (physical), 1.8 million (digital/electronic); *Serial titles:* 51,824 (physical), 154,044 (digital/electronic); *Databases:* 836. Study areas open 24 hours, 5–7 days a week; students can reserve study rooms.

STUDENT LIFE

Housing options: on-campus residence required through sophomore year; coed, special housing for students with disabilities. Campus housing is university owned and leased by the school. Freshman campus housing is guaranteed.

Activities and organizations: drama/theater group, student-run newspaper, radio station, choral group, national fraternities, national sororities.

Athletics Member NCAA. All Division III except men's and women's lacrosse (Division I). *Intercollegiate sports:* baseball M, basketball M/W, cross-country running M/W, fencing M/W, field hockey W, football M, lacrosse M(s)/W(s), soccer M/W, swimming and diving M/W, tennis M/W, track and field M/W, volleyball W, water polo M, wrestling M. *Intramural sports:* badminton M(c)/W(c), baseball M(c), basketball M/W, cheerleading W(c), equestrian sports M(c)/W(c), fencing W(c), football M/W, golf M(c)/W(c), ice hockey M(c), lacrosse M(c)/W(c), racquetball M(c)/W(c), riflery M(c)/W(c), rock climbing M/W, rugby M(c)/W(c), soccer M/W, softball W(c), squash M(c)/W(c), swimming and diving M(c)/W(c), table tennis M(c)/W(c), tennis M(c)/W(c), track and field M(c)/W(c), triathlon M(c)/W(c), ultimate Frisbee M(c)/W(c), volleyball M(c)/W(c), water polo M(c)/W(c), wrestling M(c).

Campus security: 24-hour emergency response devices and patrols, student patrols, late-night transport/escort service, controlled dormitory access, CCTV monitoring of public areas.

Student services: health clinic, personal/psychological counseling, women's center.

COSTS & FINANCIAL AID

Costs (2018–19) *One-time required fee:* $500. *Comprehensive fee:* $69,576 includes full-time tuition ($53,740) and room and board ($15,836). Part-time tuition: $1791 per credit hour. *College room only:* $9178. Room and board charges vary according to board plan and housing facility. *Payment plan:* installment. *Waivers:* employees or children of employees.

Financial Aid Of all full-time matriculated undergraduates who enrolled in 2018, 3,194 applied for aid, 2,793 were judged to have need, 2,772 had their need fully met. 2,175 Federal Work-Study jobs (averaging $2282). In 2018, 155 non-need-based awards were made. *Average percent of need met:* 100. *Average financial aid package:* $44,147. *Average need-based loan:* $1534. *Average need-based gift aid:* $41,904. *Average non-need-based aid:* $25,181. *Average indebtedness upon graduation:* $25,697. *Financial aid deadline:* 1/15.

APPLYING

Standardized Tests *Required:* SAT or ACT (for admission).

Options: electronic application, early decision, deferred entrance.

Application fee: $70.

Required: essay or personal statement, high school transcript, 2 letters of recommendation.

Application deadlines: 1/1 (freshmen), 1/1 (transfers).

Early decision deadline: 11/1.

Notification: 4/1 (freshmen), 4/1 (transfers), 12/15 (early decision).

CONTACT

Ms. Ellen Kim, Dean of Undergraduate Admissions, Johns Hopkins University, 3400 North Charles Street, Baltimore, MD 21218.

See page 357 for display ad and page 1028 for the College Close-Up.

Loyola University Maryland

Baltimore, Maryland

http://www.loyola.edu/

CONTACT

Loyola University Maryland, 4501 North Charles Street, Baltimore, MD 21210-2699. *Phone:* 410-617-2000. *Toll-free phone:* 800-221-9107.

See below for display ad and page 1034 for the College Close-Up.

Maple Springs Baptist Bible College and Seminary

Capitol Heights, Maryland

http://www.msbbcs.edu/

CONTACT

Ms. Jeannie Bowman, Assistant Director of Admissions and Records, Maple Springs Baptist Bible College and Seminary, 4130 Belt Road, Capitol Heights, MD 20743. *Phone:* 301-736-3631. *Fax:* 301-735-6507.

Maryland Institute College of Art

Baltimore, Maryland

http://www.mica.edu/

- **Independent** comprehensive, founded 1826
- **Urban** 16-acre campus with easy access to Washington, DC
- **Endowment** $90.8 million
- **Coed** 1,714 undergraduate students, 99% full-time, 75% women, 25% men
- **Very difficult** entrance level, 64% of applicants were admitted

UNDERGRAD STUDENTS

1,689 full-time, 25 part-time. Students come from 44 states and territories; 42 other countries; 74% are from out of state; 8% Black or African American, non-Hispanic/Latino; 3% Hispanic/Latino; 11% Asian, non-Hispanic/Latino; 0.1% Native Hawaiian or other Pacific Islander, non-Hispanic/Latino; 13% Two or more races, non-Hispanic/Latino; 2% Race/ethnicity unknown; 27% international; 5% transferred in; 88% live on campus.

Freshmen:

Admission: 3,702 applied, 2,379 admitted, 425 enrolled. *Average high school GPA:* 3.5.

Retention: 88% of full-time freshmen returned.

FACULTY

Total: 352, 45% full-time, 83% with terminal degrees.

Student/faculty ratio: 8:1.

ACADEMICS

Calendar: semesters. *Degrees:* bachelor's, master's, and postbachelor's certificates.

Special study options: accelerated degree program, adult/continuing education programs, advanced placement credit, distance learning, double majors, English as a second language, independent study, internships, off-campus study, services for LD students, student-designed majors, study abroad, summer session for credit. *ROTC:* Army (c).

Computers: 750 computers/terminals and 3,000 ports are available on campus for general student use. Students can access the following: campus intranet, computer help desk, free student e-mail accounts, online (class) grades, online (class) registration, online (class) schedules, Campus Portal, online gallery space, Behance image portfolio system, Google Apps, Lynda.com web-based training, network storage space, personal websites, online software training tutorials, Canvas learning management system, printing services. Campuswide network is available. 100% of college-owned or -operated housing units are wired for high-speed Internet access. Wireless service is available via entire campus.

Library: Decker Library. *Books:* 76,337 (physical), 191,873 (digital/electronic); *Serial titles:* 407 (physical); *Databases:* 41. Weekly public service hours: 70; students can reserve study rooms.

STUDENT LIFE

Housing options: on-campus residence required through sophomore year; coed, special housing for students with disabilities. Campus housing is university owned. Freshman campus housing is guaranteed.

IF IT CAN BE IMAGINED, IT CAN BE ACHIEVED AT JOHNS HOPKINS.

JOHNS HOPKINS
UNIVERSITY

APPLY.JHU.EDU

Activities and organizations: drama/theater group, student-run radio station, choral group, Haunted House, Urban Gaming Club, Oy , Korean International Student Association, MICA Design League.

Campus security: 24-hour emergency response devices and patrols, student patrols, late-night transport/escort service, controlled dormitory access, self-defense education, 24-hour building security, safety awareness programs, campus patrols by city police, Rave Guardian mobile app.

Student services: health clinic, personal/psychological counseling.

COSTS & FINANCIAL AID
Costs (2018–19) *One-time required fee:* $190. *Comprehensive fee:* $61,910 includes full-time tuition ($46,870), mandatory fees ($1760), and room and board ($13,280). Part-time tuition: $1950 per credit hour. *Required fees:* $880 per term part-time. *College room only:* $10,010. Room and board charges vary according to board plan and housing facility. *Payment plan:* installment. *Waivers:* employees or children of employees.

Financial Aid *Average indebtedness upon graduation:* $17,472.

APPLYING
Standardized Tests *Required:* SAT or ACT (for admission).

Options: electronic application, early admission, early decision, early action, deferred entrance.

Application fee: $70.

Required: essay or personal statement, high school transcript, 3 letters of recommendation, art portfolio, test scores, and a list of activities and interests. *Recommended:* interview.

Application deadlines: 2/1 (freshmen), 2/1 (out-of-state freshmen), 4/1 (transfers), 12/1 (early action).

Early decision deadline: 11/1.

Notification: 2/26 (freshmen), 3/6 (out-of-state freshmen), 4/25 (transfers), 12/1 (early decision), 1/11 (early action).

CONTACT
Kelly Teeling, Maryland Institute College of Art, 1300 Mount Royal Avenue, Baltimore, MD 21217. *Phone:* 410-225-2222. *E-mail:* admissions@mica.edu.

McDaniel College
Westminster, Maryland
http://www.mcdaniel.edu/
- **Independent** comprehensive, founded 1867
- **Suburban** 160-acre campus with easy access to Baltimore and Washington, DC
- **Endowment** $132.0 million
- **Coed** 1,558 undergraduate students, 98% full-time, 51% women, 49% men
- **Moderately difficult** entrance level, 85% of applicants were admitted

UNDERGRAD STUDENTS
1,529 full-time, 29 part-time. Students come from 39 states and territories; 35 other countries; 34% are from out of state; 14% Black or African American, non-Hispanic/Latino; 6% Hispanic/Latino; 3% Asian, non-Hispanic/Latino; 0.1% Native Hawaiian or other Pacific Islander, non-Hispanic/Latino; 0.3% American Indian or Alaska Native, non-Hispanic/Latino; 4% Two or more races, non-Hispanic/Latino; 4% Race/ethnicity unknown; 4% international; 4% transferred in; 82% live on campus.

Freshmen:
Admission: 2,814 applied, 2,392 admitted, 415 enrolled. *Average high school GPA:* 3.5. *Test scores:* SAT evidence-based reading and writing scores over 500: 91%; SAT math scores over 500: 84%; ACT scores over 18: 100%; SAT evidence-based reading and writing scores over 600: 40%; SAT math scores over 600: 32%; ACT scores over 24: 52%; SAT evidence-based reading and writing scores over 700: 7%; SAT math scores over 700: 5%; ACT scores over 30: 17%.

Retention: 81% of full-time freshmen returned.

FACULTY
Total: 564, 24% full-time, 45% with terminal degrees.
Student/faculty ratio: 11:1.

ACADEMICS

Calendar: 4-1-4. *Degrees:* bachelor's, master's, and postbachelor's certificates.

Special study options: academic remediation for entering students, adult/continuing education programs, advanced placement credit, distance learning, double majors, honors programs, independent study, internships, off-campus study, part-time degree program, services for LD students, student-designed majors, study abroad, summer session for credit. *ROTC:* Army (b).

Unusual degree programs: 3-2 gerontology, human services management, music education, secondary education, special education.

Computers: 138 computers/terminals and 1,500 ports are available on campus for general student use. Students can access the following: campus intranet, computer help desk, free student e-mail accounts, online (class) grades, online (class) registration, online (class) schedules, online billing summaries, financial aid letter, tax information. Campuswide network is available. 100% of college-owned or -operated housing units are wired for high-speed Internet access. Wireless service is available via entire campus.

Library: Hoover Library. *Books:* 181,489 (physical), 193,549 (digital/electronic); *Serial titles:* 1,440 (physical), 83,076 (digital/electronic); *Databases:* 87. Weekly public service hours: 103; study areas open 24 hours, 5–7 days a week; students can reserve study rooms.

STUDENT LIFE

Housing options: on-campus residence required through junior year; coed, special housing for students with disabilities. Campus housing is university owned. Freshman campus housing is guaranteed.

Activities and organizations: drama/theater group, student-run newspaper, radio and television station, choral group, Student Government Association, Black Student Union, International Club, Maryland State Legislature, McDaniel Allies, national fraternities, national sororities.

Athletics Member NCAA. All Division III except golf (Division II). *Intercollegiate sports:* baseball M, basketball M/W, cross-country running M/W, field hockey W, football M, golf M/W, lacrosse M/W, soccer M/W, softball W, swimming and diving M/W, tennis M/W, track and field M/W, volleyball W, wrestling M. *Intramural sports:* basketball M/W, cheerleading M(c)/W(c), football M/W, golf M/W, soccer M/W, softball M/W, ultimate Frisbee M/W, volleyball M/W.

Campus security: 24-hour emergency response devices and patrols, late-night transport/escort service.

Student services: health clinic, personal/psychological counseling.

COSTS & FINANCIAL AID

Costs (2018–19) *Comprehensive fee:* $54,690 includes full-time tuition ($43,260) and room and board ($11,430). Full-time tuition and fees vary according to course load. Part-time tuition: $1352 per credit hour. Part-time tuition and fees vary according to course load. *College room only:* $5250. Room and board charges vary according to board plan and housing facility. *Payment plan:* installment. *Waivers:* children of alumni and employees or children of employees.

Financial Aid Of all full-time matriculated undergraduates who enrolled in 2018, 1,287 applied for aid, 1,203 were judged to have need, 316 had their need fully met. In 2018, 294 non-need-based awards were made. *Average percent of need met:* 88. *Average financial aid package:* $41,454. *Average need-based loan:* $2991. *Average need-based gift aid:* $37,622. *Average non-need-based aid:* $21,698. *Average indebtedness upon graduation:* $35,569. *Financial aid deadline:* 4/1.

APPLYING

Standardized Tests *Required:* SAT or ACT (for admission).

Options: electronic application, early admission, early decision, early action, deferred entrance.

Application fee: $50.

Required: essay or personal statement, high school transcript, minimum 2.5 GPA, 2 letters of recommendation. *Recommended:* interview.

Application deadlines: rolling (freshmen), rolling (out-of-state freshmen), 8/15 (transfers), 12/15 (early action).

Early decision deadline: 11/1 (for plan 1), 1/15 (for plan 2).

Notification: continuous (freshmen), continuous (out-of-state freshmen), continuous (transfers), 12/1 (early decision plan 1), 2/1 (early decision plan 2), 1/15 (early action).

CONTACT

Mrs. Janelle Holmboe, Vice President for Enrollment Management and Dean of Admissions, McDaniel College, 2 College Hill, Westminster, MD 21157-4390. *Phone:* 410-857-2230. *Toll-free phone:* 800-638-5005. *Fax:* 410-857-2757. *E-mail:* admissions@mcdaniel.edu.

Morgan State University
Baltimore, Maryland
http://www.morgan.edu/

CONTACT

Ms. Shonda Gray, Acting Director of Admissions and Recruitment, Morgan State University, 1700 East Cold Spring Lane, Baltimore, MD 21251. *Phone:* 443-885-3000. *Toll-free phone:* 800-332-6674. *E-mail:* shantell.saunders@morgan.edu.

Mount St. Mary's University
Emmitsburg, Maryland
http://www.msmary.edu/

- **Independent Roman Catholic** comprehensive, founded 1808
- **Rural** 1500-acre campus with easy access to Baltimore and Washington, DC
- **Endowment** $50.3 million
- **Coed**
- **Moderately difficult** entrance level

FACULTY
Student/faculty ratio: 13:1.

ACADEMICS
Calendar: semesters. *Degrees:* bachelor's, master's, post-master's, and postbachelor's certificates.
Library: Phillips Library. *Books:* 149,657 (physical), 280,598 (digital/electronic); *Serial titles:* 1,207 (physical), 26,497 (digital/electronic); *Databases:* 157.

STUDENT LIFE
Housing options: on-campus residence required for freshman year; coed, special housing for students with disabilities. Campus housing is university owned. Freshman campus housing is guaranteed.

Activities and organizations: drama/theater group, student-run newspaper, radio station, choral group, Mount Students for Life, CRUX - Outdoor Adventures, Campus Ministry Student Organization, FOCUS, Mount Chorale.

Athletics Member NCAA. All Division I.

Campus security: 24-hour emergency response devices and patrols, late-night transport/escort service, controlled dormitory access.

Student services: health clinic, personal/psychological counseling.

COSTS & FINANCIAL AID
Costs (2018–19) *Comprehensive fee:* $54,425 includes full-time tuition ($39,975), mandatory fees ($1375), and room and board ($13,075). Full-time tuition and fees vary according to location and program. Part-time tuition: $1300 per credit hour. Part-time tuition and fees vary according to location and program. *College room only:* $6650. Room and board charges vary according to housing facility.

Financial Aid Of all full-time matriculated undergraduates who enrolled in 2018, 1,395 applied for aid, 1,276 were judged to have need, 313 had their need fully met. 119 Federal Work-Study jobs (averaging $1875). 505 state and other part-time jobs (averaging $1505). In 2018, 404 non-need-based awards were made. *Average percent of need met:* 75. *Average financial aid package:* $30,494. *Average need-based loan:* $4129. *Average need-based gift aid:* $26,343. *Average non-need-based aid:* $19,675. *Average indebtedness upon graduation:* $40,355. *Financial aid deadline:* 3/1.

APPLYING
Standardized Tests *Required:* SAT or ACT (for admission).
Options: electronic application, early action, deferred entrance.
Application fee: $45.

Required: high school transcript, minimum 2.0 GPA, 1 letter of recommendation. *Recommended:* essay or personal statement, minimum 3.0 GPA, interview.

CONTACT
Mr. Eric M. Danielson, Director of Admissions, Mount St. Mary's University, 16300 Old Emmitsburg Road, Emmitsburg, MD 21727. *Phone:* 301-447-5505. *Toll-free phone:* 800-448-4347. *Fax:* 301-447-5818. *E-mail:* admissions@msmary.edu.

Ner Israel Rabbinical College
Baltimore, Maryland

CONTACT
Ner Israel Rabbinical College, 400 Mount Wilson Lane, Baltimore, MD 21208. *Phone:* 410-484-7200.

Notre Dame of Maryland University
Baltimore, Maryland
http://www.ndm.edu/

CONTACT
Angela Baumler, Director of Admissions (Women's College), Notre Dame of Maryland University, 4701 North Charles Street, Baltimore, MD 21210. *Phone:* 410-532-5330. *Toll-free phone:* 800-435-0200. *E-mail:* abaumler@ndm.edu.

Peabody Conservatory of The Johns Hopkins University
Baltimore, Maryland
http://www.peabody.jhu.edu/

CONTACT
Mr. David Lane, Director of Admissions, Peabody Conservatory of The Johns Hopkins University, Peabody Conservatory Admissions Office, One East Mount Vernon Place, Baltimore, MD 21202-2397. *Phone:* 410-234-4848. *Toll-free phone:* 800-368-2521.

Purdue University Global
Hagerstown, Maryland
http://www.purdueglobal.edu/

CONTACT
Purdue University Global, 18618 Crestwood Drive, Hagerstown, MD 21742. *Phone:* 301-739-2680 Ext. 217. *Toll-free phone:* 844-PURDUE-G.

★ St. John's College
Annapolis, Maryland
http://www.sjc.edu/

- **Independent** comprehensive, founded 1696
- **Small-town** 36-acre campus with easy access to Washington, D.C. and Baltimore, MD
- **Endowment** $120.9 million
- **Coed** 474 undergraduate students, 100% full-time, 48% women, 52% men
- **Very difficult** entrance level, 58% of applicants were admitted

UNDERGRAD STUDENTS
474 full-time. Students come from 43 states and territories; 30 other countries; 60% are from out of state; 2% Black or African American, non-Hispanic/Latino; 5% Hispanic/Latino; 4% Asian, non-Hispanic/Latino; 5% Two or more races, non-Hispanic/Latino; 0.2% Race/ethnicity unknown; 23% international; 4% transferred in; 96% live on campus.

Freshmen:
Admission: 913 applied, 526 admitted, 122 enrolled. *Average high school GPA:* 3.5. *Test scores:* SAT evidence-based reading and writing scores over 500: 97%; SAT math scores over 500: 97%; ACT scores over 18: 100%; SAT evidence-based reading and writing scores over 600: 86%; SAT math scores over 600: 71%; ACT scores over 24: 93%; SAT evidence-based reading and writing scores over 700: 52%; SAT math scores over 700: 28%; ACT scores over 30: 64%.

Retention: 91% of full-time freshmen returned.

A ★ *indicates that the school has detailed information with a Premium Profile on Petersons.com.*

FACULTY
Total: 70, 90% full-time, 86% with terminal degrees.
Student/faculty ratio: 7:1.

ACADEMICS
Calendar: semesters. *Degrees:* bachelor's and master's.
Special study options: internships, off-campus study, services for LD students, study abroad.
Computers: 26 computers/terminals and 500 ports are available on campus for general student use. Students can access the following: campus intranet, computer help desk, free student e-mail accounts, free wi-fi access throughout the campus; support for bring-your-own mobile devices. Campuswide network is available. 100% of college-owned or -operated housing units are wired for high-speed Internet access. Wireless service is available via entire campus.
Library: Greenfield Library plus 1 other. *Books:* 111,240 (physical), 538 (digital/electronic); *Serial titles:* 128 (physical), 2,410 (digital/electronic); *Databases:* 14. Weekly public service hours: 94; students can reserve study rooms.

STUDENT LIFE
Housing options: on-campus residence required for freshman year; coed, special housing for students with disabilities. Campus housing is university owned. Freshman campus housing is guaranteed.
Activities and organizations: drama/theater group, student-run newspaper, choral group, King William's Players (drama), Reality (social), Delegate Council (student government), Waltz (social), Student Committee on Instruction (advisory).
Athletics Member USCAA. *Intercollegiate sports:* crew M(c)/W(c), fencing M(c)/W(c), rowing M(c)/W(c), sailing M(c)/W(c). *Intramural sports:* basketball M/W, crew M/W, fencing M, field hockey W, rowing M/W, sailing M/W, soccer M/W, swimming and diving M/W, ultimate Frisbee M/W, volleyball M/W, weight lifting M/W.
Campus security: 24-hour emergency response devices and patrols, late-night transport/escort service, controlled dormitory access.
Student services: health clinic, personal/psychological counseling.

COSTS & FINANCIAL AID
Costs (2019–20) *One-time required fee:* $100. *Comprehensive fee:* $49,271 includes full-time tuition ($35,000), mandatory fees ($635), and room and board ($13,636). *College room only:* $7000. Room and board charges vary according to board plan and housing facility. *Payment plan:* installment. *Waivers:* employees or children of employees.
Financial Aid Of all full-time matriculated undergraduates who enrolled in 2017, 385 applied for aid, 349 were judged to have need, 58 had their need fully met. 88 Federal Work-Study jobs (averaging $3000). 110 state and other part-time jobs (averaging $3000). In 2017, 96 non-need-based awards were made. *Average percent of need met:* 87. *Average financial aid package:* $44,590. *Average need-based loan:* $4605. *Average need-based gift aid:* $40,005. *Average non-need-based aid:* $21,296. *Average indebtedness upon graduation:* $20,067.

APPLYING
Standardized Tests *Required for some:* SAT or ACT (for admission). *Recommended:* SAT/ACT, TOEFL/IELTS or interview for international applicants; SAT/ACT/CLT for homeschooled students and applicants who have not and will not graduate high school.
Options: electronic application, early admission, early action, deferred entrance.
Required: essay or personal statement, high school transcript, 2 letters of recommendation. *Required for some:* outline of curriculum for home-schooled applicants. *Recommended:* interview.
Application deadlines: rolling (freshmen), rolling (transfers), 11/15 (early action).
Notification: continuous (freshmen), continuous (transfers), 12/15 (early action).

CONTACT
Mr. Benjamin Baum, Director of Admissions, St. John's College, 60 College Avenue, Annapolis, MD 21401. *Phone:* 410-626-2522. *Toll-free phone:* 800-727-9238. *Fax:* 410-269-7916. *E-mail:* annapolis.admissions@sjc.edu.

See previous page for display ad and page 1094 for the College Close-Up.

St. Mary's College of Maryland
St. Mary's City, Maryland
http://www.smcm.edu/
- **State-supported** comprehensive, founded 1840
- **Rural** 361-acre campus
- **Endowment** $36.4 million
- **Coed** 1,572 undergraduate students, 97% full-time, 58% women, 42% men
- **Moderately difficult** entrance level, 80% of applicants were admitted

UNDERGRAD STUDENTS
1,521 full-time, 51 part-time. Students come from 26 states and territories; 7 other countries; 6% are from out of state; 9% Black or African American, non-Hispanic/Latino; 7% Hispanic/Latino; 4% Asian, non-Hispanic/Latino; 0.1% Native Hawaiian or other Pacific Islander, non-Hispanic/Latino; 0.1% American Indian or Alaska Native, non-Hispanic/Latino; 5% Two or more races, non-Hispanic/Latino; 3% Race/ethnicity unknown; 0.8% international; 7% transferred in; 80% live on campus.

Freshmen:
Admission: 1,700 applied, 1,361 admitted, 376 enrolled. *Average high school GPA:* 3.4. *Test scores:* SAT evidence-based reading and writing scores over 500: 92%; SAT math scores over 500: 84%; ACT scores over 18: 97%; SAT evidence-based reading and writing scores over 600: 53%; SAT math scores over 600: 42%; ACT scores over 24: 68%; SAT evidence-based reading and writing scores over 700: 11%; SAT math scores over 700: 9%; ACT scores over 30: 17%.
Retention: 82% of full-time freshmen returned.

FACULTY
Total: 209, 65% full-time, 75% with terminal degrees.
Student/faculty ratio: 10:1.

ACADEMICS
Calendar: semesters. *Degrees:* bachelor's and master's.
Special study options: advanced placement credit, cooperative education, double majors, freshman honors college, independent study, internships, part-time degree program, services for LD students, student-designed majors, study abroad, summer session for credit.
Computers: 340 computers/terminals are available on campus for general student use. Students can access the following: campus intranet, computer help desk, free student e-mail accounts, online (class) grades, online (class) registration, online (class) schedules, learning management system. Campuswide network is available. 100% of college-owned or -operated housing units are wired for high-speed Internet access. Wireless service is available via entire campus.
Library: Library, Archives, and Media Center. *Books:* 123,704 (physical), 12,593 (digital/electronic); *Serial titles:* 1,193 (physical), 90,283 (digital/electronic); *Databases:* 112. Weekly public service hours: 106; study areas open 24 hours, 5–7 days a week; students can reserve study rooms.

STUDENT LIFE
Housing options: coed, men-only, women-only, special housing for students with disabilities. Campus housing is university owned. Freshman campus housing is guaranteed.
Activities and organizations: drama/theater group, student-run newspaper, radio station, choral group, Dance Club, Humans vs. Zombies, InterVarsity Christian Fellowship, Habitat for Humanity, Programs Board.
Athletics Member NCAA. All Division III. *Intercollegiate sports:* baseball M, basketball M/W, crew M/W, cross-country running M/W, equestrian sports M(c)/W(c), fencing M(c)/W(c), field hockey W, lacrosse M/W, rock climbing M(c)/W(c), rowing M/W, rugby M(c)/W(c), sailing M/W, soccer M/W, softball W(c), swimming and diving M/W, tennis M/W, ultimate Frisbee M(c)/W(c), volleyball W. *Intramural sports:* badminton M/W, basketball M/W, soccer M/W, volleyball M/W.
Campus security: 24-hour emergency response devices and patrols, late-night transport/escort service, controlled dormitory access.
Student services: health clinic, personal/psychological counseling.

COSTS & FINANCIAL AID
Costs (2018–19) *Tuition:* state resident $11,646 full-time, $200 per credit hour part-time; nonresident $27,097 full-time, $200 per credit hour part-

time. Full-time tuition and fees vary according to course load. Part-time tuition and fees vary according to course load. *Required fees:* $2850 full-time. *Room and board:* $12,816; room only: $7400. Room and board charges vary according to board plan and housing facility. *Payment plan:* installment. *Waivers:* senior citizens and employees or children of employees.

Financial Aid Of all full-time matriculated undergraduates who enrolled in 2017, 1,125 applied for aid, 812 were judged to have need, 24 had their need fully met. 117 Federal Work-Study jobs (averaging $893). In 2017, 433 non-need-based awards were made. *Average percent of need met:* 67. *Average financial aid package:* $13,388. *Average need-based loan:* $4324. *Average need-based gift aid:* $10,196. *Average non-need-based aid:* $3562. *Average indebtedness upon graduation:* $24,132.

APPLYING
Standardized Tests *Required:* SAT or ACT (for admission).

Options: electronic application, early decision, early action, deferred entrance.

Application fee: $50.

Required: essay or personal statement, high school transcript, 2 letters of recommendation. *Recommended:* interview.

Application deadlines: 1/15 (freshmen), 1/15 (out-of-state freshmen), 8/1 (transfers), 11/1 (early action).

Early decision deadline: 11/1.

Notification: continuous until 4/1 (freshmen), continuous (out-of-state freshmen), continuous until 5/1 (transfers), 12/1 (early decision), 1/1 (early action).

CONTACT
Kendra L. Lawrence, Director of Admissions, St. Mary's College of Maryland, 47645 College Drive, St. Mary's City, MD 20686-3001. *Phone:* 240-895-5000. *Toll-free phone:* 800-492-7181. *Fax:* 240-895-5001. *E-mail:* admissions@smcm.edu.

Salisbury University
Salisbury, Maryland
http://www.salisbury.edu/

- **State-supported** comprehensive, founded 1925, part of University System of Maryland
- **Small-town** 201-acre campus
- **Endowment** $71.3 million
- **Coed** 7,650 undergraduate students, 93% full-time, 56% women, 44% men
- **Moderately difficult** entrance level, 62% of applicants were admitted

UNDERGRAD STUDENTS
7,081 full-time, 569 part-time. Students come from 31 states and territories; 37 other countries; 13% are from out of state; 14% Black or African American, non-Hispanic/Latino; 4% Hispanic/Latino; 4% Asian, non-Hispanic/Latino; 0.2% Native Hawaiian or other Pacific Islander, non-Hispanic/Latino; 0.7% American Indian or Alaska Native, non-Hispanic/Latino; 3% Two or more races, non-Hispanic/Latino; 3% Race/ethnicity unknown; 1% international; 10% transferred in; 29% live on campus.

Freshmen:
Admission: 8,983 applied, 5,585 admitted, 1,289 enrolled. *Average high school GPA:* 3.7. *Test scores:* SAT evidence-based reading and writing scores over 500: 99%; SAT math scores over 500: 99%; ACT scores over 18: 98%; SAT evidence-based reading and writing scores over 600: 61%; SAT math scores over 600: 52%; ACT scores over 24: 37%; SAT evidence-based reading and writing scores over 700: 6%; SAT math scores over 700: 5%; ACT scores over 30: 4%.
Retention: 83% of full-time freshmen returned.

FACULTY
Total: 669, 66% full-time, 61% with terminal degrees.
Student/faculty ratio: 16:1.

ACADEMICS
Calendar: 4-1-4. *Degrees:* bachelor's, master's, doctoral, post-master's, and postbachelor's certificates.

Special study options: accelerated degree program, advanced placement credit, cooperative education, distance learning, double majors, English as a second language, freshman honors college, honors programs, independent study, internships, off-campus study, part-time degree program, services for LD students, student-designed majors, study abroad, summer session for credit. *ROTC:* Army (b), Air Force (c).

Unusual degree programs: 3-2 engineering with University of Maryland, College Park; Old Dominion University; Widener University; social work with University of Maryland Eastern Shore; biology and environmental marine science with University of Maryland Eastern Shore.

Computers: 1,000 computers/terminals and 3,552 ports are available on campus for general student use. Students can access the following: campus intranet, computer help desk, free student e-mail accounts, online (class) grades, online (class) registration, online (class) schedules, university accounts, student web hosting. Campuswide network is available. 100% of college-owned or -operated housing units are wired for high-speed Internet access. Wireless service is available via entire campus.

Library: Guerrieri Academic Commons plus 2 others. *Books:* 269,531 (physical), 347 (digital/electronic); *Serial titles:* 694 (physical), 150 (digital/electronic); *Databases:* 106. Weekly public service hours: 112; study areas open 24 hours, 5–7 days a week; students can reserve study rooms.

STUDENT LIFE
Housing options: on-campus residence required through sophomore year; coed, special housing for students with disabilities. Campus housing is university owned. Freshman applicants given priority for college housing.

Activities and organizations: drama/theater group, student-run newspaper, radio and television station, choral group, Student Government Association, Radio (WXSU) / SU TV / The Flyer Newspaper, Student Organization for Activity Planning (SOAP), Campus Crusade for Christ, Black Student Union, national fraternities, national sororities.

Athletics Member NCAA. All Division III. *Intercollegiate sports:* baseball M, basketball M/W, cross-country running M/W, field hockey W, football M, lacrosse M/W, soccer M/W, softball W, swimming and diving M/W, tennis M/W, track and field M/W, volleyball W. *Intramural sports:* basketball M/W, cheerleading M(c)/W(c), equestrian sports M(c)/W(c), fencing W(c), field hockey M(c), golf M/W, gymnastics M(c)/W(c), ice hockey M(c), lacrosse M(c)/W(c), rock climbing M/W, rugby M(c)/W(c), sailing M(c)/W(c), sand volleyball M/W, soccer M/W, softball M/W, ultimate Frisbee M(c)/W(c), volleyball M/W, weight lifting M(c)/W(c).

Campus security: 24-hour emergency response devices and patrols, student patrols, late-night transport/escort service, controlled dormitory access.

Student services: health clinic, personal/psychological counseling, veterans affairs office.

COSTS & FINANCIAL AID
Costs (2018–19) *Tuition:* state resident $7122 full-time, $292 per credit hour part-time; nonresident $16,824 full-time, $695 per credit hour part-time. Full-time tuition and fees vary according to location. Part-time tuition and fees vary according to location. *Required fees:* $2702 full-time, $100 per credit hour part-time. *Room and board:* $11,950; room only: $6950. Room and board charges vary according to board plan and housing facility. *Payment plan:* installment. *Waivers:* senior citizens and employees or children of employees.

Financial Aid Of all full-time matriculated undergraduates who enrolled in 2017, 5,853 applied for aid, 3,859 were judged to have need, 416 had their need fully met. 75 Federal Work-Study jobs (averaging $2087). In 2017, 1168 non-need-based awards were made. *Average percent of need met:* 54. *Average financial aid package:* $8726. *Average need-based loan:* $4088. *Average need-based gift aid:* $6757. *Average non-need-based aid:* $2630. *Average indebtedness upon graduation:* $26,521.

APPLYING
Standardized Tests *Required for some:* SAT or ACT (for admission).

Options: electronic application, early admission, early decision, early action, deferred entrance.

Application fee: $50.

Required: essay or personal statement, minimum 2.0 GPA, 1 letter of recommendation. *Required for some:* high school transcript.

Application deadlines: 1/15 (freshmen), 1/15 (out-of-state freshmen), rolling (transfers), 12/1 (early action).
Early decision deadline: 11/15.
Notification: 3/15 (freshmen), 3/15 (out-of-state freshmen), continuous (transfers), 12/15 (early decision), 1/15 (early action).

CONTACT
Elizabeth Skoglund, Director of Admissions, Salisbury University, Salisbury University - Admissions House, 1101 Camden Avenue, Salisbury, MD 21801. *Phone:* 410-543-6161. *Toll-free phone:* 888-543-0148. *Fax:* 410-546-6016. *E-mail:* admissions@salisbury.edu.

★ Stevenson University
Stevenson, Maryland
http://www.stevenson.edu/
- **Independent** comprehensive, founded 1952
- **Suburban** 163-acre campus with easy access to Baltimore
- **Endowment** $82.7 million
- **Coed**
- **Moderately difficult** entrance level

FACULTY
Student/faculty ratio: 16:1.

ACADEMICS
Calendar: semesters. *Degrees:* bachelor's, master's, and postbachelor's certificates.
Library: Stevenson University Learning Resource Center-Greenspring Campus plus 2 others. *Books:* 67,987 (physical), 342,648 (digital/electronic); *Serial titles:* 476 (physical), 72,885 (digital/electronic); *Databases:* 88. Weekly public service hours: 136; students can reserve study rooms.

STUDENT LIFE
Housing options: coed. Campus housing is university owned. Freshman applicants given priority for college housing.
Activities and organizations: drama/theater group, student-run newspaper, radio station, choral group, marching band, Relay for Life, Mustang Activities Programming, Black Student Union, American Chemical Society, Phi Sigma Sigma, national fraternities, national sororities.
Athletics Member NCAA. All Division III.
Campus security: 24-hour emergency response devices and patrols, late-night transport/escort service, controlled dormitory access, patrols by trained security personnel during campus hours.
Student services: health clinic, personal/psychological counseling.

COSTS & FINANCIAL AID
Costs (2018–19) *Comprehensive fee:* $49,488 includes full-time tuition ($33,690), mandatory fees ($2552), and room and board ($13,246). Full-time tuition and fees vary according to course load and degree level. Part-time tuition: $850 per credit hour. Part-time tuition and fees vary according to degree level. *Required fees:* $75 per term part-time. *College room only:* $8446. Room and board charges vary according to board plan and housing facility.
Financial Aid Of all full-time matriculated undergraduates who enrolled in 2018, 2,337 applied for aid, 2,106 were judged to have need, 296 had their need fully met. 219 Federal Work-Study jobs (averaging $1870). In 2018, 534 non-need-based awards were made. *Average percent of need met:* 68. *Average financial aid package:* $25,047. *Average need-based loan:* $4358. *Average need-based gift aid:* $22,343. *Average non-need-based aid:* $17,170. *Average indebtedness upon graduation:* $36,925.

APPLYING
Standardized Tests *Required:* SAT or ACT (for admission).
Options: electronic application, deferred entrance.
Application fee: $40.

Required: essay or personal statement, high school transcript, 1 letter of recommendation. *Required for some:* interview.

CONTACT
Mr. Mark Hergan, Vice President, Enrollment Management, Stevenson University, 1525 Greenspring Valley Road, Stevenson, MD 21153. *Phone:* 410-486-7001. *Toll-free phone:* 877-468-6852 (in-state); 877-468-3852 (out-of-state). *Fax:* 410-352-4440. *E-mail:* admissions@stevenson.edu.

Stratford University
Baltimore, Maryland
http://www.stratford.edu/

CONTACT
Admissions, Stratford University, 210 South Central Avenue, Baltimore, MD 21202. *Phone:* 410-752-4710. *Toll-free phone:* 800-624-9926 (in-state); 800-624-9926 Ext. 120 (out-of-state). *E-mail:* baadmissions@stratford.edu.

Strayer University–Anne Arundel Campus
Millersville, Maryland
http://www.strayer.edu/maryland/anne-arundel/

CONTACT
Strayer University–Anne Arundel Campus, 1520 Jabez Run, Suite 100, Millersville, MD 21108. *Toll-free phone:* 888-311-0355.

Strayer University–Owings Mills Campus
Owings Mills, Maryland
http://www.strayer.edu/maryland/owings-mills/

CONTACT
Strayer University–Owings Mills Campus, 500 Redland Court, Suite 100, Owings Mills, MD 21117. *Toll-free phone:* 888-311-0355.

Strayer University–Prince George's Campus
Suitland, Maryland
http://www.strayer.edu/maryland/prince-georges/

CONTACT
Strayer University–Prince George's Campus, 5110 Auth Way, Suitland, MD 20746. *Toll-free phone:* 888-311-0355.

Strayer University–Rockville Campus
Rockville, Maryland
http://www.strayer.edu/maryland/rockville/

CONTACT
Strayer University–Rockville Campus, 1803 Research Boulevard, Suite 110, Rockville, MD 20850. *Toll-free phone:* 888-311-0355.

Strayer University–White Marsh Campus
Baltimore, Maryland
http://www.strayer.edu/maryland/white-marsh/

CONTACT
Strayer University–White Marsh Campus, 9920 Franklin Square Drive, Suite 200, Baltimore, MD 21236. *Toll-free phone:* 888-311-0355.

Towson University

Towson, Maryland
http://www.towson.edu/

- **State-supported** university, founded 1866, part of University System of Maryland
- **Suburban** 329-acre campus with easy access to Baltimore and Washington, DC
- **Endowment** $83.5 million
- **Coed** 19,818 undergraduate students, 88% full-time, 59% women, 41% men
- **Moderately difficult** entrance level, 79% of applicants were admitted

UNDERGRAD STUDENTS
17,350 full-time, 2,468 part-time. Students come from 45 states and territories; 73 other countries; 12% are from out of state; 23% Black or African American, non-Hispanic/Latino; 8% Hispanic/Latino; 6% Asian, non-Hispanic/Latino; 0.1% Native Hawaiian or other Pacific Islander, non-Hispanic/Latino; 0.1% American Indian or Alaska Native, non-Hispanic/Latino; 5% Two or more races, non-Hispanic/Latino; 2% Race/ethnicity unknown; 2% international; 11% transferred in; 28% live on campus.

Freshmen:
Admission: 11,933 applied, 9,427 admitted, 2,996 enrolled. *Average high school GPA:* 3.6. *Test scores:* SAT evidence-based reading and writing scores over 500: 94%; SAT math scores over 500: 88%; ACT scores over 18: 97%; SAT evidence-based reading and writing scores over 600: 35%; SAT math scores over 600: 24%; ACT scores over 24: 41%; SAT evidence-based reading and writing scores over 700: 3%; SAT math scores over 700: 2%; ACT scores over 30: 4%.

Retention: 85% of full-time freshmen returned.

FACULTY
Total: 1,743, 52% full-time, 54% with terminal degrees.
Student/faculty ratio: 17:1.

ACADEMICS
Calendar: semesters. *Degrees:* bachelor's, master's, doctoral, post-master's, and postbachelor's certificates.

Special study options: academic remediation for entering students, adult/continuing education programs, advanced placement credit, cooperative education, distance learning, double majors, English as a second language, freshman honors college, honors programs, independent study, internships, off-campus study, part-time degree program, services for LD students, student-designed majors, study abroad, summer session for credit. *ROTC:* Army (c), Air Force (c).

Unusual degree programs: 3-2 engineering with University of Maryland, College Park; law with University of Baltimore School of Law.

Computers: 3,800 computers/terminals and 10,310 ports are available on campus for general student use. Students can access the following: campus intranet, computer help desk, free student e-mail accounts, online (class) grades, online (class) registration, online (class) schedules. Campuswide network is available. 100% of college-owned or -operated housing units are wired for high-speed Internet access. Wireless service is available via entire campus.

Library: Cook Library. *Books:* 396,754 (physical), 520,928 (digital/electronic); *Serial titles:* 288 (physical), 79,916 (digital/electronic); *Databases:* 312. Weekly public service hours: 108; study areas open 24 hours, 5–7 days a week; students can reserve study rooms.

STUDENT LIFE
Housing options: coed, special housing for students with disabilities. Campus housing is university owned and is provided by a third party. Freshman campus housing is guaranteed.

Activities and organizations: drama/theater group, student-run newspaper, radio and television station, choral group, marching band, University Residence Government, Latin American Student Organization, Black Student Union, Hillel, African Diaspora Club, national fraternities, national sororities.

Athletics Member NCAA. All Division I except football (Division I-A). *Intercollegiate sports:* baseball M(s), basketball M(s)/W(s), cross-country running W(s), field hockey W(s), golf M(s)/W(s)(c), gymnastics W(s), lacrosse M(s)/W(s), soccer W(s), softball W(s), swimming and diving M(s)/W(s), tennis W(s), track and field W(s), ultimate Frisbee M/W, volleyball M/W(s). *Intramural sports:* badminton M/W, basketball M/W, cheerleading M(c)/W(c), cross-country running M(c)/W(c), equestrian sports M(c)/W(c), fencing W(c), field hockey M(c)/W(c), golf M(c)/W(c), gymnastics M(c)/W(c), ice hockey M(c)/W(c), lacrosse M(c)/W(c), riflery M(c)/W(c), rugby M(c)/W(c), soccer M/W, softball M/W, swimming and diving M(c)/W(c), table tennis M/W, tennis M(c)/W(c), track and field M(c)/W(c), ultimate Frisbee M(c)/W(c), volleyball M/W, water polo M(c)/W(c), wrestling M(c)/W(c).

Campus security: 24-hour emergency response devices and patrols, late-night transport/escort service, controlled dormitory access.

Student services: health clinic, personal/psychological counseling, women's center, veterans affairs office.

COSTS & FINANCIAL AID
Costs (2019–20) *Tuition:* state resident $6962 full-time, $299 per credit hour part-time; nonresident $22,140 full-time, $888 per credit hour part-time. *Required fees:* $3344 full-time, $147 per credit hour part-time. *Room and board:* $13,034; room only: $7446.

Financial Aid Of all full-time matriculated undergraduates who enrolled in 2018, 12,988 applied for aid, 10,016 were judged to have need, 888 had their need fully met. 937 Federal Work-Study jobs (averaging $1951). In 2018, 1086 non-need-based awards were made. *Average percent of need met:* 57. *Average financial aid package:* $10,734. *Average need-based loan:* $4010. *Average need-based gift aid:* $9412. *Average non-need-based aid:* $5042. *Average indebtedness upon graduation:* $27,295.

APPLYING
Standardized Tests *Required:* SAT or ACT (for admission).

Options: electronic application, early admission, early action, deferred entrance.

Application fee: $45.

Required: essay or personal statement, high school transcript. *Required for some:* interview. *Recommended:* minimum 3.0 GPA, 2 letters of recommendation, resume or activity list.

Notification: continuous (freshmen), continuous (transfers).

CONTACT
Mr. David Fedorchak, Director of University Admissions, Towson University, 8000 York Road, Towson, MD 21252. *Phone:* 410-704-2113. *Fax:* 410-704-3030. *E-mail:* admissions@towson.edu.

United States Naval Academy

Annapolis, Maryland
http://www.usna.edu/

CONTACT
Capt. Ann Kubera, Director of Admissions, United States Naval Academy, 52 King George Street, Annapolis, MD 21402. *Phone:* 410-293-4361. *Toll-free phone:* 888-249-7707. *Fax:* 410-293-4348. *E-mail:* webmail@usna.edu.

University of Baltimore

Baltimore, Maryland
http://www.ubalt.edu/

CONTACT
David Waggoner, Associate Vice President of Admission, University of Baltimore, 1420 North Charles Street, Baltimore, MD 21201. *Phone:* 410-837-4777. *Fax:* 410-837-4793. *E-mail:* admission@ubalt.edu.

University of Maryland, Baltimore County

Baltimore, Maryland
http://www.umbc.edu/

- **State-supported** university, founded 1963, part of University System of Maryland
- **Suburban** 530-acre campus with easy access to Washington, DC
- **Endowment** $105.2 million
- **Coed** 12,471 undergraduate students, 87% full-time, 50% women, 50% men
- **Moderately difficult** entrance level, 58% of applicants were admitted

UNDERGRAD STUDENTS
10,834 full-time, 1,637 part-time. Students come from 42 states and territories; 81 other countries; 5% are from out of state; 18% Black or African American, non-Hispanic/Latino; 8% Hispanic/Latino; 22% Asian, non-Hispanic/Latino; 0.2% Native Hawaiian or other Pacific Islander, non-Hispanic/Latino; 0.2% American Indian or Alaska Native, non-Hispanic/Latino; 5% Two or more races, non-Hispanic/Latino; 3% Race/ethnicity unknown; 4% international; 9% transferred in; 35% live on campus.

Freshmen:
Admission: 11,720 applied, 6,790 admitted, 1,794 enrolled. *Average high school GPA:* 3.9. *Test scores:* SAT evidence-based reading and writing scores over 500: 99%; SAT math scores over 500: 99%; ACT scores over 18: 99%; SAT evidence-based reading and writing scores over 600: 75%; SAT math scores over 600: 73%; ACT scores over 24: 82%; SAT evidence-based reading and writing scores over 700: 16%; SAT math scores over 700: 23%; ACT scores over 30: 25%.

Retention: 87% of full-time freshmen returned.

FACULTY
Total: 830, 65% full-time, 70% with terminal degrees.
Student/faculty ratio: 18:1.

ACADEMICS
Calendar: 4-1-4. *Degrees:* bachelor's, master's, doctoral, and postbachelor's certificates.

Special study options: academic remediation for entering students, adult/continuing education programs, advanced placement credit, cooperative education, distance learning, double majors, English as a second language, external degree program, freshman honors college, honors programs, independent study, internships, off-campus study, part-time degree program, services for LD students, student-designed majors, study abroad, summer session for credit. *ROTC:* Army (c), Navy (b), Air Force (c).

Computers: 1,065 computers/terminals and 4,000 ports are available on campus for general student use. Students can access the following: campus intranet, computer help desk, free student e-mail accounts, online (class) grades, online (class) registration, online (class) schedules, billing, housing, parking, degree audit and advising. Campuswide network is available. 100% of college-owned or -operated housing units are wired for high-speed Internet access. Wireless service is available via entire campus.

Library: Albin O. Kuhn Library and Gallery. *Books:* 700,265 (physical), 175,405 (digital/electronic); *Serial titles:* 18,354 (physical), 134,280 (digital/electronic); *Databases:* 388. Weekly public service hours: 94; study areas open 24 hours, 5–7 days a week; students can reserve study rooms.

STUDENT LIFE
Housing options: coed, special housing for students with disabilities. Campus housing is university owned and is provided by a third party. Freshman campus housing is guaranteed.

Activities and organizations: drama/theater group, student-run newspaper, radio station, choral group, Student Government Association, Student Events Board, Retriever Weekly, Resident Student Association, WMBC, Campus Radio, national fraternities, national sororities.

Athletics Member NCAA. All Division I. *Intercollegiate sports:* baseball M(s), basketball M(s)/W(s), crew M(c)/W(c), cross-country running M(s)/W(s), equestrian sports M(c)/W(c), fencing M(c)/W(c), ice hockey M(c), lacrosse M(s)/W(s), rugby M(c)/W(c), sailing M(c)/W(c), soccer M(s)/W(s), softball W(s), swimming and diving M(s)/W(s), tennis M(c)/W(c), track and field M(s)/W(s), ultimate Frisbee M(c)/W(c), volleyball M(c)/W(s), wrestling M(c)/W(c). *Intramural sports:* basketball M/W, cross-country running M(c)/W(c), football M/W, lacrosse M(c)/W(c), sand volleyball M/W, soccer M/W, softball M/W, track and field M(c)/W(c), volleyball M/W(c).

Campus security: 24-hour emergency response devices and patrols, late-night transport/escort service.

Student services: health clinic, personal/psychological counseling, women's center, veterans affairs office.

COSTS & FINANCIAL AID
Costs (2018–19) *One-time required fee:* $225. *Tuition:* state resident $8534 full-time, $354 per credit hour part-time; nonresident $23,628 full-time, $981 per credit hour part-time. Full-time tuition and fees vary according to location and program. Part-time tuition and fees vary according to location and program. *Required fees:* $3244 full-time, $140 per credit hour part-time. *Room and board:* $11,696; room only: $7050. Room and board charges vary according to board plan and housing facility. *Payment plan:* installment. *Waivers:* senior citizens and employees or children of employees.

Financial Aid Of all full-time matriculated undergraduates who enrolled in 2018, 6,537 applied for aid, 5,229 were judged to have need, 585 had their need fully met. 120 Federal Work-Study jobs (averaging $3097). 121 state and other part-time jobs (averaging $10,404). In 2018, 1807 non-need-based awards were made. *Average percent of need met:* 55. *Average financial aid package:* $11,667. *Average need-based loan:* $4184. *Average need-based gift aid:* $10,031. *Average non-need-based aid:* $8164. *Average indebtedness upon graduation:* $26,862.

APPLYING
Standardized Tests *Required:* SAT or ACT (for admission).

Options: electronic application, early admission, early action, deferred entrance.

Application fee: $75.

Required: essay or personal statement, high school transcript. *Recommended:* minimum 3.0 GPA, 2 letters of recommendation.

Application deadlines: 2/1 (freshmen), 12/15 (transfers), 11/1 (early action).

Notification: continuous (freshmen), continuous (transfers), 12/15 (early action).

CONTACT
Mr. Dale Bittinger, Director of Admissions, University of Maryland, Baltimore County, 1000 Hilltop Circle, Baltimore, MD 21250. *Phone:* 410-455-2291. *Toll-free phone:* 800-UMBC-4U2 (in-state); 800-862-2402 (out-of-state). *Fax:* 410-455-1094. *E-mail:* admissions@umbc.edu.

University of Maryland, College Park

College Park, Maryland
http://www.umd.edu/

- **State-supported** university, founded 1856, part of University System of Maryland
- **Suburban** 1335-acre campus with easy access to Baltimore and Washington, DC
- **Endowment** $531.2 million
- **Coed** 30,762 undergraduate students, 93% full-time, 47% women, 53% men
- **Moderately difficult** entrance level, 47% of applicants were admitted

UNDERGRAD STUDENTS
28,501 full-time, 2,261 part-time. Students come from 49 states and territories; 66 other countries; 23% are from out of state; 12% Black or African American, non-Hispanic/Latino; 10% Hispanic/Latino; 17% Asian, non-Hispanic/Latino; 0.1% Native Hawaiian or other Pacific Islander, non-Hispanic/Latino; 0.1% American Indian or Alaska Native, non-Hispanic/Latino; 4% Two or more races, non-Hispanic/Latino; 2% Race/ethnicity unknown; 5% international; 7% transferred in; 41% live on campus.

Freshmen:
Admission: 33,461 applied, 15,760 admitted, 4,712 enrolled. *Average high school GPA:* 4.3. *Test scores:* SAT evidence-based reading and

writing scores over 500: 99%; SAT math scores over 500: 99%; ACT scores over 18: 100%; SAT evidence-based reading and writing scores over 600: 91%; SAT math scores over 600: 90%; ACT scores over 24: 95%; SAT evidence-based reading and writing scores over 700: 37%; SAT math scores over 700: 56%; ACT scores over 30: 60%.

Retention: 95% of full-time freshmen returned.

FACULTY
Total: 2,615, 70% full-time, 80% with terminal degrees.
Student/faculty ratio: 18:1.

ACADEMICS
Calendar: semesters. *Degrees:* certificates, bachelor's, master's, doctoral, post-master's, and postbachelor's certificates.

Special study options: academic remediation for entering students, accelerated degree program, adult/continuing education programs, advanced placement credit, cooperative education, distance learning, double majors, English as a second language, external degree program, honors programs, independent study, internships, off-campus study, part-time degree program, services for LD students, student-designed majors, study abroad, summer session for credit. *ROTC:* Army (b), Navy (c), Air Force (b).

Computers: Students can access the following: campus intranet, computer help desk, free student e-mail accounts, online (class) grades, online (class) registration, online (class) schedules, student account information, financial aid summary. Campuswide network is available. 100% of college-owned or -operated housing units are wired for high-speed Internet access. Wireless service is available via entire campus.
Library: McKeldin Library plus 6 others. *Books:* 2.1 million (physical), 2.8 million (digital/electronic); *Serial titles:* 2,759 (physical), 63,891 (digital/electronic); *Databases:* 164. Weekly public service hours: 140; study areas open 24 hours, 5–7 days a week; students can reserve study rooms.

STUDENT LIFE
Housing options: coed, women-only, cooperative, special housing for students with disabilities. Campus housing is university owned and is provided by a third party. Freshman applicants given priority for college housing.

Activities and organizations: drama/theater group, student-run newspaper, radio and television station, choral group, marching band, Student Government Association, Residence Hall Association, Black Student Union, Asian-American Student Union/Jewish Student Union, Commuter Students Association, national fraternities, national sororities.

Athletics Member NCAA. All Division I. *Intercollegiate sports:* baseball M(s), basketball M(s)/W(s), cross-country running W(s), field hockey W(s), football M(s), golf M(s)/W(s)(c), gymnastics W(s), lacrosse M(s)/W(s), soccer M(s)/W(s), softball W(s), swimming and diving M/W, tennis W(s), track and field M/W(s), volleyball W(s), wrestling M(s).
Intramural sports: badminton M(c)/W(c), baseball M(c), basketball M(c)/W(c), crew M(c)/W(c), cross-country running M(c)/W(c), equestrian sports M(c)/W(c), fencing M(c)/W(c), field hockey W(c), football M/W, golf M(c)/W(c), ice hockey M(c)/W(c), lacrosse M(c)/W(c), racquetball M(c)/W(c), rock climbing M(c)/W(c), rugby M(c)/W(c), sailing M(c)/W(c), soccer M(c)/W(c), softball W(c), squash M(c)/W(c), swimming and diving M(c)/W(c), table tennis M(c)/W(c), tennis M(c)/W(c), ultimate Frisbee M/W, volleyball M(c)/W(c), water polo M(c)/W(c), wrestling M(c).

Campus security: 24-hour emergency response devices and patrols, student patrols, late-night transport/escort service, controlled dormitory access.

Student services: health clinic, personal/psychological counseling, women's center, legal services, veterans affairs office.

COSTS & FINANCIAL AID
Costs (2018–19) *Tuition:* state resident $8651 full-time, $360 per credit hour part-time; nonresident $33,272 full-time, $1387 per credit hour part-time. Full-time tuition and fees vary according to location, program, and student level. Part-time tuition and fees vary according to course load, location, program, and student level. *Required fees:* $1944 full-time, $453 per term part-time. *Room and board:* $12,429; room only: $7425. Room and board charges vary according to board plan and housing facility.
Payment plans: installment, deferred payment. *Waivers:* employees or children of employees.

Financial Aid Of all full-time matriculated undergraduates who enrolled in 2017, 16,383 applied for aid, 11,560 were judged to have need, 1,631 had their need fully met. In 2017, 4196 non-need-based awards were made. *Average percent of need met:* 60. *Average financial aid package:* $12,311. *Average need-based loan:* $4393. *Average need-based gift aid:* $10,147. *Average non-need-based aid:* $5939. *Average indebtedness upon graduation:* $28,511.

APPLYING
Standardized Tests *Required:* SAT or ACT (for admission).
Options: electronic application, early admission, early action, deferred entrance.
Application fee: $75.
Required: essay or personal statement, high school transcript. *Required for some:* Resume of activities, audition for music applicants, drawing requirement for architecture applicants. *Recommended:* 2 letters of recommendation.
Application deadlines: 1/20 (freshmen), 1/20 (out-of-state freshmen), 6/1 (transfers), 11/1 (early action).
Notification: 4/1 (freshmen), 4/1 (out-of-state freshmen), continuous (transfers), 1/31 (early action).

CONTACT
Ms. Shannon Gundy, Director, Office of Undergraduate Admissions, University of Maryland, College Park, Clarence Mitchell Building, 7999 Regents Drive, College Park, MD 20742. *Phone:* 301-314-8385. *Toll-free phone:* 800-422-5867. *Fax:* 301-314-9693. *E-mail:* ApplyMaryland@umd.edu.

★ University of Maryland Eastern Shore
Princess Anne, Maryland
http://www.umes.edu/
- **State-supported** university, founded 1886, part of University System of Maryland
- **Rural** 745-acre campus
- **Endowment** $27.9 million
- **Coed** 2,603 undergraduate students, 91% full-time, 55% women, 45% men
- **Moderately difficult** entrance level, 54% of applicants were admitted

UNDERGRAD STUDENTS
2,360 full-time, 243 part-time. Students come from 31 states and territories; 31 other countries; 19% are from out of state; 71% Black or African American, non-Hispanic/Latino; 4% Hispanic/Latino; 2% Asian, non-Hispanic/Latino; 0.1% Native Hawaiian or other Pacific Islander, non-Hispanic/Latino; 0.2% American Indian or Alaska Native, non-Hispanic/Latino; 4% Two or more races, non-Hispanic/Latino; 7% Race/ethnicity unknown; 3% international; 6% transferred in; 58% live on campus.

Freshmen:
Admission: 4,923 applied, 2,664 admitted, 503 enrolled. *Average high school GPA:* 2.9. *Test scores:* SAT evidence-based reading and writing scores over 500: 40%; SAT math scores over 500: 37%; ACT scores over 18: 42%; SAT evidence-based reading and writing scores over 600: 5%; SAT math scores over 600: 3%; ACT scores over 24: 4%.
Retention: 63% of full-time freshmen returned.

FACULTY
Total: 288, 71% full-time, 67% with terminal degrees.
Student/faculty ratio: 13:1.

ACADEMICS
Calendar: semesters. *Degrees:* certificates, bachelor's, master's, and doctoral.
Special study options: part-time degree program. *ROTC:* Army (c).
Computers: 1,097 computers/terminals are available on campus for general student use. Students can access the following: computer help desk, free student e-mail accounts, online (class) grades, online (class) registration, online (class) schedules. Campuswide network is available. Wireless service is available via entire campus.

Library: Frederick Douglass Library. *Books:* 131,714 (physical), 28,157 (digital/electronic); *Serial titles:* 170 (physical), 1,152 (digital/electronic); *Databases:* 149. Study areas open 24 hours, 5–7 days a week; students can reserve study rooms.

STUDENT LIFE

Housing options: coed, men-only, women-only. Campus housing is university owned and leased by the school.

Athletics Member NCAA. All Division I. *Intercollegiate sports:* baseball M(s), basketball M(s)/W(s), bowling W(s), cheerleading M/W, cross-country running M(s)/W(s), golf M(s)/W(s), softball W(s), tennis W(s), track and field M(s)/W(s), volleyball W(s). *Intramural sports:* basketball M/W, bowling W, cheerleading M/W, cross-country running M/W, soccer M/W, softball W, swimming and diving M/W, table tennis M/W, tennis M/W, track and field M/W, volleyball M/W, wrestling M.

Campus security: 24-hour emergency response devices and patrols, student patrols, late-night transport/escort service, controlled dormitory access.

COSTS & FINANCIAL AID

Costs (2019–20) *Tuition:* area resident $5418 full-time, $224 per credit hour part-time; state resident $5418 full-time, $224 per credit hour part-time; nonresident $15,828 full-time, $583 per credit hour part-time. *Required fees:* $3140 full-time, $84 per credit hour part-time. *Room and board:* $11,189; room only: $6730.

Financial Aid Of all full-time matriculated undergraduates who enrolled in 2015, 3,133 applied for aid, 2,697 were judged to have need, 21 had their need fully met. 88 Federal Work-Study jobs (averaging $2955). In 2015, 92 non-need-based awards were made. *Average percent of need met:* 34. *Average financial aid package:* $4416. *Average need-based loan:* $3996. *Average need-based gift aid:* $3337. *Average non-need-based aid:* $4545. *Average indebtedness upon graduation:* $9861.

APPLYING

Standardized Tests *Required:* SAT or ACT (for admission).

Options: electronic application, deferred entrance.

Application fee: $35.

Required: essay or personal statement, high school transcript, minimum 2.5 GPA, 3 letters of recommendation. *Required for some:* interview.

CONTACT

Dr. Eric V. Hilton, Director of Admissions and Recruitment, University of Maryland Eastern Shore, 11868 Academic Oval, Princess Anne, MD 21853. *Phone:* 410-651-6410 Ext. 6410. *Fax:* 410-651-7922 Ext. 7922. *E-mail:* evhilton@umes.edu.

University of Maryland University College

Adelphi, Maryland

http://www.umuc.edu/

- **State-supported** comprehensive, founded 1947, part of University System of Maryland
- **Suburban** campus with easy access to Washington, DC
- **Coed** 47,253 undergraduate students, 20% full-time, 45% women, 55% men
- **Noncompetitive** entrance level, 100% of applicants were admitted

UNDERGRAD STUDENTS

9,607 full-time, 37,646 part-time. Students come from 52 states and territories; 58 other countries; 62% are from out of state; 27% Black or African American, non-Hispanic/Latino; 14% Hispanic/Latino; 5% Asian, non-Hispanic/Latino; 0.6% Native Hawaiian or other Pacific Islander, non-Hispanic/Latino; 0.5% American Indian or Alaska Native, non-Hispanic/Latino; 4% Two or more races, non-Hispanic/Latino; 10% Race/ethnicity unknown; 1% international; 23% transferred in.

Freshmen:

Admission: 2,592 applied, 2,592 admitted, 704 enrolled.

FACULTY

Total: 3,846, 5% full-time, 55% with terminal degrees.

Student/faculty ratio: 19:1.

ACADEMICS

Calendar: semesters. *Degrees:* certificates, associate, bachelor's, master's, doctoral, and postbachelor's certificates (offers primarily part-time evening and weekend degree programs at more than 30 off-campus locations in Maryland and the Washington, DC area, and more than 180 military communities in Europe and Asia with military enrollment not reflected in this profile; associate of arts program available to military students only).

Special study options: academic remediation for entering students, accelerated degree program, advanced placement credit, cooperative education, distance learning, double majors, external degree program, independent study, internships, off-campus study, part-time degree program, services for LD students, summer session for credit.

Computers: 510 computers/terminals are available on campus for general student use. Students can access the following: campus intranet, computer help desk, free student e-mail accounts, online (class) grades, online (class) registration, online (class) schedules. Campuswide network is available. Wireless service is available via entire campus.

Library: Library plus 1 other. *Books:* 1,234 (physical), 129,937 (digital/electronic); *Serial titles:* 161,585 (digital/electronic); *Databases:* 96. Weekly public service hours: 95.

STUDENT LIFE

Housing options: college housing not available.

Campus security: 24-hour emergency response devices and patrols, late-night transport/escort service.

COSTS & FINANCIAL AID

Costs (2018–19) *Tuition:* state resident $6936 full-time, $289 per credit hour part-time; nonresident $11,976 full-time, $499 per credit hour part-time. *Required fees:* $360 full-time. *Payment plan:* installment. *Waivers:* senior citizens and employees or children of employees.

Financial Aid Of all full-time matriculated undergraduates who enrolled in 2017, 6,006 applied for aid, 5,643 were judged to have need, 53 had their need fully met. *Average percent of need met:* 33. *Average financial aid package:* $7274. *Average need-based loan:* $4293. *Average need-based gift aid:* $5071.

APPLYING

Options: electronic application, early decision, deferred entrance.

Application fee: $50.

Required: high school transcript.

Application deadlines: rolling (freshmen), rolling (transfers).

Notification: continuous (freshmen), continuous (transfers).

CONTACT

Ms. Carolene Bloomfield, Senior Director of Admissions, University of Maryland University College, 3501 University Boulevard East, Adelphi, MD 20783. *Phone:* 800-888-UMUC. *Toll-free phone:* 800-888-8682. *E-mail:* enroll@umuc.edu.

Washington Adventist University

Takoma Park, Maryland

http://www.wau.edu/

CONTACT

Elaine Oliver, Associate Vice President, Enrollment Services, Washington Adventist University, 7600 Flower Avenue, Takoma Park, MD 20912. *Phone:* 301-891-4502. *Toll-free phone:* 800-835-4212. *Fax:* 301-971-4230. *E-mail:* enroll@cuc.edu.

Washington College

Chestertown, Maryland

http://www.washcoll.edu/

- **Independent** 4-year, founded 1782
- **Small-town** 140-acre campus with easy access to Baltimore and Washington, DC
- **Endowment** $220.0 million
- **Coed**
- **Moderately difficult** entrance level

FACULTY

Student/faculty ratio: 11:1.